LARGE-SAMPLE INFERENCE ($n \geq 30$)

Parameter (Population Value)	Statistic (Sample Value)	Hypothesis (Example)	Standard Error	Test Statistic	Confidence Interval
μ (Mean)	$\bar{X}$	$H_0: \mu = 50$ $H_A: \mu \neq 50$	$\sigma_{\bar{x}} = \dfrac{\sigma}{\sqrt{n}}$ or $s_{\bar{x}} \approx \dfrac{s}{\sqrt{n}}$	$Z = \dfrac{\bar{X} - \mu}{\frac{\sigma}{\sqrt{n}}}$ or $Z = \dfrac{\bar{X} - \mu}{\frac{s}{\sqrt{n}}}$	$\bar{X} \pm Z\dfrac{\sigma}{\sqrt{n}}$ or $\bar{X} \pm Z\dfrac{s}{\sqrt{n}}$
$\mu_1 - \mu_2$ (Two means)	$\bar{X}_1 - \bar{X}_2$	$H_0: \mu_1 - \mu_2 = 0$ $H_A: \mu_1 - \mu_2 \neq 0$	$\sigma_{\bar{x}_1 - \bar{x}_2} = \sqrt{\dfrac{\sigma_1^2}{n_1} + \dfrac{\sigma_2^2}{n_2}}$ or $s_{\bar{x}_1 - \bar{x}_2} \approx \sqrt{\dfrac{s_1^2}{n_1} + \dfrac{s_2^2}{n_2}}$	$Z = \dfrac{(\bar{X}_1 - \bar{X}_2) - (\mu_1 - \mu_2)}{\sqrt{\frac{\sigma_1^2}{n_1} + \frac{\sigma_2^2}{n_2}}}$ or $Z = \dfrac{(\bar{X}_1 - \bar{X}_2) - (\mu_1 - \mu_2)}{\sqrt{\frac{s_1^2}{n_1} + \frac{s_2^2}{n_2}}}$	$(\bar{X}_1 - \bar{X}_2) \pm Z\sqrt{\dfrac{\sigma_1^2}{n_1} + \dfrac{\sigma_2^2}{n_2}}$ or $(\bar{X}_1 - \bar{X}_2) \pm Z\sqrt{\dfrac{s_1^2}{n_1} + \dfrac{s_2^2}{n_2}}$
p (Proportion)	$\hat{p}$	$H_0: p \leq 0.10$ $H_A: p > 0.10$	$\sigma_p = \sqrt{\dfrac{pq}{n}}$ or $s_p = \sqrt{\dfrac{\hat{p}\hat{q}}{n}}$	$Z = \dfrac{\hat{p} - p}{\sqrt{\frac{pq}{n}}}$	$\hat{p} \pm Z\sqrt{\dfrac{\hat{p}\hat{q}}{n}}$
$p_1 - p_2$ (Two proportions)	$\hat{p}_1 - \hat{p}_2$	$H_0: p_1 - p_2 = 0$ $H_A: p_1 - p_2 \neq 0$	$\sigma_{\hat{p}_1 - \hat{p}_2} = \sqrt{\dfrac{p_1 q_1}{n_1} + \dfrac{p_2 q_2}{n_2}}$ or $s_{\hat{p}_1 - \hat{p}_2} = \sqrt{\dfrac{\hat{p}_1\hat{q}_1}{n_1} + \dfrac{\hat{p}_2\hat{q}_2}{n_2}}$	$Z = \dfrac{(\hat{p}_1 - \hat{p}_2) - (p_1 - p_2)}{\sqrt{\bar{p}(1 - \bar{p})\left(\frac{1}{n_1} + \frac{1}{n_2}\right)}}$	$\hat{p}_1 - \hat{p}_2 \pm Z\sqrt{\dfrac{\hat{p}_1\hat{q}_1}{n_1} + \dfrac{\hat{p}_2\hat{q}_2}{n_2}}$

BUSINESS STATISTICS

THIRD EDITION

BUSINESS STATISTICS
A Decision-Making Approach

DAVID F. GROEBNER
PATRICK W. SHANNON

Boise State University

Merrill Publishing Company
A Bell & Howell Information Company
Columbus   London   Toronto   Melbourne

Computer Graphic: ICOM, Inc.

Published by Merrill Publishing Company
A Bell & Howell Information Company
Columbus, Ohio 43216

This book was set in Times Roman.

Administrative Editor: John Stout
Developmental Editor: Dwayne Martin
Production Coordinator: Molly Kyle
Art Coordinator: Ruth Kimpel
Cover Designer: Cathy Watterson
Text Designer: Cynthia Brunk

Library of Congress Catalog Card Number: 88-63500
International Standard Book Number: 0-675-20977-3
Printed in the United States of America
1 2 3 4 5 6 7 8 9—93 92 91 90 89 88

PREFACE

Business Statistics introduces students to concepts and techniques that are used extensively in business decision-making activities in both the private and the public sectors. The statistical techniques described in the introductory course are used in all the functional areas of business, including accounting, finance, marketing, production, and personnel management. We feel that it is the application of statistical techniques that will enable students to understand why their statistics course is important and to appreciate the role that statistics plays in their academic education.

The first two editions of *Business Statistics: A Decision-Making Approach* represented our effort to provide a meaningful statistics text for students and professionals who are interested in learning not only how the statistical techniques are used, but also why decision makers need to use them. As with most products, the marketplace is the best judge of a textbook's worthiness. We are happy to say that both editions were adopted by many colleges and universities in the United States and Canada. The feedback we have received from both faculty and students has reinforced our belief that the teaching of business statistics from a decision-making viewpoint is the key to making the course both meaningful and enjoyable.

This third edition of *Business Statistics: A Decision-Making Approach* represents our effort to improve upon the second edition. The changes we have made were based on our own use of the text and on comments we received from our students and the many faculty members who so graciously offered to critique the second edition. We have made some significant improvements to the text in the third edition, but we tried not to disrupt the level of topic coverage and the easy-to-read writing style that proved successful in the previous editions. Throughout the third edition you will find the same emphasis on business applications that was present in the first two editions.

Several significant changes have been incorporated into the third edition. A totally new chapter on forecasting is included along with a revised chapter on time series analysis and index numbers. This edition contains an increased emphasis on computer applications. All appropriate chapters contain a section on computer applications using MINITAB and SPSS-X, with the KIVZ-Channel 5 data base. A new case study and data base are included in chapter 1, along with related computer problems and questions in all appropriate chapters.

We have also restructured the order of several topics in the third edition. We have placed the chapters on large-sample estimation together (chapters 8–10) and followed with chapter 11, which discusses small-sample estimation and hypothesis testing. The tests of one- and two-population variances have been combined with the chapter on ANOVA. The discussion of sampling techniques has been moved from chapter 2 to chapter 8.

Many new problems have been added to the text. In addition to the large number of application problems located at the end of each chapter, the third edition now has skill development problems at the end of each section. A number of new minicases have also been added to further emphasize the application of business statistics.

Along with all the improvements over the second-edition text itself, the third edition has accompanying it one of the widest range of supplementary materials on the market. First, a comprehensive study guide written by Dr. Belva Cooley is available. This guide has a complete set of notes for each chapter in the text and worked-out solutions to each of the odd-numbered problems in the text. Also included in the study guide are sample test questions pertaining to each chapter. We believe that this study guide is ideally suited to the student who wishes to obtain the maximum amount of knowledge from the statistics course.

Available for purchase with this edition is a microcomputer-based statistical software package called GS-STAT, designed by the authors and professionally programmed to be a valuable tool for beginning statistics students. This software offers students the opportunity to incorporate computerized statistical software and real data into their study of descriptive and inferential statistical techniques. The software comes with a *User's Guide* that fully explains how to use the software and gives numerous examples.

For the instructor, the third edition offers an instructor's manual that contains worked-out solutions to all the problems and cases in the text. In addition, a high-quality set of transparency masters is available. These masters are designed to be used as the basis for the course lectures from each chapter in the text. The data bases contained in both the text and the computer supplements are available in ASCII format on both magnetic tape and IBM/PC diskette form. Finally, a test bank of more than 1,000 objective test questions with correct answers is included.

The third edition of *Business Statistics: A Decision-Making Approach* contains many changes and improvements. Many of these are the result of the comments and constructive criticisms we received from the following individuals: William Notz, The Ohio State University; Clifford Hawley, West Virginia University; Ken Galchas, University of Arkansas, Little Rock; Joe Katz, Georgia State University; Joseph Williams, University of Montana; Robert Mogull, California State University, Sacramento; David Booth, Kent State University; Michael Broida, Miami University of Ohio; Pat Gaynor, Appalachian State University; Robert Balough, Clarion University; Anthony L. Casey, University of Dayton; Prem S. Mann, Eastern Connecticut State University; Joseph Longi, St. Louis Community College; Bonnie Bilant, University of Montana; Earl Williams, Northeast Oklahoma State University; Gordon Heath, Rochester Community College; Damodar Y. Golhar, Western Michigan University; and Bruce Baird, University of Utah. We are most appreciative of input we received from these people for helping us make the third edition a meaningful improvement over the second edition.

There are several other individuals that deserve special recognition for their contributions to the third edition. Nancy Ellison, V. Lyman Gallup, and Janet Weaver of Boise State University provided much valuable feedback based on their use of the book in their statistics courses. Belva Cooley at Indiana State University provided extensive suggestions that resulted in substantial improvements. We respect all these individuals as excellent teachers and weighed heavily their inputs. A special thanks to Joyce Davis, who spent countless hours proofing the manuscript and checking the accuracy of our examples. A special note of appreciation goes to Susan Fry who helped in so many ways including page proofing and preparing the index.

Finally, a text and all the supplementary materials that accompany it do not get completed without the professional assistance of the editorial staff. We are deeply grateful to Dwayne Martin for his support and expert direction throughout the work on this third edition. Thanks also to Jean Brown for her thoughtful copyediting and attention to detail.

In writing the first two editions of *Business Statistics: A Decision-Making Approach,* we said that we learned a great deal about ourselves and our attitude toward education. Working on the third edition has extended our learning process a great deal and we are grateful for the opportunity. We know that we are better teachers for having written this text; we hope that after students have had the chance to read this text they will consider themselves better off for the experience too. We hope they will understand the importance of statistics as a decision-making tool.

CONTENTS

    3–1   Measures of Location   74
    3–2   Measures of Spread   80
    3–3   Measures of Location and Spread for Grouped Data (Optional)   91
    3–4   Coefficient of Variation   97
    3–5   Computer Applications   100
    3–6   Conclusions   104
            Cases   116

4   INTRODUCTION TO PROBABILITY CONCEPTS   119

    4–1   What is Probability?   120
    4–2   Methods of Assigning Probability   123
    4–3   Counting Principles   126
    4–4   Probability Rules   134
    4–5   Conclusions   147
            Cases   158

5   DISCRETE PROBABILITY DISTRIBUTIONS   161

    5–1   Discrete Random Variables   162
    5–2   Discrete Probability Distributions   163
    5–3   Mean and Standard Deviation of a Discrete Probability
            Distribution   165
    5–4   Characteristics of the Binomial Distribution   169
    5–5   Developing a Binomial Probability Distribution   171
    5–6   Using the Binomial Distribution Table   176
    5–7   Mean and Standard Deviation of the Binomial Distribution   180
    5–8   Some Comments About the Binomial Distribution   185
    5–9   The Hypergeometric Distribution   185
    5–10   The Poisson Probability Distribution   192
    5–11   Mean, Variance and Standard Deviation of the Poisson
            Distribution   198
    5–12   Conclusions   200
            Cases   215

BUSINESS STATISTICS

DATA AND DATA COLLECTION

1

WHY DECISION MAKERS NEED TO KNOW

The production vice-president for Chrysler Motors has just completed a meeting with his United States plant managers. The emphasis of the meeting was on production quality control and plant productivity. A number of sessions were held to discuss steps being taken by the company to build the highest-quality cars possible. These sessions focused on the use of statistical quality control techniques. Everyone at the meeting knew that foreign auto makers such as Toyota are committed to statistical quality control and in the 1970s and early 1980s developed a reputation for high-quality products. They applied basic statistical techniques to help solve many forms of quality control problems. American car manufacturers such as Chrysler Motors are now making great strides toward applying these same basic statistical tools. Therefore, decision makers in this industry must understand statistics.

However, statistical quality control extends far beyond the automobile industry. Virtually every production and service industry in this country has turned its attention to quality control. Decision makers in industries such as wood products, electronics, steel, garments, and food processing must have a basic understanding of statistics to effectively deal with the quality control issues facing their organizations.

But not just quality control issues present a need for understanding statistics. Decisions such as those involving new product introductions, market identification, desired inventory levels, production volume, and financial investment strategy can be improved by using statistics. There is no functional business area that operates today without using statistics. This means that a business student who graduates without a good understanding of statistics will be at a disadvantage when hired into a decision-making position and also when trying to advance within the organization.

As the competitive nature of business increases, it is becoming apparent that to make good decisions, the decision maker must carefully analyze all alternatives in light of all available information. The primary role of statistics is to provide decision makers with methods for obtaining data and converting data into useful information. **Data** are values, facts, observations, or measurements.

This text introduces many statistical techniques that are used by decision makers in the functional areas of business. Regardless of whether you plan a career in marketing, finance, accounting, economics, management, real estate, or the public sector, you will benefit from knowing how to apply the basic statistical tools introduced in this text.

Statistics, like most academic disciplines, has its own terminology. As a student and future decision maker, you must learn the language of statistics. Throughout this and the subsequent chapters, we will present terms that have special statistical meaning. Each chapter contains a glossary that summarizes the important terms introduced in the chapter.

CHAPTER OBJECTIVES

The objectives of this chapter are to introduce business statistics and emphasize its role in the decision-making process. This chapter will focus on the process of data collection. We will point out some potential problems associated with collecting data. Our discussion will include an introduction to the more commonly used sampling techniques.

This chapter also introduces a case study that describes the data collection process and presents you with a small data base. Both the case study and data base will be referred to throughout the text.

STUDENT OBJECTIVES

After studying the material in this chapter you should

1. Understand the role of statistics in the decision-making process.
2. Be able to discuss the four levels of data measurement.
3. Be able to identify some of the more commonly used methods of data collection.
4. Know the strengths and weaknesses of the different data collection methods.
5. Understand the differences between a population and a sample.

WHAT DOES STATISTICS INVOLVE?

1-1

All too often individuals think of statistics as only numerical measures of some item of interest. For example, the unemployment rate is a statistic published monthly by the U.S. Department of Labor. The Dow-Jones Industrial Average is a statistic that interests many stock market investors. Another statistic important to everyone is the inflation rate. Although the numbers these examples yield are a type of statistics, the philosophy of statistics introduced in this text is something quite different.

Statistics can be described by three terms: (1) *data description*, (2) *probability*, and (3) *inference*.

1. Data description, or descriptive statistics, is an important area of statistics. Descriptive statistics consists of techniques and measures that help decision makers describe data. Graphs, charts, tables, and summary numerical measures

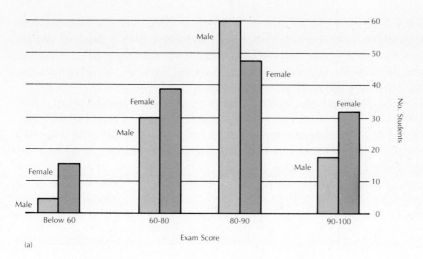

FIGURE 1–1
Descriptive statistics

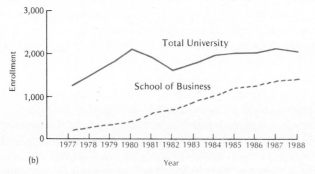

are tools that decision makers use to help turn data into meaningful information. For example, figure 1–1 illustrates two approaches for meaningfully presenting education-related data. Chapters 2 and 3 introduce some basic methods
and procedures of descriptive statistics.

2. Probability is important to statistics because it helps measure a decision maker's level of uncertainty about whether some outcome will occur. For example,
suppose an investment manager for a bank in California is considering invest-
ing $10 million of her bank's money in a government bond. The manager
recognizes that this investment may earn an acceptable rate of return or, because of increasing inflation, may result in an actual loss to the bank. Although
the investment manager is uncertain which will occur, she has analyzed the
available information and feels there is a 75 percent chance of the investment
being profitable and a 25 percent chance of a loss. These percentages, or probabilities, reflect her attitude about the chances of the two outcomes occurring
and thus measure her uncertainty about which outcome will result. The fact
that she has assigned a 0.75 probability to the profit outcome indicates that she
feels a profit is three times as likely as a loss.

3. Inference, or inferential statistics, is an area of statistics in which conclusions

about a large body of data are reached by examining only part of those data. For example, an accountant in charge of auditing a client's financial records may select a subset, or *sample,* of accounts from the ledger of all accounts. Then, based on the accuracy rate of the sampled accounts, the accountant can make inferences about the accuracy rate of all accounts.

In another instance, quality control testing relies heavily on statistical inference to accept or reject production output. Suppose a semiconductor production process is designed to produce less than 1 percent defective items. To determine if the production process is in control, the quality control manager may select a sample of items from the production process. If he finds ''too many'' defectives in the sample, he will infer that the defective rate of all items is too high. He will probably then decide that the production process needs to be adjusted.

Statistics, as defined in this text, is a collection of techniques to describe data and provide a means for making inferences about a total group based on observations from part of the total. Statistics will then allow us to make a statement about the chance that our inferences are true. The primary purpose of statistics is to provide information for the decision-making process. If you keep this in mind, you should understand why statistics is called a partner in decision making.

Probably the greatest misconception about statistics is that it is ''just another math course.'' Certainly, if statistics is approached from a theoretical viewpoint, as is the case in many mathematical statistics courses, the required mathematics can be considerable. However, the concepts introduced in this text can be discussed with a minimum amount of math. In fact, one objective in this text has been to present the statistical material at a precalculus level. The text emphasizes how statistics is applied in decision-making settings and stresses the intuitive logic of the techniques. This is not to say, however, that some basic math skills are not required, because some statistical tools have a mathematical format.

The algebra review at the end of this chapter contains the mathematical concepts required to successfully learn the statistical concepts presented in this text. We suggest you take a look at the review material and spend some time with it if you are uncertain about your math ability.

DATA LEVELS

1-2

The statistical techniques introduced in this text deal with different forms of data. The data, in turn, come from observations that can be measured. However, the level of measurement may vary greatly from application to application. In some cases the observed value can be expressed in purely numerical terms, such as dollars, pounds, inches, percentages, and so forth. In other cases the observation may be quantifiable only to the extent that it has more of some characteristic than does a second observation; such observations can be ranked only in a greater-than, equal-to, or less-than form. As an example, we may be firmly convinced that the quality of one product is greater than that of another product but be unable to state that the quality is, say, twice as great. In still other cases we may be only able to count the number of observations having a particular characteristic. For instance, we may count the number of males and females in a statistics class.

To use statistical tools, we must, in one manner or another, be able to attach some quantifiable measure to the observations we are making. Thus the measurement technique used to gather data becomes important in determining how the data can be analyzed. We shall discuss and give examples of four levels of measurements: **nominal, ordinal, interval,** and **ratio.**

Nominal

Nominal measurement is the weakest data measurement technique. In nominal measurements, numbers or other symbols are used to describe an item or characteristic. For example, when developing a computerized payroll system, designers will generally assign a number to each employee. Most of the data processing is then performed by employee number, not name. Employee numbers make up a nominal measurement scale; they are used to represent the employees but contain no additional information. Most colleges and universities require each student to have a unique student number— another example of nominal measurement.

Ordinal

Ordinal, or *rank,* measurement is one notch above nominal data in the measurement hierarchy. At this level, the data elements can be rank-ordered on the basis of some relationship between them; the assigned values indicate this order. For example, a typical market-research technique is to offer potential customers the chance to use two unidentified brands of a product. The customers are then asked to indicate which brand they prefer. The brand eventually offered to the general public depends on how often it was the preferred test brand. The fact that an ordering of items took place makes this an ordinal measure.

A corporate management hierarchy offers another example of ordinal measurement. The president, vice-president, division manager, plant manager, and so on form an ordinal scale: the president is "greater than" the vice-president, who is "greater than" the division manager, who is "greater than" the plant manager, and on down the line.

Ordinal measurement allows decision makers to equate two or more observations or to rank-order the observations. In contrast, nominal data can be compared only for equality. You cannot order nominal measurements. Thus a primary difference between ordinal data and nominal data is that ordinal data contain both an equality ($=$) and a greater-than ($>$) relationship, whereas the nominal scale contains only an equality ($=$) relationship.

Interval

If you have data with ordinal properties $(>, \ =)$ and can also measure the distance between two data items, you have an **interval** measurement. Interval measurements are preferred over ordinal measurements because, with them, decision makers can precisely determine the difference between two observations.

Frozen-food packagers have daily contact with a common interval measurement—temperature. Both the Fahrenheit and Celsius temperature scales have equal distances between points on the scales, which is an interval scale property, along with the ordinal properties of ">" and "=." For example, 32°F > 30°F, and 8°C > 4°C. The difference between 32°F and 30°F is the same as the difference between 80°F and 78°F: two degrees in either case.

Our ordinal example about the corporate hierarchy—president > vice-president > division manager > plant manager—could not be interval unless we could measure the difference between the various titles using some equal scale.

Ratio

Data that have all the characteristics of interval data but also have a unique or true zero point (where zero means "none") are called **ratio data.** Ratio measurement is the highest level of measurement.

Packagers of frozen foods encounter ratio measures when they pack their products by weight. Weight, whether measured in pounds or grams, is a ratio measurement because it has a unique zero point. Many other types of data encountered in business environments involve ratio measurements; for example, distance, money, and time.

The difference between interval and ratio measurements can be confusing because it involves the definition of a true zero. If you have five dollars and your brother has ten dollars, he has twice as much money as you. If you convert your dollars to pounds, or lire, or yen, or marks, your brother will still have twice as much as you. Money has

FIGURE 1–2
Levels of data measurement

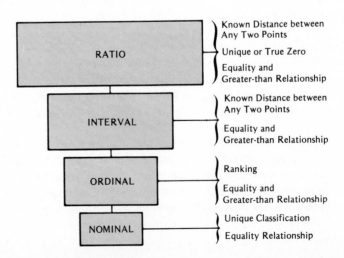

a true zero. Likewise, if you travel 100 miles today and 200 miles tomorrow, the ratio of distance traveled will be 2/1, even if you convert the distance to kilometers. Distance has a true zero. Conversely, if today's temperature is 35°F and tomorrow's is 70°F, is tomorrow twice as warm as today? The answer is no. One way to see this is to convert the Fahrenheit temperature to Celsius and the ratio will no longer be 2/1. Temperature, measured with either the Fahrenheit or Celsius scales, does not have a true zero.

Figure 1–2 illustrates the four levels of data measurement and summarizes the properties of each. The level of data measurement largely influences the type of statistical technique that can be used to analyze the data. As statistical techniques are introduced in this text, the data levels appropriate for analysis will be indicated.

METHODS OF OBTAINING DATA

1-3

Statistical tools are used to transform data into useful information. However, data must be available before the decision maker can use the statistical tools. Data are available from many sources, both within the organization and outside it.

Many data are originally generated in the day-to-day operations of the firm or from sources outside the firm such as government agencies. This type of data is extremely useful for resolving normal operational problems in an organization. However, many important decisions made in any organization involve actions that will occur in the future or that have future consequences. And, specifically, much of the information needed by decision makers can be found only in the actions or thoughts of individuals. The problems of gathering information on human actions are important for almost all managers and decision makers. This kind of information can be gathered in many ways. The following paragraphs will outline some basic techniques.

Observation

Conceptually, the simplest way to gather data on human behavior is to watch people. If you are trying to decide whether a new method of displaying your product at the supermarket will be more pleasing to customers, change a few displays and watch their reactions. If you would like some information on whether your new movie will be a success, have a preview screening and listen to the comments of patrons as they exit.

Time and motion study is actually a detailed method for watching people and determining their responses to environmental conditions. Much of what has been learned by psychologists has come from watching individuals' reactions when confronted with a new situation or a series of stimuli.

The conceptually simple method of watching human reactions or behavior patterns is not, however, without problems. The major constraints are time and money—a person or an organization never has enough of either. When time and money are considered, personal observation is a very expensive method of gathering data. For this method to be effective, trained observers must be used, and this naturally increases the cost. Personal observation is also time consuming, and to be certain that enough observations are taken, a long observation period is generally necessary. Also, since personal perception is subjective, you have no guarantee that two observers will see a situation the same, much less report it the same.

Personal Interviews

Primarily to reduce cost and time waste, personal interviews are used much more frequently than observation as a means of data collection. Individuals are asked a series of questions with the hope that they will supply useful information to the decision makers. Almost everyone has at one time or another been asked to fill out a questionnaire giving information on such items as product preference, activities, work habits, transportation choices, and so on. If these questions were asked by an interviewer, it was a personal interview.

The questions asked in personal interviews fall into two categories: *closed-ended* questions and *open-ended* questions. If the question is phrased in such a way that only certain answers are possible, it is a closed-ended question. Examples of this would be

1. Are you considering buying a new car this year?
   Yes_____ No_____
2. How would you rate the food at the student union?
   a. Excellent b. Good c. Average d. Poor e. Flushable

If the question is phrased so that the respondents are required to formulate their own answers, it is open-ended. For instance:

1. What qualities do you look for in a car?
2. Why did you decide to major in business administration?

In general, open-ended questions will gather more accurate information than closed-ended questions, but statistically analyzing open-ended answers is often difficult. When open-ended questions are analyzed, the answers are usually grouped into subjective categories. There is always room for disagreement, both about the categories and about which responses belong in which category. Data collected from closed-ended questions are much easier to analyze statistically than data from open-ended questions.

Although the time and money spent on personal interviews are generally less than for personal observations, both may still be high. This method of data gathering has additional problems:

1. Interviewers may unconsciously predetermine the answer to a question by indicating the socially acceptable answer. Consequently the interviewer can influence the response given. This problem is compounded the greater the number of interviewers used. Each interviewer may indicate different acceptable answers.
2. Many people are uncomfortable answering certain questions in person. For instance, most individuals are reluctant to give information about their incomes. However, these people may give the information on an anonymous questionnaire.
3. An increasingly common problem with using personal interviews is that many

door-to-door salespeople use questionnaires as a ploy to gain entry to a house. Individuals who have answered questions involving their children's education only to find themselves listening to a sales pitch for encyclopedias may have little sympathy for the person asking legitimate questions for the local school board.

Telephone Interviews

A common method of gathering data is the telephone interview. The main advantage of a telephone interview is that it provides a rapid method of gathering data. It has the added benefit of relatively low cost, especially when compared with personal observations and personal interviews.

In spite of the advantages of low cost and short time, the telephone interview has several disadvantages. First, people are not as likely to answer questions over the telephone as they are in person. Second, people are able to lie easily over the telephone, and unfortunately often do. During a personal interview, the interviewer can do some screening to determine if the answers given appear to be correct. This screening can be done for questions involving relative socioeconomic status, age, sex, and so forth. This screening is generally not possible over the telephone. The telephone interview generally limits the sample to people listed in the phone book. This eliminates that segment of the population who do not have phones or who are not listed in the directory.

Thus, when telephone questionnaires are used, the time and cost advantages must be weighed against the disadvantages of potentially poorer information. Since the hardest phase of telephone interviewing is holding a person's attention, only short-answer questions should be asked.

Mail Questionnaires

Certainly the cheapest method of gathering data is a mail questionnaire. Many questionnaires can be printed and sent for the cost of one personal interview. The mail questionnaire also eliminates the possibility of interviewer bias. However mail questionnaires have definite disadvantages. Probably the largest of these is a characteristically poor response. Most response rates to mail questionnaires run less than 10 percent. Also, the individuals who do answer are often those who have a particular interest in the subject, and consequently may not accurately represent the overall population. In addition, individuals will often interpret the same question differently, and so similar answers may not mean the same thing.

A poor questionnaire response can be followed up with letters, phone calls, or even personal visits. However, these procedures add greatly to the cost of data gathering.

Questionnaire writers should always remember that whenever they gather data from people, the problems of confidentiality are great. If the questions are asked incorrectly or concern sensitive information, many people will refuse to answer or will give wrong answers.

POPULATIONS AND SAMPLES

1-4

Two of the most important terms in statistics are *population* and *sample*. A **population** is a collection of all the items or observations of interest to the decision makers. Decision makers can specify the population in any manner they choose. A **sample** is a subset of the population. The following example should clarify what is meant by a population and a sample.

One of the problems a certified public accounting firm faces when auditing a business is determining the number of accounts to examine. Until recently, good accounting practice dictated that the auditors verify the balance of every account and trace through each financial transaction. Though this is still done in some audits, the size and complexity of most businesses has forced accountants to select only some accounts and some transactions to audit.

The accountant's first problem is to determine just what she wishes to examine. Suppose one part of the financial audit involves verifying the accounts-receivable balances. By definition a population includes all the items of interest to the data gatherer. The accountant defines the population of interest as all receivable accounts on record. Next she selects from this population a representative group of accounts and determines their level of accuracy or inaccuracy. The representative group of accounts is the sample. The accountant uses the sample results to make inferences about the population. How these inferences are drawn will be discussed at great length in later chapters.

The process of selecting a subset of data from the population of interest is called *sampling*. George Odiorne, a widely published author on the subject of management, makes a very intuitive analogy about sampling. He says in effect that managers will take little buckets and row their boats over an ocean of data, dipping the buckets here and there. By examining what they find in the buckets, they will be able to draw firm conclusions not only about what is in the buckets, but also about the entire ocean.[1]

This managerial process of rowing over an ocean of data and occasionally dipping in a bucket should not be viewed as unscientific. Rather, decision makers have available both a procedure to tell them where to row their boats and dip their buckets *(sampling techniques)* and a method of scientifically drawing conclusions based on what they find in the sample buckets *(statistical inference)*.

We have defined a population as all items of interest to the decision maker. If we have access to the entire population, we could collect measurements from each item. A set of measurements from the whole population is called a **census.** There are trade-offs between taking a census and a sample. Usually the trade-off is whether the cost of taking a census is worth the extra information gathered by the census. In organizations where many census-type data are stored on computer files, the additional time and effort of gathering all information are not substantial. In other cases, technology in testing equipment has advanced to the point where many companies can run a 100 percent acceptance sample. Thus, a census should not automatically be eliminated as an information-gathering technique.

Generally a census should be considered if these two factors exist: (1) the needed

---

[1]George S. Odiorne, *Management Decisions by Objectives*, 196.

information has already been gathered as a byproduct of another operation, or if technology allows information to be gathered rapidly from the population, and (2) if the gathering process will not change or destroy the item being observed. If these factors do not exist, a sample will most likely offer the best means of obtaining the needed information. Even if a decision maker can take a census, there are often reasons to sample. These reasons fall into the following four categories:

1. *Time constraints*. Obviously, asking a question of 100 people will take much less time than asking the same question of 10,000 people. Thus a major advantage of sampling is that it is much faster than taking a census. An additional advantage, and one that is often overlooked, is that sample data can be processed much faster than census information. Although actual processing of data is now almost always done by computer, coding and putting the data into machine-readable form is time consuming. For instance, it takes the U.S. Census Bureau several years to make final ten-year census data available. Most managerial decisions have a time limit. The manager must make a good decision, but often this involves making a decision now instead of next year. A manager does not want to still be gathering data when the decisions must be made.

2. *Cost constraints*. The cost of taking a census may be tremendous. Consider, for example, the cost to General Motors of determining exactly what the U.S. population thinks of its latest automobiles. Gathering that data would be an astronomical undertaking. Even the federal government, with its large financial resources, attempts a nationwide census only once every ten years, and, indeed, much of its information is based on a sample.

    This is not to say, however, that the cheapest approach is the best. In all cases the decision makers must balance the cost of obtaining information against the value of the information. Often decision makers can obtain more relevant and meaningful information from a sample than from a census. This generally occurs because more care can be taken with a sample since the data are gathered from fewer sources. Basically, if a certain amount of time is allotted to gather information, we can either gather a little information from a lot of observations, or a lot of information from a few observations. Often the value of the additional information from a few sources outweighs the advantage of having a census.

3. *Improved accuracy*. The results of a sample may be more accurate than the results of a census. A person gathering data from fewer sources tends to be more complete and thorough in both gathering and tabulating the data. There are likely to be fewer human errors. However, if these measurement errors can be eliminated, a census will be more accurate than a sample.

4. *Impossibility of a census*. Sometimes taking a complete census to gather information is economically impossible. In addition, obtaining information often requires a change in, or destruction of, the item from which information is being gathered. For instance, light-bulb manufacturers have to determine the average lifetime of their bulbs. The way to determine how long a bulb will last

is to plug it in and wait until it burns out. Once the bulb fails, they have determined how long it would have lasted, but obviously are unable to sell the bulb. Many other information-gathering methods are destructive and therefore cannot be used on a census basis.

A slightly different problem occurs when gathering information involving legal restrictions or personal freedoms. An example is testing new drugs. Ill people are generally unwilling to take a new drug until its effectiveness has been determined; certainly individuals cannot be forced to test a drug. However, you cannot determine a drug's effectiveness until it has been used. In fact, the Food and Drug Administration will not allow a drug to be sold until it has been extensively tested. Thus, using a census to test a new drug's effectiveness is difficult, if not impossible.

In practice, most important managerial decisions are made on the basis of sample data, and the whole issue of correctly selecting a sample from a population is one of the most complicated, and most important, in statistics. In a later chapter we will introduce some common sampling techniques and briefly consider potential problems found when applying these techniques. However, throughout this text we will assume any sample data given were gathered using correct sampling procedures. We will leave an in-depth consideration of the important subject of sampling to a later course.

At the end of this chapter, a case study involving a research effort conducted by a state transportation department is presented. This case study is designed to illustrate the steps taken to collect data and also to provide a *data base* that will be referred to throughout the remainder of the text.

CONCLUSIONS

1-5

Decision makers, by definition, make decisions. They are willing to use any technique that will help them make better decisions. The primary objective of the statistical tools presented in this and the remaining chapters is to provide decision makers with a means of transferring data into meaningful information that can be used to make better decisions.

Before a decision can be made, most often data must be gathered. Unfortunately, all methods used to gather data have inherent problems. This chapter has presented some methods used to gather data and some problems that can occur when data are gathered. These problems do not imply that decision makers should throw up their hands and just guess at the best decision. Rather, they should view statistical techniques as tools to be used in making decisions. We will continually emphasize, and you should never forget, that statistical techniques do not make decisions—people make decisions.

The tools presented in this text give decision makers added information to use in arriving at decisions, but the degree to which the information is useful depends on the degree to which the problems associated with data gathering have been avoided.

The chapter glossary gives the definitions of terms included in this chapter.

CHAPTER GLOSSARY

census   A measurement of each item in the population.

data   A set of values, facts, or observations.

interval data   Data with the "=" and ">" comparative relationships and known distances between any two items or numbers.

nominal data   The weakest form of data. Numbers or other symbols are used to describe an item or characteristic. The "=" relationship is the highest level of comparison.

ordinal data   Data elements that can be placed in a rank ordering based on some specific relationship between them. The relationships for comparison are "=" and ">".

population   A collection of measurements, items, or individuals that make up the total of all possible measurements within the scope of the study.

ratio data   Data with all the characteristics of interval data, but with a unique zero point. These data are considered to be the highest data level.

sample   A subset of a population. The members of a sample may be selected using either probability or nonprobability sampling.

PROBLEMS

Section 1–1

1. Look up the course description of your college statistics course. Relate this description to the basic description of statistics presented in this chapter.

2. List some examples of television and radio commentators referring to or giving descriptive statistics. When are they discussing statistical inference?

3. In connection with other classes, discuss instances when you have been exposed to descriptive statistics and when you have seen statistical inference used.

Section 1–2

4. The Ford Motor Company has been advertising a series of comparisons between its cars and competitors' cars. What level of data measurement would each of the following be?
   a. The sound level inside the car.
   b. Drivers' ratings of the handling characteristics of the car.
   c. The mileage ratings for the cars.
   d. The indication of whether a stereo radio is standard equipment on a car.

5. This chapter presented four levels of data measurement. List these four levels and provide examples of each.

6. A company financial manager recently made a presentation showing that during the

previous sixteen quarters (three months per quarter) the company showed a profit twelve times and a loss four times. What possible levels of data is the manager working with? Show what you mean with an example.

Section 1–3

7. Discuss the advantages and disadvantages of telephone surveys. As you answer this question think in terms of a survey of small business in your hometown regarding employee turnover.

8. Suppose you work at a local fast-food restaurant. The manager has asked you to begin compiling a data base which may be helpful later on in marketing decisions. Identify five internal sources of data and three external sources of data which might prove useful for the data base.

9. Suppose the U.S. Post Office is interested in obtaining feedback about how satisfied the public is with its Express Mail service. Which method of data collection would you recommend and why? Be sure to outline the procedure by which they could collect the data and discuss any potential problems.

10. Develop a short questionnaire that will be administered as a mail survey. The questionnaire will be used to collect data regarding undergraduate opinion on a proposal to institute a fee for computer usage to be paid by all undergraduate students at your college or univesity. Be sure to include both closed-ended and open-ended questions in your questionnaire.

11. Referring to question 10, modify your questionnaire so that it can be administered as a telephone survey. Also comment on how you would go about selecting the telephone numbers of those to be surveyed.

12. Comment on how it might be possible for data collected through personal interviews or observation to be inaccurate or biased. If you know of any examples of when this may have happened, discuss them.

REFERENCES

Kish, Leslie. *Survey Sampling*. Melbourn, Fla.: Krieger Publishing, 1983.

Loether, H. J., and McTavish, D. *Descriptive and Inferential Statistics*. Boston: Allyn and Bacon, 1980.

Neter, John; Wasserman, William; and Whitmore, G. A. *Applied Statistics*. Boston: Allyn and Bacon, 1982.

Odiorne, George S. *Management by Objectives*. Englewood Cliffs, N.J.: Prentice-Hall, 1969.

Siegel, S. *Nonparametric Statistics for the Behavioral Sciences*. New York: McGraw-Hill, 1956.

Yamane, Taro. *Elementary Sampling Theory*. Englewood Cliffs, N.J.: Prentice-Hall, 1967.

STATE DEPARTMENT OF TRANSPORTATION INSURANCE DIVISION CASE STUDY AND DATA BASE

This case study describes the efforts undertaken by the director of the Insurance Division for the State Department of Transportation to assess the magnitude of the uninsured motorist problem in the state. The objective of the case study is to introduce you to a data collection application and show how one organization developed a data base. The actual data base will be supplied to your instructor upon request. The data base that appears at the end of the case study is a subset of the data found by the state department. A copy of the raw data subset has been included so you can apply different statistical techniques introduced in subsequent chapters using a computer and appropriate statistical hardware.

The impetus for the case came from the Legislative Transportation Committee, which heard much testimony during the recent legislative session about the problems that occur when an uninsured motorist is involved in a traffic accident where damages to individuals and property occur. The state's law enforcement officers also testified that a large number of vehicles are not covered by liability insurance.

Because of both political pressure and a sense of duty to do what is right, the legislative committee spent many hours wrestling with what to do about drivers who don't carry the *mandatory* liability insurance. Because the magnitude of the problem was really unknown, the committee finally arrived at a compromise plan, which required the State Transportation Department's Insurance Division to perform random audits of vehicles to determine whether the vehicle was covered by liability insurance. The audits are to be performed on approximately 5 percent of the state's 1 million registered vehicles each year. If a vehicle is found not to have liability insurance, the vehicle license and

the owner's driver's license will be revoked for three months and a $250 fine will be imposed.

However, before actually implementing the audit process, which is projected to cost $1.5 million per year, Herb Kriner, director of the Insurance Division of the State Transportation Department, was told to conduct a study of the uninsured motorists problem in the state and to report back to the legislative committee in six months.

The Study

A random sample of twelve counties in the state was selected in a manner that gave the counties with higher numbers of registered vehicles proportionally higher chances of being selected. Then two locations were selected in each county and the State Police set up roadblocks on a randomly selected day. Vehicles with in-state license plates were stopped at random until approximately 100 vehicles had been stopped at each location. The target total was about 2,400 vehicles statewide.

The issue of primary interest was whether or not the vehicle was insured. This was determined by observing whether the vehicle was carrying the required certificate of insurance. If so, the officer took down the insurance company name and address and the policy number. If the certificate was not in the car, but the owner stated insurance was carried, the owner was given a postcard to return within five days supplying the required information. A vehicle was determined to be uninsured if no postcard was returned or if, subsequently, the insurance company reported that the policy was not valid on the day of the survey.

In addition to the issue of insurance coverage, Herb Kriner wanted to collect other information about the vehicle and the owner. This was done using a personal interview during which the police officer asked a series of questions and observed certain things such as seat belt usage and driver's and vehicle license expiration status. Also, the owners' driving records were obtained through the Transportation Department's computer division and added to the information gathered by the State Poice.

The Data

In all, a file consisting of 2,434 valid observations (vehicles) with all associated data was developed. Seventeen different variables were measured for each vehicle. Table 1C–1 contains a listing of the data for 100 vehicles. These data should be available from your instructor on computer diskette. The diskette also contains the data set for the entire group of 2,434 observations.

The first few variables on the data set relate to the owner's driving record:

X_1 = Number of DUI (Driving under the Influence) occurrences during the past three years

X_2 = Number of DUI points on the driving record in the past three years; different categories of DUI offenses result in different numbers of points being assigned

X_3 = Number of occurrences of failure to maintain liability insurance within the past three years

X_4 = Number of points on the driving record for failure to maintain insurance within the past three years

X_5 = Total convictions for driving-related citations within the past three years

X_6 = Total cancellations and suspensions of driver's license within the past three years

The following variables deal with the vehicle and the owner of the vehicle:

X_7 = Vehicle year

X_8 = Sex of the owner/driver; coded 1 if male, 2 if female

X_9 = Age of the owner/driver

X_{10} = Driver's seat belt status, coded
  0 = Not observed
  1 = Yes, was wearing seat belt
  2 = No, was not wearing seat belt
  3 = Not required because of age of vehicle

X_{11} = Knowledge of the state's mandatory liability insurance law, coded
  0 = No response
  1 = Yes, aware of law
  2 = No, not aware of law
  3 = Uncertain about the law

X_{12} = Employment status coded
  0 = No response
  1 = Yes, is employed
  2 = No, unemployed
  3 = Other (retired)

X_{13} = Number of years lived in this state

X_{14} = Number of vehicles registered in this state

X_{15} = Number of years of formal education

X_{16} = Insurance certificate status coded
  0 = Not observed
  1 = Yes, certificate in vehicle
  2 = No, certificate not in vehicle
  3 = Other

X_{17} = Liability insurance status coded
  0 = Uninsured
  1 = Insured

The data collected by this survey are designed to help Herb Kriner and his staff respond to the legislative committee and to provide background information that should be helpful if the decision is to continue with the random audit enforcement process currently proposed.

TABLE 1C–1
State Transportation Department Insurance Division data base

								Variable									Case No.
X_1	X_2	X_3	X_4	X_5	X_6	X_7	X_8	X_9	X_{10}	X_{11}	X_{12}	X_{13}	X_{14}	X_{15}	X_{16}	X_{17}	
0	0	0	0	0	0	60	1	29	3	1	1	4	2	12	1	1	1
0	0	0	0	0	0	69	2	24	2	1	2	17	1	10	2	1	2
0	0	0	0	0	0	77	1	50	2	1	2	0	1	12	1	1	3
0	0	0	0	0	0	82	1	64	2	2	2	37	1	12	1	1	4
0	0	0	0	0	0	77	2	18	2	1	1	9	0	11	1	1	5
0	0	0	0	0	0	87	2	18	2	1	2	10	0	11	1	1	6
0	0	0	0	0	0	81	1	52	1	1	2	52	3	17	1	1	7
0	0	0	0	0	0	79	2	38	2	1	1	7	1	2	1	1	8
0	0	0	0	2	0	87	1	31	1	1	1	30	2	12	1	1	9
0	0	0	0	0	0	82	1	58	2	1	1	57	2	9	1	1	10
0	0	0	0	1	0	74	1	69	2	1	2	4	2	10	1	1	11
0	0	0	0	0	0	78	2	45	2	1	1	12	0	13	2	1	12
0	0	0	0	0	0	86	1	35	1	1	1	10	3	14	2	1	13
0	0	0	0	0	0	80	2	42	2	1	1	13	3	12	1	1	14
0	0	0	0	0	0	85	2	22	1	1	1	21	1	12	1	1	15
0	0	0	0	1	0	87	2	20	1	1	2	17	1	12	1	1	16
0	0	0	0	0	0	79	1	36	1	1	1	35	3	12	1	1	17
0	0	0	0	0	0	0	1	23	2	0	1	11	2	12	2	1	18
0	0	0	0	0	0	82	1	55	1	1	1	45	1	13	2	1	19
0	0	0	0	0	0	68	2	61	2	1	2	7	3	16	2	1	20
0	0	0	0	1	0	87	1	68	1	1	2	9	2	12	1	1	21
0	0	0	0	0	0	86	2	65	1	1	2	2	1	18	1	1	22
0	0	0	0	0	0	80	1	61	0	1	1	59	1	16	2	1	23
0	0	0	0	0	0	86	1	37	2	1	1	25	2	14	1	1	24
0	0	0	0	1	0	76	1	38	2	1	2	37	1	14	2	1	25
0	0	0	0	0	0	79	2	49	2	1	1	48	2	13	1	1	26
0	0	0	0	5	0	79	1	21	2	1	1	20	1	12	1	1	27
0	0	0	0	0	0	77	2	39	1	1	2	1	3	12	2	1	28
0	0	0	0	2	0	74	1	38	2	1	1	21	2	1	1	1	29
0	0	0	0	0	0	78	1	18	2	1	2	17	1	10	2	1	30
0	0	0	0	1	0	0	1	27	1	1	1	2	1	10	2	0	31
0	0	0	0	0	0	84	2	58	2	1	1	57	2	12	1	1	32
0	0	0	0	0	0	78	1	26	2	1	2	10	2	10	1	1	33
0	0	0	0	0	0	82	1	37	1	1	2	9	2	12	2	1	34
0	0	0	0	1	0	79	2	31	2	1	2	9	1	15	2	1	35
0	0	0	0	1	0	85	1	56	2	1	1	55	2	10	1	1	36
0	0	0	0	1	0	72	1	18	3	1	1	16	1	12	1	1	37
0	0	0	0	0	0	78	2	61	2	1	2	60	1	12	2	1	38
0	0	0	0	0	0	78	1	42	2	1	1	17	3	14	2	1	39
0	0	0	0	0	0	84	2	41	1	1	1	26	4	12	2	1	40
0	0	0	0	2	0	79	1	19	2	1	1	14	1	12	1	1	41
0	0	0	0	0	0	79	1	55	2	3	2	30	2	6	2	1	42
0	0	0	0	0	0	83	2	67	2	1	1	66	2	12	1	1	43
0	0	0	0	0	0	78	2	50	1	1	2	49	4	18	1	1	44
0	0	0	0	0	0	79	1	48	2	1	2	47	2	8	2	1	45
0	0	0	0	0	0	68	1	49	2	1	1	46	7	12	1	1	46
0	0	0	0	0	0	75	1	38	2	1	1	11	3	12	2	1	47
0	0	0	0	0	0	77	1	27	2	1	1	26	1	12	2	1	48
0	0	0	0	1	0	84	2	22	1	1	1	21	1	13	1	1	49
0	0	0	0	1	0	86	2	23	2	1	1	20	2	13	1	1	50
0	0	0	0	3	1	81	1	20	2	1	1	18	1	12	2	0	51

TABLE 1C–1 (*Continued*)
State Transportation Department Insurance Division data base

								Variable									Case No.
X_1	X_2	X_3	X_4	X_5	X_6	X_7	X_8	X_9	X_{10}	X_{11}	X_{12}	X_{13}	X_{14}	X_{15}	X_{16}	X_{17}	
0	0	0	0	3	1	81	1	20	2	1	1	18	1	12	2	0	51
0	0	0	0	0	0	81	2	42	1	1	1	11	4	17	1	1	52
0	0	0	0	0	0	0	1	24	2	1	1	6	0	1	1	1	53
0	0	0	0	0	0	73	2	70	2	1	2	69	1	14	1	1	54
0	0	0	0	0	0	83	2	42	2	1	2	36	3	12	1	1	55
0	0	0	0	1	0	74	1	29	2	1	1	28	1	16	1	1	56
0	0	0	0	0	0	84	1	50	2	1	1	39	2	9	1	1	57
0	0	0	0	0	0	86	2	45	2	0	1	40	1	12	2	1	58
0	0	0	0	1	0	87	2	62	1	1	2	60	3	11	1	1	59
0	0	0	0	0	0	0	1	18	2	1	1	16	3	12	1	1	60
0	0	0	0	0	0	80	2	38	2	1	1	27	2	13	1	1	61
0	0	0	0	0	0	59	1	66	2	1	2	65	5	13	1	1	62
0	0	0	0	0	0	73	2	43	1	1	2	9	4	16	1	1	63
0	0	0	0	0	0	77	2	19	2	2	1	3	1	10	2	1	64
0	0	0	0	0	0	75	1	65	2	1	2	64	6	12	1	1	65
0	0	0	0	0	0	81	1	62	2	1	1	40	2	8	1	1	66
0	0	0	0	0	0	79	1	72	1	1	1	68	4	8	1	1	67
0	0	0	0	0	0	76	1	28	2	1	1	27	2	16	2	1	68
0	0	0	0	0	0	86	2	44	2	1	1	43	1	12	1	1	69
0	0	0	0	0	0	86	1	80	2	1	2	75	1	18	2	1	70
0	0	0	0	0	0	75	2	48	2	1	1	47	1	12	1	0	71
0	0	0	0	1	0	72	1	27	2	1	2	26	2	12	1	1	72
0	0	0	0	0	0	86	2	41	2	1	2	25	3	9	1	1	73
0	0	0	0	0	0	0	1	29	2	1	1	27	2	12	1	1	74
0	0	0	0	1	0	78	1	44	2	1	1	43	3	12	1	1	75
0	0	0	0	0	0	77	1	38	2	1	1	37	2	15	1	1	76
0	0	0	0	0	0	70	1	19	2	1	2	18	0	12	1	1	77
4	0	0	0	5	4	88	1	31	2	1	1	30	2	16	2	1	78
0	0	0	0	1	0	87	2	36	1	1	2	3	0	12	1	1	79
0	0	0	0	0	0	82	1	33	2	1	1	32	2	10	1	1	80
0	0	0	0	0	0	79	1	83	2	1	2	65	4	8	1	1	81
0	0	0	0	0	0	86	1	45	2	1	1	44	2	15	2	1	82
0	0	0	0	0	0	80	2	79	1	1	2	1	1	13	2	0	83
0	0	0	0	0	0	87	2	39	2	2	1	13	3	14	1	0	84
0	0	0	0	0	0	0	1	61	2	1	1	39	3	12	1	1	85
0	0	0	0	0	0	71	2	23	2	1	2	12	0	12	2	0	86
0	0	0	0	0	0	73	1	41	1	1	1	35	5	13	1	1	87
0	0	0	0	0	0	86	1	30	1	1	1	14	2	12	1	0	88
0	0	0	0	0	0	77	1	24	2	1	1	21	2	12	1	1	89
1	0	0	0	2	1	76	1	39	1	1	1	3	3	16	1	1	90
0	0	1	0	1	3	78	1	22	1	1	1	19	1	12	2	1	91
1	0	0	0	1	0	85	1	65	1	1	1	64	1	12	1	1	92
1	0	0	0	4	2	71	1	22	1	1	2	21	2	12	2	1	93
2	0	1	0	1	3	0	1	70	3	3	2	45	3	6	2	1	94
1	0	0	0	0	2	66	1	26	2	1	1	25	2	14	1	1	95
2	0	0	0	1	1	74	1	27	2	1	1	3	3	10	1	1	96
1	0	0	0	1	1	80	1	32	2	1	1	6	2	12	1	1	97
2	0	0	0	3	1	78	1	24	2	1	1	15	1	11	1	1	98
2	0	0	0	5	5	60	1	32	2	1	1	15	1	12	2	1	99
1	0	1	0	3	4	65	1	21	2	1	1	5	1	11	1	1	100

STATE DEPARTMENT OF TRANSPORTATION
CASE STUDY PROBLEMS

Most of the chapters in this text contain questions or problems that pertain to this data base and case study. It is expected that you will be using a computer and appropriate software to work these problems. The following questions for this chapter relate to the case study but do not actually require you to do any computations with the data.

1. For each of the seventeen variables in the data base, indicate level of data measurement for each variable.

2. The data collection method consisted of a combination of observation and personal interview. Indicate which of the seventeen variables were obtained through observation. What potential problems might result from collecting data through observation?

3. It would probably have been less expensive to collect the data via a telephone survey. What variables would have been difficult to collect over the telephone? Discuss.

4. If a mail questionnaire or telephone survey had been used, what would some of the problems have been and what would some of the advantages have been? Discuss.

5. Write a short statement outlining the objectives for which the data were collected. Assuming there was more than one objective, list the objectives in priority order.

ALGEBRA REVIEW

The material in this text assumes you have taken an introductory algebra course. This Appendix section contains a short review of the concepts encountered in this text.

Basic Algebra

RULE

Numbers can be substituted for letters.

EXAMPLE 1

Given

$$X = 6Y + 10$$

Let

$$Y = 5$$

Solve for X.

$$X = 6(5) + 10$$
$$= 30 + 10$$
$$= 40$$

EXAMPLE 2

Given

$$A = 20X + 7Y + 3Z$$

Let

$$X = 2 \qquad Y = 6 \qquad Z = 8$$

Solve for A.

$$A = 20(2) + 7(6) + 3(8)$$
$$= 40 + 42 + 24$$
$$= 106$$

EXAMPLE 3

Given

$$A = 3\frac{X}{Y} + Z$$

Let

$$X = 7 \qquad Y = 4 \qquad Z = 8$$

Solve for A.

$$A = 3\left(\frac{7}{4}\right) + 8$$
$$= 5.25 + 8$$
$$= 13.25$$

RULE

To add or subtract similar terms, add or subtract their coefficients.

EXAMPLE 4

$$6XY + 3XY = 9XY$$

EXAMPLE 5

$$18.5X - 13X = 5.5X$$

RULE

When numbers are contained within parentheses, the enclosed quantity is considered as one term.

EXAMPLE 6

$$10(8 - 3) = 10(5)$$
$$= 50$$

EXAMPLE 7

$$X\left(14 - \frac{33}{11}\right) = X(14 - 3) = X(11)$$
$$= 11X$$

RULE

To change a percentage to a decimal, move the decimal point two places to the left and drop the percent sign.

EXAMPLE 8

Change 10 percent to a decimal.

$$10\% = 0.10$$

EXAMPLE 9

Change 93.6 percent to a decimal.

$$93.6\% = 0.936$$

RULE

To convert a fraction to a decimal, just carry out the division.

EXAMPLE 10

Convert 3/4 to a decimal.

$$\frac{3}{4} = 0.75$$

EXAMPLE 11

Convert 4/5 to a decimal.

$$\frac{4}{5} = 0.80$$

RULE

The square of a number can be found by multiplying the number by itself.

EXAMPLE 12

Given

$$X = Y^2$$
$$= (Y)(Y)$$

Let

$$Y = 8$$

Solve for X.

$$X = Y^2 = (8)(8)$$
$$= 64$$

EXAMPLE 13

Given

$$X = (Y - Z)^2$$
$$= (Y - Z)(Y - Z)$$

Let

$$Y = 12 \qquad Z = 15$$

Solve for X.

$$X = (12 - 15)^2 = (12 - 15)(12 - 15)$$
$$= (-3)(-3)$$
$$= 9$$

One Equation, One Unknown

RULE

You can do anything you want to an equation (except divide by zero) as long as you do the same thing to both sides.

EXAMPLE 14

$$3X = 9$$

$$\frac{3X}{3} = \frac{9}{3}$$

$$X = 3$$

EXAMPLE 15

Given

$$e = \frac{ZX}{\sqrt{n}}$$

Let

$$Z = 2 \qquad X = 4 \qquad e = 0.5$$

Solve for n.

$$0.5 = \frac{2(4)}{\sqrt{n}}$$

$$\sqrt{n}(0.5) = 2(4)$$

$$\sqrt{n} = \frac{2(4)}{0.5}$$

$$n = \frac{(2)^2(4)^2}{(0.5)^2}$$

$$= 256$$

EXAMPLE 16

Given

$$e = \frac{ZX}{\sqrt{n}}$$

Let

$$e = 0.5 \qquad n = 400 \qquad X = 5$$

Solve for Z.

$$0.5 = \frac{Z(5)}{\sqrt{400}}$$

$$0.5\sqrt{400} = Z(5)$$

$$\frac{0.5\sqrt{400}}{5} = Z$$

$$Z = 2$$

Inequalities

$>$ *is read "is greater than."*
$<$ *is read "is less than."*
$\geq$ *is read "is greater than or equal to."*
$\leq$ *is read "is less than or equal to."*

EXAMPLE 17

a. $2.50 > 1.80$ is read "2.50 is greater than 1.80."
b. $-2.8 < -1.5$ is read "negative 2.8 is less than negative 1.5."
c. $3.80 \geq X$ is read "3.80 is greater than or equal to X."
d. $Z_1 \leq Z_2$ is read "Z_1 is less than or equal to Z_2."

Summation Notation

Statistics relies heavily on **summation notation** to simplify equations involving sums of numbers. Consider the following sequence of numbers in examples 18 through 20:

$$1, 2, 3, 4, 5, 6, 7, \ldots$$

EXAMPLE 18

The notation summing the first five numbers is

$$\sum_{X=1}^{5} X = 1 + 2 + 3 + 4 + 5$$
$$= 15$$

Note that we read this as "the sum of the X values where X goes from 1 through 5 is equal to 15." The capital form of the Greek letter sigma (Σ) stands for the summation of these numbers.

EXAMPLE 19

$$\sum_{X=1}^{4} X^2 = 1 + 4 + 9 + 16$$
$$= 30$$

This is read "the sum of the squared X values where X ranges from 1 through 4."

EXAMPLE 20

$$\sum_{X=1}^{3} (X - 3) = (1 - 3) + (2 - 3) + (3 - 3)$$
$$= -3$$

Subscripts and Summation Notation

Suppose we have

i	X_i
1	5
2	7
3	3
4	1
5	12
6	5

where $i = 1, 2, 3, 4, 5, 6$
$\qquad X_i = i$th value of X (i.e., $X_1 = 5$, $X_2 = 7$, etc.)

EXAMPLE 21

$$\sum_{i=1}^{3} X_i = X_1 + X_2 + X_3$$

$$= 5 + 7 + 3$$
$$= 15$$

EXAMPLE 22

$$\sum_{i=1}^{5} X_i^2 = X_1^2 + X_2^2 + X_3^2 + X_4^2 + X_5^2$$

$$= 5^2 + 7^2 + 3^2 + 1^2 + 12^2$$
$$= 25 + 49 + 9 + 1 + 144$$
$$= 228$$

EXAMPLE 23

$$\sum_{i=1}^{3} X_i - 4 = X_1 + X_2 + X_3 - 4$$

$$= 5 + 7 + 3 - 4$$
$$= 11$$

RULE

If c is a constant (an element that does not contain a subscript), the summation of the constant is

$$\sum_{i=1}^{n} c = nc$$

EXAMPLE 24

$$\sum_{i=1}^{5} c = c + c + c + c + c$$
$$= 5c$$

Note that the c value has no subscript.

If c is a constant, then

$$\sum_{i=1}^{n} cX_i = c\sum_{i=1}^{n} X_i$$

EXAMPLE 25

$$\sum_{i=1}^{5} cX_i = cX_1 + cX_2 + cX_3 + cX_4 + cX_5$$
$$= c(X_1 + X_2 + X_3 + X_4 + X_5)$$
$$= c\sum_{i=1}^{5} X_i$$

EXAMPLE 26

Suppose

i	X_i
1	11
2	14
3	3
4	9
5	15

Then

$$\sum_{i=1}^{3} 5X_i = 5\sum_{i=1}^{3} X_i = 5(X_1 + X_2 + X_3)$$
$$= 5(11 + 14 + 3)$$
$$= 140$$

RULE

The summation of two or more different elements can be found by summing each element and adding the summed quantities. That is,

$$\sum_{i=1}^{n}(X_i + Y_i) = \sum_{i=1}^{n}X_i + \sum_{i=1}^{n}Y_i$$

EXAMPLE 27

Given

i	X_i	Y_i
1	3	14
2	8	6
3	5	9
4	2	7

Then

$$\sum_{i=1}^{4}(X_i + Y_i) = (3 + 8 + 5 + 2) + (14 + 6 + 9 + 7)$$
$$= \quad 18 \quad + \quad 36$$
$$= 54$$

Factorials

Factorials are convenient means of representing a product of decreasing integers in the form $n!$; read "n factorial."

EXAMPLE 28

$$3! = (3)(2)(1)$$
$$= 6$$
$$4! = (4)(3)(2)(1)$$
$$= 24$$

RULE

$$0! = 1$$

EXAMPLE 29

$$\frac{3!}{(3 - 3)!} = \frac{(3)(2)(1)}{0!} = \frac{(3)(2)(1)}{1}$$
$$= 6$$

Exponents

Exponents are a shortcut to writing long mathematical expressions. Limiting our review to positive integer exponents of the form a^n:

EXAMPLE 30

$$a^n = \underbrace{a \cdot a \cdot a \cdot a \cdot a \cdot a \ldots a}_{n \text{ factors}}$$

EXAMPLE 31

$$4^3 = 4 \cdot 4 \cdot 4 = 64$$

RULE

$$a^m a^n = a^{m+n}$$

EXAMPLE 32

$$5^2 \cdot 5^3 = (5 \cdot 5)(5 \cdot 5 \cdot 5) = 3{,}125 = 5^5$$

RULE

$$(a^n)^m = a^{nm}$$

EXAMPLE 33

$$(3^2)^3 = (3 \cdot 3)(3 \cdot 3)(3 \cdot 3) = 729 = 3^6$$

RULE

$$(ab)^m = a^m \cdot b^m$$

EXAMPLE 34

$$(3 \cdot 2)^4 = 6 \cdot 6 \cdot 6 \cdot 6 = 1{,}296 = 3^4 \cdot 2^4$$
$$= (3 \cdot 3 \cdot 3 \cdot 3)(2 \cdot 2 \cdot 2 \cdot 2)$$

RULE

$$\left(\frac{a}{b}\right)^m = \frac{a^m}{b^m}, \, b \neq 0$$

EXAMPLE 35

$$\left(\frac{1}{2}\right)^3 = \frac{1}{2} \cdot \frac{1}{2} \cdot \frac{1}{2} = \frac{1}{8} = \frac{1^3}{2^3}$$

RULE

$$\frac{a^m}{a^n} = a^{m-n}, \, a \neq 0$$

EXAMPLE 36

$$\frac{5^3}{5^2} = \frac{5 \cdot 5 \cdot 5}{5 \cdot 5} = \frac{125}{25} = 5 = 5^{3-2}$$

ORGANIZING AND PRESENTING DATA

2

WHY DECISION MAKERS NEED TO KNOW

The element most common to the decision maker's environment is uncertainty. This is true, at least in part, because other people make up much of the managerial environment. Whenever you interact with other individuals, you can never be certain of their actions. Other parts of the managerial environment also are characterized by uncertainty. Unpredictable events such as machine breakdowns and weather changes affect output or productivity, making them anything but consistent.

The problem most decision makers must resolve is how to deal with the uncertainty that is inherent in almost all aspects of their jobs. In making decisions with uncertain results, decision makers should use all available data to analyze the possible alternatives. In many cases the data available are in *raw* form. Unfortunately, raw data are often not useful and cannot be considered to be information. Take the personnel manager who is concerned that employee absenteeism is becoming excessive. The data he has available consist of absentee rates for each of the last 500 days. Without being organized, these raw data provide little, if any, information about the pattern or growth of absenteeism in the company.

Decision makers need a means of converting the raw data into useful information. A first step in transforming data into information is to organize and present the data in a meaningful way. Therefore, decision makers must be aware of the basic techniques for effectively organizing and presenting data.

The ability to effectively organize and present data may mean a great deal to you in your advancement through the organization. Recently a vice-president for the General Motors Company spoke at his former university business school's awards banquet. During a question-and-answer period that followed his speech, he was asked what single factor he considers most important in his rise to vice-president of one of the world's largest companies. He responded that a short time after he joined General Motors he took part in a departmental presentation before a group of upper-management personnel. He indicated that he was able to *effectively organize and present* the complex data and that the upper-management people were outwardly impressed with his presentation. Further, he said that he is convinced that this presentation and several others like it were remembered by upper management when they needed a person for a special project a couple of years later. One thing led to another and he became vice-president.

The vice-president stressed the importance of knowing how to organize and present data and pointed out that no matter how high in an organization you reach, these skills are still an important part of the job.

CHAPTER OBJECTIVES

The objective of this chapter is to introduce some methods for handling the uncertainty that managers continually face. Practical managers often are not interested in attempting to eliminate the uncertainty or variation they face because they recognize that variation will always exist. Rather, managers often are mainly interested in determining if the uncertainty they face is what would normally be expected or if somehow the extent of the uncertainty or variation has changed. Production managers are interested in whether their production processes are continuing in a normal fashion or whether they have been altered. A change may indicate the need for corrective action. Personnel managers are interested in knowing if overall employee skill levels have changed over time. A change may indicate that the managers need to institute a training procedure or that a new training program is paying off.

This chapter will introduce some tools decision makers need for examining the uncertainty they face. The first tools managers need are those necessary to "picture" the situation around them. To this end, several frequently used methods of presenting data will be discussed.

STUDENT OBJECTIVES

After studying the material in this chapter, you should be able to

1. Determine how to separate large volumes of data into more workable forms.
2. Describe several different methods to graph and present data in order to transform raw data into usable information.

METHODS OF REPRESENTING DATA

2-1

The process of gathering information is often complicated not because of a lack of potential information, but because the body of raw data is too large to analyze. Consider the problems facing merchandising managers interested in sales data from a series of stores, or even from one store. They are interested in which product lines are selling best, what the inventory levels are, which store areas have the highest sales levels, and numerous related questions. Imagine the managers being given a box of sales-slip copies each day and being asked to answer the questions just presented. The data cannot be effectively used in that form and therefore must be converted to a more useful form. This section introduces several useful techniques of data presentation.

Frequency Distribution

Perhaps the easiest method of organizing data is to construct a **frequency distribution.** To do this, we first establish **classes,** where a class is simply a category of interest. In a study of weather the classes might be "clear days" and "cloudy days." In another example the categories of loan balances might be "$0 and under $500," "$500 and under $1,000," and "$1,000 and under $2,000."

The second step in developing a frequency distribution is to count the number of observations that fall into each class. Table 2–1 presents the raw data and a frequency distribution of salaries for 134 employees in a hypothetical company. We see that thirty-nine persons have salaries in the class "$10,000 and under $12,500" and that only six

TABLE 2–1
Employee salaries

Raw Data							
$ 2,525	$ 4,852	$ 4,900	$ 2,800	$ 3,300	$ 4,000	$ 7,704	$ 9,120
3,346	4,750	3,950	4,300	3,100	2,950	8,000	8,900
3,850	4,425	5,105	5,250	7,204	7,000	9,305	7,905
6,250	6,000	5,900	5,403	6,250	7,005	7,700	8,200
5,950	5,700	6,300	5,500	7,100	6,300	7,950	8,300
6,450	7,100	7,480	6,475	6,000	7,620	8,750	9,250
9,200	9,650	9,000	8,800	9,300	9,000	9,600	10,100
9,400	8,300	8,900	8,605	9,200	9,800	10,003	11,900
11,000	12,210	12,175	11,290	12,000	12,210	12,400	11,000
12,000	11,000	10,800	10,500	10,250	11,400	12,000	12,450
11,000	11,000	12,400	11,000	12,000	11,000	12,100	12,175
10,700	10,900	11,175	12,150	11,275	10,283	11,240	13,700
11,400	12,200	10,983	12,800	13,250	14,100	14,200	14,750
13,350	12,950	13,000	13,000	13,000	13,475	14,900	15,300
14,200	14,750	14,000	14,000	13,750	13,800	15,250	19,200
15,400	17,000	16,900	17,200	16,000	16,500	17,800	
19,500	20,000	21,005	19,000	10,700	11,750	8,120	

Frequency Distribution	
Salary Class	Frequency of Employees
$ 2,500 and under $5,000	14
$ 5,000 and under $7,500	21
$ 7,500 and under $10,000	27
$10,000 and under $12,500	39
$12,500 and under $15,000	19
$15,000 and under $17,500	8
$17,500 and over	6
Total	134

individuals earn $17,500 or more. Note how confusing the salary data are in their raw form.

Although developing a frequency distribution is fairly straightforward, two factors must be considered: how many classes should be used and the limits for each class. These are considered in the following paragraphs.

Decision makers want to organize data in the first place so that they can picture what the data look like. However they immediately face a dilemma. The data must be grouped into separate classes. If the number of classes is too small, much detail available in the data is lost and the amount of potential information is reduced. On the other hand, having too many classes often makes the representation as confusing as the raw data.

Consider a company that wants some information about the age of its employees. (Many organizations use this information for future hiring practices and for pension planning.) The employees would likely range in age from twenty or less to sixty-five or more. Separating the data into single-year groups would give at least forty-five categories—too many to digest and analyze. The company could, for instance, have no one in the forty-three-year category, but several people in the forty-two-year category. On the other hand, if the data were broken into two classes—those over forty and those forty and under—much potential information would be lost. Both the number of observations and their intended use must be considered in determining the number of classes.

No firm rule exists for determining the appropriate number of classes for a particular application, but one rule that is sometimes employed is that the number of classes, k, be the smallest integer such that $2^k \geq n$, where n is the number of raw data values. For instance, using this rule we get

Number of Observations	Number of Classes
9 to 16	4
17 to 32	5
33 to 64	6
65 to 128	7
129 to 256	8

Remember, this is just a rule of thumb; specific applications may require that the number of classes be more or less than implied by this rule.

Determining class size and class limits is essentially arbitrary. Two individuals will often come up with different ways of arranging data into classes. Nevertheless, certain rules and guidelines are available. The only firm rule in grouping data is that the classes be both mutually exclusive and all-inclusive. **Mutually exclusive classes** means that the classes must be arranged so that every piece of data can be placed in only one class. In particular, this means selecting class limits so that an item cannot fall into two classes. **All-inclusive classes** are classes that together contain all the data.

Every class in a frequency distribution has *expressed* class limits. Expressed class limits are those shown in the frequency distribution. For example, a frequency distribution of employee ages might have the following expressed class limits:

$$\text{Expressed lower limits} \quad \left\{ \begin{array}{l} 21\text{--}30 \\ 31\text{--}40 \\ 41\text{--}50 \\ 51\text{--}60 \end{array} \right\} \text{Expressed upper limits}$$
$$61\text{--}70$$

The **class width** is determined by counting the number of units between (and including) the lower and upper expressed class limits. For instance, the class width of the first class of the employee age frequency distribution is 10 years because 21, 22, 23, . . . , 30 gives 10 years.

To find the center of a class, called the **midpoint,** we apply the half-the-sum rule:

$$\boxed{\text{Midpoint} = \frac{(\text{lower limit} + \text{upper limit})}{2}}$$

For the employee age frequency distribution the midpoints are

Expressed Class Limits	Sum	Midpoint = Sum/2
21 to 30	51	25.5
31 to 40	71	35.5
41 to 50	91	45.5
51 to 60	111	55.5
61 to 70	131	65.5

Thus, for the first class, the value 25.5 is midway between the expressed class limits and is therefore the midpoint of this class.

As mentioned, the classes of a frequency distribution need to be developed such that they are mutually exclusive and all-inclusive. In addition, it is desirable to select class limits so that the actual observations are evenly distributed throughout the class interval. This means that if an age class has limits of "21–30," the ages within this class should be evenly spread between 21 and 30 inclusive. If most of the people are younger than 25, the limits "21–30" are not very representative of the data in this class.

An easy way to determine an approximate class width is to take the smallest and largest values in the raw data, subtract the two, and divide by the desired number of classes:

$$\boxed{\text{Class width} = \frac{\text{largest value} - \text{smallest value}}{\text{number of classes}}}$$

This will give a starting figure for class widths. You should also apply some common sense in developing the frequency distribution. For example, if the division gives class sizes of 4.817 years, round this off to 5 years. Also start your class limits at some easy-to-use value. If you have data on automobile weights, don't have 100-pound intervals starting at 1,805.6 pounds; start with 1,800 pounds.

If possible, have class intervals of equal size. Frequency distributions with equal class intervals are not only easier to understand, but will make later statistical analysis much simpler. However, constant intervals are not possible in many managerial applications because the data are **skewed.** Data are *skewed* when most observations are located relatively close together, but a few points are located in one direction far from the majority. Data that are not skewed are *symmetrical*.

Many data of interest to managers are skewed. Incomes in the United States form a skewed frequency distribution. The vast majority of incomes are less than $50,000, but a few individuals make much more than that. Class intervals wide enough to contain all observations using even twenty classes would be hundreds of thousands of dollars wide. Thus almost everyone would fall in the first interval, totally obscuring information in the data. However, if the intervals were $2,000, $5,000, or even $10,000 wide, many more than twenty intervals would be needed to contain all data points. The way out of this dilemma is to use open-ended intervals, or intervals of unequal sizes. *Open-ended intervals* occur when the first class contains no lower limit or the last data class contains no upper limit. Table 2–1 contains an open-ended interval, ''$17,500 and over.''

Data may be skewed by either direction; thus open-ended intervals or unequal intervals are common. Once again, they are necessary when the majority of data are contained within a limited range of values and a relatively few observations exist with extreme values.

Constructing a Frequency Distribution

The manager of a local department store is interested in what her store's sales values look like. Table 2–2 presents the raw data from a sample of sixty-four sales. What do the data in this form indicate to you?

The manager decides to construct a frequency distribution of the sample data. She elects to apply the $2^k \geq n$ rule. Since $n = 64$, she will start with six classes. To determine the class width, she divides the difference between the highest (74.95) and the lowest (0.97) value in the sample by the number of classes, as follows:

$$\text{Class width} = \frac{\$74.95 - \$0.97}{6}$$

$$= \$12.33$$

She rounds up to $12.50. She then picks a starting point of $0.00 and forms the following expressed classes:

$$
\begin{array}{ll}
\$ \ 0.00 \text{ and under} & \$12.50 \\
12.50 \text{ and under} & 25.00 \\
25.00 \text{ and under} & 37.50 \\
37.50 \text{ and under} & 50.00 \\
50.00 \text{ and under} & 62.50 \\
62.50 \text{ and under} & 75.00 \\
\end{array}
$$

$ 6.49	$ 8.90	$22.95	$16.30
7.19	11.97	74.95	13.39
18.63	4.44	24.99	11.99
1.29	13.88	69.99	4.44
34.98	8.12	8.99	61.98
12.95	64.88	35.95	6.99
21.25	24.99	1.26	11.99
68.99	9.97	3.97	9.97
9.98	3.99	4.35	7.49
0.97	14.99	5.99	12.49
2.19	7.75	11.99	21.50
41.69	67.29	5.25	1.69
4.65	4.50	9.85	49.99
3.19	34.95	6.50	13.89
10.45	7.49	29.97	19.97
23.85	5.69	3.57	2.77

TABLE 2–2
Raw sales data, department store example

Note that the class limits are mutually exclusive and that no overlap exists between classes. Also the classes are all-inclusive since the smallest and largest elements are included. You should also note that the decision maker could have rounded the class width to a value such as $13.00 or even $15.00. Remember that the reason for grouping raw data into a frequency distribution is to make things easier to understand, so always develop class limits that are easy to work with.

With the class limits determined as shown, the manager now counts the number of values that fall into each class. The resulting frequency distribution is shown in table 2–3. The midpoint of each class has also been recorded for future use. For example, the midpoint for the second class is found using the half-the-sum rule, as follows:

$$\text{Midpoint} = \frac{12.50 + 25.0}{2}$$

$$= \frac{37.50}{2}$$

$$= \$18.75$$

Referring to table 2–3, the frequency column shows the number of sales values falling in each class. The **relative frequency** is the ratio of observations in a class to the total observations in all classes. Thus 21.875 percent of the sample sales values were in the class $12.50 and under $25.00. The relative frequency values are very useful for comparing two or more frequency distributions that have been developed from data sets with a different number of raw data. For example, this department store manager can say that slightly over 59 percent of the individual sales were under $12.50. This percentage could be compared meaningfully with the percentage of sales under $12.50 for another store regardless of the number of raw data available from the second store. A comparison of actual frequencies would not be meaningful if the sample sizes differed.

TABLE 2–3
Frequency distribution, department store sales

Sales Class	Midpoint	Frequency	Relative Frequency	Cumulative Frequency	Relative Cumulative Frequency
$ 0 and under $12.50	6.25	38	0.59375	38	0.59375
12.50 and under 25.00	18.75	14	0.21875	52	0.81250
25.00 and under 37.50	31.25	4	0.06250	56	0.87500
37.50 and under 50.00	43.75	2	0.03125	58	0.90625
50.00 and under 62.50	56.25	1	0.01563	59	0.92188
62.50 and under 75.00	68.75	5	0.07812	64	1.00000
Total		64	1.00000		

Table 2–3 contains two other columns: the **cumulative frequency** and the **relative cumulative frequency.** The *cumulative frequency* is the sum of the frequency of a particular class and all preceding classes. For example, we see in table 2–3 that fifty-six of the sales values in the sample were under $37.50. The *relative cumulative frequency* in a class is the cumulative frequency divided by the total observations in all classes. For example, 87.5 percent of the sales values in this sample were under $37.50.

Stem and Leaf Plots

An alternate method of organizing raw data is called **stem and leaf plotting.** Consider table 2–4, which contains data collected by a production foreman at a plywood mill. The data reflect the number of truckloads of plywood shipped per day for a sample of twenty-five days.

The stem and leaf plot is developed by first determining the **stem** and then adding **leaves.** With respect to the plywood data in table 2–4, the data contain at most two digits, so the stem is formed by the "tens" digit and the leaves are the "ones" digit. Figure 2–1 shows the stem and leaf plot for these data. Note that the stem values are placed to the left of the vertical line and the individual leaves on the right.

The stem and leaf plot shows that on most days between ten and twenty trucks loaded with plywood were shipped. It also indicates that the maximum number of trucks loaded in one day was thirty-two trucks.

A frequency distribution can easily be developed from a stem and leaf plot. Table 2–5 shows a frequency distribution for the plywood data.

TABLE 2–4
Trucks loaded per day

8	15	16	15	28
14	20	24	19	26
10	31	18	30	15
11	12	32	25	19
20	12	14	25	30

Stem	Leaves
0	8
1	4, 0, 1, 5, 2, 2, 6, 8, 4, 5, 9, 5, 9
2	0, 0, 4, 5, 5, 8, 6
3	1, 2, 0, 0

FIGURE 2–1
Stem and leaf plot, plywood company example

Class	Frequency
0 and under 10 loads	1
10 and under 20 loads	13
20 and under 30 loads	7
30 and under 40 loads	4
Total days	25

TABLE 2–5
Frequency distribution, plywood company example

SKILL DEVELOPMENT PROBLEMS FOR SECTION 2–1

The following set of problems is meant to test your understanding of the material in this section. Additional problems are found at the end of this chapter under this section heading.

1. Describe briefly each of the following:
   a. Class limits
   b. Relative frequency distribution
   c. Cumulative frequency distribution

2. Describe the difference between a frequency distribution and a relative frequency distribution.

3. Assume you are trying to construct a frequency distribution for the weights of people in this class. Describe the steps you would take.

4. Think of examples of skewed distributions. How would you select class limits for these distributions?

5. Go to the library, and from the *Statistical Abstract of the United States,* construct a frequency distribution for unemployment rate by state. Justify your choice of class limits and number of classes.

6. Suppose that the loan officer at Money First National Bank wants to obtain information about the loans she has made over the past five years. She has decided to develop a distribution showing the loan frequency by size of loan. A quick look at the data indicates that the smallest loan she made was for $1,000 and the largest loan was $25,000. She has decided to have ten classes in her distribution. Define the ten classes in terms of lower and upper limits. Determine the midpoints for each class developed.

7. The following data are a sample of sixty accounts receivable balances selected from accounts at the Wallingford Department Store.

a. Decide how many classes would be appropriate for these data and justify why you selected that number.

$ 39.93	$ 72.04	$ 69.04	$ 87.00	$ 55.55	$33.33
107.56	146.93	107.33	80.00	7.50	29.59
98.05	27.50	141.88	68.00	15.00	11.05
24.88	105.19	70.00	96.07	150.00	9.47
25.00	11.41	37.73	44.09	80.05	99.99
19.95	53.72	125.00	75.55	97.94	47.09
72.50	16.18	33.97	56.25	12.11	19.58
20.00	126.12	16.47	110.00	8.00	49.00
30.72	14.50	11.01	76.47	19.33	62.50
90.05	19.33	49.99	52.52	27.05	66.05

b. Using the number of classes you selected, develop a frequency distribution for the accounts receivable.

c. Write a one-paragraph statement describing the accounts receivable balances as reflected by the sample. (Remember that in business, report writing is an important way of conveying information.)

8. Comment on using the following classes in connection with the data given in problem 7.

a. $ 9.47–$19.46
 19.47– 29.46
   etc.

b. $ 5–$15
 15– 25
 25– 30
   etc.

c. $ 5 to under $35
 35 to under 45
 45 to under 55
   etc.

d. $16 to under $30
 31 to under 45
 46 to under 60
   etc.

PRESENTING DATA

2-2

The usefulness of a body of data depends on whether the individuals working with it are able to readily understand the information it contains. Data must be arranged in the

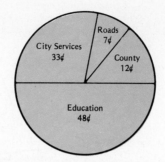

FIGURE 2–2
Pie chart, property-tax example

most understandable manner possible. In addition, the information should be arranged in an eye-catching way. Unfortunately, frequency distributions are often neither totally meaningful nor eye-catching. Because of this, *graphical representations* are often used to display statistical information. There are almost as many ways to present data as there are persons doing the presenting. The following sections discuss some of the most common forms of graphical data representation.

Pie Charts

An effective manner of presenting statistical data is with a **pie chart.** This method is often used by newspapers and magazines when national, state, or local government budgets are being determined. Pie charts are also used to show how a total has been used or divided. Perhaps the major advantage of a pie diagram is that it is extremely easy to understand. The entire circle, or ''pie,'' represents the total amount available, and the pieces are proportional to the amount of the total they represent. Figure 2–2 illustrates how a property-tax dollar was distributed in a midwestern city in 1989.

Pie charts can also be developed quite easily from a frequency distribution by using relative frequencies. Consider again the department store sales frequency distribution shown in table 2–3. Figure 2–3 shows the pie chart illustrating the percentage breakdown of sales in each of the six classes. In this example, the pie chart provides an effective picture of the relative frequency distribution.

Histograms

A **histogram** is a graphical picture of a frequency (or relative frequency) distribution. The number of observations in each class is represented by a rectangle whose base is equal to the class width and whose height is proportional to the frequency (or relative frequency) of cases belonging to that class. The vertical axis represents the class frequency and begins at the zero point. The horizontal axis represents the measure of interest, and the scale can begin with any conveniently low value.

The purpose of a histogram is to provide a visual picture of a frequency distribution. Relative differences in the areas of the rectangles correspond to relative differences in the number of observations between different classes.

When constructing a histogram, the measure for the item being considered is plot-

FIGURE 2–3
Pie chart, department store sales

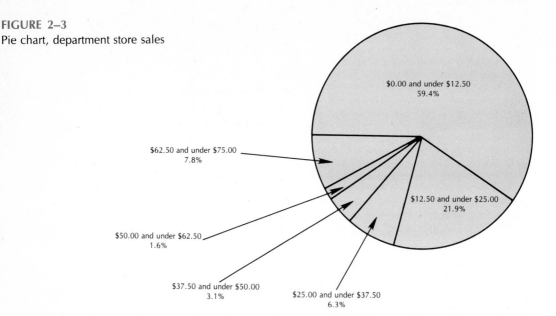

ted on the horizontal axis, and the appropriate frequency measure on the vertical axis. Figure 2–4 shows a histogram representing the frequency distribution of sales data shown in table 2–3.

Using Histograms in Decision Making

The following example demonstrates how histograms can assist a manager in a decision-making process.

Although you may not think of hospitals as business enterprises, in today's world they are very much businesses and must be operated as such to remain financially solvent. Some hospitals have decreasing patient admissions, whereas others are faced with overcrowded conditions. Those hospitals with decreasing admissions find themselves searching for new patients while at the same time trying to reduce costs without sacrificing quality health care. Overcrowded hospitals search for ways to satisfy their growing demand while at the same time maintaining high-quality care.

FIGURE 2–4

Histogram showing the distribution of daily store sales

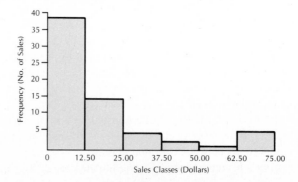

The Magic Valley Memorial Hospital is currently experiencing steady growth. By analyzing the financial records and patient admissions summaries, the administrator has concluded that the hospital is approaching full use. However, he also knows his ability to effectively allocate some resources (for instance patient rooms) is restricted. For example, if the pediatrics ward is full, the administrator cannot transfer children to the unused beds in the obstetrics department. To overcome the crowding problem, the administrator has decided to attempt to schedule admissions more effectively. Because of past resistance to advance scheduling by both patients and doctors, the administrator has decided to begin his efforts with those departments where the problem is greatest. To help identify these departments, the administrator has developed the frequency histograms shown in figure 2–5 from patient data collected during the past year. Note that for each histogram, the horizontal axis shows the number of beds used, and the vertical axis shows the number of days each number of beds was used. The capacity (total beds available) is also indicated on each histogram.

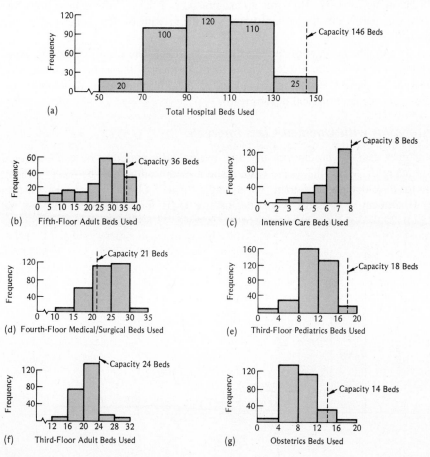

FIGURE 2–5
Histograms of patients census data, Magic Valley Memorial Hospital

TABLE 2–6
Frequency distribution with unequal-size class intervals, department store data

Sales Class	Frequency	Relative Frequency
$ 0.00– 7.49	24	0.375
7.50–14.99	19	0.297
15.00–29.99*	10	0.156
30.00–37.49	3	0.047
37.50–44.99	1	0.016
45.00–74.99*	7	0.109
Total	64	1.000

*Intervals having widths greater than $7.50.

Figure 2–5(a) is the frequency histogram for total hospital bed use (all departments combined). Based only on this distribution, it appears that the hospital is being used well below its capacity. However an examination of the bed-use distributions for each department points out the administrator's problem with overcrowding [see figures 2–5(b)–(g)].

The graphical view of the departmental patient data clearly indicates which departments are most overcrowded. Using this information, the administrator has decided to begin his patient-scheduling campaign in the fifth-floor adult department and the fourth-floor medical/surgical department.

Histograms with Unequal Class Intervals

Sometimes data can be most clearly and meaningfully presented by using *unequal-size class intervals*. When this is the case, a slight modification must be made in the procedure for developing a histogram. For example, table 2–6 shows a frequency distribution for department store sales with unequal-size class intervals. Note that the interval "15.00–29.99" is twice the width of the interval "7.50–14.99," and that the interval

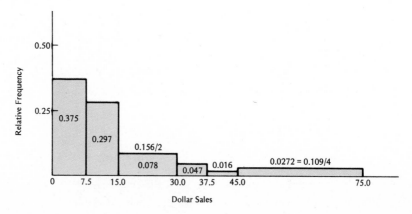

FIGURE 2–6
Relative frequency histogram with unequal class intervals, department store sales data

"45.00–74.99" is four times as wide. In developing a histogram for the relative frequency distribution, we must account for the extra width by reducing the height of the histogram proportionately. That is, for an interval having a width twice the normal size, the height of the associated frequency rectangle must be cut in half. Figure 2–6 illustrates this concept for the department store sales data.

Special care should be taken when using histograms to represent frequency distributions with unequal intervals. Even though the area of each rectangle represents the relative frequency, many people will automatically look at the height of each rectangle instead. Therefore, the possibility of misrepresenting the data always exists.

Cumulative Histogram and Ogive Graphs

Table 2–3 displays the cumulative frequency distribution for the department store sales data. Decision makers frequently find it useful to graph this cumulative frequency distribution to illustrate a particular point about the data. Two graphical methods are generally used to present cumulative frequency distributions. The first is a **cumulative frequency histogram.** Figure 2–7 shows a cumulative histogram developed from the information in table 2–3. Note that the vertical axis represents the cumulative frequency and the height of each rectangle is the cumulative frequency of the class shown on the horizontal axis and all preceding classes. Figure 2–7 shows that most of the data (52 of 64 data points) are contained in the first two classes.

A second graphical method for displaying cumulative distributions is an ogive. Figure 2–8 illustrates an ogive for the department store sales data. An **ogive** is con-

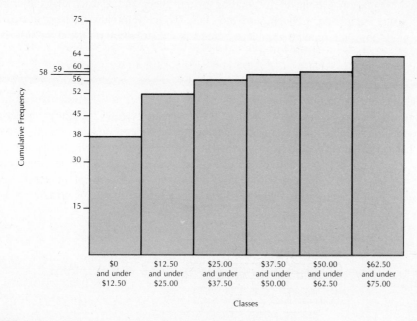

FIGURE 2–7
Cumulative frequency histogram, department store sales

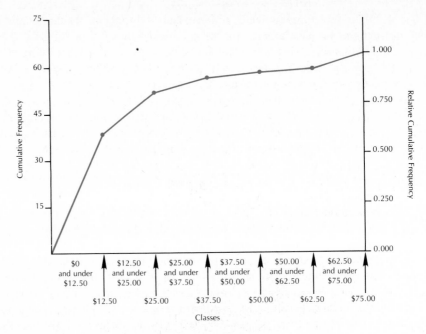

FIGURE 2–8
Cumulative ogive, department store sales

structed by placing a point corresponding to the upper end of each class at a height equal to the cumulative frequency of the class. These points then are connected. The ogive also shows the relative cumulative frequency distribution on the right-side axis.

Bar Charts

Bar charts are variations of histograms and are often used to illustrate data or to emphasize classes or categories of interest. For example, figure 2–9 shows a bar-chart representation of data collected in a recent survey of college students. In this example, each bar is the same length, representing 100 percent of those taking the course. From this we can visualize the relative rate of students passing and failing specific courses. Figure 2–10 uses a bar chart to illustrate the growth in number of homes heated by electricity in a western state. The bar chart is an effective means of presenting data to

FIGURE 2–9

Bar chart of pass/fail percentages by course

Failed	Passed
25%	English Composition
37%	Biology
40%	Math
20%	Statistics

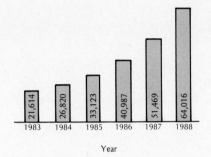

FIGURE 2–10
Bar chart of annual electricity use, number of homes with electrical heat

demonstrate a particular point. It is easy to see that electricity use has been rising rapidly in this western state since 1983. To avoid possibly misrepresenting the associated data, each bar in these graphs should be of equal width.

Time Series Plots

A **time series plot** is a graph of data that have been measured over time. For example, consider the Beltview Printing Company, which does virtually all forms of printing for businesses in the Miami, Florida, area. Table 2–7 shows data for sales and advertising expenses for the company over the ten-year period beginning in 1979. These data constitute **time series data.**

Figure 2–11 illustrates a time series plot where both sales and advertising are plotted against time. Time series plots like these are very useful for identifying how variables have changed over time. Here the plots show that both advertising and sales have increased over the ten-year period. Also, except for 1984 and 1985, relative changes in advertising and sales have been in the same direction.

Scatter Plots

A **scatter plot** is a two-dimensional graph of the ordered pairs of two variables. One variable is placed on the horizontal axis and the second variable is located on the vertical

Year	Sales	Advertising
1979	$117,000	$11,000
1980	205,000	54,000
1981	190,000	39,000
1982	300,000	65,000
1983	325,000	90,000
1984	400,000	75,000
1985	375,000	80,000
1986	340,000	70,000
1987	300,000	60,000
1988	340,000	75,000

TABLE 2–7
Time series data, Beltview Printing Company example

FIGURE 2–11
Time series plot, Beltview Printing Company example

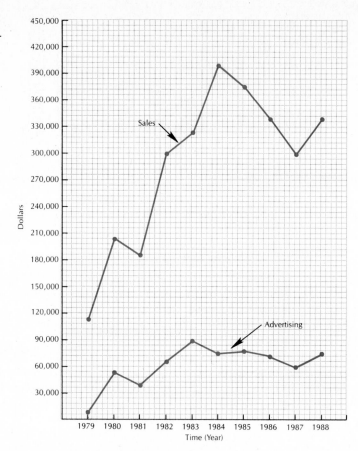

axis. For example, the J–Max Real Estate Agency has randomly selected a sample of eight homes from those that have sold during the past year in Madison, Wisconsin. For each of these eight homes, data have been recorded for the sales price, the number of square feet in the home, and the distance of the home from the airport. These data are presented in table 2–8.

TABLE 2–8
Scatter plot data, J–Max Real Estate Company example

Home	Sales Price	Square Feet	Miles to Airport
1	$ 95,000	1,750	0.50
2	117,000	2,150	1.00
3	95,000	1,500	3.00
4	145,000	2,200	2.50
5	80,000	1,900	0.25
6	70,000	1,800	0.20
7	110,000	2,000	1.50
8	77,000	1,900	0.30

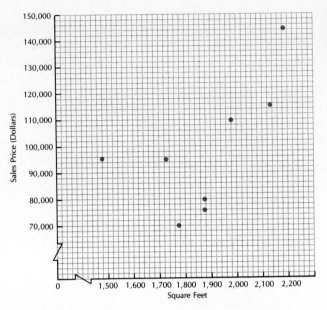

Figures 2–12 and 2–13 show the scatter plots for sales price versus square feet and for sales price versus distance to the airport, respectively. Scatter plots like these are useful for helping identify what, if any, relationship exists between two variables. For instance, figure 2–12 shows that, in general, larger homes tend to sell for more money. Figure 2–13 shows that, in general, the closer the home is to the airport, the lower the sales price.

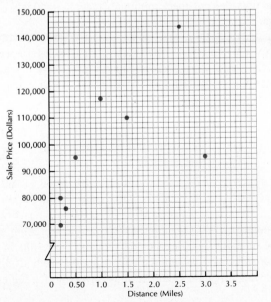

FIGURE 2–13
Sales price vs. distance scatter
plot, J–Max Real Estate Company
example

SKILL DEVELOPMENT PROBLEMS FOR SECTION 2–2

The following set of problems is meant to test your understanding of the material in this section. Additional problems are found at the end of this chapter under this section heading.

9. You work for the State Industrial Development Council. You are presently working on a financial services brochure to send to out-of-state companies. You are given the following data on banks in your state and are to present them in an eye-catching manner with a two-paragraph summary of what the data would mean to a company considering moving. Further, your boss has just said you need to include relative frequencies in your presentation.

Deposit Size (× $1 million)	Number Banks	Total Deposits (× $1 million)
Less than 5	2	7.2
5 to less than 10	7	52.1
10 to less than 25	6	111.5
25 to less than 50	3	95.4
50 to less than 100	2	166.6
100 to less than 500	2	529.8
Over 500	2	1,663.0

10. Your company is about to introduce a complete line of steel-belted radial tires. Because you are late entering the market, you are supposed to develop a new, hard-hitting advertising approach. You decide to put test tires on 100 taxis along the Alaskan pipeline. The following is a listing of how far the 100 taxis ran before one of the four tires did not meet minimum federal standards (rounded to the nearest thousand miles):

38	24	12	36	41	40	45	41	40	47
26	15	48	44	29	43	28	29	37	10
37	45	29	31	23	49	41	47	41	42
61	40	40	45	37	55	47	42	28	38
38	48	18	16	39	50	14	52	33	32
51	10	49	21	44	31	43	34	49	48
28	39	28	36	56	54	39	31	35	36
32	20	54	25	39	44	25	42	50	41
9	34	32	34	42	40	43	32	30	45
20	29	14	19	38	46	46	39	40	47

Although you don't want to be dishonest in presenting the results of your test, at the same time your job depends on showing the results in as favorable a light as possible. Organize and present the data using the methods discussed in this chapter and decide which method would be most favorable for selling the tires.

Your boss apparently delights in putting people on the spot. Make sure you can defend your choice, including how you determined the interval size and interval limits.

11. Ed Christianson has been asked by the director of marketing to make a presentation at next week's annual meeting of the Brown Manufacturing Company. The presentation concerns the company's advertising budget for the past year and the projected budget for the next year. In preparing for the meeting, Ed has obtained the following data:

Medium	This Year's Expenses	Next Year's Budget
Newspaper	$35,000	$40,000
Television	60,000	80,000
Trade Publications	25,000	20,000
Miscellaneous	10,000	10,000

Use these data to develop a bar chart that effectively shows both this year's expenses for advertising and next year's proposed budget.

12. Referring to problem 11, present the data in a pie chart. Do this presentation first using two separate pie charts, and then present both sets of data in one pie chart. Finally, develop a pie chart that shows how the increased advertising expenditure will be allocated the next year.

13. The American Accounting Association recently contracted with a consulting company to study issues pertaining to continuing education on the part of certified public accountants. As part of that study, the consulting firm selected a random sample of twenty accountants in New York state and collected data on a variety of variables, including the number of years since each accountant entered public accounting, the number of continuing education courses taken the past year, and the annual salary of the accountant. These data are shown in the following table.

Years Since Entering Public Accounting X_1	Number of Courses Taken Last Year X_2	Annual Salary X_3
11	2	$ 45,000
4	3	29,000
17	0	71,000
6	4	38,000
15	1	40,000
12	0	31,000
2	6	32,500
21	0	104,000
4	6	36,000
10	3	39,500
7	2	29,500

Continued.

Years Since Entering Public Accounting X_1	Number of Courses Taken Last Year X_2	Annual Salary X_3
11	1	54,000
13	0	44,000
15	0	47,000
4	3	29,500
9	1	37,000
23	0	41,000
10	1	36,000
14	0	56,000
3	5	23,500

a. Develop scatter plots of all three combinations of two variables. Discuss what (if anything) you can discern from the scatter plots.

b. Develop frequency distributions for each variable and then develop a histogram from each frequency distribution. Write a short report describing the data.

c. Develop a bar chart that shows (on the same chart) X_1 and X_2 by income (X_3). Discuss the advantage of presenting all these data together.

14. Discuss how bar charts and frequency histograms are similar and how they are different.

15. The following data represent expenditures on advertising over the period of 1978 to 1988 by the Swanson Lumber Company.

Year	Advertising
1978	$12,500
1979	14,600
1980	16,250
1981	19,800
1982	23,700
1983	22,700
1984	18,790
1985	23,500
1986	24,000
1987	25,600
1988	27,800

Construct a time series plot of the advertising variable and prepare a report that discusses this plot.

16. The Morrison Center for the performing arts has been operational since 1978. Below are the annual ticket sales for the center for the years 1978 through 1988.

Year	Sales
1978	$204,000
1979	275,000
1980	280,000
1981	299,000
1982	345,000
1983	368,000
1984	401,000
1985	344,000
1986	359,000
1987	405,000
1988	507,000

Prepare a time series plot for the sales data and write a short report describing what your graphs illustrate.

COMPUTER STATISTICAL SOFTWARE: AN INTRODUCTION

2-3

Most of you have probably had at least one computer course, and therefore have some knowledge of your school's computer system. Your instructor may choose to integrate a statistical software package into this course, and this likely will be your first exposure to statistical software. Although this text is not intended to provide instruction on how to use any particular statistical software, we will briefly discuss some concepts that are common to computer statistics software packages so that you will be better prepared to take advantage of the capabilities of the software package you may be asked to use.

Two terms you should know are *variable* and *case*. A **variable** is the label used to identify a factor being counted or measured. For instance, if a marketing research study is being conducted, one variable for which data might be collected is income. Thus, income is a variable. Other variables might be age and marital status. Data are usually collected for each person sampled for each variable of interest. Thus, a data set consists of data for one or more variables.

A **case** consists of data recorded for each variable of interest. For instance, in the marketing research example each person sampled would constitute a case since data would be collected for each person on each variable of interest. Thus, the number of cases is the number of people in the sample. In another example, a production manager might sample fifty items from the production line and record the weight and length of each item. Thus, he would have fifty cases and two variables (weight and length).

You can think of data as being arranged in a matrix where columns constitute the variables and rows constitute the cases. Table 2–9 illustrates this matrix concept. Most computer software packages associate the variables with a column number, so the data must be organized so that each case contains the variable data in the same order. Most statistical software also allows you to name the variable and refer to a variable by the name you have assigned.

TABLE 2–9
Data matrix concept

Cases	C1	C2	C3	Variables C4	C5	C6	. . .
1	·	·	·	·	·	·	·
2	·	·	·	·	·	·	·
3	·	·	·	DATA	·	·	·
4	·	·	·	·	·	·	·
·	·	·	·	·	·	·	·
·	·	·	·	·	·	·	·

Before the computer can perform any statistical computations, the data must be stored in the computer's memory. The software package does this by using some form of a READ command. The program will read the data for each variable case-by-case and store it in memory in matrix form. The data can be read from another computer file or the user can type in the data.

Statistical software packages can be either batch mode or interactive mode. Batch mode software requires that the user enter at one time all the commands that he or she wants the program to perform. After this list is entered, all the commands are executed in the order listed. Batch-oriented software is especially useful when the user has a large statistical analysis project that needs to be performed in one computer session. Generally, the user can issue some form of a RUN command and all the statistical commands listed will be executed.

An interactive software package operates in an interactive mode, which means that as the user issues a command, it is immediately executed. If the user needs to perform several statistical procedures, a command would be given and then executed, followed by another command which is executed, and so forth. The interactive approach is very convenient if a user has only a few procedures to perform at any one session. Further, this mode allows the results of one command to be observed before moving to the next command.

Many statistical software packages allow the user to create new variables from the original variables that were read into memory. This is accomplished in various ways depending on the software, but the end result is that new variables can be created for analysis. For instance, suppose the data set consists of forty cases with two variables, sales and advertising. We might be interested in analyzing the relationship between sales and advertising. We could do this using the data that were originally read into memory. However, we might also be interested in analyzing the relationship between sales and the square root of advertising. Because the square root of advertising was not one of the variables we initially read into memory, the new variable must be created by issuing a command that takes the square root of advertising for each of the forty cases. This new variable can be placed into a new column in the "data matrix" or can replace the original advertising variable. This process of creating new variables is called *variable transformation*.

Most statistical software packages allow you to select particular categories of cases from the total available cases. Suppose a data set representing a market survey is available. The data set contains fifteen variables and 400 cases. One variable represents sex, where if a case has a code of 1 for the sex variable, the respondent is female and if it has a code of 0, the respondent is male. You could analyze any of the remaining variables selecting only males (code = 0) or only females (code = 1).

Statistical software packages will differ somewhat in specific procedures. However, most packages will contain the programs necessary to cover the introductory techniques you will learn in this course.

A statistics software package called GS-STAT has been developed specifically to accompany this text. It is IBM PC- and PS-compatible and contains programs covering many of the topics covered in this text. Your instructor may have adopted the GS-STAT software to be used in conjunction with this course or he or she may have you use a different software package available at your university. Regardless, computers play an important role in applying statistics to decision-making situations. Thus, in many of the chapters in this text, we will present a section that illustrates the kind of computer output you can expect if you use statistical software. For most of our examples, we will use two software packages frequently found at colleges and universities. These are MINI-TAB and SPSS-X (Statistical Package for the Social Sciences). The exact form of the computer output will vary from software to software, but the same basic information will be present.

Computer Graphics and Statistical Software

Technological advances during the past several years have brought many changes to the way organizations operate. One area in which technological change has been widely implemented is in the employment of statistical techniques. Not too many years ago most statistical analysis was performed by hand or with a calculator; now virtually every decision maker has access to a mainframe and/or a microcomputer that has statistics software.

These software programs allow the user to perform statistical analyses quickly and accurately and to work with large or small data sets to do more extensive analysis than would be feasible by manual methods. This is especially true in the field of graphical analysis. Earlier in this chapter we described methods for manually developing bar charts, histograms, pie charts, and other graphical techniques for displaying data. All of these techniques and many others can be performed using a computer and the right statistical software.

To illustrate, we will use data gathered for KIVZ-Channel 5, in Middleton. KIVZ has started to slip in the Arbitron ratings. Alex McKinnon, the recently hired station manager, has decided to survey viewers in the market area to develop an information base before trying to formulate a strategy to increase viewer numbers. Table 2–10 shows the sample data for KIVZ-Channel 5, and table 2–11 provides the definition of each variable.

Figures 2–14, 2–15, and 2–16 illustrate three graphs created using a graphics package and the KIVZ-Channel 5 data. Note the level of sophistication that can be included in the bar charts shown in figures 2–14 and 2–15. Remember that the role of

TABLE 2–10
KIVZ-Channel 5 data

X_1	X_2	X_3	X_4	X_5	X_6	X_7	X_8	X_9	X_{10}	X_{11}	X_{12}	X_{13}	X_{14}	X_{15}	X_{16}	X_{17}	X_{18}	X_{19}	Respondents
2.	1.	5.	2.	4.	3.	3.	3.	1.	2.	3.	1.	2.	11.	18.	1.	60.	21,300.	12.	1
4.	4.	5.	5.	2.	2.	4.	3.	2.	1.	3.	1.	2.	6.	10.	2.	71.	22,800.	18.	2
1.	2.	3.	3.	2.	2.	4.	2.	1.	1.	3.	2.	2.	1.	7.	2.	20.	28,900.	10.	3
4.	4.	5.	5.	4.	3.	2.	2.	1.	1.	3.	2.	2.	1.	41.	4.	41.	30,100.	11.	4
1.	3.	3.	3.	3.	3.	3.	3.	2.	3.	1.	2.	1.	1.	1.	2.	26.	17,900.	21.	5
3.	2.	3.	5.	5.	4.	5.	4.	2.	1.	3.	1.	2.	15.	41.	3.	46.	27,100.	12.	6
3.	2.	1.	2.	3.	5.	4.	3.	2.	1.	3.	1.	2.	4.	34.	5.	34.	26,800.	8.	7
3.	3.	1.	3.	1.	3.	5.	2.	2.	1.	3.	1.	2.	4.	27.	4.	58.	13,600.	17.	8
1.	1.	2.	3.	4.	1.	5.	4.	2.	2.	3.	1.	2.	8.	9.	6.	31.	32,700.	6.	9
3.	2.	5.	4.	4.	4.	4.	4.	2.	2.	3.	1.	2.	11.	58.	2.	58.	24,700.	6.	10
3.	2.	3.	3.	3.	3.	3.	3.	1.	2.	3.	2.	2.	11.	41.	1.	81.	31,600.	11.	11
0.	2.	3.	4.	2.	2.	3.	3.	1.	2.	3.	1.	2.	2.	26.	3.	26.	21,100.	12.	12
3.	2.	4.	4.	4.	4.	5.	4.	2.	1.	3.	1.	2.	37.	65.	5.	65.	27,400.	15.	13
3.	2.	2.	1.	1.	3.	2.	2.	2.	1.	3.	1.	2.	11.	62.	6.	62.	23,500.	12.	14
3.	2.	3.	3.	5.	3.	3.	3.	1.	1.	3.	3.	2.	6.	59.	5.	59.	20,600.	4.	15
1.	1.	3.	3.	1.	3.	1.	3.	2.	2.	3.	1.	2.	1.	7.	2.	29.	30,300.	8.	16
3.	2.	3.	4.	2.	3.	4.	3.	1.	1.	3.	1.	2.	5.	26.	2.	28.	27,000.	13.	17
4.	2.	3.	2.	3.	4.	3.	4.	2.	2.	3.	1.	1.	3.	15.	2.	45.	39,200.	6.	18
3.	3.	3.	2.	3.	2.	5.	3.	2.	2.	3.	1.	2.	3.	10.	6.	40.	23,300.	11.	19
2.	2.	4.	4.	4.	4.	4.	1.	2.	3.	1.	2.	1.	1.	31.	4.	38.	20,000.	10.	20
4.	4.	2.	4.	3.	2.	3.	2.	2.	1.	1.	1.	1.	2.	26.	6.	26.	20,000.	10.	21
3.	2.	4.	5.	3.	5.	2.	4.	2.	2.	1.	2.	2.	35.	50.	6.	50.	34,100.	10.	22
2.	2.	3.	1.	1.	2.	3.	5.	2.	2.	3.	1.	2.	12.	21.	6.	21.	32,100.	17.	23
1.	2.	4.	1.	4.	3.	5.	3.	2.	1.	3.	2.	1.	11.	21.	2.	59.	25,600.	9.	24
3.	2.	3.	1.	4.	5.	3.	1.	3.	2.	3.	1.	2.	15.	43.	2.	43.	26,400.	12.	25
1.	3.	3.	3.	3.	3.	3.	1.	2.	3.	2.	2.	1.	1.	21.	5.	21.	24,100.	13.	26
1.	3.	4.	3.	4.	3.	4.	4.	2.	1.	3.	1.	2.	2.	2.	2.	42.	25,800.	21.	27
1.	3.	2.	5.	3.	1.	3.	1.	1.	4.	2.	2.	4.	20.	5.	51.	16,500.	6.		28
3.	2.	3.	3.	4.	3.	3.	3.	2.	2.	3.	1.	2.	10.	17.	4.	40.	22,800.	12.	29
3.	3.	2.	4.	4.	5.	5.	4.	2.	2.	3.	1.	2.	10.	35.	4.	67.	23,300.	16.	30
4.	2.	3.	3.	3.	3.	3.	3.	2.	3.	2.	2.	4.	22.	4.	24.	23,300.	7.		31
1.	3.	3.	4.	5.	3.	2.	3.	2.	1.	3.	1.	2.	11.	11.	2.	48.	22,600.	16.	32
2.	1.	5.	4.	4.	5.	5.	4.	2.	1.	3.	2.	2.	2.	11.	4.	40.	26,700.	12.	33
3.	2.	3.	3.	2.	3.	2.	3.	1.	1.	1.	3.	2.	15.	21.	6.	21.	22,500.	5.	34
2.	2.	3.	4.	2.	3.	5.	3.	2.	2.	3.	1.	2.	3.	3.	5.	47.	22,900.	12.	35
3.	3.	4.	5.	5.	5.	4.	3.	1.	2.	3.	1.	2.	12.	20.	5.	55.	24,500.	13.	36
1.	3.	3.	3.	3.	3.	3.	2.	1.	3.	2.	2.	2.	15.	61.	6.	61.	22,300.	17.	37
1.	1.	3.	4.	2.	3.	3.	3.	2.	2.	3.	1.	1.	2.	6.	5.	45.	27,600.	13.	38
3.	3.	4.	5.	1.	5.	5.	3.	2.	2.	3.	2.	1.	1.	7.	5.	37.	16,500.	20.	39
3.	2.	4.	4.	5.	4.	4.	4.	2.	2.	3.	1.	2.	22.	50.	3.	58.	24,000.	6.	40
2.	1.	4.	4.	5.	3.	3.	4.	2.	1.	3.	1.	2.	11.	15.	5.	52.	18,800.	18.	41
3.	2.	4.	5.	5.	5.	3.	5.	2.	1.	3.	2.	1.	2.	7.	5.	24.	28,000.	9.	42
1.	1.	1.	5.	2.	5.	4.	2.	2.	2.	2.	1.	1.	17.	17.	2.	31.	27,700.	14.	43
3.	2.	4.	3.	4.	5.	3.	4.	2.	1.	3.	1.	2.	12.	67.	6.	68.	22,100.	17.	44
1.	2.	4.	3.	5.	4.	4.	4.	2.	2.	3.	1.	2.	3.	3.	2.	30.	23,900.	13.	45
4.	4.	3.	3.	1.	2.	3.	2.	2.	2.	3.	1.	2.	2.	35.	6.	35.	21,500.	17.	46
3.	2.	3.	5.	3.	3.	5.	3.	2.	1.	3.	1.	1.	19.	42.	4.	66.	26,900.	15.	47
2.	1.	3.	3.	3.	3.	3.	2.	1.	3.	3.	3.	2.	17.	27.	3.	50.	25,100.	9.	48
2.	3.	3.	1.	3.	5.	1.	3.	1.	2.	3.	2.	2.	13.	40.	2.	40.	23,400.	16.	49
2.	4.	5.	2.	1.	2.	1.	4.	1.	2.	3.	1.	2.	7.	30.	5.	33.	31,400.	6.	50

TABLE 2–11
KIVZ-Channel 5, identification of variables

Variable	Question & Response
X_1:	On which of the following channels do you most frequently watch national network news at 5:30 P.M.? (1) Channel 5 (2) Channel 3 (3) Channel 8 (4) Undecided
X_2:	On which of the following channels do you most frequently watch local news at 6:00 P.M.? (1) Channel 3 (2) Channel 8 (3) Channel 5 (4) Undecided
X_3:	Considering the local news station you most frequently watch, how would you rate the station's coverage of local news? (1) Poor (2) Fair (3) Good (4) Very Good (5) Excellent
X_4:	Considering the local news station you most frequently watch, how would you rate the station's sports coverage? (1) Poor (2) Fair (3) Good (4) Very Good (5) Excellent
X_5:	Considering the local news station that you most frequently watch, how would you rate the station's weather report? (1) Poor (2) Fair (3) Good (4) Very Good (5) Excellent
X_6:	Considering the local news station that you most frequently watch, how would you rate the station's anchor newcaster? (1) Poor (2) Fair (3) Good (4) Very Good (5) Excellent
X_7:	Considering the local news station that you most frequently watch, how would you rate the station's sportscaster? (1) Poor (2) Fair (3) Good (4) Very Good (5) Excellent
X_8:	Considering the local news station that you most frequently watch, how would you rate the overall news performance? (1) Poor (2) Fair (3) Good (4) Very Good (5) Excellent
X_9:	I believe the network news station I prefer to watch at 5:30 P.M. is an important influence regarding which local news I usually watch. (1) True (2) False (3) Undecided
X_{10}:	The head of this household is: (1) Male (2) Female
X_{11}:	The head of this household is: (1) Single (2) Divorced (3) Married (4) Other
X_{12}:	How many people living in this household are employed full time? _____
X_{13}:	Are you buying or renting (leasing) the home you now live in? (1) Renting/leasing (2) Buying
X_{14}:	How many years have you lived at this residence? _____
X_{15}:	How many years have you lived in this state? _____
X_{16}:	Indicate the highest level of formal education of the head of this household: (1) Grade school (2) Some college (3) Vocational training (4) High school (5) College graduate (6) Graduate work
X_{17}:	How old is the head of this household? _____
X_{18}:	Please indicate the total household annual income. _____
X_{19}:	Approximately how many hours per week is the television turned on in your household? _____

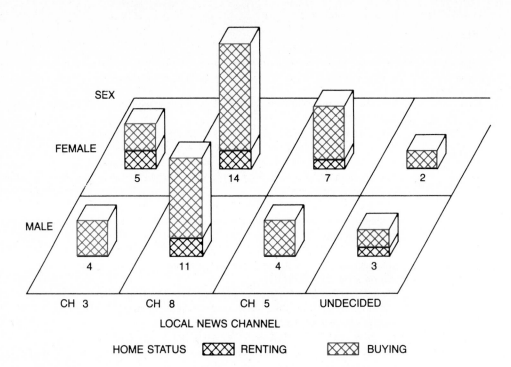

FIGURE 2–14
Three-dimensional bar chart, KIVZ-Channel 5 home ownership analysis

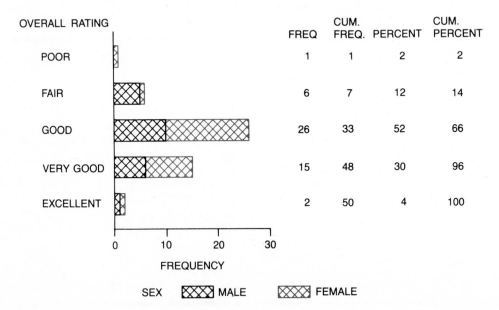

OVERALL RATING	FREQ	CUM. FREQ.	PERCENT	CUM. PERCENT
POOR	1	1	2	2
FAIR	6	7	12	14
GOOD	26	33	52	66
VERY GOOD	15	48	30	96
EXCELLENT	2	50	4	100

FIGURE 2–15
Bar chart, KIVZ-Channel 5 overall news ratings analysis

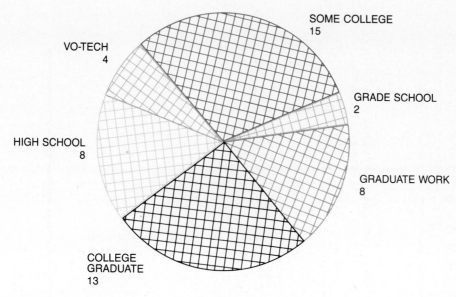

FIGURE 2–16
Pie chart, KIVZ-Channel 5 education level distribution

graphical data presentation is to help the decision maker obtain information from a data set. Computer graphics is an important tool in this process.

The graphs shown in figures 2–14, 2–15, and 2–16 are only a few examples of graphics you can create with graphics software and a plotter. In the next section we show some alternative computer applications that can be performed without the aid of special graphics capabilities.

COMPUTER APPLICATIONS

2-4

The purpose of this section is to show examples of computer output from two software programs, SPSS-X and MINITAB. We will use the KIVZ-Channel 5 data as the basis for these examples and demonstrate the type of output you can expect if you run SPSS-X, MINITAB, or a similar statistical software package. If you do not have access to a computer and statistical software, these examples provide an overview of what the computer can offer. (Other chapters in the text also have sections like this one showing computer applications based on the KIVZ-Channel 5 data.) Note that these data are arranged in matrix format, with columns representing variables and rows representing cases.

The TV station's staff conducted a survey of people in the station's viewing area. For descriptive purposes, the manager would like to see a frequency distribution and histogram for education level of the viewers. Table 2–12 shows the output obtained from the MINITAB software. Note that this program formats the histogram a little

TABLE 2-13
SPSS-X computer output, crosstabulation—KIVZ-Channel 5, variable X_2 by variable X_{16}

```
VAR02      LOCAL NEWS STATION      - - - C R O S S T A B U L A T I O N   O F - - -
                                              BY VAR16                EDUCATION

           VAR16
     COUNT I
           IGRADE SC SOME COL VOTECH HIGH SCH COLLEGE  GRADUATE  ROW
           IHOOL    LEGE             OOL      GRAD     WORK      TOTAL
           I  1.00I  2.00I   3.00I   4.00I    5.00I    6.00I
VAR02      ------+-------+-------+-------+--------+---------+---------+
      1.00 I   1 I    2 I    1 I     1 I      3 I       1 I      9
CHANNEL 3  I     I      I      I       I        I         I     18.0
           ------+-------+-------+-------+--------+---------+---------+
      2.00 I   1 I    8 I    3 I     4 I      5 I       4 I     25
CHANNEL 8  I     I      I      I       I        I         I     50.0
           ------+-------+-------+-------+--------+---------+---------+
      3.00 I     I    4 I      I     2 I      4 I       1 I     11
CHANNEL 5  I     I      I      I       I        I         I     22.0
           ------+-------+-------+-------+--------+---------+---------+
      4.00 I     I    1 I      I     1 I      1 I       2 I      5
UNDECIDED  I     I      I      I       I        I         I     10.0
           ------+-------+-------+-------+--------+---------+---------+
    COLUMN     2      15      4       8       13        8       50
    TOTAL    4.0    30.0    8.0    16.0     26.0     16.0    100.0


NUMBER OF MISSING OBSERVATIONS =      0
```

*SPSS-X Procedure
  CROSSTABS TABLES = VAR02 BY VAR16

differently than did our manual examples presented earlier in this chapter. Figure 2–17 shows the MINITAB commands that generated the output shown.

Suppose that the TV station manager also would like to see a joint frequency distribution for responses about the station watched for local news and education level. A joint frequency distribution is frequently called a *crosstabulation*. Table 2–13 shows

```
EDUCAT

MIDDLE OF        NUMBER OF
INTERVAL         OBSERVATIONS
  1.00               2      **
  2.00              15      ***************
  3.00               4      ****
  4.00               8      ********
  5.00              13      *************
  6.00               8      ********
```

TABLE 2–12
MINITAB computer output, histogram and frequency distribution—KIVZ-Channel 5, Variable X_{16} (education)

```
MTB> READ 'KIVZ5' INTO C1-C19
MTB> NAME C16 'EDUCAT'
MTB> OUTUNIT = 'PRINTER'
MTB> HISTOGRAM C16, 1, 1
```

FIGURE 2–17
MINITAB commands—frequency distribution and histogram

```
UNNUMBERED
TITLE DESCRIPTIVE STATISTICS EXAMPLES
FILE HANDLE KIVZ NAME='KIVZ DATA C'
DATA LIST FILE=KIVZ LIST/VAR01 TO VAR19
VARIABLE LABELS
   VAR01 'NATIONAL NEWS STATION'
   VAR02 'LOCAL NEWS STATION'
   VAR03 'NEWS RATING'
   VAR04 'SPORTS RATING'
   VAR05 'WEATHER RATING'
   VAR06 'ANCHOR RATING'
   VAR07 'SPORTSCASTER RATING'
   VAR08 'OVERALL RATING'
   VAR09 'NATIONAL INFLUENCE'
   VAR10 'SEX'
   VAR11 'MARITAL STATUS'
   VAR12 'NUMBER EMFLOYED'
   VAR13 'HOME STATUS '
   VAR14 'YEARS AT RESIDENCE'
   VAR15 'YEARS IN STATE'
   VAR16 'EDUCATION'
   VAR17 'AGE'
   VAR18 'INCOME'
   VAR19 'HOURS OF TV'
VALUE LABELS
   VAR01 1 'CHANNEL 5' 2 'CHANNEL 3' 3 'CHANNEL 8' 4 'UNDECIDED'/
   VAR02 1 'CHANNEL 3' 2 'CHANNEL 8' 3 'CHANNEL 5' 4 'UNDECIDED'/
   VAR03 TO VAR08 1 'POOR' 2 'FAIR' 3 'GOOD' 4 'VERY GOOD' 5 'EXCEL'/
   VAR09 1 'TRUE' 2 'FALSE' 3 'UNDECIDED'/
   VAR10 1 'MALE' 2 'FEMALE'/
   VAR11 1 'SINGLE' 2 'DIVORCED' 3 'MARRIED' 4 'OTHER'/
   VAR13 1 'RENTING' 2 'BUYING'/
   VAR16 1 'GRADE SCHOOL' 2 'SOME COLLEGE' 3 'VOTECH' 4 'HIGH SCHOOL'
         5 'COLLEGE GRAD' 6 'GRADUATE WORK'
CROSSTABS TABLES= VAR02 BY VAR16
```

FIGURE 2–18
SPSS-X commands—crosstabulation

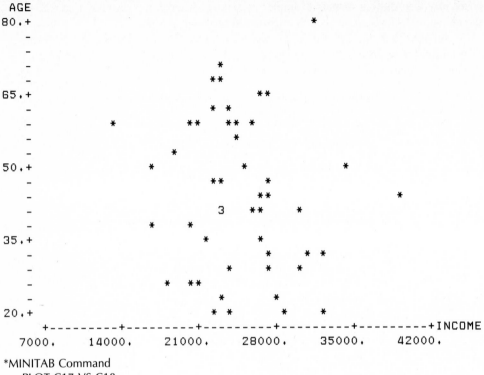

*MINITAB Command
   PLOT C17 VS C18

FIGURE 2–19
MINITAB computer output, scatter plot—KIVZ-Channel 5, variable X_{17} (age) vs. variable X_{18} (income)

the computer output using the SPSS-X software. Each square or cell in table 2–13 shows the joint frequency of response for variables X_2 and X_{16}. Figure 2–18 shows the SPSS-X program statements.

Both SPSS-X and MINITAB can produce other types of graphical output. For instance, figure 2–19 shows a scatter plot for variables X_{17} (age) and X_{18} (income) which was developed using MINITAB (see figure 2–20 for MINITAB program statements). SPSS-X was used to develop the bar chart shown in figure 2–21 for responses to variable X_8 (overall news performance rating). Figure 2–22 shows the SPSS-X program statements.

These are but a few of the possible descriptive outputs possible from these two software packages. Other software packages will have different options and likely will

FIGURE 2–20
MINITAB commands—scatter plot

```
MTB> READ 'KIVZ5' INTO C1-C19
MTB> NAME C17 'AGE'
MTB> NAME C18 'INCOME'
MTB> OUTUNIT = 'PRINTER'
MTB> PLOT C17 VS C18
```

VAR08   OVERALL RATING

VALUE LABEL	VALUE	FREQUENCY	PERCENT	VALID PERCENT	CUM PERCENT
POOR	1.00	1	2.0	2.0	2.0
FAIR	2.00	6	12.0	12.0	14.0
GOOD	3.00	26	52.0	52.0	66.0
VERY GOOD	4.00	15	30.0	30.0	96.0
EXCEL	5.00	2	4.0	4.0	100.0
		-------	-------	-------	
	TOTAL	50	100.0	100.0	

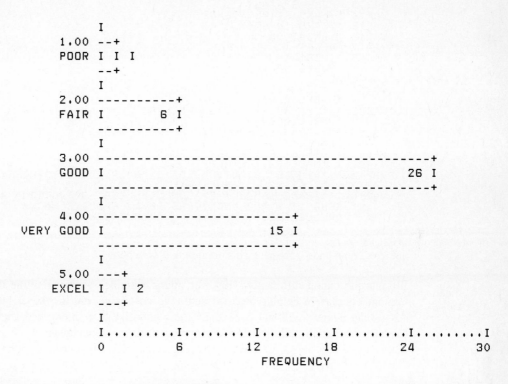

```
            I
    1.00  --+
    POOR  I I I
          --+
            I
    2.00  ----------+
    FAIR  I     6 I
          ----------+
            I
    3.00  ------------------------------------------+
    GOOD  I                                  26 I
          ------------------------------------------+
            I
    4.00  -----------------------+
VERY GOOD  I              15 I
          -----------------------+
            I
    5.00  ---+
   EXCEL  I  I 2
          ---+
            I
          I..........I..........I..........I..........I..........I
          0          6         12         18         24         30
                                FREQUENCY
```

VALID CASES   50   MISSING CASES   0

*SPSS-X Procedure
      FREQUENCIES VARIABLE = VAR08/BARCHART/

FIGURE 2–21
SPSS-X computer output, bar chart—KIVZ-Channel 5, variable X_8 (overall news rating)

```
UNNUMBERED
TITLE DESCRIPTIVE STATISTICS EXAMPLES
FILE HANDLE KIVZ NAME='KIVZ DATA C'
DATA LIST FILE=KIVZ LIST/VAR01 TO VAR19
VARIABLE LABELS
  VAR01 'NATIONAL NEWS STATION'
  VAR02 'LOCAL NEWS STATION'
  VAR03 'NEWS RATING'
  VAR04 'SPORTS RATING'
  VAR05 'WEATHER RATING'
  VAR06 'ANCHOR RATING'
  VAR07 'SPORTSCASTER RATING'
  VAR08 'OVERALL RATING'
  VAR09 'NATIONAL INFLUENCE'
  VAR10 'SEX'
  VAR11 'MARITAL STATUS'
  VAR12 'NUMBER EMPLOYED'
  VAR13 'HOME STATUS'
  VAR14 'YEARS AT RESIDENCE'
  VAR15 'YEARS IN STATE'
  VAR16 'EDUCATION'
  VAR17 'AGE'
  VAR18 'INCOME'
  VAR19 'HOURS OF TV'
VALUE LABELS
  VAR01 1 'CHANNEL 5' 2 'CHANNEL 3' 3 'CHANNEL 8' 4
        'UNDECIDED'/
  VAR02 1 'CHANNEL 3' 2 'CHANNEL 8' 3 'CHANNEL 5' 4
        'UNDECIDED'/
  VAR03 TO VAR08 1 'POOR' 2 'FAIR' 3 'GOOD' 4 'VERY GOOD' 5
        'EXCEL'/
  VAR09 1 'TRUE' 2 'FALSE' 3 'UNDECIDED'/
  VAR10 1 'MALE' 2 'FEMALE'/
  VAR11 1 'SINGLE' 2 'DIVORCED' 3 'MARRIED' 4 'OTHER'/
  VAR13 1 'RENTING' 2 'BUYING'/
  VAR16 1 'GRADE SCHOOL' 2 'SOME COLLEGE' 3 'VOTECH' 4 'HIGH
        SCHOOL' 5 'COLLEGE GRAD' 6 ' GRADUATE WORK'
        FREQUENCIES VARIABLE = VAR08/BARCHART/
```

FIGURE 2–22
SPSS-X commands—frequency distribution and bar chart

format the output differently. However, these examples demonstrate the potential that computers play in helping describe data. We encourage you to study tables 2–12 and 2–13 and figures 2–19 and 2–21 and write a narrative to go along with them. This will help you see more fully the role of graphical statistical techniques.

CONCLUSIONS

2-5 This chapter has introduced some of the most commonly used statistical techniques for organizing data and presenting them in a meaningful way to aid in the decision-making process. Just organizing raw data into a frequency distribution is a major step in transferring data into information. We have outlined the steps for developing frequency distributions and for producing histograms.

The chapter also has introduced other graphical techniques for displaying data to make them more usable to a decision maker. You are limited only by your imagination in the choices for effective graphical data displays. Bar charts, pie charts, scatter plots, and time series plots are among the more commonly used techniques.

Recent developments in statistical software packages have made graphical representation of data much easier. In this chapter we have demonstrated some possible graphical output from two commonly used software packages: SPSS-X, and MINITAB. Output from these two packages will be presented at the ends of many following chapters.

CHAPTER GLOSSARY

all-inclusive classes The frequency distribution classes that include all raw data.

bar chart A graph used to display data or to emphasize the categories into which data have been divided.

case Data recorded for each variable of interest.

class midpoint The center point between the upper and lower limits of a class in a frequency distribution.

class width The number of units between the lower class limit and upper class limit of a frequency class.

cumulative frequency distribution A distribution that represents the frequency of observations equal to or less than a particular class limit or value.

frequency distribution A way in which data are arranged, showing the number of cases in each category or class.

frequency histogram A graphical representation of a frequency or relative frequency distribution. The frequency of cases in each class is represented by a rectangle with a base equal to the class width and a height proportional to the frequency of cases belonging to the class.

mutually exclusive classes Frequency classes that have boundaries that do not overlap.

ogive A graph of a cumulative frequency distribution.

pie chart A graph drawn in the form of a circle, with slices sized proportionally to percentages that each category is of the whole.

relative frequency The percentage of observations falling within a particular class.

scatter plot A two-dimensional plot of the ordered pairs of two variables.

skewed distribution A distribution that has more than half of the observations falling above or below the midpoint of the center class.

time series data Data measured over time.

time series plot A graph of time series data. Usually the horizontal axis is the time variable and the vertical axis is the variable being measured.

variable The label used to identify a factor being counted or measured.

ADDITIONAL PROBLEMS

Section 2–1

17. The claims manager at Handover Insurance Company has been collecting data on the size of each claim paid by the company this month. A total of 500 claims were paid, with the smallest one being $44.00 and the largest one being $29,000.

    a. If a grouped data-frequency distribution is to be constructed, how many class intervals would you suggest?

    b. Based upon your answer to part a, assuming you want equal width classes, what should the class width be for each class?

    c. Based upon your responses to parts a and b, construct the intervals and determine the class midpoints.

18. The following data represent the commuting distances for employees of the Pay-and-Carry Department store. The personnel manager for Pay-and-Carry would like you to develop a stem and leaf plot and frequency distribution for these data.

Commuting Distance (Miles)

3.5	2.0	4.0	2.5	0.3	1.0	12.0	17.5	3.0	3.5	6.5	7.0	9.0
3.0	2.4	2.7	4.0	9.0	16.0	3.5	0.5	2.5	1.0	0.7	1.5	1.4
12.0	9.2	8.3	4.0	2.0	1.0	3.0	7.5	3.2	2.0	1.0	3.5	3.6
1.9	2.0	3.0	1.5	0.4	2.0	3.0	6.4	11.0	2.5			

19. The McGiven Construction Company keeps records of maintenance performed on all its construction equipment. The following frequency distribution shows the maintenance data where the classes represent the number of hours of operation until a mechanical breakdown occurred.

Class	Frequency
0 and under 20 hours	5
20 and under 40 hours	20
40 and under 60 hours	30
60 and under 80 hours	27
80 and under 100 hours	50
over 100 hours	20

    a. How many total breakdowns are represented by the data in the frequency distribution?

    b. Describe in your own words what the value 5 means in the frequency column for the class 0 and under 20 hours.

    c. Develop the relative frequency distribution for these breakdown data.

    d. Develop both the cumulative and relative cumulative frequency distributions for the breakdown data.

20. Wendy Harrington is a staff accountant at a regional accounting firm in Miami, Florida. One of her clients has had a problem with the cash register balancing at the end of the day. Because several clerks work out of the same cash register, it is not possible to determine if only one person is at fault. Wendy has made a study of the ending shortage or overages for the past thirty days when the cash register didn't balance and has recorded the following data:

Amount Over or (Under)

$12.00	(2.55)	13.05	(55.20)	10.00	(18.00)
(11.00)	6.35	(19.02)	(33.00)	11.00	14.00
(10.00)	9.50	23.00	(16.00)	8.30	2.00
(24.00)	2.38	20.01	(43.50)	17.20	(41.04)
11.00	(19.33)	23.01	(0.34)	1.01	(23.04)

a. Develop a frequency distribution for these data.

b. Write a short report describing the data. Reference the frequency distribution, relative frequency distribution, cumulative frequencies, and any other pertinent factors in your report.

21. A large supermarket in Dallas, Texas, has been having trouble with bad checks. A management intern was given the task of studying the bad checks to determine whether there was a way to anticipate which checks might be bad in advance. She began by examining 300 bad checks taken in the previous month and recording the check number of each and the amount of the check. The check numbers ranged from 0022 to 3456 and the amount of the bad checks ranged from $4.23 to $109.05. To begin with, the intern planned to develop frequency distributions for each of these two factors.

a. How many classes would you recommend that she use in developing a grouped data frequency distribution?

b. If she wants equal class widths, what should the class width be for each variable being studied?

c. In doing the analysis, do you think it would be helpful to also look at checks that were good? Explain why or why not.

Section 2–2

22. The Green Glow Lawn Company spreads liquid fertilizer on lawns. They charge by the square foot of the lawn, so they have good records of the lawn sizes for their customers. Below is a frequency distribution for lawn size:

Class	Frequency
Lawn Size (sq. ft.)	f_i
0 and under 400	8
400 and under 800	12
800 and under 1200	20
1200 and under 1600	50
1600 and under 2000	125
2000 and under 2400	103
2400 and under 2800	24

a. Develop a histogram from the frequency distribution.
b. Determine the relative frequency distribution for the lawn sizes and make a pie chart that represents the data. Be sure to label the pie chart correctly.

23. Locate two examples each of pie charts, histograms, and bar charts in current business periodicals and write a short report that summarizes what the charts are showing. Make sure you read the article associated with the charts. Then comment on how effective you feel these charts and graphs have been in displaying the data.

24. The Minnesota State Fishing Bureau has contracted with a university biologist to study the length of fish caught in Minnesota lakes. The biologist has collected data on a sample of 1,000 fish caught and developed the following relative frequency distribution.

Class	Relative Frequency
Length (inches)	Rf_i
8 and under 10	0.22
10 and under 12	0.15
12 and under 14	0.25
14 and under 16	0.24
16 and under 18	0.06
18 and under 20	0.05
20 and under 22	0.03

a. Construct a frequency distribution from this relative frequency distribution and then produce a histogram based upon the frequency distribution.
b. Construct a pie chart from the relative frequency distribution. Discuss which of the pie chart or histogram you feel is more effective in presenting the fish length data.
c. Construct a cumulative ogive graph for the fish length data and write a short paragraph to accompany the graph.

25. Michael Gordon is the regional sales manager for American Toys, Inc. Recently, he collected data on weekly sales (in dollars) for the fifteen stores in his region. He also collected data on the number of sales clerk work hours during the week for each of the stores. The data are as follows:

Store	Sales	Hours	Store	Sales	Hours
1	$23,300	120	9	$27,886	140
2	$25,600	135	10	$54,156	300
3	$19,200	96	11	$34,080	254
4	$10,211	102	12	$25,900	180
5	$19,330	240	13	$36,400	270
6	$35,789	190	14	$25,760	175
7	$12,540	108	15	$31,500	256
8	$43,150	234			

a. Develop a scatter plot of these data.

b. Based on the scatter plot, what, if any, conclusions might the sales manager reach with respect to the relationship between sales and number of clerk hours worked? Do any stores stand out as being different? Discuss.

STATE DEPARTMENT OF TRANSPORTATION CASE STUDY PROBLEMS

The following questions and problems pertain directly to the State Department of Transportation case study and data base introduced in chapter 1. The questions and problems were written assuming that you will have access to a computer and appropriate statistical software. The data base containing 100 observations and seventeen variables is shown in table 1C–1 in chapter 1.

1. Herb Kriner has asked you to develop a frequency distribution for all nominal and ordinal variables and prepare a short written report that summarizes these frequency distributions.

2. Prepare an ungrouped frequency distribution for the driving record variables, X_1–X_6. Construct a frequency histogram for each variable and then write a short report to Herb Kriner informing him of the results.

3. Variable X_9 is the age of the owner/driver. Develop a grouped data frequency distribution with six classes of equal width. Then construct a frequency histogram from this distribution.

4. Develop a crosstabulation table with X_{17}, liability insurance status, as the row variable and variable X_{11}, knowledge of the law, as the column variable. Write a report to Herb Kriner describing the results of this crosstabulation. Also indicate the advantage of using crosstabulation versus looking at the two variables individually.

5. Herb Kriner is interested in knowing the percentage of owners/drivers who are not employed who also do not carry liability insurance. Determine this percentage for the entire sample. Then do the same for males and females separately.

6. *Special Group Exercise:*

Prepare a complete presentation of the data for all seventeen variables in the data base. Use all the methods of data presentation discussed in this chapter to their best advantage. Try to make the graphs, charts, and tables as attractive as possible. Don't be afraid to expand your knowledge of the software package you are currently using or to seek out other software that can aid in the presentation. Sometimes you may find that the computer is capable of doing a certain amount and that you can take it from there manually.

Prepare a written report to accompany the graphs, charts, and tables you have prepared. This assignment is typical of the kind of activity you will be involved in when you go to work in the public or private sector, so make the most of it!

C A S E S

Case 2A   Willburn & Associates

Willburn & Associates is a regional CPA firm located in upstate New York. The managing partner, Chad Willburn, is considered one of the more progressive accountants in the area in his use of statistical analysis and quantitative methods. When he hires new staff accountants, one of the criteria is that they have a basic understanding of statistics and an interest in applying statistics to their accounting work.

Elenor Douglas joined Willburn and Associates nearly two months ago after finishing her accounting degree at a nearby state university. She plans to sit for her CPA

TABLE 2A–1

Inventory data, Willburn & Associates

Item No.	X_1	X_2	X_3	X_4
1	204	198	$3.42	8
2	18	18	89.50	34
3	44	49	49.80	2
4	7	5	2004.40	74
5	14	14	5.49	11
6	33	38	14.70	6
7	9	9	1234.50	49
8	46	49	203.99	3
9	187	175	4.33	5
10	11	11	58.00	14
11	4	6	749.00	34
12	35	35	12.49	9
13	15	15	2.45	17
14	77	89	14.25	1
15	21	21	79.50	12
16	345	372	1.25	1
17	6	6	39.78	13
18	19	16	34.00	6
19	77	80	102.50	24
20	4	5	756.40	7
21	457	478	3.04	5
22	23	13	23.50	45
23	19	19	111.34	7
24	50	56	45.79	1
25	2	1	5.50	34
26	23	23	206.00	5
27	45	46	19.90	1
28	234	244	450.00	12
29	7	7	678.99	19
30	23	23	78.98	35

examination in the spring. Currently, Elenor is assigned to an audit project for a governmental client of the firm and has been assisting in all phases of the audit.

In the course of the audit, Elenor has collected data on inventory levels for parts and materials kept by the agency for carrying out its normal business operations. She has taken a sample of thirty inventory items and recorded data on the following variables:

X_1 = number of items actually on hand

X_2 = number of items stated to be on hand on the ledger

X_3 = per unit price of each item

X_4 = number of days since last recorded withdrawal from inventory

These data are shown in table 2A–1. Elenor plans on preparing a short presentation describing these data. Knowing Chad Willburn's interest in statistical methods, Elenor wants to make effective use of statistical methods of data presentation. She knows that the conclusions reached in her report need to be supported by the tables and graphs she uses. If her report is of sufficient quality, it will be included as part of the final audit report, and conclusions about the agency's inventory control can be partially based on this study.

REFERENCES

Hamburg, Morris. *Statistical Analysis for Decision Making,* 4th Edition. Orlando, Fla.: Harcourt Brace Jovanovich, 1987.

Huntsberger, David V.; Billingsley, Patrick; Croft, D. James; and Watson, Collin J. *Statistical Inference for Management and Economics,* 3rd Edition. Boston: Allyn and Bacon, 1986.

Loether, H. J., and McTavish, D. G. *Descriptive Statistics for Sociologists.* Boston: Allyn and Bacon, 1974.

MEASURES OF LOCATION AND SPREAD 3

WHY DECISION MAKERS NEED TO KNOW

The methods for graphically presenting data discussed in chapter 2 provide a starting point for analyzing data. However, these methods do not reveal all the information contained in a set of data. Managers who want to know as much as possible about their companies' sales divisions most likely will not be satisfied with frequency distributions showing the distribution of daily sales. Even frequency histograms or other graphical techniques probably will not provide all the required information. The managers will likely want to make comparisons between sales divisions to discern whether major differences exist. Although frequency distributions and histograms provide some basis for making this type of comparison, they may be misleading. In fact, histograms from two quite different sets of data may appear very similar owing to the number and width of the class intervals selected.

To overcome some limitations in the methods discussed in chapter 2, decision makers need to become acquainted with some additional tools of descriptive statistics. Specifically, managers need to know some statistical measures that can be determined from any set of data. There are two broad categories within which these measures fall: *measures of location* and *measures of spread*.

CHAPTER OBJECTIVES

Statistics is often used to decide whether a true difference exists between two sets of data. Many statistical techniques used to test for differences between data groups attempt to determine whether the data from the two groups have the same distribution. That is, do the groups have the same central location and the same spread?

This chapter will discuss some techniques for measuring the central location of a data distribution. Although many ways of measuring data location exist, the three most common will be explored here: the arithmetic mean, the median, and the mode.

Techniques for measuring the spread, or dispersion, in a set of data will also be discussed. The measures that will receive the greatest emphasis are the range, variance, and standard deviation.

STUDENT OBJECTIVES

After studying the material in this chapter, you should be able to

1. Calculate the mean and median for both grouped and ungrouped data.
2. Determine the variance and standard deviation for grouped and ungrouped data.

MEASURES OF LOCATION

3-1

As implied by the name, the *central location* is the middle, or center, of a set of data. This section considers several common measures of central location. The important statistical properties will be discussed and some business applications for each of the measures will be introduced. The measures of location that will be covered are the mode, the median, and the arithmetic mean.

The Mode

The **mode** is the observation that occurs most frequently in a data set. Suppose two business majors have just been hired for the summer to run the T-Shirt Shop in an eastern resort hotel. This is the first summer the shop will be open; although the owner has designated the total inventory investment allowed, the two comanagers will have to determine the inventory mix. T-shirts for adults come in five sizes: small (S), medium (M), large (L), extra large (XL), and extra extra large (XXL). To help in deciding the inventory levels for each size, the managers have selected a sample of fifty potential customers and have recorded their shirt sizes, as shown in table 3–1.

Initially, the two managers might use this sample to estimate which size T-shirt will be demanded most often. Recalling that the mode is the value occurring most often,

TABLE 3–1
Adult T-shirt sizes

L	L	L	S	S
XL	L	XL	XL	M
XL	M	M	XL	M
M	M	XXL	L	M
M	M	XL	M	L
M	S	S	M	L
M	XXL	M	M	XL
S	M	M	XL	XL
XXL	M	L	XL	XL
XL	L	XL	XXL	S

the mode here is medium since this size was observed eighteen times in the sample, more than any other size. Note also the data here are ordinal. The mode can be found for data measured at any of the four levels considered in chapter 1. This will not be true for the median and mean.

A set of data may have two or more values that tie for the most frequently occurring. When this happens the distribution is *multimodal*. Also, a data set may have no mode if no one value occurs more frequently than another.

The following example illustrates how the mode can aid in the decision-making process. Fox Corporation executives saw that the existing corporate jets, such as Lear and Gulfstream, were expensive ($1 million or more each). Some of this cost was due to the fact these jets were usually built to carry eight or more passengers. A study of passenger loads for a large number of trips for different corporate jets revealed that although sometimes the jets were full, in a vast majority of trips there were empty seats. In fact, for the data studied, the number of passengers observed most often was three, including the pilot. Thus the value 3, the mode for the observed data, figured strongly into Fox Corporation's plans to build a "small," lower-priced, four-passenger jet.

The Median

The **median** is the middle observation in data that have been arranged in ascending or descending numerical sequence. A numerical sequence of data is called an *array*. For example, Midstates Bank Corp. has been conducting a campaign to get small-account customers to use automated banking machines, which can process most transactions at less cost than can tellers. The following data represent the number of times each of nine customers used the banking machines last month. (Note that the data have been arranged in numerical order.)

$$
\begin{array}{c}
2 \\
4 \\
4 \\
5 \\
7 \\
8 \\
10 \\
10 \\
13
\end{array}
$$

When the array has an *odd* number of observations, the median is $(N + 1)/2$ observations from either end. Thus the median number of banking machine uses for these nine customers is the fifth observation from either the top or bottom $[(9 + 1)/2]$. Therefore the median is 7.

If the array contains an *even* number of observations, the median is any point between the two middle values. Generally the median is taken to be the average of the middle two values. For example, a company that supplies heating oil to residential customers has collected the following data on the quantity of oil purchased by eight households in December:

42 gallons
51
53
53
59
61
75
100

Since there are eight observations, the median is the average of the fourth and fifth observations.

$$\text{Median} = \frac{53 + 59}{2}$$
$$= 56 \text{ gallons}$$

The median is most useful as a measure of central tendency, or central location, in situations where the data contain some extreme observations. For instance, incomes in a market area are often characterized by a few very high incomes, but with the majority under $40,000. Although the few high-income earners are worth noting, a person contemplating opening a drive-in restaurant would like to have a measure of central income that represents the majority of people in the area. The median might be this measure since it is relatively unaffected by extreme values.

To illustrate that the median is not sensitive to extreme cases, suppose the highest banking machine use rate for the nine customers discussed earlier was 75 rather than 13, the median would still be 7. Note also that data must be at least ordinal for the median to be determined.

The Mean

By far the most common statistical measure of location is the mean. The **mean** is often called the *arithmetic average* in nonstatistical applications and is found by summing all the observations and dividing the sum by the number of observations.

The notation used to represent the mean differs depending on whether the data represent an entire population or a sample from a population. If the data comprise an entire population, the mean is found from equation 3–1:

$$\mu_x = \frac{\sum\limits_{i=1}^{N} X_i}{N}$$

(3-1)

where μ_x = population mean (μ is pronounced mū)

N = population size

Σ = summation symbol

X_i = individual observations

Recall from your math class or from the algebra review in chapter 1 that $\sum\limits_{i=1}^{N}$ requires us to sum all the elements with an i subscript from $i = 1$ to $i = N$ inclusive.

If the data are from a sample, the sample mean is found from equation 3–2:

$$\overline{X} = \frac{\sum\limits_{i=1}^{n} X_i}{n}$$

(3-2)

where $\overline{X}$ = sample mean (pronounced X bar)

n = sample size

X_i = individual observations

Now suppose the population of interest is the total sales of the T-Shirt Shop in the resort hotel for the first ten days it is open. These sales values are listed in table 3–2. The mean sales for these ten days is

$$\mu_x = \frac{\sum\limits_{i=1}^{N} X_i}{N}$$

$$= \frac{\$216 + 255 + 330 + 254 + 348 + 317 + 292 + 267 + 310 + 295}{10}$$

$$= \frac{\$2884}{10}$$

$$= \$288.40$$

We must use equation 3–1 since we are dealing with the entire population of sales values.

Suppose we select a sample of five days' sales from this population, say, $216, $330, $348, $292, $310. The sample mean is found using equation 3–2:

$$\overline{X} = \frac{\sum\limits_{i=1}^{n} X_i}{n}$$

$$= \frac{\$216 + 330 + 348 + 292 + 310}{5}$$

$$= \frac{\$1496}{5}$$

$$= \$299.20$$

Note that the sample mean in this example does not equal the population mean. This difference is called *sampling error*. Sampling error occurs whenever the sample does not perfectly represent the population. Sampling error generally occurs any time sampling is performed. We will look at the subject of sampling error in detail beginning in chapter 7. Note also that the data must be either interval or ratio for the mean to be meaningful.

As we discussed previously, the median is not affected by extreme values. However, since the mean is determined by using all observations, it is affected by extreme values. Returning to the banking machine use rate for nine customers,

$$2, 4, 4, 5, 7, 8, 10, 10, 12$$

the mean is $\overline{X} = 62/9 = 6.889$, and the median $= (7 + 8)/2 = 7.5$. We saw that increasing the largest observation to 75 would not affect the median but it would change the mean to

$$\overline{X} = 125/9 = 13.889$$

The Mean, Median, and Mode for Skewed Data

The mean, median, and mode usually are not the same for a given set of data. Yet each of the three measures is an attempt to describe the central position of the data being considered. The only time the mean, median, and mode will all have the same value is when the data distribution is both unimodal *and* symmetrical. Several unimodal and symmetrical distributions are shown in figure 3–1.

The three measures of location do not have the same value if the data distribution is skewed. As mentioned in chapter 2 data can be skewed to the left or right depending on the direction of the tail in the distribution. Skewed distributions affect the three measures of location differently. The mode is the value that occurs most frequently. In

TABLE 3–2
Daily sales, resort hotel T-Shirt Shop

$216	$317
255	292
330	267
254	310
348	295

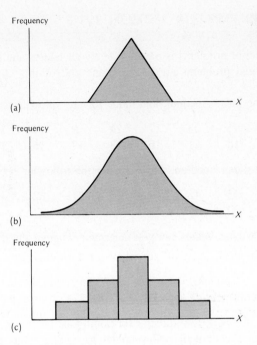

FIGURE 3–1
Unimodal and symmetrical distributions

(a)

(b)

(c)

the distribution shown in figure 3–2, the mode is at the highest point of the distribution. The median, which is the center observation, lies to the skewed side of the mode. The mean—the measure most affected by extreme values in the distribution's tail—lies beyond the median. Of the three common measures of location, the mean is most affected by a skewed distribution. For this reason, the mean, although the most commonly used statistical measure, is not always the best measure of location.

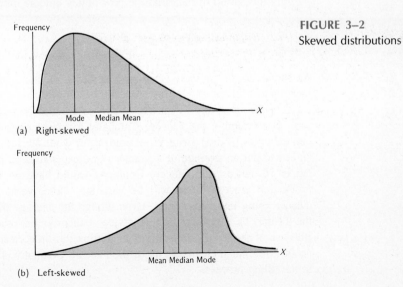

FIGURE 3–2
Skewed distributions

(a) Right-skewed

(b) Left-skewed

SKILL DEVELOPMENT PROBLEMS FOR SECTION 3–1

The following set of problems is meant to test your understanding of the material in this section. Additional problems are found at the end of this chapter under this section heading.

1. Determine the mean, median, and mode for the following set of data:

16	23	17	24	9	11	13	15
18	21	16	23	17	16	10	14

2. Compare the mean, median, and mode for the following set of data:

33	42	39	17	27	32	40	37
30	35	37	19	34	37	41	35

By looking at these values can you determine whether the data are skewed?

3. Determine the mean, median, and mode for the following sales data:

$17.87	19.95	22.95	18.74	9.95
11.22	21.98	14.52	16.65	14.98

4. Gail Pooley, the marketing director for South East Insurance, has been worried about the increasing age of their policy holder base. She wants to determine if the new advertising campaign has had the desired effect of attracting more younger customers. She has taken a sample of ten new policies and has found the following ages:

32	22	24	27	27
33	28	23	24	21

Determine the mean, median, and mode of these data. Is there any indication from this group of data that the new policy holders may lean toward younger ages?

MEASURES OF SPREAD

3-2

As shown in the previous section, the mean, median, and mode describe the central location of a distribution. However, the location is only one data characteristic of interest to decision makers. Measures of *spread* are also important.

For example, the Fabcare Company is considering a new machine for filling 16-ounce bottles of their Brite-Wool cold-water wool fabric cleaner. The machine is guaranteed to put an average of 16 ounces of cleaner in each bottle. If the machine always put in 16 ounces, the Fabcare Company would have no worries. However, as in any production process, there will be variation. Here, variation occurs in the amount of cleaner going into each bottle. Even though the average may be 16 ounces, sometimes the fill may be slightly more than sixteen ounces and at other times less than 16 ounces. Because of the legal ramifications of putting too little cleaner in bottles, and of the lost profit if too much cleaner is used, the Fabcare Company is concerned with the variation in the filling process.

You should also be aware that the mean by itself tells only part of the story in a set of data. For example, consider an oversimplified case where the fabric cleaner company selected two bottles of cleaner and measured the volume in each bottle, with the following results:

Bottle 1: 16.01 ounces
Bottle 2: 15.99 ounces

The average amount in a bottle is

$$\overline{X} = (16.01 + 15.99)/2$$
$$= 16.00 \text{ ounces}$$

Thus, these data show the desired average of 16 ounces was reached for these two bottles. Suppose a couple of weeks later the manufacturer selected two more bottles of fabric cleaner and measured these bottles, with the following results:

Bottle 1: 18 ounces
Bottle 2: 14 ounces

The average amount per bottle is still 16 ounces. Thus if the manufacturer looked only at the averages, it would conclude that the filling mechanism was performing the same as two weeks ago. Taking into account the spread in the data, there is a big difference in the filling process at present. It is important to look at both measures of location and measures of variation in analyzing a set of data.

Statistical measures of variation are also called measures of spread, or measures of dispersion. In this section we shall discuss the measures of dispersion most commonly used in statistical analysis. These measures are the *range, variance,* and *standard deviation.*

The Range

The simplest measure of spread in a set of data is the range. The *range* is the difference between the largest and smallest observations in the data. For example, table 3–3 lists the number of IBM personal System/2 computers sold by the PC Shop during its first twenty days in business. The range for these data is found by equation 3–3:

$$\boxed{\text{Range} = \text{maximum} - \text{minimum}} \qquad (3\text{–}3)$$

TABLE 3–3
Sales for twenty days, IBM System/2

8	6	7	2	6
1	2	7	4	4
1	3	5	1	12
5	4	3	4	2

Therefore

$$\text{Range} = 12 - 1$$
$$= 11 \text{ personal computers}$$

Although the range is the easiest measure of dispersion to calculate, it also conveys the least information. Since the range is determined by only the two extreme values, it provides no indication about the spread of the other values. The range is therefore very sensitive to extreme values in the data. For example, if the PC Shop had on the one day sold twenty personal computers instead of twelve, the range would have been nineteen rather than eleven, even though no other values had changed.

The range is also sensitive to the number of observations in the data set. In general, if more observations are included, there is a greater chance of having extreme values in the data set.

The Variance and Standard Deviation

As just illustrated, the range is an easy measure of spread to compute but is of limited value because it is computed from only the most extreme values in the data. This section introduces the two most frequently used measures of spread: the **variance** and the **standard deviation.** Unlike the range, the variance and the standard deviation consider all the data in their computation.

The variance and standard deviation provide numerical measures of how the data tend to vary around the mean. If the data are tightly clustered around the mean, both the variance and standard deviation will be relatively small. However, if the data are widely scattered around the mean, the variance and standard deviation will be relatively large.

Consider again the computer sales data shown in table 3–3. Assuming these data to be the population of interest, the population mean is computed as follows:

$$\mu_x = \frac{\sum_{i=1}^{N} X_i}{N}$$

$$= \frac{87}{20}$$

$$= 4.35$$

Thus, on the average, 4.35 computers were sold daily by the PC Shop during the twenty days of operation. You will note that the data in table 3–3 tend to vary. Some data are larger than 4.35; others are smaller. The variance and standard deviation can be used to provide measures of this variation. We will concentrate first on computing the variance.

The first step in computing the variance is to find the algebraic difference between each X_i value and the mean, as shown in column b of table 3–4. Note that the sum of these differences is zero. This will always be the case for any set of raw data. To overcome the problem of the negative differences cancelling with the positive differ-

a X_i	b $(X_i - \mu_x)$	c $(X_i - \mu_x)^2$
8	$(8 - 4.35) = \quad 3.65$	13.32
1	$(1 - 4.35) = -3.35$	11.22
1	$(1 - 4.35) = -3.35$	11.22
5	$(5 - 4.35) = \quad 0.65$	0.42
6	$(6 - 4.35) = \quad 1.65$	2.72
2	$(2 - 4.35) = -2.35$	5.52
3	$(3 - 4.35) = -1.35$	1.82
4	$(4 - 4.35) = -0.35$	0.12
7	$(7 - 4.35) = \quad 2.65$	7.02
7	$(7 - 4.35) = \quad 2.65$	7.02
5	$(5 - 4.35) = \quad 0.65$	0.42
3	$(3 - 4.35) = -1.35$	1.82
2	$(2 - 4.35) = -2.35$	5.52
4	$(4 - 4.35) = -0.35$	0.12
1	$(1 - 4.35) = -3.35$	11.22
4	$(4 - 4.35) = -0.35$	0.12
6	$(6 - 4.35) = \quad 1.65$	2.72
4	$(4 - 4.35) = -0.35$	0.12
12	$(12 - 4.35) = \quad 7.65$	58.52
2	$(2 - 4.35) = -2.35$	5.52
	$\Sigma = \quad 0.00$	$\Sigma = 146.50$

TABLE 3–4

Variance calculations, System/2 sales example

ences, we can square each of the differences as shown in column c of table 3–4. The sum of the differences squared is 146.50.

The final step in computing the variance of the population is to divide the sum of squared differences by the population size, $N = 20$, in equation 3–4:

$$\sigma_x^2 = \frac{\displaystyle\sum_{i=1}^{N} (X_i - \mu_x)^2}{N}$$

(3–4)

Then

$$\sigma_x^2 = \frac{146.50}{20}$$

$$= 7.33$$

The notation for the population variance is σ_x^2 (pronounced sigma sub x squared). Because we have squared all the differences between the individual data and the population mean, the variance is measured in units squared. Thus, the variance for the sales data is 7.33 computers squared. Although this terminology presents no statistical problems, we do have a problem interpreting the term computers squared!

If we take the square root of the variance, we return to the original units of measure, computers. The square root of the variance is called the **standard deviation.** We compute the standard deviation as in equation 3–5:

$$\sigma_x = \sqrt{\dfrac{\sum\limits_{i=1}^{N} (X_i - \mu)^2}{N}} \qquad (3\text{–}5)$$

Then

$$\sigma_x = \sqrt{\dfrac{146.50}{20}}$$
$$= \sqrt{7.33}$$
$$= 2.71$$

The notation for the population standard deviation is σ_x, (pronounced sigma sub x). Thus, the standard deviation for the population of the System/2 computers sold at the PC Shop dealer during the twenty days of operation is 2.71 computers.

Because the standard deviation is measured in the same units as the raw data, we generally use it as the measure of spread rather than variance. However, we will deal specifically with the variance in later chapters of this text.

The Meaning of the Standard Deviation

Because the standard deviation plays such an important role in statistical analysis, it is important that you understand what it means. The standard deviation may be thought of as a measure of distance from the mean. For instance, in figure 3–3 we see that a point on the line $1\sigma_x$ above the mean corresponds to $(4.35 + 2.71) = 7.06$ and a point on the line $2\sigma_x$ above the mean corresponds to $(4.35 + 5.42) = 9.77$. Likewise, a point on the line $2\sigma_x$ below the mean corresponds to $(4.35 - 5.42) = -1.07$.

We can also pick any point on the line and determine how many standard deviations above or below the mean that point falls. For example, suppose we pick the value 6.2. To determine how many standard deviations 6.2 is from 4.35, we perform the following:

$$Z = \dfrac{X - \mu_x}{\sigma_x}$$
$$= \dfrac{6.2 - 4.35}{2.71}$$
$$= 0.683$$

Thus, the value 6.2 falls 0.683 standard deviations above the mean value of 4.35. The Z is sometimes referred to as a Z score. A Z score is the number of standard deviations

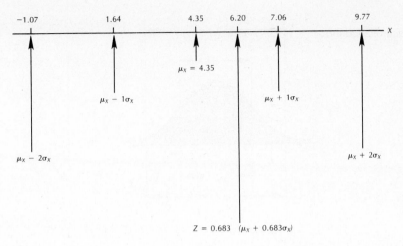

FIGURE 3–3
Standard deviation—a measure of distance, System/2 sales example

a point is above or below the mean of a set of data. We will use Z scores a great deal in our study of statistics because it is a unitless number and will allow us to make comparisons between different data sets.

Keeping in mind that the standard deviation is a measure of distance from the mean, we can use the information contained in the mean and the standard deviation to provide us with greater insight about the data from which they have been computed. Two important statistical concepts can be employed: the *empirical rule* and *Tchebysheff's theorem*.

Empirical Rule

The empirical rule holds that if the distribution of the data is bell shaped, like that shown in figure 3–4, then the interval

$(\mu_x \pm 1\sigma_x)$ contains approximately 68 percent of the values.
$(\mu_x \pm 2\sigma_x)$ contains approximately 95 percent of the values.
$(\mu_x \pm 3\sigma_x)$ contains virtually all the values.

Suppose we were to apply the empirical rule to the computer sales data in table 3–3, which have a mean of 4.35 and standard deviation of 2.71. Applying the empirical rule, (4.35 ± 2.71) should contain approximately 68 percent of the twenty values.

We find that in the interval 1.64 to 7.06 there are actually fifteen values, or 75 percent of the population. If we look at (4.35 ± 5.42) according to the empirical rule, we should find approximately 95 percent of the twenty values. We actually find exactly nineteen of the twenty, or 95 percent, of the values between -1.07 and 9.77. The more the distribution resembles the bell-shaped curve in figure 3–4, the more accurate the empirical rule is.

Suppose the time it takes to install a door on a new automobile is known to have a mean of twelve minutes and a standard deviation of two minutes. If the distribution

FIGURE 3–4
Empirical rule—bell-shaped distribution

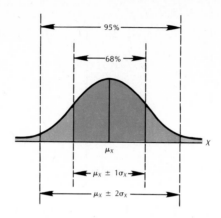

of actual times is bell shaped, like that shown in figure 3–5, then the production manager could expect about 68 percent of all doors to be mounted in ten to fourteen minutes (12 ± 2). Further, he could expect about 95 percent of all doors to take between eight and sixteen minutes to mount. Finally, he could expect virtually all doors to be mounted in between six and eighteen minutes (12 ± 6). If he begins to observe too many doors that require over eighteen minutes to mount, he might suspect that a problem exists.

Tchebysheff's Theorem

The empirical rule works best if the distribution of the data is bell shaped. However, many situations will exist in business in which the data are not bell shaped or the decision maker does not know precisely how the data are distributed. In these cases Tchebysheff's Theorem can be used.

TCHEBYSHEFF'S THEOREM

Regardless of how the data are distributed, *at least* $(1 - 1/k^2)$ of the measurements will lie within k standard deviations of the mean ($k \geq 1$).

Consider a distribution of data like the one in figure 3–5. Tchebysheff's theorem indicates that at least

$$\left(1 - \frac{1}{1^2}\right) = 0 = 0 \text{ percent of the values lie within } \pm 1\sigma_x.$$

$$\left(1 - \frac{1}{2^2}\right) = \frac{3}{4} = 75 \text{ percent of the measurements lie within } \pm 2\sigma_x.$$

$$\left(1 - \frac{1}{3^2}\right) = \frac{8}{9} = 88.9 \text{ percent of the values lie within } \pm 3\sigma_x.$$

Note that Tchebysheff's theorem is extremely conservative. It tells us nothing with respect to the number of values within $\pm 1\sigma_x$. It also tells us that *at least* 75 percent of the values will fall within ± 2 standard deviations of the mean. For a given set of

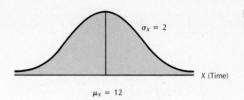

FIGURE 3–5
Distribution of door installation times

data the actual percentage may be substantially greater than 75 percent. The reason that Tchebysheff's theorem must be conservative is so that it can apply to any population or sample without regard to shape of the data distribution.

If we apply Tchebysheff's theorem to the System/2 sales data in table 3–3, which had a mean of 4.35 and a standard deviation of 2.71, we would expect a least fifteen (75 percent) of the values to lie in the range −1.07 to 9.77. A count indicates that in fact nineteen of the twenty values, or 95 percent, fall in this interval. Tchebysheff's theorem is extremely conservative in this case.

Regardless of whether we employ the empirical rule or Tchebysheff's theorem, the standard deviation plays an important role as the measure of spread.

The Standard Deviation with Sample Data

The variance and standard deviation were introduced through an example that dealt with a population of data. However, as indicated several times already, decision makers will often be dealing with a sample from the population rather than the entire population. Therefore, in describing the sample data and making inferences about the population from which the sample was selected, these decision makers will have to compute the variance and standard deviation for the sample.

The method for computing the sample variance is almost exactly the same as for computing the population variance. Consider an example involving Julie Hanson, owner of Hanson Auto, Home and Life, an insurance agency in Wichita, Kansas. Julie has selected a sample from long-term auto insurers (with the Hanson Agency for more than three years) and has determined the number of claims filed against these policies for the past three-year period. These data for a sample of ten policies are shown in table 3–5.

To analyze these sample data, we first compute the sample mean from equation 3–6:

$$\overline{X} = \frac{\Sigma X}{n}$$

(3–6)

TABLE 3–5
Auto policy claims—sample data, Hanson Agency

3	5
0	2
6	0
2	3
2	2

Then

$$\overline{X} = \frac{25}{10}$$

$$= 2.5 \text{ claims}$$

In computing the sample variance we determine the differences between the individual X values and the sample mean and then square each of these differences:

X	$X - \overline{X}$	$(X - \overline{X})^2$
3	$3 - 2.5 =$ 0.5	0.25
0	$0 - 2.5 = -2.5$	6.25
6	$6 - 2.5 =$ 3.5	12.25
2	$2 - 2.5 = -0.5$	0.25
2	$2 - 2.5 = -0.5$	0.25
5	$5 - 2.5 =$ 2.5	6.25
2	$2 - 2.5 = -0.5$	0.25
0	$0 - 2.5 = -2.5$	6.25
3	$3 - 2.5 =$ 0.5	0.25
2	$2 - 2.5 = -0.5$	0.25
	$\Sigma =$ 0.0	$\Sigma = 32.50$

To compute the variance we divide the sum of the squared differences by $n - 1$. Note the divisor is $n - 1$ for the sample variance, S_x^2. The reason that $n - 1$ is used in computing S_x^2 rather than n is that for small samples, computing S_x^2 with n as the divisor will slightly underestimate σ_x, the population variance. When $n - 1$ is used as the divisor, S_x^2 is a better estimate for the population variance. Remember, the goal of statistics is to use information in a sample to estimate what is true for a population. Because division by $n - 1$ rather than n does a "better" job of estimating the population variance, division by $n - 1$ is used when calculating sample variances. We will discuss this more fully in chapter 7. For now, just remember to divide by N when computing a population variance and by $n - 1$ when computing a sample variance.

Thus the formula for the sample variance is given by equation 3–7:

$$\boxed{S_x^2 = \frac{\Sigma(X - \overline{X})^2}{n - 1}} \tag{3–7}$$

Then for this example,

$$S_x^2 = \frac{32.50}{9}$$

$$= 3.611$$

Like the population variance, the sample variance is measured in units squared. To convert to original units, we take the square root. The *sample standard deviation* is the square root of the sample variance. This is shown in equation 3–8:

$$S_x = \sqrt{\frac{\Sigma(X - \overline{X})^2}{n - 1}} \qquad (3\text{–}8)$$

Then

$$S_x = \sqrt{\frac{32.50}{9}}$$
$$= \sqrt{3.611}$$
$$= 1.900 \text{ claims}$$

The sample standard deviation has the same meaning as the population standard deviation. It can be thought of as a measure of distance from the mean. The empirical rule or Tchebysheff's theorem can be applied in the same manner as for population data.

Note that in the equations for the sample variance and sample standard deviation we have dropped the subscript notation. We will follow this format for the remainder of the text whenever the summation involves all the data either in the sample or in a population. You should find this relaxed notation easier to work with.

Approximating the Standard Deviation

A quick approximation for the standard deviation can be made by dividing the range by 4. For instance consider the computer sales data shown in table 3–3. The range for these data is computed as follows:

$$\text{Range} = \text{High} - \text{Low}$$
$$= 12 - 1$$
$$= 11$$

Then, we approximate the standard deviation as

$$\text{Standard deviation} \approx \text{Range/4}$$
$$\approx 11/4$$
$$\approx 2.75 \text{ personal System/2 computers}$$

Recall that the actual standard deviation computed from these sales data is 2.71. In this case the approximation is good. Caution should be used in applying this approximation technique for the standard deviation, but it can be useful in some situations.

For example, consider the Morrison Construction Company. Dave Hill is the project scheduler for the stadium construction project at Kansas State University. He is in the process of putting together a critical path schedule for the project and needs values for the average and standard deviation time for each task on the construction project. To obtain these values he consults with the project foreman. The foreman can provide an average time without much difficulty based on his previous experience, but does not know what a standard deviation is. Dave can approximate the standard deviation by asking the foreman to indicate the quickest possible time and the longest possible time for each task on the project. Dave then approximates the standard deviations by taking the range for each task divided by four.

SKILL DEVELOPMENT PROBLEMS FOR SECTION 3–2

The following set of problems is meant to test your understanding of the material in this section. Additional problems are found at the end of this chapter under this section heading.

5. Determine the range, variance, and standard deviation for the following data, assuming it represents the population:

16	23	17	24	9	11	13	15
18	21	16	23	17	16	10	14

Compare the values you just found with those found if you assume the data came from a sample of the population.

6. Calculate the range, variance, and standard deviation of the following set of data. First assume the data represent a population and then that they come from a sample taken from a population.

33	42	39	17	27	32	40	37
30	35	37	19	34	37	41	35

7. Use the following set of sales data to test both the empirical rule and Tchebysheff's theorem. Assume the data represent a population.

$17.87	19.95	22.95	18.74	9.95
11.22	21.98	14.52	16.65	14.98

8. The Morgan Manufacturers Representative Company provides sales services for several small computer software developers. The company has been worried about their increasing sales force expense accounts. A sample of 15 daily expense logs shows the following total values:

$84.29	94.55	67.98	112.15	75.29
102.58	92.67	128.90	135.85	86.34
89.95	63.44	128.80	94.55	115.60

Calculate the mean, variance, and standard deviation of these data. Use both the empirical rule and Tchebysheff's theorem in a short report analyzing these sales values.

MEASURES OF LOCATION AND SPREAD FOR GROUPED DATA (OPTIONAL)

3-3

The previous sections introduced the most commonly used measures of location and spread. The formulas presented are used when you are dealing with raw data either from a population or from a sample. For most applications in business, you probably will be working with raw data and those formulas will most likely be used. Even when you have large amounts of data, calculators with memory units or computers will likely be available for you to use in performing the calculations.

However, as illustrated in chapter 2, one of the first steps that many decision makers take in transforming data into useful information is to form a frequency distribution. There may be instances in which you are given the frequency distribution but not the raw data from which it was constructed. Thus it is important to be able to compute measures of location and spread from the grouped data frequency distribution. This section introduces the methods for doing this and presents some examples.

You should note that computations made from grouped data frequency distributions are *only approximations* of the values that would be computed from the original raw data. The reason for this is that we lose detail by grouping the data into classes. We no longer know what the individual values are and must assume that the data in each class are spread evenly through each class and therefore the midpoint is used to represent each value within a given class. This concept will become clear as we look at the computations of the measures of location and spread.

Finding the Median for Grouped Data

If the data have been grouped into a frequency distribution, calculating the median requires interpolation. For example, table 3–6 gives the distribution of the last 5,000

Class	Frequency f_i	Cumulative Frequency
$ 0 and under $ 50	600	600
50 and under 100	1,000	1,600
100 and under 150	1,200	2,800
150 and under 200	800	3,600
200 and under 250	600	4,200
250 and under 300	400	4,600
300 and under 350	200	4,800
350 and under 400	200	5,000
Total	5,000	

TABLE 3–6
Distribution of awards in small claims court

awards given by the Fort Wayne, Indiana, small claims court. The *median class* contains the middle value in the array. Thus, if the frequency distribution has N items, the median class contains the $N/2$ item (in this case the 2,500th item). Starting from either the top or bottom, item 2,500 is in the class "$100 and under $150."

Although we know the class that contains the median, does it lie near $100, or is it closer to $150? This question is answered by interpolating the required distance from the lower limit of the median class, as shown in the median formula 3–9:

$$\text{Median} \approx L_{\text{median}} + \left(\dfrac{\dfrac{N}{2} - \Sigma f_{\text{prec}}}{f_{\text{median}}} \right)(W) \qquad (3\text{–}9)$$

where L_{median} = lower limit of the median class
N = total number of observations
Σf_{prec} = sum of observations in classes preceding the median class
W = *width of the median class*
f_{median} = observations in the median class

Therefore

$$\text{Median} \approx \$100 + \left(\dfrac{\dfrac{5000}{2} - 1600}{1200} \right)(\$50)$$

$$\approx \$100 + (900/1200)(\$50)$$

$$\approx \$137.50$$

We should discuss the rationale behind this procedure. Notice in table 3–6 there are 1,600 observations in the classes with awards less than $100. Because we want to find award 2,500 we need to go 900 awards into the next interval, "$100 and less than $150." Because 1,200 awards are contained in this interval, and the awards are assumed evenly spread through the interval, we need to move 900/1200 of the way through this class. Because the class width is $50, we will go 900/1200 of this $50 width. This is $37.50 through the $50 interval. Because the interval starts at $100, the median award is

$$\$100 + \$37.50 = \$137.50$$

Remember, the median is not sensitive to extreme values in a data set and thus is particularly useful as a measure of location for skewed distributions.

Finding the Mean for Grouped Data

If the data have been grouped into classes and a frequency distribution has been formed, we apply equation 3–10 to find the mean:

$$\mu_x \approx \frac{\sum_{i=1}^{c} f_i M_i}{N} \qquad (3\text{–}10)^{[1]}$$

where μ_x = population mean
c = number of classes
f_i = frequency in the ith class
M_i = midpoint of the ith class
N = population size

Using the grouped distribution of small claims awards given in table 3–6, the mean award can be found as follows:

Class	Midpoint M_i	Frequency f_i	$f_i M_i$
$ 0 and under $ 50	$ 25	600	15,000
50 and under 100	75	1,000	75,000
100 and under 150	125	1,200	150,000
150 and under 200	175	800	140,000
200 and under 250	225	600	135,000
250 and under 300	275	400	110,000
300 and under 350	325	200	65,000
350 and under 400	375	200	75,000
		$N = \sum_{i=1}^{c} f_i = 5,000$	$\sum_{i=1}^{c} f_i M_i = 765,000$

For this example,

$$\mu_x \approx \frac{\sum_{i=1}^{8} f_i M_i}{N}$$

$$\approx \frac{\$765,000}{5,000}$$

$$\approx \$153$$

Equation 3–10 also assumes the data are equally spread through the interval. Therefore, the midpoint can be assumed to be a good representative of each value.

Recall that the median for these data was $137.50. For any set of data, the mean and median need not be the same. Also, when the data are in grouped form, the calculations for the median and mean provide only approximations. When the data are

[1]Equation 3–10 can also be used to define a weighted mean, or weighted average, where

f_i = weights assigned to each category or class
N = sum of all the weights

grouped, we assume either that all observations fall at the class midpoint or that the observations are evenly spread throughout each class interval and can be represented by the midpoint. The closer these assumptions are to being true, the better the approximations will be.

The Variance and the Standard Deviation for Grouped Data

As illustrated, data are often best presented by grouping into classes. The variance and standard deviation can be calculated for grouped data in much the same manner as the mean is calculated for grouped data. The formula for calculating the variance and standard deviation for grouped data are given in equations 3–11 to 3–14:

For populations

$$\sigma_x^2 \approx \frac{\Sigma f(M - \mu_x)^2}{N} \qquad (3\text{--}11)$$

$$\sigma_x \approx \sqrt{\frac{\Sigma f(M - \mu_x)^2}{N}} \qquad (3\text{--}12)$$

where f = number of values in each class
M = midpoint of each class
μ_x = mean of the population $\approx \Sigma fM/N$
N = population size = Σf

For samples

$$S_x^2 \approx \frac{\Sigma f(M - \overline{X})^2}{n - 1} \qquad (3\text{--}13)$$

$$S_x \approx \sqrt{\frac{\Sigma f(M - \overline{X})^2}{n - 1}} \qquad (3\text{--}14)$$

where $\overline{X}$ = sample mean $\approx \dfrac{\Sigma fM}{n}$

n = sample size = Σf

Table 3–7 illustrates the frequency distribution from a sample of 100 days of production at a lumber mill. The standard deviation for this sample is found as follows.

TABLE 3–7
Lumber production sample
(board feet $\times$ 1,000)

Class	M	f	fM
15 and under 25	20	5	100
25 and under 35	30	8	240
35 and under 45	40	15	600
45 and under 55	50	20	1,000
55 and under 65	60	15	900
65 and under 75	70	10	700
75 and under 85	80	17	1,360
85 and under 95	90	5	450
95 and under 105	100	5	500
		$n = 100$	$\Sigma = 5,850$

First

$$\overline{X} \approx \frac{\Sigma fM}{n}$$

$$\approx \frac{5,850}{100}$$

$$\approx 58.50$$

Then

M	f	$(M - \overline{X})$	$(M - \overline{X})^2$	$f(M - \overline{X})^2$
20	5	$(20 - 58.50) = -38.50$	1,482.25	7,411.25
30	8	$(30 - 58.50) = -28.50$	812.25	6,498.00
40	15	$(40 - 58.50) = -18.50$	342.25	5,133.75
50	20	$(50 - 58.50) = -\ 8.50$	72.25	1,445.00
60	15	$(60 - 58.50) = \ \ \ 1.50$	2.25	33.75
70	10	$(70 - 58.50) = \ \ 11.50$	132.25	1,322.50
80	17	$(80 - 58.50) = \ \ 21.50$	462.25	7,858.25
90	5	$(90 - 58.50) = \ \ 31.50$	992.25	4,961.25
100	5	$(100 - 58.50) = \ \ 41.50$	1,722.25	8,611.25
	$n = 100$			$\Sigma = 43,275.00$

which makes the standard deviation

$$S_x \approx \sqrt{\frac{43,275}{100 - 1}}$$

$$\approx 20.91$$

Now, based on these calculations, the production manager has estimates for both the central location and dispersion in the daily lumber production. Without the information contained in the mean and standard deviation, the production manager would be hard pressed to reasonably assess and monitor the mill's daily lumber production. For example, the large standard deviation in this example indicates high variability in production output. High variability in production is generally undesirable and is an indication that better production control is needed.

SKILL DEVELOPMENT PROBLEMS FOR SECTION 3–3

The following set of problems is meant to test your understanding of the material in this section. Additional problems are found at the end of this chapter under this section heading.

9. Find the mean and median for the following set of grouped data:

Class	Frequency
0 to under 5	15
5 to under 10	22
10 to under 15	47
15 to under 20	34
20 to under 25	19
25 to under 30	9

10. Find the variance and standard deviation for the following set of grouped data. Assume the data came from a sample.

Class	Frequency
10 to under 20	29
20 to under 30	69
30 to under 40	81
40 to under 50	57
50 to under 60	44
60 to under 70	21

11. Find the mean, median, variance, and standard deviation for the following set of grouped data. Assume the data represent a population of values.

Class	Frequency
0 to less than 10	15
10 to less than 20	27
20 to less than 30	52
30 to less than 50	48
50 to less than 100	35
100 to less than 200	29

12. Several recent articles in *Fortune* and *The Wall Street Journal* about the potential health insurance problems being caused by the aging American work force have caused Harry Anderson, benefits director for AdvanceTech Manufacturing, to look at the age of its work force. He found the following values:

Class	Frequency
20 through 24	26
25 through 29	45
30 through 34	52
35 through 39	61
40 through 44	49
45 through 49	37
50 through 54	32
55 through 59	24
60 through 64	17
65 through 69	11

Find the mean, median, variance, and standard deviation of these data. Using these values write a short report analyzing the age distribution of the work force. (Assume this represents the entire work force.)

COEFFICIENT OF VARIATION

3-4

The standard deviation measures the variation in a set of data. For distributions having the same mean, the distribution with the largest standard deviation has the greatest relative spread. This is illustrated in figure 3–6, where the distribution in (b) has greater dispersion than that in (a). For decision makers, the standard deviation indicates how spread out, or uncertain, a distribution is. Given two distributions with the same mean, decision makers should feel more certain about the decisions made from the distribution with the smaller standard deviation. However, when considering distributions with different means, decision makers cannot compare the uncertainty in distributions by comparing standard deviations only.

For instance, Agra-Tech has recently introduced feed supplements for both cattle and hogs that will increase the speed at which these animals gain weight. Three years of feedlot tests indicate that cattle fed the supplement will weigh an average of 125 pounds more than those not fed the supplement. The standard deviation of the additional weight gain is ten pounds. Similar tests with hogs indicate those fed the hog supplement will gain an average of forty pounds more than hogs not fed the supplement. The standard deviation associated with the average additional weight gain for hogs is also ten pounds. Even though the standard deviation is ten pounds for both distributions, the fact the average increase in weight gain for cattle is 125 pounds and the average increase for hogs is forty pounds indicates there is a different degree of uncertainty associated with these two distributions.

The **coefficient of variation** is often used to indicate the relative uncertainty of distributions with different means. It does so by attempting to adjust the scales so they

FIGURE 3–6
Distribution spread

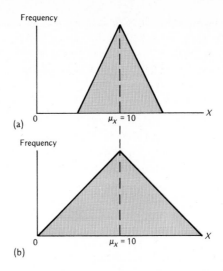

(a)

(b)

Note: The distribution in part (a) and the distribution in part (b) both
have the same mean, but that in (b) has a larger standard deviation
than that in (a) and is thus more spread out around the mean.

are comparable. This is done by dividing the standard deviation by the mean, thus
producing a unitless ratio.

The coefficients of variation for populations and samples are given in equations
3–15 and 3–16:

For populations

$$CV = \frac{\sigma_x}{\mu_x}(100)$$

where CV = coefficient of variation

For samples

$$CV = \frac{S_x}{\bar{X}}(100)$$

(3–15)

(3–16)

When the coefficients of variation for different distributions are compared, the
distribution with the largest CV value has the greatest relative spread. For the Agra-
Tech example, the two coefficients of variation are

$$CV(\text{cattle}) = \frac{10}{125}(100) = 8\%$$

$$CV(\text{hogs}) = \frac{10}{40}(100) = 25\%$$

Clearly, the distribution associated with the additional weight gain for hogs has a greater relative spread.

The coefficient of variation is an excellent example of both the advantages and disadvantages of many statistical aids to decision making. When the mean and standard deviation of a distribution are combined to form the coefficient of variation, the effect of different mean values tends to be eliminated. However, many decisions must be based on both central location *and* spread of distributions. By combining the measure of location and measure of spread into one value, decision makers lose some information. The point is that any statistical tool should be used as an aid to good managerial judgment, not in place of managerial judgment. Cases 3B and 3C at the end of the chapter reinforce this point.

SKILL DEVELOPMENT PROBLEMS FOR SECTION 3–4

The following set of problems is meant to test your understanding of the material in this section. Additional problems are found at the end of this chapter under this section heading.

13. Determine the coefficient of variation for the following set of population data:

33	42	39	17	27	32	40	37
30	35	37	19	34	37	41	35

14. Determine the coefficient of variation for the following set of sample date:

16	23	17	24	9	11	13	15
18	21	16	23	17	16	10	14

15. Determine which of the following two sets of sample data has the largest coefficient of variation.

Set A		Set B	
1.2	1.7	217	287
1.1	2.1	196	225
0.9	1.6	276	298
1.4	1.6	313	256
1.8	0.8	244	234

16. Sportway Manufacturing has been experimenting with new materials to use for golf ball covers. Two recently developed compounds have been shown to be equally resistant to cutting and the Development Lab is now looking at the distance the balls will travel during a simulated drive. However, both distance and consistency are important for a golf ball. A sample of ten balls with each type of cover was selected and the following distances were measured (in yards) using a mechanical driver that struck each ball with the same force.

Type A		Type B	
298	291	290	310
296	299	300	305
289	285	297	315
291	292	301	286
287	290	302	321

Write a report analyzing the performance of the two types of balls.

COMPUTER APPLICATIONS

3-5

This chapter has introduced several descriptive measures that can be computed from data. These measures, such as the mean, median, variance, and standard deviation, provide insight regarding the central location and spread in a data set.

The formulas for computing these measures are straightforward but the task can be burdensome if the data set has a large number of cases. Computer software is ideally suited to making computations quickly and accurately for very large data bases.

Both MINITAB and SPSS-X have routines for computing a variety of descriptive statistics. In this section, we illustrate three examples of the type of output available from these programs. Figure 3–7 shows the results of using the DESCRIBE command in MINITAB for the KIVZ-Channel 5 television data (see chapter 2, table 2–10). The output shows the sample size, mean, and standard deviation for three variables: age, income, and hours of TV watched per week. Figure 3–8 shows the MINITAB program statements.

Table 3–8 shows the results of using the BREAKDOWN procedure in SPSS-X using the data base from the KIVZ-Channel 5 data. Figure 3–9 shows the SPSS-X program statements. The output in table 3–8 shows the mean, standard deviation, and sample size for variable X_{14}, years at current residence. It also breaks down the sample by sex of the head of household and shows the mean years at the current residence for both males and females. For instance, from table 3–8 we can see that the males averaged 8.8182 years at the current residence, while females averaged slightly less time, 8.5714 years.

Table 3–8 also shows SPSS-X descriptive output for years at current residence by home status and hours of TV by sex of the head of household. These types of breakdowns are useful if the decision maker wants to understand his or her data set in greater detail than would be possible by just looking at the descriptive measures for the sample as a whole.

```
AGE        N =   50    MEAN =     44.060    ST.DEV. =     15.5
INCOME     N =   50    MEAN =     24846.    ST.DEV. =     4800.
HOURSTV    N =   50    MEAN =     12.080    ST.DEV. =     4.36
```

FIGURE 3–7
MINITAB computer output for the DESCRIBE command, KIVZ-Channel 5

FIGURE 3–8
MINITAB commands—descriptive statistics

```
MTB> READ 'KIVZ5' INTO C1-C19
MTB> NAME C17 'AGE'
MTB> NAME C18 'INCOME'
MTB> NAME C19 'HOURSTV'
MTB> OUTFILE = 'PRINTER'
MTB> DESCRIBE C17-C19
```

TABLE 3–8
SPSS-X computer output for the BREAKDOWN command, KIVZ-Channel 5

D E S C R I P T I O N   O F   S U B P O P U L A T I O N S

```
CRITERION VARIABLE    VAR14       YEARS AT RESIDENCE
   BROKEN DOWN BY     VAR10       SEX
```

- -

VARIABLE	VALUE	LABEL	MEAN	STD DEV	CASES
FOR ENTIRE POPULATION			8.6800	8.0088	50
VAR10	1.00	MALE	8.8182	8.2036	22
VAR10	2.00	FEMALE	8.5714	8.0020	28

TOTAL CASES =   50

D E S C R I P T I O N   O F   S U B P O P U L A T I O N S

```
CRITERION VARIABLE    VAR14       YEARS AT RESIDENCE
   BROKEN DOWN BY     VAR13       HOME STATUS
```

- -

VARIABLE	VALUE	LABEL	MEAN	STD DEV	CASES
FOR ENTIRE POPULATION			8.6800	8.0088	50
VAR13	1.00	RENTING	7.1250	7.4342	8
VAR13	2.00	BUYING	8.9762	8.1644	42

TOTAL CASES =   50

Continued.

TABLE 3–8 *continued*

D E S C R I P T I O N   O F   S U B P O P U L A T I O N S

CRITERION VARIABLE   VAR19   HOURS OF TV
    BROKEN DOWN BY   VAR10   SEX

- -

VARIABLE	VALUE	LABEL	MEAN	STD DEV	CASES
FOR ENTIRE POPULATION			12.0800	4.3558	50
VAR10	1.00	MALE	12.2273	4.6489	22
VAR10	2.00	FEMALE	11.9643	4.1942	28

TOTAL CASES =   50

```
UNNUMBERED
TITLE DESCRIPTIVE STATISTICS EXAMPLES
FILE HANDLE KIVZ NAME='KIVZ DATA C'
DATA LIST FILE=KIVZ LIST/VAR01 TO VAR19
VARIABLE LABELS
    VAR01 'NATIONAL NEWS STATION'
    VAR02 'LOCAL NEWS STATION'
    VAR03 'NEWS RATING'
    VAR04 'SPORTS RATING'
    VAR05 'WEATHER RATING'
    VAR06 'ANCHOR RATING'
    VAR07 'SPORTSCASTER RATING'
    VAR08 'OVERALL RATING'
    VAR09 'NATIONAL INFLUENCE'
    VAR10 'SEX'
    VAR11 'MARITAL STATUS'
    VAR12 'NUMBER EMPLOYED'
    VAR13 'HOME STATUS '
    VAR14 'YEARS AT RESIDENCE'
    VAR15 'YEARS IN STATE'
    VAR16 'EDUCATION'
    VAR17 'AGE'
    VAR18 'INCOME'
    VAR19 'HOURS OF TV'
VALUE LABELS
    VAR01 1 'CHANNEL 5' 2 'CHANNEL 3' 3 'CHANNEL 8' 4 'UNDECIDED'/
    VAR02 1 'CHANNEL 3' 2 'CHANNEL 8' 3 'CHANNEL 5' 4 'UNDECIDED'/
    VAR03 TO VAR08 1 'POOR' 2 'FAIR' 3 'GOOD' 4 'VERY GOOD' 5 'EXCEL'/
    VAR09 1 'TRUE' 2 'FALSE' 3 'UNDECIDED'/
    VAR10 1 'MALE' 2 'FEMALE'/
    VAR11 1 'SINGLE' 2 'DIVORCED' 3 'MARRIED' 4 'OTHER'/
    VAR13 1 'RENTING' 2 'BUYING'/
    VAR16 1 'GRADE SCHOOL' 2 'SOME COLLEGE' 3 'VOTECH' 4 'HIGH SCHOOL'
        5 'COLLEGE GRAD' 6 'GRADUATE WORK'
BREAKDOWN TABLES = VAR14 BY VAR10/
        TABLES = VAR14 BY VAR13/
        TABLES = VAR19 BY VAR10/
```

FIGURE 3–9
SPSS-X commands—breakdown

TABLE 3–9
SPSS-X computer output for the CONDESCRIPTIVE command, KIVZ-Channel 5

```
NUMBER OF VALID OBSERVATIONS (LISTWISE) =       50.00
VARIABLE        MEAN      STD DEV    MINIMUM    MAXIMUM VALID N   LABEL
VAR17         44.060      15.510      20.00      81.00        50   AGE
```

Table 3–9 shows output generated using SPSS-X's CONDESCRIPTIVE command for variable X_{17}, age, for the KIVZ-Channel 5 data. (See figure 3–10 for SPSS-X program statements.) This output shows the mean, standard deviation, and minimum and maximum values for this variable for the entire data set. The role of these numerical statistics is to provide the decision maker with information about a set of data. The computer is a useful tool for calculation, and almost any statistical software you might use will have the capabilities of computing the measures shown in tables 3–7 through 3–9.

```
UNNUMBERED
TITLE DESCRIPTIVE STATISTICS EXAMPLES
FILE HANDLE KIVZ NAME='KIVZ DATA C'
DATA LIST FILE=KIVZ LIST/VAR01 to VAR19
VARIABLE LABELS
  VAR01 'NATIONAL NEWS STATION'
  VAR02 'LOCAL NEWS STATION'
  VAR03 'NEWS RATING'
  VAR04 'SPORTS RATING'
  VAR05 'WEATHER RATING'
  VAR06 'ANCHOR RATING'
  VAR07 'SPORTSCASTER RATING'
  VAR08 'OVERALL RATING'
  VAR09 'NATIONAL INFLUENCE'
  VAR10 'SEX'
  VAR11 'MARITAL STATUS'
  VAR12 'NUMBER EMPLOYED'
  VAR13 'HOME STATUS '
  VAR14 'YEARS AT RESIDENCE'
  VAR15 'YEARS IN STATE'
  VAR16 'EDUCATION'
  VAR17 'AGE'
  VAR18 'INCOME'
  VAR19 'HOURS OF TV'
VALUE LABELS
  VAR01 1 'CHANNEL 5' 2 'CHANNEL 3' 3 'CHANNEL 8' 4 'UNDECIDED'/
  VAR02 1 'CHANNEL 3' 2 'CHANNEL 8' 3 'CHANNEL 5' 4 'UNDECIDED'/
  VAR03 TO VAR08 1 'POOR' 2 'FAIR' 3 'GOOD' 4 'VERY GOOD' 5 'EXCEL'/
  VAR09 1 'TRUE' 2 'FALSE' 3 'UNDECIDED'/
  VAR10 1 'MALE' 2 'FEMALE'/
  VAR11 1 'SINGLE' 2 'DIVORCED' 3 'MARRIED' 4 'OTHER'/
  VAR13 1 'RENTING' 2 'BUYING'/
  VAR16 1 'GRADE SCHOOL' 2 'SOME COLLEGE' 3 'VOTECH' 4 'HIGH SCHOOL'
        5 'COLLEGE GRAD' 6 'GRADUATE WORK'
CONDESCRIPTIVE VAR17
```

FIGURE 3–10
SPSS-X commands—descriptive statistics

CONCLUSIONS

3-6

Measures of central location and measures of variation, or spread, are statistical tools for transforming data into meaningful information. When used together, measures of location and dispersion allow managerial decision makers to compare distributions and determine whether they are statistically the same or whether a difference exists between them. Although we have discussed several measures of both location and spread for a distribution, the most widely used measures are the mean and standard deviation.

Throughout the chapter new statistical concepts have been discussed in general managerial terms. The chapter glossary presents a list of more formal statistical definitions for these concepts. To test your understanding, reconcile the managerial discussion with these definitions.

The important equations introduced in this chapter are presented in a special section following the glossary.

CHAPTER GLOSSARY

coefficient of variation A measure that can be used to compare relative dispersion between two or more data sets. It is formed by dividing the standard deviation by the mean of a data set.

mean The mean of a set of n measurements is equal to the sum of the measurements divided by n. The mean is the most commonly used measure of location.

median A measure of location. The middle item in a set of measurements that have been arranged according to magnitude.

mode A measure of location. The value in a series of measurements that appears more frequently than any other. The mode may not be unique.

range The difference between the largest and the smallest values in a set of data.

standard deviation The positive square root of the variance.

variance A measure of data dispersion. The average of the squared differences between the individual measurements and the mean.

CHAPTER FORMULAS

Median
Grouped

$$\text{Median} = L_{\text{median}} + \left(\frac{\frac{N}{2} - \Sigma f_{\text{prec}}}{f_{\text{median}}} \right)(W)$$

Mean
   Population
     Ungrouped

$$\mu_x = \frac{\Sigma X}{N}$$

     Grouped

$$\mu_x \approx \frac{\Sigma fM}{N}$$

   Sample
     Ungrouped

$$\overline{X} = \frac{\Sigma X}{n}$$

     Grouped

$$\overline{X} \approx \frac{\Sigma fM}{n}$$

Variance
   Population
     Ungrouped

$$\sigma_x^2 = \frac{\Sigma(X - \mu_x)^2}{N}$$

     Grouped

$$\sigma_x^2 \approx \frac{\Sigma f(M - \mu_x)^2}{N}$$

   Sample
     Ungrouped

$$S_x^2 = \frac{\Sigma(X - \overline{X})^2}{n - 1}$$

     Grouped

$$S_x^2 \approx \frac{\Sigma f(M - \overline{X})^2}{n - 1}$$

Standard deviation
Population
  Ungrouped

$$\sigma_x = \sqrt{\frac{\Sigma(X - \mu_x)^2}{N}}$$

  Grouped

$$\sigma_x \approx \sqrt{\frac{\Sigma f(M - \mu_x)^2}{N}}$$

Sample
  Ungrouped

$$S_x = \sqrt{\frac{\Sigma(X - \overline{X})^2}{n - 1}}$$

  Grouped

$$S_x \approx \sqrt{\frac{\Sigma f(M - \overline{X})^2}{n - 1}}$$

Coefficient of variation
Population

$$CV = \frac{\sigma_x}{\mu_x}(100)$$

Sample

$$CV = \frac{S_x}{\overline{X}}(100)$$

SOLVED PROBLEMS

1. A retail store manager has selected a sample of sales slips during the past month and now needs your assistance in answering some questions about the sample. The sixty-four sales values have been numerically ordered as follows:

$0.97	$5.69	$10.48	$22.95
1.23	5.99	11.97	23.85
1.29	6.49	11.99	24.99
1.69	6.50	11.99	24.99
2.19	6.99	11.99	29.97

2.77	7.19	12.49	34.95
3.19	7.44	12.95	34.98
3.57	7.49	13.39	35.95
3.97	7.75	13.88	41.69
3.99	8.12	13.89	49.99
4.35	8.90	14.99	61.98
4.44	8.99	16.30	64.88
4.44	9.85	18.63	67.29
4.50	9.97	19.97	68.99
4.65	9.97	21.25	69.99
5.25	9.98	21.50	74.96

a. What is the mean sales level for the sixty-four sales values?
b. What is the median sales level for these data?
c. What is the mode?
d. Note that the median and mode are fairly close but that the mean is much larger. Why is this?
e. What is the standard deviation from the sample of sales values?

Solutions:

a. The formula for finding the mean is

$$\overline{X} = \frac{\Sigma X}{n}$$

If we sum the sixty-four values, we get

$$\Sigma X = \$1,149.86$$

Dividing by $n = 64$,

$$\overline{X} = \frac{\$1,149.86}{64}$$
$$= \$17.97$$

Thus the mean sale for the sample is $17.97.
b. The median is the center item when the data have been rank-ordered. When the number of observations is an even number, the median is the average of the two middle observations. Thus the median for these data is midway between the thirty-second and thirty-third sales values.

$$\text{Median} = \frac{\$9.98 + \$10.48}{2}$$
$$= \$10.23$$

c. The mode is the value in the data that appears most often. In this data set, the value $11.99 occurred three times, which is more often than any other value. Thus the mode is $11.99.

d. Whenever the mean, median, and mode differ in value, the data distribution is skewed. The farther the mean is from the median and the mode, the greater the skewness. The mean is sensitive to extreme observations, and in this example, although the majority of the observations are less than $15.00, the few high sales values over $60.00 have pulled the mean up to $17.97.

e. The sample standard deviation is found using the following formula:

$$S_x = \sqrt{\frac{\Sigma(X - \overline{X})^2}{n - 1}}$$

Recalling that $\overline{X} = 17.97$, we can find the standard deviation as follows:

X	$(X - \overline{X})$	$(X - \overline{X})^2$
0.97	$(0.97 - 17.97) = -17.00$	289.00
1.23	$(1.23 - 17.97) = -16.74$	280.23
1.29	$(1.29 - 17.97) = -16.68$	278.22
1.69	$(1.69 - 17.97) = -16.28$	265.04
.	. .	.
.	. .	.
.	.	.
74.95	$(74.95 - 17.97) = 56.98$	3,246.72
		$\Sigma = 23,384.57$

$$S_x = \sqrt{\frac{23,384.57}{64 - 1}}$$
$$= \sqrt{371.18}$$
$$= \$19.27$$

Thus the sample standard deviation is $19.27.

ADDITIONAL PROBLEMS

Section 3–1

17. Discuss the circumstances under which you would prefer the median as a measure of location instead of the mean.

18. Considering the relative positions of the mean, median, and mode:
   a. Draw a symmetrical distribution and label the three measures of location.
   b. Draw a left-skewed distribution and label the three measures of location.
   c. Draw a right-skewed distribution and label the three measures of location.

19. The marketing manager for Sweetright Cola has just received the results of two

separate marketing studies performed in the Ohio Valley market region. One study was based on a random sample of 300 people and the study indicated that the mean income is $2,450.00 per month. The second study was based on a random sample of 400 people and indicated that the mean income in the region is $2,375.00 per month. The manager is confused. Should he have expected the two samples to yield the exact same mean? Why or why not? Also, is it reasonable to believe that a sample mean should exactly equal the mean of the population? Discuss.

20. Ivan Horton is a building contractor whose company builds many homes every year. In planning for each job, Ivan needs some idea about the direct labor hours required to build a home. He has collected sample information on the labor hours for ten jobs during the past year.

245 h	402 h
291	351
353	242
118	595
152	175

a. Calculate the mean for this sample and explain what it means.
b. Calculate the median for this sample.
c. If Ivan had to select the mean or the median as the measure of location for direct labor hours, what factors about each should he consider before making the decision?

21. The Hillside Bowling Alley manager has selected a random sample of his league customers. He asked them to record the number of lines they bowl during the month of December, including both league and open bowling. The sample of twenty people produced the following data:

13	22	12	9	16
17	16	12	12	20
11	16	15	12	12
14	32	12	18	15

a. Compute the mean for these sample data.
b. Compute the median for these sample data.
c. Compute the mode for these sample data.
d. Note that one person in the sample bowled thirty-two lines. What effect, if any, does this large value have on each of the three measures of location? Discuss.
e. For these sample data, which measure of location provides the best measure of the center of the data? Discuss.

22. The Wilnet Development Company has proposed building a new housing development in Warwick, Rhode Island. The city's planning department requires that the developer conduct a traffic study as part of the project planning. One part of that traffic study is analyzing the trips from home made by residents in the "impact area" located near the proposed project location. The Wilnet Company has selected

thirty families at random from those in the "impact area" and has asked them to keep track of their trips from home during the next week. The data returned to the Wilnet Company are

38	44	11	26	19	13
45	27	11	19	19	26
20	19	34	30	20	8
15	17	19	11	28	46
67	25	58	43	23	19

a. Compute the mean for these data and describe what it measures.
b. Compute the median for these data and compare it with the mean found in part a.
c. Compute the mode for these data.
d. Write a short report to submit to the city's planning department describing the sample data. Use any graphical techniques you think would be helpful in transforming the data into useful information, as well as any measures of location.

23. The Indiana Transportation Department recently set up a speed check station on one of the interstate highways. They collected speed data on forty vehicles selected at random during a four-hour period. The data collected (in miles per hour) are:

68	72	62	75	81	64	81	66
65	68	70	70	69	73	72	75
71	70	80	74	62	59	81	69
66	88	66	65	65	77	70	65
64	77	68	70	72	66	73	68

a. Compute the average speed for the sample.
b. Compute the median speed for the sample data.
c. Compute the mode for these sample data.
d. The speed limit on the highway where the data were collected is 65 m.p.h. Write a short report describing the sample data and include both graphical analyses and measures of location. The report should address the issue of whether the vehicles traveling on this highway tend to obey the speed limit.

24. The Norton Oil Company has twenty oil wells operating in the Gulf of Mexico. The output of these twenty oil wells has been recorded in terms of barrels per day pumped, as follows:

800	100	230	700	1900
300	400	700	250	500
340	670	340	250	450
700	500	200	75	1200

a. Compute the mean daily production for these twenty wells. Assume the data represent the population of interest.
b. What is the median oil production per day for this population of oil wells?

c. Write a short report describing the daily oil production for the Norton Oil Company wells in the Gulf of Mexico.

25. The Norton Oil Company of problem 24 had twenty wells producing in the Gulf of Mexico, with the following daily yield rates in barrels:

800	100	230	700	1900
300	400	700	250	500
340	670	340	250	450
700	500	200	75	1200

Select a random sample of six oil wells from this population.
a. Discuss the method you used to determine your sample and list the sample data.
b. Compute the median for the sample.
c. Compute the mean for the sample.
d. Write a short report comparing the sample measures of location with the population measures.

Section 3–2

26. Discuss the advantages and disadvantages of using the range as a measure of spread in a set of data.

27. The Hillside Bowling Alley manager of problem 21 selected a random sample of twenty customers and asked them to record the number of lines they bowled during December. He found the following set of sample data:

13	22	12	9	16
17	16	12	12	20
11	16	15	12	12
14	32	12	18	15

From these data, compute the variance and standard deviation.

28. In problem 22, we considered the Wilnet Development Company, which proposed building a new housing development in Warwick, Rhode Island. As part of the impact study, they asked thirty families to keep track of their trips from home during a week time period. The following data were gathered:

38	44	11	26	19	13
45	27	11	19	19	26
20	19	34	30	20	8
15	17	19	11	28	46
67	25	58	43	23	19

Compute the sample standard deviation and discuss what it measures.

29. Referring to the Wilnet Development Company of problem 28, approximate the standard deviation by dividing the range by four. Compare this value with the sample standard deviation and discuss how effective the approximation was.

30. Since deregulation has taken place, the airline industry has undergone substantial changes with respect to ticket prices. Many discount fares are available if a customer knows how to obtain the discount. Many travelers complain that they get a different price every time they call. The American Consumer Institute recently priced tickets between Spokane, Washington, and St. Louis, Missouri. The passenger was to fly coach class round trip, staying seven days. Calls were made directly to airlines and to travel agents with the following results. Note the data reflect round-trip airfare.

$229.00	$345.00	$599.00
229.00	429.00	605.00
339.00	339.00	229.00
279.00	344.00	407.00

a. Compute the mean quoted airfare.
b. Compute the variance and standard deviation in airfares quoted. Treat the data as a sample.
c. Write a short report for the American Consumer Institute describing these sample data.

31. The Indiana Highway Patrol gathered the following data at a check station that recorded the speed of forty cars:

68	72	62	75	81	64	81	66
65	68	70	70	69	73	72	75
71	70	80	74	62	59	81	69
66	88	66	65	65	77	70	65
64	77	68	70	72	66	73	68

a. Compute the mean, variance, and standard deviation of these sample data.
b. Using the values found in part a, write a report discussing whether the drivers obey the 65 m.p.h. speed limit. Incorporate either the empirical rule or Tchebysheff's theorem into this report.

32. Computerworld sells various personal computer products including hardware and software. Recently the manager at the Boston Computerworld store collected data on all sales of complete computer systems (consisting of a central processing unit, disk storage, a monitor, a keyboard, and an operating system). She specifically noted the memory volume purchased by customers and recorded these data for the thirty sales made the previous week. These data measured in 1,000-byte amounts are

64	64	128	592	64	128
192	256	64	64	128	192
256	64	64	128	128	256
128	64	64	592	64	256
256	64	128	64	128	64

a. Compute the mean memory purchased for this population of data.

b. Compute the median amount of memory purchased.

c. Compute the range and use it to approximate the standard deviation of memory purchased.

d. Compute the standard deviation and compare this result with the approximation in part c.

e. Suppose the store manager is concerned that her sales staff has not been convincing enough in selling additional memory over the basic 64k amount. Write a report using appropriate measures of location and spread and graphical techniques to describe this population of data.

Section 3–3

33. In the past few years many companies using trees as raw material have become interested in growing trees. One company has collected the following information on tree growth per year for samples from three species of trees:

Growth Class (feet)	Pine Frequency	Redwood Frequency	Cedar Frequency
0 and under 1	10	15	5
1 and under 2	5	10	10
2 and under 3	9	2	4
3 and under 4	4	2	4
4 and under 5	2	1	7
Total	30 trees	30 trees	30 trees

Write a report to management analyzing this information. Be sure to discuss the location and spread in the growth for each type of tree.

34. Suppose you are considering purchasing an apartment house. There would certainly be many things to consider in the buy/don't buy analysis. One of these would be the maintenance costs you might incur. The following frequency distribution reflects the historical weekly costs (rounded to the nearest dollar) based on the current owner's records for the past thirty weeks:

Expense Class	Frequency
$ 0–$100	12
101– 200	5
201– 300	6
301– 400	4
401– 500	3
Total	30 weeks

a. Calculate the mean weekly expense.

b. Calculate the variance and standard deviation.

35. Referring to problem 34, suppose you have made a deal with the current owner to keep the maintenance records yourself for one week. You find that $600 was spent.

Assuming this was a typical week, what would you conclude about the current owner's records? Why?

36. Explain why the mean calculated for a set of ungrouped data might differ from the mean if the same data were grouped into a frequency distribution. Would this also be the case for the standard deviation? Why?

37. The manager of the Clark Fork Station Restaurant recently selected a random sample of fifty customers and kept track of how long the customers were required to wait from the time they arrived at the restaurant until they were actually served dinner. This study resulted from several complaints the manager had received from customers saying that their wait time was unduly long and that it appeared that the objective was to keep people waiting in the lounge for as long as possible to increase the lounge business. The following data were recorded, with time measured in minutes.

34	24	43	56	74	20	19	33	55	43
45	23	43	56	67	45	26	57	78	41
30	19	36	32	65	24	54	34	27	34
36	24	54	39	43	23	56	36	34	45
67	54	32	18	40	35	67	53	23	47

a. Compute the mean waiting time for this sample of customers.

b. Compute the median waiting time for this sample of customers.

c. Compute the variance and standard deviation of waiting time for this sample of customers. Develop a frequency distribution using seven classes with class width of ten. Make the lower limit of the first class fifteen.

d. For each class, determine the class midpoint.

e. Develop a frequency histogram for the frequency distribution.

f. Compute the mean waiting time from the grouped data and compare this value with the mean computed from the raw data in part a.

g. Compute the median waiting time from the grouped data and compare this value with the median computed from the raw data in part b.

h. Compute the variance and standard deviation of the waiting times from the grouped data and compare these values with the variance and standard deviation computed from the raw data in part c.

i. Discuss whether it is preferable to compute measures of location and spread from grouped data versus raw data if a decision maker has the option.

Section 3–4

38. The C. A. Whitman Investment Company recently offered two mutual funds to its customers. A mutual fund is a group of stocks and bonds that is managed by a company such as C. A. Whitman. Individuals purchase shares of the mutual fund, and the investment company uses the money to buy stocks. Many investors feel comfortable with a mutual fund because their money is not tied up in one or two stocks but is spread over many stocks, thereby, they hope, reducing the risk.

The two mutual funds offered by C. A. Whitman currently have sixty stocks each. During the past six months the average stock in fund A has increased $3.30 in price, with a standard deviation of $1.25. The stocks in fund B have shown an average increase of $8.00, with a standard deviation of $3.50.

Based on this information, which of the two funds has stocks that have shown the greater relative variability? Compute the appropriate measures and explain why we cannot simply compare standard deviations in this case.

39. The Smithfield Agricultural Company operates in the Midwest. The company owns and leases a total of 34,000 acres of prime farmland. Most of the crops are grain. Because of the size of this company it can afford to do a great amount of testing to determine what seed types produce greatest yields. Recently the company tested three types of corn seed on test plots. The following values were observed after the first test year:

	Seed Type A	Seed Type B	Seed Type C
Mean bushels/acre	88	56	100
Standard deviation	16	15	25

a. Based on the results of this testing, which seed seems to produce the greatest average yield per acre? Comment on the type of testing controls that should have been used to make this study valid.
b. Suppose the company is interested in consistency. Which seed type shows least relative variability?
c. Using the empirical rule, describe the production distribution for each of the three seed types.

40. The B. L. Williams Company makes tennis balls. The company has two manufacturing plants. The plant in Portland, Maine, is a unionized plant with average daily production of 34,000 tennis balls. The output varies, with a standard deviation of 4,500 tennis balls per day. The San Antonio, Texas, plant is nonunion and quite a bit smaller than the Portland plant. The San Antonio plant averages 12,000 tennis balls per day, with a standard deviation of 3,000.

Recently, the production manager was giving a speech to the Association of Sporting Goods Manufacturers. In that speech he stated that the B. L. Williams Company has been having real problems with its union plant maintaining consistency in production output and that the problem was not so great at the nonunion plant.

Based on the production data, was the manager justified in drawing the conclusions he made in the speech? Discuss and support your discussion with any appropriate calculations.

41. A survey of local airline passengers shows that the mean height of male passengers is 69.5 inches, with standard deviation 2.5 inches. The mean weight is 177 pounds, and the standard deviation is twelve pounds. Which of the two distributions has the greater variability?

STATE DEPARTMENT OF TRANSPORTATION CASE STUDY PROBLEMS

The following questions and problems pertain directly to the State Department of Transportation case study and data base introduced in chapter 1. The questions and problems were written assuming that you will have access to a computer and appropriate statistical software. The data base containing 100 observations and seventeen variables is shown in table 1C–1 in chapter 1.

1. Herb Kriner is interested in determining the demographic characteristics of his sample. In particular, he would like to know the mean, median, and standard deviation for each interval or ratio level variable in the data set. Prepare one summary table that contains these statistics and write a short report describing the results.

2. Referring to problem 1, Herb Kriner would like the same type of summary prepared for two groups: those determined to have insurance and those determined not to have insurance. Make one table showing the statistics for the two groups and write a report comparing the two groups.

3. After reading the reports in problems 1 and 2, Herb Kriner has requested that the data be broken down by male and female drivers and that a report be prepared discussing the results.

4. Determine the mean, median, and standard deviation for number of years of formal education (X_{15}) and age (X_9) broken down by whether or not the driver is wearing a seat belt. (Use X_{10} with codes = 1 of 2 only.)

5. Determine whether the variation in age of insured drivers exceeds that of uninsured drivers. Remember, the standard deviations should not be compared directly if the means are different!

6. One of his staff members asked why Herb didn't request means, medians, and standard deviations for all variables (see problems 1 and 2); for instance, X_8 and X_{12}. Herb has asked you to write a letter of response indicating whether it is all right to compute this type of descriptive measure on nominal and ordinal data and to indicate what interpretation should be made if such calculations are performed.

C A S E S

3A The Association of Independent Homeowners

The Association of Independent Homeowners has been spurred into action by the success of tax-limitation efforts in many states. However, although members are not particularly happy with the property-tax levels in their states, they are more concerned with the possibility of assessment errors. They do not think the county assessors are doing anything illegal, but they have all heard stories of how some properties are assessed at a much lower rate than other properties, when in fact they are of equal value.

    The property-tax level in each county depends on the assessed valuation of all property in the county. One person's or business's property tax will depend on the levy set by the county and on the property value. Because the value of property changes from year to year, the association is particularly concerned that the assessed value accurately reflect the changing market value, as specified by state law.

Ruth Powers, an active member of the association, has heard of a recent study performed by the State Tax Commission. The commission gathers information on the sale price of recently marketed property and compares the true market price with the assessed value. Using the gathered data, the commission computes a mean assessment-to-market-value ratio for each county in the state. Since property is broken into four categories for assessment purposes ("residential," "rural investment," "business and industrial," and "other rural"), the commission also computes an adjusted mean value based on the number of parcels in each of these categories in each county. The State Tax Commission determined these values, plus the standard deviations of the individual ratios, for each county in the state. Ruth gathers the values for the seven counties nearest hers and for her own. They are as follows:

County	Ratio Mean Value	Ratio Weighted Mean	Ratio Standard Deviation
Box	18.38%	18.36%	1.96%
Elm	12.93	13.39	3.48
Canyon	15.93	15.90	6.91
Valley	11.92	13.45	7.97
Rice	15.42	16.90	6.24
Washington	20.44	19.69	11.74
Grant	13.82	17.07	2.25
Sandstone*	13.72	14.50	6.50

*Ruth's county.

Ruth wants to discuss the implications of these figures at the next meeting of the association's directors.

3B Delphi Investment Company, Part 1

The Delphi Investment Company offers financial advice for individual and corporate clients. Its clients are of course concerned with the return on investment. Jacqueline Morton, managing partner at Delphi Investment, is considering three separate investment alternatives. Summary statistics for these three are as follows:

	Alternative 1	Alternative 2	Alternative 3
μ_x	12% return	14% return	16% return
σ_x	6%	5%	6%

Jacqueline Morton needs some assistance in presenting these three investments to a client. She is particularly concerned with analyzing the relative risks of the investments.

3C Delphi Investment Company, Part 2

At 10:10 A.M. Jacqueline Morton received word about two investment opportunities. The first investment will return an average of 8 percent with a standard deviation of 0.5 percent. The second investment will return an average of 20 percent with a standard deviation of 5 percent. Jacqueline has quickly computed the coefficient of variation of each investment and has concluded that the second investment has the greater relative dispersion in the possible returns on investment. At 10:35 A.M. Jacqueline calls a client and recommends the first investment alternative based on the relative risk between the two investments.

REFERENCES

Hamburg, Morris. *Statistical Analysis for Decision Making,* 2nd Edition. New York: Harcourt Brace Jovanovich, 1977.

Iman, R. L., and Conover, W. J. *Modern Business Statistics.* New York: Wiley, 1983.

McAllister, Harry E. *Elements of Business and Economic Statistics: Learning by Objectives.* New York: Wiley, 1975.

Pfaffenberger, Roger C., and Patterson, James H. *Statistical Methods for Business and Economics.* Homewood, Ill.: Irwin, 1977.

INTRODUCTION TO PROBABILITY CONCEPTS

4

WHY DECISION MAKERS NEED TO KNOW

Decision making means selecting between two or more alternatives. To make good decisions, managers must establish general criteria for deciding among these alternatives. Certainly the criteria must somehow be related to the objective of the decision-making situation. This objective may involve a profit level, a sales level, or even creating an orderly situation from near-chaos.

Once the objective has been established, managers often assess the chances that each alternative will reach this objective. The managers may make this assessment while saying something like, "The chances are good that if we build a parking garage, we will make a higher return on our investment than if we build an office building. On the other hand, the chances are fair that building a shopping mall will produce a higher return than a parking garage."

When managers refer to the chances of something occurring, they are using *probability* in the decision-making process. The decision makers are establishing in their minds the probability that some result will occur if a particular action is taken. If the business world were a place of certainty, decision makers would have little need to understand probability; but as emphasized in the previous chapters, the world is not certain. In practice, probability assists managers in dealing with uncertainty.

Chapter 1 pointed out that managers must often operate with sample information collected from the population of interest. They are uncertain about the population, but know a great deal about the sample. Probability theory allows managers to make inferences about the population based on knowledge of the sample and to have confidence in these inferences. As you shall see in later chapters, because statistical inference is based on probability, decision makers must have a solid grasp of basic probability theory.

CHAPTER OBJECTIVES

This chapter will present the fundamentals of probability needed to understand statistical inference. It will begin by discussing the differences between subjective probability, classical probability, and relative frequency of occurrence.

It will also cover some rules and concepts associated with probability theory. Such topics as sample space, the addition rule, the multiplication rule, independent events, and conditional probability will be included in this discussion.

STUDENT OBJECTIVES

All too often decision makers, when dealing with probability, rely on intuition rather than on well-established probability principles. This intuitive approach often proves faulty. After studying the material in this chapter, you should be able to

1. Discuss the reasoning behind, and the differences between, three approaches to assessing probability.
2. Discuss and use the common rules of probability.
3. Discuss and use three methods of counting large numbers of possible outcomes.

In studying the material in this chapter, concentrate initially on how probability helps decision makers rather than on the formulas necessary to use probability. The formulas are useless unless they are applied in the correct situation, and concentrating on applications often will remove the mystery sometimes associated with probability.

WHAT IS PROBABILITY?

4-1

Before we can apply probability to the decision-making process, we must first discuss just what is meant by *probability*. The mathematical study of probability originated over three hundred years ago. A Frenchman named Gombauld, who today would probably be a dealer in Las Vegas, began asking questions about games of chance. He was mostly interested in the probability of observing various outcomes (probably 7s and 11s) when a pair of dice was repeatedly rolled. A French mathematician named Pascal (you may remember studying Pascal's triangle in a mathematics class) was able to answer Gombauld's questions. Of course Pascal began asking more and more complicated questions of himself and his colleagues, thus beginning the formal study of probability.

Several explanations of what probability is have come out of this mathematical study. Although probabilities will help managers in a decision-making process, managers often have trouble determining how to assign probabilities. Later we shall discuss three methods managers can use to assign probabilities to possible outcomes. These three methods are **relative frequency of occurrence, subjective probability,** and **classical probability.** However, first some basic probability terminology should be introduced.

As discussed in chapter 1, data come in many forms and are gathered in many ways. In a business environment, when a sample is selected or a decision is made, there are generally many possible outcomes. A **sample space** is the collection of all possible outcomes that can result from the selection or decision. In probability language, the process that produces the outcomes in an *experiment*. In business situations, the experiment can range from an investment decision to a personnel decision to a choice of warehouse location. The individual outcomes from an experiment are called **elementary events.** Thus the sample space for an experiment consists of all the elementary events that the experiment can produce. A collection of elementary events is called an *event.* An example will help clarify these terms.

Suppose the vice-president for Project Development for Spectrum Electronics is interested in analyzing the performance of her many project development teams. She is particularly interested in whether the projects are finished by the projected completion date. The vice-president can define the elementary events for one project for one team to be

$$e_1 = \text{project done early}$$
$$e_2 = \text{project done on time}$$
$$e_3 = \text{project done late}$$

The sample space for the experiment, which would be a single project, is

$$SS = (e_1, e_2, e_3)$$

where SS = the notation for sample space.

If the experiment is expanded to include two projects, the sample space is

$$SS = (e_1, e_2, e_3, e_4, e_5, e_6, e_7, e_8, e_9)$$

where the events are defined as follows:

Elementary Event	Project 1	Project 2
e_1	early	early
e_2	early	on time
e_3	early	late
e_4	on time	early
e_5	on time	on time
e_6	on time	late
e_7	late	early
e_8	late	on time
e_9	late	late

Here, each elementary event consists of the combined outcomes of project 1 and project 2.

The manager might be interested in the event "At least one project is completed late." This event *(E)* is

$$E = (e_3, e_6, e_7, e_8, e_9)$$

In another example, the Wright National Bank classifies all outstanding installment loans into one of four categories. The experiment in this case is the loan classification. The elementary events for each loan are

$$e_1 = \text{very solid}$$
$$e_2 = \text{solid}$$
$$e_3 = \text{doubtful}$$
$$e_4 = \text{uncollectable}$$

Then the sample space for a loan is

$$SS = (e_1, e_2, e_3, e_4)$$

The manager in charge of installment loans might be interested in the event "The loan is doubtful or uncollectable." If too many loans are in one or the other of these categories, the bank examiners will issue an unfavorable report. This event is

$$E = (e_3, e_4)$$

Keeping in mind the definitions for *experiment, sample space, elementary events,* and *events,* two additional concepts are introduced. The first is the concept of *mutually exclusive events.* Two events are mutually exclusive if the occurrence of one event precludes the occurrence of the other. For example, consider again the Spectrum Electronics example. The possible elementary events for different projects done by two teams are

Elementary Event	Project 1	Project 2
e_1	early	early
e_2	early	on time
e_3	on time	early
e_4	early	late
e_5	late	early
e_6	late	on time
e_7	on time	late
e_8	late	late
e_9	on time	on time

Suppose we define one event as consisting of the elementary events in which at least one of the two projects is late:

$$E_1 = (e_4, e_5, e_6, e_7, e_8)$$

Further, suppose we define two more events as follows:

$$E_2 = \text{neither project is late}$$
$$= (e_1, e_2, e_3, e_9)$$
$$E_3 = \text{both projects are done at the same time}$$
$$= (e_1, e_8, e_9)$$

Events E_1 and E_2 are mutually exclusive: if E_1 occurs, E_2 cannot occur, and conversely. That is, if at least one project is late, then it is not also possible for neither project to be late. This can be verified by observing that no elementary events in E_1 appear in E_2. This provides another way of defining mutually exclusive events: two events are mutually exclusive if they have no common elementary events.

The second additional probability concept is that of *independent* versus *dependent* events. Two events are independent if the occurrence of one event in no way influences the probability of the occurrence of the other event. For instance, again consider the Spectrum Electronics example. The experiment is to check the completion times of two projects that had been assigned to different teams. Each pair of projects would be one trial of the experiment.

Suppose that two projects are checked and the elementary event is

Elementary Event	Project 1	Project 2
e_8	late	late

If a new pair of projects were observed and the elementary event

Elementary Event	Project 1	Project 2
e_1	early	early

occurred, the two trials would be *independent* if the probability of the occurrence of e_1 for the second pair is in no way influenced by elementary event e_8 occurring for the first pair of projects. This might be the case if the problems that caused the first pair of projects to be late in no way impacted the second pair of projects. On the other hand, if the fact the first pair of projects was late caused the people on the second pair of projects to work overtime, the trials would be considered *dependent*.

Another example of dependence and independence might be an assembly-line operation. Each item produced could be an experimental trial. On each trial the outcome is either a *good* or a *defective* item. Thus the sample space is

$$SS = (\text{good, defective})$$

As long as the machine is properly adjusted, it may produce some good outcomes and some defective outcomes with no apparent pattern, or dependency, between trials. That is, one item being good has no influence on the probability of the outcome of subsequent trials. However, if the machine goes out of adjustment, problems begin. A defective item may cause still further adjustment problems and increase the chances that subsequent items will be defective. In this case the trials are dependent because the probability of the outcome on one trial is in some way influenced by the outcome of a previous trial.

METHODS OF ASSIGNING PROBABILITY

4-2

Part of the confusion surrounding probability may be due to the fact that probability means different things to different people. This section presents three ways to assign probability to events: *relative frequency of occurrence, subjective probability assessment,* and *classical probability assessment.*

Relative Frequency of Occurrence

The **relative frequency of occurrence** method defines *probability* as the number of times an event occurs divided by the total number of times an experiment is performed. Thus the relative frequency of occurrence approach is based on actual observations. For instance, if we were interested in the probability of twenty or fewer customers arriving before 9:00 A.M. to take advantage of the new breakfast menu at our hamburger franchise, we would pick a trial number of days *(n)* and count how often twenty or fewer customers actually did order breakfasts before 9:00 A.M. Our probability assessment would be the ratio of days when twenty or fewer customers arrived to the total number of days observed. More formally, the probability "assessment" for event E_1 using the relative frequency of occurrence approach is given by equation 4–1:

$$RF(E_1) = \frac{\text{number of times } E_1 \text{ occurs}}{n} \qquad (4\text{--}1)$$

where $RF(E_1)$ = relative frequency of E_1 occurring
         n = number of trials

We can use $RF(E_1)$ to represent $P(E_1)$, the probability of E_1 occurring. However some dangers exist when using a relative frequency to represent a probability. If n is small, as it often must be in business situations because of dollar and time constraints, the estimated probability may be quite different from the true probability.

Although the relative frequency approach has some limitations, it is a valuable tool for decision makers because it can be used to quantitatively represent experience. For example, if 90 percent of the ventures a firm has undertaken have proven profitable, a starting point for estimating the probability of success of a similar new venture might be 0.90.

Subjective Probability Assessment

Unfortunately, even though managers may have past experience, there will always be new factors in a decision that make that experience only an approximate guide to the future. In other cases managers may have no past experience and therefore not be able to use a relative frequency of occurrence as even a starting point in assessing the desired probability. When past experience is not available, decision makers must make a subjective probability assessment. A **subjective probability** is a measure of a personal conviction that an outcome will occur. Subjective probability rests in a person's mind and not with the physical event. Therefore, in this instance, probability represents a person's belief that an event will occur.

Classical Probability Assessment

The final method of probability measurement is **classical probability,** or **a priori probability.** Although classical probability is not as directly applicable to business decision making as are the subjective and relative frequency methods, it is an interesting and useful tool for discussing the rules of probability. You are probably already familiar with classical probability. It had its beginning with games of chance and is still most often discussed in those terms.

In those situations where all possible outcomes are *equally likely,* the classical probability measurement is defined in equation 4–2:

$$P(E_1) = \frac{\text{number of ways } E_1 \text{ can occur}}{\text{total number of ways anything can occur}} \qquad (4\text{--}2)$$

For example, if a "fair" coin is tossed one time, the probability of heads is

$$P(\text{heads}) = \frac{\text{number of ways heads can result}}{\text{number of possible outcomes from one flip}} = \frac{1 \text{ (heads)}}{2 \text{ (heads or tails)}}$$
$$= 0.50$$

Drawing cards from a "fair" deck of cards is another example of a classical probability experiment. The probability of drawing an ace from the fifty-two well-shuffled cards is

$$P(\text{ace}) = \frac{\text{number of aces}}{\text{total number of cards}} = \frac{4}{52}$$
$$= \frac{1}{13}$$

The probability of drawing an ace of hearts is

$$P(\text{ace of hearts}) = \frac{\text{number of aces of hearts}}{\text{total number of cards}}$$
$$= \frac{1}{52}$$

As you can see, the classical approach to probability measurement is fairly straightforward. However, it is difficult to apply to most business situations. The major problem is determining values for the numerator and denominator in equation 4–2. For example, if we were interested in the probability that a particular W & A Restaurant would have gross sales next year over $50,000, we really couldn't use the classical approach

$$P(\text{sales over } \$50,000) = \frac{\text{number of ways sales can exceed } \$50,000}{\text{total sales levels possible}}$$

We could not possibly define either the total ways to have sales over $50,000 or the total possible sales levels. There are too many factors not within our control. Unlike flipping a coin, the probability of sales over $50,000 depends on the persons involved and the operating environment.

Another problem with the classical approach to probability assessment is that for equation 4–2 to apply, all possible events must be *equally likely* to occur. Although decision makers may be faced with such a situation, this will rarely be the case. In the W & A Restaurant example, the possible ways of obtaining a sales level over $50,000, even if they could all be identified, certainly do not have equal chances of occurring.

As indicated, each of the three means by which probabilities are assigned to events has special advantages and applications. However, regardless of how decision makers arrive at a probability assessment, the rules by which these probabilities are used to assist in decision making are the same.

COUNTING PRINCIPLES

4-3

The previous section discussed three methods for assigning probabilities. In applications involving either the classical or relative frequency methods, you will usually have to count the number of elementary events in the sample space in order to determine a desired probability. For many applications, physically listing the sample space would prove difficult and time consuming. Instead, counting methods exist which do not require that we physically list the sample space to determine the number of elementary events. This section introduces four specific counting techniques you will need to know and discusses the conditions under which each should be used.

The Basic Counting Principle

Suppose the Top Flight Air Freight Company has its package-sorting hub in Denver, Colorado. A package sent from anywhere in the United States and destined for anywhere else in the United States is first sent to Denver, where it is sorted and sent to its destination via airline and truck. Recently a package mailed from Miami to Chicago was lost in shipment. The company has a sophisticated tracking system that logs in all packages every step of the way. In this particular instance, the package was tracked to Denver, but never reached its final destination in Chicago. Top Flight has six flights nightly to Chicago and fourteen delivery trucks on the ground in Chicago. If the manager of lost parcels wishes to check each possible route, how many routes will he have to check?

This type of question could, of course, be answered by listing all the routes. However, we can also take advantage of the basic counting principle to determine the number of routes without listing them.

BASIC COUNTING PRINCIPLE

If an event, A, can occur in n_1 ways, and if following the occurrence of event A, a second event, B, can occur in n_2 ways, regardless of which way event A occurs, then the number of ways A and B can occur in that order is $n_1 \cdot n_2$.

Thus, in our example, the package could have traveled using $n_1 = 6$ possible airlines and $n_2 = 14$ possible trucks. Thus, the total number of routes the package could have taken is

$$6 \cdot 14 = 84 \text{ ways}$$

The basic counting principle can easily be extended to a general counting principle for cases involving more than two events.

GENERAL COUNTING PRINCIPLE

If k events can occur where event A_1 can occur in n_1 ways, followed by event A_2, which can occur in n_2 ways (regardless of how A_1 occurs) . . . followed by event A_k, which can occur in n_k ways (regardless of how the previous events occur), then the events A_1 through A_k can together occur in $n_1 \cdot n_2 \cdot n_3 \cdot \ . \ . \ . \ \cdot n_k$ ways.

Suppose a state issues car license plates that have six numerical digits. The State Licensing Bureau wishes to know how many possible license plates can be made if no two have the same six-digit number. To find this number, we can employ the general counting principle.

$$\text{Number of ways} = n_1 \cdot n_2 \cdot n_3 \cdot \ . \ . \ . \ \cdot n_6$$

Since each of the digits can take on a value of zero through nine, there are ten possible values for each digit. Therefore, the total number of license plates is

$$\begin{aligned} \text{Total number} &= 10 \cdot 10 \cdot 10 \cdot 10 \cdot 10 \cdot 10 \\ &= 1,000,000 \end{aligned}$$

The state can make one million plates without duplicating a number. Most states need more than 1,000,000 license plates. Suppose the State Licensing Bureau decides to have the first three positions on the plate be letters and the next three positions be numbers. Thus the first three positions can be any one of twenty-six letters and the last three can be any numerical value. Using the general counting principle, we can find the number of possible license plates as follows:

$$\begin{aligned} \text{Total number} &= 26 \cdot 26 \cdot 26 \cdot 10 \cdot 10 \cdot 10 \\ &= 17,576,000 \end{aligned}$$

Thus the state could make 17,576,000 plates without a duplication.

Permutations and Combinations

The general counting principle forms the basis of two other useful counting techniques: **permutations** and **combinations.** An arrangement of a set of n objects in a given order is called a permutation of the n objects. An arrangement of $r \leq n$ objects in a given order is called a permutation of n objects taken r at a time. For example, suppose a movie complex has four possible theaters and four movies. How many different ways can the four movies be shown in the four theaters? We will represent the movie complex as follows:

The first theater can show any of the four possible movies. After the first movie is placed in its theater, the second theater can show any of the three remaining movies. In a like manner, the next theater can show either of the remaining two movies. Finally, there is only one choice for the last theater. This can be shown as

| 4 | 3 | 2 | 1 |

Thus, using the general counting principle, there are $4 \cdot 3 \cdot 2 \cdot 1 = 24$ possible arrangements of the four movies. Therefore, the number of permutations of four things taken four at a time is twenty-four.

A general equation for permutations can be given using factorial notation. Factorial notation refers to the practice of denoting the product of the positive integers from n down to 1 as $n!$ (read n factorial). We also define $0! = 1$. Thus, the formula for permutations of n items taken n at a time is

$$_nP_n = n!$$

For our example:

$$_4P_4 = 4! = 4 \cdot 3 \cdot 2 \cdot 1 = 24$$

Now suppose the theater complex had six movies to choose from for its four theaters. How many possible arrangements are possible? To answer this question, we recognize there are six choices for the first theater, five choices for the second, four choices for the third theater, and three choices for the last. We represent this by

| 6 | 5 | 4 | 3 |

Using the general counting principle, we get $6 \cdot 5 \cdot 4 \cdot 3 = 360$ possible arrangements. Thus there are 360 permutations of six items taken four at a time. In general notation, the number of permutations of n items taken r at a time is

$$_nP_r = n \cdot (n - 1) \cdot (n - 2) \cdot \ldots \cdot (n - r + 1)$$

Then

$$_nP_r = \frac{n!}{(n-r)!}$$

Thus, for our example,

$$_6P_4 = \frac{6!}{2!} = \frac{6 \cdot 5 \cdot 4 \cdot 3 \cdot 2 \cdot 1}{2 \cdot 1}$$

$$= 6 \cdot 5 \cdot 4 \cdot 3$$

$$= 360$$

As another example we determine the number of permutations of seven objects taken five at a time as follows:

$$_7P_5 = \frac{7!}{(7-5)!} = \frac{7 \cdot 6 \cdot 5 \cdot 4 \cdot 3 \cdot 2 \cdot 1}{2 \cdot 1}$$

$$= 7 \cdot 6 \cdot 5 \cdot 4 \cdot 3$$

$$= 2,520$$

Frequently we wish to determine the number of permutations of objects of which some are alike. When this is the case, we need a method for finding the **permutations of like items.** One example of this is sailing ships that use flags to pass messages to shore and to other ships. A ship might have flags of four colors, say red, yellow, green, and white, with three flags of each color. Suppose a message is sent by arranging the twelve flags in a particular order. For example, the order "red, red, red, white, white, white, yellow, yellow, yellow, green, green, green" may indicate the ship is carrying an injured person. Since we do not distinguish between flags of the same color, but only the difference between colors, we can use permutations of like items to determine how many different messages can be sent with the twelve flags by finding the permutations of like items as follows:

$$\frac{n!}{x_1! \cdot x_2! \cdot x_3! \cdot \ldots \cdot x_k!}$$

where $\quad x_1, x_2, x_3, \ldots x_k$ = number of items belonging to a
particular category
k = number of categories
n = total number of items

In our flag example,

$$\text{Number of messages} = \frac{12!}{3!3!3!3!}$$

$$= 369,600$$

We have seen in the previous discussion that permutations take into account the order of objects in a group, as in the example of movies and theaters in which they are shown. However, there are many applications in which the particular ordering of the objects is not a consideration. When this is the case, instead of finding the permutations of *n* items taken *r* at a time, we need to determine the number of *combinations* of *n* items taken *r* at a time. A combination of *n* objects taken *r* at a time is any subset of *r* items from the original *n*.

Consider a marketing research study in which participants are asked to select the three cars they think are of highest quality from a list of four luxury-class automobiles. How many possible groupings of three automobiles could a given participant select? To answer this, suppose we label the cars W, X, Y, and Z. Then we can list the combinations as

Combinations	*Permutations*
W, X, Y	WXY, WYX, XWY, XYW, YXW, YWX
W, X, Z	WXZ, WZX, XWZ, XZW, ZXW, ZWX
W, Y, Z	WYZ, WZY, ZWY, ZYW, YWZ, YZW
X, Y, Z	XYZ, XZY, ZXY, ZYX, YXZ, YZX

We see that for each of the four possible combinations there are $_3P_3 = 3! = 6$ permutations. Using notation for combinations like that for permutations we get

$$3!\,_4C_3 = \,_4P_3$$

Then to find the number of combinations without listing them, we use

$$_4C_3 = \frac{_4P_3}{3!}$$

$$_4C_3 = \frac{\dfrac{4!}{1!}}{3!} = \frac{4!}{3!}$$

$$= \frac{24}{6}$$

$$= 4$$

In general notation we have the following formula for combinations:

$$_nC_r = \frac{_nP_r}{r!} = \frac{\dfrac{n!}{(n-r)!}}{r!}$$

or

$$_nC_r = \frac{n!}{r!(n-r)!}$$

Suppose the list of automobiles has seven names rather than four. Now how many combinations of three can a research participant select? Using the formula for combinations we get

$$_7C_3 = \frac{7!}{3!(7-3)!}$$

$$= \frac{7!}{3!4!}$$

$$= \frac{7 \cdot 6 \cdot 5 \cdot 4 \cdot 3 \cdot 2 \cdot 1}{(3 \cdot 2 \cdot 1)(4 \cdot 3 \cdot 2 \cdot 1)}$$

$$= \frac{7 \cdot 6 \cdot 5}{6}$$

$$= 35 \text{ combinations}$$

The earlier discussion of classical probability defined the probability that event A will occur for equally likely outcomes as

$$P(A) = \frac{\text{number of ways } A \text{ can occur}}{\text{number of ways any event can occur}}$$

As we saw in the earlier section, finding $P(A)$ is straightforward when values in the numerator and denominator are known. However, in many business situations these will not be easily determined. For example, a local company has been in trouble recently over hiring male applicants rather than female applicants. The last three employees hired were all male even though the six applicants for the three positions included three females. The company personnel director claims that in each case the remaining applicants were given an equal chance of selection because the name of the person hired was drawn from a hat. One female applicant claims that if the selections were made in this fashion, the process must have been "rigged." She says that the probability of fairly selecting three consecutive males is so low that it would be extremely doubtful that it would have happened without "some assistance from the company." How do we find this probability?

To answer this, we first let A be the event of hiring three males and no females. (We must stipulate that we started with three qualified males and three qualified females.) Then

$$P(A) = \frac{\text{number of ways to hire three males}}{\text{number of ways to hire three people from six}}$$

Our problem is to determine values for the numerator and denominator. However, the "number of ways" for each may not be immediately apparent. We might approach this problem in several ways. The most elementary way is to list the sample space as shown in table 4–1. Notice that the order of hiring is not important. We are interested only in the three jobs as a group. We find by listing the entire sample space that there

TABLE 4–1
Sample space

Elementary Event	Outcomes		
1	M_1	M_2	M_3
2	M_1	M_2	F_1
3	M_1	M_2	F_2
4	M_1	M_2	F_3
5	M_1	M_3	F_1
6	M_1	M_3	F_2
7	M_1	M_3	F_3
8	M_2	M_3	F_1
9	M_2	M_3	F_2
10	M_2	M_3	F_3
11	M_1	F_1	F_2
12	M_1	F_1	F_3
13	M_1	F_2	F_3
14	M_2	F_1	F_2
15	M_2	F_1	F_3
16	M_2	F_2	F_3
17	M_3	F_1	F_2
18	M_3	F_1	F_3
19	M_3	F_2	F_3
20	F_1	F_2	F_3

where M_1 = male number 1
M_2 = male number 2
M_3 = male number 3
F_1 = female number 1
F_2 = female number 2
F_3 = female number 3

are only twenty possible ways of hiring three people from the six applicants. Of these, only one satisfies the requirement of event *A:* all three hires are male, and that is (M_1, M_2, M_3). Thus

$$P(A) = \frac{1}{20}$$

$$= 0.05$$

The probability of hiring three males and no females is 0.05 assuming the selection process followed the random selection implied by drawing names from the hat. It would now be up to the decision makers to decide whether they think the company was "fair" in the selection process. The answer to this will depend on whether the 0.05 probability is viewed as being a very small probability.

Listing the entire sample space is fine for a limited situation like that in the example. However, suppose that instead of six applicants for the three positions, there were twelve applicants, five male and seven female. Now what is the probability that all three positions would go to males if the selection process is fair? Although listing the sample space is possible, doing so would be time consuming and there would be a good chance of accidentally omitting one or more of the elementary events. To avoid listing the sample space, you can use the combinations method, as follows.

$$P(A) = \frac{\text{number of ways three males can be hired}}{\text{number of ways any three people can be hired}}$$

Using combinations we get

$$P(A) = \frac{{}_5C_3}{{}_{12}C_3} = \frac{\dfrac{5!}{3!2!}}{\dfrac{12!}{3!9!}}$$

$$= \frac{10}{220}$$

$$= 0.045$$

Thus, if all applicants received an equal chance, the probability is 0.045 that all three jobs would go to male applicants.

SKILL DEVELOPMENT PROBLEMS FOR SECTION 4–3

The following set of problems is meant to test your understanding of the material in this section. Additional problems are found at the end of this chapter under this section heading.

1. Find the number of different ordered groups of five that can be made from ten items.

2. Find the number of different groupings of four, with order not being important, that can be made from nine items.

3. Find the number of distinct permutations of six letters that can be made from a set of four As, five Bs and six Cs.

4. The year has been good to the Finch and Nagle Investment Banking Firm. At present, they have more potential new issues to place than they can accept. Although general manpower is not a problem, only five members of the firm have the necessary experience to handle the twelve possible new issues being considered. How many possible groupings of five new issues can the firm handle? Once the five are selected, how many possible ways can they be arranged between the five experienced firm members?

5. The Carlisle Medical Clinic has five doctors on staff. The doctors have agreed to keep the office open on Saturdays but with only three doctors. The office manager has decided to make up Saturday schedules in such a way that no set of three doctors will be in the office together more than once. How many weeks can be covered by this schedule?

6. The White Aviation Company runs a charter air service with eight planes. However, because of pilot availability, only four planes can be in the air at one time. The dispatcher has decided to set up a plane usage schedule that will include the planes to be used on a particular day in order of usage. How many different schedules are possible without repeating a schedule?

PROBABILITY RULES

4-4

The probability attached to an event represents the likelihood of that event occurring on a specified trial of an experiment. This probability also measures the perceived uncertainty about whether the event will occur. If we are not uncertain at all, we will assign the event a probability of zero or 1.0: $P(E_1) = 0.0$ indicates that the event, E_1, will not occur, and $P(E_1) = 1.0$ means that E_1 will definitely occur. These values represent the outside limits on a probability assessment. If, in fact, we are uncertain about the result of an experiment, we measure this uncertainty by assigning a probability between zero and 1.0. Probability rule 1 shows the range for probability assessments.

PROBABILITY RULE 1

$$0.0 \leq P(E_i) \leq 1.0 \qquad \text{for all } i$$
$$\text{for any event } E_i$$

All possible elementary events associated with an experiment form the sample space. Probability rule 2 indicates that the probabilities of all elementary events must add up to 1.0.

PROBABILITY RULE 2

$$\sum_{i=1}^{K} P(e_i) = 1.0$$

where K = number of elementary events in the sample space
e_i = ith elementary event

For example, suppose we use classical probability theory to assign probabilities to each possible outcome of a roll of one die. We can use the classical approach since the possible outcomes are equally likely. Let the sample space be

$$SS = (1, 2, 3, 4, 5, 6)$$

Then the probability the die will turn up "1" is

$$P(1) = \frac{\text{number of ways "1" can occur}}{\text{number of ways any value can occur}}$$

Since there is only one way to roll a "1" and six possible outcomes, the probability is

$$P(1) = \frac{1}{6}$$

The same is true for each elementary event in the sample space.

e_i	$P(e_i)$
1	1/6
2	1/6
3	1/6
4	1/6
5	1/6
6	1/6
	$\Sigma = 1.0$

Note that the probabilities of the individual elementary events sum to 1.0.

Closely connected with probability rules 1 and 2 is the *complement* of an event. The complement of an event E is the collection of all possible outcomes that are not contained in event E. The complement of event E is represented by $\overline{E}$. Thus a corollary to probability rules 1 and 2 is

$$\boxed{P(\overline{E_i}) = 1 - P(E_i)}$$

That is, the probability of the complement of event E is 1.0 minus the probability of event E.

Addition Rules

When making a decision involving probabilities, you will often need to combine elementary event probabilities to find the probability associated with the event of interest. *Combining probabilities requires addition.* There are three rules that govern the addition of probabilities.

Ted's Big Boy Restaurant is thinking about opening an establishment in Appleton, Wisconsin, and has recently performed a resident survey as part of their decision-making process. Probabilities are often used in analyzing the results of questionnaires and surveys. One question of particular interest is how often the respondent dines out. Table 4–2 shows the results of the survey for this question.

We can define the sample space for the experiment for each respondent as

$$SS = (e_1, e_2, e_3, e_4)$$

where e_1 = dines out 10 or more times a week
           e_2 = dines out 3 to 9 times a week
           e_3 = dines out 1 or 2 times a week
           e_4 = dines out less than once a week

TABLE 4–2
Appleton resident responses

How Often Dines Out	Frequency	Relative Frequency
10 or more times a week	2,100	0.42
3 to 9 times a week	1,500	0.30
1 or 2 times a week	1,200	0.24
Less than once a week	200	0.04
Total	5,000	1.00

Using the relative frequency of occurrence approach, we assign the following probabilities:

$$P(e_1) = 0.42$$
$$P(e_2) = 0.30$$
$$P(e_3) = 0.24$$
$$P(e_4) = \underline{0.04}$$
$$\Sigma = 1.00$$

Suppose we define an event from these elementary events as follows:

$$E_1 = \text{respondent dines out 1 to 9 times a week}$$

The elementary events that make up E_1 are

$$E_1 = (e_2, e_3)$$

We can find the probability $P(E_1)$, by using probability rule 3.

PROBABILITY RULE 3

Addition rule for elementary events
The probability of an event E_i is equal to the sum of the probabilities of the elementary events forming E_i. That is, if

$$E_i = (e_1, e_2, e_3)$$

then

$$P(E_i) = P(e_1) + P(e_2) + P(e_3)$$

The probability a respondent dines out one or two times a week or three to nine times a week is

$$P(E_1) = P(e_2) + P(e_3) = 0.30 + 0.24$$
$$= 0.54$$

Suppose the restaurant survey also contained questions about the respondent's age. Ted's Big Boy considers age an important factor in the location decision since its restaurants do better in areas with an older population base. Table 4–3 shows the break-down of the sample by age group and by number of times the respondent dines out per week. This table illustrates two important concepts in data analysis: *joint frequencies* and *marginal frequencies*. Joint frequencies are represented by the values inside the table and represent information concerning age group and dining out jointly. Marginal frequencies are the row and column totals. These values, found in the margins, represent information concerning just age group or just dining out.

For example, 2,100 people in the survey are in the 30- to 50-year age group. This column total is a marginal frequency and is represented by E_6. Also, 600 respondents are less than 30 years old and dine out from three to nine times a week. Thus, 600 is a joint frequency represented by e_4. In this table the joint frequencies are elementary events and can be represented in terms of the two marginal frequencies making up the joint frequency. Here

$$e_4 = E_2 \text{ and } E_5$$

The key word here is *and*, which indicates a joint frequency. (You may have covered this same concept as an *intersection* in a math class.)

Table 4–4 shows the relative frequencies for the data in table 4–3.

Now let E_1 be the event that the respondent dines out ten or more times a week:

$$E_1 = (e_1, e_2, e_3)$$

TABLE 4–3

Number of times dines out by age group

How Often Dines Out	Age Group			
	E_5 Less than 30	E_6 30 to 50	E_7 Over 50	$e_1 + e_2 + e_3$
E_1 10 or more times a week	e_1 200	e_2 100	e_3 100	400
E_2 3 to 9 times a week	e_4 600	e_5 900	e_6 400	1,900
E_3 1 or 2 times a week	e_7 400	e_8 600	e_9 500	1,500
E_4 less than once a week	e_{10} 700	e_{11} 500	e_{12} 0	1,200
	1,900	2,100	1,000	5,000

TABLE 4–4
Relative frequency of number of times dines out by age group

How Often Dines Out	Age Group			
	E_5 Less than 30	E_6 30 to 50	E_7 Over 50	
E_1 10 or more times a week	e_1 200/5000 = 0.04	e_2 100/5000 = 0.02	e_3 100/5000 = 0.02	400/5000 = 0.08
E_2 3 to 9 times a week	e_4 600/5000 = 0.12	e_5 900/5000 = 0.18	e_6 400/5000 = 0.08	1900/5000 = 0.38
E_3 1 or 2 times a week	e_7 400/5000 = 0.08	e_8 600/5000 = 0.12	e_9 500/5000 = 0.10	1,500/5000 = 0.30
E_4 less than once a week	e_{10} 700/5000 = 0.14	e_{11} 500/5000 = 0.10	e_{12} 0/5000 = 0.00	1,200/5000 = 0.24
	1,900/5000 = 0.38	2,100/5000 = 0.42	1000/5000 = 0.20	5,000/5000 = 1.00

Further, let event E_5 indicate the person is less than 30:

$$E_5 = (e_1, e_4, e_7, e_{10})$$

Using rule 3, we find the probabilities for E_1 and E_5 as follows (we are using the relative frequency approach for assigning probabilities):

$$P(E_1) = P(e_1) + P(e_2) + P(e_3)$$
$$= 0.08$$
$$P(E_5) = P(e_1) + P(e_4) + P(e_7) + P(e_{10})$$
$$= 0.38$$

Suppose we now wish to find the probability of a respondent dining out less than once a week *or* being in the 30 to 50 age group. That is,

$$P(E_4 \text{ or } E_6) = ?$$

To find this probability, we must use probability rule 4.

PROBABILITY RULE 4

Addition rule for any two events E_1, E_2

$$P(E_1 \text{ or } E_2) = P(E_1) + P(E_2) - P(E_1 \text{ and } E_2)$$

The key word in knowing when to use rule 4 is *or*. The word *or* indicates addition. (You may have covered this concept as a *union* in a math class.)

Table 4–5 shows the relative frequencies, with the events of interest shaded. The overlap corresponds to the *joint occurrence* of dining out less than once a week and being in the 30 to 50 age group. The relative frequency of this overlap is $P(E_4$ and $E_6)$ and must be subtracted to avoid double counting when calculating $P(E_4$ or $E_6)$. Thus

$$P(E_4 \text{ or } E_6) = 0.24 + 0.42 - 0.10$$
$$= 0.56$$

Therefore, the probability that a respondent will either be in the 30 to 50 age group or eat out less than once a week is 0.56.

What is the probability a respondent will dine out less than once a week or be in the over-50 age group? We can again use rule 4:

$$P(E_4 \text{ or } E_7) = P(E_4) + P(E_7) - P(E_4 \text{ and } E_7)$$

Table 4–6 shows the relative frequencies for these events. We have

$$P(E_4 \text{ or } E_7) = 0.24 + 0.20 - 0.00 = 0.44$$

As can be seen, no one both dines out less than once a week and is in the over-50 age

TABLE 4–5
Joint occurrence of being in the 30 to 50 age group and dining out less than once a week

How Often Dines Out	Age Group			
	E_5 Less than 30	E_6 30 to 50	E_7 Over 50	
E_1 10 or more times a week	e_1 200/5000 = 0.04	e_2 100/5000 = 0.02	e_3 100/5000 = 0.02	400/5000 = 0.08
E_2 3 to 9 times a week	e_4 600/5000 = 0.12	e_5 900/5000 = 0.18	e_6 400/5000 = 0.08	1900/5000 = 0.38
E_3 1 or 2 times a week	e_7 400/5000 = 0.08	e_8 600/5000 = 0.12	e_9 500/5000 = 0.10	1,500/5000 = 0.30
E_4 less than once a week	e_{10} 700/5000 = 0.14	e_{11} 500/5000 = 0.10	e_{12} 0/5000 = 0.00	1,200/5000 = 0.24
	1,900/5000 = 0.38	2,100/5000 = 0.42	1000/5000 = 0.20	5,000/5000 = 1.00

TABLE 4–6
Joint occurrence of being in the over-50 age group and dining out less than once a week

How Often Dines Out	Age Group			
	E_5 Less than 30	E_6 30 to 50	E_7 Over 50	
E_1 10 or more times a week	e_1 200/5000 = 0.04	e_2 100/5000 = 0.02	e_3 100/5000 = 0.02	400/5000 = 0.08
E_2 3 to 9 times a week	e_4 600/5000 = 0.12	e_5 900/5000 = 0.18	e_6 400/5000 = 0.08	1900/5000 = 0.38
E_3 1 or 2 times a week	e_7 500/5000 = 0.08	e_8 600/5000 = 0.12	e_9 500/5000 = 0.10	1,500/5000 = 0.30
E_4 less than once a week	e_{10} 700/5000 = 0.14	e_{11} 500/5000 = 0.10	e_{12} 0/5000 = 0.00	1,200/5000 = 0.24
	1,900/5000 = 0.38	2,100/5000 = 0.42	1000/5000 = 0.20	5,000/5000 = 1.00

group.[1] When the joint probability of two events is zero, the events are mutually exclusive. This is consistent with our earlier definition of mutually exclusive events. When events are mutually exclusive, a special form of rule 4 applies:

PROBABILITY RULE 5

Addition rule for mutually exclusive events E_1, E_2

$$P(E_1 \text{ or } E_2) = P(E_1) + P(E_2)$$

This section has presented three rules for adding probabilities. You should become familiar with these rules and understand how they are used. To test your understanding, use the information in table 4–6 and let

$$E_8 = (E_1, E_2)$$
$$E_9 = (E_5, E_6)$$

---

[1]This example illustrates a potential weakness in using relative frequencies to represent probabilities. In this case no person both dined out less than once a week and was over 50. Thus, using relative frequencies, we conclude the probability of the joint event is zero. A larger sample may well have included one or more persons in this joint category, in which case the true probability is not zero. However, for the purposes of this example, we will assume these events are mutually exclusive.

Find

$$P(E_8 \text{ or } E_9)$$

Your answer should be 0.82. Do you know why?

Conditional Probability

In dealing with probabilities, you will often need to determine the chances of two or more events occurring either at the same time or in succession. For example, a quality control manager for a manufacturing company may be interested in the probability of selecting two successive defectives from an assembly line. If the probability is low, this manager would be surprised at such a result and might readjust the production process.

In other instances the decision maker may know that an event has occurred and may want to know the chances of a second event occurring. For instance, suppose an oil company geologist feels oil will be found at a certain drilling site. The oil company exploration vice-president might well be interested in the probability of finding oil, given the favorable report.

These situations require tools different from those presented in the section on addition rules. Specifically, you need to become acquainted with rules for *conditional probability* and *multiplication* of probabilities.

West-Air, Inc., a regional airline, has performed a study of its customers' traveling habits. Among the information collected are the data shown in table 4–7. Lee Hansel, the operations manager, is aware the average traveler has changed over the years. Given the recent increase in discount fares, Lee is particularly interested in maintaining good relations with business travelers. However, since a business traveler is no longer necessarily dressed in a suit, or even always a man, Lee has trouble telling a business traveler from a nonbusiness traveler. Yet he wants to know the present composition of people traveling on his company's airline.

Trips per Year	Sex		
	E_4 Female	E_5 Male	
E_1 1 or 2	e_1 $f = 450$	e_2 $f = 500$	$\Sigma = 950$
E_2 3–10	e_3 $f = 300$	e_4 $f = 800$	$\Sigma = 1{,}100$
E_3 Over 10	e_5 $f = 100$	e_6 $f = 350$	$\Sigma = 450$
	$\Sigma = 850$	$\Sigma = 1{,}650$	$\Sigma = 2{,}500$

TABLE 4–7
West-Air, Inc. data

Suppose Lee knows a traveler is female and wants to know the chances this woman will travel between three and ten times a year. We let

$$E_2 = (e_3, e_4) = \text{event: person travels 3–10 times per year}$$
$$E_4 = (e_1, e_3, e_5) = \text{event: traveler is female}$$

Then Lee needs to know the probability of E_2 given E_4 has occurred. Table 4–8 shows the frequencies and relative frequencies of interest. One way to find the desired probability is as follows:

1. We know E_4 has occurred. There are 850 females in the survey.
2. Of the 850 females, 300 travel between three and ten times per year.
3. Then

$$P(E_2|E_4) = \frac{300}{850}$$
$$= 0.3529$$

The notation $P(E_2|E_4)$ is read "probability of E_2 given E_4."

Although this approach produces the desired probability, probability rule 6 offers a general rule for conditional probability.

PROBABILITY RULE 6

Conditional probability for any two events E_1, E_2

$$P(E_1|E_2) = \frac{P(E_1 \text{ and } E_2)}{P(E_2)}$$

where: $P(E_2) \neq 0$

TABLE 4–8
West-Air Inc. relative frequencies

Trips per Year	Sex		
	E_4 Female	E_5 Male	
E_1 1 or 2	e_1 $RF = 450/2{,}500 = 0.18$	e_2 $RF = 500/2{,}500 = 0.20$	$950/2{,}500 = 0.38$
E_2 3–10	e_3 $RF = 300/2{,}500 = 0.12$	e_4 $RF = 800/2{,}500 = 0.32$	$1{,}100/2{,}500 = 0.44$
E_3 Over 10	e_5 $RF = 100/2{,}500 = 0.04$	e_6 $RF = 350/2{,}500 = 0.14$	$450/2{,}500 = 0.18$
	$850/2{,}500 = 0.34$	$1.650/2{,}500 = 0.66$	$2{,}500/2{,}500 = 1.00$

Rule 6 uses a *joint probability*, $P(E_1$ and $E_2)$, and a *marginal probability*, $P(E_2)$, to calculate the conditional probability, $P(E_1|E_2)$. Note that, to find a conditional probability, we find the ratio of how frequently E_1 occurs to the total number of observations given that we restrict our observations to only those cases where E_2 has occurred.

Applying rule 6 in our previous problem,

$$P(E_2|E_4) = \frac{0.12}{0.34}$$

$$= 0.3529$$

where $P(E_2$ and $E_4) = 0.12$
$P(E_4) = 0.34$

An earlier section stated that two events are independent if one event occurring has no bearing on the probability the second event occurs. Therefore, when two events are independent, the rule for conditional probability takes a special form, as indicated in probability rule 7.

PROBABILITY RULE 7

Conditional probability for independent events, E_1, E_2

$$P(E_1|E_2) = P(E_1)$$

and

$$P(E_2|E_1) = P(E_2)$$

As rule 7 shows, the conditional probability of one event occurring, given a second independent event has already occurred, is simply the probability of the first occurring.

Table 4–9 shows some more data from the West-Air passenger survey which we can use to demonstrate rule 7.

Suppose Lee Hansel wants to know the probability a passenger will pay cash for the airline ticket given the passenger is a male. To find this probability, let

$$E_1 = (e_1, e_2) = \text{event: pay with cash}$$
$$E_4 = (e_2, e_4) = \text{event: passenger is male}$$

Then, using rule 6, $P(E_1|E_4)$ is as follows:

$$P(E_1|E_4) = \frac{P(E_1 \text{ and } E_4)}{P(E_4)} = \frac{0.2112}{0.6600}$$

$$= 0.32$$

But, from table 4–9, $P(E_1) = 0.32$. Thus

$$P(E_1|E_4) = P(E_1)$$

Therefore these two events are independent.

You should become comfortable with the rules for conditional probability since they are used heavily in statistical decision making.

Multiplication Rules

We needed the joint probability of two events in the preceding discussion. We were able to find $P(E_1$ and $E_4)$ simply by examining the frequencies in table 4–9. However, often we need to find $P(E_1$ and $E_2)$ when we do not know the joint relative frequencies. To illustrate how to find a joint probability, consider an example involving classical probability.

Suppose a game of chance involves selecting two cards from a fifty-two card deck. If both cards are aces, the participant receives a specified payoff. What is the probability of selecting two aces? To answer this question, we must recognize that two events are required to form the desired outcome. Therefore, let

$$A_1 = \text{event: ace on the first draw}$$

$$A_2 = \text{event: ace on the second draw}$$

The question really being asked is, what are the chances of observing both A_1 and A_2? The key word here is *and,* as contrasted with the addition rule, where the key word is *or.* The *and* signifies that we are interested in the joint probability of two events, as noted by

$$P(A_1 \text{ and } A_2)$$

To find this probability, we employ rule 8, the multiplication rule.

TABLE 4–9

Payment method by sex of traveler

Payment Method	Sex		
	E_3 Female	E_4 Male	
E_1 Cash	e_1 $f = 272$ $RF = 272/2{,}500 = 0.1088$	e_2 $f = 528$ $RF = 528/2{,}500 = 0.2112$	$\dfrac{800}{2{,}500} = 0.3200$
E_2 Credit card	e_3 $f = 578$ $RF = 578/2{,}500 = 0.2312$	e_4 $f = 1{,}122$ $RF = 1{,}122/2{,}500 = 0.4488$	$\dfrac{1{,}700}{2{,}500} = 0.6800$
	$850/2{,}500 = 0.3400$	$1{,}650/2{,}500 = 0.6600$	$\dfrac{2{,}500}{2{,}500} = 1.0000$

PROBABILITY RULE 8
Multiplication rule for two events E_1, E_2

$$P(E_1 \text{ and } E_2) = P(E_1)P(E_2|E_1)$$

and

$$P(E_2 \text{ and } E_1) = P(E_2)P(E_1|E_2)$$

Note that rule 8 is an algebraic rearrangement of rule 6.

We use the classical approach to probability assessment to find the value of $P(A_1$ and $A_2)$ as follows:

$$P(A_1) = \frac{\text{number of aces}}{\text{number of possible cards}}$$

$$= \frac{4}{52}$$

Then, since we are not replacing the first card, we find $P(A_2|A_1)$ by

$$P(A_2|A_1) = \frac{\text{number of remaining aces}}{\text{number of remaining cards}}$$

$$= \frac{3}{51}$$

Thus, by rule 8,

$$P(A_1 \text{ and } A_2) = P(A_1)P(A_2|A_1) = \left(\frac{4}{52}\right)\left(\frac{3}{51}\right)$$

$$= 0.0045$$

Therefore there are slightly more than four chances in 1,000 of selecting two successive aces from a fifty-two card deck *without* replacement.

Note that rule 8 requires that conditional probability be used since the result on the second draw depends on the card selected on the first draw. The chance of obtaining an ace on the second draw was lowered from 4/52 to 3/51 given that the first card was an ace. However, if the two events of interest are *independent*, the conditional aspect is not important, and the multiplication rule takes the form shown in probability rule 9.

PROBABILITY RULE 9
Multiplication rule for independent events E_1, E_2

$$P(E_1 \text{ and } E_2) = P(E_1)P(E_2)$$

Thus the joint probability of two independent events is simply the product of the marginal probabilities of the two events.

The probability rules presented in this section are vital to managers who will use statistical decision-making techniques. Remember the key words *or* and *and*. Know with what rules they are associated, and you should have little trouble with basic probability theory.

SKILL DEVELOPMENT PROBLEMS FOR SECTION 4–4

The following set of problems is meant to test your understanding of the material in this section. Additional problems are found at the end of this chapter under this section heading.

7. Find the following probabilities associated with rolling two dice:
   a. Rolling an 11.
   b. Rolling a 7.
   c. Rolling a 5.
   d. Rolling two 7s in a row.
   e. Rolling first a 7 and then a 5.
   f. Rolling first a 5 and then a 7.

8. From a population of five As, ten Bs and fifteen Cs:
   a. What is the probability of randomly selecting a B?
   b. What is the probability of randomly selecting a B and then a C if sampling is done with replacement? Is there a change if sampling is done without replacement?
   c. What is the probability of selecting either an A or a B?
   d. What is the probability of selecting three straight Cs if sampling is done without replacement?

9. Using the following joint frequency distribution table:

	A	B	C	Sum
D	20	32	18	70
E	12	28	40	80
F	8	20	22	50
	40	80	80	200

   a. What is $P(C)$?
   b. What is $P(E)$?
   c. What is $P(A$ and $F)$?
   d. What is $P(D$ or $F)$?
   e. What is $P(E$ or $B)$?
   f. What is $P(D$ and $E)$?

10. Your neighbor has just returned from a trip to Atlantic City and claims to have a foolproof method to make money on the roulette wheel. She knows the odds are slightly with the house on any single roll but claims all you need to do is to watch the wheel and any time three successive rolls have the same color bet the next roll on the opposite color. Comment on her technique.

11. In the late 1960s the U.S. government instituted a lottery system for determining how young men between the ages of eighteen and twenty-six would be drafted into military service. Three hundred sixty-five balls, each with a different day of the year, were placed in a large drum and mixed. Balls were selected from the drum randomly.
    a. What is the probability that the first two balls selected were for birthdays in March?
    b. What is the probability that the first ball selected was a December birthday or a birthday on the first of any month?
    c. If the first ball selected was a March birthday, what is the probability that the second ball selected was a June birthday.
    d. What is the probability that the first three balls selected were of birthdays in the same month?

12. The Ace Construction company has submitted a bid on a state government project in Delaware. The price of the bid was predetermined in the bid specifications. The contract is to be awarded on the basis of a blind drawing from those who have bid. Five other companies have also submitted bids.
    a. What is the probability of the Ace Construction Company winning the bid?
    b. Suppose that there are two contracts to be awarded by a blind draw. What is the probability of Ace winning both contracts?
    c. Referring to part b, what is the probability of Ace not winning either contract?
    d. Referring to part b, what is the probability of Ace winning exactly one contract?
    e. Referring to part b, what is the probability of Ace winning at least one contract?

CONCLUSIONS

4-5

Probability provides decision makers a quantitative measure of the chance an environmental outcome will occur. It allows decision makers to quantify uncertainty. The objectives of this chapter have been to discuss the various types of probability and to provide the basic rules that govern probability operations.

We have discussed many probability concepts from a managerial perspective. The chapter glossary lists a set of strict definitions for important probability concepts introduced in this chapter. To test your understanding of these concepts, reconcile the managerial definitions with the more formal definitions. The list of chapter formulas follows the glossary.

CHAPTER GLOSSARY

classical probability   A method of determining probability based on the ratio of the number of ways the event of interest can occur to the number of ways any event can occur.

combinations   The method of counting possible selections from a set of elementary events when order is not important.

$$_nC_r = \frac{n!}{r!(n-r)!}$$

elementary events   The single outcomes resulting from an experiment.

permutations   The method of counting possible arrangements from a set of elementary events when order is important.

$$_nP_r = \frac{n!}{(n-r)!}$$

permutations of like items   The method of counting possible selections from a set of elementary events when order is important but the simple events within particular categories are indistinguishable.

$$\text{Permutations of like items} = \frac{n!}{X_1!X_2!X_3!\ldots X_k!}$$

relative frequency of occurrence   The method that defines probability as the number of times an event occurs divided by the total number of times an experiment is performed.

sample space   The set of all possible elementary events, or outcomes, that can result from a single trial or experiment.

subjective probability   The method that relates probability to a decision maker's state of mind regarding the likelihood a particular event will occur.

CHAPTER FORMULAS

Probability rule 1

$$0.0 \leq P(E_i) \leq 1.0 \qquad \text{for all } i$$

for any event E_i (including elementary events)

Probability rule 2

$$\sum_{i=1}^{K} P(e_i) = 1.0$$

Probability rule 3   Addition rule for elementary events
The probability an event E_i is equal to the sum of the probabilities of the elementary events forming E_i. That is, if

$$E_i = (e_i, e_2, e_3)$$

then

$$P(E_i) = P(e_i) + P(e_2) + P(e_3)$$

Probability rule 4   Addition rule for any two events E_1, E_2

$$P(E_1 \text{ or } E_2) = P(E_1) + P(E_2) - P(E_1 \text{ and } E_2)$$

Probability rule 5   Addition rule for mutually exclusive events E_1, E_2

$$P(E_1 \text{ or } E_2) = P(E_1) + P(E_2)$$

Probability rule 6   Conditional probability for any two events E_1, E_2 $[P(E_2) \neq 0]$

$$P(E_1|E_2) = \frac{P(E_1 \text{ and } E_2)}{P(E_2)}$$

Probability rule 7   Conditional probability for independent events E_1, E_2

$$P(E_1|E_2) = P(E_1)$$

and

$$P(E_2|E_1) = P(E_2)$$

Probability rule 8   Multiplication rule for two events E_1, E_2

$$P(E_1 \text{ and } E_2) = P(E_1)P(E_2|E_1)$$

and

$$P(E_2 \text{ and } E_1) = P(E_2)P(E_1|E_2)$$

Probability rule 9   Multiplication rule for independent events E_1, E_2

$$P(E_1 \text{ and } E_2) = P(E_1)P(E_2)$$

SOLVED PROBLEMS

1. There are four defective power supplies in a package of ten. If two power supplies are randomly selected one after another, what is the probability of
   a. One defective and one good power supply being selected?
   b. Two defectives being selected?
   c. At least one defective being selected?
   d. Three good power supplies being selected?

Solutions:

a. We will solve this problem two ways. First we list the sample space as follows:

G,G
G,D
D,G
D,D

where   G = good power supply
          D = defective power supply
Then we attach probabilities to each sample event.

$$P(G_1) = P(\text{good on first draw})$$

$$= \frac{6}{10}$$

$$P(D_1) = P(\text{defective on first draw})$$

$$= \frac{4}{10}$$

Notice that the probabilities on the second draw depend on what took place on the first draw. Thus

$$P(G_2|G_1) = \frac{5}{9}$$

$$P(G_2|D_1) = \frac{6}{9}$$

$$P(D_2|G_1) = \frac{4}{9}$$

$$P(D_2|D_1) = \frac{3}{9}$$

Then we find the probability of one defective power supply and one good power supply in a sample of two by using both the addition rule and the conditional probability rule:

$$P(G_1 \text{ and } D_2) + P(D_1 \text{ and } G_2) = P(G_1)P(D_2|G_1) + P(D_1)P(G_2|D_1)$$

$$= \left(\frac{6}{10}\right)\left(\frac{4}{9}\right) + \left(\frac{4}{10}\right)\left(\frac{6}{9}\right)$$

$$= \frac{24}{90} + \frac{24}{90} = \frac{48}{90}$$

$$= \frac{8}{15}$$

A second method uses the combinations counting method. We are looking for the sample event of selecting two power supplies by picking one of the four defectives and one of the six good supplies. This is represented in the following picture.

$$P(1 \text{ defective and } 1 \text{ good}) = \frac{\text{number of ways to get 1 defective and 1 good}}{\text{number of ways to draw 2 power supplies}}$$

$$= \frac{{}_4C_1 \text{ and } {}_6C_1}{{}_{10}C_2} = \frac{\left(\dfrac{4!}{1!3!}\right)\left(\dfrac{6!}{1!5!}\right)}{\dfrac{10!}{2!8!}}$$

$$= \frac{(4)(6)}{45} = \frac{24}{45}$$

$$= \frac{8}{15}$$

b. We want the following situation:

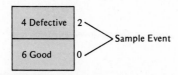

Again using combinations, we obtain

$$P(2 \text{ defective}) = \frac{\text{number of ways to draw 2 defective and 0 good}}{\text{number of ways to draw 2 power supplies}}$$

$$= \frac{{}_4C_2 \text{ and } {}_6C_0}{{}_{10}C_2} = \frac{\left(\dfrac{4!}{2!2!}\right)\left(\dfrac{6!}{0!6!}\right)}{45}$$

$$= \frac{6}{45}$$

$$= \frac{2}{15}$$

Remember, $0! = 1$.

c. We are looking for the following sample event:

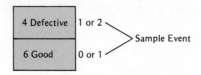

We know that

$$P(0 \text{ defective}) + P(1 \text{ defective}) + P(2 \text{ defective}) = 1$$

or

$$P(0 \text{ defective}) + P(1 \text{ or more defective}) = 1$$

So

$$P(1 \text{ or more defective}) = 1 - P(0 \text{ defective})$$

To find $P(1 \text{ or more defective})$, we find $P(0 \text{ defective})$. Using combinations,

$$P(0 \text{ defective}) \frac{(_4C_0)(_6C_2)}{_{10}C_2} = \frac{(1)(15)}{45}$$

$$= \frac{1}{3}$$

Therefore

$$P(1 \text{ or more defective}) = 1 - \frac{1}{3}$$

$$= \frac{2}{3}$$

d. $P(3 \text{ good}) = 0$ since only two power supplies are selected.

2. A small town has two ambulances. Records indicate that the first ambulance is in service 60 percent of the time and the second one is in service 40 percent of the time. What is the probability that when an ambulance is needed, one will not be available?

Solution:

The sample space is as follows:

$$A, A = \text{both available}$$
$$A, B = \text{one available}$$
$$B, A = \text{one available}$$
$$B, B = \text{both busy}$$

If we assume that the ambulances being busy are *independent* events (no large accidents), the probability of both ambulances being busy is

$$P(\text{B and B}) = (0.60)(0.40)$$
$$= 0.24$$

3. For the information given in problem 2, what is the probability that at least one ambulance will be available?

Solution:

Since

$$P(0 \text{ available}) + P(1 \text{ or more available}) = 1$$

then

$$P(1 \text{ or more available}) = 1 - P(0 \text{ available}) = 1 - 0.24$$
$$= 0.76$$

ADDITIONAL PROBLEMS

Section 4–1

13. The Goldberg Construction Company recently bid on three contracts, each of which it can either be awarded or not awarded.
   a. Define the elementary events for a given bid.
   b. List the sample space for a bid on one contract.
   c. List the sample space for all three contracts.

14. The Harrison Corporation manufactures electronic components for the U.S. government. One particular component can be made either without defect, with a minor defect, or with a major defect.
   a. If the company makes only one of these components, list the sample space.
   b. If the company makes three of the components, list the sample space.
   c. Grouping the minor defect and major defect elementary events together, list the sample space if the company makes six components.

15. The Sullivan Stables Company owns and races expensive racehorses. One of its horses placed second in the Kentucky Derby two years ago. Suppose Sullivan Stables recently purchased a new racehorse from a European breeder. Sullivan plans to race the horse four times this year.
   a. If the company is interested only in winning versus losing a particular race, list the sample space for the four races. Let W indicate win and L indicate lose.
   b. Suppose the stable is interested in the chances of the horse placing first, second, third, or lower in each race. List the sample space for the first two races.

Section 4–2

16. Discuss what is meant by the relative frequency of occurrence approach to probability assessment. Provide a business-related example other than those given in the text where this method of probability assessment might be used.

17. Discuss what is meant by *subjective probability*. Provide a business-related example in which subjective probability assessment would likely be used. Also provide an example of when you have personally used subjective probability assessment.

18. Discuss what is meant by *classical probability assessment* and indicate why classical assessment is not often used in business applications.

19. Amstar Airlines has just supplied data to the U.S. federal government indicating that out of 10,000 flights, 4,900 arrived on time (within five minutes of schedule), 4,000 arrived late, and the remaining flights arrived early.
    a. Using the relative frequency of occurrence method, provide an assessment of the chances that an Amstar Airlines flight will arrive on time.
    b. Assess the probability that a flight will be late.
    c. Assess the chances that a flight will be early.
    d. Comment on some of the potential problems associated with using relative frequency of occurrence probability assessment in cases like this one.

20. Assuming the outcomes of lottery are equally likely:
    a. What is the probability that an individual will win if he or she holds one ticket out of 500 sold?
    b. What is the probability of winning if he or she holds three tickets out of 500 sold?
    c. What method of probability assessment did you use to answer parts a and b?

21. Based on your experience thus far in the text, what is the probability that you will receive an A grade? Discuss the factors you have used in arriving at this probability assessment. Do you believe that all students in your class will arrive at the same probability assessment that you have? Why or why not?

22. How old is your statistics instructor? Rather than trying to pick an exact age, assess a probability to each of the following categories. Make sure that the sum of the probabilities you assess equals 1.0.

    Under 30
    30–40
    41–50
    51–60
    Over 60

Compare your assessments with those of some other students in the class. Why might the assessments be different? Discuss.

Section 4–3

23. A bicycle manufacturer offers five color options, three handlebar options, and four seat options on its deluxe bicycle. How many different configurations could the company possibly make?

24. A computer program designed to prepare time and billing reports for an accounting firm has six subroutines. The first subroutine has three alternative paths that the program can take depending on the type of application. The second has four paths, the third has only one path, the fourth has eleven paths, the fifth has four paths, and the final subroutine has only two paths.

    a. If the program designer were considering testing the first three subroutines, how many different tests would she have to conduct to make sure that all paths had been taken at least once? (For example, one test might be subroutine 1—path 1, subroutine 2—path 1, and subroutine 3—path 1.)

    b. If the programmer wished to test the entire program and each possible path through it, how many different tests would be required?

25. A photography studio recently ran a Christmas special for children's photographs. It offered three poses with a nature backdrop, four poses with a fireside backdrop, and four poses with a schoolroom backdrop. If the parents must purchase one picture of each backdrop, how many possible choices will each customer have per child?

26. The United Way campaign has fifteen applicants for funding this year. If the committee will fund only seven of these, how many possible lists of sucessful applicants are there?

27. The Devor Corporation recently planned to test market a new product in an Arizona community. Management decided that it could put its product in five of the ten possible stores. The manager said that he would like to see a list of the possible store combinations before he picked the five stores to be used. How long will this list be?

28. A production manager has eleven people in his crew. A special project that will require five people for about a week has been assigned to this crew. Since any of the eleven people could successfully serve on the special crew, the manager wishes to select the crew randomly. How many different possible five-person crews can he select from the eleven people?

29. The KYLT radio station program manager has started call-in request program from noon to 1 P.M. Time permits ten requested songs, news, sports, and some special features to be broadcast. Listeners place their calls before 11.00 A.M. to have them played during the hour slot.

    a. Suppose the first day, fifteen people called to request different songs. If the order the songs are played is not considered important, in how many ways can ten songs be played from the fifteen requested?

    b. If the order the songs are played is important, how many different sequences of ten records can be played from the fifteen requested?

30. The Phillips Publishing Company publishes technical manuscripts for the Defense Department. The contract specifies the allowable error rate and so the company has a policy of having three reviewers check each manuscript.
  a. If the company has eight available reviewers, how many different groupings of three reviewers are possible to assign to a particular manuscript?
  b. Suppose the payment to a reviewer depends on the order in which he or she reviewed the manuscript (the first reviewer receives the highest payment and so forth). How many different arrangements can be made with three reviewers from the eight?

Section 4-4

39. Define
  a. Mutually exclusive events.
  b. Independent events.
     List five business examples of each.

32. Suppose $P(A) = 0.50$, $P(B) = 0.40$, and $P(A \text{ and } B) = 0.20$.
  a. Are A and B mutually exclusive? Why or why not?
  b. Are A and B independent events? Why or why not?

33. If the probability of a particular stock increasing in value is assessed at 0.60 and the probability of a second stock increasing is 0.70, are the two stocks independent if the probability of both stocks increasing is 0.15? Discuss.

34. A board of directors consists of ten members, six of whom are loyal to the current company president and four of whom want to fire the president. If the chairman of the board, who is a loyal supporter of the president, decides to randomly select four other board members to serve with him on a committee to decide the president's fate,
  a. What is the probability all five members will vote to keep the president if no one changes sides?
  b What is the probability that a majority of the five members will vote to keep the president if no one changes sides? A majority vote will decide the issue.
  c. What is the probability that the vote will be four to one in favor of firing the current president if no one on the board changes sides?

35. The Town-Pump service station has performed an analysis of its gas customers and found that 80 percent pay on credit and the rest pay cash. If five customers are sampled, what is the probability that three or fewer of them will pay on credit?

36. In the sales business, repeat calls to finally make a sale are common. Suppose a particular salesperson has a 0.70 probability of selling on the first call and that the probability of selling drops by 0.10 on each successive call. If the salesperson is willing to make up to four calls on any client, what is the probability of a sale?

37. Of a batch of twenty television picture tubes, five are known to be defective. What is the probability that a sample of five without replacement will result in each of the following?
  a. Exactly one defective

b. No defectives

c. Two or fewer defectives

38. Recreational developers are considering opening a skiing area near a western U.S. town. They are trying to decide whether to open an area catering to family skiers or to some other group. To help make their decision, they gather the following information. If

$$A_1 = \text{family will ski}$$
$$A_2 = \text{family will not ski}$$
$$B_1 = \text{family has children but none in the 8–16 age group}$$
$$B_2 = \text{family has children in the 8–16 age group}$$
$$B_3 = \text{family has no children}$$

Then, for this location,

$$P(A_1) = 0.40$$
$$P(B_2) = 0.35$$
$$P(B_3) = 0.25$$
$$P(A_1|B_2) = 0.70$$
$$P(A_1|B_1) = 0.30$$

a. Use the probabilities given to construct a joint probability distribution table.

b. What is the probability a family will ski *and* have children but not any in the 8–16 age group? How do you write this probability?

c. What is the probability a family with children in the 8–16 age group will not ski?

d. Are the categories "skiing" and "family composition" independent?

39. A company is considering changing its starting hour from 8:00 A.M. to 7:30 A.M. A census of the company's 1,200 office and production workers shows 370 of its 750 production workers favor the change and a total of 715 workers favor the change. To further assess worker opinion, the region manager decides to randomly talk with workers.

a. What is the probability a randomly selected worker will be in favor of the change?

b. What is the probability a randomly selected worker will be against the change *and* be an office worker?

c. Is the relationship between job type and opinion independent? Why?

40. An investment advisor has a portfolio of eighty stocks: fifty blue-chip and thirty growth stocks. Of the fifty blue-chip stocks, thirty have increased in price during the past month, and twenty of the thirty growth stocks have increased in price.

a. If a stock is selected at random from the portfolio, what is the probability it will be a blue-chip stock that has not increased in price?

b. What is the probability of selecting a stock that has increased in price?

c. If the stock selected has not increased in price, what is the probability it is a growth stock?

41. Bill Jones and Herman Smith are long-time business associates. They know that regular exercise improves their productivity and have made a practice of playing either tennis or golf every Saturday for the past ten years. Jones enjoys tennis, but Smith prefers golf. Each Saturday they flip a coin to decide what sport to play. Jones beats Smith at tennis 80 percent of the time, whereas he beats Smith at golf only 30 percent of the time.

a. Suppose Jones walks into the Monday morning staff meeting and announces he beat Smith on Saturday. What sport do you think they played and why?

b. Assume open tennis courts are hard to find on Saturday, so instead of flipping a coin, Smith and Jones always first look for a tennis court. If they find one open, they play tennis; if not, they play golf. Further, suppose the chance of finding an open court is 30 percent. Given this, what sport do you think they played on Saturday, given that Jones won?

42. A marketing research team is considering using a mailing list for an advertising campaign. They know that 40 percent of the people on the list have only a MasterCard and that 10 percent have only an American Express card. Another 20 percent hold both MasterCard and American Express. Finally, 30 percent of those on the list have neither card.

Suppose a person on the list is known to have a MasterCard. What is the probability that person also has an American Express card?

C A S E S

4A Great Air Commuter Service

The Great Air Commuter Service Company originated in 1984 to provide efficient and inexpensive commuter travel between Boston and New York City. Peter Wilson, the principal owner and operating manager of the company, is known as "a real promoter" by people in the airline industry. Before founding Great Air, Peter operated a small regional airline in the Rocky Mountain area with varying success. When Cascade Airlines offered to buy his company. Peter decided to sell and return to the East.

Peter arrived at his office near Fenway Park in Boston a little later than usual this morning. He had stopped to have a business breakfast with Aaron Little, his longtime friend and sometimes partner in various business deals. Peter needed some advice and through the years had learned to rely on Aaron as a ready source of advice no matter what the subject.

Peter had explained to Aaron that his commuter service needed a promotional gimmick to improve its visibility among the business communities in both Boston and

New York. Peter was thinking of running some sort of contest on each flight and awarding the winner a prize of some sort. The idea would be that travelers who have to
commute between Boston and New York might just as well have fun on the way and
have a chance to win a nice prize.

As Aaron sat back listening to Peter outline his contest plans, his mind raced
through ideas for contests. Aaron thought that a large variety of contests and types of
contests would be needed since many of the passengers would likely be repeat customers
and might tire of the same old thing. In addition some of the contests should be chance-
type contests, while others should be skill-based.

"Well, what do you think?" asked Peter. Aaron finished his scrambled eggs before responding. When he did, it was completely in character. "I think it will fly,"
Aaron said and proceeded to offer a variety of suggestions.

Peter felt good about the enthusiastic response Aaron had given to the idea and
thought that the ideas discussed at breakfast presented a good basis for the promotional
effort. Now back at the office Peter did have some concerns with one part of the plan.
Aaron felt that in addition to the regular in-flight contests for prizes (such as free flights,
dictation equipment, business periodical subscriptions) each month on a randomly selected day, a major prize should be offered on all Great Air flights. This would encourage the regular business fliers to fly Great Air all the time. Aaron proposed that the
prize could be a trip to the Virgin Islands or somewhere similar or the cash equivalent.

Great Air has three flights daily to New York and three flights returning to Boston
for a total of six flights. Peter was concerned that the cost of funding six prizes of this
size each month plus six daily smaller prizes might be excessive. Peter felt that it might
be better to increase the size of the prize to something like a new car, but use a contest
that would not guarantee a winner.

But what kind of a contest could be use? Just as he was about to dial Aaron's
number, Margret Runyon, Great Air's marketing manager, entered Peter's office. He
had been waiting for her to return from a meeting so he could run the contest idea past
her and get her input.

Margret's response was not as upbeat as Aaron's had been, but she did feel the
idea was worth looking into. She offered an idea for the large prize contest which she
thought might be workable. She outlined the contest as follows.

On the first of each month she and Peter would randomly select a day for that
month on which the major contest would be run. That date would not be disclosed to
the public. Then on each flight that day, the flight attendant would ask each passenger
to write down his birthday (month and day). If any two people on the plane had the
same birthday, they would place their names in a hat and one name would be selected
to receive the grand prize.

Margret explained that since the capacity of each flight was forty passengers plus
the crew that there was a very low chance of a birthday match and, therefore, the chance
of giving away a grand prize on any one flight was small. Peter liked the idea but when
he asked Margret what the probability was that a match would occur, her response of
40/365 for a full plane and less than that when there are fewer than forty passengers
aboard didn't sound quite right.

After Margret left, Peter thought that it would be useful to know the probability of one or more birthday matches on flights with 20, 30 and 40 passengers. Further, he wanted to know what the chances were that he would end up awarding two or more major prizes during a given month, assuming that the six flights carried the same number of passengers (20, 30, or 40). He realized that he would need some help from someone with a background in statistics.

REFERENCES

Blyth, C. R. "Subjective vs. Objective Methods in Statistics." *American Statistician* 26 (June 1972): 20–22.

Hogg, R. V., and Elliot, A. T. *Probability and Statistical Inference,* 2nd Edition. New York: MacMillian Publishing, 1983.

Raiffa, Howard. *Decision Analysis,* Reading, Mass.: Addison-Wesley, 1968.

Rowntree, Dereck. *Probability,* New York: Charles Scribner's, 1984.

DISCRETE PROBABILITY DISTRIBUTIONS $\quad$ 5

WHY DECISION MAKERS NEED TO KNOW

Thus far we have seen that a frequency distribution transforms ungrouped data into more meaningful form. Therefore frequency distributions help decision makers deal with the uncertainty in their decision environments. We also learned in chapter 4 that probability is a fundamental part of statistics. Because all managers operate in an uncertain environment, they must be able to make the connection between descriptive statistics and probability. This connection is made by moving from frequency distributions to *probability distributions*.

Constructing and analyzing a frequency distribution for every decision-making situation would be time consuming. Just deciding on the correct data-gathering procedures, the appropriate class intervals, and the right methods of presenting the data is not a trivial problem. Fortunately many physical events that appear to be unrelated have the same underlying characteristics and can be described by the same probability distribution. If decision makers are dealing with an application described by a predetermined *theoretical* probability distribution, they can use a great deal of developmental statistical work already known and save considerable personal effort in analyzing their situation. Therefore decision makers need to become comfortable with probability distributions if they are to apply them effectively in the decision-making process.

CHAPTER OBJECTIVES

This chapter introduces general discrete probability distributions and then considers four commonly used discrete probability distributions: the uniform distribution, the binomial distribution, the hypergeometric distribution, and the Poisson distribution. These distributions describe situations with discrete values for the variables of interest. Many business applications can use one of these distributions.

The chapter also discusses how discrete probability distributions are developed and indicates what type of events these distributions describe. In addition, several descriptive measures that help define discrete probability distributions will be covered.

STUDENT OBJECTIVES

After studying the material in this chapter, you should be able to

1. Identify the type of processes that are represented by discrete probability distributions in general and by the uniform, binomial, hypergeometric, and Poisson distributions in particular.
2. Find the probabilities associated with particular outcomes in discrete distributions.
3. Determine the mean and standard deviation for general discrete probability distributions and for the binomial and Poisson probability distributions.

DISCRETE RANDOM VARIABLES

5-1

As discussed in chapter 4, when a random experiment or trial is performed, some outcome, or event, must occur. When the trial or experiment has a quantitative characteristic, we can associate a number with each outcome. For example, suppose the quality control manager at the American Plywood plant examines three pieces of plywood. Letting "G" stand for a good piece of plywood and "D" stand for a defective piece, the sample space is

G, G, G
G, G, D
G, D, G
D, G, G
G, D, D
D, G, D
D, D, G
D, D, D

We can let X be the number of *good* pieces of plywood in the sample of three pieces. Then X can only be 0, 1, 2, or 3, depending on how many defectives are found. Although the quality control manager knows these are the possible values of X before she samples, she would be uncertain about which would occur in any given trial; further, the value of X may vary from trial to trial. Under these conditions we say that X is a **random variable.** A *random variable* is a variable whose numerical value is determined by the outcome of a random experiment or trial.

In another example, if an accountant randomly examines fifteen accounts, the number of inaccurate account balances can be represented by the variable X. Then X is a random variable with the following values:

0
1
2
.
.
.
15

Two classes of random variables exist: *discrete* random variables and *continuous* random variables. A **discrete random variable** is a random variable that can assume only values from a distinct predetermined set. The two previous examples illustrate discrete random variables. The pieces of good plywood could assume only the values 0, 1, 2, or 3, and the number of incorrect account balances had to be one of the values 0, 1, 2, . . . , 15.

On the other hand, *continuous random variables* are random variables that may assume any value on a continuum. For example, time is often thought to be continuous. The time it takes a trainee to perform a job task may be any value between two points, say one minute and ten minutes.

This chapter discusses discrete random variables and introduces the concept of discrete probability distributions. Chapter 6 covers continuous random variables.

DISCRETE PROBABILITY DISTRIBUTIONS

5-2

A discrete probability distribution is actually an extension of the relative frequency distribution first introduced in chapter 2. For example, the Magnetic Scan Corporation has introduced a magnetic resonance scanning system for use as a medical diagnostic tool. This system is a major commitment for Magnetic Scan. Not only is the system very expensive, but some much larger companies, like General Electric, have introduced competing equipment. To keep inventory investment to the lowest possible level, the company will carry no finished units in stock but will build only to order. However, production-line limitations mean a maximum of four units can be built in any week. Cory Rickbeil, the production vice-president for Magnetic Scan, has recorded how many units were built in each of the thirty weeks the system has been on the market (see table 5–1). Note that X is a discrete random variable whose value equals the number of scanning systems built. The possible values of X are 0, 1, 2, 3, and 4.

The relative frequencies for each value of X have been computed in table 5–1. For instance, during this thirty-week period the company has built none of its systems during twelve, or 40 percent, of the weeks. During 8, or 27 percent, of the weeks one system was built. Recall from chapter 4 that one way to assess probability is to use the relative frequency of occurrence; that is, the probability of an outcome (or value of the random variable) occurring can be assessed by the relative frequency of that outcome.

Systems Built (X)	Frequency	Relative Frequency
0	12	12/30 = 0.40
1	8	8/30 = 0.27
2	4	4/30 = 0.13
3	4	4/30 = 0.13
4	2	2/30 = 0.07
	$\Sigma = 30$	$\Sigma = 1.00$

TABLE 5–1
Scanning systems built per week

The probability distribution for a discrete random variable shows each value of the random variable and its associated probability. The Magnetic Scan probability distribution is

X	$P(X)$
0	0.40
1	0.27
2	0.13
3	0.13
4	0.07
	$\Sigma = 1.00$

Since X represents all possible production values, the probability distribution must add to 1.0. Figure 5–1 shows this probability distribution in graphical form.

Consider another example involving the McMillin Manufacturing Company, which makes an efficient wood-burning stove for use in homes. It manufactures all parts of the stove except for the chimney pipe, which it purchases from a supplier in Pennsylvania. The purchasing agent for McMillin has just received notification that this supplier was no longer going to make the type of chimney pipe that McMillin needs. The notification listed another company in Maryland that could supply the chimney pipe.

A call to the Maryland company confirmed that it could be used as the source of chimney pipe. The price was comparable to that of the Pennsylvania company but it could not guarantee a fixed time between order and delivery. This time, referred to as *lead time,* would be anywhere between one and four weeks. Having nothing else to go on, the McMillin purchasing agent developed the following discrete probability distribution for lead time.

X	$P(X)$
1 week	0.25
2 weeks	0.25
3 weeks	0.25
4 weeks	0.25
	$\Sigma = 1.00$

In this example, the probability distribution for lead time was subjectively assessed by the purchasing agent. Note that the probabilities assessed to each of the discrete outcomes of the random variable, X, are the same. Since the purchasing agent had nothing other than the supplier's statement that lead time would be between one and four weeks, he chose to assign equal probabilities to each of the four outcomes. A probability distribution that has equal probabilities for all possible outcomes of the random variable is called a **uniform probability distribution.**

The uniform probability distribution is sometimes called the distribution of little

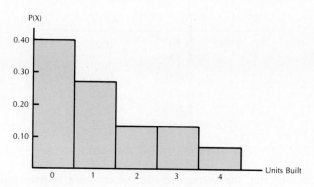

FIGURE 5–1
Probability distribution, Magnetic Scan Corporation example

knowledge. In this example, the purchasing agent is unable to reflect any information in his probability assessments other than that the lead time will be either one, two, three, or four weeks. Many instances arise in business when it is appropriate to assess a uniform probability distribution. These occur when the decision maker believes the outcomes of the random variable are equally likely.

MEAN AND STANDARD DEVIATION OF A DISCRETE PROBABILITY DISTRIBUTION

A probability distribution, like a frequency distribution, can be only partially described by a graph. Often decision makers will need to calculate the distribution's *mean* and *standard deviation*. These values measure the *central* location and spread, respectively, of the probability distribution.

5-3

Mean of a Discrete Probability Distribution

The mean of a discrete probability distribution is also called the **expected value** of the discrete random variable. The expected value is actually a *weighted average* of the random variable values, where the weights are the probabilities assigned to the values. The expected value is given in equation 5–1:

$$E(X) = \Sigma XP(X)$$ (5–1)

where $E(X)$ = expected value of X
X = values of the random variable
$P(X)$ = probability of each value of X

The mean of the random variable X for the Magnetic Scan Corporation example is found as follows:

X	P(X)	XP(X)
0	0.40	0.00
1	0.27	0.27
2	0.13	0.26
3	0.13	0.39
4	0.07	0.28
	$\Sigma = 1.00$	$\Sigma = 1.20$

$$\mu_x = E(X) = 1.2 \text{ units built}$$

Therefore, in the long run, the average number of scanning systems built per week is 1.2. Again, the expected value is just a weighted average of random variable values.

Standard Deviation of a Discrete Probability Distribution

The standard deviation measures the spread, or dispersion, in a set of data. The standard deviation also measures the spread in the values of a random variable. To calculate the standard deviation for a discrete probability distribution, we use equation 5–2:

$$\sigma_x = \sqrt{\Sigma[X - E(X)]^2 P(X)} \qquad (5\text{–}2)$$

where X = values of the random variable
      $E(X)$ = expected value of X
      $P(X)$ = probability of each value of X

As you can see, the standard deviation is a weighted average of squared differences between each value of the random variable and the expected value of the frequency distribution. The weights are the respective probabilities. For the Magnetic Scan example, the standard deviation is computed as

X	P(X)	X − E(X)	$[X - E(X)]^2$	$[X - E(X)]^2 P(X)$
0	0.40	$0 - 1.2 = -1.2$	1.44	$(1.44)(0.40) = 0.576$
1	0.27	$1 - 1.2 = -0.2$	0.04	$(0.04)(0.27) = 0.011$
2	0.13	$2 - 1.2 = 0.8$	0.64	$(0.64)(0.13) = 0.083$
3	0.13	$3 - 1.2 = 1.8$	3.24	$(3.24)(0.13) = 0.421$
4	0.07	$4 - 1.2 = 2.8$	7.84	$(7.84)(0.07) = 0.549$
				$\Sigma = 1.640$

$$\sigma_x = \sqrt{1.640}$$
$$= 1.28$$

Thus the standard deviation of the random variable, scanning systems built, is 1.28 systems built.

An alternative equation for computing the standard deviation of discrete random variables exists which reduces the required calculations. Equation 5–3 is the algebraic equivalent of equation 5–2;

$$\sigma_x = \sqrt{\Sigma X^2 P(X) - [E(X)]^2} \qquad (5\text{--}3)$$

Applying equation 5–3 to the Magnetic Scan example we find

X	X^2	$P(X)$	$X^2P(X)$
0	0	0.40	0
1	1	0.27	0.27
2	4	0.13	0.52
3	9	0.13	1.17
4	16	0.07	1.12
			$\Sigma = 3.08$

Now, recall that $E(X) = 1.20$. Then, we find the standard deviation as follows:

$$\begin{aligned}\sigma_x &= \sqrt{3.08 - (1.2)^2} \\ &= \sqrt{1.64} \\ &= 1.28 \text{ scanning systems}\end{aligned}$$

Thus, we see that equations 5–2 and 5–3 produce the same value for the standard deviation. As such, either equation is acceptable.

SKILL DEVELOPMENT PROBLEMS FOR SECTION 5–3

The following set of problems is meant to test your understanding of the material in this section. Additional problems are found at the end of this chapter under this section heading.

1. Find the mean and standard deviation of the following discrete frequency distribution.

X	Frequency
1	10
2	15
3	20
4	15
5	10

2. Find the mean and standard deviation of the following discrete probability distribution.

X	P(X)
0	0.12
1	0.20
2	0.25
3	0.18
4	0.15
5	0.06
6	0.04

3. Find the mean, expected value, variance, and standard deviation of the following discrete probability distribution.

X	P(X)
10	0.05
15	0.15
20	0.20
25	0.25
30	0.35

4. For the past four years, Armonco Manufacturing has been offering a three-year limited warranty on all appliances it manufactures. Although all appliances are given a unique serial number when manufactured, until this year Armonco had no capability of determining how often any appliance was brought to an authorized service facility. At the beginning of the year, the long-promised computer data base linking all service facilities with a central system was finally operational. A preliminary report shows the following results:

Times Brought for Repair	Probability
0	0.55
1	0.25
2	0.14
3	0.04
4	0.02

a. Find the expected number of repairs for each appliance.
b. Find the standard deviation of this repair distribution.
c. If the average service call cost is $40, how much does the average warranty cost Armonco per year?

5. The Seremonte Emergency Medical Department has recorded the number of emergency calls received each day for the past 200 days. These data are shown in frequency distribution form as follows:

Calls	Number of Days
0	22
1	20
2	40
3	55
4	28
5	20
6	5
7	10
	200

a. Determine the probability distribution based upon the above frequency distribution.
b. What is the mean of the probability distribution?
c. What is the standard deviation of the probability distribution?
d. Using Tchebysheff's theorem (see chapter 3), indicate the range of calls that will come in on at least 75 percent of the days.

6. The Nu-Look Car Wash recently opened at a new location. The manager at this location is concerned about staffing levels so he has taken a sample of 100 days from the company's other location and found the following frequency distribution.

Cars	Frequency
0 and under 10	8
10 and under 20	16
20 and under 30	35
30 and under 40	25
40 and under 50	16
	100

a. Using the midpoints of each class to reflect the values in the class, develop a probability distribution for the number of cars arriving at the car wash.
b. Determine the expected number of cars to arrive at the car wash.
c. Determine the variance and standard deviation.

CHARACTERISTICS OF THE BINOMIAL DISTRIBUTION

Managers could face innumerable discrete probability distributions such as those illustrated in the previous sections. Fortunately there are several theoretical discrete distributions that have extensive application in business decision making. A probability distribution is called *theoretical* when it is well defined and the probabilities associated with values of the random variable can be computed from a well-established equation. This section introduces the first of three such distributions presented in this chapter, the **binomial probability distribution.**

5-4

Theoretical distributions are useful because, over time, they have been well-analyzed and often provide a good approximation to the situation being studied. However, you should be aware they rarely provide perfect descriptions. In those cases where a theoretical distribution can be used, this analysis can be accomplished with many fewer data than if a distribution had to be constructed.

The simplest probability distribution we will consider is one that describes processes with only *two* possible outcomes. The physical events described by this type of process are widespread. For instance, a quality control system in a manufacturing plant labels each tested item either ''defective'' or ''acceptable.'' A firm bidding for a contract will either get the contract or it won't. A marketing research firm may receive responses to a questionnaire in the form of ''Yes, I will buy'' or ''No, I will not buy.'' The personnel manager in an organization is faced with a two-stage process each time he offers a job: the applicant will either accept the offer or not accept it.

Suppose the management of a firm that makes radio transistors feels its production process is operating correctly if 10 percent of the transistors produced are defective and 90 percent are acceptable. In a random sample of ten transistors, how often would we expect to find no defectives? Exactly one defective? Two defectives? The quality control manager may have a real reason for asking this type of question. He depends on the sample to provide the information necessary to decide whether to let the production process continue as is or to take corrective action.

A process in which each trial or observation can assume only one of two states is called a **binomial** or **Bernoulli process.** In a true Bernoulli process the following conditions are necessary:

1. The process has only two possible outcomes: successes and failures.
2. There are *n* identical trials or experiments.
3. The trials or experiments are independent of each other. In a production process, this means that if one item is found defective, this fact does not influence the chances of another being found defective.
4. The process must be consistent in generating successes and failures. That is, the probability associated with a success, *p,* remains consistent from trial to trial.
5. If *p* represents the probability of a success, then $(1 - p) = q$ is the probability of a failure.

Condition 3 states that the trials or experiments must be independent in order for a random variable to be considered a binomial random variable. This can be assured in a finite population if the sampling is performed **with replacement.** For instance, if the quality control manager for the transistor manufacturer selects his sample one transistor at a time, recording whether that item is defective or not, and then replaces it into the population before selecting a second item, and so forth, the trials can be considered independent. This also assures that the probability of a defective will remain constant from trial to trial.

However, sampling with replacement is the exception rather than the rule in business applications. Most often the sampling is performed **without replacement.** For instance, if in testing the transistor the quality control manager is forced to destroy the transistor, the item obviously should not be replaced into the population. In many other cases sampling without replacement is used because it is undesirable to potentially sample the same item more than once.

Thus, strictly speaking, when sampling is performed without replacement, the conditions for the binomial distribution cannot be satisfied. However, the conditions are approximately satisfied if the sample selected is quite small relative to the size of the population from which the sample is selected. A commonly used rule of thumb is that the binomial distribution can be applied if $n/N < 1/20$. Thus, if the sample is less than 5 percent of the size of the population, the conditions for the binomial will be approximately satisfied. An example using this rule of thumb is presented in the next section.

DEVELOPING A BINOMIAL PROBABILITY DISTRIBUTION

5-5

E. M. International produces and installs upgrade conversion units for automatic teller machines for banks. The upgrade conversion unit allows customers a wider variety of services, such as receiving checking and savings balances from remote locations and the ability to split deposits between different accounts. E. M. International prices the units to include one-day installation service by two technicians. A defective conversion unit arriving at a site will require more than one day to install. Unfortunately, defective units can be a result of either the production process or shipping.

E. M. International has completed an extensive study of its production and distribution systems. The information shows that if the company is operating at standard quality, 10 percent (0.10) of the conversion units will be defective (require more than one day to install) by the time they reach the customer's bank location. Assuming the production, inventory, and distribution process are such that the Bernoulli process applies, the following conditions are true:

1. There are only two possible outcomes when a unit is produced: the conversion unit is good or it is defective (will take more than one day to install).[1]
2. Each conversion unit is made by the same process.
3. The outcome of a conversion unit (defective or good) is independent of whether the preceding unit was good or defective.
4. The probability of a defective conversion unit, $p = 0.10$, remains constant from unit to unit.
5. The probability of a good unit, $q = (1 - p) = 0.90$, remains constant from unit to unit.

Suppose the quality assurance group at E. M. International has developed a plan for dismantling four conversion units each week to help determine whether the company is maintaining its quality standard. The sampling will be performed without replace-

---

[1]Students are often confused about the definition of success and failure. A success occurs when we observe the outcome of interest. If we are looking for defective machines, finding one is a success.

TABLE 5–2
Frequency distribution of defective units, E. M. International example

No. Defectives (n = 4)	Frequency	Relative Frequency
0	4	0.2
1	6	0.3
2	4	0.2
3	4	0.2
4	2	0.1
	Σ = 20 weeks	Σ = 1.0

ment. Since the sample ($n = 4$) is small relative to the size of the population, the conditions of independence and constant probability will be approximately satisfied.

Because this is a physical process, we would expect the number of the defective upgrade units to vary from sample to sample. Table 5–2 shows the results of the first twenty weeks of sampling. Notice the number of defectives is limited to discrete values 0, 1, 2, 3, or 4.

If we let the number of defective upgrade conversion units be the random variable of interest, we can determine the probability the random variable will have any of the discrete values. One way of finding these probabilities is to list the sample space as shown in table 5–3. We can find the probability of zero defectives, for instance, by employing the multiplication rule for independent events.

TABLE 5–3
Sample space of defective upgrade units, E. M. International example

Results	No. Defectives (n = 4)	No. Ways
G,G,G,G	0	1
G,G,G,D		
G,G,D,G		
G,D,G,G	1	4
D,G,G,G		
G,G,D,D		
G,D,G,D		
D,G,G,D	2	6
G,D,D,G		
D,G,D,G		
D,D,G,G		
D,D,D,G		
D,D,G,D	3	4
D,G,D,D		
G,D,D,D		
D,D,D,D	4	1
where	G = good unit	
	D = defective unit	

$$P(0 \text{ defective}) = P(G, G, G, G)$$

where

$$G = \text{upgrade unit is good (not defective)}$$
$$G, G, G, G = \text{four good upgrade units}$$

Since

$$P(G) = 0.90$$

and we have assumed the upgrade units are independent, then

$$P(G, G, G, G) = P(G)P(G)P(G)P(G) = (0.9)(0.9)(0.9)(0.9)$$
$$= 0.9^4 = 0.6561$$

Note that when we have more than two independent events, the joint probability is determined by multiplying each individual probability.

We can find the probability of exactly one defective in a sample of $n = 4$ using both the multiplication rule for independent events and the addition rule for mutually exclusive events:

$$P(1 \text{ defective}) = P(G, G, G, D) + P(G, G, D, G) + P(G, D, G, G)$$
$$+ P(D, G, G, G)$$

where

$$P(G, G, G, D) = P(G)P(G)P(G)P(D) = (0.9)(0.9)(0.9)(0.1)$$
$$= (0.9^3)(0.1)$$

Likewise,

$$P(G, G, D, G) = (0.9^3)(0.1)$$
$$P(G, D, G, G) = (0.9^3)(0.1)$$
$$P(D, G, G, G) = (0.9^3)(0.1)$$

Then

$$P(1 \text{ defective}) = (0.9^3)(0.1) + (0.9^3)(0.1) + (0.9^3)(0.1) + (0.9^3)(0.1)$$
$$= (4)(0.9^3)(0.1)$$
$$= 0.2916$$

Using the same method, we can find the probabilities of two, three, and four defectives:

$$P(2 \text{ defective}) = (6)(0.9^2)(0.1^2)$$
$$= 0.0486$$
$$P(3 \text{ defective}) = (4)(0.9)(0.1^3)$$
$$= 0.0036$$
$$P(4 \text{ defective}) = (0.1^4)$$
$$= 0.0001$$

Table 5–4 gives the binomial probability distribution for the number of defective conversion units in a random sample of four if the probability of a unit being defective is 0.10. If you look closely at the distribution in table 5–4 you will see that each probability is determined by (1) finding the probability of one way a particular event can occur and (2) multiplying this probability by the number of different ways that event can occur. For example,

$$P(2 \text{ defective}) = (6)(0.9^2)(0.1^2)$$
$$= 0.0486$$

One way of getting two defectives in four units from the sample space in table 5–2 is

$$G, G, D, D$$

and the probability of this happening is

$$P(G, G, D, D) = (0.9)(0.9)(0.1)(0.1)$$
$$= (0.9^2)(0.1^2)$$

Now, how many ways can we get two defectives in a sample of four? Again, from the sample space in table 5–3 we find there are six ways, each having exactly the same probability. Thus

$$P(2 \text{ defective}) = (6)(0.9^2)(0.1^2)$$

Therefore the key to developing the probability distribution for a binomial process is first to determine the probability of any one way the event of interest can occur and then to multiply this probability by the number of ways that event can occur.

One use of a theoretical distribution should become apparent after comparing table 5–3 with table 5–4. Table 5–3 lists the actual defectives and relative frequencies found by the sampling process. Table 5–4 lists the probabilities expected if a Bernoulli process applies and the probability of a good unit is 0.9. The difference between the two tables should lead a decision maker to question either the appropriateness of the binomial distribution or whether the probability of a good unit is 0.9. The methods for analyzing this type of question will be addressed in later chapters.

For small sample sizes, the binomial distribution can be generated by listing the sample space and proceeding as just described. However, when the sample size is large,

TABLE 5–4
Binomial probability distribution, E. M. International example ($n = 4$, $p = 0.10$)

No. Defectives X	Probability $P(X)$
0	$0.9^4 = 0.6561$
1	$(4)(0.9^3)(0.1) = 0.2916$
2	$(6)(0.9^2)(0.1^2) = 0.0486$
3	$(4)(0.9)(0.1^3) = 0.0036$
4	$0.1^4 = \underline{0.0001}$
	$\Sigma = 1.0000$

this method becomes tedious because the number of different events becomes very large. Fortunately we can develop any binomial probability distribution without actually listing the sample space. To do this, we use the **binomial formula,** equation 5–4:

$$P(X_1) = \frac{n!}{X_1!X_2!}p^{X_1}q^{X_2} \qquad (5\text{--}4)$$

where n = same size
   X_1 = number of successes (where a success is what we are looking for)
   X_2 = number of failures $(n - X_1)$
   p = probability of a success
   q = $1 - p$ = probability of a failure

You should recognize the quantity $n!/X_1!X_2!$ as the expression for the number of *permutations of like items* discussed in chapter 4. This expression determines the number of ways that X_1 successes can occur in a sample of size n. The expression $p^{X_1}q^{X_2}$ represents the probability of one way that X_1 successes can occur.

By applying the binomial formula to the E. M. International example with a sample size of eight rather than four, the binomial distribution shown in table 5–5 is found.

SKILL DEVELOPMENT PROBLEMS FOR SECTION 5–5

The following set of problems is meant to test your understanding of the material in this section. Additional problems are found at the end of this chapter under this section heading.

7. Develop the sample space for a situation where five products are tested and can be either good or defective.

8. Develop the sample space for a situation where five movie reviewers state whether they like or dislike a new movie.

9. Use the binomial formula to develop the probability distribution for a situation where $n = 8$ and $p = 0.2$.

10. Use the binomial formula to develop the probability distribution for a situation where $n = 10$ and $p = 0.4$.

11. Union Bank is considering opening a special teller window for corporate customers only. A recent study has shown that on the average 15 percent of the people entering the bank have corporate business. Assuming the conditions necessary for the binomial distribution apply, determine the probability distribution that describes the next twelve bank customers. What is the expected number of corporate customers? What is the standard deviation of this distribution?

TABLE 5–5
Binomial probability distribution,
E. M. International example ($n = 8$, $p = 0.10$)

No. Defectives X_1	Binomial Formula $\dfrac{n!}{X_1!X_2!}p^{x_1}q^{x_2}$		Probability $P(X_1)$
0	$\dfrac{8!}{0!8!}(0.1^0)(0.9^8)$	=	0.4305
1	$\dfrac{8!}{1!7!}(0.1^1)(0.9^7)$	=	0.3826
2	$\dfrac{8!}{2!6!}(0.1^2)(0.9^6)$	=	0.1488
3	$\dfrac{8!}{3!5!}(0.1^3)(0.9^5)$	=	0.0331
4	$\dfrac{8!}{4!4!}(0.1^4)(0.9^4)$	=	0.0046
5	$\dfrac{8!}{5!3!}(0.1^5)(0.9^3)$	=	0.0004
6	$\dfrac{8!}{6!2!}(0.1^6)(0.9^2)$	=	0.0000*
7	$\dfrac{8!}{7!1!}(0.1^7)(0.9^1)$	=	0.0000*
8	$\dfrac{8!}{8!0!}(0.1^8)(0.9^0)$	=	0.0000*
		$\Sigma =$	1.0000

*The probability is very small. Rounded to four decimal places, $P(X_1) = 0.0000$.

USING THE BINOMIAL DISTRIBUTION TABLE

5-6

Using equation 5–4 to develop the binomial distribution is not difficult, but it can be time consuming. To make binomial probabilities easier to find, you can use the binomial probability table in appendix A. This table is constructed to give individual probabilities for different sample sizes and p values. Within the table for each specified sample size you will find columns of probabilities. Each column is headed by a probability value, p, which is the probability associated with a success. The column headings correspond to p values ranging from 0.01 to 0.50. At the bottom of each column are p values corresponding to probabilities of successes ranging from 0.50 to 0.99. Down both sides of the table are integer values that correspond to the number of successes. The X_1 values on the *left* side are used with p values between 0.01 and 0.50. The X_1 values on the *right* side are used for p values greater than 0.50. Note that the values on the extreme right also correspond to the number of failures, X_2, for p values between 0.1 and 0.50.

Instead of using equation 5–4, you can find the appropriate binomial probability by turning to the part of the table with the correct sample size. Then look down the column headed by the appropriate p value until you locate the probability corresponding to the desired X_1 value. For example, if $n = 5$ and $p = 0.5$, the probability of exactly three successes is 0.3125. This is the same value we find using the binomial formula

$$P(X_1 = 3) = \frac{5!}{3!2!}(0.5^3)(0.5^2)$$

$$= 0.3125$$

Using the binomial table, we can find the probabilities of selecting zero, one, two, and three defectives in a sample of ten from a production process producing 10 percent defectives. We go to the table for $n = 10$, $p = 0.10$ and find

$$P(X_1 = 0) = 0.3487$$
$$P(X_1 = 1) = 0.3874$$
$$P(X_1 = 2) = 0.1937$$
$$P(X_1 = 3) = 0.0574$$

As another example, assume you are working for an automobile manufacturer. Based on engineering reports, 2 percent of the cars your company produces will receive a "below standard" rating from the Environmental Protection Agency (EPA) on the pollution control devices. Thus even a correctly operating production process will have variation, and not all cars will be produced exactly as designed. If twenty cars are selected at random from the inventory in Detroit, what is the probability of each of the following?

1. Finding no below-standard cars
2. Finding two or three below-standard cars
3. Finding more than three below-standard cars

The answers to these questions can be found directly from the binomial table in appendix A if we assume a binomial distribution applies.

Using the binomial table with $n = 20$ and $p = 0.02$, we find

$$P(X_1 = 0) = 0.6676$$

and

$$P(X_1 = 2 \text{ or } 3) = P(X_1 = 2) + P(X_1 = 3) = 0.0528 + 0.0065$$
$$= 0.0593$$

There are two ways to find the probability of *more than* three below-standard cars in a sample of twenty. The first way to add the probabilities of

$$P(X_1 = 4) + P(X_1 = 5) + P(X_1 = 6) + \ldots + P(X_1 = 20) = 0.0006$$

Or we could find the probability of selecting three or fewer below-standard cars and subtract this probability from one. That is,

$$P(X_1 = 3 \text{ or fewer}) = P(X_1 = 3) + P(X_1 = 2) + P(X_1 = 1) + P(X_1 = 0)$$
$$= 0.0065 + 0.0528 + 0.2725 + 0.6676$$
$$= 0.9994$$

and

$$P(X_1 = \text{more than } 3) = 1 - 0.9994$$
$$= 0.0006$$

Suppose the EPA has been given a mandate by Congress to determine if automobiles manufactured in the United States meet pollution standards. The EPA wishes to allow no more than 2 percent of the cars produced by any manufacturer to receive a substandard rating. A southern U.S. state with strict pollution control standards has decided to base its enforcement policy on the EPA 2 percent standard. Since the state enforcement agency cannot test every car sold in the state, it randomly samples twenty cars of each make and model. If it finds more than one car in the sample with a substandard pollution rating, the manufacturer receives a stiff fine and is ordered to recall all cars of that make and model sold in the state. The state's rule says that if more than one substandard car is found, the conclusion is that the automobile company is exceeding the 2 percent limit.

Of course the automobile manufacturers are concerned about the chances of being unjustly accused. That is, a company may in fact be producing 2 percent or fewer cars with substandard pollution control devices but the state could find more than one such car in its sample of twenty. The binomial probability table can be used to find the probability of this happening. The company wants

$$P(X_1 > 1) = 1 - P(X_1 \leq 1)$$

Going to the binomial table with $n = 20$ and $p = 0.02$ we find that

$$P(X_1 > 1) = 1 - [P(0) + P(1)]$$
$$= 1 - (0.6676 + 0.2725) = 1 - 0.9401$$
$$= 0.0599$$

This means that, under the proposed sampling plan, there is just under a 6 percent chance the auto makers will be unjustly accused of making too many substandard cars (by pollution standards).

Because of the high potential costs of being unjustly accused, the manufacturers would likely challenge the sample plan. They would probably argue that more cars should be sampled and that the cutoff point for recalling should be altered to reduce the probability of being unjustly accused.

So as not to look at the situation entirely from the manufacturer's perspective, let us consider the situation where 10 percent of a manufacturer's cars exceed the pollution standards. What is the probability a sample of twenty cars will have only none or one exceed the standards and thus allow the manufacturer to pass the test? This time we want

$$P(X_1 \leq 1)$$

Going to the binomial table with $n = 20$ and $p = 0.10$, we find

$$P(X_1 \leq 1) = [P(0) + P(1)]$$
$$= [0.1216 + 0.2702]$$
$$= 0.3918$$

This relatively large chance of incorrectly passing the test may lead EPA officials to argue for stricter standards.

SKILL DEVELOPMENT PROBLEMS FOR SECTION 5–6

The following set of problems is meant to test your understanding of the material in this section. Additional problems are found at the end of this chapter under this section heading.

12. Use the binomial distribution table to construct the distribution for a situation where $n = 15$ and $p = 0.35$.

13. Use the binomial distribution table to construct the distribution for a situation where $n = 20$ and $q = 0.40$.

14. For a sample of $n = 10$, assuming that the binomial probability distribution applies, find the following:
    a. The probability of $X_1 = 3$ successes if the probability of a success is 20 percent.
    b. The probability of $X_1 = 3$ successes if the probability of a success is 80 percent.
    c. The probability of $X_1 = 4$ successes if the probability of a success is 33 percent.
    d. The probability of $X_1 = 4$ successes if the probability of a success is 15 percent.

15. Assuming that the binomial distribution applies, given a sample size of $n = 25$, find the following:
    a. The probability of $X_1 = 5$ successes if the probability of a success is 75 percent.
    b. The probability of $X_1 = 4$ failures if the probability of a success is 20 percent.
    c. The probability of $X_1 = 11$ successes if the probability of a failure is 33 percent.
    d. The probability of $X_1 = 5$ successes if the probability of a success is 40 percent.

16. The Lexington School Board has agreed to help the A. P. Stevens School Furniture Company test a new type of elementary school chair. Using the present school furniture, school administrators have found that 15 percent of the chairs must be replaced each year. A. P. Stevens claims its chair will average a 10 percent replacement rate.
    a. In a sample of 100 chairs, determine the distribution that describes the number of present chairs that would be replaced each year.
    b. What is the distribution that describes the A. P. Stevens chairs if its claim of a 10 percent replacement rate is correct?
    c. Assume 100 Stevens chairs are tested for one year and twelve need to be replaced. Comment on Stevens' claim this proves its chair is superior to the present brand.

MEAN AND STANDARD DEVIATION OF THE BINOMIAL DISTRIBUTION

5-7

Recall that the mean of a discrete probability distribution is referred to as its *expected value*. The expected value of a discrete random variable, X, is found using equation 5–1:

$$E(X) = \Sigma XP(X)$$

where $E(X)$ = expected value of X
         X = value of the random variable
         $P(X)$ = probability of each value of X

Suppose we wish to find the expected number (value) of defective upgrade conversion units in a sample of $n = 4$ with a 0.10 probability of a single unit being defective. This probability distribution for E. M. International was given in table 5–4.

We find the expected value as follows:

No. Defectives X	P(X)	XP(X)
0	0.6561	0
1	0.2916	0.2916
2	0.0486	0.0972
3	0.0036	0.0108
4	0.0001	0.0004
		$\Sigma = 0.4000$

Thus

$$\mu_x = E(X) = \Sigma XP(X)$$
$$= 0.4000$$

Therefore, if the probability of a single upgrade unit being defective is 0.10, the average number of defectives found in repeated samples of four is 0.4000. Of course, for any single sample we could not find 0.4000 defective since defectives must occur in discrete values, in this case 0, 1, 2, 3, or 4.

If the sample size were increased to $n = 8$, we would use table 5–5 and calculate the mean for this probability distribution as follows:

No. Defectives X	P(X)	XP(X)
0	0.4305	0
1	0.3826	0.3826
2	0.1488	0.2976
3	0.0331	0.0993
4	0.0046	0.0184

5	0.0004	0.0020
6	0.0000	0.0000
7	0.0000	0.0000
8	0.0000	0.0000

$$\Sigma \approx 0.8000*$$

*Difference due to rounding of $P(X)$ values to four decimal places.

Thus,

$$\mu_x = E(X) = \Sigma XP(X)$$
$$= 0.8000$$

Therefore, with repeated samples of eight conversion units we would expect an average of 0.80 defective.

Mean of the Binomial Distribution

The mean, or expected value, of any discrete random variable can be found by

$$E(X) = \Sigma XP(X)$$

However, if we are working with a binomial distribution, the mean can be found much more easily. If the discrete distribution is binomial, we use equation 5–5:

$$\mu_x = np \qquad\qquad (5\text{–}5)$$

where n = sample size
p = probability of a success

Using the E. M. International example with a sample of four selected from a population with 10 percent defective upgrade units, the distribution mean is

$$\mu_x = np = (4)(0.10)$$
$$= 0.40$$

Notice that this is the same value we found earlier using the expected value equation.
When $n = 8$ and $p = 0.10$, the mean of the binomial distribution is

$$\mu_x = np = (8)(0.10)$$
$$= 0.80$$

Again, the mean agrees with the value found previously.
For the binomial distribution,

$$\mu_x = E(X) = \Sigma XP(X) = np$$

Standard Deviation of the Binomial Distribution

Recall that to calculate the standard deviation for a discrete probability distribution, we use equation 5–2.

$$\sigma_x = \sqrt{\Sigma(X - \mu_x)^2 P(X)}$$

where X = value of the random variable
σ_x = standard deviation of X
μ_x = mean = $E(X)$
$P(X)$ = probability of X

Continuing with the E. M. International example for a sample of $n = 4$ and $p = 0.10$, we find the standard deviation for the distribution of defective upgrade conversion units as follows:

$$\mu_x = E(X) = \Sigma XP(X) = np = (4)(0.10)$$
$$= 0.4000$$

X	$P(X)$	$X - \mu_x$	$(X - \mu_x)^2$	$(X - \mu_x)^2 P(X)$
0	0.6561	-0.4000	0.16	0.1050
1	0.2916	0.6000	0.36	0.1050
2	0.0486	1.6000	2.56	0.1244
3	0.0036	2.6000	6.76	0.0243
4	0.0001	3.6000	12.96	0.0013
				$\Sigma = 0.3600$

$$\sigma_x^2 = 0.3600$$
$$\sigma_x = \sqrt{0.3600}$$
$$= 0.60$$

Thus the mean and standard deviation for this distribution are 0.4000 and 0.60, respectively.

Using the distribution for E. M. International where $n = 8$ and $p = 0.10$, we find a different standard deviation:

$$\mu_x = E(X) = \Sigma XP(X) = np = (8)(0.10)$$
$$= 0.8000$$

X	$P(X)$	$X - \mu_x$	$(X - \mu_x)^2$	$(X - \mu_x)^2 P(X)$
0	0.4305	-0.8	0.64	0.276
1	0.3826	0.2	0.04	0.015
2	0.1488	1.2	1.44	0.214
3	0.0331	2.2	4.84	0.160
4	0.0046	3.2	10.24	0.047

5	0.0004	4.2	17.64	0.007
6	0.0000	5.2	27.04	0.000
7	0.0000	6.2	38.44	0.000
8	0.0000	7.2	51.84	0.000

$$\Sigma = 0.720*$$

*Difference due to rounding $P(X)$ values to four decimal places.

$$\sigma_x^2 = 0.720$$
$$\sigma_x = \sqrt{0.720}$$
$$= 0.848$$

Thus the mean and standard deviation for this distribution are 0.8000 and 0.848, respectively.

If a discrete probability distribution meets the binomial distribution conditions, the standard deviation is defined in equation 5–6:

$$\sigma_x = \sqrt{npq} \qquad (5\text{--}6)$$

where n = sample size
p = probability of a success
q = probability of a failure

For the E. M. International example with $n = 4$ and $p = 0.10$, the standard deviation is

$$\sigma_x = \sqrt{npq} = \sqrt{(4)(0.10)(0.90)}$$
$$= \sqrt{0.3600}$$
$$= 0.60$$

The standard deviation when $n = 8$ and $p = 0.10$ is

$$\sigma_x = \sqrt{(8)(0.10)(0.90)}$$
$$= \sqrt{0.7200}$$
$$= 0.848$$

We see that these values agree with those found using

$$\sigma_x = \sqrt{\Sigma(X - \mu_x)^2 P(X)}$$

SKILL DEVELOPMENT PROBLEMS FOR SECTION 5–7

The following set of problems is meant to test your understanding of the material in this section. Additional problems are found at the end of this chapter under this section heading.

17. Assuming the binomial distribution applies, find the mean and standard deviation of the distribution determined by $n = 75$ and $p = 0.3$.

18. Assuming the binomial distribution applies, find the expected value, variance, and standard deviation of the distribution determined by $n = 90$ and $q = 0.75$.

19. Assuming the binomial distribution applies, find the mean, variance, standard deviation, and coefficient of variation of the distribution determined by $n = 250$ and $p = 0.7$.

20. The A. B. C. Institute offers classes in state-of-the-art technical repair services. They have recently started teaching classes in fiber-optic repair. Because many long-distance companies have been converting to fiber-optic systems, the institute

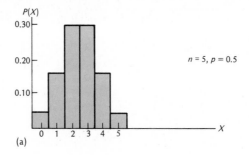

(a)

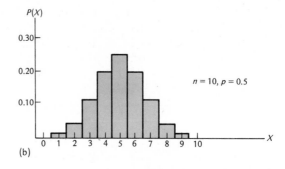

(b)

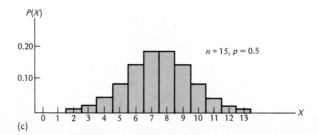

(c)

FIGURE 5–2
The binomial distribution with varying sample sizes

has been advertising that 90 percent of its graduates should expect job offers within their communities. The first class of five has just graduated.

a. Assuming the claim of 90 percent community job offers is valid, and the class of five can be considered to be a sample of all possible future graduates, develop the probability distribution describing the possible number of home community job offers.

b. Find the mean and standard deviation of the distribution found in part a.

c. If the first graduating class had four people receiving home community job offers, what would you conclude about the 90 percent claim?

SOME COMMENTS ABOUT THE BINOMIAL DISTRIBUTION

5-8

The binomial distribution has many applications, such as the elementary quality control example. In later chapters on decision making under uncertainty, we will use this distribution for applications in the other functional areas of business.

At this point, several comments about the binomial distribution are worth making. If p, the probabilty of a success, is 0.5, the binomial distribution is *symmetrical* regardless of the sample size. This is illustrated in figure 5–2, which shows frequency histograms for samples of $n = 5$, $n = 10$, and $n = 15$. Notice that all three distributions are centered at the expected value, μ_x.

When the value of p differs from 0.5 in either direction, the binomial distribution is *skewed*. This was the case for the E. M. International examples with $n = 4$ or $n = 8$ and $p = 0.10$. The skewness will be most pronounced when n is small and p approaches zero or 1.0. However, the binomial distribution approaches symmetry as n increases. The frequency histograms shown in figure 5–3 bear this out. This fact will be used in chapter 6, where we will show that the *normal distribution* (a symmetrical continuous distribution) can be used to approximate probabilities from a binomial distribution.

THE HYPERGEOMETRIC DISTRIBUTION

5-9

The Lindell Corporation manufactures high-speed line printers for computer systems. The Lindell printers are compatible with most of the major computer vendors' hardware. Because of the intense competition in the marketplace for line printers and other peripherals, Lindell has made every attempt to make a high-quality printer. However, a recent production run of twenty printers contained two printers that tested out as defective. The problem was traced to a shipment of defective cable that Lindell received shortly before the production run started.

The production manager ordered that the entire batch of twenty printers be isolated from other production output until further testing could be completed. Unfortunately, a new shipping clerk packaged ten of these isolated printers and shipped them to the California State Purchasing Department to fill an order that was already overdue. By

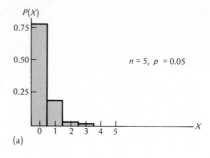

(a)

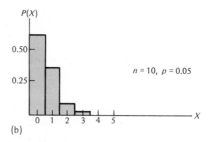

(b)

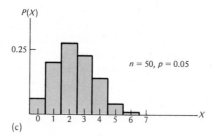

(c)

FIGURE 5–3
The binomial distribution with varying sample sizes ($p = 0.05$)

the time the production manager noticed what had happened, the printers were already in transit.

The immediate concern was whether one or more of the defectives had been included in the shipment. The new shipping clerk felt there was a good chance that no defectives were included. Short of reinspecting the remaining printers, how might the Lindell Corporation determine the chances that no defectives were actually shipped?

At first glance, it might seem that the question could be answered by employing the binomial distribution with $n = 10$ and $p = 2/20 = 0.10$. Thus

$$P(X_1 = 0) = \frac{10!}{0!10!}(0.10)^0(0.90)^{10}$$

$$= 0.3487$$

There is a 0.3487 chance that no defectives were shipped, assuming the selection process satisfied the requirements of a binomial distribution. However, for the binomial distribution to be applicable, the trials must be independent, and the probability of a success, p, must remain constant from trial to trial. In order for this to occur when the sampling is from a *finite* population, the sampling must be performed with *replacement*. This means that after each item is selected it is put back into the population and may be selected again later in the sampling.

In the Lindell example the sampling was obviously performed without replacement from a finite population of size $N = 20$. Thus, p, the probability of a defective printer, does not remain equal to 0.10 on each trial. The value of p on any particular trial depends on what has already been selected on previous trials.

To demonstrate how this works, let's list the sample space, and the associated probabilities, for the probability of shipping no defective printers in the shipment of ten. The sample space is

$$G\,G\,G\,G\,G\,G\,G\,G\,G\,G$$

The probability the first printer selected for shipment would be good would be 18/20 since there are eighteen good printers in the batch of twenty. Now, assuming the first printer selected is good, the probability the second printer will be good is 17/19 since we now have only nineteen printers to select from. The probability all ten printers selected will be good is

$$\frac{18}{20} \times \frac{17}{19} \times \frac{16}{18} \times \frac{15}{17} \times \frac{14}{16} \times \frac{13}{15} \times \frac{12}{14} \times \frac{11}{13} \times \frac{10}{12} \times \frac{9}{11} = 0.2368$$

As this example demonstrates, where sampling is performed without replacement from finite populations, the binomial distribution *cannot* be used to compute exact probabilities unless the sample is small relative to the size of the population. Under these circumstances, the value of p will not change much as the sample is selected, and the binomial distribution will be a reasonable approximation to the actual probability distribution.

In those cases where the sample is large relative to the size of the population, a discrete probability distribution, called the **hypergeometric distribution,** is the correct distribution for computing probabilities for the random variable of interest.

The *hypergeometric distribution* is formed by the ratio of the number of ways an event of interest can occur over the total ways any event can occur. The hypergeometric formula is used to determine probabilities by using the combinatorial counting technique in equation 5–7:

$$P(x) = \frac{{}_{N-X}C_{n-x} \cdot {}_{X}C_{x}}{{}_{N}C_{n}}$$

(5–7)

where N = population size
         X = number of successes in population
         n = sample size
         x = number of successes in the sample
   $n - x$ = number of failures in the sample

Note the numerator of equation 5–7 is the product of the number of ways you can select x successes out of the X number of successes in the population times the number of ways you can select $n - x$ failures out of the $N - X$ failures in the population. The denominator in the equation is just the number of ways the sample can be selected from the population.

In the Lindell example, the probability of zero defectives being shipped ($x = 0$) is

$$P(x = 0) = \frac{{}_{20-2}C_{10-0} \cdot {}_{2}C_{0}}{{}_{20}C_{10}}$$

$$= \frac{{}_{18}C_{10} \cdot {}_{2}C_{0}}{{}_{20}C_{10}}$$

Carrying out the arithmetic, we get

$$P(x = 0) = 0.2368$$

Thus, the probability that zero defectives were included in the shipment is 0.2368, or approximately 24 percent. Note that this is quite different from the 0.3487 probability we observed when the binomial distribution was employed. The difference occurs because the sampling was performed without replacement from a finite population and the sample size was greater than 5 percent of the population size.

The probabilities of $x = 1$ and $x = 2$ defectives can also be found by using equation 5–7 as follows:

$$P(x = 1) = \frac{{}_{18}C_{9} \cdot {}_{2}C_{1}}{{}_{20}C_{10}} = 0.5264$$

and

$$P(x = 2) = \frac{{}_{18}C_{8} \cdot {}_{2}C_{2}}{{}_{20}C_{10}} = 0.2368$$

Thus, the hypergeometric probability distribution for the number of defective printers in a random selection of ten is

x	$P(x)$
0	0.2368
1	0.5264
2	0.2368
	$\Sigma = 1.0000$

Using the Binomial Distribution to Approximate the Hypergeometric Distribution

As you will discover, the arithmetic associated with the hypergeometric formula can be overwhelming for problems involving large samples or large populations. For instance, suppose instead of twenty printers with two defectives the Lindell Corporation had made 100 printers, of which ten were defective. Using the hypergeometric formula, the probability of $x = 0$ defectives in a shipment of ten is

$$P(x = 0) = \frac{_{100-10}C_{10-0} \cdot {_{10}}C_0}{_{100}C_{10}}$$

$$= \frac{_{90}C_{10} \cdot {_{10}}C_0}{_{100}C_{10}}$$

$$= 0.3304$$

Recall that the binomial distribution probability for $x = 0$ defectives was 0.3487. Notice that the binomial probability is closer to the hypergeometric probability when the population size is $N = 100$ than when it is $N = 20$. It can be demonstrated that as the population size is increased relative to the sample size, the binomial distribution approaches the hypergeometric distribution. The general rule is that when the population is at least twenty times the sample size ($N \geq 20n$) the binomial distribution will serve as a reasonable approximation for the hypergeometric distribution.

The Hypergeometric Distribution with More Than Two Possible Outcomes Per Trial

Equation 5–7 assumes that on any given sample selection or trial only one of two possible outcomes will occur. However, the hypergeometric distribution can easily be extended to consider any number of possible outcomes on a given trial by employing equation 5–8:

$$P(x_1, x_2, x_3, \ldots, x_k) = \frac{x_1 C_{x1} \cdot x_2 C_{x2} \cdot x_3 C_{x3} \cdot \ldots \cdot x_k C_{xk}}{N C_n}$$

(5–8)

where $\qquad \sum_{i=1}^{k} X_i = N$

$\qquad\qquad \sum_{i=1}^{k} x_i = n$

and $\qquad N$ = population size

$\qquad n$ = total sample size

$\qquad X_i$ = number in the population with possible outcome i

$\qquad x_i$ = number in the sample with possible outcome i

Consider a marketing study which involves placing toothpaste made by four different companies in a basket at the exit to a drugstore. A sign on the basket invites customers to take one tube free of charge. At the beginning of the study, the basket contained:

5 brand A tubes
4 brand B tubes
6 brand C tubes
4 brand D tubes

The researchers were interested in the brand selection patterns for customers who could select without regard to price. Suppose six customers were observed and three selected brand B, two selected brand D, and one selected brand C. No one selected brand A. The probability of this selection mix, assuming the customers were selecting entirely at random without replacement from a finite population is:

$$
\begin{array}{lll}
X_1 = 5 & \text{(brand A)} & x_1 = 0 \\
X_2 = 4 & \text{(brand B)} & x_2 = 3 \\
X_3 = 6 & \text{(brand C)} & x_3 = 1 \\
X_4 = 4 & \text{(brand D)} & x_4 = 2 \\
\hline
N = 19 & & n = 6
\end{array}
$$

$$P(0,3,1,2) = \frac{{}_5C_0 \cdot {}_4C_3 \cdot {}_6C_1 \cdot {}_4C_2}{{}_{19}C_6}$$

$$= \frac{1 \cdot 4 \cdot 6 \cdot 6}{27132} = \frac{144}{27132}$$

$$= 0.0053$$

Thus, there are slightly over five chances in 1,000 of this exact selection occurring by random chance.

SKILL DEVELOPMENT PROBLEMS FOR SECTION 5–9

The following set of problems is meant to test your understanding of the material in this section. Additional problems are found at the end of this chapter under this section heading.

21. A sample of four is taken from a population of twenty containing four defective items. Determine the probability distribution that defines the defectives that can be found in the sample.

22. A sample of three is taken from a population of twelve engines, five of which are built to metric standards and seven of which are built to English standards. Determine the probability distribution that defines the number of English standard engines that could be found in the sample.

23. The Defense Department has recently advertised for bids for producing a new night-vision binocular. Vista Optical has decided to submit a bid for the contract. The first step was to supply a sample of binoculars for the army to test at their Kentucky development grounds. Vista makes a superior night-vision binocular. However, the four sent to the army for testing were taken from a development lab project of twenty that were 20 percent defective. The army has indicated they will reject any manufacturer that submits defective binoculars. What is the probability this mistake has cost Vista any chance at the contract?

24. An inventory of ranges contains eleven white, nine green, and six harvest gold. If five new homes are being built in a subdivision by five different builders and the ranges will be taken from this inventory,
    a. What is the probability that three of the homes will have a white range and the other two green?
    b. What is the probability that all five ranges are the same color?
    c. What is the probability that three ranges are white and the other two are of the same color but not white?

25. The Farmhill Nursery sells trees and other yard and garden items. Currently, they have ten fruit trees, eight pine trees, and fourteen maple trees. They plan to give four trees away at next Saturday's lawn and garden show in the city park. The four winners can select which type of tree they want.
    a. What is the probability that all four winners will select the same type of tree?
    b. What is the probability that three winners will select pine trees and the other tree will be a maple?
    c. What is the probability that no fruit trees and two of each of the others will be selected?

THE POISSON PROBABILITY DISTRIBUTION

5-10

To use the binomial distribution, we must be able to count the number of successes and the number of failures. Whereas in many applications you may be able to count the number of successes, you often cannot count the number of failures. For example, suppose a company builds freeways in Vermont. The company could count the number of chuckholes that develop per mile (here a chuckhole is a success since it's what we are looking for), but how could it count the number of non-chuckholes? Or what about the emergency medical service in Los Angeles? It could easily count the number of emergencies its units respond to in one hour, but how could it determine how many calls it did not receive? Obviously, in these cases the number of possible outcomes (successes + failures) is difficult, if not impossible, to determine. If the total number of possible outcomes cannot be determined, the binomial distribution cannot be applied as a decision-making aid.

Fortunately, the **Poisson probability distribution** can be applied in these situations without knowing the total possible outcomes. To apply the Poisson distribution, we need only know the *average* number of successes for a given segment. For instance, we could use the Poisson distribution for our freeway construction company if we were able to determine the average number of chuckholes per mile. Likewise, the emergency medical service in Los Angeles could apply the Poisson distribution if it could find the average number of responses per hour. Of course, before the Poisson distribution can be applied, certain conditions must be satisfied.

Characteristics of the Poisson Distribution

A physical situation must possess certain characteristics before it can be described by the Poisson distribution:

1. The physical events must be considered *rare* events. Considering all the chuckholes that could form, only a few actually do form. Considering all the medical emergencies that might result, only a few do occur.[2]
2. The physical events must be *random* and *independent* of each other. That is, an event occurring must not be predictable, nor can it influence the chances of another event occurring.

The Poisson distribution is described by a single parameter, λ (lambda), which is the average occurrence per segment. The value of λ depends on the situation being described. For instance, λ could be the average number of machine breakdowns per month or the average number of customers arriving at a checkout stand in a ten-minute period. Lambda could also be the average number of emergency responses for the emergency medical service or the average number of chuckholes in a section of freeway.

Once λ has been determined, we can calculate the average occurrence for any

---

[2]Another explanation of *rare* is that we are able to define a sufficiently small interval, perhaps of distance or time, such that at most, one occurrence of the event is possible. In addition, any increase in the width of this interval will lead to a proportional increase in the probability of an occurrence.

multiple segment, t. This is λt. Lambda and t must be in compatible units. If we have $\lambda = 20$ arrivals per hour, we cannot multiply this by a time period measured in minutes. That is, if we have

$$\lambda = 20/\text{h and } t = 30 \text{ min}$$

we must set

$$t = \text{one-half h or } \frac{1}{2}$$

Then

$$\lambda t = 10$$

The average number of occurrences is not necessarily the number we will see if we observe the process one time. We might expect an average of twenty people to arrive at a checkout stand in any given hour, but we don't expect to find that exact number arriving every hour. The actual arrivals will form a distribution with an expected value, or mean, equal to λt. So, for the Poisson distribution,

$$\mu_x = \lambda t$$

The Poisson distribution is a discrete distribution. This means that if we are dealing with airplane arrivals at the San Francisco International Airport, in any given hour only 0, 1, 2, and so on, airplanes can arrive; 1.5 airplanes cannot land.

The Poisson Distribution Formula

Once λt has been specified, the probability for any discrete value in the Poisson distribution can be found using equation 5–9:

$$P(X_1) = \frac{(\lambda t)^{X_1} e^{-\lambda t}}{X_1!} \qquad (5\text{–}9)$$

where X_1 = number of successes in segment t
   λt = expected number of successes in segment t
   e = base of the natural number system (2.71828)

Consider the case where the predetermined average number of airplane arrivals at the San Francisco International Airport is sixty per hour. Thus $\lambda = 60$. We can find the probability of exactly seven planes arriving in a ten-minute period as follows:

$$t = \text{one 10-min period} = \frac{1}{6}\text{h}$$

$$\lambda = 60/\text{h}$$

$$\lambda t = (60)\left(\frac{1}{6}\right)$$

$$= 10$$

Then

$$P(X_1 = 7) = \frac{(10)^7 e^{-10}}{7!}$$

$$= 0.0901$$

The probability of five, six, or seven airplanes arriving in the ten-minute period is calculated as follows:

$$P(X_1 = 5) = \frac{(10)^5 e^{-10}}{5!}$$

$$= 0.0378$$

$$P(X_1 = 6) = \frac{(10)^6 e^{-10}}{6!}$$

$$= 0.0631$$

$$P(X_1 = 7) = \frac{(10)^7 e^{-10}}{7!}$$

$$= 0.0901$$

Then

$$P(5 \le X_1 \le 7) = P(5) + P(6) + P(7) = 0.0378 + 0.0631 + 0.0901$$
$$= 0.1910$$

Using the Poisson Probability Tables

As was the case with the binomial distribution, a table of probabilities exists for the Poisson distribution. (This table appears in appendix B at the end of the text.) The Poisson table is easy to use, as demonstrated through the following example.

The Acme Taxi Service has studied the demand for taxis at the local airport and found that, on the average, six taxis are demanded per hour. Thus $\lambda = 6$/hour. If the company is considering locating six taxis at the airport during each hour, what is the probability that demand will exceed six and people will have to wait for taxi service?

To answer this question, we recognize that the segment of interest, t, equals one hour, so $\lambda t = 6$. We are interested in

$$P(X > 6) = 1 - P(X \le 6)$$

To use the Poisson probability tables, we turn to appendix B and locate the column with $\lambda t = 6$. Then we locate the values of X down the left-hand side of the table. We wish to first determine the sum of the probabilities for $X = 0$ to $X = 6$. This sum is found by adding the probabilities under the column for $\lambda t = 6$ from $X = 0$ through $X = 6$. These values are

X	$P(X)$
0	0.0025
1	0.0149
2	0.0446
3	0.0892
4	0.1339
5	0.1606
6	0.1606
	$\Sigma = 0.6063$

Thus

$$P(X \le 6) = 0.6063$$

Then the desired probability is

$$\begin{aligned} P(X > 6) &= 1 - P(X \le 6) \\ &= 1 - 0.6063 \\ &= 0.3937 \end{aligned}$$

Thus, there is a 0.3937 chance that demand for taxis at the airport will exceed supply if the company puts only six taxis at the airport.

Suppose the Acme Taxi Service did a similar study at the town's largest hotel and found that demand averaged four taxis per hour. If the company planned to locate two taxis during each half-hour time segment, what is the probability that demand would exceed the supply within a half-hour time segment?

We first recognize that $\lambda = 4$ and the segment of interest is 0.5 hours. Thus $t = 0.5$ and $\lambda t = 2$. Then the probability of interest is

$$P(X > 2) = 1 - P(X \le 2)$$

We go to the Poisson probability table in appendix B and look at the column headed $\lambda t = 2$. We sum the probabilities from $X = 0$ to $X = 2$ as follows:

X	$P(X)$
0	0.1353
1	0.2707
2	0.2707
	$\Sigma = 0.6767$

Then the probability of interest is

$$P(X > 2) = 1 - P(X \le 2)$$
$$= 1 - 0.6767$$
$$= 0.3233$$

As you can see, the Poisson tables allow you to determine probabilities much more quickly than when using the Poisson formula.

Applying the Poisson Probability Distribution

Consider the problem facing a Boise Cascade Corporation lumber mill manager. Logs arrive by truck and are scaled (measured to determine the number of board feet) before they are dumped into the log pond. Figure 5–4 illustrates the basic flow. The mill manager must determine how many scale stations to have open during various times of the day. If he has too many stations open, the scalers will have excessive idle time and the cost of scaling will be unnecessarily high. On the other hand, if too few scale stations are open, some log trucks will have to wait.

The manager has studied the truck arrival patterns and has determined that during the first open hour (7:00–8:00 A.M.), the trucks randomly arrive at six per hour. He knows that if eight or fewer arrive during an hour, two scale stations can keep up with the work. If more than eight trucks arrive, three scale stations are required. The manager recognizes that the distribution of log truck arrivals during this hour can be represented by a Poisson distribution with $\lambda = 6.0$ per hour. The mill manager can use the Poisson distribution table to determine the probability that three scale stations will be needed.

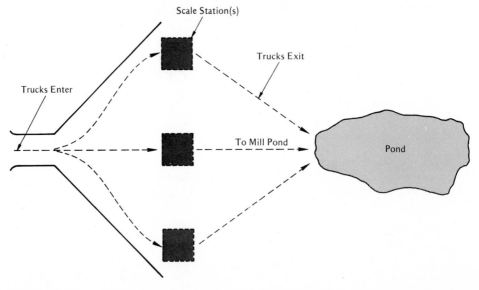

FIGURE 5–4
Truck flow, Boise Cascade mill example

The Boise Cascade mill manager would select $\lambda t = 6.0$ and find the probability that more than eight trucks will arrive during the 7:00–8:00 A.M. time slot. He could add the probabilities for $X_1 = 9, 10, 11, \ldots$ as follows:

$$
\begin{aligned}
P(9 \text{ or more trucks}) &= P(9) + P(10) + P(11) + \ldots + P(17) \\
&= 0.0688 + 0.0413 + 0.0225 + \ldots + 0.0001 \\
&= 0.1526
\end{aligned}
$$

Notice that the probability of more than seventeen trucks arriving is so small that it has been rounded to zero.

The probability of needing three scale stations is 0.1526, and the probability that only two stations will be needed is 0.8474 or $(1 - 0.1526)$. The manager must now make the decision. He must balance the cost of an additional scale station against the potential dissatisfaction of both log truck drivers and the companies they represent.

Suppose this Boise Cascade manager studies the log truck arrivals in the hour between 11:00 A.M. and 12:00 noon and finds the average number of trucks arriving is 3.5. Assuming truck arrivals can be represented by the Poisson distribution, what is the probability of eight or fewer trucks arriving? We can determine this probability using the column under $\lambda t = 3.5$ in the Poisson probability table. We sum the individual probabilities from $X_1 = 0$ to $X_1 = 8$.

$$
\begin{aligned}
P(8 \text{ or fewer trucks}) &= P(0) + P(1) + P(2) + \ldots + P(8) \\
&= 0.0302 + 0.1057 + 0.1850 + \ldots + 0.0169 \\
&= 0.9902
\end{aligned}
$$

This indicates there is a 99 percent chance of needing only two scale stations from 11:00 A.M. to 12.00 noon.

SKILL DEVELOPMENT PROBLEMS FOR SECTION 5–10

The following set of problems tests your understanding of the material in this section. Additional problems are found at the end of this chapter under this section heading.

26. Determine the Poisson probability distribution associated with a $\lambda = 6$ and $t = 2$. Find $P(X \leq 3)$.

27. Determine the Poisson probability distribution associated with $\lambda = 20$ and $t = 1/2$. Find $P(X \geq 14)$.

28. If $\lambda = 8$ and $t = 1$, and the Poisson probability distribution applies, find
   a. $P(X > 4)$
   b. $P(X \leq 9)$
   c. $P(6 \leq X \leq 12)$

29. If $\lambda = 16$ and $t = 1/2$, and the Poisson probability distribution applies, find
   a. $P(X < 10)$
   b. $P(X \leq 7)$
   c. $P(3 \leq X \leq 7)$

30. East-West Translations publishes textbooks of ancient Oriental teachings for English-speaking universities. They are presently testing a computer-based translation service. Since Oriental symbols are difficult to translate, East-West assumes the computer program will make some errors, but then so do human translations. The computer service claims their error rate will average three per 400 words of translation. East-West randomly selects a 1,200-word passage. If the computer company's claim is accurate:
a. What is the probability no errors will be found?
b. What is the probability more than fourteen errors will be found?
c. What is the probability fewer than nine errors will be found?
d. If fifteen errors are found in the 1,200-word passage, what would you conclude about the computer company's claim? Why?

MEAN, VARIANCE AND STANDARD DEVIATION OF THE POISSON DISTRIBUTION

5-11

The mean of the Poisson distribution is

$$\mu_x = \lambda t$$

Thus, for the Boise Cascade lumber mill example, the mean number of arrivals was 6.0 trucks between 7:00 A.M. and 8:00 A.M. Since the Poisson distribution is a discrete distribution, we can calculate the mean, or expected value, using

$$\mu_x = E(X) = \Sigma XP(X)$$

and the variance using

$$\sigma_x^2 = \Sigma(X - \mu_x)^2 P(X)$$

The appropriate calculations are shown in table 5–6.

Note that both the mean and the variance equal 6.0. This is no accident. The variance for the Poisson distribution always equals the mean:

$$\boxed{\sigma_x^2 = \lambda t} \tag{5-10}$$

The standard deviation of the Poisson distribution is the square root of the mean:

$$\boxed{\sigma_x = \sqrt{\lambda t}} \tag{5-11}$$

Thus, for those processes that can be assumed to follow a Poisson distribution, variance can be controlled directly by controlling the mean. If, as noted in chapter 3, the variance can be considered a measure of uncertainty, then for those applications where a Poisson distribution applies, the uncertainty can be reduced by reducing the mean. Often this can be achieved by effective scheduling.

TABLE 5–6
Poisson distribution, log truck arrivals ($\lambda t = 6.0$)

X (1)	$P(X)$ (2)	$XP(X)$ (3)	$X - \mu_x$ (4)	$(X - \mu_x)^2$ (5)	$(X - \mu_x)^2 P(X)$ (6)
0	0.0025	0	-6	36	0.0900
1	0.0149	0.0149	-5	25	0.3725
2	0.0446	0.0892	-4	16	0.7136
3	0.0892	0.2676	-3	9	0.8028
4	0.1339	0.5356	-2	4	0.5356
5	0.1606	0.8030	-1	1	0.1606
6	0.1606	0.9636	0	0	0
7	0.1377	0.9639	1	1	0.1377
8	0.1033	0.8264	2	4	0.4132
9	0.0688	0.6192	3	9	0.6192
10	0.0413	0.4130	4	16	0.6608
11	0.0225	0.2475	5	25	0.5625
12	0.0113	0.1356	6	36	0.4068
13	0.0052	0.0676	7	49	0.2548
14	0.0022	0.0308	8	64	0.1408
15	0.0009	0.0135	9	81	0.0729
16	0.0003	0.0048	10	100	0.0300
17	0.0001	0.0017	11	121	0.0121
		$\Sigma = 5.9979 \approx 6.0^*$			$\Sigma = 5.9859 \approx 6.0^*$

$$\mu_x = \Sigma XP(X) = 6.0 = \lambda t$$
$$\sigma_x^2 = \Sigma(X - \mu_x)^2 P(X) = 6.0 = \lambda t$$

*Difference due to rounding.

SKILL DEVELOPMENT PROBLEMS FOR SECTION 5–11

The following set of problems is meant to test your understanding of the material in this section. Additional problems are found at the end of this chapter under this section heading.

31. If $\lambda = 5$ and $t = 2$, determine the mean and standard deviation of the corresponding Poisson distribution.

32. If $\lambda = 18$ and $t = 1/3$, find the expected value, variance, and standard deviation of the corresponding Poisson distribution.

33. The O'Rilley Office Worker Company has agreed to supply 100 part-time office employees to Mid-East Insurance each day. The O'Rilley Company knows that on the average 7 percent of the workers they schedule for any day will not come to work for one of many reasons. Mid-East Insurance is O'Rilley's biggest customer and so O'Rilley wants to have fewer than the scheduled 100 people show up less than one day in twenty workdays per month. Assuming the Poisson distribution can be used to describe the number of workers not coming to work on any day, how many workers should O'Rilley schedule?

CONCLUSIONS

5-12   This chapter has introduced discrete random variables and showed how a probability distribution is developed for a discrete random variable. Additionally, it has showed how to compute the mean and standard deviation for any discrete distribution.

As indicated in this chapter, there is virtually no end to the possible discrete probability distributions decision makers might use. However, the binomial, hypergeometric, and Poisson distributions represent three of the most commonly used theoretical distributions. In spite of some seemingly strong restrictions on the situations these distributions represent, they can be used in a surprising number of managerial applications.

This chapter has discussed some concepts connected with discrete distributions from a managerial perspective. The chapter glossary defines these concepts in more formal terms. Test your understanding of the material in this chapter by comparing the chapter's managerial discussion with the more formal definitions.

The important statistical equations presented in the chapter are summarized following the glossary.

CHAPTER GLOSSARY

Bernoulli process   A sequence of random experiments such that the outcome of each trial has one of two complementary outcomes (success or failure), each trial is independent of the preceding trials, and the probability of a success remains constant from trial to trial.

binomial distribution   A probability distribution that gives the probability of X_1 successes in n trials of a Bernoulli process. The distribution is specified by

$$P(X_1) = \frac{n!}{X_1 X_2!} p^{X_1} q^{X_2}$$

discrete random variable   A variable that can assume only integer or specific fractional values.

expected value   A measure of location for a probability distribution. The expected value of an experiment is the weighted average of the values the outcomes of the experiments may assume. The weighting factors are the probabilities associated with each outcome.

$$E[X] = \Sigma XP(X)$$

hypergeometric distribution   A discrete probability distribution formed by the ratio of the number of ways an event of interest can occur over the total ways any event can occur.

Poisson probability distribution   A probability distribution that gives the probability of X_1 occurrences from a Poisson process when the average number of occurrences is λt. The distribution is specified by

$$P(X_1) = \frac{(\lambda t)^{X_1} e^{-\lambda^t}}{X_1!}$$

Poisson process   A process describing the random occurrences of independent rare events.

random variable   A function or rule that assigns numerical values to the possible outcomes of a trial or experiment.

sample space   A set representing the universe of all possible outcomes from a statistical experiment.

sampling with replacement   The process of replacing an item into the population before selecting the next item in the sample.

sampling without replacement   The most common type of sampling, where items are not replaced into the population until after the entire sample has been selected.

uniform probability distribution   A probability distribution that has equal probabilities for all values of the random variable.

CHAPTER FORMULAS

Binomial formula

$$P(X_1) = \frac{n!}{X_1! X_2!} p^{X_1} q^{X_2}$$

Expected value of a discrete probability distribution

$$E[X] = \Sigma X P(X)$$

Standard deviation of a discrete probability distribution

$$\sigma_x = \sqrt{\Sigma (X - \mu_x)^2 P(X)}$$

Mean of a binomial distribution

$$\mu_x = np$$

Standard deviation of a binomial distribution

$$\sigma_x = \sqrt{npq}$$

Poisson formula

$$P(X_1) = \frac{(\lambda t)^{X_1} e^{-\lambda t}}{X_1!}$$

Mean of a Poisson distribution

$$\mu_x = \lambda t$$

Variance of a Poisson distribution

$$\sigma_x^2 = \lambda t$$

Hypergeometric formula (two outcomes)

$$P(x) = \frac{{_{N-x}C_{n-x}} \cdot {_xC_x}}{{_NC_n}}$$

Hypergeometric formula (any number of outcomes)

$$P(x_1, x_2, x_3, \ldots, x_k) = \frac{{_{x_1}C_{x_1}} \cdot {_{x_2}C_{x_2}} \cdot {_{x_3}C_{x_3}} \cdot \ldots \cdot {_{x_k}C_{x_k}}}{{_NC_n}}$$

SOLVED PROBLEMS

1. The Ace Electronics Corporation produces electronic calculators and markets them on a national basis. These calculators are sent to the division warehouses in lots of 1,000. You as the warehouse manager will not accept a lot of calculators if you think more than 5 percent are defective. You sample twenty calculators ($n = 20$) and test to see how many are defective and how many are good. Using the binomial distribution, find the following if $n = 20$ and $p = 0.05$:
   a. The probability of exactly one defective.
   b. The probability of finding more than one defective.
   c. The probability of finding from one to three defectives.
   d. The variance and standard deviation.
   e. Suppose you have just found three defectives in the sample. Would your recommendation be to keep the lot of 1,000 calculators or return them?
   f. How many defectives would you expect to find in a sample of $n = 20$ if there is actually 0.05 defective in a lot?

Solutions:

a. Using the binomial equation,

$$P(1 \text{ defective}) = \frac{20!}{1!19!}(0.05)^1(0.95)^{19}$$

$$= 0.3774$$

From the binomial table in appendix A, with $n = 20$ and $p = 0.05$,

$$P(1) = 0.3774$$

b. $P(2 \text{ or more defective}) = P(2) + P(3) + P(4) + \ldots + P(20)$

or, by using the complement,

$$P(2 \text{ or more defective}) = 1 - [P(1) + P(0)]$$

From the binomial table,

$$P(2 \text{ or more defective}) = 1 - (0.3774 + 0.3585)$$
$$= 0.2641$$

c. $P(1 \leq X_1 \leq 3) = P(1) + P(2) + P(3)$

From the binomial table,

$$P(1 \leq X_1 \leq 3) = 0.3774 + 0.1887 + 0.0596$$
$$= 0.6257$$

d.

$$\sigma_x^2 = npq = (20)(0.05)(0.95)$$
$$= 0.95$$
$$\sigma_x = \sqrt{0.95}$$
$$= 0.9747$$

e. The recommendation should depend on the probability of observing three or more defective calculators if, in fact, only 5 percent are defective. If this probability is very small, we would conclude that the lot must actually contain more than 5 percent defectives and should be returned. If the probability is not small, the recommendation should be to keep the calculators. Thus, with $n = 20$ and $p = 0.05$,

$$P(3 \text{ or more defective}) = 1 - P(2 \text{ or fewer defective})$$
$$= 1 - P(2) + P(1) + P(0)$$
$$= 1 - (0.1887 + 0.3774 + 0.3585)$$
$$= 1 - 0.9246$$
$$= 0.0754$$

Thus 0.0754 is the probability of finding three or more defectives in a sample of $n = 20$ when the population is supposed to contain, at most, 5 percent defective calculators. You make the final decision. (This type of question and the complete method for analysis will be discussed in chapters 9 and 10, which cover inference and hypothesis testing.)

f. The number of expected defectives is

$$E[X] = \Sigma X P(X)$$

For a binomial distribution,

$$\mu_x = E[X] = np$$

Therefore

$$\mu_x = (20)(0.05)$$
$$= 1.0$$

2. In a study for a local hospital you have found that the average number of arrivals at the emergency room between 6 P.M. and 9 P.M. on Friday night is five patients. Using a Poisson distribution, answer the following:

a. What is the probability distribution describing emergency room arrivals?

b. Is this distribution skewed? If so, in what direction? Are all Poisson distributions skewed?

c. What is the probability that only one or two patients will arrive during the three-hour period on any Friday night?

d. What is the probability exactly five patients will arrive?

e. What is the probability more than eight patients will arrive?

f. What are the mean and standard deviation of this probability distribution?

g. Would you expect the same distribution to apply between 6 A.M. and 9 A.M. on Friday morning? Why or why not?

Solutions:

a. The probability distribution relates the discrete arrivals to the probability of each arrival occurring. The following distribution is taken from the table of Poisson probabilities in appendix B.

X_1	$P(X_1)$	X_1	$P(X_1)$
0	0.0067	8	0.0653
1	0.0337	9	0.0363
2	0.0842	10	0.0181
3	0.1404	11	0.0082
4	0.1755	12	0.0034
5	0.1755	13	0.0013
6	0.1462	14	0,0005
7	0.1044	15	0.0002

b. Yes, the distribution is skewed to the right. Looking at the probability columns in appendix B, we see that all Poisson distributions are skewed. However, as λt becomes very large, the Poisson distribution approaches a symmetrical distribution.

c. From the Poisson table,

$$P(1) + P(2) = 0.0337 + 0.0842$$
$$= 0.1179$$

d. Again, from the Poisson disbritution table,

$$P(5) = 0.1755$$

e. $\quad$ P(more than 8 arrive) $\quad = P(9) + P(10) + P(11) + P(12)$
$$+ P(13) + P(14) + P(15)$$
$$= 0.0363 + 0.0181 + 0.0082 + 0.0034$$
$$+ 0.0013 + 0.0005 + 0.0002$$
$$= 0.068$$

f. The mean is given as five per three hours. The standard deviation, by definition, is the square root of the mean; that is,

$$\sigma_x = \sqrt{\mu_x} = \sqrt{5}$$
$$= 2.236$$

g. Since the underlying conditions that give rise to the Friday night distribution would not remain constant, we would expect a different distribution to apply during the morning hours.

3. Assume you are responsible for operating a large fleet of taxis. The average number of taxis under repair during any day is four. The Poisson distribution applies.
   a. What is the probability that during any day fewer than three taxis will be under repair?
   b. What is the probability that eight or more taxis will be under repair?
   c. How many spare taxis must you have if you want the probability of not being able to assign a driver a spare taxi to be a maximum of 5 percent? Assume it takes an entire day to repair a taxi.

Solutions:

   a. Again, from the Poisson table, in the column under $\lambda t = 4.00$,

   P(fewer than 3) $= P(0) + P(1) + P(2) = 0.0183 + 0.0733 + 0.1465$
   $$= 0.2381$$

   b. P(8 or more) $= P(8) + P(9) + P(10) + P(11) + P(12) + P(13) + P(14)$
   $$= 0.0298 + 0.0132 + 0.0053 + 0.0019 + 0.0006$$
   $$+ 0.0002 + 0.0001$$
   $$= 0.0511$$

   c. To answer this part, start at the bottom of the $\lambda t = 4.00$ probability column and work toward the top in the following manner. If you have thirteen spare taxis, you will be short only when fourteen or more break down. The probability of this happening is 0.0001. If you have twelve spare taxis, you will be short if thirteen or more taxis break down. The probability of this happening is

   $$P(13) + P(14) = 0.0001 + 0.0002$$
   $$= 0.0003$$

If you have seven spare taxis, the probability of being short is the probability of eight or more taxis being under repair. This is

$$P(8 \text{ or more}) = 0.0511 \qquad \text{(See part b)}$$

Since having seven taxis gives a probability of being short of *more* than 5 percent, you will have eight spare taxis with a probability of being caught short equal to

$$P(9 \text{ or more}) = 0.0213$$

ADDITIONAL PROBLEMS

Section 5–3

34. The Harris Newspaper Company sometimes makes printing errors in its advertising and is forced to provide corrected advertising in the next issue of the paper. The managing editor has done a study of this problem and found the following data:

No. of Errors X	Relative Frequency
0	0.56
1	0.21
2	0.13
3	0.07
4	0.03

a. Using the relative frequencies as probabilities, what is the expected number of errors? Interpret what this value means to the managing editor.

b. Compute the variance and standard deviation for the number of errors and explain what these values measure.

35. The Aims Photo Company sends photographers around to various department stores in the South to take pictures of children. The company charges only $0.99 for a sitting, which consists of six poses. The company then makes up three packages which are offered to the parents, who have a choice of buying 0, 1, 2, or all 3 of the packages. Based on his experience in the business, Samuel Aims has assessed the following probabilities of the number of packages that might be purchased by a parent.

No. of Packages X	P(X)
0	0.30
1	0.40
2	0.20
3	0.10

a. What is the expected number of packages to be purchased by each parent?

b. What is the standard deviation for the random variable, X?

c. Suppose all of the picture packages are to be priced at the same level. How much should they be priced at if the Aims Company wants to break even? Assume that the production costs are $3.00 per package. Remember the sitting charge of $0.99.

36. Gossage's Beverages recently sent a special advertisement to a large number of people in its marketing area. It offered a special price on root beer for purchases of between one and four packages of six bottles or cans. In planning for the special promotion, Jane Gossage assessed the probability relative to the number of packages of six that each customer would buy during the promotion as follows:

No. of Packages of Six X	$P(X)$
0	0.30
1	0.10
2	0.10
3	0.05
4	0.45

a. Based on the probability assessments, what is the expected number of packages to be sold per customer? Comment on whether any particular customer will likely purchase exactly this amount.

b. Compute the standard deviation for the random variable X using equation 5–3, and compare it with the value computed using equation 5–2.

37. The Iverson Investment Company recently gave a public seminar in which it discussed a number of issues, including investment risk analysis. In that seminar it reminded people that the coefficient of variation many times can be used as a measure of risk of an investment. To demonstrate its point it used two hypothetical stocks as examples. It let X equal the change in assets for a $1,000.00 investment in stock 1 and Y reflect the change in assets for a $1,000.00 investment in stock 2. It showed the seminar participants the following probability distributions:

X	$P(X)$	Y	$P(Y)$
− $1,000.00	0.10	− $1,000.00	0.20
0.00	0.10	0.00	0.40
500.00	0.30	500.00	0.30
1,000.00	0.30	1,000.00	0.05
2,000.00	0.20	2,000.00	0.05

a. Compute the expected value for random variables X and Y.

b. Compute the standard deviation for random variables X and Y.

c. Recalling that the coefficient of variation is determined by the ratio of the standard deviation over the mean, compute the coefficient of variation for each random variable.

   d. Referring to part c, suppose the seminar director said that the first stock was most risky since its standard deviation was greater than the standard deviation of the second stock. How would you respond? (*Hint:* What do the coefficients of variation imply?)

38. The Bentfield Electronics Company purchases parts from a variety of vendors. In each case the company is particularly concerned with the quality of the products it purchases. Part number 34–78D is used in the company's new laser printer. The parts are sensitive to dust and can easily be damaged in shipment even if they are acceptable when they leave the vendor's plant. In a shipment of four parts, the purchasing agent has assessed the following probability distribution for the number of defective products.

X	$P(X)$
0	0.20
1	0.20
2	0.20
3	0.20
4	0.20

   a. What is the expected number of defectives in a shipment of four parts? Discuss what this value really means to Bentfield.
   b. Compute and interpret the standard deviation of the number of defective parts in a shipment of four.
   c. Examine the probabilities as assessed and indicate what this probability distribution is called. Provide some reasons why the probabilities might all be equal, as they are in this case.

Section 5–4

39. Discuss the characteristics that must be present for the binomial probability distribution to apply. Relate these to a particular business application and show how the application meets the binomial requirements.

40. Discuss why, in the strictest sense, if the sampling is performed without replacement, the binomial distribution does not apply. Also, indicate under what conditions it is considered acceptable to use the binomial distribution even when the sampling is without replacement. Identify a business application that supports your answer.

Section 5–5

41. The Question Research Company performs research work in which opinion surveys are administered. In a recent survey regarding the acceptability of a particular product, the respondents were asked to indicate (*yes* or *no*) whether they would consider using the product regularly after having tried the product. The product's manufacturer felt that the chances of an individual saying *yes* was 0.70.

a. Assuming that the 0.70 is correct, develop a probability distribution for the number of *yes* responses in a sample of five, assuming that the binomial distribution applies. Use the binomial formula.

b. Use equation 5–1 to compute the expected value of this probability distribution. Interpret what this value means.

c. Suppose the Question Research Company did survey five people and found no one that said *yes*. What is the probability of this happening, assuming the manufacturer's 0.70 probability value is correct? What might be concluded about the manufacturer's probability value? Why?

42. Suppose a study performed at St. Jude's Hospital shows that 30 percent of all patients arriving at the emergency room are subsequently admitted to the hospital for at least one night. Assuming that the number of people in a sample of seven that arrived at the emergency room needing to be admitted to the hospital meets the requirements for the binomial distribution:

a. Determine the probabilities for each of the possible values of the random variable. Use the binomial formula.

b. What is the probability that five or more in the sample of seven will require admittance to the hospital?

c. What is the expected number of patients in the sample that will require admittance to the hospital?

43. The Bayhill city council claims that 40 percent of the parking spaces in downtown are used by employees of the downtown businesses. A sample of five parking spaces was selected from the 4,000 parking spaces.

a. Assuming that the number of spaces filled by an employee can be described by the binomial distribution, develop the binomial probability distribution for the sample of size five using the binomial formula.

b. Suppose the sample results showed four or more of the spaces were actually filled by employees. What would you conclude about the council's claim? Discuss.

c. What is the expected number of employees' cars in a sample of five parking spaces?

Section 5–6

44. Suppose you were given a ten-question multiple-choice examination where each question had four optional answers.

a. What is the probability of getting a perfect score if you were forced to guess at each question?

b. Suppose it takes seven out of ten to pass the test. What is the probability of passing if you are forced to guess at each question? What does this indicate about studying for such an exam?

c. Suppose through some late-night studying you are able to correctly eliminate two answers on each question. Now answer parts a and b.

45. The Sertan Corporation makes replacement parts for video cassette recorders (VCRs) sold under a variety of name brands. The company has a contract with one of the leading VCR manufacturers to supply a certain part. The contract calls for 95 percent of all parts to be "good." Before shipping a lot of 5,000 parts, Sertan selected a random sample of fifty parts and found that four were defective.

   a. What is the probability that a sample will contain four or more defectives if the population of all parts meets the contract specifications? What conditions must be satisfied to employ the binomial distribution?

   b. Based on the probability computed in part a, would you conclude that the shipment is likely to meet the specifications in the contract? Discuss.

46. The Sertan Corporation discussed in the last problem has a contract to supply 5,000 parts to a company producing video cassette recorders. The contract specifies that 95 percent of the parts must be "good." Suppose the company sets up the following sampling plan before shipping out the parts. If a sample of fifty contains three or fewer defectives, the shipment will be considered acceptable. If it contains six or more defectives, it will be considered unacceptable. Between three and six defectives in the sample will result in a second sample of fifty items.

   a. If the shipment really does meet the 95 percent "good" requirement, what is the probability that the first sample of fifty parts will lead the company to incorrectly conclude that the shipment is unacceptable?

   b. Suppose the shipment contains only 90 percent good parts. What is the probability that the first sample will lead to the company thinking the shipment actually does meet the 95 percent requirements?

   c. Based on your answers to parts a and b, what do you think of the sampling plan and why?

   d. What is the probability that the sample results on the first sample will lead to the necessity of a second sample? (Assume 95 percent good.)

47. The Stevens Company in Seattle, Washington, recently did a study regarding customer satisfaction with its winter boots, which are marketed throughout the United States. A basic premise the company has been operating under for the past several years is that 90 percent of its customers were satisfied with the boots they purchased. However, H. B. Stevens, the company president, felt that a survey should be taken to see if this was in fact the case.

   a. Assuming that the characteristics of the binomial distribution are satisfied, what is the probability of finding fewer than ninety satisfied customers in a sample of 100 if the company's assumption about consumer satisfaction is correct?

   b. Assuming that the binomial distribution is applicable, what is the probability of finding more than ten dissatisfied customers in a sample of 100 if the probability of any one customer being satisfied is 90 percent?

   c. Suppose the sample reveals seventy-eight satisfied customers. What is the probability of exactly seventy-eight satisfied customers if the probability of a customer being satisfied is 90 percent?

48. The Telephone Company of America recently made the claim that only 10 percent of the people who have telephones in their residences make enough local calls during the month to justify paying the monthly bill if the calls were charged at the rate of twenty-five cents per call. A consumer agency decided to follow up this claim by selecting a random sample of fifteen people who have telephones.

a. Assuming the binomial distribution applies, what is the probability that the survey will show fewer than seven people actually making the necessary number of calls to justify their phone bill if in fact the true percentage in the population is 10 percent, as claimed by the Telephone Company of America?

b. If the binomial distribution applies, what is the probability that no customer in the sample will be found to be making enough calls to justify their bill at the rate of twenty-five cents per call?

49. After a recent freeze in Florida, the Sweetbrand Citrus Company was concerned about the quality of its grapefruit. Estimates by the Department of Agriculture indicated that 25 percent of the grapefruit was damaged by the freeze. The problem is that there seems to be no pattern to indicate which grapefruit suffered freeze damage. For instance, given two grapefruit growing side by side on a tree, one could be perfect and the other damaged. Suppose the Sweetbrand Company selected a random sample of fifty grapefruit.

a. What conditions must be satisfied in order that the number of damaged grapefruit has a probability distribution described by the binomial distribution?

b. Assuming that the binomial distribution does apply, what is the probability of finding less than five damaged grapefruit, given that the 25 percent estimate is correct?

c. Assuming that the binomial distribution applies, what is the probability of finding more than twenty damaged grapefruit if the 25 percent estimate is correct?

d. Referring to your answer to part c, suppose that the company did actually observe more than twenty damaged grapefruit in a sample of fifty. What might be concluded about the Department of Agriculture's 25 percent estimate? Discuss.

Section 5–7

50. The makers of Time-Tell digital watches claim that their watches are of very high quality. Specifically, they have claimed that no more than 10 percent of their watches will fail within the first six months of use. Suppose the distribution of watch failures in a sample of ten watches is binomially distributed.

a. Use the binomial tables to develop the probability distribution for the number of watch failures in a sample of ten within the first six months of ownership.

b. Based on the distribution in part a, what is the mean of the probability distribution? Interpret this value.

c. Based on the distribution developed in part a, what is the standard deviation of the random variable? Interpret this value.

51. The Milky-Way Dairy buys milk bottles in lots of 5,000. According to the supplier, 80 percent of the bottles will be acceptable for use without any additional cleaning by the company's "scrubber." Assuming that the binomial distribution applies:

a. In a sample of 200 bottles, what is the expected number of bottles that will need to be cleaned by the "scrubber"?

b. In a sample of 100 bottles, what is the expected number of bottles that will not require additional cleaning by the Milky-Way Dairy?

c. Suppose it costs the Milky-Way Dairy three cents per bottle to use the "scrubber." What is the expected cost of scrubbing for a sample of 300 bottles?

d. Compute the standard deviation of the probability distribution for a sample of $n = 100$ bottles, where X_1 is defined as the number of bottles that require scrubbing. Assume that the 80 percent acceptable clean bottles estimate applies.

Section 5–8

52. The Dade County Emergency Services dispatcher is trained to determine from the call received whether an emergency exists or whether the problem can be handled on a nonemergency basis. Past evidence indicates that 50 percent of calls are true emergencies.

a. If the binomial distribution applies, develop the probability distribution for a sample of ten, and graph the distribution in histogram form. Does the distribution appear to be symmetric? Discuss.

b. Referring to part a, suppose that the probability of a call being a true emergency is actually 70 percent. Develop the probability distribution, and graph the distribution in histogram form. Compare the distribution in part a with this one in terms of symmetry. Discuss.

53. How is the shape of a binomial distribution changed for a given sample size as p approaches 0.50 from either side? Discuss.

54. How is the shape of the binomial distribution changed for a given value of p as the sample size is increased? Discuss.

Section 5–9

55. A particular state senate finance committee has four Democrats and five Republicans. The Governor has selected four members from this committee to serve on a special task force. What is the probability that the task force will be equally composed of Democrats and Republicans? What are the chances that all four members will come from one political party?

56. Recently four women and eight men applied for a job at the Baxter Company. The personnel manager claimed that the applicants were so equally qualified that he made the selection of the three people hired totally by random process. The selection resulted in three men and no women being selected. The women have filed discrimination charges against the company. Based on probability, what would you conclude about the suit? Discuss.

57. The Morton Manufacturing Company recently received a batch of ten computer tapes for their data-processing department. Suppose that of the ten tapes, three are damaged, but the damage cannot be detected until the computer attempts to write information on the tape. Suppose the data-processing staff needs four tapes for a file back-up process this afternoon. What are the chances that they will select four good tapes from the ten? What is the probability that they will find all three bad tapes in the four they select?

58. A class at a university had three freshmen, five sophomores, six juniors, and eight seniors. The instructor randomly selected seven students to represent the class at a department meeting. What is the probability that the students selected were as follows: no freshmen or sophomores, three juniors, and four seniors?

59. Last year Fellows Table Company had fifteen tables left over. Six of the tables were slightly damaged, seven were extensively damaged, and the rest were perfect. The company decided to offer these tables to the employees at no cost. Eight people requested a table. The manager decided to randomly select the eight tables from the fifteen and give the tables to the employees in the order that people had made requests. The results of the giveaway showed four slightly damaged tables and four extensively damaged tables were selected. What is the probability of this occurring?

60. Discuss why the hypergeometric distribution is used instead of the binomial distribution when sampling is performed without replacement. Indicate under what conditions the binomial distribution can be used even if the sampling is performed without replacement.

61. The accounting firm Cash, Carry, and Post recently completed twelve tax returns for clients. All the returns were prepared by a new employee and five of them contained an error of some kind. The office policy is to sample-check 50 percent of the returns for accuracy. What is the probability that of the six returns sampled, all were found to contain no error? Assume that the check always catches an error if it exists.

Section 5–10

62. Discuss the basic differences and similarities between the binomial distribution and the Poisson distribution.

63. Assuming that the customer arrivals at the Fidelity Credit Union drive-through window is thought to be Poisson-distributed with a mean of five per hour, find
    a. The probability that in a given hour more than eight customers will arrive at the drive-through window.
    b. The probability that between three and six customers, inclusive, will arrive at the drive-through window in a given hour.
    c. The probability that fewer than three customers will arrive at the window in a given thirty-minute period.

64. The manager of a local convenience food and gasoline store has observed that the number of customers failing to pay for their gasoline is Poisson-distributed, with a mean of five per week.
    a. What is the probability that during a given week, no customers fail to pay?
    b. Suppose that during the initial week of a new employee's hire, over nine people failed to pay for their gasoline. Based on the probability of this happening, what should the store manager conclude?

65. The Hilgren Map Company produces topographical maps covering all parts of Utah, Arizona, and New Mexico. Past studies have indicated that the number of errors per map are Poisson-distributed, with an average of 0.5 errors per map.
   a. What is the probability that a map will contain no errors?
   b. What is the probability that a map will contain fewer than three errors?
   c. What is the probability that a series of three maps will contain no errors?
   d. What is the probability that a map will have five or more errors? What would you conclude if this did occur? Discuss.

66. The State of Maine has an inspector who checks all painting work performed by the state's painting crew. Past experience indicates that the average number of mistakes per 500 square feet of painting is 3.5 and the distribution of mistakes follows a Poisson distribution.
   a. What is the probability that if the inspector checks 1,000 square feet she will not find a mistake?
   b. What is the probability in an inspection of 500 square feet that over seven mistakes are observed? What could be concluded if this did occur?
   c. Suppose the 3.5 figure is considered to be a standard for good work. If the inspector wants at most a 10 percent chance on unjustly criticizing the painters, how many errors should she allow before she makes a criticism for 500 square feet of painting?

67. The manager for the Inland Food Market chain has determined that the occurrence of spoiled fruit is Poisson-distributed, with a mean of four pieces per case.
   a. What is the probability that in two cases over ten pieces of spoiled fruit will be discovered?
   b. Suppose a new employee has been assigned the task of unpacking two cases of fruit and he reports that none of the pieces were spoiled. What are some conclusions you might reach and why?

68. It has been determined that vehicles arriving at a drive-through pharmacy window arrive according to a Poisson distribution at the rate of twelve per hour.
   a. In a half-hour time period what is the probability that three or fewer cars will arrive at the window?
   b. In a fifteen-minute period, what is the probability that three or fewer cars will arrive at the window?
   c. If the pharmacist can serve four cars per half-hour, what is the probability that during the first half-hour of business a customer will not be served and will still be waiting in line when the half-hour period ends?

Section 5–11

69. A typist at Austin Company's typing pool makes errors periodically. In fact, a study has shown that errors made are random and independent of each other at an average rate of three per page ($\lambda = 3$).
   a. Develop the appropriate probability distribution for the number of errors made by the typist on a particular page.

b. Based on the distribution developed in part a, determine the average number of errors the typist will make per page.

c. Compute the variance and standard deviation for the probability distribution in part a.

70. The Askot Publishing Company publishes paperback romantic novels. At the page-proof stage, it has been determined that spelling errors appear random and independent of each other at an average rate of 1.3 errors per page ($\lambda = 1.3$). Suppose a proofreader has been hired to read a new book.

a. Develop the appropriate discrete probability distribution describing the number of errors in two pages of a book to be published.

b. If the proofreader does a perfect job, what is the average number of errors he will find for each two pages read?

c. What is the variance of the number of errors per two pages? What is the standard deviation?

d. Suppose a proofreader has just finished four pages and has found no errors. What are some of the possible conclusions you might reach and why?

71. Through an example, discuss the reason that, if the mean of Poisson distribution can be reduced, the spread of the distribution can also be reduced.

C A S E S

5A Checker Cab Company

The Checker Cab Company has just received an exclusive contract to supply taxi service for a large western United States city. This contract amounts to a monopoly for Checker and was not a popular move on the part of the city council. The council, however, had received many complaints about service when the city allowed many taxi companies and feels it will now have greater control over both equipment and drivers.

Checker currently has 176 cars. However, the company is required as part of the contract to have 210 taxis on the streets during peak rush hours. Max Winter, Checker's managing director, feels 210 cars are too many to have on the street; however, he knows the city will monitor Checker's performance closely. In particular, he is sure the council will check driver records to see that enough taxis are on the streets during the peak demand hours.

When purchasing additional cars, Max also has to consider replacement, or backup, cars. Although he disputes the frequent claim that his drivers drive without regard for life or limb, he feels they sometimes drive without regard for the company's cars. For instance, a long-time driver, Don Billings, has just driven into the garage with his left front door in the back seat. Frequent minor accidents and mechanical failures seem to be a fact of life in the taxi business.

Max Winter has been managing director of Checker Cab for seven years. His policy has been to buy good-quality two- or three-year-old used cars to use as taxis.

Checker maintains its own repair shop. However the mechanics do only minor body and mechanical repairs. If a taxi requires more than a day to repair, the car will be replaced, not repaired.

Up to now, Max has not kept comprehensive daily records on the number of cars out of commission. He also does not know exactly how many cars he has had available on a daily basis. However, he feels that over the last two years, Checker has had an average of 150 to 175 cars available, and an average of eight cars per day in the repair shop.

Max knows he will have to buy additional cars now that his company has the exclusive contract. However, he doesn't really know how many to buy, or the ramifications of buying different numbers.

5B Great Plains Oil Company

Margaret Clemonts, operations vice-president of Great Plains Oil, is putting together a proposal for the board of directors. Great Plains has several refineries in the mid-central United States. It has for years relied on crude oil from its fields in Texas and the Gulf area. However, these fields are very mature and have declining outputs. Margaret has recently been buying foreign crude delivered to eastern United States ports. In addition, she has been considering trying to buy some extra Alaska crude from the West Coast. Her main problem up until now has been the extra cost of transporting Alaska oil to Great Plains refineries.

Margaret has recently learned about an unused natural gas pipeline that would drastically reduce the cost of bringing oil from the West Coast to Great Plains refineries. Great Plains can buy the pipeline for a reasonable price and, in fact, could use the excess distribution capability to add to its cash flow by selling excess crude. The main drawback to the proposal is that the pipeline was built for gas and, therefore, may not be strong enough for the additional forces generated by transmitting crude oil. The pipe material is strong enough; however, the welds may not be.

The vast majority of the pipe is buried approximately ten feet undergound. The pipeline is made of fifty-foot sections and, since it is approximately 1,000 miles long, there are some 110,000 separate welds. If the welds were solidly made, they will be strong enough to handle the crude oil. If the welds were not carefully made, they will need to be redone.

An industrial x-ray company has recently developed a small, portable machine that will travel through a pipe and x-ray each weld. However, this machine is very expensive to rent and requires the pipe to be cut periodically to extend the machine's power cables. Margaret does not want to use the machine unless she is sure she will recommend buying the pipeline. Once the line is bought, any faulty welds will have to be located and redone.

As part of the negotiation procedure, the pipeline owners have agreed to let Great Plains dig up sections of the pipe and x-ray a sample of welds. Margaret's industrial engineers have estimated that if 1 percent or fewer of the welds need to be redone, the pipeline will be a good investment. If 2 percent or more need to be redone, the pipeline should not be bought. Unfortunately, taking the sample x-rays will not be easy, and Margaret estimates that each x-ray will cost $5,000.

Margaret recognizes the problems of sampling, but feels a respresentative random sample can be taken. She would be willing to spend up to $175,000 to determine whether the pipeline should be bought, but would not want to spend this entire amount if the pipeline should obviously not be bought. She is presently devising her sampling plan.

5C Dearborn Corporation, Part 1

The Dearborn Corporation of Palo Alto, California, makes stereo speakers and sells these speakers wholesale to several electronics companies. These companies install the Dearborn speakers in special cabinets and market them under a variety of brand names.

Dearborn's price quotations are based on the assumption that at least 95 percent of all speakers it manufactures are acceptable. The potential exists, according to Dearborn, that up to 5 percent of its speakers contain some defect.

The Dearborn production control manager has been getting a lot of pressure lately because of the customer complaints. Some customers claim the defective rate has climbed above 5 percent. In fact, one customer recently found four defective speakers in a shipment of fifty speakers. In his letter of complaint, the customer implied that something must be wrong at the Dearborn plant if the defective rate has increased to 8 percent. He demanded an adjustment on his purchase price for this shipment (Dearborn would gladly do this since it is part of the sales contract) and that the stated price on future speaker purchases reflect the higher defective rate.

The production control manager wonders how he should respond to this customer.

5D Dearborn Corporation, Part 2

A few days after receiving the first customer's letter of complaint (see case 5C), the Dearborn production control manager received a phone call from a second customer. This customer indicated that her quality control people had discovered six defective speakers in a shipment of fifty speakers. This customer indicated that Dearborn's defective rate must be higher than the stated 5 percent and that the production manager should do something about it right away.

The production manager sat down to prepare a letter to this customer but was having trouble assessing the issue.

REFERENCES

Duncan, Acheson J. *Quality Control and Industrial Statistics,* 4th Edition. Homewood, Ill.: Irwin, 1974.

Harnett, Donald L. *Introduction to Statistical Methods,* 3rd Edition. Reading, Mass.: Addison-Wesley, 1982.

Hayes, Glenn E., and Romig, Harry G. *Modern Quality Control.* Encino, Calif.: Glencoe Publishing, 1982.

Hogg, R. V., and Craig, A. T. *Introduction to Mathematical Statistics,* 4th Edition. New York: Macmillan, 1978.

CONTINUOUS PROBABILITY DISTRIBUTIONS

6

WHY DECISION MAKERS NEED TO KNOW

Chapter 5 introduced discrete random variables and discussed discrete probability distributions as they apply to the decision process. It also discussed four theoretical discrete probability distributions: the uniform, binomial, hypergeometric, and Poisson. For discrete distributions, the variable of interest can take on only specific values. For example, the number of defective tires produced by the day shift at General Tire Company can have only integer values (0, 1, 2, etc.).

In many business applications the variable of interest is not restricted to integer values. For example, checkout times through a supermarket checkout stand can take on any value between zero and some large number. And the load weight carried by a freight truck can take on values between zero and some large number. Variables that are measured in units of time, weight, volume, or distance are often assumed to be *continuous* variables. Technically, a continuous variable is one that can take on an infinite number of values (measured to as many decimal places as necessary). Because of measuring limitations, many persons argue that there is no such thing as a truly continuous variable. These individuals consider all variables discrete even though they can take on decimal values. This text defines a *continuous random variable* as a variable that can assume a large number of values between any two points.

Because many business applications involve continuous or quasi-continuous variables, decision makers need to become acquainted with continuous probability distributions and learn how to use them in decision making.

CHAPTER OBJECTIVES

This chapter will discuss the characteristics of continuous probability distributions. It will emphasize the normal distribution and illustrate how to apply this distribution in a decision-making environment.

STUDENT OBJECTIVES

After studying the material in this chapter, you should be able to

1. Discuss and apply the uniform probability distribution.
2. Discuss the important properties of the normal probability distribution.
3. Recognize when the normal distribution might apply in a decision-making process.
4. Calculate probabilities using the normal distribution table.

CONTINUOUS RANDOM VARIABLES

6-1

A discrete random variable has been defined as a variable that can have only a specific finite set of values. In many cases these discrete values are limited to integers. As illustrated in chapter 5, many decision situations can be analyzed using discrete random variables and their associated probability distributions.

In many instances decision makers will be faced with random variables that can take on a seemingly unlimited number of values. Such a random variable is a continuous random variable. Figure 6–1 illustrates a continuous random variable and contrasts it with a discrete random variable. Here, the actual waist measurement is a continuous variable because it can assume any value along the scale. However, when the scale is divided into intervals, a discrete value can be assigned to each waist size depending on where the size falls. In business decision making, many variables are defined as continuous, including

- Time measurements
- Interest rates
- Financial ratios
- Income levels
- Weight measurements

FIGURE 6–1
Classification of random variables

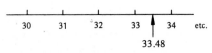

Men's Waist Measurements (Inches)

(a) Continuous Random Variable

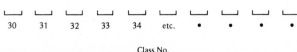

Class No.

(b) Discrete Random Variable

- Distance measures
- Volume measures

Chapter 5 discussed the problems facing the Boise Cascade Lumber mill manager when deciding how many log-scaling stations to open during a certain hour. The number of trucks arriving in that hour is a *discrete* random variable, but the time between arrivals (the interarrival time) is a *continuous* random variable. The time it takes to scale a truckload of logs is also a continuous random variable, and the amount of board feet of lumber on a truck still another.

In general, the value of a continuous random variable is found by *measuring,* whereas the value of a discrete random variable is determined by *counting*.

CONTINUOUS PROBABILITY DISTRIBUTIONS

6-2

In contrast to discrete case situations where the appropriate probability distribution can be represented by the areas of rectangles (histogram), the probability distribution of a continuous random variable is represented by a *probability density function.* Figure 6–2 illustrates a probability density function and shows its relationship to discrete probability distributions. Note that as the class width in the discrete examples becomes narrower, the top of the histogram approaches a smooth curve. This smooth curve represents the probability density function for a continuous variable.

Remember, discrete probability distributions have two characteristics. First, the rectangle representing each discrete value has an area corresponding to the probability of that value occurring. Second, the areas (probabilities) of all the rectangles must sum to 1.0. These two characteristics generally also apply to probability density functions. First of all, the total area (probability) under the density function curve must equal 1.0. In addition, the probability that the variable will have a value between any two points on the continuous scale equals the area under the curve between these two points. However, the probability that the variable will have any specific value cannot be determined because that probability would correspond to the area directly above a point. Because the area above a point is a line, and because a line has no width, it has no area and zero probability.

Since the probability of a single point on a continuous scale is zero, when dealing with continuous random variables we never consider the probability of a single value occurring. Rather, we consider the probability of a range of values occurring by finding the area under the density function for this range. For instance, we might ask "What is the probability of a student in this class weighing 160 pounds?" If we mean exactly 160.0000 . . . , the probability is zero. If we mean any weight that would round to 160 pounds, i.e., 159.5 to 160.5 pounds, the question makes sense and we could find a probability.

The next section introduces one useful continuous probability distribution called the *uniform distribution* and demonstrates how we can find a desired probability by determining the appropriate area under the density function describing that distribution.

FIGURE 6–2

Comparison of a probability density function and discrete probability distributions

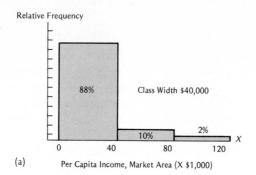

(a)   Per Capita Income, Market Area (X $1,000)

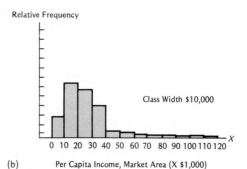

(b)   Per Capita Income, Market Area (X $1,000)

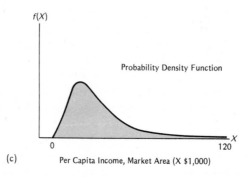

(c)   Per Capita Income, Market Area (X $1,000)

THE UNIFORM DISTRIBUTION

6-3

Chapter 5 introduced the discrete uniform distribution. The **uniform distribution** has equal probabilities for all possible values of the random variable. This is also true for the **continuous uniform probability distribution.** That is, if the uniform probability distribution applies for a continuous random variable, the corresponding probability density function is a line parallel to the X-axis.

The *continuous uniform distribution* has the probability density function shown in equation 6–1:

$$f(X) = \begin{cases} \dfrac{1}{b-a} & \text{if } a \leq X \leq b \\[2mm] 0 & \text{otherwise} \end{cases} \qquad (6\text{--}1)$$

where $f(X)$ = value of the density function at any X value
        a = lower limit of the interval from a to b.
        b = upper limit of the interval from a to b.

Figure 6–3 illustrates two examples of uniform distributions with different a to b intervals. Note that the probability of all values of X between a and b is the same for a given distribution.

Now consider a situation involving the Stern Manufacturing Company, which makes seat-belt buckles for all types of vehicles. The production scheduler just noticed that the inventory level for the spring mechanism has somehow run dangerously low. In fact, she estimates that there are only enough spring parts to last two more hours. The source of supply is located nearby, but the time it will take to replenish the inventory is uniformly distributed over the interval of one hour to four hours. The production scheduler would like to continue production without any work stoppage; however, she

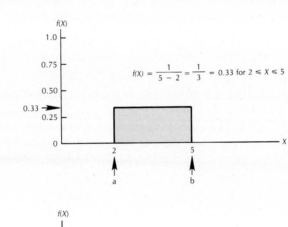

(a)

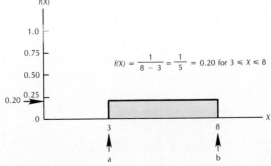

(b)

FIGURE 6–3
Uniform distributions

could plan for general maintenance by calling in the maintenance staff that generally works the 12:00 P.M. to 7:00 A.M. shift. It takes two hours to get these people to the plant, so the decision must be made promptly.

A first step in deciding whether to continue production and hope that the inventory arrives in time or to call the maintenance staff is to determine the probability of the inventory arriving late. She is specifically concerned that a work delay be no longer than a half-hour. We can determine the probability that it will require in excess of 2.5 hours to replenish the inventory of spring mechanisms as follows.

The probability of interest is the dark shaded area shown in figure 6–4. We determine the area as follows:

$$
\begin{aligned}
P(X > 2.5) &= 1 - P(X \le 2.5) \\
&= 1 - f(X)\,(2.5 - 1) \\
&= 1 - 0.33\,(1.5) \\
&= 1 - 0.50 \\
&= 0.50
\end{aligned}
$$

Thus, there is a 50 percent chance that production will be delayed for a half-hour or more because of a shortage of spring mechanisms. The production scheduler will have to weigh this probability along with the costs of a work stoppage and the costs of needlessly calling in the maintenance staff before making a decision. The final two chapters in this text present techniques for assisting with this type of decision.

The Mean and Standard Deviation for the Uniform Distribution

Chapter 5 explained that it is often useful to obtain measures of the center and the spread of a discrete probability distribution. Doing so more fully describes the probability distribution. The same is true when we are dealing with a continuous probability distribution. We usually want to know the mean or expected value of the distribution as well as the standard deviation of the distribution. For example, consider the following situation.

FIGURE 6–4
Stern Manufacturing Company, uniform distribution

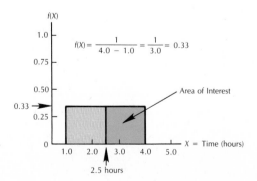

The Jones Corporation owns and operates a lumber mill in Bend, Oregon. Records indicate that the production of dimension lumber (two-by-fours, two-by-sixes, etc.) is uniformly distributed between 4,000 and 10,000 board feet per day. The production manager has been asked to deliver a presentation to the company's stockholders regarding the production distribution. He needs to discuss such things as average production and variation in production.

The density function describing his company's production is the uniform density function as follows:

$$f(X) = \begin{cases} \dfrac{1}{10,000 - 4,000} & (4,000 \le X \le 10,000) \\ 0 & \text{otherwise} \end{cases}$$

Mean

The mean or expected value of the uniform distribution is determined by equation 6–2:

$$\mu_x = E(X) = \frac{a + b}{2} \qquad (6\text{–}2)$$

Thus, the mean of the uniform distribution is found by determining the average of a and b. Remember that the mean of a probability distribution is the average occurrence of the random variable in the long run. Since all values between a and b have the same chance of occurring, the long-run average of individual outcomes will be $(a + b)/2$.

Therefore, for the Jones Company, the mean daily production is

$$\mu_x = E(X) = \frac{4,000 + 10,000}{2}$$

$$= \frac{14,000}{2}$$

$$= 7,000 \text{ board feet}$$

Thus, the Jones Company can expect to produce 7,000 board feet of lumber on the average.

The Standard Deviation

The mean provides a measure of the center of the uniform distribution. But it is also important to measure the spread in the probability distribution. The measure of spread most frequently used is the standard deviation. For the uniform distribution, the standard deviation is developed using equation 6–3. The mathematical development of this equation will not be shown, but it will be used to compute the standard deviation for the Jones Company production distribution (see equation 6–3):

$$\sigma_x = \sqrt{\frac{(b-a)^2}{12}}$$

(6–3)

Thus, for the Jones Company, the standard deviation in production is

$$\sigma_x = \sqrt{\frac{(10,000 - 4,000)^2}{12}}$$
$$= \sqrt{\frac{6,000^2}{12}}$$
$$= 1,732.05 \text{ board feet}$$

Thus, the production distribution will average 7,000 board feet, with a standard deviation of slightly more than 1,732 board feet.

SKILL DEVELOPMENT PROBLEMS FOR SECTION 6–3

The following set of problems is meant to test your understanding of the material in this section. Additional problems are found at the end of this chapter under this section heading.

1. A continuous random variable is uniformly distributed between twenty and sixty.
   a. What is the mean of the distribution?
   b. What is the standard deviation of the distribution?
   c. What is the probability a randomly selected value will be above fifty?
   d. What is the probability a randomly selected value will be exactly forty-five?

2. A continuous random variable is uniformly distributed between 100 and 400.
   a. What is the expected value of the distribution?
   b. What are the variance and standard deviation of the distribution?
   c. What is the coefficient of variation of the distribution?
   d. What is the probability a randomly selected value will be above 200?
   e. What is the probability a randomly selected value will be between 150 and 300?

3. The time it takes to build a laser printer is thought to be uniformly distributed between eight and fifteen hours.
   a. What is the average completion time for a laser printer?
   b. What are the chances that it will take longer than ten hours to build one?
   c. What is the standard deviation for the probability distribution?

4. In Oregon, the growth distribution for a pine tree is thought to be uniformly distributed between twelve and twenty-eight inches per year.
   a. What is the mean growth per year?

b. What is the standard deviation in growth per year?

c. What is the probability of a tree growing between fourteen and twenty inches in a year?

5. The Sea Pines Golf Course is preparing for a major LPGA golf tournament. Since parking near the course is extremely limited (room for only 500 cars), the course officials have contracted with the local community to provide parking and a bus shuttle service. Sunday, the final day of the tournament, will have the largest crowd and the officials estimate they will have between 8,000 and 12,000 cars needing parking spaces, but feel no value is any more likely than another.

a. Discuss why the uniform distribution is the appropriate distribution to use in this situation.

b. What is the mean of the distribution?

c. What is the standard deviation of the distribution?

d. The tournament committee is discussing how many parking spots to contract for from the city. If they want to limit the chance of not having enough provided parking to 10 percent, how many spaces do they need from the city on Sunday?

CHARACTERISTICS OF THE NORMAL DISTRIBUTION

6-4

The most important continuous distribution in statistical decision making is the **normal distribution.** The normal distribution describes many physical situations where variation in a measured value occurs due to random, or unassignable, sources. Therefore, the distribution in populations such as the average weight gain of cattle in a feed lot, the power drain in a batch of integrated circuits, the rate of growth in a cloned planting of Douglas fir trees, and the average mileage among cars of the same type could all form a normal distribution. Most importantly, the normal distribution has a special place in statistical decision making, as we shall see in later chapters.

The normal distribution has the following properties:

1. It is *unimodal;* that is, the normal distribution peaks at a single value.
2. It is *symmetrical,* with the mean, median, and mode equal. Symmetry assures us that 50 percent of the area under the curve lies left of the center and 50 percent lies right of the center.
3. It approaches the horizontal axis on either side of the mean toward plus and minus infinity ($\pm\infty$). In more formal terms, the normal distribution is *asymptotic* to the X-axis.

Figure 6–5 illustrates a typical normal distribution and highlights these three characteristics.

Although all normal distributions have the shape shown in Figure 6–5, their central locations and spreads can vary greatly depending on the situation being considered. The horizontal-axis scale is determined by the process being represented. It may be pounds, inches, dollars, or any other physical attribute with a continuous or quasi-continuous measurement. Figure 6–6 shows several normal distributions with different centers and different spreads. Note that the area under each normal "curve" equals 1.0.

FIGURE 6–5
Characteristics of a normal distribution

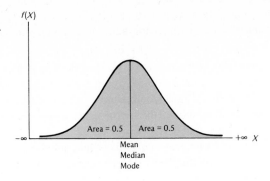

Characteristics:

1. Unimodal
2. Symmetric
3. Asymptotic to the X-axis in both directions

FIGURE 6–6
Normal distributions with different locations and spreads

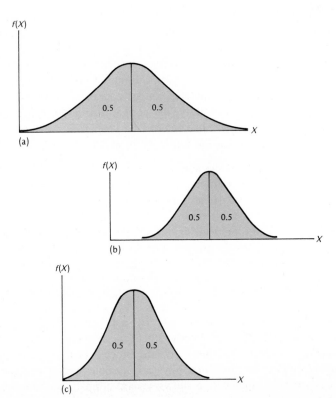

The normal distribution is defined by two parameters: μ_x, the population mean, and σ_x, the population standard deviation. Given these two values, the normal distribution is described by the probability density function of equation 6–4:

$$f(X) = \frac{1}{\sigma_x\sqrt{2\pi}}e^{-(X-\mu_x)^2/2\sigma_x^2}$$ (6–4)

where X = any value of the continuous random variable
σ_x = population standard deviation
e = base of the natural log ≈ 2.7182
μ_x = population mean

Equation 6–4 will determine the height of the normal distribution curve for each possible value of the random variable X. If we were to substitute values for μ_x and σ_x along with many values for X, the plot of $f(X)$ would be a curve similar to those shown in figures 6–5 and 6–6.

Determining $f(X)$ requires only basic algebra. However, in business applications decision makers will rarely need to plot the normal distribution.

FINDING PROBABILITIES FROM A STANDARD NORMAL DISTRIBUTION

6-5

As indicated earlier, the probability of any particular value of a discrete random variable can be represented by an area in a relative frequency histogram. For example, figure 6–7 shows a histogram for a binomial distribution with $n = 6$ and $p = 0.5$. The probabilities (areas) sum to 1.0, and the area above each value on the horizontal axis represents the probability of that value occurring. For example, the probability of exactly two successes in six trials ($n = 6$) is 0.2344. Likewise, the probability of observing values between any two points in a normal distribution is equal to the area under the normal curve between those two points. Figure 6–8 shows several examples.

Integral calculus is used to find the area under a normal distribution curve. However, we can avoid using calculus by transforming all normal distributions to fit the **standard normal distribution.** The principle behind the standard normal distribution is that all normal distributions can be converted to a common normal distribution with a common mean and standard deviation. This conversion is done by *rescaling* the normal distribution axis from its true units (time, weight, dollars, and so forth) to the standard measure referred to as a *Z value*. (Recall that Z was introduced in Chapter 3.) Thus, any value of the normally distributed continuous random variable can be represented by a unique Z value. The Z value is determined by the equation 6–5:

FIGURE 6–7

Binomial distribution ($n = 6$, $p = 0.5$)

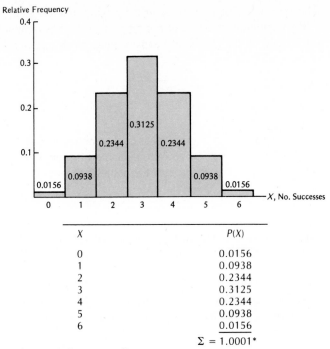

X	P(X)
0	0.0156
1	0.0938
2	0.2344
3	0.3125
4	0.2344
5	0.0938
6	0.0156
	$\Sigma = 1.0001^{*}$

*Difference due to rounding.

FIGURE 6–8

Areas and probabilities for a normal distribution

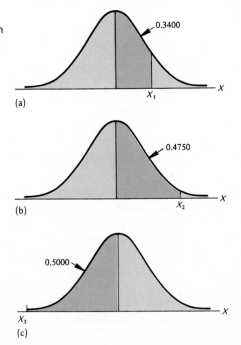

$$Z = \frac{X - \mu_x}{\sigma_x} \qquad (6\text{--}5)$$

where $\quad Z$ = scaled value

X = any point on the horizontal axis

μ_x = mean of the normal distribution

σ_x = standard deviation of the normal distribution

To use a simplified example to show how the standard normal distribution works, consider Westex Oil, which has home offices in Midland, Texas. Westex, an independent oil exploration and production company, was built by Tom Sanders after the oil embargo in the early 1970s. Tom had some initial success in finding small deposits of new oil, but most of the company's cash flow comes from wells it owns on established, and maturing, oil fields.

Even though most oil fields in the lower forty-eight states are maturing and facing declining production rates, substantial oil remains that is not recoverable by conventional means. Therefore most oil producers experiment with ways to increase production from mature wells. One method is to inject water into a well to force out additional oil. Tom Sanders is considering adding a newly developed enzyme to the injected water but will do so only if the increased production is sufficient to cover the additional costs. Suppose the new enzyme will increase oil output by an average of fifty barrels a day but because of differences in rock structures this output varies and has a standard deviation of ten barrels a day. Assuming the output increases can be represented by a normal distribution, figure 6–9 shows the distribution of potential increases in oil output.

Suppose we select an increase level $X = 50$ barrels per day. (Note that 50 is also μ_x, the mean increase.) We can find the Z value for this point using equation 6–5:

$$Z = \frac{X - \mu_x}{\sigma_x} = \frac{50 - 50}{10}$$

$$= 0$$

Thus, the Z value corresponding to the population mean, μ_x, is zero. This will be the case for all applications. Suppose we select sixty barrels per day as X. The Z value for this point is

$$Z = \frac{X - \mu_x}{\sigma_x} = \frac{60 - 50}{10} = \frac{10}{10}$$

$$= 1.00$$

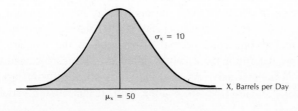

FIGURE 6–9
Distribution of increases in oil output due to adding new enzyme

FIGURE 6–10

Standard normal distribution probabilities

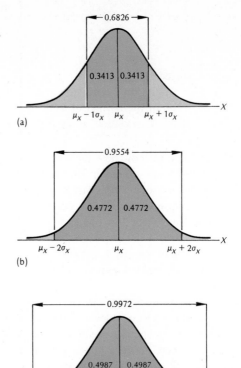

Verify for yourself that $X = 40$ barrels per day corresponds to a Z value of -1.00. Note that a negative Z value indicates only that the specified value of X is less than the mean.

If we examine equation 6–5 and the previous examples carefully, we see the Z value actually represents the number of standard deviations a point, X, is away from the population mean. In this Westex Oil example, σ_x, the standard deviation, is ten barrels per day. Therefore, an output increase of sixty barrels per day is exactly 1.00 standard deviation above $\mu_x = 50$ barrels per day. Likewise, an output increase of seventy barrels per day is 2.00 standard deviations from the mean.

Suppose Westex Oil can make an engineering change in injection techniques that will reduce the standard deviation to five barrels per day without changing the mean. Now an increase in output of sixty barrels per day is two standard deviations from the mean of fifty, and seventy barrels per day is 4.00 standard deviations from μ_x.

Thus, scaling an actual normal distribution to the standard normal distribution requires that we determine the Z values (number of standard deviations from μ_x) for any point on the horizontal axis. As shown, this is not a difficult process. Therefore, re-gardless of what situation we are dealing with, if the random variable is normally distributed, we can use the standard normal distribution, which is a special distribution with a mean of zero and a standard deviation of one. This offers some specific advantages when finding probabilities for ranges of values under the normal curve because a table of standard normal distribution probabilities has been developed. This table, which appears in appendix C, lists a series of Z values and the corresponding probability that a random variable value will fall between that Z value and the mean of the distribution. Remember that the Z value is simply the number of standard deviations a point, X, is from the mean μ_x. Therefore, if you want to know the probability that a value will lie within 1.00 standard deviation of the population mean, use the normal table as follows:

1. Go down the left-hand column of the table to $Z = 1.0$.
2. Go across the top row of the table to 0.00 for the second decimal place in $Z = 1.00$.
3. Find the value where the row and column found in steps 1 and 2 intersect.

Thus, the value 0.3413 is the probability that a value in a normal distribution will lie within 1.00 standard deviation *above* the population mean. Since the normal distribution is symmetrical, the probability that a value will lie within 1.00 standard deviation *below* the population mean is also 0.3413. Therefore the probability that a value will lie within 1.00 standard deviation of the population mean in *either* direction is 0.6826 (0.3413 + 0.3413 = 0.6826).

The same procedure is used to find the probability that a value will be within 2.00 standard deviations of the mean and within 3.00 standard deviations of the mean. Figure 6–10 illustrates these probabilities.

Let's return to the Westex Oil example. Recall that the mean increase in oil output was fifty barrels per day and the original standard deviation was ten barrels per day. However, Tom must try the enzyme on the wells he has and can't afford to play the averages. He has estimated the output level must be increased by at least forty-five barrels per day to pay for the additional cost of the enzyme injection. Therefore, if he tries the enzyme on one well, he is interested in the probability that production will be increased by forty-five or more barrels per day. This probability corresponds to the area under the curve to the right of forty-five barrels per day:

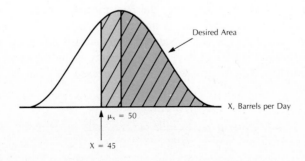

To use the standard normal table, we need to convert forty-five barrels per day to a Z value. This is equivalent to determining the number of standard deviations forty-five is from the mean.

$$Z = \frac{X - \mu_x}{\sigma_x} = \frac{45 - 50}{10}$$

$$= -0.50$$

The area corresponding to $Z = -0.50$ is 0.1915, shown under the normal curve:

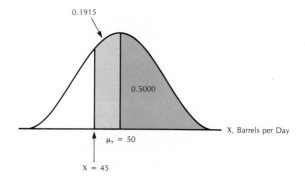

Since the normal curve is symmetrical and half the total area lies on each side of the mean, we can find $P(X \geq 45$ barrels per day$)$ by adding 0.1915 to 0.5000:

$$0.1915 + 0.5000 = 0.6915$$

Thus, the probability the well will increase production by enough to pay for the new enzyme is 0.6915.

As stressed many times in the preceding chapters, variation in a process cannot be completely avoided. Because of ever-present variation in the business world, decision makers face uncertainty. The best we can hope for is that this variation, and thus uncertainty, can be reduced. For example, we just calculated the probability as 0.6915 that introducing an enzyme in a mature oil well will be cost-effective. This means that slightly more than 30 percent of the time adding the enzyme will reduce profits. Tom Sanders, who must decide whether to try the new process, knows it will more likely increase profits than reduce them, yet is uncertain about what will happen with any single well. If he could find a way to reduce the standard deviation associated with output increases to five barrels per day, the uncertainty would be reduced because the probability of having a cost-effective well will be increased. We can calculate this probability as follows:

$$Z = \frac{X - \mu_x}{\sigma_x} = \frac{45 - 50}{5}$$

$$= -1.00$$

The following normal curve shows the area corresponding to the probability that adding the enzyme to a well will be cost-effective. Note that by developing a more consistent process, and thus reducing the standard deviation, we have increased the probability the enzyme injection will be cost-effective from 0.6915 to 0.8413:

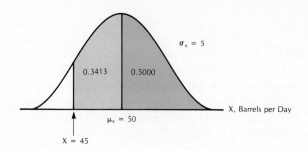

SKILL DEVELOPMENT PROBLEMS FOR SECTION 6–5

The following set of problems is meant to test your understanding of the material in this section. Additional problems are found at the end of this chapter under this section heading.

6. Assuming that we have a normal distribution, find the following probabilities if the mean is 60 and the standard deviation is 10.
   a. $P(X_1 > 60) =$
   b. $P(X_1 \geq 70) =$
   c. $P(50 \leq X \leq 70) =$
   d. $P(X_1 \leq 40) =$

7. For a normal distribution with mean $= 7.5$ and variance $= 9$, find the following probabilities:
   a. $P(X_1 \geq 8.5) =$
   b. $P(X_1 \geq 6.5) =$
   c. $P(X_1 \geq 9.5) =$
   d. $P(3 \leq X \leq 5.5) =$

8. Find the following probabilities assuming a normal distribution with a mean $= 7,450$ and a standard deviation $= 300$:
   a. $P(X_1 \leq 7,000) =$
   b. $P(X_1 \geq 8,000) =$
   c. $P(X_1 \geq 8,250) =$
   d. $P(7,400 \leq X \leq 7,700) =$

9. The average number of acres burned in August by forest and range fires in the western United States is 430,000, with a standard deviation of 75,000 acres. The distribution of acres is normal.
   a. What is the probability in any year that more than 500,000 acres will be burned?
   b. What is the probability in any year that fewer then 400,000 acres will be burned?

c. What is the probability that between 250,000 and 420,000 acres will be burned?

d. On those years when more than 550,000 acres are burned, help is needed from eastern-region fire teams. What is the probability help will be needed in any year?

OTHER APPLICATIONS OF THE NORMAL DISTRIBUTION

6-6

Suppose a consumer protection agency has decided to check packaging practices in the canned-food industry. This agency is checking to see if the manufacturers are filling cans with an amount of food about equal to that stated on the can's label. For instance, if a can of corn is supposed to weigh 16 ounces, the agency requires it to weigh at least 15.2 ounces. If it does not, the manufacturer is subject to heavy fines. Although variation is part of the filling process, each manufacturer obviously is interested in the chances of a can weighing less than 15.2 ounces. One company has set its automatic fillers so that the *average* fill is 16 ounces for a 16-ounce can. The standard deviation in weights produced by the filling machines is 0.3 ounce.

To calculate the probability of a can weighing less than 15.2 ounces, we find the appropriate area under the normal curve as follows:

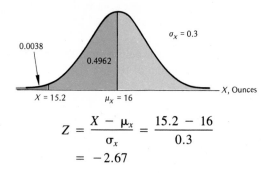

$$Z = \frac{X - \mu_x}{\sigma_x} = \frac{15.2 - 16}{0.3}$$

$$= -2.67$$

The negative 2.67 indicates that the value falls to the left of the mean. The probability corresponding to $Z = -2.67$ is 0.4962. This represents the probability that a can will weigh between 15.2 and 16 ounces. To find the probability that a can will weigh less than 15.2 ounces, we subtract 0.4962 from 0.5000, which gives 0.0038. This means the canning company has less than four chances in 1,000 of selling a can weighing less than the acceptable limit.

The normal distribution table is not used exclusively to find probabilities. For instance, suppose the scores on a company's employment exam are normally distributed with a mean of fifty points and a standard deviation of ten points. The personnel manager wants a minimum passing score such that only 15 percent of those who take the test pass. What should this minimum score be to ensure that only the top 15 percent of the applicants pass? We can solve this problem using the normal distribution table in the following manner:

1. Rather than using the normal table to find the probability associated with a particular Z value, we find the Z value associated with the known probability.

In this example, the probability of interest is 0.3500 (0.5000 − 0.1500). We look in the body of the normal table for the probability closest to 0.3500. This value is 0.3508, and the Z value corresponding to a probability of 0.3508 is 1.04.

2. We use the Z value determined in step 1 and solve for the minimum passing score, X.

$$Z = \frac{X - \mu_x}{\sigma_x}$$

$$1.04 = \frac{X - 50}{10}$$

$$X = (10)(1.04) + 50$$
$$= 60.4$$

Thus the minimum passing score that will allow at most 15 percent of the applicants to pass the employment exam is 60.4 points. The following normal distribution illustrates these results:

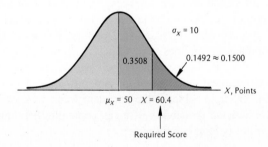

We can use the normal distribution in still another situation. We may know an X value and the standard deviation, but not μ_x. For example, suppose the production manager at the canning plant is faced with a problem. Because of the way the filling machines have been designed, the standard deviation of ounces per fill is fixed at 0.3 ounce, but the average ounces per fill can be adjusted. Under fear of reprisal by the consumer agency, the president of the canning company has ordered the production manager to set the filling machine so that there is a maximum 0.05 chance of a 16-ounce can weighing less than 15.2 ounces. To determine what the average fill should be, we perform the following analysis:

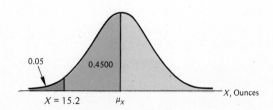

The area between 15.2 and μ_x is 0.4500. The Z value that corresponds to a probability of 0.4500 is approximately -1.64. Then, to solve for μ_x, we use

$$Z = \frac{X - \mu_x}{\sigma_x}$$

Then, substituting

$$Z = -1.64$$
$$X = 15.2 \text{ ounces}$$
$$\sigma_x = 0.3 \text{ ounce}$$

gives us

$$-1.64 = \frac{15.2 - \mu_x}{0.3}$$
$$\mu_x = 15.692 \text{ ounces}$$

Therefore, to have a probability of 5 percent or less of filling a can with less than 15.2 ounces, the average fill should be 15.692 ounces. The president of the company is faced with an ethical question here. So far, he has expressed total concern for getting caught with too little food in a can (that is, under 15.2 ounces in a 16-ounce can). To reasonably protect his company from fines, the filling machines should be set at 15.692 ounces. However, if this plan were adopted, the customer who expected 16 ounces in the can would be shortchanged over half of the time.

To continue the example, suppose the president wants to know the average filling quantity needed to reduce the probability of a can containing less than 16 ounces to 10 percent. This probability is found as follows:

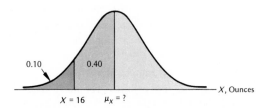

$$Z = \frac{X - \mu_x}{\sigma_x}$$

where

$$Z = -1.28$$
$$X = 16 \text{ ounces}$$
$$\sigma_x = 0.3 \text{ ounce}$$

Therefore

$$\mu_x = (1.28)(0.3) + 16$$
$$= 16.38 \text{ ounces}$$

Although the president is concerned about not filling the cans with enough food and not giving the customer the stated 16 ounces, he is also concerned about putting in more food than the customer is paying for. This last problem causes lost profits for the canning company. The president wants to know the average filling quantity such that no more than 15 percent of the 16-ounce cans actually weigh more than 16.2 ounces. To determine the setting to satisfy this requirement, we perform the following analysis:

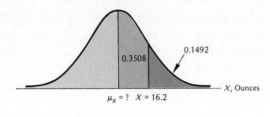

$$Z = \frac{X - \mu_x}{\sigma_x}$$

where $Z = 1.04$ (1.04 corresponds to a probability of 0.3508)
$\qquad\quad X = 16.2$ ounces
$\qquad\quad \sigma_x = 0.3$ ounces
Now solving for μ_x,

$$1.04 = \frac{16.2 - \mu_x}{0.3}$$

$$\mu_x = 15.888 \text{ ounces}$$

Therefore, to satisfy the president's requirement of a maximum 15 percent of the cans having more than 16.2 ounces, the production manager will have to adjust the filling machine to fill at an average of 15.888 ounces.

Thus, with three different criteria, three different machine settings have been determined. The president must weigh the potential economic and social costs before deciding the fill setting.

SKILL DEVELOPMENT PROBLEMS FOR SECTION 6–6

The following set of problems is meant to test your understanding of the material in this section. Additional problems are found at the end of this chapter under this section heading.

10. Assume a normal distribution with a mean of 15 and a standard deviation of 2.5.
  a. What percent of the distribution is greater than 18?
  b. What percent of the distribution is less than 13.5?
  c. 85 percent of the distribution is less than what value?
  d. 78 percent of the distribution is greater than what value?
  e. Assuming the probabilities are equally spaced on each side of the mean, 70 percent of the distribution is contained between which two values?

11. Assume a normal distribution with a mean of 22. If 75 percent of the distribution values are greater than 17, what is the standard deviation?

12. Assume a normal distribution with a standard deviation of 6.8. If 18 percent of the distribution values are less than 17.5, what is the mean?

13. J and G Painting has been gathering data on their painting speed in an effort to be more accurate in submitting bids. Based on data they have gathered after considering washing, taping, painting, and clean-up, one person can paint 100 square feet of indoor wall space per hour (because of extra taping time, doors and windows are counted as plain wall space), with a standard deviation of 40 square feet. A J and G painter has just started an 8-foot by 10-foot room at 2:00 P.M. (assume an 8-foot high ceiling). The painter will be paid overtime if she is not done by 5:00 P.M. If the ceiling is not to be painted, what is the probability overtime will not be paid?

NORMAL APPROXIMATION TO THE BINOMIAL DISTRIBUTION

6-7

The binomial distribution discussed in chapter 5 is not easy to work with when the sample size is larger than those found in the binomial table, or when the p values are not given in the table. In these cases, we would have to apply the binomial formula, which can be cumbersome. Fortunately, for large samples, an *approximation* can be used.

As a rule of thumb, the normal distribution generally provides good approximations for binomial problems if the sample size is large enough to meet the following two conditions:

> $$np \geq 5$$
> $$nq \geq 5$$
>
> where n = sample size
> p = probability of a success
> $q = 1 - p$ = probability of a failure

These conditions help ensure that the histogram formed by the binomial distribution is reasonably symmetrical and "looks like" a normal distribution. The best approximations occur when p approaches 0.5 and the sample size becomes large, because the binomial distribution approaches symmetry as p approaches 0.5. If $np \geq 5$ and $nq \geq 5$, the normal distribution can be used if we recall that for the binomial distribution, $\mu_x = np$ and $\sigma_x = \sqrt{npq}$. We can substitute these values into the Z formula and use the normal distribution table, as the following example illustrates.

A large retail store has discovered that 5 percent of its sales receipts contain some form of human error. Out of the next 1,000 sales made, the credit manager wants to know the probability that more than sixty errors will be made.

Since

$$np = (1,000)(0.05)$$
$$= 50 \geq 5$$

and

$$nq = (1,000)(0.95)$$
$$= 950 \geq 5$$

we will use the normal distribution to approximate the binomial. The first step is to determine the mean and standard deviation:

$$\mu_x = np = (1,000)(0.05)$$
$$= 50$$
$$\sigma_x = \sqrt{npq} = \sqrt{(1,000)(0.05)(0.95)}$$
$$= 6.89$$

Because the binomial distribution is a discrete distribution, we must make a slight modification when using the normal approximation. Specifically, we must treat sixty errors as the unit interval "59.5 to 60.5." Thus, the probability of exactly sixty errors will correspond to the area between 59.5 and 60.5 errors and the probability of *more* than sixty errors is found as follows:

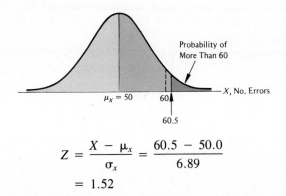

$$Z = \frac{X - \mu_x}{\sigma_x} = \frac{60.5 - 50.0}{6.89}$$
$$= 1.52$$

From the normal distribution table, the area between 60.5 and 50 ($Z = 1.52$) is 0.4357. Therefore the approximate probability of more than sixty incorrect sales slips is 0.0643 ($0.5000 - 0.4357 = 0.0643$).

Consider another example where the appropriate distribution is binomial, but we can choose to approximate the probability using the normal approximation approach. In this example, we will compute both the exact probability, using the binomial distribution, and the approximate probability, using the normal distribution.

The American Chip Company manufactures computer memory chips for use in such products as digital watches and microwave oven controls. After checking and rechecking their product, records indicate that 6 percent of the chips actually delivered to customers are faulty. Recently the company was informed that a shipment of 100 chips contained four defectives. The quality control manager was asked to determine the probability of four or more defectives being shipped if, in fact, the 6 percent defective level was still valid.

To help her answer this question, we recognize that the appropriate probability distribution might likely be the binomial distribution since the random variable is discrete, with only two possible outcomes (*defective* or *nondefective*) per chip. Assuming that the binomial distribution does apply, we can find the exact probability of four or more defectives using either the binomial formula or, preferably, the binomial tables in the appendix. We do this as follows:

$$P(X_1 \geq 4) = 1 - P(X_1 < 4)$$

Using the binomial table with $n = 100$ and $p = 0.06$, we find

$$\begin{aligned} P(X_1 \geq 4) &= 1 - (0.0021 + 0.0131 + 0.0414 + 0.0864) \\ &= 1 - 0.1430 \\ &= 0.8570 \end{aligned}$$

Thus, the exact probability of four or more defectives being shipped by the American Chip Company is 0.8570. We say this is the exact probability because we assumed the underlying distribution is binomial and we did, in fact, use the binomial distribution to compute the probability.

Suppose, however, that we did not have available the binomial tables with $n = 100$ and $p = 0.06$, and we did not wish to use the binomial formula, which could be quite cumbersome for this problem. We can instead use the normal approximation to the binomial probability since

$$np = (100)(0.06) = 6 \qquad (6 \geq 5)$$

and

$$nq = (100)(0.94) = 94 \qquad (94 \geq 5)$$

In order to use the normal approximation, we need to know the mean and standard deviation. For the binomial distribution

$$\mu_x = np = 6$$

and

$$\sigma_x = \sqrt{npq} = 2.375$$

Then we draw a normal distribution as follows. The area of interest has been labeled. Take special notice that the 0.5 unit adjustment has been made, which is required anytime we use the normal distribution to approximate a discrete distribution like the binomial.

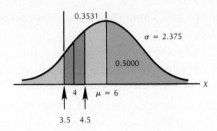

As we wish to find the probability of $X_1 \geq 4$, we will solve for the Z value using $X = 3.5$, which would include any value 4 or higher. This is shown as follows:

$$Z = \frac{3.5 - 6.0}{2.375}$$

$$= -1.0526 = -1.05$$

We next go to the normal distribution table for $Z = -1.05$ and find the area between 3.5 and the mean 6.0, which we find is 0.3531. As the diagram shows, the desired area can be found by adding 0.5000 to 0.3531, giving 0.8531. Thus, the normal approximation for the probability of four or more defective chips is 0.8531.

This approximation compares favorably with the exact probability of 0.8570 computed earlier from the binomial tables. Thus, the normal approximation can offer a good alternative under certain conditions to computing binomial probabilities using the binomial formula or the binomial tables.

SKILL DEVELOPMENT PROBLEMS FOR SECTION 6–7

The following set of problems is meant to test your understanding of the material in this section. Additional problems are found at the end of this chapter under this section heading.

14. Using the normal approximation to the binomial distribution with $n = 250$ and $p = 0.1$:

a. What is the probability a value from the distribution will have a value between twenty and thirty-five?

b. What is the probability a value from the distribution will have a value greater than eighteen?

c. What is the probability a value from the distribution will have a value less than twenty-two?

d. What is the probability a value from the distribution will have a value less than thirty-five?

15. Sun City Stages promotes three-day weekend excursions to Las Vegas. A typical promotion will be staged for 150 people, who will be transported in three buses. Historical records indicate the no-show rate for people who call in to sign up for a tour will be 20 percent. If fewer than 115 people take part in a tour, Sun City will lose money. What is the probability the next tour will be profitable?

16. A quality control process at the Guidian Manufacturing plant calls for a random sample of 150 parts to be inspected. If the defective rate in the population is thought to be 0.076 and the underlying distribution is binomial, what is the probability of finding fewer than twenty-one defectives in the sample?

17. The X-Color Lab in Los Angeles attempts to produce pictures with a 98 percent success rate. To check on the quality control, a sample of 500 pictures has been selected. The distribution is assumed to be binomial.
   a. What is the expected number of defective pictures in the sample?
   b. What is the standard deviation of the distribution?
   c. What is the probability of finding between seven and thirteen defectives in the sample if the defective level is 2 percent?

CONCLUSIONS

6-8

This chapter introduced continuous probability distributions, including uniform and normal distributions. It also showed that the normal distribution, with its special properties, is used extensively in statistical decision making. It discussed in some detail the standard normal distribution and showed how it can be adapted to any normal distribution application. It also showed that the normal distribution can be used to approximate the binomial distribution under certain circumstances.

Subsequent chapters will introduce other continuous probability distributions. Among these will be the *t distribution*, the *chi-square distribution*, and the *F distribution*. These additional distributions play important roles in statistical decision making. The basic concept that the area under a continuous curve is equivalent to probability is true for all continuous distributions.

The important statistical terms introduced in this chapter are summarized in the chapter glossary. The main statistical formulas presented in this chapter are listed following the glossary.

CHAPTER GLOSSARY

continuous probability distribution   The probability distribution of a variable that can assume an infinitely large number of values. The probability of any single value is theoretically zero.

normal distribution   A continuous distribution that is symmetrical (mean, median, and mode are all equal) and in theory has an infinite range. It is represented by

$$f(X) = \frac{1}{\sigma_x\sqrt{2\pi}}e^{-(X-\mu_x)^2/2\sigma_x^2}$$

standard normal distribution   A normal distribution with a mean equal to zero and a standard deviation equal to 1.0. All normal distributions can be standardized by forming a standard normal distribution of Z values.

$$Z = \frac{X - \mu_x}{\sigma_x}$$

where Z = scaled value
X = any point on the horizontal axis
μ_x = mean of the normal distribution
σ_x = standard deviation of the normal distribution

uniform probability distribution   A probability distribution that has probabilities for a random variable that are equal for all values of the random variable between two limits, a and b.

CHAPTER FORMULAS

Normal distribution

$$f(X) = \frac{1}{\sigma_x\sqrt{2\pi}}e^{(X-\mu_x)^2/2\sigma_x^2}$$

Standard Z value

$$Z = \frac{X - \mu_x}{\sigma_x}$$

Uniform distribution

$$f(X) = \begin{cases} \dfrac{1}{b-a} & (a \le X \le b) \\ 0 & \text{otherwise} \end{cases}$$

Mean of uniform distribution

$$\mu_x = E(X) = \frac{a+b}{2}$$

Standard deviation of uniform distribution

$$\sigma_x = \sqrt{\frac{(b-a)^2}{12}}$$

SOLVED PROBLEMS

1. The length of steel I-beams made by the Smokers City Steel Company is normally distributed, with $\mu_x = 25.1$ feet and $\sigma_x = 0.25$ foot.
   a. What is the probability that a steel beam will be less than 24.8 feet long?
   b. What is the probability that a steel beam will be more than 25.25 feet long?
   c. What is the probability that a steel beam will be between 24.9 and 25.7 feet long?
   d. What is the probability that a steel beam will be between 24.6 and 24.9 feet long?
   e. For a particular application, any beam less than 25 feet long must be scrapped. What is the probability that a beam will have to be scrapped?

Solutions:

To answer all these questions, we will use the following procedure:

1. Draw a picture to show what area we are interested in.
2. Find the desired Z value.
3. Use the normal distribution table to find the desired area under the normal distribution curve (the needed probability).

a.

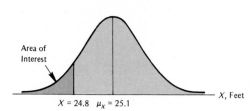

Area of Interest

$X = 24.8 \quad \mu_x = 25.1$

X, Feet

$$Z = \frac{X - \mu_x}{\sigma_x} = \frac{24.8 - 25.1}{0.25}$$

$$= \frac{-0.3}{0.25}$$

$$= -1.20$$

The negative sign means only that we are on the left half of the distribution.

From the normal distribution table, the area associated with a Z value of -1.20 is 0.3849. However, this is the area between 24.8 and 25.1 feet. We want the area less than 24.8 feet. We proceed as follows:

1. The total area under the curve (probability the beam will have some length) is 1.0.
2. The area under half the curve is 0.5.
3. The area we want is $0.5 - 0.3849 = 0.1151$.

b.

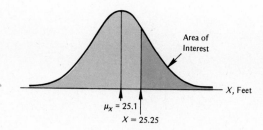

$$Z = \frac{X - \mu_x}{\sigma_x} = \frac{25.25 - 25.1}{0.25} = \frac{0.15}{0.25}$$

$$= 0.60$$

The area between 25.1 and 25.25 from the table is 0.2257. The area greater than 25.25 is $0.5 - 0.2257 = 0.2743$.

c.

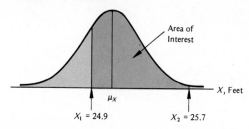

We do this problem in three steps:

1. Find the area between 25.1 and 25.7 feet.
2. Find the area between 24.9 and 25.1 feet.
3. Add the probabilities found in steps 1 and 2.

Therefore

1. $Z = \dfrac{25.7 - 25.1}{0.25} = \dfrac{0.6}{0.25}$

$\qquad = 2.40$

From the table, area $= 0.4918$.

2. $Z = \dfrac{24.9 - 25.1}{0.25} = \dfrac{-0.2}{0.25}$

$\qquad = -0.80$

From the table, area $= 0.2881$.

3. Total area $= 0.4918 + 0.2881 = 0.7799$.

d.

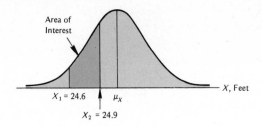

We also do this problem in three steps:

    1. Find the area between 25.1 and 24.6.
    2. Find the area between 25.1 and 24.9.
    3. Subtract the area in step 2 from the area in step 1.

Therefore

    1. $Z = \dfrac{24.6 - 25.1}{0.25}$

        $= -2.0$

    From the table, area = 0.4772.

    2. $Z = \dfrac{24.9 - 25.1}{0.25}$

        $= -0.80$

    From the table, area = 0.2881.

    3. Desired area = 0.4772 − 0.2881 = 0.1891.

e.

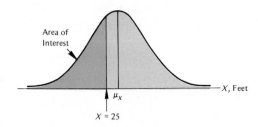

$$Z = \frac{25 - 25.1}{0.25} = \frac{-0.1}{0.25}$$

$$= -0.40$$

From the table, area = 0.1554. The probability we want is

$$0.5 - 0.1554 = 0.3446$$

Thus slightly more than 34 percent of the beams will have to be scrapped because they will not meet the required length.

2. The average absentee rate in large economics lecture sections has always been 15 percent. In a section of 200 students:
   a. What is the probability that on a given day 160 or more students will attend class?
   b. What is the probability that 180 or fewer students will attend?
   c. What is the probability that between 165 and 185 students will attend?

Solutions:

Since

$$np = (200)(0.15) = 30 \geq 5$$

$$n(1 - p) = (200)(0.85) = 170 \geq 5$$

we can use the normal approximation to the binomial. For all parts of this problem,

$$\mu_x = np = (0.15)(200)$$
$$= 30$$
$$\sigma_x = \sqrt{np(1 - p)} = \sqrt{(200)(0.15)(0.85)}$$
$$= 5.05$$

a. This part asks for the probability that forty or fewer students will be absent. We must use $X = 40.5$ because we are using a continuous distribution to approximate a discrete distribution. This is illustrated as follows:

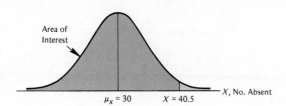

$$Z = \frac{40.5 - 30}{5.05} = 2.08$$

From the table, $Z = 2.08$ gives an area of 0.4812. We have

$$P(X \leq 40.5) = P(30 \text{ to } 40.5) + P(\text{less than } 30)$$

but since $P(\text{less than } 30) = 0.5$,

$$P(X \leq 40.5) = 0.4812 + 0.5$$
$$= 0.9812$$

b. We want the probability twenty or more will be absent.

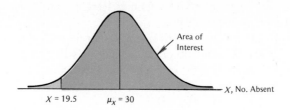

$$Z = \frac{19.5 - 30}{5.05}$$

$$= -2.08$$

From the table,

$$P(19.5 \text{ to } 30) = 0.4812$$

therefore,

$$P(X \geq 19.5) = P(19.5 \text{ to } 30) + P(\text{more than } 30) = 0.4812 + 0.5$$
$$= 0.9812$$

c. We want the probability that from fifteen to thirty-five students will be absent.

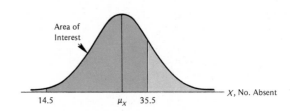

$$P(14.5 \text{ to } 35.5) = P(14.5 \text{ to } 30) + P(30 \text{ to } 35.5)$$

$$Z = \frac{14.5 - 30}{5.05} \qquad\qquad Z = \frac{35.5 - 30}{5.05}$$

$$= -3.07 \qquad\qquad\qquad = 1.09$$

$$\text{Area} = 0.4989 \qquad\qquad \text{Area} = 0.3621$$

So

$$P(14.5 \text{ to } 35.5) = 0.4989 + 0.3621$$
$$= 0.8610$$

ADDITIONAL PROBLEMS

Section 6–3

18. The American Testing Service has determined that examination scores on the Indiana real estate exam are uniformly distributed between scores of 40 and 80 percent correct.
   a. Develop a graph of the probability distribution.
   b. Determine the probability of a score under 65 percent correct on the exam.
   c. What is the probability of scoring 70 percent correct or better on the exam?
   d. What is the probability of scoring between 60 and 75 percent correct on the exam?

19. A new battery designed especially for children's toys has been found to have a lifetime between two-and-a-half hours and seven hours, with probabilities uniformly distributed between these two points.
   a. Develop a graph showing the probability distribution.
   b. Determine the probability that a battery will last over six hours.
   c. What is the probability that a battery, will last between three and a half and five and a half hours?
   d. What is the average lifetime of a battery?
   e. What is the standard deviation of battery life?

20. In a particular geographical area, the amount of annual rainfall is uniformly distributed between ten and twenty-four inches.
   a. Develop a graph of the probability distribution for annual rainfall.
   b. What is the expected value of the probability distribution?
   c. Compute the variance and standard deviation and annual rainfall in the geographical region.
   d. Using your answers to parts b and c, what is the probability of a year having rainfall within plus or minus two standard deviations of the mean?
   e. Referring to your answer to part d, how does it compare to what Tchebysheff's theorem would indicate within plus or minus two standard deviations of the mean?

21. Many computer simulation experiments use the uniform distribution in determining random numbers. For instance, an inventory simulation model requires that uniformly distributed random numbers with values between thirty and ninety be selected. These numbers will be used in the model to indicate the delivery time for merchandise once an order is placed.
   a. What is the probability that a random number will exceed eighty?
   b. On the average, what value of the random number can be expected if a large number of random numbers are generated?
   c. If a large number of random numbers are generated, what will be the standard deviation?

22. Problem 21 considers a computer program used to generate random numbers that follow a uniform distribution. You are using the program to generate numbers ranging from thirty to ninety, but the first ten values you get are all less than forty. What is the probability of this occurring? Given you have seen the ten numbers, what conclusion might you draw with respect to the program?

Section 6–4

23. Describe a business application in which the random variable of interest is normally distributed.

24. The manager of consumer loans at Swiftview National Bank has determined that the average account balance is $700.00, with a median balance of $600.00. He has indicated that the distribution of account balances is a normal distribution. Comment on whether it is possible for a distribution to be normal if the mean and median are different.

25. The time spent by patients at a particular hospital has averaged 4.2 days, which is also the number of days in a median stay. In order for the distribution of patient length of stay to be normally distributed, what must the mode for length of stay be?

Section 6–5

26. Assuming that the distribution of family incomes in a west Boston neighborhood is normally distributed, with a mean of $20,000 and a standard deviation of $4,000, find
a. The probability that a family has an income under $12,000.
b. The probability that a family's income is over $19,000.
c. The probability that a family's income is between $18,000 and $26,000.
d. The probability that a family's income exceeds $40,000.

27. Suppose personal daily water usage in California is normally distributed, with a mean of eighteen gallons and a standard deviation of six gallons.
a. What percentage of the population uses more than eighteen gallons?
b. What percentage of the population uses between ten and twenty gallons?
c. What is the probability of finding a person who uses less than ten gallons?

28. Cattle are often fattened in a feedlot before being shipped to a slaughterhouse. Suppose the weight gain per steer at a feedlot averaged 1.5 pounds per day, with a standard deviation of 0.25 pound. Assume a normal distribution.
a. What is the probability a steer will gain over two pounds on a given day?
b. What is the probability a steer will gain between one and two pounds in any given day?
c. What is the probability of selecting two steers that both gain less than 1.5 pounds on a given day, assuming the two are independent?
d. Compute the probabilities found in parts a, b, and c assuming a standard deviation of 0.2 pound. Why are these probabilities different?

29. The dollar amount of dairy products consumed per week by adults is thought to be normally distributed, with a mean of $4.50 and a standard deviation of $1.10.

a. What is the probability that an individual adult from the population will consume over $4.90 in dairy products in a week?

b. What is the probability that an individual selected at random from the population will consume less than $6.25 in dairy products in a week?

c. What is the probability that a person will consume between $3.25 and $5.75 in dairy products in a week?

30. Jamieson Airlines has a central office that takes reservations for all flights flown by the airline. The calls received during any week are normally distributed, with a mean of 12,000 and a standard deviation of 2,500.

a. During what percentage of the weeks does the airline receive more than 11,000 calls?

b. During what percentage of the weeks does it receive fewer than 12,300 calls?

c. During what percentage of the weeks does it receive between 10,800 and 13,400 calls?

d. During what percentage of the weeks does the airline receive more than 12,800 or fewer than 11,100 calls?

Section 6–6

31. Refer to problem 27, in which water usage in California was thought to be normally distributed, with a mean of eighteen gallons and a standard deviation of six gallons. Because of a perpetual water shortage in California, the governor wants to give a tax rebate to the 20 percent of the population that use the least amount of water.

a. What should the governor use as the maximum water limit for a person to qualify for a tax rebate?

b. Suppose the governor's proposed tax rebate causes a shift in the average water use from eighteen gallons to fourteen gallons per person per day, but causes no change in the variance. What limit should be set on water use if 20 percent of the population is to receive a tax rebate?

32. The Ziegler Lumber Company sets the cut length on its 2 × 12 lumber a little longer than the specified length because its trim saw is fairly old. The mill foreman had discovered the saw would cut any set length short by an average of three inches, with a standard deviation of one-and-a-half inches. Fortunately, the errors seem to be normally distributed.

a. If the foreman is setting up the trim saw to cut 2 × 12 boards ten feet long, what should the trim saw length setting be if he wants no more than a 5 percent chance of a board being shorter than ten feet?

b. Suppose the machine can be fixed so that the standard deviation in cut error can be controlled to a specified level. What would the standard deviation have to be in order that trim length could be set one inch shorter than the answer to part a?

33. Problem 32 refers to the Ziegler Lumber Company, which discovered its old trim saw would cut any set length short by an average of three inches, with a standard deviation of one-and-a-half inches. The errors seen are normally distributed. Suppose an adjustment is made to the machine that reduces the average error to two inches, but increases the standard deviation to two inches. What should the trim saw length setting be if he wants no more than a 5 percent chance of a board being cut shorter than ten feet?

34. The personnel manager for a large company is interested in the distribution of sick-leave hours for employees of her company. A recent study revealed the distribution to be approximately normal, with a mean of fifty-eight hours per year and a standard deviation of fourteen hours.

    An office manager in one division has reason to believe that during the past year, two of his employees have taken excessive sick leave relative to everyone else. The first employee used seventy-four hours of sick leave, and the second used ninety hours. What would you conclude about the office manager's claim and why?

35. Problem 34 considers a company's distribution of sick-leave hours for its employees. The personnel manager has found the distribution to be approximately normal, with a mean of fifty-eight hours per year and standard deviation of fourteen hours. Suppose the company grants forty hours of paid sick leave per year. Given the sick-leave distribution, what would you conclude about the adequacy of the company's sick-leave policy? Why?

36. The preceding two problems deal with a company's distribution of sick-leave hours for its employees. The personnel manager has found the distribution to be approximately normal, with a mean of fifty-eight hours per year and a standard deviation of fourteen hours.

    Suppose the company is considering a change in its sick-leave policy for next year. The objective is to have the number of paid sick-leave hours at a level that will require 10 percent or fewer people to incur unpaid sick time. Assuming the historical sick-leave pattern holds true next year, how many sick-leave hours should be paid by the company?

37. This is the last of several problems dealing with a company's distribution of sick-leave hours for its employees which the personnel manager has found to be approximately normal, with a mean of fifty-eight hours per year and a standard deviation of fourteen hours.

    Suppose a consultant has suggested the company hold its paid sick-leave hours to forty hours per year and hire a physician who will serve employees at the plant in an attempt to reduce the average number of sick-leave hours used to a more acceptable level. What would the mean have to be if the probability of an individual needing more than forty hours of sickleave is to be, at most, 10 percent? Assume the standard deviation remains fourteen hours and the distribution is normal.

38. The Bryce Brothers Lumber Company is considering buying a machine that planes lumber to the correct thickness. The machine is advertised to produce ''six-inch lumber'' having a thickness that is normally distributed, with a mean of six inches and a standard deviation of 0.1 inch.
    a. If building standards in the industry require a 99 percent chance of a board being between 5.85 and 6.15 inches, should Bryce Brothers purchase this machine? Why or why not?

b. To what level would the company that manufactures the machine have to reduce the standard deviation for the machine to conform to industry standards?

Section 6–7

39. Suppose light bulbs are packed in boxes of 1,000 bulbs. Although the packers try their best, 10 percent of the bulbs get broken before they reach the retail stores.
  a. Using the normal approximation to the binomial distribution, find the probability that from 110 to 130 bulbs will be broken in a box.
  b. Using the normal approximation, find the probability that more than 130 bulbs will be broken.
  c. Suppose you have just found a box with 200 broken bulbs. Would you consider this unusual? Why or why not?

40. A market-research firm was hired to determine the percentage of people in a market area who would purchase *Playboy* magazine if a door-to-door sales campaign were undertaken. The firm stated that 40 percent would buy if contacted at home. Suppose the publisher has tried the sales campaign at 300 randomly selected homes.
  a. If the market research was accurate, what is the probability that fewer than 100 individuals will buy? Use the normal approximation to the binomial distribution.
  b. Suppose the publisher actually sells *Playboy* to seventy people out of the 300 contracted. What would you conclude about the market research and about the sales campaign, respectively?
  c. Assuming the market research was done properly and the 40 percent is representative, how many sales are expected if the publisher attempts to sell to 5,000 homes?

41. The firm of Anderson, Barnhart, and DuPuis is a C.P.A. firm in Lincoln, Nebraska. When its accountants perform audits, they often use sampling as a way of reducing the cost of audits. Recently they audited an automobile dealership, including the parts inventory. The inventory has 4,000 different part numbers. For each part number there is a stated inventory quantity on a computer listing.

The accountants plan on sampling 100 part numbers and counting the actual inventory. They will then compare the actual inventory with the stated amount shown on the printout. They will record the number of "material" differences between actual and stated in the sample of 100 parts.
  a. If the true proportion of "material" errors is 10 percent, what is the probability that the sample will contain fewer than five parts with "material" errors? Use the normal approximation to the binomial.
  b. Use the binomial tables to solve part a and compare the two answers. Discuss why they are not exactly the same.

42. A market-research study indicates that 10 percent of all homes have a video-cassette recorder for recording television programs.
  a. In a sample of 500 homes, what is the probability that from forty to eighty, inclusive, will have a video-cassette recorder?

b. In a sample of 1,000 homes, what is the probability that between 80 and 100 homes will have a recorder?

43. The Internal Revenue Service (IRS) has estimated that 60 percent of their audits find that there is either no change in the individual's tax or that the individual actually paid too much.

a. If the IRS estimate is true, what is the probability that in a sample of 1,000 audits, from 500 to 600 individuals will not owe additional taxes?

b. What is the probability in a random sample of 1,500 IRS audits that fewer than 800 will owe additional tax?

CASES

6A East Mercy Medical Center

Dorothy Jacobs was recently hired as assistant administrator of the East Mercy Medical Center. She is a new graduate of a well-regarded master's degree program in hospital administration and is expected to incorporate some advanced thinking into the apparently lax practices at East Mercy.

Hospitals have recently been under increasing pressure from both government and local sources because of escalating costs. Although members of the board of directors of East Mercy feel that cost considerations are secondary to quality care, its members also are sensitive to the increasing public pressure.

East Mercy is located in a rapidly growing area and is feeling capacity limitations. In particular, according to staff personnel, the obstetrics, adult medical/surgical, and pediatric wards are "bursting at the seams." East Mercy is considering an extensive expansion program, including expansion of the obstetric, adult medical/surgical, and pediatric wards. The board has allocated a total of $400,000 for new beds in these three wards. Dorothy is presently trying to determine how many beds current demand levels justify for each ward and how many beds to actually add, given the $400,000 cost constraint.

Dorothy and her staff have computed statistics based on the current year's patient census data in each of the three wards. These figures are as follows:

Ward	Average No. Beds Used per Day	Standard Deviation
Obstetrics	24	6.1
Surgery	13	4.3
Pediatrics	19	4.7

Histogram plots of bed usage show a remarkably close approximation to a normal distribution for each department.

The present capacity of each ward is

$$\text{Obstetrics} = 30$$
$$\text{Surgery} = 20$$
$$\text{Pediatrics} = 24$$

The hospital's architects have given the following estimates for the cost of adding one bed and all necessary supporting equipment to each of the wards:

$$\text{Obstetrics} = \$20{,}000$$
$$\text{Surgery} = \$26{,}000$$
$$\text{Pediatrics} = \$15{,}500$$

It is possible for a ward to exceed its capacity, but according to state guidelines, this should not occur more than 5 percent of the time.

Dorothy is in the process of preparing a report to the administrator showing how many beds are to be added to each of the three wards.

6B American Oil Company, Inc.

Chad Williams, field geologist for American Oil Company, settled into his first-class seat on the Sun-Aire flight between Los Angeles and Oakland, California. He had left a meeting with the design engineering group at the Los Angeles New Products Division earlier that afternoon and was now on his way home to his home office in Oakland. He was looking forward to the one-hour flight as it would give him a chance to reflect on a problem that surfaced at the meeting. It would also give him a chance to think about the exciting opportunities that lay ahead in Australia.

Chad works with a small group of highly trained people at American Oil who literally walk Earth looking for new sources of oil. They make use of the latest in electronic equipment to take a wide range of measurements from many thousands of feet below Earth's surface. It was one of these electronic machines that was the source of Chad's current problem. A sophisticated enhancement that would greatly improve the equipment's ability to detect oil had been designed by the engineers in Los Angeles. The enhancement required 800 capacitors, which have to operate within $\pm$ 0.50 micron (μm) from the specified standard of 12 microns. The problem was that the supplier could provide the capacitors, which operate according to a normal distribution, with a mean of 12 microns and a standard deviation of 1.0 micron, and consequently, not all the capacitors could be expected to meet the specifications required by this new piece of exploration equipment. This would mean that in order to acquire the 800 capacitors, more than 800 would have to be purchased from the supplier. Chad knew that he would have to determine how many to buy before the next day if the project was going to remain on schedule and the exploration trip to Australia was to begin on time. As he reclined in his seat, he wondered if there was some way that basic probability could aid him in his decision.

6C Belko Equipment Company

When Andrew Wilson was hired at the Belko Equipment Company, he was considered a top prospect by the company's managers. After a short introduction period in each of the company's departments, Andrew was assigned to the production control division in the Des Moines, Iowa, plant. He reported directly to Sarah Billings, who had been in charge of production control for about three years. Sarah was excited about having Andrew in her department because the work load had been increasing very fast during the past few months. It was becoming difficult to maintain the type of control on incoming parts that Sarah wanted with the increasing volume of orders.

Sarah assigned Andrew immediately to the task of reviewing the acceptance sampling plan for a critical part (A-67890-BCD). This part has been one of those singled out because of its high failure rate. Andrew discovered that the acceptance sampling plan involved a random sample of 250 parts from each shipment. The decision rule that had been used in the past was to accept the entire shipment if the sample contained fewer than twenty defectives. If the sample contained twenty or more defectives, the shipment was rejected and returned to the supplier.

In reviewing the contract with the supplier and Belko's work notes in the contract file, Andrew learned that the negotiated price for part A-67890-BCD assumed a maximum defective rate of 4 percent. Further, the notes indicated that Belko would start losing money in significant amounts if the defective rate on a shipment reached 10 percent defective.

Andrew leaned back in his chair and looked out his window. His concern with the acceptance sampling plan was that it be both fair to the supplier by not rejecting too many good shipments, but that the plan also be fair to Belko by not letting too many shipments be accepted which contain 10 percent or more defectives. Andrew thought that he could apply the binomial probability distribution to help evaluate the sampling plan. He would submit his report on the plan to Sarah Billings the next morning.

REFERENCES

Lapin, Lawrence. *Statistics for Modern Business Decisions,* 3rd Edition. New York: Harcourt Brace Jovanovich, 1982.

Neter, John; Wasserman, William; and Whitmore, G. A. *Applied Statistics,* 2nd Edition. Boston: Allyn and Bacon, 1982.

Richards, Larry, and Lacava, Jerry. *Business Statistics: Why and When,* 2nd Edition. New York: McGraw-Hill, 1983.

SAMPLING TECHNIQUES AND THE SAMPLING DISTRIBUTION OF $\bar{X}$ AND $\hat{p}$

7

WHY DECISION MAKERS NEED TO KNOW

Many business decisions involve determining the average, or mean, of a set of data. For example, when deciding what brand of tires to purchase, the manager of a car-rental company wants to know which brand will give the longest average wear. In another example, light-bulb manufacturers are now required to indicate the average life of each type of bulb they make. These companies must somehow determine the mean life of the bulbs they manufacture.

Calculating the mean of a set of data presents no particular problem as long as the data are available. However, few business problems allow decision makers to measure the entire population of values. Either cost or time constraints limit the number of values they can use to calculate the mean. As stated in Chapter 1, these constraints are the main reason for sampling.

In practice, selecting a sample from a population in such a manner that valid statistical conclusions can be drawn about the population is a complicated task. Few managers need to be experts on sampling techniques, but all managers who rely on sample information should be aware of what is generally required for a sample to yield statistically sound results. This chapter introduces some commonly used sampling techniques.

After a sample is taken, and the mean of that sample calculated, the decision maker needs to recognize that the sample mean observed depends on which sample of the many possible samples is selected. Consequently, decision makers need to understand how the possible sample means are distributed. This chapter introduces the very important concept of *sampling distributions*.

CHAPTER OBJECTIVES

This chapter begins our discussion of how sample values are used to allow a decision maker to draw inferences about population values. But before any statistical relationships between sample values and population values can be drawn, a statistically valid sample must be taken. This chapter discusses some common sampling techniques.

This chapter also introduces the sampling distribution of $\overline{X}$. The chapter will show that the value of $\overline{X}$ obtained depends on the particular sample selected. Thus $\overline{X}$ comes from a distribution of possible sample means. The chapter also introduces one of the most important theorems in statistics—the central limit theorem—and will show how it is used in the decision-making process. Finally, this chapter introduces the sampling distribution for the sample proportion and shows how it is applied.

STUDENT OBJECTIVES

After studying the material in this chapter, you should be able to

1. Discuss the difference between statistical and nonstatistical sampling and describe four statistical sampling techniques: simple random sampling, stratified random sampling, systematic random sampling, and cluster random sampling.
2. Discuss the relationship between a population and the many samples that can be selected from it.
3. Explain why the central limit theorem is so important to statistical decision making.
4. Discuss the relationship between the sample size and the decisions that can be based on sample information.
5. Discuss how variation in the population affects decisions that can be based on sample information.

AN INTRODUCTION TO SAMPLING

7-1

Once the manager decides to gather information by sampling, there are many ways to select the sample. This section introduces several of the sampling techniques most often employed.

All sampling techniques fall into one of two categories: *statistical* or *nonstatistical*. *Statistical sampling* techniques include all those using *random* or *probability sampling*. With a random or probability sample, data items are selected by chance alone. Once the probabilities of selecting the items in the population are known, the individual selecting the sample does not change those probabilities. *Nonstatistical sampling,* or *nonprobability sampling,* is *nonrandom* in nature.

Both statistical and nonstatistical sampling techniques are commonly used by decision makers. However, nonstatistical sampling techniques have some widely recognized problems. For example, when a judgmental sample is selected, there is no objective means of evaluating the results. Because the results depend on personal judgment, their reliability cannot be measured using probability theory.

This does not imply that judgmental sampling is bad or should not be used. In fact, in many cases it represents the only feasible way to sample. For example, the J. R. Simplot Corporation, a manufacturer of frozen french fries, tests potatoes from each truck arriving at its manufacturing plant. The company uses the results of the sample to determine whether each truckload should be accepted. The quality control people judg-mentally select a few potatoes from the top of each truck rather than from throughout the load as statistical sampling would require. It just is not feasible to take a statistical sample.

The remainder of this section discusses statistical and nonstatistical sampling tech-niques. While many techniques fall within each of these categories, only the most com-mon will be covered.

Statistical (Probability) Sampling Techniques

Simple Random Sampling

The most fundamental statistical sample is called a *simple random sample*. Simple ran-dom sampling is a method of selecting items from a population such that every possible sample of a specific size has an equal chance of being selected.

As an example, suppose a new insurance salesperson wishes to estimate the per-centage of people in a local subdivision who already have life insurance policies. This would be important since the result would be an indication of the potential market in the subdivision. The population of interest consists of all families living in the subdivi-sion.

For the purposes of our example, we will simplify the situation. Suppose there are five families in the subdivision: James, Sanchez, Lui, White, and Fitzpatrick. We will let N be the population size and n be the sample size. Then, from the five families ($N = 5$), we select three ($n = 3$) for the sample. Now we list the possible samples of size three that could be selected as follows:

> James, Sanchez, Lui
> James, Sanchez, White
> James, Sanchez, Fitzpatrick
> James, Lui, White
> James, Lui, Fitzpatrick
> James, White, Fitzpatrick
> Sanchez, Lui, White
> Sanchez, Lui, Fitzpatrick
> Sanchez, White, Fitzpatrick
> Lui, White, Fitzpatrick

In a correctly performed simple random sample, each of these samples would have an equal chance of being selected.

This example did not allow for a family to be selected more than once in a given sample. This condition is *sampling without replacement* and is the most common sam-pling condition. However, sometimes after an item has been selected for the sample it is replaced into the population and may be reselected. This is called *sampling with replacement*.

In some cases we will not be able to easily count the number of possible samples that could be selected due to the nature of the population. However, from a practical point of view, if every effort is made to select the individual items in a random fashion, the decision maker can be fairly sure that the sample will have the attributes of a simple random sample.

Simple random samples can be obtained in a variety of ways. We will present several examples to illustrate how simple random samples are selected in practice.

The Lottery.   In those situations where a perception of fairness is important, simple random sampling is useful. For instance, shortly before the military draft ended, the U.S. Selective Service Commission adopted a *lottery* system to select draftees. The purpose was to eliminate any possible favoritism in determining who would be drafted. The lottery was held every year and the population each year consisted of all males who turned nineteen years old since the last lottery. Each male in this population was assigned a lottery number corresponding to his birthday. To assure a random selection of numbers, the following procedure was used:

1. A rotating drum was filled with 365 balls, each corresponding to a specific day of the year.
2. In front of a group of questioning members of Congress, news reporters, and television floodlights, the first ball (date) was selected from the drum. All individuals with this birthday were ranked number one in the draft priority system.
3. After the first date was removed, the drum was closed, turned, and the next date selected. The procedure was repeated for all 365 dates. However, constructing a fair lottery is difficult since, as in this example, you must be sure that the balls in the drum are adequately mixed.

The Random Number Table.   Another way of selecting a random sample is to use a *random number table*. Appendix H is a random number table and is reproduced as table 7–1. Random number tables are constructed by recording values from a process that produces numbers which have the properties of randomness. Generally, random numbers are generated by computer routines.

Suppose the personnel department at a large retail store in Seattle is considering changing the pay period from once a month to every two weeks. Since the decision will affect all 400 Seattle employees, the personnel manager has decided to select a simple random sample of ten employees and ask their opinion about the change.

To select a random sample, each employee is assigned a number between 000 and 399. (For this application, no two employees will be assigned the same number.) The personnel manager decides on the following procedure for using the random number table:

1. Since table 7–1 has seventy rows and forty columns, pick two numbers, the first between one and seventy and the second between one and forty.
2. Use the first number to locate the *row* for the starting random number and the second number to locate the *column*.
3. Beginning with this starting point, select ten three-digit numbers by moving

large. We could then select a simple random sample of institutions from each group and estimate the average cash on hand from this combined sample.

What we have done is break the population (Oregon's financial institutions) into *subpopulations* called *strata*. Selecting simple random samples from predetermined sub-populations, or strata, is called *stratified random sampling*. Stratified random sampling is particularly useful when some subpopulations are relatively small and may be missed in a simple random sample. A stratified random sample guarantees we will obtain sample information from these subpopulations.

Populations can be stratified if they have a readily identifiable characteristic that can be used to separate the population members into subgroups. In our example the identifiable characteristic is institution size. In other cases the characteristic may be family size, location, or disposable personal income. In looking at company employees, we may stratify on the basis of sex, age, education, or race.

If done correctly, stratified sampling can be used to estimate a population's characteristics with *less error* than the same-size simple random sample. Since sample size is directly related to cost (in both time and money), this means a stratified sample can be more cost-effective than a simple random sample. Stratification is particularly useful when the population contains extreme points that can be grouped into separate strata. This will guarantee that some of the sample values include the extremes.

Let us look at another example where stratified random sampling could be used. A manufacturer of automotive replacement parts recently landed a contract with several national retailers to manufacture parts to be sold under the retailers' brand names. Because of these large contracts, the company was forced to move from a single-shift operation to a three-shift operation. The manufacturing company has begun to receive complaints about the quality of its parts. Before operations were expanded, quality complaints were rare. The company owner is concerned about the increasing complaints and discusses the situation with her production manager. The production manager thinks the increase in complaints could be due to any one of several things. First, because the plant is now used more extensively, the machines may go out of adjustment faster than in the past. Consequently, the solution may be to increase periodic maintenance. Second, most of the quality control problems could be occurring in the two added shifts, in which case additional training is needed. Third, the complaints may be increasing because the national retailers offer well-advertised money-back guarantees, in which case the complaints will likely continue.

The production manager has some historical quality information and therefore decides to sample the present output. He has decided to perform a stratified sample by shift. With results from the stratified sample, the production manager feels he will be able to identify the cause of the complaints and to recommend the correct course of action. Note, however, that once the population has been stratified, simple random sampling is used to select items from each stratum.

Systematic Sampling

The publishers of *Anvil* magazine are faced with a growing market. They are considering changing the magazine's information content to include more worldwide news. Let us assume *Anvil* has 150,000 subscribers and the publishers wish to question 1,500 subscribers about this proposed change.

Simple random sampling would involve assigning a unique number to each subscriber and using a random number table to select the sample of 1,500. (A computer could also be used if the subscriber lists are stored on disk or tape files. The computer could be programmed to generate random numbers similar to those in the table in appendix H.)

An alternative to selecting a simple random sample would be to question every 100th subscriber from the list of subscribers. The procedure would involve using a random number table to select a number between 1 and 100 for the starting point. Using the random starting point, each 100th subscriber would be selected. If the starting point were 75, the sample would be

$$\left.\begin{array}{r} 75 \\ 175 \\ 275 \\ 375 \\ . \\ . \\ . \\ 149,975 \end{array}\right\} \quad n = 1,500$$

Selecting a sample based on this type of predetermined system is called *systematic sampling*. Systematic sampling is frequently used in business applications. Systematic sampling should be used as an alternative to simple random sampling only when the population is randomly ordered. For example, *Anvil* subscribers are no doubt listed alphabetically. To use systematic sampling in this case, we must assume opinion is randomly distributed through the alphabet.[1]

Systematic sampling, when applicable, has specific advantages. First, a systematic sample is easy to select. A highly trained expert is not needed to select, say, every 100th name from a subscription list or every third house in a subdivision. Also, depending on the characteristics of the population, a systematic sample can be more evenly distributed across the population and thus more representative.

Cluster Sampling

Taking a random sample requires not only that we randomly determine who from the population will be in the sample, but also that those selected be contacted and measured. This is not a problem when the population is an incoming shipment of transistors. This is a problem when the population members selected for the sample are scattered across the country or the world.

Suppose the Morrison-Knudsen Company, one of the largest construction companies in the world, wants to develop a new corporate bidding strategy. Upper manage-

[1]There are more statistically precise indications of when systematic sampling can be used instead of simple random sampling. See Leslie Kish, *Survey Sampling,* 113–42.

FIGURE 7–1
Number of middle-level managers at various geographical locations of Morrison-Knudsen

ment desires input on possible new strategies from its middle-level managers. Figure 7–1 illustrates the hypothetical distribution of middle-level managers throughout the world. For example, there are twenty-five middle-level managers in Algeria, forty-seven in Illinois, and so forth. The upper management decided to have personal interviews with a sample of these employees.

One sampling technique is to select a simple random sample of size n from the population of middle managers. Unfortunately, this technique would likely require that the interviewer(s) go to each state or country where Morrison-Knudsen has middle-level managers. This would prove an expensive and time-consuming process. A systematic or stratified sampling procedure would probably also require visiting each location.

A sampling technique that overcomes the traveling (time and money) problem is *simple cluster sampling*. Cluster sampling is a method by which the population is divided into groups, or clusters, and a sample of clusters is taken to represent the population. Once the clusters are chosen, sampling of items from each cluster may be undertaken. In the Morrison-Knudsen example, the clusters are the geographical locations of the middle-level managers. As shown in figure 7–1, this example has ten clusters. Notice that clusters are determined by the physical locations of the population. This is different than stratified sampling, where strata are determined by some measurable characteristic of the items in the population.

The first step in the simple cluster sampling is to randomly select various clusters (m) from the total possible clusters (M). Suppose Morrison-Knudsen randomly selects the following three clusters:

Mexico	Alaska	Algeria
76	20	25

The interview team can either question all middle managers in these three locations or select a random sample at each location, depending on the desired sample size and the cost of sampling. Suppose they randomly sample from each primary cluster, and they select the following number of managers from the chosen clusters:

$$\left.\begin{array}{lr} \text{Mexico} & 15 \\ \text{Alaska} & 8 \\ \text{Algeria} & 12 \end{array}\right\} \text{Ultimate clusters}$$

Cluster sampling can be used in a variety of ways. Table 7–2 illustrates the relationship between population, population members, and clusters for this example and several other possible clusters.

TABLE 7–2

Examples of possible clusters

Population	Variable of Interest	Individual Elements	Clusters
Middle managers	Ideas on bidding strategies	Persons	Area locations
People in Boston	Political preference	Persons	City block
San Francisco workers	Commuting distance	Persons	Office building
Houses in Atlanta	Price	Houses	Subdivisions
Automobiles produced in Detroit	Mileage	Automobiles	State of current location
Harvard University students	Parents' income	Students	Class standing

Two additional examples illustrate the potential of cluster sampling. A manufacturer of frozen bakery products, which has recently expanded into a new market area, prides itself in producing quality products and maintaining an extensive in-plant quality control system. In its original market area, the company handled its own distribution and maintained strict controls on its product. (If the frozen bakery goods begin to thaw, the quality is diminished.)

When expanding into the new market area, the firm decided to employ a regional distributor. Though the manufacturing firm has no reason to think that the distribution firm is inadequately handling its product, it decides to take a sample from retail stores to check quality. To save time and money, the frozen-product firm decides to use cluster sampling. Management decides to randomly select four population centers in the new sales area and then randomly select stores from these four centers. Once a store is selected, the company representatives will randomly select a sample of frozen bakery products.

Another example concerns a manufacturer of electronics products. The company is considering producing a new marine radio that has a signal beacon and wants to make sure there is sufficient interest before going to the expense of producing and marketing the product. Since the product is technically advanced, specially trained interviewers are needed to explain the product to prospective buyers.

The company decides to use cluster sampling to determine its potential market. The clusters are the marinas on the U.S. west coast. The company randomly selects five marinas. From each of these marinas, six registered boat owners are randomly selected and interviewed to determine the likelihood they would purchase this new radio. Based on the results of this sample, the company will decide whether to produce the new product.

A well-designed cluster sample will generally provide equal-quality information at less cost than a simple random sample. However, cluster sampling has some potential disadvantages. Ideally, each cluster should be representative of all the population and thus heterogeneous with respect to the variable of interest. But in actual practice, this may not be the case. For instance, if the clusters are determined by geographical proximity, there will likely be some degree of homogeneity in the clusters. In this situation, cluster sampling may require a *larger* sample size than a simple random sample to provide the same level of information. Since similar people and items tend to group together, more clusters will have to be sampled than if the clusters were heterogeneous. This can reduce the cost advantage associated with cluster sampling. In addition, the costs and problems associated with statistically analyzing the sample data obtained from cluster sampling are generally increased.

Because of their cost advantage, cluster samples are often used in performing surveys over a wide geographical area. For instance, many of the major polling organizations use cluster sampling when taking political polls.

Nonprobability Sampling Techniques

The simple random, stratified random, systematic, and cluster sampling techniques discussed previously are all examples of probability samples. When a probability sample is selected, there are a variety of statistical techniques available to analyze the sample data, as you will see in the remaining chapters of this text.

However, sometimes a probability sample is either not possible or not desirable. In these instances *nonprobability sampling* is used. One example of nonprobability sampling is *judgment sampling*. In judgment sampling, the person taking the sample has direct or indirect control over which items are selected for the sample. Judgment sampling is appropriate when decision makers feel that some population members have more or better information than other members.

Judgment sampling is also used when the decision makers feel that some population members are more representative of the population than others. For instance, if you had to pick only one city in the United States in which to test market a new product, you probably would not select that city randomly. You would likely pick the city for a reason, such as "Los Angeles is good for new products and it tends to lead the country," or "Never introduce anything new in the Midwest." You would probably also use a judgment sample if you could select only two cities, or three, or four. However, if you could select twenty-five cities to test market your product, you might very well choose these cities randomly.

Of course a judgment sample is only as good as the people doing the sampling. If poor judgment is used, the information gathered may be nonrepresentative and misleading. For example, a decision maker can easily bias an opinion survey by sampling only individuals who share similar opinions.

Other nonprobability samples include *quota sampling* and *convenience sampling*. In quota sampling, the decision maker requires the sample to contain a certain number of items with a given characteristic. For example, suppose an opinion survey is to be taken in a factory employing 60 percent males and 40 percent females. If the sample size is 1,000, the sampling quota might be 600 randomly selected males and 400 randomly selected females. Many political polls are, in part, quota samples.

With convenience sampling the decision maker selects a sample from the population in a manner that is relatively easy and convenient. For example, the Flathead

Cherry Association operates a cherry warehouse in Polson, Montana. During the picking season in early August, cherry growers bring truckloads of cherries to the warehouse in lugs weighing about twenty pounds each. As the trucks are unloaded, each lug moves along a conveyor and over a scale that weighs it. Next, an individual selects several cherries from the top of each lug and places them into a sack marked with the grower's name and the load number. When the truck is completely unloaded, the sample of cherries in the sack is graded by inspectors and the price per pound paid to the grower is determined for that load of cherries.

In this case the sampling process would not meet the definition of random sampling but it is a convenient method of sampling. The cherry association and the growers should be aware, however, of the risks associated with their sampling techniques. For example, it is possible that cherries on top of each lug may not be representative of the remaining cherries in the lugs. Also, the quality of cherries may not be evenly distributed throughout all lugs in the load.

Market research firms also use convenience sampling as a means of obtaining data on consumer buying habits. For example, you may have encountered individuals located outside supermarkets or department stores who ask people a series of questions related to their purchases, the store, and general demographics. No effort is made to select a statistically valid sample. Rather, the researchers rely on the convenience of the sampling technique to allow them to interview a large number of people who they hope represent the targeted population.

Although nonprobability sampling is often used in decision-making situations, it has some serious potential problems. The greatest of these is that if you use a nonprobability sample you have no way of assessing the probability of reaching a correct conclusion from the sample information.

RELATIONSHIP BETWEEN SAMPLE DATA AND POPULATION VALUES

7-2

Decision makers are faced with a problem in addition to the problems associated with correctly gathering and arranging data in an understandable manner. This problem is that two samples from the same population will likely have different sample values and therefore possibly lead to different decisions. The following example will demonstrate what this means.

Suppose the investment officer at SeaSide State Bank handles the retirement fund for all state government employees. Although most of the retirement money is invested in government bonds, the officer has been increasing the amount invested in corporate stocks.

The retirement committee, composed of state government employees, is naturally concerned with the rate of return being earned by the invested dollars. The greater this return, the larger the retirement fund will be and the greater the benefits to the employees when they retire. The committee has asked the investment officer to determine the average return for money invested in stocks only.

For the purposes of this example, assume the money has been invested in five stocks, with an equal amount in each stock. The returns on each stock last year were

Stock	Return
A	7%
B	12%
C	−3%
D	21%
E	3%

With only five stocks, the investment officer could easily report the population mean, μ_x, to the employee committee. The population mean is given in equation 7–1:

$$\mu_x = \frac{\Sigma X}{N} \qquad (7\text{–}1)$$

where X = individual returns for the stocks
          N = population size

Thus

$$\mu_x = \frac{7\% + 12\% + (-3\%) + 21\% + 3\%}{5}$$

$$= 8\%$$

To more fully describe the stock returns, the investment officer might also calculate the population standard deviation (equation 7–2):

$$\sigma_x = \sqrt{\frac{\Sigma(X - \mu_x)^2}{N}} \qquad (7\text{–}2)$$

Thus

$$\sigma_x = \sqrt{\frac{(7 - 8)^2 + (12 - 8)^2 + (-3 - 8)^2 + (21 - 8)^2 + (3 - 8)^2}{5}}$$

$$= 8.15\%$$

However, for this example, the investment officer has decided to select a simple random sample of three stocks and base her report on this sample. Although she will select only one sample, there are several possible samples from which to choose. We can determine exactly how many possible samples of three stocks can be selected with-

TABLE 7–3
Possible samples, SeaSide State Bank example

Sample Stocks	Returns	$\overline{X}$
A, B, C	7%, 12%, −3%	5.33
A, B, D	7%, 12%, 21%	13.33
A, B, E	7%, 12%, 3%	7.33
A, C, D	7%, −3%, 21%	8.33
A, C, E	7%, −3%, 3%	2.33
A, D, E	7%, 21%, 3%	10.33
B, C, D	12%, −3%, 21%	10.00
B, C, E	12%, −3%, 3%	4.00
B, D, E	12%, 21%, 3%	12.00
C, D, E	−3%, 21%, 3%	7.00

where: $\overline{X} = \dfrac{\Sigma X}{n}$

n = sample size

out replacement from a population size of five by recognizing this as a combinations problem (equation 7–3):

$$_NC_n = \frac{N!}{n!(N - n)!} \tag{7–3}$$

Thus

$$_5C_3 = \frac{5!}{3!(5 - 3)!}$$

$$= 10 \text{ possible samples}$$

Table 7–3 lists the ten possible samples and the sample mean, $\overline{X}$, of each. Since the $\overline{X}$ values range from 2.33 percent to 13.33 percent, the value of the sample mean reported to the employee committee will depend on the sample selected. The reported sample mean will also be different from the true population mean, although some samples have a mean closer to the true value than others.

SKILL DEVELOPMENT PROBLEMS FOR SECTION 7–2

The following set of problems is meant to test your understanding of the material in this section. Additional problems are found at the end of this chapter under this section heading.

1. Consider the following population of values:

33   41   17   27   35   23   24   19

a. Determine the population mean and standard deviation.

b. If you were to select a sample of four from the population, how many possible samples could you select?

c. Use a random sampling procedure to select five samples of four and determine the mean and standard deviation of each sample.

2. Consider the following population of values:

> 71   58   55   67   61   77   65   49   80   72

a. Determine the population mean and standard deviation.

b. If you were to select a sample of three from this population, how many possible samples could you select?

c. Use a random sampling procedure to select five samples of three and determine the mean and standard deviation of each sample.

3. Tom Scott Inc. distributes mining equipment made in several European Common Market countries. The company has midsize computers in each of its seven district sales offices. Last year the maintenance cost on the seven computers was

> $17,593   14,295   15,608   10,255
> 9,118   19,895   13,495

a. What is the average maintenance cost?

b. If the company auditors were to select three districts to do an extensive audit, how many different samples of three could they select?

c. Randomly select three districts and determine the sample average maintenance cost.

SAMPLING ERROR

7-3

The investment officer at SeaSide State Bank is going to select only one of the ten possible samples. Notice in table 7–3 that no sample mean equals the population mean of 8 percent. Thus her report to the employee committee will contain **sampling error.**

Sampling error is the difference between a population value and the corresponding sample value. The amount of sampling error is determined by which $\overline{X}$ value is found. In the SeaSide example, if $\overline{X} = 8.33$ percent, the sampling error is fairly small. However, if $\overline{X} = 13.33$ percent, the sampling error is quite large. Because the investment officer cannot know how large the sampling error will be before selecting the sample, she should know how the possible sample means are distributed. The distribution of possible sample means is called the **sampling distribution of $\overline{X}$.**

Sampling Distribution of $\overline{X}$

We can use the SeaSide State Bank example to illustrate two important concepts for statistical decision making. The first concerns the relationship between the population mean, μ_x, and the average of the possible sample means, $\mu_{\overline{x}}$. We often call $\mu_{\overline{x}}$ the *mean of the sample means.* We find $\mu_{\overline{x}}$ from equation 7–4:

$$\mu_{\bar{x}} = \frac{\sum_{i=1}^{K} \bar{X}_i}{K} \tag{7–4}$$

where $\bar{X}_i$ = ith sample mean
K = number of possible samples

Then

$$\mu_{\bar{x}} = \frac{5.33\% + 13.33\% + 7.33\% + \ldots + 7.00\%}{10}$$

$$= 8\%$$

We see that the $\mu_{\bar{x}}$, the average of all possible sample means, equals the true population mean, μ_x. This will always be true because $\bar{X}$ is an **unbiased estimator** of μ_x, the population mean. We will discuss the concept of unbiased estimates more fully in chapter 8.

The second important concept concerns the relationship between the population standard deviation and the *standard deviation of the sample means*. The population returns ranged from -3 percent to 21 percent. However, table 7–1 illustrates that the sample means range from 2.33 percent to 13.33 percent. The distribution of sample means is less variable than the population from which the samples were taken.

Recall that in our example, the population standard deviation, σ_x, is 8.15 percent. Since there are only ten possible samples, we can calculate the standard deviation of the sample means, $\sigma_{\bar{x}}$, as follows:

$$\sigma_{\bar{x}} = \sqrt{\frac{\sum_{i=1}^{K} (\bar{X}_i - \mu_{\bar{x}})^2}{K}}$$

Therefore

$$\sigma_{\bar{x}} = \sqrt{\frac{(5.33 - 8.0)^2 + (13.33 - 8.0)^2 + \ldots + (7.0 - 8.0)^2}{10}}$$

$$= \sqrt{11.07}$$

$$= 3.326$$

Note that $\sigma_{\bar{x}} = 3.326$ percent is less than $\sigma_x = 8.15$ percent. In fact, $\sigma_{\bar{x}}$ will be less than the population standard deviation, σ_x, for any application.

The value $\sigma_{\bar{x}}$, also called the **standard error of the mean,** indicates the spread in the distribution of all possible sample means.

SKILL DEVELOPMENT PROBLEMS FOR SECTION 7–3

The following set of problems is meant to test your understanding of the material in this section. Additional problems are found at the end of this chapter under this section heading.

4. Consider the following population of values:

39   33   47   41   30   23   28   50

 a. Determine the population mean and standard deviation.
 b. If you were to select a sample of four from this population, how many possible samples could you select?
 c. Use a random sampling procedure to select five samples of four and determine the mean and standard deviation of each sample.
 d. For each of the five samples selected in part c, determine the sampling error.

5. Consider the following population of values:

171   258   155   367   261   177   165   449   280   172

 a. Determine the population mean and standard deviation.
 b. If you were to select a sample of three from this population, how many possible samples could you select?
 c. Use a random sampling procedure to select five samples of three and determine the mean and standard deviation of each sample.
 d. For each of the five samples selected in part c, determine the sampling error.

6. Problem 3 in the preceding section considered Tom Scott Inc., which distributes mining equipment made in several European Common Market countries. The company has midsize computers in each of its seven district sales offices. Last year the maintenance cost on the seven computers was

$17,593   14,295   15,608   10,255
  9,118   19,895   13,495

The company auditors selected three districts to do an extensive audit.

Randomly select four samples of three districts and determine the average maintenance cost for each sample. Give the sampling error associated with each sample and discuss how you think the auditors should deal with this error.

SAMPLING FROM NORMAL DISTRIBUTIONS

7-4

In more realistic situations with larger populations, the number of possible $\overline{X}$ values can become very large. For example, if a sample of five is selected from a population of 100, the number of possible samples is

$$_{100}C_5 = \frac{100!}{5!95!}$$

$$= 75{,}287{,}520$$

In applications where the number of possible samples is very large, we cannot possibly calculate all the possible sample means to find $\sigma_{\bar{x}}$ and $\mu_{\bar{x}}$. However, two important theorems allow decision makers to describe the distribution of sample means for any distribution. Theorem 7–1 is the first of these.

THEOREM 7–1

If a population is normally distributed, with mean μ_x and standard deviation σ_x, the sampling distribution of $\bar{X}$ values is also normally distributed, with $\mu_{\bar{x}} = \mu_x$ and $\sigma_{\bar{x}} = \sigma_x/\sqrt{n}$.

Figure 7–2 shows a normal population distribution and two sampling distributions. As theorem 7–1 states, the average of the sample means, $\mu_{\bar{x}}$, equals the population mean, μ_x. Figure 7–1 also shows that the spread of the sampling distribution decreases as the sample size increases. From theorem 7–1, the standard error of the mean is given by equation 7–5:

FIGURE 7–2

Relationship between normal population and sampling distribution of $\bar{X}$

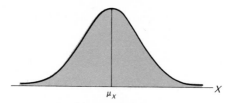

(a) Population Distribution

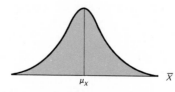

(b) Sampling Distribution, $n = 8$

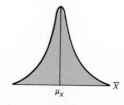

(c) Sampling Distribution, $n = 64$

$$\sigma_{\bar{x}} = \frac{\sigma_x}{\sqrt{n}}$$ (7–5)

where σ_x = population standard deviation
         n = sample size

Suppose scores for all students taking a standard college entrance examination are normally distributed, with $\mu_x = 80$ and $\sigma_x = 10$. If a random sample of 100 scores is selected, the sampling distribution of possible $\bar{X}$ values will be normally distributed, with

$$\mu_{\bar{x}} = \mu_x = 80$$

and

$$\sigma_{\bar{x}} = \frac{\sigma_x}{\sqrt{n}} = \frac{10}{\sqrt{100}} = 1.0$$

We see that the spread of the sampling distribution, $\sigma_{\bar{x}} = 1.0$, is considerably smaller than the spread of the population, $\sigma_x = 10$. Because the population standard deviation is divided by the square root of the sample size, as the sample size increases, the standard deviation of the sample means decreases. If the sample size were 400 instead of 100 scores, the mean of the sampling distribution would still be 80, but the standard deviation of the sampling distribution would be reduced to 0.50.

$$\sigma_{\bar{x}} = \frac{\sigma_x}{\sqrt{n}} = \frac{10}{\sqrt{400}} = 0.5$$

$\sigma_{\bar{x}}$ is a measure of average sampling error. Therefore, increasing the sample size will reduce the average sampling error.

SKILL DEVELOPMENT PROBLEMS FOR SECTION 7–4

The following set of problems is meant to test your understanding of the material in this section. Additional problems are found at the end of this chapter under this section heading.

7. A population is normally distributed, with a mean of 58 and a standard deviation of 10.
   a. If a sample of nine is taken from the population (assume it is less than 5 percent of the population), the mean of all possible samples is what value?
   b. What is the measure of average sampling error?
   c. How are the values changed if the sample size is changed to twenty?

8. A population is normally distributed, with a mean of 117 and a standard deviation of 30.

   a. If a sample of twenty is taken from the population (assume less than 5 percent of the population), the mean of all possible samples is what value?

   b. What is the measure of average sampling error?

   c. How are the values changed if the sample size is changed to forty?

   d. What would the sample size have to be to reduce the standard error to half that found in part b?

9. The Adam's Food King chain employs over 3,000 people. The workers ages are approximately normally distributed, with a mean of 31 and a standard deviation of 4.3 years. The company is thinking of introducing a health care package, and their insurance company wants to sample twenty-five workers before quoting a price.

   a. What is the probability the sample of twenty-five will have an average age less than 31?

   b. What is the value of the standard error associated with this sample?

   c. What can the insurance company do to reduce the standard error?

SAMPLING FROM NON-NORMAL POPULATIONS

7-5

Theorem 7–1 applies only if the population from which the sample is selected is normal. As discussed in chapter 6, there are many instances where the population of interest can be assumed to be normally distributed. However, there are many other applications where the population of interest will not be normally distributed. If the population is non-normal, theorem 7–1 cannot be used. In this case, however, theorem 7–2—the **central limit theorem**—does apply.

THEOREM 7–2

Central Limit Theorem

If random samples of n observations are taken from any population with mean μ_x and standard deviation σ_x, and if n is large enough, the distribution of possible $\overline{X}$ values will be approximately normal, with $\mu_{\overline{x}} = \mu_x$ and $\sigma_{\overline{x}} = \sigma_x/\sqrt{n}$ regardless of the population distribution. The approximation becomes increasingly more accurate as the sample size, n, increases.

An important question when using the central limit theorem is how large a "large" sample size is. Although there is no exact answer to this question, if the population is symmetric and unimodal about μ_x, sample sizes of four or five will produce approximately normal sampling distributions. In other cases where the population is extremely skewed, sample sizes of more than twenty-five are required to produce a normal sampling distribution. Many authors have adopted the rule of thumb that $n \geq 30$ will provide a distribution of sample means that is approximately normally distributed. We will also adopt this rule.

To more clearly see the relationship between increasing sample size and the application of the central limit theorem, see figures 7–3 through 7–6, which show various population distributions and the resulting sampling distributions of $\overline{X}$ for various sample

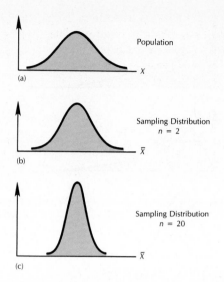

FIGURE 7–3

Central limit theorem, population normally distributed

sizes. These examples were originally developed using a computer program that could quickly select large numbers of samples and plot the sampling distributions. Note that in figure 7–3 the population itself is normal, so the sampling distribution is also normal even for sample sizes as small as two. Figure 7–4 shows, for a population that is uniformly distributed, that the sampling distribution is approximately normal for sample sizes as small $n = 5$.

The populations in figures 7–5 and 7–6 are less symmetrical and, as can be seen, larger samples are required before the sampling distribution approximates a normal distribution. Note also that figures 7–3 through 7–6 show that the spread of the sampling distribution decreases as the size of the sample is increased, which is consistent with what the central limit theorem indicates should occur.

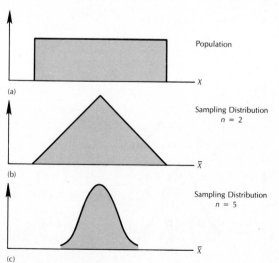

FIGURE 7–4

Central limit theorem, uniform population distribution

FIGURE 7–5
Central limit theorem, exponential population distribution

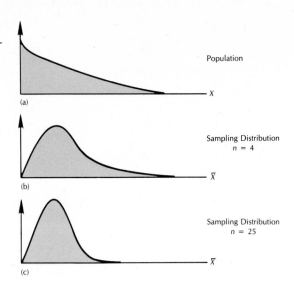

FIGURE 7–5
Central limit theorem, exponential population distribution

THE FINITE CORRECTION FACTOR

7-6   Both theorems 7–1 and 7–2 assume either that sampling is done *with replacement* or that the population is large relative to the sample size. If sampling is done *without replacement* and the sample is large relative to the population, a modification must be made in calculating $\sigma_{\bar{x}}$. If *n* is greater than 5 percent of the population size and sampling is performed without replacement, equation 7–6 applies:

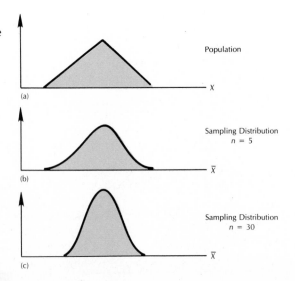

FIGURE 7–6
Central limit theorem, triangle
population distribution

$$\sigma_{\bar{x}} = \frac{\sigma_x}{\sqrt{n}} \sqrt{\frac{N-n}{N-1}}$$ (7–6)

where σ_x = population standard deviation
n = sample size
N = population size

$\sqrt{\dfrac{N-n}{N-1}}$ = finite correction factor

In the SeaSide Bank example, the population mean, μ_x, was 8 percent, and the population standard deviation, σ_x, was 8.15 percent. Owing to the small number of possible samples (10), we were able to calculate $\sigma_{\bar{x}} = 3.326$. Because $n = 3$ is greater than 5 percent of $N = 5$ and sampling was without replacement, we can also use equation 7–6 to find $\sigma_{\bar{x}}$:

$$\sigma_{\bar{x}} = \frac{\sigma_x}{\sqrt{n}} \sqrt{\frac{N-n}{N-1}} = \frac{8.15}{\sqrt{3}} \sqrt{\frac{5-3}{5-1}}$$

$$= 3.327$$

The term $\sqrt{(N-n)/(N-1)}$ is called the **finite correction factor** and is used if we are sampling without replacement and the sample size is large relative to the population. Note that the finite correction factor always is less than 1.0 and that as the population gets large relative to the sample size, the factor approaches 1.0.

SKILL DEVELOPMENT PROBLEMS FOR SECTIONS 7–5 AND 7–6

The following set of problems is meant to test your understanding of the material in these sections. Additional problems are found at the end of this chapter under these section headings.

10. A population of 100 has a mean of 17.5 and a standard deviation of 2.2. If a sample of thirty-five is taken from the population, what is the mean of the distribution of all possible samples of thirty-five? What is the standard deviation of the distribution of all possible sample means?

11. A population of 350 has a mean of 36.7 and a standard deviation of 6.3. If a sample of forty is taken from the population, what is the mean of the distribution of all possible samples of forty? What is the standard deviation of the distribution of all possible sample means?

12. SeaFair Fashions relies on their sales force of 217 to do an initial screen of all new fashions. The company is presently bringing out a new line of swimwear and has invited forty salespeople to their Orlando home office. An issue of constant concern to the SeaFair sales office is the volume of orders generated by each salesperson. Last year the overall company average was $417,330, with a standard deviation of $45,285.

a. What is the probability the sample of forty will have a sales average less than that of the entire sales force?

b. What shape do you think the distribution of all possible samples of forty will have? Discuss.

c. What is the value of the standard deviation of the distribution of all possible samples of forty?

d. How would the answers to parts a, b, and c change if the home office brought sixty salespeople to Orlando?

DECISION MAKING AND THE SAMPLING DISTRIBUTION OF $\overline{X}$

7-7   The concepts discussed in this chapter are extremely important to decision makers. The following example will demonstrate how the theorems are used in a decision environment. In this example, remember to distinguish between

1. The population distribution.
2. The distribution of all possible sample means.
3. The mean of a single sample.

These are three different factors in the decision-making situation and should not be confused with one another.

Because of legislated mileage requirements, the major U.S. automobile makers are being forced to build smaller, lighter cars. But while building cars with smaller exteriors, the auto makers want to maintain interior dimensions that are comfortable for the majority of U.S. car buyers. One important dimension for riding comfort is the distance between the floorboard and the bottom of the dashboard. If this distance is too small, the rider's knees will hit the dash. Unfortunately for the auto makers, the distance from the foot to the knee is not the same for all car buyers.

Suppose the average foot-to-knee length for the population is $\mu_x = 20$ inches and the population standard deviation is $\sigma_x = 3$ inches. One maker has decided to select a random sample of potential customers to test the riding comfort of its latest compact car. The product design manager wants the test group to represent the population as a whole. The average foot-to-knee length for the test sample of thirty-six people is 21.5 inches. The product design manager wishes to know whether this group is an unlikely selection from a population with $\mu_x = 20$ and $\sigma_x = 3$.

To help the product design manager, we employ the central limit theorem. Thus the distribution of possible $\overline{X}$ values will be approximately normal, with $\mu_{\overline{x}} = \mu_x$ and $\sigma_{\overline{x}} = \sigma_x/\sqrt{n}$. This sampling distribution is shown as follows:

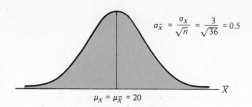

$$\sigma_{\bar{X}} = \frac{\sigma_X}{\sqrt{n}} = \frac{3}{\sqrt{36}} = 0.5$$

$\mu_X = \mu_{\bar{X}} = 20$

The sample mean selected is 21.5 inches. When the product design manager wonders if this sample mean is an unlikely selection, he is really wondering about the chances of finding an $\bar{X} \geq 21.5$ inches. This probability is represented by the darkest area in the following normal curve:

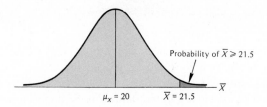

Probability of $\bar{X} \geq 21.5$

$\mu_X = 20$ $\bar{X} = 21.5$

Recall that to find areas under the normal curve, we first standardize the distribution so that we can work with Z values. Remember that Z represents the number of standard deviations a value is from the mean. When working with a sampling distribution, we find the Z value from equation 7–7 or 7–8:

$$Z = \frac{\bar{X} - \mu_x}{\sigma_{\bar{x}}} \tag{7–7}$$

or

$$Z = \frac{\bar{X} - \mu_x}{\dfrac{\sigma_x}{\sqrt{n}}} \tag{7–8}$$

If sampling is without replacement and n is greater than 5 percent of the population, equation 7–9 is used:

$$Z = \frac{\bar{X} - \mu_x}{\dfrac{\sigma_x}{\sqrt{n}} \sqrt{\dfrac{N - n}{N - 1}}} \tag{7–9}$$

In the auto maker example, the sample size, $n = 36$, is certainly small relative to the population size, so we will use equation 7–8:

$$Z = \frac{\overline{X} - \mu_x}{\frac{\sigma_x}{\sqrt{n}}} = \frac{21.5 - 20}{\frac{3}{\sqrt{36}}}$$

$$= 3.00$$

Thus an $\overline{X}$ of 21.5 is 3.00 standard deviations away from μ_x of 20. From the standard normal distribution table in appendix C, the area corresponding to $Z = 3.00$ is 0.4987:

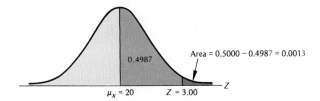

The probability of finding a sample mean equal to or greater than 21.5 inches is only 0.0013. Since this probability is so small, the product design manager would most likely not want to use these thirty-six people to test the new car's comfort because they have foot-to-knee lengths that apparently do not represent the population.

SKILL DEVELOPMENT PROBLEMS FOR SECTION 7–7

The following set of problems is meant to test your understanding of the material in this section. Additional problems are found at the end of this chapter under this section heading.

13. A sample of forty is taken from a population with a mean of 87.6 and a standard deviation of 14.4.
  a. What is the probability the sample mean will be greater than 90?
  b. What is the probability the sample mean will be less than 86.5?
  c. What is the probability the sample mean will be between 85 and 87.3?
  d. What is the probability the sample mean will be either less than 86.2 or more than 88?

14. A sample of thirty is taken from a population with a mean of 165 and a standard deviation of 25.
  a. What is the probability the sample mean will be greater than 170?
  b. What is the probability the sample mean will be less than 160?
  c. What is the probability the sample mean will be between 150 and 160?
  d. What is the probability the sample mean will be either less than 170 or more than 180?

15. The UPSAT Company markets a computerized study guide the company claims will greatly improve high school seniors' average SAT scores. In their advertising the company says that students who have once taken the test will increase their overall score by an average of forty points. The company is presently being sued in state court by an irritated student whose score did not go up at all. The company claims that their advertising refers to overall averages and so one individual score may go up by more or less than the advertised amount and that the standard deviation of the increases is fifteen points.

a. Accepting the company's claim, what is the probability a student could show no increase in overall score?

b. The student's lawyer forces the company to allow her to see a random sample of thirty test scores. The sample average increase is thirty-two. What is the probability of seeing a sample average this high or higher if the company's claim is correct?

c. Based on the available sample evidence, do you think the company's advertising claim is truthful?

DECISION MAKING AND THE SAMPLING DISTRIBUTION OF $\hat{p}$

7-8

As illustrated in chapter 5, many business applications involve random variables that have discrete distributions rather than continuous distributions. The binomial distribution, in particular, is encountered a great deal in all areas of business.

The examples in chapter 5 involving the binomial distribution always considered situations in which the decision maker was interested in the *number* of successes or failures that might occur in a sample of a given size. However, just as often the decision maker is concerned with the *proportion*, *p*, of successes or failures that would occur in the sample. Consider the following example involving the Heaton Manufacturing Company.

Heaton Manufacturing makes Christmas-tree ornaments and sells them through distributors across the United States. Because the ornaments are so fragile, they must be carefully packed. Even with this special packing, Heaton executives have observed that 15 percent of the ornaments are broken by the time they arrive at the retail outlet. Evidence indicates no particular pattern to the broken ornaments, and occurrences of breakages are apparently independent.

Figure 7–7 shows the probability density function for an individual ornament. Recall that the expected value of a binomial distribution with sample size $= n$ and probability of success $= p$ is

$$E(X) = np$$

The standard deviation is

$$\sigma = \sqrt{npq}$$

We learned in chapter 6 that if both

$$np \geq 5$$

FIGURE 7–7
Probability density function,
Heaton Manufacturing Company
example

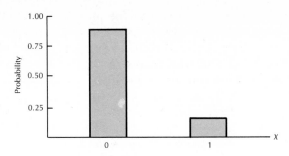

X = no. of broken ornaments in a sample of size one ornament.

and

$$nq \geq 5$$

the binomial distribution can be approximated by the normal distribution. Figure 7–8 illustrates the sampling distribution for the number of successes in a sample of size n. Note that figure 7–8 illustrates the distribution of X, the number of successes if all possible samples are selected.

However, if instead of counting the number of successes, we think in terms of the proportion of success, the sampling distribution is determined by dividing the number of successes in each possible sample by the sample size. Figure 7–9 shows the sampling distribution of $\hat{p}$, which is still approximately normally distributed.

When we convert our thinking from number of successes to proportions we must make equivalent transformations of the mean and standard deviation of the sampling distribution for $\hat{p}$ as in equations 7–10 and 7–11:

$$\text{mean} = \mu_{\hat{p}} = \frac{np}{n} = p \qquad (7\text{–}10)$$

and

$$\text{standard deviation} = \sigma_{\hat{p}} = \frac{\sqrt{npq}}{n}$$

$$= \sqrt{\frac{npq}{n^2}}$$

$$= \sqrt{\frac{pq}{n}} \qquad (7\text{–}11)$$

Now suppose the Heaton Manufacturing Company received a letter from a retailer stating that 18 percent of the 500 ornaments it purchased arrived damaged. Assuming Heaton's 15 percent damage rate is still true for the population of all ornaments, how

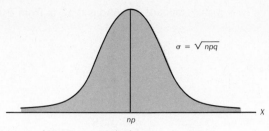

FIGURE 7–8
Sampling distribution for number
of successes (normal)

X = no. of successes in a sample of size n.

likely is it that a sample of 500 ornaments would contain 18 percent or more defectives?
We answer this by recognizing that since

$$np = (500)(0.15) = 75 \qquad (75 \geq 5)$$

and

$$nq = (500)(0.85) = 425 \qquad (425 \geq 5)$$

the sampling distribution for $\hat{p}$ will be approximately normal, with

$$\text{mean} = p = 0.15$$

and

$$\text{standard deviation} = \sqrt{\frac{pq}{n}} = \sqrt{\frac{(0.15)(0.85)}{500}} \approx 0.01597$$

The sampling distribution is shown as follows:

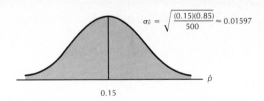

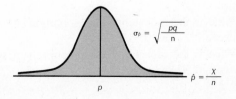

FIGURE 7–9
Sampling distribution of $\hat{p}$

We next determine how many standard deviations 0.18 is from 0.15:

$$Z = \frac{\hat{p} - p}{\sqrt{\dfrac{pq}{n}}}$$

$$= \frac{0.18 - 0.15}{0.01597}$$

$$= 1.88$$

The area under a normal curve between Z equals 1.88 and the mean is approximately 0.4699. Therefore, the probability of a sample of 500 ornaments containing 18 percent or more damaged ornaments is 0.0301, which is shown as follows:

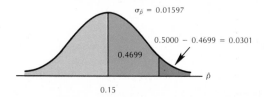

Since the probability of 18 percent or more is only 0.0301, Heaton Manufacturing might want to evaluate its packing process to determine if some unusual problems occurred during packing of that particular order.

SKILL DEVELOPMENT PROBLEMS FOR SECTION 7–8

The following set of problems is meant to test your understanding of the material in this section. Additional problems are found at the end of this chapter under this section heading.

16. Given a population where the probability of a success is $p = 0.25$, if a sample of 400 is taken:

    a. What is the expected number of successes?

    b. What is the expected proportion of successes in the sample?

    c. What is the standard deviation of the sampling distribution of $\hat{p}$?

    d. What is the probability the proportion of successes in the sample will be greater than 0.22?

    e. What is the probability the proportion of successes in the sample will be less than 0.24?

    f. What is the probability the proportion of successes in the sample will be between 0.27 and 0.31?

    g. What is the probability the proportion of successes in the sample will be between 0.20 and 0.24?

17. Given a population where the probability of a success is $p = 0.40$, if a sample of 1,000 is taken:

   a. What is the expected number of successes?

   b. What is the expected proportion of successes in the sample?

   c. What is the standard deviation of the sampling distribution of $\hat{p}$?

   d. What is the probability the proportion of successes in the sample will be less than 0.42?

   e. What is the probability the proportion of successes in the sample will be greater than 0.44?

   f. What is the probability the proportion of successes in the sample will be between 0.37 and 0.41?

   g. What is the probability the proportion of successes in the sample will be between 0.415 and 0.455?

18. Tom Marley and Jennifer Griggs have recently started a market research firm in Jacksonville, Florida. They have contacted the Florida Democratic Party with a proposal to do all political polling for the party. Since they have just started their company, the state party chairman is reluctant to sign a contract without some sort of test of their accuracy and so has asked them to do a trial poll in a central Florida county known to have 60 percent registered Democratic party voters. The poll itself had many questions, but Tom and Jennifer report back that of their 760 respondents 395 were registered Democrats. If Tom and Jennifer took a random sample of voters what is the probability they would get 395 or fewer Democrats in the sample?

CONCLUSIONS

7-9

When a manager selects a sample, it is only one of many samples that could have been selected. Consequently the sample mean, $\overline{X}$, is only one of the many possible sample means that could have been found. There is no reason to believe that the single $\overline{X}$ value will equal the population mean, μ_x. The difference between $\overline{X}$ and μ_x is called *sampling error*. Because sampling error exists, decision makers must be aware of how the sample means are distributed in order to discuss the potential sampling error.

This chapter introduced two important theorems. These theorems describe the distribution of sample means taken from any population. The more important of these theorems is the central limit theorem. Much of the material in chapters, 9, 10, and 11 is based on the central limit theorem.

The important aspect of the central limit theorem is that no matter how the population is distributed, if the sample size is large enough, the sampling distribution will be approximately normal.

This chapter has presented the development of the sampling distributions for $\overline{X}$ and $\hat{p}$. Much of the discussion in the next few chapters is based upon the concept of a normally distributed sampling distribution.

The chapter also presented several new statistical terms, which are listed in the chapter glossary. Be sure you understand each one and how it applies to the material in this chapter. You will encounter these terms many times as you continue in this text.

A summary of the statistical equations used in this chapter follows the glossary.

CHAPTER GLOSSARY

central limit theorem   For random samples of n observations selected from any population with mean μ_x and standard deviation σ_x, if n is large, the distribution of possible $\overline{X}$ values will be approximately normal with $\mu_{\overline{x}} = \mu_x$ and $\sigma_{\overline{x}} = \sigma_x/\sqrt{n}$. The approximation improves as n becomes larger.

finite correction factor   The factor used to adjust $\sigma_{\overline{x}}$ when sampling is done without replacement and the sample size is more than 5 percent of the population size. The formula is

$$\sqrt{\frac{N - n}{N - 1}}$$

sampling error   The difference between a population value and the corresponding sample value. Sampling error occurs when the sample does not perfectly represent the population from which it was selected

standard deviation of a proportion   A measure of the average sampling error when sampling from a binomial distribution. It is determined by dividing the product of the sample proportion, p, and $(1 - p)$ by the sample size. The square root of this term is then taken.

standard error of the mean   A measure of the average sampling error. It is determined by dividing the population standard deviation by the square root of the sample size.

unbiased estimator   An unbiased estimator of a population value is an estimator whose expected value equals the population values. For example, $E(\overline{X}) = \mu_x$. The average of all possible sample means will equal the population mean.

CHAPTER FORMULAS

Population mean

$$\mu_x = \frac{\Sigma X}{N}$$

Population standard deviation

$$\sigma_x = \sqrt{\frac{\Sigma(X - \mu_x)^2}{N}}$$

Combinations (number of possible samples of size *n*)

$$_NC_n = \frac{N!}{n!(N-n)!}$$

Sample mean

$$\overline{X} = \frac{\Sigma X}{n}$$

Standard error of the mean

$$\sigma_{\overline{x}} = \frac{\sigma_x}{\sqrt{n}}$$

and

$$\sigma_{\overline{x}} = \frac{\sigma_x}{\sqrt{n}} \sqrt{\frac{N-n}{N-1}}$$

Finite correction factor

$$\sqrt{\frac{N-n}{N-1}}$$

Sample proportion

$$\hat{p} = \frac{X}{n}$$

Mean of sampling distribution of $\hat{p}$

$$\mu_{\hat{p}} = p$$

Standard deviation of $\hat{p}$

$$\sigma_{\hat{p}} = \sqrt{\frac{pq}{n}}$$

Z value

$$Z = \frac{\overline{X} - \mu_x}{\sigma_{\overline{x}}}$$

or

$$Z = \frac{\overline{X} - \mu_x}{\dfrac{\sigma_x}{\sqrt{n}}}$$

If sampling is without replacement and $n > 5$ percent of the population,

$$Z = \frac{\overline{X} - \mu_x}{\dfrac{\sigma_x}{\sqrt{n}}\sqrt{\dfrac{N - n}{N - 1}}}$$

SOLVED PROBLEMS

1. In a local agriculture reporting area, the average wheat yield is known to be 60 bushels per acre, with a standard deviation of 10 bushels.
   a. If a random sample of 64 acres is selected and the wheat yield recorded, what is the probability the sample mean will lie between 59 and 61 bushels?
   b. Suppose a sample size of 49 acres is selected. What is the probability the same mean will lie between 59 and 61 bushels?
   c. Why is the probability found in part b different from that found in part a?

Solutions:

   a. The sampling distribution will be normally distributed with $\mu_{\overline{x}} = 60$ and $\sigma_{\overline{x}} = 10/\sqrt{64}$, as follows:

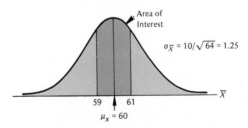

We standardize the sampling distribution by determining the Z values for $\overline{X} = 59$ and $\overline{X} = 61$.

$$Z = \frac{59 - 60}{\dfrac{10}{\sqrt{64}}} \qquad \text{and} \qquad Z = \frac{61 - 60}{\dfrac{10}{\sqrt{64}}}$$

$$= \frac{-1.0}{1.25} \qquad\qquad\qquad = \frac{1.0}{1.25}$$

$$= -0.80 \qquad\qquad\qquad\quad = 0.80$$

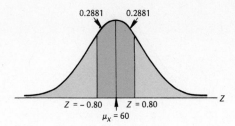

The probability can be determined by adding the areas corresponding to $Z = -0.80$ and $Z = 0.80$. From the normal table in appendix C, the area corresponding to a Z of -0.80 is 0.2881. The area corresponding to a Z of 0.80 is also 0.2881. Therefore, the probability that an $\overline{X}$ value will lie between 59 and 61 bushels for a sample of 64 acres is 0.5762 ($0.2881 + 0.2881 = 0.5762$).

b. The solution here is the same as for part a except that $\sigma_{\overline{x}}$ is increased because of the smaller sample size. Therefore

$$\mu_{\overline{x}} = 60$$

$$\sigma_{\overline{x}} = \frac{10}{\sqrt{49}}$$

$$\approx 1.429$$

Thus

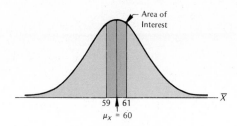

and

$$Z = \frac{59 - 60}{\dfrac{10}{\sqrt{49}}} \quad \text{and} \quad Z = \frac{61 - 60}{\dfrac{10}{\sqrt{49}}}$$

$$= \frac{-1.0}{1.429} \qquad\qquad = \frac{1.0}{1.429}$$

$$= -0.70 \qquad\qquad = 0.70$$

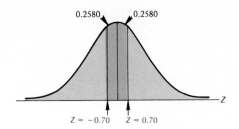

The probability, therefore, is 0.5160 (0.2580 + 0.2580 = 0.5160).

c. When the sample size is reduced (from 64 to 49), the probability of obtaining a sample mean between 59 and 61 is reduced. With a smaller sample size, the sampling distribution is spread more, giving a greater opportunity for extreme $\overline{X}$ values.

2. A local insurance company has 240 employees who have an average annual salary of $21,000. The standard deviation of annual salaries is $5,000.

   a. In a random sample of 100 employees, what is the probability the average salary will exceed $21,500?

   b. What is the probability the sample mean found in part a will be less than $22,000?

   c. Why does the finite correction factor need to be used in determining $\sigma_{\overline{x}}$?

Solutions:

   a.

$$\mu_{\overline{x}} = 21,000$$

$$\sigma_{\overline{x}} = \frac{\sigma_x}{\sqrt{n}}\sqrt{\frac{N-n}{N-1}}$$

$$= \frac{5,000}{\sqrt{100}}\sqrt{\frac{240-100}{239}}$$

$$= 382.68$$

$$Z = \frac{\overline{X} - \mu_x}{\dfrac{\sigma_x}{\sqrt{n}}\sqrt{\dfrac{N-n}{N-1}}}$$

$$= \frac{21,500 - 21,000}{382.68}$$

$$= 1.31$$

From appendix C, the area corresponding to a Z of 1.31 is 0.4049.

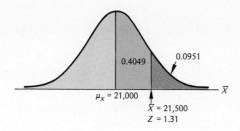

The probability of $\overline{X} \geq 21,500$ is 0.0951.

b. To find the probability the mean salary of 100 employees will be less than $22,000, we must find the following area:

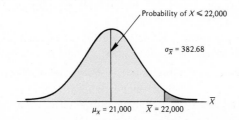

Then

$$Z = \frac{22,000 - 21,000}{382.68}$$

$$= 2.61$$

From the normal distribution table in appendix C, the area corresponding to $Z = 2.61$ is 0.4955. The probability of an $\overline{X}$ value below 22,000 is, therefore, 0.9955 $(0.5000 + 0.4955 = 0.9955)$.

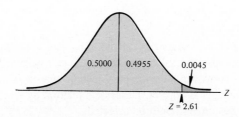

c. The finite correction factor must be used in determining $\sigma_{\overline{x}}$ because the sample size is quite large relative to the population size and the sampling is assumed to be without replacement.

ADDITIONAL PROBLEMS

Section 7–1

19. Define in your own words what a simple random sample is and provide a business example where such a sample could be used.

20. Define in your own words what a stratified random sample is and give a business example where such a sample could be used.

21. Suppose a retail store is considering expanding into a new market area. As part of the study, the store's managers wish to find out more about peoples' spending habits for the kind of goods the new store would sell. Assuming the market area is about the size of your hometown, how might the managers select a sample of individuals to talk to?

22. In problem 21, the market area was reasonably small (the size of your hometown). How might your response change in terms of the type of sampling if the market area were about the size of your state?

23. Discuss in your own words what is meant by *cluster sampling* and indicate why it might offer an advantage over other types of statistical sampling.

24. The Basin Ski Resort is planning a telephone survey of the holders of its season lift ticket to determine their level of satisfaction with services this year. Management has a list of ticket holders in alphabetical order. Devise a sampling technique that might be used to select the individuals to call.

25. Under what circumstances might a decision maker use nonprobability sampling techniques rather than probability sampling techniques?

26. The maker of Creamy Good Ice Cream is concerned about the quality of ice cream being produced by its Illinois plant. Discuss a plan by which the Creamy Good managers might determine the percentage of defective cartons of ice cream. Would it be possible or feasible to take a census?

27. A random sample of skiers at the Aspen Ski Resort was selected by the makers of a particular brand of skiing equipment. Their method for selecting the sample required that individuals waiting in one of the lift lines be asked questions about various brands of skiing equipment. Comment on the method of sampling and indicate how you would design a sampling technique that might produce more statistically valid results.

28. A beer manufacturer is considering abandoning can containers and going exclusively to bottles because the sales manager feels that beer drinkers prefer drinking beer from bottles. However the vice-president in charge of marketing is not convinced the sales manager is correct. Describe a method by which a statistical sample of the company's customers could be selected.

29. With respect to problem 28, how might a cluster sampling approach be used if it is known that the beer is marketed at stores in all fifty states?

30. If you were designing a stratified random sampling plan for a survey of city governments in your state to find out the amount of money they are spending on administrative salaries, what criteria might you use to form the strata? Provide several ideas and indicate the one that might give the best results.

31. Using the random numbers table in appendix H, discuss how a simple random sample of service station operators could be selected.

32. As this chapter indicates, a cluster sampling plan might save you time and money, yet it might also cost you more money. Why is this? What effect do homogeneous clusters have on whether a cluster sample will be more or less costly than another form of statistical sampling?

33. Discuss the circumstances under which a systematic sample might be selected and provide an example of how such a sample might be obtained.

34. Student leaders often poll students to obtain opinions on topics of interest such as athletics, library hours, and so on. Using the last such poll on your campus, discuss the methods by which the sampling was performed, pointing out the strong and weak points of the process. If necessary visit your student body officers and find out their approach to sampling student opinion.

Section 7–2

35. The McMann Company has eight vehicles, which were purchased within the past two years. The service manager has recorded the current mileage on each vehicle as shown here. Consider these data to be a population.

12,200 mi	9,200 mi
7,500	10,500
21,000	17,600
16,300	9,800

   a. Determine the mean number of miles for the population of eight vehicles.
   b. Suppose the service manager selected a random sample of six vehicles from the population. How many possible samples of size six could be selected?
   c. Referring to part b, use a random sampling procedure and select four samples of size six each. List the sample values and show the mean for each sample. Discuss why the sample means are likely to be different and why they do not necessarily equal the population mean.

36. The Doran Maintenance Company recently selected a random sample of businesses in the Dallas, Texas, area and asked the businesses to report their monthly budgets for office maintenance. The sample was randomly selected and contained 200 businesses. The mean budget for the sample was $750.00 per month. Does this indicate that the true average maintenance budget for all businesses in the Dallas area is $750.00 per month? Discuss.

37. The Doran Maintenance Company discussed in problem 36 selected a random sample of 200 businesses and found that the average amount spent on office maintenance was $750. Suppose a second sample of 200 was taken by a rival maintenance company, which found an average of $680. Would you expect to see this difference between the two sample averages or does this indicate one sample was incorrectly taken?

38. The Hardcone Baking Company recently performed a market study in which it asked people from the sample of 400 how much they spent on bakery products per week. The average of this sample was $3.45. Is it reasonable to expect that another sample of size 400 would result in the same sample mean? Discuss.

Section 7–3

39. Explain in your own words what is meant by the term *sampling distribution*.

40. Discuss why the sampling distribution will be less variable than the population. Give a short example to illustrate your answer.

41. Discuss what is meant by the term *unbiased estimator*. Provide an example involving means of the population and the sample.

42. If a researcher has collected all possible samples of a given size from a population and listed the sample means for each of these samples, and if the average of the sample means is 450.55, what would be the true population mean? Discuss.

43. In problem 42, a researcher collected all possible samples of a given size and found the average of the sample means was 450.55. The researcher recognized the sample means will vary around the true population mean. Consequently, she found the standard deviation of the sample means to be 30.56. Discuss this number and what it is called.

Section 7–4

44. Recently a school system in the Midwest performed a study of its students' performance on mathematics examinations. If the population of all examination scores is thought to be normally distributed, with a mean of 68 points and a standard deviation of 12 points:
  a. What are the mean and standard deviation for the sampling distribution of the mean if the sample size is 100? Discuss why the sampling distribution has a smaller standard deviation than the population, but the same mean.
  b. Suppose we take a second sample of size 500. What is the difference between the two sampling distributions? Illustrate using graphs.

45. If the time it takes a mechanic to tune an engine is known to be normally distributed, with a mean of forty-five minutes and a standard deviation of fourteen minutes, what are the mean and standard error of a sampling distribution for a sample size of twenty tune-ups? Show a picture of the sampling distribution.

46. Suppose we are told that the sampling distribution developed from a sample of size 400 has a mean of 56.78 and a standard error of 9.6. If the population is known to be normally distributed, what are the population mean and population standard deviation? Discuss how these values relate to the values for the sampling distribution.

47. If a population is known to be normally distributed, what size sample is required to ensure that the sampling distribution is normally distributed?

48. If the money spent by individuals for recreation in a particular target population is normally distributed, will doubling the sample size cut the standard error of the sampling distribution by 25 percent? Why or why not?

49. Discuss why the standard error of a sampling distribution is considered a measure of average sampling error.

Section 7–5

50. Suppose the interest earned on savings accounts by individuals at a particular bank has a distribution which may be skewed to the right. If the population mean is $450.00 earned per year, with a standard deviation of $67.00, describe the sampling distribution for a sample of size 100. Also show the sampling distribution in graphical form.

51. The population distribution for incomes in the St. Louis area is known to be non-normal, with a mean of $26,500 and a standard deviation of $1,700.00.
  a. Describe the sampling distribution both in terms of its general shape and descriptive measures. Assume the sample size is 200.
  b. If the sample size were actually 60 instead of 200, how would the sampling distribution be affected? Illustrate with a graph, indicating what the mean and standard error will be.

52. The central limit theorem indicates that the sampling distribution of $\overline{X}$ will have a standard deviation of $\sigma_x/\sqrt{n}$. Discuss why the sampling distribution of $\overline{X}$ should have less dispersion than the population.

Section 7–6

53. Under what conditions should the finite correction factor be used in determining the standard error of a sampling distribution?

54. The Galusha C.P.A. Firm performs auditing for the Allen Tool Company. As part of an audit, the accountant in charge of the audit selected a random sample of 300 accounts from the 2,000 accounts receivable on the Allen Company books. He was particularly interested in the average account balance.
  a. If the computer records indicate the true average balance for all 2,000 accounts is $786.98, with a standard deviation of $356.75, describe the sampling distribution of the mean. Also draw an illustration of the sampling distribution.
  b. Describe the sampling distribution for the mean if the accountant changes the sample to 500 accounts. Also discuss why we need not be concerned with the shape of the population distribution.

55. The engineering staff for the Bentrim Manufacturing Company is considering sampling 100 parts produced by the company to determine the average diameter. If the population is 200 parts and the population standard deviation is known to be 0.15 inch, what is the standard error of the sampling distribution?

56. Discuss (using examples of your own) what effect the finite correction factor has on the computation of the standard error of the sampling distribution as the sample size gets small relative to the size of the population.

57. Dan Evko works for the *Morning Star* newspaper. He recently selected a random sample of forty issues of the daily newspaper during the past year. He was interested in determining the average number of column inches devoted to hard news. If the true standard deviation for the number of inches of hard news is eight inches, what will the standard error of the sampling distribution be?

Explain the effect the finite correction factor has on the mean of the sampling distribution.

Section 7–7

58. Suppose a population is normally distributed. What is the probability of finding a sample mean, $\overline{X}$, that is greater than the population mean?

59. The Chair Company repairs old furniture and restores it to "better than original" condition. Records indicate that the time it takes to refinish and otherwise restore a standard dining room set is normally distributed, with a mean of thirty hours and a standard deviation of five hours. Recently a customer complained that he was charged too much for work performed by The Chair Company. To settle the argument, the manager of the company offered the customer the following option. The company will select a random sample of past work performed on tables similar to the customer's. If the sample mean based on five work times turns out less than hers, The Chair Company will refund her money. If the mean of this sample turns out to be greater than or equal to her billed time, she will pay the company half again the amount of the bill.

Taking into account the average and standard deviation of all work times on file, do you think the manager is wise to make such an offer if this customer's billed time was thirty-two hours? Discuss why or why not.

What would be your response if the customer's billed time was thirty-four hours?

60. The Chair Company considered in the last problem repairs and restores old furniture. Records indicate the time needed to refinish and otherwise restore a standard dining room set is normally distributed, with a mean of thirty hours and a standard deviation of five hours. A customer was billed for thirty-two hours. What is the probability of a single customer being billed for these hours or more? What is the probability a sample of five customers will average thirty-two hours or more?

61. The Swim and Racquet Club is in the process of establishing a policy for how long a court may be reserved at any one time. To help make this decision, the club managers have selected a random sample of 100 tennis matches and determined that the mean time for completion is seventy-five minutes. What is the probability of finding a sample mean as small as or smaller than this if the true average completion time is ninety minutes, with a standard deviation of ten minutes, as some members have claimed?

62. The Environmental Protection Agency (EPA) requires all U.S. automobile makers to test their cars for mileage in the city and on the highway. One company has indicated that a certain model will get 25 mpg in the city and 32 mpg on the highway. However, not all cars of a given model will get the same mileage; these mileage ratings are simply averages. Further, because there is variation among cars, the manufacturer has discovered that the standard deviation is 3 mpg for city driving, and 2 mpg for highway driving.

Given this information, suppose the San Francisco Police Department has purchased a random sample of sixty-four cars from this company. The police officers have driven these cars exclusively in the city and have recorded an average of 21 mpg. What would you conclude regarding the EPA mileage rating for this model car? Indicate the basis for your conclusion.

63. Problem 62 considered sixty-four cars bought by the San Francisco Police Department. The manufacturer advertised the cars would average 24 mpg in the city and 32 mpg on the highway. These values are, of course, averages and have standard deviations of 3 mpg for city driving and 2 mpg for highway driving. The police chief has asked his officers to drive the cars to Los Angeles and back to determine how the cars perform in highway driving. The sixty-four cars averaged 34 mpg. What can the chief conclude about the advertised highway mileage? Explain your answer.

64. The Mason Construction Company has built a total of fifty homes in the Seattle area in an average time of thirty-five days, with a standard deviation of ten days. A prospective customer has interviewed forty of the fifty homeowners about the quality of construction, and so forth. One of the questions asked of the homeowners was how long it took the builder to construct their homes. The forty responses averaged forty-six days. What would you conclude about these responses? Explain.

65. The Sullivan Advertising Agency has determined that the average cost to develop a 30-second commercial is $20,000. The standard deviation is $3,000. Suppose a random sample of fifty commercials is selected and the average cost is $20,300. What are the chances of finding a sample mean this high or higher?

66. Suppose the Sullivan Advertising Agency is interested in establishing a pricing policy for prospective customers of 30-second commercials. Given that the mean cost is $20,000, with a standard deviation of $3,000, what are the chances of a given commercial costing between $19,500 and $22,000? What is the probability of a sample of thirty-six commercials having an average cost between $19,500 and $22,000? Explain why these probabilities are different.

67. The Baily Hill Bicycle Shop sells ten-speed bicycles and offers a maintenance program to its customers. The manager has found the average repair bill during the maintenance program's first year to be $15.30, with a standard deviation of $7.00.
   a. What is the probability a random sample of forty customers will have a mean repair cost exceeding $16.00?

b. What is the probability the mean repair cost for a sample of 100 customers will be between $15.10 and $15.80?

68. As part of a marketing study, the Food King Supermarket chain has randomly sampled 150 customers. The average dollar volume purchased by the customers in this sample was $33.14.

Before sampling, the company assumed that the distribution of customer purchases had a mean of $30.00 and a standard deviation of $8.00. If these figures are correct, what is the probability of observing a sample mean of $33.14 or greater? What would this probability indicate to you?

69. The Bendbo Corporation has a total of 300 employees in its two manufacturing locations and the headquarters office. A study conducted five years ago showed that the average commuting distance to work for Bendbo employees was 6.2 miles, with a standard deviation of 3 miles.

a. Recently a follow-up study based on a random sample of 100 employees indicated an average travel distance of 5.9 miles. Assuming that the mean and standard deviation of the original study hold, what is the probability of obtaining a sample mean of 5.9 miles or less? Based on this probability, do you think the average travel distance may have decreased?

b. A second random sample of size forty was selected. This sample produced a mean travel distance of 5.9 miles. If the mean for all employees is 6.2 miles and the standard deviation is 3 miles, what is the probability of observing a sample mean of 5.9 miles or less?

c. Discuss why the probabilities differ even though the sample results were the same in each case.

70. A marketing consultant has claimed that the average family income in a certain market area is at least $18,100 per year, with a standard deviation of $4,000. A market research firm wishes to test this claim by selecting a random sample of 64 families. The process to test the claim begins with computing $\overline{X}$. If this sample mean is less than some specified value (called A), the claim will be rejected; otherwise, the claim will be accepted.

a. Suppose the market-research company wishes to set the value A such that $P(\overline{X} \le A) = 0.05$. Determine the appropriate value of A.

b. Suppose the marketing research firm were to select a random sample of size 100 rather than 64 to test the claim. Determine A such that $P(\overline{X} \le A) = 0.05$, given this change in sample sizes. Compare this answer to the one you found for problem 70.

71. An automatic saw at a local lumber mill cuts 2 × 4s to an average length of 120 inches. However, since the saw is a mechanical device, not all 2 × 4s are 120 inches. In fact, the distribution of lengths has a variance of 0.64. The saw operator took a sample of just thirty-six boards.

a. If the saw is set correctly, what is the probability the average length of the sample boards is more than 120.6 inches?

b. What is the probability the sample length is less than 119.3 inches?

c. What should the saw operator conclude if she finds the sample to have an average length of 120.3 inches?

Section 7–8

72. The manager for quality control at Bixby Electronics recently reviewed a contract the company has with one of the suppliers of a particular component part. According to the contract, the defective rate in the components is to be no more than 7 percent. A large quantity of the components has just arrived at Bixby Electronics. As part of the regular receiving process, a random sample of 100 parts was selected and 12 percent of these parts were found to be defective. What is the probability of 12 percent or more of the components being defective if the true percentage in the population is actually 7 percent? Based on the probability you have computed, what should the quality control manager conclude about the entire shipment of components with respect to the 7 percent defective limit?

73. If a random sample of 344 people is selected from the adult population in Houston, Texas, what is the probability that less than 22 percent of the sample favor a state lottery if the true percentage for the entire population who favor one is 42 percent?

74. Suppose 34 percent of the members of the AFL-CIO labor union are registered Republicans, but a random sample of 300 members shows a sample proportion of 55 percent registered Republicans. What is the difference between the 55 percent and the 34 percent called? Also how likely is it that a sample of this size would contain 55 percent or more Republicans if the 34 percent figure is accurate?

75. An insurance company in Wyoming recognizes that 30 percent of the people it insures will file a claim against their homeowner's policy within three years after taking out the policy. Suppose a random sample of policyholders who have had policies for three years or longer have been selected. What is the probability that the 246 sampled, over 40 percent will have filed a claim in the first three years? How would this probability change if the sample size is doubled to 492?

C A S E S

7A Mountain West Gas and Electric Company

Jim Kelly called the meeting of the executive committee to order promptly at 9:00 A.M. in the plush McGiven Conference Room. In his capacity as operations vice-president for Mountain West Gas and Electric, Jim has day-to-day responsibility for the company and reports directly to the president, Willis Clayborn. Jim chairs the executive committee and can call it together for special meetings like the one being held today.

The purpose of the meeting was to discuss the latest ruling by the State Public Utility Commission, the regulatory body responsible for overseeing all public utilities in the state. The PUC ruling requires that gas and electric companies in the state take into account peak day usage in setting their rates. As Jim explained to the executive committee, the ruling means that the amount of gas and electricity used on the peak day (the day with the greatest number of therms used) by the various classes of customers must be factored into the rates charged for the customer classes. The PUC logic, according to Jim, is that the company just maintain adequate capacity to meet the peak day demand. The classes of customers demanding a high share of this capacity should pay more of the capacity-related costs than those customers in classes who have a low demand on the peak day.

As Jim explained, this means the company needs a way to monitor electricity and gas usage on a daily basis. Currently, customer meters are read once a month and the total power used for the month is known for each customer class. No information is currently available on a daily basis by customer class. However, Mountain West can measure the total gas and electricity supplied by the system each day, so the peak day during a year can be identified. Every year since records have been maintained, the peak day has occurred during January.

The company has four classes of customers, RES-1, RES-2, COM-1, and COM-2. The difference between RES-1 and RES-2 is that RES-1 customers have an electric water heater and RES-2 customers have gas water heaters. Both RES-1 and RES-2 are residential classes. There are approximately 42,000 RES-1 customers and 37,000 RES-2 customers. The COM-1 customer class consists of small- to medium-size commercial customers like retail stores and small manufacturing. The COM-1 customers number approximately 6,400. The last customer class, COM-2, consists of the large industrial users. While small in number (245), this class accounts for over 23 percent of the gas and electricity used throughout the year.

After a series of comments and questions from the other executive board members, Jim outlined the alternatives as he saw them:

1. Manually read the meters for every customer every day during the month of January.
2. Manually read the meters for a sample of customers every day during January.
3. Install a microcomputer device for recording gas and electricity usage for a sample of customers.
4. Do nothing and justify the current rate structure to the Public Utilities Commission.

Options 1, 2, and 4 were easily understandable by the board members, but the microcomputer option was new to most members and Jim spent some extra time explaining what this involved. He pointed out that a California company has developed a "black box" that contains a small microprocessor capable of measuring natural gas and electricity usage in 15-minute intervals and can store up to one year's worth of data. The cost is $250.00 per unit plus installation and maintenance, figured to be another $100.00 per unit.

The board members agreed that manually reading every customer's meter each day was impractical, and they also agreed that doing nothing was not a desirable option in light of the PUC's interest in the issue. The group decided to investigate the sampling alternatives: either manually reading a sample of customer meters or using the new "black box" on a sample. Jim Kelly suggested that Elizabeth Kornfield, manager of data services, have her staff work up a report that would discuss the different sampling options available to Mountain West. The report should discuss the advantages and disadvantages of each sampling method considered.

When the meeting broke up at 11:15 A.M., Elizabeth headed back to her office. She knew who she would have to prepare the report on sampling and wanted to get it started right away!

7B Truck Safety Inspection, Part 1

The Idaho Department of Law Enforcement, in conjunction with the federal government, recently began to formulate a truck inspection program in Idaho. The current truck safety program is limited to an inspection of only those trucks that appear (visually) to have some defect when they stop at one of the weigh stations in the state. The proposed inspection program will not be limited to the trucks with visible defects, but will potentially subject all trucks to a comprehensive safety inspection.

Mr. Lund of the Department of Law Enforcement is in charge of the new program. He has stated that the ultimate objective of the new truck inspection program is to reduce the number of trucks with safety defects operating in Idaho. Ideally, all trucks passing through, or operating within, Idaho would be inspected once a month, and substantial penalties applied to operators if safety defects were discovered. Mr. Lund is confident that such an inspection program would, without fail, reduce the number of defective trucks operating on Idaho's highways. However, each safety inspection takes about an hour, and because of limited money to hire inspectors, Mr. Lund realizes that all trucks cannot be inspected. He also knows it is unrealistic to have trucks wait to be inspected until trucks ahead of them have been checked. Such delays would cause problems with the drivers.

In meetings with his staff, Mr. Lund has suggested that before the inspection program begins, the number of defective trucks currently operating in Idaho needs to be estimated. This estimate can be compared with later estimates to see if the inspection program has been effective. To arrive at this initial estimate, Mr. Lund feels that some sort of sampling plan to select representative trucks from the population of all trucks in Idaho must be developed. He has suggested that this sampling be done at the eight weigh stations near Idaho's borders, but is unsure how to establish a statistically sound sampling plan that is practical to implement.

7C Carpita Bottling Company

Don Carpita owns and operates Carpita Bottling Company in Evertown, Maryland. The company bottles soda pop and beer, and distributes the products in the counties surrounding Evertown.

The company has four bottling machines, which can be adjusted to fill bottles at any mean fill level between 2 ounces and 72 ounces. The machines do exhibit some variation in actual fill from the mean setting. For instance, if the mean setting is 16 ounces, the actual fill may be slightly more or slightly less than that amount.

Three of the four filling machines are relatively new and their fill variation is not as great as that of the older machine. Don has observed that the standard deviation in fill for the three new machines is about one percent of the mean fill level when the mean fill is set at 16 ounces or less and one half of one percent of the mean at settings exceeding 16 ounces. The older machine has a standard deviation of about 1.5 percent of the mean setting regardless of the mean fill setting. However, the older machine tends to underfill bottles more than overfill, so the older machine is set at a mean fill slightly in excess of the desired mean to compensate for the propensity to underfill. For example, when 16-ounce bottles are to be filled, the machine is set at a mean fill level of 16.05 ounces.

It is possible for the company to simultaneously fill bottles with two brands of soda pop using two machines and use the other two machines to bottle beer. Although each filling machine has its own warehouse and the products are loaded from the warehouse directly to a truck, products from two or more filling machines may be loaded on the same truck. However, an individual store almost always receives bottles on a particular day from just one machine.

Saturday morning Don received a call at home from the J. R. Summers Grocery store manager. She was very upset because the shipment of 16-ounce bottles of beer received yesterday contained several bottles that were not adequately filled. The manager wanted Don to replace the entire shipment at once.

Don gulped down his coffee and prepared to head for the store to check out the problem. He started thinking how he could determine which machine was responsible for the problem. If he could at least determine whether it was the old machine or one of the new ones, he could save his maintenance people a lot of time and effort checking all the machines.

His plan was to select a sample of 64 bottles of beer from the store and measure the contents. Don figured that he might be able to determine, on the basis of the average contents, whether it is more likely that the beer was bottled by a new machine or by the old one.

The results of the sampling showed an average of 15.993 ounces. Now, Don needs some help in determining whether a sample mean of 15.993 ounces or less is more likely to come from the new machines or the older machine.

REFERENCES

Lapin, Lawrence. *Statistics for Modern Business Decisions,* 3rd Edition. New York: Harcourt Brace Jovanovich, 1982.

Mendenhall, William, and Reinmuth, James. *Statistics for Management and Economics,* 4th Edition. North Scituate, Mass.: Duxbury, 1982.

Neter, John; Wasserman, William; and Whitmore, G. A. *Applied Statistics,* 2nd Edition. Boston: Allyn and Bacon, 1982.

STATISTICAL ESTIMATION—LARGE SAMPLES

8

WHY DECISION MAKERS NEED TO KNOW

Chapter 1 emphasized that decision makers cannot always measure an entire population but instead must often rely on information gained by sampling the population. Therefore, the decision made often depends on the sample information, which, as shown in chapter 7, is subject to sampling error. Sampling error can cause problems for decision makers who are not familiar with statistical estimation. Suppose a market-research firm needs to know the average per capita income in a city before it can advise its client whether to open a new retail outlet in that city. This firm would likely select a statistical sample and compute the mean per capita income. However, as illustrated in chapter 7, the sample mean does not have to equal the population mean. Therefore, the market-research firm has to include the possible sampling error in its estimate of the true population mean.

This chapter introduces the statistical techniques for estimating a population value with sample information if the sample is large.

CHAPTER OBJECTIVES

This chapter introduces the process of estimating population values based on samples from the population. Specifically, it introduces point estimates and interval estimates for such parameters as the population mean, the population proportion, the difference between two population means, and the difference between two population proportions. It will concentrate on estimation procedures for large sample sizes.

The chapter also introduces the concepts of precision and confidence level for an estimate and will show how to determine the sample size necessary to maintain a specified level of confidence and precision.

STUDENT OBJECTIVES

After studying the material in this chapter, you should be able to

1. Discuss the difference between a point estimate and an interval estimate.
2. Discuss the advantages of a confidence interval estimate and recognize applications of such an estimate.
3. Calculate a confidence interval estimate for each of the following:
   a. Population mean
   b. Population proportion
   c. Difference between two population means
   d. Difference between two population proportions
4. Determine the impact of sample size on the confidence interval.
5. Discuss the importance of precision in a confidence interval estimate.
6. Determine the required sample size for specific estimation problems involving population means and proportions.
7. Identify business decision applications that require statistical estimation.

THE NEED FOR STATISTICAL ESTIMATION

8-1

A large motel chain with several hundred motels throughout the United States is considering changing the brand of television set in its motel rooms. The major consideration is to select the brand with the lowest combination of initial cost and maintenance cost. Although the motel management can get complete information on the initial purchase costs for the various brands, it is uncertain about the total maintenance costs. Management plans to keep the sets in the rooms for five years regardless of the brand it decides to purchase. The managers know that for any brand of television, some sets will require more maintenance than others. They also know that regardless of the brand they select, the actual total maintenance cost will not be known until the five years have passed. Obviously the managers cannot wait for five years of cost data to make their decision.

An electronics company in Delaware has developed a new testing simulator that uses heat to age the television parts. This electronics company can record all maintenance during a simulated five years for the television set being tested. The television manufacturing industry has vouched for the simulator's accuracy, and the motel managers are confident of its results.

Since the motel chain will purchase 4,000 television sets, the only way the motel managers will be able to make a decision is to sample a few televisions for each brand. They will calculate the average maintenance cost for each brand and use the sample means to estimate what the average maintenance cost will be for all televisions of each brand.

Like these motel managers, decision makers often need to use sample information to make estimates about a population. Market research relies heavily on statistical estimation. The market researchers select a sample of potential customers for a new product or service and, from that sample, estimate the proportion of people in the entire market area who will purchase the product or service. The list of business applications is endless. You will be introduced to a variety of applications of statistical estimation throughout this chapter.

POINT ESTIMATES AND INTERVAL ESTIMATES

8-2

You have either been a respondent or have seen the results of a political poll taken during an election year. These polls attempt to determine the percentage of voters who will favor a particular candidate or a particular issue. For example, suppose a poll indicates that 62 percent of people over 18 years old in your state favor setting the legal drinking age at 21 years. The pollsters have not contacted every person in the state, but rather have sampled only a relatively few people to arrive at the 62 percent figure. In statistical terminology, the 62 percent is the *point estimate* for the true population percentage who favor the 21-year drinking age. In general, a **point estimate** is a single number determined from a sample and is used to estimate the population value.

The Environmental Protection Agency (EPA) tests automobile models sold in the United States to determine their mileage ratings. Following the testing, each model is assigned an EPA mileage rating based on the test mileage. This rating is actually a point estimate for the true average of all cars of the given model.

Cost accountants make detailed studies of their company's production process to determine the costs of producing each product. These costs are often found by selecting a sample of items and following each item through the complete production process. The costs at each step in the process are determined, and the total cost is found when the process is completed. The accountants calculate the average cost for the items sampled and use this figure as the point estimate for the true average cost of all pieces produced. The point estimate becomes the basis for assigning a selling price to the finished product.

The federal government publishes many population estimates. Among these are estimates of the median family income and the proportion of unemployed persons. These values are calculated from samples and are point estimates of the population values.

Which point estimator the decision maker uses depends on the population characteristic the decision maker wishes to estimate. However, regardless of the population value being estimated, you can expect that the estimate will not equal the true population value. We always expect some sampling error. Recall that *sampling error* is the difference between the population value (μ_x) and the sample value ($\overline{X}$). Chapter 7 discussed the distribution of potential sampling error. We can't eliminate sampling error, but we can deal with it in our decision process. Thus, for example, when cost accountants use $\overline{X}$, the average cost of a sample of pieces, to establish the total production cost, the point estimate will most likely be wrong. But they will have no way of determining how wrong it is.

To overcome this problem with point estimates, the most common procedure is to calculate an *interval* that the decision maker is fairly sure contains the true population parameter. These intervals are called **confidence intervals.** The statistical techniques used for developing confidence intervals assume that the data are interval- or ratio-scaled. Refer to chapter 1 for a discussion of levels of data measurement.

Confidence Interval Estimation

The production manager of the Valley View Canning Company is responsible for monitoring the filling operations of cans. His company has recently installed a new machine that has been carefully tested and is known to fill cans of any size with a standard deviation of $\sigma_x = 0.2$ ounce. The manager's main problem is to adjust the average fill to the level specified on the can, for instance, 16 ounces, 24 ounces, and so forth.

Suppose he has just made a setting in an attempt to fill the peach cans to an average of 16 ounces. From the cans already filled he selects a random sample of 100 and carefully weighs each one. The sample mean, $\overline{X}$, provides a point estimate of the population mean, μ_x. Suppose this value is

$$\overline{X} = 16.8 \text{ ounces}$$

Because of the nature of any point estimate, the manager does not expect to find a sample mean that exactly equals 16 ounces. He also knows from the central limit theorem that the distribution of all possible sample means will be approximately normal around the true mean. This is illustrated in figure 8–1.

Thus, although the manager does not expect a sample mean of 16 ounces, he will likely allow the process to continue if the sample mean is close to 16 ounces. To determine just what "close" is, the manager needs to determine a confidence interval.

CONFIDENCE INTERVAL ESTIMATE OF μ_x

8-3

Large Samples, σ_x Known

The Valley View Canning Company manager specifies that he wants a 95 percent confidence interval. This means that of all the intervals he might obtain, 95 percent will include the true mean. He figures that if the interval includes 16 ounces, the true mean might actually be 16 ounces and he will leave the machine setting as is. The general format for the confidence interval is

Point estimate ± (interval coefficient)(standard error)

FIGURE 8–1
Sampling distribution of $\overline{X}$, Valley View Canning Company example (peach can fill in ounces)

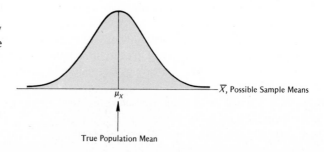

The point estimate for our canning example is $\overline{X}$. The standard error is $\sigma_{\overline{x}}$, which is determined by equation 8–1:

$$\sigma_{\overline{x}} = \frac{\sigma_x}{\sqrt{n}} \qquad (8\text{–}1)$$

The remaining factor, the **interval coefficient,** is the number of standard errors on either side of the population mean necessary to include a percentage of the possible sample means equal to the confidence level. When the sample size is *large* and the population standard deviation is *known,* the interval coefficient is a Z value from the standard normal distribution table in appendix C. For example, if the desired confidence level is 95 percent, the Z value (interval coefficent) is 1.96, as shown in figure 8–2. Recall the central limit theorem states that for sufficiently large samples, the sampling distribution will be normal.

The format for a confidence interval for estimating μ_x is given in equation 8–2:

$$\overline{X} \pm Z\sigma_{\overline{x}} \qquad (8\text{–}2)$$

For this example, the confidence interval is

$$\overline{X} \pm 1.96\,\frac{\sigma_x}{\sqrt{n}} \qquad (8\text{–}3)$$

Any value of $\overline{X}$ between $\mu_x - 1.96\sigma_{\overline{x}}$ and $\mu_x + 1.96\sigma_{\overline{x}}$ will produce a confidence interval that contains μ_x. Using $Z = 1.96$ indicates that since 95 percent of the possible sample means come from this range, 95 percent of the potential confidence intervals will include the population mean. Figure 8–3 illustrates this important concept by showing a few of the possible intervals.

For the Valley View Canning Company example, the 95 percent confidence interval with a sample mean, $\overline{X}$, of 16.8 ounces is

$$\overline{X} \pm 1.96\frac{\sigma_x}{\sqrt{n}}$$

$$16.8 \pm 1.96\frac{0.2}{\sqrt{100}}$$

$$16.8 \pm 1.96(0.02)$$

$$16.8 \pm 0.0392$$

Therefore, the 95 percent confidence interval estimate for the true average fill is

16.7608 ounces ——— 16.8392 ounces

This represents a 95 percent confidence interval because it is constructed by a procedure that will produce an interval containing μ_x 95 percent of the time. The manager is almost certain this interval *does* include the true mean. Since the desired average

FIGURE 8–2
Interval coefficient, 95 percent
confidence interval

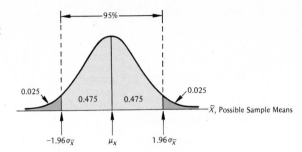

FIGURE 8–2
Interval coefficient, 95 percent
confidence interval

of 16 ounces is not contained within the limits, he will conclude (rightly or wrongly) that the true mean is not 16 ounces and will order further machine adjustment. The sampling and estimation process will be repeated.

Suppose after several adjustments the sample mean, $\overline{X}$, for a sample of size 100 cans is 16.02 ounces. The 95 percent confidence interval developed from this point estimate is

$$\overline{X} \pm 1.96\sigma_{\overline{x}}$$

$$16.02 \pm 1.96(0.02)$$

$$15.9808 \text{ ounces} \underline{\hspace{1cm}} 16.0592 \text{ ounces}$$

The production manager knows that 95 percent of all possible confidence intervals should include μ_x, the true population mean. Therefore he feels confident that the true mean is between 15.9808 ounces and 16.0592 ounces. Because 16 ounces falls in this interval, the manager should not make any further adjustments in the machine setting at this time.

Suppose the filling process is allowed to continue for eight hours. The production manager might then halt the run and select a random sample of 100 cans to determine whether the filling machine has remained in adjustment. He will calculate a 95 percent confidence interval estimate of μ_x, the average content of the cans. Suppose the sample mean is 16.01 ounces. Then the 95 percent confidence interval is

$$\overline{X} \pm 1.96\frac{\sigma_x}{\sqrt{n}}$$

$$16.01 \pm 1.96\frac{0.2}{\sqrt{100}}$$

$$16.01 \pm 0.0392$$

$$15.9708 \text{ ounces} \underline{\hspace{1cm}} 16.0492 \text{ ounces}$$

The confidence interval includes 16 ounces. Therefore, the production manager would have no reason to believe the true mean is not 16 ounces.

FIGURE 8–3
Possible confidence intervals

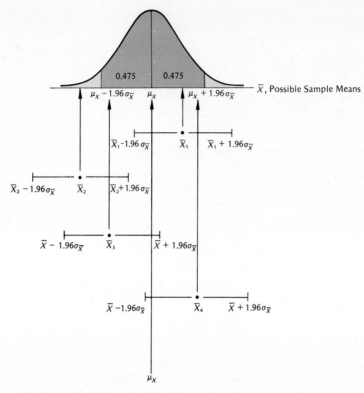

Note: Most intervals include μ_x, and some do not. Those intervals that do not contain the population mean are developed from sample means that fall in either tail of the sampling distribution.

Precision of the Estimate

The production manager for Valley View Canning is concerned about the width of his confidence interval. Though he is willing to believe, based on a sample of 100, that the true mean fill is 16 ounces because this value falls within the interval, he would also be willing to believe that the true mean fill is 16.02 ounces or 15.99 ounces because they also fall in the interval. The manager would like to decrease the width of the confidence interval estimate. The **precision** of a confidence interval estimate is inversely related to the width of the interval. As the estimate becomes more precise, the width of the interval becomes narrower.

One way to increase the precision of an estimate is to decrease the confidence level. For example, if the manager is willing to accept a 90 percent confidence level, the interval coefficient can be reduced from 1.96 to 1.645, as shown in figure 8–4. For a sample of 100 selected from the production run, the 90 percent confidence interval from a sample mean of 16.01 is

FIGURE 8–4
Interval coefficient, 90 percent
confidence interval

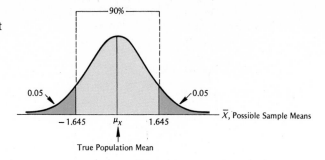

$$\overline{X} \pm Z\frac{\sigma_x}{\sqrt{n}}$$

$$16.01 \pm 1.645\frac{0.2}{\sqrt{100}}$$

$$16.01 \pm 0.0329$$

$$15.9771 \text{ ounces} \underline{\qquad} 16.0429 \text{ ounces}$$

This represents a slight *increase* in precision (narrowing the interval) from the 95 percent confidence level. A confidence level of 80 percent would increase the precision even further:

$$\overline{X} \pm Z\frac{\sigma_x}{\sqrt{n}}$$

$$16.01 \pm 1.28\frac{0.2}{\sqrt{100}}$$

$$16.01 \pm 0.0256$$

$$15.9844 \text{ ounces} \underline{\qquad} 16.0356 \text{ ounces}$$

We have increased the precision by decreasing the confidence level, but what is the trade-off? Reducing the confidence from 95 percent to 80 percent means that now only 80 percent of all intervals are expected to include the true population mean. Thus the chances of obtaining an interval that includes the true mean have been decreased. The trade-off is between obtaining a narrow, more precise interval and increasing the chances of obtaining an interval estimate that does not contain the true population mean. The extent to which a decision maker is willing to reduce the confidence level depends upon the cost associated with an interval that does not contain μ_x. The higher this cost, the less willing the decision maker will be to reduce the confidence level.

A second alternative for increasing the precision of an interval estimate is to increase the sample size. Since an increase in sample size will reduce the standard error, $\sigma_{\overline{x}}$, it will also reduce the confidence interval width. For example, suppose the production manager at Valley View Canning selects a random sample of 400 cans from the production run. Further, suppose the sample mean, $\overline{X}$, for this larger sample is also 16.01 ounces. The 95 percent confidence interval would be

$$\overline{X} \pm Z\frac{\sigma_x}{\sqrt{n}}$$

$$16.01 \pm 1.96\frac{0.2}{\sqrt{400}}$$

$$16.01 \pm 0.0196$$

$$15.9904 \text{ ounces} \underline{\hspace{1cm}} 16.0296 \text{ ounces}$$

This interval is more precise than the 95 percent interval for a sample of 100 cans, which was calculated previously to be

$$15.9708 \text{ ounces} \underline{\hspace{1cm}} 16.0492 \text{ ounces}$$

If the sample size is increased to 800, precision can be increased further:

$$\overline{X} \pm Z\frac{\sigma_x}{\sqrt{n}}$$

$$16.01 \pm 1.96\frac{0.2}{\sqrt{800}}$$

$$16.01 \pm 0.0139$$

$$15.9961 \text{ ounces} \underline{\hspace{1cm}} 16.0239 \text{ ounces}$$

There are obvious trade-offs associated with selecting a larger sample size, generally in terms of time and money. Decision makers must decide the benefit to be gained from increased precision and balance this gain against the increased costs.

Sample Size Determination (Simple Random Sample)

Often a decision maker has a desired confidence level and a specified precision level, but is unsure about what sample size to select. For example, suppose an economist wishes to estimate the average annual family income of the residents in an agricultural county in Nebraska. Assume that the population standard deviation, σ_x, is known to be $1,000. The economist wants 95 percent confidence and a precision of $300. Therefore, she needs a confidence interval with a total width of no more than $300. How large a sample size is required to satisfy the economist's confidence and precision requirements?

To answer this question, we must introduce a new concept, *tolerable error*. **Tolerable error** is one-half the width of the confidence interval. Recall that

$$\overline{X} \pm Z\frac{\sigma_x}{\sqrt{n}}$$

is the format of a confidence interval estimate of μ_x. Then tolerable error can be calculated from equation 8–4:

$$e = Z\frac{\sigma_x}{\sqrt{n}} \qquad (8\text{--}4)$$

where e = tolerable error
$\quad\quad\quad Z$ = interval coefficient
$\quad\quad\quad \sigma_x$ = population standard deviation
$\quad\quad\quad n$ = sample size

Since tolerable error is half the width of a confidence interval, the economist, who wishes an interval width of $300, will accept a tolerable error of $150. We can solve equation 8–4 for *n,* the sample size, by equation 8–5:

$$e = Z\frac{\sigma_x}{\sqrt{n}}$$
$$n = \frac{Z^2\sigma_x^2}{e^2} \qquad (8\text{--}5)$$

Equation 8–5 applies to problems where the population can be considered infinite or where the sampling is performed with replacement and simple random sampling is used.

For the economist's problem,

$$e = Z\frac{\sigma_x}{\sqrt{n}}$$

$$150 = 1.96\frac{1,000}{\sqrt{n}}$$

$$n = \frac{(1.96)^2(1,000)^2}{(150)^2} = 170.74$$

$$= 171 \text{ families}$$

Thus, to obtain a 95 percent confidence with a tolerable error of $150 (precision = $300), the economist would need to sample 171 families from the county.

What would be the impact on the sample size of increasing the required precision to $200? This means the tolerable error is reduced to $100. The required sample size would be calculated as follows:

$$e = Z\frac{\sigma_x}{\sqrt{n}}$$

$$100 = 1.96\frac{1,000}{\sqrt{n}}$$

$$n = \frac{(1.96)^2(1,000)^2}{(100)^2} = 384.16$$

$$= 385 \text{ families}$$

The economist may or may not be able to afford increasing the sample size from 171 to 385. As indicated earlier, decision makers will be forced, in practical applications, to strike a balance between required confidence and precision and the sample size they can afford.

Large Samples, σ_x Unknown

The previous section discussed confidence interval estimates for large samples with a known population standard deviation. Although the population standard deviation may be known, in most business applications, if μ_x is not known, neither is σ_x. When σ_x is not known, it must also be estimated. The appropriate estimator is S_x, the *sample standard deviation*, calculated by equation 8–6:

$$S_x = \sqrt{\frac{\Sigma(X - \overline{X})^2}{n - 1}} \qquad (8\text{--}6)$$

where S_x = sample standard deviation
              $\overline{X}$ = sample mean
              n = sample size

If the sample size is *large*, the confidence interval estimate of the population mean, μ_x, is approximated by equation 8–7:

$$\overline{X} \pm Z\frac{S_x}{\sqrt{n}} \qquad (8\text{--}7)$$

Suppose the Ohio State Department of Transportation has undertaken a study of highway accidents and their causes. As one part of the study, the administrators need to estimate the average speed of vehicles around a dangerous curve on the interstate highway. They have selected a random sample of 500 vehicles and used radar to measure the vehicles' speed, finding

$$\overline{X} = 52.31/\text{m.p.h.}$$
$$S_x = 6.30/\text{m.p.h.}$$

The administrators want a 98 percent confidence interval. Therefore,

$$\overline{X} \pm Z\frac{S_x}{\sqrt{n}}$$

$$52.31 \pm 2.33\frac{6.30}{\sqrt{500}}$$

$$52.31 \pm 0.66$$

$$51.65 \text{ m.p.h.} \underline{\quad\quad} 52.97 \text{ m.p.h.}$$

For the purposes of their report, the administrators are confident that the actual average speed for all cars traveling on this curve is between 51.65 and 52.97 miles per hour.

In another example, the postmaster at a large New York post office was required to report the average weight per package mailed at her post office and the number of packages mailed during September. The post office auditors could then multiply the average weight by the number of packages to determine the total weight of all packages. Then they could multiply the total weight by the mailing rate to provide a rough estimate of what the income should have been from package mailing.

Because of the time it would take to record the weight of all 49,007 packages mailed, the postmaster was granted permission to select a sample of packages. She reported the following information to the auditors:

$$N = 49,007$$
$$n = 100$$
$$\overline{X} = 3.12 \text{ lb}$$
$$S_x = 2.8 \text{ lb}$$

The auditors then used this information to construct a 95 percent confidence interval for estimating μ_x, the true average package weight:

$$\overline{X} \pm 1.96\sigma_{\bar{x}}$$

$$3.12 \pm 1.96\frac{2.8}{\sqrt{100}}$$

$$3.12 \pm 0.55$$

$$2.57 \text{ lb} \underline{\quad\quad} 3.67 \text{ lb}$$

A rough estimate for total weight is found by multiplying the lower limit and upper limit by 49,007 packages, which gives

$$125,947.99 \text{ lb} \underline{\quad\quad} 179,855.69 \text{ lb}$$

The auditors might multiply these limits by the appropriate rate to arrive at an interval estimate for income from package mailing. They will compare the post office's reported income with this estimate. If the reported income is within that interval, no formal audit will be conducted. Otherwise, the department will conduct a full-scale audit.

Estimating a Population Total

In the previous example, the postmaster developed a rough confidence interval estimate for the total weight of the 49,007 packages by first developing an interval estimate of the average package weight and then multiplying the upper and lower limits by the population size. A more statistically correct procedure exists for estimating the total of a population, as illustrated in equation 8–8:

$$(N)(\overline{X}) \pm Z \sqrt{N^2 \frac{S^2}{n}\left(\frac{N-n}{N}\right)} \qquad (8\text{--}8)$$

where
$\overline{X}$ = sample mean
N = population size
S^2 = sample variance
n = sample size

For the post office example, the 95 percent confidence interval is

$$(49,007)(3.12) \pm 1.96 \sqrt{(49,007)^2 \frac{(2.8)^2}{100}\left(\frac{49,007-100}{49,007}\right)}$$

$$152,901.84 \pm (1.96)(13,707.95)$$

$$152,901.84 \pm 26,867.59$$

$$126,034.25 \text{ pounds} \underline{\quad\quad} 179,769.43 \text{ pounds}$$

Thus the auditors can be confident that the total weight falls within the interval of 126,034.25 pounds to 179,769.43 pounds. Note that this is a slightly more precise estimate (narrower interval) than the estimate computed from the interval estimate for mean package weight.

SKILL DEVELOPMENT PROBLEMS FOR SECTION 8–3

The following set of problems is meant to test your understanding of the material in this section. Additional problems are found at the end of this chapter under this section heading.

1. Given the following information:

$$\overline{X} = 350$$
$$\sigma_x = 45$$
$$n = 200$$

   a. Compute and interpret the 90 percent confidence interval estimate for the population mean.

b. Compute and interpret the 95 percent confidence interval estimate for the population mean.

2. Given the following information:

$$\overline{X} = 2{,}700$$
$$\sigma_x = 400$$
$$n = 500$$

a. Compute and interpret the 99 percent confidence interval estimate for the population mean.
b. Compute and interpret the 95 percent confidence interval estimate for the population mean.

3. Given the following information:

$$Z = 1.96$$
$$\sigma_{\overline{x}} = 20$$

a. What is the required sample size necessary to estimate the population mean if the tolerable error = 3?
b. Determine the sample size necessary to estimate the population mean with a tolerable error of 2.
c. Discuss why there is a difference in the sample sizes determined in part a and part b.

4. Given the following information:

$$N = 40{,}000$$
$$n = 200$$
$$\overline{X} = 450$$
$$S_x^2 = 3{,}000$$

a. Compute and interpret the 95 percent confidence interval estimate for the population total.
b. Compute and interpret the 90 percent confidence interval estimate for the population total.
c. Discuss the difference between the two estimates computed in parts a and b and indicate why this difference exists.

5. Agri-Beef Inc. is a large midwestern farming operation. The company has been a leader in employing statistical analysis techniques in its business. Recently, John Goldberg, operations manager, requested that a random sample of cattle be selected and that these cattle be fed a special diet. The cattle were weighed before the start of the new feeding program and at the end of the feeding program. He wished to estimate the average daily weight gain for cattle on the new feed program. Two hundred cattle were tested, with the following sample results:

$$\overline{X} = 1.2 \text{ pounds per day gain}$$
$$S_x = 0.50 \text{ pound}$$

a. Develop the 95 percent confidence interval estimate for the true average daily weight gain.

b. Develop the 90 percent confidence interval estimate for the true average daily weight gain.

c. Discuss the difference between the two estimates found in parts a and b and indicate the advantages and disadvantages of each.

6. The Filmont Company operates retail pharmacies in ten eastern states. Recently, the company's internal audit department selected a random sample of 300 prescriptions issued throughout the system. The objective of the sampling was to estimate the average dollar value of all prescriptions issued by the company. The following data were collected:

$$\overline{X} = \$14.23$$
$$S_x = 3.00$$

Determine the 90 percent confidence interval estimate for the true average sales value for prescriptions issued by the company. Interpret the interval estimate.

7. The State National Bank is considering a survey of their customers for the purposes of estimating the number of checks written per month. The manager wishes to have the estimate be within plus or minus one check of the true average and wants a confidence level of 95 percent. If the standard deviation is assumed to be 5.0 checks, how many customers should be sampled?

8. Marine World-Africa USA is a facility located near San Francisco, California, where people can see animals from the ocean and from Africa on display and performing in shows. Customers pay for a day ticket and can stay as long as they wish. The management is interested in determining the average length of time customers spend at the park per day. They plan to select a simple random sample of customers and ask them, as they leave the park, what time they arrived. The estimate is desired to be within plus or minus five minutes, with a 90 percent confidence level. A previous pilot sample indicated that the standard deviation is twenty-eight minutes. Given this information, how many customers need to be sampled?

9. The American-Savings Rent-A-Car Company is interested in estimating the total miles their cars are driven on a particular holiday. They have 23,000 cars nationwide and plan to sample 200 cars on this particular holiday. The mileage for each car will be recorded. The following data were computed from the sample data:

$$\overline{X} = 54.5 \text{ miles}$$
$$S_x = 14.0 \text{ miles}$$

Develop a 95 percent confidence interval estimate for the total miles driven by all 23,000 vehicles owned by the company.

10. The Swiftmore Company owns and operates movie theaters in Wyoming. The president of the company is concerned that home video recorders are hurting business because people can simply rent a movie and watch it at home. He has directed a staff member to estimate the total number of movies rented by people in Wyoming in December. A phone survey involving a random sample of 300 homes in Wyoming was conducted, with the following results:

$$\overline{X} = 2.4 \text{ movies}$$
$$S_x = 1.6 \text{ movies}$$

Develop and interpret the 90 percent confidence interval estimate for the total movies rented per month by the 211,000 homes in Wyoming in December.

CONFIDENCE INTERVAL ESTIMATION OF A POPULATION PROPORTION

8-4

Chapter 5 introduced the binomial distribution. Recall that the binomial distribution applies when the following conditions are satisfied:

1. There are n identical trials, each of which results in one of two possible outcomes, success or failure.
2. The n trials are *independent* and the probability of a success remains constant from trial to trial.

Also recall that the *average* of the binomial distribution is as given by equation 8–9:

$$\mu_x = np \qquad (8\text{–}9)$$

where n = sample size (number of trials)
         p = probability of a success

and that the standard deviation of the binomial distribution is as given by equation 8–10:

$$\sigma_x = \sqrt{npq} \qquad (8\text{–}10)$$

where $q = 1 - p$

The binomial distribution has many applications. However, rather than attempting to count the number of successes, decision makers will often want to determine the proportion or percentage of successes in the population. A Republican candidate for the U.S. Senate is concerned about the proportion of voters who will vote Republican. The quality control manager for a large toy manufacturer is concerned about the proportion of defective toys his company produces. The president of the United States and his economic advisors are concerned about the proportion of the labor force that is unemployed. These are but a few of the situations in which decision makers need to know the *population proportion*. The population proportion is determined by equation 8–11:

$$p = \frac{X}{N}$$ (8–11)

where p = population proportion
X = total number of successes in the population
N = population size

If decision makers have access to the entire population, the calculated p value is a **parameter.** However, rarely can decision makers measure the entire population. Consequently, a random sample must be selected and the population proportion estimated. The point estimate for the population proportion is given by equation 8–12:

$$\hat{p} = \frac{x}{n}$$ (8–12)

where $\hat{p}$ = sample proportion
x = number of successes in the sample
n = sample size

As shown in chapter 7, the sampling distribution of $\hat{p}$ values can be approximated by a normal distribution if the sample size is large and the population proportion, p, is not too close to zero or 1.0. The expected value and standard deviation of the sampling distribution are given by equations 8–13 and 8–14:

$$E(\hat{p}) = \mu_{\hat{p}} = p$$ (8–13)

$$\sigma_{\hat{p}} = \sqrt{\frac{pq}{n}}$$ (8–14)

where $\mu_{\hat{p}}$ = expected proportion of successes
$\sigma_{\hat{p}}$ = standard error of the sampling distribution of $\hat{p}$
$q = 1 - p$
n = sample size

There is a problem with equations 8–13 and 8–14. The mean and standard deviation of the sampling distribution, $\mu_{\hat{p}}$ and $\sigma_{\hat{p}}$, are determined by knowing p, the population proportion. But we want to estimate p in the first place. We overcome this problem by substituting $\hat{p}$ and $\hat{q}(\hat{q} = 1 - \hat{p})$ for p and q in equation 8–14 (as shown in equation 8–15):

$$S_{\hat{p}} = \sqrt{\frac{\hat{p}\hat{q}}{n}} \qquad (8\text{–}15)$$

With this equation, we can construct a confidence interval estimate for the population proportion as in equation 8–16:

$$\hat{p} \pm ZS_{\hat{p}} \qquad (8\text{–}16)$$

where $\hat{p}$ = point estimate
   Z = interval coefficient
   $S_{\hat{p}}$ = estimated standard error of the sampling distribution

The Top-Down Construction Company operates in several western U.S. states. This company sells cedar shake roofs to people who currently have a different type of roof, but want a more aesthetically pleasing look. Top-Down is considering opening an outlet in a Utah city, but before doing so the manager wishes to estimate the proportion of homes in the city that already have cedar shake roofs. If this percentage is too high, the company will not operate in that city. The manager wants a 90 percent confidence interval and has selected a random sample of 200 homes, with the following results:

$\hat{p}$ = 0.36 (sample proportion of homes with cedar shakes)

$$S_{\hat{p}} = \sqrt{\frac{(0.36)(0.64)}{200}}$$

$$= 0.0339$$

The 90 percent confidence interval estimate for the true proportion of homes currently with cedar shake roofs is

$$\hat{p} \pm 1.645 S_{\hat{p}}$$
$$0.36 \pm (1.645)(0.0339)$$
$$0.36 \pm 0.0558$$
$$0.3042 \underline{\qquad} 0.4158$$

Based on this interval, the manager is confident that the true proportion is between 0.3042 and 0.4158. From this estimate, she will have to decide whether to open an outlet in this city.

Sample Size Requirements

Suppose the manager of Top-Down Construction is unhappy with the precision of the confidence interval just calculated. She indicates that the precision (interval width) should be no greater than 0.05. Assuming the manager wishes to retain the 90 percent confidence level, how many houses should be included in the sample?

The appropriate sample size is found using equation 8–17:

$$e = Z\sqrt{\frac{pq}{n}}$$

where e = tolerable error = $\dfrac{\text{precision}}{2}$

(8–17)

Solving for n, we get equation 8–18:

$$n = \frac{Z^2 pq}{e^2}$$

(8–18)

Equation 8–18 assumes that sampling is with replacement or that the sample size is less than 5 percent of the population and that the decision maker knows p. Of course, if p were already known, there would be no need to sample. There are two recommended ways of getting around this problem:

1. Use $p = 0.5$, since this will give the largest possible $\sigma_{\hat{p}}$, and thus a conservatively large sample size.
2. Select a *pilot* sample smaller than the expected sample size and calculate $\hat{p}$ for this sample.

Using the first approach, the required sample size for Top-Down Construction is

$$n = \frac{(1.645)^2(0.5)(0.5)}{(0.025)^2} = 1{,}082.41$$
$$= 1{,}083 \text{ houses}$$

Thus, a sample of 1,083 houses will guarantee the desired precision and confidence.

Under the pilot sample approach, the Top-Down manager may use the results of the sample of 200 homes to determine the required sample size. That is, she will use the $\hat{p} = 0.36$ value as a pilot estimate of p for determining the sample size as follows:

$$n = \frac{(1.645)^2(0.36)(0.64)}{(0.025)^2} = 997.55$$
$$= 998 \text{ houses}$$

Given the pilot sample information, the required sample size is 998 houses. Note that the 200 homes in the pilot sample can be included in the 998, meaning that only 798 additional homes need to be sampled.

SKILL DEVELOPMENT PROBLEMS FOR SECTION 8–4

The following set of problems is meant to test your understanding of the material in this section. Additional problems are found at the end of this chapter under this section heading.

11. Given the following information:

$$n = 100$$
$$x = 23$$

  a. Determine the 90 percent confidence interval for the population proportion.
  b. Determine the 95 percent confidence interval for the population proportion.

12. Given the following information:

$$n = 300$$
$$x = 221$$

  a. Determine the 80 percent confidence interval estimate for the population proportion.
  b. Determine the 95 percent confidence interval estimate for the population proportion.

13. Determine the sample size necessary to estimate the population proportion with a tolerable error of plus or minus 0.04 with 90 percent confidence. Assume $p = 0.50$ for the purpose of computing the required sample size.

14. What is the required sample size for estimating the population proportion with plus or minus 0.02 of the true value at 90 percent confidence. Assume that $p = 0.50$ for the purposes of determining the required sample size.

15. In determining the required sample size when estimating the population proportion, it is often recommended that the p value be set at 0.50. Discuss why this is and what the impact is on the computed sample size.

16. The makers of Stuffing-Puffing, the most popular childrens' toy of the year, are interested in estimating the proportion of parents who would buy a "Chattie-Wettie Stuffing-Puffing" if the company decided to market such a product. They have selected 200 customers who purchased the original Stuffing-Puffing toy and asked them whether they would buy the new toy. A total of 125 said "yes." Based on these data, what is the 90 percent confidence interval estimate for the true proportion of all former customers who will buy the new toy? Interpret your result.

17. The McGulp Company sells franchise fast-food stores throughout the southeast. As part of the franchise service provided to the individual stores, McGulp managers provide a variety of marketing research services. Recently they selected a random sample of 400 customers and asked them whether they would be interested in a new product called "finger-food." Of the 400 people surveyed, 45 indicated an interest in the new product. Based upon these results, determine the 95 percent confidence interval estimate for the true population proportion of customers who would be interested. Interpret the estimate.

18. KRTV-Channel 6 is the local ABC television affiliate in Denver, Colorado. The station manager is interested in estimating the percentage of her customers who watch the local news on Channel 6 and then switch to another network for the national news. An old survey indicated that the percentage was about 30 percent. She wishes to have her estimate be within plus or minus 0.03 of the true value and have 95 percent confidence in her estimate. How large a sample size is necessary?

19. United Airlines is interested in the percentage of its fliers who feel that the service aboard their flights is either very good or excellent. They wish the estimate to be within plus or minus 0.02 of the true percentage and they wish to have 98 percent confidence. How large a sample size is necessary?

20. The Minnesota Department of Lands has recently selected a sample of 100 taxpayers. The taxpayers were asked whether the state should provide more state parks and camping facilities. A total of sixty indicated "yes" to the question. A 95 percent confidence interval estimate was developed and provided to the director. However, the director was not satisfied with the precision of the estimate and asked that the width of the interval be cut in half. What size sample is necessary to achieve these results? How many new taxpayers need to be surveyed?

CONFIDENCE INTERVALS FOR ESTIMATING THE DIFFERENCE BETWEEN TWO POPULATION PARAMETERS—LARGE SAMPLES

8-5

Managers often have to estimate either the mean of a single population or the proportion of successes in a population. The tools we have discussed up to now are very useful for these estimates. However, managers will often have to estimate either the difference between two population means or the difference between two population proportions. These situations involve two populations and require random samples to be selected *independently* from each.

Difference between Two Population Means

The training director of a large industrial corporation is considering adopting one of two alternative training methods, referred to as "reward-based" and "motive-goal." The director has used each method on trial groups in the company and has maintained records on employee productivity after each training method. The manager would like to know the difference in average productivity scores for employees trained under the two methods.

The point estimator for the difference between population means, $(\mu_{x_1} - \mu_{x_2})$ is $(\overline{X}_1 - \overline{X}_2)$, the difference in sample means. As with a single sample mean, for large samples the sampling distribution of the difference, $(\overline{X}_1 - \overline{X}_2)$, will be normally distributed, with the center of the sampling distribution determined by equation 8–19:

$$E(\overline{X}_1 - \overline{X}_2) = \mu_{x_1} - \mu_{x_2}$$

(8–19)

The standard deviation of the difference between two sample means is determined by equation 8–20:

$$\sigma_{\bar{x}_1 - \bar{x}_2} = \sqrt{\frac{\sigma_{\bar{x}_1}^2}{n_1} + \frac{\sigma_{\bar{x}_2}^2}{n_2}} \qquad (8\text{--}20)$$

Suppose the training manager selects a random sample of 100 employee records for each training method and obtains the following results on productivity scores:

Reward-Based	Motive-Goal
$\overline{X}_1 = 94$ points	$\overline{X}_2 = 89$ points
$n_1 = 100$	$n_2 = 100$

From industry experience and federal government reports, the manager knows that the standard deviation for the reward-based method, σ_{x_1}, is 12 and that the standard deviation for the motive-goal method, σ_{x_2}, is 9.

The format for developing a confidence interval for estimating the difference between population means is the same as that for a single population mean. That is,

Point estimate ± (interval coefficient)(standard error of the estimate)

Thus, the 95 percent confidence interval for estimating the difference in average productivity for all employees in the reward-based versus the motive-goal programs is given by equation 8–21:

$$(\overline{X}_1 - \overline{X}_2) \pm Z \sqrt{\frac{\sigma_{x_1}^2}{n_1} + \frac{\sigma_{x_2}^2}{n_2}} \qquad (8\text{--}21)$$

Then,

$$(94 - 89) \pm 1.96 \sqrt{\frac{144}{100} + \frac{81}{100}}$$

$$5 \pm 2.94$$

$$2.06 \text{ points} \underline{\quad\quad} 7.94 \text{ points}$$

Therefore, the training director is confident that the average difference in productivity scores from the two training techniques is between 2.06 and 7.94 points. This indicates that the reward-based method tends to produce higher productivity scores on the average than does the motive-goal method. Based on these results, the training manager might decide to go with the reward-based system.

In the previous example, the population standard deviations (and variances) were assumed known. This will occasionally be the case, but in most decision situations, the standard deviations will not be known and will need to be estimated from the sample data. When the sample sizes are sufficiently large (n_1 and n_2 greater than 30), the sample standard deviations (or variances) can be substituted for population values, as shown in equation 8–22:

$$(\bar{X}_1 - \bar{X}_2) \pm Z \sqrt{\frac{S_{x_1}^2}{n_1} + \frac{S_{x_2}^2}{n_2}} \qquad (8\text{–}22)$$

Suppose a bus company has tested ninety tires from each of two brands and has found the following mileage information:

Brand A	Brand B
$\bar{X}_1 = 33{,}000$ mi	$\bar{X}_2 = 29{,}400$ mi
$S_{x_1} = 1{,}100$ mi	$S_{x_2} = 750$ mi
$n_1 = 90$	$n_2 = 90$

The 90 percent confidence interval for estimating the difference in tire mileage is

$$(\bar{X}_1 - \bar{X}_2) \pm 1.645 \sqrt{\frac{S_{x_1}^2}{n_1} + \frac{S_{x_2}^2}{n_2}}$$

$$(33{,}000 - 29{,}400) \pm 1.645 \sqrt{\frac{1{,}210{,}000}{90} + \frac{562{,}500}{90}}$$

$$3{,}600 \pm 230.85$$

$$3{,}369.15 \text{ miles} \underline{\qquad} 3{,}830.85 \text{ miles}$$

The bus company might use this information to help decide which brand of tires to buy for its fleet of buses. Based on these sample data, brand A tires seem to last longer than brand B tires, on the average.

Difference between Two Population Proportions

The quality control manager for Morgan electronics has been experimenting with two quality control systems. System 1 has been used on one assembly line, which has produced 15,000 computer power supplies. System 2 has been used on a second assembly line, which has produced 25,000 computer power supplies. The manager is interested in determining the difference in the proportion of defectives produced under each quality control system.

Although the quality control manager wants to know ($p_1 - p_2$), he cannot test every power supply unit. Instead, he will select a sample of units produced under each system and calculate ($\hat{p}_1 - \hat{p}_2$), the point estimate for the difference in population proportions. If the sample sizes are sufficiently large, the sampling distribution of ($\hat{p}_1 - \hat{p}_2$) will be approximately normally distributed with a mean and standard error as shown in equations 8–23 and 8–24.

$$E(\hat{p}_1 - \hat{p}_2) = (p_1 - p_2) \tag{8-23}$$

and

$$\sigma_{\hat{p}_1 - \hat{p}_2} = \sqrt{\frac{p_1 q_1}{n_1} + \frac{p_2 q_2}{n_2}} = \text{standard error of the sampling distribution} \tag{8-24}$$

Equation 8–24, the standard error of the sampling distribution, contains p_1 and p_2, the population proportions. The quality control manager can substitute the estimates, $\hat{p}_1$ and $\hat{p}_2$, for these values (equation 8–25):

$$S_{\hat{p}_1 - \hat{p}_2} = \sqrt{\frac{\hat{p}_1 \hat{q}_1}{n_1} + \frac{\hat{p}_2 \hat{q}_2}{n_2}} \tag{8-25}$$

Given equation 8–25, the quality control manager can develop a confidence interval estimate of $(p_1 - p_2)$ (equation 8–26):

$$(\hat{p}_1 - \hat{p}_2) \pm Z \sqrt{\frac{\hat{p}_1 \hat{q}_1}{n_1} + \frac{\hat{p}_2 \hat{q}_2}{n_2}} \tag{8-26}$$

As you can see, the format of equation 8–26 is the same as for all other confidence intervals. That is,

Point estimate ± (interval coefficient)(standard error of the sampling distribution)

Suppose the quality control manager has selected a sample of 400 computer power supplies from each assembly line and tested them, with the following results:

Line 1	Line 2
$\hat{p}_1 = 0.08$	$\hat{p}_2 = 0.06$
$\hat{q}_1 = 0.92$	$\hat{q}_2 = 0.94$
$n_1 = 400$	$n_1 = 400$

The manager wants a 98 percent confidence interval estimate for the difference in the proportion of defectives produced under the two systems. He would find the estimate as follows:

$$(\hat{p}_1 - \hat{p}_2) \pm 2.33 \sqrt{\frac{\hat{p}_1 \hat{q}_1}{n_1} + \frac{\hat{p}_2 \hat{q}_2}{n_2}}$$

$$(0.08 - 0.06) \pm 2.33 \sqrt{\frac{(0.08)(0.92)}{400} + \frac{(0.06)(0.94)}{400}}$$

$$0.02 \pm 0.042$$

$$-0.022 \underline{\hspace{1cm}} + 0.062$$

The manager is very confident that this interval includes the true difference between the proportion of defectives produced under the two quality control systems. Since the interval contains zero, the manager will conclude that, even though there is a difference between the two sample proportions, this difference is not large enough to conclude there is a significant difference between the two population proportions.

SKILL DEVELOPMENT PROBLEMS FOR SECTION 8–5

The following set of problems is meant to test your understanding of the material in this section. Additional problems are found at the end of this chapter under this section heading.

21. Given the following information:

$$n_1 = 100 \qquad n_2 = 150$$
$$\overline{X}_1 = 20 \qquad \overline{X}_2 = 25$$
$$S_1 = 6 \qquad S_2 = 9$$

a. Determine the 90 percent confidence interval estimate for the difference between population means. Interpret the estimate.

b. Determine the 98 percent confidence interval estimate for the difference between population means. Interpret the estimate.

22. Given the following information:

$$n_1 = 300 \qquad n_2 = 400$$
$$\overline{X}_1 = 120 \qquad \overline{X}_2 = 100$$
$$S_1 = 24 \qquad S_2 = 20$$

a. Determine the 95 percent confidence interval estimate for the difference between population means. Interpret the estimate.

b. Determine the 90 percent confidence interval estimate for the difference between population means. Interpret the estimate.

23. Given the folllowing information:

$$n_1 = 200 \qquad n_2 = 200$$
$$x_1/n_1 = 0.30 \qquad x_2/n_2 = 0.27$$

a. Determine the 90 percent confidence interval estimate for the difference between population proportions. Interpret the estimate.

b. Determine the 95 percent confidence interval estimate for the difference between population proportions. Interpret the estimate.

24. Given the following information:

$$n_1 = 100 \qquad n_2 = 200$$
$$x_1/n_1 = 0.60 \qquad x_2/n_2 = 0.67$$

a. Determine the 95 percent confidence interval estimate for the difference between population proportions. Interpret the estimate.

b. Determine the 80 percent confidence interval estimate for the difference between population proportions. Interpret the estimate.

25. The Shell Oil Company is interested in estimating the difference in the population proportions of customers who purchase unleaded gasoline in eastern states versus western states. They have selected a random sample of 1,200 eastern-state customers and 900 western-state customers; 852 of the eastern-state customers and 643 of the western-state customers purchased unleaded gasoline. Using a 95 percent confidence level, determine the estimate for difference in population proportions and interpret the estimate.

26. A marketing consulting firm was recently hired by a large retail hardware chain to study the buying habits of the chain's customers. As part of the study, the consultant selected a random sample of male customers and another random sample of female customers. The sampled customers were observed to determine how long they spent in the store per visit. The following data were recorded:

Male	*Female*
$n_1 = 250$	$n_2 = 350$
$\overline{X}_1 = 24$ minutes	$\overline{X}_2 = 53$ minutes
$S_{x_1} = 13$	$S_{x_2} = 34$

Based upon these sample data, what is the 90 percent confidence interval estimate for the difference between true average shopping times for males and females? Interpret your estimate.

27. Two companies that manufacture batteries for toys and other small electronics products have submitted their products to an independent testing agency. The agency tested 200 of each company's batteries and recorded the length of time the batteries lasted before failure. The following results were determined:

Company A	*Company B*
$\overline{X}_1 = 43.5$ hours	$\overline{X}_2 = 41.0$ hours
$S_1 = 3.6$	$S_2 = 5.0$

Based upon these data, determine the 95 percent confidence interval; estimate the difference in average life of the batteries for the two companies. Do these data indicate that one company's batteries will outlast the other company's batteries on average? Explain.

28. The Acme Cleaning Company is considering opening its next branch location in one of two cities in Texas. Before making a decision, they have done some market research. A sample of 200 homes in city 1 was selected and the residents were asked whether they would use a professional cleaning service at least once a year. Residents of two hundred homes in city 2 were asked the same question. In city 1, forty-five residents said "yes"; in city 2, 56 said "yes."

Based upon these sample data, determine the 98 percent confidence interval estimate for the difference in proportion of customers who will use a cleaning service at least once a year. Does this estimate provide the company with evidence to help in selecting between the two cities? Discuss.

COMPUTER APPLICATIONS

8-6

This chapter has introduced large-sample estimation. We have demonstrated how confidence intervals can be developed based upon sample data. If you are provided the summary statistics from a sample, such as the mean and standard deviation, the computations involved in developing a confidence interval are not too difficult. However, in many applications, a decision maker will have only the raw sample data. In these cases, a computer and appropriate statistical software can be very useful.

In this section, two computer applications for developing large sample confidence intervals are shown. In both cases, we use the MINITAB software package and the KIVZ-Channel 5 survey data (see table 2–10 in chapter 2). First, we develop a 95 percent confidence interval estimate of the population's mean income (VAR18). Table 8–1 shows the MINITAB output. Figure 8–5 shows the MINITAB commands used to generate the output. You should review the printout and make sure that you can interpret the interval estimate.

In the second example, we want to estimate the difference in average income (VAR18) between males and females (VAR10). Table 8–2 shows the computer output generated when the MINITAB commands in Figure 8–6 were used. Be sure that you can interpret the 95 percent confidence interval estimate.

TABLE 8–1
MINITAB output—95 percent confidence interval for income

```
THE ASSUMED SIGMA = 95.0
  N      MEAN      STDEV     SE MEAN      95.0 PERCENT INCOME
 50    24846.0    4800.5      13.4        (24819.6, 24872.4)
```

```
MTB> READ 'KIVZ5' into C1-C19
MTB> NAME C18 'INCOME'
MTB> OUTFILE = 'PRINTER'
MTB> ZINTERVAL 95 C18
```

FIGURE 8–5
MINITAB commands—confidence interval estimation

TABLE 8–2
MINITAB output—two-sample estimation, males vs. females income (C10 = 2 = female; C10 = 1 = male)

C10	N	MEAN	STDEV	SE MEAN
2	28	25661	5188	981
1	22	23809	4141	883

FIGURE 8–6
MINITAB commands—confidence interval estimation, income by sex

```
MTB> READ 'KIVZ5' into C1-C19
MTB> OUTFILE = 'PRINTER'
MTB> TWOT 95 C18 C10
```

CONCLUSIONS

$8\text{-}7$ Many decision-making applications involve estimating a population value from a sample of the population. This chapter introduced the concepts of statistical estimation for large samples. We discussed two types of estimates: point estimates and interval estimates.

Point estimates are values such as $\overline{X}$, S_x^2, $\hat{p}$, $(\overline{X}_1 - \overline{X}_2)$, and $(\hat{p}_1 - \hat{p}_2)$, which are calculated from a sample. Confidence interval estimates are recommended when a decision maker wants to estimate a population value and have an idea of the estimate's error. The decision maker can control the estimate's level of confidence and precision, but constantly faces a trade-off between these two factors and the required sample size.

Even if a confidence interval that meets the decision maker's precision and confidence requirements is developed, there is no guarantee the calculated interval will actually include the population value of interest. The decision maker must recognize that there is always a chance of error any time sampling and statistical estimation are involved. The best that can be said is that the decision maker has a measure of the chance the interval includes the true population value. If the confidence level is increased, the decision maker can be even more confident. Formulas were presented for estimating population values when the population standard deviation is known and when it is unknown. Generally, the standard deviation will not be known, so the formulas that employ estimates of σ will be used most frequently.

The chapter glossary presents a summary of several new terms that were presented in this chapter. Several equations that can be used to develop interval estimates of various population parameters are listed immediately following the glossary.

CHAPTER GLOSSARY

confidence interval An interval developed from sample values such that if all possible intervals were calculated, a percentage equal to the confidence level would contain the population value of interest.

interval coefficient The table value (Z value in this chapter) associated with a particular level of confidence. For example:

Confidence	Interval Coefficient
90	$Z = 1.645$
95	$Z = 1.96$
98	$Z = 2.33$
99	$Z = 2.58$

parameter A descriptive measure of the population that has a fixed value. Examples are the population mean, μ_x, and the population standard deviation, σ_x.

precision The width of the confidence interval.

point estimate A single number determined from a sample used to estimate a population parameter.

tolerable error One-half the width of the confidence interval. Tolerable error is used in determining required sample size.

unbiased estimator An estimator whose expected value equals the population parameter. If μ_x is the population parameter, $\overline{X}$ is an unbiased estimate if $E(\overline{X}) = \mu_x$.

CHAPTER FORMULAS

Standard error of the mean

σ_x *known*

$$\sigma_{\overline{x}} = \frac{\sigma_x}{\sqrt{n}}$$

σ_x *unknown*

$$S_{\overline{x}} = \frac{S_x}{\sqrt{n}}$$

Sample mean

$$\overline{X} = \frac{\Sigma X}{n}$$

Sample variance

$$S_x^2 = \frac{\Sigma(X - \overline{X})^2}{n - 1}$$

Sample standard deviation

$$S_x = \sqrt{\frac{\Sigma(X - \overline{X})^2}{n - 1}}$$

Confidence interval for μ_x

$$\overline{X} \pm Z\sigma_{\overline{x}}$$

Standard error of the difference between two means

Population variances known

$$\sigma_{\overline{x}_1 - \overline{x}_2} = \sqrt{\frac{\sigma_{x_1}^2}{n_1} + \frac{\sigma_{x_2}^2}{n_2}}$$

Population variances unknown

$$S_{\overline{x}_1 - \overline{x}_2} = \sqrt{\frac{S_{x_1}^2}{n_1} + \frac{S_{x_2}^2}{n_2}}$$

Confidence interval for $\mu_{x_1} - \mu_{x_1}$

$$(\overline{X}_1 - \overline{X}_2) \pm Z\sqrt{\frac{\sigma_{x_1}^2}{n_1} + \frac{\sigma_{x_2}^2}{n_2}}$$

Sample proportion

$$\hat{p} = \frac{x}{n}$$

Standard error of proportions

$$\sigma_{\hat{p}} = \sqrt{\frac{pq}{n}}$$

and

$$S_{\hat{p}} = \sqrt{\frac{\hat{p}\hat{q}}{n}}$$

Confidence interval for p

$$\hat{p} \pm ZS_{\hat{p}}$$

Standard error of the difference between two proportions

p_1 and p_2 *known*

$$\sigma_{\hat{p}_1 - \hat{p}_2} = \sqrt{\frac{p_1 q_1}{n_1} + \frac{p_2 q_2}{n_2}}$$

p_1 and p_2 *unknown*

$$S_{\hat{p}_1 - \hat{p}_2} = \sqrt{\frac{\hat{p}_1 \hat{q}_1}{n_1} + \frac{\hat{p}_2 \hat{q}_2}{n_2}}$$

Confidence interval for $(p_1 - p_2)$

$$(\hat{p}_1 - \hat{p}_2) \pm Z S_{\hat{p}_1 - \hat{p}_2}$$

Sample size
One population mean

$$n = \frac{Z^2 \sigma_x^2}{e^2}$$

One population proportion

$$n = \frac{Z^2 pq}{e^2}$$

Confidence interval for population total

$$N(\overline{X}) \pm Z \sqrt{N^2 \frac{S^2}{n} \left(\frac{N - n}{N}\right)}$$

SOLVED PROBLEMS

1. The manager at a major U.S. airport wishes to estimate the population of flights that arrived late at the airport last year for a report she must submit to the Civil Aeronautics Administration. She has indicated that a 95 percent confidence interval is required with precision of percent?
   a. How large a sample should the airport manager select? (*Hint:* Use $\hat{p} = 0.5$ and explain why you can use this value.)
   b. Using the sample size determined in part a, suppose the sample proportion, $\hat{p}$, is 0.24. Develop the confidence interval and provide the appropriate interpretation for the airport manager.

Solutions:

   a. To determine the appropriate sample size, we need the following information:

$$\text{Confidence level} = 95\%$$
$$\text{Interval coefficient} = 1.96$$
$$\text{Precision} = 0.04$$

$$\text{Tolerable error} = 0.02$$
$$\hat{p} = 0.5$$

(Note that using $\hat{p} = 0.5$ implies the greatest possible variance in the sampling distribution. Consequently the sample size we find will always be large enough to meet the confidence level and precision requirements.) Then

$$e = Z \sqrt{\frac{\hat{p}\hat{q}}{n}}$$

$$0.02 = 1.96 \sqrt{\frac{(0.5)(0.5)}{n}}$$

$$n = \frac{(1.96)^2(0.5)(0.5)}{(0.02)^2}$$

$$= 2{,}401$$

b. The 95 percent confidence interval is

$$\hat{p} \pm 1.96 \sqrt{\frac{(0.24)(0.76)}{2{,}401}}$$

$$0.24 \pm 0.017$$

$$0.223 \underline{\qquad} 0.257$$

Note that this interval is more precise than that required by the airport manager. The reason for this is that $\hat{p}$ calculated is lower than the $\hat{p} = 0.5$ which was used to find the required sample size.

2. Suppose the airport manager in solved problem 1 wishes to estimate the difference in proportion of late flights for two airlines that use the airport. She has indicated that a 95 percent confidence interval is required, with precision equal to 0.03.

a. What sample size is needed from each airline to provide an interval estimate with this confidence and precision? Let the sample sizes from the two airlines be equal. Also, use $\hat{p} = 0.24$ for both airlines since this value was calculated for a sample from all airlines using this airport.

b. Using the sample size determined in part a, the airport manager found the following:

$$\hat{p}_1 = 0.22 \quad \text{and} \quad \hat{p}_2 = 0.27$$

Develop the 95 percent confidence interval estimate for the difference between population proportions.

Solutions:

a. To determine the required sample size, we must perform the following calculation:

$$e = 1.96 \sqrt{\frac{\hat{p}_1 \hat{q}_1}{n_1} + \frac{\hat{p}_2 \hat{q}_2}{n_2}}$$

Since $n_1 = n_2 = n$, we get

$$0.015 = 1.96 \sqrt{\frac{(0.24)(0.76)}{n} + \frac{(0.24)(0.76)}{n}}$$

$$n = 6{,}228.5$$
$$= 6{,}229$$

Thus the airport manager needs to study 6,229 flights from each airline. This is quite a large sample. Chances are the manager will have to decrease the confidence level, the desired precision, or both.

b. The 95 percent confidence interval is

$$(\hat{p}_1 - \hat{p}_2) \pm 1.96 \sqrt{\frac{\hat{p}_1 \hat{q}_1}{n_1} + \frac{\hat{p}_2 \hat{q}_2}{n_2}}$$

$$(0.22 - 0.27) \pm 1.96 \sqrt{\frac{(0.22)(0.78)}{6{,}229} + \frac{(0.27)(0.73)}{6{,}229}}$$

$$(0.22 - 0.27) \pm 0.015$$

$$-0.065 \underline{\qquad} -0.035$$

Thus the manager is confident that the true difference is between -0.065 and -0.035 (airline 2 has a higher proportion of late flights).

ADDITIONAL PROBLEMS

Section 8–2

29. Discuss in your own words the difference between a point estimator and an interval estimator.

30. Give at least one business-related example for which a point estimate would be used rather than an interval estimate.

31. Give at least one business-related example for which an interval estimate would be preferred over a point estimate.

32. Discuss in your own words the general advantage of an interval estimate over a point estimate.

Section 8–3

33. The service manager for Hyatt Motors in Kansas City is interested in estimating the average miles people drive between oil changes. Suppose the standard deviation is known to be 300 miles. A sample of 200 car owners was selected from among those that had their car serviced at Hyatt Motors at least twice during the past year. The sample mean was 2,250 miles between oil changes.
   a. Define the population of interest and identify which population parameter the manager is interested in estimating.
   b. Determine the point estimate of interest. Do you think the point estimate is equal to the actual population mean?
   c. Develop a 90 percent confidence interval estimate for the population mean and provide an interpretation of this interval.

34. The United Automobile Association recently selected a random sample of 400 people who had purchased a new car three years ago. The U.A.A. is interested in estimating the average mileage for three-year-old cars. If the sample showed a mean of 26,355 miles and a standard deviation of 4,250 miles:
   a. What is the point estimate for the population mean?
   b. Develop a 95 percent confidence interval estimate for the population mean and interpret this estimate.
   c. Develop a 90 percent confidence interval estimate and compare this estimate with the one developed in part b.

35. Referring to problem 34, suppose the same sample results had been derived from a sample of 800 car owners:
   a. Develop a 95 percent confidence interval estimate for the population mean and interpret this value.
   b. Compare this interval estimate to the one developed in problem 34b. Which interval would be preferred and why?

36. The Florida Highway Department is studying traffic patterns on a busy highway near Miami. As part of the study, the department needs to estimate the average number of vehicles that pass an off-ramp each day. A random sample of sixty-four days gives $\overline{X} = 14,205$ and $S_x = 1,010$. Develop the 90 percent confidence interval estimate for μ_x, the average number of cars per day, and interpret your results.

37. Referring to problem 36, suppose the Highway Department officials after careful analysis decide they really need 99 percent confidence. What is the 99 percent confidence interval estimate of μ_x, the average number of cars passing the off-ramp? Interpret your results.

38. After calculating the confidence interval in problem 37, the Highway Department officials feel the precision is too low for their needs. They feel the precision should be 300. Given this precision and 99 percent confidence, what size sample is required?

39. At a recent board meeting a district manager made the following statement: "We have selected a sample of potential customers and calculated a 95 percent confidence interval for the estimate of those who will purchase our new product. Based on these results, I am 95 percent sure the true proportion is between 0.52 and 0.71." Comment on this manager's statement.

40. For each of the following confidence levels, determine the appropriate interval coefficient:
   a. 90 percent
   b. 95 percent
   c. 99 percent
   d. 94 percent
   e. 50 percent
   f. 89 percent
   g. 80 percent

41. This chapter stated that an increase in sample size will improve the precision of a confidence interval estimate. Discuss in your own words what the term *precision* means.

42. Would you agree that an increase in sample size will increase the confidence level of an interval estimate? Why or why not?

43. What is the effect on an estimate's precision of increasing the confidence level of the estimate? What is the reason for this change?

44. You have determined that the sample size necessary to estimate the average major league baseball game attendance with 90 percent confidence and tolerable error of 500 people is $n = 40$ games. Suppose the baseball commissioner states the precision is too low. What are his alternatives for increasing precision? Discuss the advantages and disadvantages of each.

45. The Felton State Bank vice-president of operations is considering doing a study to estimate the average number of monthly transactions to savings accounts at the bank. A previous study indicated that the standard deviation is about 2.8 transactions. If she desires a tolerable error of no more than plus or minus 0.30 transaction and 90 percent confidence, how large a sample is required?

   Further suppose the Felton Bank vice-president of operations feels that her first requirement for precision of plus or minus 0.30 transaction needs to be changed to plus or minus 0.20 transaction. Keeping the confidence level at 90 percent, how large a sample will be required?

46. The Illinois State Revenue Department is interested in estimating the total income earned by corn farmers per acre of land farmed in the state. To obtain a 95 percent confidence interval for the total income, he selected a random sample of 150 farmers from the 8,200 in the population. The sample mean showed $38.00 per acre income, with a standard deviation of $12.00.

   a. Develop a 95 percent confidence interval estimate for the mean per acre income and interpret this estimate.

   b. Develop a 95 percent confidence interval estimate for the total income per acre for all farmers within the population and interpret this estimate.

47. A recent study was commissioned by the New Jersey Gaming Commission, an organization that oversees the legalized gambling operations in New Jersey. It was interested in estimating the total tips earned by blackjack dealers in Atlantic City. To arrive at this estimate, a sample of forty dealers was selected on one randomly selected day. The average for the sample was $55.80, with a standard deviation of $9.30.

   a. What is the 95 percent confidence interval estimate for the mean tips earned per day by a blackjack dealer? Interpret this estimate.

   b. Assuming there are 2,400 blackjack dealers in Atlantic City, what is the 95 percent confidence interval estimate for the total daily dollars earned in tips by blackjack dealers?

48. Each January an independent polling company conducts a survey of television viewers to provide an estimate of the average number of hours spent by Americans watching television per day. The January 1984 report showed that for a random sample of 1,700 people the mean time spent watching television was 7.2 hours, with a standard deviation of 2.3 hours.

   a. What is the point estimate for the average number of hours Americans spend watching television per day?

   b. What is the 97 percent confidence interval estimate for the average number of hours Americans spend watching television per day?

   c. A representative for the polling company said that this survey sampled 400 more people than the previous year's survey. He said that the reason the point estimate jumped to 7.2 hours per day from 6.5 hours per day may have been because the larger sample might have included more extremes on the high side of the viewing time distribution. Therefore, the 7.2 value might be an "aberration." Comment on this statement and the soundness of the reasoning behind it.

49. Suppose the following confidence intervals estimating the mean age in a southern retail market area have been constructed from three different simple random samples. Assume the age distribution is normal.

Sample	Lower Limit	Upper Limit
1	39.0	50.0
2	40.0	51.9
3	42.0	50.0

   a. If the three samples had the same value for S_x^2 and all three intervals were constructed with a 95 percent confidence level, which sample was the largest? Explain how you know this. Which sample was the smallest? How do you know this?

b. Suppose the size of sample 2 was thirty-six and had a sample variance of 256. Approximately what level of confidence should be associated with this interval?

c. Suppose each of the three samples contained sixty observations and all three intervals were constructed with an 80 percent confidence level. Which sample had the smallest standard deviation? Explain.

d. Compute the standard error for each sample, assuming the values in part c apply. Then determine what change in sample size would be necessary to cut the tolerable error by one half.

e. Which sample had the smallest mean? How do you know?

50. The manager at the Chart House Restaurant has started receiving complaints about the waiting time before being served in the dining room. The manager takes a sample of 120 diners and finds that the mean time from entrance to serving is 17.56 minutes, with a standard deviation of 4.5 minutes.

a. What is the confidence interval estimate of average serving time if the manager specifies a 94 percent confidence level?

b. What should the manager say to the next irate customer who enters his office claiming to have waited in the dining room for forty-five minutes without being served?

c. Can you see any sampling problems that may affect the conclusions you can draw from the interval calculated in part a?

51. The Government Accounting Office (GAO) wants to estimate the average yearly repair cost for government copying machines. In some regions the government has bought a repair contract that costs $500 per year for each machine. The GAO wants to know whether this is a fair price. Fortunately, government offices in several sections of the country do not have the repair contract and have been repairing the machines on an individual basis. The GAO has taken a random sample of 250 annual repair invoices and has found the average cost to be $426.78, with a sample standard deviation of $167.18.

Based on these sample data, would you recommend discontinuing the repair contract?

52. Great Northern Chemical has developed a new, effective insect repellent. The leading spray on the market now advertises an effective time of eight hours. From past experience, Great Northern knows that the time a spray is effective is a function of personal skin chemistry, and the variability remains the same no matter what the type of spray. This variability gives a variance of 2.3. Great Northern field tests its spray on sixty-five volunteers and finds it to be effective for an average of 8.85 hours.

Can Great Northern state, based on a 90 percent confidence level estimate, that its spray is more effective than the leading brand?

Section 8–4

53. The makers of Word-Smart, a word-processing package for microcomputers, are interested in estimating the proportion of their packages that are being used in business settings rather than for personal uses. The sales manager believes the figure is close to 70 percent.

a. If the sales manager's figure is used, what random-sample size should the company select if it wishes to estimate the true proportion with 95 percent confidence with a tolerable error of plus or minus 0.03?

b. Suppose that the company does select a sample of the size computed in part a, and the $\hat{p}$ value equaled 0.60. Comment on whether the sample size computed in part a was large enough to allow for a tolerable error of plus or minus 0.03 with 95 percent confidence.

54. The manager of the North Saw Mill needs to estimate the percentage of clear and standard redwood contained in a recent shipment of logs. She samples a random selection of logs before they go to the drying kilns.

a. If out of a sample of 350 boards she finds 89 clear, what is the 97 percent confidence level estimate of the overall proportion of clear boards?

b. Suppose, in an effort to increase the estimate's precision, the manager looks at an additional 350 boards and finds 249 of standard quality. What is her new estimate for the proportion of clear boards? (Standard boards have knots in them.)

55. The federal government has mandated that to qualify for federal highway funds, states must ensure that at least 70 percent of the cars traveling on their highways are obeying the 55-mile-per-hour speed limit where required. A team of federal inspectors has gone to a southern state and randomly checked the speed of 180 cars. They found 117 obeying the limit where required. Based on this evidence, and using a 96 percent confidence level, can the inspectors make a case for denying the state highway funds?

56. The district manager, upon reviewing the report submitted by the inspectors in problem 55, objects strongly. He claims the sample size was much too small to draw any meaningful conclusions. Do you agree or disagree? If the district manager wants to limit the tolerable error of all future estimates to 0.02, how large a sample size is needed?

57. A consumer organization has recently mounted a campaign to make using seat belts mandatory in a southern state. As part of the argument, the organization has sampled 1,000 accident records and found that in 140 cases, people were thrown from their vehicles. Based on this sample evidence, calculate and interpret a 90 percent confidence interval estimate for the true proportion of accidents in which people are thrown from their vehicles.

58. You have just completed a poll for a political candidate and have estimated the percentage of voters who will vote for her at 0.51 ± 0.029. She is not happy with this estimate and would like a precision of 0.02. If each interview costs $1.75, how much will it cost to give her the interval width she wants? She will accept a 95 percent confidence level.

Section 8–5

59. The Kingfield Service Corporation provides technical support for typewriters and word-processing equipment in the Detroit area. Recently the company's manager for service was asked to recommend a word-processing system to an automaker in Detroit. Although there were many systems she could have recommended, she narrowed the choice down to two brands: the Hawk/System 8000 and the Mercury–D750. Both systems are priced about the same, but the manager was uncertain about maintenance costs.

She decided to select a random sample of forty owners of each system and obtain their maintenance records for the first year of ownership. She recorded repair costs for each brand as follows:

Hawk/System 8000	Mercury–D750
$\overline{X}_1 = \$1375.00$	$\overline{X}_2 = \$1190.00$
$S_1 = \$201.00$	$S_2 = \$308.00$
$n_1 = 40$	$n_2 = 40$

a. Determine the point estimate for the difference in average repair costs for the two brands of word-processing systems.

b. Develop and interpret the 95 percent confidence interval for estimating the difference in population means for repair costs.

c. Based on your estimate in part b, what should the manager conclude with respect to word-processing-system average repair costs for the two systems? All other things being equal, which, if either, of these two systems should the manager recommend? Discuss.

60. Referring to problem 59, the Kingfield Service Corporation knows the automaker is also concerned with system down time. Suppose the service manager for Kingfield also recorded the down time during the first year for the systems owned by each of the businesses sampled, and arrived at these summary statistics:

Hawk/System 8000	Mercury—D750
$\overline{X}_1 = 16.3$ hours	$\overline{X}_2 = 12.8$ hours
$S_1 = 2.0$ hours	$S_2 = 3.8$ hours
$n_1 = 40$	$n_2 = 40$

a. Develop a 90 percent confidence interval estimate for the difference in average down time for the two machines. Interpret this estimate.

b. Referring to the interval developed in part a, assuming all other things are equal, do the sample data provide evidence to support one system over the other based on average down time?

c. Referring to your answers to part a and b of this problem and also to parts b and c of problem 59, what conclusions might be reached with respect to the word-processing systems? Discuss.

61. The Army purchasing department is seeking suppliers of black oxfords because the previous supplier has stopped making this type of shoe. Since these shoes are issued to new recruits and these recruits do a lot of marching, the Army is particularly concerned with the durability of the soles. They have devised a shoe tester that rubs the shoe bottom against a slab of concrete. The testers monitor the time needed to rub a hole in the sole.

The Army asks for a sample of 100 from each of two shoe manufacturers, but part of one shipment is lost. The following results are found:

	Manufacturer A	Manufacturer B
Sample size	100	80
Average time	3.2 hours	2.9 hours
Standard deviation	0.86 hours	0.79 hours

a. What is the 98 percent confidence level estimate for the difference between the average wear times for the shoes of the two manufacturers?
b. Based on this interval, should the Army prefer one manufacturer over the other?

62. A small metal fabricator is developing a new material to use on stove tops in place of stainless steel. Although initial appearance is important, so is hardness. The fabricator has developed a measure of hardness based on resistance to scrubbing. Since the field has been limited to two materials based on previous tests, the fabricator has decided to market the material with the higher average hardness coefficient. The following test results are found:

	Material 1	Material 2
Sample size	64	64
Hardness coefficient average	0.66	0.64
Standard deviation	0.08	0.063

The manufacturing department has a slight preference for material 2. Is there any reason this material should not be the one marketed? You must pick your own confidence level.

63. The manager whose department operates a fleet of company cars is trying to decide on which brand of tires to use. Her choices are brand F and brand M, and the price per tire is the same for both brands. The manager takes a sample of sixty-four tires from brand F and fifty-five tires from brand M. She finds the following values:

	Brand F	Brand M
Average mileage	42,156	43,414
Sample standard deviation	3,455	2,981

Based on this sample information, is there any reason to prefer one brand of tires based on its average mileage? Use a confidence level of 94 percent.

64. The Early Dawn Egg Farm is trying to decide between two brands of egg containers. The major consideration is to prevent breakage during shipment. Early Dawn Egg Farm ships 500 eggs in each type of container, with the following results:

	Brand 1	Brand 2
Percent broken	1.7	2.2

Using 95 percent confidence, can one brand be concluded to be better than the other in preventing breakage?

65. The research department of an appliance manufacturing firm has developed a solid-state switch for its blender which the department claims will reduce from 6 percent to 3 percent the percentage of appliances being returned under the one-year full warranty. To test this claim, the testing department selects a group of the blenders manufactured with the new switch and subjects them to a normal year's worth of wear.

   a. If out of 250 blenders tested with the new switch, nine would have been returned, can you accept the research department's claim? Use a 95 percent confidence level.
   b. The testing department also tests 250 blenders with the old switch and finds that sixteen fail. Is there reason to believe the new switch outperforms the old switch?

66. The personnel director at a large southern electronics plant is not satisfied with the present training program. He feels that although the present program is extensive and expensive, too many people must be released because of inadequate work even after completing training. Unfortunately, he really doesn't know what percentage are released for inadequate work and what percentage are released for some other reason.

   In any event, he has been considering implementing a new training program and would like to compare the results of the new program with those of the old. He decides to randomly separate the next group of new trainees into two groups, train each group entirely by one of the two methods, and monitor the results. After several months, he has found the following:

	New Method	Old Method
Group size	214	215
No. released for poor work	63	72

   a. Using a 96 percent confidence level, is there any reason to change training methods?
   b. Suppose both methods are equivalent in cost, but trainees seem to like the new method better than the old. Is there any reason not to change training methods?

STATE DEPARTMENT OF TRANSPORTATION CASE STUDY PROBLEMS

The following questions and problems pertain directly to the State Department of Transportation case study and data base introduced in chapter 1. The questions and problems were written assuming that you will have access to a computer and appropriate statistical software. The data base containing 100 observations and seventeen variables is shown in table 1C–1 in chapter 1. *In the following problems, assume that the sampling was performed according to a simple random sampling procedure.*

1. Herb Kriner would like an estimate of the average age of the drivers in the state. He would like you to provide the estimate in the form of a 95 percent confidence level. Be sure to interpret your estimate.

2. Variable X_5 is the total convictions for driving-related citations in the past three years. Herb Kriner would like a 90 percent confidence interval estimate for the average number of convictions for drivers in the state. Be sure to interpret the interval.

3. For those drivers who were insured ($X_{17} = 1$), provide a 95 percent confidence interval estimate for the number of years of formal education. Interpret the interval estimate.

4. Referring to problem 3, suppose the interval estimate is not precise enough to satisfy Herb Kriner. What must the sample size be to reduce the width by half without changing the confidence level? Show your calculations and prepare a short letter to Herb discussing your results.

5. Develop a 95 percent confidence interval estimate for the percentage of vehicles in the state which are insured. Interpret the interval.

6. Determine a 90 percent confidence interval estimate for the percentage of drivers in the state who use their seat belts.

7. Based on those drivers in the sample who were wearing a seat belt, what is the 90 percent confidence interval for the percentage of vehicles insured and driven by belted drivers? Interpret the interval estimate.

C A S E S

8A Amalgamated Trucking Company

The Amalgamated Trucking Company has just lost a labor arbitration suit in which it was accused of wrongly dismissing Al Farr, one of its drivers. The dismissal was ruled to be a violation of the union contract. In the current labor contract both parties (union and management) agreed that all disputes that cannot be settled directly between the two parties be placed in binding arbitration. In the past few months there have been other cases arbitrated, and Amalgamated has always been the victor. However, in this case the ruling states that Al Farr must be rehired and given back pay equivalent to the amount he would have earned in the nine months since he was dismissed. The arbitrator stated, as is common in the case of this sort, that Al Farr must be ''made whole.''

Amalgamated Trucking pays its drivers an hourly wage with time-and-a-half for overtime and double-time for holidays. The hours worked each week depend on the routes assigned. The assignment of routes is done randomly. Thus in some weeks cer-

TABLE 8C–1

	Quarter 1	Quarter 2	Quarter 3
Regular hours per week			
$\overline{X}$	39.4	39.7	39.6
S_x	1.6	2.1	1.3
Overtime hours per week			
$\overline{X}$	10.3	9.1	11.0
S_x	3.7	2.9	4.4
Holiday hours per quarter			
$\overline{X}$	12.7	6.2	8.8
S_x	3.1	4.7	2.6

tain drivers receive substantial overtime work and therefore more pay, while other drivers receive no overtime pay at all.

Dan Thomas, supervisor of Amalgamated Trucking personnel relations, has been assigned the task of determining the amount of back pay that should be awarded to Al Farr. The arbitrator will determine whether the amount proposed by Amalgamated Trucking is adequate, so Dan knows that he must be able to substantiate his figures.

The issue of back pay is complicated. The union has suggested a maximum-hours method in which Al Farr would receive pay equivalent to his pay rate multiplied by the maximum number of hours worked by any employee during the same nine-month period at Amalgamated Trucking. Dan is resisting this plan because of the precedent it would set. At the same time, he has admitted that he does not know the exact amount that Al Farr should receive.

Because he must have a figure by Wednesday, Dan has decided to use personnel records to attempt to arrive at a dollar amount for Al that will be fair. During the first six months that Al Farr was out of work, he would have been paid $7.75 per hour, and $8.10 per hour during the final three months. Personnel department records show hourly work records for all Amalgamated Trucking drivers. A sampling procedure Dan selected required him to pull a random sample of fifty employee records for each of the last three quarters (one quarter = three months). Table 8C–1 shows the results of the sampling after several calculations have been made.

Dan faces a long evening trying to make sense out of this information so he can make an effective presentation to the arbitrator.

8B The Harris Collection Agency

The Harris Collection Agency, located in Tempe, Arizona, is owned by L. C. Harris and his aging mother, Agnes. The company buys aged accounts receivable from other firms at a fraction of the face value with the hopes of collecting more dollars of the accounts receivable than they paid for the accounts.

On small deals, L. C. relies on his past experience with this particular type of business in knowing what to offer. In most cases, the Harris Collection Agency is able to turn a small profit this way. However, for large deals, L. C. likes to approach the issue of how much to pay on a somewhat more scientific basis.

Recently the Harris Collection Agency was made aware of an opportunity of a lifetime. To hear L. C. tell it, if the right price could be negotiated, the opportunity existed to "heal the company and Mama too." The Vernlee Sales and Distribution Company of Providence, Rhode Island, was being bought out by a large conglomerate, and the existing accounts receivable were to remain as an asset of the current owners of the Vernlee Company. These owners, however, planned to sell the accounts receivable to a collection agency since they would not have the organization required to collect the accounts themselves.

On the flight to Providence, L. C. reviewed in his mind the proposal he would make to the Vernlee owners. He would ask for permission to randomly select fifty accounts from the ledger of accounts receivable. The Harris Collection Agency would then go through its usual means to collect the accounts within a one-month period. Whatever money collected during this time from the accounts sampled would be returned to the Vernlee owners. But L. C. would use the information obtained from the same data to determine his bid price.

As he sipped on an iced tea somewhere over Nebraska he reasoned to himself that this would be a good deal for both himself and the current owners of the accounts because typically the discount rate is around 90 percent. However, since these accounts are not necessarily delinquent or difficult to collect, Harris might be able to pay substantially more than ten cents on the dollar and still make a good profit. As the plane touched down, L. C. felt quite confident that he would convince the owner that it was in both their best interests to approach the sale this way.

Steven Langly, representing the owners of the accounts receivable at the meeting with L. C. Harris, indicated that as of the latest computer run there were 78,255 accounts receivable with an average age of seventy-eight days and a total dollar value of $15,278,325.00. Further, the owners had already received an offer of 22 percent, which they were considering. This latter news further upset L. C. Harris. This meant that if he were to be successful he would need to bid in excess of $3.5 million. L. C. thought that maybe the deal was just too big for his company, but thought that as long as he was there he might as well present his approach to Langly.

It was clear by the time he concluded his presentation that Langly was impressed. After discussing the details a little more, Langly said that he would call Tempe, Arizona, in two days with an answer one way or another, but as far as he was concerned the one-month wait was a no-lose situation for the owners since the 22 percent offer was good for sixty days.

When the call came, L. C. was both relieved and nervous. The Vernlee people had agreed to the terms, and as L. C. looked out his office window, he knew all that was required now was for the random sample to be selected and for his collection staff to go to work.

With the assistance of a disinterested third party trained in sampling procedures, a sample of fifty accounts was selected. The following data reflect the dollars actually collected by the Harris Collection Agency for each account sampled.

$311.00	$ 0.00	$ 25.00	$475.00	$146.00
46.00	71.00	0.00	112.00	18.00
133.00	0.00	0.00	0.00	55.00
55.00	0.00	14.00	120.00	125.00
90.00	302.00	106.00	80.00	140.00
127.00	155.00	245.00	50.00	26.00
219.00	11.00	0.00	0.00	0.00
27.00	0.00	15.00	17.00	55.00
0.00	95.00	12.00	90.00	30.00
18.00	100.00	33.00	0.00	275.00

L. C. needs some assistance in analyzing these data. In particular, in light of the new bid of 22 percent of the accounts' value, should he bother to submit a bid? Write a short report to him explaining why or why not, and discuss if a bid is justified. Provide some guidance for L. C. in determining what the bid should be.

REFERENCES

Hayes, Glenn E., and Romig, Harry G. *Modern Quality Control.* Enrico, Calif.: Glencoe Publishing, 1982.

Pfaffenberger, Roger C., and Patterson, James H. *Statistical Methods for Business and Economics,* Revised Edition. Homewood, Ill.: Irwin, 1981.

Winkler, Robert L., and Hayes, William L. *Statistics: Probability, Inference, and Decision,* 2nd Edition. New York: Holt, Rinehart and Winston, 1975.

Wonnacott, Thomas H., and Wonnacott, Ronald J. *Introductory Statistics for Business and Economics,* 3rd Edition. New York: Wiley, 1984.

INTRODUCTION TO HYPOTHESIS TESTING— LARGE SAMPLES

9

WHY DECISION MAKERS NEED TO KNOW

Chapter 8 introduced the basic techniques of large-sample statistical estimation. These techniques have many business applications. All applications, however, have a common bond: sample information is used to help decision makers determine what the population is like. Although the marketing researcher, the accountant, and the operating manager all have their particular uses for statistical sampling, they all start out knowing very little about the population of interest. Through random sampling they are able to estimate population values such as the mean, variance, and proportion. This process of using sample information to statistically decide on the state of a population is called **statistical inference.**

The estimation process of going from sample to population is useful and so is often applied. However, there is another class of problems where sampling and statistical techniques are employed. In this class decision makers are faced with a claim, or **hypothesis,** about the population and must be able to substantiate or refute this claim. For example, a producer of electronic components claims that no more than 3 percent of its components are defective. Before you buy 100,000 electronic components, you would want to test the manufacturer's claim. Since you could not feasibly test each component, you would select a sample and use the sample information to decide whether there really are fewer than 3 percent defectives in the shipment.

This chapter introduces statistical techniques used to test claims about population values. All decision makers need to have a solid understanding of these techniques if they are to be able to use the information available in a sample effectively.

CHAPTER OBJECTIVES

This chapter will introduce statistical hypothesis testing for large-sample applications. Hypothesis testing requires that decision makers first formulate a position or make a claim regarding the decision environment they are dealing with. Then they select a sample and, based on its contents, either affirm that this position is correct or conclude it is wrong. This chapter will demonstrate how these predetermined positions or claims are formulated and how data are used to substantiate or refute the positions. The two types of errors that can be made in hypothesis testing will be discussed. The material in this chapter will also show how to establish decision-making rules in light of the chances of making each type of error.

STUDENT OBJECTIVES

After studying the material in this chapter, you should be able to

1. Discuss three forms of statistical hypotheses and know how to use sample information to test each.
2. Correctly identify and formulate a decision rule to accompany each statistical hypothesis.
3. Identify the two forms of potential error in hypothesis testing and discuss these errors and their consequences.
4. Develop the operating characteristic curve and power curve associated with each decision rule.
5. Recognize business applications in which statistical hypothesis testing can be performed.

REASONS FOR TESTING HYPOTHESES

9-1   Most managers would greatly increase their decision-making accuracy if they knew the exact values of all the measures in their environments. Unfortunately they seldom do. Previous chapters have spent considerable time discussing why managers need to gather data by sampling. Many times managers know what a population value should be because of company policy or contract specification and must be able to use sample information to determine whether the policy or contract specification is being satisfied. For example, the Rock-Dee Corporation has a contract to produce a worm gear that will be used in Army helicopters. The contract specifies that the gears must have an average diameter of 3.4 inches. Further, 99 percent of all gears must be within 0.05 inch of this average. Certainly the Rock-Dee Corporation is interested in knowing whether it is satisfying the contract. A sample of gears could be selected, and based on the sample information, the production and quality control managers would decide whether or not to ship the last batch of gears.

Because information contained in a sample is always subject to sampling error, the decision regarding the gear production may be incorrect. Decision makers must recognize that the chance of making the wrong decision always exists.

Statistical hypothesis testing allows managers to use a structured analytical method to make decisions. It lets them make the decisions in such a way that the chances of decision errors can be controlled, or at least measured. Even though statistical hypothesis testing does not eliminate the uncertainty in the managerial environment, the techniques involved often allow managers to identify and control the level of uncertainty.

The techniques presented in this chapter assume that the data were selected using a statistical sampling process and that the data are interval or ratio level.

THE HYPOTHESIS-TESTING PROCESS

Denise Fitzgerald has been hired as head of production for the Seltzer Bottling Company. Some soft-drink bottlers have recently been under pressure from consumer groups, which claim that bottlers have been increasing the price of soda and filling the bottles with less than the advertised amounts. Although Denise feels no manufacturer would purposely short-fill a bottle, she knows that filling machines sometimes fail to operate properly and fill the bottles less than full.

Since Denise is responsible for making sure the filling machines at her company operate correctly, she samples bottles every hour and, based on the sample results, decides whether to adjust the machines. If she is *not* interested in whether the bottles are filled with too much soft drink, she can identify two possible **states of nature** for 16-ounce bottles:

1. The bottles are filled with 16 or more ounces of soft drink on the average (machine is operating correctly).
2. The bottles are filled with less than 16 ounces on the average (machine is not operating correctly).

Denise must base her decision about the filling process on the results of her hourly sample. As indicated earlier, when a decision is based on sample results, sampling error must be expected. Therefore, sometimes when the process is operating correctly, the sample will indicate that the average soda bottle contains less than 16 ounces. And sometimes the process will actually need adjustments when the sample results indicate it is operating correctly. To analyze such a situation and best select among the possible states of nature, decision makers need to formulate the problem such that a hypothesis test can be conducted. The first step is to restate the states of nature in hypothesis-test notation. For example, for our Seltzer example,

$$\text{Null hypothesis—} H_0: \mu_x \geq 16 \text{ ounces}$$

$$\text{Alternate hypothesis—} H_A: \mu_x < 16 \text{ ounces}$$

where μ_x is the mean fill level for bottles. The state of nature picked as the *null hypothesis* depends on the decision problem. The null hypothesis, H_0, is the hypothesis being tested and traditionally contains the equality sign. The *alternative hypothesis, H_A*, represents population values other than those contained in the null hypothesis.

Depending on the sample information, the null hypothesis will either be supported or refuted. Careful thought should be given to establishing the null and alternative hypotheses since the conclusion reached may depend on the hypotheses being tested. Many examples throughout this and subsequent chapters will illustrate how to develop proper statistical hypotheses.

If Denise decides the filling process is operating correctly, she will allow it to continue, but if she decides it is operating incorrectly, she will adjust the filling machines. The decision will be based on the results of her sample. She can make two possible errors when testing a hypothesis based on sample information:

1. She may decide that the process is filling bottles with an average less than 16 ounces when, in fact, the average fill is 16 or more ounces. In this case she will *reject* a true null hypothesis. This error is a **Type I statistical error.**
2. She may decide the process is filling bottles with an average of 16 or more ounces when, in fact, it is not. Thus she might accept the null hypothesis when it is false. This error is a **Type II statistical error.**

Figure 9–1 shows the possible actions and possible states of nature associated with all hypothesis-testing problems. As you can see, there are three possible outcomes; no error, Type I error, and Type II error. Only one of these outcomes will occur for each test of a null hypothesis. Note that from figure 9–1 we can conclude that if the null hypothesis is true and an error is made, it must be a **Type I error.** On the other hand, if the null hypothesis is false and an error is made, it must be a **Type II error.**

Many statisticians argue that you should never accept the null hypothesis, but instead you should simply *not reject* it. Thus, the only two hypothesis-testing decisions would be *reject* H_0 or *do not reject* H_0. The implication is that if the sample information leads you to not reject H_0, then you have not yet committed to accept the null hypothesis, and thus a Type II error cannot occur.

This thinking is appropriate when hypothesis testing is employed in situations where some future action is not dependent on the results of the hypothesis test. However, in most business applications, the purpose of the hypothesis test is to direct the decision maker to take one action or another based on the results of the test. For instance, Denise Fitzpatrick will decide to shut down the filling machine if H_0 is rejected and will decide to keep the machine running if H_0 is accepted.

For this reason, this text will adopt the policy of either rejecting H_0 or accepting H_0 and will deal with Type II errors in greater depth than do some basic statistics texts.

Establishing the Decision Rule

The objective of a hypothesis test is to use sample information to decide whether to accept or reject the null hypothesis about a population value. But how do decision

FIGURE 9–1
Hypothesis-testing outcome possibilities

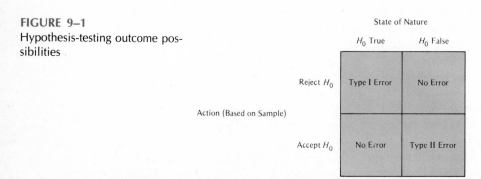

| | State of Nature | |
	H_0 True	H_0 False
Reject H_0	Type I Error	No Error
Accept H_0	No Error	Type II Error

Action (Based on Sample)

makers determine whether the sample information supports or refutes the null hypothesis? The answer to this question is the key to understanding statistical hypothesis testing.

Returning to the Seltzer Bottling Company example, the null and alternative hypothesis are as follows:

Hypotheses:

Null hypothesis—H_0: $\mu_x \geq 16$ ounces

Alternative hypothesis—H_A: $\mu_x < 16$ ounces

Recall from the central limit theorem that for large samples, the distribution of possible sample means will be approximately normal with a center at the population mean, μ_x. The null hypothesis in the Seltzer Bottling Company example is $\mu_x \geq 16$ ounces; but even if the null hypothesis is true, we may get a sample mean less than 16 ounces due to sampling error. Assume that the population mean is exactly 16 ounces. Figure 9–2 shows the distribution of possible sample means for the company if μ_x equals 16 ounces.

Values of $\overline{X}$ greater than or equal to 16 ounces would tend to support the null hypothesis. However, values of $\overline{X}$ below 16 ounces would tend to refute the null hypothesis. The smaller the value of $\overline{X}$, the greater the evidence that the null hypothesis should be rejected.

However, since we expect some sampling error, do we want to reject H_0 any time $\overline{X}$ is found to be less than 16 ounces? Probably not, since the chances of $\overline{X}$ being less than 16 when the population mean, μ_x, is 16 ounces is 50 percent. But what if the sample mean is only 15 ounces, or 14 ounces, or 13 ounces? Just how much sampling error do we expect to observe in our sampling?

The job of the decision maker is to establish a cut-off point that can be used to separate sample results that should lead to rejecting H_0 from sample results that will lead to accepting H_0. This cut-off point is called a **critical value** and in this text is labeled A.

For example, the critical value, A, in the Seltzer example might be located as shown in figure 9–3. The darkest area represents the rejection region. When $\overline{X}$ is less than A, H_0 is rejected. When $\overline{X}$ is greater than or equal to A, H_0 will be accepted. Since it is possible to observe $\overline{X}$ less than A even if H_0 is true ($\mu_x \geq 16$), the area in the rejection region represents the maximum probability of a Type I statistical error. This probability is called **alpha (α).** If A is moved farther to the left, the chances of committing a Type I error can be reduced. Figure 9–4 illustrates this point.

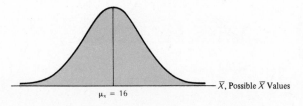

FIGURE 9–2
Sampling distribution of $\overline{X}$, Seltzer Bottling Company example

$\overline{X}$, Possible $\overline{X}$ Values

$\mu_x = 16$

FIGURE 9–3

Critical value, Seltzer Bottling Company example

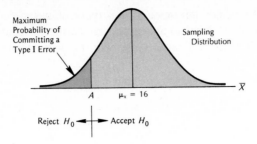

FIGURE 9–4

Type I error probabilities, Seltzer Bottling Company example

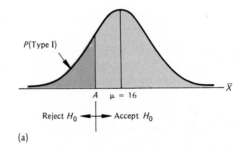

(a)

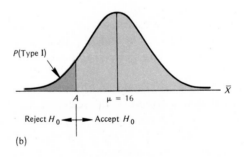

(b)

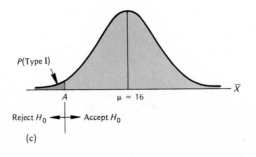

(c)

Ideally, we would like to make the chance of making both a Type I and a Type II error small. Unfortunately, if you make the chance of making a Type I error small, the chance of making a Type II error, is increased. The decision maker must balance his or her choice for alpha against the probability of making a Type II error. This trade-off between the probabilities of making Type I and Type II errors is perhaps the most important part of hypothesis testing. We will discuss this more fully in section 9–4.

To determine the appropriate value for A, decision makers must determine how large an alpha they want, keeping in mind the smaller the alpha, the larger the chance of making a Type II error.

Ultimately, decision makers must select the value of alpha in light of the costs involved in committing a Type I error relative to the Type II error cost. For example, if Denise Fitzgerald rejects the null hypothesis when it is true, she will needlessly shut down production and incur the cost of machine adjustment. In addition, the adjustment might be incorrect, and future production could be affected. Calculating these costs and determining the probability of incurring them is a subjective management decision. Any two managers might well arrive at different alpha levels. The important thing is that each would specify his or her alpha level for the hypothesis test.

Suppose Denise decides that she is willing to incur a 0.10 chance of committing a Type I error. Assume the standard deviation of the production process is 0.5 ounce and the sample size is sixty-four bottles.

The critical value can be stated in either of two ways. First we can establish the critical value as the number of standard deviations the critical value, A, is from μ_x. Figure 9–5 shows that if the rejection region on the lower end of the sampling distribution has an area of 0.10, the Z value from the standard normal table corresponding to the critical value is -1.28. Thus, if the sample mean lies more than 1.28 standard deviations below the population mean, 16, H_0 should be rejected.

The second way we can state the critical value is in the same terms as the sample mean is measured. In the seltzer example, A could be stated in terms of ounces such that if $\overline{X}$ is less than A ounces, we should reject H_0, and if $\overline{X}$ is greater than or equal to

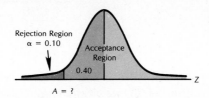

FIGURE 9–5
Establishing the critical value as a Z value

From the standard normal table,*

$$Z_{0.40} \approx -1.28$$

Then

$$A = Z_{critical} \approx -1.28$$

*The Z value from the standard normal table is used because the sampling distribution of X is approximately normal according to the central limit theorem for samples size $n \geq 30$. Remember also from chapter 6 that if $Z_{critical}$ is to the left of the mean, it will be negative.

A ounces, we should accept H_0. Figure 9–6 shows how the value of A is determined using this method. Thus, if $\overline{X}$ is less than 15.92 ounces, H_0 should be rejected and the machine stopped for adjustment; otherwise, H_0 should be accepted and the machine left running.

It makes no difference which approach you use in establishing the critical value. This text will mix the use of the methods throughout so that you become familiar with both.

Suppose the sample yields a sample mean of 15.75 ounces. We can test the null hypothesis two ways, depending on the procedure we used to establish the critical value. First using the Z value method, we establish the following decision rule:

Hypotheses:

H_0: $\mu \geq 16$ ounces

H_A: $\mu < 16$ ounces

$\alpha = 0.10$

Decision Rule:

If $Z < Z_{\text{critical}}$, reject H_0.

If $Z \geq Z_{\text{critical}}$, accept H_0

where $\quad Z_{\text{critical}} = -1.28$

Z is computed by what we call a test statistic as follows:

$$Z = \frac{\overline{X} - \mu}{\dfrac{\sigma_x}{\sqrt{n}}}$$

$$= \frac{15.75 - 16}{\dfrac{0.50}{\sqrt{64}}}$$

$$= -4$$

Thus, the sample mean is 4 standard deviations below the hypothesized mean. Since $Z = -4$ is less than -1.28, we clearly reject H_0.

Now we use the second approach, which established a decision rule as follows:

Decision Rule:

If $\overline{X} < 15.92$ ounces, reject H_0.

If $\overline{X} \geq 15.92$ ounces, accept H_0.

Then since 15.75 is less than 15.92, H_0 should be rejected.

Note that the two methods yield the same conclusion, which they always will if you perform your calculations correctly.

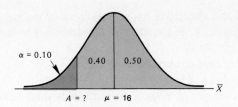

From the standard normal table,

$$Z_{0.40} \approx -1.28$$

Then

$$Z = \frac{A - \mu_x}{\dfrac{\sigma_x}{\sqrt{n}}}$$

Solving for A,

$$A = \mu_x + Z\frac{\sigma_x}{\sqrt{n}} = 16 + (-1.28)\left(\frac{0.5}{\sqrt{64}}\right)$$

$$= 15.92 \text{ oz.}$$

Summary of Hypothesis Testing

The hypothesis-testing process discussed in this section can be summarized in six steps:

1. Determine the null hypothesis and the alternative hypothesis.
2. Determine the desired alpha level (α).
3. Choose a sample size.
4. Determine the critical value, A, or Z_{critical}.
5. Establish the decision rule.
6. Select the sample and perform the test.

These six steps can be followed to test any null hypothesis. Become well acquainted with the hypothesis-testing process, as it is a fundamental part of statistical decision making.

One-Tailed Hypothesis Tests

In the Seltzer Company example the null hypothesis could be refuted only if the sample mean was too small (that is, too far to the left of $\mu_x = 16$ ounces). Consequently the critical value, A, was placed in the left-hand (lower) tail of the normal curve. This example illustrates a **one-tailed hypothesis test.**

A one-tailed hypothesis test will assume one of two forms, depending on the way the null and alternative hypotheses are stated. Examples of these two forms are

1	*2*
$H_0: \mu_x \leq 50$	$H_0: \mu_x \geq 16$
$H_A: \mu_x > 50$	$H_A: \mu_x < 16$

If the first set of null and alternative hypotheses is used, we use a one-tailed hypothesis test with the critical value, A, in the right-hand (upper) tail of the normal curve, and we reject H_0 when $\overline{X}$ is greater than A. However, if the second set of null and alternative hypotheses is used (our Seltzer example), the critical value, A, is placed in the left-hand tail, and we reject H_0 when $\overline{X}$ is less than A.

The Marwick Chemical Company manufactures many different chemicals in an eastern U.S. state. The firm uses vast amounts of water in its processing and has a conditional-use permit from the Environmental Protection Agency. Marwick is allowed to return its waste water to the nearby river if it lowers the pollutant levels to allowable amounts. For a common toxic chemical, Marwick is required to reduce the amount in the waste water to twenty parts per million (p.p.m.) or less.

Marwick's pollution-abatement equipment will easily reduce the toxic chemical levels below the upper limit of twenty parts per million when working correctly, but like much pollution equipment it needs checking and adjustment to maintain the standards. The waste water is continually monitored, and based on the periodic sample results, the pollution equipment is either adjusted—a costly process—or allowed to continue as is. The appropriate hypotheses and decision rule for this situation are stated as follows:

Hypotheses:

H_0: $\mu_x \leq 20$ p.p.m., process can continue.

H_A: $\mu_x > 20$ p.p.m., process requires adjustment.

Decision Rule:

Take a random sample of size n and calculate $\overline{X}$.

If $\overline{X} \leq A$, accept H_0.

If $\overline{X} > A$, reject H_0.

Marwick decides to limit alpha to a maximum of 3 percent and base the decision on a sample of forty trials. The decision rule is determined as shown in figure 9–7. Note that the standard deviation, σ_x, is assumed to be five parts per million. If the standard deviation is not known, we use S_x from the sample.

Suppose the Marwick Chemical Company has selected a sample of forty units of water that is scheduled to go into the river and has found an average of 23.4 parts per million of the toxic chemical. What should they do based on this information? As with any hypothesis test, the sample results are compared to the decision rule and H_0 is either rejected or accepted. In this case we formed two equivalent decision rules:

Option 1	*Option 2*
If $\overline{X} \leq 21.485$ p.p.m., accept H_0.	If $Z \leq 1.88$, accept H_0.
If $\overline{X} > 21.485$ p.p.m., reject H_0.	If $Z > 1.88$, reject H_0.

Hypotheses:

H_0: $\mu_x \leq 20$ p.p.m.
H_A: $\mu_x > 20$ p.p.m.

$\alpha = 0.03$

FIGURE 9–7
Decision rule, Marwick
Chemical Company example

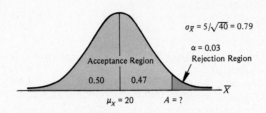

$\sigma_{\bar{x}} = 5/\sqrt{40} = 0.79$

$\alpha = 0.03$
Rejection Region

Acceptance Region

0.50 | 0.47

$\mu_x = 20$ $A = ?$

From the standard normal table,

$$Z_{0.47} \approx 1.88$$

Then

$$Z = \frac{\bar{X} - \mu_x}{\sigma_{\bar{x}}} = \frac{A - \mu_x}{\dfrac{\sigma_x}{\sqrt{n}}}.$$

Solving for A,

$$A = \mu_x + Z\frac{\sigma_x}{\sqrt{n}} = 20 + 1.88(0.79)$$

$$= 21.485 \text{ p.p.m.}$$

Decision Rule:

If $\bar{X} \leq 21.485$ p.p.m., accept H_0.
If $\bar{X} > 21.485$ p.p.m., reject H_0.
   or
If $Z \leq 1.88$, accept H_0.
If $Z > 1.88$, reject H_0.

Using option 1, our decision is to reject H_0, since the sample mean, 23.4, is greater than 21.485 p.p.m. Thus, the company would conclude that an adjustment is needed.

If the second decision rule is used, we will reject H_0 if the sample mean is more than 1.88 standard deviations greater than the mean of 20 p.p.m. Based on the sample results, we compute the test statistic as follows:

$$Z = \frac{\bar{X} - \mu_x}{\dfrac{\sigma_x}{\sqrt{n}}}$$

$$= \frac{23.4 - 20}{\dfrac{5}{\sqrt{40}}}$$

$$\approx 4.30$$

Since 4.30 is greater than 1.88, we reject H_0. The sample mean is approximately 4.30 standard deviations above the hypothesized mean. This is beyond what we would attribute to sampling error at an alpha of 0.03.

Thus, again we see that regardless of which approach we take to test the hypothesis, the same conclusion is reached.

Hypothesis Testing—Population Standard Deviation Unknown, Large Sample

In the previous example, we assumed that the population standard deviation was known. When we discussed statistical estimation, we stated that in most cases, the population standard deviation is not known. In estimation, our solution to an unknown standard deviation was to estimate the population standard deviation, σ_x, by the sample standard deviation, S_x. As you might suspect, we will also make this change for hypothesis testing. For example, engineers at the American Lighting Company recently developed a new three-way light bulb that it says is more energy efficient than the company's existing three-way bulb. It also claims that the bulb will outlast the current bulb, which has an average lifetime of 700 hours.

The American Lighting Company has decided that before it begins full-scale production on the new light bulbs, it should build a test sample of 1,000 light bulbs (assumed to be a random sample) and determine whether the mean life of the new three-way bulb *exceeds* the old bulb's average of 700 hours. The sample results for the 1,000 bulbs were as follows:

$$\overline{X} = 704 \text{ h}$$
$$S_x = 150 \text{ h}$$

To test the claim about the bulbs, we formulate the null and alternative hypotheses as follows:

Hypotheses:

H_0: $\mu_x \leq 700$ h
H_A: $\mu_x > 700$ h
$\alpha = 0.05$

Note that we have placed the claim in the alternative hypothesis. This puts the burden on the new product to "prove" it is superior to the old product. If the claim contains the equality, it becomes the null hypothesis; if not, it becomes the alternative hypothesis.

Figure 9–8 shows the results of the hypothesis test. Note that S_x, the sample standard deviation, is used in place of σ_x in computing the test statistic. As figure 9–8 shows, the null hypothesis is accepted, which means that the sample results (only 0.84 standard deviations from the hypothesized mean) are not sufficient to reject H_0. Thus,

Hypotheses:

H_0: $\mu_x \leq 700$ h
H_A: $\mu_x > 700$ h

$\alpha = 0.05$

FIGURE 9–8
Hypothesis test, American Lighting Company example

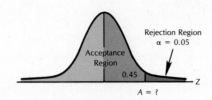

From the standard normal table

$$Z_{0.45} \approx 1.65 = Z_{critical}$$

Decision Rule:

If $Z > 1.65$, reject H_0.
If $Z \leq 1.65$, accept H_0.

Test Statistic:

$$Z = \frac{\overline{X} - \mu_x}{\frac{S_x}{\sqrt{n}}}$$

$$= \frac{704 - 700}{\frac{150}{\sqrt{1,000}}}$$

$$\approx 0.84$$

Since $0.84 \leq 1.65$, accept H_0.

American Lighting may have a superior bulb energywise but, based on these sample data, it cannot say the same for average lifetime.

Two-Tailed Hypothesis Tests

The hypothesis-testing examples presented thus far have been one-tailed. The entire rejection region (alpha) has been located in either the upper or the lower tail of the sampling distribution. However, there are many instances in which a one-tailed hypothesis test is not appropriate. In these cases you will need to use a **two-tailed hypothesis test.** In a two-tailed test, the rejection region (alpha) is split into the two tails of the sampling distribution.

Consider the example involving the Creme N' Smooth Ice Cream plant in Pittsburgh, Pennsylvania. The plant produces ice cream sold under the Creme N' Smooth brand and a number of store brands in the East. The production process is highly automated. The filling machine for the 64-ounce cartons is good but not perfect. There is some variation in the actual volume of ice cream that goes into the 64-ounce carton.

The machine can go out of adjustment and put either less than 64 ounces or more than 64 ounces in a carton.

To monitor the filling process, the production manager selects a sample of 100 ice cream cartons at the end of each day. The sample information is used to test the following null and alternative hypotheses:

$$H_0: \mu_x = 64 \text{ ounces}$$

$$H_A: \mu_x \neq 64 \text{ ounces}$$

In any hypothesis-testing situation, there will likely be sampling error. In this case, this means that the sample mean may exceed 64 ounces or be less than 64 ounces. The production manager will not reject the null hypothesis as long as the difference appears to be due to sampling error. If the difference becomes too extreme, however, the null hypothesis will be rejected and the machine will be readjusted.

In establishing the decision rule, the production manager must decide which values of $\overline{X}$ will tend to refute the null hypothesis. In this example, values of $\overline{X}$ either too large or too small should lead to rejecting the null hypothesis. This situation is referred to as a **two-tailed hypothesis test,** meaning that the rejection region is divided into two tails. (Although not required, the general convention is to divide the rejection region equally between the two tails of the sampling distribution. The examples and problems in this text will follow this pattern.)

The correct decision rule to apply for a two-tailed hypothesis test about a population mean is

Decision Rule:

Select a sample of size n and determine $\overline{X}$.

If $A_L \leq \overline{X} \leq A_H$, accept H_0.
If $\overline{X} > A_H$, reject H_0.
If $\overline{X} < A_L$, reject H_0.

where A_L = critical value in the lower tail
               A_H = critical value in the upper tail

Suppose the production manager specifies an alpha level of 0.06 ($\alpha = 0.06$), meaning that she is willing to accept a 6 percent chance of rejecting the null hypothesis when it is really true. At the end of a particular day, the sample of 100 cartons resulted in a sample mean of 64.12 ounces, with a sample standard deviation of 0.50 ounce. Figure 9–9 illustrates how the decision rule is developed. It shows that if $\overline{X} > 64.094$ ounces or if $\overline{X} < 63.906$ ounces, the null hypothesis should be rejected. For this particular day, the sample mean $\overline{X} = 64.12 > 64.094$, so the production manager should reject the null hypothesis and conclude that the machine is not filling the cartons with an average of 64 ounces of ice cream.

Hypotheses:

H_0: μ_x = 64 oz.
H_A: μ_x ≠ 64 oz.

α = 0.06

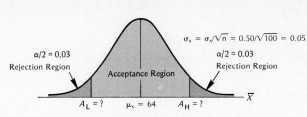

FIGURE 9–9

Decision rule for a two-tailed
test, Creme 'N' Smooth example

From the standard normal table,

$$Z_{0.47} \approx \pm 1.88$$

Then, solving for A_L and A_H,

$$Z = \frac{A_L - \mu_x}{\sigma_{\bar{x}}} \qquad \text{and} \quad Z = \frac{A_H - \mu_x}{\sigma_{\bar{x}}}$$

$A_L = \mu_x + Z\sigma_{\bar{x}} = 64 + (-1.88)(0.05)$ $A_H = \mu_x + Z\sigma_{\bar{x}} = 64 + 1.88(0.05)$
   = 63.906   = 64.094

Decision Rule:

If 63.906 ≤ X ≤ 64.094, accept H_0.
If X < 63.906, reject H_0.
If X > 64.094, reject H_0.

SKILL DEVELOPMENT PROBLEMS FOR SECTION 9–2

The following set of problems is meant to test your understanding of the material in this section. Additional problems are found at the end of this chapter under this section heading.

1. Given the following null and alternative hypotheses:

$$H_0: \mu \leq 300$$
$$H_A: \mu > 300$$
$$\alpha = 0.05$$

and $\bar{X} = 304.50$
    $\sigma_x = 45.00$
    $n = 200$

a. Establish the appropriate decision rule.
b. Indicate the appropriate decision based upon the sample information and the decision rule.

2. Given the following null and alternative hypotheses:

$$H_0: \mu \leq 24.78$$
$$H_A: \mu > 24.78$$
$$\alpha = 0.03$$

and $\overline{X} = 24.85$
       $\sigma = 9.00$
       $n = 50$

a. Establish the appropriate decision rule.
b. Indicate the appropriate decision based upon the sample information and the decision rule.

3. Given the following null and alternative hypotheses:

$$H_0: \mu \geq 1{,}000$$
$$H_A: \mu < 1{,}000$$
$$\alpha = 0.05$$

and $\overline{X} = 980$
       $S_x = 205$
       $n = 100$

a. Establish the appropriate decision rule.
b. Indicate the appropriate decision based upon the sample information and the decision rule.

4. Given the following null and alternative hypotheses:

$$H_0: \mu = 346$$
$$H_A: \mu \neq 346$$
$$\alpha = 0.05$$

and $\overline{X} = 338$
       $\sigma_x = 90$
       $n = 36$

a. Establish the appropriate decision rule.
b. Indicate the appropriate decision based upon the sample information and the decision rule.

5. Given the following null and alternative hypotheses:

$$H_0: \mu = 1{,}450$$
$$H_A: \mu \neq 1{,}450$$
$$\alpha = 0.10$$

and $\overline{X} = 1{,}475.60$
       $S_x = 340$
       $n = 70$

a. Establish the appropriate decision rule.
b. Indicate the appropriate decision based upon the sample information and the decision rule.

6. The makers of a new home furnace system claim that if the furnace is installed, homeowners will observe an average fuel bill of no more than $90.00 per month during January if their house has between 2,200 and 2,400 square feet of heated living space. A consumer agency plans to test this claim by taking a random sample of this size homes where the new furnace has just been installed.
   a. Establish the appropriate null and alternative hypotheses.
   b. If the desired alpha level for the test is 0.05, what should be concluded about the company's claim if the following sample results are observed?

$$\overline{X} = \$91.40$$
$$S_x^2 = 625$$
$$n = 64$$

Be sure to set up the appropriate decision rule.

7. A mail order business prides itself in its ability to fill customers' orders in five calendar days or less on the average. Periodically, the operations manager selects a random sample of customer orders and determines the number of days actually taken to fill their orders. Based upon this sample information, he concludes whether the desired standard is being met.
   a. Establish the appropriate null and alternative hypotheses.
   b. On one occasion where a sample of 100 customers was selected, the average number of days was 5.65, with a sample standard deviation of 1.5 days. If an alpha level of 0.08 is to be used, what is the appropriate decision rule to use and what should the operations manager conclude? Discuss.

8. The makers of Tini-Oats Cereal have an automated packaging machine that can be set at any targeted fill level between twelve and thirty-two ounces. It is expected that not every box of cereal will contain exactly the targeted weight, but the average of all boxes filled should. At the end of every shift (eight hours), 100 boxes are selected at random and the mean and standard deviation of the sample are computed. Based upon these sample results, the production control manager determines whether the filling machine needs to be readjusted or whether it remains okay to operate. Use an alpha = 0.05.
   a. Establish the appropriate null and alternative hypotheses to be tested.
   b. At the end of a particular shift during which the machine was filling 24-ounce boxes of Tini-Oats, the sample mean of 100 boxes was 24.32 ounces, with a standard deviation of 0.70 ounce. Determine the appropriate decision rule and indicate what should be concluded about this machine based upon these sample data.
   c. Why do you suppose the production control manager would prefer to make this hypothesis test a two-tailed test? Discuss.

TYPE II ERRORS AND THE POWER OF THE HYPOTHESIS TEST

9-3 The previous examples have shown how decision rules for hypothesis tests of the population mean are determined and how the appropriate decision is based on the results of a sample from the population. In these examples we have determined the critical values by first specifying alpha, the probability of committing a Type I error. As we indicated, if the cost of committing a Type I error is high, the decision maker should specify a small alpha. A small alpha results in a small rejection region. If the rejection region is small, the sample mean is less likely to fall there, and the chances of rejecting a true null hypothesis are small.

This logic provides a basis for establishing the critical value for the hypothesis test. However it completely ignores the possibility of committing a Type II error. Recall that accepting a false null hypothesis is a Type II decision error. If the rejection region is made small by selecting a small alpha level, the acceptance region will be large since the rejection region plus the acceptance region must add to 1.0. This is illustrated in figure 9–10.

To complete the logic, if the acceptance region is large, the probability of committing a Type II error [called **beta (β)**] will also tend to be large. This is a point many decision makers often forget in their efforts to control Type I errors. A decrease in alpha

FIGURE 9–10
Acceptance and rejection regions

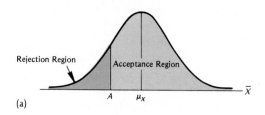

(a)

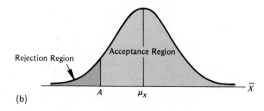

(b)

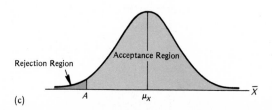

(c)

will increase beta. However, as will be shown, the increase in beta will not equal the decrease in alpha.

Decision makers must examine carefully the costs of committing Type I and Type II errors and, in light of these costs, attempt to establish acceptable values for alpha and beta. Generally the decision of what values of Type I and Type II errors are acceptable depends on the relative cost associated with making each type of error. For instance, in the Marwick Chemical Company example considered in the last section, committing a Type I error would cause the pollution equipment to be adjusted needlessly, a costly process, and therefore alpha was limited to 3 percent. However, we did not consider the probability of making a Type II error, which would involve continuing a process producing too much pollution. Here, making a Type II error might have disastrous consequences. We will delay our discussion of how decision makers can simultaneously control the chances of making a Type I and a Type II error until the next section. You will now learn how to calculate the probability of committing a Type II error.

Calculating Beta (Probability of Committing a Type II Error)

Once alpha has been specified for a hypothesis test involving a particular sample size, beta cannot also be specified, Rather, the beta value is fixed, and all the decision maker can do is calculate it. This does not imply that beta is a single value, because it is not. Since a Type II error occurs when a false null hypothesis is accepted (refer to figure 9–1), there is a beta value for each possible population value for which the null hypothesis is false. For example, for the Marwick Chemical Company, the null and alternative hypotheses were

$$H_0: \mu_x \leq 20 \text{ p.p.m.}$$
$$H_A: \mu_x > 20 \text{ p.p.m.}$$

Therefore, the null hypothesis is false for all possible values of $\mu_x > 20$ parts per million. Thus, for each of these infinite number of possibilities, a value of beta can be determined. Suppose we assume that μ_x is actually 21 parts per million. If we use the alpha level of 0.03 and the decision rule determined in figure 9–7, we can calculate beta using the following steps:

1. Draw a picture of the hypothesized sampling distribution showing the rejection region(s) and the acceptance region found by specifying an alpha level.
2. Immediately below the hypothesized sampling distribution, draw the true sampling distribution based on the assumed true population mean. Note that the shape of the true distribution will be the same as the shape of the hypothesized distribution. Only the central location will be different.
3. Extend the critical value(s) from the hypothesized distribution down to the true distribution and shade the rejection region on the true distribution.
4. The unshaded area in the true distribution is beta, the probability of committing a Type II error.

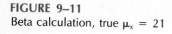

FIGURE 9–11
Beta calculation, true $\mu_x = 21$

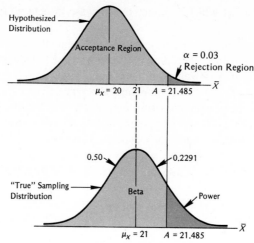

$$Z = \frac{\overline{X} - \mu_x}{\sigma_{\overline{x}}} \quad \text{(From the ''true'' distribution)}$$

$$= \frac{21.485 - 21}{0.79}$$

$$= 0.61$$

The area between $Z = 0.61$ and μ_x is 0.2291. Therefore

$$\text{Beta} = 0.5000 + 0.2291$$
$$= 0.7291$$
$$\text{Power} = 1 - \text{beta} = 1 - 0.7291$$
$$= 0.2709$$

Figure 9–11 shows how beta is determined if the true value of μ_x is 21 parts per million. Thus, by holding alpha to 0.03, the chance of committing a Type II error is approximately 0.7291. However, what if the true mean is actually 22? Figure 9–12 shows how to calculate beta for this case.

The shaded area in the true distribution has also been calculated. This area is called the *power* of the hypothesis test. **Power** is the probability of rejecting a false hypothesis.[1] Naturally, decision makers want power to be as large as possible, and this occurs if beta is made as small as possible, since power and beta are inversely related. Power is determined by equation 9–1:

$$\boxed{\text{Power} = 1 - \text{beta}} \qquad (9\text{--}1)$$

Like beta, power changes depending on what the ''true'' value for μ_x is assumed to be. In the calculation shown in Figure 9–11, for instance, power is 0.2709. This would

---

[1]Although this is a common definition of power, it is not universal. Some authors define power as the probability of rejecting the null hypothesis. For the purposes of an introductory text, this difference is not important.

FIGURE 9–12
Beta calculation true $\mu_x = 22$

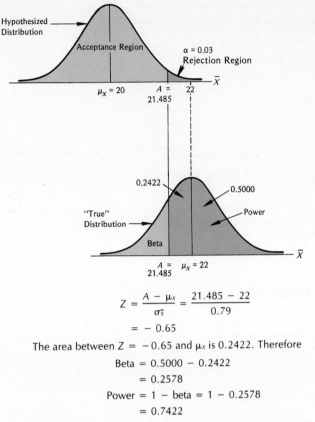

$$Z = \frac{A - \mu_x}{\sigma_{\bar{x}}} = \frac{21.485 - 22}{0.79}$$

$$= -0.65$$

The area between $Z = -0.65$ and μ_x is 0.2422. Therefore

$$\text{Beta} = 0.5000 - 0.2422$$

$$= 0.2578$$

$$\text{Power} = 1 - \text{beta} = 1 - 0.2578$$

$$= 0.7422$$

likely be an unacceptably low value if it was important to be able to reject the null hypothesis when the true average pollution level is as high as 21.

Figures 9–11 and 9–12 show that as the true μ_x value is moved farther away from the hypothesized μ_x, beta becomes smaller. The greater the difference between the true mean and the hypothesized mean, the easier it is to tell the two apart, and the less likely we are to accept the null hypothesis when it is actually false. Of course the opposite is also true. As the true mean moves increasingly closer to the hypothesized mean, the harder it is for the hypothesis test to recognize the difference between the two.

Operating Characteristic Curves and Power Curves

As indicated earlier, there are an infinite number of possible values for μ_x when the null hypothesis is false, and it would not be practical to calculate beta and power for each one. Instead we select several possible values for μ_x and find both beta and power. These values are plotted on separate graphs to form an **O.C. (operating characteristic) curve** for the beta values and a **power curve** for the power values. For example, the Marwick Chemical Company might be interested in values for beta and power for the

TABLE 9–1

Beta and power values, Marwick
Chemical Company example

True μ_x	Beta	Power
20.10	0.9599	0.0401
20.50	0.8944	0.1056
21.00	0.7291	0.2709
21.50	0.4920	0.5080
22.00	0.2578	0.7422
22.50	0.1003	0.8997
23.00	0.0274	0.9726

possible values of μ_x shown in table 9–1. Make sure you can calculate these values also.

Figure 9–13 illustrates the O.C. curve and the power curve constructed from the values shown in table 9–1. Notice that the several points have been plotted and connected with a smooth curve. Thus, by using the O.C. curve and power curve in figure 9–13, you can approximate both power and beta for any possible value of μ_x.

Impact of Sample Size on Power and Beta

Previous chapters have emphasized that the size of the sample influences the spread in the sampling distribution of $\overline{X}$. As the sample size increases, $\sigma_{\overline{x}}$ decreases. The smaller

FIGURE 9–13

O.C. curve and power curve,
hypothesized $\mu_x = 20$

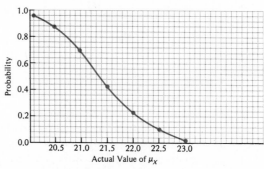

(a) O. C. Curve (Plot of Beta Values)

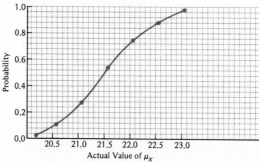

(b) Power Curve

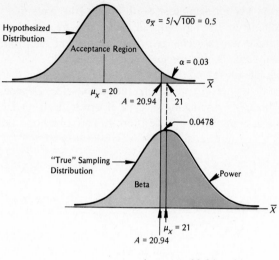

$$Z = \frac{A - \mu_x}{\sigma_{\bar{x}}} = \frac{20.94 - 21}{0.50}$$

$$= -0.12$$

The area between $Z = -0.12$ and μ_x is 0.0478. Therefore

$$\text{Beta} = 0.5000 - 0.0478$$

$$= 0.4522$$

$$\text{Power} = 1 - \text{beta} = 1 - 0.4522$$

$$= 0.5478$$

$\sigma_{\bar{x}}$ becomes, the less the chance of extreme sampling error. This same concept applies in hypothesis testing and determining power and beta. As more information is available (larger sample size), with alpha held constant, the smaller beta (and the larger power) will be for any value of μ_x.

For example, the values of power and beta in table 9–1 were determined assuming a sample size of forty ($n = 40$). Suppose the sample size is increased to 100. Figure 9–14 shows how beta and power are determined for $\mu_x = 21$. Table 9–2 presents the

True μ_x	Beta		Power	
	$n = 40$	$n = 100$	$n = 40$	$n = 100$
20.10	0.9599	0.9535	0.0401	0.0465
20.50	0.8944	0.8106	0.1056	0.1894
21.00	0.7291	0.4522	0.2709	0.5478
21.50	0.4920	0.1314	0.5080	0.8686
22.00	0.2578	0.0170	0.7422	0.9830
22.50	0.1003	0.0009	0.8997	0.9991
23.00	0.0274	0.0000*	0.9726	1.0000

TABLE 9–2
Power and beta values, Marwick Chemical Company example (H_0: $\mu_x = 20$).

*The true value is small but positive.

values of beta and power for sample sizes of 40 and 100. Note that in all cases, a shift in sample size from 40 to 100 has reduced beta and increased power. Notice also that the increase in sample size has changed the critical value, A, from 21.485 to 20.94. The reduced critical value occurs because $\sigma_{\bar{x}}$ has decreased.

This example has illustrated that for a given level of alpha, the chances of making a Type II error can be reduced by increasing the sample size. Depending on the decision being made and the costs of making a Type II error, decision makers may want to control the chances of committing a Type II error. This problem is addressed in the next section.

SKILL DEVELOPMENT PROBLEMS FOR SECTION 9–3

The following set of problems is meant to test your understanding of the material in this section. Additional problems are found at the end of this chapter under this section heading.

9. You are given the following null and alternative hypotheses:

$$H_0: \mu \leq 200$$
$$H_A: \mu > 200$$
$$\alpha = 0.05$$

a. If the true population mean is 204, what is the value of beta? Assume that the population standard deviation is known to be twenty and the sample size is forty.

b. Indicate clearly the decision rule that would be used to test the null hypothesis and determine what decision should be made if the sample mean was 201.3.

10. You are given the following null and alternative hypotheses:

$$H_0: \mu \leq 88$$
$$H_A: \mu > 88$$
$$\alpha = 0.10$$

a. If the true population mean is 90, what is the value of beta? Assume that the population standard deviation is known to be twelve and the sample size is sixty-four.

b. Indicate clearly the decision rule that would be used to test the null hypothesis and determine what decision should be made if the sample mean was 90.34.

11. You are given the following null and alternative hypotheses:

$$H_0: \mu \geq 1,350$$
$$H_A: \mu < 1,350$$
$$\alpha = 0.05$$

a. If the true population mean is 1,345, what is the value of beta? Assume that the population standard deviation is known to be 200 and the sample size is 100.

b. Indicate clearly the decision rule that would be used to test the null hypothesis and determine what decision should be made if the sample mean was 1,337.50.

12. You are given the following null and alternative hypotheses:

$$H_0: \mu = 2,000$$
$$H_A: \mu \neq 2,000$$
$$\alpha = 0.05$$

a. If the true population mean is 2,004, what is the value of beta? Assume that the population standard deviation is known to be 500 and the sample size is 100. (*Hint:* Look at solved problem 3 at the end of this chapter to see the methodology for finding beta for a two-tailed hypothesis test.)

b. If the true population mean is 1,995, what is the value of beta? Assume that the population standard deviation is known to be 500 and the sample size is 100.

c. Find power for the conditions expressed in parts a and b.

d. Indicate clearly the decision rule that would be used to test the null hypothesis and determine what decision should be made if the sample mean was 1,987.40.

13. The Franklin Bicycle Tire Company plans to warranty their new Mountain Bike Tire for twelve months. However, before they do this, they want to be sure that the average tire will last at least eighteen months under normal operations. They plan to test this statistically using a random sample of tires. Specify an alpha level and justify why you picked that value.

a. If the true average is actually 16.8 months, what is the probability that the hypothesis test will lead to accepting the null hypothesis incorrectly? Assume that the population standard deviation is known to be 2.4 months and the sample size is sixty tires.

b. Determine the decision rule and test the hypothesis assuming that the sample mean turns out to be 17.4 months.

14. The union negotiations between labor and management at the Stone Container paper mill in Minnesota hit a snag when management asked labor to take a cut in health insurance coverage. As part of their justification, management claimed that the average dollars of insurance claims filed by union employees did not exceed $250 per employee. The union's chief negotiator requested a sample of 100 employees' records be selected and this claim tested statistically. Specify an alpha level and justify why you picked that value.

a. State the null and alternative hypotheses.

b. Before the sample was selected, the negotiator was interested in the chances that her statistical test would incorrectly accept the null hypothesis if the true mean was $275. (Note that it was assumed the standard deviation in claims is $70.00, as determined in a similar study of another plant location.) Determine the value of beta.

c. Referring to part b, suppose the negotiator was concerned about the value of beta if the true mean was really $260. Calculate the beta under this condition.

d. Based upon your findings in parts b and c, would you recommend that the negotiator go ahead with the test as it is currently structured? Discuss.

CONTROLLING TYPE I AND TYPE II ERRORS

9-4

The Sleepware Company manufactures and sells waterbeds in several areas of the United States. The company has been purchasing the waterbed mattresses from a southern California firm, but it manufactures its own wood frames at an Oregon plant.

To compete in the waterbed market, Sleepware must guarantee its product. The chief competitor is currently offering a 36-month, money-back guarantee, and Sleepware feels that it must match or exceed this guarantee. To do this profitably, Sleepware's cost accountant and production manager have determined that the mattresses must have a strength rating that averages at least 1,200.

The production manager has suggested that a sample of mattresses be selected to determine whether the company should introduce the 36-month guarantee for its product. Thus, he wishes to test the hypothesis that the strength rating average is at least 1,200 versus the alternative that the rating average is less than 1,200. Although the mean strength rating may vary, the standard deviation of strength ratings is an assumed known value of forty.

The testing process destroys the mattress since pressure is applied until the vinyl tears. Consequently the production manager wants to hold the sample size to a minimum. However, he also knows that hypothesis tests involve the risk of committing either a Type I or a Type II error. If a Type I error is committed, Sleepware will incorrectly conclude that its mattresses are not strong enough and consequently will not offer the 36-month guarantee. The company will then be at a marketing disadvantage and may spend money to improve the quality when it is not necessary. Thus, if a Type I error is committed, Sleepware will needlessly lose sales and spend money. The potential costs are very high, so the company president wants a small probability of a Type I error. Specifically, she is willing to accept a probability of a Type I error no larger than 2 percent.

However, if the sample leads to accepting the null hypothesis, a Type II error might be made. The Type II error occurs if a false hypothesis is accepted. In this case, the company would incorrectly believe that the mattresses are strong enough to make the guarantee profitable. Depending on how low the true average strength rating is, a Type II error could be very costly due to an excessive number of required replacements.

After a careful study of the costs involved, the cost accountant and the production manager have agreed that if the true average strength rating is equal to or less than 1,180, the company would be hit hard financially by making the 36-month guarantee. Because of this, the president is willing to accept only a 0.05 chance of committing a Type II error if the true average strength rating is 1,180.

The minimum sample size required to hold both Type I and Type II errors to the levels specified is determined by the following procedure:

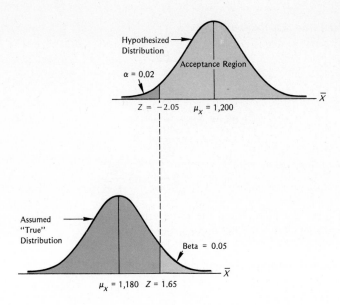

Hypotheses:

H_0: $\mu_x \geq 1,200$

H_A: $\mu_x < 1,200$

Constraints:

1. The probability of a Type I error must be less than or equal to 0.02.
2. If the true mean strength rating is 1,180, the chances of a Type II error must not exceed 0.05.

Figure 9–15 illustrates these contraints.

The first step is to solve for the critical value, A. We can do this two ways. *For the hypothesized distribution:*

$$Z = \frac{A - \mu_x}{\dfrac{\sigma_x}{\sqrt{n}}}$$

$$-2.05 = \frac{A - 1,200}{\dfrac{40}{\sqrt{n}}}$$

$$A = 1,200 - 2.05 \frac{40}{\sqrt{n}}$$

For the assumed true distribution:

$$Z = \frac{A - \mu_x}{\dfrac{\sigma_x}{\sqrt{n}}}$$

$$1.65 = \frac{A - 1{,}180}{\dfrac{40}{\sqrt{n}}}$$

$$A = 1{,}180 + 1.65\,\frac{40}{\sqrt{n}}$$

Both of these equations equal the same critical value, A. Thus, we can set one equal to the other and solve for the optimal sample size n.

$$1{,}200 - 2.05\,\frac{40}{\sqrt{n}} = 1{,}180 + 1.65\,\frac{40}{\sqrt{n}}$$

$$20 - 2.05\,\frac{40}{\sqrt{n}} = 1.65\,\frac{40}{\sqrt{n}}$$

$$20\sqrt{n} - 2.05\,(40) = 1.65(40)$$

$$20\sqrt{n} - 82.0 = 66.0$$

$$20\sqrt{n} = 148.0$$

$$n = \left(\frac{148.0}{20}\right)^2 = 54.76$$

$$\approx 55$$

Thus the Sleepware Company should test fifty-five mattresses to limit the Type I and Type II errors to the desired levels. If the cost of sampling fifty-five mattresses is high, either the Type I or the Type II error constraint, or both, will have to be relaxed.

The process of solving for the correct sample size to control alpha and beta at the desired levels can be reduced to equation 9–2:

$$n = \left[\frac{(Z_\alpha - Z_\beta)\sigma_x}{\mu_h - \mu_t}\right]^2 \qquad (9\text{–}2)$$

where n = required sample size
   Z_α = critical Z corresponding to the desired alpha
   Z_β = critical Z corresponding to the desired beta
   μ_h = hypothesized mean
   μ_t = assumed true mean
   σ_x = standard deviation

Thus, for the Sleepware Company we apply equation 9–2 as follows:

$$n = \left[\frac{(-2.05 - 1.65)40}{1200 - 1180} \right]^2$$
$$= 54.76$$
$$\approx 55$$

This is the same result we arrived at by going through algebraic calculations.

SKILL DEVELOPMENT PROBLEMS FOR SECTION 9–4

The following set of problems is meant to test your understanding of the material in this section. Additional problems are found at the end of this chapter under this section heading.

15. Given the following null and alternative hypotheses:

$$H_0: \mu \leq 3,000$$
$$H_A: \mu > 3,000$$

and the following conditions:

   1. Alpha = 0.05
   2. Beta = 0.05 if the population mean is 3,005
   3. Beta = 0.10 if the population mean is 3,008

   a. If the population standard deviation is thought to be 80, what is the required sample size to meet the conditions stated?
   b. Based upon the sample size computed in part a, determine the appropriate decision rule.

16. Given the following null and alternative hypotheses:

$$H_0: \mu \geq 230$$
$$H_A: \mu < 230$$

and the following conditions:

   1. Alpha = 0.10
   2. Beta = 0.08 if the population mean is 227
   3. Beta = 0.14 if the population mean is 225

   a. If the population standard deviation is thought to be 100, what is the required sample size to meet the conditions stated?
   b. Based upon the sample size computed in part a, determine the appropriate decision rule.

17. Given the following null and alternative hypotheses:

$$H_0: \mu \geq 198$$
$$H_A: \mu < 198$$

and the following conditions:

1. Alpha = 0.05
2. Beta = 0.20 if the population mean is 196
3. Beta = 0.10 if the population mean is 192

   a. If the population standard deviation is thought to be fifty, what is the required sample size to meet the conditions stated?
   b. Based upon the sample size computed in part a, determine the appropriate decision rule.

18. Given the following null and alternative hypotheses:

$$H_0: \mu \leq 33.50$$
$$H_A: \mu > 33.50$$

and the following conditions:

1. Alpha = 0.10
2. Beta = 0.05 if the population mean is 34
3. Beta = 0.10 if the population mean is 35

   a. If the population standard deviation is thought to be 3.2, what is the required sample size to meet the conditions stated?
   b. Based upon the sample size computed in part a, determine the appropriate decision rule.

19. The *Regional Gazette* newspaper circulation department is considering having their customers mail in their monthly payments for the newspapers instead of having the carriers do the collecting. The carriers are concerned that they will lose the tips they receive from customers when they collect each month. The carriers claim that the average tip is at least $1.00 per customer per month. Based upon this, the newspaper is considering adding $12.00 per year per customer to the pay received by the carrier and passing this along to the customer. But first, the newspaper plans to test the carriers' claim and the manager wants a sampling plan that will meet the following conditions:

1. No more than a 5 percent chance of rejecting the claim if it is true.
2. No more than a 5 percent chance of accepting the claim if in fact the actual average is $0.90 per customer per month.
3. No more than a 7 percent chance of accepting the claim if in fact the actual average is $0.85 per month

   a. State the null and alternative hypotheses.
   b. What is the required sample size to control both types of statistical errors ac-

cording to the specified conditions if the standard deviation in tips is assumed to be $0.25?

c. State the decision rule and indicate what decision should be reached if the sample mean (based on the sample size determined in part b) is $0.96?

20. The Hilbert City Water Company is considering a change in summer water rates. The basis for this change is the claim that the average daily household use within the city has increased at least eighty gallons since the summer of 1987. The company's data analysis section has been assigned the task of verifying this claim. They wish to establish a sampling plan that will reasonably protect against both Type I and Type II statistical errors. Specifically, they wish to satisfy the following conditions:

1. No more than a 5 percent chance of rejecting the claim if it is true.
2. No more than a 3 percent chance of accepting the claim if in fact the actual average increase is seventy-four gallons per day.
3. No more than a 6 percent chance of acepting the claim if in fact the actual average increase is seventy gallons per day.

a. State the null and alternative hypotheses.
b. What is the required sample size to control both types of statistical errors according to the specified conditions if the standard deviation is assumed to be ten gallons?
c. State the decision rule and indicate what decision should be reached if the sample mean (based on the sample size determined in part b) is 76.4 gallons.

CONCLUSIONS

9-5

This chapter has introduced the fundamentals of hypothesis testing. The focus has been on hypothesis tests for decisions with large sample sizes. The concepts presented in this chapter provide decision makers with tools for using sample information to decide whether a given null hypothesis should be rejected or accepted.

In this chapter we have concentrated on examples of large-sample hypothesis tests involving a single population mean. In following chapters you will see the hypothesis-testing methodology is basically the same for all situations. The central issue is always to determine whether the sample information tends to support or refute the null hypothesis.

We have emphasized the importance of recognizing that when a hypothesis is tested, an error might occur. Type I and Type II statistical errors have been discussed, and we have shown how to calculate the probability of committing either type of error for applications involving a single population mean.

You have probably noticed that the statistical estimation techniques discussed in chapter 8 and hypothesis testing have a lot in common. Both estimation and hypothesis testing are used extensively by business decision makers. Estimation procedures are most useful when the decision makers have little or no idea of the value of a population parameter and are primarily interested in determining these values. On the other hand, hypothesis testing is used when a claim about a population value needs to be tested. Estimation and hypothesis testing are the central components of statistical inference and will be used throughout the remaining chapters of this text.

The chapter glossary contains important terms introduced in this chapter, and the chapter formulas are summarized following the glossary.

CHAPTER GLOSSARY

alpha (α)   The maximum probability of committing a Type I error.

beta (β)   The probability of committing a Type II error.

critical value   The value(s) in a hypothesis test that separate the rejection region from the acceptance region. The critical value can be in the same units as the population mean or it can be in standardized units.

hypothesis   A supposition about a true state of nature.

O.C. (operating characteristic) curve   The plot of the probability of accepting a false null hypothesis over the range of the alternative parameter values.

one-tailed hypothesis test   A hypothesis test in which the entire rejection region is located in one tail of the sampling distribution.

power   The probability of rejecting a null hypothesis when it is false. Power is the complement of beta.

power curve   The plot of the probability of rejecting a false hypothesis.

states of nature   The uncertain events over which decision makers have no direct control.

statistical inference   The process by which decision makers reach conclusions about a population based on sample information collected from the population.

two-tailed hypothesis test   A hypothesis test in which the rejection region is split between the two tails of the sampling distribution.

Type I error   Rejecting the null hypothesis when it is, in fact, true.

Type II error   Accepting the null hypothesis when it is, in fact, false.

CHAPTER FORMULAS

Critical value

$$A = \mu_x + Z \frac{\sigma_x}{\sqrt{n}}$$

$$Z = \frac{11.520 - 12}{\frac{2}{\sqrt{40}}}$$

$$= -1.52$$

The area between $Z = -1.52$ and μ_x is 0.4357, so

$$P(\text{firing}) = 0.5000 + 0.4357$$
$$= 0.9357$$

This means there is greater than 93 percent chance of firing Robinson when, in fact, he is actually producing the pieces in a time averaging twelve minutes. Note that beta $= 1 -$ power is $1 - 0.9357 = 0.0643$. This means there is slightly over a 6 percent chance this decision rule will lead to keeping Robinson if he is really producing at an average rate of twelve minutes per piece.

2. The Convoy Truck Company has been faced with steadily increasing fuel, labor, repair, and equipment costs. Although the company has raised rates as much as possible to reflect increased costs, many of the rates are subject to governmental regulation.

Four years ago Convoy completed an extensive study of the costs and revenues associated with its operations. The average profit per truckload shipment was found to be $158.12. Convoy doesn't want to go through such an extensive study again because of the costs involved and doesn't feel the need to because it hasn't altered operations. Rather than a complete study, the managers decide to select a random sample of invoices, determine the average profitability of this sample, and see if the per-run profitability has changed. The results of this sample are as follows:

$$\text{Sample size} = 800 \text{ invoices}$$
$$\text{Average sample profit} = \$149.76$$
$$\text{Sample standard deviation} = \$189.90$$

a. Formulate the null hypothesis and decision rule for Convoy if the company wants to limit the chance of making a Type I error to 4 percent.

b. Based on your decision rule and the sample data, what conclusions should the Convoy Truck Company reach?

Solutions:

a. **Hypotheses:**

H_0: $\mu_x = \$158.12$

H_A: $\mu_x \neq \$158.12$

Note that this is a two-tailed hypothesis text.

Decision Rule:

Take a sample of 800 and determine $\overline{X}$.

If $A_L \leq \overline{X} \leq A_H$, accept H_0.
If $\overline{X} < A_L$, reject H_0.
If $\overline{X} > A_H$, reject H_0.

The appropriate figure is

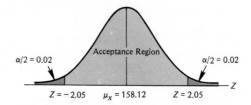

Note that we have split the rejection region into both tails.

$$A_L = \$158.12 + (-ZS_{\overline{x}}) \qquad \text{and} \qquad A_H = \$158.12 + ZS_{\overline{x}}$$

$$= \$158.12 - 2.05 \frac{\$189.90}{\sqrt{800}} \qquad\qquad\qquad = \$158.12 + 2.05 \frac{\$189.90}{\sqrt{800}}$$

$$= \$144.36 \qquad\qquad\qquad\qquad\qquad = \$171.88$$

The decision rule becomes
Decision Rule:

If $\$144.36 \leq \overline{X} \leq \$171.88$, accept H_0.
If $\overline{X} < \$144.36$, reject H_0.
If $\overline{X} > \$171.88$, reject H_0.

b. Since $\overline{X} = \$149.76$, we should not reject H_0 and conclude, based on the sample data, that the average profit has not changed.

3. The manager of a Chicago meat-packing plant has established a standard which says that from a 900-pound steer (live weight), the company should obtain an average of 550 pounds of meat (cut and wrapped). Past experience indicates that even though the average may change, the standard deviation remains fairly constant at forty pounds. To determine whether current work deviates from the standard, the manager selects a sample of 100 ($n = 100$) 900-pound steers and compares the sample average with the standard.

   a. Establish the null and alternative hypotheses.

   b. If the manager wishes to have no more than a 0.05 chance of committing a Type I error, specify the appropriate decision rule for this hypothesis test.

   c. Given an alpha level of 0.05 and the decision rule found in part b, what is the probability of committing a Type II error if an average of 547 pounds are cut and wrapped from the 900-pound steers?

d. Calculate the power of this hypothesis test if the true mean is 547 pounds. Discuss what power means in this example.

Solutions:

a. Hypotheses:

H_0: μ_x = 550 lb
H_A: $\mu_x \neq$ 550 lb

Note that because the manager is concerned with detecting departures from the mean in either direction, the hypothesis is two-tailed.

b. The appropriate decision rule is determined as follows:

Hypotheses:

H_0: μ_x = 550 lb
H_A: $\mu_x \neq$ 550 lb
α = 0.05

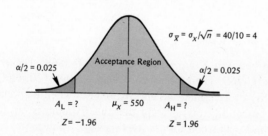

$\sigma_{\bar{x}} = \sigma_x/\sqrt{n} = 40/10 = 4$

$\alpha/2 = 0.025$ Acceptance Region $\alpha/2 = 0.025$

$A_L = ?$ $\mu_x = 550$ $A_H = ?$
$Z = -1.96$ $Z = 1.96$

Solve for critical values.

$$A_L = \mu_x + (-Z)\sigma_{\bar{x}} \quad \text{and} \quad A_H = \mu_x + Z\sigma_{\bar{x}}$$
$$= 550 - 1.96(4) \qquad\qquad = 550 + 1.96(4)$$
$$= 542.16 \qquad\qquad\qquad = 557.84$$

Decision Rule:

If $542.16 \leq \bar{X} \leq 557.84$, accept H_0.
If $\bar{X} < 542.16$, reject H_0.
If $\bar{X} > 557.84$, reject H_0.

c. To determine the probability of committing a Type II error if μ_x is actually 547 pounds, we use the following procedure:

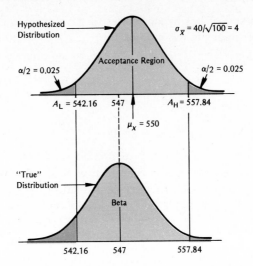

To find beta,

$$Z = \frac{A_L - \mu_x}{\sigma_{\bar{x}}} \qquad \text{and} \qquad Z = \frac{A_H - \mu_x}{\sigma_{\bar{x}}}$$

$$= \frac{542.16 - 547}{4} \qquad\qquad = \frac{557.84 - 547}{4}$$

$$= -1.21 \qquad\qquad\qquad = 2.71$$

The area between $Z = -1.21$ and μ_x is 0.3869. The area between $Z = 2.71$ and μ_x is 0.4966. Therefore, beta equals $0.3869 + 0.4966 = 0.8835$. Beta is the probability of accepting the null hypothesis when it is actually false.

d. Power is the probability of rejecting the null hypothesis. In this case, if μ_x is really 547 pounds, and not 550 as hypothesized, power $= 1 -$ beta $= 1 - 0.8835 = 0.1165$. Thus the chance of rejecting H_0 when μ_x is actually 547 pounds is only 0.1165. If this probability is too low, either alpha or the sample size can be increased.

ADDITIONAL PROBLEMS

Section 9–2

21. Discuss the two types of statistical errors that can occur when a hypothesis is tested. Illustrate what you mean by using a business example.

22. What is meant by the term *critical value* in a hypothesis-testing situation? Illustrate what you mean with a business example.

23. What is the probability of committing a Type I error called? How is this probability determined? Discuss.

24. The Main Street Burger Station recently ran a coupon advertisement in the local newspaper in which it offered a free soft drink with the purchase of a meal. Since the store did not define precisely what a meal was in the advertisement, the store manager was concerned with whether the average meal purchased using the coupon was less than or equal to $2.75.

    a. If the store manager wished to know whether the average meal purchase with a coupon was less than or equal to $2.75 without examining every cash receipt for the week, describe the procedure he might use to make a statistical inference about the average amount spent with the coupon.

    b. Formulate the appropriate null and alternative hypotheses and discuss in the terms of the problem what a Type I error would be and what a Type II error would be.

    c. Suppose the manager wished to select a random sample of fifty cash register receipts. What would the critical value be if the population standard deviation were somehow known to be $0.50? Express the critical value in the same terms as the sample mean. Assume alpha equals 0.05.

    d. Referring to parts b and c, suppose the sample results showed a sample mean of $2.83. What conclusion should be reached and why if the test were performed with an alpha level of 0.05?

25. The Sergo Company operates coin-operated candy machines in Lincoln, Nebraska. When the company first started using the so-called "talking" machines it expected daily revenue per machine to be at least $62, on the average. Suppose the standard deviation in daily sales per machine is known to be $10.

    a. Formulate the appropriate null and alternative hypotheses for this situation.

    b. Establish the critical value and decision rule using the Z value approach, assuming the alpha level is 0.05.

    c. Suppose a sample of 100 observations ($n = 100$) was taken in the Lincoln area over a period of time after the new machines had been installed and the average revenue per machine was $59.35. Compute the appropriate test statistic and indicate what inference should be made about the population mean.

26. The Zurker Chemical Company develops and manufactures pharmaceutical drugs for distribution and sale in the United States. The pharmaceutical business can be very lucrative when useful and safe drugs are introduced into the market. Whenever Zurker research lab considers putting a drug into production, the company must actually establish the following sets of null and alternative hypotheses:

Set 1	Set 2
H_0: The drug is safe.	H_0: The drug is effective.
H_A: The drug is not safe.	H_A: The drug is not effective.

    Taking each set of hypotheses separately, discuss the considerations that should be made in establishing alpha and beta.

27. The Coopers Insurance Company provides insurance coverage for automobile owners at a fixed premium. If customers are poor risks, Coopers would like to deny

them coverage. However, if the customers are good risks, Coopers would like to have the business. Each time an individual applies for insurance, Coopers is faced with the following null and alternative hypotheses:

H_0: The applicant is a good risk.
H_A: The applicant is a poor risk.

Given that Coopers has recently been suffering decreasing profits, how would you go about assessing levels for alpha and beta? Discuss the factors that you consider important in arriving at this decision. How would your responses change if Coopers were a new company anxious to grow and expand? Discuss your reasoning.

28. The Softsoap Company recently developed a new soap product designed for use in automatic washing machines. The marketing department would like to claim in its advertisements that the new soap will save the average homeowner at least ten ounces of soap per month. Before setting up the advertising plan, it decided to test the product in a random sample of seventy-five homes for a period of one month. Homeowners selected were asked to record how much soap they had used the month before. Then they were asked to keep track of their soap usage with the new Softsoap product. They were asked to keep their washing procedures the same as before the test.
    a. Establish the null and alternative hypotheses to be tested considering the objectives of the marketing department.
    b. Assuming that the population standard deviation is known to be three ounces saved per month, what is the decision rule for the hypothesis test if the test is to be conducted with an alpha level of 0.05?
    c. Suppose the sample shows that the average savings is 9.5 ounces. What conclusion should the Softsoap marketing department reach with respect to its desired advertising claim? Discuss.
    d. With respect to the decision reached in part c, comment on which statistical error may have been committed and what it would mean to the Softsoap Company.

29. The C. C. Jaynes Speedreading Course advertises that the average increase in reading speed for graduates of the course is at least 200 words per minute. Assuming that the standard deviation for the population is known to be forty words per minute, what should an independent reviewer conclude if a sample of 110 graduates showed an average improvement of 195 words per minute? Test at the alpha level of 0.05.

    Suppose the true population standard deviation is twenty words per minute rather than forty. Assuming that the sample results were the same and alpha was held to 0.05, what conclusion should be reached with respect to the speedreading course offered by C. C. Jaynes? Discuss why the change in standard deviation would have this effect on the conclusion reached, considering that the sample information did not change.

30. The J. H. Smith & Sons Company sells dwarf fruit trees through the mail. It claims that the average pear tree will produce at least 2.5 bushels of pears the second year after it has been planted. If the standard deviation in production is known to be 0.70 bushel and the desired alpha level is 0.10, what should be concluded if the following data were recorded for a sample of forty trees showing the number of bushels produced the second year after planting?

1.5	3.3	4.0	2.6
2.6	2.8	3.2	2.7
3.4	2.4	3.6	3.9
2.7	3.1	2.6	1.9
2.8	3.0	2.8	1.5
3.0	2.5	1.9	3.0
3.0	4.5	1.0	2.3
1.8	2.9	0.4	3.6
2.0	2.5	2.7	2.6
2.4	1.3	3.5	2.0

31. The Jamison Secretarial Service claims that its typists average at least 3.4 pages per hour. Before placing this information in its advertising brochures, Jamison wishes to determine if this claim is true. A random sample of 400 records indicating typing productivity shows a mean of 3.2 pages per hour. Assuming the population standard deviation is known to be 0.5 page per hour and the desired alpha level is 0.05:

a. Establish the appropriate null and alternative hypotheses.

b. Develop the decision rule and test the null hypothesis. Indicate what the decision means to Jamison.

c. Would the decision rule change if the same sample results had been obtained from a sample of thirty-six records? Discuss why or why not.

d. Suppose the sample mean from a sample of size 300 is 3.34 pages per hour. What decision should Jamison make based on these sample data? Explain what this means to Jamison.

32. A manufacturer of computer terminals claims that its product will last at least fifty hours without needing repairs. The Bo-Little Corporation is considering purchasing a great many of these computer terminals. Bo-Little's data-processing manager has determined that given the price of the terminal and the total dollars involved, Bo-Little should ask for some quality control records from the manufacturer.

Suppose the manufacturer produces records of a random sample of 100 terminals. The average time before the first breakdown was forty-eight hours. Assume the population standard deviation is known to be twenty-five hours.

a. Set up the appropriate null and alternative hypotheses.

b. Determine the appropriate decision rule and indicate whether the sample information justifies rejecting the manufacturer's claim. Use an alpha level of 0.10.

c. Discuss the ramifications of this decision and the potential costs of being wrong.

33. Referring to problem 32, suppose the sample mean of 100 terminals had been forty-five hours rather than forty-eight.
    a. What is the probability of finding a sample mean as small or smaller than forty-five if the true mean is fifty hours?
    b. Now that you have determined the probability in part a, what does this mean to you with respect to whether or not the terminals can be expected to average at least fifty hours before the first breakdown?
    c. "If the probability of a sample result, given the null hypothesis, is too small, the null hypothesis should be rejected." Comment on this statement with respect to your answers in parts a and b.
    d. What relationship does alpha have with a "too small" sample result, as discussed in part c?

34. In a recent management-union negotiating process at a large national tire manufacturing company, one of the points made by management was that the average number of dollars in health-care benefits used per worker was $411 per year. They also indicated that the standard deviation was $200 per employee. Assuming that the standard deviation figure is correct, the union decided to select a random sample of 100 employee health records and test to determine whether the management assertion was correct. It planned to test at an alpha level of 0.08.
    a. Set up the correct null and alternative hypotheses.
    b. Discuss why this hypothesis test is considered a two-tailed hypothesis test.
    c. If the sample mean for the 100 workers was $402, what should the union conclude about the claim made by management? Discuss.

35. The All Star Testing service prepares real estate license examinations for several states. Wisconsin officials are considering hiring this company to devise a test for their real estate brokers' license requirements. Wisconsin requires that the average test score be exactly 70 points. In order to evaluate the test prepared by All Star Testing, Wisconsin officials have selected a random sample of sixty potential brokers and have administered the exam. They found that the mean score was 68.75 points.
    a. State the appropriate null and alternative hypotheses.
    b. Assuming that the true standard deviation is 10 points and the hypothesis is to be tested at an alpha level of 0.05, what conclusions should be reached based on the sample data? Discuss.

36. The Rice Krackle Cereal Company has a machine that automatically fills 16-ounce boxes of cereal. This machine may be set to any mean fill, but the standard deviation of fill is known to be 0.5 ounce. The machine gets out of adjustment sometimes, even though the mean has been set at the desired fill level. The production manager has the responsibility of testing samples of filled cereal boxes to see whether the average fill has deviated from the desired level.
    a. Suppose the average fill level has been set at 16.2 ounces. If a sample of fifty boxes is tested and found to average 16.26 ounces, what should the production manager conclude about the machine's adjustment? Test at an alpha level of 0.05.

b. Suppose the average fill setting is 16.2 ounces, but instead of a sample of fifty boxes, the sample size is 400 boxes. What conclusion should the production manager reach if the sample mean is the same as before, 16.26 ounces? Test at an alpha level of 0.05.

c. Why are the conclusions different even though the sample mean was the same for both parts a and b? Discuss.

37. The Ribold Company has a contract to produce a part for Boeing Corporation which must have an average diameter of 5 inches and a standard deviation of 0.10 inch. The Ribold Company has developed the process, which will meet the specifications with respect to the standard deviation, but it is still trying to meet the mean specifications. A test run (considered a random sample) of parts was produced and the company wishes to determine whether this latest process that produced the sample will produce parts meeting the requirement of average diameter equal to 5 inches.

a. Specify the appropriate null and alternative hypotheses.

b. Develop the decision rule, assuming that the sample size is 200 parts and the alpha level is 0.01.

c. What should the Ribold Company conclude if the sample mean diameter for the 200 parts is 5.016 inches? Discuss.

38. At a recent meeting of the budget committee at the Beltline Corporation, the marketing manager made a pitch for a larger department budget by stating that more money was needed in advertising to improve the company's image. This prompted the president of the company to establish a task force to measure public opinion about the company.

   This task force planned to use a well-established instrument for measuring public perception of companies like Beltline. Past studies using this particular instrument indicated that a company should receive at least an average forty point overall rating to consider that it has a positive image by the public.

   The task force randomly sampled 400 people within the market area and found that the average rating received was 38.95, with a sample standard deviation of 5.2 points.

a. Establish the appropriate null and alternative hypotheses.

b. Assuming that the test is to be conducted with an alpha equal to 0.10, what conclusion should the Beltline Company reach with respect to its average company rating by all the members of the population? Discuss.

39. The Inland Empire Food Store Company has stated in its advertising that the average shopper will save $5.00 or more per week by shopping at Inland stores. A consumer group has decided to test this assertion by sampling fifty shoppers who currently shop at other stores. It selects the customers and then notes each item purchased at their regular store. These same items are then priced at the Inland store and the total bill is compared. The following data reflect savings at Inland for the fifty shoppers. Note that those cases where the bill was higher at Inland are marked with a minus sign.

$14.00	$2.54	$11.33	$12.02	$ 4.55
12.00	8.45	−0.75	1.33	12.04
− 5.04	2.80	2.09	− 3.10	8.07
12.10	3.21	2.70	4.65	1.03
2.13	9.75	1.73	− 1.54	9.80
3.56	3.29	1.34	− 4.08	9.70
10.02	1.13	4.56	− 1.52	3.23
− 0.65	−5.02	2.19	− 3.45	0.65
1.90	2.43	0.43	2.54	0.03
2.10	−0.56	7.89	− 0.65	1.34

a. Set up the appropriate null and alternative hypotheses to test Inland's claim.

b. Using an alpha level of 0.05, develop the decision rule and test the hypothesis. Discuss the results.

40. Ted Parker operates a gas station in a suburban area of Detroit. He is thinking of installing a mechanism on his self-service pumps that won't allow more than ten gallons to be pumped without having the pump restarted. He hopes this will cut down on theft without making the honest customers angry.

The marketing representative for the new mechanism claims that if Ted's station is typical, the average fill-up is no more than ten gallons. Ted has decided to select a random sample of 100 customers and test to determine whether the marketing man's claim is true.

a. Establish the appropriate null and alternative hypotheses.

b. If the sample results show a mean of 10.22 gallons per fill-up, with a sample standard deviation of 2.7 gallons, what should Ted conclude about the population mean? Use an alpha level of 0.05. Discuss your results.

41. The United States federal government has issued requests for proposals to cities around the country that might wish to serve as the site of a wind energy research facility. This facility would employ about 100 people and would be a boost to the economy of any city, but especially smaller cities.

The government required that the average wind speed year round in the selected city be at least 10 m.p.h. In response to this bid, Cheyenne, Wyoming, submitted a bid for the research facility. Its proposal reached the finalist stage. The last step in the selection process was for the federal government to select a random sample of 300 days from the National Weather Service records for the city to determine whether the city met the average wind-speed requirements.

If the average wind speed for the sampled days was 9.58 m.p.h., with a standard deviation of 4.6 m.p.h., what should the federal government conclude about the average wind speed in Cheyenne? Use an alpha level of 0.03. Discuss your conclusions.

42. The Maine State Tax Commission attempts to set up payroll-tax withholding tables such that by the end of the year, an employee's income tax withholding is about $100 below his actual income tax owed to the state. The commission director claims that when all the Maine returns are in, the average additional payment will be less than or equal to $100.

A random sample of forty accounts revealed an average additional payment of $114 with a sample variance of $2,400. Testing at an alpha level of 0.10, do the sample data refute the director's claim?

Section 9–3

43. The Cherry Hill Growers Association operates a fruit warehouse in California. Because of the volume of cherries that arrive at the warehouse during the picking season, the growers have agreed that instead of weighing each box of cherries, they would assume that the average box weighs twenty pounds. The total weight is then simply the number of boxes times twenty pounds.

Past studies have shown that the standard deviation of weight from box to box is 0.5 pound. Suppose the manager of the warehouse has decided to select a random sample of fifty boxes of cherries from a particular grower's crop. He feels that the grower may be underfilling the boxes and is concerned with detecting this if it is the case. He is not concerned if the average box contains more than twenty pounds.
   a. State the appropriate null and alternative hypotheses.
   b. Establish the decision rule that the warehouse manager should use if he wishes to have at most a 10 percent chance of committing a Type I error.
   c. What is the probability of the warehouse manager making a Type II error if the true average weight is 19.75 pounds per box?
   d. What is the probability of the warehouse manager making a Type II error if the true average weight of a box is 19.85 pounds. Explain why the probability of a Type II error is larger in part d than in part c.

44. The personnel manager for a large airline has claimed that on the average workers are asked to work no more than three hours overtime per week. Past studies show the standard deviation in overtime hours per worker to be 1.2 hours.

Suppose the union negotiators wish to test this claim by sampling payroll records for 150 employees. They feel that the personnel manager's claim is untrue, but want to base their conclusion on the sample results.
   a. State the null and alternative hypotheses and discuss the meaning of Type I and Type II errors in this case.
   b. Establish the appropriate decision rule if the union wishes to have no more than a 0.01 chance of a Type I error.
   c. Determine the value of beta if the true mean overtime is 3.02 hours.
   d. Compute the Type II error probability under the assumption that the true mean is 3.05 hours.

45. The Pell Corporation is the parent corporation that franchises automobile lube and oil change centers around the United States. The standard set forth by the Pell Corporation is that the average time to lube and change oil in a car is ten minutes or less.

Periodically, representatives from the Pell Company visit the franchises and perform a compliance test on this standard. They randomly select 100 cars (without the local operator's knowledge) and record how long it takes to service each car. Then, based on the sample mean, they will determine whether the franchise is operating within the standard. (The standard deviation is known to be 2.0 minutes.)

a. Establish the appropriate null and alternative hypotheses.

b. Determine the decision rule assuming that the company performs the compliance test using an alpha level of 0.05.

c. Determine the probability of committing a Type II error if the true average service time is 10.30 minutes.

d. Referring to part c, calculate power and explain what it means.

e. Develop an operating characteristic curve with values of beta obtained for the following values of the true mean:

$$\mu = 10.10 \text{ min}$$
$$\mu = 10.20 \text{ min}$$
$$\mu = 10.30 \text{ min}$$
$$\mu = 10.40 \text{ min}$$
$$\mu = 10.50 \text{ min}$$
$$\mu = 10.60 \text{ min}$$

Explain why a decision maker might be interested in developing an operating characteristic curve. Also based on this O.C. curve, comment on the sampling procedure employed by the Pell Corporation in evaluating performance of its franchises.

46. Suppose the manager in charge of compliance auditing for the Pell Corporation (see problem 45) has decided that a larger sample size is necessary and thus has decided to select a random sample of 150 cars rather than 100. What general impact will this have on the probability of committing a Type II error for any level of the true mean? What impact will this have on the probability of committing a Type I error? Discuss.

47. The makers of Super Cover paint advertise that their product will average at least 900 square feet a gallon coverage. A consumers' group which regularly tests these types of claims has budgeted enough money to sample fifty gallons of paint. It uses an alpha level of 0.10 to test claims like the one made by Super Cover. The consumers' group will base its analysis on findings of a previous study which showed the standard deviation in area covered to be 200 square feet.

a. State the null and alternative hypothesis to be tested.

b. Establish the appropriate decision rule for this hypothesis test.

c. Determine the probability of accepting the null hypothesis when, in fact, the true average area covered is 875 square feet.

d. Referring to part c, what is the probability of a Type II error if the sample size could be increased to seventy-five gallons? Discuss why the increase in sample size reduces the Type II error probability.

48. The managing partner of Brookings and Associates, a CPA firm, has a basic knowledge of hypothesis testing. One of his clients, a retail store, would like Brookings to perform an audit of the daily cash register tape against the actual dollar amount in the till.

The client recognizes that occasionally an error is going to occur. As long as the error is in the store's favor, the store manager is not concerned. However, when the store comes up short, the store manager is very concerned.

The Brookings managing partner has indicated that he will perform the audit via sampling and hypothesis testing with the following hypotheses:

H_0: $\mu_x \geq$ \$0 error, store at least comes out even on the average
H_A: $\mu_x <$ \$0 error, the store loses some money on the average

From past experience in this kind of audit, the CPA feels that A, the critical value, should be set at $-$\$2. Therefore, if the average discrepancy between cash register tape and actual dollars is \$2 or more at the store's expense, the null hypothesis will be rejected. If the null hypothesis is rejected, the clerk will be dismissed.

The CPA partner realizes that his client wants to be very sure any such employee is fired, but only if the firing is truly justified. Consequently he is concerned with knowing beta for various values of the true, but unknown, population mean.

a. If the sample size is forty-nine days and the standard deviation is known to be \$4.00, what is beta if the true mean is actually $-$\$1.50?

b. Calculate beta for a sample size of sixty-four. The standard deviation remains \$4, and the critical value, A, is held at $-$\$2.

c. Why has an increase in sample size caused an increase, rather than a decrease, in beta? Discuss how this undesirable event happened and how you could have prevented it from happening in this case. (Consult the following article if you need some help: Herbert H. Tsang, "The Effects of Changing Sample Size on the Alpha and Beta Errors: A Pedagogic Note," *Decision Sciences* 8 (October 1977): 757–59.)

Section 9–4

49. The Television Advertising Institute claims that, on the average, adults spend 2.4 hours or more watching television on Thursday nights during the prime time hours of 8:00 to 11:00. Past studies have shown that the standard deviation is 0.6 hour. The National Educational Association wishes to test this claim, but is uncertain how large the sample size should be to meet the following requirements: (1) no more than a 0.10 chance of rejecting the null hypothesis when it is true; and (2) no more than a 0.20 chance of accepting the null hypothesis when in fact the true mean is 2.28 hours. Determine the sample size sufficient to meet both of these restrictions.

Also, develop the appropriate decision rule and test the hypothesis, assuming the sample information provides a sample mean of 2.35 hours. Which type of error may have been committed in this case? Discuss.

50. The L. G. and Associates firm performs market research work for clients primarily located along the eastern United States seaboard. Recently it was hired by a firm to perform a review of some work done by the company's own marketing department. The marketing department estimated that the average income in a particular market area was $21,600, with a standard deviation of $500. In reviewing this work, L. G. and Associates plans to select a sample of people in the market area and, based on the sample mean, either refute or support the $21,600 hypothesis. However, before issuing a review report, L. G. and Associates has set the following requirements, which will impact on its sample size requirements.

(a) No more than a 0.05 chance of a Type I error; (b) a 0.10 chance of accepting the null hypothesis when in fact the true average income is $21,450; and (c) no more than a 0.05 chance of accepting that the mean is $21,600 when in fact it really is $21,400. Assuming that the population standard deviation is $500.00, determine the sample size required to meet these restrictions.

51. The Consumer Information Company is interested in performing a test to validate an advertising claim made by the Tremco Drill Company that the average useful life of its electronic drill equipment is at least 400 hours. A prior study has shown the standard deviation to be twenty hours. What size sample should Consumer Information select if it wishes to satisfy the following constraints?

a. No more than a 0.05 chance of committing a Type I error.

b. No more than a 0.10 chance of committing a Type II error when $\mu_x = 390$ hours.

c. No more than a 0.14 chance of committing a Type II error when $\mu_x = 395$ hours.

d. Suppose the standard deviation for the population is thirty hours, not twenty as previously thought. Compute the required sample size to control alpha and beta. Comment on why the sample size requirements are greater when the population standard deviation is larger.

52. Suppose a fast-food chain is considering expanding into a new community but management knows from past experience that the chances of success are limited if the income level in the community is too low. To justify expansion, management feels that the average per capita income must be at least $8,100 per year.

To determine the feasibility of expansion, the chain wishes to select a sample to test the hypothesis that the income is at least $8,100. Suppose another study has indicated that the standard deviation of income in this community is $1,900. What decision rule should the company adopt if it will accept the following:

a. No more than a 0.0735 chance of a Type I error when $\mu_x = \$8,100$. No more than a 0.10 chance of committing a Type II error if $\mu_x = \$8,000$. Remember, the decision rule includes the required sample size and the appropriate critical value.

b. Show the impact on the required sample size if the probability of the Type II error is held to 0.05 when $\mu_x = \$8,000$. State why the sample size changed in this manner.

c. Suppose the cost of the sample sizes determined in parts a and b is too great.

What alternatives do the decision makers have? Discuss why each will likely lower the required sample size.

C A S E S

9A   Campbell Brewery, Inc., Part 1

Don Campbell and his younger brother Edward purchased Campbell Brewery from their father in 1983. The brewery makes and bottles beer under two labels and distributes throughout the Southwest. Since purchasing the brewery, Don has been instrumental in modernizing operations.

One of the latest acquisitions is a filling machine, which can be adjusted to fill at any average fill level desired. Since the bottles and cans filled by the brewery are exclusively the 12-ounce size, when they received the machine Don set the fill level to 12 ounces and left it that way. According to the manufacturer's specifications, the machine would fill bottles or cans around the average, with a standard deviation of 0.15 ounce.

Don just returned from a brewery convention where he attended a panel discussion related to problems with filling machines. One brewery representative discussed a problem her company had when it failed to learn that its machine's average fill went out of adjustment until several months later when its cost accounting department reported some problems with beer production in bulk not matching output in bottles and cans. It turns out that the machine's average fill had slipped from 12 ounces to 12.07 ounces. With large volumes of production, this deviation meant substantial loss in profits.

Another brewery reported on the same type of problem, but in the opposite direction. Its machine began filling bottles with slightly less than 12 ounces on the average. Although the consumers could not detect the shortage in a given bottle, the state and federal agencies responsible for checking the accuracy of packaged products discovered the problem in their testing and fined the brewery substantially for the underfill.

These problems were a surprise to Don Campbell. He had not considered that the machine might go out of adjustment and pose these types of problems. In fact he became very concerned because both problems of losing profits and potentially being fined by the government were ones that he wished to avoid if possible. Following the convention, Don and Ed decided to hire a consulting firm with expertise in these matters to assist them in setting up a procedure for monitoring the performance of the filling machine.

The consultant suggested that they set up a sampling plan whereby once a month they sample some number of bottles and measure their volume precisely. If the average of the sample deviates too much from 12 ounces, they should shut the machine down and make necessary adjustments. Otherwise, they should let the filling process continue. The consultant identified two types of problems that can occur from this sort of sampling plan:

1. They may incorrectly decide to adjust the machine when it was not really necessary to do so.

2. They may incorrectly decide to allow the filling process to continue when, in fact, the true average has deviated from 12 ounces.

After carefully considering what the consultant told them, Don indicated that he wanted no more than a 0.02 chance of the first problem occurring because of the costs involved. He also decided that if the true average fill had slipped to 11.99 ounces, he wanted no more than a 0.05 chance of not detecting this with his sampling plan. He wanted to avoid problems with the state and federal agencies. Finally, if the true average fill had actually risen to 12.007 ounces, he wants to be able to detect this 98 percent of the time with his sampling plan. Thus, he wants to avoid the lost profits that would result from such a problem.

Don needs to determine how large a sample size is necessary to meet his requirements.

9B   Campbell Brewery, Inc., Part 2

Don and Ed Campbell (see case 9A) received assistance in setting up a sampling plan for helping them detect whether their filling machine had gone out of adjustment. Upon hearing the results of the sample size calculations, both Don and Ed were shocked. It was simply not feasible to sample that many bottles and cans each month.

Don's letter to the consultant expressed his dissatisfaction with the sample size requirements. He requested a report back from the consultant advising him of his options regarding how the sample size could be reduced. The report was to contain specific options and the resulting sample sizes as well as an overall review of the general trade-offs involved in this type of situation. You have been assigned the task by the consulting firm to prepare this report to the Campbell Brewery.

ADDITIONAL LARGE SAMPLE HYPOTHESIS TESTS

10

WHY DECISION MAKERS NEED TO KNOW

Chapter 9 introduced the topic of hypothesis testing. Although it may initially appear to be only a statistical procedure, you should recognize the process as common in many decision-making situations. For instance:

- On the basis of initial discussions with state party officials, a politician tentatively decides to run for office (hypothesizes she could win). She commissions a political poll to gauge her strength with voters (gathering sample information). Based on the results of the poll, she will make her final decision.
- A bioengineering firm has developed a strain of corn that, in laboratory tests, appears to be more resistant to frost than current strains. The new strain appears to have commercial value (the hypothesis). The firm decides to perform a field trial (gather sample information) before making the final decision on whether to market the seeds.
- A travel agency with many branches in Florida has been notified the printing firm supplying its office forms is going out of business. Two competing firms are bidding for the agency's business. The travel agency's central office manager sees no reason to favor one firm over the other (the hypothesis) but asks to see samples of both firms' work (gather sample information) before making a decision between the two.
- After listening to the weather report on the nightly news, you decide tomorrow may be rainy (the hypothesis) and so place your umbrella by the door. Before leaving in the morning you look up at the sky (gather sample information) and decide not to take the umbrella after all.

Clearly the hypothesis-testing procedure fits in well with the way many decisions are made. Just as clearly, based on the discussion of chapter 9, a correctly executed statistical hypothesis depends on more than a seat-of-the-pants look at the situation. This chapter extends the hypothesis-testing discussion started in the last chapter.

CHAPTER OBJECTIVES

Chapter 9 introduced the steps taken when performing a statistical hypothesis test. These steps were discussed when considering only hypothesis tests about a population mean. This chapter will extend the hypothesis-testing discussion to include hypothesizing about a population proportion, about the difference between two population means, and about the difference between two population proportions. In each situation, this chapter will emphasize the use of the following steps in conducting a statistical hypothesis test:

1. Determine the null and alternative hypotheses.
2. Determine the desired alpha (α).
3. Choose a sample size.
4. Determine the critical value, A, or $Z_{critical}$.
5. Establish the decision rule.
6. Select the sample and perform the test.

STUDENT OBJECTIVES

After studying the material in this chapter, you should be able to extend the hypothesis-testing procedure to

1. Performing hypothesis tests about a population proportion.
2. Performing hypothesis tests about the difference between two population means.
3. Performing hypothesis tests about the difference between two population proportions.

HYPOTHESIS TESTING ABOUT A POPULATION PROPORTION

10-1 The discussion in chapter 9 involved hypotheses tests about a single population mean. Although there are many decision problems that can be limited to a test of population mean, there are many other cases where the value of interest is the **population proportion.** For example, the percentage of defective items produced on an assembly line might determine whether the assembly process should be restructured or left as it is, or the success of a life insurance salesperson might be measured by the percentage of renewals generated from his or her existing customers.

The Burns and Williams C.P.A. firm has been asked to perform an audit on the brokerage account balances of customers of a large Seattle, Washington, stockbroker. Managers of the brokerage firm are concerned that their internal control procedures may be inadequate and that one percent or more of the customer account balances may be incorrect.

The Burns and Williams firm has selected a random sample of 600 customer accounts and has determined that four have actual balances that differ from those stated on the customer records. Does this sample information indicate that one percent or more of the entire population of client files are in error?

To answer this question statistically, we need to recall our work in chapters 7 and 8, in which we indicated that the sampling distribution for the population proportion is approximately normal for large sample sizes. Then we perform the hypothesis test at an alpha level of 0.02 by taking the following steps:

Hypotheses:

$H_0: p \geq 0.01$

$H_A: p < 0.01$

$\alpha = 0.02$

Next, a decision rule is formulated as shown in figure 10–1. Thus if the proportion of incorrect account balances in the sample, $\hat{p}$, is less than 0.00176, the auditors will conclude that the internal controls are doing their job and no further auditing is required (i.e., $p < 0.01$). Otherwise, they will conclude that the proportion of incorrect accounts is 0.01 or greater. Note that this formulation of H_0 and H_A protects against the more costly error of continuing to operate with faulty internal controls.

The sample results are

$$n = 600$$
$$X = 4 \text{ errors}$$
$$\hat{p} = \frac{4}{600} \approx 0.0067$$

Thus, since 0.0067 is greater than or equal to 0.00176, H_0 is accepted. The inference based on the sample data is that the accounting firm should perform a complete audit of the internal controls.

An important point to consider when testing hypotheses about a population proportion is that the standard deviation of the sampling distribution, σ_p, is formed using the hypothesized proportion rather than the sample proportion. Equation 10–1 illustrates this:

$$\sigma_p = \sqrt{\frac{p(1 - p)}{n}} \qquad \text{(10–1)}$$

where p = hypothesized proportion
n = sample size

Hypotheses:

$H_0: p \geq 0.01$
$H_A: p < 0.01$

$\alpha = 0.02$

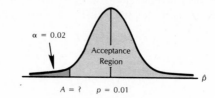

$$Z_{0.48} = -2.06$$

$$\sigma_p = \sqrt{\frac{(p)(1 - p)}{n}} = \sqrt{\frac{(0.01)(0.99)}{600}} = 0.004$$

The critical value, A, is 2.06 standard deviations below $p = 0.01$. Thus, the critical value is

$$A = p + Z \sqrt{\frac{p(1 - p)}{n}}$$

or

$$A = p + Z\sigma_p$$
$$= 0.01 - (2.06)(0.004)$$
$$= 0.00176$$

Decision Rule:

If $\hat{p} < 0.00176$, reject H_0.
If $\hat{p} \geq 0.00176$, accept H_0.

FIGURE 10–1
Decision rule, Burns and Williams example

SKILL DEVELOPMENT PROBLEMS FOR SECTION 10–1

The following set of problems is meant to test your understanding of the material in this section. Additional problems are found at the end of this chapter under this section heading.

1. Given the following null and alternative hypotheses:

$$H_0: p \leq 0.24$$

$$H_A: p > 0.24$$

Test the null hypothesis based upon a random sample of $n = 100$ where $\hat{p} = 0.267$. Assume an alpha $= 0.05$ level. Be sure to show clearly the decision rule.

2. Given the following null and alternative hypotheses:

$$H_0: p \geq 0.50$$
$$H_A: p < 0.50$$

Test the null hypothesis based upon a random sample of $n = 200$ where $\hat{p} = 0.469$. Assume an alpha $= 0.10$ level. Be sure to show clearly the decision rule.

3. Given the following null and alternative hypotheses:

$$H_0: p = 0.20$$
$$H_A: p \neq 0.20$$

Test the null hypothesis based upon a random sample of $n = 100$ where $\hat{p} = 0.225$. Assume an alpha $= 0.05$ level. Be sure to show clearly the decision rule.

4. A shopping center developer claims in a presentation to a potential client that at least 40 percent of the adult female population in a community visit the mall one or more times a week. To test this claim, the developer selected a random sample of 100 households with an adult female present and asked whether they visit the mall at least one day per week. Thirty-eight of the 100 respondents indicated "yes" to the question. Based upon the sample data and an alpha $= 0.05$ level, what should be concluded about the developer's claim? Show the decision rule and your analysis clearly.

5. A large number of complaints have been received in the past six months regarding airlines losing fliers' baggage. The airlines claim the problem is nowhere near as great as the newspaper articles have indicated. In fact, one airline spokesman claimed that no more than 1 percent of all bags fail to arrive at the destination with the passenger. To test this claim, 200 bags were randomly selected at various airports in the United States when they were checked with this airline. Of these, six failed to reach the destination when the passenger (owner) arrived. Is this sufficient evidence to refute the airline spokesman's claim? Test at an alpha $= 0.05$ level. Discuss.

HYPOTHESIS TESTING ABOUT THE DIFFERENCE BETWEEN TWO POPULATION MEANS

10-2

Many business decision problems require analyzing values from two or more populations. This section introduces methods to test hypotheses about the *difference between two population means*. These methods, however, are merely extensions of hypothesis tests for one population mean.

The Peterson Toy Company designs and manufactures games for children and adults. The company has several popular games currently in production, but still finds itself with excess production capacity. Consequently the company introduces new games as fast as they are designed and at the same time eliminates poor sellers from production. The marketing people push for games with recognizable themes and attempt to time their introduction for a holiday season, particularly Christmas.

The Peterson marketing people have performed extensive market research to determine what factors are most influential in a game's success or failure. A critical factor in children's games is the length of time needed to play the game. Games that are too complicated and too long are generally poor sellers, as are games that can be finished too quickly and are considered unchallenging.

After a new children's game has been designed, the company selects a sample of typical children to play it on a trial basis to determine the average time needed to finish. When the new game is similar to an existing game, the two are compared to determine whether they are equal with respect to average playing time.

For example, Peterson is currently developing an advertising plan for a game with the company identification "1." Some marketing department members fear that game 1 requires too much time to play. Recently the research and design department has developed a game that is similar to game 1 in design but which it claims should take less time to play. However, the new game contains other features that are important in selling games. The new game is assigned the identification "2."

The marketing department at Peterson wishes to test the following hypotheses:

Hypotheses:

H_0: $\mu_1 \leq \mu_2$ or $\mu_1 - \mu_2 \leq 0$

H_A: $\mu_1 > \mu_2$ or $\mu_1 - \mu_2 > 0$

To simplify notation, we let μ_1 and μ_2 equal the population means, μ_{x_1}, and μ_{x_2}, respectively. Also, we let σ_1^2 and σ_2^2 represent the population variances, $\sigma_{x_1}^2$ and $\sigma_{x_2}^2$, respectively. We shall follow this notation pattern throughout the remainder of the text whenever two or more populations are considered.

The null hypothesis states that the average playing time for game 2 is *as long as or longer than* the average for game 1. If this is accepted, the company will continue with its marketing efforts for game 1. If the null hypothesis is rejected, the company will conclude that the average playing time for game 2 is *less than the average* time for game 1. In this case, Peterson will abandon game 1 in favor of game 2.

The decision rule for the Peterson hypothesis is as follows:

Decision Rule:

Select two samples, n_1 and n_2, and calculate $\overline{X}_1$ and $\overline{X}_2$.

If $\overline{X}_1 - \overline{X}_2 \leq A$, accept H_0.

If $\overline{X}_1 - \overline{X}_2 > A$, reject H_0.

In chapter 7 we introduced the central limit theorem for the sampling distribution of $\overline{X}$. The central limit theorem also applies for the sampling distribution of the difference between two sample means. Thus, if the sample sizes are sufficiently large, the sampling distribution of $(\overline{X}_1 - \overline{X}_2)$ will be approximately normally distributed, with a mean and standard error as shown in equations 10–2 and 10–3:

$$\mu_{\bar{x}_1 - \bar{x}_2} = \mu_1 - \mu_2 \qquad \text{(10–2)}$$

and

$$\sigma_{\bar{x}_1 - \bar{x}_2} = \sqrt{\frac{\sigma_1^2}{n_1} + \frac{\sigma_2^2}{n_2}} \qquad \text{(10–3)}$$

where $\overline{X}_1$ and $\overline{X}_2$ = sample means for population 1 and population 2, respectively

$\mu_1 - \mu_2$ = hypothesized difference between population means

σ_1^2 and σ_2^2 = variances of population 1 and population 2, respectively

n_1 and n_2 = sample sizes from population 1 and population 2, respectively

Thus the critical value for the large-sample statistical test of the difference between two population means is found by solving equation 10–4 for A:

$$Z = \frac{A - (\mu_1 - \mu_2)}{\sqrt{\dfrac{\sigma_1^2}{n_1} + \dfrac{\sigma_2^2}{n_2}}} \qquad \text{(10–4)}$$

Then, solving for A,

$$A = (\mu_1 - \mu_2) + Z\sqrt{\frac{\sigma_1^2}{n_1} + \frac{\sigma_2^2}{n_2}}$$

Suppose the variances of the times needed to complete the games are 900 minutes for game 1 and 900 minutes for game 2. The company is willing to accept a 0.07 chance of a Type I error ($\alpha = 0.07$) and selects a sample of 100 for each game. Figure 10–2 shows the results of the sampling and the decision rule.

The decision, based on the sample results, is that game 2 takes as long or longer to play on the average than game 1. The company should continue to market game 1.

Before the hypothesis test is performed, the decision maker should consider the chances of committing both Type I and Type II errors. Calculating beta for the two-sample tests follows the same procedure as for the one-sample case discussed in section 9–3. Further, alpha and beta are interpreted the same as for the one-sample test.

Hypotheses:

$H_0: \mu_1 - \mu_2 \leq 0$
$H_A: \mu_1 - \mu_2 > 0$

$\alpha = 0.07$
$n_1 = 100, n_2 = 100$
$\sigma_1^2 = 900, \sigma_2^2 = 900$
$\bar{X}_1 = 50, \bar{X}_2 = 46$

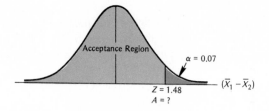

Decision Rule:

If $(\bar{X}_1 - \bar{X}_2) \leq A$, accept H_0.
If $(\bar{X}_1 - \bar{X}_2) > A$, reject H_0.

Solving for the critical level, A,

$$A = (\mu_1 - \mu_2) + Z \sqrt{\frac{\sigma_1^2}{n_1} + \frac{\sigma_2^2}{n_2}} = 0 + 1.48 \sqrt{\frac{900}{100} + \frac{900}{100}}$$

$$= 6.279$$

Since $(\bar{X}_1 - \bar{X}_2) = 4 < 6.279$, accept H_0.

FIGURE 10–2
Two-sample decision rule, Peterson Toy Company example

When the Population Variances Are Unknown

As in decisions involving one population, often the variances for a two-population hypothesis test are not known. However, if the sample sizes are reasonably large (generally over thirty), the sample variances can be substituted for the population variances. Then, the critical value in the decision rule is found by solving for A in equations 10–5:

$$Z = \frac{A - (\mu_1 - \mu_2)}{\sqrt{\dfrac{S_1^2}{n_1} + \dfrac{S_2^2}{n_2}}}$$ (10–5)

The decision rule is found exactly as in the previous examples. For example, in the Peterson Toy Company problem, instead of assuming that $\sigma_1^2 = 900$ and $\sigma_2^2 = 900$, suppose we found the sample variances $S_1^2 = 808$ and $S_2^2 = 933$. Figure 10–3 shows this situation. Thus, using the sample variances in place of the unknown population variances is the only change in the hypothesis-testing procedure. Is this case, the decision to accept H_0 is unchanged from the previous example.

Hypotheses:

$H_0: \mu_1 - \mu_2 \leq 0$
$H_A: \mu_1 - \mu_2 > 0$

$\alpha = 0.07$
$Z = 1.48$
$n_1 = 100, n_2 = 100$
$\bar{X}_1 = 50, \bar{X}_2 = 46$
$S_1^2 = 808, S_2^2 = 933$

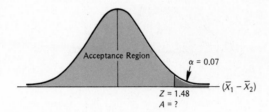

Decision Rule:

If $(\bar{X}_1 - \bar{X}_2) \leq A$, accept H_0.
If $(\bar{X}_1 - \bar{X}_2) > A$, reject H_0.

$$Z = \frac{A - (\mu_1 - \mu_2)}{\sqrt{\dfrac{S_1^2}{n_1} + \dfrac{S_2^2}{n_2}}}$$

$$A = (\mu_1 - \mu_2) + Z\sqrt{\frac{S_1^2}{n_1} + \frac{S_2^2}{n_2}} = 0 + 1.48\sqrt{\frac{808}{100} + \frac{933}{100}}$$

$$= 6.175$$

Since $(\bar{X}_1 - \bar{X}_2) \leq 6.175$, accept H_0.

FIGURE 10–3
Two-sample decision rule, variances unknown, Peterson Toy Company example

Hypothesis tests involving two population means for large samples can also be performed using the Z-test statistic approach. Consider an example involving the Jacobson Textile Company. Harmon Phillips, the personnel manager, recently studied a sample of eighty employees (forty men and forty women) following a letter the Jacobson Company received from an insurance company offering its group health insurance to the company's 4,200 employees. As part of the study Mr. Phillips hypothesized that there is no difference in the average hours of sick leave taken during the past year by men versus women employees. The sample results were as follows:

Men	Women
$n_1 = 40$	$n_2 = 40$
$\bar{X}_1 = 23$	$\bar{X}_2 = 30$
$S_1^2 = 36$	$S_2^2 = 49$

Figure 10–4 shows the results of the hypothesis test using the Z-statistic approach. The test is performed using an alpha level of 0.05 and is a two-tailed test.

Hypotheses:

$H_0: \mu_1 - \mu_2 = 0$
$H_A: \mu_1 - \mu_2 \neq 0$

$\alpha = 0.05$

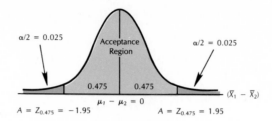

$\alpha/2 = 0.025$

Acceptance Region

$\alpha/2 = 0.025$

0.475   0.475

$\mu_1 - \mu_2 = 0$

$(\overline{X}_1 - \overline{X}_2)$

$A = Z_{0.475} = -1.95$ $A = Z_{0.475} = 1.95$

Decision Rule:

If $Z > 1.96$, reject H_0.
If $Z < -1.96$, reject H_0.
Otherwise, accept H_0.

Test Statistic:

$$Z = \frac{(\overline{X}_1 - \overline{X}_2) - (\mu_1 - \mu_2)}{\sqrt{\dfrac{S_1^2}{n_1} + \dfrac{S_2^2}{n_2}}} = \frac{(23 - 30) - 0}{\sqrt{\dfrac{36}{40} + \dfrac{49}{40}}}$$

$$= -4.80$$

Since $Z = -4.80 < -1.96$, reject H_0.

FIGURE 10–4
Hypothesis test—difference between population means, Jacobson Textile Company example

Harmon Phillips should infer from the sample that there is a difference in population means and that women employees took more hours of sick leave last year, on the average, than men.

Other Considerations

The three basic forms for the null and alternative hypotheses for the two-sample test are

$$H_0: \mu_1 \leq \mu_2 \quad \text{or} \quad \mu_1 - \mu_2 \leq 0$$
$$H_A: \mu_1 > \mu_2 \quad \text{or} \quad \mu_1 - \mu_2 > 0$$

$$H_0: \mu_1 = \mu_2 \quad \text{or} \quad \mu_1 - \mu_2 = 0$$
$$H_A: \mu_1 \neq \mu_2 \quad \text{or} \quad \mu_1 - \mu_2 \neq 0$$

$$H_0: \mu_1 \geq \mu_2 \quad \text{or} \quad \mu_1 - \mu_2 \geq 0$$
$$H_A: \mu_1 < \mu_2 \quad \text{or} \quad \mu_1 - \mu_2 < 0$$

Also, the hypothesized difference between two population means need *not* be zero. For example, we might hypothesize that the average difference in attendance at two movie theaters is at least 120 people per day. In this case, the null and alternative hypotheses would be

$$H_0: \mu_1 - \mu_2 \geq 120$$
$$H_A: \mu_1 - \mu_2 < 120$$

Another consideration is that the sample sizes selected from the two populations need *not* be equal. In the theater example, we might randomly sample 50 days ($n_1 = 50$) from theater 1 and 75 days ($n_2 = 75$) from theater 2. Generally, if the population variances are not equal, the larger sample size should be selected from the population with the larger variance.

SKILL DEVELOPMENT PROBLEMS FOR SECTION 10–2

The following set of problems is meant to test your understanding of the material in this section. Additional problems are found at the end of this chapter under this section heading.

6. Given the following null and alternative hypotheses:

$$H_0: \mu_1 - \mu_2 = 0$$
$$H_A: \mu_1 - \mu_2 \neq 0$$

and the following sample information:

Sample 1	Sample 2
$n = 100$	$n = 120$
$S = 20$	$S = 24$
$\overline{X} = 230$	$\overline{X} = 205$

a. Develop the appropriate decision rule, assuming an alpha level of 0.05 is to be used.
b. Test the null hypothesis and indicate whether the sample information leads you to reject or accept the null hypothesis.

7. Given the following null and alternative hypotheses:

$$H_0: \mu_1 - \mu_2 = 0$$
$$H_A: \mu_1 - \mu_2 \neq 0$$

and the following sample information:

Sample 1	Sample 2
$n = 400$	$n = 400$
$S = 120$	$S = 130$
$\overline{X} = 2,302.5$	$\overline{X} = 2,295.7$

a. Develop the appropriate decision rule, assuming an alpha level of 0.10 is to be used.

b. Test the null hypothesis and indicate whether the sample information leads you to reject or accept the null hypothesis.

8. Given the following null and alternative hypotheses:

$$H_0: \mu_1 - \mu_2 = 100$$
$$H_A: \mu_1 - \mu_2 \neq 100$$

and the following sample information:

Sample 1	Sample 2
$n = 100$	$n = 100$
$S = 50$	$S = 40.5$
$\overline{X} = 2,200$	$\overline{X} = 2,346$

a. Develop the appropriate decision rule, assuming an alpha level of 0.05 is to be used.

b. Test the null hypothesis and indicate whether the sample information leads you to reject or accept the null hypothesis.

9. Given the following null and alternative hypotheses:

$$H_0: \mu_1 - \mu_2 \geq 0$$
$$H_A: \mu_1 - \mu_2 < 0$$

and the following sample information:

Sample 1	Sample 2
$n = 64$	$n = 91$
$S = 30$	$S = 32$
$\overline{X} = 2,456$	$\overline{X} = 2,460$

a. Develop the appropriate decision rule, assuming an alpha level of 0.05 is to be used.

b. Test the null hypothesis and indicate whether the sample information leads you to reject or accept the null hypothesis.

10. Given the following null and alternative hypotheses:

$$H_0: \mu_1 - \mu_2 \leq 0$$
$$H_A: \mu_1 - \mu_2 > 0$$

and the following sample information:

Sample 1	Sample 2
$n = 200$	$n = 220$
$S = 5.5$	$S = 4.8$
$\overline{X} = 345$	$\overline{X} = 344.50$

a. Develop the appropriate decision rule, assuming an alpha level of 0.05 is to be used.

b. Test the null hypothesis and indicate whether the sample information leads you to reject or accept the null hypothesis.

11. The State College registrar is interested in determining whether there is a difference between male and female students in average number of credit hours taken during a term. She has selected a random sample of sixty males and sixty females and observed the following sample information:

Male	Female
$\overline{X} = 14.24$ credits	$\overline{X} = 15.65$ credits
$S = 1.2$ credits	$S = 1.56$ credits

a. State the appropriate null and alternative hypotheses to be tested.

b. Develop the decision rule, based upon an alpha $= 0.05$ level, and indicate whether the null hypothesis should be accepted or rejected.

12. The Rogiers Product Testing Service in Detroit, Michigan, recently worked with a client who wished an independent determination of whether customers preferred their product to a particular competitor's product. The Rogiers staff set up a rating scale and selected a random sample of 100 individuals to rate the client's product. A second random sample of 100 individuals was selected and asked to rate the competitor's product. The client felt that its product would be rated at least as high as the competitor's.

The following sample data were observed:

Client	Competitor
$\overline{X} = 88.5$	$\overline{X} = 90.05$
$S = 6.5$	$S = 5.0$

a. State the appropriate null and alternative hypotheses to be tested.

b. Based upon the sample information and an alpha level $= 0.10$, what should be concluded about the average ratings? Be sure to state clearly the decision rule.

HYPOTHESIS TESTING ABOUT THE DIFFERENCE BETWEEN TWO POPULATION PROPORTIONS

10-3

Section 10–1 introduced the methodology for testing hypotheses involving population proportions. This section extends the analysis to testing hypotheses about the difference between two population proportions.

Pomona Fabrication, Inc., produces hand-held hair dryers which several major retailers sell as their house brands. Pomona was an early entrant into this market and has developed substantial manufacturing and technological skills. However, in recent years the firm has faced increased competition from both domestic and foreign manufacturers. Pomona has been forced to reduce its prices, and this, coupled with ever-increasing production costs, has caused a substantial reduction in the company's profit margin.

A critical component of a hand-held hair dryer is the motor-heater unit. This component accounts for the majority of the dryer's cost and also for a majority of the product's reliability problems. Product reliability is extremely important to Pomona since the company currently offers a standard one-year warranty. Of course Pomona is also interested in reducing production costs.

Pomona's research and development department has recently developed a new motor-heater unit that will offer a 15 percent cost savings. However, the company's vice-president of product development is unwilling to authorize the new component unless it is at least as reliable as the motor-heater currently being used.

The research and development department has decided to test samples of both units to see whether there is a difference in the proportions that will fail in one year. Two hundred and fifty units of each type will be tested under conditions that simulate one year's use. Thus, the following hypotheses are formed:

Hypotheses:

H_0: $p_{new} \leq p_{old}$ or $p_{new} - p_{old} \leq 0$
H_A: $p_{new} > p_{old}$ or $p_{new} - p_{old} > 0$

where p = proportion of dryers that fail before 1 year

Decision Rule:

Select two samples, n_1 and n_2, and calculate $\hat{p}_1$ and $\hat{p}_2$, respectively, where $\hat{p}_1$ and $\hat{p}_2$ are estimates of the two population proportions, p_{new} and p_{old}, respectively.

If $Z \leq Z_{critical}$, accept H_0.
If $Z > Z_{critical}$, reject H_0.

If the null hypothesis is rejected, the company will continue to use the old motor-heater unit. Otherwise, the new motor-heater will be installed.

As with a hypothesis test of a single population proportion, the normal distribution can be used to test hypotheses about the difference between two population proportions, providing the sample sizes are sufficiently large. In this case, the critical value is found by solving the equation 10–6 for Z:

$$Z = \frac{(\hat{p}_1 - \hat{p}_2) - (p_1 - p_2)}{\sqrt{\dfrac{p_1(1 - p_1)}{n_1} + \dfrac{p_2(1 - p_2)}{n_2}}} \tag{10–6}$$

Note that the standard deviation of the sampling distribution for the difference between proportions is given by equation 10–7:

$$\sigma_{p_1 - p_2} = \sqrt{\frac{p_1(1 - p_1)}{n_1} + \frac{p_2(1 - p_2)}{n_2}} \tag{10–7}$$

However, equation 10–7 requires that we know p_1 and p_2. Since these values are unknown and we have hypothesized zero difference between the two population proportions, we must calculate a **pooled estimator** $(\bar{p})$ by taking a weighted average of the observed sample proportions as in equation 10–8:

$$\bar{p} = \frac{n_1\hat{p}_1 + n_2\hat{p}_2}{n_1 + n_2} \tag{10–8}$$

The reason for taking a weighted average is to give more weight to the larger sample. Note that the numerator is the total number of successes in the two samples and the denominator is the total sample size.

The standard deviation is given by equation 10–9:

$$S_{\hat{p}_1 - \hat{p}_2} = \sqrt{(\bar{p})(1 - \bar{p})\left(\frac{1}{n_1} + \frac{1}{n_2}\right)} \tag{10–9}$$

Thus the Z formula is given by equation 10–10:

$$Z = \frac{(\hat{p}_1 - \hat{p}_2) - (p_1 - p_2)}{\sqrt{(\bar{p})(1 - \bar{p})\left(\dfrac{1}{n_1} + \dfrac{1}{n_2}\right)}} \tag{10–10}$$

Assume that Pomona is willing to accept an alpha level of 0.05 and that seventy-five of the new motor-heaters and sixty-five of the originals failed the one-year test.

Hypotheses:

H_0: $p_{new} - p_{old} \leq 0$
H_A: $p_{new} - p_{old} > 0$

$\alpha = 0.05$

$n_{new} = 250$, $n_{old} = 250$
$x_{new} = 75$, $x_{old} = 65$
$\hat{p}_{new} = 75/250 = 0.30$, $\hat{p}_{old} = 65/250 = 0.26$

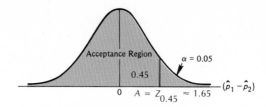

Decision Rule:

If $Z > 1.65$, reject H_0.
If $Z \leq 1.65$, accept H_0.

Test Statistic:

$$Z = \frac{(\hat{p}_1 - \hat{p}_2) - (p_1 - p_2)}{\sqrt{\bar{p}(1 - \bar{p})\left(\frac{1}{n_1} + \frac{1}{n_2}\right)}} = \frac{(0.30 - 0.26) - 0}{\sqrt{(0.28)(0.72)\left(\frac{1}{250} + \frac{1}{250}\right)}} = 0.996$$

where: $\bar{p} = \dfrac{250(0.30) + 250(0.26)}{250 + 250}$
$= 0.28$

Since $0.996 < 1.65$, accept H_0.

FIGURE 10–5
Hypothesis test for two proportions, Pomona Fabrication, Inc., example

Figure 10–5 illustrates the decision rule development and the null hypothesis test. As you can see in the figure, Pomona should *not* reject the null hypothesis. Rather, based on the sample information, the firm should conclude that the new motor-heater is at least as reliable as the old one. Since the new one is less costly, it should be used.

SKILL DEVELOPMENT PROBLEMS FOR SECTION 10–3

The following set of problems is meant to test your understanding of the material in this section. Additional problems are found at the end of this chapter under this section heading.

13. Given the following null and alternative hypotheses:

$$H_0: p_1 - p_2 = 0$$
$$H_A: p_1 - p_2 \neq 0$$

and the following sample information:

Sample 1	Sample 2
$n = 100$	$n = 100$
$x = 30$	$x = 34$

Based upon an alpha level = 0.05 and the sample information, what should be concluded with respect to the null and alternative hypotheses? Be sure to clearly show the decision rule.

14. Given the following null and alternative hypotheses:

$$H_0: p_1 - p_2 = 0$$
$$H_A: p_1 - p_2 \neq 0$$

and the following sample information:

Sample 1	Sample 2
$n = 200$	$n = 150$
$x = 87$	$x = 80$

Based upon an alpha level = 0.10 and the sample information, what should be concluded with respect to the null and alternative hypotheses? Be sure to clearly show the decision rule.

15. Given the following null and alternative hypotheses:

$$H_0: p_1 - p_2 \geq 0$$
$$H_A: p_1 - p_2 < 0$$

and the following sample information:

Sample 1	Sample 2
$n = 100$	$n = 100$
$x = 70$	$x = 75$

Based upon an alpha level = 0.05 and the sample information, what should be concluded with respect to the null and alternative hypotheses? Be sure to clearly show the decision rule.

16. Given the following null and alternative hypotheses:

$$H_0: p_1 - p_2 \leq 0$$
$$H_A: p_1 - p_2 > 0$$

and the following sample information:

Sample 1	Sample 2
$n = 60$	$n = 80$
$x = 30$	$x = 24$

Based upon an alpha level = 0.02 and the sample information, what should be concluded with respect to the null and alternative hypotheses? Be sure to clearly show the decision rule.

17. The United Way Organization raises money for community charity activities. Recently in one community, the fund raising committee was concerned whether there is a difference in the proportion of employees who give to United Way depending on whether the employer is a private business or a government agency. It was decided to select a random sample of people who had been contacted about contributing last year. Seventy of those contacted worked for a private business and fifty worked for a government agency. Of the seventy private sector employees, twenty-two had contributed some amount to United Way and nineteen of the government employees in the sample had contributed.

    Based upon these sample data and an alpha level = 0.05, what should be concluded? Be sure to show the decision rule.

18. The Idaho Transportation Department recently conducted a study that dealt with the issue of uninsured motorists. Vehicles were stopped at random and the driver was asked to show his or her registration and proof of insurance certificate. It was noted whether the car was registered to a single individual or whether it was a joint registration (for example, a husband and wife). The investigators recorded the registration information and whether or not the motorist had proof of insurance. The following sample data were observed:

Single	Joint
$n = 80$	$n = 200$
$x = 68$	$x = 191$

    If x indicates the number who did have proof of insurance, what should the Transportation Department conclude about the difference in proportions of single versus joint registered vehicles with insurance? Test at the alpha = 0.05 level and show the decision rule.

ADDITIONAL COMMENTS

10-4

Some additional comments are in order now with respect to hypothesis testing. First, as a decision maker, if you have the choice in setting up your null and alternative hypotheses, it is generally preferable to formulate them so that the Type I error is the most costly. The reason for this is that you have direct control over the maximum probability of committing the Type I error since you can set alpha at any desired level. By making

Hypotheses:

H_0: $\mu_x \leq 400$
H_A: $\mu_x > 400$

$\alpha = 0.05$

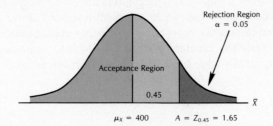

Decision Rule:

If $Z > 1.65$, reject H_0.
If $Z \leq 1.65$, accept H_0.

Test Statistic:

$$Z = \frac{\overline{X} - \mu_x}{\dfrac{S_x}{\sqrt{n}}}$$

$$= \frac{425 - 400}{\dfrac{100}{\sqrt{60}}}$$

$$= 1.936$$

Since $1.936 > 1.65$, reject H_0.

FIGURE 10–6
Hypothesis test, Finley Automobile Dealership example

the most costly error the Type I error, the Type II error probabilities can be allowed to be somewhat greater. This means that sample sizes can be reduced and sampling costs can be reduced.

Another topic to be aware of is the way in which some computer programs print out results of a hypothesis test. Many programs print something called a **p value** or **prob value.** A p value is the probability of observing a sample value as extreme, or more extreme, than the value actually observed, given that the null hypothesis is true. You can compare the p value to your alpha level and

If $p <$ alpha, reject H_0.
If $p \geq$ alpha, accept H_0.

An example (figure 10-6) illustrates this concept. Suppose the sales manager for the Finley Automobile Dealership claims that the average expenditure on new car accessories exceeds $400 for each new car sold by the dealership. A sample of sixty sales records shows an average of $425, with a sample standard deviation of $100. If the sales manager wishes to test her claim with an alpha level equal to 0.05, what should she conclude? Using the methods presented in this chapter, the hypothesis test is performed as in figure 10–6. Thus, the sample results indicate that the null hypothesis should be rejected. Note that the test statistic was computed to be $Z = 1.936$. To arrive at the p value printed out by many computer programs, we recognize that $Z = 1.936$ indicates that the sample mean was 1.936 standard deviations above the hypothesized mean. The p value represents the probability of Z being greater than or equal to 1.936 standard deviations from the standard normal distribution, which we determined by going to the standard normal table for 1.94 (≈ 1.936), shown as follows:

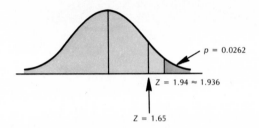

Thus, the p value associated with the sample results is 0.0262. Since $0.0262 < \alpha = 0.05$, we reject H_0. This decision agrees with our earlier conclusion. (Note that if the test is two-tailed, you should compare p with $\alpha/2$; if p is less than $\alpha/2$, you should reject H_0; and if p is greater than or equal to $\alpha/2$, you should accept H_0.)

Finally, two-tailed hypotheses tests are sometimes performed by developing a $1 - \alpha$ confidence interval. If the interval includes the hypothesized value, H_0 is accepted. If the interval does not include the hypothesized value, H_0 is rejected.

CONCLUSIONS

10-5   This chapter has expanded on the hypothesis-testing procedure introduced in chapter 9. Again the focus has been on applications with large sample sizes.

You have seen examples of large-sample hypothesis tests involving the difference between two population means, a single population proportion, and the difference between two population proportions. If you paid close attention, you should have seen the hypothesis-testing methodology is basically the same for all these situations. The central issue is always to determine whether the sample information supports or refutes the null hypothesis.

CHAPTER GLOSSARY

population proportion   The percentage of items in a population that possess a desired attribute.

p value   A value output by some computer software packages that indicates the probability of a sample result being as extreme or more extreme than the one observed, given the hypothesized parameter is true.

prob value Same as p value.

Critical value

One population proportion

$$A = p + Z \sqrt{\frac{p(1 - p)}{n}}$$

Difference between means

$$A = (\mu_1 - \mu_2) + Z \sqrt{\frac{\sigma_1^2}{n_1} + \frac{\sigma_2^2}{n_2}}$$

Pooled estimator

$$\bar{p} = \frac{n_1 \hat{p}_1 + n_2 \hat{p}_2}{n_1 + n_2}$$

Z value

One population proportion

$$Z = \frac{\hat{p} - p}{\sqrt{\frac{p(1 - p)}{n}}}$$

Two population proportions

$$Z = \frac{(\hat{p}_1 - \hat{p}_2) - (p_1 - p_2)}{\sqrt{\bar{p}(1 - \bar{p})\left(\frac{1}{n_1} + \frac{1}{n_2}\right)}}$$

One population mean

$$Z = \frac{\bar{X} - \mu_x}{\frac{\sigma_x}{\sqrt{n}}}$$

Two population means

$$Z = \frac{(\overline{X}_1 - \overline{X}_2) - (\mu_1 - \mu_2)}{\sqrt{\dfrac{\sigma_1^2}{n_1} + \dfrac{\sigma_2^2}{n_2}}}$$

Two population means, variances unknown

$$Z = \frac{(\overline{X}_1 - \overline{X}_2) - (\mu_1 - \mu_2)}{\sqrt{\dfrac{S_1^2}{n_1} + \dfrac{S_2^2}{n_2}}}$$

Standard deviation of the proportion

$$\sigma_p = \sqrt{\frac{p(1 - p)}{n}}$$

Standard deviation of difference between means

$$\sigma_{\overline{X}_1 - \overline{X}_2} = \sqrt{\frac{\sigma_1^2}{n_1} + \frac{\sigma_2^2}{n_2}}$$

SOLVED PROBLEMS

1. Property taxes are based on the assessed valuation of real estate. The higher the valuation the greater the tax on that property. In one southern county, a controversy is taking place between some citizens and the county tax appraiser. The citizens claim that during a recent reappraisal, the residential property was increased in value by a greater average percentage than commercial property. If the citizens' claim is true, they will end up paying a greater relative share of property taxes than owners of commercial property.

   An outside consulting firm has been hired to study the situation. As part of their study, the consultants have selected a sample of 400 residential properties and 300 commercial properties and determined the average percent increase in assessed valuation for each class of property. The sample means along with the sample variances are

	Residential	*Commercial*
	$n_R = 400$	$n_C = 300$
	$\overline{X}_R = 108\%$	$\overline{X}_C = 102\%$
	$S_R^2 = 1,400$	$S_C^2 = 1,650$

Does this sample evidence support the citizens' claim? Test at the 0.10 alpha level.

Solution:

Even though this problem deals with percentages, the problem is still one of hypothesis testing about two population means.

Hypotheses:

$H_0: \mu_R - \mu_C \leq 0$

$H_A: \mu_R - \mu_C > 0$

The sampling distribution and the acceptance and rejection regions are as follows:

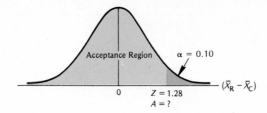

We can test the null hypothesis two ways. First, we can solve for Z, using

$$Z = \frac{(\overline{X}_R - \overline{X}_C) - 0}{\sqrt{\dfrac{S_R^2}{n_R} + \dfrac{S_C^2}{n_C}}}$$

Note that we use the normal distribution even though the population variances are unknown since the samples are large. Therefore

$$Z = \frac{(108 - 102) - 0}{\sqrt{\dfrac{1,400}{400} + \dfrac{1,650}{300}}}$$

$$= 2.00$$

Since $Z = 2.00 > Z_{\text{critical}} = 1.28$, we reject the null hypothesis and conclude that the citizens' claim is true.

A second approach is to solve for A and then compare the difference between the two sample means to the decision rule.

$$A = 0 + 1.28 \sqrt{\frac{1,400}{400} + \frac{1,650}{300}}$$

$$= 3.84$$

Decision Rule:

If $(\overline{X}_R - \overline{X}_C) \leq 3.84\%$, accept H_0.

If $(\overline{X}_R - \overline{X}_C) > 3.84\%$, reject H_0.

Since $(\overline{X}_R - \overline{X}_C) = 6$ percent, we reject H_0. Rejecting the null hypothesis does not mean that the assessments are incorrect. They may actually reflect the change in market values or an adjustment from previous inequalities against commercial property.

2. The state legislature is deciding whether to remove the investment tax credit for capital investments. The Democrats in the legislature are generally in favor of removing the credit and the Republicans in favor of keeping the credit. Both parties have taken polls and claim the results support their position as shown:

Republican	Democratic
$n = 300$	$n = 350$
keep credit $= 165$	keep credit 165

Both parties claim the other has taken a biased poll. Assuming the polls are both taken by simple random sampling techniques, from the same population, could we expect to see the above results?

Solution:

Since the question is whether both samples could have come from the same population, we formulate the following hypotheses:

Hypotheses

$H_0: p_r = p_d$

$H_A: p_r \neq p_d$

Since we have specified an equal-to hypothesis, we have a two-tailed test. The sampling distribution and the acceptance and rejection regions for an alpha of 0.02 are as follows:

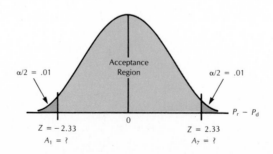

We can test the null hypothesis two ways. First we can solve for Z, using

$$Z = \frac{(\hat{p}_r - \hat{p}_d) - 0}{\sqrt{\dfrac{\hat{p}_r(1 - \hat{p}_r)}{n_r} + \dfrac{\hat{p}_d(1 - \hat{p}_d)}{n_d}}}$$

Since $\hat{p}_r = 165/300 = 0.55$
and $\hat{p}_d = 165/350 = 0.47$ (rounded)
the Z value is

$$Z = \frac{(0.55 - 0.47) - 0}{\sqrt{\dfrac{0.55(1 - 0.55)}{300} + \dfrac{0.47(1 - 0.47)}{350}}}$$

$$= \frac{0.08}{\sqrt{0.000825 + 0.000712}}$$

$$= 2.04$$

Since this value of Z falls in the acceptance region (it is less than 2.33), we would accept the hypothesis that the two population means are equal. Note that if we had specified a different alpha value, say 10 percent, our conclusion would have been different.

A second approach is to solve for A_1 and A_2 and then compare the difference between the two sample means to the range defined by the decision rule. Again assuming an alpha of 0.02,

$$A_1 = 0 - Z\sqrt{\frac{\hat{p}_r(1 - \hat{p}_r)}{n_r} + \frac{\hat{p}_d(1 - \hat{p}_d)}{n_d}}$$

$$= 0 - 2.33\sqrt{\frac{0.55(1 - 0.55)}{300} + \frac{0.47(1 - 0.47)}{350}}$$

$$= -0.0912$$

Since the distribution is symmetrical,

$$A_2 = 0.0912$$

Decision Rule:

If $-0.0912 \le (p_r - p_d) \le 0.0912$, accept H_0
If $(p_r - p_d) < -0.0912$ or
  $(p_r - p_d) > 0.0912$, reject H_0

Since $(p_r - p_d) = 0.08$, we accept the null hypothesis. Remember, accepting the null hypothesis does not "prove" the two populations are equal. It simply means the observed difference could have occurred because of chance variation or sampling error.

ADDITIONAL PROBLEMS

Section 10–1

19. A recent National Collegiate Athletic Association (NCAA) ruling requires that athletes progress toward a degree to remain eligible to play varsity sports. One athletic conference is considering defining *progress* as a situation under which, of the credits taken by the student, at least 75 percent of the credit hours are taken in courses leading toward the declared major at his or her institution.

    One of the college officials from this conference complained that this was too strict a requirement because for the student body as a whole less than 75 percent of the credit hours taken would be counted toward the declared major for the student taking those credits. To test this, a random sample of 400 individual three-credit hour courses taken by students at the university was selected by going to the computerized transcript file. Each of the three-credit-hour courses was evaluated to determine whether it would apply toward the degree program for the student involved. It was found that in 368 instances the course did apply toward degree requirements.

a. State the appropriate null and alternative hypotheses to be tested.

b. Based on the sample results, what should be concluded if the hypotheses are tested at an alpha level of 0.05?

20. The manager of a local engine repair service is considering mailing out a large number of coupons that offer substantial discounts on engine tune-ups. An industry trade publication indicates that no more than 20 percent of all such coupons will be used. He has decided to send out a test mailing of 200 coupons.

a. State the null and alternative hypotheses to be tested based on the random sample.

b. Suppose that of the 200 coupons mailed out, forty-six are used within the specified period. At an alpha level of 0.10, what should the shop owner conclude?

c. Discuss in terms that the shop owner can understand what Type I and Type II errors are as they relate to this situation. Also discuss the relative costs associated with each type of error.

21. The Dodge City town council members have attempted to deal with the downtown parking problem by increasing the fines for overtime parking. They have done this partly because they believe that many of the people using the parking spaces are employees of downtown business who would rather pay the parking fine than ride the bus or park a considerable distance from where they work. The council has claimed that at any given time at least 40 percent of the spaces are occupied by employees.

    The downtown business association dislikes the idea of increased fines because it will discourage people from coming downtown to shop. As part of its preparation to fight the proposed plan it has hired a local statistician to select a random sample of parking spaces occupied by cars and determine whether the percentage of spaces occupied by employees in the sample supports or refutes the claim by the council.

a. State the null and alternative hypotheses to be tested.

b. If the desired alpha level is 0.10, what conclusion should be reached if the sample proportion is 0.37? Assume that the sample size is 100 parking spaces ($n = 100$).

c. Discuss in terms related to this problem what the Type I and Type II errors mean. Which may have been committed in this case?

22. Parking at State University during Thursday-night basketball games is a subject that has received great attention lately as season-ticket holders find themselves having to park substantial distances from the field house and walking to the game in cold winter weather. Many complaints have been received and on many occasions these irate customers ask why they cannot park on the nearby recreation field that will not be used until spring.

In response to these complaints, the campus parking manager has issued a strong statement that there are plenty of parking spaces on campus the night of the ball games and that people would find them if they would "give it half a try." He followed this up with the claim that at least 20 percent of the spaces are open between 6:30 and 7:30 P.M. on game nights.

To test this claim the alumni association has randomly sampled 100 parking spaces and checked these spaces on a game night. It found fifteen spaces open. Using an alpha level of 0.05, what conclusion should be reached based on these data?

23. In planning for the university graduation, the chairperson based her timetable on the assumption that no more than 65 percent of the graduates would actually go through graduation. One new member of the graduation committee felt that the committee should test to determine if the 65 percent figure was safe to use in the planning. The decision was made to select a random sample of fifty graduating seniors and ask them whether they would be attending graduation. Thirty-two said "yes."

a. State the null and alternative hypotheses to be tested.

b. Establish the appropriate decision rule based on an alpha level of 0.03.

c. Based on the sample results, what should be concluded with respect to the proportion of graduates who will attend graduation? Discuss.

24. The Utah Department of Transportation conducted a study of bridges in the state. To receive a federal grant, the department had to show that at least 40 percent of the bridges need repair, as claimed in its grant proposal. A random sample of forty-nine bridges revealed eighteen bridges in need of repair. Do these data support or refute the claim made in the grant proposal? Use an alpha level of 0.01.

Section 10–2

25. The Clargor Service Company provides financial services for people in Wisconsin and Ohio. Recently at a sales meeting the statement was made that there is no difference in the average whole life insurance coverage for clients in the two states. It was decided that a test of this should be made as the conclusion could affect the sales promotion that was being planned.

To test the claim, a random sample of sixty clients was selected from Wisconsin and another sample of eighty clients was selected from Ohio, with the following sample results:

Wisconsin	Ohio
$n_W = 60$	$n_O = 80$
$\overline{X}_W = \$25,600$	$\overline{X}_O = \$32,300$
$S_W = \$\ 8,100$	$S_O = \$\ 9,200$

   a. State the appropriate null and alternative hypotheses.
   b. Using an alpha level of 0.05, test the null hypothesis and discuss the conclusions that should be reached based on the sample data.

26. The makers of Ever-Bounce glass backboards for basketball gymnasiums have claimed that their board is at least as durable, on the average, as the leading backboard made by Clearview Company. Products Testing Services of Des Moines, Iowa, was hired to verify this claim. It selected a random sample of forty backboards of each type and subjected the boards to a pressure test to determine the breaking point in terms of how much weight it would take to break the fiberglass backboard as it hung from a basketball rim. The following results were determined from the testing process:

Clearview	Ever-Bounce
$n_C = 40$	$n_E = 40$
$\overline{X}_C = 675$ lbs	$\overline{X}_E = 643$ lbs
$S_C = 102$ lbs	$S_E = \ \ 95$ lbs

   a. Assuming that the more pounds it takes to break the backboard, the better it is, state the appropriate null and alternative hypotheses.
   b. At an alpha level of 0.01, what conclusion should be reached with respect to the claim made by the Ever-Bounce Company? Discuss.
   c. Suppose the hypothesis test was conducted at an alpha of 0.10 instead of 0.01. Would this change the conclusion reached based on the sample data? If so, discuss why, if not, discuss why not.

27. The makers of a new chemical fertilizer claim that hay yields will average at least 0.40 ton more per acre if this fertilizer is used than if the leading brand is used. The agricultural testing service at Oregon State University was retained to test this claim. Fifty-two one-acre plots were selected at random and the new fertilizer was applied. A second sample of forty one-acre plots was selected and the leading fertilizer was used. The following sample data were observed in tons per acre:

Old	New
$n_O = 40$	$n_N = 52$
Total = 126	Total = 205
$S_O^2 = 0.36$	$S_N^2 = 0.49$

a. State the appropriate null and alternative hypotheses.
b. If alpha is set at 0.05, what conclusion should be reached with respect to the claim made by the new fertilizer's company? Discuss.

28. The manufacturer of one type of microcomputer has two options for the way in which the floppy disk drives are configured. One option is the horizontal configuration, in which the disk drives are laid flat and the disks are inserted horizontal to the table on which the microcomputer sits. The second is the vertical option, in which the diskettes are put into the disk drives in a position that is at right angles with the table top.

Engineers at the company feel that there is no difference in maintenance problems with either configuration, but have never collected any data to support that contention. They have decided to select a random sample of 200 users of each option and determine their maintenance costs. The data are as follows:

Horizontal	Vertical
$n_H = 200$	$n_V = 200$
$\overline{X}_H = \$75.25$	$\overline{X}_V = \$40.10$
$S_H = \$20.00$	$S_V = \$17.80$

a. State the null and alternative hypotheses for this problem facing the microcomputer company.
b. Using an alpha level of 0.02, what conclusion should the engineers reach with respect to average maintenance costs for the two disk-drive configurations?

Section 10–3

29. The Fraiser Company sells breakable china through a mail-order system, which has been very profitable. One of its major problems is freight damage. It insures the items at shipping, but the inconvenience to the customer when a piece gets broken can cause the customer to not make another order in the future. Thus, packaging is important to the Fraiser Company.

In the past the company has purchased two different packaging materials from two respective suppliers. The assumption was that there would be no difference in proportion of damaged shipments resulting from use of either packaging material.

It occurred to the sales manager that a study of this issue should be done. Therefore, a random sample of 300 orders ($n = 300$) using shipping material 1 and a random sample of 250 orders ($n = 250$) which used material 2 were pulled from the files. The number of damaged parcels was recorded for each material as follows:

Material 1	Material 2
$n = 300$	$n = 250$
$x = 15$	$x = 9$

a. State the appropriate null and alternative hypotheses.
b. Using an alpha level of 0.05, what conclusion should be reached with respect to the two packaging materials?
c. Referring to the conclusions reached in part b, what type of statistical error may have been committed? Discuss.

30. United States automakers have been criticized in some circles for poor quality of U.S. cars compared with their foreign competitors. In fact, one trade publication has indicated that the percentage of U.S.-made cars having serious mechanical troubles within two years from purchase is greater than that for foreign cars after five years of ownership. If this allegation were to be substantiated, it would be a severe blow to the U.S. automakers' efforts to contradict their poor quality image.

   To test this claim, a random sample of sixty U.S. car owners and another sample of seventy foreign car owners were selected. It was found that eleven owners of U.S. cars had severe mechanical problems within the first two years and twelve foreign car owners had severe mechanical problems within the first five years of ownership.
   a. State the appropriate null and alternative hypotheses.
   b. Discuss what a Type I and a Type II error would be in this situation and attempt to provide an assessment of the relative costs of each.
   c. Based on an alpha level of 0.01, what conclusion should be reached. Discuss.

31. Last year the city of Bellingham in Selina County, Georgia, undertook a campaign to consolidate the city and county governments. The premise was that proportionately more people in the city would favor the concept than in the outlying county area; this was because the county people might expect a tax increase from the consolidation even though the proponents of the plan promised a tax reduction in the long run.

   A polling agency was hired to conduct a study of this issue. It randomly selected 100 people in the city and seventy people in the county. It found sixty city dwellers favoring the idea and thirty-five county residents favoring the plan.
   a. State the appropriate null and alternative hypotheses to be tested.
   b. Based on the sample results, what should be concluded about the proportions favoring the consolidation when the city residents are compared with the county residents? Use an alpha level of 0.10. Discuss.

32. A book publisher claims that undergraduates are more likely to buy used text-books than are graduate students. The publisher's marketing department selected two random samples of 200 undergraduate students and 100 graduate students, respectively, at The Ohio State University. The students were asked whether they had

purchased a used textbook this term. Sixty-one of the undergraduates said "yes" while forty-two of the graduates said "yes." Using an alpha level of 0.03, what should the publisher conclude?

Based on the results of this survey should the publisher extend its conclusions to all undergraduates and graduates at any university? Discuss.

33. The makers of Tex/Mex Chili in San Antonio, Texas, have a product which, by seasoning standards, is one of the hottest on the market. They have marketed this product under the assumption that there is no difference between men's and women's preference for spicy foods. The marketing manager decided that she would test this assumption by taking two samples of 200 men and 200 women, respectively, and letting them taste Tex/Mex Chili and a milder variety offered by a competitor. The people were asked to select which chili they liked better based on the criteria of seasoning.

The results showed that eighty-one men prefered Tex/Mex Chili and seventy-four women preferred Tex/Mex Chili. Using an alpha level of 0.05, what conclusions should the marketing manager reach based on these sample data?

C A S E S

10–A   Green Valley Assembly Company

The Green Valley Assembly Company assembles consumer electronics products for manufacturers that need temporary extra production capacity. As such, it has periodic product change. Since the products Green Valley assembles are marketed under the label of well-known manufacturers, high quality is a must.

Tom Bradley of the Green Valley personnel department has been very impressed by recent research concerning job-enrichment programs. In particular, he has been impressed with the increases in quality that seem to be associated with these programs. However, some studies have shown no significant increase in quality and imply that the money spent on such programs has not been worthwhile.

Tom has talked to Sandra Hansen, the production manager, about instituting a job-enrichment program in the assembly operation at Green Valley. Sandra was somewhat pessimistic about the potential, but agreed to introduce the program. The plan was to implement the program in one wing of the plant and continue with the current method in the other wing. The procedure was to be in effect for six months. Following that period, a test would be made to determine the effectiveness of the job-enrichment program.

After the six-month trial period, a random sample of employees from each wing produced the following output measures:

	Old		Job-Enriched
	$n_1 = 50$ employees		$n_2 = 50$ employees
	$\overline{X}_1 = 11/h$		$\overline{X}_2 = 9.7/h$
	$S_1 = 1.2/h$		$S_2 = 0.9/h$

Both Sandra and Tom wonder whether the job-enrichment program has affected production output. They would like to use these sample results to determine if the average output has been changed and to determine if the consistency of the employees was affected by the new program.

A second sample from each wing was selected. The measure was the quality of the products assembled. In the "old" wing, seventy-nine products were tested and 12 percent were found to be defectively assembled. In the "job-enriched" wing, 123 products were examined and 9 percent were judged defectively assembled.

With all these data, Sandra and Tom are beginning to get a little confused, but they realize that they must be able to use the information somehow in order to make a judgment about the effectiveness of the job-enrichment program.

10–B Downtown Development: Bayview, North Dakota

Bayview, North Dakota, is a rapidly growing city with a high number of corporate headquarters. In addition, Bayview has a substantial amount of light industry and an increasing number of service businesses to support the population.

The city government has been involved in a controversy for the past five years over the issue of whether to build a regional shopping center in the downtown area or in the suburbs. The city council has gone on record as favoring the downtown site, but has received heavy opposition from a citizens' group called KNOW (Keep Nice Our World), which feels that the best site is in the suburbs. KNOW's argument is that less energy will be needed to reach the shopping center if it is placed closer to the people. The city council, on the other hand, has passed a "Metro" plan, calling for downtown development and mass transit of people to the downtown area, which it argues would save energy.

Endless meetings and hearings have been held on the issue, but a vote or poll of the people has not been taken. The city council and the KNOW representatives have agreed to hire a marketing consultant from Rock Springs, Wyoming, to select a random sample of citizens and ask which location is favored for the shopping center.

The city council claims that at least 50 percent of the population favor the downtown site and feels quite confident that the sample will bear this out. However, the KNOW group claims that 50 percent or fewer prefer the downtown location and is equally confident in its claim.

The Rock Springs consultant selected a random sample of 384 persons and found 188 in favor of the downtown site and 196 opposed to the downtown site.

The day following the tabulation of the sample results, the *Bayview Gazette* ran a headline story relating the sample results and statements from the city council and

KNOW, both of which stated that the results proved their claims. The story mentioned something about both parties testing their hypotheses at the 0.05 alpha level.

One citizen was heard that morning to say, "What does this mean? How can they both be right? This just doesn't make sense. It can't be."

REFERENCES

Duncan, Acheson J. *Quality Control and Industrial Statistics,* 4th Edition. Homewood, Ill.: Irwin, 1974.

Lapin, Lawrence L. *Statistics for Modern Business Decisions,* 3rd Edition. New York: Harcourt Brace Jovanovich, 1982.

Neter, John; Wasserman, William; and Whitmore, G. A. *Applied Statistics,* 2nd Edition. Boston: Allyn and Bacon, 1982.

Rozeboom, William W. "The Fallacy of the Null-Hypothesis Significance Test." *Psychological Bulletin* 57 (September 1960): 416–28.

Wilson, Warner; Miller, Howard L.; and Lower, Jerold S. "Much Ado about the Null Hypothesis." *Psychological Bulletin* 67 (March 1967): 188–96.

Wonnacott, Thomas H., and Wonnacott, Ronald J. *Introductory Statistics for Business and Economics,* 3rd Edition. New York: Wiley, 1984.

STATISTICAL ESTIMATION AND HYPOTHESIS TESTING— SMALL SAMPLES

11

WHY DECISION MAKERS NEED TO KNOW

Chapter 8 introduced the fundamental concepts of statistical estimation. It emphasized the difference between point estimators and confidence interval estimators and showed how to calculate each. The discussion in chapter 8 assumed that the decision makers were dealing with large samples of measurements from the populations of interest.

However, in many applications, obtaining measurements from large samples is not possible. Often the costs in time or money are prohibitive. In these instances decision makers must rely on small samples from the populations of interest, so the estimation techniques presented in chapter 8 are inappropriate. Yet decision makers still need to be able to estimate various population values. Thus they need to understand the techniques for small-sample statistical estimation presented in this chapter.

Chapters 9 and 10 introduced the basics of hypothesis testing for large samples. When circumstances make it infeasible to work with large samples, decision makers need techniques for testing hypotheses based upon data from small samples. This chapter presents the fundamentals of hypothesis testing using small samples.

The small-sample estimation and hypothesis-testing techniques are very similar to those for large samples. If you understood the logic of estimation and hypothesis testing presented in chapters 8, 9, and 10, you will have little trouble with the material in this chapter.

CHAPTER OBJECTIVES

This chapter introduces statistical estimation based on small samples. It will consider the Student t distribution and develop confidence intervals for estimates of the population mean, the difference between two population means for independent samples, and the difference between two population means for paired samples. This chapter will also show how hypothesis tests are carried out for each of the above population values when the decision maker is employing a small-size sample.

STUDENT OBJECTIVES

After studying the material presented in this chapter, you should

1. Know what the Student t distribution is.
2. Understand the fundamental differences between the t distribution and the normal distribution.
3. Be aware of the conditions under which the t distribution rather than the normal distribution should be used to determine the confidence interval estimate of a population value.
4. Know how to develop a small-sample confidence interval for estimating the population mean and how to test a small-sample hypothesis for this parameter.
5. Know how to develop a small-sample confidence interval and hypothesis test for estimating the difference between two population means for independent samples.
6. Know how to develop a small-sample confidence interval and hypothesis test for estimating the difference between two population means for paired samples.
7. Understand the trade-offs between sample size, confidence level, and precision.

SMALL SAMPLE ESTIMATION

11-1   Chapter 8 introduced statistical estimation for several population values. The common bond for all the confidence intervals developed in that chapter was that the sample sizes were large and the interval coefficient was a Z value from the standardized normal distribution. Although differentiating between a large sample and a small sample is to some extent arbitrary, a widespread convention is to consider the sample large if the sample size is greater than or equal to 30 ($n \geq 30$).

Although many business applications involve large sample sizes, others do not. The cost in terms of dollars and time often prevents a large sample from being used to estimate a population value. In other instances, a large sample cannot be obtained because the population items are difficult to observe or few in number. And, in these cases, the large-sample procedures presented in chapter 8 are simply not appropriate.

A major insurance company is conducting a study to determine if a downward change in its automobile collision rates can be justified. As part of the study, the company needs to estimate the average damage in dollars to a new car that hits a barricade head-on at 15 miles per hour. Because of the high cost of this type of sampling, the insurance company has decided to crash only ten cars.

Since 10 is less than 30, the insurance company does not have a large sample, and therefore, cannot employ the methods presented in chapter 8. Rather, the company needs to use statistical techniques that are appropriate when dealing with small samples. Before these small-sample techniques are introduced, let's review four basic principles of interval estimation:

1. The format for any confidence interval is

   Point estimate $\pm$ (interval coefficient)(standard error of the estimate)

2. The higher the confidence, the lower the precision for a given sample size.
3. An increase in sample size will increase the precision of the estimate for a given confidence level. This occurs because an increase in sample size decreases the standard error of the estimate.
4. A confidence interval carries with it the following interpretation: If all possible samples of a given size are selected, and all possible confidence intervals for a given confidence level are calculated, the percentage of intervals containing the true population value will equal the confidence level.

These four principles were introduced in connection with large-sample estimation. They also apply to small-sample estimation. If you understand these four concepts, you should have little trouble understanding and applying the material presented in the remaining section of this chapter.

THE STUDENT t DISTRIBUTION

11-2

The interval estimates in chapter 8 were based on large samples. In developing the intervals, no concern was expressed about the shape of the population distribution because the central limit theorem tells us the sampling distribution will be approximately normal for large samples. Consequently, the interval coefficient we used for each interval was a Z value from the standard normal distribution. For example, the confidence interval estimate for μ_x is given by equation 11–1:

$$\overline{X} \pm Z\frac{\sigma_x}{\sqrt{n}} \qquad (11–1)$$

Even if σ_x is not known and must be estimated, the sampling distribution of $\overline{X}$ is still approximately normal if the sample size is large. The confidence interval estimate for μ_x with an unknown population standard deviation and a large sample size is given by equation 11–2:

$$\overline{X} \pm Z\frac{S_x}{\sqrt{n}} \qquad (11–2)$$

However, when σ_x is unknown and both μ_x and σ_x must be estimated from a small sample, the interval coefficient in equation 11–2 cannot be determined using the standard normal distribution.

an exact solution to the problem of small-sample interval estimation is available. W. S. Gosset discovered the properties governing the sampling distribution of $\overline{X}$ for small samples. Gossett published his findings in 1908 under the pen name "Student" and called the sampling distribution the **t distribution.** He showed for small samples that the quantity of equation 11–3,

$$t = \frac{\overline{X} - \mu_x}{\dfrac{S_x}{\sqrt{n}}} \qquad (11\text{–}3)$$

follows a t distribution. "Student" (Gosset) set forth the following theorem:

> If the population from which the sample is being selected is *normally distributed* with *unknown standard deviation,* the sampling distribution for $(\overline{X} - \mu_x)/(S_x/\sqrt{n})$ will be described by a t *distribution* with $n - 1$ degrees of freedom.

The t distribution is similar to the Z distribution in that both distributions are symmetrical and range from $-\infty$ to $+\infty$. Both standardized distributions have a mean of zero. The basic difference is in the spread of the two distributions. The variance of the standard normal distribution is 1.0, whereas the variance of the t distribution is always greater than 1.0. The variance of the t distribution is determined by the following formula:

$$\frac{n - 1}{n - 1 - 2}$$

for $n \geq 4$. The exact variance of the t distribution depends on the sample size. If $n = 10$, the variance is 1.285. The variance for $n = 15$ is 1.167. The variance for $n = 25$ is 1.091.

Figure 11–1 illustrates the relationship between the t distribution and the Z distribution and shows how the variance of the t distribution changes as the sample size changes. When the sample size increases, the variance approaches 1.0. Thus, for large sample sizes, the t distribution approaches the standard normal distribution.

FIGURE 11–1
Comparison of t and Z distributions

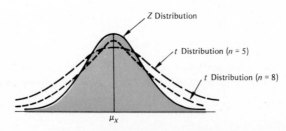

Chapter 7 showed that

$$Z = \frac{\overline{X} - \mu_x}{\dfrac{\sigma_x}{\sqrt{n}}}$$

and emphasized that Z represents the number of standard deviations $\overline{X}$ is from μ_x. Likewise,

$$t = \frac{\overline{X} - \mu_x}{\dfrac{S_x}{\sqrt{n}}}$$

where the t value is the number of standard deviations $\overline{X}$ is from μ_x.

As with the Z distribution, tables of t values have been developed. The standardized t-distribution table is contained in appendix D. Across the top of the table are probabilities corresponding to areas in one tail and two tails and for various confidence levels. Down the left side is a column headed "d.f." (degrees of freedom).[1] You will learn how to determine the degrees of freedom for all statistical procedures introduced in this text. For example, when we are developing a confidence interval for estimating μ_x, the number of degrees of freedom is $n - 1$.

The t value for a 90 percent confidence level with sample size 10 is 1.833. Note that we find this value by reading across the top to 0.90 and down the d.f. column to 9. The value found at the row and column intersection is the appropriate t value. As another example, the t value corresponding to a 95 percent confidence level and sample size 19 is 2.101. The t value for 95 percent confidence and sample size 14 is 2.160. Make sure you can locate these values in the t-distribution table in appendix D. You will be required to use the t-distribution table extensively in this chapter.

SKILL DEVELOPMENT PROBLEMS FOR SECTION 11–2

The following set of problems is meant to test your understanding of the material in this section. Additional problems are found at the end of this chapter under this section heading.

1. Referring to the t-distribution table in Appendix D, find the t value for each of the following:
   a. $n = 10$, confidence level $= 0.99$; $t =$ 3.250
   b. $n = 19$, confidence level $= 0.90$; $t =$ 1.734
   c. $n = 22$, confidence level $= 0.95$; $t =$ 2.080
   d. $n = 9$, confidence level $= 0.90$; $t =$ 1.860

---

[1]The statistical concept of *degrees of freedom* is one of the most difficult for beginning students because of its many possible interpretations. The general expression for degrees of freedom is $n - k$, where n is the number of observations and k is the number of constants that must be calculated from the sample data to estimate the variance of the sampling distribution.

2. Referring to the t-distribution table in Appendix D, find the t value for each of the following:
   a. $n = 12$, confidence level $= 0.90$; $t =$
   b. $n = 23$, confidence level $= 0.95$; $t =$
   c. $n = 29$, confidence level $= 0.80$; $t =$
   d. $n = 14$, confidence level $= 0.90$; $t =$

3. Given the following information:

$$\overline{X} = 300$$
$$\mu = 320$$
$$S_x = 8$$
$$n = 20$$

Find the t statistic and indicate what it measures.

4. Given the following information:

$$\overline{X} = 19.7$$
$$\mu = 18.0$$
$$S_x = 3.0$$
$$n = 25$$

Find the t statistic and indicate what is measures.

5. Discuss the difference between the standard normal distribution and the t distribution.

ESTIMATING THE POPULATION MEAN— SMALL SAMPLES

11-3

Let's return to the insurance company that needs to estimate the average damage to an automobile that crashes at 15 miles per hour.

The automobile industry in general has been attempting to build sturdier cars. Because of this, many insurance companies are examining their collision rates. The insurance company in our example needs to estimate each model's average damage for a 15-mile-per-hour crash to help the actuaries develop a premium rate for the model's owners.

Because of the costs involved, the company has selected a random sample of ten new cars and has crashed each one at 15 miles per hour. The resulting damage costs are shown in table 11–1. Assuming the true distribution of damages is *normal*, the insurance actuaries can use these data to develop an interval estimate for the true average damage level by use of equation 11–4:

$$\overline{X} \pm t\frac{S_x}{\sqrt{n}} \qquad\qquad (11\text{--}4)$$

where $\overline{X}$ = point estimate
           t = interval coefficient from the t distribution
           S_x = estimate of σ_x
           n = sample size

Assuming a 95 percent confidence interval is specified, and using the values for $\overline{X}$ and S_x shown in table 11–1, the interval is

$$\overline{X} \pm 2.262\,\frac{S_x}{\sqrt{n}}$$

$$\$3,121.5 \pm 2.262\,\frac{\$1,357.62}{\sqrt{10}}$$

$$\$3,121.5 \pm \$971.12$$

$$\$2,150.38 \underline{\qquad} \$4,092.62$$

Therefore the actuaries are confident that the true average repair cost will be between $2,150.38 and $4,092.62.

Of course, the true mean either will or will not fall in this interval. If this precision is too low (interval is too wide), the insurance company has two ways of increasing it. The company can increase the sample size *or* decrease the confidence level.

$1,954.00	$6,109.00
2,702.00	3,311.00
3,605.00	3,702.00
1,627.00	2,151.00
4,105.00	1,949.00

TABLE 11–1
Mean and standard deviation of automobile damage at 15 miles per hour

$$\overline{X} = \frac{\Sigma X}{n}$$

$$= \$3,121.50$$

$$S_x^2 = \frac{\Sigma(X - \overline{X})^2}{n - 1}$$

$$= 1,843,142.7$$

$$S_x = \sqrt{1,843,142.7}$$

$$= 1,357.62$$

Suppose because of the costs involved, the number of cars tested cannot be increased. If the confidence level is reduced to 90 percent, the interval coefficient, t, is reduced, giving the following confidence interval estimate for μ_x:

$$\bar{X} \pm 1.833 \frac{S_x}{\sqrt{n}}$$

$$\$3,121.50 \pm 1.833 \frac{\$1,357.62}{\sqrt{10}}$$

$$\$3,121.50 \pm \$786.94$$

$$\$2,334.56 \underline{\hspace{1cm}} \$3,908.44$$

Thus, decreasing the confidence level from 95 percent to 90 percent has decreased the interval width from $1,942.24 to $1,573.88.

As another example, consider the Quality Fitness Company, which operates the Health Fitness Center in Tulsa, Oklahoma. The company selected a sample of twelve new members and put them on a special weight loss/conditioning program for six months at no cost to the members. The purpose of this test was to estimate the average weight typical new members could expect to lose on this plan.

After six months, the company determined that the sample mean weight loss was 13.5 pounds, with a sample standard deviation of 3.6 pounds. They assumed the population distribution for weight loss would be normally distributed around the true mean.

The point estimate for average weight loss is the sample mean, 13.5 pounds. However, company officials recognize that this estimate is subject to sampling error. Thus they wish to develop a 99 percent confidence interval estimate for the true mean weight loss. They could do this as follows:

$$\bar{X} \pm 3.106 \, S_x/\sqrt{n}$$

$$13.5 \pm 3.106 \, (3.6/\sqrt{12})$$

$$13.5 \pm 3.23$$

$$10.27 \underline{\hspace{1cm}} 16.73$$

Thus, based upon these sample data, the company officials can be confident that the true average weight loss by typical new members during the initial six-month period on this new program will be 10.27 to 16.73 pounds. (Note that the t value is found in the t table with 99 percent confidence and $12 - 1 = 11$ degrees of freedom.)

SKILL DEVELOPMENT PROBLEMS FOR SECTION 11–3

The following set of problems is meant to test your understanding of the material in this section. Additional problems are found at the end of this chapter under this section heading.

6. Given the following sample information and assuming that the population is normally distributed:

$$n = 20$$
$$\overline{X} = 96.5$$
$$S_x = 7.4$$

   a. Develop and interpret the 95 percent confidence interval estimate for the population mean.
   b. Develop and interpret the 90 percent confidence interval estimate for the population mean.

7. Given the following sample information and assuming that the population is normally distributed:

$$n = 11$$
$$\overline{X} = 123.5$$
$$S_x = 16.0$$

   a. Develop and interpret the 95 percent confidence interval estimate for the population mean.
   b. Develop and interpret the 90 percent confidence interval estimate for the population mean.

8. Given the following sample information and assuming that the population is normally distributed:

$$n = 30$$
$$\overline{X} = 2,340.9$$
$$S_x = 220.50$$

   a. Develop and interpret the 99 percent confidence interval estimate for the population mean.
   b. Develop and interpret the 90 percent confidence interval estimate for the population mean.

9. Given the following sample information and assuming that the population is normally distributed:

$$n = 13$$
$$\overline{X} = 4.23$$
$$S_x = 1.20$$

   a. Develop and interpret the 90 percent confidence interval estimate for the population mean.
   b. Develop and interpret the 80 percent confidence interval estimate for the population mean.

10. Schwartz Lumber Company wishes to estimate the average number of board feet of lumber sold per day at their Eugene, Oregon, store. A random sample of fifteen days of sales data has been collected, with the following results:

$$\overline{X} = 14,600$$
$$S_x = 3,005$$

    a. If a small sample interval estimate is to be made, what assumption is required? What distribution will be used to obtain the interval coefficient for an interval estimate?

    b. Develop and interpret the 95 percent interval estimate for the average board feet of lumber sold per day at the Eugene store.

11. The U.S. Golf Association is interested in estimating the average number of times its members play golf during the month of September. In a pilot study, a random sample of twenty-five USGA members were polled, with the following results:

$$\overline{X} = 3.45$$
$$S_x = 2.4$$

Determine the 90 percent confidence interval estimate for the true average number of rounds played by members in September. Interpret this estimate.

12. The Ajax Taxi company is interested in estimating the average time per eight-hour shift that its drivers are waiting for a fare. A sample of eighteen drivers was observed for one eight-hour shift, with the following results:

$$\overline{X} = 4.7 \text{ hours}$$
$$S_x = 2.0 \text{ hours}$$

Based upon these sample data, what is the 90 percent confidence interval estimate for the true average number of idle hours per shift for Ajax taxi drivers? Interpret and indicate what assumptions you have made.

13. The U.S. National Park Service sells annual passes good for an unlimited number of visits to the country's national parks. Recently, a student intern for the Park Service surveyed ten randomly selected tourists holding passes and asked how many prior visits he or she had made to a national park. The following data were collected:

$$2 \quad 0 \quad 3 \quad 6 \quad 0 \quad 4 \quad 2 \quad 1 \quad 0 \quad 3$$

Based upon these sample data, develop the 95 percent confidence interval estimate for the average number of prior visits to a national park made by the population members. Interpret.

ESTIMATING THE DIFFERENCE BETWEEN TWO POPULATION MEANS—SMALL SAMPLES

11-4

The C. J. Milne Corporation manufactures and distributes power hand tools in the Midwest. The plant managers at the two Milne locations have been responsible for their own quality control. They have always assumed that the quality of the tools coming from the two locations was the same. Recently, Milne has received more customer complaints than usual. A corporate vice-president thinks that one plant may have lost some control on quality. Since the finished goods from the two locations are mixed at a central warehouse before they are distributed to the retailers, she cannot tell which plant is producing the inferior product. Consequently, she has hired a testing company to examine twelve tools from each plant and assign a quality rating to each. The vice-president is interested in estimating the difference in the average ratings for tools produced at the two plants.

Chapter 8 discussed estimating the difference between two population means for large samples. We can estimate this difference for small samples using the t distribution, provided we make the following assumptions:

1. The two populations are normally distributed and independent.
2. The two populations have equal standard deviations.

If these two assumptions are satisfied, the small-sample confidence interval estimate of the difference between population means is shown by equation 11–5:

$$(\overline{X}_1 - \overline{X}_2) \pm tS_{\text{pooled}} \sqrt{\frac{1}{n_1} + \frac{1}{n_2}} \qquad (11\text{–}5)$$

where $\overline{X}_1$ = sample mean from population 1
$\overline{X}_2$ = sample mean from population 2
t = interval coefficient from the t distribution with d.f.
$= (n_1 + n_2 - 2)$

$$S_{\text{pooled}} = \sqrt{\frac{S_{x_1}^2(n_1 - 1) + S_{x_2}^2(n_2 - 1)}{n_1 + n_2 - 2}}$$

n_1 and n_2 = sample sizes from populations 1 and 2, respectively

Note that the small-sample confidence interval for estimating the difference between two population means follows the usual format, that is,

Point estimate $\pm$ (interval coefficient)(standard error of the estimate)

As can be seen, the standard error of the estimate involves *pooling* the variances from each sample. The **pooled standard deviation**, S_{pooled}, is the square root of a weighted average of the sample variances, where the weights are $n_1 - 1$ and $n_2 - 1$. This pooled value is a better estimate of the common variance than either individual estimate.

The interval coefficient is a t value from the Student t distribution. An important point about this t value is that the appropriate degrees of freedom are $n_1 + n_2 - 2$. Note that this is equal to the denominator in the equation for the pooled standard deviation. This is also the sum of the individual degrees of freedom; that is, $n_1 + n_2 - 2 = (n_1 - 1) + (n_2 - 1)$.

Suppose the ratings for the twelve tools from each plant in our example give the following results:

	Plant 1	*Plant 2*
	$n_1 = 12$	$n_2 = 12$
	$\overline{X}_1 = 49$	$\overline{X}_2 = 46$
	$S_{x_1}^2 = 147$	$S_{x_2}^2 = 154$

Notice the two sample variances are nearly equal. This adds validity to the assumption of equal variances. We will introduce a technique for determining whether two population variances are equal in chapter 12. In section 11–6 of this chapter, we will comment on what can be done if we cannot assume the variances are equal.

The 90 percent confidence interval for estimating the difference between the mean ratings for tools from plants 1 and 2 is

$$(\overline{X}_1 - \overline{X}_2) \pm 1.717 S_{pooled} \sqrt{\frac{1}{n_1} + \frac{1}{n_2}}$$

$$(49 - 46) \pm 1.717 S_{pooled} \sqrt{\frac{1}{12} + \frac{1}{12}}$$

where

$$S_{pooled} = \sqrt{\frac{(12 - 1)(147) + (12 - 1)(154)}{22}}$$

$$= 12.27$$

Note that the interval coefficient, t, is found in the t-distribution table with $n_1 + n_2 - 2 = 22$ degrees of freedom.

The confidence interval is

$$(49 - 46) \pm (1.717)(12.27)(0.4082)$$

$$3 \pm 8.60$$

$$-5.60 \text{ points} \underline{\qquad} 11.60 \text{ points}$$

The vice-president is confident, based on this interval estimate, that the true difference between the average quality ratings for the two plants is between 5.60 in favor of plant 2 and 11.60 in favor of plant 1. Since she believes that this interval contains the true mean difference, and since this interval includes zero, she would make no judgment about the quality control at either plant. However, she may dislike the low precision (wide interval) and suggest a larger sample size or a decreased confidence level to increase the precision.

Note that the two sample sizes need not be equal when equation 11–5 is used to estimate the difference between two population means.

SKILL DEVELOPMENT PROBLEMS FOR SECTION 11–4

The following set of problems is meant to test your understanding of the material in this section. Additional problems are found at the end of this chapter under this section heading.

14. Independent random samples from each of two populations have been selected, with the following results:

Sample 1	Sample 2
$n = 10$	$n = 10$
$\overline{X} = 43.5$	$\overline{X} = 52.4$
$S_x = 10$	$S_x = 9.6$

a. Determine the point estimate for the difference between the two population means.

b. Develop the 95 percent confidence interval estimate for the difference between the two population means. Be sure to provide an interpretation of the interval estimate.

15. Independent random samples from each of two populations have been selected, with the following results:

Sample 1	Sample 2
$n = 8$	$n = 12$
$\overline{X} = 1{,}234.6$	$\overline{X} = 1{,}198.45$
$S_x = 33.45$	$S_x = 35.70$

a. Determine the point estimate for the difference between the two population means.

b. Develop the 90 percent confidence interval estimate for the difference between the two population means. Be sure to provide an interpretation of the interval estimate.

16. Independent random samples from each of two populations have been selected, with the following results:

	Sample 1	Sample 2
	$n = 9$	$n = 7$
	$\overline{X} = 2.38$	$\overline{X} = 3.20$
	$S_x = 1.12$	$S_x = 1.05$

a. Determine the point estimate for the difference between the two population means.

b. Develop the 95 percent confidence interval estimate for the difference between the two population means. Be sure to provide an interpretation of the interval estimate.

17. The owner of a fast-food franchise outlet is considering two different promotions. In the first case, she will give out coupons that make the Big-Bite Burger half-price. The second alternative gives two Big-Bites for the price of one. She is interested in estimating the difference in average dollars spent on other products (such as fries, soft drinks, etc.) for the two alternatives. This estimate will help her decide which promotion to go with.

   The manager has selected a random sample of ten households and has mailed half-price coupons to each. A second sample of ten households was selected and two-for-one coupons were sent to each of these. By week's end, eight half-price coupons and nine two-for-one coupons had been redeemed, with the following data for extra purchases:

	Half-Price	Two-for-One
	$n = 8$	$n = 9$
	$\overline{X} = \$2.45$	$\overline{X} = \$2.10$
	$S_x = 0.72$	$S_x = 0.86$

a. Develop a 95 percent confidence interval estimate for the difference in average dollar purchases between the two coupon offers. Interpret.

b. Based upon the estimate in part a, can the manager conclude that a difference exists between the two promotions in terms of average extra dollar purchases? Discuss.

18. The Virginia Department of Highways recently conducted a study to estimate the difference in average damage to vehicles that crashed into an unprotected bridge abutment versus those that crashed into an experimental padded bridge abutment. Eight "identical" cars traveling 45 m.p.h. were crashed into the unprotected abutment; a second sample of seven "identical" cars were crashed into the experimental protected bridges. The following sample data were recorded based upon figures supplied by the department's maintenance crew. The data are in thousands of dollars.

Unprotected		Experimental	
$4.34	4.23	$3.65	4.01
3.98	5.02	4.10	3.33
4.12	4.23	3.76	4.23
4.11	3.56	3.45	

a. Develop the 95 percent confidence interval estimate of the difference in average dollar damage to vehicles for crashes into the two types of bridges. Interpret your estimate.

b. Based upon the estimate developed in part a, is there sufficient evidence to say that the experimental padding reduces average dollar damages? Discuss.

ESTIMATING THE DIFFERENCE BETWEEN TWO POPULATION MEANS—PAIRED SAMPLES

11-5

Comparing two population means often involves situations where the two samples are *not* independent. For example, the O. T. Herman Company makes tractor tires under two different processes. The quality assurance department wishes to estimate the difference in average wear of tires from the two processes. The test plan is to place a tire made from each process on the rear wheels of ten tractors and to measure tire wear after one month. The quality control people realize that tractor tire wear depends on the driver, the type of work performed, the amount of time the tractor is driven, and the tractor's age and type, so they place one tire from each process on each tractor to eliminate these factors. However, when they do this, the samples can no longer be considered independent. Instead they are paired samples, and the confidence interval estimate for the difference in population means is given in equation 11–6:

$$\bar{d} \pm t\frac{S_d}{\sqrt{n}} \qquad (11–6)$$

where $\bar{d}$ = average of the paired differences
    t = interval coefficient
    S_d = standard deviation of the paired differences
    n = number of pairs

Table 11–2 presents the wear measurements for ten tires made under each process.

Using equation 11–6, we can develop a 95 percent confidence interval in the following manner. (Note that the degrees of freedom associated with the interval coefficient, t, are $n - 1$. Here, degrees of freedom equals $10 - 1 = 9$.)

TABLE 11-2
Tire wear measurements, O. T. Herman Tire Company example (wear = tire tread depth in inches)

Tractor	Process 1	Process 2	d	$(d - \bar{d})^2$
1	3.25	3.14	0.11	$(0.11 - 0.309)^2 = 0.0396$
2	3.86	3.20	0.66	$(0.66 - 0.309)^2 = 0.1232$
3	7.15	6.93	0.22	$(0.22 - 0.309)^2 = 0.0079$
4	8.00	7.90	0.10	$(0.10 - 0.309)^2 = 0.0437$
5	1.14	1.01	0.13	$(0.13 - 0.309)^2 = 0.0320$
6	4.77	3.95	0.82	$(0.82 - 0.309)^2 = 0.2611$
7	5.24	4.93	0.31	$(0.31 - 0.309)^2 = 0.0000$
8	6.17	6.02	0.15	$(0.15 - 0.309)^2 = 0.0253$
9	8.32	8.13	0.19	$(0.19 - 0.309)^2 = 0.0142$
10	4.80	4.40	0.40	$(0.40 - 0.309)^2 = 0.0083$
			$\bar{d} = 3.09/10 = 0.309$	$\Sigma = 0.5553$

$$S_d = \sqrt{\frac{\Sigma(d - \bar{d})^2}{n - 1}}$$
$$= 0.2484$$

$$\bar{d} \pm 2.262 \frac{S_d}{\sqrt{n}}$$

$$0.309 \pm 2.262 \frac{0.2484}{\sqrt{10}}$$

$$0.1313 \text{ inch} \underline{\qquad} 0.4867 \text{ inch}$$

Thus, the department management is confident that the true difference between the average wear for tires made under the two processes is between 0.1313 and 0.4867 inch, with process 1 showing less wear.

Note that this estimate was obtained by pairing observations *before* the measurements were taken. The reason for this was to control for differences that might result because of the tractor, the driver, or working conditions.

The previous example involved the need to control for factors pertaining to individual tractors before we could reasonably test to determine whether the two tire-making processes yielded tires with the same or different average wear. If the need actually does exist to provide this type of control, there are clear advantages to doing so, as the next example illustrates.

The Simmons Company makes and markets soap and soap products for use in the home. It markets its product primarily in supermarkets and grocery stores. The marketing department is currently considering a new sales campaign, but cannot decide between two store layout arrangements. A store layout arrangement consists of space allocated to the product on the store's shelf and the manner in which the product is arranged on the shelf. The marketing people feel strongly that layout is vital to the success of the new sales campaign. Consequently, they want to use the layout that will result in the most sales.

The vice-president of marketing has decided that both layouts should be tested in a sample of stores to determine what the difference is in average store sales of the product from the two layouts. One option would be to select a random sample of stores and in these set up layout 1 and in a second sample of stores set up layout 2. The company would then determine the number of sales in each store over a period of a week and estimate the difference in average sales per store based on the sample data.

However, it was suggested that store size and the stores' overall sales volume might influence soap sales more than the layout. For instance, a large store might sell more of the soap products than a very small store regardless of layout used. Thus, to control for store size, it was decided to select a random sample of stores and first use one layout for one week and then the other layout during the second week. Officials would randomly determine which layout was used first in each store. By having the layouts tested in the same set of stores, the company can control for the potential differences that might occur due just to store size. However, in doing this the samples are considered paired samples instead of two independent samples. Table 11–3 shows the sales data (in cases) for the two layouts and also shows the necessary calculations for providing a paired-sample confidence interval estimate for the difference in average store sales for the two layouts.

The 95 percent confidence interval estimate for the paired difference is

$$\bar{d} \pm t\left(\frac{S}{\sqrt{n}}\right)$$

$$2 \pm 2.365 \left(\frac{4.54}{\sqrt{8}}\right)$$

$$2 \pm 3.796$$

Thus, the 95 percent confidence interval for the paired difference in average store sales for the two layouts is

$$-1.796 \underline{\qquad} 5.796$$

This interval crosses zero, which means that based on these sample data the Simmons Company should not infer that the layouts affect average store sales.

Remember that the previous interval estimate was developed under the assumption that a paired sample was used. Suppose that we now treat the data as two independent samples and that we develop a 95 percent confidence interval estimate for the difference in population means, using the approach outlined in section 11–4. Table 11–4 presents the data and the calculations required to arrive at the interval estimate.

TABLE 11-3
Product layout test data, Simmons Company example

Store	Layout 1	Layout 2	d	$(d - \bar{d})^2$
1	35	26	9	49
2	17	11	6	16
3	15	17	-2	16
4	20	16	4	4
5	30	35	-5	49
6	8	6	2	0
7	12	13	-1	9
8	15	12	3	1
			$\bar{d} = 2$	$\Sigma = 144$

$$S_d = \sqrt{\frac{\Sigma(d - \bar{d})^2}{n - 1}}$$

$$= \sqrt{\frac{144}{7}}$$

$$= 4.54$$

TABLE 11-4
Estimation assuming independent samples, Simmons Company example

Layout 1		Layout 2	
X_1	$(X - \bar{X}_1)^2$	X_2	$(X - \bar{X}_2)^2$
35	256	26	81
17	4	11	36
15	16	17	0
20	1	16	1
30	121	35	324
8	121	6	121
12	49	13	16
15	16	12	25
$\Sigma = 152$	$\Sigma = 584$	$\Sigma = 136$	$\Sigma = 604$

$$\bar{X}_1 = \frac{152}{8} = 19 \qquad \bar{X}_2 = \frac{136}{8} = 17$$

$$S_1^2 = \frac{\Sigma(X - \bar{X}_1)^2}{n - 1} \qquad S_2^2 = \frac{\Sigma(X - \bar{X}_2)^2}{n - 1}$$

$$= \frac{584}{7} \qquad\qquad = \frac{604}{7}$$

$$= 83.42 \qquad\qquad = 86.29$$

$$S_p = \sqrt{\frac{83.42(7) + 86.29(7)}{14}}$$

$$= 9.21$$

Using the values computed in table 11–4, we can develop the 95 percent confidence interval estimate for difference in population means as follows:

$$\overline{X}_1 - \overline{X}_2 \pm tS_{\text{pooled}}\sqrt{\frac{1}{n_1} + \frac{1}{n_2}}$$

$$2 \pm 2.145 \, (9.21)(0.5)$$

$$2 \pm 9.88$$

Thus, under the assumptions of independent samples, normal populations, and equal variances, the estimate for the difference in average store sales is -7.88 cases to 11.88 cases. Since the interval crosses zero, the marketing managers cannot conclude that a difference exists in average store sales from the two layouts.

Note that the 95 percent confidence interval just computed has a tolerable error of plus or minus 9.88 cases. This is substantially greater than the tolerable error we observed when the paired-sample approach was used earlier. Recall that the tolerable error for that 95 percent confidence interval was 3.796 cases. This is due to the fact that the pooled standard deviation developed under the assumption of independent samples is substantially greater than the standard deviation of the paired differences (see tables 11–3 and 11–4).

Controlling for outside factors like store size in this case is called **blocking.** Blocking is often done when the observations can be naturally grouped into clusters of similar observations (the blocks). Observations within a block are often more homogeneous than those from different blocks. In the previous example, we blocked on store.

Blocking may or may not be desired. In this product layout example, we know that blocking was effective because it produced a more precise estimate of the difference in average store sales than did the two-independent-sample approach. We can check this after the fact by computing confidence intervals both ways and comparing interval widths. If blocking is not effective, the paired-sample approach can actually yield a wider interval since the degrees of freedom are reduced. Note that the t value from the t-distribution table is larger for the paired-sample interval (2.365 to 2.145). Thus, unless the blocking results in reduction in standard deviation sufficient to offset the loss in degrees of freedom, the paired approach will actually produce a wider, less precise interval.

Thus, if you are considering whether to use a paired-sample approach to estimate the difference in population means, you must realize that once you have collected the data in that format and developed the confidence interval, you may not change to the independent-samples approach without throwing out the data already collected and starting over. Of course the opposite is also true.

SKILL DEVELOPMENT PROBLEMS FOR SECTION 11–5

The following set of problems is meant to test your understanding of the material in this section. Additional problems are found at the end of this chapter under this section heading.

19. Given two dependent samples with the following information:

Item	Sample 1	Sample 2
1	234	245
2	221	224
3	196	194
4	245	267
5	234	230
6	204	198

Develop a 90 percent confidence interval estimate for the paired difference between population means. Interpret.

20. Given two dependent samples with the following information:

Item	Sample 1	Sample 2
1	19.6	21.3
2	22.1	17.4
3	18.5	19.0
4	20.0	21.2
5	21.5	20.1
6	20.2	23.5
7	17.9	18.9
8	23.0	22.4
9	12.5	14.3
10	19.0	17.8

Develop a 95 percent confidence interval estimate for the paired difference between population means. Interpret.

21. Given two dependent samples with the following information:

Item	Sample 1	Sample 2
1	3.4	2.8
2	2.5	3.0
3	7.0	5.5
4	5.9	6.7
5	4.0	3.5
6	5.0	5.0
7	6.2	7.5
8	5.3	4.2

Develop a 99 percent confidence interval estimate for the paired difference between population means. Interpret.

22. Given two dependent samples with the following information:

Item	Sample 1	Sample 2
1	1004	1045
2	1245	1145
3	1360	1400
4	1150	1000
5	1300	1350
6	1450	1350
7	900	1140

Develop a 90 percent confidence interval estimate for the paired difference between population means. Interpret.

23. Discuss the circumstances under which a paired sample estimate is desirable instead of taking two independent random samples.

24. The publisher of a microcomputer magazine regularly features a comparison between two different makes of microcomputers. The usual practice is to run the same set of sample applications on each machine and record speed. Suppose one such issue contained the following data measured in seconds:

Application	Microcomputer A	Microcomputer B
1	4.5 s	5.6 s
2	10.4	12.3
3	23.4	20.6
4	10.0	11.4
5	12.0	13.4
6	27.5	24.3
7	3.0	4.2

Based upon these sample data, determine the 95 percent confidence interval estimate for the difference in average time to perform applications. Also discuss why this estimate should be based upon a paired-sample test instead of using two random samples of applications to test the microcomputers independently.

25. A publisher of technical books on subjects like computer documentation is considering going to a new publishing format. Before doing so, they are interested in getting some opinion about the old versus the new method. They have selected twenty people randomly from the population and have asked them to review a book in the old format and a book in the new format. Then they are to assign a point rating to each book between 1 and 1,000. The following results were obtained:

$$\bar{d} = -24.5$$
$$S_d = 40$$
$$n = 20$$

Considering this sampling to be paired sampling, construct the 95 percent confidence interval estimate for the true average paired difference in rating for the two publishing formats.

EFFECT OF VIOLATING THE ASSUMPTIONS FOR SMALL-SAMPLE ESTIMATION

11-6   When using the t distribution for statistical estimation with small samples, we assume that

1. The populations are normally distributed.
2. The populations have equal variances if two independent populations are involved.

Although applications may exist for which these assumptions are strictly satisfied, experience indicates this rarely happens. Fortunately, however, the estimation methods presented in this chapter are fairly robust. That is, for small departures from the assumptions of normality and equal variances, the t distribution is still appropriate. However, if the populations differ extensively from normality (the populations are extremely skewed) or the variances are far from equal, the decision maker will need to employ different statistical procedures or select a large sample size and use the large-sample estimation techniques presented in chapter 8.

In chapter 12 we will consider techniques used to test whether two population variances are equal. Then, in chapter 15, we will introduce goodness-of-fit tests, which can be used to test a distribution for normality. Chapter 15 will also present techniques called nonparametric statistical tests. Several of these tests are specifically designed to handle problems where the sample sizes are small and the decision maker does not feel justified in making the assumptions required by the t distribution.

One other comment is in order here. You will note that this chapter has not presented examples for estimating a single population proportion or the difference between two population proportions when the sample sizes are small. The reason for this is that the underlying distribution for proportions is the binomial distribution. The binomial is discrete and is approximated by the normal distribution only for reasonably large sample sizes. To calculate a small-sample confidence interval for a population proportion, the binomial distribution would have to be used. We have chosen to restrict our discussion of proportions to large-sample estimation procedures.

HYPOTHESIS TESTING WITH SMALL SAMPLES AND σ_x UNKNOWN

11-7

In many business applications involving sampling, the time and costs of collecting the sample data restrict the sample size. The hypothesis-testing techniques introduced thus far are appropriate if the sample size is large. This section considers hypothesis-testing techniques that can be used when the sample size is small and the population standard deviation is unknown. In particular, these techniques use the t distribution, which was also used in small-sample estimation in previous sections. You will find little difference between the small-sample hypothesis tests requiring the t distribution and the large-sample tests, which use the standard normal distribution, just as there were only small differences between small- and large-sample confidence interval estimation procedures.

Hypothesis Testing About the Population Mean— Small Samples

Samantha Edwards and Julie Adamson left high-level engineering design jobs several years ago to form their own company. They have recently been working on a new type of bumper system for automobiles. The federal government has specified a very strict crash standard for automobile bumpers. However, the bumpers that currently meet the federal crash standard add weight to the car, which reduces gas mileage. Samantha and Julie think they have designed a lightweight bumper system that meets the federal crash standard.

The automobile manufacturers have expressed interest in the new bumper system. However, the only way to make sure the bumper meets the standard is to perform crash tests with new automobiles. The damage from the tests is measured, and the average damage is compared with the standard of $150 average damage at 15 miles per hour.

The two enterpreneurs claim their bumper system will exceed the standard (i.e., $\mu < \$150$). Thus, the null hypothesis must contain the equality.

Hypotheses:

H_0: $\mu_x \geq \$150$

H_A: $\mu_x < \$150$

Decision Rule:

Take a sample of size n and determine $\overline{X}$.

If $\overline{X} \geq A$, accept H_0.

If $\overline{X} < A$, reject H_0.

One of the large automakers has agreed to cosponsor the crash tests. It will furnish fifteen cars for the test and will accept no more than a 0.05 chance of committing a Type I error.

The first step is to perform the crash test for the fifteen cars. Suppose the tests result in an average damage of $145 and a standard deviation of $80.

The next step is to arrive at the appropriate critical value for deciding whether to accept or reject the null hypothesis. Because the sample size is small and the population standard deviation is unknown, we must use the t distribution in developing the decision rule, as shown in figure 11–2. Note that the appropriate test statistic if the population of possible crash values is normally distributed is as in equation 11–7:

$$t = \frac{\overline{X} - \mu_x}{\frac{S_x}{\sqrt{n}}} \qquad (11\text{–}7)$$

Based on the sample results, the conclusion is that the new bumper does *not* yield an average cost below the $150 government standard.

Hypotheses:

H_0: $\mu_x \geq \$150$
H_A: $\mu_x < \$150$

$\alpha = 0.05$

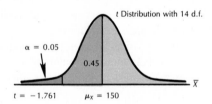

t Distribution with 14 d.f.

$\alpha = 0.05$

0.45

$t = -1.761$ $\mu_x = 150$

Decision Rule:

If $\overline{X} \geq A$, accept H_0.
If $\overline{X} < A$, reject H_0.

The critical value is

$$A = \mu_x - t\frac{S_x}{\sqrt{n}} = \$150 - 1.761\frac{\$80}{\sqrt{15}}$$
$$= \$113.62$$

Since $\overline{X} = \$145 > \$113.62$, accept H_0.

FIGURE 11–2
Small-sample hypothesis test for μ_x, bumper example

Hypothesis Tests Involving Two Population Means— Small Samples

Among the fastest-growing investment alternatives in the United States are the tax-sheltered annuity (TSA) programs offered by large insurance companies. Certain people qualify to deposit part of their paychecks in the TSA and pay no federal income tax on this money until it is withdrawn. While the money is on deposit, the insurance companies invest it in stock or bond portfolios. If the portfolios perform well, the TSA accounts grow.

Some organizations with conventional retirement plans are concerned the TSAs may have an advantage in terms of growth. As part of a comparative study, a random sample of fifteen TSAs and fifteen retirement plans is selected.

If we assume that the growth rates of the two populations are approximately normally distributed and that the population variances are equal, a t statistic is appropriate for testing the following null and alternative hypotheses:

Hypotheses:

H_0: $\mu_1 - \mu_2 = 0$

H_A: $\mu_1 - \mu_2 \neq 0$

where μ_1 = average growth rate for population 1 (TSAs)
          μ_2 = average growth rate for population 2 (retirement plans)

The sample results are

	TSA	Retirement Plan
	$n_1 = 15$	$n_2 = 15$
	$\overline{X}_1 = 8.9\%$	$\overline{X}_2 = 7.8\%$
	$S_1^2 = 58$	$S_2^2 = 61$

If we wish to test the null hypothesis using an alpha level of 0.05, we perform the analysis shown in figure 11–3. The test statistic is given in equation 11–8:

$$t = \frac{(\overline{X}_1 - \overline{X}_2) - (\mu_1 - \mu_2)}{S_{\text{pooled}}\sqrt{\dfrac{1}{n_1} + \dfrac{1}{n_2}}} \qquad (11\text{--}8)$$

where $\overline{X}_1$ and $\overline{X}_2$ = the sample means
          $\mu_1 - \mu_2$ = the hypothesized difference
          n_1 and n_2 = the sample sizes from the two populations
          S_{pooled} = pooled standard deviation

Hypotheses:

$H_0: \mu_1 - \mu_2 = 0$
$H_A: \mu_1 - \mu_2 \neq 0$

$\alpha = 0.05$

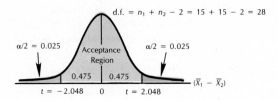

$\alpha/2 = 0.025$ Acceptance Region $\alpha/2 = 0.025$

d.f. $= n_1 + n_2 - 2 = 15 + 15 - 2 = 28$

0.475 | 0.475

$t = -2.048$ 0 $t = 2.048$ $(\overline{X}_1 - \overline{X}_2)$

Decision Rule:

If $t > 2.048$, reject H_0.
If $t < -2.048$, reject H_0.
Otherwise, accept H_0.

Test Statistic:

$$t = \frac{(\overline{X}_1 - \overline{X}_2) - (\mu_1 - \mu_2)}{S_{pooled}\sqrt{\dfrac{1}{n_1} + \dfrac{1}{n_2}}} = \frac{(8.9 - 7.8) - 0}{7.71\sqrt{\dfrac{1}{15} + \dfrac{1}{15}}} = 0.391$$

where: $S_{pooled} = \sqrt{\dfrac{(n_1 - 1)S_1^2 + (n_2 - 1)S_2^2}{n_1 + n_2 - 2}} = \sqrt{\dfrac{(14)(58) + (14)(61)}{28}}$

$= 7.71$

Since $-2.048 < 0.391 < 2.048$, accept H_0

FIGURE 11–3

Hypothesis test of the two population means—small samples, tax shelter annuities example

From our work with small-sample estimation, we get equation 11–9:

$$S_{pooled} = \sqrt{\frac{(n_1 - 1)S_1^2 + (n_2 - 1)S_2^2}{n_1 + n_2 - 2}} \qquad (11\text{--}9)$$

Note that the degrees of freedom associated with the t distribution for the two sample tests is $n_1 + n_2 - 2$.

Referring to figure 11–3, we see that the difference in sample means is 0.391 standard deviation from zero. This clearly falls into the acceptance region, which means that the sample data do not provide sufficient evidence to conclude there is a difference in average performance between tax shelter annuities and conventional retirement plans.

The previous hypothesis test used the t distribution and thus assumed that the populations were normal with equal variances.[2] In the next chapter, you will be introduced to a procedure for determining whether two populations have equal variances. Also, in chapter 15 on nonparametric statistics, you will encounter a technique for testing whether a population is normally distributed.

SKILL DEVELOPMENT PROBLEMS FOR SECTION 11–7

The following set of problems is meant to test your understanding of the material in this section. Additional problems are found at the end of this chapter under this section heading.

26. Given the following null and alternative hypotheses:

$$H_0: \mu = 300$$
$$H_A: \mu \neq 300$$

and the following sample information:

$$n = 13$$
$$\overline{X} = 344.2$$
$$S = 56.75$$

Is there sufficient evidence at the alpha $= 0.05$ level to reject the null hypothesis? Clearly show the decision rule used.

27. Given the following null and alternative hypotheses:

$$H_0: \mu \geq 25$$
$$H_A: \mu < 25$$

---

[2]In those situations where we believe the population variances are not equal, but the two distributions are normally distributed, we can still use the t distribution. However, we have to adjust the degrees of freedom for the t value. Instead of using $n_1 + n_2 - 2$ as the degrees of freedom, we compute the degrees of freedom using

$$D = \left[\frac{\dfrac{S_1^2}{n_1} + \dfrac{S_2^2}{n_2}}{\left(\dfrac{S_1^2}{n_1}\right)^2 \left(\dfrac{1}{n_1 + 1}\right) + \left(\dfrac{S_2^2}{n_2}\right)^2 \left(\dfrac{1}{n_2 - 1}\right)} \right] - 2$$

If this value becomes a fraction, we round to the nearest integer. The test statistic is now

$$t_D = \frac{(\overline{X}_1 - \overline{X}_2) - (\mu_1 - \mu_2)}{\sqrt{\dfrac{S_1^2}{n_1} + \dfrac{S_2^2}{n_2}}}$$

The critical value from the t distribution for the specified alpha has D degrees of freedom.

and the following sample information:

$$n = 26$$
$$\overline{X} = 24.28$$
$$S = 5.10$$

Is there sufficient evidence at the alpha $= 0.10$ level to reject the null hypothesis? Clearly show the decision rule used.

28. Given the following null and alternative hypotheses:

$$H_0: \mu \leq 1,980$$
$$H_A: \mu > 1,980$$

and the following sample information:

$$n = 17$$
$$\overline{X} = 1,984.20$$
$$S = 109$$

Is there sufficient evidence at the alpha $= 0.05$ level to reject the null hypothesis? Clearly show the decision rule used.

29. Given the following null and alternative hypotheses:

$$H_0: \mu_1 - \mu_2 = 0$$
$$H_A: \mu_1 - \mu_2 \neq 0$$

and the following sample information:

Sample 1	Sample 2
$n = 10$	$n = 12$
$\overline{X} = 234$	$\overline{X} = 281$
$S = 19.5$	$S = 21.4$

Is there sufficient evidence at the alpha $= 0.05$ level to reject the null hypothesis? Clearly show the decision rule used.

30. Given the following null and alternative hypotheses:

$$H_0: \mu_1 - \mu_2 \geq 0$$
$$H_A: \mu_1 - \mu_2 < 0$$

and the following sample information:

Sample 1	Sample 2
$n = 11$	$n = 9$
$\overline{X} = 21.5$	$\overline{X} = 22.4$
$S = 5.2$	$S = 4.7$

Is there sufficient evidence at the alpha = 0.10 level to reject the null hypothesis? Clearly show the decision rule used.

31. Given the following null and alternative hypotheses:

$$H_0: \mu_1 - \mu_2 \leq 0$$
$$H_A: \mu_1 - \mu_2 > 0$$

and the following sample information:

Sample 1	Sample 2
$n = 12$	$n = 10$
$\overline{X} = 4,567$	$\overline{X} = 4,540$
$S = 203.5$	$S = 215.7$

Is there sufficient evidence at the alpha = 0.01 level to reject the null hypothesis? Clearly show the decision rule used.

PAIRED-SAMPLE HYPOTHESIS TESTS

11-8

Section 11–7 outlined the methods by which decision makers can determine whether two populations have equal means if small samples are selected from normally distributed populations. The procedures presented there assumed that the samples were independent. For instance, in the tax-shelter example, one sample of tax-sheltered annuities was selected as well as a second independent sample of conventional retirement plans, and the means from the two samples were compared.

However, as illustrated earlier in this chapter in section 11–5, there exist instances in business where it is desirable to select samples from two populations that are not independent. For example, if a major oil company was interested in estimating the difference in average mileage for automobiles using two brands of engine oil, one procedure would be to test both types of oil on a sample of cars and drivers. Each oil would be used in the same sample of cars and drivers to control possible variations that might affect the results of the estimation.

When the sampling is performed in this manner, the samples are called *paired samples*. We showed how to develop confidence-interval estimates using paired samples in section 11–5. The same procedure can be used if we are concerned with testing hypotheses involving paired samples, as the following example illustrates.

The Donavan Company in Clearfield, Utah, makes and markets scales used by businesses (such as grocery stores, meat markets, livestock sales yards, and grain elevators) which have a need to accurately weigh products as part of their sales efforts. The scale, which the company has been marketing for several years, has been well accepted by business because of its accuracy. However, the scale is expensive to manufacture and thus must be sold at a high price.

Recently, Donavan Company engineers have developed a new digital scale that makes extensive use of electronic circuits and costs much less to make. If this scale can be shown to be as accurate as the old scale, Donavan officials plan to begin producing this scale as an alternative to the old one. The following null and alternative hypotheses have been established:

Hypotheses:

$H_0: \mu_1 - \mu_2 = 0$

$H_A: \mu_1 - \mu_2 \neq 0$

To perform this test for the grocery-store-type scales, company officials have selected a random sample of produce and meat items and have weighed these items on both scales. The data and some required calculations are shown in table 11–5.

Note that the samples are not independent since the same items are weighed on each scale. This means that the samples are considered paired samples. It seems reasonable to select paired samples in this case to control for variation in weights that might affect the hypothesis test if independent samples were used. Therefore we can reformulate the null and alternative hypotheses as follows:

Hypotheses:

$H_0: \mu_d = 0$

$H_A: \mu_d \neq 0$

Figure 11–4 shows the paired-sample test of the hypotheses based on the data in table 11–5. Thus, based on these data, the Donavan Company should conclude that there is no difference in the average weights provided by the two scales at an alpha level of 0.05.

If you are concerned that an outside source of variation might adversely affect your hypothesis test, it is often desirable to set up the test as a paired-sample test as was done here.

TABLE 11–5

Paired-sample data, Donavan Company example

Old Scale	New Scale	d	$(d - \bar{d})^2$
3.40	3.50	−0.10	0.008836
1.40	1.51	−0.11	0.010816
7.80	7.75	0.05	0.003136
4.60	4.55	0.05	0.003136
2.05	2.00	0.05	0.003136
1.04	1.03	0.01	0.000256
5.16	5.18	−0.02	0.000196
6.04	6.00	0.04	0.002116
9.12	9.15	−0.03	0.000576
4.14	4.14	0.00	0.000036
		$\Sigma = -0.06$	$\Sigma = 0.032240$

$$\bar{d} = -0.06/10 = -0.006$$

$$S_d = \sqrt{0.032240/9} = 0.0599$$

Hypotheses:

H_0: $\mu_d = 0$
H_A: $\mu_d \neq 0$

$\alpha = 0.05$

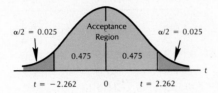

Decision Rule:

If $t > 2.262$, reject H_0.
If $t < -2.262$, reject H_0.
Otherwise, do not reject H_0.

Test Statistic:

$$t = \frac{\bar{d} - 0}{S_d/\sqrt{n}}$$
$$= \frac{-0.006 - 0}{0.0599/\sqrt{10}}$$
$$= -0.3168$$

Since $-2.262 < -0.3166 < 2.262$, accept H_0

FIGURE 11–4
Paired-sample t test, Donavan Company example

SKILL DEVELOPMENT PROBLEMS FOR SECTION 11–8

The following set of problems is meant to test your understanding of the material in this section. Additional problems are found at the end of this chapter under this section heading.

32. Given two dependent samples with the following information:

Item	Sample 1	Sample 2
1	234	245
2	221	224
3	196	194
4	245	267
5	234	230
6	204	198

Based upon these paired samples, test at the alpha = 0.05 level whether there is a difference in the true average paired differences.

33. Given two dependent samples with the following information:

Item	Sample 1	Sample 2	*d*
1	19.6	21.3	*1·7*
2	22.1	17.4	*-4·7*
3	19.5	19.0	*-o·5*
4	20.0	21.2	*1·2*
5	21.5	20.1	*-1·4*
6	20.2	23.5	*3·3*
7	17.9	18.9	*1·o*
8	23.0	22.4	*-o·6*
9	12.5	14.3	*1·8*
10	19.0	17.8	*-1·2*

Based upon these paired samples, test at the alpha = 0.10 level whether there is a difference in the true average paired differences.

34. Given two dependent samples with the following information:

Item	Sample 1	Sample 2
1	3.4	2.8
2	2.5	3.0
3	7.0	5.5
4	5.9	6.7
5	4.0	3.5
6	5.0	5.0
7	6.2	7.5
8	5.3	4.2

Based upon these paired samples, test at the alpha = 0.05 level whether there is a difference in the true average paired differences.

35. Given two dependent samples with the following information:

Item	Sample 1	Sample 2
1	1004	1045
2	1245	1145
3	1360	1400
4	1150	1000
5	1300	1350
6	1450	1350
7	900	1140

Based upon these paired samples, test at the alpha $= 0.05$ level whether there is a difference in the true average paired differences.

COMPUTER APPLICATIONS

11-9

In this chapter, we have introduced the techniques for small-sample estimation and hypothesis testing. The t distribution is used to develop the confidence intervals and as the test statistic for testing hypotheses. In this section, we show through two examples how a computer can assist in developing small-sample confidence intervals and in test-

```
UNNUMBERED
TITLE DESCRIPTIVE STATISTICS EXAMPLES
FILE HANDLE KIVZ NAME='KIVZ DATA C'
DATA LIST FILE=KIVZ LIST/VAR01 to VAR19
VARIABLE LABELS
    VAR01 'NATIONAL NEWS STATION'
    VAR02 'LOCAL NEWS STATION'
    VAR03 'NEWS RATING'
    VAR04 'SPORTS RATING'
    VAR05 'WEATHER RATING'
    VAR06 'ANCHOR RATING'
    VAR07 'SPORTSCASTER RATING'
    VAR08 'OVERALL RATING'
    VAR09 'NATIONAL INFLUENCE'
    VAR10 'SEX'
    VAR11 'MARITAL STATUS'
    VAR12 'NUMBER EMPLOYED'
    VAR13 'HOME STATUS '
    VAR14 'YEARS AT RESIDENCE'
    VAR15 'YEARS IN STATE'
    VAR16 'EDUCATION'
    VAR17 'AGE'
    VAR18 'INCOME'
    VAR19 'HOURS OF TV'
VALUE LABELS
    VAR01 1 'CHANNEL 5' 2 'CHANNEL 3' 3 'CHANNEL 8'
          4 'UNDECIDED'/
    VAR02 1 'CHANNEL 3' 2 'CHANNEL 8' 3 'CHANNEL 5'
          4 'UNDECIDED'/
    VAR03 TO VAR08 1 'POOR' 2 'FAIR' 3 'GOOD' 4 'VERY GOOD'
          5 'EXCEL'/
    VAR09 1 'TRUE' 2 'FALSE' 3 'UNDECIDED'/
    VAR10 1 'MALE' 2 'FEMALE'/
    VAR11 1 'SINGLE' 2 'DIVORCED' 3 'MARRIED' 4 'OTHER'/
    VAR13 1 'RENTING' 2 'BUYING'/
    VAR16 1 'GRADE SCHOOL' 2 'SOME COLLEGE' 3 'VOTECH' 4 'HIGH
          SCHOOL'
          5 'COLLEGE GRAD' 6 'GRADUATE WORK'
T-TEST GROUPS=VAR10(1,2)/VARIABLES=VAR17 TO VAR19
```

FIGURE 11–5
SPSS-X commands—small-sample t test

TABLE 11–6
SPSS-X output—t test

GROUP 1 - VAR10   EQ   1.00
GROUP 2 - VAR10   EQ   2.00

- - - - - - - - T - TEST - - - - - - - -

VARIABLE	NUMBER OF CASES	MEAN	STANDARD DEVIATION	STANDARD ERROR	F VALUE	2-TAIL PROB.	POOLED VARIANCE ESTIMATE T VALUE	DEGREES OF FREEDOM	2-TAIL PROB.	SEPARATE VARIANCE ESTIMATE T VALUE	DEGREES OF FREEDOM	2-TAIL PROB.
VAR17 AGE												
GROUP 1	22	46.6364	15.789	3.366	1.07	0.857	1.04	48	0.303	1.04	44.50	0.305
GROUP 2	28	42.0357	15.264	2.885								
VAR18 INCOME												
GROUP 1	22	23809.0909	4141.188	882.904	1.57	0.292	-1.37	48	0.178	-1.40	47.98	0.167
GROUP 2	28	25660.7143	5188.330	980.502								
VAR19 HOURS OF TV												
GROUP 1	22	12.2273	4.649	0.991	1.23	0.607	0.21	48	0.835	0.21	42.83	0.837
GROUP 2	28	11.9643	4.194	0.793								

```
MTB> READ 'KIVZ5' INTO C1-C19
MTB> NAME C17 'AGE'
MTB> CHOOSE 2 C10 C17 C20 C21
MTB> OUTFILE = 'PRINTER'
MTB> TINTERVAL 95 C21
```

FIGURE 11–6

MINITAB commands—small-sample estimation, age for females

TABLE 11–7

MINITAB output—small-sample estimation, age for females

	N	MEAN	STDEV	SE MEAN	95.0 PERCENT C.I.
AGE	28	42.04	15.26	2.88	(32.12, 47.96)

ing hypotheses based on small samples. Both examples use the KIVZ-Channel 5 data presented in tables 2–10 and 2–11 in chapter 2.

Table 11–6 shows the output from SPSS-X where a t test is used to determine whether there is a difference in average age, average income, and average hours of television for males versus females. Figure 11–5 shows the SPSS-X commands that produced the output. Note that this output shows both "T VALUE" and "2-Tail Prob." In these three hypothesis tests, the null hypothesis of equal population means would be accepted for an alpha $= 0.178$ or less.

Table 11–7 shows a MINITAB output for an interval estimate for the average age (VAR17) for women in the population. Figure 11–6 shows the MINITAB commands necessary to produce this output.

HYPOTHESIS TESTING SUMMARY

11-10

This chapter has extended the discussion of hypothesis testing started in chapter 9. By now you should have discovered that the same basic logic is used to test hypotheses regardless of the parameter of interest and regardless of whether the sample is large or small. The problem most students have at this point is deciding "what to use when." To help you with this problem a set of tables has been included in the front inside cover of the text. To use these tables of equations as an aid in hypothesis testing and confidence interval estimation, you should ask yourself the following questions each time you approach a homework problem and later when you approach a decision situation in business.

1. *Are you working with large or small sizes?*
   Your answer here will determine whether you can rely on the central limit theorem and thus the standard normal distribution, or whether you will need to use a different distribution, such as the t distribution.
2. *What is the parameter of interest?*
   Are you dealing with a single population mean, difference between population means, a single population variance, or something else? The answer to this

along with the sample-size answer will allow you to locate the appropriate row in the table of equations.

3. *Is this an estimation or hypothesis testing problem?*
   The answer to this question further allows you to locate the appropriate equation to apply to the problem at hand.

These tables are not meant to encourage a "cookbook" approach to statistical inference. However, if you can concentrate on answering these three questions, you will be able to get to the heart of the decision problem and can devote your efforts to interpreting your results and applying those results to the decision situation.

Two further ideas should be stressed relative to hypothesis testing.

1. If you are in position to set up the null and alternative hypotheses, it is generally desirable to formulate them in such a manner that the Type I error is the most costly. We do this because we can directly control the Type I error probability by setting alpha to a desired level.

2. If you are in the position of testing someone else's claim about a population value, put the claim in the null hypothesis if it contains the equality, and put the claim in the alternative hypothesis if the claim does not contain the equality. The reason for this centers on the requirement that the null hypothesis must contain the equality. Review the examples presented in chapters 9 and 10 and you will see that in every case the null hypothesis contains the equality.

CONCLUSIONS

11-11

Decision makers often need to estimate population values based on a small sample from the populations. Providing the populations are normally distributed (or at least not highly skewed), the t distribution forms the basis for statistical estimation with a small sample size.

The t distribution has a larger variance than the standard normal distribution, but approaches the normal distribution as the sample size becomes large. The t distribution is symmetrical and has degrees of freedom that depend on the application. We have indicated, for each use, how to calculate the degrees of freedom.

We have also introduced small-sample confidence interval estimation for μ_x, for $(\mu_{x_1} - \mu_{x_2})$ with independent samples and for $(\mu_{x_1} - \mu_{x_2})$ with dependent samples.

This chapter has also extended our discussion of statistical hypothesis testing beyond the basic concepts introduced in chapter 9. It has introduced the methods necessary to test hypotheses involving samples using the t distribution.

You have probably noticed that statistical estimation and hypothesis testing, for large and small samples have a lot in common. Some decision makers and statistical authors seem to favor one technique over the other. Both have their place and both should be learned. Estimation procedures are most useful when decision makers have little idea about the population values and are primarily concerned with determining these values. On the other hand, if the decision makers have some idea about the parameter's value, the hypothesis-testing format is most useful.

You should make sure you are familiar with the terminology and equations at the end of this chapter before moving to chapter 12. The chapter glossary and chapter formulas summarize the concepts and techniques presented in this chapter.

CHAPTER GLOSSARY

interval estimator   An interval within which a population parameter may fall. The width of the interval is determined by a combination of sample size, confidence level, and variance.

large sample   In this text, a sample of size $n \geq 30$.

one-tailed test   A hypothesis test in which the entire rejection region is placed in one tail of the sampling distribution.

parameter   A measure of the population, such as μ_x, the population mean.

precision   The width of the confidence interval. The narrower the interval, the greater the precision, and vice versa.

point estimator   A single value calculated from a sample to be used to estimate a population parameter.

pooled variance   A weighted average of two sample variances where the weights are the degrees of freedom associated with each variance.

population   A finite or infinite collection of measurements, items, or individuals of all possible measurements, items, or individuals within the scope of the study.

sample   A subset of the population.

small sample   In this text, a sample of size $n < 30$.

statistic   A value computed from sample measures, such as $\overline{X}$, the sample mean. The statistic is usually a point estimator of the corresponding population parameter.

Student _t_ distribution   A sampling distribution of

$$t = \frac{\overline{X} - \mu_x}{\dfrac{S_x}{\sqrt{n}}}$$

for samples selected from a normally distributed population with σ_x estimated by S_x, and based on a small sample. The standardized t distribution has a mean of zero and a variance equal to $(n - 1)/[(n - 1) - 2]$.

two-tailed test   A hypothesis test in which the rejection region is split between the two tails of the sampling distribution.

Type I error   Rejecting a true null hypothesis.

Type II error   Accepting a false null hypothesis.

CHAPTER FORMULAS

Sample mean

$$\overline{X} = \frac{\Sigma X}{n}$$

Sample variance

$$S_x^2 = \frac{\Sigma(X - \overline{X})^2}{n - 1}$$

Sample standard deviation—shortcut formula

$$S_x = \sqrt{\frac{\Sigma X^2 - \dfrac{(\Sigma X)^2}{n}}{n - 1}}$$

Confidence interval estimate for the population mean—small sample

$$\overline{X} \pm t\frac{S_x}{\sqrt{n}}$$

where t has $n - 1$ d.f.

Confidence interval estimate for the difference between two population means—independent small samples

$$(\overline{X}_1 - \overline{X}_2) \pm tS_{\text{pooled}}\sqrt{\frac{1}{n_1} + \frac{1}{n_2}}$$

where t has $n_1 + n_2 - 2$ d.f.

Pooled standard deviation

$$S_{\text{pooled}} = \sqrt{\frac{S_{x_1}^2(n_1 - 1) + S_{x_2}^2(n_2 - 1)}{n_1 + n_2 - 2}}$$

t value
   One population mean

$$t = \frac{\overline{X} - \mu_x}{\dfrac{S_x}{\sqrt{n}}}$$

Two population means

$$t = \frac{(\overline{X}_1 - \overline{X}_2) - (\mu_1 - \mu_2)}{S_{\text{pooled}} \sqrt{\dfrac{1}{n_1} + \dfrac{1}{n_2}}}$$

Paired samples

$$t = \frac{\overline{d} - \mu_d}{S_d / \sqrt{n}}$$

Paired-sample confidence interval—small sample

$$\overline{d} \pm t \frac{S_d}{\sqrt{n}}$$

where t has $n - 1$ d.f., and n = number of pairs.

SOLVED PROBLEMS

1. The ARTEE Corporation makes glass basketball backboards. The company has made ten boards using a new technique. Before it makes any more for commercial sale, ARTEE needs to estimate the average strength of the new boards. To determine the strength of a board, pressure is applied to each corner until the glass shatters. The pressure at which the glass shatters is recorded.

   Suppose that for the ten glass backboards tested, the mean was 1,526 pounds per square inch and the standard deviation was 15.25 pounds per square inch (psi).

   a. Determine the 90 percent confidence interval for estimating μ_x, assuming the population is normally distributed.

   b. Determine the 99 percent confidence interval for estimating μ_x, assuming the population is normally distributed.

   c. Why are the precisions of the intervals calculated in parts a and b different?

Solutions:

   a. The 90 percent confidence interval for μ_x is determined as follows:

$$\overline{X} \pm t \frac{S_x}{\sqrt{n}}$$

   where t with 90 percent confidence and $n - 1 = 9$ degrees of freedom $= 1.833$.

Then

$$1,526 \pm 1.833 \frac{15.25}{\sqrt{10}}$$

1,517.16 psi ———— 1,534.84 psi

The ARTEE Corporation therefore can be confident that the average pressure at which a board will break is between 1,517.16 and 1,534.84 pounds per square inch.

b. The 99 percent confidence interval is

$$\bar{X} \pm 3.250 \frac{S_x}{\sqrt{n}}$$

$$1,526 \pm 3.250 \frac{15.25}{\sqrt{10}}$$

1,510.33 psi ———— 1,541.67 psi

c. The interval calculated in part a is more precise than the interval calculated in part b because the confidence level is higher in part b. When confidence is increased, the interval width is increased, and thus precision is decreased.

2. Referring to solved problem 1, suppose the ARTEE Corporation wishes to estimate the difference in average strength between the original glass backboards and the new glass backboards. Suppose the company has data for twenty original backboards and the ten new backboards. The available information is as follows:

Original	New
$\bar{X}_1 = 1,500$ psi	$\bar{X}_2 = 1,526$ psi
$S_1 = 45.00$ psi	$S_2 = 15.25$ psi
$n_1 = 20$	$n_2 = 10$

a. Calculate the 95 percent confidence interval estimate of the difference between the two population means, assuming each population is normally distributed and the population variances are equal.

b. Calculate the 90 percent confidence interval estimate for the difference between the two population means, assuming each population is normally distributed and the population variances are equal.

Solutions:

a. The 95 percent confidence interval is

$$(\bar{X}_1 - \bar{X}_2) \pm tS_{pooled} \sqrt{\frac{1}{n_1} + \frac{1}{n_2}}$$

where

$$S_{pooled} = \sqrt{\frac{S_1^2(n_1 - 1) + S_2^2(n_2 - 1)}{n_1 + n_2 - 2}}$$

$$= \sqrt{\frac{2,025(19) + 232.56(9)}{28}}$$

$$= 38.06$$

Note that the degrees of freedom for the interval coefficient are $n_1 + n_2 - 2 = 28$ for this problem. Then the interval is

$$(1,500 - 1,526) \pm (2.048)(38.06)\sqrt{\frac{1}{20} + \frac{1}{10}}$$

$$-56.19 \text{ psi} \underline{\quad\quad} 4.19 \text{ psi}$$

The ARTEE Corporation could be confident that the true difference between the average strengths of the original and new boards is between -56.19 pounds per square inch (new backboard is stronger) and 4.19 pounds per square inch (old backboard is stronger). Since zero falls within the limits, the company could conclude that the true difference might be zero. This could then provide justification for the claim that the two types of backboards are no different with respect to average strength.

b. The 90 percent confidence interval is

$$(\overline{X}_1 - \overline{X}_2) \pm 1.701 S_{pooled}\sqrt{\frac{1}{n_1} + \frac{1}{n_2}}$$

$$(1,500 - 1,526) \pm (1.701)(38.06)\sqrt{\frac{1}{20} + \frac{1}{10}}$$

$$-51.07 \text{ psi} \underline{\quad\quad} -0.93 \text{ psi}$$

The ARTEE Corporation is confident that the true difference in average strength is between -51.07 (new is stronger) and -0.93 (new is stronger) pounds per square inch.

3. A major television manufacturer claims that its average set will be defect-free for more than two years of use. A consumer reporting service has decided to test this claim. The service finds a random sample of twenty set owners and determines the time to the sets' first repair. The sample results, in years, are

1.97	2.87	3.01	2.75
2.09	1.34	1.62	1.10
2.24	1.79	2.81	0.57
3.17	3.89	3.10	2.05
1.01	4.16	2.59	1.67

Based on these sample data, is the manufacturer's claim supported, assuming the burden of proof is on the manufacturer to justify its advertising claim?

Solution:

Hypotheses:

H_0: $\mu_x \leq 2$ yr, claim is not true

H_A: $\mu_x > 2$ yr, claim is true

Decision Rule:

Take a sample of size n and determine $\overline{X}$.

If $\overline{X} \leq A$, accept H_0.

If $\overline{X} > A$, reject H_0.

The alpha level is 0.05.

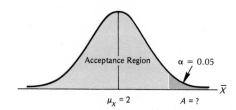

Since σ_x is unknown and the sample size is small, we use the sample standard deviation and the t distribution to determine the A value if we assume the distribution of time to the first breakdown is normally distributed. Then

$$A = \mu_x + t\frac{S_x}{\sqrt{n}}$$

Next, we calculate $\overline{X}$ and S_x.

$$\overline{X} = \frac{\Sigma X}{n}$$

$$= 2.29$$

$$S_x = \sqrt{\frac{\Sigma(X - \overline{X})^2}{n - 1}}$$

$$S_x = \sqrt{\frac{17.115}{19}}$$

$$= 0.949$$

The t value for $\alpha = 0.05$ for a one-tailed test with $n - 1 = 19$ degrees of freedom is 1.729. Thus

$$A = 2 + 1.729\frac{0.949}{\sqrt{20}}$$

$$= 2.3669$$

Decision Rule:

If $\overline{X} > 2.3669$ yr, reject H_0.

If $\overline{X} \leq 2.3669$ yr, accept H_0.

Since $\overline{X} = 2.29 < 2.3669$, we should accept the null hypothesis and conclude that the manufacturer's claim cannot be supported. Note that the manufacturer would no doubt argue for a larger alpha level or that the burden of proof be shifted to the reporting service.

ADDITIONAL PROBLEMS

Section 11–2

36. The following questions are included to provide you with practice in locating t values from the t-distribution table. Each question provides the number of degrees of freedom and the confidence level. You are asked to find the corresponding t value.

a. d.f. = 8, confidence = 90 percent, $t =$
b. d.f. = 14, confidence = 95 percent, $t =$
c. d.f. = 17, confidence = 98 percent, $t =$
d. d.f. = 24, confidence = 99 percent, $t =$
e. d.f. = 6, confidence = 80 percent, $t =$

37. Take a good look at the t-distribution table in appendix D at the back of this text. For a specific level of confidence, what could be said about the value of t as the degrees of freedom increase? Discuss why this occurs.

38. Discuss the basic similarities and differences between the standard normal distribution and the t distribution.

39. Discuss how the t distribution is used in small-sample confidence interval estimation.

40. A drug manufacturer has asked you to help decide how to test a new drug designed to lower blood pressure. The drug has been tested on animals and found theoretically sound, but has not yet been tested on humans.

a. Discuss some major considerations in using statistics in this situation. Do you expect to be able to use a large-sample statistical test or a small-sample test?

b. How important do you expect precision to be in your results and recommendations? Why?

Section 11–3

41. The Phillips Accounting Firm has a branch office in San Jose, California. This branch office works primarily with individual tax returns. The managing partner of the Phillips Accounting Firm is in the process of restructuring the rate structure for the San Jose office. In doing this he needs an estimate of the average time it takes to do an individual tax return by employees in that office.

    To obtain this estimate, he selected a random sample of twenty-three tax returns and consulted office records to determine the time spent on each return.
    a. If we assume that the population of times is normally distributed, what is the 90 percent confidence interval estimate for the population mean if $\overline{X} = 1.2$ hours and $S_x = 0.4$ hour? Interpret this interval.
    b. If the manager decides that he would like a 95 percent confidence level rather than 90 percent, what would the advantages and disadvantages of this be?
    c. Referring to part b, develop the 95 percent confidence interval and interpret it.

42. The Ohio Power Company recently went before the Ohio Regulatory Commission to propose a rate increase. As part of its testimony, it presented the following data, which reflect the results of a random sample of Ohio Power customers who were asked to indicate the dollar amount of money spent on energy conservation measures in their homes during the past year.

$240.00	$ 0.00	$ 76.00
119.00	33.00	0.00
17.00	400.00	100.00

    a. What is the point estimate for the average amount spent on energy conservation by all Ohio Power customers?
    b. Assuming the population of expenditures is normally distributed, what is the 98 percent confidence interval estimate for the mean expenditures on energy conservation? Interpret this interval.
    c. Comment on whether it would be reasonable to assume that the population of interest here is normally distributed.

43. A congressional committee concerned about highway safety has assigned an investigator to check into complaints that long-distance truckers have been violating the federal law limiting the hours they can drive each day. The investigator has arrived in your state and randomly selects trucker log books from twenty-two long-distance haulers. Looking at the driving time for the last full day, he finds a mean of 11.3 hours, with a standard deviation of 2.69 hours.
    a. What is his 95 percent confidence level estimate of the true average driving time per day for truckers going through your state?
    b. What is the 80 percent confidence level estimate?

c. What practical problems in using these data might make these conclusions invalid?

44. A local television station has added a consumer spot to its nightly news. The consumer reporter has recently bought ten bottles of aspirin from a local drugstore and has counted the aspirins in each bottle. Although the bottles advertised 500 aspirins, the reporter found the following numbers:

491	490
487	497
496	507
504	481
483	495

The consumer reporter claims this is an obvious case of the public being taken advantage of. Comment. (*Hint:* What is the 95 percent confidence interval estimate for the average number of aspirins?)

45. Health Care, Inc., is a nonprofit company that provides health-care treatment to patients with heart conditions. Health Care, Inc., relies heavily on contributions from around the state to fund its operation. Recently the company initiated a fund-raising campaign in which it hoped for 15,000 contributions totaling $1.5 million.

In preparation for a board of directors meeting, the treasurer selected a random sample of twenty contributions that had already arrived and found the mean contribution to be $88.00 and the standard deviation to be $25.00.

a. Assuming the organization will receive 15,000 contributions, what is the 95 percent confidence interval estimate for the total dollars this campaign will generate? Based on this estimate, what should the treasurer report with respect to the $1.5 million goal? Assume the population is normally distributed.

b. How would the treasurer's report differ if the interval estimate were based on a 99 percent confidence level?

Section 11–4

46. Kent Billings, a political-science instructor at State University, is experimenting with a different method of teaching introductory political science. He is teaching two sections this term and decides to use the old method in one section and the new, objective-based method in the other section. At the end of the term he gives a standardized test to each section and wants to estimate the difference in average scores between the two methods. The standardized test gives the following results:

	Old Method	New Method
Class size	17	13
Average score	78.9 points	81.3 points
Sample standard deviation	7.2 points	6.9 points

a. Develop and interpret a 95 percent confidence interval estimate for the difference in average test scores.

b. Suppose Kent wishes to improve the precision of this estimate. Discuss his alternatives.

47. The Wild West Exploration Company has recently started drilling exploratory gas wells. The company expects to buy over one hundred quick-assembly drill platforms over the next several years, so it is receiving lots of attention from platform manufacturers. Wild West has narrowed the possible suppliers to two, but cannot decide between them. Wild West management has placed an initial order for ten platforms from each manufacturer and will choose the type of platform that takes less time to assemble. Management randomly ships the two types of platforms to the next twenty sites and measures the time it takes to assemble them. The results are summarized as follows:

	Type A	*Type B*
Average time to assemble	5.2 days	4.90 days
Sample standard deviation	0.6 days	0.48 days

Based on this sample information, from which manufacturer should Wild West buy the other platforms? Base your response on a 90 percent confidence interval estimate for the difference in means.

48. The Heavenly Cake Mix Company has recently developed a new angel food cake mix. The company is certain that this mix is "lighter" than the mix of its leading competitor. To test the contention, Heavenly sends twenty-two numbered, but unidentified, boxes of mix to its testing lab (eleven boxes of its new mix and eleven of the competitor's mix). The cakes are baked, and the weights per square unit (in grams) are determined. The following values are found:

New	*Competition*
$\overline{X} = 2.14$ g	$\overline{X} = 2.27$ g
$S_{\overline{x}}^2 = 0.29$ g	$S_{\overline{x}}^2 = 0.32$ g

Based on these results, would Heavenly be justified in claiming that its cake is "lighter" than its leading competitor's? Analyze using a 95 percent confidence level.

49. The Stilmand Corporation personnel director is interested in determining how effective the company's preventive health care program has been. As part of her analysis, she selected a random sample of employees and recorded the hours of work missed by each employee due to illness in the year immediately preceding the start of the new program. She also selected another random sample of employees and recorded their hours missed during the new program's first year. The data collected are shown as follows:

Before Plan (hrs)			After Plan (hrs)		
16	11	28	30	72	102
72	44	80	5	16	
5	16	90	45	25	

   a. What assumptions must be made in order that a 95 percent confidence interval estimate for the difference in mean hours can be made and interpreted?

   b. Develop and interpret the 95 percent confidence interval estimate for the difference in population mean before versus after.

   c. Based on the results of part b, what conclusions could the personnel director reach? Discuss.

50. A company personnel director is interested in estimating the difference in absenteeism between the day and night shifts at her company's East Coast distribution center. She takes a random sample of fifteen days from the day shift, but only eleven days from the night shift. She finds an average of 7.8 days for the day shift and an average of 9.3 days for the night shift. Based on this evidence, the personnel director concludes that the night supervisor is being lax in hiring practices and recommends a possible change in supervisors. Comment on this conclusion. Should such a conclusion be reached without incorporating the standard deviations into the analysis?

51. The night supervisor in problem 50, hearing about this possible action, comments strongly about the "evidence." In particular, she states that drawing a conclusion based on this small a sample is just plain wrong. She says, "Anyone who knows anything about statistics knows you have to have a sample size of at least thirty before you can draw any conclusions." Comment on this statement.

52. A worker in the personnel department finds that the data used by the director in problem 50 have the following standard deviations: 4.3 days for the day shift and 4.1 days for the night shift.

   a. Should this additional information change the conclusion the personnel director has drawn?

   b. What assumptions do you have to make before you are justified in using the procedures in this chapter to make conclusions based on the information contained in these data?

Section 11–5

53. In recent years there has been a major shift in data processing from batch-oriented systems to on-line systems. One of the possible reasons for this is that programming is more efficient in the on-line environment.

    A recent study by one large computer software company involved six senior programmers. Each programmer wrote the same two programs. The programs were judged to be of comparable difficulty. The first program was developed in a batch environment, and the second was developed in the on-line environment. The manager overseeing the study recorded the actual work hours from start to finish as follows:

Programmer	Batch	On-Line
1	9.8 h	8.5 h
2	11.7	10.0
3	5.6	5.8
4	10.5	8.6
5	14.3	13.0
6	9.2	11.0

a. Develop a 90 percent confidence interval estimate for the mean difference in programming time under the two approaches for these two programs. What conclusions can you make about batch versus on-line systems based on these data?

b. Develop a 95 percent confidence interval estimate for the mean difference in programming time for the two approaches. Interpret your results.

c. Explain how the two confidence intervals differ and why. Also point out any similarities between the two interval estimates.

d. Compute a 90 percent confidence interval estimate for the difference in means, assuming the samples are independent rather than paired. Interpret this interval and then discuss whether it was appropriate to use blocking as was done in part a.

54. The Olvime Corporation is considering two word-processing systems for its microcomputers. One factor which will influence its decision is the ease of use in preparing a business report. Consequently, Belva Olvime selected a random sample of nine typists from the clerical pool and asked them to type a typical report using both word-processing systems. The typists then rated the systems on a scale of 0 to 100. The results were as follows:

Typist	System 1	System 2
1	82	75
2	76	80
3	90	70
4	55	58
5	49	53
6	82	75
7	90	80
8	45	45
9	70	80

a. Discuss why it might be appropriate to set up this analysis as a paired-sample estimation problem.

b. Develop a 95 percent confidence interval estimate for the difference between population means and interpret it. Do these sample data help Belva Olvime select between the two word-processing systems? Explain.

55. The Charles Athletic Shoe Company has a promotional agreement with the Trail-markers professional basketball team. Charles will supply shoes and monetary consideration to each team member in exchange for rights to feature team members in its advertising. Charles has recently developed a new shoe sole material it thinks provides superior wear compared with the old material. The company gives each of the ten team members one shoe of each material and monitors wear until the shoe, for playing purposes, is worn out. The following times (in hours) are found:

Player	New Material	Old Material
1	47.0	45.5
2	51.0	50.0
3	42.0	43.0
4	46.0	45.5
5	58.0	58.5
6	50.5	49.0
7	39.0	29.5
8	53.0	52.0
9	48.0	48.0
10	61.0	57.5

Based on these data, and assuming a 95 percent confidence interval, does the evidence indicate there is a difference between the two shoe materials?

Section 11–7

56. The makers of a particular brand of dot-matrix-type printers claim that the average repair costs during the first two years of ownership will be less than $40. To test this claim, a random sample of people who have owned this type of printer for at least two years was selected. The people were asked to record their total repair bills during the first two years of ownership. These data are as follows for the sample of eight owners:

$52.00 $17.50 $0.00 $0.00
$ 8.75 $32.00 $6.50 $0.00

a. State the appropriate null and alternative hypotheses to be tested.
b. What assumption is required if you are to perform the hypothesis test using the t distribution?
c. Perform the hypothesis test at an alpha level of 0.05 and discuss the conclusion that should be reached based on the sample data.

57. An insurance company was interested in knowing whether the average dollar damage sustained in a 30 m.p.h. head-on crash between a car and a solid wall is less than or equal to $1800 for the new front-wheel-drive station wagon being marketed by Ford Motor Company. To test this, it has selected a sample of eight vehicles and crashed them under controlled conditions. It found that the average damage for the sample was $1875, with a standard deviation of $200. At an alpha level of 0.10, what conclusion should be reached based on the sample data?

58. The Northern Furnace Company has just designed a new furnace system that, if it works the way its engineers predict, will allow people to save an average of $40 or more per month on heating. The furnace has been tested at the factory, but Northern production engineers feel that it should be tested under actual conditions. This means that the company will have to install the furnace in a sample of homes and then compare heating bills for the current month with heating bills for the same month the year before. Although not a perfect test because of possible variations in temperature, the company feels it can test the claim about the savings in this manner. The following data, reflecting the dollar savings, were collected for a random sample of fifteen homes in which the furnace was installed without charge to the homeowner:

$18.50	$21.75	$11.40	$63.00	$34.10
45.00	37.60	52.05	27.60	20.05
35.90	21.76	18.90	41.65	36.84

   a. State the appropriate null and alternative hypotheses.
   b. Using an alpha level of 0.10, develop the appropriate decision rule. What assumption must be made about the population distribution?
   c. Referring to part b, what conclusion should be reached regarding the furnace based on the sample data? Discuss.

59. The U.S. Defense Department has issued a contract with the Smithfield Corporation of San Diego, California, to produce an important component for a fighter jet plane. Each of these components costs Smithfield $50,000 to produce.

   The contract calls for these components to have an average operating life exceeding 1,000 hours. Smithfield engineers have devised a method for simulating operating conditions so they can test the components to determine whether they meet government specifications. The testing budget allows for only eight of these components to be tested since testing destroys the components. The following sample data represent the results of the test in number of hours:

950	1,402	1,051	987
1,069	1,123	967	1,054

   a. If these data represent the time before the component wore out in testing, test whether the data can be used to infer that the contract specification with respect to average lifetime is being satisfied. Use an alpha level of 0.05.
   b. Discuss the ramifications involved with a Type I error and a Type II error in this situation. Which may have been committed in this instance?

60. The Allentown Fire Department has come under pressure from the city council because many citizens have complained about poor response rates. Last year the town had 1,525 fires. The required average response time is five minutes or less.

   A random sample of twenty-five fires is selected and the results show a mean of seven minutes and a variance of thirty-six. Testing at the alpha level of 0.05, determine whether the council should chastise the fire department or if it should conclude that the standard is being satisfied.

61. The Altus Park and Recreation Department has claimed that the city parks are being used by adults rather than children. In fact, a recent report claims that the average age of park users is at least thirty years. If this claim is true, the city council plans to institute a research study to determine whether a children's park is needed.

In an effort to verify whether the recreation department's claim is true, a sample of park users has been selected and ages recorded. A random sample of people entering the park was used, giving the following results in years of age:

11	5
17	66
31	59
59	14
18	18

Based on this sample evidence, should the department's claim be supported? Assume the sample was random. Test at the alpha level of 0.05.

62. As purchasing agent for the Tanner Company, you have primary responsibility for securing high-quality raw materials at the best possible price. One particular material that the Tanner Company uses a great deal is molded plastic. After careful study, you have been able to reduce the prospective vendors to two. It is unclear whether these two vendors produce molded plastics that are equally durable.

To compare durability, the recommended procedure is to put pressure on the plastic molding until it breaks. The vendor whose plastic requires the greatest average pressure will be judged the one that provides the most durable product.

To carry out this test, fourteen pieces from vendor 1 are selected at random and fourteen pieces from vendor 2 are selected at random. The following results in pounds per square inch were noted:

Vendor 1	Vendor 2
$n_1 = 14$	$n_2 = 14$
$\overline{X}_1 = 2{,}345$ psi	$\overline{X}_2 = 2{,}411$ psi
$S_1 = 300$	$S_2 = 250$

a. State the appropriate null and alternative hypotheses.
b. What assumptions are required to test the null hypothesis for small samples?
c. What conclusions should be reached regarding the two vendors based on the sample results? Use an alpha level of 0.05. Discuss.

63. Campbell Electronics has decided to place an advertisement on television to be shown three times during a live broadcast of the local university's football game. The sales for each of the seven days after the ad was placed are to be compared with the sales for the seven days immediately prior to running the ad. The following data representing the total dollar sales each day were collected:

Sales before the ad	Sales after the ad
$1,765	$2,045
1,543	2,456
2,867	2,590
1,490	1,510
2,800	2,850
1,379	1,255
2,097	2,255

a. State the appropriate null and alternative hypotheses to be tested.
b. What assumptions must be made about the population distributions in order to test the hypothesis using the t distribution?
c. Based on the sample data, what conclusions should be reached with respect to average sales before versus after the advertisement? Test using an alpha level of 0.01.

64. The American Tax Institute at Providence, Rhode Island, offers courses for individuals in preparing income tax returns. The courses are designed to prepare individuals to complete their own income tax returns rather than taking their tax materials to an accountant or other tax preparer. The course is also designed to help those people who already fill out their own tax returns, but would like to learn to be more efficient in doing the task.

   Recently the institute recruited a sample of fifteen individuals and had them bring their tax materials to the institute. They were asked to work on their own tax returns and spend as long as they wanted doing so. The actual time spent completing the forms was recorded for each individual. A second sample of individuals was selected and these people were provided with the institute's short course free of charge. Then the time it took each of these people to complete their tax returns was recorded. Two people dropped out of this second sample.

   The following summary statistics were recorded for each of the samples in hours:

No Tax Course	Short Course
$n_N = 15$	$n_S = 13$
$\overline{X}_N = 5.3$ h	$\overline{X}_S = 4.9$ h
$S_N = 2.0$ h	$S_S = 2.8$ h

a. State the appropriate null and alternative hypotheses.
b. Based on the sample data, what should be concluded about the average time it takes to complete an individual's income taxes with and without the short course offered by the American Tax Institute? Test using an alpha level of 0.01.
c. Discuss the assumptions that are necessary in order to use the t distribution to test the null hypothesis.

Section 11–8

65. The BMI Corporation is in the design stages for a new microcomputer that will be portable, yet very powerful. BMI plans to market the product primarily to businesses that wish to have very powerful word-processing capabilities in a portable computer. One specific application would be for the secretary to have a way of taking typing work home on evenings and weekends. Thus, it is extremely important that the keyboard layout and touch be acceptable to professional typists.

BMI is currently considering two companies for the production of the keyboard. The two companies have developed prototypes, and BMI plans to test these using a random sample of professional typists from the BMI Corporation. The plan is for each typist to try each keyboard and then provide a rating of the keyboard layout and touch on a 100-point scale, with 100 being the highest rating. The following data were obtained for the twelve typists who participated in the study:

Typist	Keyboard 1	Keyboard 2
1	67	72
2	56	60
3	80	84
4	60	55
5	90	88
6	40	46
7	75	75
8	65	64
9	80	82
10	30	34
11	48	47
12	70	70

a. State the appropriate null and alternative hypotheses.
b. Based on the sample data, what should be concluded about the preferences of typists for the two keyboards? Test using an alpha level of 0.10. Discuss.
c. Discuss why it would be desirable to set up the study of microcomputer keyboards using a paired-sample approach like this. What are the advantages and potential disadvantages?

66. The Blazer Company manufactures and distributes cosmetics in the United States and Canada. One of the most difficult problems for the company is forecasting regional demand for its products. The procedure it often uses is to select a random sample of potential customers and ask the people to estimate the number of dollars they will spend on Blazer cosmetics in the next forecast period. The marketing vice-president feels that, on the average, there will be no difference between what the customers forecast and what they actually buy.

To test this contention, the marketing department selected a random sample of twenty-five people in Illinois and asked the people to provide forecasts of their

Blazer cosmetics purchases during the next month. It then did a follow-up survey with these same people and determined the actual expenditure on Blazer cosmetics. Since this situation reflects a paired sample test, the following statistics from the sample data were computed:

$$\bar{d} = \frac{\Sigma(\text{forecast} - \text{actual})}{25}$$

$$= \$2.80$$

$$S_d = \$4.50$$

What should the Blazer Company conclude about the customers' forecasts, on the average? Test at the alpha level of 0.05. Discuss.

67. The Essex Insurance Company is considering purchasing a computer. One factor the company is concerned with is a given computer's throughput, or how quickly it can process a job under a specific set of conditions. To compare the two leading computers, a series of benchmark runs were performed where seven production jobs were processed through each machine under the same general load conditions. The total processing time was recorded for each computer to determine whether a difference in average processing time for the two machines could be found. The following data were collected:

				job			
	1	*2*	*3*	*4*	*5*	*6*	*7*
Machine 1	20	45	103	56	204	56	109
Machine 2	14	36	134	54	200	50	112

Based on these sample data, what should Essex conclude about the average processing speed of these two computers? Test using an alpha level of 0.05. [Note that the data represent CPU (central processing unit) seconds.]

68. In Pittsburg, California, a tax protest group has charged the local real estate appraiser with appraising property higher than the market value, on the average. To refute this claim, the city offered to work with the tax protest group in selecting a random sample of properties sold during the last six months. Together they agreed that the sales price would be considered the market value at the time the house sold. They then would compare the market value with the value assessed by the appraiser to determine whether the appraised values exceeded market values, on the average. The following data were obtained:

Property	Appraised Value	Market Value
1	$87,500	$ 84,400
2	76,200	78,900
3	43,750	38,000
4	96,000	101,000
5	56,400	52,500

6	44,700	44,600
7	88,300	90,100
8	56,000	52,800
9	77,000	76,500
10	83,200	84,700

a. State the appropriate null and alternative hypotheses to be tested.

b. Based on these sample data and an alpha level of 0.10, what should be concluded with respect to the average difference in market value and appraised value for homes in the Pittsburg area? Discuss.

69. Referring to problem 68, there are two chief appraisers in Pittsburg that do most of the residential appraising. There has been some concern that the older appraiser tends to underappraise homes, on the average, compared to the younger appraiser. If this is true, then, on the average, residents that have the younger appraiser end up paying an unfair share of the taxes in the city. To test this, each appraiser was asked to appraise a sample of six homes. The following appraisals were recorded in thousands of dollars:

| | *Home* | | | | | |
	1	*2*	*3*	*4*	*5*	*6*
Older Person	40.5	89.6	41.5	98.0	75.5	88.0
Younger Person	46.5	90.0	43.0	97.0	80.6	94.2

What should be concluded about the difference in average appraisals by the two appraisers, using an alpha level of 0.10? If you conclude that the older person does appraise property on average lower than the younger appraiser, would you recommend that the older appraiser's values be adjusted upward? Discuss.

STATE DEPARTMENT OF TRANSPORTATION CASE STUDY PROBLEMS

The following questions and problems pertain directly to the State Department of Transportation case study and data base introduced in chapter 1. The questions and problems were written assuming that you will have access to a computer and appropriate statistical software. The data base, containing 100 observations and seventeen variables, is shown in table 1C–1 in chapter 1. *Please assume that the data were collected using a simple random sampling process.*

1. Develop and interpret a 95 confidence interval estimate for average age of uninsured motorists in the state. Interpret this estimate.

2. Determine a 90 percent confidence interval estimate for the average years of formal education for those drivers whose vehicles are not insured.

3. Determine a 95 percent confidence interval estimate for the difference in average age of drivers of vehicles that are uninsured versus those that are insured.

4. Determine the 90 percent confidence interval estimate for the difference in average years lived in the state for drivers of vehicles that are insured versus those that are uninsured.

5. Develop a 95 percent confidence interval estimate for the average number of total convictions for drivers of vehicles that are insured versus those that are uninsured. Be sure to interpret the interval.

6. Determine a 90 percent confidence interval estimate for the average number of vehicles registered in the state for those who were driving an uninsured vehicle.

C A S E S

11A   Midcentral Warehousing

Midcentral Warehousing is a contract warehouse operation with locations in several large southern cities. It is open twenty-four hours a day and services many middle-size manufacturing and distributing companies that are not large enough to individually afford the extensive inventory control and security provided by Midcentral.

Midcentral has been using a large number of diesel-operated forklifts, but recently has been considering changing to battery-operated lifts. The purchasing chief, Georgeanne Andrews, has been asked to consider the relative merits of battery versus diesel lifts. Georgeanne feels that diesel lifts have definite cost advantages for the moment, but that battery-powered lifts may be more efficient in the future. However, she is worried about how long battery-operated lifts can operate before they need to be recharged. The battery lifts require one hour of down time to charge. Naturally Georgeanne is concerned that there will be too much down time during the three shifts. Her dilemma is whether to start replacing the older-model diesels with battery-operated lifts or with new diesels.

Georgeanne has decided that the critical factor is the time the lifts can operate between charges. The manufacturer's specifications indicate the lifts will operate for at least two shifts, but Georgeanne, having been in the purchasing game for a long time, has learned to distrust specifications.

The lift manufacturer has agreed to supply Midcentral with records from fifty of its customers. The data consist of measurements on the number of hours between charges. Because of the large volume of data, Georgeanne has selected a random sample of eighteen values from all of the data. These values are

8 hr	12 hr	7 hr
10	11	9
13	10	8
3	9	10
12	9	12
11	10	11

Georgeanne reasons that she ought to be able to get an idea about the lasting power of the battery lifts from the sample data without looking at all the data.

11B   U-NEED-IT Rental Agency

Richard Fundt has operated the U-NEED-IT rental agency in a northern Wisconsin city for the past five years. One of the biggest rental items has always been chain saws, and lately the demand for these saws has increased dramatically. Richard buys chain saws at a special industrial rate and then rents them for $10 per day. The average chain saw is used between fifty and sixty days per year. Although Richard makes money on any chain saw, he obviously makes more on those saws that last the longest.

Richard worked for a time as a repairperson and can make most repairs on the equipment he rents, including the chain saws. However, he would also like to limit the time he spends making repairs. U-NEED-IT is presently stocking two types of saws—North Woods and Accu-Cut. Richard has a vague feeling that one of the models, Accu-Cut, doesn't seem to break down as much as the other. Richard presently has eight North Woods saws and eleven Accu-Cut saws. He decides to keep track of the number of hours each saw is used between major repairs. He finds the following values:

Accu-Cut		North Woods	
48 hr	46 hr	48 hr	78 hr
39	88	44	94
84	29	72	59
76	52	19	52
41	57		
24			

The North Woods salesperson has stated that North Woods may be raising the price of its saws in the near future. This will make them slightly more expensive than the Accu-Cut models. However, the prices have tended to move with each other in the past.

REFERENCES

Hayes, Glen E., and Romig, Harry G. *Modern Quality Control.* Encino, Calif.: Glencoe Publishing, 1982.

Pfaffenberger, Roger C., and Patterson, James H. *Statistical Methods for Business and Economics.* Homewood, Ill.: Irwin, 1977.

Winkler, Robert L., and Hayes, William. *Statistics: Probability, Inference, and Decision.* New York: Holt, Rinehart and Winston, 1975.

Wonnacott, Thomas H., and Wonnacott, Ronald J. *Introductory Statistics for Business and Economics,* 3rd Edition. New York: Wiley, 1984.

TESTS OF VARIANCES AND AN INTRODUCTION TO ANOVA 12

WHY DECISION MAKERS NEED TO KNOW

As we have continually emphasized, the reason to know statistical techniques is that they assist decision makers. The previous four chapters have introduced some of the more commonly used decision-making aids. An advantage to using both statistical estimation and hypothesis testing is not that they allow decision makers to always make correct decisions, but that they will increase the likelihood of the decisions being correct. The techniques will not eliminate the uncertainty a decision maker faces, but they will allow the uncertainty to be incorporated in the process. However, you may be able to think of decision-making situations that cannot be addressed using the techniques introduced to this point. For instance:

1. Almco Fabricated Parts has just signed a contract to supply parts for the power windows in Ford Thunderbirds. Each part has specified dimensions, including a tolerance: i.e., 10 ± 0.003 in. Almco wishes to know whether their production output meets the standard.

2. Elko Electronics is designing a ground-sensing radar unit to be used when landing newly built jumbo jets. The unit must be able to sense the ground and report the distance to within six inches. The design lab has developed two designs and is interested in whether both meet the specifications and in which of the two is most accurate.

3. Farber Rubber Products makes a household product line at each of six manufacturing facilities across the country. It has just recently started receiving an excessive number of customer complaints about poor quality. The question is whether the problem is at all of the six plants or is confined to one or two facilities.

4. Biotech, Inc., a genetic engineering company, has just developed a new strain of soybeans. Although the product is clearly superior to present strains of soybeans, Biotech scientists have been asked which of eight possible levels of fertilizer to recommend to farmers buying the product.

The statistical tools introduced in previous chapters will not help in any of these situations. Both the hypothesis testing and estimation techniques we have considered so far are limited to dealing with measures of the location of a distribution such as μ, $\mu_1 - \mu_2$, p, and $p_1 - p_2$. In situations 1 and 2, the decision makers are interested in the spread in a distribution. Therefore, we need tools for dealing with population variances (or standard deviations). In addition, the tools considered up to now were limited to dealing with one or two populations. Decision makers often need a way to consider more than two populations.

CHAPTER OBJECTIVES

This chapter introduces methods for testing hypotheses involving a single population variance. The test procedure uses a distribution called the chi-square distribution. This chapter will show you how to use this distribution. This chapter will also introduce the method for testing hypotheses involving the difference between two population variances and will illustrate how the F distribution is used in this process.

The chapter also introduces an important statistical technique called analysis of variance and shows how it can be used by business decision makers. The chapter will show how analysis of variance is used to test hypotheses involving three or more population means. For cases when the analysis of variance leads us to conclude that population means are not all equal, three techniques are introduced to help you decide which population means are different.

STUDENT OBJECTIVES

After studying the material in this chapter, you should be able to

1. Recognize applications that require a hypothesis test of a single population variance and perform the test correctly.
2. Realize when an application calls for a hypothesis test involving the difference between two population variances and perform the test correctly.
3. Discuss why using multiple two-sample t tests is not an appropriate alternative to analysis of variance.
4. Describe what is meant by partitioning the sum of squares.
5. Perform an analysis of variance for a one-way experimental design.
6. List the assumptions necessary to use analysis of variance.
7. Apply Tukey's method for pairwise comparisons of population means.
8. Apply Scheffé's method for pairwise comparisons of population means.
9. Perform two-way analysis of variance tests and apply the least significant difference test to determine which populations have different means.
10. Recognize business applications for which analysis of variance is the appropriate statistical tool.

HYPOTHESES ABOUT A SINGLE POPULATION VARIANCE

12-1

The discussions in chapters 9, 10, and 11 concentrated on the population center as the value of interest. As shown, the population center is often of interest when a decision is made. However, in some cases decision makers are more interested in the spread of a population than in its central location. For instance, military planes designed to penetrate enemy defenses have a ground-following radar system. The radar tells the pilot exactly how far the plane is above the ground. A radar unit that is correct *on the average* is useless if the readings are distributed widely around the true value. As a second example, many automatic transportation systems have stopping sensors to deposit passengers at the correct spot in a terminal. An automated stopping sensor that *on the average* lets passengers off at the correct point could leave many irritated people long distances up and down the track. Therefore, many product specifications involve both an average value and some limit on the dispersion these values can have. These specifications are called *tolerances*. For example, the specification for a steel push-pin may be an average length of 1.78 inches plus or minus 0.01 inch. The manufacturer using these pins would be interested in both the average length and how much these pins vary in length.

The Fly-Way Airline Company has long had a reputation within the industry for meeting its schedules. One of the factors that has allowed the company to earn this reputation is the baggage handling process. For example, for a particular flight scheduled to arrive in Chico, California, at 11:40 A.M. and depart at 12:05 P.M., the company standards call for the average time to unload and load baggage to be twelve minutes or less, with a standard deviation of four minutes or less. Suppose management is particularly interested in the standard deviation and wishes to test whether the ground crew is performing the unloading and loading process according to the time-consistency goal of a standard deviation of four or fewer minutes.

They are interested in testing the following null and alternative hypotheses:

$$H_0: \sigma \leq 4$$
$$H_A: \sigma > 4$$

There is no statistical technique for directly testing hypotheses about a population standard deviation. However, a test is available for testing about a population variance. Thus, the previous hypothesis must be converted to:

$$H_0: \sigma^2 \leq 16$$
$$H_A: \sigma^2 > 16$$

As with all the hypothesis tests introduced in chapters 9, 10 and 11, the decision to reject or accept the null hypothesis will be based upon the statistic computed from a sample. In testing hypotheses about a single population variance, the appropriate statistic is S^2, the sample variance, given in equation 12–1:

$$S^2 = \frac{\Sigma(X - \bar{X})^2}{n - 1}$$

(12–1)

To test a null hypothesis about a population variance, we compare S^2 with the hypothesized population variance, σ^2. To do this, we need to be able to standardize the distribution of sample variances in much the same way we used the Z distribution and the t distribution when hypothesizing about population means. The standardized distribution for sample variances is a *chi-square distribution*. The standardized chi-square variable is computed by equation 12–2:

$$\chi^2 = \frac{(n - 1)(S^2)}{\sigma^2}$$

(12–2)

where χ^2 = standardized chi-square variable
          n = sample size
          S^2 = sample variance
          σ^2 = hypothesized variance

The shape of the standardized chi-square distribution depends on the hypothesized variance and the degrees of freedom, $n - 1$. Figure 12–1 illustrates chi-square distributions for various degrees of freedom. Note that as the degrees of freedom increase, the chi-square distribution approaches a normal distribution.

Returning to the Fly-Way example, suppose the manager took a sample of twenty flights and found a variance of 18 minutes squared. Figure 12–2 presents the hypothesis test at an alpha level of 0.10.

Appendix E contains a table of chi-square values for various probabilities and degrees of freedom. The chi-square table is used in a manner similar to use of the t-distribution table. For example, to find χ^2_{critical} for the Fly-Way Airlines example, we first determine that the degrees of freedom equal $n - 1$ ($20 - 1 = 19$) and that the

FIGURE 12–1
Chi-square distributions

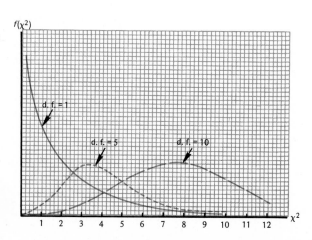

Hypotheses:

H_O: $\sigma^2 \leq 16$
H_A: $\sigma^2 > 16$
$\alpha = 0.10$

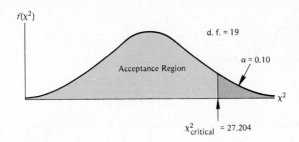

Decision Rule:

If $\chi^2 > \chi^2_{critical} = 27.204$, reject H_0.
Otherwise, do not reject H_0.

The chi-square test is as follows:

$$\chi^2 = \frac{(n-1)(S^2)}{\sigma^2} = \frac{19(16)}{15}$$

$$= 21.375$$

Since $\chi^2 = 21.375 < \chi^2_{critical} = 27.204$, accept H_0.

FIGURE 12–2
Chi-square test for one population variance, Fly-Way Airlines example

desired alpha level is 0.10. Now we go to the chi-square table under the column headed "0.10" (corresponding to the desired alpha) and find the χ^2 value in this column that intersects the row corresponding to the appropriate degrees of freedom. Table 12–1 illustrates how the chi-square table is used to find $\chi^2_{critical} = 27.204$. If the calculated χ^2 exceeds $\chi^2_{critical}$, the null hypothesis should be rejected.

As you can see in figure 12–2, the sample variance is not *enough larger* than the hypothesized variance to cause the manager to reject the null hypothesis. He will conclude, based on these results, that the baggage handling crew does meet the requirement of a standard deviation of four minutes or less.

In most applications, decision makers are concerned about the variance being too large. However, there are instances in which decision makers are concerned with knowing whether the variance is *higher* or *lower* than a specified level. For instance, the ACME Assembly Company assembles clock radios. The number assembled from day to day varies because of several factors, such as parts availability and employee attitudes. From past records, the production supervisor knows that the assembly variance should be fifty. She has selected twenty-five days at random from this year's production reports and found a sample variance of twenty. Figure 12–3 shows the statistical test using an alpha level of 0.20. As the test indicates, this sample information is so different from past information that the production supervisor should infer that the true variance

TABLE 12–1
Finding critical values in the chi-square table

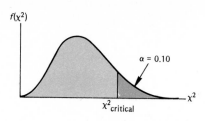

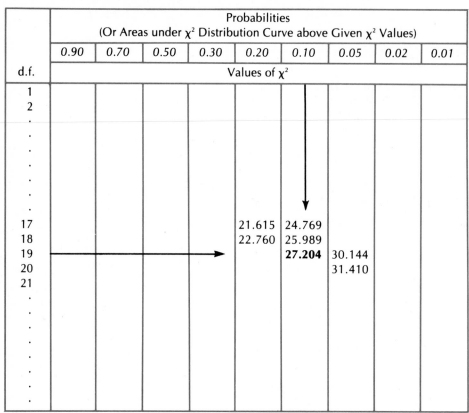

	Probabilities (Or Areas under χ^2 Distribution Curve above Given χ^2 Values)								
	0.90	*0.70*	*0.50*	*0.30*	*0.20*	*0.10*	*0.05*	*0.02*	*0.01*
d.f.	Values of χ^2								
1									
2									
.									
.									
.									
.									
.									
.									
.									
17					21.615	24.769			
18					22.760	25.989			
19						**27.204**	30.144		
20							31.410		
21									
.									
.									
.									
.									
.									
.									
.									
.									

Hypotheses:

$H_0: \sigma^2 = 50$
$H_A: \sigma^2 \neq 50$

$\alpha = 0.20$

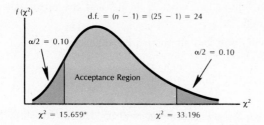

Decision Rule:

If $\chi^2 > \chi^2_{critical} = 33.196$, reject H_0.
If $\chi^2 < \chi^2_{critical} = 15.659$, reject H_0.
If $15.659 \leq \chi^2 \leq 33.196$, accept H_0.

The chi-square test is

$$\chi^2 = \frac{(n-1)(S^2)}{\sigma^2} = \frac{24(20)}{50}$$
$$= 9.6$$

Since calculated $9.6 < 15.659$, reject H_0.

*Since the hypothesis test is two-tailed, the lower critical value is found from the chi-square table under the column for an area $1 - \alpha/2 = 1 - 0.10 = 0.90$. The upper critical value is found from the chi-square table under the column for an area $\alpha/2 = 0.10$.

FIGURE 12–3
Chi-square test for one population variance, ACME Assembly Company example

has decreased. Based on this conclusion, the supervisor would, no doubt, try to find out what caused the improved consistency in an effort to ensure that it continues. Of course she would also want to determine if the assembly process is meeting the standard for average output.

SKILL DEVELOPMENT PROBLEMS FOR SECTION 12–1

The following set of problems is meant to test your understanding of the material in this section. Additional problems are found at the end of this chapter under this section heading.

1. Find the value of chi-square when $n = 10$ and the upper tail area (alpha) of the distribution $= 0.05$.

2. Find the value of chi-square when $n = 20$ and the upper tail area (alpha) of the distribution $= 0.10$.

3. Find the value of chi-square when $n = 22$ and the upper tail area (alpha) of the distribution $= 0.20$.

4. Find the value of chi-square when $n = 18$ and the upper tail area (alpha) of the distribution $= 0.05$.

5. Given the following null and alternative hypotheses:

$$H_0: \sigma^2 \leq 40$$
$$H_A: \sigma^2 > 40$$

   a. Test if $n = 10$, $S = 7$, and alpha $= 0.05$. Be sure to show the decision rule.
   b. Test if $n = 30$, $S^2 = 54$, and alpha $= 0.10$. Show the decision rule.

6. Given the following null and alternative hypotheses:

$$H_0: \sigma^2 \leq 300$$
$$H_A: \sigma^2 > 300$$

   a. Test if $n = 20$, $S = 20$, and alpha $= 0.05$. Be sure to show the decision rule.
   b. Test if $n = 15$, $S^2 = 420$, and alpha $= 0.10$. Show the decision rule.

7. Given the following null and alternative hypotheses:

$$H_0: \sigma^2 \leq 12$$
$$H_A: \sigma^2 > 12$$

   a. Test if $n = 13$, $S = 4$, and alpha $= 0.10$. Be sure to show the decision rule.
   b. Test if $n = 30$, $S^2 = 21$ and alpha $= 0.05$. Show the decision rule.

8. The Haglund Corporation manufactures paint and stain products for interior and exterior home and commercial applications. The new "Apple Wood Stain" product is thought to be a real improvement over some of the company's previous products. One criterion of a quality stain is the consistency of coverage per gallon. Haglund hopes that the standard deviation in coverage will not exceed twenty square feet per gallon. To test this, they have selected a random sample of twelve gallons and found the following coverage in square feet:

   245 302 240 280 255 300 290 240 300 270 230 300

   a. State the null and alternative hypotheses.
   b. State the decision rule, assuming an alpha $= 0.05$.
   c. Perform the test and write a one-paragraph conclusion for the Haglund manager.

9. The National Football League is in the process of renegotiating their television contracts with the networks. At issue is concern over what happens if a game goes too long and runs into the time slot reserved for other programs. As part of the negotiations, the NFL commissioner claimed that the game-time standard deviation does

not exceed eight minutes. To test this claim, a random sample of fifteen past games was selected, with the following times (in minutes) recorded:

145	136	123	109	145
125	137	134	140	138
120	146	129	135	134

a. State the appropriate null and alternative hypotheses.
b. Determine the decision rule, assuming an alpha level of 0.10.
c. Test the null hypothesis and comment on the result.

HYPOTHESES ABOUT TWO POPULATION VARIANCES

12-2

Just as decision makers are often interested in testing hypotheses regarding two population means, they are often faced with decision problems involving *two population variances*. For example, the Midlands Asphalt and Grading Company is considering purchasing a new paving machine. The company has two machines from which to choose. Midlands has decided to select the paver that provides the lesser variation in paving thickness. Variations in asphalt depth can have effects on both material cost and road strength. In addition, penalties are often assessed if testers find the road too thin.

One machine is considerably less expensive than the other, and although Midlands will buy the more expensive model if necessary, the company does not want to miss out on a good deal if the less expensive machine will spread asphalt with a comparable variation.

The purchasing agent at Midlands has arranged to sample eleven surfaces made by each machine to see whether he can detect a difference in thickness variation between the two. The hypotheses are

Hypotheses:

$$H_0: \sigma_1^2 = \sigma_2^2$$
$$H_A: \sigma_1^2 \neq \sigma_2^2$$

Since the population variances are not known, they must be estimated from the sample variances S_1^2 and S_2^2. Intuitively, you might reason that if the two population variances are actually equal, the sample variances should be nearly equal also.

If the samples are selected from two normally distributed populations with σ_1^2 equal to σ_2^2, the ratio of the sample variances, S_1^2/S_2^2, has a probability distribution known as an F distribution. The F statistic is given in equation 12–3:

$$F = \frac{S_1^2}{S_2^2}$$

(12–3)

Hypotheses:

$H_0: \sigma_1^2 = \sigma_2^2$
$H_A: \sigma_1^2 \neq \sigma_2^2$

$\alpha = 0.10$

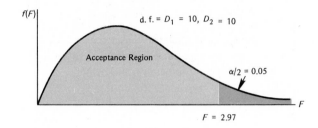

Decision Rule:

If $F \leq F_{critical} = 2.97$, accept H_0.
If $F > F_{critical}$, reject H_0.

The F test is

$$F = \frac{S_1^2}{S_2^2} = \frac{0.025}{0.017}$$

$$= 1.47$$

Since $F = 1.47 < F_{critical}$ with $D_1 = 10$ and $D_2 = 10$ degrees of freedom $= 2.97$, accept H_0.

Note: The right-hand tail of the F distribution always contains an area of $\alpha/2$ if the hypothesis test is two-tailed.

FIGURE 12–4

F test for two population variances, Midlands Asphalt and Grading Company example

Because S_1^2 and S_2^2 have $n_1 - 1$ and $n_2 - 1$ degrees of freedom, respectively, the F distribution formed by the ratio of sample variances has $D_1 = n_1 - 1$ and $D_2 = n_2 - 1$ degrees of freedom.

The calculated F value gets larger if S_1^2 is greater than S_2^2. Since we have control over which population we label as "1" and which we label as "2," we always select as population 1 the population with the larger sample variance. Therefore, if the calculated F gets too large, we conclude that the two populations have unequal variances.

Suppose the samples for the two paving machines yield variances of $S_1^2 = 0.025$ and $S_2^2 = 0.017$. Figure 12–4 presents the test of the hypothesis that the two machines have equal variances. As was the case with the normal, t, and chi-square distributions, the F distribution has been tabulated. The F-distribution values for upper-tail areas of 0.05 and 0.01 are provided in appendix F.

The relationship between the specified alpha level and the appropriate F table is important. Two situations can occur:

1. If the hypothesis test is two-tailed (that is, $H_0: \sigma_1^2 = \sigma_2^2$), the appropriate F table is the one with an upper-tail area (area above the critical value) equal to one-half alpha. For example, if you have a two-tailed test with an alpha level of 0.10, you should use the F-distribution table containing values of F for the

TABLE 12–2
Finding critical values in the F table (values of F for upper 5 percent)

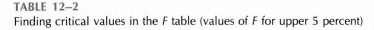

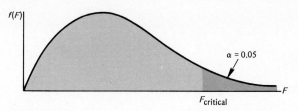

D_2 \ D_1	1	2	3	4	5	6	7	8	10	12
1										
2										
3										
4										
5										
6										
7										
8										
10								3.07	2.97	
12								2.85	**2.76**	
14									2.60	2.53
16										
20										
24										
.										
.										
.										
.										
.										
.										
.										

upper 5 percent of the distribution. If the alpha level is 0.02, you should use the F table containing values of F for the upper 1 percent.

2. If the hypothesis test is one-tailed (that is, H_0: $\sigma_1^2 \leq \sigma_2^2$), the appropriate F table is the one with the upper-tail area equal to alpha. For example, if the alpha level is 0.05, use the F table containing values of F for the upper 5 percent of the distribution.

Thus, to determine which F table to use, you must know the alpha level and also whether the test is one- or two-tailed. We can illustrate this concept with two examples. First, take the case of a two-tailed test with a stated alpha level of 0.10 and degrees of freedom D_1 equal to 10 and D_2 equal to 12. We can use table 12–2 to illustrate how $F_{critical}$ is determined. First, because it is a two-tailed test, go to the F table having an

TABLE 12–3
Finding critical values in the F table (values of F for upper 1 percent)

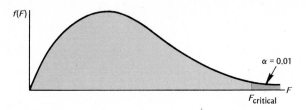

$D_2 \diagdown D_1$	1	2	3	4	5	6	7	8	10	12
1										
2										
3										
4										
5										
6										
7										
8							6.37			
10					5.64	5.39	5.21			
12					5.06	4.82				
14										
.										
.										
.										
.										
.										
.										
.										
.										

upper-tail area equal to one-half alpha (in this case, $0.10/2 = 0.05$). Next, go to the column corresponding to $D_1 = 10$ and read down to the row corresponding to $D_2 = 12$. The value at the intersection of the row and column is the desired F_{critical} (2.76).

As a second example, take the case of a one-tailed test with a stated alpha level of 0.01 and degrees of freedom D_1 equal to 6 and D_2 equal to 10. Because the test is one-tailed, we use the F table having an upper-tail area equal to alpha. Table 12–3 illustrates how we find the appropriate critical value. Figure 12–4 illustrates the hypothesis test for the Midlands Asphalt and Grading Company example. Since the F test leads to accepting the null hypothesis, Midlands should conclude, at the alpha level of 0.10, that there is no difference between the two machines with respect to variability in paving thickness.

The following set of problems is meant to test your understanding of the material in this section. Additional problems are found at the end of this chapter under this section heading.

10. Find the appropriate F value from the F-distribution table for each of the following:
   a. $D_1 = 10$, $D_2 = 14$, alpha $= 0.05$
   b. $D_1 = 8$, $D_2 = 8$, alpha $= 0.01$
   c. $D_1 = 14$, $D_2 = 10$, alpha $= 0.05$

11. Find the appropriate F value from the F-distribution table for each of the following:
   a. $D_1 = 16$, $D_2 = 14$, alpha $= 0.01$
   b. $D_1 = 5$, $D_2 = 12$, alpha $= 0.05$
   c. $D_1 = 16$, $D_2 = 20$, alpha $= 0.01$

12. Given the following null and alternative hypotheses:

$$H_0: \sigma_1^2 = \sigma_2^2$$
$$H_A: \sigma_1^2 \neq \sigma_2^2$$

and the following sample information:

Sample 1	Sample 2
$n = 11$	$n = 21$
$S = 19$	$S = 23$

   a. If alpha $= 0.02$, state the decision rule for the hypothesis.
   b. Test the hypothesis and indicate whether the null hypothesis should be rejected.

13. Given the following null and alternative hypotheses:

$$H_0: \sigma_1^2 = \sigma_2^2$$
$$H_A: \sigma_1^2 \neq \sigma_2^2$$

and the following sample information:

Sample 1	Sample 2
$n = 15$	$n = 11$
$S = 230$	$S = 210$

   a. If alpha $= 0.10$, state the decision rule for the hypothesis.
   b. Test the hypothesis and indicate whether the null hypothesis should be rejected.

14. Given the following null and alternative hypotheses:

$$H_0: \sigma_1^2 \leq \sigma_2^2$$
$$H_A: \sigma_1^2 > \sigma_2^2$$

and the following sample information:

Sample 1	Sample 2
$n = 13$	$n = 21$
$S^2 = 1450$	$S^2 = 1320$

a. If alpha $= 0.05$, state the decision rule for the hypothesis.

b. Test the hypothesis and indicate whether the null hypothesis should be rejected.

15. Given the following null and alternative hypotheses:

$$H_0: \sigma_1^2 \geq \sigma_2^2$$
$$H_A: \sigma_1^2 < \sigma_2^2$$

and the following sample information:

Sample 1	Sample 2
$n = 21$	$n = 13$
$S^2 = 345.7$	$S^2 = 745.2$

a. If alpha $= 0.01$, state the decision rule for the hypothesis.

b. Test the hypothesis and indicate whether the null hypothesis should be rejected.

16. The McBurger Company operates fast-food stores throughout the United States and in fourteen other countries. Management is very concerned about making sure that a standard quality of service is achieved. For instance, they are interested in whether there is a difference in variance in service times for customers who use the drive-up window versus those who go inside to the service counter.

   The McBurger store in Knoxville, Tennessee, recently was the subject of evaluation. A sample of thirteen drive-through customers was selected and a sample of nine inside-counter customers was selected. The time it took each customer to be serviced was recorded. The following statistics were computed from the sample data:

Drive Through	Walk In
$\overline{X} = 4.5$	$\overline{X} = 4.0$
$S = 2.0$	$S = 1.2$

a. State the appropriate null and alternative hypotheses for testing about equality of variances.

b. Based on an alpha level of 0.10, determine the appropriate decision rule and test the null hypothesis.

c. Suppose the managers are also interested in testing whether there is a difference in average time it takes to service the two types of customers. State the appropriate null and alternative hypotheses and test at an alpha $= 0.05$ level.

17. A national TV telethon committee is interested in determining whether males give donations that have greater variability in amount than do those of females. To test this, a random sample of twenty-five males and twenty-five females was selected from people who donated during last year's telethon. The following statistics were computed from the sample data:

Males	Females
$\overline{X} = \$12.40$	$\overline{X} = \$8.92$
$S = \$2.50$	$S = \$1.34$

a. State the null and alternative hypotheses to be tested.
b. Based upon an alpha level of 0.05, determine the decision rule and test the null hypothesis.
c. Suppose the committee is also interested in determining whether there is a difference in average donations between men and women. State the appropriate null and alternative hypotheses and test at the alpha = 0.05 level.

ANALYSIS OF VARIANCE—ONE-WAY DESIGN

12-3

The national sales manager for Ambell, Inc. was recently asked by the company's president whether there is a difference in the average weekly sales per salesperson among the four regions covered by the sales force. The president suspects that average sales productivity has not been equal in the four regions. If his suspicions are true, he will recommend that the national sales manager direct more effort to the regions with lower average sales. In addition, the company will increase advertising to the regions with significantly lower average sales.

To answer this question, Pam Burke, the national manager, selected a random sample of eight salespeople from each region and calculated each person's sales level for the past year. Pam has formulated the following null and alternative hypotheses:

H_0: $\mu_1 = \mu_2 = \mu_3 = \mu_4$

H_A: Not all means are equal

She has also established an alpha level of 0.05 for this test.

Why Two Sample t Tests Will Not Work

One method to test the null hypothesis involving four population means would be to use the two-sample t test discussed in chapter 10. Pam Burke could set up a series of null and alternative hypotheses involving *all* possible pairs of sales regions. The two-sample t test could be used to test each null hypothesis. With four populations, there are

$$_4C_2 = \frac{4!}{2!(4-2)!}$$

$$= 6$$

separate pairs of regions. Thus, to test the null hypothesis that all four population means are equal would require six separate t tests of the form

$$H_0: \mu_1 = \mu_2$$
$$H_A: \mu_1 \neq \mu_2$$

with the test statistic as in equation 12–4:

$$t = \frac{(\overline{X}_1 - \overline{X}_2) - 0}{S_{pooled}\sqrt{\dfrac{1}{n_1} + \dfrac{1}{n_2}}} \qquad (12\text{–}4)$$

If the six separate t tests are performed, and the null hypothesis is accepted in each case, we could conclude that all four population means are equal. However, the problem with using a series of two-sample t tests is that although each test has an alpha level of 0.05, the true alpha level for all tests combined is greater than 0.05. If we consider the six tests to be independent, the probability of committing an alpha error in six tests is

$$\begin{aligned} \alpha_{actual} &\leq [1 - (1 - \alpha_1)(1 - \alpha_2)(1 - \alpha_3) \ldots (1 - \alpha_6)] \qquad (12\text{–}5) \\ &\leq [1 - (0.95)(0.95)(0.95)(0.95)(0.95)(0.95)] \\ &\leq 1 - 0.7351 \\ &\leq 0.2649 \end{aligned}$$

Thus the maximum probability of committing one or more Type I errors using a series of six t tests, each with an alpha level of 0.05, is, at most, 0.2649. The logic behind this increase in alpha is that *as more tests are performed, the risk of rejecting a true hypothesis is increased.*

Due to this problem, a series of two-sample t tests is not generally considered adequate to test hypotheses involving more than two populations. However, a statistical tool known as *analysis of variance* (ANOVA) can be used without ''compounding'' the probability of committing a Type I error.

The Rationale of One-Way Analysis of Variance

In the Ambell example, Pam Burke needs to determine whether the average sales output per salesperson is equal between regions. Analysis of variance is a statistical procedure which, as its name implies, is used to examine population variances to determine whether the population means are equal.

Three assumptions (the same ones as for a two-sample t test) must be satisfied before analysis of variance can be applied:

1. The sample must be independent random samples.
2. The samples must be selected from populations with normal distributions.

TABLE 12–4

Sales data, Ambell, Inc. example (units sold by each salesperson)

Salesperson	Region 1	Region 2	Region 3	Region 4	
1	3	9	7	12	
2	5	8	5	8	
3	9	8	4	7	
4	10	7	9	7	
5	7	10	9	8	
6	3	9	6	10	Grand
7	5	9	8	5	total
8	6	4	8	7	↓
Total	48	64	56	64	232

$$\overline{X}_1 = 6 \qquad \overline{X}_2 = 8 \qquad \overline{X}_3 = 7 \qquad \overline{X}_4 = 8$$

$$\text{Grand mean } (\overline{\overline{X}}) = \frac{232}{32}$$

$$= 7.25$$

3. The populations must have equal variances (that is, $\sigma_1^2 = \sigma_2^2 = \ldots = \sigma_k^2 = \sigma^2$).

The rationale behind analysis of variance might best be understood by studying table 12–4, which presents the sales data Pam Burke has collected. You should notice several things about these data. First, the salespeople in the sample did *not* sell exactly the same number of units. Thus variation exists in the units sold by the thirty-two people. This is called the **total variation** in the data. Second, within any particular region, the salespeople did *not* all sell an equal number of units. Thus variation exists within regions. This variation is called **within-sample variation.** Finally, the sample means for the four regions are not all equal. Thus variation exists between the regions. As you might have guessed, this is called **between-sample variation.**

The basic principle of one-way analysis of variance is that

Total sample variation = between-sample variation + within-sample variation

From our discussion of variance in chapter 3, we know that the variability in a set of measurements is proportional to the sum of the squared deviations of the measurements from the mean, as given by equation 12–6:

$$\Sigma(X - \overline{X})^2 \qquad\qquad (12\text{–}6)$$

Therefore the total sample variation in the data shown in table 12–4 is proportional to the sum of the squared deviations of the thirty-two sales figures around the *grand mean*. This is called the *total sum of squares (TSS)* and is calculated by equation 12–7:

$$TSS = \sum_{i=1}^{K} \sum_{j=1}^{n_i} (X_{ij} - \overline{\overline{X}})^2 \qquad (12\text{--}7)$$

where   TSS = total sum of squares
K = number of populations (columns)
n_i = sample size from population i
X_{ij} = jth measurement from population i (in the present example, the thirty-two different measurements)
$\overline{\overline{X}}$ = grand mean (here, the mean of all thirty-two measurements)

The total sum of squares for the Ambell example is

$$TSS = (3 - 7.25)^2 + (5 - 7.25)^2 + (9 - 7.25)^2 + \ldots + (7 - 7.25)^2$$
$$= 148$$

As was stated earlier, total variation equals the between-sample variation plus the within-sample variation. Equation 12–8 states this:

$$\underbrace{\sum_{i=1}^{K} \sum_{j=1}^{n_i} (X_{ij} - \overline{\overline{X}})^2}_{TSS} = \underbrace{\sum_{i=1}^{K} n_i(\overline{X}_i - \overline{\overline{X}})^2}_{SSB} + \underbrace{\sum_{i=1}^{K} \sum_{j=1}^{n_i} (X_{ij} - \overline{X}_i)^2}_{SSW} \qquad (12\text{--}8)[1]$$

Equation 12–8 shows that TSS can be *partitioned* into two parts: the *sum of squares between (SSB)* and the *sum of squares within (SSW)*. For the Ambell example, we get

$$TSS = SSB + SSW$$
$$148 = 22 + 126$$

where

$$SSB = 8(6 - 7.25)^2 + 8(8 - 7.25)^2 + 8(7 - 7.25)^2 + 8(8 - 7.25)^2$$
$$= 22$$
$$SSW = TSS - SSB = 148 - 22$$
$$= 126$$

Pam Burke wants to determine whether the mean sales in the four regions are equal. However, she must decide this based on a sample from each region. Pam wants to know if the four distributions shown in figure 12–5 best describe the sales distribu-

---

[1]The chapter glossary contains calculation formulas for each of the sum of squares formulas contained in this section.

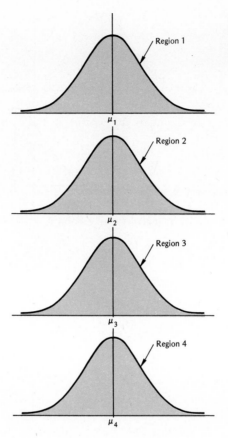

FIGURE 12–5
Normal populations with equal means and equal variances

tions, or whether figure 12–6 applies. If figure 12–5 applies, a null hypothesis that all means are equal should be accepted. If figure 12–6 is the case, the null hypothesis should be rejected. Note that these figures illustrate the assumptions of normal populations and equal population variances.

To determine whether to accept or reject the null hypothesis using analysis of variance, we perform the following:

1. Establish the null hypothesis to be tested:

$$H_0: \mu_1 = \mu_2 = \mu_3 = \ldots$$

$$H_A: \text{Not all means are equal}$$

2. Make two estimates of the population variance, one based on individual regions and one based on differences in regional averages.

3. If the two estimates are about the same, we conclude that figure 12–5 applies and that the means are equal.

FIGURE 12–6
Normal populations with unequal means and equal variances

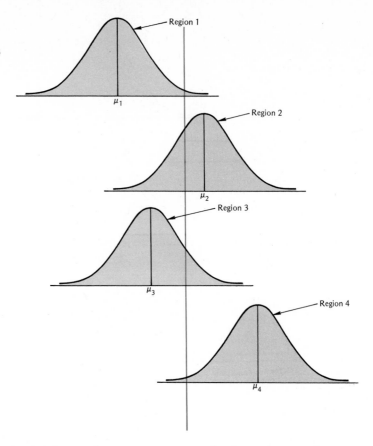

The computational procedures necessary to make the variance estimates are not
complicated. Remembering that any variance is a sum of squares divided by degrees of
freedom, the first estimate is given by equation 12–9:

$$\text{MSW} = \frac{\text{SSW}}{N - K} = \text{unbiased estimate of } \sigma^2 \qquad (12\text{–}9)$$

where   MSW = mean square within
      SSW = sum of squares within
         N = total number of measurements from all samples
        K = number of groups (here, four regions)

Also, if the region means are truly equal (the null hypothesis is true), the second estimate is given by equation 12–10:

$$MSB = \frac{SSB}{K-1} = \text{unbiased estimate of } \sigma^2 \qquad (12\text{--}10)$$

where $MSB = \text{mean square between}$
$SSB = \text{sum of squares between}$
$K = \text{number of groups}$

Thus, if the null hypothesis is true (that is, all means are equal), MSW and MSB are both estimates of the population variance, σ^2, and we would expect MSW and MSB to be nearly equal.

However, because of the way SSB is calculated, the more the sample means differ, the *larger* SSB becomes. As SSB is increased, MSB begins to differ from MSW. When this difference gets too large, our conclusion will be that the population means are not all equal. Therefore we would reject the null hypothesis. But how do we determine what "too large" is?

TABLE 12–5
ANOVA, Ambell, Inc. example

Hypotheses:

$H_0: \mu_1 = \mu_2 = \mu_3 = \mu_4$
$H_A:$ Not all means are equal.

$\alpha = 0.05$

Source of Variation	SS	d.f.	MS	F Ratio
Between samples	22	$K - 1 = 3$	MSB $= 7.33$	MSB/MSW $= 1.629$
Within samples	126	$N - K = 28$	MSW $= 4.5$	
Total	148	$N - 1 = 31$		

d. f. $= D_1 = 3, D_2 = 28$

Acceptance Region

$\alpha = 0.05$

$CV \approx 2.92$

$F = 1.628$

Decision Rule:

If $F > F_{critical} \approx 2.92$, reject H_0.
Otherwise, do not reject H_0.

Since $1.628 < 2.92$, do not reject H_0.

TABLE 12–6
Response data by fire district (number of responses)

Day	District 1	District 2	District 3
1	3	4	2
2	2	4	2
3	1	4	1
4	0	4	0
5	0	3	0
6	0	5	0
7	2	4	3
8	2	4	0
9	1	4	2
10	4	4	0
Total	15	40	10

$$\bar{X}_1 = 1.5 \qquad \bar{X}_2 = 4 \qquad \bar{X}_3 = 1$$

$$\text{TSS} = \sum_{i=1}^{K}\sum_{i=1}^{n_i}(X_{ij} - \bar{\bar{X}})^2 = (3 - 2.1667)^2 + (2 - 2.1667)^2 + \ldots +$$
$$(0 - 2.1667)^2$$
$$= 82.17$$

$$\text{SSB} = \sum_{i=1}^{K}n_i(\bar{X}_i - \bar{\bar{X}})^2 = 10(1.5 - 2.16)^2 + 10(4 - 2.16)^2 + 10(1 - 2.16)^2$$
$$= 51.67$$

$$\text{SSW} = \text{TSS} - \text{SSB}$$
$$= 30.50$$

Recall the test of two population variances presented in Section 12–2. There we saw that the ratio of two unbiased estimates of the same variance, σ^2, forms an F distribution with D_1 and D_2 degrees of freedom. If the population means are equal, MSW and MSB are both unbiased estimates of σ^2. Their ratio should produce a statistic that is F-distributed when H_0 is true, as shown in equation 12–11:

$$F = \frac{\text{MSB}}{\text{MSW}} \qquad (12–11)$$

The calculated F comes from an F distribution with $D_1 = K - 1$ and $D_2 = N - K$ degrees of freedom if H_0 is true.

A common means of illustrating analysis of variance calculations is in table format. Pam Burke has formulated table 12–5 (p. 515). Notice that she has listed the null and alternative hypotheses, and has shown the F distribution and the decision rule for an alpha level of 0.05.

The ratio of MSB to MSW for this example is 1.629. This value is smaller than the critical F value of approximately 2.92 found in the F-distribution table in appendix

TABLE 12–7
ANOVA, Arizona fire districts

Hypotheses:

H_0: $\mu_1 = \mu_2 = \mu_3$
H_A: Not all means are equal.

$\alpha = 0.05$

Source of Variation	SS	d.f.	MS	F Ratio
Between districts	51.67	2	25.84	22.87
Within districts	30.50	27	1.13	
Total	82.17	29		

f(F)

d. f. = $D_1 = 2, D_2 = 27$

Acceptance Region

$\alpha = 0.05$

CV = 3.36

F

Decision Rule:

If $F > F_{critical} = 3.36$, reject H_0.
Otherwise, do not reject H_0.

Since $F = 22.87 > 3.36$, reject H_0.

*The critical F value denoted CV is found by interpolating the F distribution for values of F between degrees of freedom $D_1 = 2, D_2 = 24$ and $D_1 = 2, D_2 = 30$.

F. Note that we have used degrees of freedom $D_1 = 3$ and $D_2 = 30$ to obtain the critical F value. The exact F value could be found from an F table that contains entries for degrees of freedom $D_1 = 3$ and $D_2 = 28$. Since the calculated F value is smaller than the critical F value, Pam should *not* reject the null hypothesis. She would conclude that the average sales per salesperson in the four regions could, in fact, be equal. There is no justification for individual treatment in any one region based on these results. The president's concern seems unfounded.

The analysis of variance has allowed Pam to test a null hypothesis involving four population means without compounding alpha above the 0.05 level.

One-Way Analysis of Variance—A Second Example

A city in Arizona has recently received a federal grant to purchase two new fire trucks and hire six additional firefighters. The city manager, in compliance with the grant, will assign the trucks and firefighters to the two busiest fire districts in the city. However, the city manager doesn't know which districts are the busiest or, for that matter, if there is a difference between the city's three districts.

The city manager develops the following null hypothesis:

H_0: There is no difference in the average number of responses per day among the three fire districts.

To test this hypothesis (and help determine which districts will get the firefighters and equipment), the city manager selected a random sample of ten days during the current year. He asked the district fire marshals to supply the number of responses made in their districts on each day. These data are shown in table 12–6 (p. 516).

Assuming the populations are normally distributed, with equal variances, analysis of variance can be used to test the hypothesis of equal means. Table 12–7 (p. 517) shows the null and alternative hypotheses, as well as the analysis of variance calculations and decision rule for this example.

Based on the analysis of variance shown in table 12–7, the city manager should conclude that the average number of responses is not equal for the three districts.

Given this conclusion, the next logical step is to determine which means are different. Several statistical procedures exist to help the city manager accomplish this and decide which districts get the trucks and firefighters. We will introduce two of these techniques: *Tukey's method* and *Scheffé's method*.

SKILL DEVELOPMENT PROBLEMS FOR SECTION 12–3

Below are several exercises and problems designed to help you understand the material presented in section 12–3. A number of additional application problems are presented at the end of the chapter to provide you with additional practice in applying the statistical tools presented in this section. (Don't forget to review the solved problem section at the end of the chapter for worked-out examples of the material in this chapter.)

18. Given the following sample data:

Item	Group 1	Group 2	Group 3
1	10	8	13
2	9	6	12
3	11	8	12
4	12	9	11
5	13	10	13
6	12	10	15

    a. State the appropriate null and alternative hypotheses for determining whether a difference exists in the average value for the three populations.

    b. Compute the sum of squares between for the above sample data.

    c. Compute the sum of squares within for the above sample data.

d. Based upon the computations in parts b and c, develop the ANOVA table and test the null hypothesis using an alpha = 0.05 level.

19. Given the following sample data:

Item	Group 1	Group 2	Group 3	Group 4
1	20	28	17	21
2	27	26	15	23
3	26	21	18	19
4	22	29	20	17
5	25	30	14	
6	30	25		
7	23			

a. State the appropriate null and alternative hypotheses for determining whether a difference exists in the average value for the four populations.
b. Compute the sum of squares between for the above sample data.
c. Compute the sum of squares within for the above sample data.
d. Based upon the computations in parts b and c, develop the ANOVA table and test the null hypothesis using an alpha = 0.05 level.

20. Given the following sample data:

Item	Group 1	Group 2	Group 3
1	100	98	113
2	69	96	102
3	110	88	120
4	112	99	110
5	55	100	100

a. State the appropriate null and alternative hypotheses for determining whether a difference exists in the average value for the three populations.
b. Compute the sum of squares between for the above sample data.
c. Compute the sum of squares within for the above sample data.
d. Based upon the computations in parts b and c, develop the ANOVA table and test the null hypothesis using an alpha = 0.01 level.

21. The Green-Checker Cab Company operates twelve taxis in Seattle, Washington. The manager is interested in determining whether there is a difference in average fares collected for the day, swing, and graveyard shifts. To test whether a difference exists, she has collected a random sample of ten observations from each shift. The following summary values have been computed from the sample data:

$$TSS = 156,764 \qquad SSB = 55,600$$

a. State the appropriate null and alternative hypotheses.
b. Develop the appropriate ANOVA table and test the hypotheses using an alpha level = 0.01.

22. The American Beef Growers Association is trying to promote the consumption of beef products. The organization performs numerous studies, the results of which are often used in advertising campaigns. One such study involved a quality perception test. Three levels of beef gradings—choice, standard, and economy—were involved. A random sample of people was provided a piece of choice-grade beefsteak and asked to rate its quality on a scale of 1 to 100. A second sample of people was given a piece of standard-grade beefsteak and a third sample was given a piece of economy-grade beefsteak, with instructions to rate the beef on the 100-point scale. The following data were obtained:

Choice	Standard	Economy
78	67	65
87	80	62
90	78	70
87	80	66
89	67	70
90	70	73

Based upon the sample data, is there sufficient evidence to conclude that there is a difference in perceived quality for the three grades of beefsteak? Test at the alpha = 0.05 level; make sure to state the null and alternative hypotheses and provide the ANOVA table.

TUKEY'S AND SCHEFFÉ'S METHODS OF MULTIPLE COMPARISONS

12-4   Once the analysis of variance leads to rejecting the null hypothesis of equal means, decision makers need a method to determine which means are not equal and which will not compound the alpha error. (Remember that t tests are not acceptable; they compound the probability of Type I errors.) One method, developed by John W. Tukey, can be used when the samples from the populations are the same size. Tukey's method involves establishing a T range according to equation 12–12:

$$T \text{ range} = T\sqrt{\text{MSW}} \qquad (12\text{--}12)$$

where $T = \dfrac{1}{\sqrt{n}} q$

q = value from the Studentized range table (appendix G), given the alpha level and $D_1 = K$ and $D_2 = N - K$ d.f.

n = common sample size

If any pair of sample means has an *absolute difference*, $|\bar{X}_1 - \bar{X}_2|$, greater than the T range, we can conclude that the population means are not equal. For example, our Arizona city has three fire districts. The possible *pairwise* comparisons (formally referred to as *contrasts*) are

$$|\overline{X}_1 - \overline{X}_2| = |1.5 - 4.0| = 2.5$$
$$|\overline{X}_1 - \overline{X}_3| = |1.5 - 1.0| = 0.5$$
$$|\overline{X}_2 - \overline{X}_3| = |4.0 - 1.0| = 3.0$$

The calculated T range for this example with an alpha level of 0.05 is

$$T \text{ range} = T\sqrt{\text{MSW}}$$

where $T = \dfrac{1}{\sqrt{n}} q_{(1-\alpha),\, D_1 = K = 3,\, D_2 = N - K = 27}$

$= \dfrac{1}{\sqrt{10}} 3.51$ Note that q is from the Studentized range table in appendix G (value interpolated)

$= 1.110$

Then

$$T \text{ range} = 1.110 \sqrt{1.13}$$
$$= 1.180$$

And thus

$$|\overline{X}_1 - \overline{X}_2| = |1.5 - 4.0| = 2.5 > 1.180$$
$$|\overline{X}_2 - \overline{X}_3| = |4.0 - 1.0| = 3.0 > 1.180$$
$$|\overline{X}_1 - \overline{X}_3| = |1.5 - 1.0| = 0.5 < 1.180$$

Therefore, based on Tukey's method, the city manager can conclude that the mean number of responses for district 1 is *not* equal to the mean for district 2 and that the mean for district 2 is *not* equal to the mean for district 3. However, he doesn't have enough statistical evidence to conclude that the means of district 1 and district 3 are different.

By examining the sample means, the city manager can infer that district 2 has more responses on the average than district 1 and more than district 3. Thus, district 2 should receive some new firefighters and at least one truck. However, based on this study, the city manager has no statistical basis for assigning a truck or crew to a second district. He cannot conclude that districts 1 and 3 differ with respect to average responses. Some other factor will have to be used to make the final decision.

Tukey's method of multiple comparisons allows decision makers to determine which population means are not equal once analysis of variance leads to rejecting the null hypothesis of equal population means. This method does not compound the alpha level, but only applies when the sample sizes are equal.

The main restriction of Tukey's method is that it requires equal sample sizes. In some controlled applications managers can guarantee equal sample sizes from each population. However, in many other applications equal sample sizes are not possible. When

TABLE 12–8
Calculator assembly data, Bend River Corporation example (number of calculators assembled)

Sequence 1	Sequence 2	Sequence 3	Sequence 4	Sequence 5
47	86	65	58	49
52	85	63	62	51
46	81	67	63	47
49	90	64	64	55
53	84	59	59	54
39	88	67	55	42
51	77	70	70	53
	79	59	59	57
	82		60	59
			61	58

$n_1 = 7$ $n_2 = 9$ $n_3 = 8$ $n_4 = 10$ $n_5 = 10$ $N = 44$

$\bar{X}_1 = 48.14$ $\bar{X}_2 = 83.55$ $\bar{X}_3 = 64.25$ $\bar{X}_4 = 61.10$ $\bar{X}_5 = 51.50$ $\bar{\bar{X}} = 62.02$

$$\text{TSS} = \sum_{i=1}^{K} \sum_{j=1}^{n_i} (X_{ij} - \bar{\bar{X}})^2 = (47 - 62.02)^2 + (52 - 62.02)^2 + \ldots + (48 - 62.02)^2$$

$$= 7,446.97$$

$$\text{SSB} = \sum_{i=1}^{K} n_i (\bar{X}_i - \bar{\bar{X}})^2 = 7(48.14 - 62.02)^2 + \ldots + 10(51.50 - 62.02)^2$$

$$= 6,675.40$$

$$\text{SSW} = \text{TSS} - \text{SSB}$$

$$= 771.57$$

decision makers have unequal sample sizes, the analysis of variance equations still apply, as does the interpretation of results. But, since Tukey's method does not apply, decision makers need a method of multiple comparisons that allows unequal sample sizes. Henry Scheffé has developed such a procedure.

The Bend River Corporation assembles calculators for several calculator manufacturers. The assembly process is completely manual. The company has become successful by steadily improving its productivity level. A large part of the improvement is due to the production supervisors, who are always looking for ways to improve the work flow.

Recently the supervisors identified five possible sequences by which new-model calculators could be assembled. To determine which sequence or sequences are best, they selected a random sample of fifty workers. Ten workers were randomly assigned to each sequence. At the end of a two-week training period, the workers began assembling calculators for twenty consecutive days using their assigned sequences. Table 12–8 shows the number of calculators assembled by each worker for each sequence. As

TABLE 12–9
ANOVA, Bend River Corporation example

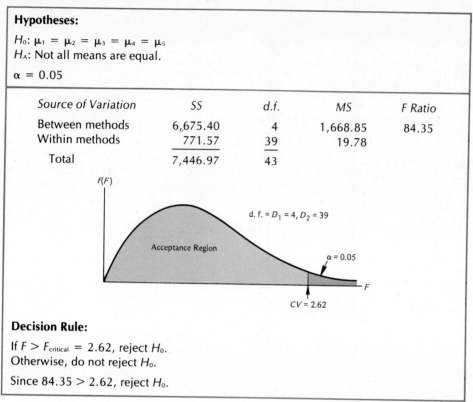

Hypotheses:

H_0: $\mu_1 = \mu_2 = \mu_3 = \mu_4 = \mu_5$
H_A: Not all means are equal.

$\alpha = 0.05$

Source of Variation	SS	d.f.	MS	F Ratio
Between methods	6,675.40	4	1,668.85	84.35
Within methods	771.57	39	19.78	
Total	7,446.97	43		

$f(F)$

d. f. $= D_1 = 4, D_2 = 39$

Acceptance Region

$\alpha = 0.05$

F

$CV = 2.62$

Decision Rule:

If $F > F_{critical} = 2.62$, reject H_0.
Otherwise, do not reject H_0.

Since $84.35 > 2.62$, reject H_0.

might be expected in a study of this kind, several workers missed days of work and had to be eliminated from the study. Therefore unequal sample sizes resulted, as shown in table 12–8.

Table 12–9 presents the analysis of variance results, the null and alternative hypotheses, and the decision rule. The null hypothesis that the five assembly sequences are equal with respect to the average number of calculators produced is clearly rejected. The production supervisors should conclude that not all assembly sequences will produce equal average outputs.

Once the analysis of variance indicates that the null hypothesis should be rejected, *Scheffé's method of multiple comparisons* can determine which means are different. Like Tukey's method, Scheffé's method produces a range to which the absolute differences in pairs of sample means (called contrasts) can be compared. This range is given in equation 12–13:

$$S \text{ range} = S\hat{\sigma} \qquad (12\text{--}13)$$

where

$$S = \sqrt{(K - 1)(F_{\alpha, D_1 = K-1, \, D_2 = N-K})}$$

$$\hat{\sigma} = \sqrt{\left(\frac{1}{n_i} + \frac{1}{n_j}\right)(\text{MSW})}$$

One contrast for an alpha level of 0.05 is

$$|\overline{X}_1 - \overline{X}_2| = |48.14 - 83.55| = 35.41$$

If 35.41 is greater than the S range, the production supervisors should conclude that sequences 1 and 2 differ significantly with respect to average output. In this case the S range is

$$S \text{ range} = S\hat{\sigma}$$

where

$$S = \sqrt{(K - 1)(F_{\alpha, D_1, D_2})} = \sqrt{4(2.62)}$$
$$= 3.23$$

$$\hat{\sigma} = \sqrt{\left(\frac{1}{n_1} + \frac{1}{n_2}\right)(\text{MSW})} = \sqrt{\left(\frac{1}{7} + \frac{1}{9}\right)(19.78)}$$
$$= 2.24$$

Therefore

$$S \text{ range} = 3.23(2.24)$$
$$= 7.235$$

TABLE 12–10
Scheffé test, Bend River Corporation example

Contrast	S Range	Significant?
$\|\overline{X}_1 - \overline{X}_2\| = \|48.14 - 83.55\| = 35.41$	7.235	yes
$\|\overline{X}_1 - \overline{X}_3\| = \|48.14 - 64.25\| = 16.11$	7.434	yes
$\|\overline{X}_1 - \overline{X}_4\| = \|48.14 - 61.10\| = 12.96$	7.079	yes
$\|\overline{X}_1 - \overline{X}_5\| = \|48.14 - 51.50\| = 3.36$	7.079	no
$\|\overline{X}_2 - \overline{X}_3\| = \|83.55 - 64.25\| = 19.30$	6.980	yes
$\|\overline{X}_2 - \overline{X}_4\| = \|83.55 - 61.10\| = 22.45$	6.600	yes
$\|\overline{X}_2 - \overline{X}_5\| = \|83.55 - 51.50\| = 32.05$	6.600	yes
$\|\overline{X}_3 - \overline{X}_4\| = \|64.25 - 61.10\| = 3.15$	6.814	no
$\|\overline{X}_3 - \overline{X}_5\| = \|64.25 - 51.50\| = 12.75$	6.814	yes
$\|\overline{X}_4 - \overline{X}_5\| = \|61.10 - 51.50\| = 9.60$	6.424	yes

Since the absolute difference of 35.41 is greater than 7.235, the supervisors will conclude that the mean levels for these sequences do differ. Based on the sample means, they infer that assembly sequence 2 will give significantly higher average output than sequence 1.

The Scheffé method can be applied to any or all possible pairwise contrasts. The S range will differ slightly from contrast to contrast if the sample sizes differ. Table 12–10 shows all possible pairwise contrasts and their associated S ranges for our calculator example. The only contrasts for which we can conclude that the population means are not different are μ_1 and μ_5, and μ_3 and μ_4. Based on the sample means, the production supervisors infer that sequence 2 will produce a higher average output than the other four sequences.

SKILL DEVELOPMENT PROBLEMS FOR SECTION 12–4

Below are several exercises and problems designed to help you understand the material presented in section 12–4. A number of additional application problems are presented at the end of the chapter to provide you with additional practice in applying the statistical tools presented in this section. (Don't forget to review the solved problem section at the end of the chapter for worked-out examples of the material in this chapter.)

23. Under what conditions would Tukey's method of multiple comparison be used and for what purpose is it used?

24. Under what conditions would Scheffé's method of multiple comparison be used and for what purpose is it used?

25. Given the following sample data:

Item	Group 1	Group 2	Group 3
1	12	8	16
2	15	5	12
3	21	7	12
4	15	8	14
5	17	10	15
6	12	10	15

  a. State the appropriate null and alternative hypotheses for determining whether a difference exists in the average value for the three populations.
  b. Compute the sum of squares between for the above sample data.
  c. Compute the sum of squares within for the above sample data.
  d. Based upon the computations in parts b and c, develop the ANOVA table and test the null hypothesis using an alpha $= 0.05$ level.
  e. Employ the appropriate method for detecting which means are different, using an alpha $= 0.05$ level.

26. Given the following sample data:

Item	Group 1	Group 2	Group 3	Group 4
1	20	28	17	21
2	27	26	15	23
3	26	21	18	19
4	22	29	20	17
5	25	30	14	
6	30	25		
7	23			

a. State the appropriate null and alternative hypotheses for determining whether a difference exists in the average value for the four populations.
b. Compute the sum of squares between for the above sample data.
c. Compute the sum of squares within for the above sample data.
d. Based upon the computations in parts b and c, develop the ANOVA table and test the null hypothesis using an alpha = 0.05 level.
e. Use the appropriate method of multiple comparison to determine which populations have different means. Use an alpha = 0.05 level.

27. Given the following sample data:

Item	Group 1	Group 2	Group 3
1	105	88	113
2	69	86	102
3	110	88	120
4	112	99	110
5	55	90	100

a. State the appropriate null and alternative hypotheses for determining whether a difference exists in the average value for the three populations.
b. Compute the sum of squares between for the above sample data.
c. Compute the sum of squares within for the above sample data.
d. Based upon the computations in parts b and c, develop the ANOVA table and test the null hypothesis using an alpha = 0.01 level.
e. Using the appropriate method of multiple comparison, determine which populations have different means. Use an alpha = 0.01 level.

28. The Green-Checker Cab Company (see problem 21) operates twelve taxis in Seattle, Washington. The manager is interested in determining whether there is a difference in average fares collected for the day, swing, and graveyard shifts. To test whether a difference exists, she has collected a random sample of ten observations from each shift. The following summary values have been computed from the sample data:

$$\text{TSS} = 156{,}764 \qquad \text{SSB} = 55{,}600$$

a. State the appropriate null and alternative hypotheses.

b. Develop the appropriate ANOVA table and test the hypothesis using an alpha level = 0.01.

c. Determine which populations have different means. Using an alpha = 0.01 level, indicate the appropriate decision rule to use.

29. The American Beef Growers Association (see problem 22) is trying to promote the consumption of beef products. The organization performs numerous studies, the results of which are often used in advertising campaigns. One such study involved a quality perception test. Three levels of beef gradings—choice, standard, and economy—were involved. A random sample of people were provided a piece of choice-grade beefsteak and asked to rate its quality on a scale of 1 to 100. A second sample of people was given a piece of standard-grade beefsteak and a third sample was given a piece of economy-grade beef, with instructions to rate it on the 100-point scale. The following data were observed:

Choice	Standard	Economy
78	67	65
87	80	62
90	78	70
87	80	66
89	67	70
90	70	73

Based upon the sample data, is there sufficient evidence to conclude that there is a difference in perceived quality for the three grades of beefsteak? Test at the alpha = 0.05 level; make sure to state the null and alternative hypotheses and provide the ANOVA table. Also, if appropriate, determine which populations have different means, using a method of multiple comparison.

TWO-WAY ANALYSIS OF VARIANCE (OPTIONAL)

12-5

In the previous sections you were introduced to the one-way analysis of variance statistical procedure for testing hypotheses involving three or more population means. One-way analysis of variance is appropriate as long as we are interested in analyzing one factor at a time and we select independent random samples from the populations. For instance, our example involving calculator assembly at the Bend River Company (table 12–8) illustrated a situation in which we were interested in only one factor—number of calculators assembled by different sequences. To test the hypothesis that the five assembly sequences were equal with respect to average number of calculators assembled in a twenty-day period, five groups of people were assigned to each sequence independently. Thus the one-way ANOVA design was appropriate.

TABLE 12–11

Sample data, real estate appraisers example (in thousands of dollars)

Property	Appraisers 1	2	3	$\overline{X}_j$
1	78.0	82.0	79.0	79.67
2	102.0	102.0	99.0	101.00
3	68.0	74.0	70.0	70.67
4	83.0	88.0	86.0	85.67
5	95.0	99.0	92.0	95.33
$\overline{X}_i$	85.2	89.0	85.2	

$$\overline{\overline{X}} = 86.47$$

There are, however, situations in which the one-way design may not be appropriate. Chapter 11 introduced you to the concept of paired samples and indicated that there are instances when it is desirable to test for differences in two population means by employing paired samples. The reason for using paired samples is to control for sources of variation that might adversely affect the analysis. For instance, in testing average lifetime for automobile shock absorbers, we might put one shock absorber of each type on a car and then repeat this for a sample of cars. We would be attempting to control for the variation in cars while testing the average lifetime of the shock absorbers.

The same kind of concerns can arise in hypothesis tests involving more than two population means. For instance, suppose we wish to test the hypothesis that there is no difference in the average house appraisal by three different appraising companies. We would likely want to control for the variation in size, quality, and location of homes that were appraised in order to fairly test that the three companies' appraisals are equal on the average. To do this we would select a random sample of properties and have each company appraise the same properties. The properties are called blocks and the test design is called a blocked design. The blocked design is merely an extension of the paired-sample t test introduced in chapter 11.

Table 12–11 illustrates appraisals for five properties by each appraisal company. We are interested in testing the following hypothesis:

$$H_0: \mu_1 = \mu_2 = \mu_3$$
$$H_A: \text{Not all population means are equal}$$

Because we have chosen a blocked design, we must employ **two-way analysis of variance** to test the hypothesis. Two-way ANOVA is similar in concept to one-way ANOVA in that we can partition the total sum of squares into component parts.

Once again, the total variation in the data is represented by equation 12–14:

$$TSS = \sum_{i=1}^{K} \sum_{j=1}^{r} (X_{ij} - \overline{\overline{X}})^2 \qquad (12\text{–}14)$$

where
  K = number of columns (appraisers)
  r = number of rows or blocks (properties)
  X_{ij} = individual appraisals
  $\overline{\overline{X}}$ = grand mean (86.47)

Then

$$TSS = (78.0 - 86.47)^2 + (102.0 - 86.47)^2 + \ldots + (92.0 - 86.47)^2$$
$$= 1829.73$$

When discussing one-way ANOVA we showed that

$$TSS = SSW + SSB$$

With two-way ANOVA we partition the total sum of squares into three parts instead of two:

$$TSS = SSB + SSBL + SSW$$

where

  TSS = total sum of squares
  SSB = sum of squares between groups
  SSBL = sum of squares between blocks
  SSW = sum of squares within groups

Now, SSB is given by equation 12–15:

$$SSB = \sum_{i=1}^{K} r(\overline{X}_i - \overline{\overline{X}})^2 \qquad (12\text{–}15)$$

where $\overline{X}_i$ = mean of each group

Since r is the number of blocks (in this case properties):

$$SSB = 5(85.2 - 86.47)^2 + 5(89.0 - 86.47)^2 + 5(85.2 - 86.47)^2$$
$$= 48.13$$

TABLE 12–12
Two-way analysis of variance table

Source	SS	d.f.	MS	F
Between	SSB	$K - 1$	SSB/$(K - 1)$	MSB/MSW
Blocks	SSBL	$r - 1$	SSBL/$(r - 1)$	MSBL/MSW
Within	SSW	$(K - 1)(r - 1)$	SSW/$(K - 1)(r - 1)$	
Total	SST	$N - 1$		

Substituting numerical values yields the following				

Source	SS	d.f.	MS	F
Between	48.13	2	48.13/2 = 24.065	8.31
Blocks	1758.42	4	1758.42/4 = 439.605	151.72
Within	23.18	8	23.18/8 = 2.898	
Total	1829.73	14		

Test for Blocking Effectiveness	Test for Difference between Companies
$H_0: \mu_1 = \mu_2 = \mu_3 = \mu_4 = \mu_5$ H_A: Not all means are equal $\alpha = 0.05$	$H_0: \mu_1 = \mu_2 = \mu_3$ H_A: Not all means are equal $\alpha = 0.05$

$f(F)$ $D_1 = 4$ $D_2 = 8$ $\alpha = 0.05$ Acceptance Region $F = 3.84$ F	$f(F)$ $D_1 = 2$ $D_2 = 8$ $\alpha = 0.05$ Acceptance Region $F = 4.46$ F
Since $F = 151.72 > 3.84$, reject H_0; conclude that blocking is effective.	Since $F = 8.31 > 4.46$, reject H_0; conclude that not all population means are equal.

Also, SSBL is given by equation 12–16:

$$\text{SSBL} = \sum_{j=1}^{r} K(\overline{X}_j - \overline{\overline{X}})^2 \qquad (12\text{–}16)$$

where K = number of groups
$\overline{X}_j$ = mean for each block across groups

SSBL is the **between-block variation.** As you can see from equation 12–16, the SSBL value is the weighted sum of the difference between the block means and the grand mean. Then

$$SSBL = 3(79.67 - 86.47)^2 + \ldots + 3(95.33 - 86.47)^2$$
$$= 1758.42$$

Finally,

$$SSW = TSS - SSB - SSBL \qquad (12-17)$$
$$= 1829.73 - 48.13 - 1758.42$$
$$= 23.18$$

You should note that the computation for SSB is performed exactly as with one-way ANOVA. However, the within-group variation has been broken into two parts, SSBL and SSW. Table 12–12 shows the ANOVA table for the two-way analysis of variance.

Note that in table 12–12 we have computed two F values. This is because there is a secondary hypothesis to be tested; this deals with the effectiveness of blocking.

Effective blocking in this case would mean that the property appraisals are in fact influenced by the property being appraised. The blocks then form a second factor of interest and we formulate a secondary hypothesis dealing with this factor as follows:

$$H_0: \mu_1 = \mu_2 = \mu_3 = \mu_4 = \mu_5$$
$$H_A: \text{Not all block means are equal}$$

Thus, in performing the two-way ANOVA we also test to see whether the average appraisals for each property are equal. If the null hypothesis is rejected, this means that blocking was effective and the block design was justified. Referring to table 12–12, we see that the F ratio formed by

$$F = MSBL/MSW = 151.72$$

is substantially larger than the $F_{critical}$ for $D_1 = 4$ and $D_2 = 8$ degrees of freedom of 3.84 at an alpha level of 0.05. Thus, we reject the secondary hypothesis and conclude that the blocking design was appropriate; now we go on to the primary hypothesis involving whether the companies appraise properties at equal values on the average. (Note that if we conclude that blocking is not effective and if the main hypothesis is not rejected, then we should begin again by selecting independent samples and analyze using one-way analysis of variance.)

The main factor of interest is whether the companies appraise properties at values that are equal on the average. Table 12–12 shows the F ratio formed as

$$F = MSB/MSW = 8.31$$

exceeds the $F_{critical}$ for $D_1 = 2$ and $D_2 = 8$ degrees of freedom from the F-distribution table of 4.46 at an alpha level of 0.05. Thus, we should conclude that the mean appraisals by the three companies do differ, on the average.

As was the case with one-way ANOVA, once the null hypothesis is rejected we conclude that not all means are equal. The next step is to determine which means are not equal and which, if any, are equal. We earlier learned that Tukey's or Scheffé's method was useful for making such conclusions with one-way ANOVA. *Fisher's least significant difference* is a way for testing multiple comparisons when two-way ANOVA is used. This test also avoids the problem of compounding the Type I error probability.

If the null hypothesis has been rejected, then we can compare the absolute differences in sample means from any two populations to the *least significant difference (LSD)* and reject that the means for the two populations are equal if equation 12–18 is true:

$$|\bar{X}_i - \bar{X}_j| > \text{LSD} \qquad (12\text{–}18)$$

where

$$\text{LSD} = t\sqrt{\text{MSW}} \sqrt{\frac{1}{n_i} + \frac{1}{n_j}}$$

and where

$t = t$ value for $\alpha/2$ and $(K - 1)(r - 1)$ degrees of freedom from the Studentized t distribution

MSW = mean square within from the two-way analysis of variance

n_i and n_j = sample sizes from populations i and j, respectively

Since we have equal sample sizes from all three populations, the common LSD is computed as follows:

$$\text{LSD} = t_{0.25,8} \sqrt{\text{MSW}} \sqrt{\frac{1}{5} + \frac{1}{5}}$$

$$= 2.306 \sqrt{2.898} \sqrt{\frac{1}{5} + \frac{1}{5}}$$

$$= 2.483$$

Then we form the three possible comparisons as follows:

Absolute Difference $|\bar{X}_i - \bar{X}_j|$	Conclusion
$|85.2 - 89.0| = 3.8$	$\mu_1 \neq \mu_2$
$|85.2 - 85.2| = 0.0$	$\mu_1 = \mu_3$
$|89.0 - 85.2| = 3.8$	$\mu_2 \neq \mu_3$

Therefore, from the sample data we can infer that the mean appraisals of company 1 and company 3 both differ significantly from that of company 2, but not from each other.

Interactive Effects

This section has introduced two-way analysis of variance and showed how it is applied in a case where there are actually two factors of interest. The procedures presented in that section rely on the basic assumption that the blocks are *additive*. This means that the difference between any two blocks means is a constant amount regardless of which population we are considering.

For instance, consider again the example where we are testing about the mean appraisals for three appraisal companies. The additivity assumption implies, for example, that the average difference between assessments of property 3 and property 5 by company 1 will be the same as the average difference in assessments for the same two properties if company 2 or company 3 did the assessment. Since each company made only one assessment of each property we have no choice but to make this assumption.

However, in many instances, instead of additivity there is **interaction** between the factors. For instance, suppose we have three types of glues that can be used in making plywood (Brand 1, Brand 2, and Brand 3). We are interested in determining whether there is a difference in the mean strength of the plywood. One factor thought to affect the strength of plywood in addition to glue type is the species of wood that is used to construct the plywood. If one species of wood tends to work better with one brand of glue while another species makes stronger plywood when a different glue is used, we call this interaction between the wood and the glue. If no interaction exists, then the species of wood that is superior for one type of glue will be superior for all types of glue and the degree of superiority on the average will be a constant when compared with other wood species.

Thus, when interaction is suspected, it is necessary to control for it when analyzing the main factor of study. We do this by employing two-way ANOVA with interaction. This topic, also referred to as factorial ANOVA, is beyond the scope of this text. However, if you take a course in experimental design or analysis of variance, substantial time will be spent interpreting the meaning when interaction is present in the analysis.

SKILL DEVELOPMENT PROBLEMS FOR SECTION 12–5

Below are several exercises and problems designed to help you understand the topics presented in section 12–5. More application problems have been placed at the end of the chapter. We encourage you to work as many of these as possible to help you gain a better understanding of how to apply these statistical tools. The solved problem section at the end of the chapter provides worked-out examples for your reference.

30. A two-way ANOVA experiment has been performed, with the following sample data resulting:

Case	Group 1	Group 2	Group 3
1	20	24	30
2	17	26	28
3	15	24	29
4	30	35	40
5	12	16	21
6	20	25	29
7	17	29	31

a. State the appropriate null and alternative hypotheses to be tested.
b. Compute TSS, SSBL, SSB, and SSW.
c. Develop the ANOVA table and test the hypotheses. Be sure to indicate whether blocking was effective. Use alpha = 0.05.
d. If you concluded that the three population means are different, use the LSD method to determine which populations have different means. Use an alpha = .05 level.

31. A two-way ANOVA experiment has been performed, with the following sample data resulting:

Case	Group 1	Group 2	Group 3	Group 4
1	10	7	16	21
2	12	3	13	26
3	10	9	17	23
4	9	10	20	25
5	10	5	22	30
6	13	8	17	24
7	11	7	16	22
8	14	12	23	21

a. State the appropriate null and alternative hypotheses to be tested.
b. Compute TSS, SSBL, SSB, and SSW.
c. Develop the ANOVA table and test the hypotheses. Be sure to indicate whether blocking was effective. Assume an alpha = 0.05 level.
d. If you concluded that the four population means are different, use the LSD method to determine which populations have different means.

32. The *Buying Guide* is similar to other sales catalogs but instead of carrying a wide line of merchandise in one edition, each edition of *Buying Guide* contains many colors and styles of only a few brands of merchandise. Recently, the sales manager decided to perform a study to determine whether there is a difference in average purchases per order from three of the editions. Because she was concerned that the variability from customer to customer might mask a real difference between catalog editions, she set up the study as a two-way ANOVA problem. She sampled 100 customers and sent each one a copy of each of the three editions. The following data reflect the orders from those who placed orders from all three catalog editions:

Customer	Edition 1	Edition 2	Edition 3
1	$ 44	$ 27	$ 90
2	67	36	80
3	50	20	112
4	80	40	230
5	36	18	60
6	50	30	80
7	110	140	209
8	80	40	140
9	20	12	40
10	30	12	58

a. State the null and alternative hypotheses to be tested.
b. Develop the appropriate ANOVA table and test the hypotheses at the alpha = 0.01 level.
c. If you have concluded that there is a difference in mean order sizes for the three editions, use the LSD method to determine which editions have different means.

33. The Goodmonth Tire Company has four plants where they make the XG-99 all-season radial tire. The production control staff is concerned about whether the four plants are producing tires that will provide the same average mileage for the customers. To test this, they have selected a random sample of twenty car owners and mounted one tire from each plant on the car. The tires were then used for 12,000 miles (with rotation every 500 miles) and at the end of the period the amount of remaining tread was measured.

The following values were computed from the sample data:

$$TSS = 200 \quad SSB = 50 \quad SSBL = 70$$

a. State the appropriate null and alternative hypotheses.
b. Develop the ANOVA table and test the hypotheses at the alpha = 0.05 level. Discuss the results of your test in terms of what they mean to Goodmonth Tire Company.
c. Indicate why it was appropriate to use a two-way ANOVA design in this case.

COMPUTER APPLICATIONS

12-6

This chapter has introduced analysis of variance, which is used to test hypotheses involving means of three or more populations. The computations involved can be performed using a calculator, but when sample sizes become large, the effort required and the chance for error increase. Computers and statistical software are ideally suited to the task of performing analysis of variance calculations.

TABLE 12–13
MINITAB computer output—one-way ANOVA, KIVZ-Channel 5 case study

```
ANALYSIS OF VARIANCE

DUE TO          DF            SS       MS=SS/DF      F-RATIO
FACTOR           4     26511992,      6627998,          ,27
ERROR           45   1102671872,    24503820,
TOTAL           49   1129183744,


LEVEL       N            MEAN      ST, DEV,
0           1          21100,          0,
1          13          25069,       4613,
2           9          24633,       4706,
3          21          24605,       4503,
4           6          26150,       7276,

POOLED ST, DEV, =         4950,
1


INDIVIDUAL 95 PERCENT C, I, FOR LEVEL MEANS
(BASED ON POOLED STANDARD DEVIATION)
        +---------+---------+---------+---------+---------+---------+
0         I************************I************************I
1                               I******I******I
2                            I*********I*******I
3                              I*****I****I
4                            I*********I**********I
        +---------+---------+---------+---------+---------+---------+
     8000,    12000,    16000,    20000,    24000,    28000,    32000,
```

The purpose of this section is to illustrate the type of computer output you can expect when you use statistical software to perform one-way analysis of variance. As in earlier chapters the examples presented use the MINITAB and SPSS-X software systems and the data for the examples come from the KIVZ-Channel 5 survey used in earlier chapters and which appears in table 2–10.

Table 12–13 shows the MINITAB output for a one-way analysis of variance for testing the null hypothesis that the average income (X_{18}) is equal for viewers regardless of which station they prefer for their national news coverage (X_1). The F ratio of 0.27 is so small it falls in the acceptance region for any reasonable alpha level. (See figure 12–7 for MINITAB commands.)

Table 12–14 shows the SPSS-X computer output for a one-way analysis of variance for testing the hypothesis that mean hours of television watched (X_{19}) is equal for all categories of marital status (X_{11}). Note that the F Prob. value can be compared

TABLE 12–14
SPSS-X computer output—one-way ANOVA KIVZ-Channel 5 case study and data base

- - - - - - - - - - - - - - - - - O N E W A Y - - - - - - - - - -

```
    Variable   VAR19      HOURS OF TV
 By Variable   VAR11      MARITAL STATUS
```

ANALYSIS OF VARIANCE

SOURCE	D.F.	SUM OF SQUARES	MEAN SQUARES	F RATIO	F PROB.
BETWEEN GROUPS	2	50.3147	25.1574	1.3750	.2630
WITHIN GROUPS	46	841.6444	18.2966		
TOTAL	48	891.9592			

GROUP	COUNT	MEAN	STANDARD DEVIATION	STANDARD ERROR	MINIMUM	MAXIMUM	95 PCT CONF INT FOR MEAN
Grp 1	3	8.3333	2.8868	1.6667	5.0000	10.0000	1.1622 TO 15.5045
Grp 2	1	14.0000					
Grp 3	45	12.4222	4.3301	.6455	4.0000	21.0000	11.1213 TO 13.7231
TOTAL	49	12.2041	4.3107	.6158	4.0000	21.0000	10.9659 TO 13.4423

- - - - - - - - - - - - - - - - - O N E W A Y - - - - - - - - - -

FIGURE 12–7

MINITAB commands—analysis of variance, income by national news station

```
MTB> READ 'KIVZ5' INTO C1-C19
MTB> OUTFILE = 'PRINTER'
MTB> ONEWAY C18 C1
```

directly with the selected alpha level. If the *F* Prob. is smaller than alpha, the null hypothesis of equal means can be rejected. If the *F* Prob. exceeds the alpha level, the null hypothesis should not be rejected. In this case, the *F* Prob. is 0.2630. Assuming an alpha of 0.05, these results show that the television viewers in the KIVZ market area may watch television an equal number of hours, on average, regardless of marital status of the head of household. (Figure 12–8 shows the SPSS-X program statements.)

The computer output examples shown in tables 12–13 and 12–14 are indicative of the type of output you can expect from most statistical software packages for one-way analysis of variance. Programs such as MINITAB and SPSS-X also can be used to run two-way analysis of variance applications.

```
UNNUMBERED
TITLE DESCRIPTIVE STATISTICS EXAMPLES
FILE HANDLE KIVZ NAME='KIVZ DATA C'
DATA LIST FILE=KIVZ LIST/VAR01 TO VAR19
VARIABLE LABELS
   VAR01 'NATIONAL NEWS STATION'
   VAR02 'LOCAL NEWS STATION'
   VAR03 'NEWS RATING'
   VAR04 'SPORTS RATING'
   VAR05 'WEATHER RATING'
   VAR06 'ANCHOR RATING'
   VAR07 'SPORTSCASTER RATING'
   VAR08 'OVERALL RATING'
   VAR09 'NATIONAL INFLUENCE'
   VAR10 'SEX'
   VAR11 'MARITAL STATUS'
   VAR12 'NUMBER EMPLOYED'
   VAR13 'HOME STATUS'
   VAR14 'YEARS AT RESIDENCE'
   VAR15 'YEARS IN STATE'
   VAR16 'EDUCATION'
   VAR17 'AGE'
   VAR18 'INCOME'
   VAR19 'HOURS OF TV'
VALUE LABELS
   VAR01 1 'CHANNEL 5' 2 'CHANNEL 3' 3 'CHANNEL 8' 4
        'UNDECIDED'/
   VAR02 1 'CHANNEL 3' 2 'CHANNEL 8' 3 'CHANNEL 5' 4
        'UNDECIDED'/
   VAR03 TO VAR08 1 'POOR' 2 'FAIR' 3 'GOOD' 4 'VERY GOOD' 5
        'EXCEL'/
   VAR09 1 'TRUE' 2 'FALSE' 3 'UNDECIDED'/
   VAR10 1 'MALE' 2 'FEMALE'/
   VAR11 1 'SINGLE' 2 'DIVORCED' 3 'MARRIED' 4 'OTHER'/
   VAR13 1 'RENTING' 2 'BUYING'/
   VAR16 1 'GRADE SCHOOL' 2 'SOME COLLEGE' 3 'VOTECH' 4 'HIGH
        SCHOOL'
        5 'COLLEGE GRAD' 6 'GRADUATE WORK'
ONEWAY VAR19 BY VAR11(1,3)
```

FIGURE 12–8

SPSS-X program commands—analysis of variance

CONCLUSIONS

There are many decision-making situations in which the spread of the distribution is as important or more important than its center. This chapter has introduced techniques for testing hypotheses involving a single population variance and involving the difference between two population variances. The chi-square and F distributions were used in these two hypothesis-testing applications.

Managers are also often faced with comparing alternatives involving more than two populations. Because hypothesis testing is such a powerful decision-making tool, managers need to be able to extend the hypothesis-testing procedure to more than two populations. Analysis of variance allows this extension.

By using analysis of variance, managers are able to determine whether the sample observations come from the same population or from different populations. Analysis of variance allows managers to separate observations into categories and see whether this separation explains some of the variation in the sample observations. The ability to test for significant relationships between sample observations falling into different categories makes analysis of variance a powerful decision-making tool.

CHAPTER GLOSSARY

between-sample variation (SSB)   The variation that exists between the sample means selected from the populations of interest in an analysis of variance test.
between-blocks variation (SSBL)   The variation that exists between the second factor sample means in a two-way analysis of variance.
interaction   The non-additive effect exhibited by each block and population mean.
one-way ANOVA   The analysis of variance design in which only one factor is analyzed and the samples selected from the populations are independent.
total variation (TSS)   The variation that exists in the data as a whole.
two-way ANOVA   The analysis of variance design which simultaneously analyzes two factors.
within-sample variation (SSW)   The variation that exists within the sample data from a given population.

CHAPTER FORMULAS

Chi-square test statistic

$$\chi^2 = \frac{(n-1)S^2}{\sigma^2}$$

F-distribution test statistic

$$F = \frac{S_1^2}{S_2^2}$$

Total sum of squares

$$TSS = \sum_{i=1}^{K} \sum_{j=1}^{n_i} (X_{ij} - \overline{\overline{X}})^2$$

Sum of squares between

$$SSB = \sum_{i=1}^{K} n_i(\overline{X}_i - \overline{\overline{X}})^2$$

Sum of squares within

$$SSW = \sum_{i=1}^{K} \sum_{j=1}^{n_i} (X_{ij} - \overline{X}_i)^2$$

Mean square within

$$MSW = \frac{SSW}{N - K}$$

Mean square between

$$MSB = \frac{SSB}{K - 1}$$

F statistic for one-way analysis of variance

$$F = \frac{MSB}{MSW}$$

One-way analysis of variance (calculation formulas)

$$TSS = \sum_{i=1}^{K} \sum_{j=1}^{n_i} X_{ij}^2 - \frac{\left(\sum_{i=1}^{K} \sum_{j=1}^{n_i} X_{ij}\right)^2}{N}$$

$$SSB = \sum_{i=1}^{K} \frac{\left(\sum_{j=1}^{n_i} X_{ij}\right)^2}{n_i} - \frac{\left(\sum_{i=1}^{K} \sum_{j=1}^{n_i} X_{ij}\right)^2}{N}$$

$$SSW = TSS - SSB$$

Two-way ANOVA—No interaction

$$\text{TSS} = \sum_{i=1}^{K}\sum_{j=1}^{r}(X_{ij} - \overline{\overline{X}})^2 = \sum_{i=1}^{K}\sum_{j=1}^{r} X_{ij}^2 - \frac{\left(\sum_{i=1}^{K}\sum_{j=1}^{r} X_{ij}\right)^2}{(K)(r)}$$

$$\text{SSB} = \sum_{i=1}^{K} r(\overline{X}_i - \overline{\overline{X}})^2 = \sum_{i=1}^{K} \frac{\left(\sum_{j=1}^{r} X_{ij}\right)^2}{r} - \frac{\left(\sum_{i=1}^{K}\sum_{j=1}^{r} X_{ij}\right)^2}{(K)(r)}$$

$$\text{SSBL} = \sum_{j=1}^{r} K(\overline{X}_j - \overline{\overline{X}})^2 = \sum_{j=1}^{r} \frac{\left(\sum_{i=1}^{K} X_{ij}\right)^2}{K} - \frac{\left(\sum_{i=1}^{K}\sum_{j=1}^{r} X_{ij}\right)^2}{(K)(r)}$$

SOLVED PROBLEMS

1. The plant manager of a small Midwest fishing-equipment manufacturing plant is convinced that he can come up with a method of determining why his workers are sometimes very accurate and at other times very careless. Although he hasn't had much luck up to this point in determining causes, he has recently completed a book dealing with biorhythms. This seems to be the final explanation, so he has biorhythm charts prepared for all assembly employees. He divides the employees into four groups according to their positions on their charts: high, low, going up, or going down. He monitors the error per hundred rate for each employee and finds the following results:

High	Low	Going Up	Going Down
2.3	3.2	3.6	1.7
3.1	1.8	2.7	2.5
1.9	2.2	2.9	2.0
2.7	2.5	3.0	1.8
2.1	1.9	3.8	2.1
3.3	2.0	3.4	2.6

a. Formulate the null hypothesis and decision rule necessary to test this situation if you want to control Type I error probability at the 1 percent level.
b. How many degrees of freedom are associated with the between-group estimates? How do you determine this value?
c. How many degrees of freedom are associated with the within-group estimate?

d. Set up the appropriate analysis of variance table and formulate a conclusion about the possible relationship between error rate and biorhythm level.

e. What is meant by *MSW* and *MSB?* What do they estimate?

Solutions:

a. Hypotheses:

H_0: $\mu_{high} = \mu_{low} = \mu_{up} = \mu_{down}$
H_A: Not all means are equal

Decision Rule:

If $F > F_{critical}$, reject H_0.
If $F \leq F_{critical}$, accept H_0.

where $F_{critical} = 4.94$ (from appendix F).

b. The degrees of freedom for the between-group estimate equal the number of groups minus 1. In this problem,

$$\text{d.f.} = K - 1 = 4 - 1$$
$$= 3$$

c. For the within-group estimate, the degrees of freedom equal the total sample size minus the number of groups. Here,

$$\text{d.f.} = N - K = 24 - 4$$
$$= 20$$

d.

Source of Variation	SS	d.f.	MS	F Ratio
Between groups	4.411	3	1.470	6.504
Within groups	4.528	20	0.226	
Total	8.939	23		

Since $6.504 > F_{critical} = 4.94$, the null hypothesis is rejected.

e. MSW is the population variance estimate based on the variation found within the groups after partitioning. MSB is the population variance estimate based on the average values found for each group.

2. An equipment rental firm is trying out three new types of oil in the transmissions of its rental front-end loaders. The maintenance manager is interested in whether any of the oils reduce the time before the transmissions have to be repaired. The oils were randomly distributed among a set of new loaders; however, the numbers with each type of oil are not equal. The following data show the hours of use until repair for each front-end loader:

Oil 1	Oil 2	Oil 3
314	401	426
423	307	377
298	267	450
267	217	479
298		503
		532

a. Formulate the appropriate null hypothesis and decision rule to test this situation. Assume an alpha level of 0.01.

b. Construct the analysis of variance table for this situation and either accept or reject your hypothesis.

c. If you conclude one or more oils are associated with a longer average time to repair, determine which oils result in different means.

Solutions:

a. Hypotheses:

H_0: $\mu_1 = \mu_2 = \mu_3$
H_A: Not all means are equal

Decision Rule:

If $F \leq F_{critical}$, accept H_0.
If $F > F_{critical}$, reject H_0.

where $F_{critical} = 6.93$ (from appendix F).

b.

Source of Variation	SS	d.f.	MS	F Ratio
Between groups	81,477	2	40,738.50	10.41
Within groups	46,957	12	3,913.08	
Total	128,434	14		

Since $F = 10.41 > 6.93$, the null hypothesis should be rejected.

c. Since the number of observations differs between groups, we have to use Scheffé's method, where

$$S \text{ range} = S\hat{\sigma}$$
$$S = \sqrt{(K - 1)F_{critical}}$$
$$\hat{\sigma} = \sqrt{\left(\frac{1}{n_1} + \frac{1}{n_2}\right)(MSW)}$$

We have

$$F_{critical} = 6.93$$

so

$$S = \sqrt{(3 - 1)(6.93)} = 3.723$$

For groups 1 and 2:

$$\hat{\sigma} = \sqrt{\left(\frac{1}{5} + \frac{1}{4}\right)(3{,}913.08)} = 41.96$$

$$S \text{ range } = 3.723(41.96) = 156.23$$

For groups 1 and 3:

$$\hat{\sigma} = \sqrt{\left(\frac{1}{5} + \frac{1}{6}\right)(3{,}913.08)} = 37.88$$

$$S \text{ range } = 3.723(37.88) = 141.02$$

For groups 2 and 3:

$$\hat{\sigma} = \sqrt{\left(\frac{1}{4} + \frac{1}{6}\right)(3{,}913.08)} = 40.38$$

$$S \text{ range } = 3.723(40.38) = 150.33$$

Also, $\overline{X}_1 = 320$, $\overline{X}_2 = 298$, and $\overline{X}_3 = 459.667$.

Contrasts			S Range	Significant?
$\lvert\overline{X}_1 - \overline{X}_2\rvert = \lvert320 - 298\rvert$	$= 22$		156.23	no
$\lvert\overline{X}_1 - \overline{X}_3\rvert = \lvert320 - 459.667\rvert$	$= 139.667$		141.02	no
$\lvert\overline{X}_2 - \overline{X}_3\rvert = \lvert298 - 459.667\rvert$	$= 161.667$		150.33	yes

ADDITIONAL PROBLEMS

Section 12–1

34. The Cranston Company has a contract to provide ball bearings that average 1.25 inches in diameter, with a standard deviation not to exceed 0.04 inch. To monitor their production, a random sample of ball bearings was selected and Cranston quality control people found the mean bearing to be 1.2552 inches with a standard deviation of 0.061 inch. If the sample size was twenty ball bearings, is Cranston meeting the requirements of the contract? Test the hypotheses using an alpha level of 0.05. Discuss your results.

35. The Phillips Company makes basketball rims used in most college arenas and professional facilities. The basketball standard calls for the rim diameters to have a standard deviation no greater than 0.10 inch. A random sample of twenty-four rims selected from the inventory in the Phillips warehouse showed a variance of 0.032. Given these sample data, what should be concluded about the variation of rim diameters? Be sure to specify the correct null and alternative hypotheses and test at an alpha level of 0.05.

36. The makers of a cattle feed supplement claim that if cattle feeders use the supplement as directed, cattle will gain an average of 1.2 pounds per day over a thirty-day period. Further, they say that the range in weight gain will be 12 pounds per cow over this period.

   A test situation has been developed where a random sample of cattle will be checked for weight gain at the end of thirty days. The results of the test involving ten cattle showed a mean gain of 37 pounds, with a standard deviation of 5.2 pounds. What conclusions should be reached with respect to the two claims made by the cattle feed supplement maker? Test at the alpha level of 0.10. (*Hint:* Recall that the standard deviation can be approximated by the range/4.) Discuss your answer.

37. Hospitals tend to build facilities to support peak demand for their services. Without proper scheduling of patients, these peak demand periods can prove excessive. To help reduce the propensity to overbuild, hospitals in Idaho must have a coefficient of variation in daily patient demand not exceeding 20 percent. Periodically, a state agency will select a sample of daily patient census figures to verify whether the hospital is meeting the coefficient of variation requirement.

   At one hospital, average daily demand is 100 patients. A sample of twenty days showed a standard deviation of twenty-five patients. What should be concluded with respect to this hospital meeting the coefficient of variation requirement? Test at the alpha level of 0.10. (*Hint:* Review the section on coefficient of variation in chapter 3.)

Section 12–2

38. As purchasing agent for the Horner-Williams Company, you have primary responsibility for securing high-quality raw materials at the best possible price. One particular material that the Horner-Williams Company uses a great deal is aluminum. After careful study, you have been able to reduce the prospective vendors down to two. It is unclear whether these two vendors produce aluminum that is equally durable.

   To compare durability, the recommended procedure is to put pressure on the aluminum until it cracks. The vendor whose aluminum requires the greatest average pressure will be judged the one that provides the most durable product.

   To carry out this test, fourteen pieces from vendor 1 are selected at random and fourteen pieces from vendor 2 are selected at random. The following results in pounds per square inch were noted:

Vendor 1	Vendor 2
$n_1 = 14$	$n_2 = 14$
$\overline{X}_1 = 2{,}345$ psi	$\overline{X}_2 = 2{,}411$ psi
$S_1 = 300$	$S_2 = 250$

Before testing the hypothesis about difference in population means, suppose the purchasing agent for the company was concerned whether the assumption of equal population variances was satisfied. Based on the sample data, what would you tell him if you tested at the alpha level of 0.10? Would your conclusion differ if you tested at the alpha level of 0.02? Discuss.

39. Campbell Electronics has decided to place an advertisement on television to be shown three times during a live broadcast of the local university's football game. The sales for each of the seven days after the ad was placed are to be compared with the sales for the seven days immediately prior to running the ad. The following data representing the total dollar sales each day were collected:

Sales before the Ad	Sales after the Ad
$1,765	$2,045
1,543	2,456
2,867	2,590
1,490	1,510
2,800	2,850
1,379	1,255
2,097	2,255

a. State the appropriate null and alternative hypotheses to be tested.
b. What assumptions must be made about the population distributions in order to test the hypothesis using the t distribution?
c. Based on the sample data, what conclusions should be reached with respect to average sales before versus after the advertisement?
d. Suppose the Campbell Electronics Company wished to verify whether the assumption of equal population variances was satisfied when it performed the two-sample t test. Based on the sample data, what should it conclude if the alpha level 0.02 is used?

40. Explain in your own terms why, in a two-tailed F test for equal population variances, the alpha level is divided by two before the F critical value is looked up in the F-distribution table.

41. The Fister Corporation makes ribbons for computer printers. They are currently considering changing from the current model to a new model expected to last just as long on the average as the current model. However, the new model is thought to be more consistent in terms of how long the individual ribbons will last.

To test this claim, a random sample of twenty-one current-model and seventeen new-model ribbons were selected and tested on the company's quality testing equipment. The following results (measured in tens of thousands of characters) were recorded:

Current	New
$n = 21$	$n = 17$
$S = 3.45$	$S = 2.87$

a. State the null and alternative hypotheses to be tested.
b. Test the hypotheses at the alpha $= 0.05$ level. Be sure to state clearly the decision rule and also discuss the results.

42. The production control manager at Ashmore Manufacturing is interested in determining whether there is a difference in standard deviation of product diameter for part #XC-343 for units made at the Trenton, New Jersey, plant versus those made at the Atlanta, Georgia, plant. The Trenton plant is highly automated and thought to provide better quality control. Thus the parts produced there should be less variable than those made in Atlanta.

   A random sample of fifteen parts was selected from those produced last week at Trenton. The standard deviation for these parts was 0.14 inch. A sample of thirteen parts was selected from those made in Atlanta. The sample standard deviation for these parts was 0.202 inch.

   Based upon these sample data, is there sufficient evidence to conclude that the Trenton plant produces parts that are less variable than those of the Atlanta plant? Test at the alpha $= 0.05$ level.

43. Bach Photographs is a large regional photography business with studios in two locations. The owner is interested in monitoring business activity closely at the two locations. Among the factors in which he is interested is the variation in customer orders per day for the two locations. A random sample of eleven days' orders for the two locations showed the following data:

Location A			Location B		
$444	$478	$501	$233	$127	$230
200	400	350	299	250	300
167	250	300	800	340	400
300	600		780	370	

a. State the appropriate null and alternative hypotheses.
b. Based upon the sample data, test the hypotheses, using an alpha $= 0.02$ level. Be sure to state clearly the decision rule.

44. Consider decision-making situations in your major and describe two or more in which tests of one or more population variances is important.

Section 12–3

45. Discuss in your own words each of the following:
   a. Within-group variation
   b. Between-group variation
   c. Total sum of squares
   d. Degrees of freedom

46. You are responsible for installing emergency lighting in a series of state office buildings. You have bids from four manufacturers of battery-operated emergency lights. The costs are about equal, so you decide to base your decision to buy on which type lasts the longest. You receive a sample of four lights from each manufacturer, turn on the lights, and record the time it takes before each light fails. You find the following values in hours:

Type A	Type B	Type C	Type D
24	27	21	23
21	25	20	23
25	26	25	21
22	22	22	21

Based on this evidence, can you conclude that the mean times to failure of the four types are equal? You will have to specify an alpha level.

47. A large metropolitan police force is considering changing from full-size cars to intermediates. The force purchases fifteen cars, five from each of three manufacturers. Each car is driven for 5,000 miles, and the operating cost per mile computed. Unfortunately one car is involved in an accident, one is run into a river during a high-speed chase, and one is "lost" due to a paperwork mix-up. The operating costs for the remaining twelve cars are distributed as follows in cents per mile:

Car A	Car B	Car C
13.3	12.4	13.9
14.3	13.4	15.5
13.6	13.1	14.7
12.8		14.5
14.0		

Perform an analysis of variance on these data. Assume an alpha level of 0.01. Do the experimental data provide evidence that the operating costs per mile for the three types of police cars are different?

48. A nationwide moving company is considering three different types of nylon tie-down straps. The purchasing department randomly selects straps of each type and determines their breaking strengths. The following values are found, in pounds:

Type 1	Type 2	Type 3
1,950	2,210	1,820
1,870	2,300	1,730
1,900	1,990	1,760
1,880	2,190	1,700
2,010	2,250	1,810

a. Construct the analysis of variance table for this set of data.

b. Based on your analysis, with a Type I error of 0.05, can you conclude that a difference exists between the types of nylon ropes?

49. A leading manufacturer of beer is considering five different types of advertising displays for a new low-calorie beer. The displays are each tested in five different randomly selected stores. A total of twenty-five stores are in the sample. The average monthly sales and variances for the first three months for each type of display are as follows:

Display Type	Mean	Variance
A	98 cases	10
B	77	8
C	84	8
D	103	11
E	91	9

Can the manufacturer conclude that it really doesn't matter which type of display is used? Assume an alpha level of 0.01.

50. Channel 9 television in Bextfort, Washington, recently conducted a study of television news viewers. One item of interest to Channel 9 management was whether the average age of viewers watching Channel 9 was the same as for the other two stations in Bextfort. The sample included twenty-four viewers of each station, with the results TSS = 2,900 and SSW = 700.

   Using an alpha level of 0.05, what should Channel 9 conclude about the average ages of news viewers of the three stations? Why?

51. Discuss in your own words why decision makers should use analysis of variance rather than multiple two-sample t tests when testing hypotheses involving more than two populations.

52. Ajax Mountain Ski Company operates a small snow-skiing operation with two chair lifts. Recently some customers have complained that the lines at chair 1 are too long. The Ajax manager has collected the following data, which represent the number of people in line at the two chair lifts at randomly observed times during a week:

Chair 1	Chair 2
10	14
3	13
14	19
7	7
19	11
33	9
28	12
11	13
26	15

a. Use a two-sample t test to determine whether there is a significant difference in the average numbers of people waiting at the two lifts. Test this at the alpha level of 0.05.

b. Use analysis of variance to test the null hypothesis that the average numbers waiting at the two chair lifts are equal.

c. What observations can you make about the relationship between the two-sample t test and two-sample analysis of variance?

53. The Savouy Corporation recently purchased a bicycle manufacturing plant formerly owned by the American Traveling Company. American had been outfitting its bikes with tires produced by the Leach Corporation. Savouy management is considering whether to stay with Leach tires or to change to another brand. Three other brands are being considered, all of which cost about the same as the Leach tire. The criterion for tire selection will be average tread life.

   Samples of twenty have been selected from the Leach tires and from brands, A, B, and C. The following results were found:

$$\overline{X}_{Leach} = 111\ h \qquad \overline{X}_A = 126\ h \qquad \overline{X}_B = 100\ h \qquad \overline{X}_C = 105\ h$$
$$TSS = 19,620$$

(Note that $\overline{X}$ indicates the average hours of use until the tread was reduced to a specified level.) Using an alpha level of 0.05, test that there is no difference in average tread life for the four brands.

54. A ski resort in Idaho has been charged with discriminating against some nationalities of ski instructors in the amount they are allowed to earn from private lessons. Three nationalities teach at this resort: Canadians, Austrians, and Germans. Random samples of six Canadians, eight Austrians, and seven Germans were selected. The following statistics were recorded:

$$\overline{X}_{Canadian} = \$3,111 \qquad \overline{X}_{Austrian} = \$2,005 \qquad \overline{X}_{German} = \$3,511$$
$$TSS = 18,328,128$$

   Based on these values, what do you conclude about average salaries for ski instructors at this ski resort? Use an alpha level of 0.05.

Section 12–4

55. A recent study performed by a marketing consultant hired by State University to determine the best use for empty space in the student union surveyed fifty students selected at random from the student body. Among other questions, the consultant asked the students to indicate how much money they spent in the school bookstore the last month on items other than textbooks. The following data represent the sample results broken down by student class ranks. (Note that the data have been rounded to the nearest dollar.)

Freshman	Sophomore	Junior	Senior	Graduate
$12	$15	$13	$27	$14
9	13	15	19	10
12	14	17	23	7
14	15	14	23	26
12	13	21	25	14
14	11	19	16	10
5	12	15	32	16
10	14	17	26	17
13	17	20	23	19
13	16	19	27	19

a. Based on these sample data, what can be concluded with respect to the average purchases at the bookstore by students with these class rankings? Test using an alpha level of 0.05.

b. If the conclusion is reached that the population means are not all equal, perform the appropriate method of multiple comparison to determine which pairs of populations have different means. Discuss the results of your test in a short memo to the vice-president of operations at the university.

56. The Xerox Company makes a wide variety of office products, including a line of copying machines. Recently the marketing directors at Xerox did a study of governmental users of Xerox copiers. They selected a random sample of twelve clients each from city, county, and state government units. Data were collected on the number of copies made each month by the agencies sampled. The following calculation results were reported to the director of marketing services:

$$\text{TSS} = 204,500,000$$
$$\overline{X}_{\text{County}} = 16,900 \text{ copies}$$
$$\overline{X}_{\text{City}} = 21,300 \text{ copies}$$
$$\overline{X}_{\text{State}} = 18,700 \text{ copies}$$

a. Based on these sample results, what can you conclude about the average number of copies made by units in the three government sectors? Base your analysis on an alpha level of 0.01.

b. Which pairs of populations have different means? Discuss.

57. Referring to problem 56, suppose Xerox decided to expand its study to include private-sector companies with 200 or more employees. The company uses the same government data collected earlier and combines this with the sample data collected from a sample of twelve private companies. In addition to those means found in problem 56, the following values are now available:

$$\text{TSS} = 267,333,780$$
$$\overline{X}_{\text{Private}} = 20,000 \text{ copies}$$

a. What should Xerox conclude about the average number of copies made per month for these four classes of organizations? Test using an alpha level of 0.05.
b. Which pairs of populations have different means based on the sample data? Show the appropriate calculations.

58. The Environmental Protection Agency (EPA) performs various tests on automobiles for mileage analysis. Recently the EPA selected a random sample of people who had purchased a new car within the previous six-month period. Of the twenty-four people surveyed, eight had purchased big luxury cars, eight medium-sized cars, and eight compact cars. The following data represent the difference between these car owners' mileage compared with the EPA mileage rating as posted on the car window when the car was bought:

Luxury Cars	Medium-Sized Cars	Compact Cars
3.5	3.8	1.5
7.4	4.5	2.3
5.0	3.5	0.5
2.0	3.0	−2.0
3.6	2.7	2.5
5.8	4.0	−3.0
8.0	5.0	3.0
7.0	−1.5	−2.0

Note that positive values indicate that the owner received lower actual mileage than advertised by the sticker on the car window; negative values indicate the actual mileage exceeded the EPA rating on the sticker.

a. Based on an alpha level of 0.05, what can you conclude about the three types of cars with respect to the average differences between actual mileage and EPA-sticker mileage ratings?
b. If a difference in means is indicated by the test performed in part a, which populations of cars have different means? Discuss.

59. A Midwestern U.S. city has four radio stations. Radio stations run a fine line between having enough commercial time versus having too much. A study was conducted in which a random sample of hours was selected for each station over a one-month period. The actual minutes of commercial time in each of these hours was recorded. The following values represent calculations that were performed on the raw data:

$$\overline{X}_1 = 14.6 \qquad \overline{X}_2 = 9.7 \qquad \overline{X}_3 = 13.5 \qquad \overline{X}_4 = 7.9$$
$$\text{TSS} = 3456.80$$

a. What can you conclude about the average minutes per hour of commercial time for the four stations if the sample size was twenty hours for each station? Test at the alpha level of 0.05.

b. Based on the appropriate method for multiple comparisons, what can be determined with respect to the mean commercial time for the four stations? Discuss.

60. Why is Tukey's procedure for multiple comparisons used instead of performing several t tests?

61. The Wicks Advertising Agency recently ran a coupon marketing campaign for one of its retail clients in Denver. Coupons were mailed to several thousand households. In addition, coupons were placed in two daily papers. The coupon offered a 15 percent discount on any purchases made with the coupon. The Wicks Agency is interested in knowing whether the volume of purchases differs on the average depending on the source from which the customer obtained the coupon. The marketing executive in charge of this client had one of her staff personnel select a random sample of coupons from each source and keep track of the volume of the purchases that accompanied that coupon. The following data represent the dollar amounts rounded to the nearest dollar:

Mailing	Paper 1	Paper 2
38	20	14
27	19	16
33	20	11
12	10	9
33	15	
21	14	
13		
25		

a. Based on the sample data, what can be concluded about the average purchase amounts by customers using coupons from the three sources? Test using an alpha level of 0.05.

b. Which pairs of coupon sources have different population means? Use the appropriate method of multiple comparisons to answer this question.

62. Referring to problem 59, form the S range using Scheffé's method of multiple comparison and compare this with the T range computed in problem 59. Which method is appropriate to use and why? Also compare the values of the T range and the S range and comment on what the difference means.

63. The National Basketball Association (NBA) recently performed a survey of fans attending a Celtics game at the Boston Garden Arena. The survey collected data on money spent on concessions at the game. Four types of respondents were identified by the survey: students under 18 years, students over 18 years, professional people, and blue-collar workers. These people, who were selected at random, were observed and the dollar volume spent on concessions at the game recorded. These data are shown as follows:

Under 18	Over 18	Professional	Blue Collar
3.10	2.40	2.80	4.20
2.45	2.70	1.25	3.75
3.00	1.75	0.00	5.90
4.50	2.00	2.30	4.20
3.00	0.00	1.50	2.80
	3.00	1.20	6.20
	2.30	0.00	3.00
		2.10	4.00
		0.00	1.25
		4.10	

a. Based on these data, what should the NBA conclude about the average expenditures on concessions by the four groups represented? Test at the alpha level of 0.05.
b. If the test performed in part a concluded that there is a difference in the mean amount spent on concessions among the four groups, which groups have different means? Perform the appropriate pairwise test method. Discuss.

64. The Blainville Police Department has four patrol regions in which officers are assigned for traffic detail. The chief is interested in whether the average dollar amounts in traffic fines were different among the four regions during the previous year. To answer his question, a random sample of court records was selected for tickets issued in each of the four regions. The following data represent the dollar amount of the fine:

Region 1	Region 2	Region 3	Region 4
$25.00	$18.00	$45.00	$30.00
10.00	25.00	36.00	29.00
14.50	22.00	26.00	33.00
13.00	15.00	26.00	27.00
14.00	20.00	75.00	40.00
15.00	15.00	40.00	80.00
14.00	20.00	60.00	
	10.00	30.00	
	14.00	28.00	
	17.00		
	24.00		

a. Based upon the sample data, what should the chief conclude about the average fines per ticket in the four regions? Test using an alpha level of 0.05.
b. Use the appropriate method of multiple comparisons to determine which regions

have different means. Write a short report to the chief describing your results and offering some explanations for the findings.

65. A one-way analysis of variance test has just been performed. The conclusion reached is that the null hypothesis stating that the population means are equal is to be accepted. What would you expect the Scheffés multiple comparison method to show if it were performed for all pairwise comparisons? Discuss.

Section 12–5

66. Weekly cash sales records have been collected for four drive-in restaurants in Topeka, Kansas, for a six-week period, and the following data were collected.

Week	Drive-in			
	1	*2*	*3*	*4*
1	1,430	980	1,780	2,300
2	2,200	1,400	2,890	2,680
3	1,140	1,200	1,500	2,000
4	880	1,300	1,470	1,900
5	1,670	1,300	2,400	2,540
6	990	550	1,600	1,900

a. Assuming that the assumptions of a one-way ANOVA design are satisfied in this case, what should be concluded about the average sales at the four drive-in restaurants in Topeka? Use an alpha level of 0.05.

b. Discuss whether you think the assumptions of a one-way ANOVA test are satisfied in this case and indicate why or why not. If they're not, what design is appropriate? Discuss.

67. Referring to problem 66, perform a two-way analysis of variance test using an alpha level of 0.05 to determine whether the mean sales for the four drive-ins are equal. Comment on the difference in any of the results.

68. With reference to problem 67, determine whether the blocking on week was effective. Test at the alpha level of 0.05 and discuss what is meant by effective blocking.

69. With reference to problems 67 and 68, use Fisher's least significant difference procedure to determine which, if any, drive-ins have different true average weekly sales.

70. The Felton City Automobile Dealers Association recently authorized an independent testing firm to study the four Felton City dealers' service facilities. One of the tests the firm conducted involved the selection of seven vehicles at random that needed repairs of various kinds. The vehicles were taken to each of the dealers, and estimates for repair costs were made without the service department knowing that the vehicle was part of the test. The following data were collected. The values represent the dollar estimates rounded to the nearest dollar for each of the seven vehicles at each of the four dealers.

Car	Dealer 1	Dealer 2	Dealer 3	Dealer 4
1	114	156	65	126
2	224	203	156	188
3	430	379	290	290
4	55	103	30	120
5	240	133	110	190
6	500	490	300	609
7	160	200	80	195

a. Based on these sample data, was the testing agency justified in using a two-way analysis of variance? Test at the alpha level of 0.05.

b. What should the testing agency conclude about the average service costs at the four dealers? State the appropriate null and alternative hypotheses and test at the alpha level of 0.05.

c. Use the LSD approach to determine which pairs of dealers have different average service costs. Write a short memo explaining your results.

71. There are three commercial tax preparing offices in Benboe, Minnesota. The local Better Business Bureau has been receiving some complaints that one of the offices does not understand tax law well enough to provide expert advice. The complaints state that to safeguard itself, the preparing office overstates the tax due by the payer and thus avoids later problems.

The Better Business Bureau has decided to invest several hundred dollars in grant money to test the claim. It has selected eight people at random and asked that they allow each of the three offices to prepare their taxes using the same information. The following data show the tax bills as figured by each preparer:

Return	Office 1	Office 2	Office 3
1	$ 4,376.20	$ 5,100.10	$ 4,988.03
2	5,678.45	6,234.23	5,489.23
3	2,341.78	3,342.60	2,121.90
4	9,875,33	10,300.30	9,845.60
5	7,650.20	8,002.90	7,590.88
6	1,324.80	1,450.90	1,356.89
7	2,345.90	2,356.90	2,345.90
8	15,468.75	16,080.78	15,376.70

a. Assuming that the data meet the assumptions of the one-way analysis of variance, what conclusions should be made about the difference in average taxes figured by the three offices? Test at the alpha level of 0.05.

b. Recognizing that the design is a blocked design, determine whether blocking was effective. Test at the alpha level of 0.05.

c. What conclusions should be reached with respect to the average tax computed by the three offices? Test using an alpha level of 0.05. Discuss.

d. Determine which, if any, of the offices have different mean tax computations and write a short report outlining the position the Better Business Bureau should take in this case.

STATE DEPARTMENT OF TRANSPORTATION CASE STUDY PROBLEMS

The following questions and problems pertain directly to the State Department of Transportation case study and data base introduced in chapter 1. The questions and problems were written assuming that you will have access to a computer and appropriate statistical software. The data base containing 100 observations and seventeen variables is shown in table 1C–1 in chapter 1. *Please assume that the data were collected using a simple random sampling process.*

1. Herb Kriner attended a conference last fall that indicated that female drivers tended to be relatively less variable in the number of convictions (X_5) than male drivers. He would like you to test this claim at the alpha = 0.05 level and prepare a short letter confirming or rejecting the claim based upon the sample information from this state. Indicate whether your conclusion can be applied to other states and indicate why or why not.

2. Herb Kriner would like you to test the hypothesis that there is no difference in average years of education for drivers with various employment statuses. Test using an alpha = 0.05 level.

3. Use analysis of variance to test whether there is a difference in average age of male versus female drivers in this state. Then do the same test using a two-sample t test. Compare the results and write a short memo that discusses the relationship between the two approaches.

4. Considering only those drivers who have insured vehicles, is there a difference in average years lived in the state depending on their knowledge of the law? Test at the alpha = 0.05 level and discuss your results.

5. Is there a difference in average age for those drivers operating insured vehicles versus those operating uninsured vehicles? Test at an alpha = 0.01 level and discuss the conclusions of the test. Use both ANOVA and the t test and comment on the relationship between the two procedures with respect to this problem.

C A S E S

12A   Consumer Information Association

Yolanda Carson is a newly hired research assistant for the Consumer Information Association. The association is a nonprofit group whose major purpose is to supply information necessary to help consumers make better-informed decisions. Yolanda has been assigned to work with the group studying consumer practices in the banking industry.

Yolanda is aware of studies that indicate that the interest banks charge for loans is related to demographic factors such as the size of the city in which the banks are located and whether the state allows branch banks. She has been asked to determine whether there is a difference in consumer loan charges between major sections of the country.

Yolanda has been assured the cooperation of the American Banking Institute and has been given access to any data the institute has. However, she knows that loan charges may depend on many factors and feels compelled to study banks firsthand. In particular, she has decided to randomly select banks in all parts of the country and apply for an automobile loan at each bank selected. She has decided to make the test during two time periods six months apart.

Since consumer interest rates have been changing rapidly lately, Yolanda has recorded all rates in terms of the prime rate plus a certain percent. (The prime rate is the rate large banks charge their largest corporate customers.) In the first test, Yolanda found the following values charged:

Northeast	Southeast	Midwest	West
prime + 3.2%	prime + 2.7%	prime + 3.4%	prime + 3.7%
2.9	2.9	3.5	3.6
2.8	3.0	2.9	3.6
3.5	2.9	3.7	3.9
3.4	2.8	3.4	4.0
4.0	2.5	3.5	3.8
3.2	2.7	3.0	3.4
	2.9		3.8

The executive director of the Consumer Information Association is going to be holding a news conference in a few days to discuss the work the organization has been doing. He would like to be able to cite Yolanda's study as an example of its services.

12B   Singleaf Department Store, Part 1

The Singleaf Department Store operates in several large eastern U.S. cities. Singleaf was one of the first department stores to offer customers its own credit card, and since then the profits on its credit operations have approached those of its sales operations.

Since credit sales are such an important part of operations, the Singleaf board of directors monitors the credit area closely. In particular, the board demands a quarterly report on the age of the account receivable. ("Aging" accounts is a common practice. The accounts are arranged into a distribution according to the time since a payment has been made to the accounts.)

The board has noticed a trend toward older accounts. Although outstanding balances mean extra interest on the accounts, they also increase the chance of having to write off the account as a bad debt. Beth Hansen, staff assistant to the president in charge of customer relations, has been considering methods to reduce the age of the accounts while at the same time not alienating the credit customers and losing future sales.

Many financial concerns turn old accounts over to a professional collection agency, but Singleaf does not. Singleaf's management feels the good will lost when a customer is called on by a professional bill collector may be more than the potential loss if the account is written off. While Singleaf makes an effort to collect on delinquent accounts, this effort has been handled by each of its stores individually.

Beth Hansen has been asked to supervise a study of collecting on delinquent accounts. She has decided to start by determining if the type of collection letter sent to the customer makes a difference in the response received. She has devised the following letter system:

1. Reminder letter
2. Reminder letter with return envelope included
3. "Tough" letter
4. "Tough" letter with return envelope included

Beth has had forty letters (ten of each type) sent to randomly selected credit customers with old accounts of approximately the same balance. The following amounts of money were collected from the customers in the two weeks following the date the collection letter was mailed:

Letter Type

1	2	3	4
$45	$48	$56	$59
0	0	18	28
39	43	58	63
0	0	0	15
33	44	63	57
0	12	0	9
35	36	11	72
5	0	0	41
41	44	0	73
0	0	20	0

The president is anxious to report the findings to the board, along with any conclusions that can be drawn.

12C   American Testing Services

When P. T. Miller formed American Testing Services he anticipated that there was a market for consulting services in the market-research area. By the amount of work that his firm has had during the past three years, he is sure he was correct.

Recently P. T. was approached by the Convestal Corporation to perform an analysis of the five running shoes Convestal makes. The basic research question to be answered was whether people who own Convestal running shoes share an equal opinion (on the average) of the shoes without regard to the particular type or style of Convestal shoe they own. If not, then the company wants to determine which styles seem to be most liked, and which seem to be most disliked, by the customers.

P. T. suggested that Convestal ask a random sample of shoe customers to rate their shoes on a scale of 1 to 100, with 100 being the highest. The following data represent the results of the sampling:

Style 1	Style 2	Style 3	Style 4	Style 5
84	67	78	60	88
54	56	79	64	79
88	70	89	60	84
90	67	84	72	78
88	59	78	77	68
76	66	84	70	70
	70	90	66	80
	56	85	70	80
	70		59	78
	67		70	84
				75

What should P. T. Miller conclude?

REFERENCES

Guenther, W. C. *Analysis of Variance*. Englewood Cliffs, N.J.: Prentice Hall, 1964.

Mendenhall, W. *An Introduction to Linear Models and the Design of Experiments*. Belmont, Calif.: Wadsworth, 1968.

Neter, John and Wasserman, William. *Applied Linear Statistical Models*. Homewood, Ill.: Irwin, 1974.

SIMPLE LINEAR REGRESSION AND CORRELATION ANALYSIS

13

WHY DECISION MAKERS NEED TO KNOW

The statistical techniques discussed thus far have all dealt with a single variable. For example, in chapter 8, where the fundamentals of statistical estimation were introduced, decision makers were interested in estimating values such as the average weight of a can of corn or the average income of families in a certain geographical area. Chapters 9 through 12 introduced the basic concepts of hypothesis testing. Again the hypothesis involved a single variable from one or more populations.

Although many business applications involve only one variable, in other instances decision makers need to consider the relationship between two or more variables. For example, the sales manager for a tool company may notice his sales are not the same each month. He also knows that the company's advertising expenditures vary from month to month. This manager would likely be interested in whether a relationship exists between tool sales and advertising. If he could successfully define the relationship, he might use this information to improve predictions of monthly sales and, therefore, do a better job of planning for his company.

This chapter introduces simple linear regression and correlation analysis. These techniques are important to decision makers who need to determine the relationship between two variables. Regression and correlation analysis are two of the most often applied statistical tools for decision making.

CHAPTER OBJECTIVES

This chapter will introduce simple linear regression and correlation techniques. Examples will be used to demonstrate the uses of regression analysis for prediction and description.

This chapter will also show how decision makers can determine whether a significant linear relationship exists between two variables. It shows how to determine whether regression analysis is actually useful in a practical decision-making situation.

In addition, it shows how to develop confidence intervals for the estimates made using regression analysis.

Finally, this chapter will introduce the assumptions behind regression analysis and discuss some problems that might occur if regression analysis is incorrectly used.

STUDENT OBJECTIVES

After studying the material in this chapter, you should be able to

1. Calculate the simple correlation between two variables.
2. Determine if the correlation is significant.
3. Calculate the simple linear regression equation for a set of data and know the basic assumptions behind regression analysis.
4. Determine whether a regression model is significant.
5. Develop confidence intervals for the regression coefficients.
6. Interpret the confidence intervals for the regression coefficients.
7. Recognize regression analysis applications for purposes of prediction and description.
8. Recognize some potential problems if regression analysis is used incorrectly.
9. Recognize several nonlinear relationships between two variables and be able to introduce the appropriate transformation to apply linear-regression analysis.

STATISTICAL RELATIONSHIPS BETWEEN TWO VARIABLES

13-1 Clint Brown has just taken over as general manager for the Madison Furniture Company. The owners have been concerned about the company's varying monthly sales. Variation in sales causes cash-flow and inventory-stocking problems. To get a handle on the extent of sales variation, Clint has tabulated sales data for twelve randomly selected months. Table 13–1 shows that monthly sales do vary. The company's sales

Table 13–1
Sales, Madison Furniture Company example (x$1,000)

Month	Sales
1	22
2	28
3	22
4	26
5	34
6	18
7	30
8	38
9	30
10	40
11	50
12	46

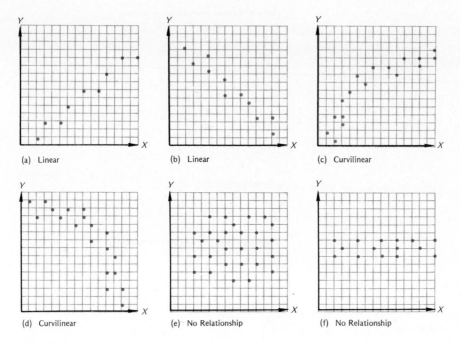

FIGURE 13-1
Two-variable relationships

manager claims the sales variability occurs because the marketing department constantly changes its advertising expenditures. He is quite certain there is a relationship between sales and advertising but doesn't know what the relationship is.

Figure 13–1 shows **scatter plots,** which depict several potential relationships between a dependent variable, Y, and an independent variable, X. A **dependent variable** is the variable whose variation we wish to explain. An **independent variable** is a variable used to explain variation in the dependent variable. Figures 13–1 (a) and (b) are examples of *linear* relationships between X and Y. This means that as the independent variable, X, changes, the dependent variable, Y, tends to change systematically in a straight-line manner. Note that this systematic change can be positive (Y increases as X increases) or negative (Y decreases as X increases). Also notice that the points do not need to fall on an exact straight line for a linear relationship to be exhibited.

Figures 13–1(c) and (d) are examples of *curvilinear* statistical relationships between variables X and Y. And figures 13–1 (e) and (f) are examples showing *no relationship* between X and Y. That is, when X increases, sometimes Y decreases, and other times Y increases.

The three situations shown in figure 13–1 are all possibilities for describing the relationship between sales and advertising for the Madison Furniture Company. The first step in determining the appropriate relationship is to collect advertising expenditure data

Table 13–2
Sales and advertising data, Madison Furniture Company example (×$1,000)

Month	Sales Y	Advertising X
1	22	0.8
2	28	1.0
3	22	1.6
4	26	2.0
5	34	2.2
6	18	2.6
7	30	3.0
8	38	3.0
9	30	4.0
10	40	4.0
11	50	4.0
12	46	4.6

FIGURE 13–2
Plot of sales versus advertising expense, Madison Furniture Company example

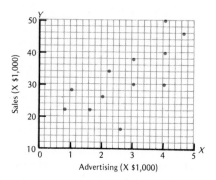

for each month for which sales data are available. These values are shown in table 13–2. Next, the scatter plot shown in figure 13–2 should be constructed.

Figure 13–2 indicates that advertising and sales seem to be linearly related. However, the strength of this relationship is questionable. That is, how close do the points come to falling on a straight line? The scatter plot provides a visual feel for the answer to this question but we also need a quantitative measure of the strength of the linear relationship between two variables. The next section introduces a measure called the *correlation coefficient*.

SKILL DEVELOPMENT PROBLEMS FOR SECTION 13–1

Additional exercises and application problems relating to the material in section 13–1 appear at the end of this chapter.

1. Develop a scatter plot for the following data:

Y	X
100	88
200	120
150	200
75	100
140	100
160	90
230	125

Based upon the scatter plot, describe what, if any, relationship exists between these two variables.

2. Develop scatter plots for the variable Y against variables X_1 and X_2

Y	X_1	X_2
25	4	7
29	3	9
40	1	13
20	6	6
24	5	8
18	7	5
30	3	11
25	3	5

Describe what, if any, relationship is present in each of the scatter plots.

3. If two variables have a negative linear relationship, what will the value of X tend to do when the corresponding value Y increases substantially? Show with an example.

4. If the scatter plot of two variables shows a weak positive linear relationship, what will be the general change in Y associated with a downward change in X? Show with an example.

5. If a scatter plot shows that two variables have a curvilinear relationship showing Y increasing at a decreasing rate as X increases, what might the scatter plot look like? Can you think of two variables that might exhibit such a relationship?

CORRELATION ANALYSIS

The quantitative measure of strength in the linear relationship between two variables is called the **correlation coefficient.** The correlation coefficient for two variables (here, sales and advertising expenditures) can be estimated from sample data using equation 13–1:

13-2

$$r = \frac{\Sigma(X - \bar{X})(Y - \bar{Y})}{\sqrt{[\Sigma(X - \bar{X})^2][\Sigma(Y - \bar{Y})^2]}}$$ (13–1)

or by using an algebraic equivalent formula (equation 13–2) more suited to calculators:

$$r = \frac{n\Sigma XY - \Sigma X \Sigma Y}{\sqrt{[n(\Sigma X^2) - (\Sigma X)^2][n(\Sigma Y^2) - (\Sigma Y)^2]}}$$ (13–2)

where r = simple correlation coefficient
n = sample size
X = value of the independent variable
Y = value of the dependent variable

The correlation coefficient can range from a perfect positive correlation, $+1.0$, to a perfect negative correlation, -1.0. If two variables have no linear relationship, the correlation between them is zero. Consequently, the more the correlation differs from zero, the stronger the linear relationship between the two variables. The sign of the correlation coefficient indicates the direction of the relationship, but does not aid in determining the strength.

Figure 13–3 illustrates some possible correlations between two variables. Note that for the correlation coefficient to equal plus or minus 1.0, all the (X, Y) points must be perfectly aligned. The more the points depart from a straight line, the weaker (closer to 0.0) the correlation between the two variables.

The scatter plot of sales and advertising values for Madison Furniture (figure 13–2) indicates a *positive* linear relationship, but *not* a *perfect* linear relationship. Table 13–3 lists the calculations necessary to determine the correlation coefficient for Madison Furniture. The calculated correlation coefficient, r, is 0.7343.

Although a correlation coefficient of 0.7343 seems quite high (relative to zero), remember that this value is based on a sample of twelve data points and there is always a chance that the sample may provide misleading information due to extreme sampling error. To determine whether the linear relationship between sales and advertising is significant, we must test whether the sample data support or refute the hypothesis that the population correlation coefficient, ρ, is zero. The hypothesis that the population correlation coefficient is zero is tested by computing the t statistic by equation 13–3:

$$t = \frac{r}{\sqrt{\dfrac{1 - r^2}{n - 2}}}$$ (13–3)

where t = number of standard deviations r is from 0
r = sample correlation coefficient
n = sample size

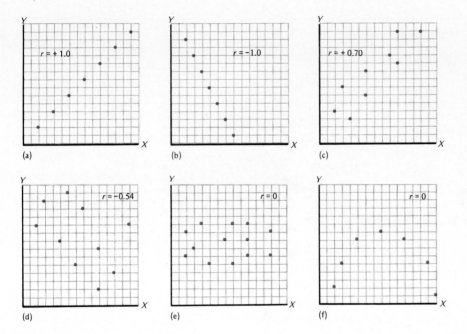

FIGURE 13–3
Correlations between two variables

TABLE 13–3
Correlation coefficient calculations, Madison Furniture Company example

Sales Y	Advertising X	YX	Y^2	X^2
22	0.8	17.6	484	0.64
28	1.0	28.0	784	1.00
22	1.6	35.2	484	2.56
26	2.0	52.0	676	4.00
34	2.2	74.8	1,156	4.84
18	2.6	46.8	324	6.76
30	3.0	90.0	900	9.00
38	3.0	114.0	1,444	9.00
30	4.0	120.0	900	16.00
40	4.0	160.0	1,600	16.00
50	4.0	200.0	2,500	16.00
46	4.6	211.6	2,116	21.16
$\Sigma = 384$	$\Sigma = 32.8$	$\Sigma = 1,150.0$	$\Sigma = 13,368$	$\Sigma = 106.96$

$$r = \frac{n\Sigma XY - \Sigma X \Sigma Y}{\sqrt{[n(\Sigma X^2) - (\Sigma X)^2][n(\Sigma Y^2) - (\Sigma Y)^2]}} = \frac{12(1,150.0) - 384(32.8)}{\sqrt{[12(106.96) - (32.8)^2][12(13,368) - (384)^2]}}$$
$$= 0.7343$$

Hypotheses:

H_0: $\rho = 0$
H_A: $\rho \neq 0$

$\alpha = 0.05$

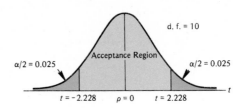

Decision Rule:

If $t > t_{critical} = 2.228$, reject H_0.
If $t < t_{critical} = -2.228$, reject H_0.
Otherwise, do not reject H_0.

Since $3.421 > 2.228$, reject H_0.
The calculated t value is

$$t = \frac{r}{\sqrt{\dfrac{1 - r^2}{n - 2}}} = \frac{0.7343}{\sqrt{\dfrac{1 - 0.5392}{10}}}$$

$$= 3.421$$

FIGURE 13–4
Correlation significant test, Madison Furniture Company example

The degrees of freedom for this test are $n - 2$.

Figure 13–4 shows the test for an alpha level of 0.05. Based on these sample data, we should conclude there is a significant linear relationship between Madison Furniture Company's advertising and sales.

The t test for determining whether the population correlation is significantly different from zero assumes that the data are interval or ratio level and that two variables (Y and X) are distributed as a *bivariate normal*. Although the formal mathematical representation is beyond the scope of this text, *two variables are bivariate normal if their joint distribution is normally distributed*. Although the t test assumes a bivariate normal distribution, it is robust—that is, correct inferences can be reached even with slight departures from the normal-distribution assumption. (See Neter and Wasserman's *Applied Linear Statistical Models* for further discussion of bivariate normal distributions.)

Cause-and-Effect Interpretations

Care must be used when interpreting the correlation results. Even though we found a significant linear relationship between Madison Furniture's sales and advertising, the correlation does not imply cause and effect. Although a change in advertising may, in fact, cause sales to change, simply because the two variables are correlated does not guarantee a cause-and-effect situation. Two seemingly unconnected variables will often be highly correlated. For example, over a period of time, teachers' salaries in North Dakota might be highly correlated with the price of grapes in Spain. Yet, we doubt that a change in grape prices will *cause* a corresponding change in salaries for teachers in North Dakota, or vice versa. When a correlation exists between two seemingly unrelated variables, the correlation is **spurious.** You should take great care to avoid basing conclusions on spurious correlations.

Clint Brown has a logical reason to believe that advertising and sales are related. In fact, marketing theory holds that a change in advertising expenditure might well cause a change in sales by enticing customers to purchase from Madison rather than some other store. However, the correlation alone does not prove that this cause-and-effect situation exists.

SKILL DEVELOPMENT PROBLEMS FOR SECTION 13–2

The following exercises will help you learn the concepts presented in section 13–2. There are additional application problems at the end of this chapter which will further aid in your understanding this material.

6. You are given the following data for variables X and Y:

X	Y
20	16
18	12
24	18
20	17
22	21
14	10
18	10

a. Plot these variables in scatter plot format. Based upon this plot, what type of relationship appears to exist between the two variables?

b. Compute the correlation coefficient for these sample data. Indicate what the correlation coefficient measures.

c. Test to determine whether the population correlation coefficient is zero. Use the alpha = 0.05 level to conduct the test. Be sure to state the null and alternative hypotheses and show the test and decision rule clearly.

7. You are given the following data for variables X and Y:

X	Y
3.0	1.5
2.0	0.5
2.5	1.0
3.0	1.8
2.5	1.2
4.0	2.2
1.5	0.4
1.0	0.3
2.0	1.3
2.5	1.0

a. Plot these variables in scatter plot format. Based upon this plot, what type of relationship appears to exist between the two variables?

b. Compute the correlation coefficient for these sample data. Indicate what the correlation coefficient measures.

c. Test to determine whether the population correlation coefficient is zero. Use the alpha = 0.05 level to conduct the test. Be sure to state the null and alternative hypotheses and show the test and decision rule clearly.

8. You are given the following data for variables X and Y:

X	Y
100	80
110	90
90	75
100	90
110	80
80	60
90	90
90	70

a. Plot these variables in scatter plot format. Based upon this plot, what type of relationship appears to exist between the two variables?

b. Compute the correlation coefficient for these sample data. Indicate what the correlation coefficient measures.

c. Test to determine whether the population correlation coefficient is zero. Use the alpha = 0.05 level to conduct the test. Be sure to state the null and alternative hypotheses and show the test and decision rule clearly.

9. A sample of thirty-two people was randomly selected and height and weight measurements were made for each person. The correlation coefficient for the two variables was 0.80.

a. Discuss in your own words what the $r = 0.80$ means with respect to the variables height and weight.

b. Using an alpha = 0.10 level, test to determine whether the population correlation coefficient is significantly different from zero. Be sure to state the null and alternative hypotheses.

10. A random sample of fifty bank accounts was selected from a local branch bank. The account balance and the number of deposits and withdrawals during the past month were the two variables recorded. The correlation coefficient for the two variables was −0.23.

a. Discuss what the $r = -0.23$ measures. Make sure to frame your discussion in terms of the two variables discussed here.

b. Using an alpha = 0.05 level, test to determine whether there is a significant linear relationship between account balance and the number of transactions to the account during the past month. State the null and alternative hypotheses and show the decision rule.

11. Suppose it has been determined that the number of new workers hired per week in your county has a high positive correlation with the average weekly temperature. Is it safe to conclude that an increase in temperature causes an increase in the number of the new hires? Discuss.

SIMPLE LINEAR REGRESSION ANALYSIS

13-3

Clint Brown has determined that the relationship between advertising expenditures and sales is linear based on the correlation analysis of the previous section. Clint would very much like to use this information to help predict his company's sales. Predicted sales levels would make his whole planning and budgeting process much easier.

The statistical method Clint uses for prediction is *regression analysis*. Where there are only two variables, a dependent variable such as sales and an independent variable such as advertising, the technique is **simple regression analysis.** And, when the relationship between the dependent variable and the independent variable is linear, the technique is *simple linear regression*.

The objective of simple linear regression (which we shall call regression analysis) is to represent the relationship between X and Y with a model of the form shown in equation 13–4:

$$Y_i = \beta_0 + \beta_1 X_i + e_i \qquad (13\text{–}4)$$

where Y_i = value of the dependent variable
X_i = value of the independent variable
β_0 = Y-intercept
β_1 = slope of the regression line
e_i = error term, or residual (i.e., the difference between the actual Y value and the value of Y predicted by the model)

The simple linear regression model described in equation 13–4 has four assumptions:

1. Individual values of the dependent variable, Y, are statistically independent of one another.
2. For a given X value, there can exist many values of Y. Further, the distribution of possible Y values for any X value is normal.
3. The distributions of possible Y values have equal variances for all values of X.
4. The means of the dependent variable, Y, for all specified values of the independent variable, $(\mu_Y|X)$, can be connected by a straight line called the *population regression model*

Figure 13–5 illustrates assumptions 2, 3, and 4. The regression model (straight line) connects the averages of Y for each level of the independent variable, X. The regression line (like any other straight line) is determined by two values, β_0 and β_1. These values are the **regression coefficients.** Value β_0 identifies the Y-intercept and β_1 the slope of the regression line. Under the regression assumptions, the coefficients define the true population model. For each observation, the actual value of the dependent variable, Y, for any X, is the sum of two components, as shown by equation 13–5:

$$Y = A + BX + e.$$

$$Y_i = \beta_0 + \beta_1 X_i + \qquad e_i \qquad (13\text{–}5)$$

Linear component   Random component

The random component, e_i, may be positive or negative, depending on whether a single value of Y for a given X falls above or below the regression line.

Meaning of the Regression Coefficients

Coefficient β_1, the slope of the regression line, measures the average change in the dependent variable, Y, for each unit change in X. The slope can be either positive or negative, depending on the relationship between X and Y. For example, a positive slope of 12 ($\beta_1 = 12$) means that for a one-unit increase in X, we can expect an average twelve-unit increase in Y. Correspondingly, if the slope is a negative 12 ($\beta_1 = -12$), we can expect an average decrease of twelve units in Y for a one-unit increase in X.

The Y-intercept, β_0, indicates the mean value of Y when X is zero. However, this interpretation holds only if the population could have X values of zero. When this cannot occur, β_0 does not have a meaningful interpretation in the regression model.

FIGURE 13–5
Graphical display of linear regression assumptions

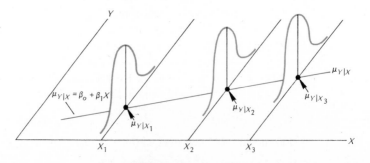

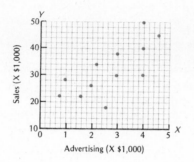

Estimating the Simple Regression Model— the Least Squares Approach

Clint Brown of the Madison Furniture Company has only a sample of monthly data available, yet he has been able to establish a significant linear relationship between advertising and sales using correlation analysis. Now he would like to estimate the *true* linear relationship between advertising and sales by determining the regression model for the twelve months of data he has available.

Figure 13–6 shows the scatter plot for advertising and sales. Clint needs to use the sample points to estimate β_0 and β_1, the true intercept and slope of the line representing the relationship between the two variables. Statistical theory shows that the best estimates for β_0 and β_1 are the intercept and slope formed from the available sample data. Thus, the *regression line* through the sample data is the estimate of the population regression line. However, there are an infinite number of possible regression lines for a set of points. For example, figure 13–7 shows three different lines that pass through Madison Furniture's advertising and sales points. These are but a few of the lines that could have been drawn. Which line should be used to estimate the true regression model?

Since so many possible regression lines exist for a sample of data, we must establish a criterion for selecting the best line. The criterion used is the **least squares criterion.** According to the least squares criterion, the best regression line is the one that minimizes the sum of squared distances between the observed (X, Y) points and the regression line. Note that the distance between an (X, Y) point and the regression line is called the *residual* or error.

Figure 13–8 shows how the error is calculated when X equals 4.6 and the regression line is $\hat{Y} = 20 + 5X$ (where $\hat{Y}$ is estimated sales value). Notice that when X equals 4.6, the difference between the regression line value $\hat{Y}$ (43) and the observed Y (46) is $Y - \hat{Y} = 3$. Thus the residual for this line when X is 4.6 is 3.

Table 13–4 (p. 576) shows the calculated errors and sum of squared errors for each of the three regression lines shown in figure 13–7. Of these three potential regression models, the line with the equation $\hat{Y} = 20 + 5X$ has the smallest sum of squared errors. However, is this line the best of all possible lines? That is, would

$$\sum_{i=1}^{n}(Y_i - \hat{Y}_i)^2 = 542$$

FIGURE 13–7

Potential regression lines, Madison Furniture Company example

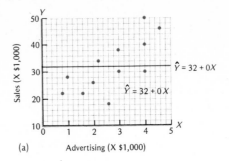

(a)

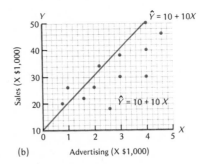

(b)

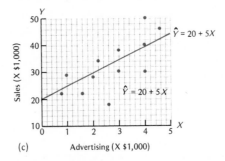

(c)

be smaller than for any other line? One way to determine this is to calculate the sum of squared errors for other regression lines. However, since there are an infinite number of these lines, this approach is not feasible. Fortunately through the use of calculus, equations that can be used to directly determine the slope and intercept estimates such that $\Sigma(Y_i - \hat{Y})^2$ is minimized can be derived.

Let the estimated regression model be of the form shown in equation 13–6:

$$\hat{Y}_i = b_0 + b_1 X_i \qquad (13\text{–}6)$$

where $\hat{Y}_i$ = estimated, or predicted, Y value
b_0 = unbiased estimate of the regression intercept
b_1 = unbiased estimate of the regression slope
X_i = value of the independent variable

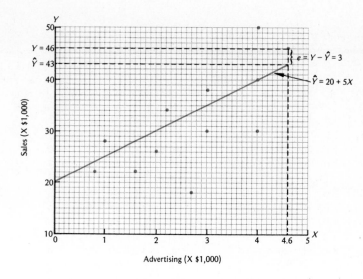

FIGURE 13–8
Computation of regression error,
Madison Furniture Company example; see figure 13–7(c).

Then the values of b_0 and b_1 are calculated by equations 13–7, 13–8, and 13–9:[1]

$$b_1 = \frac{\Sigma (X - \bar{X})(Y - \bar{Y})}{\Sigma (X - \bar{X})^2} \qquad (13\text{–}7)$$

$$b_1 = \frac{\Sigma XY - \dfrac{\Sigma X \Sigma Y}{n}}{\Sigma X^2 - \dfrac{(\Sigma X)^2}{n}} \qquad (13\text{–}8)$$

and

$$b_0 = \bar{Y} - b_1 \bar{X} \qquad (13\text{–}9)$$

Table 13–5 shows the calculations necessary to estimate the population line for the Madison Furniture Company. Here the best regression line, given the least squares criterion, is

$$\hat{Y}_i = 16.143 + 5.801 X_i$$

Table 13–6 shows the predicted sales values and the errors and squared errors associated with this best regression line. The errors are called **residuals.** From table 13–6, the sum of the squared residuals is 497.556. This is the smallest sum of squared residuals possible. Any other regression line through these twelve (X, Y) points will produce a larger sum of squared residuals.

---

[1] The derivation of these least squares regression values for b_0 and b_1 is presented in a technical appendix at the end of this chapter.

TABLE 13–4
Sum of squared errors, Madison Furniture Company example

Figure 13–7(a) $\hat{Y} = 32 + 0X$					Figure 13–7(b) $\hat{Y} = 10 + 10X$					Figure 13–7(c) $\hat{Y} = 20 + 5X$				
X	$\hat{Y}$	Y	$Y - \hat{Y}$	$(Y - \hat{Y})^2$	X	$\hat{Y}$	Y	$Y - \hat{Y}$	$(Y - \hat{Y})^2$	X	$\hat{Y}$	Y	$Y - \hat{Y}$	$(Y - \hat{Y})^2$
0.8	32	22	−10	100	0.8	18	22	4	16	0.8	24	22	−2	4
1.0	32	28	−4	16	1.0	20	28	8	64	1.0	25	28	3	9
1.6	32	22	−10	100	1.6	26	22	−4	16	1.6	28	22	−6	36
2.0	32	26	−6	36	2.0	30	26	−4	16	2.0	30	26	−4	16
2.2	32	34	2	4	2.2	32	34	2	4	2.2	31	34	3	9
2.6	32	18	−14	196	2.6	36	18	−18	324	2.6	33	18	−15	225
3.0	32	30	−2	4	3.0	40	30	−10	100	3.0	35	30	−5	25
3.0	32	38	6	36	3.0	40	38	−2	4	3.0	35	38	3	9
4.0	32	30	−2	4	4.0	50	30	−20	400	4.0	40	30	−10	100
4.0	32	40	8	64	4.0	50	40	−10	100	4.0	40	40	0	0
4.0	32	50	18	324	4.0	50	50	0	0	4.0	40	50	10	100
4.6	32	46	14	196	4.6	56	46	−10	100	4.6	43	46	3	9
				Σ = 1,080					Σ = 1,144					Σ = 542

Figure 13–9 shows the scatter plot of sales and advertising and the least squares regression line for the Madison Furniture Company.

Least Squares Regression Properties

Table 13–6 and figure 13–9 illustrate several important properties of least squares regression:

1. The sum of the residuals from the least squares regression line is zero (equation 13–10):

$$\sum_{i=1}^{n} (Y_i - \hat{Y}_i) = 0 \qquad (13\text{–}10)$$

2. The sum of the squared residuals is a minimum (equation 13–11):

$$\sum_{i=1}^{n} (Y_i - \hat{Y}_i)^2 = \text{minimum} \qquad (13\text{–}11)$$

This property provided the basis for developing the equations for b_0 and b_1.

3. The simple regression line always passes through the mean of the Y variable, $\overline{Y}$, and the mean of the X variable, $\overline{X}$. This is illustrated in figure 13–9. Thus,

TABLE 13–5

Least squares regression coefficients, Madison Furniture Company example

X	Y	XY	X^2
0.8	22	17.6	0.64
1.0	28	28.0	1.00
1.6	22	35.2	2.56
2.0	26	52.0	4.00
2.2	34	74.8	4.84
2.6	18	46.8	6.76
3.0	30	90.0	9.00
3.0	38	114.0	9.00
4.0	30	120.0	16.00
4.0	40	160.0	16.00
4.0	50	200.0	16.00
4.6	46	211.6	21.16
$\Sigma = 32.8$	$\Sigma = 384$	$\Sigma = 1{,}150.0$	$\Sigma = 106.96$

$$b_1 = \frac{\Sigma XY - \dfrac{\Sigma X \Sigma Y}{n}}{\Sigma X^2 - \dfrac{(\Sigma X)^2}{n}} = \frac{1{,}150.0 - \dfrac{32.8(384)}{12}}{106.96 - \dfrac{(32.8)^2}{12}}$$

$$= 5.801$$

Then

$$b_0 = \overline{Y} - b_1\overline{X} = 32 - 5.801(2.733)$$
$$= 16.143$$

The least squares regression line is, therefore,

$$\hat{Y} = 16.143 + 5.801X$$

X	Y	$\hat{Y}$	Residuals $Y - \hat{Y}$	Squared Residuals $(Y - \hat{Y})^2$
0.8	22	20.784	1.216	1.4786
1.0	28	21.944	6.056	36.6751
1.6	22	25.425	− 3.425	11.7306
2.0	26	27.746	− 1.746	3.0485
2.2	34	28.906	5.094	25.9488
2.6	18	31.226	− 13.226	174.9271
3.0	30	33.547	− 3.548	12.5883
3.0	38	33.547	4.453	19.8292
4.0	30	39.348	− 9.348	87.3851
4.0	40	39.348	0.652	0.4251
4.0	50	39.348	10.652	113.4651
4.6	46	42.829	3.170	10.0489
			$\Sigma = 0.000$	$\Sigma = 497.5560$

TABLE 13–6

Residuals and squared residuals, Madison Furniture Company example

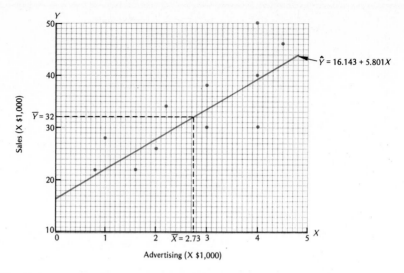

FIGURE 13–9
Least squares regression line, Madison Furniture Company example

to draw any simple linear regression line, all you need to do is connect the least squares Y-intercept with the $(\overline{X}, \overline{Y})$ point.

4. The least squares coefficients are unbiased estimates of β_0 and β_1. Thus the expected values of b_0 and b_1 are β_0 and β_1, respectively.

SKILL DEVELOPMENT PROBLEMS FOR SECTION 13–3

The exercises and problems listed below will help you learn the concepts presented in section 13–3. There are additional application problems at the end of this chapter which will further help you to understand this material.

12. You are given the following sample data for variables Y and X:

Y	140	120	80	100	130	90	110	120	130	130	100
X	5	3	2	4	5	4	4	5	6	5	4

a. Develop a scatter plot for these data and describe what, if any, relationship exists.
b. Compute the correlation coefficient. Test to determine whether the correlation is significant at the alpha $= 0.05$ level.
c. Compute the regression equation based upon these sample data and interpret the regression coefficients.

13. You are given the following sample data for variables Y and X:

Y	12.5	9.0	13.0	7.5	9.0	6.2	3.5	14.0	15.0
X	100	120	100	90	110	160	200	95	80

a. Develop a scatter plot for these data and describe what, if any, relationship exists.

b. Compute the correlation coefficient. Test to determine whether the correlation is significant at the alpha = 0.05 level.

c. Compute the regression equation based upon these sample data and interpret the regression coefficients.

14. The APEX Telephone Company recently performed a study in which they surveyed ten households to determine the number of phone calls made per week (Y) and the number of people living at the residence (X). The following sample data were determined:

Calls (Y)	37	23	67	21	10	33	46	67	44	38
People (X)	4	2	3	1	2	3	4	5	3	4

a. Develop a scatter plot for these data and describe what, if any, relationship exists.

b. Compute the correlation coefficient. Test to determine whether the correlation is significant at the alpha = 0.05 level.

c. Compute the regression equation based upon these sample data and interpret the regression coefficients.

15. At a recent Beach Boys concert, a survey was conducted that asked those sampled their age (X) and how many concerts they have attended since the first of the year (Y). The following data were collected with eleven respondents:

Age (X)	24	21	34	45	23	34	47	29	20	37	42
Concerts (Y)	3	2	1	3	5	2	1	3	5	2	3

a. Develop a scatter plot for these data and describe what, if any, relationship exists.

b. Compute the correlation coefficient. Test to determine whether the correlation is significant at the alpha = 0.05 level.

c. Compute the regression equation based upon these sample data and interpret the regression coefficients.

d. Compute the residuals and the sum of squared errors. Also compute the sum of squares for the Y variable and compare the sum of squared errors to this sum. Why do you suppose the sum of squared errors is smaller? Discuss.

16. At State University, a study was done to establish whether a relationship existed between student graduating GPA and the SAT score when the student originally entered the university. The following sample data are reported:

GPA (Y)	2.5	3.2	3.5	2.8	3.0	2.4	3.4	2.9	2.7	3.8
SAT (X)	640	700	550	540	620	490	710	600	505	710

a. Develop a scatter plot for these data and describe what, if any, relationship exists.

b. Compute the correlation coefficient. Test to determine whether the correlation is significant at the alpha $= 0.05$ level.

c. Compute the regression equation based upon these sample data and interpret the regression coefficients.

d. Compute the residuals and the sum of squared errors. Also compute the sum of squares for the Y variable and compare the sum of squared errors to this sum. Why do you suppose the sum of squared errors is smaller? Discuss.

SIGNIFICANCE TESTS IN REGRESSION ANALYSIS

13-4   If you recall, Clint Brown found that his company's sales varied from month to month. The amount of total variation in the dependent variable (sales) is TSS (total sum of squares). TSS is computed using equation 13–12:

$$TSS = \sum_{i=1}^{n} (Y_i - \bar{Y})^2 \tag{13–12}$$

where   TSS = total sum of squares
n = sample size
Y_i = ith value of the dependent variable
$\bar{Y}$ = average value of the dependent variable

TABLE 13–7
Calculation of total sum of squares, Madison Furniture Company example

Month	Y	Y^2
1	22	484
2	28	784
3	22	484
4	26	676
5	34	1,156
6	18	324
7	30	900
8	38	1,444
9	30	900
10	40	1,600
11	50	2,500
12	46	2,116
	$\Sigma = 384$	$\Sigma = 13,368$

$$TSS = \Sigma(Y - \bar{Y})^2 = \Sigma Y^2 - \frac{(\Sigma Y)^2}{n}$$

$$= 13,368 - \frac{(384)^2}{12}$$

$$= 1,080$$

The total sum of squares for Madison Furniture's sales is calculated in table 13–7. As you can see, the total variation in sales that needs to be explained is 1,080.

The least squares regression line minimized the sum of squared residuals. This value (see table 13–6) is called the *sum of squares error (SSE)* and is calculated by equation 13–13:

$$SSE = \sum_{i=1}^{n} (Y_i - \hat{Y}_i)^2 \qquad (13\text{–}13)$$

where
n = sample size
Y_i = ith value of the dependent variable
$\hat{Y}_i$ = least squares estimated value for the average of Y for each given X value

The SSE represents the amount of variation in the dependent variable that is not explained by the least squares regression line. For Madison Furniture, the amount of unexplained variation is 497.556. The amount of variation in the dependent variable that is explained by the regression line is called the *sum of squares regression (SSR)* and is calculated by equation 13–14:

$$SSR = TSS - SSE \qquad (13\text{–}14)$$

where
SSR = sum of squares regression
TSS = total sum of squares
SSE = sum of squares error

For the Madison Furniture Company, the least squares regression line calculated in table 13–5 produces a sum of squares regression of

$$SSR = 1,080 - 497.556$$
$$= 582.444$$

The percentage of the total variation in the dependent variable which is explained by the independent variable is called the *coefficient of determination* or R^2. We compute R^2 by equations 13–15, 13–16, or 13–17:

$$R^2 = 1 - \frac{\Sigma (Y - \hat{Y})^2}{\Sigma (Y - \bar{Y})^2} \qquad (13\text{–}15)$$

$$R^2 = 1 - \frac{SSE}{TSS} \qquad (13\text{–}16)$$

or, alternatively,

$$R^2 = \frac{SSR}{TSS} \qquad (13\text{–}17)$$

Then, for the Madison Furniture Company example, the percentage of variation in sales which can be explained by the level of advertising is

$$R^2 = 1 - \frac{497.556}{1,080}$$

$$= 1 - 0.4607$$

$$= 0.5393$$

This means that 53.93 percent of the variation in the sales data for this sample can be explained by knowing the level of advertising that accompanied the sales amount.

R^2 can be a value between zero and 1.0. If there is perfect linear relationship between two variables, the coefficient of determination, R^2, will be 1.0. This would correspond to a situation in which the least squares regression line would pass through each of the points in the scatter plot.

R^2 is the measure used by many decision makers to indicate how well the linear regression line fits the (X, Y) data points. The better the fit, the closer R^2 will be to 1.0. R^2 will be close to zero when there is a weak linear relationship or no linear relationship at all.

Finally, when you are employing *simple linear regression* (one independent variable in the model) there is an alternative way of computing R^2, as shown in equation 13–18:

$$R^2 = r^2 \tag{13–18}$$

where R^2 = coefficient of determination
         r = simple correlation coefficient

Thus, by squaring the correlation coefficient we can get R^2 for the simple regression model. This is verified for the Madison Furniture Company example as follows:

$$R^2 = r^2$$

$$= 0.7343^2$$

$$= 0.5392 \text{ (difference from 0.5393 due to rounding)}$$

Significance of the Regression Model

Before he uses the regression model to predict sales values, Clint should find out if the model itself is statistically significant. To test this, he uses the analysis of variance approach shown in figure 13–10. Based on the analysis of variance F test, he concludes that the proportion of sales variation explained by the least squares regression line is greater than zero. The analysis of variance test has shown that the sample coefficient of determination is significantly greater than zero. This means that the regression model we have developed is statistically significant. That is, predictions for sales based on advertising using the least squares model would be generally preferable to just using $\overline{Y}$.

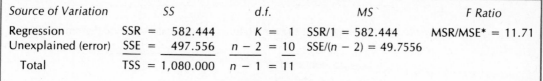

Hypotheses:

H_0: The regression model does not explain any of the total variation in the dependent variable.

H_A: The regression model does explain a proportion of the total variation in the dependent variable greater than 0.0.

$\alpha = 0.05$

Source of Variation	SS	d.f.	MS	F Ratio
Regression	SSR = 582.444	K = 1	SSR/1 = 582.444	MSR/MSE* = 11.71
Unexplained (error)	SSE = 497.556	n − 2 = 10	SSE/(n − 2) = 49.7556	
Total	TSS = 1,080.000	n − 1 = 11		

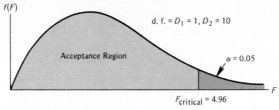

Decision Rule:

If $F > F_{critical} = 4.96$, reject H_0.
Otherwise, do not reject H_0.

Since $11.71 > 4.96$, we reject H_0 and conclude that the regression model explains a significant amount of variation in the dependent variable.

*MSR = mean square regression; MSE = mean square error.

FIGURE 13–10

Significance test of the regression model, Madison Furniture Company example

Significance of the Slope Coefficient

To test the significance of the simple linear regression model, we test whether the true regression slope is zero. A slope of zero would imply that the X variable is of no use in explaining the variation in Y. If the X variable is useful, then we should reject that the regression slope is zero. Because the b_1 value is calculated from a sample, it is subject to sampling error. Thus, even though b_1 is not zero, we must determine whether its difference from zero is greater than would generally be attributed to sampling error.

If we selected several samples from the same population, and for each sample determined the least squares regression line, we would likely get lines from different slopes and different Y-intercepts. This is analogous to getting different sample means from different samples. And, just as the distribution of possible sample means has a standard deviation, the possible regression slopes have a standard deviation, which is given in equation 13–19:

$$\sigma_{b1} = \frac{\sigma_e}{\sqrt{\Sigma(X - \bar{X})^2}} \qquad (13\text{--}19)$$

where σ_{b1} = standard deviation of the regression slope
(called the *standard error of the slope*)
σ_e = *standard error of the estimate*

Because we are sampling from the population, we estimate σ_{b1} by equation 13–20:

$$S_{b1} = \frac{S_e}{\sqrt{\Sigma(X - \bar{X})^2}} = \frac{S_e}{\sqrt{\Sigma X^2 - \dfrac{(\Sigma X)^2}{n}}} \qquad (13\text{--}20)$$

where S_{b1} = estimate of the standard error of the least squares
slope

$S_e = \sqrt{\dfrac{\text{SSE}}{n - 2}}$ = sample **standard error of the estimate**
(the measure of deviation of the actual
Y values around the regression line)

For Madison Furniture Company, the estimate of the standard error of the slope is

$$S_{b1} = \frac{\sqrt{\dfrac{497.556}{10}}}{\sqrt{106.96 - \dfrac{(32.8)^2}{12}}}$$

$$= 1.6955$$

If the standard error of the slope is large, the value of b_1 will be quite variable from sample to sample. On the other hand, if S_{b1} is small, the slope will be less variable. However, regardless of the standard error, the average value of b_1 will equal β_1, the true regression slope, if the assumptions of the regression analysis are satisfied. Figure 13–11 illustrates what this means. Notice that when the standard error is large, the sample slopes can take on values *much* different from the true population slope. As figure 13–11(a) shows, a sample slope and the true population slope can even have different signs. However, when S_{b1} is small, the sample regression lines will cluster closely around the true population line (figure 13–11(b)).

Because the sample regression slope will most likely not equal the true population slope, we must test to determine if the true slope could possibly be zero. A slope of zero in the linear model means that the independent variable will not explain any varia-

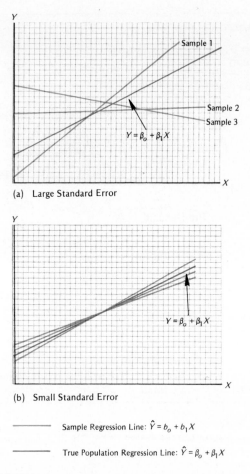

FIGURE 13–11
Standard error of the slope

(a) Large Standard Error

(b) Small Standard Error

———— Sample Regression Line: $\hat{Y} = b_o + b_1 X$

———— True Population Regression Line: $\hat{Y} = \beta_o + \beta_1 X$

tion in the dependent variable. To test the significance of a slope coefficient, we use the t test of equation 13–21:

$$t = \frac{b_1 - \beta_1}{S_{b_1}} \qquad (13\text{–}21)$$

where t = number of standard errors b_1 is from β_1
           b_1 = sample regression slope coefficient
           β_1 = hypothesized slope
           S_{b_1} = estimate of the standard error of the slope

This test has $n - 2$ degrees of freedom. Figure 13–12 illustrates this test for the Madison Furniture Company example, which indicates we should reject the hypothesis that

Hypotheses:

H_0: $\beta_1 = 0$
H_A: $\beta_1 \neq 0$

$\alpha = 0.05$

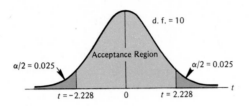

The calculated t is

$$t = \frac{b_1 - \beta_1}{S_{b_1}} = \frac{5.801 - 0}{1.6955}$$
$$= 3.421$$

Decision Rule:

If $t > t_{critical} = 2.228$, reject H_0.
If $t < t_{critical} = -2.228$, reject H_0.
Otherwise, do not reject H_0.

Since $3.421 > 2.228$, we should reject the null hypothesis and conclude that the true slope is not zero.

FIGURE 13–12
Significance test for the regression slope, Madison Furniture Company example

the true regression slope is zero. Thus advertising can be used to help explain the variation in Madison Furniture Company sales.

Figure 13–13 outlines the steps involved in developing a simple linear regression model and reviews the various tests of significance. You should recognize that the three tests used thus far to test the significance of the linear relationship between X and Y are actually equivalent. Therefore, the decision maker needs to perform only one of these tests, since they will all lead to the same conclusion. However, you should be familiar with all three since they are each used. When we introduce multiple regression analysis in chapter 14, the three tests serve different purposes.

Computer Application

The calculations required to develop a simple linear regression model can be performed with a calculator. However, many computer programs have been developed that will perform the calculations quickly and with great accuracy. These computer programs will

Step 1. Develop a scatter plot of Y and X. You are looking for a linear relationship between the two variables.

Step 2. Calculate the correlation coefficient, r. This measures the strength of the linear relationship between the two variables.

Step 3. Test to see whether r is significantly different from zero. The test statistic is

$$t = \frac{r}{\sqrt{\dfrac{1 - r^2}{n - 2}}}$$

Step 4. Calculate the least squares regression line for the sample data.

Step 5. Calculate the simple coefficient of determination, r^2. This value measures the proportion of variation in the dependent variable explained by the independent variable.

Step 6. Test to see whether the model is significant. The test statistic is

$$F = \frac{\dfrac{\text{SSR}}{1}}{\dfrac{\text{SSE}}{n - 2}} = \frac{\text{MSR}}{\text{MSE}}$$

Step 7. Test to determine whether the true regression slope is zero. The test statistic with d.f. = $n - 2$ is

$$t = \frac{b_1 - \beta_1}{S_{b_1}}$$

Note: Steps 3, 6, and 7 are equivalent tests for the simple regression model. Only one of these tests needs to be performed.

FIGURE 13–13
Summary of simple regression steps

also calculate the values necessary to test the significance of the regression model. Table 13–8 is a sample computer printout for the Madison Furniture Company example.

As you look at the computer output in table 13–8, you will note the printout labels things a little differently than the text has been doing. For instance, the standard error of the estimate on the printout is $s = 7.054$, the standard deviation of the regression slope is Stdev = 1.696. The intercept is shown on the printout as the Constant = 16.143. Other software packages will use still different labels for the regression statistics. However, the documentation that accompanies the various software will indicate what the output labels mean.

SKILL DEVELOPMENT PROBLEMS FOR SECTION 13–4

The following exercises are included to help you gain a firm understanding of the concepts presented in this section. There are further application problems at the end of the chapter which you should work to add to your understanding.

TABLE 13–8
MINITAB computer output—
Madison Furniture Company example

```
MTB > print c1-c2
  ROW     advertis      sales
   1        0.8          22
   2        1.0          28
   3        1.6          22
   4        2.0          26
   5        2.2          34
   6        2.6          18
   7        3.0          30
   8        3.0          38
   9        4.0          30
  10        4.0          40
  11        4.0          50
  12        4.6          46

MTB > regression c2 1 c1

The regression equation is
sales = 16.1 + 5.80 advertis

Predictor        Coef       Stdev     t-ratio
Constant        16.143      5.062       3.19
advertis         5.801      1.696       3.42

s = 7.054     R-sq = 53.9%     R-sq(adj) = 49.3%

Analysis of Variance

SOURCE          DF         SS          MS
Regression       1       582.44      582.44
Error           10       497.56       49.76
Total           11      1080.00
```

17. You are given the following results from computations pertaining to a simple linear regression application:

$$\hat{Y} = 23.0 + 1.45X$$
$$\text{SSE} = 45{,}000$$
$$n = 25$$
$$\Sigma(X - \bar{X})^2 = 4{,}000$$

a. Based on the statistics supplied, can you conclude there is a significant linear relationship between X and Y? Test at the alpha = 0.05 level.
b. Interpret the slope coefficient.

18. The following data have been collected by an accountant who is performing an audit of parts inventory for a machinery company. The dependent variable, Y, is the actual number of units counted by the accountant. The independent variable, X, is the number of units on the computer inventory record.

Y	233	10	24	56	78	102	90	200	344	120	18
X	245	12	22	56	90	103	85	190	320	120	23

a. Develop a scatter plot for these data.

b. Compute the correlation coefficient and test to determine if a significant linear relationship exists between the two variables. Test at an alpha = 0.05 level.

c. Compute the regression model based upon the sample data. Compute also the standard error of the estimate. Test to determine whether the regression slope is significantly different from zero. Use an alpha = 0.05 level.

d. Referring to parts b and c, comment on the relationship between the two hypothesis tests.

19. The Skelton Manufacturing Company recently did a study of their customers. A random sample of $n = 50$ customer accounts was pulled from the computer records. Two variables were observed:

$$Y = \text{the total dollar volume of business this year}$$
$$X = \text{miles customer is from corporate headquarters}$$

The following statistics were computed:

$$\hat{Y} = 2140.23 - 10.12X$$
$$S_b = 3.12$$

a. Interpret the regression slope coefficient.

b. Using an alpha = 0.05 level, test to determine whether the true regression slope is different from zero. Discuss the conclusions.

20. The National Football League is concerned about the injuries suffered by its players. A sample of players was selected prior to last season. At the end of the year, two variables were measured:

$$Y = \text{number of days out with an injury}$$
$$X = \text{weight of the player}$$

The following data were observed:

Y	17	9	0	3	26	18	2	8	19	38	20	0	2
X	221	198	234	256	278	197	206	224	234	278	220	199	234

a. Develop a scatter plot for these data.

b. Compute the correlation coefficient and test to determine if a significant linear relationship exists between the two variables. Test at an alpha = 0.05 level.

c. Compute the regression model based upon the sample data. Compute also the standard error of the estimate. Test to determine whether the regression slope is significantly different than zero. Use an alpha = 0.05 level.

d. Referring to parts b and c, comment on the relationship between the two hypothesis tests.

REGRESSION ANALYSIS FOR DESCRIPTION

13-5

Regression and correlation analysis is often used as a descriptive tool. For example, the loan manager at a savings and loan might be interested in describing the relationship between a loan's term (number of months) and its dollar value. Although the loan manager has never studied this, she thinks a positive linear relationship exists between time and amount. Smaller loans would tend to be associated with shorter lending periods, whereas larger loans would be for longer periods.

A descriptive analysis using linear regression requires the same steps described in figure 13–13. Using regression for description, the decision maker concentrates on the significance of the **regression slope coefficient,** and its sign, size, and standard error.

For example, suppose the loan manager sampled sixty accounts and found the following information:

$$Y = \text{length of loan period (months)}$$
$$X = \text{dollar amount of loan}$$
$$\Sigma(X - \overline{X})^2 = \$42{,}000$$
$$b_0 = 7.5$$
$$b_1 = 0.120$$
$$\text{SSE} = 972$$
$$\text{d.f.} = n - 2 = 60 - 2 = 58$$

In performing the descriptive analysis, the loan officer might first test to see whether the slope coefficient is significantly different from zero.

$$t = \frac{b_1 - \beta_1}{S_{b_1}} = \frac{b_1 - \beta_1}{\sqrt{\dfrac{\text{SSE}/(n-2)}{\Sigma(X - \overline{X})^2}}}$$

$$= \frac{0.120 - 0}{\sqrt{\dfrac{972/58}{42{,}000}}}$$

$$= 6.007$$

For any reasonable level of alpha, $t = 6.007$ will exceed the critical value from the t table. Thus the loan officer can reject the hypothesis that the true regression slope is zero. Further, since the sign on the regression slope is positive, she can infer there is a positive linear relationship between the loan's term and size.

Also, the loan officer would no doubt be interested in developing a confidence interval estimate for the regression slope and interpreting this interval. This would be done by use of equation 13–22:

$$b_1 \pm t_{\alpha/2}S_{b1}$$

or, equivalently,

$$b_1 \pm t_{\alpha/2} \sqrt{\dfrac{\dfrac{\text{SSE}}{n-2}}{\Sigma(X-\overline{X})^2}} \qquad (13\text{--}22)$$

$$\text{d.f.} = n - 2$$

So, for a 95 percent confidence interval, she would arrive at

$$0.120 \pm 2.0 \sqrt{\dfrac{\dfrac{972}{58}}{42{,}000}}$$

$$0.120 \pm 2.0(0.0199)$$

$$0.120 \pm 0.0399$$

$$0.0801 \underline{\qquad} 0.1599$$

The loan officer would be quite confident that, if the amount of a loan is increased by one dollar, the term will be increased by an average of from 0.0801 to 0.1599 month.

There are many other situations where the prime purpose of regression analysis is description. Economists use regression analysis for descriptive purposes as they search for a means of explaining the economy. Market researchers also use regression analysis, among other techniques, in an effort to describe the factors that influence the demand for products.

Consider again the Madison Furniture Company example. The regression equation developed between the dependent variable, Y = sales and the independent variable, X = advertising, is

$$\hat{Y} = 16.143 + 5.801X$$

We would interpret the slope coefficient to mean that for a one-unit (one thousand dollars) increase in advertising, we would expect an average increase in sales of 5.801 units (5,801 dollars). However, the slope coefficient is a *point estimate* for the true regression slope. In section 13–4 we found that the potential variation in the value of the regression slope coefficient from sample to sample is measured by the *standard error of the slope*. This is

$$S_{b_1} = 1.6955$$

Then, to develop a 90 percent confidence interval estimate for the true regression slope, we use equation 13–22 as follows:

$$5.801 \pm 1.812 \,(1.6955)$$

$$5.801 \pm 3.072$$

$$2.729 \underline{\hspace{1cm}} 8.873$$

SKILL DEVELOPMENT PROBLEMS FOR SECTION 13–5

The following exercises are included to help you gain a firm understanding of the concepts presented in this section. There are further application problems at the end of the chapter which you should work to add to your understanding.

21. You are given the following results from computations pertaining to a simple linear regression application:

$$\hat{Y} = 5723.0 + 145X$$

$$n = 25$$

$$S_{b_1} = 10.80$$

   a. Based on the statistics supplied, can you conclude there is a significant linear relationship between X and Y? Test at the alpha = 0.05 level.
   b. Interpret the slope coefficient.
   c. Develop a 95 percent confidence interval estimate for the true regression slope and interpret the estimate.

22. The following data have been collected by an accountant who is performing an audit of paper products at a large office supply company. The dependent variable, Y, is the actual number of units counted by the accountant. The independent variable, X, is the number of units on the computer inventory record.

Y	23	100	242	56	178	10	94	200	44	128	180
X	24	120	228	56	190	13	85	190	32	120	230

   a. Develop a scatter plot for these data.
   b. Compute the regression model based upon the sample data. Compute also the standard error of the estimate. Test to determine whether the regression slope is significantly different from zero. Use an alpha = 0.05 level.
   c. Develop a 90 percent confidence interval estimate for the true regression slope and interpret this interval estimate.

23. The Wilson Manufacturing Company recently did a study of its customers. A random sample of $n = 50$ customer accounts was pulled from the computer records. Two variables were observed:

Y = the total dollar volume of business this year

X = miles customer is from corporate headquarters

The following statistics were computed:

$$\hat{Y} = 2140.23 - 10.12X$$
$$S_{b_1} = 3.12$$

a. Interpret the regression slope coefficient.

b. Develop a 95 percent confidence interval estimate for the true slope and interpret this interval.

24. The State Department of Transportation has conducted a study of 100 randomly selected vehicles in which they measured the speed of the vehicle and age of the driver. A regression model was developed, with vehicle speed as the dependent variable and age as the independent variable. The following results were obtained:

$$\hat{Y} = 56.78 + 0.124X$$
$$S_{b_1} = 2.88$$

a. Develop a 95 percent interval estimate for the true regression slope and interpret.

b. Based upon your response to part a, can you conclude that age and speed are linearly related? Discuss.

REGRESSION ANALYSIS FOR PREDICTION

13-6

One of the main uses of regression analysis is *prediction*. In the Madison Furniture Company example, Clint Brown wanted to predict sales by knowing advertising expenditures. Regression is used for predictive purposes in applications ranging from predicting demand to predicting production and output levels. For example, your state government may use regression to forecast annual tax revenues so that elected officials can establish state department budgets.

Using a regression model to predict the dependent variable is quite straightforward once the model has been found. The regression model for Madison Furniture Company sales is

$$\hat{Y} = 16.143 + 5.801X$$

where

$\hat{Y}$ = point estimate for the average sales in thousands of dollars, given X

X = level of advertising in thousands of dollars

To find $\hat{Y}$, the point estimate of expected sales, we substitute the specified advertising level into the regression model. For example, suppose Clint Brown learns that the company's marketing department has decided to spend $2,500 ($X = 2.5$) on advertising during the next quarter. Then the point estimate of sales, $\hat{Y}$, is

$$\hat{Y} = 16.143 + 5.801(2.5) = 30.6455$$
$$= \$30,645.50$$

Confidence Interval for the Average Y, Given X

In chapter 8, we stated that decision makers cannot be confident of the accuracy of any point estimate. In fact, the best they can hope for is that the point estimate is close to the true value being estimated.

In some cases only a point estimate of the expected value of the dependent variable is required. However, in many other cases the decision maker will want a *confidence interval estimate*. For example, Clint Brown might like a 95 percent confidence interval estimate for average sales, given that $2,500 is spent on advertising. The prediction interval for the expected value of a dependent variable, given a specific level of the independent variable, is determined by equation 13–23:

$$\hat{Y} \pm t_{\alpha/2} \sqrt{\frac{SSE}{n-2}} \sqrt{\frac{1}{n} + \frac{(X_p - \overline{X})^2}{\Sigma X^2 - \dfrac{(\Sigma X)^2}{n}}} \qquad (13\text{–}23)$$

where $\hat{Y}$ = point estimate of the dependent variable
  t = interval coefficient with $n - 2$ d.f.
  n = sample size
  X_p = value of the independent variable used to arrive at $\hat{Y}$
  $\overline{X}$ = mean of the independent variable observations in the sample

Thus, if X_p equals 2.5, we get

$$30.6455 \pm 2.228 \sqrt{\frac{497.556}{10}} \sqrt{\frac{1}{12} + \frac{(2.5 - 2.733)^2}{106 - \dfrac{(32.8)^2}{12}}}$$

$$30.6455 \pm 4.626$$

$$26.019 \underline{\hspace{2cm}} 35.271$$

Therefore Clint Brown can be 95 percent confident that the average sales for a $2,500 advertising expenditure will be between $26,019 and $35,271. He might use this information to help establish future budgeting policies and inventory levels.

Confidence Interval for a Single Y, Given X

The prediction interval just calculated is for the expected, or average, sales level, given a $2,500 advertising expenditure. Clint Brown would likely be more interested in predicting the actual sales next month if his company spends $2,500 on advertising. Developing the interval within which he can be 95 percent confident next month's sales will fall requires only a slight modification of equation 13–23. This predictive interval is given by equation 13–24:

$$\hat{Y} \pm t_{\alpha/2} \sqrt{\frac{\text{SSE}}{n-2}} \sqrt{1 + \frac{1}{n} + \frac{(X_p - \bar{X})^2}{\Sigma X^2 - \frac{(\Sigma X)^2}{n}}} \qquad (13\text{–}24)$$

For the Madison Furniture Company, the 95 percent confidence interval estimate for next month's sales, given that $2,500 is spent on advertising, is

$$30.6455 \pm 2.228 \sqrt{\frac{497.566}{10}} \sqrt{1 + \frac{1}{12} + \frac{(2.5 - 2.733)^2}{106 - \frac{(32.8)^2}{12}}}$$

$$30.6455 \pm 16.3820$$

$$14.2635 \underline{\quad\quad} 47.0275$$

Thus, Clint can be 95 percent confident that sales next month will be between $14,263.50 and $47.027.50 if his company spends $2,500 on advertising. As you can see, this estimate has extremely poor precision. Although the regression model explains

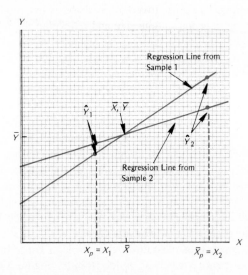

FIGURE 13–14
Regression lines, illustrating the increase in the potential variation in Y as X_p moves farther from $\bar{X}$

FIGURE 13–15
Confidence intervals for $Y|X_p$ and $\overline{Y}|X_p$

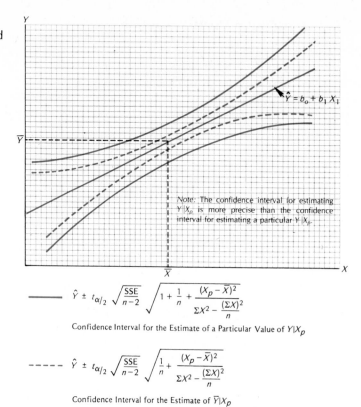

$$\underline{\qquad\qquad}\quad \hat{Y} \pm t_{\alpha/2} \sqrt{\frac{SSE}{n-2}} \sqrt{1 + \frac{1}{n} + \frac{(X_p - \overline{X})^2}{\Sigma X^2 - \frac{(\Sigma X)^2}{n}}}$$

Confidence Interval for the Estimate of a Particular Value of $Y|X_p$

$$----\quad \hat{Y} \pm t_{\alpha/2} \sqrt{\frac{SSE}{n-2}} \sqrt{\frac{1}{n} + \frac{(X_p - \overline{X})^2}{\Sigma X^2 - \frac{(\Sigma X)^2}{n}}}$$

Confidence Interval for the Estimate of $\overline{Y}|X_p$

a significant proportion of variation in the dependent variable, it is relatively imprecise for predictive purposes. To improve the precision, Clint might decrease his confidence requirements or increase the sample size and redevelop the model.

Note that the prediction interval for a single value of the dependent variable is wider (less precise) than the interval for predicting the average value of the dependent variable. This will always be the case, as seen in equations 13–23 and 13–24. From an intuitive viewpoint, we should expect to come closer to predicting an average value than a single value (for example, although the average weight of the U.S. population will not be above 250 pounds, many people weigh more than that).

Note that the term $(X_p - \overline{X})^2$ has a particular effect on the confidence interval determined by both equations 13–23 and 13–24. The farther X_p (the value of the independent variable used to predict Y) is from $\overline{X}$, the greater $(X_p - \overline{X})^2$. Figure 13–14 shows two regression lines developed from two samples with the same set of X values. We have made both lines pass through the same $(\overline{X}, \overline{Y})$ point; however, they have different slopes and intercepts. At $X_p = X_1$, the two regression lines give predictions of Y that are close to each other. However, for $X_p = X_2$, the predictions of Y are quite different. Thus, when X_p is close to $\overline{X}$, the problems caused by variations in regression slopes are not as great as when X_p is far from $\overline{X}$. Figure 13–15 shows the prediction intervals over the range of possible X_p values. The band around the estimated regression line bends away from the regression line as X_p moves in either direction from $\overline{X}$.

Things to Consider

Decision makers often use regression analysis as a predictive tool. When doing so, they should keep several important things in mind. One consideration is that the conclusions and inferences made from a regression line apply only over the range of data contained in the sample used to develop the regression line. For instance, in the Madison Furniture Company example, advertising expenditures ranged from 0.8 to 4.6. Therefore predictions for sales based on advertising expenditures between $800 and $4,600 are justified because the regression model was formed with data within that range. However, if Clint Brown attempts to predict sales with advertising levels outside the range of $800 to $4,600, he should understand that the relationship between advertising and sales may be different. Since no observations were taken outside the $800 to $4,600 range, he has no information about what might happen outside that range. For example, figure 13–16 shows a case where the true relationship between advertising and sales is not linear but curvilinear. If a linear regression line were used to predict sales based on advertising values beyond the relevant range of data, large overpredictions would result. Thus, the range of data in the sample, if at all possible, should cover the range of data in the population. If this can be done, decision makers are more apt to recognize the true relationship between the two variables and be able to develop the appropriate regression model.

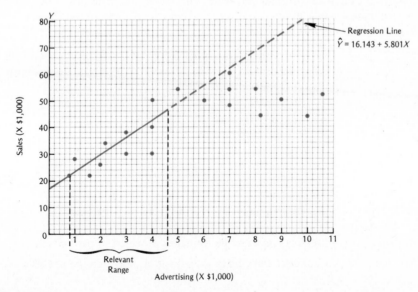

FIGURE 13–16
Problems with extrapolation in the least squares regression model, Madison Furniture Company example

A second important consideration, one that was discussed earlier, involves correlation and causation. The fact that a significant linear relationship exists between two variables does not imply that one variable causes the other. Although there may be a cause-and-effect relationship, decision makers should not infer such a relationship is present based only on regression and/or correlation analysis.

Decision makers should also recognize that a cause-and-effect relationship between two variables is not necessary for regression analysis to be used for prediction. What matters is that the regression model accurately reflects the relationship between the two variables and that the relationship remains stable.

Finally, many users of regression analysis mistakenly believe that a high coefficient of determination (R^2) guarantees that the regression model will be a good predictor. You should remember that R^2 measures the percentage of variation in the dependent variable explained by the independent variable. While the least squares criterion assures us that R^2 will be maximized, the R^2 applies only to the sample data used to develop the model. Thus R^2 measures the fit of the regression line to the sample data. There is no guarantee that there will be an equally good fit with new data. The only true test of a regression model's predictive ability is how well the model actually predicts.

SKILL DEVELOPMENT PROBLEMS FOR SECTION 13–6

The following exercises will help you better understand the materials presented in this section. Additional application problems are included at the end of the chapter.

25. You are given the following summary statistics from a regression analysis:

$$\hat{Y} = 200 + 150X$$
$$S_e = 25.25$$
$$\text{SSX} = \text{sum of squares } X = 99,645$$
$$n = 18$$
$$\overline{X} = 52.0$$

a. Determine the point estimate for estimating Y if $X_p = 48$ is used.

b. Provide a 95 percent prediction interval estimate for the average Y, given $X_p = 48$. Interpret this interval.

c. Provide a 95 percent prediction interval estimate for a particular Y, given $X_p = 48$. Interpret.

d. Discuss the difference between the estimates provided in parts b and c.

26. You are given the following summary statistics from a regression analysis:

$$\hat{Y} = 9784 - 345.50X$$
$$S_e = 800.25$$
$$\text{SSX} = \text{sum of squares } X = 145,789$$

$$\bar{X} = 67.20$$
$$n = 20$$

a. Determine the point estimate for estimating Y if $X_p = 48$ is used.
b. Provide a 90 percent prediction interval estimate for the average Y, given $X_p = 80$. Interpret this interval.
c. Provide a 90 percent prediction interval estimate for a particular Y, given $X_p = 80$. Interpret.
d. Discuss the difference between the estimates provided in parts b and c.

27. You are given the following summary statistics from a regression analysis:

$$\hat{Y} = 1200 + 0.878X$$
$$S_e = 145.40$$
$$SSX = \text{sum of squares } X = 134,679$$
$$\bar{X} = 40,000$$
$$n = 8$$

a. Determine the point estimate for estimating Y if $X_p = 48$ is used.
b. Provide a 95 percent prediction interval estimate for the average Y, given $X_p = 40,000$. Interpret this interval.
c. Provide a 95 percent prediction interval estimate for a particular Y, given $X_p = 40,000$. Interpret.
d. Discuss the difference between the estimates provided in parts b and c.
e. What would happen to the precision of the estimate if the value of X_p were increased to 43,000? Discuss.

28. The following data have been collected by an accountant who is performing an audit of account balances for a major retail company. The population from which the data were collected represented those accounts for which the customer had indicated the balance was incorrect. The dependent variable, Y, is the actual account balance as verified by the accountant. The independent variable, X, is the computer account balance.

Y	233	10	24	56	78	102	90	200	344	120	18
X	245	12	22	56	90	103	85	190	320	120	23

a. Prepare a regression analysis where Y is the dependent variable and X is the independent variable. Show the following results:
   ▪ Regression equation
   ▪ SSX
   ▪ S_e
b. Determine the point estimate for Y, given $X_p = 100$.
c. Develop a 95 percent prediction interval estimate for the average value of Y, given $X_p = 100$. Interpret.
d. Develop a 95 percent prediction interval estimate for the particular value of Y, given $X_p = 100$. Interpret.

REGRESSION ANALYSIS FOR CURVILINEAR
RELATIONSHIPS (OPTIONAL)

13-7

Section 13–1 showed that there are a variety of ways in which two variables can be related. Correlation and regression analysis techniques are tools for modeling linear relationships between variables. Many situations in business have linear relationships between two variables, and regression equations that model that relationship will be appropriate to use in these situations.

However, there are also many instances where the relationship between two variables will be curvilinear rather than linear. For instance, demand for electricity has grown at an almost exponential rate relative to the population growth in some areas. Advertisers believe that a diminishing-returns relationship will occur between sales and advertising if advertising is allowed to grow too large. These two situations are shown in figures 13–17 and 13–18, respectively. They represent just two of a great many possible curvilinear relationships that could exist between two variables.

This section shows how linear regression analysis can be used in dealing with curvilinear relationships. The following examples illustrate two of the most common instances where curvilinear relationships can be used in decision making, and they should give you an idea of how to approach similar situations.

The Beemon Brothers Manufacturing Company makes camper trailers. Recently the cost accounting department for Beemon Brothers did a study of overtime hours and production output. A sample of data from ten months of production was selected and

FIGURE 13–17
Exponential relationship, increased demand for electricity versus population growth

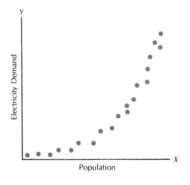

FIGURE 13–18
Diminishing returns relationship, advertising versus sales

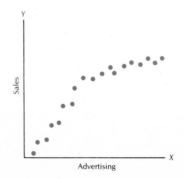

Period	Production (units) X	Overtime (hours) Y
1	200	25
2	500	25
3	1,000	75
4	1,300	175
5	1,300	200
6	800	75
7	200	50
8	1,400	225
9	600	75
10	1,100	125
11	900	75
12	900	75
13	1,200	175
14	400	50
15	300	50
16	1,600	250
17	1,100	250
18	1,200	150
19	700	50
20	1,000	100

TABLE 13–9
Production and overtime data, Beemon Brothers Manufacturing example

personnel records were checked to determine the number of overtime hours in each of the months. The data are shown in table 13–9.

Figure 13–19 presents a scatter plot of the data with the dependent variable, overtime hours, on the vertical axis and the independent variable, production units, on the horizontal axis. At first glance it appears that there is a fairly strong linear relationship between the two variables. We have employed a computer and regression analysis soft-

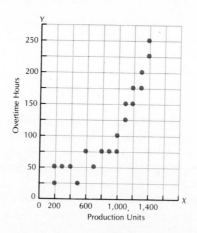

FIGURE 13–19
Scatter plot–overtime hours versus production units, Beemon Brothers Manufacturing example

```
*****************************************************

REGRESSION EQUATION

    VARIABLE        B        ST. ERROR B    T VALUE

    X             .15260      .01858        8.20

 - - - - - - - - - - - - - - - - - - - - - - - - - - - -

 INTERCEPT    -24.78

 - - - - - - - - - - - - - - - - - - - - - - - - - - - -

 CORRELATION COEFFICIENT        .888

 R SQUARE                       .789

 STANDARD ERROR OF ESTIMATE     32.06

*****************************************************
```

ware to analyze the linear relationship between overtime hours and production volume. Table 13–10 presents a summary of the computer output.

We see in table 13–10 that the correlation between the two variables is 0.888 ($r = 0.888$). Recall that the correlation coefficient measures the strength of the linear relationship between two variables. The test to determine if the correlation is significant is the t test, as follows:

$$t = \frac{r}{\sqrt{\frac{1 - r^2}{n - 2}}}$$

$$= \frac{0.888}{\sqrt{\frac{1 - 0.789}{18}}}$$

$$= 8.20$$

With 18 degrees of freedom, the critical t value from the t distribution with an alpha level of 0.05 is 2.101. Since 8.20 is greater than 2.101, we conclude that there is a significant linear relationship between the two variables.

Table 13–10 also shows that the regression equation is

$$\hat{Y} = -24.78 + 0.1526X$$

Figure 13–20 shows the linear regression equation plotted along with the sample data. The line appears to fit the data. However, a close inspection indicates that there seem to be instances where several consecutive points lie above or below the line instead of having the points randomly dispersed around the regression line as we would expect given the regression analysis assumptions.

This indicates that the relationship between the two variables could probably be better modeled as a curvilinear relationship than a linear one. It appears from looking

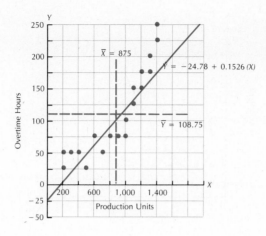

FIGURE 13–20
Plot of linear regression line, Beemon Brothers Manufacturing example

at the scatter plots in figures 13–19 and 13–20 that there is an exponential relationship between overtime hours and production output; that is, as production increases, overtime is increasing at an exponential rate.

One approach to analyzing curvilinear relationships is to *transform* either the independent variable or the dependent variable to make the relationship between the two variables appear linear rather than curvilinear. For instance, in the Beemon Brothers Manufacturing example we might transform the X variable from X to X^2 and run a regression analysis with Y and X^2, using the procedures outlined in this chapter.

Table 13–11 shows the regression results from the computer analysis of Y and X^2. In comparing the results in table 13–11 with the results in table 13–10, it is clear that this transformation has resulted in an improved model. The correlation has increased from 0.888 to 0.951, and the standard error of the estimate has decreased from 32.06 to 21.55; R^2 has likewise increased from 0.789 to 0.905. All of these differences imply

```
**************************************************
REGRESSION EQUATION

    VARIABLE       B       ST. ERROR B     T VALUE

    X SQUARE     .0001     .000007649      13.09

- - - - - - - - - - - - - - - - - - - - - - - - - - -

INTERCEPT    17.224

- - - - - - - - - - - - - - - - - - - - - - - - - - -

CORRELATION COEFFICIENT      .9513

R SQUARE                     .905

STANDARD ERROR OF ESTIMATE   21.55

**************************************************
```

TABLE 13–11
Regression results using X^2, Beemon Brothers Manufacturing example

FIGURE 13–21

Plot of regression curve, Beemon Brothers Manufacturing example

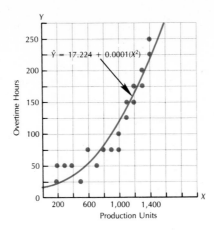

that the second regression results are superior to our initial attempt with Y and X. The new regression equation is:

$$\hat{Y} = 17.224 + 0.0001X^2$$

Figure 13–21 shows the plot of this regression equation against the original (X, Y) data. Note that the regression equation is a curve that appears to fit the data more closely than the straight line in figure 13–20. The higher R^2 value supports this observation.

Thus, in the Beemon Brothers Manufacturing example, the linear regression between overtime hours and production level is improved by transforming the X variable into X^2 and doing the regression analysis again. The improvement occurs because the relationship between the two variables is better represented by a curvilinear relationship than by a linear relationship.

However, squaring the independent variable is not the only type of transformation which may be appropriate. The required transformation depends on the relationship between the two variables. Consider the Electro-Ram Software firm located in Orem, Utah. It produces computer software for both microcomputers and mainframes. Table 13–12 gives collected data showing sales volumes in units for a particular software package and the number of advertisements appearing in national publications for it. In each instance the data represent a month's activity.

Figure 13–22 shows the scatter plot of the data and the least squares linear regression line. Table 13–13 shows a summary of the regression results that were computed using a computer and regression software. These results indicate that a significant linear relationship exists between the two variables and that a significant linear regression model can be developed. The model explains 86.8 percent of the variation in sales.

Although the linear regression results are significant, a close look at figure 13–22 illustrates the same problem we saw earlier with the Beemon Brothers example. The points do not appear to be randomly scattered around the regression line. The relationship between sales and advertising might be better modeled as a curvilinear relationship showing the diminishing returns that seem to take place as advertising is increased to large levels.

TABLE 13–12

Number of Advertisements X	Sales in Units Y
25	2,500
50	3,750
50	5,000
75	7,500
75	10,000
100	12,500
100	15,000
150	17,500
150	20,000
175	20,000
200	22,500
225	23,700
250	22,500
250	25,000
275	25,000
300	22,500
300	27,500
350	25,000
350	27,500

Sales and Advertising Data, Elec-tro-Ram Software Example

This calls for a transformation of the independent variable to account for the cur-vilinear relationship. The appropriate transformation is to take the square root of X and regress these new data against the Y values. Table 13–14 shows the results of the com-puter calculations. If you compare the output in table 13–13 with that shown in table 13–14, you will see that the transformation improved the regression results. R^2 has been

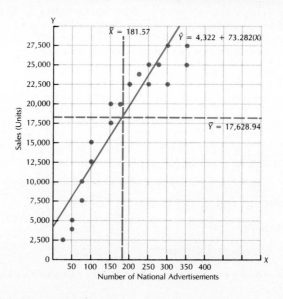

FIGURE 13–22

Plot of regression line (linear), Electro-Ram Software example

TABLE 13–13
Linear regression computer output, Electro-Ram Software example

```
***************************************************
REGRESSION EQUATION

    VARIABLE        B        ST. ERROR B     T VALUE
      X           73.282       6.943          10.56
-------------------------------------------
INTERCEPT    4322.0
-------------------------------------------
CORRELATION COEFFICIENT        .9316
R SQUARE                       .868
STANDARD ERROR OF ESTIMATE     3123
***************************************************
```

increased from 86.8 percent to 93.3 percent. The standard error of the estimate has decreased from 3,123 to 2,224.

The improvements brought about by the transformations are reflected in the graph of the regression equation against the original data shown in figure 13–23. Note that the graph of the equation using the square root of X is a curve which more accutely reflects the relationship between the two variables.

The preceding examples are just two of many possible transformations which

TABLE 13–14
Regression analysis computer output (square root of X), Electro-Ram Software example

```
***************************************************
REGRESSION EQUATION

    VARIABLE         B        ST. ERROR B     T VALUE
    SQ. ROOT X     1890.0       123.0          15.37
----------------------------    --------------
INTERCEPT    -6602
-------------------------------------------
CORRELATION COEFFICIENT      .9659
R SQUARE                     .933
ST. ERROR OF ESTIMATE        2224
***************************************************
```

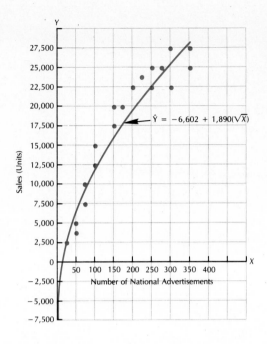

FIGURE 13–23
Plot of regression line (curvilinear), Electro-Ram Software example

might prove useful depending on the particular curvilinear relationship between the two variables of interest. As you encounter different situations in which there appears to be a curvilinear relationship between the two variables, you will need to try different transformations to determine which is the most appropriate for the situation you are modeling.

The application problems for section 13–7 at the end of the chapter will help you better understand how to deal with curvilinear relationships.

COMPUTER APPLICATIONS

13-8

This chapter has introduced simple linear regression analysis. We manually worked through an example to show how the regression model was developed and how various statistics were computed. Although regression analysis can be performed by hand, using a computer and appropriate statistical software is obviously preferred. In this section, we provide several computer applications based on the KIVZ-Channel 5 data presented in table 2–10. As in previous chapters, we will use the MINITAB and SPSS-X software packages.

Figure 13–24 shows the SPSS-X output produced when the SCATTERGRAM command is used with INCOME as the dependent variable and YEARS IN THE STATE as the independent variable. Both a scatter plot and regression results are shown.

The scatter plot shows little relationship between the two variables. This is confirmed by the regression output at the bottom of figure 13–24, which shows a correlation of 0.02202 and a R^2 value of 0.00045. The regression line itself has an intercept of

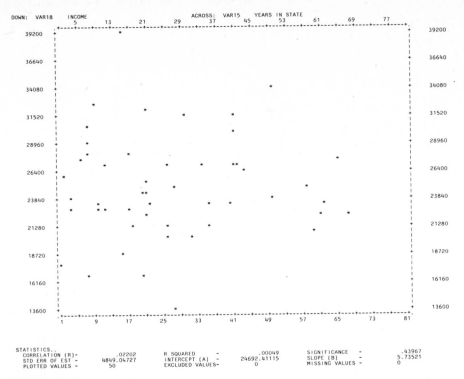

STATISTICS..
CORRELATION (R)-   .02202   R SQUARED   -   .00049   SIGNIFICANCE -   .43967
STD ERR OF EST - 4849.04727   INTERCEPT (A) - 24692.41115   SLOPE (B)   -   5.73521
PLOTTED VALUES -   50   EXCLUDED VALUES-   0   MISSING VALUES -   0

FIGURE 13–24
SPSS-X output—scatter plot and regression

TABLE 13–15
MINITAB output—regression analysis

```
The regression equation is
INCOME = 26233 - 31.5 AGE

Predictor        Coef      Stdev      t-ratio
Constant        26233      2074        12.65
AGE            -31.47      44.44       -0.71

s = 4825     R-sq = 1.0%     R-sq(adj) = 0.0%

Analysis of Variance

SOURCE         DF            SS            MS
Regression      1      11673632      11673632
Error          48    1117510400      23281468
Total          49    1129184000

Unusual Observations
Obs.      AGE     INCOME        Fit     Stdev.Fit     Residual     St.Resid
  8      58.0      13600      24407          922       -10807       -2.28R
 11      81.0      31600      23683         1778         7917        1.76 X
 18      45.0      39200      24816          684        14384        3.01R

R denotes an obs. with a large st. resid.
X denotes an obs. whose X value gives it large influence.
```

```
UNNUMBERED
TITLE DESCRIPTIVE STATISTICS EXAMPLES
FILE HANDLE KIVZ NAME='KIVZ DATA C'
DATA LIST FILE=KIVZ LIST/VAR01 TO VAR19
VARIABLE LABELS
    VAR01 'NATIONAL NEWS STATION'
    VAR02 'LOCAL NEWS STATION'
    VAR03 'NEWS RATING'
    VAR04 'SPORTS RATING'
    VAR05 'WEATHER RATING'
    VAR06 'ANCHOR RATING'
    VAR07 'SPORTSCASTER RATING'
    VAR08 'OVERALL RATING'
    VAR09 'NATIONAL INFLUENCE'
    VAR10 'SEX'
    VAR11 'MARITAL STATUS'
    VAR12 'NUMBER EMPLOYED'
    VAR13 'HOME STATUS '
    VAR14 'YEARS AT RESIDENCE'
    VAR15 'YEARS IN STATE'
    VAR16 'EDUCATION'
    VAR17 'AGE'
    VAR18 'INCOME'
    VAR19 'HOURS OF TV'
VALUE LABELS
    VAR01 1 'CHANNEL 5' 2 'CHANNEL 3' 3 'CHANNEL 8' 4
          'UNDECIDED'/
    VAR02 1 'CHANNEL 3' 2 'CHANNEL 8' 3 'CHANNEL 5' 4
          'UNDECIDED'/
    VAR03 TO VAR08 1 'POOR' 2 'FAIR' 3 'GOOD' 4 'VERY GOOD' 5
          'EXCEL'/
    VAR09 1 'TRUE' 2 'FALSE' 3 'UNDECIDED'/
    VAR10 1 'MALE' 2 'FEMALE'/
    VAR11 1 'SINGLE' 2 'DIVORCED' 3 'MARRIED' 4 'OTHER'/
    VAR13 1 'RENTING' 2 'BUYING'/
    VAR16 1 'GRADE SCHOOL' 2 'SOME COLLEGE' 3 'VOTECH' 4 'HIGH
          SCHOOL'
SCATTERGRAM VAR18 VAR15
OPTIONS 4 7
STATISTICS ALL
```

FIGURE 13–25

SPSS-X commands—scattergram

24692.41115 and a slope of 5.73521. The stated significance of 0.43967 means the regression model would be significant if alpha were this value or greater. Figure 13–25 shows the SPSS-X commands that produced the output in figure 13–24.

Table 13–15 shows the MINITAB regression results when INCOME is used as the dependent variable and AGE is the independent variable.

The regression line, with an intercept of 26233 and a slope of -31.5, explains only 1 percent of the variation in the dependent variable. This can be seen by looking at either the R square value or the sum of squares column in the analysis of variance table. Figure 13–26 shows the MINITAB commands necessary to produce this output.

```
MTB> READ 'KIVZ5' into C1-C19
MTB> NAME C17 'AGE'
MTB> NAME C18 'INCOME'
MTB> OUTFILE = 'PRINTER'
MTB> REGRESS C18 1 C17
```

FIGURE 13–26

MINITAB commands—regression analysis

If you have access to a statistical package, you can do many of the homework problems in this chapter on the computer. This frees you from the computational burden and allows you to focus on interpretation of results. We suggest that you prepare a short report that fully describes the output in figure 13–24 and table 13–15.

CONCLUSIONS

13-9 This chapter has introduced the fundamental concepts of simple linear regression and correlation analysis. The techniques of regression and correlation analysis are widely used in business decision making and data analysis. Regression analysis can be applied as a tool for prediction, description, and control within an organization.

Correlation measures the strength of the linear relationship between two variables. The closer the correlation coefficient is to ± 1.0, the stronger the linear relationship between the two variables. When a dependent and an independent variable are highly correlated, the resulting simple linear regression model will tend to explain a substantial proportion of the variation in the dependent variable.

A wide variety of statistical tests has been presented in this chapter. As indicated, many of these tests are equivalent. This chapter has limited discussion to the simple regression model. The next chapter introduces multiple regression analysis (more than one independent variable).

CHAPTER GLOSSARY

coefficient of determination   The square of the correlation coefficient. A measure of the percentage of variation in the dependent variable explained by the independent variable in the regression model.

correlation coefficient   A quantitative measure of the linear relationship between two variables. The correlation ranges from $+1.0$ to -1.0. A correlation of ± 1.0 indicates a perfect linear relationship, whereas a correlation of zero indicates no linear relationship.

dependent variable   The variable to be predicted or explained in a regression model. This variable is assumed to be functionally related to the independent variable.

independent variable   A variable related to a dependent variable in a regression equation. The independent variable is used in a regression model to estimate the value of the dependent variable.

least squares criterion   The criterion for determining a regression line that minimizes the sum of squared residuals.

regression coefficients   In the simple regression model there are two coefficients; the intercept and the slope.

regression slope coefficient   The average change in the dependent variable for a unit change in the independent variable. The slope coefficient may be positive or negative depending on the relationship between the two variables.

residual The difference between the actual value of the dependent variable and the value predicted by the regression model.

scatter plot A two-dimensional plot showing the (X, Y) value for each observation. The scatter plot is used as a picture of the relationship between two variables.

simple regression analysis A regression model that uses one independent variable to explain the variation in the dependent variable. The model takes the form

$$Y_i = \beta_0 + \beta_1 X_i + e_i$$

spurious correlation Correlation between two variables that have no known cause-and-effect connection.

standard error of the estimate A measure of the dispersion of the actual Y values around the regression line.

CHAPTER FORMULAS

Correlation coefficient

$$r = \frac{n\Sigma XY - \Sigma X \Sigma Y}{\sqrt{[n(\Sigma X^2) - (\Sigma X)^2][n(\Sigma Y^2) - (\Sigma Y)^2]}}$$

Test statistic for significance of the correlation coefficient

$$t = \frac{r}{\sqrt{\dfrac{1 - r^2}{n - 2}}}$$

Coefficient of determination

$$R^2 = \frac{\text{SSR}}{\text{TSS}} = 1 - \frac{\text{SSE}}{\text{TSS}}$$

Least squares estimate of the regression slope coefficient

$$b_1 = \frac{\Sigma XY - \dfrac{\Sigma X \Sigma Y}{n}}{\Sigma X^2 - \dfrac{(\Sigma X)^2}{n}} = \frac{\Sigma(X - \bar{X})(Y - \bar{Y})}{\Sigma(X - \bar{X})^2}$$

Least squares estimate of the regression intercept coefficient

$$b_0 = \bar{Y} - b_1 \bar{X}$$

Standard error of the slope coefficient

$$S_{b1} = \frac{S_e}{\sqrt{\Sigma(X - \bar{X})^2}}$$

Standard error of the estimate

$$S_e = \sqrt{\frac{SSE}{n-2}}$$

Sum of squares error

$$SSE = \sum_{i=1}^{n}(Y_i - \hat{Y}_i)^2$$

Total sum of squares

$$TSS = \sum_{i=1}^{n}(Y_i - \bar{Y})^2$$

Test statistic for significance of the slope coefficient

$$t = \frac{b_1 - \beta_1}{S_{b1}}$$

Test statistic for significance of the simple regression model

$$F = \frac{\dfrac{SSR}{1}}{\dfrac{SSE}{n-2}}$$

Prediction interval for average Y, given X_p

$$\hat{Y} \pm t_{\alpha/2}\sqrt{\frac{SSE}{n-2}}\sqrt{\frac{1}{n} + \frac{(X_p - \bar{X})^2}{\Sigma X^2 - \dfrac{(\Sigma X)^2}{n}}}$$

Prediction interval for a particular Y, given X_p

$$\hat{Y} \pm t_{\alpha/2}\sqrt{\frac{SSE}{n-2}}\sqrt{1 + \frac{1}{n} + \frac{(X_p - \bar{X})^2}{\Sigma X^2 - \dfrac{(\Sigma X)^2}{n}}}$$

TECHNICAL APPENDIX

Derivation of Least Squares Equations
Objective:

$$\min \Sigma(Y_i - \hat{Y}_i)^2$$

where

$$\hat{Y}_i = b_0 + b_1 (X_i)$$

Thus the objective is

$$\min\Sigma[Y_i - (b_0 + b_1 X_i)]^2$$

Then let

$$Q = \Sigma [Y_i - (b_0 + b_1 X_i)]^2$$

Then to minimize Q, we take partial derivatives with respect to b_0 and b_1 as follows:

$$\delta Q/\delta b_0 = -2\Sigma [Y_i - b_0 - b_1 X_i]$$

and

$$\delta Q/\delta b_1 = -2\Sigma X_i [Y_i - b_0 - b_1 X_i]$$

Then to determine b_0 and b_1 such that Q is minimized, we set the derivatives equal to zero and formulate them as a system of two equations and two unknowns as follows:

$$-2\Sigma(Y_i - b_0 - b_1 X_i) = 0$$
$$-2\Sigma X_i(Y_i - b_0 - b_1 X_i) = 0$$

Reformulating these equations, the -2 values cancel and we get

$$\Sigma Y_i - nb_0 - b_1\Sigma X_i = 0$$
$$\Sigma X_i Y_i - b_0\Sigma X_i - b_1\Sigma X_i^2 = 0$$

Then

$$\Sigma Y_i = nb_0 + b_1\Sigma X_i$$
$$\Sigma X_i Y_i = b_0\Sigma X_i + b_1\Sigma X_i^2$$

Solving for b_0 and b_1 we get

$$b_1 = \frac{\Sigma X_i Y_i - \dfrac{\Sigma X_i \,\Sigma Y_i}{n}}{\Sigma X_1^2 - \dfrac{(\Sigma X_i)^2}{n}} = \frac{\Sigma(X_i - \overline{X})(Y_i - \overline{Y})}{\Sigma(X_i - \overline{X})^2}$$

$$b_0 = \overline{Y} - b_1\overline{X}$$

SOLVED PROBLEMS

1. The Cal-Pit Water Company, located in Pittsburg, California, has selected a random sample of fifteen customers to see if it can develop a model for predicting water

usage. Because of the short supply of water in the area, predicting water usage is an important part of the company's planning activities.

The company wants to see whether a simple linear regression model with family size as the independent variable, and water used as the dependent variable, can be a valid predictive tool. The data based on the past month's water usage are

Customer	Water Used (gals) Y	Family Size X
1	1,100	3
2	1,425	5
3	785	2
4	950	3
5	1,200	4
6	1,152	4
7	973	3
8	1,525	5
9	1,600	4
10	700	3
11	1,100	5
12	1,414	4
13	700	2
14	953	2
15	1,063	2

Solution:

The first step is to develop the scatter plot.

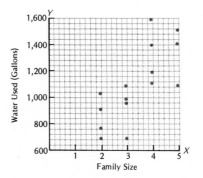

Although not perfect, there does appear to be a positive linear relationship between water used and family size. The next step is to calculate the correlation coefficient, r. Recall that r is a measure of the strength of the linear relationship between two variables and is calculated with the following equation:

$$r = \frac{n\Sigma XY - \Sigma X \Sigma Y}{\sqrt{[n(\Sigma X^2) - (\Sigma X)^2][n(\Sigma Y^2) - (\Sigma Y)^2]}}$$

Instead of calculating this value by hand, a computer was used, and the resulting printout is

```
*****************************************************************
VARIABLE SELECTED IS......X
SUM OF SQUARES REDUCED IN THIS STEP............622130
R-SQUARE..................................551986
CORRELATION COEFFICIENT...................742958
F FOR ANALYSIS OF VARIANCE (D.F. = 1, 13)........16.1069
STANDARD ERROR OF ESTIMATE...........197.084
VARIABLE     REG. COEFF.     STD. ERR.-COEFF.     COMPUTED T
X            188.011            46.978                4.00212
INTERCEPT 470.094
*****************************************************************
```

The correlation coefficient in this computer output is $r = 0.743$. The test of significance is

$$H_0: \rho = 0$$

$$H_A: \rho \neq 0$$

$$\alpha = 0.05$$

$$t = \frac{r}{\sqrt{\dfrac{1 - r^2}{n - 2}}} = \frac{0.743}{\sqrt{\dfrac{1 - (0.743)^2}{13}}}$$

$$= 4.002$$

The critical t for an alpha level of 0.05 and 13 degrees of freedom is 2.160, and, since 4.002 is greater than 2.160, we conclude that there is a significant linear relationship between the two variables.

The next step is to calculate the regression coefficients. This was also done by the computer. The estimates are

$$\hat{Y} = 470.094 + 188.011X$$

The standard error of the estimate is 197.084. The table of residuals printed by the computer program is

OBS. NO.	Y OBSERVED	Y ESTIMATED	RESIDUAL
1	1100	1034.13	65.8713
2	1425	1410.15	14.8486
3	785	846.117	-61.1173
4	950	1034.13	-84.1287
5	1200	1222.14	-22.1401
6	1152	1222.14	-70.1401
7	973	1034.13	-61.1287
8	1525	1410.15	114.849
9	1600	1222.14	377.860
10	700	1034.13	-334.129
11	1100	1410.15	-310.151
12	1412	1222.14	191.860
13	700	846.117	-146.117
14	953	846.117	106.883
15	1063	846.117	216.883

Although our test of significance has indicated that family size has a positive linear relationship to water usage, note that family size explained only 55 percent of the variation in water usage for the sample data. Also, the standard error of the estimate, 197.084, is quite large, indicating that any prediction interval developed will be imprecise.

2. Referring to solved problem 1, suppose a family of five is going to be added to the Cal-Pit Water Company's customer list. Using the regression model developed in problem 1, determine the 90 percent confidence interval for the number of gallons of water this family will use.

Solution:

The desired prediction interval format is

$$\hat{Y} \pm t_{\alpha/2} \sqrt{\frac{SSE}{n-2}} \sqrt{1 + \frac{1}{n} + \frac{(X_p - \bar{X})^2}{\Sigma X^2 - \frac{(\Sigma X)^2}{n}}}$$

To obtain the value of $\hat{Y}$, we substitute 5 for X in the regression model.

$$\hat{Y} = 470.097 + 188.011(5)$$
$$= 1,410.152$$

Thus the point estimate of water used by this family of five is roughly 1,410 gallons.

To determine the confidence interval, you should recall that $\sqrt{SSE/(n-2)}$ is the standard error of the estimate. This value is 197.084, and appeared on the computer printout shown earlier. Thus we have

$$1,410 \pm 1.771(197.084) \sqrt{1 + \frac{1}{15} + \frac{(X_p - \bar{X})^2}{\Sigma X^2 - \frac{(\Sigma X)^2}{n}}}$$

Our next step is to complete the calculations under the square root.

Family Size X	X^2	Family Size X	X^2
3	9	4	16
5	25	3	9
2	4	5	25
3	9	4	16
4	16	2	4
4	16	2	4
3	9	2	4
5	25	$\Sigma = 51$	$\Sigma = 191$

Then

$$\overline{X} = \frac{51}{15}$$

$$= 3.4$$

Thus the 90 percent prediction interval given $X_p = 5$ is

$$1,410 \pm 1.771(197.084) \sqrt{1 + \frac{1}{15} + \frac{(5 - 3.4)^2}{191 - \frac{2,601}{15}}}$$

$$1,410 \pm 384.28$$

$$1,025.72 \text{ gal} \underline{\hspace{1cm}} 1,794.28 \text{ gal}$$

The Cal-Pit Water Company can be confident that this family of five will use between 1,026 and 1,794 gallons of water per month. Although this might be helpful information, the precision of the estimate is poor.

ADDITIONAL PROBLEMS

Section 13–1

29. The Farmington City Council recently commissioned a study of the park users. Data were collected on the age of the person surveyed and the number of times he or she has been to the park in the past month. The following data were collected:

Park Visits Y	Age X
7	16
3	15
6	28
5	16
1	29
2	38
4	48
8	18
4	24
5	33
1	56

Develop a scatter plot for these data and discuss what, if any, relationship appears to be present between the two variables.

30. A marketing research study performed by the marketing division of the Klondike Company surveyed the income levels and expenditures on recreation for a sample of twenty people. Measurements recorded for Y were the expenditures on recreation during the previous year and X equaled the total family income.

Y	X	Y	X
$1,425	$21,300	900	17,600
1,675	30,200	1,000	16,890
1,356	31,500	2,450	28,000
4,530	45,900	650	14,300
3,200	34,600	300	9,800
1,060	17,800	1,500	24,700
4,090	53,600	890	20,500
1,200	17,400	2,300	31,700
1,800	26,800	3,100	47,800
700	15,700	100	8,400

Develop a scatter plot for these data and discuss what, if any, relationship between the variables appears to exist based on the scatter plot.

31. Think of two variables that you believe would be negatively related in a somewhat linear manner. Describe what is meant by a negative linear relationship.

32. The Harris Corporation has recently done a study of homes that have sold in the Detroit area within the past eighteen months. Data were recorded for the asking price and the number of weeks the home was on the market before it sold. The following data were collected:

Weeks on the Market Y	Asking Price X
23	$ 76,500
48	102,000
9	53,000
26	84,200
20	73,000
40	125,000
51	109,000
18	60,000
25	87,000
62	94,000
33	76,000
11	90,000
15	61,000
26	86,000
27	70,000
56	133,000
12	93,000

Develop a scatter plot for these data and indicate what, if any, relationship exists between the variables based on your analysis of the scatter plot.

33. The Savemore Brokerage Firm of Spokane, Washington, recently studied a random sample of companies whose stock is sold on the New York Stock Exchange. Among other things, it collected data on stock price, Y, and previous years's profits, X. The following data were collected. (The X variable is measured in thousands of dollars.)

Y	X	Y	X
$18.70	$ 40,000	12.60	12,500
34.50	24,900	43.60	9,000
25.70	102,000	33.50	23,900
8.90	44,000	71.80	15,000
25.90	123,700	15.00	45,000
11.11	36,900	6.78	99,500
21.00	3,700	21.70	45,300
3.50	145,900	44.70	23,600

Develop a scatter plot for these data and discuss what, if any, relationship appears to exist between the two variables. Also comment on what other factors might be important to consider when studying stock price and earnings of the company.

34. A national retail chain is experimenting with methods to increase sales of its house brand of cosmetics. A local store has been asked to help determine whether sales level is related to shelf space allocated to the house brand. The shelf space is randomly varied over the next ten weeks, and sales levels are recorded. The following data points are found:

Sales	Shelf Length
$ 868	4 ft
697	3
1,125	6
970	5
742	3
1,035	5
1,203	6
967	5
853	4
730	3

Plot these values as a scatter plot. Analyze your graph.

Section 13–2

35. Referring to problem 29, compute the correlation between age and the number of visits to the park. Write a letter to the Farmington City Council explaining what the correlation measures. Test to determine if the true correlation might actually equal zero. Use an alpha level of 0.10. Discuss.

36. One statistics student was recently working on a class project that required him to compute a correlation coefficient for two variables. After careful work he arrived at a correlation coefficient of 2.45. Interpret this correlation coefficient for the student who did the calculations.

37. Referring to problem 36, another student in the same class computed the correlation between the two variables to be -0.45 ($r = -0.45$). After trying several times and always coming up with the same result, she felt that she must be doing something wrong since the value was negative and she knew that this couldn't be right. Comment on this student's conclusion.

38. Refer to problem 30 and compute the correlation coefficient for the two variables *income* and *dollars spent on recreation*. Test to determine whether the true correlation is different from zero, using an alpha level of 0.05.

39. The Penrose Consulting Company performs studies for universities that want to raise money through their alumni associations. As part of its work, it recently sampled eighteen universities across the United States and determined the number of alumni and the total dollars in gifts received from alumni during the previous academic year. The following data were recorded:

School	Number of Alumni X	Gift Money Y
1	987	$ 234,700
2	1,350	769,000
3	2,345	1,230,000
4	1,300	450,780
5	12,569	6,450,000
6	8,560	2,650,000
7	3,450	1,430,000
8	1,890	230,000
9	23,456	4,560,000
10	12,700	2,678,900
11	4,600	800,000
12	5,700	2,780,000
13	23,600	7,000,000
14	33,450	8,900,000
15	28,900	8,600,000
16	1,800	133,000
17	12,800	5,790,000
18	20,540	2,400,300

a. Develop a scatter plot of these two variables. Based on this plot only, does it appear that a linear relationship exists between the two variables?
b. Compute the correlation coefficient and discuss what it measures.
c. Test to determine whether the population correlation coefficient is actually zero, using an alpha level of 0.05.

40. Refer to problem 32 and compute the correlation coefficient for number of weeks the house has been on the market and the asking price of the house. Test at an alpha level of 0.10 to determine whether the sample data support or refute the null hypothesis that states that the true correlation is zero. Discuss your results.

41. A company that makes a cattle feed supplement has studied 335 cattle and found the correlation between the amount of supplement fed and the daily weight gain to be 0.104 ($r = 0.104$). Based on these results, what should be concluded about the true correlation between these two variables? Test using an alpha level of 0.05. Comment on the results.

42. The Smithfield Tobacco Company recently studied a random sample of thirty of its distributors and found the correlation between sales and advertising dollars to be 0.67. Can it conclude that there is a significant linear relationship between sales and advertising? If so, is it fair to conclude that advertising causes sales to increase?

43. If we select a random sample of data for two variables and, after computing the correlation coefficient, conclude that the two variables may have zero correlation, can we say that there is no relationship between the two variables? Discuss.

44. The Grinfield Service Company marketing director is interested in analyzing the relationship between her company's sales and the advertising dollars spent. In the course of her analysis she selected a random sample of twenty weeks and recorded the sales for each week and the amount spent on advertising. These data are shown as follows:

Sales	Advertising	Sales	Advertising
$2,050	$180	3,250	300
3,760	243	4,680	402
1,897	204	4,200	399
2,567	199	2,400	209
4,330	356	1,890	245
5,670	605	3,600	190
2,356	200	5,700	480
3,456	304	5,690	515
1,254	105	2,300	300
4,300	379	1,700	145

    a. Identify the independent and dependent variables.

    b. Develop a scatter plot with the dependent variable on the vertical axis and the independent variable on the horizontal axis.

    c. Compute the correlation coefficient for these two variables and test to determine whether the true population correlation is different from zero at the alpha level of 0.05.

    d. Develop the least squares regression equation for these variables. Plot the regression line on the scatter plot.

45. A regional farm equipment distributor has experienced great variability in yearly sales. Conventional industry wisdom states this variability is caused by the variability in farm family income. The distributor wants to know if this explanation applies to his sales. He has gathered data on his sales and farm family income since 1977. Note in the following that the income variables have also been expressed in 1977 constant dollars:

Year	Sales (× $1 million)	Income— Current $	Income— 1977 $
1977	412	$ 4,790	$4,202
1978	428	5,030	4,263
1979	531	6,504	5,288
1980	789	11,727	8,817
1981	674	9,232	6,114
1982	621	8,637	5,203
1983	581	7,203	4,093
1984	577	7,870	4,186

    a. Develop a scatter plot for both relations.

    b. Determine a least squares line for both relationships. Plot these lines on the scatter plots. Based on your least squares line and scatter plot, which relationship do you feel provides the best explanation of sales variability?

46. The Rio-River Railroad, headquartered in Santa Fe, New Mexico, is trying to devise a method for allocating fuel costs to individual railroad cars on a particular route between Denver and Santa Fe. The railroad feels that fuel consumption will increase as more cars are added to the train, but it is uncertain how much cost should be assigned to each additional car. In an effort to deal with this problem, the cost-accounting department has randomly sampled ten trips between the two cities and recorded the following data:

Rail Cars X	Fuel (units/mile) Y
18	55
18	50
35	76
35	80
45	117
40	90
37	80
50	125
40	100
27	75

a. Develop a scatter plot for these two variables and comment on the apparent relationship between fuel consumption and the number of rail cars on the train.

b. Compute the correlation coefficient between fuel consumption and train cars. Test statistically the hypothesis that the true correlation is zero, using an alpha level of 0.05. Comment on the results of this test. Do these results necessarily indicate that adding more cars will increase the fuel usage?

c. Develop the least squares regression model to help explain the variation in fuel consumption. Interpret the results and clearly show the least squares equation.

Section 13–4

47. The College Placement Council prepares documents that contain data pertaining to many aspects of job placement for college graduates. The January 1988 report contains the following data on January 1988 job offers and average salary per month for those job offers. Each case is from a particular degree area selected at random from the entire list of possible degree programs.

Number of Offers	Average Salary per Offer
1,570	$1,616
808	1,496
381	1,462
91	1,374
1,460	2,155
55	1,472
482	1,979
87	2,502
2,843	2,140
196	2,011

a. Develop a scatter plot for these data using *average salary* as the dependent variable and *number of offers* as the independent variable.

b. Develop the least squares regression equation for explaining the variation in salary using the number of job offers.

c. Based on these sample data, can it be concluded that number of job offers is positively linearly related to the average salary offered? Test at the alpha level of 0.05.

48. Referring to problem 47, what percentage of the variation in salary is explained by knowing the number of job offers made? From this, compute the correlation between the two variables and test to see if the correlation is significant at the alpha level of 0.05. Compare this test result with the significance test performed in part c in problem 47.

49. Referring to problem 46, test to determine if the regression model is significant at the alpha level of 0.10. In performing this test, be sure to show clearly the standard error of the slope and interpret what this means.

50. Referring to problems 46 and 49, calculate the standard error of the estimate and explain what it means. Also compute the coefficient of determination and discuss what it measures.

TABLE 13P–1
Study 1 computer printout

```
******************************************************************************
CØRRELATIØN CØEFFICIENTS

                        Y           X

              Y    1.0000     − .4926

              X   − .4926      1.0000
------------------------------------------------------------------------------
DEPENDENT VARIABLE   Y   GRADE PØINT AVERAGE

INDEPENDENT VARIABLE   X   TV HØURS
------------------------------------------------------------------------------
MEAN X   20.0
------------------------------------------------------------------------------
R SQUARE                  .2426

STANDARD ERRØR ØF ESTIMATE   .5200

----------------------VARIABLES IN THE EQUATIØN-------------------
VARIABLE                     B      STD. ERRØR B     T VALUE

X                         − .0015     .000382

(CØNSTANT)                2.5300
******************************************************************************
```

TABLE 13P–2
Study 2 computer printout

****

DEPENDENT VARIABLE   Y   GRADE PØINT AVERAGE

INDEPENDENT VARIABLE   X   HØURS WØRKED

- -

R SQUARE   .1600

- -

ANALYSIS ØF VARIANCE	D.F.	SUM ØF SQUARES	MEAN SQUARE	F
REGRESSIØN				
RESIDUAL (UNEXPLAINED)	—	——		
	99	550.0		

- - - - - - - - - - - - - - - -VARIABLES IN THE EQUATIØN- - - - - - - - - - - - - - - -

VARIABLE	B
X	.0100
(CØNSTANT)	2.2500

****

51. Henry Prince has served as a consultant to the federal government for several years. Recently he was asked to make a study of high school students to obtain information about how television viewing habits are related to academic performance. Possibly because Henry is always paid by the hour, he has decided to perform two studies. In the first he collected data from fifty randomly selected students for two variables: *hours of television watched per week* and *grade-point average during a given period*. In the second study he collected data from 100 students for two variables: *number of hours per week working at a paying job* and *grade-point average during a given period*.

Table 13P–1 shows a partial computer printout for the first study. Table 13P–2 shows a partial computer printout for the second study. Using the information in these printouts, and some insight of your own, answer problems 51 through 55. Your responsibility in *this* problem is to fill in the missing values in tables 13P–1 and 13P–2.

52. In his report, Henry Prince (see problem 51) has indicated that the number of hours a student watches television each week is not a significant variable for explaining the variation in student grade-point average. He states that he tested this at the alpha level of 0.05. Based on the information provided, do you agree with Henry's conclusion? Discuss why or why not.

53. In the random sample of fifty students in study 1 (see problem 51), the number of hours of television ranged from a low of eight to a high of forty per week. In his report, Henry states that based on the regression model, if no hours are spent watching television, students will have an average grade-point average of 2.530. Why do you suppose he came to this conclusion? Discuss whether you agree or disagree with him and indicate why.

54. In study 2 (see problem 51), where hours worked ranged from zero hours to twenty hours, Henry Prince concluded that the independent variable, *hours worked,* and the dependent variable, *grade-point average,* are significantly correlated at the alpha level of 0.05. Therefore, he has stated that a student can increase his or her grade-point average by working at a paying job and should be encouraged to do so. Further, the more hours the student works, the higher the grade-point average will be. Support or refute Henry's statement.

55. In his report on study 2 (see problem 51), Henry has indicated that he tested the significance of the model using the analysis of variance approach. However, he failed to include the results of the test in his report. Using the information in table 13P–2, test the null hypothesis that the regression model is not significant, using the analysis of variance approach. Use an alpha level of 0.05. Discuss why a large F ratio should lead to the rejection of the null hypothesis. Also, using the information in the analysis of variance table, determine the standard error of the estimate and discuss briefly what it measures.

56. If you have tested for the significance of the correlation between two variables and found that the true correlation may be zero, is it feasible to develop a regression model using the same variables and data? Discuss.

Section 13–5

57. Consider the regression model developed in problem 44. Develop a 90 percent confidence interval for the true regression slope and interpret this interval.

58. The American Airline Company recently performed a customer survey in which it asked a random sample of 100 passengers to indicate their income and the number of times they have flown on any airline for pleasure during the past year. A regression model was developed for the purposes of determining if income could be used as a variable to explain the variation in number of times individuals fly on airlines in a year. The following regression results were obtained:

$$\hat{Y} = 0.25 + 0.0003X$$
$$S_e = 1.44$$
$$R^2 = 0.65$$
$$S_{b_1} = 0.0000222$$

a. Develop a 95 percent confidence interval estimate for the true regression slope and interpret this interval estimate.

b. Can the intercept of the regression equation be interpreted in this case, assuming that no one that was surveyed had an income of zero dollars? Explain.

c. Use the information provided to perform an analysis of variance test of the significance of the regression model. Discuss your results, assuming the test is performed at the alpha level of 0.05.

59. Referring to problem 32, develop a 90 percent confidence interval estimate for the true regression slope for the model having *asking price of a home* as the independent variable and *weeks on the market* as the dependent variable.

60. A manager for a major manufacturing company recently delivered a speech to other managers from around the United States. During the course of the speech he was explaining a study his company had done with respect to sales and price of a particular product. He said that it had developed a simple regression model and found the regression slope coefficient to be -3456.98. He then said that this means that increasing price by one dollar will cause sales to drop by 3456.98 units. Comment on this statement, indicating what, if anything, about the statement you agree with.

61. The Briggs Bank and Trust recently performed a study of their checking account customers. One objective of the study was to determine whether it is possible to explain the variation in average checking account balance by knowing the number of checks written per month. The following sample data were selected:

Average Account Balance	Checks Written
1202	46
789	67
233	23
908	52
1233	23
1098	34
345	76
1609	18
407	25
300	53
1190	33

  a. Develop a scatter plot for these data.
  b. Develop the least squares regression equation for these data.
  c. Develop the 90 percent confidence interval estimate for the true regression slope coefficient and interpret this interval.
  d. Test to determine whether the true regression slope is different from zero. Use alpha = 0.05. Comment on this result and the result of part c.

Section 13–6

62. The Sanders Company production manager is in the process of performing a productivity study of the employees at the Black Hills plant. In the process of performing this study he has selected a random sample of twenty employees who have worked for the company for four years or more. For each employee, he measured the number of hours of special training the employee has taken and the production rate for the employee in pieces per day produced. The following summary data are available:

$$Y = \text{pieces produced per day}$$
$$X = \text{hours of special training}$$
$$\overline{X} = 13.50$$
$$S_e = 11.0$$
$$\overline{Y} = 125.0$$
$$\hat{Y} = 88.5 + 1.5X$$
$$\Sigma(X - \overline{X})^2 = 1,245.0$$

a. Develop a 95 percent prediction interval for the average daily production for people who have taken 15.0 hours of training. Interpret this prediction interval estimate.

b. Develop a 95 percent prediction interval for a particular individual who has taken eight hours of special training courses. Interpret these results.

c. Comment on whether you believe the prediction interval computed in part b is satisfactory for predicting productivity for individual employees with eight hours of courses. Discuss.

63. A company is considering recruiting new employees from a particular college and plans to place a great deal of emphasis on college grade-point average. However, the company is aware that not all schools have the same grading standards, so it is possible that a student at this school might have a lower (or higher) grade-point average than a student from another school, yet really be on par with the other student. To make this comparison between schools, the company has devised a test which it has administered widely on a sample size of 400. With the results of the test, it has developed a regression model which it uses to predict student grade-point average. The following equation represents the model:

$$\hat{Y} = 1.0 + 0.028X$$

The R^2 for this model is 0.88 and the standard error of the estimate is 0.20, based on the sample data used to develop the model. Note that the dependent variable is the grade-point average and the independent variable is test score, where this score can range from zero to 100. For the sample data used to develop the model, the following values are known:

$$\overline{Y} = 2.76$$
$$\overline{X} = 68$$
$$\Sigma(X - \overline{X})^2 = 148,885.73$$

a. Based on the information contained in this problem, can you conclude that the regression slope coefficient is significantly different from zero, using an alpha level of 0.05?

b. Suppose a student interviews with this company, takes the company test, and scores 80 percent correct. What is the 90 percent prediction interval estimate for this student's grade-point average? Interpret the interval.

c. Suppose the student in part b actually has a 2.90 grade-point average at this school. Based on this evidence, what might be concluded about this person's actual grade-point average compared with other students at other schools with the same grade-point average? Discuss the limitations you might place on this conclusion.

64. Referring to problem 63, suppose a second student with a 2.45 grade-point average took the test and scored 65 percent correct. What is the 90 percent prediction interval for this student's "real" grade-point average? Interpret.

65. Suppose the company that developed the test discussed in problem 63 is interested in developing a 95 percent prediction interval estimate for the average grade-point average for students who score 88 percent correct on this test. Calculate this interval and interpret it.

66. Discuss why prediction intervals which attempt to predict a particular Y value are less precise than prediction intervals for predicting an average Y.

Section 13–7

67. An economist for the state government of Mississippi recently collected the following data on percentage of people unemployed in the state and the interest rate of treasury bills offered by the federal government.

Unemployment Percentage	Treasury Bill Interest Rate Percentage
4.4	8.1
7.8	9.8
4.7	8.2
5.0	8.4
3.9	7.9
5.1	8.3
9.5	10.2
8.8	10.0
4.5	8.4
5.0	8.5
10.2	10.2
9.0	10.1
6.0	8.8
5.0	8.3
9.5	10.1
13.4	10.7
15.0	11.4
4.0	7.8

Assuming that these data were selected as a random sample of weeks from the past five years, develop a plot showing the relationship between the two variables. Describe the relationship as being either linear or curvilinear.

68. Referring to problem 67,

    a. Develop a linear regression model with *unemployment rate* as the dependent variable. Write a short report describing the model and indicating the important measures. Can it be concluded that the linear regression model is statistically significant? Test at the alpha level of 0.05.

    b. Determine what appropriate transformation should be made to the independent variable to improve the regression results. Make this transformation and compute the new regression equation. Write a short report that compares the regression results obtained in part a with those obtained with this transformation. Perform any necessary statistical tests, using an alpha level of 0.05.

    c. Substitute the values for the independent variable into each of the regression equations and plot these on a graph with *Y* on the vertical axis and *X* on the horizontal axis. Describe the two regression lines.

69. The Cooley Service Center polishes and cleans automobiles. It has major accounts such as the Bayview Taxi Service and Bayview Police Department. It also does work for the general public by appointment. Recently, the manager decided to survey customers to determine how satisfied they were with the work performed by the Cooley Service Center. He devised a rating scale between 0 and 100, with 0 being poor and 100 being excellent service. He selected a random sample of fourteen customers and asked the customers when they picked up their cars to rate the service. He also recorded the amount of time spent on each customer's car. These data are shown as follows:

Rating Y	Time (in hours) X
85	1.5
60	0.2
70	0.3
72	0.35
80	1.0
65	0.23
70	0.32
90	2.5
84	1.6
70	0.27
82	1.6
75	0.40
77	0.45
89	2.0

Develop a scatter plot showing these two variables, with the Y variable on the vertical axis and the X variable on the horizontal axis. Describe the relationship between these two variables.

70. Referring to problem 69,

a. Develop a linear regression model to explain the variation in the service rating. Write a short report describing the model and showing the results of pertinent hypothesis tests, using an alpha level of 0.10. Comment on whether you think the model could be improved by transforming the independent variable. Discuss.

b. Determine what transformation to the independent variable might be appropriate. Then develop a regression model, using the transformed independent variable, and write a short report comparing this model to the one developed in part a. Discuss which model you prefer and why.

STATE DEPARTMENT OF TRANSPORTATION CASE STUDY PROBLEMS

The following questions and problems pertain directly to the State Department of Transportation case study and data base introduced in chapter 1. The questions and problems were written assuming that you will have access to a computer and appropriate statistical software. The data base containing 100 observations and seventeen variables is shown in table 1C–1 in chapter 1. *Please assume that the data were collected using a simple random sampling process.*

1. Develop a scatter plot for the variables X_6 and X_9. Compute the correlation coefficient for these two variables and test statistically whether a significant linear relationship exists between these two variables. Use an alpha = 0.05 level.

2. Develop a scatter plot and correlation coefficient for the variables, age, and total number of convictions, X_5. Test to determine whether there is a significant linear relationship between these two variables, using an alpha = 0.05 level.

3. Referring to problem 1, develop a simple linear regression model using X_6 and the dependent variable and X_9 as the independent variable. Test the significance of the slope coefficient and develop a 95 percent confidence interval estimate for the true regression slope coefficient. Indicate the R^2 and the standard error.

4. Determine the simple linear regression equation where variable X_{15} is the dependent variable and X_{13} is the independent variable. Make sure you test the appropriate hypotheses and that you develop a 90 percent confidence interval estimate for the regression slope. Indicate what the R^2 is and the standard error. Write a short letter describing the model and indicate whether it would be useful in predicting the number of years of formal education an individual would have. Test all hypotheses at the alpha = 0.10 level.

5. Develop a simple linear regression model using X_5 as the dependent variable and X_{15} as the independent variable. Is the model statistically significant at the alpha = 0.05

level? How much of the variation in X_5 has been explained by the model? Write a report that fully analyzes the regression results. Your report should include a scatter plot of the variables.

C A S E S

13A State Social Services

The State Social Services Department has been affected by a recent tax limitation bill passed by the state legislature. Although the director, Allan Bixby, made a logical defense of the department's increased needs, his budget was not increased this year. At the same time, the legislative committee overseeing the Social Services Department indicated it expected the level of services to remain the same. The exact words of one senator were: "You guys will have to learn to get more out of your people."

Unfortunately Allan and all other department heads are constrained by very stringent civil-service regulations. Once a person has been hired and has been on the job a year, he or she cannot be fired easily. Allan has concluded that his best chance to increase the productivity of the work force is to hire better people. Fortunately, the turnover in his department is high enough that this could be a relatively effective method. The major problem is in devising a method to hire better people.

Claudette Chambers, chief researcher for the department, has devised an entrance examination she claims will separate good workers from poor workers. This test is designed to determine a person's attitude toward work and whether he or she is attracted by secure conditions or is result-oriented. Claudette claims the higher a person scores on the test, the more effective he or she will be on the job.

Claudette has given her test to a sample of workers presently with the department. As a measure of their productivity level, she used an average of their last two job evaluations. She found the following results:

Test Score (100 points possible)	Job Evaluation (50 points possible)
71	43
58	37
91	47
86	42
97	48
65	38
78	40
82	42
89	49
74	43
69	38

Claudette claims these figures show an obvious relationship between her test and job performance and recommends the test be used to screen all future applicants.

13B Continental Trucking

Norm Painter is the newly hired cost analyst for Continental Trucking. Continental is a nationwide trucking firm, and until recently most of its routes were driven under regulated rates. These rates were set to allow small trucking firms to earn an adequate profit, and there was little incentive to work to reduce costs by efficient management techniques. By far the greatest effort was trying to influence regulatory agencies to grant rate increases.

A recent rash of deregulation moves has made the long-distance trucking industry more competitive. Norm has been hired to analyze Continental's whole expense structure. As part of this study, Norm is looking at truck repair costs. Since the trucks are involved in long hauls, they inevitably break down. Up until now, little preventive maintenance has been done, and if a truck broke down in the middle of a haul, either a replacement tractor was sent or the haul was finished by an independent contractor. The truck was then repaired at the nearest local shop. Norm is sure this procedure has been much more expensive than if major repairs had been made before they caused trucks to fail.

Norm feels some method needs to be found for determining when preventive maintenance is needed. He feels that fuel consumption is a good indicator of possible breakdowns, and that as the trucks begin running badly, they will consume more fuel. Unfortunately, the major determinants of fuel consumption are the weight of the truck and head winds. Norm picks a sample of a single truck model and gathers data relating fuel consumption to truck weight. All trucks in the sample were in good condition. He separates the data by direction of the haul, feeling winds tend to blow predominantly out of the west.

East-West Haul		West-East Haul	
Miles/Gallon	Haul Weight	Miles/Gallon	Haul Weight
4.1	41,000 lb	4.3	40,000 lb
4.7	36,000	4.5	37,000
3.9	37,000	4.8	36,000
4.3	38,000	5.2	38,000
4.8	32,000	5.0	35,000
5.1	37,000	4.7	42,000
4.3	46,000	4.9	37,000
4.6	35,000	4.5	36,000
5.0	37,000	5.2	42,000
		4.8	41,000

Although he can gather future data on fuel consumption and haul weight rapidly, now that Norm has these data, he is not quite sure what to do with them.

REFERENCES

Aaker, David. *Multivariate Analysis in Marketing: Theory and Applications,* 2nd Edition. Palo Alto, Calif: Science Press, 1981.

Draper, N. R., and Smith, H. *Applied Regression Analysis,* New York: Wiley, 1966.

Kleinbaum, David G., and Kupper, Lawrence L. *Applied Regression Analysis and Other Multivariate Methods.* North Scituate, Mass.: Duxbury, 1978.

Neter, John, and Wasserman, William. *Applied Linear Statistical Models.* Homewood Ill.: Irwin, 1974.

Richards, Larry, and Lacava, Jerry. *Business Statistics: Why and When,* 2nd Edition. New York: McGraw-Hill, 1983.

INTRODUCTION TO MULTIPLE REGRESSION ANALYSIS

14

WHY DECISION MAKERS NEED TO KNOW

Chapter 13 illustrated that decision makers often need to consider the relationship between two variables when analyzing a problem. Simple linear regression and correlation analysis provide a basis for analyzing two variables and their relationship to each other.

As you might expect, decision makers' problems are not limited to only two variables. Most practical situations involve analyzing the relationship between three or more variables. For example, a vice-president of planning for an automobile manufacturer would be interested in the relationship between her company's automobile sales and the variables that influence those sales. Included in her analysis might be such independent or explanatory variables as automobile price, competitors' sales, and advertising; and such economic variables as disposable personal income, the inflation rate, and the unemployment rate. The simple regression and correlation analysis techniques discussed in chapter 13 do not allow analysis of more than two variables. This chapter introduces the extension of the simple regression methods—*multiple regression analysis*.

CHAPTER OBJECTIVES

This chapter will introduce multiple regression analysis. It will discuss how a multiple regression model is developed and how it should be applied and interpreted in a business setting.

It will also discuss how to incorporate both qualitative and quantitative variables in a multiple regression model. Finally, it will consider some potential problems in using multiple regression analysis and the possible consequences if a regression model is improperly developed.

STUDENT OBJECTIVES

After studying the material in this chapter, you should be able to

1. Recognize the need for multiple regression analysis in a decision-making situation.
2. Analyze the computer output for a multiple regression model and interpret the regression statistics.
3. Test hypotheses about the significance of a multiple regression model and test the significance of the independent variables in the model.
4. Recognize potential problems when using multiple regression analysis, including the problems of multicollinearity.
5. Incorporate qualitative variables into the regression model by using dummy variables.
6. Perform residual analysis to determine the aptness of the model.

DEVELOPING A MULTIPLE REGRESSION MODEL

14-1

Most states have provisions allowing the counties to raise revenue through property taxes. The amount of property taxes a real estate owner will pay depends on the class of property, the appraised value of the property, and the tax rate. Typically, the appraised value for tax purposes is supposed to be the market value for the property. The market value is the value the property would sell for if it were put on the open market. Usually, the county assessor is charged with the responsibility of making property appraisals. Obviously, making a correct property appraisal is important, but trying to determine how much each property would sell for if it were placed on the market is a difficult task, and many assessors are faced with irate taxpayers disputing their property taxes.

American County, located in the Midwest, is just now in the process of changing its appraisal system. The assessor has selected a sample of 531 residential properties that have sold recently in American County. Data for the following variables were obtained for each property:

$$Y = \text{sales price}$$
$$X_1 = \text{square feet}$$
$$X_2 = \text{age of house}$$
$$X_3 = \text{number of bedrooms}$$
$$X_4 = \text{number of bathrooms}$$
$$X_5 = \text{number of fireplaces}$$

The assessor has decided to develop an appraisal model based on multiple regression, an extension of the simple regression techniques discussed in the previous chapter.

You will remember from chapter 13 that a simple regression model has the form shown in equation 14-1:

$$Y_i = \beta_0 + \beta_1 X_i + e_i \qquad\qquad (14\text{--}1)$$

where $\quad \beta_0 = $ regression intercept
$\beta_1 = $ regression slope
$e_i = $ error

If we assume that the expected value of e_i equals zero, the regression model is given by equation 14–2:

$$E[Y] = \beta_0 + \beta_1 X \qquad\qquad (14\text{--}2)$$

The simple regression model is characterized by two variables: Y, the *dependent variable*, and X, the *independent* or *explanatory variable*. The single independent variable explains some variation in the dependent variable, but unless X and Y are perfectly correlated, the proportion explained will be less than 100 percent. This means the error term, e_i, will be present. Recall that e_i is the *residual* and is the difference between the true regression line and the actual Y value (i.e., residual $= Y_i - \hat{Y}_i$). In chapter 13, we assumed that these e_i values have a mean of zero and a standard deviation called the **standard error of the estimate.** If this standard error is too large, the regression model may not be very useful for prediction.

In multiple regression analysis, additional independent variables are added to the regression model to explain some of the yet-unexplained variation in the dependent variable. Adding appropriate additional variables should thereby reduce the standard error of the estimate.

You will note as we proceed that multiple regression is merely an extension of simple regression analysis. However, as we expand the model from one independent variable to two or more there are some new considerations.

The general format of a **multiple regression model** is given by equation 14–3:

$$Y_i = \beta_0 + \beta_1 X_{1i} + \beta_2 X_{2i} + \ldots + \beta_K X_{Ki} + e_i \qquad\qquad (14\text{--}3)$$

where $\quad \beta_0 = $ regression constant
$\beta_1 = $ regression coefficient for variable X_1
$\beta_K = $ regression coefficient for variable X_K
$K = $ number of independent variables
$e_i = $ error (residual)

There are three general assumptions of the linear multiple regression model:

1. The errors are normally distributed.
2. The mean of the error terms is zero.
3. The error terms have a constant variance, σ^2, for all combined values of the independent variables.

FIGURE 14–1

Simple regression model (dependent variable—house price; independent variable—square feet)

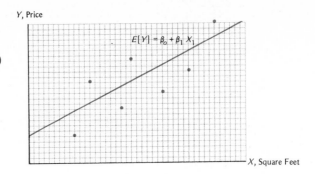

Since the error terms have a mean of zero, the expected value of Y for given values of $X_1, X_2, X_3 \ldots , X_K$ is given by equation 14–4:

$$E[Y] = \beta_0 + \beta_1 X_1 + \beta_2 X_2 + \beta_3 X_3 + \ldots + \beta_K X_K \qquad (14\text{–}4)$$

This model is an extension of the simple regression model of chapter 13 and equation 14–2. The principal difference is that, whereas equation 14–2 for the simple model is the equation for a straight line in a two-dimensional space (see figure 14–1), the multiple regression model forms a *hyperplane* (or *response surface*) through multi-dimensional space. Each regression coefficient represents a slope. When there are only two independent variables, the **regression plane** can be drawn as shown in figure 14–2. If there are more than two independent variables, the regression model cannot be visually represented, but the concept remains intact. The next section shows how a multiple regression model is developed.

FIGURE 14–2

Illustration of a regression plane

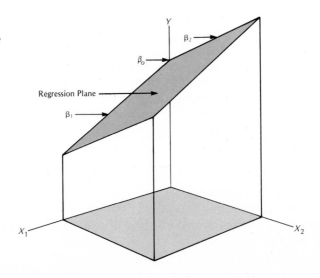

When a decision maker has sample data available for the dependent variable and for K independent variables, the least squares regression coefficients are estimated, forming the sample regression model of the form shown in equation 14–5:

$$\hat{Y}_i = b_0 + b_1X_1 + b_2X_2 + \ldots + b_KX_K \qquad (14\text{–}5)$$

where:
$$b_0 = Y\text{-intercept (constant)}$$
$$b_1, b_2, \ldots, b_K = \text{regression slope coefficients}$$
$$\hat{Y}_i = i\text{th estimated value of the dependent variable}$$
$$X_1, X_2, \ldots, X_K = \text{independent variables}$$

The estimates of the regression coefficients are determined mathematically so that $\Sigma(Y_i - \hat{Y}_i)^2$ is minimized. You should recall from chapter 13 that this is referred to as the *least squares objective*. The actual procedure for determining the values for the regression coefficients involves matrix algebra. The mathematical derivation is beyond the scope of this text, but the algebraic equation 14–6 illustrates how the least squares regression coefficients are determined:

$$\mathbf{B} = (X'X)^{-1}X'Y \qquad (14\text{–}6)$$

where
$$X = n \times (K + 1) \text{ matrix of values for the independent variables, with the first column all 1s}$$
$$Y = n \times 1 \text{ matrix of the dependent variable values}$$
$$\mathbf{B} = (K + 1) \times 1 \text{ matrix of regression coefficients}$$

(For a more complete treatment of the matrix algebra approach for estimating the multiple regression coefficients, consult *Applied Linear Statistical Models* by Neter and Wasserman.)

Almost exclusively, multiple regression analysis is performed with the aid of a computer and appropriate software. The following presentation of examples will be based on output from a computer program. Note that each software package presents the results in a slightly different format; however, the same basic information will appear in all regression output.

Before a multiple regression analysis example is introduced, you should understand this important point: the sample size required to compute a regression model must be at least one greater than the number of independent variables. Thus, if we are thinking of developing a regression model with five independent variables, the absolute minimum number of cases required is six. Otherwise the computer program will indicate an error has been made or will print out meaningless values.

As a practical matter, the sample size should be at least four times the number of independent variables. Thus if we have five independent variables ($K = 5$), we would want at least twenty cases to develop the regression model.

AMERICAN COUNTY APPRAISAL MODEL

14-2

We indicated earlier that the assessor in American County wanted to use multiple regression to develop an appraisal model for residential property in the county.

The assessor gathered data on the following residential property variables for 531 houses:

$$Y = \text{sales price}$$
$$X_1 = \text{square feet}$$
$$X_2 = \text{age of house}$$
$$X_3 = \text{number of bedrooms}$$
$$X_4 = \text{number of bathrooms}$$
$$X_5 = \text{number of fireplaces}$$

Note, that sales price is the dependent variable and the other five variables are the independent variables. The assessor hopes to be able to use the variables to predict the market value (price) of residential properties in American County. Table 14–1 illustrates how the data would be arranged. Table 14–2 presents the computer output of the mean and standard deviation for each variable. The standard deviation for the variable price is high, indicating a large variation in selling prices for houses.

TABLE 14–1
American County data

Observation	Y	X_1	X_2	X_3	X_4	X_5
1	21,400	1,410	3.0	2.0	1.0	0
2	37,275	1,725	5.0	3.0	2.5	1
.	.	.	.	.	.	.
.	.	.	.	.	.	.
.	.	.	.	.	.	.
$n = 531$	47,175	2,250	1.0	4.0	2.75	2

TABLE 14–2
Means and standard deviations, American County example

```
*********************************************************************************
```

VARIABLE	MEAN	STD. DEV.	CASES
Y	45009.6139	14290.2132	531
X1	1715.5273	588.1123	531
X2	4.3936	7.7781	531
X3	3.4038	.0555	531
X4	1.9143	.6094	531
X5	.9209	.5608	531

```
*********************************************************************************
```

Correlation Matrix

The first step in developing the appraisal model is to examine the relationship between each independent variable and the dependent variable, *sales price*. As with simple regression analysis, we can measure the strength of the linear relationship between any two variables by calculating the correlation coefficient for each pair of (X, Y) variables using equation 14–7:

$$r = \frac{\Sigma(X_i - \overline{X})(Y_i - \overline{Y})}{\sqrt{\Sigma(X_i - \overline{X})^2 \Sigma(Y_i - \overline{Y})^2}} \qquad (14\text{--}7)$$

The **correlation matrix** found by the computer program is shown in table 14–3. Note that the correlation between each X and Y variable is given, plus the correlation between each pair of independent variables. For example, the correlation between Y and X_2 is -0.068 and between X_3 and X_5 is 0.338. The correlation matrix is very useful for determining which independent variables are likely to help explain variation in the dependent variable. We look for correlations close to ± 1.0 since that indicates changes in the independent variable are linearly related to changes in the dependent variable.

Also, we can use the correlation matrix to determine the extent to which independent variables are correlated with one another. This can be useful in determining if certain independent variables are redundant and not needed in the model.

Notice the correlation matrix has 1.000s running down the main diagonal, indicating the variables are perfectly correlated with themselves. Finally, notice the matrix is symmetrical about its diagonal. For example, the correlation between X_2 and X_5 (0.086) is the same as for X_5 and X_2 (0.086).

The Regression Model

The county assessor's goal is to develop a regression model to predict the appropriate selling price for a home, using certain measurable characteristics. The first attempt at developing the model will be to run a multiple regression computer program using all

TABLE 14–3

Correlation matrix computer output, American County example

	Y	X1	X2	X3	X4	X5
Y	1.000	.841	− .068	.494	.720	.599
X1	.841	1.000	.054	.644	.680	.589
X2	− .068	.054	1.000	.007	− .149	.086
X3	.494	.644	.007	1.000	.551	.338
X4	.720	.680	− .149	.551	1.000	.518
X5	.599	.589	.086	.338	.518	1.000

TABLE 14–4

Regression model computer output, American County example

****

R SQUARE	.76686
ADJUSTED R SQUARE	.76509
STANDARD ERRØR	6926.16662

ANALYSIS ØF VARIANCE	D.F.	SUM ØF SQUARES	MEAN SQUARE	F
REGRESSIØN	4	82998243602.67404	20749560900.66851	432.53678
RESIDUAL (UNEXPLAINED)	526	25233158443.18288	47971784.11251	

---------------VARIABLES IN THE EQUATIØN-----------------

VARIABLE	B	STD. ERRØR B	T
X1 SQ. FT.	16.43956	.84287	19.504
X3 BEDRØØMS	− 2845.89318	616.91611	− 4.613
X4 BATHS	6599.24009	604.46151	9.367
X5 FIREPLACES	2507.93424	681.93968	3.677
(CØNSTANT)	11549.14261		

****

available independent variables except X_2, age. Age (X_2) was excluded in this run since the correlation between age and price was only -0.088 (see table 14–3). The resulting output is shown in table 14–4. Thus the multiple regression model (rounding to two significant digits) is

$$Y = 11,549.14 + 16.44X_1 - 2,845.89X_3 + 6,599.24X_4 + 2,507.93X_5$$

These values come from the B column of the variables in the equation section of table 14–4.

To obtain a sales price point estimate for any house, we could substitute values for X_1, X_3, X_4, and X_5 into this regression model. For example, suppose a property with the following characteristics is considered:

$$X_1 = \text{square feet} = 2,100$$
$$X_3 = \text{number of bedrooms} = 4$$
$$X_4 = \text{number of baths} = 1.75$$
$$X_5 = \text{Number of fireplaces} = 2$$

The point estimate for the sales price is

Price $= 11,549.14 + 16.44(2,100) - 2,845.89(4) + 6,599.24(1.75) + 2,507.93(2)$
$= \$51,253.19$

The computer output in table 14–4 shows a number of other regression statistics. As we proceed, we will discuss these values. Our emphasis will be on interpreting the computer regression results.

Inferences about the Regression Model

Before the American County assessor actually uses this regression model to determine the value of a house, there are several questions that should be answered:

1. Is the overall model significant?
2. Are the individual variables significant?
3. Is the standard error of the estimate too large to provide meaningful results?
4. Is multicollinearity a problem?[1]

We shall answer each of these questions in order.

Is the Overall Model Significant?

Chapter 13 introduced the coefficient of determination, which measures the percentage of variation in the dependent variable that can be accounted for by the independent variable. With multiple regression, we also use *R square,* which is calculated by equation 14–8:

$$R \text{ square} = R^2 = \frac{\text{sum of squares regression}}{\text{total sum of squares}} = \frac{SSR}{TSS} \qquad (14\text{–}8)$$

The *R* square (**multiple coefficient of determination**) for the appraisal model is given in the computer printout in table 14–4 as 0.76686. Therefore almost 77 percent of the variation in sales price can be explained by the four independent variables in the regression model.

Chapter 13 showed that an analysis of variance *F* test can be used to test whether the regression model explains a significant proportion of variation in the dependent variable. The computer printout in table 14–4 provides the analysis of variance test for this example. To test the model's significance, we compare the calculated *F* value, 432.54, with a table *F* value for a given alpha level and 4 and 526 degrees of freedom. If we specify an alpha level of 0.01, the test is as shown in figure 14–3.

Clearly, based on the analysis of variance *F* test, we should conclude that the regression model *does* explain a significant proportion of the variation in sales price.

The computer printout in table 14–4 also provides a measure called the **adjusted *R* square.** This is calculated by equation 14–9:

---

[1]**Multicollinearity** occurs when two independent variables are correlated with each other and therefore contribute redundant information to the model. When highly correlated independent variables are included in the regression model, they can affect the regression results.

Hypotheses:

H_0: The regression model does not explain a significant proportion of the total variation in the dependent variable (model is not significant). ($\beta_1 = \beta_3 = \beta_4 = \beta_5 = 0$), $R^2 = 0$

H_A: The regression model does explain a significant proportion of the total variation in the dependent variable (model is significant). (At least one $\beta_j \neq 0$; $j = 1, 3, 4, 5$), $R^2 > 0$

$\alpha = 0.01$

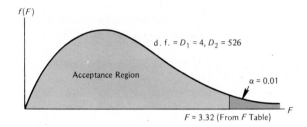

Decision Rule:

If $F > F_{critical} = 3.32$, reject H_0.
Otherwise, do not reject H_0.

The calculated F (see Table 14–4) is 432.54. Since 432.54 > 3.32, the null hypothesis should be rejected.

FIGURE 14–3
Significance test, American County example

$$\text{Adjusted } R \text{ square} = R_A^2 = 1 - (1 - R^2)\left(\frac{n - 1}{n - K - 1}\right) \qquad (14\text{–}9)$$

where $n =$ sample size
$K =$ number of independent variables in the model

In the appraisal example,

$$R_A^2 = 1 - (1 - 0.76686)\left(\frac{531 - 1}{531 - 4 - 1}\right)$$

$$= 0.76509$$

Adding more independent variables to the regression model can only increase R^2. However, the cost in terms of losing degrees of freedom may not justify adding an additional variable. The R_A^2 value takes into account this cost and adjusts the R^2 value accordingly. Therefore, if a variable is added that does not contribute its fair share, the R_A^2 will actually decline.[2] R_A^2 is particularly important when the number of independent variables is large relative to the sample size. It takes into account the relationship between sample size and number of variables. R^2 may appear artificially high if the number of variables is high compared to the sample size.

---

[2] You might think of R_A^2 as similar to the net income on an income statement and R^2 as the total revenue. Thus R_A^2 is total revenue less expenses.

Are the Individual Variables Significant?

We have concluded that the overall model is significant. This means that *at least* one independent variable explains a significant proportion of the variation in sales price. This does not mean that *all* the variables are significant.

We can test the significance of each independent variable using a *t* test, as discussed in chapter 13. The calculated *t* value for each variable is provided on the computer printout in table 14–4. Recall that the *t* statistic is determined by dividing the regression coefficient by the standard deviation of the regression coefficient. The test for each variable is performed in figure 14–4. These *t* tests are *conditional* tests. This means the hypothesis that states that *the value of each slope coefficient is zero* is made recognizing that the other independent variables are already in the model.[3] Based on the *t* tests in figure 14–4, we conclude that all four independent variables in the model are significant. When a regression model is to be used for prediction, the model should contain no insignificant variables. If insignificant variables are present, they should be dropped and the regression model rerun before it is used for prediction purposes.

Is the Standard Error of the Estimate Too Large?

The purpose of developing the American County regression model is to be able to determine values of the dependent variable when corresponding values of the independent variables are known. An indication of how good the regression model is can be found by looking at the relationship between the measured values of the dependent variable and those values that would be predicted by the regression model. The sample standard deviation of the regression model, often referred to as the **standard error of the estimate** (S_e), measures the dispersion of observed sale values, Y, around values predicted by the regression model. The standard error of the estimate, listed simply as STANDARD ERROR in table 14–4, is found by

$$S_e = \sqrt{\frac{\text{SSE}}{n - K - 1}}$$

where

$$\text{SSE} = \text{sum of squares error}$$
$$n = \text{sample size}$$
$$K = \text{number of independent variables}$$

Notice also in table 14–4 that the standard error is the square root of the mean square error of the residuals found in the analysis of variance table.

Sometimes, even though the model has a high R^2, the standard error of the esti-

---

[3]Note that the *t* tests may be affected if the independent variables in the model are themselves correlated. A procedure known as the *sum of squares drop F test*, discussed by Neter and Wasserman in *Applied Linear Statistical Models*, should be used in this situation. Each *t* test considers only the marginal contribution of the independent variables and may indicate that none of the variables in the model are significant even though the ANOVA procedure indicates otherwise.

Hypotheses:

H_0: $\beta_i = 0$, given all other variables are already in the model
H_A: $\beta_i \neq 0$, given all other variables are already in the model

$\alpha = 0.01$

Decision Rule:

If $-2.576 \leq t \leq 2.576$, accept H_0.
Otherwise, reject H_0.

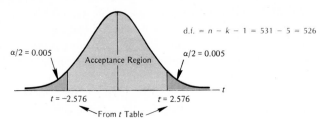

The test is:

For β_1: Calculated t (from printout) = 19.504.
       Since 19.504 > 2.576, reject H_0.

For β_3: Calculated $t = -4.613$.
       Since $-4.613 < -2.576$, reject H_0.

For β_4: Calculated $t = 9.367$.
       Since 9.367 > 2.576, reject H_0.

For β_5: Calculated $t = 3.677$.
       Since 3.677 > 2.576, reject H_0.

Note: the degrees of freedom for the t-distribution
is $n - k - 1$, where k is the total number of independent
variables in the model.

FIGURE 14–4

Significance test for a single independent variable, American County example

mate will be too large to provide adequate precision for the prediction interval. A rule of thumb we have found useful is to examine the range $\pm 2S_e$.[4] If this range is acceptable from a practical viewpoint, the standard error of the estimate might be considered acceptable.

In the American County example, as shown in table 14–4, the standard error is 6,926.17. Thus the rough prediction range is

---

[4]The actual confidence interval for prediction of a new observation requires the use of matrix algebra as follows:

$$\hat{Y}_p \pm S_e \sqrt{1 + [(X_p')(X'X)^{-1}(X_p)]}$$

where $\hat{Y}_p$ = point estimate given values for the independent variables
            X_p = vector of independent variable values used to calculate $\hat{Y}_p$
            X = matrix of independent variable values used to develop the regression model

Refer to *Applied Linear Statistical Models* by Neter and Wasserman (1974) for further discussion.

$$\pm 2(6{,}926.17)$$
$$\pm \$13{,}852.34$$

From a practical viewpoint, this range is *not* acceptable. The error is over $13,000 in either direction. Not many homeowners would be willing to have their appraisal value set by a model with this possible error. The county assessor needs to take steps to reduce the standard error of the estimate. Subsequent sections of this chapter discuss some ways to reduce this value.

Another measure of whether S_e is too large is the *coefficient of variation*, which is

$$CV = \frac{S_e}{\overline{Y}}(100)$$

where

$$\overline{Y} = \text{mean of the } Y \text{ variable}$$

In this case,

$$CV = \frac{6{,}926.17}{45{,}009.6139}(100)$$
$$= 15.3\%$$

As a rule, we like to see a *CV* of 10 percent or less. However, each application must be analyzed on an individual basis.

Is Multicollinearity a Problem?

Even if a regression is significant, and if each independent variable is significant, decision makers should still examine the regression model to determine whether it appears reasonable. That is, does any coefficient have an unexpected sign?

Before answering this question for our appraisal example, we should review what the regression coefficients mean. First, the constant term, β_0, is the model's Y-intercept. If the data used to develop the regression model contain values of X_1, X_3, X_4, and X_5 that are simultaneously zero (such as would be the case for vacant land), the constant is the mean value of Y, given that X_1, X_3, X_4, and X_5 all equal zero. Under these conditions β_0 would equal the average value of a vacant lot. However, in the American County example no vacant land was in the sample, so the constant has no particular meaning.

The coefficient for square feet, β_1, indicates the average change in sales price corresponding to a change in house size of one square foot, holding the other independent variables constant. The value shown in table 14–4 for β_1 is 16.44. The coefficient is positive, indicating that an increase in house size is associated with an increase in sales price. This relationship is expected.

Likewise, the coefficients for X_4, number of bathrooms, and X_5, number of fireplaces, are positive, indicating that an increase in their numbers is also associated with an increase price. This is also expected. However, the coefficient on variable X_3, number of bedrooms, is $-2,845.89$, meaning that if we hold the other variables constant but increase the number of bedrooms by one, the average price will *drop* by $2,845.89. This relationship may not be reasonable given the real estate market and buyers' attitudes.

Referring to the correlation matrix in table 14–3, the correlation between variable X_3 and Y, the sales price, is $+0.494$. This indicates that without considering the other independent variables, the linear relationship between number of bedrooms and sales price is positive. But why does the regression coefficient turn out negative? The answer lies in what is called *multicollinearity*. **Multicollinearity** occurs when the independent variables are themselves correlated. For example, X_3 and the other independent variables have the following correlations:

$$r_{X_3,X_1} = 0.644$$
$$r_{X_3,X_4} = 0.551$$
$$r_{X_3,X_5} = 0.338$$

In each case, the correlation is significant. Therefore the other variables in the model are overlapping X_3; hence, to some extent, making X_3 unnecessary to the model once X_1, X_4, and X_5 are included. This overlapping is multicollinearity. Multicollinearity can cause problems like those we have seen in this example, where the regression coefficient sign is clearly opposite of what we would expect.

The problems caused by multicollinearity, and how to deal with them, continue to be of prime concern to theoretical statisticians. From a decision maker's viewpoint, you should be aware that multicollinearity can (and usually does) exist and recognize the basic problems it can cause. Some of the most obvious problems and indications of severe multicollinearity are

1. Incorrect signs on the coefficients.
2. A change in the values of the previous coefficients when a new variable is added to the model.
3. The change to insignificant of a previously significant variable when a new variable is added to the model.
4. An increase in the standard error of the estimate when a variable is added to the model.

Mathematical approaches exist for dealing with multicollinearity and reducing its impact. Although these procedures are beyond the scope of this text, one suggestion is to eliminate the variables that are the chief cause of the multicollinearity problems. In the American County example, we would drop X_3 from the analysis. This variable is highly correlated with X_1, X_4, and X_5 and has low correlation with Y.

Dealing with multicollinearity problems requires a great deal of experience. This text simply aims to make you aware that such problems may exist and should be considered before the regression model is used.

SKILL DEVELOPMENT PROBLEMS FOR SECTION 14–2

The following exercises are included to help you gain a more complete understanding of the material presented in section 14–2. There are additional application problems located at the end of the chapter which pertain to the material in this section. If possible, use a computer and statistical software to solve the problems and exercises.

1. The Western State Tourist Association gives out pamphlets, maps, and other tourist-related information to people who call a toll-free number and request the information. The association orders the packets of information from a documents printing company and they like to have enough available to meet the immediate need without having too many sitting around taking up space. The marketing manager decided to develop a multiple regression model to be used in predicting the number of calls that will be received in the coming week. A random sample of eleven weeks is selected, with the following variables:

$$Y = \text{number of calls}$$
$$X_1 = \text{number of advertisements placed this week}$$
$$X_2 = \text{number of calls received last week}$$
$$X_3 = \text{number of airline tour bookings into western cities}$$
$$\text{for this week}$$

The following data were collected:

i	Y	X_1	X_2	X_3
1	345	12	297	3,456
2	456	14	502	2,456
3	356	13	340	3,600
4	605	16	450	3,500
5	209	14	350	2,400
6	306	10	340	2,890
7	457	15	401	3,457
8	259	12	340	2,590
9	540	13	400	3,240
10	460	16	440	3,560
11	378	14	348	2,460

Develop a correlation matrix for these variables and write a short report describing the various correlations. Comment on whether you feel a multiple regression model will be effectively developed from these data.

2. Referring to the data in problem 1, compute three simple linear regression models, one for each of the independent variables. Write a report that fully describes each of the models. Indicate in your report which of these models is best.

3. Referring to the data in problem 1 and to your work in problem 2, develop a multiple regression model that contains all three independent variables.

    a. Indicate the regression equation.

    b. How much of the total variation in the dependent variable is explained by the three independent variables in the model?

    c. Test to determine whether the overall model is statistically significant. Use alpha $= 0.05$ to conduct this test.

    d. Which, if any, of the independent variables is statistically significant? Test using alpha $= 0.05$.

    e. Determine the adjusted R square and comment on what it means.

    f. As the model stands, comment on whether it will be a useful model for predicting the number of calls to the Western State Tourist Association.

4. Referring to problems 1–3, prepare a short report that addresses the following points:

    a. Defines the term multicollinearity.

    b. Indicates the potential problems that multicollinearity can cause.

    c. Indicates what, if any, evidence there is of multicollinearity problems with this multiple regression model.

5. The athletic director of State University is interested in developing a multiple regression model that might be used to explain the variation in attendance at football games at his school. A sample of sixteen games was selected from home games played during the past ten seasons. Data for the following factors were determined:

$$Y = \text{game attendance}$$
$$X_1 = \text{team win/loss percentage to date}$$
$$X_2 = \text{opponent win/loss percentage to date}$$
$$X_3 = \text{games played this season}$$
$$X_4 = \text{temperature at game time}$$

The following data were collected:

i	Y	X_1	X_2	X_3	X_4
1	14,502	33.3	80.0	6	47
2	12,459	25.0	50.0	4	56
3	15,600	80.0	66.6	5	55
4	16,780	75.0	100.0	8	60
5	14,600	60.0	80.0	10	55
6	19,300	100.0	60.0	10	49
7	14,603	66.6	25.0	3	67
8	15,789	50.0	50.0	6	55
9	17,800	80.0	40.0	10	53
10	19,450	75.0	100.0	8	48
11	13,890	20.0	75.0	5	65
12	15,097	70.0	70.0	10	56
13	17,666	83.3	66.6	6	60
14	12,500	20.0	20.0	5	59
15	16,780	80.0	100.0	8	46
16	17,543	80.0	70.0	10	50

Develop a correlation matrix for these variables and write a short report describing the various correlations. Comment on whether you feel a multiple regression model will be effectively developed from these data.

6. Referring to the data in problem 5, compute four simple linear regression models, one for each of the independent variables. Write a report that fully describes each of the models. Indicate in your report which of these models is best.

7. Referring to the data in problem 5 and to your work in problem 6, develop a multiple regression model that contains all four independent variables.
   a. Indicate the regression equation.
   b. How much of the total variation in the dependent variable is explained by the four independent variables in the model?
   c. Test to determine whether the overall model is statistically significant. Use alpha = 0.05 to conduct this test.
   d. Which, if any, of the independent variables is statistically significant? Test using alpha = 0.05.
   e. Determine the adjusted R square and comment on what it means.
   f. Develop 95 percent confidence interval estimates for the regression coefficients and interpret these intervals. Write a short report to the athletic director describing the regression model.

8. Referring to problems 5–7, prepare a short report that addresses the following points:
   a. Defines the term multicollinearity.
   b. Indicates the potential problems that multicollinearity can cause.
   c. Indicates what, if any, evidence there is of multicollinearity problems with this multiple regression model.

DUMMY VARIABLES IN REGRESSION ANALYSIS

14-3

In many cases decision makers may want to use a nominal or ordinal variable (see chapter 1, section 1–2) as an independent variable in a regression model. If so, the variable is called a *qualitative variable*. For example, in a model for predicting individual income, a potential variable might be sex—male or female. In another example with GNP (gross national product) as the dependent variable, an interesting independent variable might be the U.S. president's political party—Republican or Democrat. In still another example, where the dependent variable is the number of dollars spent by women on cosmetics, such independent variables as marital status—single, married, widowed, divorced, or separated—and employment status—full time, part time, retired, unemployed, or other—are variables that may help to explain the variation in the dependent variable.

The problem with qualitative variables in a regression analysis is in assigning values to the outcomes. What value should we assign to a male as opposed to a female? What about assigning values for Republican versus Democrat? These classifications do not have unique numerical values, and different decision makers might well assign different values, which could affect the regression analysis.

To overcome this problem, qualitative variables are incorporated into a regression analysis by using **dummy variables.** For example, for the qualitative variable sex, which has two categories—male or female—a single dummy variable is created as follows:

$$\text{If sex } = \text{ male, } X_2 = 0.$$

$$\text{If sex } = \text{ female, } X_2 = 1.$$

For the political party variable, the dummy variable is

$$\text{If party } = \text{ Republican, } X_2 = 1.$$

$$\text{If party } = \text{ Democrat, } X_2 = 0.$$

Although the qualitative variable is coded (0, 1), it makes no difference which attribute is assigned zero and which is assigned 1.

When the qualitative variable has more than two possible categories, a series of dummy variables must be used. For example, since marital status could have five categories—single, married, separated, divorced, and widowed—we would develop four (5 − 1 = 4) dummy variables as follows:

$$\text{If single, } X_2 = 1$$
$$\text{Otherwise, } X_2 = 0$$

$$\text{If married, } X_3 = 1$$
$$\text{Otherwise } X_3 = 0$$

$$\text{If separated, } X_4 = 1$$
$$\text{Otherwise, } X_4 = 0$$

$$\text{If divorced, } X_5 = 1$$
$$\text{Otherwise, } X_5 = 0$$

For a widowed person, X_2, X_3, X_4, and X_5 would all be zero. By default, the person must belong to the remaining category, "widowed."[5]

To illustrate the effect of incorporating dummy variables into a regression model, consider the data displayed in the scatter plot in figure 14–5. The population from which these data were selected consists of executives between the ages of twenty-four and sixty who are working in U.S. manufacturing business. The simple linear regression line is also shown in figure 14–5. Data for the dependent variable, annual salary, and the independent variable, age, are available. Even though this model might be statistically significant, we would likely search for other independent variables that could help us to further explain the variation in annual salary.

Suppose we know which of the sixteen people in the sample had an MBA degree. Figure 14–6 shows the scatter plot for these same data with the MBA data circled. We can create a new variable, X_2, which is a dummy variable coded

---

[5]The mathematical reason that the number of dummy variables must be one less than the number of possible responses is called the **dummy variable trap.** Perfect multicollinearity is introduced, and the least squares regression estimates cannot be obtained if the number of dummy variables equals the number of possible categories.

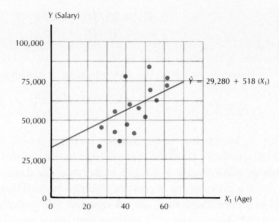

Income versus age

$$X_2 = 0 \text{ if no MBA}$$
$$X_2 = 1 \text{ if MBA}$$

Now we develop a two-variable multiple regression model of the form

$$\hat{Y} = b_0 + b_1X_1 + b_2X_2$$

After employing a computer and statistical software, we get the following model:

$$\hat{Y} = 25,002 + 625X_1 + 7,123X_2$$

Since the dummy variable, X_2, has been coded 0 or 1 depending on degree status, incorporating it into the regression model is like having two simple linear regression lines with the same slopes but different intercepts. For instance, when $X_2 = 0$, the regression equation is

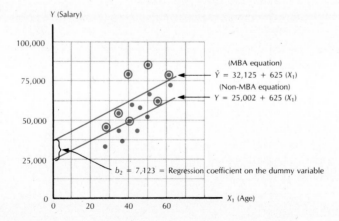

FIGURE 14–6
Impact of dummy variables on regression analysis

$$\hat{Y} = 25,002 + 625X_1 + 7,123(0)$$
$$= 25,002 + 625X_1$$

This line is shown in figure 14–6.

However, when $X_2 = 1$ (the executive has an MBA), the regression equation is

$$\hat{Y} = 25,002 + 625X_1 + 7,123(1)$$
$$= 32,125 + 625X_1$$

This regression line is also shown in figure 14–6. As you can see, the effect of the dummy variable is on the regression intercept. In this case, the intercept for executives with an MBA degree is $7,123 higher than for those without an MBA.

We interpret the regression coefficient on this degree dummy variable as follows: "Based upon these data, on the average and controlling for age (X_1), executives with an MBA degree make $7,123 per year more in salary than their non-MBA counterparts."

Of course, we could develop confidence interval estimates for this regression coefficient and test its significance just as we can with a quantitative variable.

We can also show the effect of including a dummy variable in the American County regression model by starting with the following simple regression equation:

$$\text{Sales price} = 9,915.78 + 20.45(\text{square feet})$$

Figure 14–7 illustrates this regression line for sales price as a function of square feet.

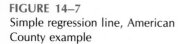

FIGURE 14–7
Simple regression line, American County example

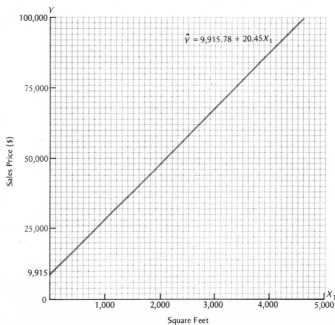

TABLE 14–5

Regression model with dummy variable, American County example

****

R SQUARE	.7583	
ADJUSTED R SQUARE	.7573	
STANDARD ERRØR	7038.7899	

- -

ANALYSIS ØF VARIANCE	D.F.	SUM ØF SQUARES	MEAN SQUARE	F
REGRESSIØN	2	82071871520.3	41035935760.1	828.44
RESIDUAL (UNEXPLAINED)	528	26159530525.8	49544563.5	

- - - - - - - - - - - - - - - - VARIABLES IN THE EQUATIØN - - - - - - - - - - - - - - - -

VARIABLE	B	STD. ERRØR B	T
X1 SQ. FT.	18.11	.70240	25.78
X6 AIR	2455.16	651.32152	3.76
(CØNSTANT)	8739.21		

****

Now, suppose a qualitative variable defining whether or not the house has central air conditioning is added. The variable would be

$$\text{If air conditioning, } X_6 = 1$$
$$\text{If no air conditioning, } X_6 = 0$$

Then the regression model would be

$$\hat{Y} = b_0 + b_1 X_1 + b_6 X_6$$

Table 14–5 shows the computer output for the American County regression model with square feet and air conditioning as the independent variables. The model is

$$\hat{Y} = 8,739.21 + 18.11 X_1 + 2,455.16 X_6$$

Since variable X_6 can be only zero or 1, incorporating a dummy variable is equivalent to finding two regression equations with *equal* slopes but *different* intercepts:

$$\hat{Y} = 8,739.21 + 18.11 X_1 \qquad \text{if } X_6 = 0$$

and

$$\hat{Y} = 11,194.37 + 18.11 X_1 \qquad \text{if } X_6 = 1$$

The inpact of the dummy variable is illustrated in figure 14–8. The difference in intercepts indicates that, holding square feet constant, the price of a house is on the average $2,455.16 higher if it has central air conditioning.

FIGURE 14–8

Impact of a dummy variable on the regression model, American County example

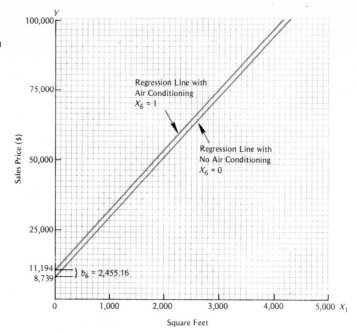

Improving the American County Appraisal Model

The real estate appraisal model we developed earlier was statistically significant, but because of the relatively large standard error of the estimate, the model was judged to be of little practical use. It might prove to be impossible to develop a regression appraisal model that is practically significant. However, before abandoning the idea, we might attempt to improve the model by *respecifying the model*. If a model is incorrectly specified, it is generally due to either of the following two factors:

1. Useful independent variables have been omitted from the model.
2. Independent variables have been included in the model which should not have been included.

There is no sure way of determining the correct model specification. However, a recommended approach is for the decision maker to try adding new variables or removing variables from the model in an attempt to improve the results.

Two variables that might affect sales price of a residential property are the location and whether the house has central air conditioning. If we can identify whether a house has air conditioning, we can use the dummy-variable concept just discussed and code this variable

$$\text{If air conditioning, } X_6 = 1$$

$$\text{If no air conditioning, } X_6 = 0$$

TABLE 14–6
Improved regression model, American County example
****

R SQUARE   .7940

ADJUSTED R SQUARE   .7920

STANDARD ERROR   6514.1353

- -

ANALYSIS OF VARIANCE	D.F.	SUM OF SQUARES	MEAN SQUARE	F
REGRESSION	5	859535732448.3	17190714649.6	405.5
RESIDUAL (UNEXPLAINED)	525	22277828797.0	42433959.6	

- - - - - - - - - - - - - - - -VARIABLES IN THE EQUATION- - - - - - - - - - - - - - - -

VARIABLE	B	STD. ERROR B	T
X1 SQ. FT.	16.93	.82041	20.63
X4 BATHS	4154.21	612.30521	6.78
X5 FIREPLACES	2010.45	692.57183	2.90
X6 AIR	1972.11	604.21073	3.26
X7 SCHOOLS	− 692.20	1304.52751	− .53

****

Data for the location variable are more difficult to come by. There are two high schools in the county. We can determine in which high school district each house is located. This breakdown of location should improve the regression model. The location variable is coded

$$\text{If Douglas High, } X_7 = 1$$
$$\text{If Biltmore High (not Douglas High), } X_7 = 0$$

Table 14–6 presents the computer output for the latest regression run with variables X_6 and X_7 included and variable X_3, number of bedrooms, excluded. Recall that X_3 was apparently giving rise to multicollinearity problems.

This latest regression model has a smaller standard error and higher R^2 than the original model shown in table 14–4. However, the dummy variable for location, X_7, has a t value of -0.53. We must conclude that the regression coefficient on this variable is not different from zero since -0.53 does not exceed the critical t value for an alpha level of 0.01 and 525 degrees of freedom of -2.576. Therefore, the location variable (high school district) is not helpful in determining the sales price of houses. In fact, the model as it now stands is still of little use since the standard error is again large. However, the standard error of the estimate should be judged on a *relative* rather than an *absolute* basis. A standard error of the estimate that is too large in one situation may be quite acceptable in another. For instance, although $S_e = \$6,514$ may be too large in an appraisal model, this same value would be viewed as exceptional in a model where U.S. GNP was the dependent variable.

This example illustrates that although a regression model may pass the statistical tests of significance, it may not be functional. Good appraisal models can be developed using multiple regression analysis provided more detail is available about such characteristics as finish quality, landscaping, location, neighborhood characteristics, and so forth. The cost and effort required to obtain these data can be relatively high.

Developing a multiple regression model is more an art than a science. The real decisions revolve around how to select the best set of independent variables for the model.

SKILL DEVELOPMENT PROBLEMS FOR SECTION 14–3

The following exercises are included to help you gain a better understanding of the material presented in this section. There are additional application problems at the end of the chapter to provide you with further opportunity to apply what you have learned.

9. A manager is considering incorporating a new variable into her regression model. This variable measures education level of the respondent. The variable has been measured on four levels as follows:

   1. No high school degree
   2. High school degree
   3. Some college courses
   4. College degree

   a. She is considering this variable and plans to use the codes 1, 2, 3, and 4 to determine which educational level the respondent has achieved. Comment on this.
   b. How many dummy variables would you set up to handle this situation? Describe each dummy variable.

10. The Polk Utility Corporation is developing a multiple regression model which they plan to use to predict customers' utility usage. They currently have three quantitative variables in the model but are unsatisfied with the R square and the standard error of the estimate. Two variables they think might be useful are whether the house has a gas water heater or an electric water heater and whether the house was constructed after the 1974 energy crisis or before.

    Provide the utility with the proper means of including these qualitative variables in their analysis.

11. A study was recently performed by the American Automobile Association in which they attempted to develop a regression model to explain variation in EPA mileage ratings of new cars. At one stage of the analysis, the model took the following form:

$$\hat{Y} = 34.20 - 0.003X_1 + 4.56X_2$$

where

$$X_1 = \text{vehicle weight}$$
$$X_2 = 1 \text{ if standard transmission}$$
$$= 0 \text{ if automatic transmission}$$

a. Interpret the regression coefficient on variable X_1.
b. Interpret the regression coefficient on variable X_2.
c. Discuss the effect of a dummy variable being incorporated in a regression model like this one. Use a graph if it is helpful.

12. A recent study by the U.S. Department of Agriculture attempted to develop a multiple regression model to explain variation in farm income. At one stage of development, the model took the following form:

$$\hat{Y} = -23{,}200 + 4.2X_1 + 2{,}345X_2 + 4{,}670X_3$$

where

$$X_1 = \text{number of acres farmed}$$
$$X_2 = 1 \text{ if land is row-irrigated}$$
$$= 0 \text{ if not}$$
$$X_3 = 1 \text{ if land is sprinkler-irrigated}$$
$$= 0 \text{ if not}$$

a. Interpret the regression coefficient on variable X_1.
b. Interpret the regression coefficient on variable X_2.
c. Interpret the regression coefficient on variable X_3.

13. The following data were collected by the Gilmore Accounting Firm in an effort to explain variation in client profitability:

Y	X_1	X_2
2,345	45	1
4,200	56	2
278	26	3
1,211	56	2
1,406	24	2
500	23	3
−700	34	3
3,457	45	1
2,478	47	1
1,975	24	2
206	32	3

where

$$Y = \text{net profit earned from the client}$$
$$X_1 = \text{number of hours spent working with the client}$$
$$X_2 = \text{type of client:}$$
1 if manufacturing
2 if service
3 if governmental

a. Develop a plot of each independent variable against the client income variable. Comment on what, if any, relationship appears to exist.
b. Run a simple linear regression analysis using only variable X_1 as the independent variable. Describe this model fully.
c. Now, incorporate the client type variable into the regression analysis and describe the resulting multiple regression model. Test all appropriate hypotheses, using an alpha = 0.05 level. (*Hint:* You will have to develop dummy variables.)
d. Holding the other factors constant, what is the average difference in profit if the client is governmental? Also state this in terms of a 95 percent confidence interval estimate.

STEPWISE REGRESSION ANALYSIS

14-4

In the American County example, we began with five independent variables plus the dependent variable, sales price. After examining the correlation matrix, we eliminated the age variable, X_2 since it had such a low correlation with price. Finally, we used a computer routine to develop the multiple regression model shown in table 14-4. Once the model had been developed, we were left to analyze its statistical and functional validity. We use the term *ordinary regression* for this approach of bringing all independent variables into the model at one step.

Another method for developing a regression model is called *stepwise regression*. Stepwise regression, as the name implies, develops the least squares regression equation in steps, either through *backward elimination* or through *forward selection*.

Backward Elimination

The backward elimination stepwise method begins by developing an ordinary regression model using all independent variables. Then a t test for significance is performed on each regression coefficient at a specified alpha level. Provided at least one t value is in the acceptance region (H_0: $\beta_i = 0$ is accepted), the variable with the t value closest to zero is removed, and another ordinary regression model is developed with the remaining independent variables. The backward elimination continues until all independent variables remaining in the model have coefficients that are significantly different from zero. The models at each step are printed by the computer routine.[6]

The advantage of backward elimination is that the decision maker has the opportunity to look at all the independent variables in the model before removing the variables that are not significant.

Forward Selection

Whereas the backward elimination procedure begins with a regression model containing all variables and eliminates insignificant variables in a stepwise fashion, the forward selection procedure works in the opposite direction. The forward selection procedure begins by selecting a single independent variable from all available. The independent variable selected at step 1 is the variable that is most highly correlated with the dependent variable. At step 2, a second independent variable is selected based on its ability to explain the remaining unexplained variation in the dependent variable.

The independent variable selected at each step is the variable with the highest *coefficient of partial determination*. The coefficient of determination measures the proportion of variation explained by all the independent variables in the model. By contrast, the coefficient of partial determination measures the marginal contribution of a single independent variable, given that other independent variables are in the model.

Thus, after the first variable (say, X_1) is selected, R^2 will indicate the percentage of variation explained by this variable. The forward selection routine will then compute all possible two-variable regression models with X_1 included and determine the R^2 for each model. The coefficient of partial determination at step 2 is the proportion of unexplained variation (after X_1 is in the model) that is explained by the additional variable. The independent variable that adds the most to R^2, given the variables already in the model, is the one selected. This process continues until either all independent variables have been entered or the remaining independent variables do not add appreciably to R^2. This procedure is outlined in figure 14–9.

The forward selection stepwise method serves one more important function. If two or more variables overlap, a variable selected in an early step may become insignificant when other variables were added at later steps. The forward selection procedure will drop this insignificant variable from the model. Stepwise regression also offers a means of observing multicollinearity problems since we can see how the regression model changes as each new variable is added to the model.

The forward selection stepwise procedure is widely used in decision-making applications and is generally recognized as a useful regression method. However, care should be exercised when using this procedure since it is easy to rely too heavily on the automatic selection process. Remember, the order of variable selection is conditional, based on the variables already in the model. There is no guarantee that stepwise regression will lead you to the best set of independent variables from those available. Decision

---

[6]Most software packages allow the user to override the default and force variables from the model even though they may be statistically significant.

(a) No independent variables in the model.

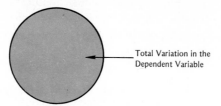

(b) Enter the variable with the highest correlation.

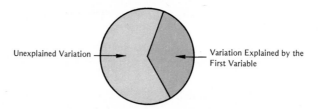

(c) Enter the variable that explains the most of the unexplained variation (has the highest coefficient of partial determination).

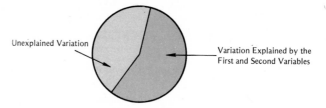

(d) Continue adding variables based on how much of the unexplained variation they account for until the next variable explains an insignificant proportion.

FIGURE 14–9
Graphical representation of the forward stepwise procedure

makers still must use common sense in applying regression analysis to make sure they have usable regression models.

A Stepwise Regression Example

The B. T. Longmont Company operates a large retail department store in San Francisco. Like other department stores, Longmont has incurred heavy losses due to shoplifting and employee pilferage. The store's security manager wants to develop a regression model to explain the monthly dollar loss from these factors. The variables the security manager is interested in are

$$X_1 = \text{average monthly temperature (°F)}$$
$$X_2 = \text{number of sales transactions}$$

X_3 = number of days per month the store is open

X_4 = number of persons on the store's monthly payroll

Y = monthly dollar loss due to shoplifting and pilferage

Table 14–7 lists the data for these variables for a random sample of seventeen months. The correlation matrix of the data is presented in table 14–8.

Note that variable X_2, number of sales transactions, is most highly correlated with dollars lost. Using the forward stepwise selection procedure, X_2 will be the first variable selected. The computer output for the model at step 1 is shown in table 14–9.

At step 1, variable X_2, number of monthly sales transactions, explains 0.3942 of the variation in the dependent variable. The overall model is significant at the 0.05 alpha level because the calculated $F = 9.764$ exceeds the table F value with 1 and 15 degrees of freedom.

Now, look at the bottom of table 14–9 to the section "variables not in the equation." The next variable added is the one that can contribute most to R^2, given that variable X_2 is already in the model. This variable will be the one with the highest coefficient of partial determination. As you can see, the variable selected in step 2 should be X_4, number of employees, since it can explain almost 29 percent of the remaining unexplained variation in the dependent variable. Tables 14–10, 14–11, and 14–12 shows steps 2, 3, and 4 of the stepwise regression.

The model at step 4 explains 74.8 percent of the variation and is significant at the 0.05 level ($F = 8.90$). In analyzing the independent variables, using the t test, we find

TABLE 14–7

Data, B. T. Longmont Company example

	Temperature X_1	No. Sales Made X_2	No. Days X_3	No. Employees X_4	Dollars Lost Y
1	58.8	7,107	21	129	3,067
2	65.2	6,373	22	141	2,828
3	70.9	6,796	22	153	2,891
4	77.4	9,208	20	166	2,994
5	79.3	14,792	25	193	3,082
6	81.0	14,564	23	189	3,898
7	71.9	11,964	20	175	3,502
8	63.9	13,526	23	186	3,060
9	54.5	12,656	20	190	3,211
10	39.5	14,119	20	187	3,286
11	44.5	16,691	22	195	3,542
12	43.6	14,571	19	206	3,125
13	56.0	13,619	22	198	3,022
14	64.7	14,575	22	192	2,922
15	73.0	14,556	21	191	3,950
16	78.9	18,573	21	200	4,488
17	79.4	15,618	22	200	3,295

TABLE 14-8
Correlation matrix, B. T. Longmont Company example

	X1	X2	X3	X4	Y
X1	1.000	− .024	.438	− .082	.286
X2		1.000	.096	.920	.628
X3			1.000	.032	− .089
X4				1.000	.413
Y					1.000

all four significant at the alpha level of 0.05. However, we find some evidence of multicollinearity in the model. For instance, at step 4 the coefficient of X_4, number of employees, is negative, yet the correlation matrix shows a positive correlation between dollar loss and number of employees. Also, as we move from step to step in the output, the regression coefficients change. In addition, the significance of variable X_1 improves

TABLE 14-9
Step 1 of the regression model, B. T. Longmont Company example

****

STEP NUMBER 1

VARIABLE ENTERED   X2

R SQUARE   .3942

ADJUSTED R SQUARE   .3538

STANDARD ERROR   359.0574

- -

ANALYSIS OF VARIANCE	D.F.	SUM OF SQUARES	MEAN SQUARE	F
REGRESSION	1	1258790.00	1258790.0	9.764
RESIDUAL (UNEXPLAINED)	15	1933835.00	128922.3	

- - - - - - - - - - - - - - - - - VARIABLES IN THE EQUATION - - - - - - - - - - - - - - - - -

VARIABLE	B	STD. ERROR B	T
X2 SALES	.07687	.02460	3.12
(CONSTANT)	2316.51855		

- - - - - - - - - - - - - - - - - VARIABLES NOT IN THE EQUATION - - - - - - - - - - - - - -

VARIABLE	PARTIAL R SQUARE
X1 TEMP.	.14932
X3 DAYS	.03704
X4 EMPLOYEES	.28828

****

TABLE 14-10

Step 2 of the regression model, B. T. Longmont Company example

****

STEP NUMBER 2

VARIABLE ENTERED	X4
R SQUARE	.5689
ADJUSTED R SQUARE	.5073
STANDARD ERROR	313.5452

- -

ANALYSIS OF VARIANCE	D.F.	SUM OF SQUARES	MEAN SQUARE	F
REGRESSION	2	1816276.0	908138.0	9.23
RESIDUAL (UNEXPLAINED)	14	1376349.0	98310.6	

- - - - - - - - - - - - - - - VARIABLES IN THE EQUATION - - - - - - - - - - - - - - -

VARIABLE	B	STD. ERROR B	T
X2 SALES	.19661	.05468	3.59
X4 EMPLOYEES	− 21.60054	9.07085	−2.38
(CONSTANT)	4706.38203		

- - - - - - - - - - - - - - - VARIABLES NOT IN THE EQUATION - - - - - - - - - - - - - - -

VARIABLE	PARTIAL R SQUARE
X1 TEMP.	.13306
X3 DAYS	.10452

****

when variable X_3 is added in the final step. These are all signs of correlation between the independent variables. We suggest the security manager be cautious about any conclusions he might reach based on this model.

This example has illustrated stepwise regression analysis and has shown what a computer output for such an analysis looks like. The model was developed using the forward selection procedure; however the model at step 4 is exactly the same as it would be using the ordinary approach with all four independent variables. The order in which variables enter makes no difference as long as all variables are in the model.

SKILL DEVELOPMENT PROBLEMS FOR SECTION 14-4

The following exercises have been included to help you gain a solid understanding of the material discussed in this section. There are additional application problems at the end of this chapter for you to work.

TABLE 14–11
Step 3 of the regression model, B. T. Longmont Company example
****

STEP NUMBER 3

VARIABLE ENTERED   X1

R SQUARE   .6263

ADJUSTED R SQUARE   .5400

STANDARD ERROR   302.9600

ANALYSIS OF VARIANCE	D.F.	SUM OF SQUARES	MEAN SQUARE	F
REGRESSION	3	1999422.0	6664740.0	7.26
RESIDUAL (UNEXPLAINED)	13	1193203.0	91784.8	

----------------- VARIABLES IN THE EQUATION ----------------

VARIABLE		B	STD. ERROR B	T
X2	SALES	.18667	.05330	3.50
X4	EMPLOYEES	− 19.67947	8.86950	− 2.21
X1	TEMP.	8.01620	5.67487	1.41
(CONSTANT)		3964.87085		

--------------- VARIABLES NOT IN THE EQUATION ---------------

VARIABLE		PARTIAL R SQUARE
X3	DAYS	.32490

****

14. Referring to the data collected by the Western State Tourist Association (see problem 1), develop the multiple regression model for predicting the number of calls received, using stepwise regression.
   a. At the final step of the analysis, how many variables are in the model?
   b. Indicate the regression model by showing the intercept and regression coefficients.
   c. Test to determine whether the overall regression model is statistically significant at the alpha = 0.05 level.
   d. Discuss why the variables entered the model in the order shown by the stepwise regression.

15. In problem 5, the athletic director at State University was interested in developing a multiple regression model for explaining the variation in home-game football attendance. Use stepwise regression to develop the model.
   a. Which variable entered the model at step 1? Discuss why this variable entered.
   b. Indicate the order of variables entering the stepwise regression model. What

TABLE 14–12

Step 4 of the regression model, B. T. Longmont Company example

****

STEP NUMBER 4

VARIABLE ENTERED	X3
R SQUARE	.7480
ADJUSTED R SQUARE	.6640
STANDARD ERROR	258.9106

ANALYSIS OF VARIANCE	D.F.	SUM OF SQUARES	MEAN SQUARE	F
REGRESSION	4	2388207.0	597051.7	8.90
RESIDUAL (UNEXPLAINED)	12	804417.0	67034.7	

------------------ VARIABLES IN THE EQUATION ------------------

VARIABLE		B	STD. ERROR B	T
X2	SALES	.20053	.04591	4.36
X4	EMPLOYEES	− 21.25937	7.60824	− 2.79
X1	TEMP.	13.57066	5.37026	2.52
X3	DAYS	− 119.80313	49.74646	− 2.41
(CONSTANT)		6286.20703		

------------------ VARIABLES NOT IN THE EQUATION ------------------

VARIABLE	PARTIAL R SQUARE

****

    happens to R square and the standard error of the estimate for each variable entering?

    c. Indicate the regression model at the final step. Also indicate why the model stopped at this step.

    d. Test the overall significance of the regression model at the final step. Also test whether each regression coefficient is statistically significant. Use an alpha = 0.05 level.

16. Comment on the statement, "Stepwise regression is the way to go. It will always give you the best subset of independent variables from the original list of variables. R square will be maximized by using stepwise regression."

17. We have four potential independent variables, X_1, X_2, X_3, and X_4, from which we wish to develop a multiple regression model. Using stepwise regression, X_2 and X_4 entered the model.

    a. Why did only two variables enter the model? Discuss.

    b. Suppose an ordinary regression with variables X_2 and X_4 had been run. Would the resulting model be different than the stepwise model? Discuss.

    c. Comment on the statement, ''The stepwise regression with the two variables will have a higher R square than an ordinary regression with all four variables included.''

DETERMINING THE APTNESS OF THE MODEL (OPTIONAL)

14-5

When we develop a simple linear or multiple regression model, we can't be sure that the model is proper for the application. That is, the model we have developed may not be suited to the available data. In chapter 13, we outlined the assumptions associated with linear regression analysis. To summarize, the regression assumptions are

    1. The relationship between the dependent and independent variables is linear.

    2. The residuals are independent.

    3. The variance of the residuals is constant over the range of the independent variables.

    4. The residuals are normally distributed.

The degree to which the regression model satisfies the assumptions is called its *aptness*.

Analysis of residuals

The residual, the difference between the actual value of the dependent variable and the value predicted by the regression model, is defined by equation 14–10:

$$\boxed{\text{Residual} = (Y_i - \hat{Y}_i)} \qquad \text{(14–10)}$$

A residual value can be computed for each observation in the data set. A great deal can be learned about the *aptness* of the regression model by analyzing the residuals. The principal means of residual analysis is study of residual plots. The following problems can be discovered through graphical analysis of residuals:

    1. The regression function is not linear.

    2. The residuals do not have a constant variance.

    3. The residuals are not independent.

    4. The error terms are not normally distributed.

We will address each of these in order.

The Regression Function Is Not Linear

A plot of the residuals (on the vertical axis) against the independent variable (on the horizontal axis) is useful for detecting whether a linear function is the appropriate

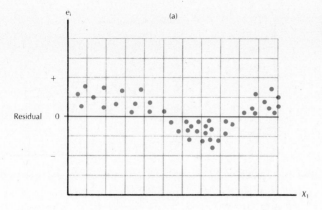

FIGURE 14–10
Residual plot—linear versus nonlinear

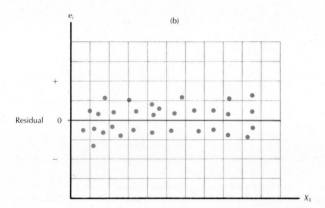

regression function. Figure 14–10 illustrates two different residual plots. Figure 14–10(a) shows residuals that systematically depart from zero. When X_1 is small, the residuals are positive. When X_1 is in the midrange, the residuals are negative, and for large X_1 values, the residuals are positive again. This type of plot suggests the relationship between Y and X_1 is nonlinear. Figure 14–10(b) shows a plot where the residuals do not show a systematic variation from zero, implying the relationship between X_1 and Y is linear.

Thus, if a linear model is appropriate, we expect the residuals to band around zero with no systematic pattern displayed.

The Residuals Do Not Have a Constant Variance

Residual plots can also be used to determine whether the residuals have a constant variance. Consider figure 14–11, in which the residuals are plotted against the independent variable. The plot in figure 14–11(a) shows an example in which, as X_1 increases, the residuals become less variable. Figure 14–11(b) shows the opposite situation. When X_1 is small, the residuals are tightly packed around zero, but as X_1 increases, the resid-

FIGURE 14–11
Constant and nonconstant variance

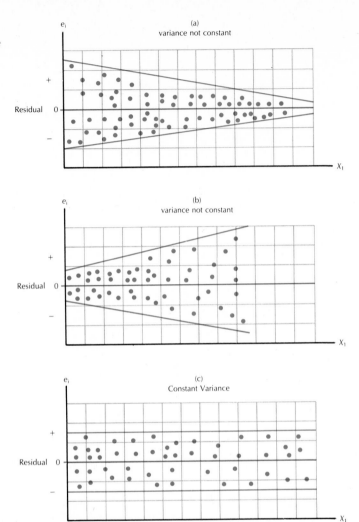

uals become more variable. Figure 14–11(c) shows an example in which the residuals exhibit a constant variance around the zero mean.

When the residual plot is cone-shaped, as in either figure 14–11(a) or 14–11(b), it suggests the assumption of constant variance has been violated. When a multiple regression model has been employed, we can analyze the constant variance assumption by plotting the residuals against the predicted values, as shown in figure 14–12. Because the plot is cone-shaped, we conclude that the constant variance assumption has not been satisfied.

The Residuals Are Not Independent

If the data used to develop the regression model are measured over time, a plot of the residuals against time is used to determine whether the residuals are correlated. Figure

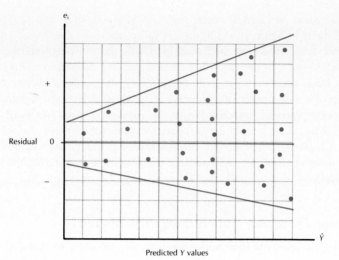

FIGURE 14–12
Plot of residuals against $\hat{Y}$

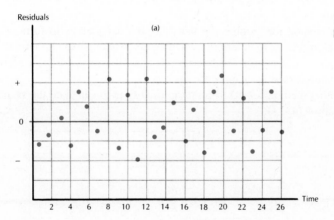

FIGURE 14–13
Plot of residuals against time

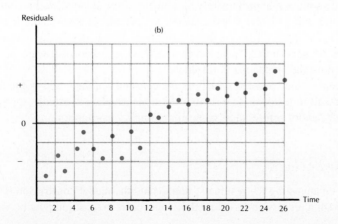

14–13(a) shows an example where the residual plot against time suggests independence. The residuals in figure 14–13(a) appear to be randomly distributed around the mean of zero over time. However, in figure 14–13(b), the plot suggests the residuals are not independent since in the early time periods the residuals are negative and in later time periods the residuals are positive. This, or any other pattern in the residuals over time, indicates the assumption of independent residuals has been violated. Generally, this means some variable associated with the passage of time has been omitted from the model. Often, time is used as surrogate for other time-related variables in a regression model. Chapters 16 and 17 will discuss time series data analysis and forecasting techniques in more detail and will address the issue of incorporating the time variable into the model.

The Error Terms Are Not Normally Distributed

The need for normally distributed residuals occurs when we want to test a hypothesis on the regression model. Small departures from normality don't cause serious problems. However, if the residuals depart dramatically from normal distribution, there is cause for concern.

   One method for graphically analyzing the residuals is to form a frequency histogram of the residuals to determine whether the general shape is normal. The chi-square goodness of fit test can be used to test whether the residuals fit a normal distribution. This test is discussed in chapter 15.

   Another method for determining normality is to calculate the **standardized residuals** (equation 14–11):

$$\frac{e_i}{\sqrt{MSE}} \tag{14–11}$$

where e_i = ith residual
   $MSE = \Sigma(Y_i - Y_i)^2/(n - K - 1)$

We then determine if approximately 68 percent of the standardized residuals have values between $+1$ and -1 and whether about 95 percent of the standardized residuals fall between $+1.96$ and -1.96. If these criteria are satisfied, we can assume that no gross departures from normality have occurred. Most regression software packages have an option to print the standardized residuals.

   Because other problems such as nonconstant variance and nonindependent residuals can result in residuals that seem to be nonnormal, it is usually appropriate to check these other factors before addressing the normality assumption.

Corrective Actions

If, based on analyzing the residuals, you decide the model constructed is not appropriate but still want a regression-based model, some corrective action may be warranted. There are two approaches that may work: transform some variables or use a different regression model.

Section 13–7 of Chapter 13 outlined the steps involved in variable transformation. The transformations of the independent variables (such as raising X to a power, taking the square root of X, or taking the log of X) are used to make the data conform to a linear relationship. If our model suffers from both nonlinearity and from the residuals having a nonconstant variance, it may be helpful to transform both the independent and dependent variables. In cases where the normality assumption is not satisfied, it is often helpful to try transformations of the dependent variable. In many instances, a log transformation is useful.

The alternative of using a different regression model means that we respecify the model to include new independent variables or remove existing variables from the model. In most modeling applications, we are in a continual state of model respecification. We are always seeking to improve the regression model by finding new independent variables.

SKILL DEVELOPMENT PROBLEMS FOR SECTION 14–5

The following exercises are included to help you gain a more complete understanding of the material presented in this section. There are additional applications problems at the end of the chapter which will provide more practice in applying these concepts.

18. Listed below are data collected on an independent variable and a dependent variable:

Y	X
200	23.4
180	19.5
210	20.3
230	26.9
219	21.0
195	16.6
267	27.0
290	27.5
304	28.1
240	25.7

a. Develop a simple linear regression model using the above data. Show the regression equation, R square, and the standard error of the estimate.

b. Compute the residuals for each observation.

c. Plot the residuals against the X variable. What conclusions could be reached about the aptness of the model based upon this plot? Discuss.

d. Plot the residuals against the predicted values of Y and comment on what this plot says about the aptness of the model.

19. Referring to problem 1 in section 14–2, compute the residuals.
   a. Based upon the appropriate residual plot, what can you conclude about the constant variance assumption?
   b. Based upon the appropriate residual analysis, does it appear that the residuals are independent? Discuss.

20. Referring to problem 5 in section 14–2, compute the residuals.
   a. Based upon the appropriate residual plot, what can you conclude about the constant variance assumption?
   b. Based upon the appropriate residual analysis, does it appear that the residuals are independent? Discuss.

21. Discuss what is meant by the term aptness of the model. Use some examples to illustrate your answer.

22. Under what conditions is it desirable to plot the residuals against the predicted Y values? Discuss.

23. In a multiple regression model, if we wish to determine whether the residuals have a constant variance, is it appropriate to plot the residuals against each X variable individually? If not, what should be done?

TABLE 14–13

SPSS-X output—correlation coefficients

```
- - - - - - - -   PEARSON    CORRELATION   COEFFICIENTS - - - - - - - -
            VAR12      VAR13      VAR14      VAR15      VAR17      VAR18      VAR19
VAR12     1.0000      .0037      .0511      .0996     -.0615     -.0323     -.3307
          (    0) (     50) (     50) (     50) (     50) (     50) (     50)
          P=  .     P= .490   P= .362   P= .246   P= .336   P= .412   P= .009

VAR13      .0037     1.0000      .0856      .2189      .0692     -.1462      .0081
          (   50) (      0) (     50) (     50) (     50) (     50) (     50)
          P= .490   P=  .     P= .277   P= .063   P= .316   P= .156   P= .478

VAR14      .0511      .0856     1.0000      .5754      .4410      .2276     -.0104
          (   50) (     50) (      0) (     50) (     50) (     50) (     50)
          P= .362   P= .277   P=  .     P= .000   P= .001   P= .056   P= .472

VAR15      .0996      .2189      .5754     1.0000      .5199      .0220     -.1307
          (   50) (     50) (     50) (      0) (     50) (     50) (     50)
          P= .246   P= .063   P= .000   P=  .     P= .000   P= .440   P= .183

VAR17     -.0615      .0692      .4410      .5199     1.0000     -.1017      .1398
          (   50) (     50) (     50) (     50) (      0) (     50) (     50)
          P= .336   P= .316   P= .001   P= .000   P=  .     P= .241   P= .166

VAR18     -.0323     -.1462      .2276      .0220     -.1017     1.0000     -.3408
          (   50) (     50) (     50) (     50) (     50) (      0) (     50)
          P= .412   P= .156   P= .056   P= .440   P= .241   P=  .     P= .008

VAR19     -.3307      .0081     -.0104     -.1307      .1398     -.3408     1.0000
          (   50) (     50) (     50) (     50) (     50) (     50) (      0)
          P= .009   P= .478   P= .472   P= .183   P= .166   P= .008   P=  .
```

COMPUTER APPLICATIONS

14-6

This chapter has presented an introduction to multiple regression analysis. Although multiple regression can be done manually, we doubt that anyone would attempt it in this age of computers. In fact, the examples presented in this chapter have been done using a computer and statistical software. In this section, we present some further computer applications of multiple regression analysis. The data used are the KIVZ-Channel 5 survey data originally introduced in chapter 2. We suggest you refer to tables 2–10 and 2–11 for a listing of the data and a description of the variables. The software used here are the MINITAB and SPSS-X packages.

Table 14–13 shows the correlation matrix for several of the variables in the KIVZ-Channel 5 survey. This correlation matrix, which was developed using SPSS-X, shows the correlation between each pair of variables. Also shown are the *p* values referred to earlier in this text. The *p* values indicate the level of significance of the correlation coefficients. For instance, the correlation between VAR13 and VAR14 is 0.0856, and

```
UNNUMBERED
TITLE DESCRIPTIVE STATISTICS EXAMPLES
FILE HANDLE KIVZ NAME='KIVZ DATA C'
DATA LIST FILE=KIVZ LIST/VAR01 TO VAR19
VARIABLE LABELS
   VAR01 'NATIONAL NEWS STATION'
   VAR02 'LOCAL NEWS STATION'
   VAR03 'NEWS RATING'
   VAR04 'SPORTS RATING'
   VAR05 'WEATHER RATING'
   VAR06 'ANCHOR RATING'
   VAR07 'SPORTSCASTER RATING'
   VAR08 'OVERALL RATING'
   VAR09 'NATIONAL INFLUENCE'
   VAR10 'SEX'
   VAR11 'MARITAL STATUS'
   VAR12 'NUMBER EMPLOYED'
   VAR13 'HOME STATUS '
   VAR14 'YEARS AT RESIDENCE'
   VAR15 'YEARS IN STATE'
   VAR16 'EDUCATION'
   VAR17 'AGE'
   VAR18 'INCOME'
   VAR19 'HOURS OF TV'
VALUE LABELS
   VAR01 1 'CHANNEL 5' 2 'CHANNEL 3' 3 'CHANNEL 8' 4
         'UNDECIDED'/
   VAR02 1 'CHANNEL 3' 2 'CHANNEL 8' 3 'CHANNEL 5' 4
         'UNDECIDED'/
   VAR03 TO VAR08 1 'POOR' 2 'FAIR' 3 'GOOD' 4 'VERY GOOD' 5
         'EXCEL'/
   VAR09 1 'TRUE' 2 'FALSE' 3 'UNDECIDED'/
   VAR10 1 'MALE' 2 'FEMALE'/
   VAR11 1 'SINGLE' 2 'DIVORCED' 3 'MARRIED' 4 'OTHER'/
   VAR13 1 'RENTING' 2 'BUYING'/
   VAR16 1 'GRADE SCHOOL' 2 'SOME COLLEGE' 3 'VOTECH' 4 'HIGH
         SCHOOL' 5 'COLLEGE GRAD' 6 'GRADUATE WORK'
PEARSON CORR VAR12 TO VAR15, VAR 17 TO VAR19
```

FIGURE 14–14
SPSS-X commands—correlation matrix

TABLE 14–14

MINITAB output—regression analysis

```
The regression equation is
INCOME = 24824 + 1844 SEX + 32.3 YEARS - 42.6 AGE

Predictor       Coef      Stdev    t-ratio
Constant       24824       2333      10.64
SEX             1844       1395       1.32
YEARS          32.31      43.92       0.74
AGE           -42.57      52.12      -0.82

s = 4819    R-sq = 5.4%    R-sq(adj) = 0.0%

Analysis of Variance

SOURCE          DF           SS           MS
Regression       3      60945584     20315196
Error           46    1068238592     23222580
Total           49    1129184256

SOURCE      DF      SEQ SS
SEX          1    42239232
YEARS        1     3217043
AGE          1    15489310

Unusual Observations
Obs.    SEX    INCOME     Fit    Stdev.Fit   Residual   St.Resid
   8   0.00    13600   23227        1227      -9627      -2.07R
  18   1.00    39200   25237        1040      13963       2.97R

R denotes an obs. with a large st. resid.
```

this is significant at the 0.277 level. This means that the correlation would be significant if our alpha level is more than 0.277. Figure 14–14 (p. 675) shows the SPSS-X commands used to generate the correlation matrix in table 14–13. The table also shows the labels for each variable.

Table 14–14 shows a MINITAB multiple regression output where INCOME is the dependent variable and AGE, YEARS in the state, and SEX are the independent variables. Figure 14–15 shows the MINITAB commands used to generate the output. Note that the SEX variable was originally coded 1 = Males, 2 = Females. We have recoded it to be 0 = Males, 1 = Females, and it is used as a dummy variable in the regression model. (This recoding is not necessary except to be consistent with the presentation in this chapter.)

FIGURE 14–15

MINITAB commands—multiple regression analysis

```
MTB> READ 'KIVZ5' INTO C1-C19
MTB> NAME C18 'INCOME'
MTB> NAME C10 'SEX'
MTB> NAME C17 'AGE'
MTB> NAME C15 'YEARS'
MTB> SUBTRACT 1 C10 C10
MTB> OUTFILE = 'PRINTER'
MTB> REGRESS C18 3 C10 C15 C17
```

CONCLUSIONS

14-7

Multiple regression is an extension of simple regression analysis. In multiple regression, two or more independent variables are used to explain the variation in the dependent variable. Just as a manager searches for the best combination of employees to perform a job, the decision maker using multiple regression analysis searches for the best combination of independent variables to explain variation in the dependent variable.

The presentation of multiple regression analysis has largely been an analysis of computer printouts. As a decision maker, you will almost assuredly not be required to manually develop the regression model, but you will have to judge its applicability based on a computer printout. The programs we have used in chapters 13 and 14 are representative of the many available. You no doubt will encounter printouts that look somewhat different from those shown in this text, and some of the terms used may differ slightly. However, the basic information will be the same, as will be the inferences you can make from the model.

This chapter has discussed the difference between R^2 and adjusted R^2, and also the difference between statistical significance and practical significance. As a decision maker, you must recognize that a regression model can be statistically significant yet have no practical use because the standard error of the estimate is too large or multicollinearity impacts too heavily.

CHAPTER GLOSSARY

adjusted R square (R_A^2)   A measure of the percentage of explained variation in the dependent variable that takes into account the relationship between the number of cases and the number of independent variables in the regression model. Whereas R^2 will always increase when an independent variable is added, adjusted R^2 (R_A^2) will decrease if the added variable does not reduce the unexplained variation enough to offset the loss of degrees of freedom.

correlation matrix   A table showing the pairwise correlations between all variables (dependent and independent).

dummy variables   Variables in a regression model that have two categories, valued zero and 1. If a qualitative variable has v multiple categories, $v - 1$ dummy variables are formed to represent the qualitative variable in the analysis.

multicollinearity   Correlation among the independent variables. Usually the term is used when the intercorrelation is high.

multiple coefficient of determination (R^2)   The percentage of variation in the dependent variable explained by the independent variables in the regression model.

multiple regression model   A regression model having two or more independent variables with a regression equation of the form

$$Y_i = \beta_0 + \beta_1 X_{1i} + \beta_2 X_{2i} + \beta_3 X_{3i} + \ldots + \beta_K X_{Ki} + e_i$$

regression plane   The multiple regression equivalent of the simple regression line. The plane has a different slope for each independent variable.

> **standard error of the estimate**   The square root of the mean square residual in the analysis of variance table for a regression model. The standard error measures the dispersion of the actual values of the dependent variable around the fitting regression plane.
>
> **standardized residual**   The residual divided by the standard error of the estimate.

CHAPTER FORMULAS

Standard error of the estimate

$$S_e = \sqrt{\text{MSE}} = \sqrt{\frac{\text{SSE}}{n - K - 1}}$$

Correlation coefficient

$$r = \frac{\Sigma(X_i - \bar{X})(Y_i - \bar{Y})}{\sqrt{\Sigma(X_i - \bar{X})^2 \Sigma(Y_i - \bar{Y})^2)}}$$

Coefficient of multiple determination

$$R^2 = \frac{\text{SSR}}{\text{TSS}}$$

Adjusted R^2

$$R_A^2 = 1 - (1 - R^2)\left(\frac{n - 1}{n - K - 1}\right)$$

Standardized residual

$$\frac{e_i}{\sqrt{\text{MSE}}}$$

ADDITIONAL PROBLEMS

The problems in this chapter are written with the assumption that you will be solving them with the aid of a computer and appropriate software.

Section 14–1

24. A financial analyst for a Wall Street firm recently collected a random sample of twenty-four companies and recorded their year-end stock prices. She hopes to be able to develop a regression model that can be used to explain the variation in stock prices for these twenty-four firms. She plans on using financial ratios like the debt/equity ratio as independent variables. What would you suggest to her as the maximum number of independent variables to use in the model? Discuss.

25. Discuss in your own terms the similarities and differences between simple linear regression analysis and multiple regression analysis.

26. Discuss the assumptions associated with regression analysis.

27. Discuss what is meant by the least squares objective as it pertains to multiple regression analysis. Is the least squares objective any different for simple regression analysis? Discuss.

Section 14–2

28. The managerial development director of a major corporation is trying to determine what personal abilities are necessary for a manager to move from middle- to upper-level management. Although she has been relatively successful predicting who will move rapidly from lower- to middle-management levels, she has had difficulty determining the characteristics necessary to move to the next major level. For a long time the director has heard that the most glaring deficiency in college graduates entering the company is in communication skills, so she decides to measure whether these skills may be a determining factor.

   The director decides to try to develop a multiple regression relationship between job ratings and communication ability. She picks a random sample of middle-level managers who have been in their present positions less than five years but more than one year. These managers are given a series of cases to analyze and asked to present both written and verbal recommendations. They are rated by a group of top-level managers on their analyses and on their written and verbal presentations. These ratings are then compared with the latest employee rating. The data are as follows:

Employee	Job Rating	Case Analysis Score	Written Presentation Score	Verbal Presentation Score
1	87	8.4	8.7	9.2
2	93	8.2	9.4	9.4
3	91	9.3	9.7	9.5
4	85	7.9	8.1	8.7
5	86	8.1	8.3	8.8
6	97	9.4	9.3	9.6
7	90	9.1	9.0	9.2
8	93	8.9	9.2	9.5
9	88	8.6	8.4	8.5
10	96	9.7	9.5	9.6
11	86	8.3	7.9	8.4
12	89	8.7	8.5	8.7
13	94	9.2	9.1	9.6
14	91	8.1	9.5	9.2
15	95	9.3	9.1	9.7

Use a computer routine available at your school to determine the multiple regression equation for these data.

Problem 29 through 36 refer to the data given in problem 28.

29. One of the assumptions of multiple regression is that the independent variables are not correlated with each other. Is this assumption satisfied for these data? What do you check to see if multicollinearity is a problem? Use an alpha level of 0.05.

30. Does the multiple regression model you have estimated show a significant relationship between job ratings and the three independent variables measured? How did you measure this significance? Test with an alpha level of 0.05.

31. If you were a middle-level manager, would you be willing to have your job rating determined just on the basis of your performance on these three independent variables? Explain in statistical terms why or why not.

32. Discuss how much of the variation in job rating is explained by the three independent variables. How do you measure this factor?

33. Are all the independent variables significant in your multiple regression relationship? How can you tell?

34. As a test, the development director gives the same cases to a group of middle-level managers without knowing their job ratings. One of the managers received the following scores:

Case analysis	9.1
Written presentations	9.4
Verbal presentations	9.3

Based on these data, what is the best estimate of the job rating this manager received?

35. The personnel director comments that perhaps the regression model just developed would be a good tool to use before hiring new employees. What do you think of this idea?

36. One manager who participated in this study is concerned with his job rating and would like to know how much his job rating should change if his written presentation score increased by a full point. You are to develop a 95 percent confidence interval for the regression coefficient for the independent variable written presentation. Be sure to interpret this interval.

37. A publishing company in New York is attempting to develop a model that it can use to help predict textbook sales for books it is considering for future publication. The marketing department has collected data on several variables from a random sample of fifteen books. These data are

Volumes Sold Y	Pages X_1	Competing Books X_2	Advertising Budget X_3	Age of Author X_4
15,000	176	5	$25,000	49
140,000	296	10	83,000	57
75,000	483	7	40,000	29
100,000	811	14	29,000	37
26,000	302	9	52,000	35
33,000	411	15	33,000	43
59,000	333	7	19,000	51
103,000	602	4	37,000	62
88,000	504	12	51,000	33
10,000	204	3	30,000	50
9,000	376	4	19,000	26
77,000	600	7	41,000	40
59,000	400	3	26,000	44
183,000	597	8	51,000	59
16,000	126	1	27,000	38

Use an available computer routine to develop the correlation matrix showing the correlation between all possible pairs of variables. Test statistically to determine which independent variables are significantly correlated with the dependent variable, book sales. Use an alpha level of 0.05.

38. Referring to problem 37, develop a multiple regression model containing all four independent variables. Show clearly the regression coefficients.

39. Referring to problems 37 and 38, how much of the total variation in book sales can be explained by these four independent variables? Would you conclude that the model is significant at the 0.05 level?

40. Referring to problems 37 and 38, develop a 95 percent confidence interval for each regression coefficient and interpret these confidence intervals.

41. Referring to problem 40, which of the independent variables can be concluded to be significant in explaining the variation in book sales? Test using an alpha level of 0.05.

42. The publishing company in problems 37 through 41 recently came up with some additional data for the fifteen books in the original sample. Two new variables, production expenditures (X_5) and number of prepublication reviewers (X_6), have been added. These additional data are

Book	X_5	X_6	Book	X_5	X_6
1	$38,000	5	9	51,000	4
2	86,000	8	10	34,000	6
3	59,000	3	11	20,000	2
4	80,000	9	12	80,000	5
5	29,500	3	13	60,000	5
6	31,000	3	14	87,000	8
7	40,000	5	15	29,000	3
8	69,000	4			

Calculate the correlation between each of these additional variables and the dependent variable, book sales. You will have to use the data from problem 37.

43. Referring to problem 42, test the significance of the correlation coefficients, using an alpha level of 0.05. Comment on your results.

44. Referring to problems 37 through 43, develop a multiple regression model that includes all six independent variables. Which, if any, variables would you recommend be retained if this model is going to be used to predict book sales for the publishing company? For any statistical tests you might perform, use an alpha level of 0.05. Discuss your results.

45. Referring to problem 44, use the analysis of variance approach to test the null hypothesis that all slope coefficients are zero. Test with an alpha level of 0.05. What do these results mean? Discuss.

46. Referring to problems 37 through 45, does it appear that multicollinearity problems are present in the model? Discuss the potential consequences of multicollinearity with respect to the regression model.

Section 14–4

The following information applies to problems 47 through 56.

The J. J. McCracken Company has authorized its marketing research department to make a study of customers who have been issued a McCracken charge card. The marketing research department hopes to be able to identify the significant variables that explain the variation in purchases. Once these variables are determined, the department intends to try to attract new customers who would be predicted to have a high volume of purchases.

Twenty-five customers were selected at random and values for the following variables were recorded:

$$Y = \text{average monthly purchases at McCracken}$$
$$X_1 = \text{customer age}$$
$$X_2 = \text{customer family income}$$
$$X_3 = \text{family size}$$

No. Purchases Y	Age X_1	Family Income X_2	Family Size X_3
75	42	$29,000	4
129	36	25,000	2
105	38	25,000	2
42	54	17,000	3
17	49	15,000	5
26	55	19,500	3
144	25	24,000	2
100	24	14,000	1
92	30	11,000	1
58	35	12,000	2
111	27	29,000	3
146	29	38,000	2
93	38	19,500	4
68	40	24,000	3
11	36	22,500	2
50	22	10,200	1
55	25	14,000	3
88	69	19,200	4
100	54	52,000	4
86	48	21,400	3
105	30	26,000	2
121	27	18,250	3
14	62	10,250	3
37	50	18,100	2
43	26	24,500	4

TABLE 14P–1
Data, McCracken Company example

Table 14P–1 illustrates the data.

A computer program was used to perform the multiple regression analysis. Tables 14P–2 through 14P–5 show the results of the computer run.

47. A first step in regression analysis often involves developing a scatter plot of the data. Develop the scatter plots of all the possible pairs of variables and with a brief statement indicate what each plot says about the relationship between the two variables.

48. Table 14P–2 illustrates the correlation matrix. Develop the decision rule for testing the significance of each coefficient. Which, if any, correlations are not significant? Use an alpha level of 0.05.

	Y	X1	X2	X3
Y	1.000	-.4057	.4591	-.2444
X1		1.000	.0512	.5037
X2			1.000	.2718
X3				1.000

TABLE 14P–2
Correlation matrix, McCracken Company example

TABLE 14P–3
Step 1 of stepwise regression, McCracken Company example

****

STEP NUMBER 1

VARIABLE ENTERED   X2

R SQUARE   .2107

ADJUSTED R SQUARE   .1763

STANDARD ERRØR   36.3553

- -

ANALYSIS ØF VARIANCE	D.F.	SUM ØF SQUARES	MEAN SQUARE	F
REGRESSIØN	1	8118.48	8118.48	6.14
RESIDUAL (UNEXPLAINED)	23	30399.32	1321.70	

- - - - - - - - - - - - - - - VARIABLES IN THE EQUATIØN - - - - - - - - - - - - - - -

VARIABLE	B	STD. ERRØR B	T
X2 INCØME	.00199	.000803	2.478
(CØNSTANT)	33.7544		

****

TABLE 14P–4
Step 2 of stepwise regression, McCracken Company example

\^******

STEP NUMBER 2

VARIABLE ENTERED   X1

R SQUARE   .3955

ADJUSTED R SQUARE   .3405

STANDARD ERRØR   32.5313

- -

ANALYSIS ØF VARIANCE	D.F.	SUM ØF SQUARES	MEAN SQUARE	F
REGRESSIØN	2	15235.4	7617.7	7.19
RESIDUAL (UNEXPLAINED)	22	23282.4	1058.29	

- - - - - - - - - - - - - - - VARIABLES IN THE EQUATIØN - - - - - - - - - - - - - - -

VARIABLE	B	STD. ERRØR B	T
X2 INCØME	.00208	.00u/19	2.899
X1 AGE	− 1.31807	.508267	− 2.593
(CØNSTANT)	82.8875		

****

49. At step 1 of the output (see table 14P–3), the variable X_2, family income, was brought into the model. Discuss why this happened.

50. Test the significance of the regression model at step 1 of the computer printout. Justify the alpha level you have selected.

51. Develop a 95 percent confidence level for the slope coefficient for the family income variable at step 1 of the model. Be sure to interpret this confidence interval.

52. Describe the regression model at step 2 (see table 14P–4) of the analysis. In your discussion, be sure to discuss the effect of adding a new variable on the standard error of the estimate and on R^2.

53. Suppose the manager of McCracken's marketing department questions the appropriateness of adding a second variable. How would you respond to her question? Use the information in table 14P–4 in your response.

54. Table 14P–5 presents the third and final step in the regression analysis. Test statistically the significance of each independent variable in the model at an alpha level of 0.05. Also test the hypothesis that all slope coefficients are zero at the alpha level of 0.05. Why can the overall model be significant while some individual variables are not significant?

55. If you look carefully at the results shown in tables 14P–3 through 14P–5, you can

TABLE 14P–5
Step 3 of stepwise regression, McCracken Company example

```
*********************************************************************************
```

STEP NUMBER 3

VARIABLE ENTERED	X3
R SQUARE	.4322
ADJUSTED R SQUARE	.3510
STANDARD ERRØR	32.2724

- -

ANALYSIS ØF VARIANCE	D.F.	SUM ØF SQUARES	MEAN SQUARE	F
REGRESSIØN	3	16646.1	5548.6	5.33
RESIDUAL (UNEXPLAINED)	21	21871.7	1040.5	

- - - - - - - - - - - - - - - - VARIABLES IN THE EQUATIØN - - - - - - - - - - - - - - - -

VARIABLE	B	STD. ERRØR B	T
X2 INCØME	.00233	.000745	3.132
X1 AGE	− .97047	.586042	− 1.655
X3 FAMILY	− 8.7233	7.49549	− 1.163
(CØNSTANT)	87.7897		

```
*********************************************************************************
```

see that the value of the slope coefficient for variable X_2, family income, changes each time a new variable is added to the regression model. Discuss why this change takes place.

56. Analyze the regression model at step 3 and the intermediate results at steps 1 and 2. Write a report to the marketing manager pointing out the strengths and weaknesses of the model. Be sure to comment on the department's goal of being able to use the model to predict customers who will purchase high volumes from Mc-Cracken.

57. The P.G.A. (Professional Golf Association) publishes statistics on the performance of the players on the tour each year. A random sample of twenty-five players was selected following the 1983 season and the data in table 14P–6 were collected for the variables indicated.

TABLE 14P–6
Data for twenty-five players on the Professional Golf Association's 1983 tour

Case	1983 Winnings	1983 Finishes 1st	2nd	3rd	Tour Events	Scoring Average	1982 Ranking
1	$237,571	6	2	2	13	69.46	2
2	231,008	4	3	2	16	70.15	1
3	136,749	1	3	0	13	70.75	5
4	130,002	2	2	0	13	70.81	7
5	120,367	1	2	1	14	71.15	105
6	106,590	1	1	1	12	70.93	4
7	93,636	0	3	1	13	70.88	10
8	72,757	0	1	0	15	71.71	19
9	70,661	0	0	3	14	71.82	16
10	69,582	0	0	1	14	71.86	6
11	69,547	0	1	1	11	71.28	30
12	68,738	0	1	0	15	71.78	18
13	68,121	1	1	0	7	70.44	102
14	59,758	0	0	1	12	71.27	13
15	54,973	0	0	2	11	72.24	21
16	39,869	0	0	1	16	73.14	20
17	39,487	0	1	0	6	72.00	63
18	35,837	0	0	1	16	73.73	26
19	35,577	0	0	0	15	73.64	22
20	35,085	0	0	0	15	72.80	27
21	32,941	0	0	0	16	73.37	24
22	32,172	0	0	0	16	73.25	23
23	31,404	0	1	0	7	72.26	44
24	31,154	0	0	0	16	73.10	11
25	30,649	0	0	0	14	72.88	8

Source: *Golf Digest,* January 1984, vol. 35, no. 1, 92.

Develop a stepwise regression model which could be used to explain the variation in 1983 tour winnings. Also develop a correlation matrix for these variables.

58. Refer to the correlation matrix developed in problem 57. Write a short report discussing the correlation matrix and indicating which variables might be effective independent variables in a multiple regression analysis.

59. Refer to problem 57 and the stepwise regression model that was developed. At step 1 of the model, which variable entered the model? Test to determine whether this variable is significant at the alpha level of 0.05. Show the regression equation at this step and interpret the slope coefficient.

60. Referring to the stepwise regression model developed in problem 57, prepare a short report which discusses the results at each step of the model. Point out such things as R^2, the standard error of the estimate, and the overall model significance at each step. Discuss whether there are any effects of multicollinearity and show what these are.

61. Comment on whether the regression model developed as an ordinary model with six independent variables would be any different than the stepwise regression model after six independent variables have been entered in a forward stepwise process.

Section 14–5

62. List the basic assumptions of regression analysis and discuss in your own terms what each means.

63. What does it mean if we have developed a multiple regression model and have concluded that the model is apt?

64. Refer to the McCracken Company data (see table 14P–1). Develop a multiple regression model using the three independent variables.
   a. Show the regression equation.
   b. Compute the residuals and print these out.
   c. Plot the residuals against the predicted value of Y and comment on what this plot means relative to the aptness of the model.
   d. Compute the standardized residuals and form these in a frequency histogram. What does this indicate about the normality assumption?
   e. Comment on the overall aptness of this model and indicate what might be done to improve the model.

65. Refer to the textbook data in problems 37 and 42. Develop a multiple regression model using all six independent variables.
   a. Show the regression equation.
   b. Compute the residuals and print these out.
   c. Plot the residuals against the predicted value of Y and comment on what this plot means relative to the aptness of the model.
   d. Compute the standardized residuals and form these in a frequency histogram. What does this indicate about the normality assumption?
   e. Comment on the overall aptness of this model and indicate what might be done to improve the model.

66. Special Problem:

Refer to the textbook data in problems 37 and 42. Take any and all steps necessary to develop the best possible regression model using these data. Show each step of your process in a clear and concise manner. Prepare a written narrative describing what steps you have taken.

Once you have what you consider to be the best model, determine its aptness, using the appropriate methods of residual analysis. If corrective actions are warranted, take those actions. Remember to document all your efforts in your narrative report.

STATE DEPARTMENT OF TRANSPORTATION CASE STUDY PROBLEMS

The following questions and problems pertain directly to the State Department of Transportation case study and data base introduced in chapter 1. The questions and problems were written assuming that you will have access to a computer and appropriate statistical software. The data base containing 100 observations and seventeen variables is shown in table 1C–1 in chapter 1. *Assume that the data were collected using a simple random sampling process.*

1. Develop the best possible linear regression model using X_7, vehicle year, as the dependent variable and any or all of the other variables as potential independent variables. Assume that your objective is to develop a predictive model. Write a report that discusses the steps you took to develop the final model. Include a correlation matrix and all appropriate statistical tests. Use an alpha = 0.05. If you are using a nominal or ordinal variable, remember you must make sure it is in the form of one or more dummy variables. The number of dummy variables will be one fewer than the number of categories for the original variable.

2. Develop the best possible linear regression model using X_6, total cancellations and suspensions, as the dependent variable and any or all of the other variables as potential independent variables. Assume that your objective is to develop a predictive model. Write a report that discusses the steps you took to develop the final model. Include a correlation matrix and all appropriate statistical tests. Use an alpha = 0.05. If you are using a nominal or ordinal variable, remember, you must make sure it is in the form of one or more dummy variables. The number of dummy variables will be one fewer than the number of categories for the original variable.

3. Develop the best possible linear regression model using X_{15}, number of years of formal education, as the dependent variable and any or all of the other variables as potential independent variables. Assume that your objective is to develop a predictive model. Write a report that discusses the steps you took to develop the final model. Include a correlation matrix and all appropriate statistical tests. Use an alpha = 0.05. If you are using a nominal or ordinal variable, remember, you must make sure it is in the form of one or more dummy variables. The number of dummy variables will be one fewer than the number of categories for the original variable.

C A S E S

14A   Dynamic Scales, Inc.

In 1975 Stanley Ahlon and three financial partners formed Dynamic Scales, Inc. The company was based on an idea Stanley had for developing a scale to weigh trucks in motion and thus eliminate the need for every truck to stop at weigh stations along

TABLE 14C–1
Test data, Dynamic Scales, Inc. example

Month	Front-Axle Static Weight	Front-Axle Dynamic Weight	Truck Speed	Temperature	Moisture
January	1,800 lb	1,625 lb	52 mi/h	21°F	0.00%
	1,311	1,904	71	17	0.15
	1,504	1,390	48	13	0.40
	1,388	1,402	50	19	0.10
	1,250	1,100	61	24	0.00
February	2,102	1,950	55	26	0.10
	1,410	1,475	58	32	0.20
	1,000	1,103	59	38	0.15
	1,430	1,387	43	24	0.00
	1,073	948	59	18	0.40
March	1,502	1,493	62	34	0.00
	1,721	1,902	67	36	0.00
	1,113	1,415	48	42	0.21
	978	983	59	29	0.32
	1,254	1,149	60	48	0.00
April	994	1,052	58	37	0.00
	1,127	999	52	34	0.21
	1,406	1,404	59	40	0.40
	875	900	47	48	0.00
	1,350	1,275	68	51	0.00
May	1,102	1,120	55	52	0.00
	1,240	1,253	57	57	0.00
	1,087	1,040	62	63	0.00
	993	1,102	59	62	0.10
	1,408	1,400	67	68	0.00
June	1,420	1,404	58	70	0.00
	1,808	1,790	54	71	0.00
	1,401	1,396	49	83	0.00
	933	1,004	62	88	0.40
	1,150	1,127	64	81	0.00

highways. This dynamic scale would be placed in the highway approximately one-quarter mile from the regular weigh station. The scale would have a minicomputer which would automatically record truck speed, axle weights, and climate variables, including temperature, wind, and moisture. Stanley Ahlon and his partners felt that state transportation departments in the United States would be the primary market for such a scale.

Like many technological advances, developing the dynamic scale has been difficult. When the scale finally proved accurate for trucks traveling forty miles per hour, it would not perform for trucks traveling at higher speeds. However, eight months ago Stanley announced that the dynamic scale was ready to be field-tested by the Nebraska State Department of Transportation under a grant from the federal government.

Stanley explained to his financial partners, and to Nebraska transportation officials, that the dynamic weight would not exactly equal the static weight (truck weight on a static scale), but that he was sure a statistical relationship between dynamic weight and static weight could be determined, which would make the dynamic scale useful.

Nebraska officials, along with people from Dynamic Scales, Inc., installed a dynamic scale on a major highway in Nebraska. Each month for six months, data were collected for a random sample of trucks weighed on both the dynamic scale and a static scale. Table 14C–1 (p. 689) presents these data.

Once the data were collected, the next step was to determine if, based on this test, the dynamic scale measurements could be used to predict static weights. A complete report will be submitted to the U.S. government and to Dynamic Scales, Inc.

REFERENCES

Demmert, Henry, and Medoff, Marshall. "Game Specific Factors and Major League Baseball Attendance: An Econometric Study." *Santa Clara Business Review* (1977): 49–56.

Draper, N. R., and Smith, H. *Applied Regression Analysis*. New York: Wiley, 1966.

Gloudemans, Robert J., and Miller, Dennis. "Multiple Regression Analysis Applied to Residential Properties." *Decision Sciences* 7 (April 1976):294–304.

Johnson, J. *Econometric Methods,* New York: McGraw-Hill, 1972.

Neter, John, and Wasserman, William. *Applied Linear Statistical Models,* Homewood, Ill.: Irwin, 1974.

AN INTRODUCTION TO HYPOTHESIS TESTING USING NONPARAMETRIC TESTS

15

WHY DECISION MAKERS NEED TO KNOW

Chapters 8 through 12 presented an introduction to estimation and hypothesis testing. There, we discussed tests for one sample, two samples, and more than two samples. We also constructed tests for large and small samples. However, all of these tests have a common bond: they all assume that the data are at least interval-scaled. Additionally, for the t test and analysis of variance, the population distributions are assumed to be normal.

For many applications, the data are at least interval-scaled, and the populations can be assumed normally distributed. Production and financial situations often correspond to these assumptions. However, there are many other applications where these conditions do not hold; for instance, in many marketing and personnel situations. For situations where the assumptions do not hold, decision makers still need a set of statistical techniques to assist in decision making. The techniques that can be employed without the strict data and distribution assumptions are called **nonparametric statistics.**

CHAPTER OBJECTIVES

This chapter will introduce several useful nonparametric statistical tests, including the chi-square goodness of fit test, the Mann-Whitney U test, contingency analysis, the Kruskal-Wallis one-way analysis of variance, and the Spearman rank correlation coefficient. These are but a few of many nonparametric tests that are available. The chapter will emphasize how the tests can be applied to assist the decision-making process. This chapter will show you how to recognize when a nonparametric test is required, as well as how to use several popular nonparametric tests.

STUDENT OBJECTIVES

After studying the material in this chapter, you should be able to

1. Apply the chi-square goodness of fit test and the Mann-Whitney U test in a decision application.
2. Use the chi-square test in a contingency analysis application.
3. Employ the Kruskal-Wallis one-way analysis of variance in a decision-making setting.
4. Compute and interpret the Spearman rank correlation coefficient.

CHI-SQUARE GOODNESS OF FIT TEST

15-1

Rebecca Sweetlittle is the managing partner of Sweetlittle and Associates Dry Cleaners. Sweetlittle is open six days a week and performs virtually every available dry cleaning service for its customers. Rebecca has always believed that good service brings customers back. Because of this belief, she has always had fifteen employees working each day the cleaners is open. Her assumption has been that the day of the week does not influence business volume. However, a few customers have recently complained that on some days, the service seems slower than on other days.

Over the past twenty-four weeks, Rebecca collected the data shown in table 15–1. The frequencies indicate the total number of customers served during each day of this twenty-four week period.

Under her assumption that the day of the week should make no difference in customer volume, Rebecca would expect an equal number of customers on each of the six days. In this case, since there were 9,792 customers in all, she would expect 1,632 customers each day. As seen in table 15–1, the observed number of customers was not 1,632 on each day. However, Rebecca wonders if the difference between what she has observed and what she would expect is great enough to offset her assumption that the day of the week makes no difference in customer volume.

A statistical test known as the *chi-square goodness of fit test* has been developed to help answer this type of question. As the name implies, the chi-square goodness of fit test measures how well observed data fit what would be expected under specified conditions. Suppose Rebecca establishes the following null and alternative hypotheses:

TABLE 15–1
Customer frequency by day of week, Sweetlittle and Associates Dry Cleaners example

Day	Observed Frequency
Monday	1,525
Tuesday	1,711
Wednesday	1,655
Thursday	1,497
Friday	1,603
Saturday	1,801
Total	9,792

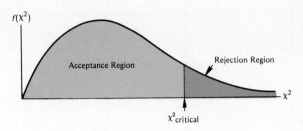

FIGURE 15–1
Chi-square probability distribution

H_0: The number of customers is evenly spread over the six working days (distribution is the uniform distribution).

H_A: The number of customers is not evenly spread over the six working days.

The chi-square goodness of fit test statistic is given in equation 15–1:

$$\chi^2 = \Sigma \frac{(f_o - f_e)^2}{f_e}$$

(15–1)

where f_o = observed frequency
f_e = expected frequency

The chi-square test statistic is distributed as a chi-square variable with $K - 1$ degrees of freedom, where K is the number of categories, or cells, specified in the null hypothesis. Figure 15–1 illustrates a chi-square probability distribution and shows the acceptance and rejection regions. The chi-square goodness of fit test is one-tailed, and the rejection region is determined by the alpha level selected.

As you can see from figure 15–1, if the calculated χ^2 gets large, the null hypothesis should be rejected. This makes sense when we examine equation 15–1. When the expected frequencies differ from the observed frequencies by a large amount, χ^2 will become large.

Figure 15–2 presents the chi-square goodness of fit test for Sweetlittle. Calculated χ^2 is 40.345, and the critical value for five degrees of freedom and the alpha level of 0.10 is 9.236 from the chi-square table is appendix E. Based on these results, Rebecca Sweetlittle should conclude that her company's customer volume is not spread evenly over the six working days. She will no doubt want to explore the possibility of adding more employees on some days or shifting the work schedule to accommodate the heavier customer days, such as Saturday.

Chi-Square Goodness of Fit Limitations

In instances when the samples are small, the *expected* cell frequencies can be very small. If the expected cell frequencies are *too* small, the calculated χ^2 may be overstated, which can lead to rejecting the null hypothesis more often than the data justify. Two generally accepted rules of thumb can be used to decide whether the expected cell frequencies are too small:

Hypotheses:

H_0: The number of customers is evenly spread over six working days (uniform).
H_A: The number of customers is not evenly spread over six working days (not uniform).

$\alpha = 0.10$

Day	f_o	f_e	$(f_o - f_e)^2$	$(f_o - f_e)^2/f_e$
Monday	1,525	1,632	11,449	7.015
Tuesday	1,711	1,632	6,241	3.824
Wednesday	1,655	1,632	529	0.324
Thursday	1,497	1,632	18,225	11.167
Friday	1,603	1,632	841	0.515
Saturday	1,801	1,632	28,561	17.500
				$\chi^2 = 40.345$

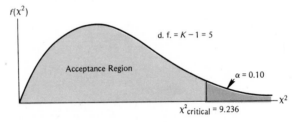

Decision Rule:

If $\chi^2 \leq \chi^2_{critical}$, accept H_0.
If $\chi^2 > \chi^2_{critical}$, reject H_0.

Since $40.345 > 9.236$, reject H_0. Conclude that the customers are not spread evenly over the six working days. Thus, the distribution is not uniform.

FIGURE 15–2
Chi-square goodness of fit test, Sweetlittle and Associates Dry Cleaners example

1. When the degree of freedom equals 1 (cells = 2), the expected cell frequencies should be at least 5.0
2. When the degrees of freedom exceed 1, at least 80 percent of the cells should have expected frequencies greater than 5.0, and all cells should have expected cell frequencies greater than 1.0.

If neither of these two conditions is satisfied, the chi-square goodness of fit test should not be used, or the expected frequencies can be increased by combining cells. However, combining should be done only if the combined cells are meaningful. For example, the regional safety manager for the U.S. Soil Conservation Service has hypothesized that the number of workers having accidents would be spread evenly among workers' grade levels. Table 15–2 presents the accident data for the previous year. If

Job Grade	Observed Accidents
GS-9	3
GS-7	7
GS-5	4
GS-3	4
Total	18

TABLE 15–2
Accident records. U.S. Soil Conservation Service example

the safety manager's claim is true, we would expect 4.5 accidents in each cell, or job grade. Since the expected frequency is below 5.0 in all cells, we should conclude either that the chi-square goodness of fit test should not be used or that some cells (job grades) must be combined to increase the expected cell frequencies. Figure 15–3 illustrates the grouping performed by the safety manager, and also the statistical test. Now the ex-

Hypotheses:

H_0: The frequency of accidents is spread evenly between the GS-9, GS-7, and the combination of GS-5 and GS-3 employees.
H_A: The frequency of accidents is not spread evenly between the job grades.

$\alpha = 0.05$

Job Grade	f_o	f_e	$(f_o - f_e)^2$	$(f_o - f_e)^2/f_e$
GS-9	3	6	9	1.500
GS-7	7	6	1	0.167
GS-5 and below	8	6	4	0.667
				$\chi^2 = 2.334$

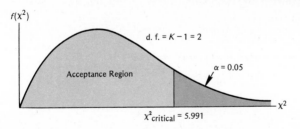

d. f. = $K - 1 = 2$

$\alpha = 0.05$

Acceptance Region

$\chi^2_{critical} = 5.991$

Decision Rule:

If $\chi^2 \leq \chi^2_{critical}$, accept H_0.
If $\chi^2 > \chi^2_{critical}$, reject H_0.

Since $\chi^2 = 2.334 < \chi^2_{critical} = 5.991$, do not reject H_0.

FIGURE 15–3
Chi-square goodness of fit test, Soil Conservation Service example

pected cell frequencies are all greater than 5.0, and the chi-square goodness of fit test is applicable. However, to use the chi-square distribution, we had to change the hypothesis slightly. Now we are no longer hypothesizing that accidents are equally spread among the grades but that GS-9 = GS-7 = GS-5 + GS-3.

As shown in figure 15–3, the safety manager, using this information, must conclude that accidents are spread evenly over the grade levels.

Another limitation of the chi-square goodness of fit test is that the data must be grouped in meaningful categories. As such, when this test is applied to continuous distributions, the results are only approximations and are sensitive to the manner in which the data have been grouped. Therefore two decision makers might apply the chi-square goodness of fit test to the same data, but because of a difference in the way they grouped the data, arrive at different conclusions.

Consider another example in which D. A. Weber and Associates, a computer service bureau, is involved in a study of the demand for its computer services. The customers have computer terminals, located at their own establishments, that are connected to the D. A. Weber and Associates mainframe computer by telephone data transmission lines.

When the mainframe computer was originally purchased, a study was done showing that during any given hour, the demand for an access port to the computer was Poisson distributed, with an average of five users. Thus, D. A. Weber purchased a computer system that has eleven ports, ten of which are available to the service bureau customers. Shelly Winters, manager of customer service, recently indicated that there appears to be a problem since she often receives calls from customers claiming that they have attempted to access the computer, but found that a port was not available. She feels that the demand distribution may be changing because the ten ports were sufficient to handle a Poisson-distributed demand with mean equal to 5 per hour.

To determine whether the demand distribution has changed, Shelly has collected data available from the phone company on the number of attempts to access the D. A. Weber computer during 200 randomly selected hours during the past two months. These data are shown in table 15–3.

TABLE 15–3
Computer access data, D. A. Weber and Associates example

No. of Access Requests	Frequency
0	2
1	4
2	7
3	12
4	15
5	30
6	35
7	55
8	20
9 and over	20
Total	200 h

Hypotheses:

H_0: The demand distribution is Poisson distributed with a mean equal to 5.
H_A: The demand distribution is not Poisson distributed with a mean equal to 5.

$\alpha = 0.05$

No. of Access Attempts	f_o	Probability*	f_e**	$(f_o - f_e)^2/f_e$
0	2	0.0067	1.34	0.325
1	4	0.0337	6.74	1.114
2	7	0.0842	16.84	5.750
3	12	0.1404	28.08	9.208
4	15	0.1755	35.10	11.510
5	30	0.1755	35.10	0.741
6	35	0.1462	29.24	1.135
7	55	0.1044	20.88	55.755
8	20	0.0653	13.06	3.688
9 and over	20	0.0681	13.62	2.989
Total	200	1.0000		$\chi^2 = 92.215$

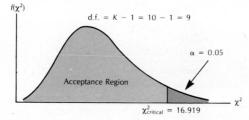

$f(\chi^2)$

d.f. $= K - 1 = 10 - 1 = 9$

$\alpha = 0.05$

Acceptance Region

$\chi^2_{critical} = 16.919$

Decision Rule:

If $\chi^2 \leq \chi^2_{critical}$, accept H_0.
If $\chi^2 > \chi^2_{critical}$, reject H_0.

Since $92.215 > 16.919$, reject H_0.

*From Poisson table, $\lambda = 5$.
**f_e = probability $\cdot$ 200.

FIGURE 15–4
Chi-square goodness of fit test, D. A. Weber and Associates example

To test whether the demand distribution continues to be Poisson distributed with a mean equal to 5, the chi-square goodness of fit test can be used. Figure 15–4 presents the chi-square goodness of fit test for the D. A. Weber and Associates example.

As figure 15–4 shows, Shelly Winters should reject the hypothesis that the demand distribution for her company's computer services is Poisson distributed with a mean equal to 5. Note that the first expected frequency is less than 5. This represents

Hypotheses:

H_0: Demand distribution is Poisson distributed.
H_A: Demand distribution is not Poisson distributed.

$\alpha = 0.05$

No. of Access Requests	f_o	Probability	f_e	$(f_o - f_e)^2/f_e$
1 and under	6	0.0146	2.92	3.248
2	7	0.0390	7.80	0.082
3	12	0.0806	16.12	1.053
4	15	0.1249	24.98	3.987
5	30	0.1549	30.98	0.031
6	35	0.1601	32.02	0.277
7	55	0.1418	28.36	25.024
8	20	0.1099	21.98	0.178
9 and over	20	0.1742	34.84	6.321
Total	200	1.0000		$\chi^2 = 40.201$

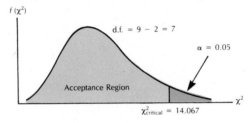

Decision Rule:

If $\chi^2 \leq \chi^2_{critical}$, accept H_0.
If $\chi^2 > \chi^2_{critical}$, reject H_0.

Since $40.201 > 14.067$, reject H_0.

Note: Degrees of freedom are computed by the number of cells minus 2 since we estimated λ rather than specifying it as part of the null hypothesis.

FIGURE 15–5
Chi-square goodness of fit test—parameter estimated from sample, D. A. Weber and Associates example

only 10 percent of the cells and since no frequency is less than 1.0, we need not combine the cells any further.

Another point should be made with respect to employing the chi-square goodness of fit test. If the distribution and parameters are specified in the hypothesis, degrees of freedom is the number of cells minus one. This was the case in the D. A. Weber example since the null hypothesis involved the distribution type (Poisson) and the parameter, λ. However, if one or more parameters is left unspecified in the null hypothesis, they must be estimated from the sample data, and the degrees of freedom are reduced by one for each parameter estimated.

To illustrate, suppose Shelly had originally hypothesized that the demand distribution was Poisson distributed, but did not specify the mean of the distribution. We shall again use the data in table 15–3 to test this latest hypothesis. But first we must estimate the mean of the distribution from the sample data. Suppose from the raw data the sample mean equals 6.2. This estimated mean is then used to determine the probabilities in figure 15–5 from the Poisson table in the appendix.

The test results shown in figure 15–5 indicate that Shelly Winters should conclude that the demand distribution is not Poisson distributed since the chi-square goodness of fit test indicates that the null hypothesis should be rejected. Note that in figure 15–5 we have combined access requests 0 and 1 because the expected cell frequency for 0 requests, given a Poisson distribution with a mean equal to 6.2, is less than 1.0. Note also that degrees of freedom is computed as the number of cells less two in this case since we estimated the mean of the distribution from the sample data. We lose an additional degree of freedom for each parameter we have to estimate.

The chi-square goodness of fit test can be employed to determine whether a set of sample data come from any specified distribution. You are encouraged to read the solved problems section at the end of this chapter for an example involving the normal distribution.

SKILL IMPROVEMENT PROBLEMS FOR SECTION 15–1

The following exercises are included to help you gain a better understanding of the material presented in this section. Additional application problems are included at the end of this chapter.

1. The Computer Warehouse sells computer equipment through mail-order advertisements in national computer magazines. Currently they offer four word-processing software packages. In determining how many of each to stock, the product manager has claimed that Word Perfect is demanded twice as often as Word Star and four times as often as Letter-Write and Writing Assistant. To test this, a sample of 1,000 sales invoices was collected, with the following results:

Package	Frequency of Demand
Word Perfect	405
Word Star	287
Letter-Write	112
Writing Assistant	196

At the alpha = 0.05 level, are these data sufficient to refute the product manager's claim?

2. The site selection manager for a national fast-food chain believes that the arrival rate for cars on a roadway has to average at least five per minute to warrant further investigation of sites along the road as potential locations for a new fast-food store. She further assumes that traffic on roadways is Poisson distributed.

For a particular roadway, the following sample data were collected:

No. of Vehicles in 1-Minute Segments	Frequency
0	3
1	2
2	3
3	8
4	11
5	30
6	34
7	19
8	18
9	13
10 and over	14
	Total 155

Based upon these data, can we conclude that the vehicles are Poisson distributed, with a mean of five vehicles per minute? Test at an alpha = 0.05 level.

3. Referring to the data in problem 2, suppose that another site analysis indicated that the vehicles should be normally distributed, with a mean of five and a standard deviation of three vehicles. Based upon these sample data, what conclusions should be reached regarding this claim? Test at the alpha = 0.05 level. (Hint: See solved problem 1.)

4. The Whitewater Hotel offers three classes of rooms: regular, standard, and deluxe. A prospective purchaser of the hotel has asked about the distribution of demand for these rooms. However, the hotel management has not kept good records so no historical information is available. The manager has stated that he feels the demand is about the same for each type of room.

To test this, a random sample of fifty customers was selected and their room preference was recorded. The resulting data are as follows:

Room Type	Frequency
Regular	18
Standard	21
Deluxe	11

Based upon these data, can it be concluded that the distribution is uniform over the three types of rooms? Test at the alpha = 0.01 level.

CONTINGENCY ANALYSIS

Wilt Roderick, the loan manager at State Bank, is interested in developing a set of criteria that he and other loan officers can use in determining whether a customer should be granted an automobile loan. During the past two years, State Bank has made 400 automobile loans. Upon careful analysis of these loans, Wilt has classified them as follows:

15-2

Class	Frequency
Good loan (payments made on time)	300
Fair loan (payments made but consistently late)	60
Poor loan (repossession required)	40

For each loan, Wilt has data on a number of variables. One variable is whether the borrower is buying or renting a home. Wilt is interested in determining whether a relationship exists between the buy-rent variable and the loan class variable. *Contingency analysis,* also called the *chi-square test of independence,* offers a means by which the loan manager can test to see whether the two variables are statistically *independent.* We begin by developing a **contingency table** from the available data as follows:

		Rent	Buy	
	Good	140	160	300
Loan Class	Fair	20	40	60
	Poor	20	20	40
		180	220	400 = N

The row and column totals in the contingency table correspond to the number of individuals in each category. For example, 180 borrowers are renting their homes and the remaining 220 are buying. The values inside the table represent the joint occurrence of two variables. For instance, 140 borrowers are renting and also have a good loan. The null and alternative hypotheses are

H_0: The row and column variables are independent.

H_A: The row and column variables are *not* independent.

If the null hypothesis is true, the probability of a good loan for a person renting a house should equal the probability of a good loan for a person buying. These two probabilities should also equal the probability of a good loan without considering the buy-rent variable. To illustrate, we can find the probability of a good loan as follows:

$$P_{good} = \frac{\text{number of good loans}}{\text{number of loans granted}} = \frac{300}{400}$$

$$= 0.75$$

Then, if the null hypothesis is true,

$$P(\text{good}|\text{rent}) = 0.75$$
$$P(\text{good}|\text{buy}) = 0.75$$

Thus we would expect 75 percent of the 180 renters, or 135 people, to have good loans, and 75 percent of the 220 buyers, or 165 people, to have good loans. We can use this same reasoning to determine the expected number of borrowers in each cell in the contingency table.

		Rent	*Buy*
Loan Class	*Good*	Actual = 140 Expected = 135	Actual = 160 Expected = 165
	Fair	Actual = 20 Expected = 27	Actual = 40 Expected = 33
	Poor	Actual = 20 Expected = 18	Actual = 20 Expected = 22

If the null hypothesis of independence is true, we would expect to find the observed frequencies in the cells equal to the corresponding expected frequencies. The greater the difference between the observed and expected, the more likely that the null hypothesis of independence is false and should be rejected. If you think this sounds like a chi-square goodness of fit problem, you are right. The appropriate test statistic is given in equation 15–2:

$$\chi^2 = \sum_{i=1}^{r} \sum_{j=1}^{c} \frac{(fo_{ij} - fe_{ij})^2}{fe_{ij}} \quad \text{with d.f.}$$

$$= (r - 1)(c - 1)$$

(15–2)

where f_o = observed cell frequency
f_e = expected cell frequency
r = number of rows
c = number of columns

Don't be confused by the double summation in equation 15–2; it merely indicates that all rows and columns must be used in calculating χ^2.

Figure 15–6 presents the hypotheses and the test results. We see that the calculated χ^2 value is less than the critical value from the chi-square probability table. Therefore Wilt Roderick *cannot* conclude, based on these data, that buying or renting makes a difference in the resulting loan classification, and he should not attempt to use this variable as a screening criterion.

Hypotheses:

H_0: Loan class is independent of buying or renting.
H_A: Loan class is not independent of buying or renting.

$\alpha = 0.01$

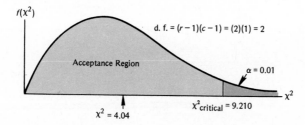

		Rent	Buy
		$f_o = 140$	$f_o = 160$
Loan Class	Good	$f_e = 135$	$f_e = 165$
	Fair	$f_o = 20$	$f_o = 40$
		$f_e = 27$	$f_e = 33$
	Poor	$f_o = 20$	$f_o = 20$
		$f_e = 18$	$f_e = 22$

$$\chi^2 = \sum_{i=1}^{r} \sum_{j=1}^{c} \frac{(f_{o_{ij}} - f_{e_{ij}})^2}{f_{e_{ij}}}$$

$$= \frac{(140 - 135)^2}{135} + \frac{(160 - 165)^2}{165} + \frac{(20 - 27)^2}{27} + \ldots + \frac{(20 - 22)^2}{22}$$

$$= 4.04$$

$f(\chi^2)$

d. f. = $(r-1)(c-1) = (2)(1) = 2$

Acceptance Region

$\alpha = 0.01$

χ^2

$\chi^2 = 4.04$

$\chi^2_{critical} = 9.210$

Decision Rule:

If $\chi^2 \leq \chi^2_{critical}$, accept H_0.
If $\chi^2 > \chi^2_{critical}$, reject H_0.

Since $\chi^2 = 4.04 < \chi^2_{critical} = 9.210$, we cannot reject the null hypothesis of independence.

FIGURE 15–6
Chi-square test of independence, State Bank example

Another variable for which Wilt has data is family income. The contingency table for income crossed with loan class is as follows:

		Income Level				
		$0– *$10,000*	*$10,000–* *$20,000*	*$20,000–* *$30,000*	*Over* *$30,000*	
	Good	12	43	87	158	300
Loan Class	Fair	18	20	18	4	60
	Poor	20	10	7	3	40
		50	73	112	165	400 = N

As is always the case with contingency analysis, the null hypothesis is that the rows and columns are independent. To test this hypothesis, we must compare the observed cell frequencies to the expected cell frequencies. A shortcut formula for determining the expected frequencies is as follows:

$$fe_{ij} = \frac{\text{sum of row } i \cdot \text{sum of column } j}{\text{total no. of observations}}$$

For example,

$$fe_{11} = \frac{300(50)}{400} = 37.50$$

$$fe_{12} = \frac{300(73)}{400} = 54.75$$

The completed contingency table and the null hypothesis test for the State Bank example are shown in figure 15–7. Clearly, the hypothesis of independence between income level and loan classification must be rejected. Based on the data, Wilt might infer that individuals with higher incomes tend to end up with loans in a higher classification.

Certainly, Wilt will want to explore other variables before arriving at his loan-screening criteria. When large numbers of data are involved, and when many crosstabulations are required, computer programs can be of great assistance.

Limitations of Contingency Analysis

The chi-square test of independence requires that the expected frequencies in all cells be at least 5.0. To ensure this, either the rows or columns may have to be combined, as was illustrated for the chi-square goodness of fit test. However, remember to make sure that there is a basis for grouping categories and that the meaning of the results is not lost when the grouping is performed. Note that the degrees of freedom are reduced when rows and/or columns are combined.

Hypotheses:

H_0: Loan classification is independent of income level.
H_A: Loan classification is not independent of income level.

$\alpha = 0.01$

		Income Level			
		$0–$10,000	$10,000–$20,000	$20,000–$30,000	Over $30,000
Loan Class	Good	$f_o = 12.00$ $f_e = 37.50$	$f_o = 43.00$ $f_e = 54.75$	$f_o = 87.00$ $f_e = 84.00$	$f_o = 158.00$ $f_e = 123.75$
	Fair	$f_o = 18.00$ $f_e = 7.50$	$f_o = 20.00$ $f_e = 10.95$	$f_o = 18.00$ $f_e = 16.80$	$f_o = 4.00$ $f_e = 24.75$
	Poor	$f_o = 20.00$ $f_e = 5.00$	$f_o = 10.00$ $f_e = 7.30$	$f_o = 7.00$ $f_e = 11.20$	$f_o = 3.00$ $f_e = 16.50$

$$\chi^2 = \sum_{i=1}^{r} \sum_{j=1}^{c} \frac{(f_{o_{ij}} - f_{e_{ij}})^2}{f_{e_{ij}}} = \frac{(12.00 - 37.50)^2}{37.50} + \frac{(43.00 - 54.75)^2}{54.75} + \cdots + \frac{(3.00 - 16.50)^2}{16.50}$$

$$= 127.72$$

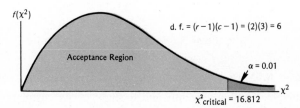

$f(\chi^2)$

Acceptance Region

d. f. $= (r-1)(c-1) = (2)(3) = 6$

$\alpha = 0.01$

$\chi^2_{critical} = 16.812$

Decision Rule:

If $\chi^2 \leq \chi^2_{critical}$, accept H_0.
If $\chi^2 > \chi^2_{critical}$, reject H_0.

Since $\chi^2 = 127.72 > \chi^2_{critical} = 16.812$, we reject the hypothesis of independence and conclude that a relationship exists between the two variables.

FIGURE 15–7
Chi-square test of independence, State Bank example

SKILL DEVELOPMENT PROBLEMS FOR SECTION 15–2

The following problems have been included to help you better understand the material in this chapter. There are additional application problems at the end of the chapter.

5. In a recent study of college graduates, it was hypothesized that income was independent of number of different employers the person has worked for since graduation. The following data were collected:

Income Level	Number of Employers				
	1	*2*	*3*	*4*	*5 or more*
Under $20,000	3	4	3	2	3
20,000–30,000	5	3	7	3	2
30,000–40,000	2	5	3	6	1
40,000–50,000	1	7	9	3	4
Over 50,000	1	3	11	7	4

Assuming that these data reflect observed frequencies, what can be concluded about the hypothesis? Test at an alpha = 0.05 level.

6. A study of automobile drivers was conducted to determine whether the number of traffic citations issued during a three-year period was independent of the sex of the driver. The following data were collected:

Citations Issued	Sex of Driver	
	Male	*Female*
0	240	160
1	80	40
2	32	18
3	11	9
Over 3	5	4

Using an alpha = 0.05 level, determine whether the two variables are independent.

7. A bank in Midvale, Oregon, recently did a study of its customers to determine whether the number of transactions in a checking account was independent of the marital status of the customer. The following data were obtained:

Marital Status	Number of Transactions				
	0–10	*11–20*	*21–30*	*31–40*	*Over 40*
Single	13	23	19	20	11
Married	6	15	33	45	27
Divorced	4	19	22	20	15
Other	2	11	8	5	2

Based upon these data what should the bank conclude? Test at an alpha = 0.05 level.

8. In a recent labor negotiation, the union officials collected data from a sample of their members regarding how long they had been with the company and how long they would be willing to stay out on strike if a strike were called. The following data were collected:

Time with Company	Strike Duration		
	Under 1 Week	*1–4 Weeks*	*Over 4 Weeks*
Under 1 year	23	6	3
1–2 years	19	15	8
2–5 years	20	23	19
5–10 years	4	21	29
Over 10 years	2	5	18

Based upon these data, can the union conclude that the strike length toleration is independent of time with the company? Test at the alpha = 0.05 level.

MANN-WHITNEY *U* TEST

15-3

The Ada County Highway District (ACHD) was recently formed to consolidate the street and highway maintenance and construction activities in Ada County. Formerly, the urban division took care of all the streets and roads in the county's largest city, and the rural division handled all street and road work outside that city. The urban and rural divisions had separate managements, and because of the perceived duplication of managerial activities, the consolidation was mandated by the Ada County commissioners. However, the working force of the ACHD at present remains divided in the divisions, rural and urban.

A few months following the consolidation, several rural division supervisors began claiming that the urban division employees waste gravel from the county gravel pit. They claimed that the urban division uses more gravel per mile of road maintenance than the rural division.

In response to these claims, Dennis Millier, the ACHD materials manager, decided to perform a test. He selected a random sample of weeks from the district's job cost records from work performed by the urban (U) division and a random sample of work performed by the rural (R) division. The data in table 15–4 represent the yards of gravel used per mile of road for each week sampled.

Even though the data are of a ratio-level measurement, Dennis Millier is not willing to make the normality assumptions necessary to employ the two-sample *t* test discussed in chapter 11. However, a nonparametric technique called the *Mann-Whitney U test* will allow Dennis to compare the gravel use of the two divisions.

The Mann-Whitney *U* test is one of the most popular nonparametric tests and can be used to compare samples from two populations in those cases where the following assumptions are satisfied:

1. The two samples are independent and random.
2. The value measured is a continuous variable.
3. The measurement scale used is at least ordinal.
4. If they differ, the distributions of the two populations will differ only with respect to location.

TABLE 15–4

Yards of gravel per mile, Ada County Highway District example

Urban	Rural
460	600
830	652
720	603
930	594
500	1,402
620	1,111
703	902
407	700
1,521	827
900	490
750	904
800	1,400

The null hypothesis for the Mann-Whitney U test is always the same:

H_0: The two populations (A and B) have identical distributions.

The alternate hypothesis can take three different forms, depending on the situation.

H_A: The two populations differ with respect to location.

The values from population A tend to be smaller than the values from population B.

The values from population A tend to be larger than the values from population B.

In this situation Dennis has decided to test the following hypotheses:

H_0: The two divisions have equal gravel use distributions.
H_A: The urban division tends to use larger amounts of gravel than the rural division.

$$\alpha = 0.05$$

The first step in testing this hypothesis using the Mann-Whitney U test is to combine the raw data from the two samples into one set of numbers, then rank the numbers in this set from low to high, which leads to the rankings as shown in table 15–5. The logic of the Mann-Whitney U test centers around the idea that if the sum of the rankings of one group differs greatly from the sum of the rankings of the second group, we should conclude that there is a difference in central locations of the populations.

We calculate a U value for each sample as shown in equations 15–3 and 15–4:

TABLE 15–5
Ranking of yards of gravel per mile, Ada County Highway District example

Urban ($n_1 = 12$)		Rural ($n_2 = 12$)	
Yards of Gravel	*Rank*	*Yards of Gravel*	*Rank*
460	2	600	6
830	16	652	9
720	12	603	7
930	20	594	5
500	4	1,402	23
620	8	1,111	21
703	11	902	18
407	1	700	10
1,521	24	827	15
900	17	490	3
750	13	904	19
800	14	1,400	22
Sum of ranks$_1$ = 142		Sum of ranks$_2$ = 158	

$$U_U = n_1 n_2 + \frac{n_1(n_1 + 1)}{2} - \text{sum of ranks}_1 \qquad (15\text{–}3)$$

$$U_R = n_1 n_2 + \frac{n_2(n_2 + 1)}{2} - \text{sum of ranks}_2 \qquad (15\text{–}4)$$

where n_1 and n_2 are the two sample sizes. Thus, for our example using the ranks in table 15–5:

$$U_U = 12(12) + \frac{12(13)}{2} - 142$$
$$= 80$$
$$U_R = 12(12) + \frac{12(13)}{2} - 158$$
$$= 64$$

Note that $U_R + U_U = n_1 n_2$. This is always the case and provides a good check on the correctness of the rankings in table 15–5.

We select either U_R or U_U and call this U_{test}. When the samples are large (n_1 and n_2 both equal at least 10), the distribution of U_{test} will be approximately normally distributed, with mean and standard deviation as shown in equations 15–5 and 15–6:

$$\text{Mean} = \frac{n_1 n_2}{2} \tag{15-5}$$

and

$$\text{Standard deviation} = \sqrt{\frac{n_1 n_2 (n_1 + n_2 + 1)}{12}} \tag{15-6}$$

Therefore the Mann-Whitney U test can use the normal distribution in a manner similar to the hypothesis tests presented in earlier chapters.

If the hypothesis test is *one-tailed*, and the alternate hypothesis indicates the rejection region is in the *lower* tail of the distribution, U_{test} should be set equal to whichever of U_R or U_U will be *smaller* if the alternate hypothesis is true. Conversely, if the test is *one-tailed*, and the alternate hypothesis says the rejection region is in the *upper* tail of the distribution, U_{test} should be set equal to whichever of U_R or U_U will be *larger* if the alternate hypothesis is true. Finally, if the test is *two-tailed*, U_{test} can be set equal

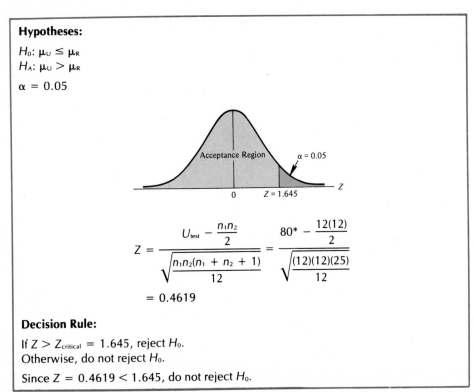

Hypotheses:

$H_0: \mu_U \leq \mu_R$
$H_A: \mu_U > \mu_R$

$\alpha = 0.05$

Acceptance Region $\alpha = 0.05$

0      $Z = 1.645$ Z

$$Z = \frac{U_{\text{test}} - \dfrac{n_1 n_2}{2}}{\sqrt{\dfrac{n_1 n_2 (n_1 + n_2 + 1)}{12}}} = \frac{80^* - \dfrac{12(12)}{2}}{\sqrt{\dfrac{(12)(12)(25)}{12}}}$$

$$= 0.4619$$

Decision Rule:

If $Z > Z_{\text{critical}} = 1.645$, reject H_0.
Otherwise, do not reject H_0.

Since $Z = 0.4619 < 1.645$, do not reject H_0.

*One-tailed upper tail; U_{test} is set equal to U_U since it should be larger if the alternative hypothesis is true.

FIGURE 15–8
Mann-Whitney U test, large samples

to *either* U_R or U_U. In our example, Dennis should set U_{test} equal to U_U since it will be larger if the alternative hypothesis is true.

The Z value is given in equation 15–7:

$$Z = \frac{U_{test} - \dfrac{n_1 n_2}{2}}{\sqrt{\dfrac{n_1 n_2 (n_1 + n_2 + 1)}{12}}} \tag{15-7}$$

Figure 15–8 presents the test for the ACHD example. We see that the sample evidence does not lead to rejecting the null hypothesis, so Dennis Millier must conclude that the urban division is no more wasteful than the rural division in the use of gravel on construction jobs. However, this test does not indicate whether both divisions are wasteful.

The normal approximation for the Mann-Whitney U test improves as the sample sizes increase. For sample sizes smaller than ten, a small-sample Mann-Whitney U test must be employed. You should consult Conover (1980) or Marascuilo and McSweeney (1977) for the details of these tests. You should also consult these sources for a discussion of the procedures necessary for adjusting the Mann-Whitney U test when there are tied rankings in the data.

SKILL DEVELOPMENT PROBLEMS FOR SECTION 15–3

The following exercises have been included to help you better understand the material in this section. There are additional application problems at the end of the chapter.

9. From a recent study we have collected the following data from two independent random samples:

Population 1	Population 2
405	300
450	340
290	400
370	250
345	270
460	410
425	435
275	390
380	225
330	210
500	395
215	315

a. Based upon these sample data, can it be concluded that the two populations have equal means? Use an alpha = 0.05 and test using the t distribution. What assumptions are needed to use this distribution?

b. Suppose we don't wish to make the assumptions indicated in part a. Use the appropriate nonparametric test to determine whether the populations have equal means. Test at the alpha = 0.05 level.

10. The makers of the Plus 20 Hardcard, a plug-in hard disk unit on a PC board, have recently done a marketing research study in which they asked two independently selected groups to rate the Hardcard on a scale of 1 to 100, with 100 being perfect satisfaction. The first group consisted of professional computer programmers. The second group consisted of home computer users. The company hoped to be able to say that the product would receive the same average ranking from each group. The following summary data were recorded:

Professionals	Home Users
$n = 27$	$n = 24$
sum of ranks = 348	sum of ranks = 300

Based upon these data, what should the company conclude? Test at the alpha = 0.01 level.

11. The Acme Speed Reading Company claims that graduates of their program have a higher average reading speed per minute than people who did not take the course. An independent agency conducted a study to determine whether this claim was justified. They selected a random sample of people who had taken the speed reading course and another random sample of people who had not taken the course. The agency was unwilling to make the assumption that the populations were normally distributed. Therefore, a nonparametric test was needed. The following summary data were observed:

With Course	Without Course
$n = 15$	$n = 15$
sum of ranks = 180	sum of ranks = 45

Assuming that higher ranks imply more words per minute being read, what should the testing agency conclude based upon the sample data? Test at an alpha = 0.05 level.

12. The Internal Revenue Service for a midwestern state recently conducted a study to determine whether there is a difference in average deductions taken for charitable contributions depending on whether the tax return was filed as a single or joint return. A random sample from each category was selected, with the following results:

	Single		*Joint*
	$n = 100$		$n = 110$
sum of ranks =	4,680	sum of ranks =	6,320

Based upon these data, what should the IRS conclude? Use an alpha = 0.05 level.

KRUSKAL-WALLIS ONE-WAY ANALYSIS OF VARIANCE

15-4

As shown, the Mann-Whitney U test is a useful nonparametric procedure for determining whether two samples are from populations with the same mean. However, as discussed in chapter 12, many decisions involve comparing more than two populations. That chapter introduced one-way analysis of variance and showed how, if certain assumptions are satisfied, the F distribution can be used to test the hypothesis of equal population means. However, what if the decision makers are not willing to assume normally distributed populations? In that case, they must turn to a nonparametric procedure to compare the populations. *Kruskal-Wallis one-way analysis of variance* is the nonparametric counterpart to the analysis of variance procedure presented in chapter 12. It is applicable any time the variable in question has a continuous distribution, the data are at least ordinal, the samples are independent, and the samples come from populations whose only possible difference is that at least one may have a different location than the rest.

The Bartholomew Company is considering acquiring a new computer system to handle its on-line data-processing activities, including inventory management, production scheduling, and general accounting and billing applications. Based on cost and performance standards, Gladys Coil, Bartholomew's data-processing manager, has reduced the possible suppliers to three. One critical factor for Gladys is down time (the time when the computer is nonoperational). When the computer goes down, the on-line applications are halted and normal business activities are interrupted. Gladys has received, from each supplier, a list of firms that are using the computer system Bartholomew is considering. From these lists Gladys selected random samples of nine users of each computer system. In a telephone interview, she found the number of hours of down time in the previous month for each system. The down times are shown in table 15–6.

To use the Kruskal-Wallis analysis of variance here, we first replace each downtime measurement by its *relative ranking* within all groups combined. The smallest down time is given a rank of 1, the next smallest a rank of 2, and so forth, until all down times for the three systems have been replaced by their relative rankings. Table 15–7 shows these rankings for the thirty observations. Notice that the rankings are summed for each computer system. The Kruskal-Wallis test will determine whether these sums are so different that it is not likely they came from populations with equal means.

If the samples actually do come from populations with equal means (that is, the three systems have the same per-month average down time), then the H statistic calcu-

TABLE 15–6
Computer down times, Bartholomew Company example (hours/month)

System A	System B	System C
4.0	6.9	0.5
3.7	11.3	1.4
5.1	21.7	1.0
2.0	9.2	1.7
4.6	6.5	3.6
9.3	4.9	5.2
2.7	12.2	1.3
2.5	11.7	6.8
4.8	10.5	14.1

lated as follows will be distributed as a chi-square variable with $K - 1$ degrees of freedom, where K equals the number of samples under study:

$$H = \frac{12}{N(N + 1)} \sum_{i=1}^{K} \frac{R_i^2}{n_i} - 3(N + 1) \tag{15–8}$$

where
N = total of all observations
K = number of samples
R_i = sum of the ranks in the ith sample
n_i = size of the ith sample

If H is larger than χ^2_{critical}, the hypothesis of equal means is rejected, and Gladys would conclude that the populations from which the samples were selected have different means. Figure 15–9 presents the hypotheses and statistical test for the Bartholomew example. The Kruskal-Wallis one-way analysis of variance shows that Gladys Coil should conclude that the three computer systems *do not* have equal average down times. From this analysis, the supplier of computer system B would most likely be eliminated from consideration unless other factors such as price or service offset the apparent longer down times.

TABLE 15–7
Rankings of computer down times, Bartholomew Company example

System A	System B	System C
11	19	1
10	23	4
15	27	2
6	20	5
12	17	9
21	14	16
8	25	3
7	24	18
13	22	26
Sum of ranks = 103	Sum of ranks = 191	Sum of ranks = 84

Hypotheses:

H_0: The mean down times are equal for all three computer systems.

H_A: The mean down times are not equal for all three computer systems.

$\alpha = 0.10$

Using the rankings and sums in table 15–7,

$$H = \frac{12}{N(N + 1)} \sum_{i=1}^{K} \frac{R_i^2}{n_i} - 3(N + 1)$$

$$= \frac{12}{27(27 + 1)} \left[\frac{(103)^2}{9} + \frac{(191)^2}{9} + \frac{(84)^2}{9} \right] - 3(27 + 1)$$

$$= 11.49$$

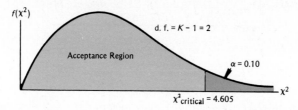

Decision Rule:

If $H \leq \chi^2_{critical}$, accept H_0.

If $H > \chi^2_{critical}$, reject H_0.

Since $H = 11.49 > \chi^2_{critical} = 4.605$, reject H_0.

FIGURE 15–9

Kruskal-Wallis one-way analysis of variance test, Bartholomew Company example

Limitations and Other Considerations

The Kruskal-Wallis one-way analysis of variance does *not* require the assumption of normality and is therefore often used instead of the analysis of variance technique discussed in chapter 12. However, the Kruskal-Wallis test as discussed here applies only if the sample sizes from each population are at least five, the samples are independently selected, and each population has the same distribution except for a possible difference in location.

When ranking observations, decision makers will sometimes encounter ties. When ties occur, each observation is given the mean rank for which it is tied. The H statistic is influenced by ties and should be corrected by dividing equation 15–8 by equation 15–9:

$$1 - \frac{\sum_{i=1}^{g} (t_i^3 - t_i)}{N^3 - N} \qquad (15\text{--}9)$$

where g = number of different groups of ties
t = number of tied observations in the tied group of scores
N = total number of observations

Thus the correct formula for calculating the Kruskal-Wallis H statistic when ties are present is equation 15–10:

$$H = \frac{\dfrac{12}{N(N + 1)} \sum_{i=1}^{K} \dfrac{R_i^2}{n_i} - 3(N + 1)}{1 - \dfrac{\sum_{i=1}^{g} (t_i^3 - t_i)}{N^3 - N}} \qquad (15\text{--}10)$$

Correcting for ties increases H and thus makes rejecting the null hypothesis more likely than if the correction is not used. A rule of thumb is that if no more than 25 percent of the observations are involved in ties, the correction factor is not required. Solved problem 3 at the end of this chapter illustrates the use of the correction for ties for the Kruskal-Wallis test.

SKILL DEVELOPMENT PROBLEMS FOR SECTION 15–4

The following exercises have been included to help you gain a better understanding of the material in this section. Additional application problems are found at the end of the chapter.

13. A consumer testing agency has been contracted to test user ratings for the three leading brands of running shoes. The rating scale is 1 to 40, with 40 being perfect. The following results were recorded:

Shoe 1	Shoe 2	Shoe 3
21	17	29
25	15	38
36	34	28
35	22	27
33	16	14
23	19	26
31	30	39
32	20	36

a. What assumptions are required to employ the analysis of variance methods discussed in chapter 12?

b. If the testing agency does not want to make the assumptions stated in your answer to part a, based upon these sample data, what should the testing agency conclude about the average ratings for the three brands of shoes? Test at an alpha = 0.05 level.

14. A study was conducted by the sports department of a national network television station in which the objective was to determine if a difference exists between average annual salaries of NBA basketball players, NFL football players, and major league baseball players. The analyst in charge of the study feels that the normal distribution assumption is violated in this study. Thus, she feels a nonparametric test is in order.

The following summary data have been collected:

NBA	NFL	Baseball
$n = 20$	$n = 30$	$n = 40$
$R = 1710$	$R = 1100$	$R = 1340$

Based upon these what can be concluded about the average salaries for the three sports? Test at the alpha = 0.05 level. Assume no ties.

15. Referring to problem 14, suppose that there were forty ties at eight different salary levels. The following shows how many scores were ties at each salary level:

Level	t
1	2
2	3
3	2
4	4
5	8
6	10
7	6
8	5

Use the appropriate adjustment for ties and adjust the test conducted in problem 14.

SPEARMAN RANK CORRELATION COEFFICIENT

15-5

Chapter 13 introduced you to a measure of the strength of the linear relationship between two variables called the *correlation coefficient*. Recall that the correlation coefficient ranges between ±1.0, with a value of zero indicating no linear relationship between the two variables. Recall also that chapter 13 introduced a test for the statistical significance of the correlation coefficient. This test assumes that the data for the two variables are at least interval scaled and the joint distribution of the variables is bivariate normal. However, in cases where the level of data measurement is ordinal or when the

TABLE 15–8

Sample data, Porter Company example

No. Copies Used (000s) Y	Employees X
23.0	140
11.0	101
9.5	43
3.5	55
20.0	79
14.5	134
6.3	75
42.0	211
3.1	78
2.0	36
15.0	45
5.5	11

bivariate normal distribution assumption seems not to be satisfied, an alternative nonparametric measure of correlation called *Spearman's rho* can be used.

Consider, for example, the Porter Company, which markets photocopiers in the eastern United States. Recently, the company's marketing department undertook a study of its clients to determine if there is a significant correlation between the number of copies made per month and the number of employees working for the company. It hoped this information would be useful in helping clients evaluate their copier needs.

Table 15–8 presents data collected by the marketing department from twelve clients selected at random. The individual in charge of the study wishes to determine whether there is significant correlation, but does not feel justified in making the assumption of bivariate normal distributions. Thus, he has decided to calculate the nonparametric Spearman correlation coefficient. The first step is to convert the data in table

TABLE 15–9

Data in ranked form, Porter Company example

No. Copies Used (000s) Y	Employees X
11	11
7	9
6	3
3	5
10	8
8	10
5	6
12	12
2	7
1	2
9	4
4	1

15–8 to ranks, as shown in table 15–9. Note that the ranks are down separately for each variable.

The Spearman correlation coefficient is computed using equation 15–11:

$$\text{rho} = r_s = 1 - \frac{6 \sum_{i=1}^{n} d_i^2}{n^3 - n} \qquad (15\text{–}11)$$

where $d_i = Y_i - X_i$ (difference in ranks)
        n = sample size

Table 15–10 shows the calculations for the Spearman correlation coefficient. The correlation is positive 0.699 for these sample data. Now the question remains whether the true population correlation is zero. If the sample size exceeds ten, the test statistic is approximated by a t statistic with $n - 2$ degrees of freedom, as shown in equation 15–12:

$$t = r_s \sqrt{\frac{n - 2}{1 - r_s^2}} \qquad (15\text{–}12)$$

Y	X	d		d^2
11	11	0		0
7	9	-2		4
6	3	3		9
3	5	-2		4
10	8	2		4
8	10	-2		4
5	6	-1		1
12	12	0		0
2	7	-5		25
1	2	-1		1
9	4	5		25
4	1	3		9
			Sum of squared differences =	86

$$r_s = 1 - \frac{6 \sum d^2}{n^3 - n}$$

$$= 1 - \frac{6\,(86)}{1728 - 12}$$

$$= 1 - 0.301$$

$$= 0.699$$

TABLE 15–10
Spearman correlation coefficient computation, Porter Company example

The hypotheses to be tested are

$$H_0: \rho = 0.0$$

$$H_A: \rho \neq 0.0$$

Thus, for the Porter Company example, we compute the test statistic as follows:

$$t = 0.699 \sqrt{\frac{12 - 2}{1 - 0.699^2}}$$

$$= 3.092$$

To test the null hypothesis using the t statistic, we go to the t-distribution table with $n - 2 = 10$ degrees of freedom for the appropriate level of alpha. Using an alpha level of 0.05, we get a critical t value equal to 2.228.

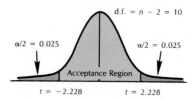

Decision Rule:

If $t > 2.228$, reject H_0.

If $t < -2.228$, reject H_0.

Otherwise, do not reject H_0.

Since $t = 3.092 > 2.228$, reject H_0 and conclude that there exists a significant positive correlation between the number of copies used and the number of employees working at the company.

Note that we have employed the t distribution to test the significance of the Spearman correlation coefficient. However, the assumption of bivariate normal populations is not necessary since we used rank data to compute the Spearman rho value.

Note also that the use of the t distribution for testing the significance of the Spearman correlation coefficient is limited to cases where the sample size is at least ten. Finally, ties are handled by giving each tied value the mean of the rank positions for which it is tied. Therefore, if the ranked observations were 10, 12, 12, 13, the rankings would be 1, 2.5, 2.5, 4.

SKILL DEVELOPMENT PROBLEMS FOR SECTION 15–5

The following exercises have been included to help you gain a better understanding of the material presented in this section. There are additional application problems at the end of this chapter.

16. Under what conditions would you recommend the Spearman correlation coefficient be used as opposed to the correlation coefficient introduced in chapter 13?

17. The following data were collected for two variables, X and Y:

X	Y
112	3.8
98	2.7
123	3.5
146	4.1
130	3.4
100	2.9
110	3.7
113	3.9
133	4.0
149	4.4
90	2.5
146	4.5

a. Compute the Spearman correlation coefficient for these two sets of data. Indicate what it measures.

b. Test whether the correlation is significant at the alpha = 0.05 level.

18. The State Golf Association recently performed a study in which data were collected on golfers' handicaps and the number of rounds played during the year. The following sampling data were collected:

Handicap	Rounds Played
13	24
23	34
17	23
6	22
2	40
15	35
18	11
4	46
8	25
10	17
16	42

a. Based upon these data, what is the Spearman correlation coefficient?

b. Test at the alpha = 0.05 level whether the correlation is statistically significant.

19. Executives were asked to rate the Federal Reserve Board relative to its handling of monetary policy. These ratings were made on a scale of 1 to 20. The ratings were then to be correlated with the age of the executive. The sample data are shown as follows:

Rating	Age
11	35
17	47
11	29
15	53
16	45
13	30
17	50
19	62
12	32
10	34
13	41
14	50
19	55
17	45
18	63

a. Compute the correlation coefficient and interpret what it means with respect to these data.

b. Using an alpha = 0.01 level, test to determine whether the true correlation is zero.

COMPUTER APPLICATIONS

15-6

This chapter has introduced several important nonparametric statistical tests. The examples presented were solved manually to show how each test is performed. Like most other areas of statistics, however, a computer and statistical software are used when dealing with nonparametric statistics. In this section, we present several computer applications based on the KIVZ-Channel 5 data introduced in chapter 2 (see tables 2–10 and 2–11). As has been our practice through this text, SPSS-X and MINITAB are the software packages used.

The Spearman correlation coefficient is the nonparametric equivalent of the correlation coefficient introduced in chapter 13. Like most nonparametric statistics, it is based on the ranks of the data rather than the raw data. Table 15–11 shows the results of using SPSS-X to generate a correlation matrix for variables VAR12 to VAR19. The "SIG" values are the same as the p values discussed earlier. They represent the significance level of the correlation coefficient. For instance, the correlation between VAR12 and VAR19 is -0.3095. The significance level (SIG) is 0.014. This means that the correlation is statistically significant at alpha levels above 0.014. Figure 15–10 shows the SPSS-X commands that generated the correlation matrix in table 15–11.

Table 15–12 shows a contingency analysis table developed using the CROSS-TABS command in SPSS-X. This table shows SEX crossed with EDUCATION. The chi-square statistic is printed. Note, in this example, eight of twelve cells have expected frequencies less than five. This is too many and may result in an inflated chi-square

TABLE 15–11
SPSS-X output—correlation matrix

```
- - -  S P E A R M A N   C O R R E L A T I O N   C O E F F I C I E N T S - - -
VAR13     -.0301
        N(   50)
        SIG .418

VAR14     -.0187       .0950
        N(   50)     N(   50)
        SIG .449     SIG .256

VAR15      .0967       .2214       .5570
        N(   50)     N(   50)     N(   50)
        SIG .252     SIG .061     SIG .000

VAR16      .1055      -.0233      -.0222       .0987
        N(   50)     N(   50)     N(   50)     N(   50)
        SIG .233     SIG .436     SIG .439     SIG .248

VAR17     -.0889       .0662       .5066       .4656      -.1790
        N(   50)     N(   50)     N(   50)     N(   50)     N(   50)
        SIG .270     SIG .324     SIG .000     SIG .000     SIG .107

VAR18      .0119      -.1512       .1632       .0114      -.0816      -.1344
        N(   50)     N(   50)     N(   50)     N(   50)     N(   50)     N(   50)
        SIG .467     SIG .147     SIG .129     SIG .469     SIG .287     SIG .176

VAR19     -.3095       .0171       .0003      -.1369      -.1261       .1628      -.2916
        N(   50)     N(   50)     N(   50)     N(   50)     N(   50)     N(   50)     N(   50)
        SIG .014     SIG .453     SIG .499     SIG .172     SIG .191     SIG .129     SIG .020

            VAR12       VAR13       VAR14       VAR15       VAR16       VAR17       VAR18
```

TABLE 15–12
SPSS-X output—contingency analysis

```
- - - - - - - - -   C R O S S T A B U L A T I O N   O F   - - - - - - - - -
  VAR10      SEX                    BY  VAR16      EDUCATON
- - - - - - - - - - - - - - - - - - - - - - - - - - - - - - PAGE 1 OF 1
                  VAR16
          COUNT
                 |GRADE   SOME      VOTECH   HIGH     COLLEGE  GRADUATE  ROW
                 |SCHOOL  COLLEGE            SCHOOL   GRAD     WORK      TOTAL
                 | 1.00 |  2.00 |   3.00 |   4.00 |   5.00 |   6.00|
VAR10      -------|------+-------+--------+--------+--------+-------|
           1.00  |      |   7   |   2    |   3    |   7    |   3   |   22
   MALE          |      |       |        |        |        |       |   44.0
                 |------+-------+--------+--------+--------+-------|
  FEMALE   2.00  |  2   |   8   |   2    |   5    |   6    |   5   |   28
                 |      |       |        |        |        |       |   56.0
                 |------+-------+--------+--------+--------+-------|
           COLUMN    2      15       4        8       13        8      50
           TOTAL    4.0    30.0     8.0     16.0     26.0     16.0   100.0

CHI-SQUARE  D.F.  SIGNIFICANCE  MIN E.F.  CELLS WITH E.F. < 5
----------  ----  ------------  --------  -------------------
  2.45900    5      0.7827       0.880    8 OF    12 ( 66.7%)

NUMBER OF MISSING OBSERVATIONS =        0
```

```
UNNUMBERED
TITLE DESCRIPTIVE STATISTICS EXAMPLES
FILE HANDLE KIVZ NAME='KIVZ DATA C'
DATA LIST FILE=KIVZ LIST/VAR01 to VAR19
VARIABLE LABELS
    VAR01 'NATIONAL NEWS STATION'
    VAR02 'LOCAL NEWS STATION'
    VAR03 'NEWS RATING'
    VAR04 'SPORTS RATING'
    VAR05 'WEATHER RATING'
    VAR06 'ANCHOR RATING'
    VAR07 'SPORTSCASTER RATING'
    VAR08 'OVERALL RATING'
    VAR09 'NATIONAL INFLUENCE'
    VAR10 'SEX'
    VAR11 'MARITAL STATUS'
    VAR12 'NUMBER EMPLOYED'
    VAR13 'HOME STATUS '
    VAR14 'YEARS AT RESIDENCE'
    VAR15 'YEARS IN STATE'
    VAR16 'EDUCATION'
    VAR17 'AGE'
    VAR18 'INCOME'
    VAR19 'HOURS OF TV'
VALUE LABELS
    VAR01 1 'CHANNEL 5' 2 'CHANNEL 3' 3 'CHANNEL 8' 4
        'UNDECIDED'/
    VAR02 1 'CHANNEL 3' 2 'CHANNEL 8' 3 'CHANNEL 5' 4
        'UNDECIDED'/
    VAR03 TO VAR08 1 'POOR' 2 'FAIR' 3 'GOOD' 4 'VERY GOOD' 5
        'EXCEL'/
    VAR09 1 'TRUE' 2 'FALSE' 3 'UNDECIDED'/
    VAR10 1 'MALE' 2 'FEMALE'/
    VAR11 1 'SINGLE' 2 'DIVORCED' 3 'MARRIED' 4 'OTHER'/
    VAR13 1 'RENTING' 2 'BUYING'/
    VAR16 1 'GRADE SCHOOL' 2 'SOME COLLEGE' 3 'VOTECH' 4 'HIGH
        SCHOOL' 5 'COLLEGE GRAD' 6 'GRADUATE WORK'
NONPAR CORR VAR12 TO VAR19
```

FIGURE 15–10

SPSS-X commands—nonparametric correlation

statistic. However, since the calculated chi-square is only 2.459, with a significance level of 0.7827, we would ''not reject'' the hypothesis of independence. This means that collapsing the cells to reduce the occurrence of small expected cell frequencies is not necessary. Figure 15–11 shows the SPSS-X commands for generating a contingency table.

Table 15–13 presents the SPSS-X output when the Mann-Whitney U test is performed. The variable of interest is INCOME and the hypothesis is no difference in average income for males and females. The Z value is -0.9871, which would clearly fall in the acceptance region. This means that we would ''not reject'' the hypothesis of equal means. Figure 15–12 shows the SPSS-X commands used to perform a Mann-Whitney U test.

MINITAB also supports several nonparametric tests. Among these is the Kruskal-Wallis one-way ANOVA test. Table 15–14 displays the MINITAB output for a Kruskal-Wallis one-way ANOVA where we hypothesize that viewers of the three local news stations have the same average age. Based upon the results in table 15–14, we would not reject the null hypothesis. Figure 15–13 shows the MINITAB commands.

```
UNNUMBERED
TITLE DESCRIPTIVE STATISTICS EXAMPLES
FILE HANDLE KIVZ NAME='KIVZ DATA C'
DATA LIST FILE=KIVZ LIST/VAR01 to VAR19
VARIABLE LABELS
  VAR01 'NATIONAL NEWS STATION'
  VAR02 'LOCAL NEWS STATION'
  VAR03 'NEWS RATING'
  VAR04 'SPORTS RATING'
  VAR05 'WEATHER RATING'
  VAR06 'ANCHOR RATING'
  VAR07 'SPORTSCASTER RATING'
  VAR08 'OVERALL RATING'
  VAR09 'NATIONAL INFLUENCE'
  VAR10 'SEX'
  VAR11 'MARITAL STATUS'
  VAR12 'NUMBER EMPLOYED'
  VAR13 'HOME STATUS '
  VAR14 'YEARS AT RESIDENCE'
  VAR15 'YEARS IN STATE'
  VAR16 'EDUCATION'
  VAR17 'AGE'
  VAR18 'INCOME'
  VAR19 'HOURS OF TV'
VALUE LABELS
  VAR01 1 'CHANNEL 5' 2 'CHANNEL 3' 3 'CHANNEL 8' 4
        'UNDECIDED'/
  VAR02 1 'CHANNEL 3' 2 'CHANNEL 8' 3 'CHANNEL 5' 4
        'UNDECIDED'/
  VAR03 TO VAR08 1 'POOR' 2 'FAIR' 3 'GOOD' 4 'VERY GOOD'
        5 'EXCEL'/
  VAR09 1 'TRUE' 2 'FALSE' 3 'UNDECIDED'/
  VAR10 1 'MALE' 2 'FEMALE'/
  VAR11 1 'SINGLE' 2 'DIVORCED' 3 'MARRIED' 4 'OTHER'/
  VAR13 1 'RENTING' 2 'BUYING'/
  VAR16 1 'GRADE SCHOOL' 2 'SOME COLLEGE' 3 'VOTECH' 4 'HIGH
        SCHOOL' 5 'COLLEGE GRAD' 6 'GRADUATE WORK'
CROSSTABS TABLES = VAR10 BY VAR16
STATISTICS 1
```

FIGURE 15–11
SPSS-X commands—CROSSTABS

TABLE 15–13
SPSS-X output—Mann-Whitney U test

```
- - - - - MANN-WHITNEY U - WILCOXON RANK SUM W TEST
    VAR18     INCOME
 BY VAR10     SEX
   MEAN RANK       CASES
        23.20      22 VAR10 = 1.00 MALE
        27.30      28 VAR10 = 2.00 FEMALE
                   --
                   50 TOTAL
                        CORRECTED FOR TIES
       U         W        Z       2-TAILED P
     257.5     510.5   -0.9871     0.3236
```

```
UNNUMBERED
TITLE DESCRIPTIVE STATISTICS EXAMPLES
FILE HANDLE KIVZ NAME='KIVZ DATA C'
DATA LIST FILE=KIVZ LIST/VAR01 to VAR19
VARIABLE LABELS
  VAR01 'NATIONAL NEWS STATION'
  VAR02 'LOCAL NEWS STATION'
  VAR03 'NEWS RATING'
  VAR04 'SPORTS RATING'
  VAR05 'WEATHER RATING'
  VAR06 'ANCHOR RATING'
  VAR07 'SPORTSCASTER RATING'
  VAR08 'OVERALL RATING'
  VAR09 'NATIONAL INFLUENCE'
  VAR10 'SEX'
  VAR11 'MARITAL STATUS'
  VAR12 'NUMBER EMPLOYED'
  VAR13 'HOME STATUS '
  VAR14 'YEARS AT RESIDENCE'
  VAR15 'YEARS IN STATE'
  VAR16 'EDUCATION'
  VAR17 'AGE'
  VAR18 'INCOME'
  VAR19 'HOURS OF TV'
VALUE LABELS
  VAR01 1 'CHANNEL 5' 2 'CHANNEL 3' 3 'CHANNEL 8' 4
        'UNDECIDED'/
  VAR02 1 'CHANNEL 3' 2 'CHANNEL 8' 3 'CHANNEL 5' 4
        'UNDECIDED'/
  VAR03 TO VAR08 1 'POOR' 2 'FAIR' 3 'GOOD' 4 'VERY GOOD' 5
        'EXCEL'/
  VAR09 1 'TRUE' 2 'FALSE' 3 'UNDECIDED'/
  VAR10 1 'MALE' 2 'FEMALE'/
  VAR11 1 'SINGLE' 2 'DIVORCED' 3 'MARRIED' 4 'OTHER'/
  VAR13 1 'RENTING' 2 'BUYING'/
  VAR16 1 'GRADE SCHOOL' 2 'SOME COLLEGE' 3 'VOTECH' 4 'HIGH
        SCHOOL' 5 'COLLEGE GRAD' 6 'GRADUATE WORK'
NPAR TESTS M-W = VAR18 BY VAR10 (1,2)
```

FIGURE 15–12
SPSS-X commands—Mann-Whitney U test

FIGURE 15–13
MINITAB commands—Kruskal-Wallis one-way ANOVA

```
MTB> READ 'KIVZ5' into C1-C19
MTB> NAME C17 'AGE'
MTB> NAME C2 'LOCAL'
MTB> OUTFILE = 'PRINTER'
MTB> KRUSKAL-WALLIS C17 C2
```

TABLE 15–14
MINITAB output—Kruskal-Wallis one-way ANOVA

LEVEL	NOBS	MEDIAN	AVE. RANK	Z VALUE
1	9	45.00	26.6	0.25
2	25	45.00	25.6	0.04
3	11	42.00	25.7	0.06
4	5	35.00	22.6	-0.47
OVERALL	50		25.5	

```
H = 0.2536
H(ADJ. FOR TIES) = 0.2539
```

Many people make the mistake of learning one or two statistical techniques and then using these techniques in all situations. Surprisingly, some people even get emotional about being able to analyze a particular problem using their favorite technique. As future managerial decision makers, you cannot afford the luxury of defining a problem situation so you can apply your favorite technique. Statistics should be an aid to decision making, not an end in itself.

Many powerful statistical tools discussed in this book rest on the assumptions that the data being analyzed can be measured by at least an interval scale and that the underlying populations being analyzed are normal. If these assumptions come close to being satisfied, many of the tools discussed prior to this chapter apply and are useful. However, in many practical situations these assumptions just do not apply, in which case the tools discussed in this chapter may be appropriate. In any case, nonparametric statistical tests should be part of every decision maker's tools. There are many other nonparametric statistical techniques which have been developed for specific applications. Many are aimed at situations involving small samples. You should consult the references at the end of the chapter for further reading.

CHAPTER GLOSSARY

contingency table   A table used to classify sample observations according to two or more identifiable characteristics.

nonparametric statistics   Statistical techniques that do not depend on the population conforming to a predetermined distribution.

CHAPTER FORMULAS

Chi-square goodness of fit statistic

$$\chi^2 = \Sigma \frac{(f_o - f_e)^2}{f_e}$$

Kruskal-Wallis H statistic

$$H = \frac{12}{N(N + 1)} \sum_{i=1}^{K} \frac{R_i^2}{n_i} - 3(N + 1)$$

Kruskal-Wallis adjustment factor

If 25 percent of the ranked observations are ties, divide H by

$$1 - \frac{\sum_{i=1}^{R} (t_i^3 - t_i)}{N^3 - N}$$

Mann-Whitney U mean

$$\text{Mean} = \frac{n_1 n_2}{2}$$

Mann-Whitney U standard deviation (no ties)

$$\text{Standard deviation} = \sqrt{\frac{n_1 n_2 (n_1 + n_2 + 1)}{12}}$$

Spearman's rho

$$r_s = 1 - \frac{6 \sum_{i=1}^{n} d_i^2}{n^3 - n}$$

SOLVED PROBLEMS

1. Burtco Incorporated designs and manufactures gears for heavy-duty construction equipment. One such gear, #9973, has the following specifications:

   1. Mean diameter 3 inches
   2. Standard deviation 0.001 inch
   3. Output normally distributed around the mean

   The production control manager has selected a random sample of 500 gears from the inventory and found the following distribution:

Gear Diameter (inches)	Frequency
Under 2.995	3
2.995 and under 2.996	4
2.996 and under 2.997	5
2.997 and under 2.998	19
2.998 and under 2.999	98
2.999 and under 3.000	146
3.000 and under 3.001	124

3.001 and under 3.002	83
3.002 and under 3.003	11
3.003 and over	7
Total	500

Based upon this sample information, does gear #9973 meet specifications? Use a significance level of 0.05.

Solution:

This is an example of a one-sample goodness of fit problem. We can hypothesize as follows:

H_0: Gear #9973 is normally distributed with a mean diameter of 3 inches and standard deviation 0.001 inch.
H_A: Gear #9973 is not within specifications.

$\alpha = 0.05$

An appropriate statistical procedure is the chi-square goodness of fit test. This test calculates the expected frequencies for each interval and compares the expected to the observed frequencies. If the calculated χ^2 gets too large, we will conclude that the fit is not good and reject the null hypothesis.

To determine the expected frequencies, we calculate the probability of a gear having a diameter in each of the intervals, assuming the gear meets the required specifications. Then we multiply the probability by 500 to obtain the expected frequency. The procedure is as follows:

P(less than 2.995) = area under normal curve to the left of 2.995.

$$Z = \frac{X - \mu_x}{\sigma_x} = \frac{2.995 - 3}{0.001}$$

$$= -5.00$$

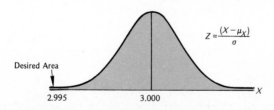

The area to the left of $Z = -5.00$ is essentially zero. Therefore, the expected frequency is $(0)(500) = 0$.

As another example,

$$P(2.997 \leq X \leq 2.998) = \text{area under the normal curve between 2.997}$$
$$\text{and 2.998}$$

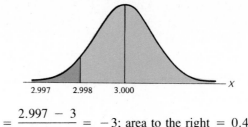

$$Z = \frac{2.997 - 3}{0.001} = -3; \text{ area to the right} = 0.4987$$

$$Z = \frac{2,998 - 3}{0.001} = -2; \text{ area to the right} = 0.4772$$

Therefore the desired probability is $0.4987 - 0.4772 = 0.0215$, and the expected frequency is $(0.0215)(500) = 10.75$.

In a like manner, we find the expected frequencies for each interval:

Gear Diameter (inches)	f_o	f_e
Under 2.995	3	0
2.995 and under 2.996	4	0.015
2.996 and under 2.997	5	0.635
2.997 and under 2.998	19	10.750
2.998 and under 2.999	98	67.950
2.999 and under 3.000	146	170.650
3.000 and under 3.001	124	170.650
3.001 and under 3.002	83	67.950
3.002 and under 3.003	11	10.750
3.003 and over	7	0.650

Because the chi-square goodness of fit test does not work well when more than 20 percent of the cells have expected cell frequencies below 5.0, as is the case in this example, we must combine the cells.

Gear Diameter (inches)	f_o	f_e	$(f_o - f_e)^2$	$(f_o - f_e)^2/f_e$
Under 2.998	31	11.4	384.16	33.70
2.998 and under 2.999	98	67.95	903.00	13.29
2.999 and under 3.000	146	170.65	607.62	3.56
3.000 and under 3.001	124	170.65	2,176.22	12.75
3.001 and under 3.002	83	67.95	226.50	3.33
3.002 and over	18	11.40	43.56	3.82
				$\chi^2 = 70.45$

$$\chi^2 = \sum_{i=1}^{K} \frac{(f_{oi} - f_{ei})^2}{f_{ei}}$$

$$= 70.45$$

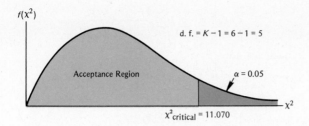

Since $\chi^2 = 70.45 > \chi^2_{critical} = 11.070$, we reject the null hypothesis and conclude that the gears are *not* within specifications. The production manager would most likely want to halt production and attempt to adjust the process to bring the gears within specifications. However, as often happens, he may discover that the specifications are unreachable with the machinery he has to work with, in which case either new machinery will be required or the specifications will have to be renegotiated.

2. Automobile insurance companies have for a number of years used age, sex, and marital status for determining rates. For example, single males under 25 years of age are considered the highest risk and are charged the highest premiums. Single females in the same age group are charged somewhat lower premiums.

   Recently the National Ranch Insurance Company studied 1,000 of its policyholders. The purpose of the study was to determine whether such factors as age, sex, and marital status are independent of whether the policyholder has filed an accident claim. With regard to age for all drivers, both male and female, National Ranch found the following:

	Age				
	Under 25	*25–40*	*40–55*	*Over 55*	
Reported Claim	93	72	53	63	281
No Claim	115	155	265	184	719
	208	227	318	247	$1,000 = N$

   Based on these data, what should National Ranch conclude about age and claim status?

Solution:

The basic question facing National Ranch is whether age is independent of claim status. Therefore we set up our null and alternative hypotheses as follows:

H_0: Whether or not an insurance claim has been filed by a policyholder is independent of the policyholder's age.

H_A: Age and claim status are not independent.

$\alpha = 0.05$

   An appropriate test is the chi-square test of independence.

$$\chi^2 = \sum_{i=1}^{r} \sum_{j=1}^{c} \frac{(fo_{ij} - fe_{ij})^2}{fe_{ij}}$$

The expected frequencies are

$$fe_{11} = \frac{281(208)}{1,000} = 58.44$$

$$fe_{12} = \frac{281(227)}{1,000} = 63.78$$

$$fe_{13} = \frac{281(318)}{1,000} = 89.35$$

.
.
.

$$fe_{24} = \frac{719(247)}{1,000} = 177.59$$

The completed contingency table is as follows:

	Age			
	Under 25	25–40	40–55	Over 55
Reported Claim	f_o = 93.00 f_e = 58.44	f_o = 72.00 f_e = 63.78	f_o = 53.00 f_e = 89.35	f_o = 63.00 f_e = 69.40
No Claim	f_o = 115.00 f_e = 149.55	f_o = 155.00 f_e = 163.21	f_o = 265.00 f_e = 228.64	f_0 = 184.00 f_e = 177.59

Then

$$\chi^2 = \frac{(93.00 - 58.44)^2}{58.44} + \frac{(72.00 - 63.78)^2}{63.78} + \ldots + \frac{(184.00 - 177.59)^2}{177.59}$$

$$= 51.28$$

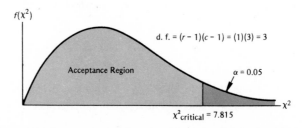

d. f. = $(r - 1)(c - 1)$ = (1)(3) = 3

Acceptance Region

α = 0.05

χ^2_{critical} = 7.815

Since $\chi^2 = 51.28 > \chi^2_{\text{critical}} = 7.815$, National Ranch should reject the hypothesis of independence. Based on the data, the insurance company might infer that young drivers have more accident claims than expected, and therefore higher rates might be justified.

3. The Bixby Company operates in three states. Its primary business is to give review seminars for individuals who plan to sit for the CPA (certified public accountant) examination. Bixby has three teams that put on the seminars, one for each state. Michelle Bixby is quite concerned that there is consistent performance by the three teams. She feels she can measure the success of her teams by the CPA exam scores received by persons who have taken the seminars.

   Michelle wishes to determine whether the average score received by those who took the seminar is the same in the three states. Because of the way the test is scored, she is *not* willing to assume the populations are normally distributed. A sample of twelve scores from each state provided the following data:

Maine	New York	New Jersey
90	90	55
65	88	55
72	83	90
83	83	83
65	65	65
50	65	65
65	83	60
83	83	55
83	90	65
55	90	72
72	65	90
65	72	65

   Based on these data, what should Michelle conclude about the average scores of the three states? Use an alpha level of 0.10. Assume the population variances are equal.

Solution:

This problem involves three independent samples and can be analyzed using Kruskal-Wallis one-way analysis of variance. We begin by establishing the null and alternative hypotheses as

H_0: The average CPA exam score for seminar students will be the same in the three states.

H_A: The average CPA exam score for seminar students will not be the same in all three states.

$\alpha = 0.10$

   The first step in the Kruskal-Wallis procedure is to change the raw scores to ranks. Note that there are many ties in these data. Thus we will give each tied value the average of the ranks for which it is tied. Also, we will calculate the Kruskal-Wallis H statistic, using the correction factor.

The rankings are as follows:

Maine	New York	New Jersey
33.5	33.5	3.5
12.0	30.0	3.5
19.5	25.5	33.5
25.5	25.5	25.5
12.0	12.0	12.0
1.0	12.0	12.0
12.0	25.5	6.0
25.5	25.5	3.5
25.5	33.5	12.0
3.5	33.5	19.5
19.5	12.0	33.5
12.0	19.5	12.0
Sum of ranks = 201.5	Sum of ranks = 288.0	Sum of ranks = 176.5

Then

$$H = \cfrac{\cfrac{12}{N(N+1)} \sum \cfrac{R^2}{n} - 3(N+1)}{1 - \cfrac{\Sigma(t^3 - t)}{N^3 - N}}$$

$$= \cfrac{\cfrac{12}{(36)(37)}\left[\cfrac{(201.5)^2}{12} + \cfrac{(288.0)^2}{12} + \cfrac{(176.5)^2}{12}\right] - 3(37)}{1 - \cfrac{[(4^3 - 4) + (11^3 - 11) + (4^3 - 4) + (8^3 - 8) + (6^3 - 6)]}{36^3 - 36}}$$

$$= \frac{5.1400}{0.9538}$$

$$= 5.389$$

Note that the denominator in the Kruskal-Wallis H equation is the correction factor for the ties in the rankings. The closer this correction factor is to zero, the greater impact it has on the calculated H value.

The null hypothesis test is a chi-square test with $K - 1 = 2$ degrees of freedom. If H exceeds the critical value from the chi-square table, we will reject the null hypothesis of equal means. Since $H = 5.389 > \chi^2_{critical} = 4.605$, we reject the null hypothesis and conclude that the mean scores in the three states are not equal. Michelle Bixby would infer that the seminar team in New York is turning out students who do better on the average than New Jersey or Maine students. Of course this does not automatically mean the New York team is superior to the others.

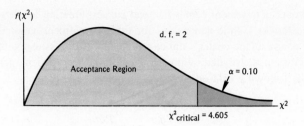

Section 15–1

20. Ramona Lane, the manager of Rapid Way Super Discount, always keeps four checkout stands open. However, she frequently notices lines for registers 1 and 2. She isn't sure whether the layout of the store channels customers into these registers or whether the check-out clerks in these lines are simply slower than the other two.

Ramona kept a record of which stands 1,000 shoppers checked out through. The shoppers checked out of the four stands according to the following pattern:

Stand 1	Stand 2	Stand 3	Stand 4
292	281	240	187

Based on these data, can Ramona conclude that an equal number of shoppers are likely to use each of the stands? (Use an alpha level of 0.05.)

21. A manufacturer of packaged food has decided to market a new quick brownie mix. This venture is rather risky since the new mix will compete with three established brands. The production manager argues that quality will sell the new mix. The marketing manager states that the average consumer can't tell the difference between brands and that the critical factor in selling the mix will be the advertising campaign.

To test the marketing manager's contention, the four types of brownies were baked under equal conditions. Shoppers were randomly stopped in several supermarkets and asked to sample each brownie and indicate which of the four tasted the best. Which brownie was tasted first was randomly determined, and the production manager and the marketing manager felt the process yielded representative results. The following data show how many shoppers rated each brand the tastiest:

	Brand		
A	B	C	New
37	23	27	41

Which contention do these data support? Use a Type I error of 0.01.

22. A regional cancer treatment center has had success treating localized cancers with a linear accelerator. While admissions for further treatment nationally average 1.1 per patient per year, the center's director feels that readmissions with the new treatment are Poisson distributed, with a mean of 0.5 per patient per year. He has collected the following data on a random sample of 300 patients:

Readmissions Last Year	Patients
0	139
1	87
2	48
3	14
4	8
5	1
6	1
7	0
8	2
	300

a. Formulate the null hypothesis to test the director's claim.
b. Calculate the test statistic to test this claim.
c. Assume the Type I error is to be controlled at 0.05. Do you agree with the director's claim? Why?

23. Cooper Manufacturing, Inc. of Dallas, Texas, has a contract with the U.S. Air Force to produce a part for a new fighter plane being manufactured. The part is a bolt that has specifications requiring that the length be normally distributed with a mean of 3.5 inches and a standard deviation of 0.15 inch. As part of the company's quality control efforts, each day Cooper's engineers select a random sample of 100 bolts produced that day and carefully measure the bolts to determine if the production is within specifications. The following data were collected the past day:

Length (inches)	Frequency
Under 3.30	5
3.30 and under 3.35	16
3.35 and under 3.40	7
3.40 and under 3.50	20
3.50 and under 3.60	36
3.60 and under 3.65	8
Over 3.65	8

Based on these sample data, what should Cooper's engineers conclude about the production output if they test using an alpha level of 0.01? Discuss.

24. The Cooper Company discussed in problem 23 has a second contract with a private firm for which it makes fuses for an electronic instrument. The quality control department at Cooper periodically selects a random sample of five fuses and tests each fuse to determine if it is defective. Based on these findings, the production process is either shut down (if too many defectives are observed) or allowed to run. The quality control department believes that the sampling process follows a binomial distribution and it has been using the binomial distribution to compute the probabilities associated with the sampling outcomes.

The contract allows for at most 5 percent defectives. The head of quality control recently compiled a list of the sampling results for the past 300 days in which five fuses were tested, with the following frequency distribution for the number of defectives observed. She is concerned that the binomial distribution with a sample size of five and a probability of defectives of 0.05 may not be appropriate.

Number of Defectives	Frequency
0	209
1	33
2	43
3	10
4	5
5	0

Using an alpha level of 0.10, what should the quality control manager conclude based on these sample data? Discuss.

25. An instructor at a major university indicates that test scores in an introductory sociology class have been normally distributed since he started using a graduate student to grade his tests. To test this claim, a random sample of 300 test scores were selected from the previous academic year. These are shown as follows.

Test Score	Frequency
Under 30	20
30 and under 40	35
40 and under 50	40
50 and under 60	35
60 and under 70	105
70 and under 80	60
Over 80	5

Based on these sample data, can it be concluded that the test scores are normally distributed at an alpha level of 0.05? Note that you need to compute the sample mean and standard deviation.

Section 15–2

26. Ralph Rogers has developed a highly successful practice as a black-market acupuncture specialist. Ralph's success is built on his money-back guarantee. If his treatment wears off, he'll treat you again. His accountant, in trying to set up an allowance for future visits account, hypothesizes that whether or not a patient will

demand a retreatment is related to the price of the original treatment. The following data show the relationship between price and return treatment:

		Price		
		High	*Medium*	*Low*
	In Less than 2 Years	26	13	16
Retreatment	*In 2–5 Years*	43	35	52
	None in 5 Years	87	79	103

a. What should the accountant conclude regarding the hypothesis? (Use an alpha level of 0.05.)

b. What factors that the accountant apparently has not considered might be important to the analysis?

27. Jack O'Connell, chief of officials for the National Basketball League, reviews films of all games to evaluate calls made by the referees. Jack rates each call "good" or "bad." During a week's worth of games, Jack found the following distribution of calls for two officials:

Call	Official A	Official B
Good	463	518
Bad	51	38

a. Do these data indicate that the proportion of bad calls is the same for each official?

b. Test the data using a chi-square statistic with an alpha level of 0.05.

c. Compare the test in part b with the Z test for the difference between two population proportions.

28. The J. Scholten CPA firm performed a study of last year's income-tax business. In one part of the study the accountants collected data on their client's gross taxable incomes and the associated tax payments. These data are shown in the following table, where, for example, there are twenty-five clients whose gross incomes were below $10,000 and who paid $3,000 or less in taxes.

	Taxes			
	$0–$3,000	*$3,001–$5,000*	*$5,001–$10,000*	*Over $10,000*
$0–$10,000	25	0	0	0
$10,001–$20,000	17	5	0	0
Gross Income *$20,001–$40,000*	15	40	8	3
Over $40,000	3	27	22	14

Based on these data, can Scholten conclude that its clients' gross incomes are independent of the income taxes paid? Test at the alpha level of 0.05. What comment would you have made had independence been concluded?

29. Referring to problem 28, Scholten also studied the time it took its accountants to complete each client's tax return, and related this time to the taxes paid by the client. Scholten managers were interested in determining whether a relationship exists between these two variables or whether they could consider the two variables independent. The following data are available:

		$0–$3,000	$3,001–$5,000	$5,001–$10,000	Over $10,000
No. Work Hours	0–2	27	30	5	2
	2–4	22	30	5	6
	Over 4	10	12	20	10

Based on these data, what should the Scholten firm conclude? Use an alpha level of 0.10.

Section 15–3

30. McDougals is a nationwide fast-food company with corporate headquarters in Bellview, Washington. For the past few months the company has undertaken a new advertising study. Initially, company executives selected twenty-two of their retail outlets that were similar with respect to sales volume, profitability, location, climate, economic status of customers, and experience of store management. Each of the outlets was randomly assigned one of two advertising plans promoting a new sandwich product. The following data represent the number of the new sandwiches sold during the specific test period at each retail outlet:

Advertising Plan 1	Advertising Plan 2
1,711	2,100
1,915	2,210
1,905	1,950
2,153	3,004
1,504	2,725
1,195	2,619
2,103	2,483
1,601	2,520
1,580	1,904
1,475	1,875
1,588	1,943

McDougals executives want you to determine whether these data indicate that the two advertising plans lead to significantly different average sales levels for the new product. They ask you to test this at the alpha level of 0.05, but are not willing to make the assumptions necessary for you to use the t test.

31. Two small regional life insurance companies are being studied by the Triangle Life Insurance Company as candidates for a possible merger. Triangle can merge with only one of these regional companies at this time and, as part of its study, wishes to determine if there is a difference in the average annual premiums received by the two regional companies. The following data represent sample policy premiums for each company:

Company 1	Company 2
$246	$300
211	305
235	308
270	325
411	340
310	295
450	320
502	330
311	240
200	360

Do these data indicate a difference in mean annual premiums for the two companies? Apply the Mann-Whitney U test with an alpha level of 0.10.

32. Referring to problem 31, apply the t test to determine whether the data indicate a difference between annual premiums for the two regional companies. Use an alpha level of 0.10. Also indicate what assumptions must be made to apply the t test.

33. The Style-Rite Company of Spokane, Washington, makes windbreaker jackets for people who play golf and who are active outdoors during the spring and fall months. The company recently developed a new material and is in the process of test marketing jackets made from the material. As part of this test-marketing effort, ten people were each supplied with a jacket made from the original material, asked to wear it for two months, and wash it at least twice during that time. A second group of ten people were given a jacket made from a new material and asked to wear it for two months with the same washing requirements.

Following the two-month trial period, the individuals were asked to rate the jackets on a scale of 0 to 100, with 0 being the worst performance rating and 100 being the best. The ratings for each material are shown as follows:

Original Material	New Material
76	55
34	90
70	72

23	17
45	56
80	69
10	91
46	95
67	86
75	74

It is expected that, on the average, the performance ratings will be superior for the new material. Do the sample data support this belief at an alpha level of 0.05? Discuss.

34. A study was recently conducted by the Bonniville Power Association to determine attitudes regarding the association's policies in western U.S. states. One part of the study asked respondents to rate the performance of the BPA on its responsiveness to environmental issues. The following responses were obtained for a sample of twelve urban residents and ten rural residents. The ratings are on a 1 to 100 scale, with 100 being perfect:

Urban	Rural
76	55
90	80
86	94
60	40
43	85
96	92
50	77
20	68
30	35
82	59
75	
84	

Based on the sample data, should the BPA conclude that there is no difference between the urban and rural residents with respect to average environmental rating? Test using an alpha level of 0.01.

35. Referring to problem 34, perform the appropriate parametric statistical test and indicate the assumptions necessary to use this test that were not required by the Mann-Whitney tests. Use an alpha level of 0.01.

Section 15–4

36. The Miltmore Corporation performs consulting services for companies that think they have image problems. Recently Miltmore was approached by the Bluedot Beer Company. Bluedot executives were concerned that the company's image relative to its two closest competitors' had diminished. Miltmore conducted an image study in which a random sample of eight people were asked to rate Bluedot's image. Five people were asked to rate competitor A's image, and ten people were asked to rate competitor B's image. The image ratings were made on a 100-point scale, with 100 being the best possible rating. The results of the sampling were

Bluedot	Competitor A	Competitor B
40	95	50
60	53	80
70	55	82
40	92	87
55	90	93
90		51
20		63
20		72
		96
		88

a. Based on these sample results, should Bluedot conclude that there is an image difference between the three companies? Select your own alpha level and justify it.

b. Should Bluedot infer that its image has been damaged by last year's federal government recall of its product? Discuss why or why not.

c. Why might the decision maker wish to use parametric analysis of variance rather than the corresponding nonparametric test? Discuss.

37. A major car manufacturer is experimenting with three new methods of pollution control. The testing lab must determine whether the three methods produce equal pollution reductions. Readings from a calibrated carbon monoxide meter are taken from groups of engines randomly equipped with one of the three control units. The following data are found:

Method 1	Method 2	Method 3
45	39	26
49	37	31
48	31	32
50	42	40
33	43	44
46	47	41
46	46	34
47	27	28
46	29	30
39	31	34
	36	35
		38

Use the Kruskal-Wallis test to determine whether the three pollution-control methods will produce equal results.

Section 15–5

38. The Luguna Hills Golf Club recently conducted a study of its playing members to determine whether a linear relationship exists between frequency of play and golf handicap. Data were collected over a three-month period for twelve golfers selected at random from the club's membership list. Variable Y is handicap at the end of the three-month period and variable X is the number of times the member played golf during the three-month period. All golfers started with a 20 handicap.

Y	X
22	13
18	30
15	19
20	24
13	33
29	15
16	20
12	31
17	44
21	10
23	12
14	28

  a. Plot these data on a scatter plot and verbally describe what, if any, relationship is present in the data.
  b. Referring to chapter 12, compute the correlation coefficient and test for significance at the alpha level of 0.05. Indicate what assumptions are required to test for statistical significance.

39. Referring to problem 38, suppose the decision maker in charge of the golf study is not willing to make the assumptions necessary to test significance of the correlation coefficient. As an alternative, compute the Spearman correlation coefficient and test for statistical significance, using an alpha level of 0.05. Comment on the results.

40. The financial analyst for Shafer and Associates regularly attempts to correlate stock prices for companies trading on the New York Stock Exchange with various financial variables from the company's financial records. One such study involved a random sample of fourteen companies in which stock price was related to earnings per share. The data collected in that study are shown as follows:

Stock Price	Earnings per Share
8.125	1.43
11.500	2.08
33.375	4.19
21.125	1.90
55.625	4.78
23.625	2.56
33.500	5.12
14.000	0.75
67.750	3.59
72.125	5.23
4.625	0.89
19.000	1.43
26.750	2.90
30.875	3.01

Plot the two variables on a scatter plot and describe the apparent relationship between the two variables.

41. Referring to problem 40, compute the Spearman correlation coefficient for the two variables and test to determine whether the true correlation is significantly different from zero. Use an alpha level of 0.10.

42. A group of ten financial experts was recently asked to select a company at random from those selling shares on the New York Stock Exchange. Each expert then was asked to rate on a scale from 1 to 100 the financial position of the company by looking at the company's financial statement by the year ended 1986. They were then asked to examine the same company's financial statements for the year ended 1988 and provide still another rating of the company's financial position but this time on a scale of 1 to 1,000. The ratings are shown as follows.

1986	1988
55	690
89	900
45	200
50	500
69	980
70	750
80	770
90	940
75	850
95	950

a. Develop a scatter plot for these data and describe the apparent relationship between the two variables based on what you see in the scatter plot.

b. Would it be appropriate to compute the parametric correlation coefficient based on these data? Discuss why or why not.

c. Compute the Spearman correlation coefficient for these two variables and indicate whether the two variables are significantly correlated using an alpha level of 0.05.

STATE DEPARTMENT OF TRANSPORTATION CASE STUDY PROBLEMS

The following questions and problems pertain directly to the State Department of Transportation case study and data base introduced in Chapter 1. The questions and problems were written assuming that you will have access to a computer and appropriate statistical software. The data base containing 100 observations and seventeen variables is shown in table 1C–1 in chapter 1. *Assume that the data were collected using a simple random sampling process.*

1. Herb Kriner is interested in determining if seat belt status is independent of insurance status. Test this at the alpha = 0.05 level. Show the contingency table and the test statistic.

2. Herb Kriner would like to determine whether the average age of drivers in this state is the same for males and females. Herb recognizes that he could test using a two-sample t test but he is unwilling to make the necessary assumptions. Therefore, he would like you to use the appropriate nonparametric test at an alpha = 0.05 level. Be sure to discuss your results and indicate what assumptions are required by the t test that are not required by the nonparametric test.

3. Can Herb Kriner conclude that knowledge of the liability insurance law is independent of sex of the respondent? Test at the alpha = 0.05 level.

C A S E S

15A   Bentford Electronics, Part 1

On Saturday morning Jennifer Bentford received a call at her home from the production supervisor at Bentford Electronics Plant #1. The supervisor indicated that she and the supervisors from Plants #2, #3, and #4 had agreed that something must be done to improve company morale and, thereby, increase the production output of their plants. Jennifer Bentford, president of Bentford Electronics, agreed to set up a Monday morning meeting with the supervisors to see if together they could arrive at a plan for accomplishing these objectives.

By Monday each supervisor had compiled a list of several ideas, including a four-day work week and interplant competition of various kinds.

After listening to the discussion for some time, Jennifer Bentford asked if anyone knew if there were a difference in average daily output for the four plants. When she heard no positive response, she told the supervisors to select a random sample of daily production reports from each plant and test whether there was a difference. They were to meet again on Wednesday afternoon with test results.

By Wednesday morning the supervisors had collected the following data on units produced:

Plant #1	Plant #2	Plant #3	Plant #4
4,306	1,853	2,700	1,704
2,852	1,948	2,705	2,320
1,900	2,702	2,721	4,150
4,711	4,110	2,900	3,300
2,933	3,950	2,650	3,200
3,627	2,300	2,480	2,975

The supervisors had little trouble collecting the data, but were at a loss how to determine if there was a difference in the output of the four plants. Jerry Gibson, the company's research analyst, told the supervisors that there were statistical procedures that could be used to test hypotheses regarding multiple samples if the daily output was distributed in a bell shape (normal distribution) at each plant. The supervisors expressed dismay because none thought his or her output was normal. Jerry Gibson indicated that there were techniques that didn't require the normality assumption, but he didn't know what they were.

The meeting with Jennifer Bentford was scheduled to begin in three hours.

15B   Bentford Electronics, Part 2

Following the Wednesday afternoon meeting (see case 15A), Jennifer Bentford and her plant supervisors agreed to implement a weekly contest called the NBE Game of the Week. The plant turning out the most production each week would be considered the NBE Game of the Week winner and would receive ten points. The second-place plant would receive seven points, and the third- and fourth-place plants would receive three points and one point, respectively. The contest would last twenty-six weeks. At the end of that period, a $200,000 bonus would be divided among the employees in the four plants proportional to the total points accumulated by each plant.

The announcement of the contest created a lot of excitement and enthusiasm at the four plants. No one complained about the rules since the four plants were designed and staffed to produce equally.

At the close of the contest, Jennifer Bentford called the supervisors into a meeting, at which time she asked for data to determine whether the contest had significantly improved productivity. She indicated that she had to know this before she could authorize a second contest. The supervisors, expecting this response, had put together the following data:

Units Produced (4 plants combined)	Before-Contest Frequency	During-Contest Frequency
0– 2,500	11	0
2,501– 8,000	23	20
8,001–15,000	56	83
15,001–20,000	15	52
	105 days	155 days

Jennifer examined the data and indicated that it looked like the contest was a success, but she wanted to base her decision to continue the contest on more than just an observation of the data. "Surely there must be some way to statistically test the worthiness of this contest," Jennifer stated. "I have to see the results before I will authorize the second contest."

15C   Singleaf Department Store, Part 2

Beth Hansen has completed her study of different types of collection letters (see case 12B). However she is also concerned about the effect of the collection efforts on the goodwill of Singleaf stores. As mentioned previously, Singleaf does not sell the past-due accounts to a collection agency because of the potential loss of goodwill.

Beth has decided to use a telephone interview system to determine customer attitudes toward the Singleaf stores. She has devised a series of questions to measure customer attitudes on many factors connected with the stores: clerk helpfulness, billing procedures, merchandise selection, and so on. The scores on each question are combined to give an overall measure of the customer attitude toward the Singleaf organization (ten points maximum). In an effort to determine what customers in general think about the store and the effect of the collection letters, Beth has decided to randomly select customers from the following categories:

1. Frequent customers with nondelinquent accounts
2. Infrequent customers with nondelinquent accounts
3. Delinquent customers who have received reminder collection letters
4. Delinquent customers who have received "tough" collection letters
5. Delinquent customers who have not received collection letters

Since the telephone questionnaire will be expensive, Beth would like to have an idea about the potential findings before asking the president in charge of customer relations to authorize spending the money. The sample telephone survey gave the following overall ratings for Singleaf stores:

Customer Category					Customer Category				
1	2	3	4	5	1	2	3	4	5
9	3	5	4	5	9	7	9	6	3
8	5	9	9	4	8	8	7	1	7
8	5	6	9	4	8	9	10	3	3

Beth has an appointment with the Singleaf president tomorrow morning.

15D   American Oil Company

Chad Williams sat back in his airline seat to enjoy the hour flight between Los Angeles and Oakland, California. The hour would give him time to reflect upon his upcoming trip to Australia and the work he had been doing the past week in Los Angeles.

Chad is one man on a six-man crew for the American Oil Company who literally walks the earth searching for oil. His college degrees in geology and petroleum engineering landed him the job with American, but he never dreamed he would be doing the exciting work he now does. Chad and his crew spend several months in special locations around the world using highly sensitive electronic equipment for oil exploration purposes.

The upcoming trip to Australia is one that Chad has been looking forward to since it was announced that his crew would be going there to search the Outback for oil. In preparation for the Australia trip the crew has been in Los Angeles at American's engineering research facility working on some new equipment that would be used in Australia in search of oil.

Chad's thoughts centered on the problem he was having with a particular component part on the new equipment. The specifications called for 200 of the components, each having a diameter of between 0.15 and 0.18 inch. The only available supplier of the component in New Jersey manufactures the components to specifications calling for normally distributed output with a mean of 0.16 inch and a standard deviation of 0.02 inch.

Chad faces two problems. First, he is unsure that the supplier actually does produce parts with the mean of 0.16 inch and standard deviation of 0.02 inch according to a normal distribution. Second, if that is the case, he needs to determine how many components to purchase if enough acceptable components are to be received to make two oil exploration devices.

The supplier has sent Chad the following data for 330 randomly selected components. Chad believes that the supplier is honest and that he can rely on the data.

Diameter (inch)	Frequency
Under 0.14	5
0.14 and under 0.15	70
0.15 and under 0.16	90
0.16 and under 0.17	105
0.17 and under 0.18	50
Over 0.18	10
Total	330

Chad needs to have a report ready for Monday indicating whether he believes the supplier delivers at its stated specifications and, if so, how many of the components American should order to have enough acceptable components to outfit two oil exploration devices.

Conover, W. J. *Practical Nonparametric Statistics,* 2nd Edition. New York: Wiley, 1980.

Daniel, Wayne W. *Applied Nonparametric Statistics.* Boston: Houghton Mifflin, 1978.

Marascuilo, Leonard A., and McSweeney, Maryellen, *Nonparametric and Distribution-free Methods for Social Sciences.* Monterey, Calif.: Brooks/Cole, 1977.

SPSS-X *User's Guide (Statistical Package for the Social Sciences).* New York: McGraw-Hill, 1983.

TIME SERIES ANALYSIS AND INDEX NUMBERS

16

WHY DECISION MAKERS NEED TO KNOW

Forecasting the future of an organization is somewhat like forecasting the weather. What the weather will be like tomorrow is related to what it is like today. The corporate "weather" is generally measured as profit, earnings per share, price/earnings ratio, or some other quantitative characteristic of the industry within which the business functions. The historical record of a firm's performance can be charted to provide an indication of the past "weather" conditions as measured over time. Whether or not this historical record will provide insight about what the future holds depends on many factors. However, decision makers should understand how to analyze the past if they expect to incorporate past information into future decisions.

CHAPTER OBJECTIVES

This chapter will introduce the fundamentals of time series analysis. Time series analysis is the process by which a set of data measured over time is analyzed. The goals of this chapter include describing the four components of a time series, indicating how to recognize these components, and providing business examples of each component. In addition, the chapter will point out what the components mean to decision makers who intend to use information from the time series in decision making.

The chapter will also introduce the increasingly important subject of index numbers. We will discuss several different kinds of index numbers, demonstrate how they are calculated, and show how they can be used in decision-making situations.

STUDENT OBJECTIVES

After studying the material in this chapter, you should be able to

1. Define a trend component and recognize if a trend component is present in a time series.

2. Define a seasonal component and determine if a seasonal component is present in a time series.
3. Define a cyclical component and determine whether the time series contains a cyclical component.
4. Define a random or irregular component.
5. Produce appropriate index numbers for applications requiring comparisons involving changes over time.
6. Be able to discuss the general manner in which index numbers are constructed and their importance in managerial decision making.

TIME SERIES COMPONENTS

16-1

The world is filled with forecasters, ranging from business people and government officials who try to predict financial outlooks to common people who might try to forecast outcomes such as the weather. If we spray weed killer on our lawns just before an unexpected rain, the consequences are not devastating; we are out a few dollars for the weed killer. Unfortunately the results of a poor managerial forecast are often more severe and cannot be rectified by an additional application of "weed spray." When faced with trying to predict the future, a manager, like all of us, would like to connect what is going to happen with something that can be seen happening now.

A large number of factors can affect the results of a managerial decision. Identifying these factors, and then measuring them, is in many cases impossible since their importance changes and new factors are continually added. However, although the factors that affect the future are uncertain, often the past offers a good indication of what the future will hold. Before decision makers use past information to make a decision about the future, they must recognize how to extract the meaningful information from all the available past data. This chapter discusses the basic components of a **time series** and illustrates, through example, what each means.

All time series contain at least one of four time series components:

1. Long-term trend components
2. Seasonal components
3. Cyclical components
4. Irregular or random components

Time series analysis involves breaking down data measured over time into one or more of these components.

Long-Term Trend Component

The **trend component** is the long-term increase or decrease in a variable being measured over time. For example, annual sales of a greeting card company in Tulsa, Oklahoma, has shown an increasing trend over the past 15 years (see figure 16–1). Figure 16–2 shows a decreasing trend in percentage of defective tires produced annually by a major tire producer. In these two cases, not much variation exists in addition to the

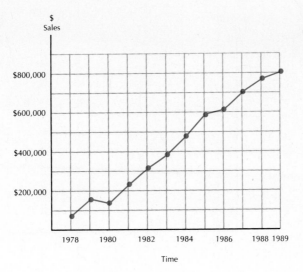

FIGURE 16–1
Greeting card sales trend

trend. In other cases, a strong trend component is evident, but variation exists around the long-term increase or decrease. Figure 16–3 shows an example of basketball attendance at a major university over the past twelve years.

In today's world, organizations are facing increasing planning problems caused mainly by changing technology, complicated government regulations, and uncertain foreign competition. A combination of these and other factors has forced most organizations into increasing the time spans of their planning cycles. Most organizations, when considering capital expenditures, look at a time frame of from three to seven years into the future. When you are planning to start spending money now to meet a demand existing in three to seven years, you had better have a reason to believe the demand will be there. Because long-term forecasting is becoming increasingly important, the trend component in time series analysis is important to all organizations.

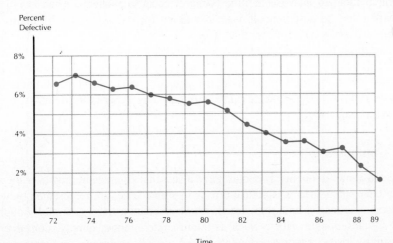

FIGURE 16–2
Percentage of defective tires

FIGURE 16–3
Annual basketball attendance

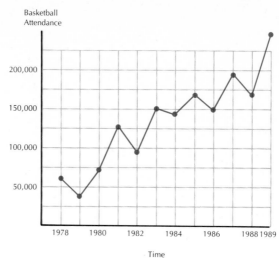

Seasonal Component

Some organizations and industries are affected not only by long-term trends but also by *seasonal* variation. The **seasonal component** represents those changes in a time series that occur at the same time every year. Figure 16–4 shows demand for automotive parts manufactured by a U.S. auto parts producer. The time series seems to have two yearly peaks, one in the spring and one in the fall.

Organizations facing seasonal variations, such as the motor vehicle industry, are often interested in knowing how well, or poorly, they are doing relative to the normal seasonal variation. For instance, while most retailers expect sales volume to be higher in December than November, they are interested in whether December sales are higher or lower than normal relative to November sales. The Department of Employment expects unemployment to increase in June because recent graduates are just arriving on the job market and because schools have dismissed for the summer. The question is whether the increase is more or less than expected.

Organizations that are affected by seasonal variation need to identify and measure this seasonality to help with planning for temporary increases or decreases in labor requirements, inventory, training, periodic maintenance, and so forth. In addition, these organizations need to know if the seasonal variation they experience occurs at more or less than the average rate.

Cyclical Component

Data collected annually obviously cannot have a seasonal component; however they can contain certain *cyclical* effects. Cyclical effects in a time series are represented by wave-like fluctuations around a long-term trend. These fluctuations are generally thought to be caused by pulsations in factors such as interest rates, money supply, consumer demand, inventory levels, national and international market conditions, and other govern-

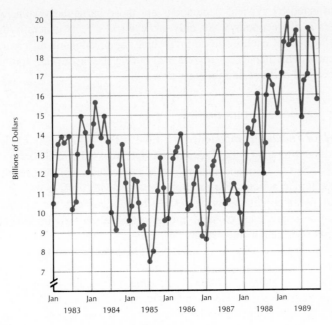

FIGURE 16–4
Automotive parts manufactured (1983–1989)

ment policies. Cyclical fluctuations repeat themselves in a general pattern in the long term, but occur with differing frequencies and intensities. Thus they can be isolated, but not *totally* predicted. Figure 16–5 shows new private housing starts in the United States from 1962 through 1987. Note the strong cyclical effect, with periods of high starts and periods of low starts.

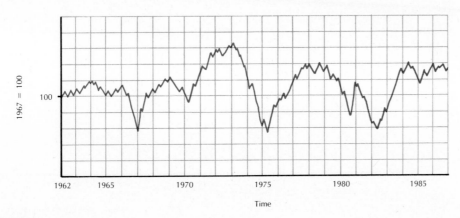

FIGURE 16–5
New private housing starts in the U.S. (1962–1987)

Source: *Business Conditions Digest.*

Firms affected by cyclical fluctuations are those particularly vulnerable to unexpected changes in the economy. Not only are cyclical effects generally unpredictable, but the overall effect of each cycle on individual organizations is different. Thus, even though you know what happened to your firm during the last cycle, you have no guarantee the effect will be the same the next time.

Irregular or Random Component

The **irregular** or *random* **component** in a time series is that part of the series that cannot be attributed to any of the three previously discussed components. Random fluctuations can be caused by many factors, such as weather, political events, and other human and nonhuman actions. For example, severe winters affect vast segments of the economy, and political statements or actions of governments or regulatory agencies often introduce an unpredicted element into an organization's environment.

Two types of irregular fluctuations may exist in a time series. *Minor* irregularities show up as sawtoothlike patterns around the long-term trend. These minor irregular fluctuations are caused by many factors and individually are not significant in an organization's long-term operations. *Major* irregularities are significant one-time, unpredictable changes in the time series due to such external and uncontrollable factors as an oil embargo, war, droughts, and so forth. Figure 16–6 shows wages paid in the mining, manufacturing, and construction industries in 1982 dollars. Note the definite cyclical component to these data, reflecting the nature of these industries. The irregular component is clearly seen as the seemingly random variations around the obvious cycles.

Almost all industries and organizations are affected by irregular components. Obviously organizations dealing with products that can be influenced by variations in the weather are interested in this component. This includes most agricultural and mining

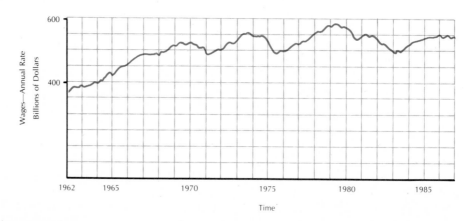

FIGURE 16–6
Wages paid in the mining, manufacturing, and construction industries (1962–1987) in 1982 dollars

concerns. Some organizations, such as insurance companies and certain governmental agencies, are directly concerned with eliminating the risk to other organizations caused by unforeseen irregular factors.

SKILL DEVELOPMENT PROBLEMS FOR SECTION 16–1

The following set of problems is included to test your understanding of the material in this section. Additional problems are found at the end of this chapter under this section heading.

1. Consider the following set of sales data given in millions of dollars.

1984		*1986*	
1st quarter	152	1st quarter	217
2nd quarter	162	2nd quarter	209
3rd quarter	157	3rd quarter	202
4th quarter	167	4th quarter	221
1985		*1987*	
1st quarter	182	1st quarter	236
2nd quarter	192	2nd quarter	242
3rd quarter	191	3rd quarter	231
4th quarter	197	4th quarter	224

Plot these data and discuss which of the time series components you see.

2. Consider the following set of inventory data given in hundreds of thousands of dollars.

1984		*1986*	
1st quarter	109	1st quarter	118
2nd quarter	95	2nd quarter	103
3rd quarter	115	3rd quarter	126
4th quarter	108	4th quarter	120
1985		*1987*	
1st quarter	115	1st quarter	130
2nd quarter	110	2nd quarter	127
3rd quarter	120	3rd quarter	138
4th quarter	116	4th quarter	135

Plot these data and discuss which of the time series components you see.

3. Don Glidden opened Video Excitement at the beginning of the VCR movie boom. Originally he charged customers a membership fee of $49.95, which allowed them to rent four movies a month for $4.95 each, with additional movies rented at $6.95 each. Don's business boomed in the New Orleans area and soon he had ten stores. Unfortunately, more and more video stores opened and soon supermarkets and convenience stores were renting movies. To maintain the sales volume necessary to remain profitable, Don soon started selling VCRs in his stores and soon moved to home entertainment centers. Don is at present analyzing the sales volume at his original location for the first five years of operation:

Sales Volume (×1,000)

	1983	1984	1985	1986	1987
January	23	67	72	76	81
February	34	63	64	75	72
March	45	65	64	77	71
April	48	71	77	81	83
May	46	75	79	86	85
June	49	70	72	75	77
July	60	72	71	80	79
August	65	75	77	82	84
September	67	80	79	86	91
October	60	78	78	87	86
November	71	89	87	91	94
December	76	94	92	96	99

Plot these sales data and prepare a short report for Don discussing which of the time series components you see.

ANALYZING THE VARIABILITY OF HISTORICAL DATA

16-2   Decision makers can think about time series analysis in much the same manner they can think about analysis of variance and regression analysis. The time series they are analyzing has some inherent variability, and they would like to explain as much of that variability as possible. The four types of components—long-term trend, seasonal, cyclical, and irregular—help explain that variability. The purpose of time series analysis is to use these components to explain the total variability in past data. This situation can be represented graphically as shown at the top of page 759.

The problem is how to best separate each component from the others so that each can be analyzed. Some general approaches to this problem will be addressed in the remainder of this chapter. Only the most basic methods are presented. Refer to *Applied Time Series Analysis* by Nelson (1973) for discussions of more sophisticated approaches to analyzing a time series.

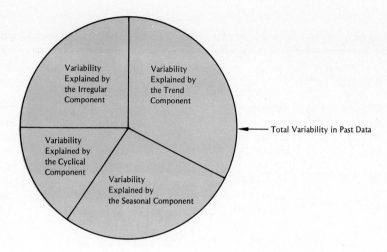

ANALYZING THE TREND COMPONENT

The trend component identifies the long-term growth or decline in the time series. Long-term growth patterns have a wide variety of shapes. The *first-degree, exponential, modified exponential,* and *Gompertz curves* are some of the most common trend patterns. Figure 16–7 illustrates these curves and indicates some areas where these curves have been used to describe long-term trends.

16-3

Many methods are available to fit trend lines to a series of data. The easiest is simply to graph the data points and draw the trend line freehand. This approach often provides adequate information about the long-term trend.

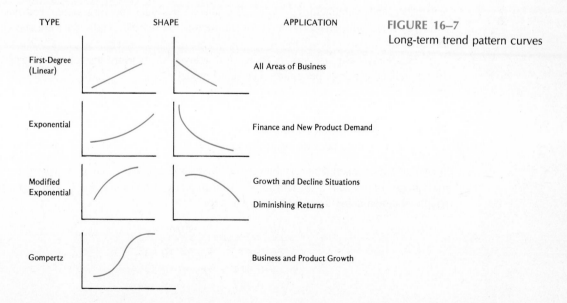

FIGURE 16–7
Long-term trend pattern curves

TABLE 16–1
Annualized quarterly net incomes per share for employment firm A and employment firm B

Firm A		Firm B	
1983	1986	1983	1986
1st—10.50	1st—16.30	1st—11.50	1st—18.30
2nd—10.80	2nd—16.60	2nd—12.10	2nd—18.70
3rd—11.30	3rd—17.30	3rd—12.50	3rd—19.40
4th—11.60	4th—17.70	4th—13.20	4th—20.00
1984	1987	1984	1987
1st—12.00	1st—18.10	1st—13.60	1st—20.70
2nd—12.50	2nd—18.70	2nd—14.20	2nd—21.20
3rd—13.10	3rd—19.20	3rd—15.00	3rd—22.00
4th—13.60	4th—19.60	4th—15.80	4th—22.60
1985	1988	1985	1988
1st—14.10	1st—20.30	1st—16.40	1st—23.10
2nd—14.70	2nd—21.00	2nd—16.80	2nd—23.90
3rd—15.10	3rd—21.70	3rd—17.40	3rd—24.50
4th—15.60	4th—22.40	4th—17.80	4th—25.00

Note: The net income was calculated quarterly. The table shows this quarterly income represented on an annual basis (annualized).

Another way of fitting a trend line to a set of data is to use least squares regression, as discussed in chapters 13 and 14. For example, suppose a financial analyst is comparing the performance of two large firms that provide temporary employees with both office and manufacturing skills. The analyst has data showing annualized net income per share on a quarterly basis for the period 1983–1988. These data are shown in table 16–1.

The analyst can use simple regression analysis to measure the long-term trend of the annualized earnings per share. The fitted model is

$$\hat{Y} = b_0 + b_1 t$$

where $\hat{Y}$ = estimated annualized earnings per share
t = time periods in quarters ($t = 1, 2, 3, \ldots, 24$)

Note that the independent variable in the regression analysis is time, t, where for the first quarter of 1983, $t = 1$, and for the fourth quarter of 1988, $t = 24$. The regression results obtained using a computer program are

Firm A	*Firm B*
$b_0 = 9.57$	$b_0 = 10.83$
$b_1 = 0.514$	$b_1 = 0.586$
$r^2 = 0.997$	$r^2 = 0.998$

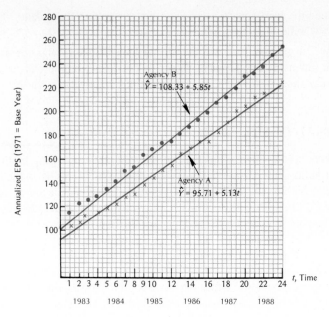

FIGURE 16–8
Annualized earnings per share for employment agencies A and B

The high r^2 values for both firms indicate that the simple linear model, with time as the independent variable, fits the annualized earnings per share well. Figure 16–8 shows the time series plots for the two temporary employment firms and the least squares trend lines. As can be seen, the earnings-per-share time series for both firms during the time period studied exhibit little seasonal or cyclical variation.

The analyst would conclude from the least squares trends not only that firm B begins with a higher annualized earnings per share than firm A, but also that growth has been faster for firm B than for firm A.

SKILL DEVELOPMENT PROBLEMS FOR SECTION 16–3

The following set of problems is included to test your understanding of the material in this section. Additional problems are found at the end of this chapter under this section heading.

4. Refer to the sales data given in problem 1 in section 16–1.
  a. Determine the least squares regression line describing these data.
  b. Discuss whether the regression line is a good fit to the data.

5. Refer to the inventory data given in problem 2 in section 16–1.

a. Determine the least squares regression line describing these data.

b. Discuss whether the regression line is a good fit to the data.

6. In problem 3 in section 16–1 we introduced Don Glidden, who operates the Video Excitement chain in New Orleans. Refer to the sales volume data in that problem and prepare a short report for Don discussing any trend you see in his data.

ANALYZING THE SEASONAL COMPONENT

16-4

Decision makers would have a much easier time if their operating environment contained no variation, but most often variation does exist. This is particularly true of industries and firms that are affected by a seasonal factor. For instance, although food processors would like to have a continual supply of fresh products, the supply is tied to the growing season. Lumber mill operators would like to have a continual supply of trees; however, tree harvesting is affected by snow depths and muddy ground during the winter and early spring. Toy store owners have a very seasonal business, with the majority of sales occurring in the two or three months immediately before Christmas.

For many organizations, either the demand for their product or service, or their source of supply, is highly dependent on the time of year. Since seasonal variation is considered normal in many businesses, the real questions are how this variation affects the planning process and whether the observed variation is more or less than expected. A **seasonal index** known as the *ratio to moving average* can be calculated to measure seasonal variation in a time series.

For example, Sunbird Tours specializes in selling Caribbean cruise tour packages. Although tour packages are sold throughout the year, because of a yearly sales campaign sales peak sharply during September, October, and November, as people plan their winter vacations, and fall off drastically during the rest of the year. The number of tour packages sold each month during the three-year period 1986 through 1988 is shown in table 16–2. Figure 16–9 shows the time series sales data for Sunbird Tours.

TABLE 16–2
Monthly tour package sales, Sunbird Tours Company example (number of packages)

Month	1986	1987	1988
January	3,200	3,500	3,500
February	3,300	3,600	3,700
March	3,400	3,300	3,400
April	3,200	3,400	3,200
May	3,500	3,900	4,000
June	3,400	4,000	4,400
July	3,700	4,000	5,000
August	4,000	3,900	4,800
September	4,800	4,900	5,900
October	5,600	5,800	6,400
November	5,900	6,200	7,200
December	6,600	7,000	7,800

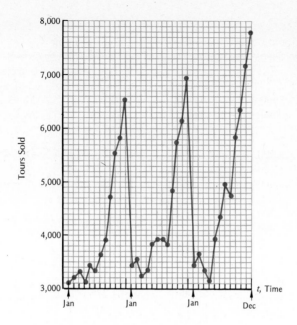

FIGURE 16–9
Monthly tour package sales, Sunbird Tours example

The ratio to moving average is only one of several methods of determining a seasonal index, but it is widely used because of its statistical and practical advantages. The ratio to moving average method begins with what is called a *multiplicative model:*

$$Y = T \cdot S \cdot C \cdot I$$

where
Y = value of the time series
T = trend value
S = seasonal value
C = cyclical value
I = irregular value

The multiplicative model assumes that each time series value is determined by the relationships between the four components. The ratio to moving average first attempts to estimate $T \cdot C$ by calculating a *twelve-month moving average*. A twelve-month moving average is computed from twelve successive monthly time series values. The moving average is then located in the middle of the twelve values. The next moving average value is determined by dropping the first time series value and adding the next, yet-unused value. Table 16–3 contains the moving averages for Sunbird Tours.

Once the twelve-month moving average is calculated, the next step is to find a *centered twelve-month moving average*. We do this by finding the mean of each successive pair of moving averages. For example, the first centered twelve-month moving average, corresponding to the seventh period (that is, July 1986), is the average of 4,217 and 4,242.

TABLE 16–3
Computation of ratio to moving average, Sunbird Tours example

Year and Month	Units Sold	12-Month Moving Total	12-Month Moving Average	Centered 12-Month Moving Average	Ratio to Moving Average (%)
1986					
January	3,200				
February	3,300				
March	3,400				
April	3,200				
May	3,500				
June	3,400	50,600	4,217		
July	3,700	50,900	4,242	4,229.5	87.5
August	4,000	51,200	4,267	4,254.5	94.0
September	4,800	51,100	4,258	4,262.5	112.6
October	5,600	51,300	4,275	4,266.5	131.3
November	5.900	51,700	4,308	4,291.5	137.5
December	6,600	52,300	4,358	4,333.0	152.3
1987					
January	3,500	52,600	4,383	4,370.5	80.0
February	3,600	52,500	4,375	4,379.0	82.2
March	3,300	52,600	4,383	4,379.0	75.4
April	3,400	52,800	4,400	4,391.5	77.4
May	3,900	53,100	4,425	4,412.5	88.4
June	4,000	53,500	4,458	4,441.5	90.0
July	4,000	53,500	4,458	4,458.0	89.7
August	3,900	53,600	4,467	4,462.5	87.4
September	4,900	53,700	4,475	4,471.0	109.6
October	5,800	53,500	4,458	4,466.5	129.9
November	6,200	53,600	4,467	4,462.5	138.9
December	7,000	54,000	4,500	4,483.5	156.1
1988					
January	3,500	55,000	4,583	4,541.5	77.1
February	3,700	55,900	4,658	4,620.5	80.1
March	3,400	56,900	4,742	4,700.0	72.3
April	3,200	57,500	4,792	4,767.0	67.1
May	4,000	58,500	4,875	4,833.5	82.7
June	4,400	59,300	4,942	4,908.5	89.6
July	5,000				
August	4,800				
September	5,900				
October	6,400				
November	7,200				
December	7,800				

The next step is to divide the original data by the corresponding centered twelve-month moving average. This ratio is called the *ratio to moving average*. These ratios approximate the $S \cdot I$ factor in the multiplicative model and are listed in table 16–3. For example, the ratio corresponding to July 1986 is found by

$$S \cdot I = \frac{T \cdot S \cdot C \cdot I}{T \cdot C}$$

$$= \frac{3700}{4229.5} = 0.875 = 87.5\%$$

Before attempting to separate the irregular component, we must determine whether the ratio to moving averages are stable from year to year. If they do not appear to be stable, there is little value in trying to arrive at an index value for a particular month. In fact, such a value might be misleading.

In the Sunbird Tours example, we have only two years of ratios to examine. Figure 16–10 shows the lines connecting the ratios for each year. As can be seen in figure 16–10, the seasonal ratios for the two years have the same basic turning points. December is the seasonal high, and March and April represent the seasonal low. Because of the consistency in the ratios between years, we will extract the irregular influences.

One method to eliminate the irregular component is to take the normalized average of the ratio to moving averages as shown in table 16–4. The *normalization* is performed

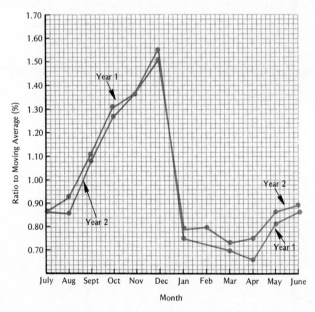

FIGURE 16–10
Seasonal patterns, Sunbird Tours (July 1986 to June 1988)

TABLE 16–4
Seasonal index, Sunbird Tours example

Year	July	Aug	Sept	Oct	Nov	Dec	Jan	Feb	Mar	Apr	May	June
July 1980–June 1981	87.5	94.0	112.6	131.3	137.5	152.3	80.0	82.2	75.4	77.4	88.4	90.0
July 1981–June 1982	89.7	87.4	109.6	129.9	138.9	156.1	77.1	80.1	72.3	67.1	82.7	89.6
Total	177.2	181.4	222.2	261.2	276.4	308.4	157.1	162.3	147.7	144.5	171.1	179.6
Average seasonal index (%) =	88.6	90.7	111.1	130.6	138.2	154.2	78.5	81.1	73.8	72.2	85.5	89.8 Σ = 1,194.3
Normalization factor = 1,200/1,194.3 = 1.0047												
Normalized average seasonal index (%) =	89.0	91.1	111.6	131.1	138.8	154.9	78.9	81.6	74.1	72.6	85.9	90.2 Σ = 1,200.0

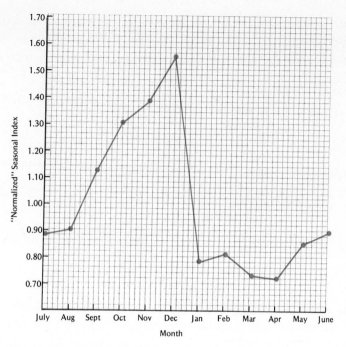

FIGURE 16–11
Seasonal index, Sunbird Tours example

by multiplying each average seasonal index by the ratio of 1,200 over the sum of these seasonal indexes. This forces the normalized indexes to sum to 1,200 (12 months × an average of 100).

Figure 16–11 graphs the seasonal index values for each month for Sunbird Tours. Looking at figure 16–11 and table 16–4, we can see that December's normalized seasonal pattern is about 55 percent greater than the yearly average, whereas April's pattern is about 27 percent below the yearly average.

This method of eliminating irregular fluctuations should be applied only when we are willing to assume that the irregular fluctuations are caused by purely random circumstances. In cases where this assumption cannot be made, more sophisticated methods must be used. Chou (1975) presents a more detailed treatment of the methods for separating irregular influences from the seasonal component in a time series.

SKILL DEVELOPMENT PROBLEMS FOR SECTION 16–4

The following set of problems is included to test your understanding of the material in this section. Additional problems are found at the end of this chapter under this section heading.

7. Extract the seasonal component from the set of quarterly data given in problem 1 in section 16–1.

8. Extract the seasonal component from the following set of monthly data.

	1985	1986	1987
January	5.4	5.8	7.0
February	10.4	12.8	14.6
March	18.6	20.1	22.6
April	4.8	8.2	7.6
May	12.2	15.6	16.2
June	14.6	14.8	15.9
July	13.0	11.0	13.0
August	19.4	19.2	17.8
September	26.8	27.0	28.6
October	21.2	21.4	23.0
November	10.2	9.9	13.1
December	6.7	5.6	7.9

9. In the last section you analyzed the trend component of Don Glidden's Video Excitement sales volume data from problem 3 in section 16–1. Now analyze the seasonal component of these data.

ANALYZING THE CYCLICAL COMPONENT

16-5

Cyclical variations in time series data do not repeat themselves in a regular pattern as do seasonal factors, but they cannot be considered random variations in the data either. Although cyclical variations generally show some recognizable pattern and are repetitious, they always differ in both intensity and timing. By *intensity* of a cycle, we mean the height from its crest to its trough. *Timing* is the frequency with which the crests and troughs occur. Therefore cyclical components can be isolated and analyzed, but, unfortunately, cannot be accurately predicted.

Many industries are influenced by cyclical patterns in their environment. The most important cyclical factor for most organizations is the cycle of economic factors, generally referred to as the *business cycle*. While some economists previously thought governmental action could essentially eliminate cyclical swings in the economy, this component still apparently exists and is very important for many organizations. The organizations hardest hit by the cyclical component are those connected with items purchased with discretionary income (appliances, cars, travel, and so forth). These are items people can often postpone purchasing and consequently are those most affected by a downturn in the economy.

The cyclical component is isolated by first removing the trend and seasonal factors from the time series data. While many complicated methods exist to isolate the cyclical component, the general procedure can be demonstrated graphically using sales data for the Apex Appliance Company (see figure 16–12).

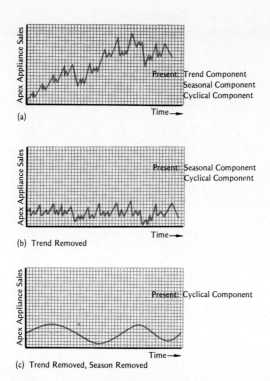

FIGURE 16–12

Isolating the cyclical component, Apex Appliance example

We will use the sales data for Sunbird Tours to illustrate one method for isolating the cyclical component in a time series. Table 16–5 shows the values involved in the calculations. The monthly sales data for the three years 1986–1988 are contained in column 1.

Column 2 contains the trend values determined by the least squares regression trend line,

$$\hat{Y} = 3,353.17 + 64.09t$$

Note that this line is calculated using units sold as the dependent variable and $t = 1$, 2, 3, . . . , 36 as the independent variable. Thus, for example, June 1986, which is the sixth time period ($t = 6$), has a trend value of

$$\hat{Y} = 3,353.17 + 64.09(6)$$
$$= 3,737.7$$

$$\text{Trend value} = 3,738$$

Column 3 contains the seasonal index for the month, as determined in table 16–4. Note that the seasonal index for July 1986 is the same as for July 1987 and July 1988.

The next step in separating the cyclical component from the trend and seasonal components is to calculate the statistical normal values ($T \cdot S$) by multiplying the trend value by the seasonal index values.

TABLE 16–5
Cyclical component index, Sunbird Tours example

Year and Month	Tours Sold Y (1)	Trend Value T (2)	Seasonal Index Ratio S (3)	Statistical Normal $T \cdot S$ (4)	Cyclical-Irregular Component (%) $\dfrac{Y}{T \cdot S}100$ (5)
1986					
January	3,200	3,417	0.789	2,696.0	118.7
February	3,300	3,481	0.815	2,837.0	116.3
March	3,400	3,545	0.741	2,626.8	129.4
April	3,200	3,610	0.725	2,617.3	122.3
May	3,500	3,674	0.859	3,156.0	110.9
June	3,400	3,738	0.902	3,371.7	100.8
July	3,700	3,802	0.890	3,383.8	109.3
August	4,000	3,866	0.911	3,521.9	113.6
September	4,800	3,930	1.116	4,385.9	109.4
October	5,600	3,994	1.311	5,236.1	106.9
November	5,900	4,058	1.388	5,632.5	104.8
December	6,600	4,122	1.549	6,385.0	103.4
1987					
January	3,500	4,186	0.789	3,302.8	106.0
February	3,600	4,250	0.815	3,463.8	103.9
March	3,300	4,314	0.741	3,196.7	103.2
April	3,400	4,379	0.726	3,179.2	106.9
May	3,900	4,443	0.859	3,816.5	102.2
June	4,000	4,507	0.902	4,065.3	98.4
July	4,000	4,571	0.890	4,068.2	98.3
August	3,900	4,635	0.911	4,222.5	92.4
September	4,900	4,699	1.116	5,244.1	93.4
October	5,800	4,763	1.311	6,244.3	92.9
November	6,200	4,827	1.388	6,699.9	92.5
December	7,000	4,891	1.549	7,576.2	92.4
1988					
January	3,500	4,955	0.789	3,909.5	89.5
February	3,700	5,019	0.815	4,090.5	90.5
March	3,400	5,084	0.741	3,767.2	90.3
April	3,200	5,148	0.726	3,737.4	85.6
May	4,000	5,212	0.859	4,477.1	89.3
June	4,400	5,276	0.902	4,759.0	92.5
July	5,000	5,340	0.890	4,752.6	105.1
August	4,800	5,404	0.911	4,923.0	97.5
September	5,900	5,468	1.116	6,102.8	96.7
October	6,400	5,532	1.311	7,252.5	88.2
November	7,200	5,596	1.388	7,767.2	92.7
December	7,800	5,661	1.549	8,768.9	89.0

The cyclical component, which also contains the irregular fluctuations, is determined for each time period by dividing the statistical normal values into the original units sold (column 1) $[Y/(T \cdot S)]$. To transfer this ratio to a percent form, we multiply by 100. These percentages are shown in column 5 of table 16–5.

SKILL DEVELOPMENT PROBLEMS FOR SECTION 16–5

The following set of problems is included to test your understanding of the material in this section. Additional problems are found at the end of this chapter under this section heading.

10. Refer to the sales data in problem 8 in section 16–4. Isolate the cyclical-irregular component of the sales data by constructing a table like table 16–5.

11. Isolate the cyclical-irregular component of the following quarterly inventory data given in hundreds of thousands of dollars by constructing a table like table 16–5.

1984		1986	
1st quarter	218	1st quarter	244
2nd quarter	190	2nd quarter	228
3rd quarter	236	3rd quarter	263
4th quarter	218	4th quarter	240

1985		1987	
1st quarter	250	1st quarter	229
2nd quarter	220	2nd quarter	221
3rd quarter	265	3rd quarter	248
4th quarter	241	4th quarter	231

12. If you have done problems 6 and 9, you have analyzed the trend and seasonal data for the original Video Excitement store. Now find the cyclical-irregular component for the sales data from problem 3, section 16–1.

ANALYZING THE IRREGULAR COMPONENT

16-6

Irregular components are those fluctuations in a time series that cannot be attributed to any of the three previously discussed components. Irregular influences may be caused by any number of one-time factors. For instance, a severe winter, a summer drought, a civil war in a country supplying raw materials, and many other factors can cause irregular changes in the time series. These events would likely cause a large irregular fluctuation, but many small, unrelated events can combine to cause random variation around the time series.

Extreme irregular variations can cause organizations a great deal of trouble. In fact, if the irregularities are severe enough, they can cause the organization to go out of business. When possible, most organizations buy insurance against the monetary effects of severe irregular effects.

Small irregular variations cause lesser problems. One of these problems crops up when the time series is being analyzed. Decision makers will generally attempt to smooth out the minor irregularities, using a moving average approach as discussed earlier. The goal is to eliminate as much as possible the irregular influences so that the true trend, seasonal, and cyclical components can be recognized.

PERCENTAGE PRICE INDEXES

16-7

"The dollar's not worth what it used to be" is a saying everyone has heard. The problem is, for all organizations, nothing is worth what is used to be; sometimes it's worth more and other times it's worth less. For instance, a barrel of oil was worth less in both 1985 and 1975 than it was in 1980. The problem for decision makers is that when evaluating data collected over time, they must often compare one figure or data point with others measured at different times. A common procedure for making relative comparisons is to construct a series of *index numbers,* using a base to which all other values can be compared.

The Armstrong Corporation is considering purchasing a small textile mill in Georgia. The present mill owners stress as a positive attribute the mill's rapid sales growth over the past ten years. While conceding the sales growth, Ann Armstrong, who is negotiating the purchase, is concerned with the increase in per hour labor rates for production workers.

Table 16–6 shows the mill hourly wage data for the years 1979 to 1988. Since she is dealing with price changes of a single item, Ann can construct an index number called a *percentage price relative.* To do this, she must first select a base year. Suppose she chooses 1979 as the base year. She will set the 1979 wage rate equal to 100, which means that 1979 hourly wages were 100 percent of 1979 hourly wages. Next, she can compute each subsequent year's wage rate as a percentage of the 1979 wage rate. To

TABLE 16-6
Hourly wage rates, Armstrong Corporation example

Year	Hourly Wages
1979	$ 8.50
1980	9.10
1981	10.00
1982	10.80
1983	11.55
1984	12.15
1985	12.85
1986	13.70
1987	14.75
1988	15.45

Year	Hourly Wages	Index Numbers
1979	$ 8.50	100.0
1980	9.10	107.1
1981	10.00	117.6
1982	10.80	127.1
1983	11.55	135.9
1984	12.15	142.9
1985	12.85	151.2
1986	13.70	161.2
1987	14.75	173.5
1988	15.45	181.8

TABLE 16–7
Wage rate index, Armstrong Corporation example

do this, divide each year's wage rate by the rate in the base period and multiply by 100, as shown in equation 16–1:

$$\text{Percentage price relatives index} = I_n = \frac{P_n}{P_b}100 \qquad (16\text{–}1)$$

where P_b = price (wage rate here) in the base year
P_n = price (wage rate here) in a given year

The index numbers for the textile mill's wage rate are shown in table 16–7.

By examining the index numbers in table 16–7, Ann Armstrong can see that 1988 hourly wages are up 81.8 percent over 1979 hourly wages. However, she cannot compare two index numbers, such as those for 1987 and 1988, to each other. That is, wages were not up 8.2 percent between 1987 and 1988, simply because this is the difference between the index numbers for the two years. The true percent increase between 1987 and 1988 is found by dividing the difference in index numbers by the earlier index number and then multiplying by 100.

$$\frac{181.8 - 173.5}{173.5}100 = 4.7\%$$

SKILL DEVELOPMENT PROBLEMS FOR SECTION 16–7

The following set of problems is included to test your understanding of the material in this section. Additional problems are found at the end of this chapter under this section heading.

13. The following data represent United Way collections for a medium-sized southern city. Use 1975 as the base year to construct a relative index showing how donations have increased.

Year	Donations (in millions)
1975	19.4
1976	22.6
1977	23.7
1978	25.5
1979	27.8
1980	28.1
1981	30.0
1982	32.2
1983	33.8
1984	35.3
1985	36.1
1986	38.9
1987	40.7

14. Analyze the donation data given in problem 13, using 1980 as the base year.

AGGREGATE PRICE INDEXES

16–8 In the previous section, Ann Armstrong was analyzing the increase in hourly wage rates for production workers at a textile mill her company was interested in purchasing. She knows, however, that she should also consider office wage rates in her analysis. Average hourly office wage rates, and the same production worker rates, are shown in table 16–8.

Ann can use these two wage rates to calculate three common aggregate indexes.

TABLE 16-8
Hourly wage rates, Armstrong Corporation example

Year	Production Hourly Wages	Office Hourly Wages
1979	$ 8.50	$ 9.10
1980	9.10	9.45
1981	10.00	9.80
1982	10.80	10.25
1983	11.55	10.60
1984	12.15	10.95
1985	12.85	11.45
1986	13.70	11.90
1987	14.75	12.55
1988	15.45	13.45

Year	Production Hourly Wages	Office Hourly Wages	Index Numbers
1979	$ 8.50	$ 9.10	100.0
1980	9.10	9.45	105.4
1981	10.00	9.80	112.5
1982	10.80	10.25	119.6
1983	11.55	10.60	125.9
1984	12.15	10.95	131.3
1985	12.85	11.45	138.1
1986	13.70	11.90	145.5
1987	14.75	12.55	155.1
1988	15.45	13.45	164.2

TABLE 16–9
Unweighted aggregate indexes, Armstrong Corporation example

The Unweighted Aggregate Index

To find an unweighted index of wages, Ann would simply divide the sum of the wages in the two categories in each year by the sum of the wages in the base year. In notation form, this is:

$$I_n = \frac{\Sigma P_n}{\Sigma P_b}100 \qquad (16\text{–}2)$$

The sum of the wages in the base year is $P_{79} = \$8.50 + 9.10 = \$17.60$. The sum of the wages in 1980 is $18.55, so I_{80} will be $(18.55/17.60)100 = 105.4$. The unweighted aggregate indexes for years 1979 through 1988 are shown in table 16–9.

The unweighted index may distort the true movement of wage rates. It assumes equal weighting for both groups, and to the extent to which this is not the case—for instance, if the company has more production employees than office employees—the index number will not represent actual wage movements. Two common indexes incorporate group weighting.

The Paasche Index

If Ann knew the work force in 1988 was 60 percent office workers and 40 percent production workers, she could use these values to weight the index numbers constructed for all ten years. She would be constructing a Paasche index, which is defined by equation 16–3:

TABLE 16–10

Paasche indexes, Armstrong Corporation example

Year	Production Hourly Wages	Office Hourly Wages	Index Numbers
1979	$ 8.50	$ 9.10	100.0
1980	9.10	9.45	105.1
1981	10.00	9.80	111.5
1982	10.80	10.25	118.2
1983	11.55	10.60	123.9
1984	12.15	10.95	129.0
1985	12.85	11.45	135.6
1986	13.70	11.90	142.4
1987	14.75	12.55	151.6
1988	15.45	13.45	160.8

$$I_n = \frac{\Sigma Q_n P_n}{\Sigma Q_n P_b} 100 \qquad (16\text{–}3)$$

where P_b = price (here wage rate) in the base year
           P_n = price in a given year
           Q_n = weighting percentages from a given year

Note that the percentages from the current period are used for all years in calculating the Paasche index.

In analyzing the wage rate increases using the Paasche index, the weighted wage rate for the base year, 1979, would be

$$0.6 \times \$9.10 + 0.4 \times \$8.50 = \$8.86$$

The weighted wage rate for 1980 would be

$$0.6 \times \$9.45 + 0.4 \times \$9.10 = \$9.31$$

and the Paasche index for 1980 is (9.31/8.86)100 = 105.1. The Paasche indexes for the years 1979 through 1988 are shown in table 16–10. Notice the index numbers calculated using the 1988 weights in table 16–10 are different from the unweighted indexes found in table 16–9.

The Laspeyres Index

Ann Armstrong was able to use the percentage weights from 1988 to determine the appropriate values for the Paasche index. If she knew the labor mix in the base year, 1979, was 60 percent production workers and 40 percent office workers she could construct a Laspeyres Index, which is defined by equation 16–4:

$$I_n = \frac{\Sigma Q_b P_n}{\Sigma Q_b P_b} 100$$ (16–4)

where P_b = price (here wage rate) in the base year
P_n = price in a given year
Q_b = weighting percentages from the base year

Note that the percentages from the base year are used for all years in calculating the Laspeyres Index.

The Laspeyres index is similar to the Paasche index, with the difference that percentages are found from the base year mix as opposed to the current year mix. The weighted wage rate for the base year, 1979, would be

$$0.4 \times \$9.10 + 0.6 \times \$8.50 = \$8.74$$

The weighted wage rate for 1980 would be

$$0.4 \times \$9.45 + 0.6 \times \$9.10 = \$9.24$$

and the Laspeyres index for 1980 is $(9.24/8.74)100 = 105.7$. The Laspeyres indexes for the years 1979 through 1988 are shown in table 16–11. Notice that the index numbers calculated using the 1979 weights in table 16–11 are different from those found in both table 16–10 and table 16–9.

The purpose of this section was to demonstrate how to determine three commonly used techniques to find index numbers for groups of values *and* to show that the same data can yield different index numbers depending on how they are analyzed. We will make more of this point in the next section.

TABLE 16–11
Laspeyres indexes, Armstrong Corporation example

Year	Production Hourly Wages	Office Hourly Wages	Index Numbers
1979	$ 8.50	$ 9.10	100.0
1980	9.10	9.45	105.7
1981	10.00	9.80	113.5
1982	10.80	10.25	121.1
1983	11.55	10.60	127.8
1984	12.15	10.95	133.5
1985	12.85	11.45	140.6
1986	13.70	11.90	148.5
1987	14.75	12.55	158.7
1988	15.45	13.45	167.6

SKILL DEVELOPMENT PROBLEMS FOR SECTION 16–8

The following set of problems is included to test your understanding of the material in this section. Additional problems are found at the end of this chapter under this section heading.

15. The following values represent advertising rates paid by a regional catalog retailer which advertises either on radio or in newspapers.

Year	30-Second Radio Advertisement	1/4-Page Newspaper Ad
1980	150	200
1981	155	210
1982	165	230
1983	173	260
1984	181	290
1985	190	320
1986	198	330

Determine a relative index for each type of advertisement, using 1980 as the base year.

16. Using the values given in problem 15, determine an unweighted aggregate index for the two types of advertisement.

17. In 1980 the retailer spent 30 percent of the advertisement budget on radio advertising and 70 percent on newspaper advertising. Use these values to construct a Laspeyres index for the data in problem 15.

18. In 1986 the advertising had changed to 45 percent radio and 55 percent newspaper. Use these values to construct a Paasche index for the data in problem 15.

COMMONLY USED INDEX NUMBERS

16-9
In addition to determining their own index numbers, decision makers will encounter a variety of index numbers in their normal activities. Federal and state governmental agencies produce index numbers that help measure such economic variables as retail prices, wholesale prices, stock market activity, production output, inventory levels, and the value of the dollar.

The Consumer Price Index

To most of us, inflation has come to mean increased prices and less purchasing power for our dollar. The *Consumer Price Index (CPI)*, constructed by the U.S. Department of Labor, Bureau of Labor Statistics, attempts to measure the overall change in retail prices for goods and services.

The consumer price index is a complicated attempt to provide a measure of changes in the relative price of a "market basket" of goods and services used by a typical wage earner living in a city. In fact, in 1977, two indexes were constructed. The first, the index for wage earners and clerical workers, was the same as had been constructed in previous years. The second, the index for all urban households, was a new index created to better represent this major segment of the economy. The purpose of having two indexes is to provide more useful economic information; however, changing consumption patterns will undoubtedly cause future revisions in the index. Therefore, any short discussion of the index will leave out important facts. The market basket consists of about 400 items a city dweller would purchase grouped into seven major categories. The items in the basket are determined by sampling and are therefore subject to all the problems associated with sampling error. In addition, the basket of 400 items is a limited representation of the thousands of items households consume. On top of that, average prices for these goods and services are determined by measuring all large urban areas and a selected sample of smaller communities. The major categories used in determining this index are

- Food and beverages
- Housing
- Apparel and upkeep
- Transportation
- Medical care
- Entertainment
- Other goods and services

The CPI was first published in 1913. Because the purpose of the index was to measure cost of living, the "market basket" has, of necessity, changed over the years as new consumer items like televisions, stereos, and video cassette recorders have become available. Since 1945 the base period used in the index has been updated, using values in base periods of 1947–1949, 1957–1959, 1967, and 1982–1984.

Table 16–12 shows the percent of the market basket devoted to the seven categories in June 1977 and June 1987. These percentages, or weighting factors, are periodically changed. Recently, the percentage of the market basket devoted to food and beverages has decreased while that devoted to housing has increased.

Categories	June 1977 Percent	June 1987 Percent
Food and beverages	23.667	17.824
Housing	34.202	42.947
Apparel and upkeep	9.194	6.335
Transportation	13.548	17.217
Medical care*	9.288	5.420
Entertainment*	5.143	4.403
Other goods and services	4.582	5.855

TABLE 16–12

Weightings for major categories in the Consumer Price Index

*These categories changed between 1977 and 1987.

TABLE 16–13
End-of-year historical Consumer
Price Index values

Year	Index Values	Year	Index Values
1952	26.9	1970	40.0
1953	27.0	1971	41.3
1954	26.9	1972	42.7
1955	27.0	1973	46.5
1956	27.8	1974	52.2
1957	28.6	1975	55.8
1958	29.1	1976	58.5
1959	29.5	1977	62.5
1960	30.0	1978	68.1
1961	30.2	1979	77.2
1962	30.6	1980	86.9
1963	31.1	1981	94.4
1964	31.4	1982	98.0
1965	32.0	1983	101.2
1966	33.1	1984	104.8
1967	34.1	1985	108.6
1968	35.7	1986	109.3
1969	37.9	1987	114.2

The consumer price index is similar to the Laspeyres index in that percent weightings, once established, are used for future time periods. The percent weightings may change between base periods; however, this would not happen with a true Laspeyres index. In addition, the CPI tries to consider product improvements and quantity decreases. For instance, if base model Pontiacs increase by $200 this year, but a stereo cassette player that was a $200 option becomes a standard feature this year, there would be no actual price increase. On the other hand, if the price of a Snickers candy bar remains the same this year, but the weight is decreased by 10 percent, there would be a price increase.

The CPI values based on the base years of 1982–1984 are shown in Table 16–13. Remember, you cannot determine the inflation rate simply by subtracting the values for two successive years. You instead must divide the difference by the value in the first of the two years.

Wholesale Price Index

The U.S. Department of Labor, Bureau of Labor Statistics, also constructs an index of prices of goods sold in U.S. primary markets. Primary markets are those where the first significant large-volume purchase for each item is made. Their measure determines the *Wholesale Price Index*.

Many groups—governmental, industrial, and academic—study the relationship between the Wholesale Price Index and the CPI. Generally, increases in the Wholesale Price Index are followed by a delayed increase in the CPI.

Industrial Production Index

The Federal Reserve Board constructs the *Industrial Production Index*. This index measures change in the volume of industrial production, including manufacturing, mining, and utilities. The purpose of this index is to keep us apprised of productivity levels through various groupings of products and materials.

Stock Market Indexes

Probably the best known stock market index is the *Dow-Jones Industrial Average*. This index is computed each day the New York Stock Exchange is open and indicates the condition of the market in general. The Dow-Jones Industrial Average is determined by the daily closing stock prices for thirty selected industrial companies, adjusted for any dividends or mergers that take place for these companies. Of course, stocks not included in the DOW may perform much differently than would be indicated by the index.

Another stock market index is the *Standard and Poor's 425*. This index is determined by stock prices of 425 industrials, not all of which are blue-chip companies. Many market analysts prefer the Standard and Poor's 425 to the DOW because they feel it better represents the market as a whole.

USING INDEX NUMBERS TO DEFLATE A TIME SERIES

A common use of index numbers is to convert values measured at different times into more directly comparable measurements. For instance, if your wages increase, but at a rate less than inflation, you will in fact be earning less in "real terms." A company experiencing increasing sales, but with an increase of less than the inflation rate, would actually be doing less well over time. Simpson Quick Stop is a regional chain of convenience stores/self service gas stations. Gary Simpson started the chain after leaving

16-10

Year	Sales in Millions
1975	50.7
1976	62.3
1977	73.4
1978	82.6
1979	88.5
1980	101.2
1981	115.9
1982	134.6
1983	140.2
1984	155.8
1985	170.0
1986	185.4

TABLE 16–14
Simpson Quick Stop yearly sales

TABLE 16–15
Simpson Quick Stop yearly sales

Year	Sales in Millions (current dollars)	Sales in Millions (1982–84 dollars)
1975	50.7	90.9
1976	62.3	106.5
1977	73.4	117.4
1978	82.6	121.3
1979	88.5	114.6
1980	101.2	116.5
1981	115.9	122.8
1982	134.6	137.3
1983	140.2	138.5
1984	155.8	148.7
1985	170.0	156.5
1986	185.4	169.6

his position as a regional manager for 7-Eleven in 1974. Yearly sales for the Quick Stop chain are shown in table 16–14 (p. 781). Gary realizes part of the sales growth is due to inflation and he can use an index number to convert the yearly sales figures, which have been measured in current dollars, to sales measured in "real" dollars.

This conversion is done simply by dividing the current value by the appropriate index value and then multiplying by 100. Therefore, Gary can use an index like that for consumer prices to convert sales measured in current dollars into sales measured in 1982–84 dollars. Using the CPI value from table 16–13 for 1975, the "real" sales figure for that year is ($50.7/55.8)100 = $90.86 million. Table 16–15 shows current dollar sales and 1982–84 dollar sales for Simpson Quick Stop. Notice in some years sales did not increase as fast as the inflation rate and so an increase in current dollars was in fact a decrease in deflated dollars.

SKILL DEVELOPMENT PROBLEMS FOR SECTION 16–10

The following set of problems is included to test your understanding of the material in this section. Additional problems are found at the end of this chapter under this section heading.

19. Use the consumer price index values given in table 16–13 to deflate the following sales values:

Year	Sales (in millions)
1980	10.4
1981	11.2
1982	12.1

1983	14.2
1984	15.0
1985	16.7
1986	18.3

20. Use the consumer price index values given in table 16–13 to deflate the following inventory levels:

Year	Inventory (times $100,000)
1975	4.3
1976	4.7
1977	5.1
1978	4.8
1979	6.2
1980	7.1
1981	6.6
1982	7.5
1983	8.2
1984	8.0
1985	7.7
1986	8.1

CONCLUSIONS

16-11

This chapter introduced the basics of time series analysis, and defined the four components of a time series: long-term trend, seasonal component, cyclical component, and irregular component.

Decision makers need to examine variables measured over time in an effort to learn about the past. We study the past to make better decisions about the future. However, the future may or may not reflect the past, and care should be used in making conclusions about the future based solely on historical data.

We have illustrated some basic techniques for extracting the long-term trend, seasonal, and cyclical components from a time series. The techniques discussed here represent only a few of the many time series analytic procedures that have been developed and are applied in decision-making situations.

We can look backward by analyzing the time series data. This analysis will provide good information about the future as long as the future looks pretty much like the past. However time series analysis is of little help if the future departs drastically from the past. No matter how sophisticated our analysis, we cannot use the past to foresee new and unusual events of the future. Decision makers should recognize both the strengths and weaknesses of time series analysis. If they do, they will find it a valuable tool in decision making.

In the past few decades, one of the disturbing factors on the decision-making scene has been the problem of inflation. A common method for trying to eliminate the effect of inflation when comparing data gathered in different time periods is to use an index number. This chapter has discussed how index numbers are constructed and has looked at some commonly used indexes.

CHAPTER GLOSSARY

cyclical component   The periodic movements in a time series usually caused by economic factors. The frequency and intensity of the cyclical components are not totally predictable.

irregular component   The changes in the time series that are unpredictable and cannot be attributed to a trend, seasonal, or cyclical factor.

seasonal component   The increases and decreases in the time series that occur at predetermined times of the year with predictable intensities.

seasonal index   The ratio found by dividing the observed value of a period by the value of an average period.

time series   A series of measurements taken of a variable at different times. In most applications, the time periods are uniform.

trend component   The long-run average increase or decrease in the time series.

CHAPTER FORMULAS

Paasche index

$$I_n = \frac{\Sigma Q_n P_n}{\Sigma Q_n P_b} 100$$

where P_b = price in the base year
P_n = price in a given year
Q_n = weighting percentages from a given year

Lespeyres index

$$I_n = \frac{\Sigma Q_b P_n}{\Sigma Q_b P_b} 100$$

where P_b = price in the base year
P_n = price in a given year
Q_b = weighting percentages from the base year

Percentage price relatives index

$$I_n = \frac{P_n}{P_b} 100$$

Unweighted aggregate index

$$I_n = \frac{\Sigma P_n}{\Sigma P_b} 100$$

ADDITIONAL PROBLEMS

Section 16–1

21. Identify three businesses in your community which might be expected to have sales that exhibit a seasonal component. Discuss.

22. If enrollments at a particular university have steadily declined over the past ten years, which time series component would be illustrated if enrollments were graphed for this period of time? Discuss.

23. The Willow Manufacturing Company has been in operation for twenty years. Records of annual sales have been maintained over this time period. If we graphed the data, would it be likely that the data would contain a seasonal component? Discuss.

24. Discuss the difference between a cyclical component and a seasonal component.

25. Which component is more predictable, seasonal or cyclical? Discuss and illustrate with examples.

Section 16–3

26. The Chesterfield Company in Omaha, Nebraska, manufactures airplane parts. Sales data for the past sixteen years are shown as follows:

Year	Sales
1973	$ 133,000
1974	128,000
1975	202,000
1976	278,000
1977	388,000
1978	376,000
1979	504,000
1980	613,000
1981	745,000
1982	975,000
1983	1,233,900
1984	1,335,000
1985	1,567,000
1986	1,234,000
1987	1,897,000
1988	2,300,000

Graph these data and indicate whether they appear to have a linear trend.

27. Referring to the sales data for the Chesterfield Company in problem 26, develop a simple linear regression model with *time* as the independent variable. Using this regression model, describe the trend and the strength of the linear trend over the sixteen years. Is the trend line statistically significant? Plot the trend line against the actual data.

28. Considering the data in problem 26, does it apper that an exponential trend may be more descriptive of the sales pattern for the Chesterfield Company than a linear trend? Develop a least squares regression model using the square of time as the independent variable. Plot this regression line against the original data. Based on the regression statistics, would you conclude that the exponential trend is more representative of the sales data than the linear trend? Discuss. (*Hint:* see chapter 13.)

29. Sunrise Sports has experienced rapidly expanding retail sales. Its sales levels for the past twelve years are

Year	Sales (millions)	Year	Sales (millions)
1975	$1.9	1981	$ 8.6
1976	3.1	1982	9.3
1977	2.8	1983	11.0
1978	4.5	1984	13.9
1979	5.7	1985	16.6
1980	5.8	1986	19.4

Plot this series on ordinary graph paper and describe the trend in the data. Construct a least squares regression line to fit the data. How does this line explain the variation in past sales data? Comment on any patterns you see in the relationship between the actual sales values and those values predicted by the regression analysis.

30. The following are birth rates (per 1,000) in the United States between 1930 and 1984. Develop a time series plot of the data.

Year	Birth rate	Year	Birth rate
1930	21.3	1942	22.2
1931	20.2	1943	22.7
1932	19.5	1944	21.3
1933	18.4	1945	20.4
1934	19.0	1946	24.1
1935	18.7	1947	26.5
1936	18.4	1948	24.8
1937	18.7	1949	24.5
1938	19.2	1950	23.9
1939	18.8	1951	24.8
1940	19.4	1952	25.0
1941	20.3	1953	24.9

Year	Birth rate	Year	Birth rate
1954	25.2	1970	18.4
1955	24.9	1971	17.2
1956	25.1	1972	15.6
1957	25.3	1973	14.8
1958	24.5	1974	14.8
1959	24.3	1975	14.6
1960	23.7	1976	14.6
1961	23.5	1977	15.1
1962	22.6	1978	15.0
1963	21.9	1979	15.6
1964	21.2	1980	15.9
1965	19.4	1981	15.8
1966	18.4	1982	15.9
1967	17.8	1983	15.5
1968	17.5	1984	15.7
1969	17.8		

Develop a linear trend regression model and plot this trend line against the actual data. Is there a significant linear trend using an alpha level of 0.05?

Section 16–4

31. Blackman's Furniture Store has maintained monthly sales records for the past forty-eight months. These sales data pertain only to furniture and not to its carpet sales. These sales data are listed as follows:

Month		Sales	Month	Sales
Jan	1	23,500	18	29,700
	2	21,700	19	31,100
	3	18,750	20	32,400
	4	22,000	21	34,500
	5	23,000	22	35,700
	6	26,200	23	42,000
	7	27,300	24	42,600
	8	29,300	Jan 25	31,000
	9	31,200	26	30,400
	10	34,200	27	29,800
	11	39,500	28	32,500
	12	43,400	29	34,500
Jan	13	23,500	30	33,800
	14	23,400	31	34,200
	15	21,400	32	36,700
	16	24,200	33	39,700
	17	26,900	34	42,400

Month	Sales	Month	Sales
35	43,600	42	35,700
36	47,400	43	37,500
Jan 37	32,400	44	40,000
38	35,600	45	43,200
39	31,200	46	46,700
40	34,600	47	50,100
41	36,800	48	52,100

a. Considering the multiplicative model, estimate the $T \cdot C$ portion by computing a twelve-month moving average and then the centered twelve-month moving average.

b. Estimate the $S \cdot I$ portion of the multiplicative model by finding the ratio to moving average for the time series data. Determine whether these ratios to moving average values are stable from year to year.

c. Extract the irregular component by taking the normalized average of the ratio to moving averages. Present a table that shows the normalized seasonal indexes. Interpret what the index for January means relative to the index for July.

32. The Maiden Theater Company operates a chain of movie theaters in the Midwest. The company recently purchased a theater in Rapid City, South Dakota. The new manager obtained ticket-sales records for the previous thirty-six months. She hoped to analyze these data and use them in her planning for the next twelve months. The data are as follows:

Month	Tickets Sold	Month	Tickets Sold
Jan 1	1,580	19	1,580
2	1,608	20	1,680
3	1,370	21	1,560
4	1,260	22	1,520
5	1,125	23	1,670
6	1,306	24	1,920
7	1,240	Jan 25	1,960
8	1,340	26	1,880
9	1,090	27	1,820
10	980	28	1,750
11	1,260	29	1,690
12	1,680	30	1,730
Jan 13	1,630	31	1,690
14	1,700	32	1,780
15	1,610	33	1,670
16	1,590	34	1,560
17	1,498	35	1,760
18	1,540	36	2,040

a. Plot these data on a time series plot and describe in a short report what these three years of ticket sales have been like for this theater.

b. Develop seasonal indexes for theater ticket sales at the Rapid City theater based on the three years of data.

33. Ellial's Quality Discount Store has applied for a line of credit with the First National Bank. This line of credit is to be used primarily for financing inventory purchases. As part of the financial application, Ellial's has been asked to provide monthly inventory levels for the past five years. These levels (in millions of dollars) are

Month	1984	1985	1986	1987	1988
Jan	5.2	4.7	6.6	7.1	7.0
Feb	3.3	2.9	4.0	4.0	6.2
Mar	2.8	3.0	3.6	2.6	4.3
Apr	5.3	6.3	7.2	8.0	9.5
May	9.4	10.0	11.4	7.8	12.5
June	2.6	4.3	4.0	5.4	6.4
July	6.2	7.7	8.0	9.3	8.6
Aug	7.2	7.5	6.8	8.2	8.4
Sept	6.8	5.8	6.8	7.9	6.9
Oct	9.7	9.6	8.9	9.3	9.8
Nov	13.6	13.9	14.2	16.1	16.5
Dec	11.8	11.9	12.7	13.8	14.6

a. Determine the seasonal index number for each month using the ratio to moving average method.

b. Is there enough consistency between years to make you comfortable using seasonal index numbers?

c. Ellial's will finance 90 percent of its monthly inventory through bank borrowing. The company has been able to get money at the prime rate plus 2 percent. However, the interest must be paid monthly, and the value of the loan can change monthly. Estimate the value of interest payments for the next year.

Section 16–5

34. Refer to the data for Ellial's Quality Discount Store in problem 33. Determine the combined cyclical and irregular components using the approach discussed in section 16–5.

35. Refer to the Maiden Theater data in problem 32. Extract the combined cyclical and irregular components from the time series and plot these on a graph.

36. Refer to the Blackman Furniture data of problem 31. Use the methods discussed in section 16–5 to extract the combined cyclical and irregular components from the time series. Plot these index values on a graph.

Section 16–7

37. Discuss some of the advantages of using index numbers.

38. The following data represent expenditures on advertising over the period 1978 to 1988 by the Swanson Lumber Company.

Year	Advertising
1978	$12,500
1979	14,600
1980	16,250
1981	19,800
1982	23,700
1983	22,700
1984	18,790
1985	23,500
1986	24,000
1987	25,600
1988	27,800

a. Construct an advertising index for these data using 1978 as the base year. Write a short report analyzing this index.

b. Would it be appropriate to say that advertising was up 31.2 percent between years 1981 and 1982? Discuss why or why not.

c. What percentage increase in advertising took place between 1987 and 1988?

39. The Quarter-Tron Company is considering the acquisition of two companies to add to its already large list of holdings. Sales records are available for seven years for company 1 and five years for company 2. These data are shown as follows.

Company 1		Company 2	
Year	Sales	Year	Sales
1978	$1,345,790	1980	$2,456,800
1979	1,468,900	1981	2,567,800
1980	1,780,000	1982	2,809,800
1981	1,906,700	1983	3,001,100
1982	2,178,000	1984	3,457,000
1983	2,345,600		
1984	2,569,900		

Develop a sales index for each company, using the first available year as the base year.

40. Referring to problem 39, make the appropriate conversions so that the two indexes can be compared with respect to sales growth of the two companies.

Section 16–8

41. U.S. Homes is a major developer of housing communities in the New England area. The company has kept a record of the relative cost of labor (including fringe benefits) and materials in its market area since 1976. These data are as follows:

Year	Average Hourly Wage for Labor	Average Material Cost per House
1976	$13.45	$37,500
1977	15.60	39,000
1978	17.80	40,500
1979	18.90	43,200
1980	20.10	46,500
1981	20.50	48,900
1982	21.70	50,600
1983	22.50	50,900
1984	24.00	51,200
1985	24.50	51,700
1986	25.10	52,050

Using 1976 as the base year, construct a separate index for each component in the construction cost of a house.

42. Construct a Paasche index using the data in problem 41 and assuming that in 1986 60 percent of the cost of a house was labor and 40 percent was materials. Use 1976 as the base year.

43. Construct a Laspeyres index using the data in problem 41 and assuming that in 1976 40 percent of the cost of a house was labor and the rest materials.

44. Lamar Construction Materials has two divisions, the northwest region and the southwest region. Annual sales expenses for the two divisions since 1978 are as follows:

Year	Sales Expense Northwest Region ($\times$ $100,000)	Sales Expense Southwest Region ($\times$ $100,000)
1978	3.4	2.9
1980	3.7	3.4
1981	3.9	4.1
1982	4.4	4.8
1983	4.9	5.5
1984	5.2	5.9
1985	5.5	6.4
1986	5.9	7.1

Construct an unweighted aggregate index for Lamar's overall expenses.

45. In 1978 the northwest region accounted for 55 percent of Lamar Construction's total sales (see problem 44). Use this percentage to construct a Laspeyres index for the sales expense.

46. In 1986 the southwest region accounted for 60 percent of Lamar Construction's total sales (see problem 44). Use this percentage to construct a Paasche index for total sales expense.

Section 16–10

47. In problem 29, twelve years of sales data for Sunrise Sports are given. Deflate this data using the CPI values given in table 16–13. Then fit a simple linear regression line to both the original data and the deflated data. Discuss the differences between these two lines.

48. Use the values given in table 16–13 to deflate the Chesterfield Company sales data given in problem 26. Fit a linear regression line to both the original and deflated data. Discuss the differences between these two lines.

REFERENCES

Anderson, O. D. *Time Series Analysis and Forecasting.* Boston: Butterworths, 1975.

Anderson, T. W. *The Statistical Analysis of Time Series.* New York: Wiley, 1971.

Chou, Ya-Lun. *Statistical Analysis with Business and Economic Applications,* 2nd Edition. New York: Holt, Rinehart and Winston, 1975.

Chou, Ya-Lun, and Bauer, Bertrand. *Applied Business Statistics.* New York: Random House, 1983.

Gross, Charles W., and Peterson, Robin T. *Business Forecasting.* Boston: Houghton Mifflin, 1976.

Hamburg, Morris. *Statistical Analysis for Decision Making,* 2nd Edition. New York: Harcourt Brace Jovanovich, 1977.

Johnston, J. *Econometric Methods.* New York: McGraw-Hill, 1972.

Lapin, Lawrence, *Statistics for Modern Business Decisions,* 3rd Edition. New York: Harcourt Brace Jovanovich, 1982.

Mendenhall, William, and Reinmuth, James. *Statistics for Management and Economics,* 4th Edition. North Scituate, Mass.: Duxbury, 1982.

Montgomery, D. C., and Johnson, L. A. *Forecasting and Time Series Analysis.* New York: McGraw-Hill, 1976.

Nelson, Charles R. *Applied Time Series Analysis,* San Francisco: Holden-Day, 1973.

INTRODUCTION TO FORECASTING TECHNIQUES

17

WHY DECISION MAKERS NEED TO KNOW

No organization, large or small, can function effectively without a forecast for the goods and services it provides. A supermarket needs to forecast the demand for different types of dairy products. A farmer in Iowa must forecast the demand for corn when deciding what to plant in the spring. The concessionaire at Tiger Stadium in Detroit must forecast each game's attendance to determine how many soft drinks and hot dogs to have at hand. Your state's elected officials must forecast tax revenues in order to establish a budget each year. These are only a few instances in which business forecasting is required, but they should give you an idea of how important forecasting is in the decision-making process. In many cases, the success of the forecasting effort will play a major role in determining the general success of the organization.

CHAPTER OBJECTIVES

Although entire texts have been written about forecasting (see the Anderson and Armstrong books cited in the references), in this chapter we will introduce some of the most frequently used forecasting models. We will first consider the difference between judgmental and statistical forecasts, but will concentrate on statistical models. All statistical models use data gathered for past time periods to forecast future values. Many types of forecasting models may be used, but constructing a statistical model involves following a three-step procedure to be discussed in this chapter. The statistical models considered fall into four general categories. First, we will look at trend-based forecasting models. You will find these an extension of our time series discussion in chapter 16. Second, we will introduce some simple regression-based forecasting models. These will extend the ideas considered in chapters 13 and 14. Third, we will consider smoothing-based models, including a moving average, weighted moving average, and single and double exponential smoothing models. Finally, we will finish with a brief discussion of the Box-Jenkins forecasting model.

STUDENT OBJECTIVES

After studying the material in this chapter you should be able to

1. Discuss the differences between judgmental and statistical forecasts.
2. Discuss the steps needed to build a statistical forecasting model.
3. Extend the time series discussion of the previous chapter to make forecasts using the trend component of the time series.
4. Use both the trend and seasonal components of a time series to forecast future values of a variable of interest.
5. Construct and use autoregressive and indicator variable regression-based models.
6. Employ several kinds of smoothing models to make short-term forecasts.
7. Discuss the concepts involved in the Box-Jenkins forecasting model.

CATEGORIES OF FORECASTS

17-1   Experts agree that good planning is essential for an organization to be effective. Because forecasts are an important part of the planning process, decision makers need to be familiar with **forecasting** methods. In this section, we introduce some important terminology pertaining to forecasting and provide a basis for your study of the remaining sections in this chapter.

There are two broad categories of forecasting techniques:

1. Judgmental techniques
2. Statistical techniques

Judgmental forecasting techniques are based upon expert opinion and judgment. *Statistical* forecasting techniques are based on statistical methods for analyzing historical data. In general, statistical forecasting techniques are employed when

1. historical data relating to the variable to be forecasted exists,
2. the historical data can be quantified, and
3. you can assume the historical pattern will continue into the future.

If these conditions do not exist, judgmental forecasting techniques will be used.

In practice, the primary factor that determines the extent to which statistical and judgmental forecasts are used in a given situation seems to be how much uncertainty the decision maker sees in the future. When the decision maker sees the future as mostly an extension of the past, statistical models should be used. The more the future is expected to differ from the past, the more judgment should be incorporated into the decision. Many practical situations involve a combination of both techniques.

JUDGMENTAL FORECASTS

17-2   The advantage of judgmental forecasting is that it employs the experience base of the decision maker along with qualitative and quantitative data. A *judgmental forecast* has no specific data requirements and is not tied directly to the past. The major disadvantage of judgmental forecasting is that there are no statistical means to test the methodology used to arrive at the forecast.

Once a decision maker has decided a judgmental forecast is needed, the question is whose judgment to use. Although many people have knowledge that will aid in making a forecast, most managers would like to base their decisions on the forecast of experts in a field. From an organizational point of view, these experts seem to fall into four main groups:

1. *Top Management.* In many organizations, top-level managers are a good source of forecast information. This is particularly true if the manager has a lot of experience in the field or the organization.
2. *The Sales Force.* All organizations ultimately exist because they supply a product or service to meet a demand. Since demand keeps changing, the sales force often gets a feel for this demand faster than any other group.
3. *Consumers.* The people who ultimately buy the product or service of an organization are often the experts on their perceived future needs.
4. *Consultants.* Often what is a new situation for one organization has been experienced closely by another organization. Consultants are often familiar with what was tried, and often worked, someplace else and can provide the company with the necessary experience base.

This list is not all-inclusive. For many organizations, the expert chosen depends on the product or service being sold. Pharmaceutical manufacturers seek the judgment of physicians; electronics manufacturers seek the judgment of electrical engineers: textbook publishers seek the judgment of instructors; and so on. The point is, judgmental forecasting may be the best, or even the only, forecasts that can be made.

In this section, we introduce two of the most commonly used qualitative forecasting methods. These are the *Delphi method* and *scenario projection*.

The Delphi Method

Decision makers who employ the Delphi method attempt to arrive at a consensus forecast from a group of experts through a systematic procedure involving a series of questionnaires. The experts are purposely kept separated throughout the process. This reduces the potential problems associated with interpersonal exchanges in which dominant personalities might sway the opinion of other experts. Although the precise steps in implementing the Delphi method depend on the situation, the following example demonstrates the general procedure.

1. An issue is identified and a study coordinator appointed. For instance, Artistic Concerns, a company located in Dallas, Texas, is considering building a manufacturing facility to construct steel-framed modular homes the company has recently invented and patented. Management is interested in forecasting total industry demand for this new product over the next ten years.
2. A group of experts with potential insight in this area would be hired to com-

plete an initial questionnaire relating to the building industry and the prospects for this new product. Suppose three experts make up the panel. Their responses to two key questions are as follows:

Question 1: What will the total number of new housing starts be over the next ten years?

Expert A	Expert B	Expert C
1,500,000	2,500,000	4,500,000

Question 2: What number of new housing starts will be built with the steel-frame modular construction over the next ten years?

Expert A	Expert B	Expert C
150,000	40,000	500,000

3. Next, the panel of experts would be shown these responses without knowing which forecasts were associated with which expert. They would be given the opportunity to adjust their own responses to the questionnaire. Suppose the revised responses were

Question 1:

Expert A	Expert B	Expert C
2,000,000	2,700,000	3,200,000

Question 2:

Expert A	Expert B	Expert C
200,000	150,000	300,000

4. These results would be shared with the panel, along with responses to any other questions on the questionnaire, and the revision process would be repeated. Management would continue the process until either a general consensus is reached or until the experts cease to revise their forecasts. You should note that the objective is not to arrive at a single forecast value, but to achieve a reasonably narrow spread among the experts.

The Delphi method has some drawbacks, many of which are common to all judgmental forecasts. The most common complaint is the difficulty of evaluating the actual expertise of the "experts." The process may also be sensitive to the questionnaire. However, perhaps because of its structured nature, it is the most widely used qualitative forecasting technique.

Scenario Projection

This technique is much less structured than the Delphi method. A company using scenario projection will take a set of well-defined and self-contained assumptions and develop a statement of what the future will likely be if these assumptions hold. In an actual application, many sets of assumptions would be formulated and a corresponding number of future scenarios would be determined. The decision maker would have to choose which set of assumptions are most likely and determine whether the related scenario is realistic.

BUILDING A STATISTICAL FORECASTING MODEL

17-3

Decision makers who are actively involved in forecasting will frequently say that forecasting is a mix of art and science. Determining the appropriate forecasting model is a challenging task but can be made manageable by employing a model-building strategy composed of the following three steps:

1. Model specification
2. Model fitting
3. Model diagnosis

Model specification, or model identification, involves selecting the forecasting technique to be used in the current application. As we will point out in later sections, guidelines exist for determining which techniques may be more appropriate than others for certain situations. However, it may be necessary to specify (and try) several model forms for a given application before determining an acceptable model.

Model fitting is the process of determining how well the specified model fits the past data. The idea is that if the future tends to look like the past, a model must adequately fit the past data to have a reasonable chance of forecasting the future. The forecaster will spend much time adjusting the model specification and estimating its *parameters* so as to reach an acceptable fit of the past data.

Model diagnosis relates to analyzing the quality of the model employed. You will determine how well the model fits the past data, how well it performs in mock forecasting trials, and how well the assumptions of the model appear to be satisfied. If the model fails on any count, you will be forced to revert to the model specification step and begin again.

An important consideration to keep in mind when you are developing a forecasting model is to use the simplest available model that will meet your forecasting needs. The objective of forecasting is to provide good forecasts. You do not need to feel that a sophisticated approach is necessarily required if a simpler one will provide acceptable forecasts.

As in football, where some players specialize in defense and others in offense, forecasting techniques have been developed for special situations, generally dependent on the forecasting horizon. The **forecasting horizon** is the number of periods in the future covered by the forecast. This is referred to as *forecast lead time* by some forecasters. For the purpose of categorizing forecasting techniques, the horizon, or lead time, is typically divided into four categories:

1. **Immediate term horizon**—less than one month
2. **Short term horizon**—one to three months

3. Medium term horizon—three months to two years

4. Long term horizon—two years or more

As we introduce different forecasting techniques, we will indicate the forecast horizon(s) for which each is best suited.

In addition to determining the desired forecasting horizon, the forecaster must determine the forecasting period. The **forecasting period** is the unit of time for which forecasts are made. For instance, the forecasting period might be a day, a week, a month, a quarter, or a year. Thus, the forecasting horizon is composed of one or more forecasting periods. If statistical forecasting techniques are to be used, historical data must be available on a forecast-period basis. If we want weekly forecasts, historical data must be measured on a weekly basis, and so forth.

The frequency with which new forecasts are prepared is called the **forecasting interval.** The forecasting interval is generally the same length as the forecast period. That is, if the forecast period is one week, then we will provide a new forecast each week.

TREND-BASED FORECASTING TECHNIQUES

17-4

As discussed in chapter 16, some time series exhibit an increasing or decreasing trend, which may be a **linear trend** or a **nonlinear trend.** A plot of the data will usually help identify which, if any, trend exists.

In this section, we introduce trend-based forecasting techniques, which, as you will see, are based on the time series discussion of the last chapter. Once the *trend model* has been defined, it is used to provide forecasts for future time periods. Trend-based forecasts are very flexible and may be used for lead times ranging from immediate term to long term.

Linear Trend Forecasting

Figure 17–1 shows the plot of sales for temperature control units produced by the Robinson Control Company during the ten-year period between 1979 and 1988. Table 17–1 displays these same sales data. Executives at the Robinson Control Company are considering expanding their manufacturing facilities. A look at the time series plot in figure 17–1 shows an increasing trend during the ten-year period.

Recall that there are three steps in the forecasting process: model specification, model fitting, and model diagnosis. Model specification consists of identifying the appropriate forecasting technique for a given application; in the case of the Robinson Control Company example, we propose a linear trend (straight-line) model. In the model fitting step, the specified model is actually fit to the historical data. Since we have specified a linear trend model, fitting can be done by either ''eyeballing'' the trend line through the data or by least squares regression analysis.

To use the ''eyeballing'' method, the manager places a straight line through the data so as to ''fit'' the data. This method has great appeal since it requires no formal

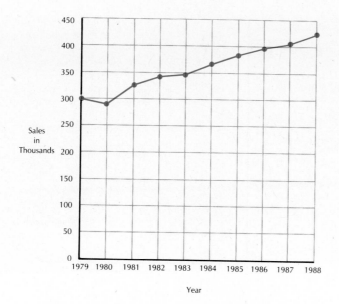

FIGURE 17–1
Temperature control unit sales data, Robinson Control Company example

training and can be done quickly. But because different decision makers may well "eye-ball" different trend lines, this method can lead to many possible trend lines, as shown in Figure 17–2. As you might expect, forecasts would differ depending on which trend line is selected. The "eyeball" approach is a "quick-and-dirty" method for modeling the trend; using *least squares regression* is generally preferred. When the model specification calls for a linear trend model, a trend line can be described as a function of time, as shown by equation 17–1:

Year	Sales (000)
1979	300
1980	295
1981	330
1982	345
1983	350
1984	370
1985	390
1986	400
1987	410
1988	430

TABLE 17–1
Temperature control unit sales data, Robinson Control Company example

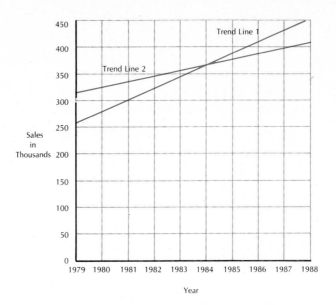

FIGURE 17–2
Trend lines ("eyeball"), Robinson Control Company example

$$\hat{Y}_t = b_0 + b_1 t \qquad (17\text{–}1)$$

where $\hat{Y}_t$ = value of the trend at time t
b_0 = Y intercept of the trend line
b_1 = slope of the trend line
t = time

We let the first period in the time series be $t = 1$, the second period be $t = 2$, and so forth.

Now, let's look at the time series data for the Robinson Control Company in table 17–1. The least squares equation for the trend line is determined in the following calculations. Note that the equation for b_1 is the same as indicated in chapter 13 except that here we substitute t for X. Also, we will let Y = actual values and $\hat{Y}$ = forecast values.

Year	t	Sales (000) Y_t	tY_t	t^2
1979	1	300	300	1
1980	2	295	590	4
1981	3	330	990	9
1982	4	345	1,380	16
1983	5	350	1,750	25

1984	6	370	2,220	36
1985	7	390	2,730	49
1986	8	400	3,200	64
1987	9	410	3,690	81
1988	10	430	4,300	100
	55	3,620	21,150	385

$$\bar{t} = 55/10 = 5.5$$

$$\bar{Y} = 3620/10 = 362.0$$

$$b_1 = \frac{\Sigma t Y_t - \dfrac{\Sigma t \Sigma Y}{n}}{\Sigma t^2 - (\Sigma t)^2/n}$$

$$= \frac{21150 - (55)(3620)/10}{385 - (55)^2/10}$$

$$= 15.03$$

$$b_0 = \bar{Y} - b_1 \bar{t}$$

$$= 362.0 - 15.03(5.5)$$

$$= 279.335$$

The least squares trend line for the Robinson Control Company is

$$\hat{Y}_t = 279.335 + 15.03t$$

The model has an $R^2 = 0.98$, which indicates the linear model provides a good fit to the data. The calculated t statistic is 14.07, which means the regression slope is statistically significant. Figure 17–3 shows this trend line plotted against the actual sales data.

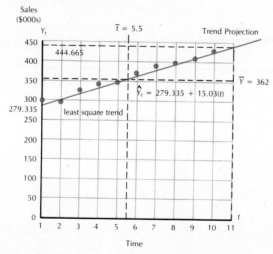

FIGURE 17–3
Least squares trend line, Robinson Control Company example

Comparing the Trend Line with Past Data

The predicted sales values for periods $t = 1$ through $t = 10$ can be found by substituting for t in the forecast equation

$$\hat{Y}_t = 279.335 + 15.03t$$

For example, for $t = 1$, we get

$$\hat{Y}_1 = 279.335 + 15.03(1)$$
$$= 294.365 \text{ control units}$$

Note that the actual sales, Y_1, for period 1 (1979) was 300. The difference between the actual sales in time t and the values found using the trend model is called the **forecast error** or **residual**. You might review section 14–5 for further discussion of residuals. Table 17–2 shows the predicted values for periods 1 through 10 and the residuals.

Finding the residuals by comparing the trend-line values with actual past data is an important part of the **model diagnosis** step. The residuals measure how close the model fits the actual data at each point. A perfect fit would lead to residuals of zero each time. Beyond that, we would like to see "small" residuals and an "overall good fit." Two commonly used measures of fit based on the residual are available:

1. Mean squared residual or mean square error (MSE) (equation 17–2):

$$MSE = \sum_{t=1}^{n} (Y_t - \hat{Y}_t)^2 / n \qquad (17\text{–}2)$$

where Y_t = actual value at time t
$\hat{Y}_t$ = predicted value at time t.
n = number of time periods

TABLE 17–2
Forecasts and residuals (000), Robinson Control Company example

Year	t	Actual Sales Y_t	Forecast Sales $\hat{Y}_t$	Residual $(Y_t - \hat{Y}_t)$
1979	1	300	294.365	5.635
1980	2	295	309.395	−14.395
1981	3	330	324.425	5.575
1982	4	345	339.455	5.545
1983	5	350	354.485	−4.485
1984	6	370	369.515	0.485
1985	7	390	384.545	5.455
1986	8	400	399.575	0.425
1987	9	410	414.605	−4.605
1988	10	430	429.635	0.365
				0.000

2. Mean absolute deviation (MAD) (equation 17–3):

$$MAD = \sum_{t=1}^{n} |Y_t - \hat{Y}_t|/n$$

(17–3)

Table 17–3 shows the MSE and MAD calculations for the Robinson Control Company example. These measures are particularly helpful when comparing two or more forecasting techniques. We can compute the MSE and/or the MAD for each forecasting technique. The forecasting technique that gives the smallest MSE or MAD is generally considered to provide the best fit.

Once we are satisfied that the linear trend model provides acceptable predictions for the historical data, we can obtain forecasts for future time periods by substituting values of t into the trend equation. This is called *extrapolation*. For example, the forecast for 1989 is developed by substituting $t = 11$ into the trend equation as follows:

$$\hat{Y}_{11} = 279.335 + 15.03(11)$$
$$= 444.67$$

You should be aware that forecasting techniques that use extrapolation work well only as long as the future tends to look like the past. If the future trend changes, the trend forecasting model may yield large forecast errors.

Adjusting Trend-Based Forecasts for Seasonality

In chapter 16 we discussed *seasonality* in a time series. The *seasonal component* represents those changes in the time series that occur at the same time every year. Most

TABLE 17–3
MSE and MAD computations, Robinson Control Company example

Year	t	Residual $(Y_t - \hat{Y}_t)$	Squared Residual $(Y_t - \hat{Y}_t)^2$	Absolute Residual $|Y_t - \hat{Y}_t|$
1979	1	5.635	31.7532	5.635
1980	2	−14.395	207.2160	14.395
1981	3	5.575	31.0806	5.575
1982	4	5.545	30.7470	5.545
1983	5	−4.485	20.1152	4.485
1984	6	0.485	0.2352	0.485
1985	7	5.455	29.7570	5.455
1986	8	0.425	0.1806	0.425
1987	9	−4.605	21.2060	4.605
1988	10	0.365	0.1332	0.365
		0.000	372.4240	46.970

MSE = 372.4240/10 = 37.2424
MAD = 46.970/10 = 4.6970

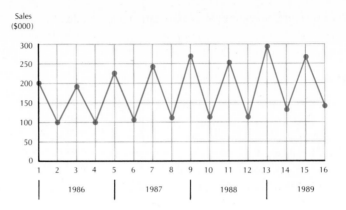

FIGURE 17–4
Sales time series plot, Rocky Mountain Sports example

businesses connected with the tourist industry find that their sales are seasonal. For example, at Rocky Mountain Sports in Aspen, Colorado, business peaks at two times during the year: winter for skiing and summer for fishing and backpacking. These peaks can be identified in a time series if the sales data are measured on at least a quarterly basis. Figure 17–4 shows total sales in each quarter over the past four years. The data are displayed in table 17–4. The time series plot clearly shows the summer and winter quarters are the busy times. There has also been an increasing linear trend in sales over the four years.

TABLE 17–4
Quarterly sales, Rocky Mountain Sports example

Year	Quarter	t	Sales ($000)
1986	Winter	1	205
	Spring	2	96
	Summer	3	194
	Fall	4	102
1987	Winter	5	230
	Spring	6	105
	Summer	7	245
	Fall	8	120
1988	Winter	9	272
	Spring	10	110
	Summer	11	255
	Fall	12	114
1989	Winter	13	296
	Spring	14	130
	Summer	15	270
	Fall	16	140

Suppose Rocky Mountain Sports wishes to forecast sales for each quarter of the upcoming year and hopes to use a linear trend model. If the data as given in Table 17–4 were used to construct the trend model, it would be

$$\hat{Y}_t = 155.075 + 2.962t$$

with an F statistic $= 0.5499$ and $R^2 = 0.038$—not a very good fit.

When the historical data reflect both a trend and seasonality, the trend-based forecasting model needs to be adjusted to incorporate the seasonality. As we saw in the last chapter, dealing with seasonality involves calculating **seasonal indexes.** Since we have quarterly data, we can develop four seasonal indexes; for winter, spring, summer, and fall. A seasonal index below 1.00 indicates the quarter has values typically below the normal values for the year. On the other hand, an index greater than 1.00 indicates the quarter is a higher than normal quarter.

Computing the Seasonally Adjusted Forecast

Assuming the actual time series data can be represented as a product of the four time series components, as we did in the last chapter, we will use the *multiplicative model* to generate our forecast. The multiplicative model is represented by equation 17–4:

$$Y_t = T_t \cdot S_t \cdot C_t \cdot I_t \qquad (17\text{–}4)$$

where $Y_t =$ value of the time series at time t
   $T_t =$ trend value at time t
   $S_t =$ seasonal value at time t
   $C_t =$ cyclical value at time t
   $I_t =$ irregular, or random, value at time t

Remember, the **ratio to moving average** method removes the seasonal and irregular components, S_t and I_t, from the data, leaving the combined trend and cyclical components, T_t and C_t. The **moving averages** and *centered moving averages,* found as we did in chapter 16, are shown in table 17–5. We use a four-period moving average because we have quarterly data. These centered moving average values estimate the $T_t \cdot C_t$ part of the multiplicative model.

The ratio to moving average value, $S_t \cdot I_t$, is found by dividing the actual sales value for each quarter by the corresponding centered moving average, as shown in equation 17–5:

$$S_t \cdot I_t = \frac{Y_t}{T_t \cdot C_t} \qquad (17\text{–}5)$$

Table 17–6 shows these values for the Rocky Mountain Sports data.

TABLE 17–5
Centered moving averages, Rocky Mountain Sports example

Year	Quarter	t	Sales ($000)	4-Period Moving Average	Centered Moving Average $T \cdot C$
1986	Winter	1	205		
	Spring	2	96	149.25	
	Summer	3	194	155.50	152.375
	Fall	4	102	157.75	156.625
1987	Winter	5	230	170.50	164.125
	Spring	6	105	175.50	173.000
	Summer	7	245	185.50	180.500
	Fall	8	120	186.75	186.125
1988	Winter	9	272	189.25	188.000
	Spring	10	110	187.75	188.500
	Summer	11	255	193.75	190.750
	Fall	12	114	198.75	196.250
1989	Winter	13	296	202.50	200.625
	Spring	14	130	209.00	205.750
	Summer	15	270		
	Fall	16	140		

TABLE 17–6
Ratio to moving averages, Rocky Mountain Sports example

Year	Quarter	t	Sales ($000)	Centered Moving Average $T \cdot C$	Ratio to Moving Average $S \cdot I$
1986	Winter	1	205		
	Spring	2	96		
	Summer	3	194	152.375	1.273
	Fall	4	102	156.625	0.651
1987	Winter	5	230	164.125	1.401
	Spring	6	105	173.000	0.607
	Summer	7	245	180.500	1.357
	Fall	8	120	186.125	0.645
1988	Winter	9	272	188.000	1.447
	Spring	10	110	188.500	0.584
	Summer	11	255	190.750	1.337
	Fall	12	114	196.250	0.581
1989	Winter	13	296	200.625	1.475
	Spring	14	130	205.750	0.632
	Summer	15	270		
	Fall	16	140		

The seasonal indexes for this data are shown as follows for each of the four quarters:

	Winter	Spring	Summer	Fall
1986			1.273	0.651
1987	1.401	0.607	1.357	0.645
1988	1.447	0.584	1.337	0.581
1989	1.475	0.632		
Total	4.323	1.823	3.967	1.877
Average	1.441	0.608	1.322	0.626
Normalized average	1.442	0.608	1.323	0.626

Thus, the seasonal index for winter is 1.442. This indicates that winter quarter sales at Rocky Mountain Sports are 44.2 percent above normal for the year. Likewise, sales in the spring quarter are only 60.8 percent of normal for the year.

The deseasonalized sales values are found by dividing Y_t by the appropriate seasonal index, S_t (equation 17–6):

$$Y_t/S_t = T_t \cdot C_t \cdot I_t \qquad (17\text{–}6)$$

Table 17–7 contains the deseasonalized values for the Rocky Mountain Sports sales data. Figure 17–5 shows the graph of these deseasonalized sales data.

TABLE 17–7
Deseasonalized time series sales data, Rocky Mountain Sports example

Year	Quarter	t	Y_t	$Y_t/S_t = T_t \cdot C_t \cdot I_t$
1986	Winter	1	205	142.16
	Spring	2	96	157.89
	Summer	3	194	146.64
	Fall	4	102	162.94
1987	Winter	5	230	159.50
	Spring	6	105	172.70
	Summer	7	245	185.19
	Fall	8	120	191.69
1988	Winter	9	272	188.63
	Spring	10	110	180.92
	Summer	11	255	192.74
	Fall	12	114	182.11
1989	Winter	13	296	205.27
	Spring	14	130	213.82
	Summer	15	270	204.08
	Fall	16	140	223.64

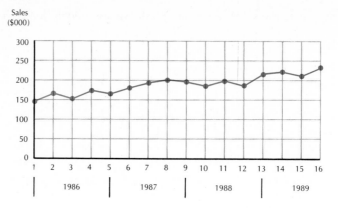

FIGURE 17–5

Deseasonalized sales data, Rocky Mountain Sports example

Once the data have been deseasonalized, the next step is to determine the trend of these deseasonalized data. As in previous examples, we use the least squares regression method to compute the linear trend equation:

$$\hat{Y}_t = b_0 + b_1(t)$$

The resulting trend line equation is

$$\hat{Y}_t = 142.1128 + 4.685t$$

This model has an F statistic $= 109.72$ and $R^2 = 0.8868$. Obviously, deseasonalizing the data has improved the model.

We can use this trend line and the trend projection method to forecast period $t = 17$:

$$\hat{Y}_{17} = 142.1128 + 4.685(17)$$
$$= 221.76$$

This forecast is a **seasonally unadjusted forecast.** We need to adjust the forecast for period 17 to reflect the quarterly fluctuations. We do this by multiplying the unadjusted forecast by the appropriate seasonal index. In this case, period 17 corresponds to the winter quarter, so the adjusted forecast is

$$\hat{Y}_{17} = (221.76)(1.442)$$
$$= 319.78$$

The seasonally adjusted forecasts for each quarter in 1990 are

Year	Quarter	t	Unadjusted Forecast	Seasonal Index	Adjusted Forecast
1990	Winter	17	221.76	1.442	319.78
	Spring	18	226.44	0.608	137.68
	Summer	19	231.13	1.323	305.78
	Fall	20	235.82	0.626	147.62

Review of the Seasonal Adjustment Process

We can summarize the steps required in performing a seasonal adjustment to a trend-based forecast as follows:

Step 1. Compute an *n* period moving average where *n* is the number of periods in a year or season.

Step 2. Compute the centered moving averages.

Step 3. Isolate the seasonal component by computing the ratio to moving average values.

Step 4. Compute the seasonal indexes by averaging the ratio to moving averages for comparable periods.

Step 5. Deseasonalize the time series by dividing the actual data by the appropriate seasonal index.

Step 6. Use least squares regression to develop the trend line, using the deseasonalized data.

Step 7. Develop the unadjusted forecasts, using trend projection.

Step 8. Seasonally adjust the forecasts by multiplying the unadjusted forecasts by the appropriate seasonal index.

Autocorrelation

If the residuals, $Y_t - \hat{Y}_t$, resulting from a regression model constructed on time series data, are correlated, **autocorrelation** of the residuals exists. The statistical tests of significance for a regression-based forecasting model are based on the assumption that there is no autocorrelation. If autocorrelation exists, the least squares estimation techniques will not provide unbiased estimates of the regression coefficients and the sample standard error of the regression slope may seriously underestimate the standard deviation of the population regression slope. There is some controversy over the issue, but many statisticians believe forecasts should not be made using models that contain autocorrelated residuals.

A widely-used test for determining whether autocorrelation exists is the *Durbin-Watson test*. In most business and economics applications, if autocorrelation exists it will be positive. Therefore, we will use the following null and alternative hypotheses to test for positive autocorrelation:

$$H_0: \rho = 0$$
$$H_A: \rho > 0$$

where

$$\rho = \text{true autocorrelation between adjacent residuals}$$

The Durbin-Watson test statistic is calculated by equation 17–7:

$$D = \frac{\displaystyle\sum_{t=2}^{n} (e_t - e_{t-1})^2}{\displaystyle\sum_{t=1}^{n} e_t^2} \tag{17–7}$$

where e_t = residual at time period t
e_{t-1} = residual at time $t - 1$

The Durbin-Watson test is not an exact test but instead provides lower and upper limits, d_l and d_u, to which we compare the calculated D value in equation 17–7. If D is less than d_l, we reject H_0 and conclude that we have positive autocorrelation.

If D is greater than d_u, we accept H_0 and conclude that no autocorrelation exists. However, if D falls in between d_l and d_u, no conclusion can be reached with respect to autocorrelation, and a larger sample size is required.

A table of Durbin-Watson d_l and d_u values appears in appendix I of this text. The limits are shown for different sample sizes and for regression models with different numbers of independent variables for alpha levels of 0.05 and 0.01.

The Harrisburg City Council instituted a meals-on-wheels program in 1969 based on the recommendation of the Senior Citizens' Advisory Council. The program has proved popular and the number of requests for meals is shown in table 17–8. Figure 17–6 shows the time series plot of these data. To provide the City Council with a demand forecast for the next four years, we could specify a linear trend model. Fitting the twenty data points with a least squares line we find

$$\text{demand} = -663.274 + 546.574t$$

The model has an $R^2 = 0.913$, an F statistic = 188.496, and a standard error of 1,026.61. The model explains a significant amount of variation in the demand over time for meals-on-wheels.

Before using the linear trend model to forecast demand, we should test for autocorrelation. Table 17–9 shows the calculations for the Durbin-Watson D statistic. (These calculations are tedious, but this is eased by the fact that most computer regression software print out the Durbin-Watson D statistic as part of the regular output.)

From table 17–9, we find that the D statistic is 0.217. We next go to the Durbin-Watson table in appendix I and find the alpha level of 0.05, sample size twenty, and number of independent variables equal to 1. The values from the table for d_l and d_u are

Time period t	Year	Requests
1	1969	1,459
2	1970	1,620
3	1971	1,783
4	1972	1,794
5	1973	2,191
6	1974	2,423
7	1975	2,677
8	1976	2,815
9	1977	3,093
10	1978	3,190
11	1979	4,550
12	1980	5,166
13	1981	5,820
14	1982	5,809
15	1983	6,622
16	1984	8,092
17	1985	9,426
18	1986	10,554
19	1987	10,998
20	1988	11,433

TABLE 17–8
Requests for meals-on-wheels, Harrisburg City Council example (1969–1988)

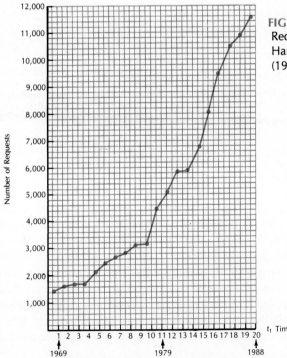

FIGURE 17–6
Requests for meals-on-wheels, Harrisburg City Council example (1969–1988)

TABLE 17–9

Computations for Durbin-Watson D statistic, meals-on-wheels, Harrisburg City Council example

t	Y	e_t	$(e_t - e_{t-1})$	$(e_t - e_{t-1})^2$	e^2
1	1,459	1,575.70			2,482,830.5
2	1,620	1,190.13	− 385.574	148,667.31	1,416,409.4
3	1,783	806.55	− 383.574	147,129.01	650,522.9
4	1,794	270.98	− 535.574	286,839.51	73,430.2
5	2,191	121.41	− 149.574	22,372.38	14,740.4
6	2,423	− 193.17	− 314.574	98,956.80	37,314.6
7	2,677	− 485.74	− 292.574	85,599.54	235,943.3
8	2,815	− 894.32	− 408.574	166,932.71	799,808.3
9	3,093	− 1,162.89	− 268.574	72,131.99	1,352,313.2
10	3,190	− 1,612.46	− 449.574	202,116.78	2,600,027.3
11	4,550	− 799.04	813.426	661,661.86	638,464.9
12	5,166	− 729.61	69.426	4,819.97	532,330.7
13	5,820	− 622.18	107.460	11,547.65	387,107.9
14	5,809	− 1,179.76	− 557.574	310,888.77	1,391,833.7
15	6,622	− 913.33	266.426	70,982.81	834,171.7
16	8,092	10.09	923.426	852,715.58	101.8
17	9,426	797.52	787.426	620,039.71	636,038.2
18	10,554	1,378.95	581.426	338,056.19	1,901,503.1
19	10,998	1,276.37	− 102.574	10,521.43	1,629,120.4
20	11,433	1,164.80	− 111.574	12,448.76	1,356,759.0
				4,124,428.80	18,970,852.0

$$D = 4,124,428.80/18,970,852.0$$
$$= 0.217$$

$$d_l = 1.20$$
$$d_u = 1.41$$

Since $D = 0.217$ is less than $d_l = 1.20$, we must reject the null hypothesis and therefore conclude that significant autocorrelation exists in the regression model. This means that the assumption of uncorrelated residuals has been violated in this case.

There are some techniques for dealing with the problem of autocorrelation which are beyond the scope of this text. (Refer to books by Johnson and Nelson.) However, one basic step might be taken in this case to potentially alleviate the autocorrelation problem. If we look closely at figure 17–6, the relationship between admissions (Y) and the independent variable, time (t), appears nonlinear rather than linear. Chapter 13 introduced the idea of transforming the independent variable in certain circumstances when a curvilinear relationship appears to exist between the dependent and independent variables.

One such transformation that we presented in chapter 13 involves squaring the independent variable. If we perform this transformation in the Harrisburg City Council example, the regression model would take the form of equation 17–8:

$$\hat{Y} = b_0 + b_1\, t^2 \qquad\qquad (17\text{–}8)$$

With the aid of a computer and appropriate software, the new regression model is determined to be

$$\hat{Y} = 1{,}302.3 + 26.296 t^2$$

Figure 17–7 shows a graph of this regression line against the original data for twenty years. The new model appears to provide a superior fit to the data and this is supported by an increased R^2 of 0.988. However, the question remains as to whether transforming the variable eliminated the problem of correlated residuals.

The computer was used to calculate the Durbin-Watson D value equal to 1.041. From the Durbin-Watson tables for an alpha level of 0.05, sample size of twenty, and variables equal to 1, the values of d_l and d_u are

$$d_l = 1.20$$
$$d_u = 1.41$$

Then since $D = 1.041$ is less than $d_l = 1.20$, we should reject the null hypothesis of no autocorrelation and conclude that there is significant positive autocorrelation between adjacent residuals from this revised regression model. (Note that if the alpha level of 0.01 were used, the D value would fall in the range of uncertainty and a larger sample size would be required to reach a conclusion.)

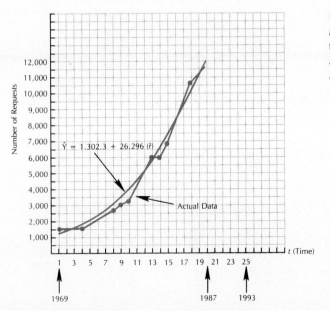

FIGURE 17–7
Meals-on-wheels forecast model, transformed independent variable, Harrisburg City Council example

The *D* statistic has been reduced but the problem of autocorrelation still persists. As stated previously, some statisticians believe that models exhibiting autocorrelation should not be used for forecasting purposes; others stress that only the statistical hypotheses tests are affected and not the forecasting results. This text holds to the latter argument, but you should be careful any time a regression-based forecasting model is used. If the past does not reflect the future, the forecasts will almost certainly be in substantial error.

SKILL DEVELOPMENT PROBLEMS FOR SECTION 17–4

The following set of problems is meant to test your understanding of the material in this section. Additional problems are found at the end of this chapter under this section heading.

1. Consider the following set of sales data, given in millions of dollars:

1984		*1986*	
1st quarter	242	1st quarter	307
2nd quarter	252	2nd quarter	299
3rd quarter	257	3rd quarter	292
4th quarter	267	4th quarter	311
1985		*1987*	
1st quarter	272	1st quarter	326
2nd quarter	285	2nd quarter	332
3rd quarter	281	3rd quarter	321
4th quarter	287	4th quarter	314

Fit a least squares regression line to these data and use the regression equation to forecast sales for the next four quarters. How much confidence would you have in this forecast?

2. Consider the following set of inventory data, given in hundreds of thousands of dollars:

1984		*1986*	
1st quarter	109	1st quarter	118
2nd quarter	95	2nd quarter	103
3rd quarter	115	3rd quarter	126
4th quarter	108	4th quarter	120

	1985			1987	
1st quarter	115		1st quarter	130	
2nd quarter	110		2nd quarter	127	
3rd quarter	120		3rd quarter	138	
4th quarter	116		4th quarter	135	

Fit a least squares regression line to these data and use the regression equation to forecast the inventory level for the next four quarters. How much confidence would you have in this forecast?

3. Using the same data given in problem 1, adjust the time series for seasonality. Prepare a new forecast for sales for the next four quarters. Do you feel adjusting for seasonality improves your forecast? Why?

4. Using the same data given in problem 2, adjust the time series for seasonality. Prepare a new forecast for inventory for the next four quarters. Do you feel adjusting for seasonality improves your forecast? Why?

5. In the last chapter we introduced Don Glidden, who opened Video Excitement at the beginning of the VCR movie boom. Originally he charged customers a membership fee of $49.95, which allowed them to rent four movies a month for $4.95 each, with additional movies rented at $6.95 each. Don's business boomed in the New Orleans area and soon he had ten stores. Unfortunately, more and more video stores opened and soon supermarkets and convenience stores were renting movies. To maintain the sales volume necessary to remain profitable, Don started selling VCRs in his stores and soon moved to home entertainment centers. Don is presently analyzing the sales volume at his original location for the first five years of operation.

		Sales Volume ($\times 1,000$)			
	1983	1984	1985	1986	1987
January	23	67	72	76	81
February	34	63	64	75	72
March	45	65	64	77	71
April	48	71	77	81	83
May	46	75	79	86	85
June	49	70	72	75	77
July	60	72	71	80	79
August	65	75	77	82	84
September	67	80	79	86	91
October	60	78	78	87	86
November	71	89	87	91	94
December	76	94	92	96	99

a. Use a least squares regression line to forecast sales for each month of the next year.

b. Determine the appropriate seasonal adjustment factors for these data and use them to prepare a monthly forecast for next year.

c. Which forecast developed in parts a and b would you feel most confidence in? Discuss in statistical terms, using the MSE, MAD, and coefficient of determination.

REGRESSION-BASED FORECASTING MODELS

17-5

Section 17–4 introduced trend-based forecasting where least squares regression was used to determine the trend. The trend-based forecasting models used two variables: a dependent variable, Y_t, and an independent variable, time. Regression analysis determined the trend line which "best fit" the time series data. An equation of the form

$$\hat{Y}_t = b_0 + b_1 t$$

was formed. Forecasts were obtained by substituting the appropriate value for time into the trend equation.

This use of regression analysis is common, but regression analysis has a much broader application in forecasting. We will consider two additional regression model forms commonly used by forecasters: regression models with indicator variables and autoregressive models.

You should find the discussion in this section familiar since you have considered regression analysis extensively in chapters 13 and 14. A brief review of section 13–6 should make the following discussion easier to follow.

The major difference found in using regression analysis specifically for forecasting is in the relationship between the dependent and independent variables, not in the statistical techniques used. If a company is trying to forecast sales for next year, it will try to find a relationship between something measurable this year and sales next year. The company is specifically interested in finding variables that "lead" the dependent variable. These variables are often called **indicator variables.**

Regression Using Leading Indicator Variables

Consider the Mike Pope Aerobics Equipment Company. The production manager is interested in forecasting monthly sales for an exercise unit produced at the Midland, Texas, plant. The manager has monthly sales data for this production for the past twelve months. He also has available monthly data on product advertising expenditures. These data are shown in table 17–10. Notice that the product's sales, Y_t, vary from month to month. Some people in the company think the variation in advertising spending one month might be partially responsible for changes in sales the next month. Thus, in this example, advertising is considered a *leading indicator variable*.

Month t	Sales (units) Y_t	Advertising (\$000) X_t
1	100	23
2	250	16
3	150	15
4	120	20
5	200	25
6	240	20
7	180	26
8	300	24
9	250	22
10	180	20
11	220	25
12	230	24

TABLE 17–10
Sales data, Mike Pope Aerobics Equipment Company example

A regression-based forecasting model could be specified of the form of equation 17–9:

$$\hat{Y}_t = b_0 + b_1(X_{t-1}) \tag{17–9}$$

where
$\hat{Y}_t$ = forecast value of sales for month t
b_0 = regression intercept
b_1 = regression slope
X_{t-1} = value of advertising at time $t - 1$

We can use least squares regression to determine the "best" values for b_0 and b_1. Be careful when calculating the regression equation for an indicator variable model. In this case the one-period lagged relationship means sales in month 2 will be associated with advertising in month 1, and so forth. Therefore, we will have only eleven data pairs to build the model. Using these eleven data points, we find

$$\hat{Y}_t = -61.5343 + 12.6986(X_{t-1})$$

This model has an F statistic = 39.40859, with 1 and 9 degrees of freedom and R^2 = 0.8141. Table 17–11 shows the MAD calculation when the indicator variable regression model output is compared with historical data.

To employ the model to forecast sales for period 13, the production manager would need to measure the level of product advertising for month 12. Suppose the company spends 24,000 ($X_{12} = 24$) for advertising. Then the sales forecast for period 13 is

$$\hat{Y}_{13} = -126.7397 + 14.8904(24)$$
$$= 230.63$$

Thus, the manager might plan on selling about 230 exercise units in month 13.

TABLE 17–11
MAD calculations, Mike Pope Aerobics Equipment Company example

Month t	Sales (units) Y_t	Advertising ($000) X_1	Forecast $\hat{Y}_t$	Absolute Error $|Y_t - \hat{Y}_t|$
1	100	23		
2	250	16	230.5335	19.4665
3	150	15	141.6433	8.3567
4	120	20	128.9447	8.9447
5	200	25	192.4377	7.5633
6	240	20	255.9309	15.9303
7	180	26	192.4377	12.4377
8	300	24	268.6293	31.3707
9	250	22	243.2321	6.7679
10	180	20	217.8349	37.8349
11	220	25	192.4377	27.5633
12	230	24	255.9309	25.9309
				202.1675

$$\text{MAD} = 202.1675/11$$
$$= 18.3788$$

Multiple Regression Models with Indicator Variables

Realistically, in forecasting applications like the Mike Pope Aerobics example, there may be several potential explanatory variables which could be included in the model. A regression model with more than one independent (indicator) variable would be a *multiple regression forecasting model*. The forecast equation would take the form of equation 17–10:

$$\hat{Y}_t = b_0 + b_1 X_{1t-m1} + b_2 X_{2t-m2} + \cdots \cdot b_k X_{kt-mk} \qquad (17\text{–}10)$$

where
$\hat{Y}_t$ = forecast value for period t
b_0 = regression intercept
mi = number of periods ith variable is lagged
b_i = ith regression slope
X_{it-mi} = value of ith indicator variable measured at time $t - mi$

The model described in equation 17–10 shows the X_i variables measured with different lead times, $t - mi$, corresponding to when the dependent variable is measured. Thus, to forecast for time $t + 1$, we would need to know values for each variable at the appropriate lead points.

In some cases we can use regression forecasting models without a lead time relationship between the independent and dependent variables. This would be possible when the indicator variable can be controlled. For instance, the marketing director of SuperMart Discount Stores may be looking for a model to forecast the weekly customer traffic in her stores. Since she knows how many radio commercials SuperMart is buying next week in each store's market area, she could include this variable in a forecasting model for next week without a lagged relationship. However, when an explanatory variable cannot be controlled and its value is not known in advance, we must lag the data to have a viable forecasting equation.

Autoregressive Forecasting Models

Another type of regression-based forecasting approach involves using indicator variables that are lagged values of the dependent variable. For instance, we might formulate a model like that of equation 17–11:

$$\hat{Y}_t = b_0 + b_1 Y_{t-1} + b_2 Y_{t-2} \qquad (17\text{–}11)$$

where $\hat{Y}_t$ = forecast value in time t
Y_{t-1} = value of the time series at time $t-1$
Y_{t-2} = value of the time series at time $t-2$

Equation 17–11 illustrates a case where the two most recent time periods are used as independent variables. The success of an autoregressive model depends on how closely past data are related to current data.

Other Regression-Based Models

You should be aware that there are other regression-based forecasting models. For the most part, these are variations of those discussed in the previous sections. For instance, the trend-projection models that use time as the independent variable can be extended to a multiple regression model of the form of equation 17–12:

$$\hat{Y}_t = b_0 + b_1 t + b_1 t^2 + b_2 t^3 \qquad (17\text{–}12)$$

where $\hat{Y}_t$ = forecast value of the time series at time t
t = value of time at time t
t^2 = time squared
t^3 = time cubed

This format could be appropriate for time series that exhibit nonlinear movements.

The distinguishing feature of each regression-based model is the form of the independent variable(s). We get a mixed regression model when the independent variables included in the model are mixed. For instance, we might determine a model of the following form:

$$\hat{Y}_t = b_0 + b_1 Y_{t-1} + b_2 t^2 + b_3 X_{1t-1}$$

In this instance, we have a combined autoregressive, trend-projection, and indicator variable regression model.

The "art" of forecasting is to determine the most appropriate form for the forecasting model. Guard against the tendency to use the same model format in all applications. What worked well in one situation may not be appropriate in others.

SKILL DEVELOPMENT PROBLEMS FOR SECTION 17–5

The following set of problems is meant to test your understanding of the material in this section. Additional problems are found at the end of this chapter under this section heading.

6. Consider the following data:

Period	Dependent Variable	Independent 1	Independent 2
1	101	19	202
2	120	18	210
3	129	17	208
4	122	20	210
5	126	22	212
6	131	23	211
7	133	22	215
8	139	21	214
9	136	24	218
10	140	26	219
11	141	27	220

a. If you were to construct a one-period leading indicator simple regression forecasting model to predict values of the dependent variable, which independent variable would you choose? Why?

b. Use the model you developed in part a to forecast the value of the dependent variable for the next three periods.

7. Refer to the sales data given in problem 1 in section 17–4.

a. Construct autoregressive forecasting models with time lags of 1, 2, 3, and 4 periods.

b. If you were to forecast sales for the next four periods, which model would you choose? Why?

c. Use the model you picked in part b to forecast the next year's sales.

8. Refer to the inventory data given in problem 2 in section 17–4.

a. Construct autoregressive forecasting models with time lags of 1, 2, 3, and 4 periods.

b. Use the models you constructed in part a to forecast the next quarter's sales.

9. Let's return to the Don Glidden Video Excitement example last considered in problem 5 in section 17–4. Refer to the five years of sales volume data given in that problem.
   a. Prepare a one-month and twelve-month lag autoregressive model for these data. Which model do you think is best for forecasting?
   b. Select the best model from part a to forecast next year's sales on a monthly basis.

FORECASTING USING SMOOTHING-BASED METHODS

17-6

Our earlier discussion of trend-based forecasting models applies to situations where the historical time series exhibits a trend. The least squares approach offers a method for modeling the trend and, by using trend projection, a forecast for future time periods can be developed. When the time series does not exhibit a trend, however, we need a different forecasting method.

If we are interested in forecasting one or two periods into the future, a class of forecasting techniques called *smoothing models* exists for situations in which there is no significant trend or cyclical or seasonal components in the time series data. These models attempt to "smooth out" the **random,** or irregular, **component** in the time series by an averaging process. In this section we discuss four smoothing techniques: moving average, weighted moving average, single exponential weighted smoothing, and double exponential weighted smoothing.

The Moving Average Technique

You were actually introduced to a moving average earlier when we discussed how to seasonally adjust the trend-based forecasting model. Consider an example involving the First Fidelity Bank. Bank managers are interested in forecasting the number of new accounts the bank will obtain next month. Table 17–12 contains historical data for the last twelve months. Figure 17–8 shows a graph of the time series. No apparent trend or seasonal components are present in these data.

An *n-period moving average* forecast model is developed as in equation 17–13:

$$\text{Moving average} = \frac{\Sigma n \text{ consecutive } Y \text{ values}}{n} \qquad (17\text{–}13)$$

For instance, in the First Fidelity Bank example, the first four-period moving average is found by averaging the values of Y_1 through Y_4:

$$\text{Moving average} = \frac{40 + 30 + 45 + 50}{4}$$

$$= 41.25$$

TABLE 17–12
New accounts, First Fidelity Bank example

Month t	New Accounts Y_t
1	40
2	30
3	45
4	50
5	60
6	40
7	40
8	35
9	45
10	50
11	40
12	50

This becomes the forecast for period 5. The next moving average is determined by dropping Y_1 and picking up Y_5:

$$\text{Moving average} = \frac{30 + 45 + 50 + 60}{4}$$

$$= 46.25$$

Thus, the forecast for period 6 is 46.25 new accounts. Table 17–13 shows the four-period moving averages through period 12. Note, the forecast for period 13 is the average of the last four data values in the time series.

$$\hat{Y}_{13} = \frac{45 + 50 + 40 + 50}{4}$$

$$= 46.25$$

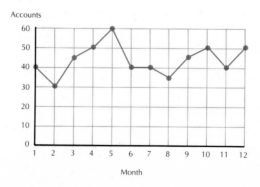

FIGURE 17–8
New accounts, First Fidelity Bank example

TABLE 17–13
Four-period moving average,
First Fidelity Bank example

Month t	New Accounts Y_t	Forecast $\hat{Y}_t$	|Error| $\|Y_t - \hat{Y}_t\|$
1	40		
2	30		
3	45		
4	50		
5	60	41.25	18.75
6	40	46.25	6.25
7	40	48.75	8.75
8	35	47.50	12.50
9	45	43.75	1.25
10	50	40.00	10.00
11	40	42.50	2.50
12	50	42.50	7.50
			67.50

$$\text{MAD} = 67.50/8$$
$$= 8.4375$$

Thus, using a four-period moving average model, the bank managers forecast approximately forty-six new accounts for next month.

Figure 17–9 shows a plot of the actual new accounts versus the forecasted values. The forecasts follow a much smoother pattern than do the original data.

The basic question when using a moving average model is how many periods to include in the moving average. We used four periods in the First Fidelity Bank example. However, the forecast for period 13 will depend on how many periods are included. A five-period moving average model will give a different forecast for period 13:

$$\hat{Y}_{13} = \frac{35 + 45 + 50 + 40 + 50}{5}$$

$$= 44$$

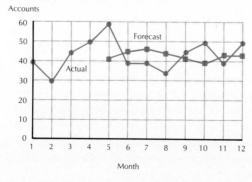

FIGURE 17–9
Plot of actual versus forecast four-period moving average, First Fidelity Bank example

This forecast, produced from the average of the last five periods in the time series, is lower than the forecast from a four-period moving average.

To determine the "best" number of periods to include in a moving average model, try various values and pick the one that gives the smallest MAD. Keep in mind that more smoothing will occur as the number of periods increases. Also be aware that the presence of trends, seasonal patterns, or cycles tends to diminish the effectiveness of the moving average model.

Weighted Moving Average

The **weighted moving average** model is a variation of the moving average approach. The weighted moving average method assigns different weights to the time series values. This might be practical if the decision maker believes the more-current values are more important in determining the forecast.

Consider again the First Fidelity Bank example. Suppose, in a four-period moving average model, the managers believe the most recent value should be considered four times as important as the oldest value. Further, the next most recent value should be considered three times as important as the oldest, with the third most recent value weighted twice the oldest value. In forecasting for period 13, the weighted average for periods 9 through 12 is

$$\hat{Y}_{13} = (1/10)45 + (2/10)50 + (3/10)40 + (4/10)50$$
$$= 46.50$$

Note, the sum of the weights must be 1.0. Note also that this model is simply an extension of the four-period moving average model where the weights are actually 1/4 for each value.

Exponential Smoothing

The trend-based forecasting methods discussed earlier are used in many applications. Least squares regression has the advantage of providing a trend line that "best fits" the historical data. As we showed, the trend line is computed using all available historical data. Each observation is given equal input in establishing the trend line. If the future pattern looks like the past, the forecast should be reasonably acceptable.

In many applications involving time series data, however, the more recent the observation, the more indicative it is of what the future values will be. For example, last month's sales are probably a better indicator of next month's sales than would be sales twenty months ago. However, with regression analysis, the data from twenty periods ago will have the same weight as data from this period in developing a forecasting model. This can be a drawback to the trend-based forecasting approach. A weighted moving average forecast offers one means of overcoming this problem. **Exponential smoothing** is another.

We will introduce two classes of exponential smoothing models: **single exponential smoothing** and **double exponential smoothing.** Although the models are similar in some respects, the double smoothing model is used when the time series exhibits a linear trend. Single smoothing is used when no linear trend is present in the time series. Both single and double exponential smoothing are appropriate for *short-term* forecasting for one or two periods into the future.

Single Exponential Smoothing

Exponential smoothing gets its name from the manner in which the influence of past data is reduced. If the most recent observation is given a weight of 0.20, the observation just before that will have a weight of $0.20(1 - 0.20) = 0.16$, and the observation before that a weight of $0.16(1 - 0.20) = 0.1328$, and so forth. As figure 17–10 shows, the weight assigned to past observations declines exponentially. In the example shown in figure 17–10, data from eight periods back have a weight of 0.03355 compared with the most current period's weight of 0.20. The weight assigned to the most recent observation is called the **smoothing constant,** or **alpha.** In single exponential smoothing, we use just one smoothing constant; double smoothing models use two smoothing constants.

Single exponential smoothing is given by equation 17–14:

$$\hat{Y}_{t+1} = \alpha Y_t + (1 - \alpha)Y_t \qquad (17\text{–}14)$$

where $\hat{Y}_{t+1}$ = forecast value for period $t + 1$
Y_t = actual value for period t
$\hat{Y}_t$ = forecast value for period t
α = alpha (smoothing constant) $(0 \leq \alpha \leq 1)$

Note that the smoothing constant is between 0 and 1. The closer alpha is to zero, the less influence the current observation has in determining the forecast. Small alpha

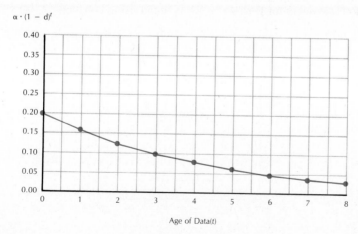

$\alpha \cdot (1 - d)^t$

Age of Data(t)

FIGURE 17–10
Weighting of past observations, exponential smoothing ($\alpha = 0.20$)

TABLE 17–14
Printed circuit sales data,
Humbolt Electronics Company
example

Week t	Sales Y_t
1	400
2	430
3	420
4	440
5	460
6	440
7	470
8	430
9	440
10	420

values will result in greater smoothing of the time series. Likewise, when alpha is near one, the current observations have greater impact in determining the forecast, and less smoothing will occur. There is no firm rule for selecting the appropriate value for the smoothing constant. However, in general, if the time series is quite stable, a small alpha should be used to lessen the impact of random or irregular fluctuations. If the time series contains increases and decreases that are not considered purely random, a larger alpha should be selected to allow the model to more quickly adapt to the changes in the time series.

To demonstrate how the single exponential smoothing model is used, consider the ten weekly sales figures for printed circuits at the Humbolt Electronics Company in northern California. These data are shown in table 17–14 and are graphed in figure 17–11. Suppose the current time period is the end of week 10 and we wish to forecast sales for week 11. We start by selecting an alpha smoothing constant value. We will use $\alpha = 0.20$ in this example.

The forecast value for period $t = 11$ is found using equation 17–14:

$$\hat{Y}_{11} = 0.20\, Y_{10} + (1 - 0.20)\hat{Y}_{10}$$

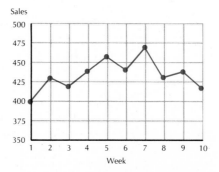

FIGURE 17–11
Printed circuit sales data, Humbolt Electronics Company example

The forecast for period 11 is a weighted average of the actual sales in period 10 and the forecast for period 10. The forecast for period 10 is determined by

$$\hat{Y}_{10} = 0.20 \, Y_9 + (1 - 0.20)\hat{Y}_9$$

Again, this forecast is a weighted average of the actual sales in period 9 and the forecast sales for period 9. We would continue in this manner until we get

$$\hat{Y}_2 = 0.20 \, Y_1 + (1 - 0.20)\hat{Y}_1$$

This requires a forecast for period 1. Since we have no sales data prior to week 1, we assume that $\hat{Y}_1 = Y_1$. This assumption is necessary to set the *starting value*. Because setting the starting value is somewhat arbitrary, you should obtain as many historical data as possible to *warm* the model and *dampen* the effect of the starting value. In our example, we have ten periods of data to warm the model before the forecast for period 11 is made. Note that, because of the form of the exponential smoothing model, the effect of the initial forecast is reduced by $(1 - \alpha)$ in the forecast for period 2, then reduced again for period 3, and so on. After sufficient periods, any error due to the initial forecast will be very small.

Before we would actually use the forecast from the exponential smoothing for decision-making purposes, we would want to determine how successfully the model fits the historical data. Table 17–15 contains the results of using the single exponential smoothing equation for weeks 1 through 10. The column headed $\hat{Y}_{t+1}$ represents the forecast from period t for the next period, $t + 1$. Thus, the last figure in that column, 432.48, is the forecast for week 11. The column headed $\hat{Y}_t$ contains the actual forecasts for periods 2 through 10. These two columns sometimes cause unneeded confusion. Simply, the 406 in week two of the $\hat{Y}_{t+1}$ column is the forecast made in week two *for* week three. It is therefore the forecast value for week three in the $\hat{Y}_t$ column.

Table 17–16 shows the MAD computation for the forecast model with alpha = 0.20. Figure 17–12 shows the plot of the forecast values and the actual values. This plot shows that smoothing has occurred.

Week t	Sales Y_t	Forecast for This Period $\hat{Y}_t$	Forecast for Next Period $\hat{Y}_{t+1}$	
1	400	400	400	**TABLE 17–15**
2	430	400	406	Single exponential smoothing
3	420	406	408.8	results ($\alpha = 0.20$), Humbolt
4	440	408.8	415.04	Electronics Company example
5	460	415.04	424.03	
6	440	424.03	427.22	
7	470	427.22	435.62	
8	430	435.62	434.50	
9	440	434.50	435.60	
10	420	435.60	432.48	

TABLE 17–16
MAD computation, single exponential smoothing ($\alpha = 0.20$), Humbolt Electronics Company example

Week t	Sales Y_t	Forecast $\hat{Y}_t$	Absolute Forecast Error $|Y_t - \hat{Y}_t|$
1	400	400	
2	430	400	30
3	420	406	14
4	440	408.8	31.2
5	460	415.04	44.96
6	440	424.03	15.97
7	470	427.22	42.78
8	430	435.62	5.62
9	440	434.50	5.50
10	420	435.60	15.60
			205.63

$$\text{MAD} = 205.63/10$$
$$= 20.563$$

Our next step would be to try a different alpha and repeat the process. Table 17–17 shows the results of using single exponential smoothing, using an alpha = 0.40. Note that the MAD has been reduced from 20.563 to 17.563 by changing the alpha from 0.20 to 0.40. Thus, if we use the smallest MAD as the selection criterion, alpha = 0.40 will be the better choice. The forecast for period 11, using this latest model, is

$$\hat{Y}_{11} = 0.40(420) + (1 - 0.40)441.80$$
$$= 433.08$$

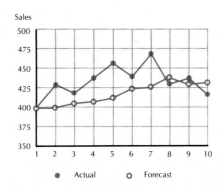

FIGURE 17–12
Plot of forecast versus actual sales, single exponential smoothing, Humbolt Electronics Company example

Week t	Sales Y_t	Forecast $\hat{Y}_t$	Absolute Forecast Error $\lvert Y_t - \hat{Y}_t \rvert$
1	400	400	
2	430	400	30.00
3	420	412	8.00
4	440	415.2	24.80
5	460	425.12	34.88
6	440	439.07	.93
7	470	439.44	30.56
8	430	451.66	21.66
9	440	443.00	3.00
10	420	441.80	21.80
			175.63

TABLE 17–17
MAD computation, single exponential smoothing ($\alpha = 0.40$), Humbolt Electronics Company example

$$\text{MAD} = 175.63/10$$
$$= 17.563$$

This is slightly higher than the forecast produced by the exponential smoothing model with an alpha $= 0.20$ value.

In an actual application you may want to try several different alphas and pick the one that fits the data best based on a MAD or MSE calculation. In fact, many commercial forecasting packages will try a range of alpha values and state which one fits the data best.

The exponential model is easy to update when new data become available. For instance, assume sales for week 11 were actually 440 units. The forecast for week 12, using the model with alpha $= 0.40$, is

$$\hat{Y}_{12} = 0.40(440) + (1 - 0.40)433.08$$
$$= 435.85$$

As you can see, we do not need to go back and recompute the entire model as would have been necessary with a trend-based regression model.

Double Exponential Smoothing

When the time series has an increasing linear trend, forecasts developed using a single exponential smoothing model will constantly be lower than actual sales. When the trend is decreasing, the forecasts will exceed the actual values. A double exponential smoothing model will eliminate this problem.

In double smoothing, a second smoothing constant, beta, is included to account for the trend. Three equations are needed to provide the forecasts. These are equations 17–15, 17–16, and 17–17:

$$C_t = \alpha Y_t + (1 - \alpha)(C_{t-1} + T_{t-1}) \qquad (17\text{--}15)$$
$$T_t = \beta(C_t - C_{t-1}) + (1 - \beta)T_{t-1} \qquad (17\text{--}16)$$
$$\hat{Y}_{t+1} = C_t + T_t \qquad (17\text{--}17)$$

where Y_t = actual value in time t

α = constant process smoothing constant

β = trend-smoothing constant

C_t = smoothed constant process value for period t

T_t = smoothed trend value for period t

$\hat{Y}_{t+1}$ = forecast value for period $t + 1$

t = current time period

Equation 17–15 is used to smooth the time series data. Equation 17–16 is used to smooth the trend, and equation 17–17 combines the two smoothed values to form the forecast for period $t + 1$.

The Billingsly Insurance Company has maintained data on the number of automobile claims filed at their Denver office over the past twelve months. These data are presented in table 17–18 and are graphed in figure 17–13. The claims manager is interested in forecasting claims for month 13. The time series contain a strong upward trend, so a double exponential smoothing model might be selected.

As was the case with single smoothing, we must select starting values for C_t and T_t and values for the smoothing constants α and β. With respect to C_t and T_t, initial values for period $t = 2$ are determined as follows:

$$C_2 = Y_1$$
$$= 38$$

TABLE 17–18
Claims data, Billingsly Insurance Company example

Month t	Claims Y_t
1	38
2	44
3	40
4	48
5	55
6	68
7	64
8	70
9	75
10	70
11	78
12	82

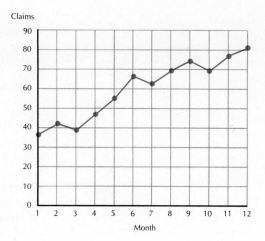

FIGURE 17–13
Claims data, Billingsly Insurance Company example

and

$$T_2 = Y_2 - Y_1$$
$$= 44 - 38$$
$$= 6$$

Then, the forecast for period 3 made at the end of period 2 is

$$\hat{Y}_3 = 38 + 6$$
$$= 44$$

The choice for smoothing constant values revolves around the same issues as discussed earlier with respect to single smoothing. That is, use smoothing constants closer to 1.0 when less smoothing is desired and values closer to 0.0 when more smoothing is desired. The larger the value, the more impact current data have on the forecast. Suppose, we use $\alpha = 0.20$ and $\beta = 0.30$ in this example.

At the close of period 3, in which actual claims were forty, the smoothing equations are updated as follows:

$$C_3 = 0.20(40) + (1 - 0.20)(38 + 6)$$
$$= 43.2$$
$$T_3 = 0.30(43.2 - 38) + (1 - 0.30)(6)$$
$$= 5.76$$

Then, the forecast for period 4 is

$$\hat{Y}_4 = 43.2 + 5.76$$
$$= 48.96$$

TABLE 17–19

Double exponential smoothing ($\alpha = 0.20$, $\beta = 0.30$), Billingsly Insurance Company example

t	Y_t	C_t	T_t	$\hat{Y}_t$	$|Y_t - \hat{Y}_t|$
1	38	—	—	—	—
2	44	38	6	38	—
3	40	43.2	5.76	44	4.00
4	48	48.768	5.7024	48.96	0.96
5	55	55.57632	5.734175	54.4704	0.5296
6	68	61.3464	6.195547	60.3105	7.6895
7	64	67.23516	5.952912	68.04395	4.04395
8	70	72.55046	5.761626	73.18808	3.18808
9	75	77.64968	5.562904	78.31209	3.31209
10	70	80.57006	4.770149	83.21256	13.21258
11	78	83.87217	4.329736	85.34021	7.34021
12	82	86.96152	3.957622	88.20191	6.20191
					50.47792

$$\text{MAD} = 50.47792/10$$
$$= 5.0478$$

We then repeat the process through period 12 to find the forecast for period 13. Table 17–19 shows the results of the computations and the MAD value. Figure 17–14 shows the actual time series and forecasts. The forecast for period 13 is

$$\hat{Y}_{13} = C_{12} + T_{12}$$
$$= 90.91914$$

Thus, based upon this double exponential smoothing model, the Billingsly Insurance Company would forecast the number of claims for period 13 to be about 91. Before they settle on this forecast, different smoothing constants would be tried to determine if a smaller MAD can be found.

Double Exponential Smoothing or Linear Trend Analysis?

Double exponential smoothing is used when the time series data show an increasing trend. But earlier in this chapter we discussed linear trend analysis as a forecasting tool to use in the same situation. Is there a way to decide between the two forecasting techniques? Yes, but it is often an art. Some points for the decision maker to consider are

1. The best fit double exponential smoothing model can be compared, using the MAD or MSE, with the linear trend model. The model with the smaller MAD (or MSE) value has fit the past data better and *may* fit future data better.
2. If the environment in which the data were gathered in the past was stable, and

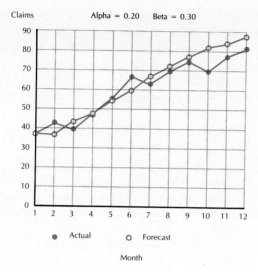

FIGURE 17–14
Plot of actual versus forecast double exponential smoothing ($\alpha = 0.20$, $\beta = 0.30$), Bill-ingsly Insurance Company example

no changes are foreseen in the immediate future, the linear trend model may be appropriate.

3. If the environment the decision maker is trying to forecast in is changing rapidly, more recent data may be more important than past data. In this case double exponential smoothing may be appropriate because it allows us to weight the more recent observations heavier.

SKILL DEVELOPMENT PROBLEMS FOR SECTION 17–6

The following set of problems is meant to test your understanding of the material in this section. Additional problems are found at the end of this chapter under this section heading.

10. Refer to the sales data given in problem 1 in section 17–4. You have worked with these data in each of the last two sections.

a. Prepare a four-period moving average forecast for the next quarter.

b. Prepare a weighted moving average forecast for the next period, with successive weights being 0.1, 0.2, 0.3, and 0.4.

c. Prepare a single exponential smoothing model forecast for the next period with an alpha value of 0.25.

d. Use the MAD value to determine which of the forecasts prepared in parts a, b, and c is best.

11. Refer to the inventory data given in problem 2 in section 17–4. You have worked with these data in the last two sections.
   a. Prepare a four-period moving average forecast for the next quarter.
   b. Prepare a weighted moving average forecast for the next period, with successive weights being 0.2, 0.2, 0.3, and 0.3.
   c. Prepare a single exponential smoothing model forecast for the next period, using an alpha value of 0.3.
   d. Prepare a double exponential smoothing model forecast for the next period, using an alpha of 0.2 and a beta of 0.3.
   e. Use the MAD value to determine which of the four forecasts prepared is best.

12. Let's return to the Don Glidden Video Excitement example last considered in problem 9. Refer to the five years of sales volume data in problem 5, section 17–4.
   a. Prepare single exponential smoothing models from these data, using alpha values of 0.2 and 0.3.
   b. Prepare double exponential smoothing models from these data, using an alpha of 0.25 and a beta of 0.3 and then an alpha of 0.4 and a beta of 0.5.
   c. Use the MAD value to determine which of the models developed in parts a and b best fit the sales data. (You might want to use a computer program to solve this problem.)

A BRIEF LOOK AT BOX-JENKINS FORECASTING

17-7   Several times in this chapter we have stated that forecasting is an art, not a science. Let's outline some factors that make it an art.

1. In any forecasting situation, choosing the model to use is generally a judgment call, as is the amount of past data to use and the forecasting period. Often, using different amounts of past data will lead to different forecasting models and someone must decide how much past data to use.

2. For many forecasting models there is really no way to determine whether the model developed is optimal. Often model determination involves trial and error, with a little luck thrown in.

3. Those models that use regression analysis are generally used in situations that violate assumptions necessary to apply regression. In particular, there is no guarantee the underlying distributions of time series data are normal, which is required for regression analysis. In addition, the distributions are probably not stable from one observation period to the next, which is also required for regression analysis. Finally, a regression model is valid only over the range contained in the observed data, and time series trend forecasts extend beyond this range.

4. In earlier chapters on estimation we emphasized that realistic estimates should contain an indication of how accurate the estimate is; therefore we developed confidence interval estimates. Yet, so far in forecasting, we have been using only point estimates. The reason is that for the models considered up to now

we have no guarantee the forecasting errors are normally distributed and thus cannot develop realistic interval estimates.

At this point you may be wondering, with all these problems with statistical models, why bother? The reason, of course, is that forecasts made using imperfect models are vastly superior to no forecasts at all. However, these problems with most statistical forecasting models caused enough worry that the Box-Jenkins model technique, introduced in 1970, caused widespread excitement.

A full development of Box-Jenkins modeling is beyond the scope of this book. However, since many organizations have begun to implement the Box-Jenkins approach, you should be generally aware of the model. In this section we will limit our discussion to considering its advantages and disadvantages and to outlining its general form.

Advantages of Box-Jenkins Models

Box-Jenkins models address many of the concerns raised in the last section about conventional time series models:

1. For any particular time series the Box-Jenkins forecasting model will be optimal in terms of fitting the data pattern and minimizing the forecast error measured by MSE.
2. The Box-Jenkins approach allows for a systematic procedure for model development. It will determine the model that is best for any given set of time series data.
3. The forecasting errors generated by a Box-Jenkins model will be normally distributed, and therefore confidence interval estimates can be made.
4. The model can be extended to allow for forecasting in those cases where the time series distributions are not stationary.

As you can see, this forecasting technique has some impressive advantages.

Disadvantages of Box-Jenkins Forecasting

The disadvantages of Box-Jenkins forecasting models generally fall into two categories:

1. A wide variety of studies have shown that the forecasts generated by Box-Jenkins models are not, in all cases, significantly better than those generated by forecasting techniques considered earlier in this chapter.
2. A practical test of how useful a forecasting model is to operational organizations is
   a. the model must be simple enough to be understood by those using it, or
   b. the model must be so good that people can simply use its output without understanding it.

A Box-Jenkins model will almost never be the simplest model available and is certainly difficult to understand. In addition, its forecasts are often not better than those generated by simpler models. Therefore, at this point in time, although organizations are beginning to employ the Box-Jenkins model, it is not the dominant forecasting technique for most of them.

Types of Box-Jenkins Models

Forecasting models generated by Box-Jenkins techniques can be placed into one of three categories: autoregressive models, moving average models, and mixed autoregressive and moving average models.

Autoregressive models

The autoregressive model has a generalized form of equation 17–9:

$$\hat{Y}_t = \phi_0 + \phi_1 Y_{t-1} + \phi_2 Y_{t-2} + \phi_3 Y_{t-3} + \cdot\cdot\cdot + \phi_k Y_{t-k} + E_t$$

where (similar to our previous regression models)

$$\phi_0 = \text{the intercept value}$$
$$\phi_{t-i} = \text{the slope coefficients for } i = 1 \text{ to } k$$
$$E_t = \text{the error term}$$

Moving-Average Models

The generalized moving-average model has the following form:

$$\hat{Y}_t = \theta_0 + \theta_1 E_{t-1} + \theta_2 E_{t-2} + \theta_3 E_{t-3} + \cdot\cdot\cdot + \theta_k E_{t-k} + E_t$$

where $\theta_0 = \text{the intercept value}$
$\theta_{t-i} = \text{the slope coefficients for periods } t - 1 \text{ to } t - k$
E_{t-1} through $E_{t-k} = \text{forecasting errors for the past } k \text{ periods}$
$E_t = \text{the error term for the most recent period}$

Mixed Autoregressive and Moving Average Models

As you might suspect, the mixed model has the following form:

$$\hat{Y}_t = \phi_0 + \phi_1 Y_{t-1} + \phi_2 Y_{t-2} + \phi_3 Y_{t-3} + \cdot\cdot\cdot + \phi_k Y_{t-k}$$
$$+$$
$$+ \theta_1 E_{t-1} + \theta_2 E_{t-2} + \theta_3 E_{t-3} + \cdot\cdot\cdot + \theta_k E_{t-k} + E_t$$

where the previous intercept, coefficient, and error term definitions continue to hold.

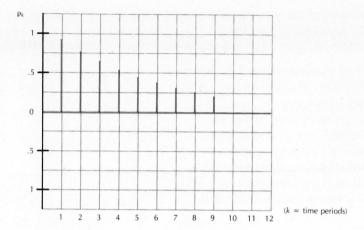

FIGURE 17–15
Hypothetical autocorrelogram

Identifying the Appropriate Model and Estimating Its Parameters

Identifying the appropriate Box-Jenkins model to use in any situation is difficult and at present involves considerable judgment based on experience. However, the identification involves calculating correlations and partial correlations (you might want to review the discussion of correlation coefficients and partial correlation coefficients from chapter 13). For instance, we could determine the correlation existing between all possible values of Y_t and Y_{t-1}, all possible values of Y_t and Y_{t-2}, and so forth. These correlations can be used to identify patterns in the time series data. If higher than average Y values are followed by higher than average values k periods later, the correlation will be positive. However, if higher than average Y values are followed by lower than average values k periods later, the correlation will be negative.

These correlation values are then graphed as an autocorrelogram. The pattern of correlations shown on the autocorrelogram indicates which of the three types of Box-Jenkins model should be used for a particular set of time series data. A hypothetical autocorrelogram is shown in figure 17–15.

In a manner similar to that of determining the correlations between all values of Y_t and all possible lagged values of Y, partial correlations could be found for the same lagged relationships. These partial correlations are plotted as a partial autocorrelogram, which is also used in the model identification stage.

CONCLUSIONS

17-8

This chapter has introduced a variety of forecasting techniques, both judgmental and statistical; our discussion, however, is not complete. An entire semester or more could be devoted to the subject and still not do it justice. Our objective has been to provide insight into some of the more frequently used techniques and to acquaint you with some terminology pertaining to forecasting.

A number of statistical forecasting techniques were introduced, including

- Trend projection (linear and nonlinear)
- Seasonally adjusted trend projection
- Moving average
- Single exponential smoothing
- Double exponential smoothing
- Indicator variable regression models
- Autoregressive regression models
- Mixed autoregression models
- Box-Jenkins forecasting models

Regardless of which model is considered, you should recognize that the success of the model is determined by two factors:

1. How well the model fits the historical time series
2. How much the future time series looks like the past

Ultimately, the best forecasting method is the one that provides the best forecasts.

We have observed that when a short-term forecast is needed on a fairly regular basis, a heavy reliance is placed on statistical techniques. For example, a company determining how many units of materials to purchase for its fabrication plant on a weekly basis will tend to use a statistical model such as exponential smoothing and may have the forecasting process tied in with the inventory system. A periodic review will be conducted to determine whether the model is performing satisfactorily. When the planning horizon is longer term, we have observed that decision makers tend to incorporate some qualitative judgment along with the statistical models. For instance, in the annual budgeting process, you will likely see a manager obtain a sales forecast from a technique such as a regression-based model and then adjust this forecast according to the judgment of his or her managers. When long-term forecasts of five or more years are involved, the tendency has been to place greater reliance on qualitative judgment methods and less reliance on statistical models.

Finally, regardless of the length of the planning horizon, our experience is that decision makers generally combine forecasting methods to arrive at a final forecast. This generally involves using some form of statistical forecasting to arrive at a base forecast, which is then adjusted through a qualitative judgment process. This practice is consistent with the premise we have set forth in this text that statistical models should be used to provide information for the decision process *but the decisions are made by people*.

CHAPTER GLOSSARY

alpha   The smoothing constant used in exponential smoothing to indicate the relative weight placed on the most recent observations versus the historical observations.

autocorrelation   Correlation between adjacent residuals in a time series regression model.

deseasonalizing   The process of removing the seasonal component from a time series.

double exponential smoothing   An exponential smoothing forecasting model that incorporates a second smoothing statistic to account for the trend in the time series.

exponential smoothing   A forecasting technique that weights the current data more heavily than the past data. The weights placed on the older observations decrease exponentially over time.

forecast error   The difference between the actual value of a time series and the forecasted value. This is also referred to as the residual.

forecasting   The process of predicting what the future will be like.

forecasting horizon   The number of periods in the future covered by the forecasting model. Sometimes referred to as the forecast lead time.

forecasting interval   The frequency with which new forecasts are prepared.

forecasting period   The unit of time for which forecasts are made. The period may be a day, week, month, quarter, or year.

immediate term horizon   Less than one month into the future.

indicator variable   An independent variable in a regression model measured at time $t - m$ used in forecasting the dependent variable in time t.

linear trend   A long-term increase or decrease in a time series in which the rate of change is relatively constant.

long-term horizon   Two years or more into the future.

mean absolute deviation   The average of the absolute differences between the actual time series value and the forecast value.

medium-term horizon   Three months to two years into the future.

model diagnosis   The process of analyzing the quality of the model employed.

model fitting   The process of determining how well a specified model fits past data.

model specification   The process of selecting the forecasting technique to be used in a particular application.

moving average   The average of n consecutive values of a time series.

nonlinear trend   An increase or decrease in a time series where the rate of change is not constant.

random component   Changes in the time series data that are unpredictable and cannot be associated with the trend, seasonal, or cyclical components.

ratio to moving average   The actual value of the time series divided by the centered moving average. This is a step in the process of constructing seasonal indexes.

residual   The difference between the actual value of the time series and the forecast value. This is also called the forecast error.

seasonal index   A number used to quantify the effect of seasonality in time series data. Indexes exceeding 1.0 imply that the period has values higher than normal; values less than 1.0 imply values for the period are typically lower than normal.

seasonally unadjusted forecast   A forecast, made for seasonal data, that does not include an adjustment for the seasonal component in the time series.

short-term horizon   One to three months into the future.

smoothing constant   The value (also called alpha) that determines the weight placed on the most current observation in an exponential smoothing model.

weighted moving average   A moving average with weights assigned to the time series values.

CHAPTER FORMULAS

Linear trend projection

$$\hat{Y}_t = b_0 + b_1 t$$

Multiplicative model

$$Y_t = T_t \cdot S_t \cdot C_t \cdot I_t$$

Deseasonalizing

$$Y_t/S_t = T_t \cdot C_t \cdot I_t$$

Nonlinear trend projection

$$\hat{Y}_t = b_0 + b_1 t + b_2 t^2 + b_3 t^3$$

Moving average

$$\text{Moving average} = \frac{\Sigma n \text{ consecutive } Y \text{ values}}{n}$$

Single exponential smoothing

$$\hat{Y}_{t+1} = \alpha Y_t + (1 - \alpha)\hat{Y}_t$$

Double exponential smoothing

$$C_t = \alpha Y_t + (1 - \alpha)(C_{t-1} + T_{t-1})$$
$$T_t = \beta(C_t - C_{t-1}) + (1 - \beta)T_{t-1}$$
$$\hat{Y}_{t+1} = C_t + T_t$$

Indicator variable regression model—one variable

$$\hat{Y}_t = b_0 + b_1 (X_{1t})$$

Indicator variable regression model—multiple variables

$$\hat{Y}_t = b_0 + b_1 X_{1t} + b_2 X_{2t} + \ldots b_k X_{kt}$$

Autoregressive model

$$\hat{Y}_t = b_0 + b_1 Y_{t-1} + b_2 Y_{t-2}$$

SOLVED PROBLEMS

1. The annual sales for Safeway, the grocery retailing giant, for twelve years are

Year	t	Sales (Y) (billions of dollars)
1974	1	8.185
1975	2	9.717
1976	3	10.443
1977	4	11.249
1978	5	12.551
1979	6	13.718
1980	7	15.103
1981	8	16.580
1982	9	17.633
1983	10	18.585
1984	11	19.642
1985	12	19.651

a. Fit a least squares regression line to these data, using time as the independent variable.

b. Discuss whether the linear regression line seems to be a good model to use on these data.

c. Use the regression line developed in part a to forecast sales for the next two years. How would you feel about using this as a forecasting model?

Solutions:

a. Using equations 13–8 and 13–9 to determine the slope and intercept of the regression line, we find

$$b_1 = \frac{\Sigma S_t - (\Sigma S \Sigma t)/n}{\Sigma t^2 - (\Sigma t)^2/n}$$

$$= \frac{1283.789 - (173.057)(78)/12}{650 - (6084)/12}$$

$$= 158.919/143$$

$$= 1.111$$

$$b_0 = \Sigma S/n - b_1 \Sigma t/n$$
$$= 173.057/12 - (1.111)(78)/12$$
$$= 7.198$$

b. We can best answer this question by comparing the values predicted by the regression line with the actual observed values:

Year	Sales	Predicted Sales
	(billions of dollars)	
1974	8.185	8.311
1975	9.717	9.422
1976	10.443	10.533
1977	11.249	11.644
1978	12.551	12.755
1979	13.718	13.866
1980	15.103	14.977
1981	16.580	16.088
1982	17.663	17.199
1983	18.585	18.310
1984	19.642	19.420
1985	19.651	20.500

By comparing the actual sales values with the predicted values, we see the model does quite a good job of tracking the actual sales. Some concern may be caused by the fact the increase in sales between 1984 and 1985 is very small. Since we know some firms experience a leveling off in sales, we might well question whether the predicted 1.111 billion increase per year would continue in the future.

c. Assuming the model will work for the next two years, we would predict sales to be

$$\text{Sales (86)} = 7.198 + 1.11(13) = 21.6 \text{ billion}$$

$$\text{Sales (87)} = 22.7 \text{ billion}$$

This forecast would be subject to the concern expressed in part b.

2. Below are the quarterly sales figures, in thousands, for keyboards the Datakey Company makes and sells to personal computer manufacturers. Datakey has decided to try exponential smoothing as a forecasting technique:

1985	1	14.7
	2	17.3
	3	15.5
	4	15.5
1986	1	21.2
	2	27.1
	3	25.9
	4	23.0
1987	1	33.1

a. Using an alpha of 0.2, use a single smoothing model to prepare a forecast for the next quarter. Assume your forecast for the first period is correct.

b. Use a double smoothing model with a trend smoothing constant of 0.3 and a process smoothing constant of 0.2 to prepare a forecast for next period.

c. If you were to recommend one of the two models, which would you choose and why?

Solutions

a. The forecast for the next quarter is found by using equation 17–14 and determining the values in the following table.

Period t	Demand Y_t	Forecast for This Period $\hat{Y}_t$	Forecast for Next Period $\hat{Y}_{t+1}$
85–1	14.7	14.7	14.7
–2	17.3	14.7	15.22
–3	15.5	15.22	15.28*
–4	15.5	15.28	15.32
86–1	21.2	15.32	16.50
–2	27.1	16.50	18.62
–3	25.9	18.62	20.08
–4	23.0	20.08	20.66
87–1	33.1	20.66	23.15

*Values from this point rounded to nearest 0.01.

b. Using equations 17–15, 17–16, and 17–17, with an alpha of 0.2 and a beta of 0.3, we find the following table of values:

t	Y_t	C_t	T_t	$\hat{Y}_t$
85–1	14.7	—	—	—
–2	17.3	14.7	2.6	—
–3	15.5	16.94	2.49*	17.3
–4	15.5	18.64	2.25	19.43
86–1	21.2	20.95	2.27	20.89
–2	27.1	24.00	2.50	23.22
–3	25.9	26.38	2.46	26.5
–4	23.0	27.67	2.11	28.84
87–1	33.1	30.44	2.31	29.78
				32.75

c. When comparing the results of the two smoothing models, we see the single smoothing model lags the increasing sales. The double smoothing model does a much better job following the sales figures. This should not surprise you since the double smoothing model is designed to be used in situations where a trend exists.

ADDITIONAL PROBLEMS

Section 17–4

13. Circle Manufacturing in Lincoln, Nebraska, manufactures center-point pivot irrigation systems. Sales for the past fifteen years are

Year	Sales
1974	$ 266,000
1975	256,000
1976	404,000
1977	556,000
1978	776,000
1979	1,008,000
1980	1,226,000
1981	1,490,000
1982	1,950,000
1983	2,467,000
1984	2,671,000
1985	3,334,000
1986	2,463,000
1987	3,395,000
1988	4,660,000

a. Develop a linear trend forecasting model for these data. Use this model to forecast sales for the next three years.

b. Develop a least squares regression model, with the square of time as the independent variable. Use this model to forecast sales for the next three years.

c. Which of the two models just developed would you feel most comfortable with? Discuss.

d. Use the Durbin-Watson test statistic to determine whether either of the models shows signs of autocorrelation.

14. Fast-In-N-Out opened its breakfast and lunch restaurant near a midwestern university fifteen years ago. Since that time the organization has been rapidly expanding by offering a limited menu of low-cost meals. Sales for the past fifteen years are

Year	Sales	Year	Sales
1975	$2,400,000	1983	$11,300,000
1976	3,700,000	1984	12,400,000
1977	3,900,000	1985	14,000,000
1978	4,100,000	1986	15,900,000
1979	5,800,000	1987	18,600,000
1980	7,500,000	1988	23,400,000
1981	8,700,000	1989	25,200,000
1982	8,600,000		

a. Develop a linear trend forecasting model for these data. Use this model to fore-cast sales for the next three years.

b. Would you feel comfortable with the forecast made in part a? Discuss.

c. Use the Durbin-Watson test statistic to determine whether the model shows signs of autocorrelation.

15. Sal's Books has had a store in the Towne Square Mall for the past four years. Sally Rodgers, the owner, has kept records on monthly sales for the four years. These data are

Month	Sales	Month	Sales
Jan 1	$33,500	Jan 25	$41,000
2	31,700	26	40,400
3	28,750	27	39,800
4	32,000	28	42,500
5	33,000	29	44,500
6	36,200	30	43,800
7	37,300	31	44,200
8	39,300	32	46,700
9	41,200	33	49,700
10	44,200	34	52,400
11	49,500	35	53,600
12	53,400	36	57,400
Jan 13	33,500	Jan 37	42,400
14	33,400	38	45,600
15	31,400	39	41,200
16	34,200	40	44,600
17	36,900	41	46,800
18	39,700	42	45,700
19	41,100	43	47,500
20	42,400	44	50,000
21	44,500	45	53,200
22	45,700	46	56,700
23	52,000	47	60,100
24	52,600	48	62,100

a. Determine the $T \cdot C$ portion of the multiplicative model of this time series by computing a twelve-month and then a centered twelve-month moving average.

b. Estimate the $S \cdot I$ portion of the multiplicative model by finding the ratio to moving average for the time series. Indicate whether these values are stable from year to year.

c. Calculate the normalized monthly indexes for these data. Discuss the meaning of these indexes.

d. Use the values found in part c to adjust a trend forecast for next year's sales. How much confidence would you have in this forecast?

16. Ned Thayer is the recently appointed service manager for Sundance Motors in Jacksonville, Florida. Ned has been told by the owner the service department will be considered as a profit center and part of Ned's salary will be determined by just how profitable the department is. Ned reasons that forecasting the demand in his department will help him control costs, and therefore increase profits. Unfortunately, Ned can find records only on the number of cars repaired monthly for the last three years. These data are

Month	Cars Serviced	Month	Cars Serviced
Jan 1	2,691	19	2,730
2	2,810	20	2,850
3	2,260	21	2,640
4	2,150	22	2,610
5	2,035	23	2,890
6	2,517	24	3,005
7	2,245	Jan 25	2,960
8	2,480	26	2,865
9	2,076	27	2,810
10	1,880	28	2,685
11	2,465	29	2,560
12	2,925	30	2,730
Jan 13	2,740	31	2,620
14	2,908	32	2,770
15	2,780	33	2,650
16	2,570	34	2,475
17	2,390	35	2,905
18	2,580	36	3,240

a. Determine the $T \cdot C$ portion of the multiplicative model for this time series by computing a twelve-month and then a centered twelve-month moving average.
b. Estimate the $S \cdot I$ portion of the multiplicative model by finding the ratio to moving average for the time series. Indicate whether these values are stable from year to year.
c. Calculate the normalized monthly indexes for these data. Discuss the meaning of these indexes.
d. Use the values found in part c to adjust a trend forecast for next year's service demand. How much use do you think this forecast will be for Ned?

17. Bob Stickle has just purchased the franchise for three fish and chips restaurants in Bridgeport, Maine. The negotiated price called for payments of $5,000 per month plus 1 percent of monthly sales. Sales data for the last five years are (× $100,000)

Month	1984	1985	1986	1987	1988
Jan	5.2	4.7	6.6	7.1	7.0
Feb	3.3	2.9	4.0	4.0	6.2
Mar	2.8	3.0	3.6	2.6	4.3
Apr	5.3	6.3	7.2	8.0	9.5
May	9.4	10.0	11.4	7.8	12.5
June	10.6	12.3	12.0	11.4	12.4
July	9.2	10.7	11.0	11.3	11.6
Aug	7.2	7.5	6.8	8.2	8.4
Sept	6.8	5.8	6.8	7.9	6.9
Oct	9.7	9.6	8.9	9.3	9.8
Nov	13.6	13.9	14.2	16.1	16.5
Dec	11.8	11.9	12.7	13.8	14.6

a. Determine the seasonal index number for each month, using the ratio to moving average method.

b. Is there enough consistency between years to make you comfortable using index numbers?

c. Use a linear trend model adjusted for seasonality to estimate the monthly payments Bob will have to make next year. Discuss factors that make you think this is, or is not, a good forecasting model.

Section 17–5

18. You have been hired by the vice-president of your university to develop a forecasting model for admissions for fall term. The vice-president wants a regression-based model with explanatory variables. Provide a list of potential explanatory variables and show the form of the regression model.

19. Referring to problem 18, collect data for the variables you have proposed, going back at least ten years. Remember that you need at least four times the number of observations as you have independent variables in the model.

Develop a regression model and provide a forecast one year ahead. (*Note.* A computer and a statistical package will be required to do this problem.)

20. In problem 16 you prepared a forecast for service manager Ned Thayer on the following data indicating cars serviced per month.

Month	Cars Serviced	Month	Cars Serviced
Jan 1	2,691	7	2,245
2	2,810	8	2,480
3	2,260	9	2,076
4	2,150	10	1,880
5	2,035	11	2,465
6	2,517	12	2,825

Month	Cars Serviced	Month	Cars Serviced
Jan 13	2,740	Jan 25	2,960
14	2,908	26	2,865
15	2,780	27	2,810
16	2,570	28	2,685
17	2,390	29	2,560
18	2,580	30	2,730
19	2,730	31	2,620
20	2,850	32	2,770
21	2,640	33	2,650
22	2,610	34	2,475
23	2,890	35	2,905
24	3,005	36	3,240

a. Analyze these data using a one-month lagged autoregressive model
b. Analyze these data using twelve-month lagged autoregressive model.
c. Using MSE and MAD measurements of how well a model fits data, indicate which of the models found in parts a and b you would recommend to Ned.
d. If you were assigned problem 16 also, compare the model found there with the two autoregressive models. Which technique seems to work best on these data?

21. In problem 17, you prepared a forecast of monthly franchise fees for Bob Stickle. Refer to the monthly sales data in that problem.
a. Analyze these data using a one-month lagged autoregressive model.
b. Analyze these data using a twelve-month lagged autoregressive model.
c. Using MSE and MAD measurements of how well a model fits data, indicate which of the models found in parts a and b you would recommend to Bob.
d. If you were assigned problem 17 also, compare the model found there with the two autoregressive models. Which technique seems to work best on these data?

Section 17–6

22. What factors should be considered when choosing a smoothing constant in exponential smoothing? Discuss.

23. The Acme Computer Corporation has been operating for twenty-four months and has maintained monthly sales records for this entire period. These data are

Month	Sales	Month	Sales
1	$145,000	8	$178,000
2	95,000	9	130,000
3	135,000	10	190,000
4	206,000	11	98,000
5	176,000	12	135,000
6	90,000	13	234,000
7	126,000	14	176,000

Month	Sales	Month	Sales
15	$78,000	20	$145,000
16	150,000	21	189,000
17	180,000	22	80,000
18	89,000	23	140,000
19	167,000	24	178,000

Use a first-order exponential smoothing model with a smoothing constant equal to 0.10 and develop a forecasting model for forecasting ahead one period. Evaluate the model by computing both the MSE and MAD. The smaller these are, the better the forecast model generally is.

24. Using the Acme Computer data from problem 23, use first-order exponential smoothing to develop a one-period-ahead forecasting model with a smoothing constant of 0.50. Compute the MSE and MAD as described in problem 23.

25. Again using the Acme Computer data, construct a four-period moving average model from problem 23.

26. Refer to the Circle Manufacturing data from problem 13.
    a. Construct a three-year moving average model, using the same data, and use this model to forecast sales for the next period.
    b. Construct a first-order exponential smoothing model, using an alpha of 0.3, and use this model to forecast sales for the next year.
    c. Construct a second-order exponential smoothing model, with a beta of 0.2 and an alpha of 0.25, to forecast next year's sales.
    d. Use the MAD values for the three models to determine which has the best fit to the past data.

27. Refer to the Fast-In-N-Out data from problem 14.
    a. Construct a four-year moving average model, using the same data, and use this model to forecast sales for the next period.
    b. Construct a first-order exponential smoothing model, using an alpha of 0.4, and use this model to forecast sales for the next year.
    c. Construct a second-order exponential smoothing model, with a beta of 0.3 and an alpha of 0.2, to forecast next year's sales.
    d. Use the MAD values for the three models to determine which has the best fit to the past data.

28. Refer to the Ned Thayer data from problem 16.
    a. Construct a four-month moving average model, using the same data, and use this model to forecast sales for the next period.
    b. Construct a first-order exponential smoothing model, using an alpha of 0.2, and use this model to forecast sales for the next year.
    c. Construct a second-order exponential smoothing model, with a beta of 0.2 and an alpha of 0.2, to forecast next year's sales.

d. Use the MAD values for the three models to determine which has the best fit to the past data.

29. The building permit section for a medium-size midwestern city has issued the following numbers of single-family building permits over the past ten years:

Year	Permits	Year	Permits
1979	1500	1984	1350
1980	1470	1985	1180
1981	2100	1986	1550
1982	2380	1987	2000
1983	2050	1988	2040

a. Construct single exponential smoothing models for these data, using alpha values of 0.2, 0.5, and 0.8. The city council is asking for a permit forecast for next year. Which value would you use to forecast permits to be issued?
b. Construct double exponential smoothing models, using the alpha values given in part a for the constant process smoothing values and trend smoothing values of 0.2, 0.4, and 0.6. What conclusions can you draw about the relation between the two smoothing constants?

30. For the permit section data contained in problem 29, if you had to forecast levels for next year, would you use a single or double smoothing model? Discuss.

C A S E S

17A   Medical Center Hospital

R. T. Trusty, the administrator of Medical Center Hospital, recently hired U. R. Regis Consulting Firm to study the medical center's admissions and develop a model for predicting future admissions. Because of the emphasis on long-range planning, Mr. Trusty needs a good admissions forecasting model. U. R. Regis collected data for the past ten years on the following variables:

VAR01	Admissions in year t
VAR02	Area population in year t
VAR03	Number of doctors in the area in year t
VAR04	Crime rate per 1,000 people in year t
VAR05	Average annual temperature in year t
VAR06	Number of vehicles registered in the county in year t
VAR07	Hospital capacity in year t
VAR08	Average daily patient cost in year t

TABLE 17C–1
Means and standard deviations

****

VARIABLE	MEAN	STD. DEV.	CASES
VAR01	5545.2000	2392.0319	10
VAR02	35860.0000	12655.9779	10
VAR03	22.8000	6.5625	10
VAR04	2.9700	1.0338	10
VAR05	65.6000	3.6878	10
VAR06	18563.5000	7398.9617	10
VAR07	6940.0000	2531.6661	10
VAR08	109.4000	23.3248	10

****

U. R. Regis Consulting provided a printout of its work but no written report or evaluation of the model's usefulness.

Since Mr. Trusty is a little shaky on regression analysis, he would like you to write a short, but accurate synopsis of the printouts in tables 17C–1 through 17C–4. Be sure to indicate any attributes the model has relative to Medical Center Hospital's needs, as well as any potential problems with the model.

TABLE 17C–2
Correlation matrix

	VAR01	VAR02	VAR03	VAR04	VAR05	VAR06	VAR07	VAR08
VAR01	1.000	.948	.932	.280	.308	.945	.944	.962
VAR02	.948	1.000	.955	.175	.060	.922	.892	.913
VAR03	.932	.955	1.000	.191	.239	.836	.869	.905
VAR04	.280	.175	.191	1.000	.460	.207	.378	.298
VAR05	.308	.060	.239	.460	1.000	.167	.294	.387
VAR06	.945	.922	.836	.207	.167	1.000	.856	.893
VAR07	.944	.892	.869	.378	.294	.856	1.000	.940
VAR08	.962	.913	.905	.298	.387	.893	.940	1.000

TABLE 17C–3
Step 1 of the regression output

****************************** MULTIPLE REGRESSIØN *****************************

DEPENDENT VARIABLE   VAR01   ADMISSIØNS

VARIABLE(S) ENTERED ØN STEP NUMBER 1   VAR08   CØST

- -

MULTIPLE R	.96258
R SQUARE	.92657
ADJUSTED R SQUARE	.91739
STANDARD ERRØR	687.51747

- -

ANALYSIS ØF VARIANCE	D.F.	SUM ØF SQUARES	MEAN SQUARE	F
REGRESSIØN	1	47714909.45544	47714909.45544	100.94542
RESIDUAL (UNEXPLAINED)	8	3781442.14456	472680.26807	

- - - - - - - - - - - - - - VARIABLES IN THE EQUATIØN - - - - - - - - - - - - - -

VARIABLE	B	STD. ERRØR B	F
VAR08	98.71624	9.82529	100.945
(CØNSTANT)	− 5254.35671		

- - - - - - - - - - - - - - VARIABLES NØT IN THE EQUATIØN - - - - - - - - - - - - - -

VARIABLE	PARTIAL	F
VAR02	.62262	4.431
VAR03	.53046	2.741
VAR04	− .02570	.005
VAR05	− .25797	.499
VAR06	.70780	7.028
VAR07	.43235	1.609

** *******

TABLE 17C–4

Step 2 of the regression output

****************************** MULTIPLE REGRESSIØN ******************************

VARIABLE(S) ENTERED ØN STEP NUMBER 2   VAR06   VEHICLES

MULTIPLE R	.98151
R SQUARE	.96336
ADJUSTED R SQUARE	.95289
STANDARD ERRØR	519.20279

ANALYSIS ØF VARIANCE	D.F.	SUM ØF SQUARES	MEAN SQUARE	F
REGRESSIØN	2	49609350.84590	24804675.42295	92.01519
RESIDUAL (UNEXPLAINED)	7	1887000.75410	269571.53630	

---------------- VARIABLES IN THE EQUATIØN ----------------

VARIABLE	B	STD. ERRØR B	F
VAR08	59.67294	16.49146	13.093
VAR06	.13782	.05199	7.028
(CØNSTANT)	− 3541.42269		

---------------- VARIABLES NØT IN THE EQUATIØN ----------------

VARIABLE	PARTIAL	F
VAR02	.36412	.917
VAR03	.61276	3.607
VAR04	.10130	.062
VAR05	.07230	.032
VAR07	.50339	2.036

****

17B   The St. Louis Companies

An irritated Roger Hatton finds himself sitting in the St. Louis airport after hearing his flight to Chicago has been delayed and, if the storm in Chicago continues, possibly cancelled. Since he must get to Chicago if possible, Roger is stuck sitting in the airport and so figures he might as well try to get some work done. He opens his lap-top computer and calls up the CLAIMNUM file.

Roger is a recently assigned analyst in the worker compensation section of the St. Louis Companies, one of the biggest issuers of worker compensation insurance in the country. Up to this year the revenues and claim costs of each part of the company were grouped together to determine any yearly profit or loss. Therefore, no one in any department of the company really knew if their department was profitable or not. However, the St. Louis Companies have a new president who is looking at each part of the company as a profit center. The clear implication is that money-losing centers may not have a future unless they can develop a clear plan to become profitable.

Roger has asked the accounting department for a listing, by client, of all policy payments and claims filed and paid. He was told that information is available but he may have to wait two or three months to get it. He was able to determine, however, that the department has been keeping track of the clients who file frequent (at least one a month) claims and the total number of firms that purchase worker compensation insurance. Roger takes this report and divides the number filing frequent claims by the corresponding number of clients. These ratios are kept in the CLAIMNUM file in his computer and are as follows:

Year	Ratio	Year	Ratio
1967	3.8%	1978	6.1%
1968	3.6	1979	7.8
1969	3.5	1980	7.1
1970	4.9	1981	7.6
1971	5.9	1982	9.7
1972	5.6	1983	9.6
1973	4.9	1984	7.5
1974	5.6	1985	7.9
1975	8.5	1986	8.3
1976	7.7	1987	8.4
1977	7.1		

Roger stares at these figures and feels there should be some way to use them to project what the next several years may hold if the company doesn't change its underwriting policies.

17C   Wagner Machine Works

Mary Lindsey has recently agreed to leave her upper-level management job at a major paper manufacturing firm and return to her home town to take over the family machine products business. The machine products industry in the United States had a strong position of world dominance until recently when the industry has been devastated by foreign competition, particularly from Germany and Japan. Among the many problems facing the American industry is that it is traditionally made up of many small firms and faces competition from major foreign industrial giants.

Wagner Machine Works, the company Mary is taking over, is one of the few survivors in its part of the state, but faces increasing competitive pressure. Mary's father let the business slide as he approached retirement and Mary sees the need for an immediate modernization of their plant. Mary has arranged for a loan from the local bank but now must forecast sales for the next three years to ensure the company has enough cash flow to repay the debt. Surprisingly, Mary has found her father has no forecasting system in place and she cannot afford the time, or money, to install a system like that used at her previous company.

Wagner Machine Works sales for the last fifteen years, on a quarterly basis, are (in millions) as follows:

	Quarter			
Year	1	2	3	4
1974	10,490	11,130	10,005	11,058
1975	11,424	12,550	10,900	12,335
1976	12,835	13,100	11,660	13,767
1977	13,877	14,100	12,780	14,738
1978	14,798	15,210	13,785	16,218
1979	16,720	17,167	14,785	17,725
1980	18,348	18,951	16,554	19,889
1981	20,317	21,395	19,445	22,816
1982	23,335	24,179	22,548	25,029
1983	25,729	27,778	23,391	27,360
1984	28,886	30,125	26,049	30,322
1985	30,212	33,702	27,907	31,096
1986	31,715	35,720	28,554	34,326
1987	35,533	39,447	30,046	37,587
1988	39,093	44,650	32,035	40,877

While looking at these data Mary wonders whether they can be used to forecast sales for the next three years. She wonders how much, if any, confidence she can have in a forecast made with these data. And she also wonders if the increase in sales seen is due to growing business or just to inflationary price increases.

REFERENCES

Anderson, O. D. *Time Series Analysis and Forecasting*. Boston: Butterworths, 1975.
Anderson, T. W. *The Statistical Analysis of Time Series*. New York: Wiley, 1971.

Armstrong, J. S. *Long Range Forecasting: From Crystal Ball to Computer*. New York: Wiley, 1978.

Box, G. E. P., and Jenkins, G. M. *Time Series Analysis, Forecasting and Control*. San Francisco: Holden-Day, 1969.

Chou, Ya-Lun. *Statistical Analysis with Business and Economic Applications*, 2nd Edition. New York: Holt, Rinehart and Winston, 1975.

Chou, Ya-Lun, and Bauer, Bertrand. *Applied Business Statistics*. New York: Random House, 1983.

Gross, Charles W., and Peterson, Robin T. *Business Forecasting*. Boston: Houghton Mifflin, 1976.

Johnston, J. *Econometric Methods*. New York: McGraw-Hill, 1972.

Lapin, Lawrence. *Statistics for Modern Business Decisions*, 3rd Edition. New York: Harcourt Brace Jovanovich, 1982.

Mendenhall, William, and Reinmuth, James. *Statistics for Management and Economics*, 4th Edition. North Scituate, Mass.: Duxbury, 1982.

Montgomery, D. C., and Johnson, L. A. *Forecasting and Time Series Analysis*. New York: McGraw-Hill, 1976.

Nelson, Charles R. *Applied Time Series Analysis*. San Francisco: Holden-Day, 1973.

Winters, P. R. "Forecasting Sales by Exponentially Weighted Moving Averages." *Management Science* 6 (1960): 324–42.

INTRODUCTION TO DECISION ANALYSIS

18

WHY DECISION MAKERS NEED TO KNOW

A concept repeated many times in this text is that business decision makers must make decisions in an environment packed with uncertainty. Production managers face uncertainty in areas such as quality control, production scheduling, and inventory control. Marketing managers cross paths with uncertainty any time they make a decision to enter a new market area with an established product or when introducing a new product. Accounting auditors deal with uncertainty when they base their audit on a sample of their client's financial transactions.

Chapters 1 through 17 introduced the fundamentals of classical statistics. The techniques presented, if applied properly, should help decision makers deal more effectively with uncertainty. The classical statistical methods are useful tools for managers making objective decisions about a population after measuring a sample from the population.

The classical approach assumes that the only pertinent information about the population of interest is contained in the sample. However, many decision makers feel that the sample is only one source of information and that subjective forms of information such as expert opinion and personal experience can, and should, be included in the decision process. The formal means by which subjectivity is included in the decision process is known as *Bayesian decision analysis*. This process is named after the mathematician the Reverend Thomas Bayes, who formulated Bayes' rule for conditional probability. Pioneering work in the area of decision analysis was performed by Professors Ronald Howard, Howard Raiffa, and Robert Schlaifer. These men are primarily responsible for making the theory of decision analysis available to business decision makers.

Chapters 18 and 19 introduce some concepts of decision analysis and illustrate how these concepts can be used to help managers make better decisions under conditions of uncertainty.

CHAPTER OBJECTIVES

The objective of this chapter is to introduce three different decision-making environments: decision making under certainty, decision making under risk, and decision making under uncertainty. Managers who can classify their decision environments correctly will have taken a large step in choosing among the available set of decision tools.

This chapter will discuss how to include subjective probability assessments in the decision process. It will also introduce the expected value criterion for deciding between alternatives in a business decision framework and show how decision tree analysis can be used in making decisions under risk and uncertainty.

STUDENT OBJECTIVES

After studying the material presented in this chapter, you should be able to

1. Recognize the limitations of making decisions under certainty.
2. Understand the difference between making decisions under certainty, risk, and uncertainty.
3. Understand the basic differences and similarities between the risk environment and the uncertainty environment.
4. Understand the principles behind the expected value criterion and be able to apply it in a decision-making problem.
5. Set up a problem in a decision tree format.

DECISION-MAKING ENVIRONMENTS

18-1

Certainty

Sometimes managers can make decisions when they are certain of the results of selecting each alternative. When this is the case, the decision makers are operating in a certain environment. The following example demonstrates a certainty decision environment.

The Spudnick Corporation produces frozen french fries for many large fast-food chains. Jack Dale, the production manager at the Spudnick eastern region plant, has just received a mailgram from Teresa Powers, a company salesperson. Powers has negotiated an order from a new customer for one million pounds of french fries at $0.50 per pound. However, this customer wants crinkle-cut fries rather than the regular fries that Spudnick now produces. Powers points out that Spudnick already has the equipment necessary to modify the cutting process to produce crinkle-cuts. Her mailgram indicates that she needs a decision soon or the customer will take its business elsewhere. She reminds Dale that Spudnick has spent a great deal of money trying to sell to this customer and all will be lost if Dale decides not to take the order.

To make a decision, Dale checks with his industrial engineering and accounting staffs and learns that production costs, including raw materials, will be $0.44 per pound after the process modification is made.

Dale's performance evaluation is based to a large extent on his plant's profit-and-loss statement. Thus Dale might use the certainty model presented in table 18–1 for

TABLE 18–1
Profit-or-loss decision table, Spudnick example

Revenues and Expenses	Alternative	
	Accept Order	Do Not Accept Order
Revenue (1 million lb at $0.50/lb)	$500,000	0
Production cost (1 million lb at $0.44/lb)	440,000	0
Selling cost (5% of revenue)*	25,000	0
Administrative overhead (1% of revenue)*	5,000	0
Profit or loss	$ 30,000	0

*These are variable costs that are allocated to any order based on corporate policy and therefore impact the plant's income statement.

making his decision. Note that each item in table 18–1 is assumed to be known with certainty. Thus, if the actual expenditures and revenues occur as expected, Dale's decision is straightforward: he should accept the order. Some managers may not be logical in their decisions, but decision analysis assumes that the decision makers are logical and will act accordingly. Therefore, once the certainty model has been correctly specified, the best decision is evident.

Risk

A second decision environment involves decision making under risk. In a risk environment, decision makers must decide among alternative actions while faced with several states of nature, or possible outcomes. Decision makers have no control over which state of nature will occur, but the chances of each state occurring are assumed known.

For example, the Barton Construction Company is considering whether to bid on a project for the state of Maryland. State officials have specified the bid price at $300,000. To avoid vendor pressure, the state will make the selection by a random drawing from the submitted proposals. Only four companies are authorized bidders on this type of project.

After several phone calls, Dan Barton, owner-manager of Barton Construction, learns that only two other companies will submit a bid. If Barton bids, the chance of winning the contract is one-third. Dan Barton has calculated the following costs:

Cost of submitting a bid $ 10,000
Cost of performing the work $250,000

Thus Barton Construction faces two possible outcomes if it submits a bid:

1. *If Barton wins the bid:*

$$\text{Profit} = \$300,000 - \$250,000 - \$10,000$$
$$= \$40,000$$

2. *If Barton loses the bid:*

$$\text{Loss} = -\$10{,}000$$

The probability of making \$40,000 is one-third, and the probability of losing \$10,000 is two-thirds. Although Dan Barton can determine the probability associated with each possible outcome, he has no way of knowing which payoff will actually occur. Thus a **risk** environment is an environment in which the decision maker knows the possible outcomes and their probabilities, but does not know which outcome will occur.

Decisions made using classical statistics are often considered examples of decision making under risk. For example, suppose the credit manager in a bank wishes to know the average account balance for her bank's 10,000 MasterCard accounts. As discussed in chapter 8, the manager would likely select a random sample of accounts and develop a statistical confidence interval. The credit manager would know (based on the central limit theorem) that the distribution of possible sample means will be approximately normal with, mean μ_x and standard deviation of $\sigma_x/\sqrt{n}$. Thus she would know the probability distribution associated with her estimation problem. However, before she selects the sample, she does not know which sample mean will actually occur. Figure 18–1 illustrates the distribution of possible sample means. Figure 18–1 also shows the range within which a sample mean will produce a 95 percent confidence interval that includes the population mean, μ_x. The chance of the confidence interval not including the true value of μ_x is 0.05. Thus the credit manager knows the probabilities of getting both a good confidence interval and a bad confidence interval but does not know which of the two she actually has. Therefore the credit manager is making an estimate under risk.

Uncertainty

Uncertainty exists for decisions where the possible outcomes are known, but the probabilities associated with the outcomes are not known. For example, the manager of Big Sky Lumber Company in Ronan, Montana, was recently forced to make a decision under uncertainty. Big Sky Lumber sells virtually all types of building supplies to contractors and do-it-yourself builders. In the spring, Bill Dickson, the owner-manager, received a special order of 1,500 board feet of 2" × 6" knotty pine, tongue-and-groove decking. The special-order customer paid \$675 when placing the order. This represented

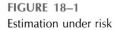

FIGURE 18–1
Estimation under risk

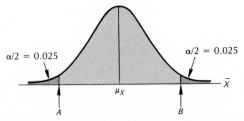

An $\overline{X}$ between A and B will produce a 95% confidence interval that actually includes the true population mean.

complete payment. However, the buyer said he would not pick up the material until October. Bill Dickson guaranteed the material would be available by October.

In July another customer, who was building a cabin at a nearby lake, arrived at Big Sky Lumber. He was looking for 1,200 board feet of 2″ × 6″ knotty pine, tongue-and-groove decking material. Because decking requires special setups, lumber mills make it only on special order. No other local lumber store had any decking material in stock. However, Big Sky Lumber had just received the special order of 1,500 board feet. The new customer was desperate for the decking because his cabin construction was stopped until the decking was installed. He was willing to pay cash for 1,200 board feet.

Bill Dickson hates to lose sales about as much as any struggling small-business person. He is faced with two alternatives:

1. Sell 1,200 board feet to the new customer and hope he can get the reorder in by October.
2. Don't sell to the new customer and lose out on this sale and maybe future sales from that customer.

Many factors affect Bill's decision:

1. He is uncertain whether he can replace the decking by October. He really has no past experience to use to accurately measure his uncertainty.
2. If he can replace the decking, he is uncertain about what its price will be relative to what he paid for the special-order material. Therefore, if he *does* sell to the new customer, he doesn't know for sure what price to charge.
3. He is uncertain how the original customer will react if the material (already paid for) is not available in October.

As you can see, what might appear to be a simple problem actually involves a decision in an extremely uncertain environment. Instances involving uncertainty abound in the business world. Most decisions made in a rapidly changing environment involve uncertainty. This chapter and chapter 19 discuss decision situations under uncertainty. Our objective is to present some basic techniques for making decisions in such situations.

SUBJECTIVE PROBABILITY ASSESSMENT

18-2

We have discussed three decision environments: certainty, risk, and uncertainty. For each environment, decision makers must know the outcomes that can result from a decision. In a certainty environment, there is only one outcome associated with each decision (with a probability of occurrence of 1.0). However, in both the risk and uncertainty environments more than one possible outcome exists.

The decision-making tools employed when dealing with risk and uncertainty environments are basically the same. These tools require that probabilities be assigned to possible decision outcomes. In a risk environment, the outcome probabilities are known.

In an uncertain environment, the probabilities must be subjectively assessed. There are four requirements for subjective probability assessments:

1. The probabilities must be nonnegative.
2. The probabilities must sum to 1.0.
3. The outcomes must be mutually exclusive.
4. The probabilities must accurately reflect the decision maker's state of mind about the chance of each outcome occurring.

The first two requirements are restatements of probability rules 1 and 2 from chapter 4. The third requirement specifies there is no overlap between outcomes, so each can be analyzed separately. The fourth requirement states that decision makers must quantify all available information about the possible outcomes in the form of a probability. If the information is based primarily on past history (or a sample), the assessed probabilities should be formed as relative frequency of occurrence statements. For example, suppose the golf pro at Toke-a-Tee Golf Club has determined that the number of pairs of golf shoes he will set on any day can vary from zero to four. A history of the last 200 days' sales is given in table 18–2. If all days are the same, the golf pro might make the sales assessments using only the relative frequencies shown in the table.

In other cases decision makers have little or no sample information and must make purely subjective probability assessments. These subjective assessments must still include all available relevant information.

If decision makers understand probability, they might assign probabilities directly to the possible outcomes. For example, in deciding whether to drill a new gas well, the exploration manager for Intermountain Gas Company might be able to assign a 70 percent chance to finding gas and a 30 percent chance to not finding gas. Some managers can think more easily in terms of betting odds. Such statements as ''I think the odds are 4 to 1 that we will find natural gas if we drill'' can be translated to probabilities by the relationship in equation 18–1:

$$P(X) = \frac{a}{a + b} \qquad (18\text{–}1)$$

where X = event of interest

odds of X happening are a to b

TABLE 18–2
Relative frequency approach to probability assessments, Toke-a-Tee Golf Club example

Demand	Days	Probability
0	100	0.50
1	30	0.15
2	30	0.15
3	20	0.10
4	20	0.10
	200	1.00

Then, for the natural gas example, the probability of finding gas is

$$P(\text{gas}) = \frac{4}{4 + 1}$$

$$= \frac{4}{5}$$

$$= 0.80$$

Sometimes decision makers have trouble pinpointing an exact probability. Suppose the exploration manager feels the probability of finding gas if Intermountain drills is somewhere between 60 percent and 90 percent, but cannot identify a single probability value. Nothing seems to remove vagueness faster than placing a bet. So when a single probability value cannot be identified, the decision maker could be asked whether he or she would place a bet on finding gas with 4 to 1 odds. If the decision maker would bet, the probability is 80 percent or higher. If not, the probability is below 80 percent. The decision maker would continue in this manner until finding the betting odds for which he or she is totally indifferent. These odds would then reflect the true subjective probability.

This presentation of probability assessment is only a basic discussion. More advanced texts on Bayesian inference and analysis by Winkler (1972), Schlaifer (1978), and Raiffa (1968) present more in-depth treatments of subjective probability assessment methods.

As stated earlier, the subjective probability assessment that a specific outcome will occur must reflect the decision maker's state of mind. Thus, there can be no right or wrong subjective probability assessment. In addition, different decision makers can arrive at different probability assessments.

DECISION-MAKING CRITERIA

18-3

The prime managerial concern is the future outcome of today's decisions. Since no one can predict the future, managers can rarely predict with certainty the outcome of their decisions. This is what makes decisions risky or uncertain. A basic premise in decision analysis is that *a good decision does not ensure a good outcome*. Decision makers who cannot accept this premise will end up with ulcers from second-guessing their own decisions.

A good decision is one that is made using all available information to satisfy criteria established by the decision maker. The final decision depends on the decision criteria. Here, two classes of decision-making criteria are introduced: *nonprobabilistic* and *probabilistic*.

Nonprobabilistic Criteria for Decisions under Uncertainty

The Ajax Electronics Company must decide how many television sets to produce this year. The firm's cost accountants have determined that the annual fixed costs are

$350,000. The variable cost of producing each television set is $300, and the sale price is $700. Company market analysts have determined that demand will be one of the following levels:

$$700$$
$$800$$
$$900$$
$$1,000$$
$$1,100$$

Because of yearly model changes, there is no market for unsold television sets.

The production manager has to establish a production level and therefore must determine the profits for each possible production level. She uses the format of equation 18–2 to arrive at these profits, or *payoffs:*

$$Payoff = TR - FC - VC \qquad (18\text{–}2)$$

where TR = total revenue = (sales price)(number of units sold)
FC = fixed cost
VC = variable cost = (cost per unit)(number of units produced)

For example, if demand is 700 television sets and 700 are produced, the payoff is

$$Payoff = \$700(700) - \$350,000 - \$300(700)$$
$$= \$490,000 - \$350,000 - \$210,000$$
$$= -\$70,000$$

If 800 sets are produced and 1,000 demanded, the payoff is

$$Payoff = \$700(800) - \$350,000 - \$300(800)$$
$$= \$560,000 - \$350,000 - \$240,000$$
$$= -\$30,000$$

TABLE 18–3
Payoff table, Ajax Electronics Company example

		Demand Level (State of Nature)				
		700	800	900	1,000	1,100
	700	−$ 70,000	−$ 70,000	−$70,000	−$70,000	−$70,000
	800	−$100,000	−$ 30,000	−$30,000	−$30,000	−$30,000
Production Level	900	−$130,000	−$ 60,000	$10,000	$10,000	$10,000
	1,000	−$160,000	−$ 90,000	−$20,000	$50,000	$50,000
	1,100	−$190,000	−$120,000	−$50,000	$20,000	$90,000

The production manager can find a payoff for each combination of output and demand and can construct the **payoff table** shown in table 18–3. Notice the different demand levels in table 18–3 are referred to as **states of nature.** This terminology is common in decision analysis theory and refers to a condition outside the decision maker's control.

Nonprobabilistic decision rules are used when the manager has the payoff table but cannot assess probabilities for the possible demand levels. Several rules exist to help the manager make a good decision about how many television sets to produce. The **maximin criterion** rule is one.

MAXIMIN RULE

For each option, find the minimum possible payoff and then select the option that has the greatest minimum payoff.

Table 18–3 shows that the minimum payoffs for the Ajax Electronics production levels are

Production Level	Minimum Payoff
700	− $ 70,000
800	− 100,000
900	− 130,000
1,000	− 160,000
1,100	− 190,000

According to the maximin criterion, the best decision is to produce 700 sets because the worst possible outcome (− $70,000) is greater than for any other production level. Note that the maximin rule is very pessimistic. It assumes the worst will happen, and the decision maker's goal is to cut the losses. Managers might choose to use the maximin criterion if their firms are in financial trouble and they must make certain that even if the worst possible outcome occurs, further operations are possible.

The **maximax criterion** is the opposite of the maximin criterion. The maximax criterion assumes the best is going to happen and that the decision maker seeks to maximize the good fortune.

MAXIMAX RULE

For each option, find the maximum possible payoff and then select the option that has the greatest maximum payoff.

The maximum profits for the Ajax Electronics production levels are

Production Level	Maximum Payoff
700	− $70,000
800	− 30,000
900	10,000
1,000	50,000
1,110	90,000

Thus the best decision under the maximax criterion is to produce 1,100 television sets.

The maximin and the maximax criteria are straightforward and easy to use. Choosing one over the other depends on whether you are a pessimist or an optimist when making the choice. However, both criteria are often criticized because they fail to include any information about the probabilities of the possible outcomes. To use this information, the decision maker should employ probabilistic criteria to make the best decision.

Probabilistic Criteria for Decisions under Uncertainty

Ajax Electronics' production manager is informed by the marketing department that the following probabilities have been assessed for the demand levels:

Demand Level	Probability
700	0.05
800	0.10
900	0.20
1,000	0.40
1,100	0.25
	1.00

These probabilities reflect the marketing department manager's state of mind and were subjectively determined.

The fundamental probabilistic criterion is the **expected value criterion.** The concept of expected value was discussed in chapter 5. The expected value of a probability distribution is the *long-run* average value of that distribution. Thus, the expected value criterion is based on the long-run average of a probability distribution.

> **EXPECTED VALUE CRITERION**
> Given a probability distribution of payoffs, select the option that yields the greatest expected payoff or the minimum expected loss.

To incorporate the demand-level probabilities into his decision-making process, the manager would calculate the expected payoff for each production level. For example, the expected payoff for a production level of 900 television sets is found by equation 18–3:

$$E[X] = \sum_{i=1}^{S} X_i P(X_i) \qquad (18\text{--}3)$$

where $\quad E[X] =$ expected value of X(payoff or loss)
$\quad\quad\quad S =$ number of different payoff levels
$\quad\quad\quad X_i =$ ith possible payoff
$\quad\quad P(X_i) =$ probability of the ith payoff

TABLE 18–4
Expected values, Ajax Electronics example

		Demand Level					Expected
		700	800	900	1,000	1,100	Value
				Probability			↓
		0.05	0.10	0.20	0.40	0.25	
	700	−$ 70,000	−$ 70,000	−$70,000	−$70,000	−$70,000	−$70,000
	800	−$100,000	−$ 30,000	−$30,000	−$30,000	−$30,000	−$33,500
Production Level	900	−$130,000	−$ 60,000	$10,000	$10,000	$10,000	−$ 4,000
	1,000	−$160,000	−$ 90,000	−$20,000	$50,000	$50,000	$11,500*
	1,100	−$190,000	−$120,000	−$50,000	$20,000	$90,000	−$ 1,000

*Highest expected value—produce 1,000.

If the production level is 900,

$$E[\text{payoff}] = -\$130,000(0.05) + (-\$60,000)(0.10) + \$10,000(0.20)$$
$$+ \$10,000(0.40) + \$10,000(0.25)$$
$$= -\$4,000$$

Therefore, on the average, Ajax Electronics can expect to lose $4,000 if it decides to produce 900 television sets. Table 18–4 illustrates the expected payoffs associated with each possible production level. Using the expected value criterion, the best decision is to produce 1,000 television sets.

The expected value criterion allows decision makers to incorporate additional information, in the form of probabilities, into a decision. Because of this feature, expected value analysis plays a key role in decisions under risk or uncertainty.

SKILL DEVELOPMENT PROBLEMS FOR SECTION 18–3

The following exercises have been included to help you gain a better understanding of the material presented in this section. There are additional problems at the end of this chapter.

1. The manager of The Book House is trying to decide how many copies of the new best-selling mystery to order. Based on past sales of mysteries, she feels that she can sell fifteen to twenty copies. Each copy costs $3 and she can sell them for $4. If there are any books that do not sell, she can get a $1 credit by returning the cover. Regardless of how many books she orders, there will be a $5 fee to cover handling and delivery. Set up a payoff table for each combination of demand and orders possible. Use the maximax decision rule to decide how many books to order.

2. Referring to problem 1, would you change your decision if the maximin criterion were used?

3. Referring to problem 1, use the expected value criterion to arrive at a decision if the manager has determined the following probabilities based on past sales:

Demand Level	Probability
15	0.05
16	0.10
17	0.20
18	0.40
19	0.15
20	0.10
	1.00

4. The Scandinavian Bakery has always rented a booth at the Annual Christmas Bazaar to sell special bread wreaths. In order to participate, they must rent a booth at a cost of $500 and donate $1 for each wreath they sell to the sponsoring charity. The wreaths can be sold for $6 and there is $3 worth of ingredients in each. Unsold wreaths can be sold the next week at the bakery for $2. Past experience has helped in making estimates for this year's demand. Based on the following information, set up a payoff table for each demand and production level. Use the maximax decision rule to help the manager decide how many wreaths to make.

Demand	Probability
500	0.1
700	0.3
900	0.4
1100	0.15
1300	0.05

5. Based on the information given in problem 4, what decision should the bakery manager make if she uses the maximin decision criterion?

6. Referring to problem 4, how many wreaths should the bakery make to sell at the Annual Christmas Bazaar? Use the expected value criterion to help make the decision.

7. An enterprising student at the university has decided to set up a stand in the lobby of the Student Union Building and sell roses on Valentine's Day. It will cost him $50 to rent the cart and obtain the necessary permits. He also plans on advertising his product in the campus paper at a cost of $40. If the student is willing to place his order by December 10th, he can obtain a substantial savings. He can get the roses at this time for $20 a dozen if he orders in lots of twelve dozen. He feels he can sell the roses for $2.50 apiece, or $30.00 a dozen. After getting some advice from a local florist, he estimates demand for the roses would be one to four lots

(12, 24, 36, or 48 dozen). Any roses that did not sell could only be given away. Use the expected value criterion to make a decision on how many lots of roses he should order if he feels the probabilities associted with each level of demand are equal.

8. Referring to problem 7, suppose the student has been overly optimistic about his chances of selling the roses. His pessimistic best friend points out that there is always a chance that he will not sell any roses and that the probabilities for each demand level are not equal. What decision should the student make based on the expected value criterion if he decides to use his friend's advice about demand and his estimates for probability levels?

Demand	Probability
0	0.2
1	0.3
2	0.2
3	0.2
4	0.1
	1.0

9. Referring to problem 7, the student suddenly finds out that there is a new permit required by the university in order to use space in any building. What effect will this have on the student's decision if the cost of the additional permit is $100? Use the expected value decision rule to construct the payoff table.

10. The buyer for The Trendsetters, a local clothing store specializing in trendy clothes for teens, is trying to decide how many sweaters she should order of the latest fad style. The manufacturer will sell only in lots of 50. Based on past sales, she thinks she can sell 50, 100, 150, or 200 sweaters. Each sweater wholesales for $20 and retails for $35. Unsold sweaters can be put on the sale rack for $15. There is always a chance that the sweaters will arrive too late to sell and have to all be sold on the discount rack. Use the maximin decision criteria to help make this decision.

11. Referring to problem 10, use the maximax decision rule to see if the buyer's decision would change.

12. Referring to problem 10, if the buyer makes the following estimates for the probability of each demand level, how many sweaters should she order?

Demand	Probability
0	0.10
50	0.35
100	0.25
150	0.20
200	0.10
	1.00

DECISION TREE ANALYSIS

18-4   When decision analysis is applied to an actual problem, the process can become quite complex. The decision maker must identify the outcomes for each decision alternative and must also assess probabilities associated with each outcome, assign cash flows in the form of payoffs and costs, and somehow keep the sequence of outcomes and decisions in the proper chronological order. *Decision tree analysis* is a technique to aid the decision maker in this process. The **decision tree** provides a "road map" of the decision problem.

Few managerial situations allow single isolated decisions. Most decisions are made in a dynamic, evolving environment. For instance, Squelch Electronics Corporation designs and manufactures a variety of electronic components. Recently a salesperson in the new-products division approached his vice-president with a proposition from ACR Television, Inc. If Squelch will pay to build a prototype color television tuner, ACR will test the tuner and may purchase 5,000 of them. ACR buys its current tuners for $40 each. Based on Squelch's reputation and the salesperson's persuasiveness, ACR has agreed to test the prototype tuner if Squelch decides to produce it. If the prototype outperforms the current tuner, ACR will purchase 5,000 tuners at $40 each.

Squelch engineers have informed the vice-president there is a 60 percent chance they can design a tuner that will outperform ACR's current tuner. The engineers also estimate that the prototype design cost will be about $25,000 and the construction cost about $10,000. The engineers further estimate that if the 5,000 tuners are produced using primarily manual labor, the fixed setup cost will be $20,000 and the per-unit variable production cost will be $24. The engineers are sure that tuners assembled by hand will perform as well as the prototype. However, the variable production cost can be reduced to $22 if a flow-solder technique is used. Squelch will have to invest $10,000 in equipment for this flow-solder technique.

If flow-solder is used, there is a 30 percent chance the production tuner will not perform as well as the prototype. Fortunately the engineers are confident that any problems in the flow process would be discovered in time to switch to hand assembly and still meet the ACR deadline.

The first decision facing Squelch's vice-president is whether to produce the prototype. However, this decision will likely depend on the following decision about whether to use flow-solder assembly. This simplified example has the *act–event–act–event* sequence typical of many managerial decisions. Whereas the vice-president has control over the acts, or decisions, she has no control over the subsequent events. But these events determine the appropriate following act. For instance, if the vice-president decides to build the prototype, she may or may not get a model that will outperform the competition, but she will have to consider the flow-solder process only if the prototype is good.

Constructing the Decision Tree

Decision trees help the decision maker logically structure the decision problem. Structuring involves properly sequencing the acts and events in the decision problem. An *act*

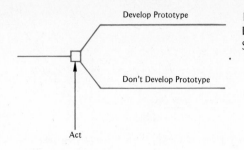

FIGURE 18–2
Initial act in the decision tree,
Squelch Corporation example

is a decision or alternative within the decision maker's control. An *event* is a state of nature beyond the decision maker's control.

To construct the decision tree, the decision maker must analyze the possible acts and events chronologically. The tree will be formed by a series of branches that represent the chronological order of the acts and events. The first act in the decision problem facing Squelch's vice-president is whether to build the prototype. This act is shown in figure 18–2. The small square at the fork represents an act, or decision, for the decision maker.

The decision tree is completed for each initial branch by adding all other acts and events in their chronological order. For example, if the lower branch ("don't develop prototype") is selected, ACR will not purchase tuners from Squelch. Figure 18–3 shows the tree with the lower branch completed. A small circle indicates an event.

Figure 18–4 shows the completed upper act branch ("develop prototype") with the correct sequence of acts and events. As the tree shows, if a prototype is developed, it will either be better than the existing tuner, in which case ACR will order 5,000, or the prototype will not be better, and ACR will not order. If ACR does not order the tuners, Squelch has no further acts or events. However, if ACR orders the tuners, Squelch must decide (an act) whether to use manual assembly or the flow-solder process. If the decision is to use manual assembly, all tuners will be satisfactory, and no further acts or events exist. However, if the flow-solder alternative is selected, it will either work satisfactorily, or it won't (an event). If the flow process doesn't work, Squelch will have to switch to the manual alternative. Eventually ACR will receive 5,000 tuners, and the Squelch Corporation will receive payment.

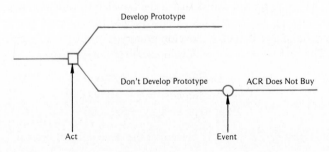

FIGURE 18–3
Complete lower branch in the decision tree, Squelch Corporation example

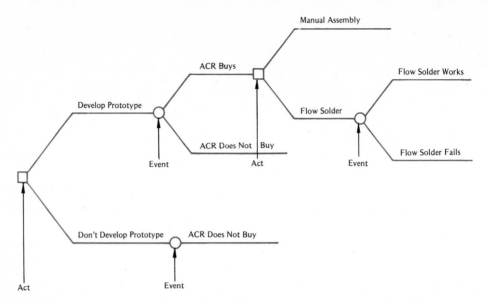

FIGURE 18–4
Complete upper act branch in the decision tree, Squelch Corporation example

As you can see, constructing a decision tree is not a complex process. If you begin on the left and add the appropriate act and event branches toward the right, when the tree is completed it should include all possible decision paths.

In an actual application, once you have formulated the initial decision tree, have someone else familiar with the problem review it to make sure no branches have been left out. This is especially important if the tree is complex. An accurate decision tree is essential. However, constructing the tree is only the first step in decision tree analysis.

Assigning Cash Flows

A decision tree is useful for visualizing the problem at hand, but by itself is not a complete decision-making tool. The next step is to assign cash flows to each tree segment and arrive at a cash value for each branch. These final cash values are called *end values* since they represent the values at the ends of the decision branches.

Figure 18–5 shows the cash flows for each act and event branch in the Squelch decision tree. The lower branch shows that if the Squelch Corporation does not develop a prototype, there is no cost or revenue. Consequently the net cash flow, or end value, is $0. However, the upper branch ("develop prototype") involves several cash inflows and outflows. The first outflow is the development (prototype) cost.

$$\begin{array}{ll} \text{Design cost} = & -\$25,000 \\ \text{Construction cost} = & -\ \underline{\ 10,000} \\ \text{Prototype cost} = & -\$35,000 \end{array}$$

The development cost (−$35,000) is placed on the development branch.

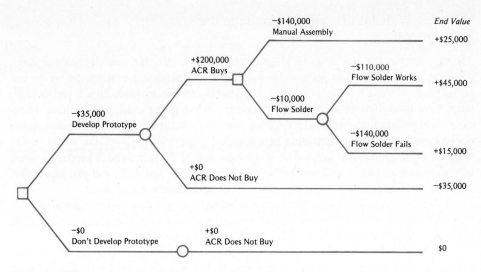

FIGURE 18–5
Cash-flow assignments, Squelch Corporation example

Next comes the event of ACR buying or not buying. If the prototype fails, ACR will not buy, and the end value is − $35,000. However, if ACR does buy, the cash inflow is

$$(5,000 \text{ tuners})(\$40/\text{tuner}) = \$200,000$$

The $200,000 cash inflow is placed on the appropriate branch in figure 18–5.

Following the "ACR buys" branch comes the act associated with whether to use manual or flow-solder assembly. If manual assembly is used, the production cash outflow is

$$\text{Fixed cost} = -\$ \ 20,000$$
$$\text{Variable cost (5,000 units} \times \$24/\text{unit)} = \underline{- \ 120,000}$$
$$\text{Total production cost} = -\$140,000$$

The − $140,000 cash outflow is shown in the "manual assembly" branch. If flow-solder assembly is used, there is a − $10,000 cash outflow for equipment, and the process will either prove successful or it won't. If flow solder works, the production cost becomes

$$(5,000 \text{ units})(\$22/\text{unit}) = \$110,000$$

This cash outflow is also shown in figure 18–5. However, if the flow-solder parts prove inadequate, Squelch will be forced to manually assemble all the tuners, as we showed earlier. In this case, the cash outflow, or production cost, is − $140,000.

Figure 18–5 also shows the end value for each branch. The end value is the sum of the cash inflows and outflows for the branch. The end values range from a high of + $45,000 to a low of − $35,000 and represent the possible cash results from the decisions facing the Squelch vice-president.

Assigning Probabilities and Determining the Expected Value

The next step in the process is to assign probabilities to the decision's events, or states of nature. As discussed in section 18–4, subjectively assessing probabilities is an important part of decision analysis under uncertainty. In this example, the Squelch engineers have used their experience and abilities to arrive at the event probabilities. However these probabilities reflect the decision makers' state of mind, and, of course, other decision makers could assign other probabilities. Figure 18–6 shows the decision tree with the event probabilities included. Remember that if the prototype is produced, there is a 60 percent chance it will successfully pass ACR's test and ACR will place an order. If flow-solder assembly is used, there is a 70 percent chance it will work.

The best decision using the expected value criterion is to select the alternative with the highest expected profit or the lowest expected cost. However, finding this alternative requires the decision maker to *fold back* the decision tree.

The folding back process involves starting at the right-hand side of the tree and moving to the left until the first act fork is reached. There are two rules for folding back a decision tree:

1. For all event forks, find the expected value.
2. For all act forks, pick the alternative with the larger expected value.

To see how these rules apply, consider figure 18–7, which is part of Squelch's overall decision tree.

The end value associated with the manual-assembly alternative is +$25,000. Since there are no events after this decision, its expected value is +$25,000. However, to find the expected value for the flow-solder alternative, we must weight the two possible payoffs, +$45,000 and +$15,000, by their probabilities.

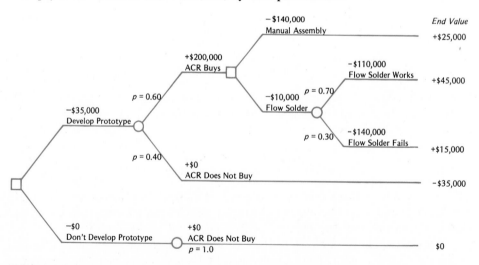

FIGURE 18–6
Subjective probabilities, Squelch Corporation example

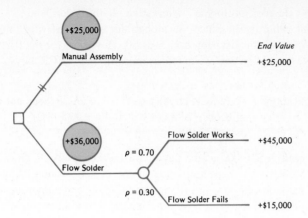

FIGURE 18–7
Step 1 in folding back the decision tree, Squelch Corporation
example

$$E[\text{payoff flow}] = 0.70(+\$45,000) + 0.30(+\$15,000)$$
$$= +\$36,000$$

Since $+\$36,000$ exceeds $+\$25,000$, if the Squelch vice-president ever has to decide between using manual or flow-solder construction, her best decision is to use flow-solder. (The two hashmarks through the manual alternative indicate that this branch should be ignored.)

The next step is to move farther left and determine the expected value of each alternative at the next act fork. From figure 18–8, this fork involves the ''develop pro-

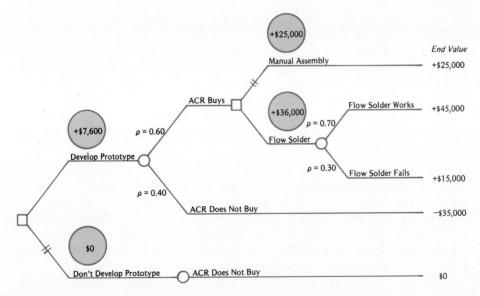

FIGURE 18–8
Final step in folding back the decision tree, Squelch Corporation example

totype''/''don't develop prototype'' alternative. If the ''don't build'' alternative is selected, the end value is $0. Since the probability associated with this outcome is 1.0, the expected value of this decision branch is $0. However, for the ''develop prototype'' alternative, we must find the weighted average of the ''ACR buys''/''ACR does not buy'' event:

$$
\begin{aligned}
E[\text{payoff}|\text{prototype}] &= P(\text{ACR buys})(\text{payoff}) + P(\text{ACR does not buy})(\text{payoff}) \\
&= 0.60(+\$36,000) + 0.40(-\$35,000) \\
&= +\$7,600
\end{aligned}
$$

Note that we used $+\$36,000$ as the payoff for the event ''ACR buys.'' This was done because $+\$36,000$ is the expected value of the best decision (''flow-solder''), given this branch. This is the essence of folding back the tree and shows clearly that the initial decision about building the prototype is dependent on the later production decision.

We have placed the $+\$7,600$ and $0 in circles to show that they are the expected values of the alternatives. Since $+\$7,600$ is greater than $0, the best decision for the vice-president is to develop the prototype. Later, if the prototype is acceptable, flow-solder production should be used.

SKILL DEVELOPMENT PROBLEMS FOR SECTION 18–4

The following exercises have been included to help you gain a better understanding of the material presented in this section. There are additional problems at the end of this chapter.

13. Tom and Joe operate a rock quarry that provides local stone for landscaping. They currently have an offer for $50,000 to sell the quarry. They are hesitant to sell because they feel there will be an increase in demand in the next two years that would improve their financial situation. If they decide to keep the quarry, the present buyer would be willing to pay $30,000 in two years regardless of the situation. Tom and Joe feel there is a 60 percent chance of an increase, at which point they could operate at a profit of $75,000 or sell the quarry to a new buyer for $60,000. If demand does not increase, they would operate at a profit of only $10,000. What should they do?

14. Vegetable Farms is a small, family-operated ranch that sells produce to local markets. The owners are currently trying to decide if they should expand their operation next year. Since this is a fairly new business, the owners have estimated the demand for their produce next year to be high (50 percent), medium (30 percent), or low (20 percent). The payoffs they expect for each demand/acreage scenerio are listed below. Use a decision tree to help decide whether or not to expand the farm.

Acreage	High	Medium	Low
Expanded	$100,000	$40,000	− $40,000
Same size	50,000	40,000	30,000

15. The owner of the College Deli is trying to plan for the future needs of his company. He is faced with the decision to expand the deli or try to cope with demand in his present, crowded location. If he chooses to expand, he can rent the location next door and remodel for a cost of $10,000. Another alternative is to move into a larger location in the next block, at a cost of $20,000. He has established the following tables to assist him in making the decision:

Demand	Probability
High	0.5
Medium	0.3
Low	0.2

Location	High	Medium	Low
Same	$30,000	$20,000	$10,000
Expand	60,000	35,000	20,000
New	70,000	40,000	10,000

The dollar values he has determined are expected revenue and do not include the cost of expansion or moving. Should he stay in the same quarters, expand, or move?

16. Aquatech currently holds the lease to a site with good potential for geothermal development to generate electricity. Aquatech is now looking at three options for the site: (1) sell the rights to the property for $1.5 million, (2) extend the lease for twenty-five years at a cost of $0.5 million, with the possibility of selling later, or (3) extend the lease and drill exploratory wells at a total cost of $2 million.

If the company decides to extend the lease in order to drill, future revenue from the site would be determined by the pressure and temperature of the water. The following chart lists the probabilities associated with the three states of nature possible, along with a projected drill revenue:

Water Temperature	Probability	Drill Revenue (in millions)
High	0.4	$5
Medium	0.4	3
Low	0.2	1

If the company extends the lease in order to sell the property later without drilling, the sale price will be determined by the demand for electricity. The following chart lists the probabilities associated with the three levels of demand and the projected drill revenue:

Demand	Probability	Drill Revenue (in millions)
High	0.3	$2.5
Medium	0.6	2.0
Low	0.1	1.5

Use a decision tree to diagram Aquatech's possible solutions and determine which option management should choose.

17. Paradise Springs is in the position of having to decide what size of cross-country ski resort to build. The majority owners are adamant that a resort be built and that future plans for the resort should be determined by revenues generated during the first two years of the project.

The developer has the option of building a small complex now and later expanding, if demand warrants, to a large complex. The expansion project would increase the size of a small complex to that of the large and could be completed in the off season to allow the resort to function as a large resort the second season. The costs of construction are as follows:

Size	Cost (in millions)
Small	$2.0
Expansion	1.5
Large	3.0

The developer believes that demand for the resort will be either high or low and thinks there will be a fifty-fifty chance the resort will be popular in its first season. If demand is high the first year, she feels there is a sixty percent chance the resort will be popular its second season. If demand is low, she would not want to expand. She feels if demand is low the first year, there is 70 percent chance it will remain low for the second season. The expected annual revenues for the resort are as follows:

Size	Expected Annual Revenues (in millions)	
	High	Low
Small	$2	$1
Large	3	2

Revenue figures do not include the cost of construction. Use a decision tree to determine which size of resort the developer should build.

CONCLUSIONS

This chapter discussed the three environments in which business decisions are made: certainty, risk, and uncertainty. When uncertainty exists, not only do decision makers have no control over which state of nature will occur, they do not even know for sure the probability that any state of nature will occur. To incorporate probability into the uncertainty environment, decision makers must be willing to introduce subjectivity into the process. However, the subjective probabilities managers assess must reflect their states of mind about the chances any particular state of nature will occur.

This chapter also introduced some nonprobabilistic decision criteria and illustrated the expected value criterion for decision making when probabilities are employed.

This chapter also indicated that the best decision does not always result in the best outcome if the decision is made under conditions of uncertainty or risk. However, by using the appropriate tool, decision makers can increase the chances the decision will have good results. One such tool is the decision tree, which provides a framework for more complex decision analysis.

A listing of statistical terms introduced in this chapter is presented in the chapter glossary. You should understand these terms before you go on to chapter 19.

CHAPTER GLOSSARY

certainty   A decision environment in which the results of selecting each alternative are known before the decision is made.

decision tree   A diagram that illustrates the chronological ordering of actions and events in a decision analysis problem. Each act and event is depicted by a branch on the decision tree.

expected value criterion   A decision criterion that employs probability: select the alternative that will produce the greatest long-run average payoff or minimum long-run average loss.

maximax criterion   An optimistic decision criterion for dealing with uncertainty when probability is not employed: for each option, find the maximum possible payoff and select the option that produces the greatest maximum payoff.

maximin criterion   A conservative decision criterion for dealing with uncertainty without using probabilities: for each option, find the minimum possible payoff and select the option with the greatest minimum payoff.

payoff table   A two-way table that shows the payoff (profit or loss) for each combination of alternative and state of nature.

risk   A decision environment in which the possible outcomes are known for each alternative. Although decision makers have no control over which outcome will occur, they do know the probability of each outcome occurring.

states of nature   The possible outcomes in a decision-making situation over which the decision maker has no control.

uncertainty   A decision environment in which the possible outcomes are known, but the decision makers do not know the probability of each outcome actually occurring.

SOLVED PROBLEMS

1. Korman Industries produces record albums that are sold to the public through the mail. Because of economies of scale and scheduling problems, Korman's policy is to produce all copies of a given record in one production run. If the demand exceeds the amount produced, the customer's money is returned along with a coupon good for $0.40 on any future Korman album. If Korman makes too many albums, the extras are sold to a department store chain for $0.50 each. This price is half the variable production cost of a record.

   Korman has recently agreed to pay $200,000 for the rights to a particular record. The company will sell this record for $4.98. Its market-research department predicts that one of the following demand levels will occur:

   $$20,000$$
   $$40,000$$
   $$60,000$$
   $$80,000$$

   a. Set up a payoff table showing the payoff for each combination of production and demand.
   b. Use the maximin rule to arrive at the appropriate decision. Contrast this decision with the one made if the maximax rule is used.
   c. The following probabilities have been subjectively assessed for the various demand levels:

Demand Level	Probability
20,000	0.10
40,000	0.30
60,000	0.40
80,000	0.20
	1.00

   Use the expected value criterion to arrive at the best decision for Korman.

Solutions:

   a. To set up the payoff table, we determine the payoff for each combination of production and demand. The following formula can be used:

   Payoff = − fixed cost − variable cost + revenue + salvage − penalty

where

$$
\begin{aligned}
\text{Fixed cost} &= \$200{,}000 \\
\text{Variable cost} &= \$1.00/\text{record} \\
\text{Revenue} &= \$4.98/\text{record sold} \\
\text{Salvage} &= \$0.50/\text{unsold record} \\
\text{Penalty} &= \$0.40/\text{unfilled demand}
\end{aligned}
$$

The payoff table is

	Demand Level (State of Nature) 20,000	40,000	60,000	80,000
Production Level 20,000	−$120,400	−$128,400	−$136,400	−$144,400
40,000	−$130,400	−$ 40,800	−$ 48,800	−$ 56,800
60,000	−$140,400	−$ 50,800	$ 38,800	$ 30,800
80,000	−$150,400	−$ 60,800	$ 28,800	$118,400

b. The maximin rule states that for each alternative, find the minimum possible payoff and then select the option that has the greatest minimum payoff. If we do this for the Korman payoff table, we find the following values:

Production Level	Minimum Payoff
20,000	−$144,400
40,000	− 130,400
60,000	− 140,400
80,000	− 150,400

Using the maximin rule, we should produce 40,000 records since this level minimizes the maximum losses. However, if we use the maximax rule, which says to find the maximum possible return for each alternative and select the alternative with the greatest maximum payoff, we find the following values:

Production Level	Maximum Payoff
20,000	−$120,400
40,000	− 40,800
60,000	38,800
80,000	118,400

The decision using the maximax rule is to produce 80,000 records. This level will produce the maximum possible payoff.

The primary difference between the maximin and the maximax decision criteria is that the maximin is conservative and the maximax is optimistic. They are both nonprobabilistic criteria.

c. The expected value criterion uses probability assessments to arrive at the decision that maximizes average payoffs. The formula for finding the expected payoff for each alternative is

$$E[\text{payoff}] = \Sigma X P(X)$$

where

$$X = \text{payoff for each demand level}$$
$$P(X) = \text{probability for each demand level occurring}$$

Consequently, we find the following payoff for each alternative:

Production Level	Expected Payoff
20,000	− $134,000
40,000	− 56,160
60,000	− 7,600
80,000	1,920

For example, for the production level of 60,000,

$$E[\text{payoff}] = (-\$140,400)(0.10) + (-\$50,800)(0.30) + \$38,800(0.40)$$
$$+ \$30,800(0.20)$$
$$= -\$7,600$$

The best decision is to pick the production level with the highest expected payoff. Therefore Korman should produce 80,000 records because that production level yields the greatest expected payoff.

2. The S. Claus Tree Company has acquired the lease rights to a large timber area in western Oregon from which it can cut up to one million Christmas trees. The problem is how many trees to cut and ship to retail outlets during the coming December; if the company doesn't cut enough, it loses potential business; if it cuts more than are demanded, it is out the costs of cutting and shipping these unused trees. As you might guess, there is not a big market for unsold Christmas trees after Christmas.

S. Claus's lease costs $50,000 per year and $2 per tree cut. Cost accountants have determined that the cost of cutting and shipping a tree averages another $1. Marketing experts have estimated this year's demand and its probability distribution as follows:

Demand Level	Probability
50,000	0.10
100,000	0.40
125,000	0.20
150,000	0.20
200,000	0.10
	1.00

Assuming the S. Claus trees sell for an average of $8 each, determine the payoff table and use the expected value criterion to find the number of trees the company should cut this year.

Solution:

To construct a payoff table for the S. Claus Tree Company, we use the following equation:

Payoff = revenue − fixed lease cost − variable lease cost − variable cut cost

where

$$\text{Revenue} = \$8/\text{tree sold}$$
$$\text{Lease fixed cost} = \$50,000$$
$$\text{Variable lease cost} = \$2/\text{tree cut}$$
$$\text{Variable cut cost} = \$1/\text{tree cut}$$

		Demand Level				
		50,000	100,000	125,000	150,000	200,000
	50,000	$200,000	$200,000	$200,000	$200,000	$200,000
	100,000	$ 50,000	$450,000	$450,000	$450,000	$450,000
Cut Level	125,000	−$ 25,000	$375,000	$575,000	$575,000	$575,000
	150,000	−$100,000	$300,000	$500,000	$700,000	$700,000
	200,000	−$250,000	$150,000	$350,000	$550,000	$950,000

The expected payoff associated with each cut alternative is

Cut Level	Expected Payoff
50,000	$200,000
100,000	$410,000
125,000	$435,000
150,000	$420,000
200,000	$310,000

For example, if the cutting level is 125,000 trees, the expected payoff is

$$E[\text{payoff}] = (-\$25,000)(0.10) + \$375,000(0.40) + \$575,000(0.50)$$
$$= \$435,000$$

Then, according to the expected value criterion, the S. Claus Tree Company should cut 125,000 trees because this level produces the highest expected profit.

ADDITIONAL PROBLEMS

Section 18–1

18. In your own words, discuss the three decision-making environments and provide a business example of each.

19. How are decision making under risk and decision making under uncertainty similar? Show an example to demonstrate.

Section 18–2

20. In making subjective probability assessments, what three requirements must be satisfied? Illustrate with an example.

21. What is meant when we say that subjective probabilities must reflect a decision maker's state of mind? Discuss.

22. At the Goldman Company, Harry Evers was recently criticized by his superiors for his poor subjective probability assessments. In one case, he assessed the chances of a shipment of raw materials arriving in less than five days to be 70 percent, but it later turned out that the shipment took eight days to arrive. This resulted in unexpected production delays. If the 70 percent assessment reflected Harry's state of mind, were the superiors justified in criticizing Harry? Discuss.

23. Gilbert Smith of the Deerfield Oil Refining Company said the odds of running short of crude oil this month are 8 to 3. Translate these odds into a subjective probability assessment for the chances that the company will run short of crude oil.

24. Andria Worden works for one of the large stock brokerage firms in New York City. Recently she performed extensive research on a particular stock. She then issued a probability statement regarding the future performance of the stock. Her assessments were

$$P(\text{increase in value}) = 0.82$$
$$P(\text{no increase in value}) = 0.24$$

Comment on Andria's probability assessments.

25. The Pick-It-Up Garbage Company has an option to take over the garbage collection in a new neighborhood. There are 450 customers who will pay $4 per month for service. Pick-It-Up will have to hire a new person at $900 per month and lease a new truck at $300 per month. Gas and other expenses will run $200 per month.

Given the information presented here, what decision environment is indicated? Why? What are Pick-It-Up's alternatives?

Section 18–3

26. Discuss what is meant by the term *nonprobabilistic decision criteria*. Provide an example.

27. Discuss the difference between the maximin and the maximax decision criteria.

28. The Fairviews Development Company is considering building homes on some property it owns in Little Rock, Arkansas. Zoning will permit up to six homes to be built on the property. However, the city planning department requires that the builder submit a plan in advance showing the exact number of units to be constructed on the property. It also requires that all homes be built within a six-month period (essentially at the same time). Thus, it will not be possible for the development company to build homes one at a time until the demand is saturated.

    If Fairviews builds more homes than are demanded in the regular market, it will be possible for them to sell the homes at 50 percent of the building cost. For those homes sold in the regular market, the developer will earn 30 percent over his building cost, which is $80,000. Using the maximax decision rule, how many homes should the developer build?

29. Referring to problem 28, how many homes should be built if the maximin decision rule is used? Be sure to construct a payoff table.

30. Referring to problem 28, suppose the developer is considering three cost levels for homes in the development. One cost is the $80,000 already considered in problem 28 and 29. A second cost level is a less expensive $60,000 home. If supply exceeds demand for these lower-cost homes, the builder can recover $40,000 through condemnation and will earn a 20 percent profit over cost for all homes sold on the regular market.

    A third cost level is $100,000 for each home. If supply exceeds demand, the builder can recover 55 percent of his costs and he also stands to make 28 percent on each house sold on the regular market.

    Using payoff tables, indicate the number of homes that the developer should build under each cost assumption. Provide a separate answer based on the maximin and maximax decision criteria.

31. Referring to problem 30, suppose the developer assesses the following probability distributions for the number of homes sold at each cost level.

$60,000		$80,000		$100,000	
Demand	P(Demand)	Demand	P(Demand)	Demand	P(Demand)
0	0.05	0	0.06	0	0.09
1	0.10	1	0.10	1	0.15
2	0.15	2	0.20	2	0.25
3	0.25	3	0.40	3	0.40
4	0.30	4	0.10	4	0.05
5	0.10	5	0.10	5	0.05
6	0.05	6	0.04	6	0.01

    For each cost alternative, determine the best production level using the expected payoff criterion. Then determine which cost level the developer should use for building homes on this parcel of land.

32. The Home-Sweet-Home Corporation builds condominiums in Dallas, Texas. At

present, the firm is considering a new condominium complex. The question is how many units to build.

Assume that the land cost will be $100,000 and that the cost of building will be $120,000, plus $48,000 for each unit. Because of design problems, Home-Sweet-Home must build the units in blocks of ten. Given that the company has decided to build, the production levels are

10
20
30
40
50

Each unit sells for $80,000 if sold in the regular market. However, if demand does not meet supply, Home-Sweet-Home will be forced to auction the units, and the average price will be $21,000.

Set up a payoff table assuming the possible demand levels are

0
10
20
30
40
50

33. Referring to problem 32, what is the best decision if the maximin criterion is used? Show how you arrived at your answer.

34. Referring to problem 32, what is the best decision if the maximax criterion is used? Show how you arrived at your answer.

35. Referring to problem 32, assume that the real estate marketing consultants Home-Sweet-Home has hired have assessed the following probability distribution for condominium demand:

Demand	Probability
0	0.05
10	0.10
20	0.25
30	0.25
40	0.20
50	0.15
	1.00

Using the expected value criterion, how many units should Home-Sweet-Home build?

36. The production manager for a beer company has been asked to help upper management in deciding whether or not to market a new dark beer. If the new beer is

successful, the company will make $1 million, but if the beer is a failure, the company stands to lose $625,000. The production manager feels that there is a 60 percent chance that the new beer will be successful. Construct the payoff table for the decision facing the beer company.

37. Referring to problem 36, what decision should the company make if it wishes to maximize its expected payoff?

38. Referring to problems 36 and 37, suppose marketing personnel have determined that there are several levels of success and failure possible with the new beer. These possibilities (states of nature) and the assessed probabilities are

Success Level	Probability
Excellent ($1,200,000)	0.30
Good ($1,000,000)	0.30
Fair ($100,000)	0.20
Poor ($-$625,000)	0.20
	1.00

Develop the payoff table that reflects these states of nature.

39. Given the payoff table in problem 38, what decision should the company make if it wishes to maximize its expected payoff?

40. The owner of a large service station must decide before winter arrives how many gallons of antifreeze to order and have in inventory. Demand for antifreeze will depend on the winter's temperatures. The service station is located in an area with usually mild temperatures, but if cold weather hits, the car owners in the area panic and immediately demand antifreeze.

   The antifreeze costs the station owner $2.50 per gallon and is sold for $6.25 a gallon. Any antifreeze left over after the winter season will be sold to a wholesaler for $1.00 per gallon. Based on past history, the owner feels that the demand will be one of the following, with the associated probability:

Demand Level	Probability
500	0.10
1,000	0.30
1,500	0.40
2,000	0.20
	1.00

   Develop a payoff table that indicates the possible alternatives and associated payoffs for each state of nature.

41. Referring to problem 40, what level of antifreeze should the station owner stock in inventory if he wishes to maximize his expected profit?

42. The bakery manager at a large supermarket must decide how many large, expensive, fancy cakes to have the bakers make each morning. The cakes cost $2.25 each to make and sell for $8.00. Any leftover cakes can be sold for $1.25 each.

Past sales records indicate that demand should have the following probability distribution:

Demand Level	Probability
0	0.10
1	0.30
2	0.25
3	0.20
4	0.10
5	0.05
6 or more	0
	1.00

Develop a payoff table for this decision problem.

43. Referring to problem 42, how many expensive cakes should the manager tell the bakers to prepare each day?

Section 18–4

44. The Continental Automobile Agency of Levelport, Washington, is considering two alternative advertising plans. The first plan will take advantage of the radio and television media and is projected to cost $40,000. The marketing department has analyzed this advertising approach and, based on a joint meeting with Continental's sales managers, believes that the following probability distribution on revenue increases is accurate:

Increased Revenue	Probability
$ 20,000	0.10
30,000	0.10
40,000	0.20
60,000	0.20
80,000	0.20
90,000	0.10
100,000	0.10
	1.00

The second plan is to use billboard and poster advertising at a cost of $12,000. However, the marketing department feels that this approach would not be as effective in generating added revenue as the first approach. This is reflected in the following probability distribution:

Increased Revenue	Probability
$ 4,000	0.10
5,000	0.10
10,000	0.25

20,000	0.25
30,000	0.10
40,000	0.10
50,000	0.10
	1.00

Because of the fear of "overkill," the company has decided not to try both approaches simultaneously. However, the managers did agree that if the billboard approach was chosen and it resulted in $10,000 or less in added revenues, they could switch to the television-radio approach at the original cost but with all potential revenue levels reduced by $5,000. They assume the probabilities would not be affected.

a. Set up the appropriate decision tree for the decision problem facing the Continental Automobile Agency.

b. Using the criterion of maximizing expected increase in net revenues, what decision strategy should Continental take?

45. The Balbado Corporation owns and operates a large orchard on the West Coast. Before the apple season, Balbado was approached by a grocery chain which proposed that Balbado sell 300,000 pounds of apples at a fixed price of $0.10 per pound. The grocery chain would pay for all shipping costs to get the apples to its central warehouse. The problem facing Balbado is whether to accept this offer or to attempt to market its entire crop on the open market.

An uncertainty exists regarding the size of the upcoming crop. If such factors as weather are good, the crop will be large (600,000 pounds). However, bad weather could cause the crop to be small (400,000 pounds). Based on available information. Balbado executives have assessed a 60 percent probability that the season will be good.

The price of apples on the open market depends on the size of the crop on both the West Coast and the East Coast. The following matrix indicates the possible open-market prices along with the assessed probabilities. Assume that the crop size on the East Coast is independent of the crop size on the West Coast.

		East Coast Crop Size	
		Large	Small
West Coast Crop Size	Large	$0.04 \\ p = 0.18	$0.08 \\ p = 0.42
	Small	$0.07 \\ p = 0.12	$0.15 \\ p = 0.28

Assuming that Balbado will be able to sell its entire crop in any case, should it accept the grocery chain's offer if it wishes to maximize its expected revenue?

46. Referring to problem 45, suppose Balbado feels it will be able to negotiate the following new deal with the grocery chain. The contract price paid to Balbado would be reduced to $0.09 per pound. Balbado commits to deliver 150,000 pounds

at this price with the option of committing to supply the remaining 150,000 pounds at $0.09 per pound after it determines what the West Coast crop size will be. This decision must be made before the size of the East Coast crop is known, however.

To negotiate this deal, Balbado would have to retain the services of legal council for a fee estimated to be $2,000.

Using any applicable information from problem 45, determine whether Balbado should propose this new deal to the grocery chain. Base your decision on expected revenues.

47. Referring to problems 45 and 46, if you were the purchasing manager for the grocery chain and Balbado did make the offer outlined in problem 46, would you recommend that it be accepted if your only other alternative were to buy 300,000 pounds of apples on the open market? Assume that you have assessed the same probabilities as Balbado regarding crop size. Base your conclusion on expected costs.

C A S E S

18A   Rockstone International, Part 1

Rockstone International is one of the world's largest diamond brokers. The firm purchases stones from South Africa which must be cut and polished for sale in the United States and Europe. The diamond business has been very profitable, and from all indications it will continue that way. However, R. B. Penticost, president and chief executive officer for Rockstone International, has stressed the need for effective management decisions throughout the organization if Rockstone is to continue to be profitable and competitive.

Normally R. B. does not involve herself in personnel decisions, but today's decision is not typical. Beth Harkness, Rockstone's personnel manager, is considering whether or not to hire Hans Marquis, "world-famous diamond cutter," to fill the opening left when Omar Barboa, "former world-famous diamond cutter," broke both his hands in a freak skateboard accident almost one month ago. Hans Marquis, if hired, will be paid on a commission basis at the rate of $5,000 per stone he successfully cuts. Because of professional pride, Hans will accept nothing if he unsuccessfully cuts a stone (smashes it to bits).

In the past, the decision to hire Hans would have been simple. If he was available, he would be hired. However, within the last six months, the Lictenstien Corporation, located in Pretoria, South Africa, developed the world's first diamond-cutting machine. This machine, which can be leased for $1 million per year, is guaranteed to successfully cut 90 percent of the stones.

Although Hans Marquis has an excellent reputation, Rockstone International cannot be sure about his percentage of successful cuts due to the extreme secrecy in the diamond business. Hans claims that his success rate is 95 percent, but he has been known to exaggerate. Rockstone executives, including Penticost, have made the following assessments based on all the information they could obtain:

Success Rate	Probability
0.97	0.10
0.95	0.40
0.90	0.30
0.85	0.10
0.80	0.10
	1.00

Rockstone purchases each stone at a cost of $15,000. If a stone is successfully cut, four diamonds can be salvaged at an average sales price of $35,000 each. Harry Winkler, sales and purchasing manager, has indicated that 100 stones will need to be cut this year.

R. B. Penticost figures there must be some way to decide whether to hire Hans Marquis or to lease the new machine.

REFERENCES

Baird, Bruce F. *Introduction to Decision Analysis.* North Scituate, Mass.: Duxbury, 1978.

Brown, R. V.; Kahr, A. S.; and Peterson, C. *Decision Analysis for the Manager.* New York: Holt, Rinehart and Winston, 1974.

Brown, Rex V. "Do Managers Find Decision Theory Useful?" *Harvard Business Review* 48 (May–June 1970): 78–89.

Kristy, James E. "Managing Risk and Uncertainty." *Management Review,* September 1978, pp 15–22.

Magee, J. F. "Decision Trees for Decision Making." *Harvard Business Review* 42 (July–August 1974): 126–38.

Raiffa, Howard. *Decision Analysis: Introductory Lectures on Choices under Uncertainty.* Reading, Mass.: Addison-Wesley, 1968.

Schlaifer, Robert. *Analysis of Decisions under Uncertainty,* New York: McGraw-Hill, 1978.

Winkler, Robert L. *Introduction to Bayesian Inference and Decision.* New York: Holt, Rinehart and Winston, 1972.

BAYESIAN POSTERIOR ANALYSIS

19

WHY DECISION MAKERS NEED TO KNOW

Chapter 18 introduced the three basic decision-making environments and the expected value criterion as a tool for making decisions in an environment of risk or uncertainty. Peter F. Drucker, who has probably written more about business management than any other person, emphasizes that the normal management operating environments are risk and uncertainty. He also states that managers need quantitative tools to help use the continual flow of information they receive about their risky or uncertain environment.

Bayesian decision makers accept the premise that their states of mind (and therefore subjective probabilities) can and should change as new information affecting the decision is obtained. Decision makers need a formal basis for combining prior information and new information to make the best decision. *Bayesian posterior analysis* provides such a basis and is the subject of this chapter.

CHAPTER OBJECTIVES

The objective of this chapter is to introduce the Bayesian approach to revising the probabilities assigned to states of nature in a decision environment. It will use examples to show how added information is used with the Bayesian technique to revise prior information.

STUDENT OBJECTIVES

After studying the material presented in this chapter, you should be able to

1. Recognize applications of Bayesian posterior analysis in the business world.
2. Apply the revision process to find new probabilities based on new information.
3. Understand how the Bayesian revision procedure incorporates new information into a decision process.

BAYES' RULE

19-1

Chapter 4 introduced the concept of conditional probabilities. **Conditional probabilities** are important in many decision-making situations. For instance, medical researchers are interested in determining the probability of a person getting cancer, given that the person was exposed to hazardous chemicals; that is,

$$P(\text{cancer}|\text{hazardous chemicals})$$

Educators are interested in the probability a student learns math skills, given that the student completed certain background work:

$$P(\text{learning skills}|\text{background work})$$

Managers are interested in the probability a worker will develop superior skills, given that the worker receives a certain job advancement sequence:

$$P(\text{work skills}|\text{advancement sequence})$$

Such conditional probabilities are calculated using probability rule 6 found in chapter 4.

$$P(E_1|E_2) = \frac{P(E_1 \text{ and } E_2)}{P(E_2)}$$

However, in many practical applications, decision makers may know for certain an event has occurred but not know what the chances were of that event occurring before the fact and thus will not be able to use probability rule 6 directly. For example, suppose an oil exploration company wants to determine the probability that its geologist's report will be favorable, given there is oil at the site; that is,

$$P(\text{favorable report}|\text{oil}) = ?$$

If the company applied probability rules 6 and 8, this probability would be

$$P(\text{favorable report}|\text{oil}) = \frac{P(\text{favorable report and oil})}{P(\text{oil})}$$

$$= \frac{P(\text{favorable report})P(\text{oil}|\text{favorable report})}{P(\text{oil})}$$

In this case the exploration company might have information to supply the probabilities in the numerator, but would not know the probability of oil needed in the denominator.

For these types of problems, an extension of conditional probability called **Bayes' rule** can be used. Bayes' rule might best be developed through the following example.

Winner Bakery makes and distributes frozen bread loaves. The company has one production plant and one central warehouse, where all products are stored until they can be moved to sales distribution points. The production plant has two lines, A and B. Line A produces 60 percent of all loaves, and line B produces the remaining 40 percent. Winner has had quality control problems. The production manager, after extensive testing, has determined that 5 percent of the loaves produced on line A are defective and that 10 percent of the loaves produced on line B are defective.

The two production lines use different combinations of equipment and workers, and the accounting department keeps cost records on each line. Winner Bakery offers a money-back guarantee on any defective loaves, and the plant manager wants to allocate these costs to the two production lines. However, she cannot identify which line produced any specific defective loaf and therefore decides to prorate the cost of honoring guarantees between the two lines. She wants to determine the following:

a. If a defective loaf is returned, what is the probability it came from line A?
b. If a defective loaf is returned, what is the probability the loaf came from line B?

She can then allocate the cost of defective loaves based on these probabilities.

This problem can be solved using conditional probabilities in the following manner:

1. Using conditional probability statements, the manager wants to determine
   a. P(loaf came from line A|loaf is defective)
   b. P(loaf came from line B|loaf is defective)
2. Using the conditional probability rule (rule 6),

$$P(\text{line A}|\text{defective loaf}) = \frac{P(\text{line A and defective loaf})}{P(\text{defective loaf})}$$

Although we do not know any of these probabilities directly, we know

$$P(\text{line A}) = 0.6$$
$$P(\text{defective loaf}|\text{line A}) = 0.05$$

and so

$$P(\text{line A}|\text{defective loaf}) = \frac{(0.6)(0.05)}{P(\text{defective loaf})}$$

3. The only trouble now is that we don't know the overall probability of a loaf being defective. To find P(defective loaf), we ask how a defective loaf can be produced. The answer is that a loaf can be defective and produced by line A or defective and produced by line B. The next step is to find the probability of each:

$$
\begin{aligned}
P(\text{line A and defective loaf}) &= P(\text{line A})P(\text{defective loaf}|\text{line A}) \\
&= (0.6)(0.05) \\
&= 0.03 \\
P(\text{line B and defective loaf}) &= P(\text{line B})P(\text{defective loaf}|\text{line B}) \\
&= (0.4)(0.1) \\
&= 0.04
\end{aligned}
$$

Then, because we can get a defective loaf from *either* line A or line B, we use the addition rule to get

$$P(\text{defective loaf}) = P(\text{defective loaf and line A})$$
$$+ P(\text{defective loaf and line B})$$
$$= 0.03 + 0.04$$
$$= 0.07$$

4. Thus the probability that a defective loaf was actually produced on line A is

$$P(\text{line A}|\text{defective loaf}) = \frac{P(\text{line A and defective loaf})}{P(\text{defective loaf})}$$
$$= \frac{(0.6)(0.05)}{0.07}$$
$$= 0.428$$

and, since a defective loaf must come from either line A or line B,

$$P(\text{line B}|\text{defective loaf}) = 1 - P(\text{line A}|\text{defective loaf})$$
$$= 1 - 0.428$$
$$= 0.572$$

This conditional probability application has used Bayes' rule, which we now formally define:

BAYES' RULE

Let A_i ($i = 1, 2, 3, \ldots, n$) be a complete set of mutually exclusive events. Let B be another event which is preceded by an A_i event. And $P(A_i)$ and $P(B|A_i)$ must be known. Then

$$P(A_1|B) = \frac{P(A_1)P(B|A_1)}{\sum_{i=1}^{n} P(A_i)P(B|A_i)}$$

Using Bayes' rule directly in our bread example, let

$$A_1 = \text{event: loaf came from line A}$$
$$A_2 = \text{event: loaf came from line B}$$
$$B = \text{event: loaf is defective}$$

The manager knows the following probabilities:

$$P(A_1) = 0.6$$
$$P(B|A_1) = 0.05$$
$$P(A_2) = 0.4$$
$$P(B|A_2) = 0.1$$

Therefore

$$P(A_1|B) = \frac{P(A_1)P(B|A_1)}{P(A_1)P(B|A_1) + P(A_2)P(B|A_2)} = \frac{(0.6)(0.05)}{(0.6)(0.05) + (0.4)(0.1)}$$

$$= \frac{0.03}{0.03 + 0.04}$$

$$= 0.428$$

Remember, we began with the plant manager who was trying to allocate costs of defective loaves between the production lines. Her problem has been solved. She should allocate 42.8 percent of all costs to line A and 57.2 percent to line B.

Consider another example using Bayes' rule. Merrit Electronics manufactures electronic calculators at three locations; 50 percent of the calculators are produced at location A, 30 percent at location B, and 20 percent at location C. Thus

$$P(A) = 0.50$$
$$P(B) = 0.30$$
$$P(C) = \underline{0.20}$$
$$1.00$$

The quality control systems differ at the three locations, and the proportions of defective calculators produced also differ: location A produces 5 percent defectives, and location B and location C produce 7 and 12 percent defectives, respectively. Thus

$$P(\text{defective}|A) = 0.05$$
$$P(\text{defective}|B) = 0.07$$
$$P(\text{defective}|C) = 0.12$$

Merritt Electronics requires each manufacturing location to be a profit center. Therefore the cost of replacing or repairing defective calculators must be allocated to the three locations. Once a defective calculator has been returned for replacement or repair, Merrit must determine the probability it was made at location A, B, or C. Although Merrit knows $P(\text{defective}|A)$, what the firm really wants is

$$P(A|\text{defective}) = ?$$
$$P(B|\text{defective}) = ?$$
$$P(C|\text{defective}) = ?$$

Once these probabilities are known, Merrit could allocate costs on a percentage basis as determined by these probabilities. Using Bayes' rule, we can find the following allocation percentages:

$$P(A|\text{defective}) = \frac{P(A)P(\text{defective}|A)}{P(\text{defective})}$$

$$P(B|\text{defective}) = \frac{P(B)P(\text{defective}|B)}{P(\text{defective})}$$

$$P(C|\text{defective}) = \frac{P(C)P(\text{defective}|C)}{P(\text{defective})}$$

First, we find $P(\text{defective})$ by summing the **joint probabilities** of defective calculators and plants:

$$P(\text{defective}) = P(A \text{ and defective}) + P(B \text{ and defective}) + P(C \text{ and defective})$$
$$= P(A)P(\text{defective}|A) + P(B)P(\text{defective}|B) + P(C)P(\text{defective}|C)$$

Therefore

$$P(\text{defective}) = 0.50(0.05) + 0.30(0.07) + 0.20(0.12)$$
$$= 0.025 + 0.021 + 0.024$$
$$= 0.07$$

so

$$P(A|\text{defective}) = \frac{P(A)P(\text{defective}|A)}{P(\text{defective})} = \frac{0.50(0.05)}{0.07}$$
$$= 0.3571$$

$$P(B|\text{defective}) = \frac{P(B)P(\text{defective}|B)}{P(\text{defective})} = \frac{0.30(0.07)}{0.07}$$
$$= 0.3000$$

$$P(C|\text{defective}) = \frac{P(C)P(\text{defective}|C)}{P(\text{defective})} = \frac{0.20(0.12)}{0.07}$$
$$= 0.3429$$

Thus the appropriate allocation of replacement or repair costs should be

Location A—35.71%

Location B—30.00%

Location C—34.29%

Bayesian Statistics and the Human Thought Process

Bayes' rule allows decision makers to incorporate new information into the decision-making process. When most people make nonrepetitive decisions in a changing environment they follow a relatively constant decision process. They make a tentative decision, gather new information, use this new information to modify the tentative decision, gather more new information, use this new information to update the decision, and so on until the time comes to act. Then they follow the course of action dictated by their decision criteria.

Suppose that before going to bed at night a contractor hears the weather forecaster predict that a cold front will move in the next morning and the chance of rain will increase to 50 percent through the day. The contractor may tentatively decide to cancel the concrete he had ordered for tomorrow. However, he will modify this decision based on the weather conditions in the morning. If the sky is dark and overcast the next day, he most likely will decide to cancel the concrete; if the sky is clear and blue, he will likely decide not to cancel. Thus he will either affirm or change his tentative decision based on new information. Up until the point at which he must make the final decision, he will most likely be watching the sky to collect current information.

As another example, the transportation manager for a large corporation has tentatively decided to change the brand of tires she specifies on the company's fleet of sales cars. She has based this decision on an article in a trade journal. However, before making the decision final, she decides to test a few new tires. If the test indicates that the new brand is more economical, the manager may decide, based on the journal article and the test, to change the brand of tires. However, if the test results are negative, she may revise her original decision and decide not to change brands.

A major strength of Bayesian decision analysis is that it provides managers with a systematic method for using new information to revise prior opinions. The next section discusses how to revise prior opinions (or probabilities) based on new information.

SKILL DEVELOPMENT PROBLEMS FOR SECTION 19–1

The following exercises have been included to help you gain a better understanding of the material presented in this section. There are additional problems at the end of this chapter.

1. The Skiwell Manufacturing Company gets materials for its cross-country skis from two suppliers. Supplier A's materials make up 40 percent of what is used, with Supplier B providing the rest. Past records indicate that 15 percent of Supplier A's materials are defective and 10 percent of B's are defective. Since it is impossible to tell which supplier the materials came from once they are in inventory, the manager is wondering which supplier most likely supplied the defective materials the foreman has brought to his attention.

2. Alpine Cannery is currently processing vegetables from the summer harvest. The manager has found a case of cans that has not been properly sealed. There are three lines that processed cans of this type and the manager wants to know which line is responsible for this mistake.

Line	Contribution to Total	Percent Defective
1	0.40	0.05
2	0.35	0.10
3	0.25	0.07

3. Cascade Paint mixes paint in three separate plants and then ships the unmarked cans to a central warehouse. Plant A supplies 50 percent of the paint, and past records indicate that the paint is incorrectly mixed 10 percent of the time. Plant B contributes 30 percent, with a defective rate of 5 percent. Plant C supplies 20 percent, with paint mixed incorrectly 20 percent of the time. If Cascade guarantees its product and spent $10,000 replacing improperly mixed paint last year, how should the cost be distributed among the three plants?

4. The Chocolate House specializes in hand-dipped chocolates for special occasions. Recently several long-time customers have complained about the quality of the chocolates. It seems there are several partially covered chocolates in each box. The defective chocolates should have been caught when the boxes were packed. The manager is wondering which of the three packers is not doing the job properly. Clerk 1 packs 40 percent of the boxes and usually has a 2 percent defective rate, number 2 packs 30 percent, with a 2.5 percent defective rate. Clerk 3 boxes 30 percent of the chocolates and her defective rate is 1.5 percent. Which clerk is most likely responsible for the boxes that have raised the complaints?

5. As the owner of the GreenThumb Nursery, Kelly is concerned about the quality of some of the plants purchased from a local wholesaler, but is not certain why the problem has suddenly cropped up. The company has been buying plants from this particular wholesaler for years and the quality has always been excellent. A new employee has been working for the wholesaler and explains that just before he left his previous position, the wholesaler had started purchasing plants from a new grower in order to meet demand. The old grower has a good reputation and only 2 percent of his plants are unusable. The new grower's plants are of poor quality 30 percent of the time. The old grower currently supplies 80 percent of the wholesaler's plants. If Kelly receives another shipment of unsalable plants, which grower most likely supplied the plants?

BAYESIAN POSTERIOR ANALYSIS

19-2   The Bartlett Corporation supplies fluorescent lights to office buildings in California. Because of its efforts over the past twenty years to stress a quality product at a fair price, Bartlett has developed a large clientele. Like most other organizations, Bartlett continually seeks to improve its profit situation. Thus Bartlett's purchasing agent seeks fluorescent light sources that will produce higher profits.

   Bartlett currently buys its lights from Brightday, Inc., a U.S. firm. Brightday has produced a good product that, based on historical records, has the following probability distribution for defectives:

Proportion Defective	Probability
0.01	0.50
0.02	0.40
0.03	0.10
	1.00

Bartlett guarantees the fluorescent lights it supplies and replaces any defectives at no cost to the customer. Bartlett accountants estimate the overall cost of each replaced defective, including damaged goodwill, at $5.

Bartlett's marketing department has used multiple regression analysis to forecast an expected demand of 100,000 lights for the coming year. If Bartlett purchases all 100,000 lights from Brightday, the probability distribution for defective lights is

No. Defective	Cost	Probability
1,000	$ 5,000	0.50
2,000	10,000	0.40
3,000	15,000	0.10
		1.00

Since Bartlett ultimately will be interested in costs, we have also determined the probability distribution for the cost of replacing defective lights:

$$\text{Cost} = \$5 \times \text{number of defectives}$$

Using the cost distribution, we can find the expected replacement cost if Bartlett buys 100,000 lights from Brightday:

Cost	$P(X)$	$XP(X)$
$ 5,000	0.50	$2,500
10,000	0.40	4,000
15,000	0.10	1,500
	1.00	$8,000 = expected cost

While attending an international convention for fluorescent light dealers, Bartlett representatives were approached by a West German light manufacturer. The West German offered to supply Bartlett with 100,000 lights at a cost, including shipping, which was $0.25 per light less than the current price charged by Brightday. Although the cost of the German manufacturer's lights is less than that of Brightday's lights, Bartlett must still consider replacement costs for defective lights. They have no direct records to use to determine the German's defective rate. Therefore, through other inquiries and their personal experience with European fluorescent light manufacturers, the Bartlett representatives developed the following subjective probability distribution for defectives from this manufacturer:

Proportion Defective	Subjective Probability
0.01	0.10
0.02	0.10
0.04	0.30
0.08	0.30
0.10	0.10
0.15	0.10
	1.00

This distribution indicates that the Bartlett representatives feel the West German lights will likely contain more defectives than the Brightday lights.

Assuming these two suppliers are Bartlett's only alternatives, which one should Bartlett select if it uses the expected value criterion? To make this decision, Bartlett must find the expected cost of the West German alternative. The expected cost of replacing defective lights is found by determining the costs associated with each projected defective level and then using the subjectively assigned probabilities to calculate the expected costs. This is shown in the following table (assume a $5 replacement cost).

Proportion Defective	No. Defective	Cost X	Probability P(X)	XP(X)
0.01	1,000	$ 5,000	0.10	$ 500
0.02	2,000	10,000	0.10	1,000
0.04	4,000	20,000	0.30	6,000
0.08	8,000	40,000	0.30	12,000
0.10	10,000	50,000	0.10	5,000
0.15	15,000	75,000	0.10	7,500
			1.00	$32,000 = expected cost

If we compare only expected replacement costs, we find

$$E[\text{cost}|\text{Brightday}] = \$8,000$$
$$E[\text{cost}|\text{West German}] = \$32,000$$

Since $8,000 is less than $32,000, the choice clearly is to stay with Brightday. This decision assumes no difference in the price Bartlet pays per light. However, the West German lights are $0.25 less than the Brightday lights. One hundred thousand lights purchased from Brightday would cost $25,000 (100,000 × $0.25) more than the same number of lights from the West German manufacturer. Therefore we must add the purchase price difference to Brightday's $8,000 expected replacement cost. Now

$$E[\text{cost}|\text{Brightday}] = \$8,000 + \$25,000$$
$$= \$33,000$$
$$E[\text{cost}|\text{West German}] = \$32,000$$

Since $33,000 is greater than $32,000, the best decision, using expected values, is to purchase from the West German manufacturer. This decision leads to an expected savings of $1,000.

Note that this decision process is consistent with the expected value criterion discussed in chapter 18. However, suppose the long-term business relationship with Brightday has been important to the Bartlett Corporation, and, before this relationship is severed, Bartlett's management would like a little more information. Specifically, Bartlett would like to sample some of the West German supplier's lights and combine the sample information with the subjective prior assessments to make a better decision. The method of incorporating sample information into the decision process is called *Bayesian posterior analysis*. This desire to use both subjectively determined probabilities and sample information together in a decision model makes this a *Bayesian analysis*.

Constructing a Posterior Table

Bartlett representatives decide to test fifty lights before making their final decision, and they find six defectives. Assuming the binomial probability distribution represents the process that produces fluorescent lights, we can use Bayesian posterior analysis through the following steps:

1. We start with the predefined set of possible outcomes, in terms of proportion defectives. These values are

Proportion Defective
0.01
0.02
0.04
0.08
0.10
0.15

2. The **prior probabilities,** which are the probabilities assessed before any other information is obtained, were subjectively determined by Bartlett representatives as follows:

Proportion Defective	Prior Probability
0.01	0.10
0.02	0.10
0.04	0.30
0.08	0.30
0.10	0.10
0.15	0.10
	1.00

3. The sample of $n = 50$ lights produced $X_1 = 6$ defectives.
4. The probability of observing six defectives in a sample of fifty depends, of course, on the fraction of defective lights in the lot of 100,000. But according to step 1, this fraction is estimated to range from 0.01 to 0.15. Therefore we must determine the conditional probability of finding six defectives in a sample of fifty for each possible defective rate. Since the production process can be represented by a binomial distribution, the table in appendix A can be used to determine these conditional probabilities:

Proportion Defective p	Prior Probability	Conditional Probability $P(n = 50, X_1 = 6 \mid$ proportion defective)
0.01	0.10	0.0000
0.02	0.10	0.0004
0.04	0.30	0.0108

Proportion Defective p	Prior Probability	Conditional Probability $P(n = 50, X_1 = 6\|$ proportion defective)
0.08	0.30	0.1063
0.10	0.10	0.1541
0.15	0.10	0.1419
	1.00	

The conditional probabilities in this table are all found in the usual way:

1. Go to the binomial table for $n = 50$.
2. Find the row for $X_1 = 6$.
3. In the column headed $p = 0.04$, find $P(n = 50, X_1 = 6|p = 0.04) = 0.0108$. In a like manner, find $P(n = 50, X_1 = 6|p = 0.08) = 0.1063$; $P(n = 50, X_1 = 6|p = 0.10) = 0.1541$; and so forth.

5. The next step is to find the joint probabilities of the defective levels based on the prior probabilities and the observed sample results. To do this, we apply the multiplication rule of probability.

$$\begin{aligned} \text{Joint probability} &= P(\text{proportion defective and sample result}) \\ &= P(\text{proportion defective})P(\text{sample results}| \\ &\quad \text{proportion defective}) \\ &= (\text{prior probability})(\text{conditional probability}) \end{aligned}$$

This is the numerator in Bayes' rule. We find the joint probabilities as follows:

Proportion Defective	Prior Probability	Conditional Probability	Joint Probability
0.01	0.10	0	0(0.10) = 0
0.02	0.10	0.0004	0.0004(0.10) = 0.00004
0.04	0.30	0.0108	0.0108(0.30) = 0.00324
0.08	0.30	0.1063	0.1063(0.30) = 0.03189
0.10	0.10	0.1541	0.1541(0.10) = 0.01541
0.15	0.10	0.1419	0.1419(0.10) = 0.01419
	1.00		0.06477

By summing the joint probabilities, we find the overall probability of six defective lights in a sample of fifty, given the possible defective levels listed in the left column. Thus 0.06477 is the overall probability of finding six defectives in a sample of fifty, given the prior states of nature. This probability is the divisor in Bayes' rule.

6. The last step in combining the prior probabilities and the sample information is to find the posterior probability for each possible outcome. These posterior probabilities are the revised probabilities of the possible defective levels given the new sample information. They are found by dividing each joint probability by the sum of the joint probabilities:

Proportion Defective	Prior Probability	Conditional Probability	Joint Probability	Posterior Probability
0.01	0.10	0	0	0
0.02	0.10	0.0004	0.00004	$\dfrac{0.00004}{0.06477} = 0.000618$
0.04	0.30	0.0108	0.00324	$\dfrac{0.00324}{0.06477} = 0.050023$
0.08	0.30	0.1063	0.03189	$\dfrac{0.03189}{0.06477} = 0.492358$
0.10	0.10	0.1541	0.01541	$\dfrac{0.01541}{0.06477} = 0.237918$
0.15	0.10	0.1419	0.01419	$\dfrac{0.01419}{0.06477} = 0.219083$
	1.00		0.06477	1.000000

What we have done in these six steps is to go from a prior distribution of proportion defectives, in this case determined subjectively, to an updated version of the distribution of proportion defectives, based on information gained from the sample. These posterior probabilities contain both subjective and sample information and reflect Bartlett's revised state of mind about the proportion of defectives produced by the West German manufacturer. These probabilities incorporate both new and prior information. From the Bayesian viewpoint, it makes sense to use these to reevaluate the purchase decision. We therefore find a new expected value:

Proportion Defective	No. Defective	Cost X	Posterior Probability P(X)	XP(X)
0.01	1,000	$ 5,000	0	$ 0
0.02	2,000	10,000	0.000618	6.18
0.04	4,000	20,000	0.050023	1,000.46
0.08	8,000	40,000	0.492358	19,694.32
0.10	10,000	50,000	0.237918	11,895.90
0.15	15,000	75,000	0.219083	16,431.22
				$49,028.08

Thus, the expected cost of selecting the West German manufacturer is $49,028.08. Since $33,000 is less than $49,028.08, this posterior analysis indicates that the best decision, using expected values, is to buy from Brightday.

Note that the original decision has changed based on this Bayesian posterior analysis. The sample information (six defectives in a sample of fifty) indicated that the probability of finding either 8, 10, or 15 percent defectives is greater than the Bartlett representatives originally thought.

The Manufacturer Asks for a Recount

As indicated throughout this text, whenever sampling occurs we can expect sampling error. Suppose the West German manufacturer believes he has been victimized by an unlucky sample. He is willing to pay for another sample of fifty lights in the hope that Bartlett will change its decision. Of course, since there is no cost to Bartlett, Bartlett is happy to obtain more information. However, Bartlett managers assure the manufacturer that they will not ignore the first sample. In fact, Bartlett will view the posterior probabilities just calculated as the new prior probabilities in the subsequent analysis. Suppose the second sample of fifty lights contains four defectives. The new revised probabilities are determined by using the same six steps just discussed. The results are

Proportion Defective	Prior Probability	Conditional Probability $P(n = 50, X_2 = 4\|$ proportion defective)	Joint Probability	Posterior Probability
0.01	0	0.0015	0	0
0.02	0.000618	0.0145	0.000009	0.000055
0.04	0.050023	0.0902	0.004512	0.027795
0.08	0.492356	0.2037	0.100293	0.617819
0.10	0.237918	0.1809	0.043039	0.265126
0.15	0.219083	0.0661	0.014481	0.089205
	1.000000		0.162334	

These posterior probabilities can now be used to determine the expected cost of purchasing 100,000 bulbs from the West German manufacturer:

Proportion Defective	No. Defective	Cost X	Posterior Probability $P(X)$	$XP(X)$
0.01	1,000	$ 5,000	0	$ 0
0.02	2,000	10,000	0.000055	0.55
0.04	4,000	20,000	0.027795	555.90
0.08	8,000	40,000	0.617819	24,712.76
0.10	10,000	50,000	0.265126	13,256.30
0.15	15,000	75,000	0.089205	6,690.38
				$45,215.89 = expected cost

Since $33,000 is less than $45,215.89, using expected values, Bartlett should still continue to purchase from Brightday.

Two Small Samples or One Large Sample?

In the example, Bartlett selected two successive samples of fifty bulbs. Bartlett used the results from the first sample to revise the probabilities for the possible defective rates. These revised, or posterior, probabilities became the prior probabilities for the second sample. Using results from the second sample, Bartlett representatives again revised the probabilities. Note that selecting two successive samples of fifty and finding six ($X_1 = 6$) and four ($X_2 = 4$) defectives, respectively, provides no more (or no less) information that if one sample of 100 had been selected and ten ($X_1 = 10$) defectives had been found. This is shown as follows:

Proportion Defective	Prior Probability	Conditional Probability $P(n = 100, X_1 = 10\|$ proportion defective)	Joint Probability	Posterior Probability
0.01	0.10	0	0	0
0.02	0.10	0	0	0
0.04	0.30	0.0046	0.00138	0.02775
0.08	0.30	0.1024	0.03072	0.61774
0.10	0.10	0.1319	0.01319	0.26523
0.15	0.10	0.0444	0.00444	0.08928
	1.00		0.04973	

These posterior probabilities (with small differences due to rounding) are the same as the posterior probabilities found after the second sample of fifty lights was selected. Thus the expected cost of buying from the West German manufacturer is the same regardless of whether Bartlett selected one sample of 100 and found ten defectives or two samples of fifty and found six and four defectives, respectively.

A Nonbinomial Example

In the previous example we assumed that the binomial distribution could be used to determine the conditional probabilities of observing the sample information. However, not all decision-making situations can be described by the binomial distribution. Suppose we use another example to demonstrate how Bayesian posterior analysis can be used when the underlying process is not binomial.

The Hamilton-Rock Company sells tax-sheltered annuities (TSAs). A tax-sheltered annuity allows employees who qualify to have part of their monthly paychecks deposited directly with an authorized company. These deposits are not subject to income taxes until the money is withdrawn.

The marketing manager for Hamilton-Rock is concerned each time she hires a new salesperson. She would like to hire only successful salespeople. Based on her past experience, the marketing manager feels TSA salespeople can be divided into four categories: "excellent," "good," "fair," and "poor." By her definition, an "excellent" salesperson will average one TSA sales per day, a "good" salesperson will average one sale every two days, a "fair" salesperson will average one TSA every five days, and a "poor" salesperson will average only one sale every ten days. If we assume that the number of tax-sheltered annuities sold can be reasonably approximated by a Poisson probability distribution, we can describe each salesperson category by λ, the average sales per day. Thus we get

Salesperson Classification	λ
Excellent	1.0
Good	0.5
Fair	0.2
Poor	0.1

Suppose the marketing manager has hired a new salesperson. Based on a complete review of this person's credentials, and a lengthy personal interview, the manager feels the new salesperson has a 20 percent chance of being "excellent," a 40 percent chance of being "good," a 30 percent chance of being "fair," and a 10 percent chance of being "poor." Thus the manager's prior distribution for λ is

λ	Prior Probability
1.0	0.20
0.5	0.40
0.2	0.30
0.1	0.10
	1.00

The standard agreement Hamilton-Rock has with each new employee is that the position is temporary for the first ten working days. After the ten-day trial the employee either will be given a permanent contract or released, as determined by the marketing manager. Of course, during the ten-day trial, sample information is collected on the new person's sales ability.

Suppose the new person sells seven TSA accounts during the first ten days. Bayesian posterior analysis can be used to incorporate this sample information into the decision-making process by using it to revise the prior probabilities. The procedure is as follows:

1. After the prior probability distribution has been assessed, the Poisson distribution table in appendix B can be used to arrive at the following conditional probabilities:

Class	λ	Prior Probability	Conditional Probability $P(X_1 = 7\|\lambda t)$
Excellent	1.0	0.20	0.0901
Good	0.5	0.40	0.1044
Fair	0.2	0.30	0.0034
Poor	0.1	0.10	0.0001
		1.00	

The conditional probabilities in this table are all found in the same way:

1. Go to the Poisson table.
2. Find the row for $X_1 = 7$.
3. In the column headed $\lambda t = 10$(one per day $\times$ ten days), find $P(X_1 = 7|\lambda t = 10) = 0.0901$. In a like manner, find $P(X_1 = 7|\lambda t = 0.5(10) = 5) = 0.1044$; $P(X_1 = 7|\lambda t = 0.2(10) = 2) = 0.0034$; and so forth.

2. Find the joint probability of the salesperson making seven sales, given each possible state of nature. This joint probability is found by multiplying the prior probability by the associated conditional probability:

Class	Prior Probability	Conditional Probability	Joint Probability
Excellent	0.20	0.0901	0.01802
Good	0.40	0.1044	0.04176
Fair	0.30	0.0034	0.00102
Poor	0.10	0.0001	0.00001
	1.00		0.06081

3. Develop each revised or posterior probability by dividing each joint probability by the sum of the joint probabilities:

Class	λ	Prior Probability	Conditional Probability	Joint Probability	Posterior Probability
Excellent	1.0	0.20	0.0901	0.01802	$\dfrac{0.01802}{0.06081} = 0.29633$
Good	0.5	0.40	0.1044	0.04176	$\dfrac{0.04176}{0.06081} = 0.68673$
Fair	0.2	0.30	0.0034	0.00102	$\dfrac{0.00102}{0.06081} = 0.01677$
Poor	0.1	0.10	0.0001	0.00001	$\dfrac{0.00001}{0.06081} = 0.00017$
		1.00		0.06081	1.00000

The sample information has almost totally convinced the marketing manager that the new salesperson is neither "fair" nor "poor." Before the ten-day trial period, the expected daily sales for the new person were

$$E[\lambda] = \Sigma\lambda P(\lambda) = 1.0(0.20) + 0.5(0.40) + 0.2(0.30) + 0.1(0.10)$$
$$= 0.4700$$

After the trial period, the expected sales per day are

$$E[\lambda] = \Sigma\lambda P(\lambda) = 1.0(0.29633) + 0.5(0.68673) + 0.2(0.01677)$$
$$+ 0.1(0.00017)$$
$$= 0.6431$$

Hamilton-Rock pays all new salespeople $40 per day regardless of their sales level. Hamilton-Rock's profit on each TSA sale is $100. The expected daily profit or loss for a new salesperson is

$$E[\text{profit}] = E[\lambda](\$100) - \$40$$

Thus, before the ten-day trial, the expected daily profit from the new salesperson was

$$\begin{aligned} E[\text{profit}] &= 0.47(\$100) - \$40 \\ &= \$47 - \$40 \\ &= \$7 \end{aligned}$$

After ten days, the expected profit is

$$\begin{aligned} E[\text{profit}] &= 0.6431\ (\$100) - \$40 \\ &= 64.31 - \$40 \\ &= \$24.31 \end{aligned}$$

Thus, if the marketing manager was willing to hire the new salesperson based on the prior probabilities (expected profit = $7.00), she should be even more willing after the ten-day trial (expected profit = $24.31).

To test your intuitive understanding of Bayesian posterior analysis, what do you think would happen to the expected profit value if the new person sold only two TSA accounts during the ten-day trial? The expected profit under this condition can be determined precisely:

Class	λ	Prior Probability	Conditional Probability $P(X_1 = 2\|\lambda t)$	Joint Probability	Posterior Probability
Excellent	1.0	0.20	0.0023	0.00046	0.00344
Good	0.5	0.40	0.0842	0.03368	0.25183
Fair	0.2	0.30	0.2707	0.08121	0.60722
Poor	0.1	0.10	0.1839	0.01839	0.13751
		1.00		0.13374	1.00000

The expected sales and profit, given these posterior probabilities, are

$$\begin{aligned} E[\text{sales}] &= 1.0(0.00344) + 0.5(0.25183) + 0.2(0.60722) + 0.1(0.13751) \\ &= 0.2645 \end{aligned}$$

$$\begin{aligned} E[\text{profit}] &= 0.2645(\$100) - \$40 \\ &= \$26.45 - \$40 \\ &= -\$13.55 \quad (\text{loss}) \end{aligned}$$

Thus, if only two sales were made during the trial period, the marketing manager most likely would not want to retain the new salesperson.

On your own, determine the minimum number of sales that must be made during the trial period before a person will be retained. The only requirement for retention is that the expected profit must exceed $0.

SKILL DEVELOPMENT PROBLEMS FOR SECTION 19–2

The following exercises have been included to help you gain a better understanding of the material presented in this section. There are additional problems at the end of this chapter.

6. The owner of a new factory that produces glassware is trying to decide which of two machines to purchase. Machine A has a cost of $5,000 and machine B costs $7,000. The machines both make pressed glass vases. The cost of manufacturing with machine A is $4; B has some different options and the process will cost only $3 per vase. Since this is a new product, the owner has estimated demand levels and probabilities for each. Regardless of which machine is selected, the glassware sells for $8.50 per unit.

Demand Level	Probability
1,000	0.10
2,000	0.20
3,000	0.40
4,000	0.20
5,000	0.10
	1.00

Construct a payoff table listing the decision alternatives and the payoff associated with each.

7. Refer to problem 6. What decision should the owner make if his goal is to maximize the expected payoff? Justify your answer.

8. Referring to problems 6 and 7, the owner has asked a friend with some expertise in marketing to assess demand and give him some input on the levels of demand he can expect for the new product. The information the friend found was combined with the owner's assessment to give the following conditional probabilities:

Demand Level	Conditional Probability P(survey|demand)
1,000	0.05
2,000	0.10
3,000	0.30
4,000	0.40
5,000	0.60

Using this information, compute the revised or posterior probability associated with each level of demand.

9. Using the posterior probabilities computed in problem 8, which machine should the owner purchase?

10. Fresh Fruit Farms has apple orchards on both the north and south sides of the valley. The apples are brought to the packing house on the south ranch in identical crates and once they are stored in the cool house it is impossible to tell where they came from. The foreman has just sampled a crate of apples and found that of the ten apples sampled, three were damaged. The foreman knows that 70 percent of the total apples come from the south ranch and normally 10 percent show some signs of damage. The north ranch contributes 30 percent of the apples and has a damage rate of 25 percent. Use the sample information to revise the probabilities about which orchard the damaged fruit came from.

11. Referring to problem 10, suppose the foreman decides to take a second sample of ten apples and this time comes up with four damaged apples. Combine this sample information with the revised probabilities from problem 10 to arrive at new posterior probabilities.

12. How would the posterior probabilities calculated in problem 11 differ from posterior probabilities that would have been determined if the foreman had chosen one sample of twenty and found seven damaged apples? Discuss.

BAYESIAN POSTERIOR ANALYSIS WITH SUBJECTIVE CONDITIONALS

19-3

The previous section discussed Bayesian posterior analysis and showed how prior probabilities can be revised using sample information. Whereas the prior probabilities were subjectively assessed, the conditional probabilities were based on known probability distributions: the binomial in one case and the Poisson in another. This section shows how Bayesian posterior analysis can be used when the conditional probabilities are also subjectively assessed.

Several project managers at the Actal Corporation are considering writing a proposal for an atomic breeder-reactor. This proposal, which will be submitted to the Department of Energy, will be extremely expensive to develop. These managers are concerned that the federal government may decide to place a moratorium on new atomic power production. If this happens, the money spent to develop the proposal will be wasted. Based on all information available on March 1, the managers assess the following probabilities:

Event	Prior Probability
Moratorium	0.20
No moratorium	0.80
	1.00

Based on these prior probabilities, the managers decide to develop the proposal. However, two weeks later the managers learn that the Department of Energy has transferred two atomic energy experts. These experts had worked in the proposal review department. Although this could mean nothing, there is a great deal of speculation within Actal that it means the moratorium is going to be ordered.

At the weekly progress meeting, the decision to develop the breeder-reactor proposal is reevaluated. After careful consideration, the managers agree that if the moratorium is going to occur, there is a 90 percent chance these employees would have been transferred. In addition they feel that if the moratorium does not occur, the chances the employees would have been transferred is 40 percent. The managers have subjectively assessed the conditional probabilities of this new information, given each possible event. Bayesian posterior analysis can be used as follows:

Event	Prior Probability	Conditional Probability	Joint Probability	Posterior Probability
Moratorium	0.20	0.90	0.18	0.36
No moratorium	0.80	0.40	0.32	0.64
	1.00		0.50	1.00

The new information has changed the managers' thinking about the chances of a moratorium; however, the decision is still to continue preparing the proposal.

Subjective conditional probabilities can be assessed at any time and are dependent upon all previous information. For example, suppose these managers later learn that the Department of Energy has hired five geothermal experts. The managers then assess the following conditional probabilities:

$$P(\text{hiring 5 geothermal}|\text{transferred 2 atomic, moratorium}) = 0.70$$

$$P(\text{hiring 5 geothermal}|\text{transferred 2 atomic, no moratorium}) = 0.10$$

These assessments reflect the fact that two atomic energy specialists were transferred before the five geothermal experts were hired.

To include this latest information in the analysis, the posterior probabilities from the previous step become the prior probabilities at this step, leading to the following table:

Event	Prior Probability	Conditional Probability	Joint Probability	Posterior Probability
Moratorium	0.36	0.70	0.252	0.797
No moratorium	0.64	0.10	0.064	0.203
	1.00		0.316	1.000

With this information, the assessed probability is almost 80 percent that a moratorium on atomic power production will take place. Based on this assessment, the managers might elect to stop the proposal and channel their resources in another direction. (Keep in mind that future information might once again cause Actal to revive the proposal.)

THE VALUE OF INFORMATION

19-4

The previous sections indicated how new information, either objective (that is, sample data) or subjective, can be combined with prior information in the decision-making situation. This new information can cause a decision to change or can support the decision that would have been made with the prior information only. However, obtaining new information is costly, and to determine whether the new information is cost-justified, we must have some idea of its value. This section provides an overview of how the value of new information can be determined.

Certainty is the ideal decision-making environment. Under certainty, managers can make the best decisions and know that the best outcomes will result. However, decision makers forced to act under risk or uncertainty must expect that good decisions will not always be associated with good outcomes. In the managerial world, the difference between a good and a poor outcome is often measured in terms of revenues or costs. Since poor outcomes can occur from good decisions, there is a cost associated with being uncertain. This cost is the *cost of uncertainty* (this term will be formally defined later).

The Best Decision with No Sample Information

The Tree-Light Corporation supplies Christmas-tree ornaments to retail stores across the United States. This year the company has two potential sources of ornaments. One supplier guarantees that in lot sizes of 50,000 ornaments, no more than 3 percent will be defective. The second supplier makes no guarantee, but will sell the ornaments for $0.02 less per ornament than the first supplier. The Tree-Light managers have assessed the following probabilities for defectives produced by the second supplier:

Proportion Defective	Probability
0.02	0.40
0.03	0.20
0.10	0.30
0.20	0.10
	1.00

Tree-Light offers free replacement for any defective ornament. The replacement cost is $0.50 per defective.

Using this information, we can determine which supplier Tree-Light should select if the criterion is to minimize expected cost. For the first supplier, the expected cost has two terms: the expected cost of replacing defective ornaments and a cost differential because the ornaments are more expensive. If we take the 3 percent maximum defective level as the true level, the expected cost for a lot of 50,000 is calculated as follows:

$$\text{Expected replacement cost} = (0.03)(50,000)(\$0.50)$$
$$= \$750$$

and

$$\text{Cost of being more expensive} = 50,000(\$0.02)$$
$$= \$1,000$$

so

$$E[\text{cost first supplier}] = \$750 + \$1,000$$
$$= \$1,750$$

The expected cost for the second supplier is only the expected replacement cost. Since the percentage of defectives for the second supplier is not known, we must use the assessed probabilities:

Proportion Defective	No. Defective in 50,000	Cost	Probability
0.02	1,000	$ 500	0.40
0.03	1,500	750	0.20
0.10	5,000	2,500	0.30
0.20	10,000	5,000	0.10
			1.00

Therefore the expected cost for the second supplier is

$$E[\text{cost second supplier}] = \$500(0.40) + \$750(0.20) + \$2,500(0.30)$$
$$+ \$5,000(0.10)$$
$$= \$1,600$$

Since the criterion is the lowest expected cost, the best decision is to select the second supplier.

The Best Decision with Perfect Information

While the best decision with no sample information for Tree-Light has an expected cost of $1,600, for any lot of 50,000 the actual cost will be $500, $750, $2,500, or $5,000 (see the previous cost table). Therefore, if Tree-Light had some perfect source of information, the ideal decision would be

- If the second supplier will ship a lot with 2 percent or 3 percent defectives, buy from that supplier.
- However, if the second supplier will ship a lot with 10 percent or 20 percent defectives, buy from the first supplier.

Even the ideal decision, made with perfect information, has a cost. This is

$$E[\text{cost}] = \$500(0.40) + \$750(0.20) + \$1,750(0.30) + \$1,750(0.10)$$
$$= \$1,050$$

Perfect information will not eliminate defects; it will simply tell us what level of defectives we can expect. Thus 40 percent of the time, the second supplier will produce 2 percent defectives; 10 percent of the time, it will produce 20 percent defectives; and so forth.

The Expected Value of Perfect Information

The expected cost with perfect information is less than the expected cost of the best decision under uncertainty ($1,600 in the Tree-Light example). The *cost of uncertainty* is the difference between the expected cost under uncertainty and the expected cost given perfect information:

> Cost of uncertainty $= E$[cost|best decision under uncertainty] $- E$[cost| best decision under certainty]

For the Tree-Light example,

$$\text{Cost of uncertainty} = \$1,600 - \$1,050$$
$$= \$550$$

If someone offered to provide perfect information to Tree-Light (maybe the second supplier will count the defectives before shipping), Tree-Light would be willing to spend a maximum of $550 for the perfect information. Any more than $550 would increase the total perfect information cost above the cost of the best decision under uncertainty. This $550 is also called the *expected value of perfect information.*

Cost of Uncertainty for Profit Maximization

The previous example was a cost-minimization problem. The cost of uncertainty also applies when we are dealing with payoff maximization.

Chapter 18 discussed a decision facing Ajax Electronics. The firm was trying to decide how many television sets to produce. The payoff table constructed in chapter 18 is reproduced as table 19–1. This table shows the payoffs for levels of production and demand. The expected payoff for each production level is listed in the right-hand column.

If Ajax Electronics can receive perfect information about which demand level will occur, it can always select the optimal production level. For example, if the production manager knew 700 televisions were going to be demanded, she would produce 700. (*Note:* Ajax would lose $70,000 on each production run and obviously could not stay in business long.) However, if demand were known to be 1,100, Ajax would produce 1,100 sets for a profit of $90,000. Table 19–2 lists the profit associated with the optimal action for each demand level.

TABLE 19–1
Expected payoffs, Ajax Electronics example

		Demand Level 700	800	900 Probability	1,000	1,100	Expected Payoff ↓
		0.05	0.10	0.20	0.40	0.25	
	700	−$ 70,000	−$ 70,000	−$70,000	−$70,000	−$70,000	−$70,000
	800	−$100,000	−$ 30,000	−$30,000	−$30,000	−$30,000	−$33,500
Production Level	900	−$130,000	−$ 60,000	$10,000	$10,000	$10,000	−$ 4,000
	1,000	−$160,000	−$ 40,000	−$20,000	$50,000	$50,000	$11,500
	1,100	−$190,000	−$120,000	−$50,000	−$20,000	$90,000	$ 5,000

Then, given that Ajax Electronics had perfect information about demand, the expected profit would be

$$E[\text{profit}|\text{perfect information}] = -\$70,000(0.05) - \$30,000(0.10)$$
$$+ \$10,000(0.20) + \$50,000(0.40)$$
$$+ \$90,000(0.25)$$
$$= \$38,000$$

Once again, the actual demand level is out of Ajax's control. However, since the expected payoff for the best decision under uncertainty (produce 1,000 television sets) is $11,500, the cost of being uncertain is $38,000 − $11,500 = $26,500. This is also the expected value of perfect information.

Value of Sample Information

The value of perfect information is the maximum amount decision makers should pay to be told which state of nature will occur. In practice, perfect information is rare.

TABLE 19–2
Optimal payoffs, Ajax Electronics example

Demand	Production	Profit	Probability
700	700	−$70,000	0.05
800	800	− 30,000	0.10
900	900	10,000	0.20
1,000	1,000	50,000	0.40
1,100	1,100	90,000	0.25
			1.00

Consequently, the only real use for the value of perfect information is as an upper limit on what we would be willing to pay for less-than-perfect information, such as that which would be derived from a sample.

A prime source of information is a random sample. As discussed in chapter 7, random sampling is always subject to error. Therefore, less-than-perfect information will be generated from a sample. Gathering sample information takes both time and money; thus, before decision makers agree to pay for the sample, they should know its actual value.

Although the calculations involved in determining the value of a sample will not be discussed, the basic steps will be outlined. The value of a sample is the difference between the cost of uncertainty before the sample is observed (*prior cost of uncertainty*) and the cost of uncertainty after the sample (*posterior cost of uncertainty*). The prior cost of uncertainty is computed using prior probabilities, as discussed in this section. The posterior cost of uncertainty is computed in the same manner except that the Bayesian revision process is employed and the posterior probabilities are used in computing the posterior cost of uncertainty.

The method described here deals with finding the value of a sample after that sample has been taken. The problem of computing the value of a sample before the results are known is much more involved. More involved yet is determining the sample size that will maximize the net gain from sampling. Texts by Parsons (1974) and Winkler (1972) contain excellent discussions of these situations (see the reference section at the end of this chapter).

SKILL DEVELOPMENT PROBLEMS FOR SECTION 19–4

The following exercises have been included to help you gain a better understanding of the material presented in this section. There are additional problems at the end of this chapter.

13. The owner of Cynthia's Interiors is trying to decide between two options. She has an offer to sell her business for $25,000 but she is not sure she wants to sell. She currently has a bid in to decorate the new mall in town and if she is awarded the contract, she will make a profit of $70,000. If she does not get the contract, she will lose the $10,000 she has invested in time and samples. She feels there is a 40 percent chance she will be awarded the contract. Based on prior probabilities, what decision should Cindy make if she wishes to maximize expected profit?

14. Referring to problem 13, suppose it were possible to obtain perfect information about whether or not she would be awarded the contract. What is the maximum amount that she should be willing to pay for this information?

15. Referring to problem 13, suppose Cindy had felt that the probability associated with being awarded the contract was 0.60 rather than 0.40. What effect would this have on her decision about how much to pay for perfect information?

16. An investor is currently looking at two projects for investment potential. The first is a new resort facility offering year-round recreational facilities, and the second is an existing sporting goods chain. The sporting goods chain has an excellent reputation and is extremely popular. They need an investor in order to expand into a neighboring city. The owner has guaranteed a profit of $500,000 on the investment. The recreational facility is an unknown quantity but its backers have formulated the following probabilities for profit:

State of Nature	Probabilities
Very successful ($1,000,000)	0.25
Successful ($750,000)	0.40
Marginally successful ($500,000)	0.30
Failure (−$1,000,000)	0.05
	1.00

Based on this information, which of the two alternatives should the investor choose if he wished to maximize expected profit?

17. Referring to problem 16, if it were possible to obtain perfect information on the resort facility, of what value would this be to the investor?

18. The Richlawn Country Club is planning a fundraising dinner to remodel the pool area. The club currently has 2,000 members and the planning committee has decided that the following distribution represents the number of members expected to attend.

Proportion Attending	Probability
0.10	0.10
0.30	0.20
0.50	0.40
0.70	0.30
	1.00

Tickets for the dinner would be sold for $50 and the cost of preparing each meal would be $20. There would also be a fixed fee of $19,000 for extra staff, decorations, and so forth. Should the committee go ahead with the plans for the gala based only on this information?

19. If the committee conducts a survey of club members to find out how many will attend, what would the value of perfect information be in problem 18?

CONCLUSIONS

19-5

This chapter has introduced Bayesian posterior analysis and illustrated how sample information can be used to revise subjectively assessed prior distributions. The Bayesian decision maker feels that this revision process is the core of the managerial decision-making process.

The chapter's discussion has been limited to decisions involving discrete events and discrete probability distributions. More advanced texts, such as *Introduction to Bayesian Inference and Decisions* by Robert Winkler (1972), present the techniques for dealing with continuous events.

This chapter introduced several new terms that are frequently used during Bayesian posterior analysis. These are listed in the chapter glossary. You should become familiar with each one.

CHAPTER GLOSSARY

Bayes' rule   Let A_i ($i = 1, 2, 3, \ldots, n$) be a complete set of mutually exclusive events. Let B be another event which is preceded by an A_i event. And $P(A_i)$ and $P(B|A_i)$ must be known. Then

$$P(A_1|B) = \frac{P(A_1)P(B|A_1)}{\displaystyle\sum_{i=1}^{n} P(A_i)P(B|A_i)}$$

conditional probability   The probability of event A occurring given that another event, B, has occurred. The conditional probability represents the chances of observing the sample information, given each possible state of nature.

joint probability   The probability of the simultaneous occurrence of two or more events. For example, joint probability represents the likelihood of observing the sample information and each state of nature.

prior probability   The probability of an event occurring before sample evidence relevant to the event has been observed.

posterior probability   The probability of an event modified in light of experimental evidence. Posterior probabilities are usually determined by employing Bayes' rule.

posterior table   A table showing the states of nature, the prior probability of each state; the conditional probability of each state, given the sample information; the joint probability of each state, given the prior and conditional probabilities; and the posterior probability for each state.

subjective conditional probability   A probability that represents the chances of observing A given that B has occurred. This probability is assessed subjectively.

SOLVED PROBLEMS

1. The Batlow Newspaper Corporation is considering setting up a division to publish a weekly magazine that summarizes the major news stories of the previous week. Batlow estimates that the weekly fixed cost of establishing the division will be $300,000 and that the variable cost per magazine printed will be $0.50. The maga-

zine will sell for $1.50. Further, the marketing department estimates that of Batlow's one million customers, the following possibilities exist with respect to the percentage who will buy this new magazine:

Proportion Buying	Prior Probability
0.20	0.10
0.30	0.30
0.40	0.40
0.50	0.20
	1.00

a. Based only on this prior information, should Batlow go ahead with the magazine if its goal is to maximize expected profits?

b. Suppose a random sample of twenty newspaper customers is selected and five indicate they will buy the new magazine if it is published. Assuming the binomial distribution applies, determine the revised or posterior probability for each possible proportion of customers who will buy the magazine.

c. Given the sample information, what should the Batlow Corporation do?

Solutions:

a. The first step is to determine the payoff for each possible level of demand as follows:

Proportion Buying	Payoff	Probability
0.20	− $100,000	0.10
0.30	0	0.30
0.40	100,000	0.40
0.50	200,000	0.20
		1.00

The expected payoff, or profit, associated with publishing the new magazine is

$$
\begin{aligned}
E[\text{profit}] &= -\$100,000(0.10) + \$0(0.30) + \$100,000(0.40) \\
&\quad + \$200,000(0.20) \\
&= \$70,000
\end{aligned}
$$

Since $70,000 is greater than $0, Batlow should publish the magazine if its objective is to maximize expected profits.

b. To revise the prior probabilities, we set up the following table and calculate the conditional probabilities using the binomial distribution:

Proportion Buying	Prior Probability	Conditional Probability $P(n = 20, X_1 = 5 \mid$ proportional buying)	Joint Probability	Posterior Probability
0.20	0.10	0.1746	0.01746	0.1680
0.30	0.30	0.1789	0.05367	0.5164
0.40	0.40	0.0746	0.02984	0.2871
0.50	0.20	0.0148	0.00296	0.0285
	1.00		0.10393	1.0000

c. To determine the best decision for Batlow using posterior analysis, we find the expected profit of the magazine alternative using the posterior probabilities.

$$E[\text{profit}] = -\$100,000(0.1680) + \$0(0.5164) + \$100,000(0.2871)$$
$$+ \$200,000(0.0285)$$
$$= \$17,610$$

Although the Bayesian posterior analysis has produced a smaller expected profit, $17,610 is greater than $0, so the best decision is to publish the news summary magazine.

2. The Telephone Company is considering whether to install a new computerized telephone system in Central City. The new system will offer several services such as call forwarding and conference call capability. The new computer can be leased for $1 million per year, and the annual incremental cost per user is estimated at $72. The Telephone Company will charge each customer served $10 per month, or $120 per year.

There are currently 400,000 telephone customers in Central City, and for the Telephone Company to break even, 20,834 customers, or 5.2 percent of all customers, will have to purchase the extra services. The company's marketing department has assessed the following probability distribution for the proportion who will buy the service:

Proportion Buying	Probability
0.02	0.20
0.04	0.30
0.06	0.40
0.08	0.10
	1.00

a. Determine the payoffs for each possible proportion buying.
b. Analyze the problem facing the Telephone Company, using only prior information. Determine the "best" decision using the expected value criterion.

Solutions:

a. $$\text{Payoff} = (P)(400,000)(\$120 - \$72) - \$1,000,000$$

where P = proportion buying the new service

	Alternative 1	Alternative 2
Proportion Buying	Payoff if New System Is Implemented	Payoff if New System Is Not Implemented
0.02	−$616,000	$0
0.04	− 232,000	0
0.06	152,000	0
0.08	536,000	0

b. Using the expected value criterion, we weight the payoff for each possible proportion by the associated probability:

$$E[\text{payoff alternative 1}] = -\$616,000(0.20) + (-\$232,000)(0.30)$$
$$+ \$152,000(0.40) + \$536,000(0.10)$$
$$= -\$78,400$$

$$E[\text{payoff alternative 2}] = \$0$$

Thus the best decision, using only prior information, is not to install the new system since the expected annual payoff for the new system is −$78,400, compared to $0 for not installing.

ADDITIONAL PROBLEMS

Section 19–1

20. A cement company has two suppliers of the raw materials used in making cement. Vendor 1 supplies 30 percent of the raw materials, and vendor 2 supplies 70 percent. Tests have shown that 40 percent of vendor 1's materials are poor quality and 5 percent of vendor 2's materials are poor quality. The cement company's manager has just found some poor-quality materials in inventory. Which company most probably supplied these materials?

21. The Germaine L. Jones Manufacturing Company produces automobile windshields at three plants in the Detroit area. The windshields are sent to a centralized warehouse, where they are so mixed up that the identity of the particular plant is lost.

Plant A makes 50 percent of the windshields, of which 10 percent contain some defect. Plant B accounts for 30 percent of the windshields, and of these 12 percent are defective. Finally, plant C makes 20 percent of the windshields, and of these only 5 percent are defective.

Last year the Germaine L. Jones Company incurred a replacement cost of $400,000 on windshields produced. The cost accountants want to divide this cost between the three plants based on the ratio of defectives produced by each plant. Provide this breakdown in costs for the accountants.

22. The Upland Paving Company has three locations where it mixes its paving material. Forty percent of all material is mixed at plant A, 50 percent at plant B, and 10 percent at plant C. Although Upland would like to believe it has a good quality control system at each plant, sometimes bad batches do get mixed. For instance, in the past, 15 percent of plant A's batches, 10 percent of plant B's batches, and 25 percent of plant C's batches have been bad.

   Suppose a bad batch has just been discovered at a construction project. Which plant most likely provided the bad batch?

23. The Internal Revenue Service (IRS) has selected an individual taxpayer at random for a basic audit from an area in which it is thought that 20 percent of the taxpayers have filed incorrect federal income tax returns. Basic audits are not perfect in that they sometimes indicate a problem when no problem exists and other times indicate no problem when, in fact, a problem does exist. The chance of the basic audit indicating no problem when, in fact, there is a problem, is 90 percent. The probability that the basic audit indicates a problem when, in fact, no problem exists, is thought to be 10 percent. Suppose that a basic audit reveals that there is a problem. What is the probability that there really will be a problem with this tax return?

24. As part of a camera company's quality control procedures, an inspector selects a sample of instant cameras to be thoroughly inspected. Past experience showed that 15 percent of all cameras are defective. The inspector judgmentally selects 55 percent of all cameras to go through a complete inspection. Past records show that of those items selected for inspection, 24 percent are actually good. This means that the inspector does provide some value in the selection process since proportionally fewer good cameras (24 percent) than the population as a whole (85 percent) actually get inspected needlessly. Suppose that a camera which was recently purchased proves to be good. What is the probability that the camera went through a complete inspection?

Section 19–2

25. The operations manager of a toy-manufacturing plant is faced with the decision of whether to buy a new assembly machine or to have the current machine repaired at a cost of $2,800. The new machine will cost $11,000 but can decrease the cost of assembling each toy to $1.00 per unit. The current machine, after repair, will assemble the toys at a cost of $1.50 each. The toy for which the machine will be used sells for $3.25 each. Because of unpredictable consumer buying habits, the demand for this toy is not known with certainty. The demand is expected to occur according to the following probability distribution:

Demand Level	Probability
10,000	0.05
15,000	0.15

20,000	0.20
30,000	0.40
50,000	0.20
	1.00

Construct a payoff table listing the decision alternatives and the payoff associated with each.

26. Refer to problem 25. What decision should the operations manager make if the objective is to maximize the expected payoff? Provide a practical justification for your answer.

27. Referring to problems 25 and 26, suppose an independent market-research firm has been hired by the toy manufacturer. The results of the marketing study are examined by the toy company managers. Basically the report is optimistic, but the managers don't want to ignore their prior assessments. Rather, they wish to include both the prior assessments and the market survey. Consequently, the toy manufacturer assesses the conditional probability of observing the results of the market survey, given each possible demand level. These conditional probabilities are

Demand Level	Conditional Probability P(optimistic survey|demand)
10,000	0.05
15,000	0.10
20,000	0.30
30,000	0.50
50,000	0.80

Using this information, determine the revised or posterior probability associated with each demand level.

28. Using the posterior probabilities calculated in problem 27, what decision should the operations manager make about fixing the current machine or buying the new one?

29. When the Arkansas Milling Company has correctly set up its manufacturing process, 5 percent of the products are defective. When the process is set up incorrectly, 20 percent of the products are defective. Past experience indicates that the chance the process will be set up properly is 85 percent.

Suppose a sample of ten items has been randomly selected and four have been found defective. Use this sample information to revise the probability that the machine is set up correctly.

30. Referring to problem 29, suppose a second sample of fifteen was selected and six were found defective. Combine this sample information with the revised probabilities found in problem 29 to arrive at new posterior probabilities.

31. How would the posterior probabilities calculated in problem 30 differ from the posterior probabilities that would be determined if one sample of twenty-five was selected and ten defectives observed? Discuss.

32. The Lubtree Corporation has just developed a drug called Bedsorine. If the drug is a "good" product, improvement will be shown by 80 percent of the users. If the drug is a "fair" product, 60 percent of the users will show improvement, and if it is a "poor" product, 30 percent will show improvement. Based on laboratory study, the Lubtree Corporation feels that the following probabilities apply:

Quality Level	Probability
Good	0.30
Fair	0.30
Poor	0.40
	1.00

   Suppose a random sample of twenty-five patients is given the drug and fourteen show improvement. Determine the posterior probability for each state of nature.

33. Referring to problem 32, if two more samples of twenty-five were selected, with the results that twelve improved and fifteen improved, respectively, determine the posterior probability for each state of nature.

34. With respect to problems 32 and 33, the Lubtree Corporation has a policy of not putting a drug on the market unless it has in excess of a 90 percent chance of being at least "fair." Using the posterior probabilities determined in problem 33, should Lubtree market the drug Bedsorine?

Section 19–4

35. The King Construction Company has the opportunity to undertake a major development project in the inner city of Washington, D.C. If the project is successful, King Construction will net $2.3 million. If the project is a failure, King Construction will lose $1.2 million. The engineering and planning departments have worked out the following probability assessments for the possible outcomes:

State of Nature	Prior Probability
Successful ($2,300,000)	0.30
Marginally successful ($250,000)	0.30
Failure (−$1,200,000)	0.40
	1.00

   If the King Construction Company does not take this development opportunity, it will select a second project with a sure profit of $125,000.
   Based only on the prior probabilities, what decision should the King Construction Company make if it wishes to maximize expected profit?

36. Referring to problem 35, suppose it were possible to obtain perfect information about this inner-city development project. What would its value be to the King Construction Company? What is the cost to King Construction of being uncertain?

37. Referring to problems 35 and 36, if King Construction could hire consultants to

provide some information about the outcomes of the proposed project, what is the absolute maximum King should be willing to pay for this information? Under what conditions would the company pay this much?

38. One of the major automobile manufacturers is considering purchasing windshields for one car model from the Acme Glass Company. Currently this auto manufacturer is buying the windshields for Windpro, Inc.

Because of the way they are installed, windshields have to be able to withstand a specific level of impact without breaking. Windpro charges $201 for each windshield. Over the past few years 5 percent of Windpro windshields have broken during installation. Glass companies do not refund for broken windshields because the price is set to reflect the possibility of breakage.

Acme proposes to charge $200 for each windshield and claims its product is more reliable than Windpro's. Based on initial testing, the automobile manufacturer has assessed the following probability distribution for the fraction of defectives produced by Acme:

Proportion Defective	Prior Probability
0.03	0.20
0.04	0.30
0.05	0.20
0.06	0.20
0.07	0.10
	1.00

If the auto maker wants to buy 100,000 windshields, what decision should it make using only prior information?

39. With reference to problem 38, suppose it is possible to obtain perfect information about the proportion of defective windshields produced by Acme. What would be the value of the perfect information?

40. Referring to problems 38 and 39, suppose Acme has offered a free sample of 100 windshields to the automaker for testing. The test results in six windshields failing. Given this sample information, what is the best decision for the automaker?

41. Considering the information in problem 40, what is the value of this sample information after the sample has been selected?

42. Bogie Basin Ski Resort managers are considering whether to have a year-end party at the main lodge for their season lift ticket customers. They have 4,000 season lift ticket holders and figure the following distribution represents those who would attend the party:

Proportion Attending	Probability
0.20	0.30
0.25	0.40
0.30	0.20
0.35	0.10
	1.00

Cost estimates indicate a fixed setup and advertising cost of $10,000 plus a variable cost of $10 per person attending. Tickets will be sold for $20.

Using only this information, should the party be held? Also determine the expected value of perfect information.

CASES

19A   Quality Bakery

Quality Bakery, managed by R. D. Poteet, makes specialty breads for distribution in retail outlets in several western U.S. states. Poteet has recently read an article in a trade magazine that described a sequential quality control sampling system. The sequential sampling system involves a process whereby a specified number of loaves are tested and the numbers of good and defective loaves are recorded. Based on the results of this sample, the bakery can decide to test more loaves in the batch or stop sampling and make an accept/reject decision regarding the batch. Depending on the cost of sampling and the time available, the sequential sampling can take on any number of stages with any number of loaves tested at each stage until the sample information indicates that a terminal decision should be made.

Poteet has been somewhat concerned that his bakery's quality control is not what it once was. A suggestion in the journal article was to introduce the system by sampling one loaf and, if required, one more. Thus, initially the sampling system would be limited to two stages and a total of two loaves tested.

At Quality Bakery, a batch contains 400 loaves. Cost accountants have determined that each loaf costs Quality $0.10 to make, including labor and raw materials. Packaging and shipping account for an additional $0.01 per loaf. (If a batch is rejected, the loaves are not packaged or shipped.) The selling price of the loaves is $0.25 each.

If a defective loaf is sold, the cost to Quality in lost goodwill is estimated to be $1 per loaf. Based on past experience, the following percent defectives are possible and should occur with a frequency represented by the associated probabilities:

Proportion Defective	Prior Probability
0.00	0.40
0.01	0.30
0.02	0.20
1.00	0.10
	1.00

This probability distribution indicates that a batch will be either good, fairly good, or completely defective. This results because of the mixing process. A totally bad batch will occur if an ingredient is left out or if bad yeast is used in the mixing process.

R. D. Poteet is attempting to establish the decision rules under the two-stage sampling plan, with a sample size of one loaf at each stage. He has decided to ignore sampling costs.

19B Artistic Americans, Inc.

Artistic Americans, Inc. is a company that has been formed to produce television specials. Artistic has just been approached with an idea for a new special. The cost of producing this special is estimated at $825,000. To finance this type of special, Artistic must secure television advertising contracts to underwrite part or all of the cost. Because of past performance, the advertisers have formed the following financing policy:

Show Rating	Percent Financing
A	100
B	80
C	40
D	0

If the show is given an "A" rating by Troody and Good's Rating Service, Artistic will be able to contract with the advertisers for the full $825,000. (Note that the advertisers pay for the right to advertise and receive no other money if the show is a success.) If the rating is a "B" or "C," Artistic will be forced to finance the production cost itself. Unfortunately rating cannot be determined until after the show has been taped.

The television networks will accept the show for a one-time presentation if it has an "A," "B," or "C" rating by Troody and Good's, with the following payment schedule:

Show Rating	Payment
A	$500,000
B	400,000
C	150,000

Thus, if the special receives an "A" rating, it will be 100 percent financed by the advertisers, and the network will pay Artistic $500,000 for rights to a one-time showing.

Suppose Artistic's management has assessed the following probabilities with respect to the potential ratings for the latest proposed special:

Show Rating	Prior Probability
A	0.20
B	0.30
C	0.40
D	0.10
	1.00

A. L. MacMillan is responsible for making a decision for Artistic and wishes to present the analysis in a logical way to the other members of the management team.

19C   American National, Part 1

American National provides consumer credit to people all over the world in the form of an American National credit card. Eligible persons receive an American National card for a small annual fee.

Each month American National encloses a "special purchase" offer in its card-holder statement. Currently American National is considering offering its customers the opportunity to purchase a set of fancy carving knives at a "reduced" price of $15. (Customers can have the amount added to their next statement.)

American National must pay $100,000 for the right to sell the knives plus $10 per set sold. Currently American National has 100,000 customers. The marketing department has assessed the following probabilities for potential demand:

Proportion Buying	Probability
0.10	0.10
0.15	0.30
0.20	0.30
0.25	0.20
0.30	<u>0.10</u>
	1.00

Fred Turner, American National's executive vice-president, is currently trying to determine whether to offer the knives and also the absolute maximum he would be willing to pay for a market-research study.

19D   American National, Part 2

The marketing department at American National has stated that the cost of sampling the customers to estimate the proportion who will buy the carving knives (see case 19C) is $3,000 fixed and $25 per person sampled if the work is done by American National employees.

Fred Turner wants his eventual decision to be based on as much information as possible. He has asked his executive assistant to determine whether a sample of $n = 50$ would produce information worth its cost.

19E   American National, Part 3

After hearing his executive assistant's report (see case 19D), Fred Turner received a phone call from an old Army pal. This friend is now a market-research consultant with Elmers, Smith, and O'Brady of Dallas, Texas. During the call, Fred mentioned his problem with the knives (cases 19C and 19D). The consultant friend offered to randomly sample twenty of American National's customers and report back with the percentage who will buy.

Fred has agreed to call back later that day with a price he is willing to pay for the information that could be obtained from the sample of twenty customers.

19F   Rockstone International, Part 2

Charley O'Finley, Rockstone's corporate controller, happened to walk into the conference room just as R. B. Penticost had made the decision whether to hire Hans Marquis (see case 18A). R. B. filled O'Finley in on the analysis he and Beth Harkness had used in arriving at the decision.

O'Finley was impressed by the methods used. However, he offered the following suggestion: "Why not hire Marquis on a temporary basis and have him cut five stones? Then, after seeing these results, you could make the decision." He added, "It seems to me that this approach could reduce our cost of uncertainty."

R. B. liked the idea but wondered how this could be done. He also wondered whether the costs involved would be worth the added information.

REFERENCES

Baird, Bruce F. *Introduction to Decision Analysis.* North Scituate, Mass: Duxbury 1978.

Green, Paul. "Bayesian Decision Theory in Advertising." *Journal of Advertising Research* 2 (1962): 33–41.

Hartley, H. O. "In Dr. Bayes' Consulting Room." *American Statistician* 17 (1963): 22–24.

Jones J. M. *Introduction to Decision Theory,* Homewood, Ill.: Irwin, 1977.

Parsons, Robert. *Statistical Analysis.* New York: Harper and Row, 1974.

Raiffa, Howard. *Decision Analysis: Introductory Lectures on Choices under Uncertainty.* Reading, Mass.: Addison-Wesley, 1968.

Schlaifer, Robert. *Analysis of Decisions under Uncertainty,* New York: McGraw-Hill, 1978.

Schlaifer, Robert. *Computer Programs for Elementary Decision Analysis.* Cambridge, Mass.: Harvard University Press, 1971.

Sorenson, J. E. "Bayesian Analysis in Auditing." *Accounting Review 44* (1969): 555–61.

Winkler, R. L. *Introduction to Bayesian Inference and Decision,* New York: Holt, Rinehart and Winston, 1972.

APPENDICES

APPENDIX A   BINOMIAL DISTRIBUTION TABLE

$$P(X_1) = \frac{n!}{X_1!(n - X_1)!} p^{X_1}(q)^{n - X_1}$$

n = 1

P=.01	P=.02	P=.03	P=.04	P=.05	P=.06	P=.07	P=.08	P=.09	P=.10	
X1										**n−X1**
0 .9900	.9800	.9700	.9600	.9500	.9400	.9300	.9200	.9100	.9000	1
1 .0100	.0200	.0300	.0400	.0500	.0600	.0700	.0800	.0900	.1000	0
q=.99	q=.98	q=.97	q=.96	q=.95	q=.94	q=.93	q=.92	q=.91	q=.90	

P=.11	P=.12	P=.13	P=.14	P=.15	P=.16	P=.17	P=.18	P=.19	P=.20	
X1										**n−X1**
0 .8900	.8800	.8700	.8600	.8500	.8400	.8300	.8200	.8100	.8000	1
1 .1100	.1200	.1300	.1400	.1500	.1600	.1700	.1800	.1900	.2000	0
q=.89	q=.88	q=.87	q=.86	q=.85	q=.84	q=.83	q=.82	q=.81	q=.80	

P=.21	P=.22	P=.23	P=.24	P=.25	P=.26	P=.27	P=.28	P=.29	P=.30	
X1										**n−X1**
0 .7900	.7800	.7700	.7600	.7500	.7400	.7300	.7200	.7100	.7000	1
1 .2100	.2200	.2300	.2400	.2500	.2600	.2700	.2800	.2900	.3000	0
q=.79	q=.78	q=.77	q=.76	q=.75	q=.74	q=.73	q=.72	q=.71	q=.70	

P=.31	P=.32	P=.33	P=.34	P=.35	P=.36	P=.37	P=.38	P=.39	P=.40	
X1										**n−X1**
0 .6900	.6800	.6700	.6600	.6500	.6400	.6300	.6200	.6100	.6000	1
1 .3100	.3200	.3300	.3400	.3500	.3600	.3700	.3800	.3900	.4000	0
q=.69	q=.68	q=.67	q=.66	q=.65	q=.64	q=.63	q=.62	q=.61	q=.60	

P=.41	P=.42	P=.43	P=.44	P=.45	P=.46	P=.47	P=.48	P=.49	P=.50	
X1										**n−X1**
0 .5900	.5800	.5700	.5600	.5500	.5400	.5300	.5200	.5100	.5000	1
1 .4100	.4200	.4300	.4400	.4500	.4600	.4700	.4800	.4900	.5000	0
q=.59	q=.58	q=.57	q=.56	q=.55	q=.54	q=.53	q=.52	q=.51	q=.50	

n = 2

P=.01	P=.02	P=.03	P=.04	P=.05	P=.06	P=.07	P=.08	P=.09	P=.10	
X1										**n−X1**
0 .9801	.9604	.9409	.9216	.9025	.8836	.8649	.8464	.8281	.8100	2
1 .0198	.0392	.0582	.0768	.0950	.1128	.1302	.1472	.1638	.1800	1
2 .0001	.0004	.0009	.0016	.0025	.0036	.0049	.0064	.0081	.0100	0
q=.99	q=.98	q=.97	q=.96	q=.95	q=.94	q=.93	q=.92	q=.91	q=.90	

P=.11	P=.12	P=.13	P=.14	P=.15	P=.16	P=.17	P=.18	P=.19	P=.20	
X1										**n−X1**
0 .7921	.7744	.7569	.7396	.7225	.7056	.6889	.6724	.6561	.6400	2
1 .1958	.2112	.2262	.2408	.2550	.2688	.2822	.2952	.3078	.3200	1
2 .0121	.0144	.0169	.0196	.0225	.0256	.0289	.0324	.0361	.0400	0
q=.89	q=.88	q=.87	q=.86	q=.85	q=.84	q=.83	q=.82	q=.81	q=.80	

P=.21	P=.22	P=.23	P=.24	P=.25	P=.26	P=.27	P=.28	P=.29	P=.30	
X1										**n−X1**
0 .6241	.6084	.5929	.5776	.5625	.5476	.5329	.5184	.5041	.4900	2
1 .3318	.3432	.3542	.3648	.3750	.3848	.3942	.4032	.4118	.4200	1
2 .0441	.0484	.0529	.0576	.0625	.0676	.0729	.0784	.0841	.0900	0
q=.79	q=.78	q=.77	q=.76	q=.75	q=.74	q=.73	q=.72	q=.71	q=.70	

	P=.31	P=.32	P=.33	P=.34	P=.35	P=.36	P=.37	P=.38	P=.39	P=.40	
X1											n-X1
0	.4761	.4624	.4489	.4356	.4225	.4096	.3969	.3844	.3721	.3600	2
1	.4278	.4352	.4422	.4488	.4550	.4608	.4662	.4712	.4758	.4800	1
2	.0961	.1024	.1089	.1156	.1225	.1296	.1369	.1444	.1521	.1600	0
	q=.69	q=.68	q=.67	q=.66	q=.65	q=.64	q=.63	q=.62	q=.61	q=.60	

	P=.41	P=.42	P=.43	P=.44	P=.45	P=.46	P=.47	P=.48	P=.49	P=.50	
X1											n-X1
0	.3481	.3364	.3249	.3136	.3025	.2916	.2809	.2704	.2601	.2500	2
1	.4838	.4872	.4902	.4928	.4950	.4968	.4982	.4992	.4998	.5000	1
2	.1681	.1764	.1849	.1936	.2025	.2116	.2209	.2304	.2401	.2500	0
	q=.59	q=.58	q=.57	q=.56	q=.55	q=.54	q=.53	q=.52	q=.51	q=.50	

n = 3

	P=.01	P=.02	P=.03	P=.04	P=.05	P=.06	P=.07	P=.08	P=.09	P=.10	
X1											n-X1
0	.9703	.9412	.9127	.8847	.8574	.8306	.8044	.7787	.7536	.7290	3
1	.0294	.0576	.0847	.1106	.1354	.1590	.1816	.2031	.2236	.2430	2
2	.0003	.0012	.0026	.0046	.0071	.0102	.0137	.0177	.0221	.0270	1
3	.0000	.0000	.0000	.0001	.0001	.0002	.0003	.0005	.0007	.0010	0
	q=.99	q=.98	q=.97	q=.96	q=.95	q=.94	q=.93	q=.92	q=.91	q=.90	

	P=.11	P=.12	P=.13	P=.14	P=.15	P=.16	P=.17	P=.18	P=.19	P=.20	
X1											n-X1
0	.7050	.6815	.6585	.6361	.6141	.5927	.5718	.5514	.5314	.5120	3
1	.2614	.2788	.2952	.3106	.3251	.3387	.3513	.3631	.3740	.3840	2
2	.0323	.0380	.0441	.0506	.0574	.0645	.0720	.0797	.0877	.0960	1
3	.0013	.0017	.0022	.0027	.0034	.0041	.0049	.0058	.0069	.0080	0
	q=.89	q=.88	q=.87	q=.86	q=.85	q=.84	q=.83	q=.82	q=.81	q=.80	

	P=.21	P=.22	P=.23	P=.24	P=.25	P=.26	P=.27	P=.28	P=.29	P=.30	
X1											n-X1
0	.4930	.4746	.4565	.4390	.4219	.4052	.3890	.3732	.3579	.3430	3
1	.3932	.4015	.4091	.4159	.4219	.4271	.4316	.4355	.4386	.4410	2
2	.1045	.1133	.1222	.1313	.1406	.1501	.1597	.1693	.1791	.1890	1
3	.0093	.0106	.0122	.0138	.0156	.0176	.0197	.0220	.0244	.0270	0
	q=.79	q=.78	q=.77	q=.76	q=.75	q=.74	q=.73	q=.72	q=.71	q=.70	

	P=.31	P=.32	P=.33	P=.34	P=.35	P=.36	P=.37	P=.38	P=.39	P=.40	
X1											n-X1
0	.3285	.3144	.3008	.2875	.2746	.2621	.2500	.2383	.2270	.2160	3
1	.4428	.4439	.4444	.4443	.4436	.4424	.4406	.4382	.4354	.4320	2
2	.1989	.2089	.2189	.2289	.2389	.2488	.2587	.2686	.2783	.2880	1
3	.0298	.0328	.0359	.0393	.0429	.0467	.0507	.0549	.0593	.0640	0
	q=.69	q=.68	q=.67	q=.66	q=.65	q=.64	q=.63	q=.62	q=.61	q=.60	

	P=.41	P=.42	P=.43	P=.44	P=.45	P=.46	P=.47	P=.48	P=.49	P=.50	
X1											n-X1
0	.2054	.1951	.1852	.1756	.1664	.1575	.1489	.1406	.1327	.1250	3
1	.4282	.4239	.4191	.4140	.4084	.4024	.3961	.3894	.3823	.3750	2
2	.2975	.3069	.3162	.3252	.3341	.3428	.3512	.3594	.3674	.3750	1
3	.0689	.0741	.0795	.0852	.0911	.0973	.1038	.1106	.1176	.1250	0
	q=.59	q=.58	q=.57	q=.56	q=.55	q=.54	q=.53	q=.52	q=.51	q=.50	

n = 4

	P=.01	P=.02	P=.03	P=.04	P=.05	P=.06	P=.07	P=.08	P=.09	P=.10	
X1											n-X1
0	.9606	.9224	.8853	.8493	.8145	.7807	.7481	.7164	.6857	.6561	4
1	.0388	.0753	.1095	.1416	.1715	.1993	.2252	.2492	.2713	.2916	3
2	.0006	.0023	.0051	.0088	.0135	.0191	.0254	.0325	.0402	.0486	2
3	.0000	.0000	.0001	.0002	.0005	.0008	.0013	.0019	.0027	.0036	1
4	.0000	.0000	.0000	.0000	.0000	.0000	.0000	.0000	.0001	.0001	0
	q=.99	q=.98	q=.97	q=.96	q=.95	q=.94	q=.93	q=.92	q=.91	q=.90	

P=.11	P=.12	P=.13	P=.14	P=.15	P=.16	P=.17	P=.18	P=.19	P=.20	
X1										n-X1
0 .6274	.5997	.5729	.5470	.5220	.4979	.4746	.4521	.4305	.4096	4
1 .3102	.3271	.3424	.3562	.3685	.3793	.3888	.3970	.4039	.4096	3
2 .0575	.0669	.0767	.0870	.0975	.1084	.1195	.1307	.1421	.1536	2
3 .0047	.0061	.0076	.0094	.0115	.0138	.0163	.0191	.0222	.0256	1
4 .0001	.0002	.0003	.0004	.0005	.0007	.0008	.0010	.0013	.0016	0
q=.89	q=.88	q=.87	q=.86	q=.85	q=.84	q=.83	q=.82	q=.81	q=.80	

P=.21	P=.22	P=.23	P=.24	P=.25	P=.26	P=.27	P=.28	P=.29	P=.30	
X1										n-X1
0 .3895	.3702	.3515	.3336	.3164	.2999	.2840	.2687	.2541	.2401	4
1 .4142	.4176	.4200	.4214	.4219	.4214	.4201	.4180	.4152	.4116	3
2 .1651	.1767	.1882	.1996	.2109	.2221	.2331	.2439	.2544	.2646	2
3 .0293	.0332	.0375	.0420	.0469	.0520	.0575	.0632	.0693	.0756	1
4 .0019	.0023	.0028	.0033	.0039	.0046	.0053	.0061	.0071	.0081	0
q=.79	q=.78	q=.77	q=.76	q=.75	q=.74	q=.73	q=.72	q=.71	q=.70	

P=.31	P=.32	P=.33	P=.34	P=.35	P=.36	P=.37	P=.38	P=.39	P=.40	
X1										n-X1
0 .2267	.2138	.2015	.1897	.1785	.1678	.1575	.1478	.1385	.1296	4
1 .4074	.4025	.3970	.3910	.3845	.3775	.3701	.3623	.3541	.3456	3
2 .2745	.2841	.2933	.3021	.3105	.3185	.3260	.3330	.3396	.3456	2
3 .0822	.0891	.0963	.1038	.1115	.1194	.1276	.1361	.1447	.1536	1
4 .0092	.0105	.0119	.0134	.0150	.0168	.0187	.0209	.0231	.0256	0
q=.69	q=.68	q=.67	q=.66	q=.65	q=.64	q=.63	q=.62	q=.61	q=.60	

P=.41	P=.42	P=.43	P=.44	P=.45	P=.46	P=.47	P=.48	P=.49	P=.50	
X1										n-X1
0 .1212	.1132	.1056	.0983	.0915	.0850	.0789	.0731	.0677	.0625	4
1 .3368	.3278	.3185	.3091	.2995	.2897	.2799	.2700	.2600	.2500	3
2 .3511	.3560	.3604	.3643	.3675	.3702	.3723	.3738	.3747	.3750	2
3 .1627	.1719	.1813	.1908	.2005	.2102	.2201	.2300	.2400	.2500	1
4 .0283	.0311	.0342	.0375	.0410	.0448	.0488	.0531	.0576	.0625	0
q=.59	q=.58	q=.57	q=.56	q=.55	q=.54	q=.53	q=.52	q=.51	q=.50	

n = 5

P=.01	P=.02	P=.03	P=.04	P=.05	P=.06	P=.07	P=.08	P=.09	P=.10	
X1										n-X1
0 .9510	.9039	.8587	.8154	.7738	.7339	.6957	.6591	.6240	.5905	5
1 .0480	.0922	.1328	.1699	.2036	.2342	.2618	.2866	.3086	.3280	4
2 .0010	.0038	.0082	.0142	.0214	.0299	.0394	.0498	.0610	.0729	3
3 .0000	.0001	.0003	.0006	.0011	.0019	.0030	.0043	.0060	.0081	2
4 .0000	.0000	.0000	.0000	.0000	.0001	.0001	.0002	.0003	.0004	1
5 .0000	.0000	.0000	.0000	.0000	.0000	.0000	.0000	.0000	.0000	0
q=.99	q=.98	q=.97	q=.96	q=.95	q=.94	q=.93	q=.92	q=.91	q=.90	

P=.11	P=.12	P=.13	P=.14	P=.15	P=.16	P=.17	P=.18	P=.19	P=.20	
X1										n-X1
0 .5584	.5277	.4984	.4704	.4437	.4182	.3939	.3707	.3487	.3277	5
1 .3451	.3598	.3724	.3829	.3915	.3983	.4034	.4069	.4089	.4096	4
2 .0853	.0981	.1113	.1247	.1382	.1517	.1652	.1786	.1919	.2048	3
3 .0105	.0134	.0166	.0203	.0244	.0289	.0338	.0392	.0450	.0512	2
4 .0007	.0009	.0012	.0017	.0022	.0028	.0035	.0043	.0053	.0064	1
5 .0000	.0000	.0000	.0001	.0001	.0001	.0001	.0002	.0002	.0003	0
q=.89	q=.88	q=.87	q=.86	q=.85	q=.84	q=.83	q=.82	q=.81	q=.80	

P=.21	P=.22	P=.23	P=.24	P=.25	P=.26	P=.27	P=.28	P=.29	P=.30	
X1										n-X1
0 .3077	.2887	.2707	.2536	.2373	.2219	.2073	.1935	.1804	.1681	5
1 .4090	.4072	.4043	.4003	.3955	.3898	.3834	.3762	.3685	.3601	4
2 .2174	.2297	.2415	.2529	.2637	.2739	.2836	.2926	.3010	.3087	3
3 .0578	.0648	.0721	.0798	.0879	.0962	.1049	.1138	.1229	.1323	2
4 .0077	.0091	.0108	.0126	.0146	.0169	.0194	.0221	.0251	.0283	1
5 .0004	.0005	.0006	.0008	.0010	.0012	.0014	.0017	.0021	.0024	0
q=.79	q=.78	q=.77	q=.76	q=.75	q=.74	q=.73	q=.72	q=.71	q=.70	

P=.31	P=.32	P=.33	P=.34	P=.35	P=.36	P=.37	P=.38	P=.39	P=.40	
X1										n-X1
0 .1564	.1454	.1350	.1252	.1160	.1074	.0992	.0916	.0845	.0778	5
1 .3513	.3421	.3325	.3226	.3124	.3020	.2914	.2808	.2700	.2592	4
2 .3157	.3220	.3275	.3323	.3364	.3397	.3423	.3441	.3452	.3456	3
3 .1418	.1515	.1613	.1712	.1811	.1911	.2010	.2109	.2207	.2304	2
4 .0319	.0357	.0397	.0441	.0488	.0537	.0590	.0646	.0706	.0768	1
5 .0029	.0034	.0039	.0045	.0053	.0060	.0069	.0079	.0090	.0102	0
q=.69	q=.68	q=.67	q=.66	q=.65	q=.64	q=.63	q=.62	q=.61	q=.60	

P=.41	P=.42	P=.43	P=.44	P=.45	P=.46	P=.47	P=.48	P=.49	P=.50	
X1										n-X1
0 .0715	.0656	.0602	.0551	.0503	.0459	.0418	.0380	.0345	.0312	5
1 .2484	.2376	.2270	.2164	.2059	.1956	.1854	.1755	.1657	.1562	4
2 .3452	.3442	.3424	.3400	.3369	.3332	.3289	.3240	.3185	.3125	3
3 .2399	.2492	.2583	.2671	.2757	.2838	.2916	.2990	.3060	.3125	2
4 .0834	.0902	.0974	.1049	.1128	.1209	.1293	.1380	.1470	.1563	1
5 .0116	.0131	.0147	.0165	.0185	.0206	.0229	.0255	.0282	.0313	0
q=.59	q=.58	q=.57	q=.56	q=.55	q=.54	q=.53	q=.52	q=.51	q=.50	

n = 6

P=.01	P=.02	P=.03	P=.04	P=.05	P=.06	P=.07	P=.08	P=.09	P=.10	
X1										n-X1
0 .9415	.8858	.8330	.7828	.7351	.6899	.6470	.6064	.5679	.5314	6
1 .0571	.1085	.1546	.1957	.2321	.2642	.2922	.3164	.3370	.3543	5
2 .0014	.0055	.0120	.0204	.0305	.0422	.0550	.0688	.0833	.0984	4
3 .0000	.0002	.0005	.0011	.0021	.0036	.0055	.0080	.0110	.0146	3
4 .0000	.0000	.0000	.0000	.0001	.0002	.0003	.0005	.0008	.0012	2
5 .0000	.0000	.0000	.0000	.0000	.0000	.0000	.0000	.0000	.0001	1
6 .0000	.0000	.0000	.0000	.0000	.0000	.0000	.0000	.0000	.0000	0
q=.99	q=.98	q=.97	q=.96	q=.95	q=.94	q=.93	q=.92	q=.91	q=.90	

P=.11	P=.12	P=.13	P=.14	P=.15	P=.16	P=.17	P=.18	P=.19	P=.20	
X1										n-X1
0 .4970	.4644	.4336	.4046	.3771	.3513	.3269	.3040	.2824	.2621	6
1 .3685	.3800	.3888	.3952	.3993	.4015	.4018	.4004	.3975	.3932	5
2 .1139	.1295	.1452	.1608	.1762	.1912	.2057	.2197	.2331	.2458	4
3 .0188	.0236	.0289	.0349	.0415	.0486	.0562	.0643	.0729	.0819	3
4 .0017	.0024	.0032	.0043	.0055	.0069	.0086	.0106	.0128	.0154	2
5 .0001	.0001	.0002	.0003	.0004	.0005	.0007	.0009	.0012	.0015	1
6 .0000	.0000	.0000	.0000	.0000	.0000	.0000	.0000	.0000	.0001	0
q=.89	q=.88	q=.87	q=.86	q=.85	q=.84	q=.83	q=.82	q=.81	q=.80	

P=.21	P=.22	P=.23	P=.24	P=.25	P=.26	P=.27	P=.28	P=.29	P=.30	
X1										n-X1
0 .2431	.2252	.2084	.1927	.1780	.1642	.1513	.1393	.1281	.1176	6
1 .3877	.3811	.3735	.3651	.3560	.3462	.3358	.3251	.3139	.3025	5
2 .2577	.2687	.2789	.2882	.2966	.3041	.3105	.3160	.3206	.3241	4
3 .0913	.1011	.1111	.1214	.1318	.1424	.1531	.1639	.1746	.1852	3
4 .0182	.0214	.0249	.0287	.0330	.0375	.0425	.0478	.0535	.0595	2
5 .0019	.0024	.0030	.0036	.0044	.0053	.0063	.0074	.0087	.0102	1
6 .0001	.0001	.0001	.0002	.0002	.0003	.0004	.0005	.0006	.0007	0
q=.79	q=.78	q=.77	q=.76	q=.75	q=.74	q=.73	q=.72	q=.71	q=.70	

P=.31	P=.32	P=.33	P=.34	P=.35	P=.36	P=.37	P=.38	P=.39	P=.40	
X1										n-X1
0 .1079	.0989	.0905	.0827	.0754	.0687	.0625	.0568	.0515	.0467	6
1 .2909	.2792	.2673	.2555	.2437	.2319	.2203	.2089	.1976	.1866	5
2 .3267	.3284	.3292	.3290	.3280	.3261	.3235	.3201	.3159	.3110	4
3 .1957	.2061	.2162	.2260	.2355	.2446	.2533	.2616	.2693	.2765	3
4 .0660	.0727	.0799	.0873	.0951	.1032	.1116	.1202	.1291	.1382	2
5 .0119	.0137	.0157	.0180	.0205	.0232	.0262	.0295	.0330	.0369	1
6 .0009	.0011	.0013	.0015	.0018	.0022	.0026	.0030	.0035	.0041	0
q=.69	q=.68	q=.67	q=.66	q=.65	q=.64	q=.63	q=.62	q=.61	q=.60	

P=.41	P=.42	P=.43	P=.44	P=.45	P=.46	P=.47	P=.48	P=.49	P=.50	
X1										n-X1
0 .0422	.0381	.0343	.0308	.0277	.0248	.0222	.0198	.0176	.0156	6
1 .1759	.1654	.1552	.1454	.1359	.1267	.1179	.1095	.1014	.0937	5
2 .3055	.2994	.2928	.2856	.2780	.2699	.2615	.2527	.2436	.2344	4
3 .2831	.2891	.2945	.2992	.3032	.3065	.3091	.3110	.3121	.3125	3

4	.1475	.1570	.1666	.1763	.1861	.1958	.2056	.2153	.2249	.2344	2
5	.0410	.0455	.0503	.0554	.0609	.0667	.0729	.0795	.0864	.0938	1
6	.0048	.0055	.0063	.0073	.0083	.0095	.0108	.0122	.0138	.0156	0

q=.59 q=.58 q=.57 q=.56 q=.55 q=.54 q=.53 q=.52 q=.51 q=.50

n = 7

X1	P=.01	P=.02	P=.03	P=.04	P=.05	P=.06	P=.07	P=.08	P=.09	P=.10	n−X1
0	.9321	.8681	.8080	.7514	.6983	.6485	.6017	.5578	.5168	.4783	7
1	.0659	.1240	.1749	.2192	.2573	.2897	.3170	.3396	.3578	.3720	6
2	.0020	.0076	.0162	.0274	.0406	.0555	.0716	.0886	.1061	.1240	5
3	.0000	.0003	.0008	.0019	.0036	.0059	.0090	.0128	.0175	.0230	4
4	.0000	.0000	.0000	.0001	.0002	.0004	.0007	.0011	.0017	.0026	3
5	.0000	.0000	.0000	.0000	.0000	.0000	.0000	.0001	.0001	.0002	2
6	.0000	.0000	.0000	.0000	.0000	.0000	.0000	.0000	.0000	.0000	1
7	.0000	.0000	.0000	.0000	.0000	.0000	.0000	.0000	.0000	.0000	0

q=.99 q=.98 q=.97 q=.96 q=.95 q=.94 q=.93 q=.92 q=.91 q=.90

X1	P=.11	P=.12	P=.13	P=.14	P=.15	P=.16	P=.17	P=.18	P=.19	P=.20	n−X1
0	.4423	.4087	.3773	.3479	.3206	.2951	.2714	.2493	.2288	.2097	7
1	.3827	.3901	.3946	.3965	.3960	.3935	.3891	.3830	.3756	.3670	6
2	.1419	.1596	.1769	.1936	.2097	.2248	.2391	.2523	.2643	.2753	5
3	.0292	.0363	.0441	.0525	.0617	.0714	.0816	.0923	.1033	.1147	4
4	.0036	.0049	.0066	.0086	.0109	.0136	.0167	.0203	.0242	.0287	3
5	.0003	.0004	.0006	.0008	.0012	.0016	.0021	.0027	.0034	.0043	2
6	.0000	.0000	.0000	.0000	.0001	.0001	.0001	.0002	.0003	.0004	1
7	.0000	.0000	.0000	.0000	.0000	.0000	.0000	.0000	.0000	.0000	0

q=.89 q=.88 q=.87 q=.86 q=.85 q=.84 q=.83 q=.82 q=.81 q=.80

X1	P=.21	P=.22	P=.23	P=.24	P=.25	P=.26	P=.27	P=.28	P=.29	P=.30	n−X1
0	.1920	.1757	.1605	.1465	.1335	.1215	.1105	.1003	.0910	.0824	7
1	.3573	.3468	.3356	.3237	.3115	.2989	.2860	.2731	.2600	.2471	6
2	.2850	.2935	.3007	.3067	.3115	.3150	.3174	.3186	.3186	.3177	5
3	.1263	.1379	.1497	.1614	.1730	.1845	.1956	.2065	.2169	.2269	4
4	.0336	.0389	.0447	.0510	.0577	.0648	.0724	.0803	.0886	.0972	3
5	.0054	.0066	.0080	.0097	.0115	.0137	.0161	.0187	.0217	.0250	2
6	.0005	.0006	.0008	.0010	.0013	.0016	.0020	.0024	.0030	.0036	1
7	.0000	.0000	.0000	.0000	.0001	.0001	.0001	.0001	.0002	.0002	0

q=.79 q=.78 q=.77 q=.76 q=.75 q=.74 q=.73 q=.72 q=.71 q=.70

X1	P=.31	P=.32	P=.33	P=.34	P=.35	P=.36	P=.37	P=.38	P=.39	P=.40	n−X1
0	.0745	.0672	.0606	.0546	.0490	.0440	.0394	.0352	.0314	.0280	7
1	.2342	.2215	.2090	.1967	.1848	.1732	.1619	.1511	.1407	.1306	6
2	.3156	.3127	.3088	.3040	.2985	.2922	.2853	.2778	.2698	.2613	5
3	.2363	.2452	.2535	.2610	.2679	.2740	.2793	.2838	.2875	.2903	4
4	.1062	.1154	.1248	.1345	.1442	.1541	.1640	.1739	.1838	.1935	3
5	.0286	.0326	.0369	.0416	.0466	.0520	.0578	.0640	.0705	.0774	2
6	.0043	.0051	.0061	.0071	.0084	.0098	.0113	.0131	.0150	.0172	1
7	.0003	.0003	.0004	.0005	.0006	.0008	.0009	.0011	.0014	.0016	0

q=.69 q=.68 q=.67 q=.66 q=.65 q=.64 q=.63 q=.62 q=.61 q=.60

X1	P=.41	P=.42	P=.43	P=.44	P=.45	P=.46	P=.47	P=.48	P=.49	P=.50	n−X1
0	.0249	.0221	.0195	.0173	.0152	.0134	.0117	.0103	.0090	.0078	7
1	.1211	.1119	.1032	.0950	.0872	.0798	.0729	.0664	.0604	.0547	6
2	.2524	.2431	.2336	.2239	.2140	.2040	.1940	.1840	.1740	.1641	5
3	.2923	.2934	.2937	.2932	.2918	.2897	.2867	.2830	.2786	.2734	4
4	.2031	.2125	.2216	.2304	.2388	.2468	.2543	.2612	.2676	.2734	3
5	.0847	.0923	.1003	.1086	.1172	.1261	.1353	.1447	.1543	.1641	2
6	.0196	.0223	.0252	.0284	.0320	.0358	.0400	.0445	.0494	.0547	1
7	.0019	.0023	.0027	.0032	.0037	.0044	.0051	.0059	.0068	.0078	0

q=.59 q=.58 q=.57 q=.56 q=.55 q=.54 q=.53 q=.52 q=.51 q=.50

n = 8

X1	P=.01	P=.02	P=.03	P=.04	P=.05	P=.06	P=.07	P=.08	P=.09	P=.10	n−X1
0	.9227	.8508	.7837	.7214	.6634	.6096	.5596	.5132	.4703	.4305	8
1	.0746	.1389	.1939	.2405	.2793	.3113	.3370	.3570	.3721	.3826	7

2	.0026	.0099	.0210	.0351	.0515	.0695	.0888	.1087	.1288	.1488	6
3	.0001	.0004	.0013	.0029	.0054	.0089	.0134	.0189	.0255	.0331	5
4	.0000	.0000	.0001	.0002	.0004	.0007	.0013	.0021	.0031	.0046	4
5	.0000	.0000	.0000	.0000	.0000	.0000	.0001	.0001	.0002	.0004	3
6	.0000	.0000	.0000	.0000	.0000	.0000	.0000	.0000	.0000	.0000	2
7	.0000	.0000	.0000	.0000	.0000	.0000	.0000	.0000	.0000	.0000	1
8	.0000	.0000	.0000	.0000	.0000	.0000	.0000	.0000	.0000	.0000	0

q=.99 q=.98 q=.97 q=.96 q=.95 q=.94 q=.93 q=.92 q=.91 q=.90

X_1	P=.11	P=.12	P=.13	P=.14	P=.15	P=.16	P=.17	P=.18	P=.19	P=.20	$n-X_1$
0	.3937	.3596	.3282	.2992	.2725	.2479	.2252	.2044	.1853	.1678	8
1	.3892	.3923	.3923	.3897	.3847	.3777	.3691	.3590	.3477	.3355	7
2	.1684	.1872	.2052	.2220	.2376	.2518	.2646	.2758	.2855	.2936	6
3	.0416	.0511	.0613	.0723	.0839	.0959	.1084	.1211	.1339	.1468	5
4	.0064	.0087	.0115	.0147	.0185	.0228	.0277	.0332	.0393	.0459	4
5	.0006	.0009	.0014	.0019	.0026	.0035	.0045	.0058	.0074	.0092	3
6	.0000	.0001	.0001	.0002	.0002	.0003	.0005	.0006	.0009	.0011	2
7	.0000	.0000	.0000	.0000	.0000	.0000	.0000	.0000	.0001	.0001	1
8	.0000	.0000	.0000	.0000	.0000	.0000	.0000	.0000	.0000	.0000	0

q=.89 q=.88 q=.87 q=.86 q=.85 q=.84 q=.83 q=.82 q=.81 q=.80

X_1	P=.21	P=.22	P=.23	P=.24	P=.25	P=.26	P=.27	P=.28	P=.29	P=.30	$n-X_1$
0	.1517	.1370	.1236	.1113	.1001	.0899	.0806	.0722	.0646	.0576	8
1	.3226	.3092	.2953	.2812	.2670	.2527	.2386	.2247	.2110	.1977	7
2	.3002	.3052	.3087	.3108	.3115	.3108	.3089	.3058	.3017	.2965	6
3	.1596	.1722	.1844	.1963	.2076	.2184	.2285	.2379	.2464	.25441	5
4	.0530	.0607	.0689	.0775	.0865	.0959	.1056	.1156	.1258	.1361	4
5	.0113	.0137	.0165	.0196	.0231	.0270	.0313	.0360	.0411	.0467	3
6	.0015	.0019	.0025	.0031	.0038	.0047	.0058	.0070	.0084	.0100	2
7	.0001	.0002	.0002	.0003	.0004	.0005	.0006	.0008	.0010	.0012	1
8	.0000	.0000	.0000	.0000	.0000	.0000	.0000	.0001	.0001	0

q=.79 q=.78 q=.77 q=.76 q=.75 q=.74 q=.73 q=.72 q=.71 q=.70

X_1	P=.31	P=.32	P=.33	P=.34	P=.35	P=.36	P=.37	P=.38	P=.39	P=.40	$n-X_1$
0	.0514	.0457	.0406	.0360	.0319	.0281	.0248	.0218	.0192	.0168	8
1	.1847	.1721	.1600	.1484	.1373	.1267	.1166	.1071	.0981	.0896	7
2	.2904	.2835	.2758	.2675	.2587	.2494	.2397	.2297	.2194	.2090	6
3	.2609	.2668	.2717	.2756	.2786	.2805	.2815	.2815	.2806	.2787	5
4	.1465	.1569	.1673	.1775	.1875	.1973	.2067	.2157	.2242	.2322	4
5	.0527	.0591	.0659	.0732	.0808	.0888	.0971	.1058	.1147	.1239	3
6	.0118	.0139	.0162	.0188	.0217	.0250	.0285	.0324	.0367	.0413	2
7	.0015	.0019	.0023	.0028	.0033	.0040	.0048	.0057	.0067	.0079	1
8	.0001	.0001	.0001	.0002	.0002	.0003	.0004	.0004	.0005	.0007	0

q=.69 q=.68 q=.67 q=.66 q=.65 q=.64 q=.63 q=.62 q=.61 q=.60

X_1	P=.41	P=.42	P=.43	P=.44	P=.45	P=.46	P=.47	P=.48	P=.49	P=.50	$n-X_1$
0	.0147	.0128	.0111	.0097	.0084	.0072	.0062	.0053	.0046	.0039	8
1	.0816	.0742	.0672	.0608	.0548	.0493	.0442	.0395	.0352	.0312	7
2	.1985	.1880	.1776	.1672	.1569	.1469	.1371	.1275	.1183	.1094	6
3	.2759	.2723	.2679	.2627	.2568	.2503	.2431	.2355	.2273	.2187	5
4	.2397	.2465	.2526	.2580	.2627	.2665	.2695	.2717	.2730	.2734	4
5	.1332	.1428	.1525	.1622	.1719	.1816	.1912	.2006	.2098	.2188	3
6	.0463	.0517	.0575	.0637	.0703	.0774	.0848	.0926	.1008	.1094	2
7	.0092	.0107	.0124	.0143	.0164	.0188	.0215	.0244	.0277	.0313	1
8	.0008	.0010	.0012	.0014	.0017	.0020	.0024	.0028	.0033	.0039	0

q=.59 q=.58 q=.57 q=.56 q=.55 q=.54 q=.53 q=.52 q=.51 q=.50

n = 9

X_1	P=.01	P=.02	P=.03	P=.04	P=.05	P=.06	P=.07	P=.08	P=.09	P=.10	$n-X_1$
0	.9135	.8337	.7602	.6925	.6302	.5730	.5204	.4722	.4279	.3874	9
1	.0830	.1531	.2116	.2597	.2985	.3292	.3525	.3695	.3809	.3874	8
2	.0034	.0125	.0262	.0433	.0629	.0840	.1061	.1285	.1507	.1722	7
3	.0001	.0006	.0019	.0042	.0077	.0125	.0186	.0261	.0348	.0446	6
4	.0000	.0000	.0001	.0003	.0006	.0012	.0021	.0034	.0052	.0074	5
5	.0000	.0000	.0000	.0000	.0000	.0001	.0002	.0003	.0005	.0008	4
6	.0000	.0000	.0000	.0000	.0000	.0000	.0000	.0000	.0000	.0001	3
7	.0000	.0000	.0000	.0000	.0000	.0000	.0000	.0000	.0000	.0000	2
8	.0000	.0000	.0000	.0000	.0000	.0000	.0000	.0000	.0000	.0000	1
9	.0000	.0000	.0000	.0000	.0000	.0000	.0000	.0000	.0000	.0000	0

q=.99 q=.98 q=.97 q=.96 q=.95 q=.94 q=.93 q=.92 q=.91 q=.90

	P=.11	P=.12	P=.13	P=.14	P=.15	P=.16	P=.17	P=.18	P=.19	P=.20	
X1											n−X1
0	.3504	.3165	.2855	.2573	.2316	.2082	.1869	.1676	.1501	.1342	9
1	.3897	.3884	.3840	.3770	.3679	.3569	.3446	.3312	.3169	.3020	8
2	.1927	.2119	.2295	.2455	.2597	.2720	.2823	.2908	.2973	.3020	7
3	.0556	.0674	.0800	.0933	.1069	.1209	.1349	.1489	.1627	.1762	6
4	.0103	.0138	.0179	.0228	.0283	.0345	.0415	.0490	.0573	.0661	5
5	.0013	.0019	.0027	.0037	.0050	.0066	.0085	.0108	.0134	.0165	4
6	.0001	.0002	.0003	.0004	.0006	.0008	.0012	.0016	.0021	.0028	3
7	.0000	.0000	.0000	.0000	.0000	.0001	.0001	.0001	.0002	.0003	2
8	.0000	.0000	.0000	.0000	.0000	.0000	.0000	.0000	.0000	.0000	1
9	.0000	.0000	.0000	.0000	.0000	.0000	.0000	.0000	.0000	.0000	0
	q=.89	q=.88	q=.87	q=.86	q=.85	q=.84	q=.83	q=.82	q=.81	q=.80	

	P=.21	P=.22	P=.23	P=.24	P=.25	P=.26	P=.27	P=.28	P=.29	P=.30	
X1											n−X1
0	.1199	.1069	.0952	.0846	.0751	.0665	.0589	.0520	.0458	.0404	9
1	.2867	.2713	.2558	.2404	.2253	.2104	.1960	.1820	.1685	.1556	8
2	.3049	.3061	.3056	.3037	.3003	.2957	.2899	.2831	.2754	.2668	7
3	.1891	.2014	.2130	.2238	.2336	.2424	.2502	.2569	.2624	.2668	6
4	.0754	.0852	.0954	.1060	.1168	.1278	.1388	.1499	.1608	.1715	5
5	.0200	.0240	.0285	.0335	.0389	.0449	.0513	.0583	.0657	.0735	4
6	.0036	.0045	.0057	.0070	.0087	.0105	.0127	.0151	.0179	.0210	3
7	.0004	.0005	.0007	.0010	.0012	.0016	.0020	.0025	.0031	.0039	2
8	.0000	.0000	.0001	.0001	.0001	.0001	.0002	.0002	.0003	.0004	1
9	.0000	.0000	.0000	.0000	.0000	.0000	.0000	.0000	.0000	.0000	0
	q=.79	q=.78	q=.77	q=.76	q=.75	q=.74	q=.73	q=.72	q=.71	q=.70	

	P=.31	P=.32	P=.33	P=.34	P=.35	P=.36	P=.37	P=.38	P=.39	P=.40	
X1											n−X1
0	.0355	.0311	.0272	.0238	.0207	.0180	.0156	.0135	.0117	.0101	9
1	.1433	.1317	.1206	.1102	.1004	.0912	.0826	.0747	.0673	.0605	8
2	.2576	.2478	.2376	.2270	.2162	.2052	.1941	.1831	.1721	.1612	7
3	.2701	.2721	.2731	.2729	.2716	.2693	.2660	.2618	.2567	.2508	6
4	.1820	.1921	.2017	.2109	.2194	.2272	.2344	.2407	.2462	.2508	5
5	.0818	.0904	.0994	.1086	.1181	.1278	.1376	.1475	.1574	.1672	4
6	.0245	.0284	.0326	.0373	.0424	.0479	.0539	.0603	.0671	.0743	3
7	.0047	.0057	.0069	.0082	.0098	.0116	.0136	.0158	.0184	.0212	2
8	.0005	.0007	.0008	.0011	.0013	.0016	.0020	.0024	.0029	.0035	1
9	.0000	.0000	.0000	.0001	.0001	.0001	.0001	.0002	.0002	.0003	0
	q=.69	q=.68	q=.67	q=.66	q=.65	q=.64	q=.63	q=.62	q=.61	q=.60	

	P=.41	P=.42	P=.43	P=.44	P=.45	P=.46	P=.47	P=.48	P=.49	P=.50	
X1											n−X1
0	.0087	.0074	.0064	.0054	.0046	.0039	.0033	.0028	.0023	.0020	9
1	.0542	.0484	.0431	.0383	.0339	.0299	.0263	.0231	.0202	.0176	8
2	.1506	.1402	.1301	.1204	.1110	.1020	.0934	.0853	.0776	.0703	7
3	.2442	.2369	.2291	.2207	.2119	.2027	.1933	.1837	.1739	.1641	6
4	.2545	.2573	.2592	.2601	.2600	.2590	.2571	.2543	.2506	.2461	5
5	.1769	.1863	.1955	.2044	.2128	.2207	.2280	.2347	.2408	.2461	4
6	.0819	.0900	.0983	.1070	.1160	.1253	.1348	.1445	.1542	.1641	3
7	.0244	.0279	.0318	.0360	.0407	.0458	.0512	.0571	.0635	.0703	2
8	.0042	.0051	.0060	.0071	.0083	.0097	.0114	.0132	.0153	.0176	1
9	.0003	.0004	.0005	.0006	.0008	.0009	.0011	.0014	.0016	.0020	0
	q=.59	q=.58	q=.57	q=.56	q=.55	q=.54	q=.53	q=.52	q=.51	q=.50	

n = 10

	P=.01	P=.02	P=.03	P=.04	P=.05	P=.06	P=.07	P=.08	P=.09	P=.10	
X1											n−X1
0	.9044	.8171	.7374	.6648	.5987	.5386	.4840	.4344	.3894	.3487	10
1	.0914	.1667	.2281	.2770	.3151	.3438	.3643	.3777	.3851	.3874	9
2	.0042	.0153	.0317	.0519	.0746	.0988	.1234	.1478	.1714	.1937	8
3	.0001	.0008	.0026	.0058	.0105	.0168	.0248	.0343	.0452	.0574	7
4	.0000	.0000	.0001	.0004	.0010	.0019	.0033	.0052	.0078	.0112	6
5	.0000	.0000	.0000	.0000	.0001	.0001	.0003	.0005	.0009	.0015	5
6	.0000	.0000	.0000	.0000	.0000	.0000	.0000	.0000	.0001	.0001	4
7	.0000	.0000	.0000	.0000	.0000	.0000	.0000	.0000	.0000	.0000	3
8	.0000	.0000	.0000	.0000	.0000	.0000	.0000	.0000	.0000	.0000	2
9	.0000	.0000	.0000	.0000	.0000	.0000	.0000	.0000	.0000	.0000	1
10	.0000	.0000	.0000	.0000	.0000	.0000	.0000	.0000	.0000	.0000	0
	q=.99	q=.98	q=.97	q=.96	q=.95	q=.94	q=.93	q=.92	q=.91	q=.90	

	P=.11	P=.12	P=.13	P=.14	P=.15	P=.16	P=.17	P=.18	P=.19	P=.20	
X1											n-X1
0	.3118	.2785	.2484	.2213	.1969	.1749	.1552	.1374	.1216	.1074	10
1	.3854	.3798	.3712	.3603	.3474	.3331	.3178	.3017	.2852	.2684	9
2	.2143	.2330	.2496	.2639	.2759	.2856	.2929	.2980	.3010	.3020	8
3	.0706	.0847	.0995	.1146	.1298	.1450	.1600	.1745	.1883	.2013	7
4	.0153	.0202	.0260	.0326	.0401	.0483	.0573	.0670	.0773	.0881	6
5	.0023	.0033	.0047	.0064	.0085	.0111	.0141	.0177	.0218	.0264	5
6	.0002	.0004	.0006	.0009	.0012	.0018	.0024	.0032	.0043	.0055	4
7	.0000	.0000	.0000	.0001	.0001	.0002	.0003	.0004	.0006	.0008	3
8	.0000	.0000	.0000	.0000	.0000	.0000	.0000	.0000	.0001	.0001	2
9	.0000	.0000	.0000	.0000	.0000	.0000	.0000	.0000	.0000	.0000	1
10	.0000	.0000	.0000	.0000	.0000	.0000	.0000	.0000	.0000	.0000	0
	q=.89	q=.88	q=.87	q=.86	q=.85	q=.84	q=.83	q=.82	q=.81	q=.80	

	P=.21	P=.22	P=.23	P=.24	P=.25	P=.26	P=.27	P=.28	P=.29	P=.30	
X1											n-X1
0	.0947	.0834	.0733	.0643	.0563	.0492	.0430	.0374	.0326	.0282	10
1	.2517	.2351	.2188	.2030	.1877	.1730	.1590	.1456	.1330	.1211	9
2	.3011	.2984	.2942	.2885	.2816	.2735	.2646	.2548	.2444	.2335	8
3	.2134	.2244	.2343	.2429	.2503	.2563	.2609	.2642	.2662	.2668	7
4	.0993	.1108	.1225	.1343	.1460	.1576	.1689	.1798	.1903	.2001	6
5	.0317	.0375	.0439	.0509	.0584	.0664	.0750	.0839	.0933	.1029	5
6	.0070	.0088	.0109	.0134	.0162	.0195	.0231	.0272	.0317	.0368	4
7	.0011	.0014	.0019	.0024	.0031	.0039	.0049	.0060	.0074	.0090	3
8	.0001	.0002	.0002	.0003	.0004	.0005	.0007	.0009	.0011	.0014	2
9	.0000	.0000	.0000	.0000	.0000	.0000	.0001	.0001	.0001	.0001	1
10	.0000	.0000	.0000	.0000	.0000	.0000	.0000	.0000	.0000	.0000	0
	q=.79	q=.78	q=.77	q=.76	q=.75	q=.74	q=.73	q=.72	q=.71	q=.70	

	P=.31	P=.32	P=.33	P=.34	P=.35	P=.36	P=.37	P=.38	P=.39	P=.40	
X1											n-X1
0	.0245	.0211	.0182	.0157	.0135	.0115	.0098	.0084	.0071	.0060	10
1	.1099	.0995	.0898	.0808	.0725	.0649	.0578	.0514	.0456	.0403	9
2	.2222	.2107	.1990	.1873	.1757	.1642	.1529	.1419	.1312	.1209	8
3	.2662	.2644	.2614	.2573	.2522	.2462	.2394	.2319	.2237	.2150	7
4	.2093	.2177	.2253	.2320	.2377	.2424	.2461	.2487	.2503	.2508	6
5	.1128	.1229	.1332	.1434	.1536	.1636	.1734	.1829	.1920	.2007	5
6	.0422	.0482	.0547	.0616	.0689	.0767	.0849	.0934	.1023	.1115	4
7	.0108	.0130	.0154	.0181	.0212	.0247	.0285	.0327	.0374	.0425	3
8	.0018	.0023	.0028	.0035	.0043	.0052	.0063	.0075	.0090	.0106	2
9	.0002	.0002	.0003	.0004	.0005	.0006	.0008	.0010	.0013	.0016	1
10	.0000	.0000	.0000	.0000	.0000	.0000	.0000	.0001	.0001	.0001	0
	q=.69	q=.68	q=.67	q=.66	q=.65	q=.64	q=.63	q=.62	q=.61	q=.60	

	P=.41	P=.42	P=.43	P=.44	P=.45	P=.46	P=.47	P=.48	P=.49	P=.50	
X1											n-X1
0	.0051	.0043	.0036	.0030	.0025	.0021	.0017	.0014	.0012	.0010	10
1	.0355	.0312	.0273	.0238	.0207	.0180	.0155	.0133	.0114	.0098	9
2	.1111	.1017	.0927	.0843	.0763	.0688	.0619	.0554	.0494	.0439	8
3	.2058	.1963	.1865	.1765	.1665	.1564	.1464	.1364	.1267	.1172	7
4	.2503	.2488	.2462	.2427	.2384	.2331	.2271	.2204	.2130	.2051	6
5	.2087	.2162	.2229	.2289	.2340	.2383	.2417	.2441	.2456	.2461	5
6	.1209	.1304	.1401	.1499	.1596	.1692	.1786	.1878	.1966	.2051	4
7	.0480	.0540	.0604	.0673	.0746	.0824	.0905	.0991	.1080	.1172	3
8	.0125	.0147	.0171	.0198	.0229	.0263	.0301	.0343	.0389	.0439	2
9	.0019	.0024	.0029	.0035	.0042	.0050	.0059	.0070	.0083	.0098	1
10	.0001	.0002	.0002	.0003	.0003	.0004	.0005	.0006	.0008	.0010	0
	q=.59	q=.58	q=.57	q=.56	q=.55	q=.54	q=.53	q=.52	q=.51	q=.50	

n = 11

	P=.01	P=.02	P=.03	P=.04	P=.05	P=.06	P=.07	P=.08	P=.09	P=.10	
X1											n-X1
0	.8953	.8007	.7153	.6382	.5688	.5063	.4501	.3996	.3544	.3138	11
1	.0995	.1798	.2433	.2925	.3293	.3555	.3727	.3823	.3855	.3835	10
2	.0050	.0183	.0376	.0609	.0867	.1135	.1403	.1662	.1906	.2131	9
3	.0002	.0011	.0035	.0076	.0137	.0217	.0317	.0434	.0566	.0710	8
4	.0000	.0000	.0002	.0006	.0014	.0028	.0048	.0075	.0112	.0158	7
5	.0000	.0000	.0000	.0000	.0001	.0002	.0005	.0009	.0015	.0025	6
6	.0000	.0000	.0000	.0000	.0000	.0000	.0000	.0001	.0002	.0003	5
7	.0000	.0000	.0000	.0000	.0000	.0000	.0000	.0000	.0000	.0000	4
8	.0000	.0000	.0000	.0000	.0000	.0000	.0000	.0000	.0000	.0000	3
9	.0000	.0000	.0000	.0000	.0000	.0000	.0000	.0000	.0000	.0000	2

10	.0000	.0000	.0000	.0000	.0000	.0000	.0000	.0000	.0000	.0000	1
11	.0000	.0000	.0000	.0000	.0000	.0000	.0000	.0000	.0000	.0000	0

q=.99	q=.98	q=.97	q=.96	q=.95	q=.94	q=.93	q=.92	q=.91	q=.90

X1	P=.11	P=.12	P=.13	P=.14	P=.15	P=.16	P=.17	P=.18	P=.19	P=.20	n-X1
0	.2775	.2451	.2161	.1903	.1673	.1469	.1288	.1127	.0985	.0859	11
1	.3773	.3676	.3552	.3408	.3248	.3078	.2901	.2721	.2541	.2362	10
2	.2332	.2507	.2654	.2774	.2866	.2932	.2971	.2987	.2980	.2953	9
3	.0865	.1025	.1190	.1355	.1517	.1675	.1826	.1967	.2097	.2215	8
4	.0214	.0280	.0356	.0441	.0536	.0638	.0748	.0864	.0984	.1107	7
5	.0037	.0053	.0074	.0101	.0132	.0170	.0214	.0265	.0323	.0388	6
6	.0005	.0007	.0011	.0016	.0023	.0032	.0044	.0058	.0076	.0097	5
7	.0000	.0001	.0001	.0002	.0003	.0004	.0006	.0009	.0013	.0017	4
8	.0000	.0000	.0000	.0000	.0000	.0000	.0001	.0001	.0001	.0002	3
9	.0000	.0000	.0000	.0000	.0000	.0000	.0000	.0000	.0000	.0000	2
10	.0000	.0000	.0000	.0000	.0000	.0000	.0000	.0000	.0000	.0000	1
11	.0000	.0000	.0000	.0000	.0000	.0000	.0000	.0000	.0000	.0000	0

q=.89	q=.88	q=.87	q=.86	q=.85	q=.84	q=.83	q=.82	q=.81	q=.80

X1	P=.21	P=.22	P=.23	P=.24	P=.25	P=.26	P=.27	P=.28	P=.29	P=.30	n-X1
0	.0748	.0650	.0564	.0489	.0422	.0364	.0314	.0270	.0231	.0198	11
1	.2187	.2017	.1854	.1697	.1549	.1408	.1276	.1153	.1038	.0932	10
2	.2907	.2845	.2768	.2680	.2581	.2474	.2360	.2242	.2121	.1998	9
3	.2318	.2407	.2481	.2539	.2581	.2608	.2619	.2616	.2599	.2568	8
4	.1232	.1358	.1482	.1603	.1721	.1832	.1937	.2035	.2123	.2201	7
5	.0459	.0536	.0620	.0709	.0803	.0901	.1003	.1108	.1214	.1321	6
6	.0122	.0151	.0185	.0224	.0268	.0317	.0371	.0431	.0496	.0566	5
7	.0023	.0030	.0039	.0050	.0064	.0079	.0098	.0120	.0145	.0173	4
8	.0003	.0004	.0006	.0008	.0011	.0014	.0018	.0023	.0030	.0037	3
9	.0000	.0000	.0001	.0001	.0001	.0002	.0002	.0003	.0004	.0005	2
10	.0000	.0000	.0000	.0000	.0000	.0000	.0000	.0000	.0000	.0000	1
11	.0000	.0000	.0000	.0000	.0000	.0000	.0000	.0000	.0000	.0000	0

q=.79	q=.78	q=.77	q=.76	q=.75	q=.74	q=.73	q=.72	q=.71	q=.70

X1	P=.31	P=.32	P=.33	P=.34	P=.35	P=.36	P=.37	P=.38	P=.39	P=.40	n-X1
0	.0169	.0144	.0122	.0104	.0088	.0074	.0062	.0052	.0044	.0036	11
1	.0834	.0744	.0662	.0587	.0518	.0457	.0401	.0351	.0306	.0266	10
2	.1874	.1751	.1630	.1511	.1395	.1284	.1177	.1075	.0978	.0887	9
3	.2526	.2472	.2408	.2335	.2254	.2167	.2074	.1977	.1876	.1774	8
4	.2269	.2326	.2372	.2406	.2428	.2438	.2436	.2423	.2399	.2365	7
5	.1427	.1533	.1636	.1735	.1830	.1920	.2003	.2079	.2148	.2207	6
6	.0641	.0721	.0806	.0894	.0985	.1080	.1176	.1274	.1373	.1471	5
7	.0206	.0242	.0283	.0329	.0379	.0434	.0494	.0558	.0627	.0701	4
8	.0046	.0057	.0070	.0085	.0102	.0122	.0145	.0171	.0200	.0234	3
9	.0007	.0009	.0011	.0015	.0018	.0023	.0028	.0035	.0043	.0052	2
10	.0001	.0001	.0001	.0001	.0002	.0003	.0003	.0004	.0005	.0007	1
11	.0000	.0000	.0000	.0000	.0000	.0000	.0000	.0000	.0000	.0000	0

q=.69	q=.68	q=.67	q=.66	q=.65	q=.64	q=.63	q=.62	q=.61	q=.60

X1	P=.41	P=.42	P=.43	P=.44	P=.45	P=.46	P=.47	P=.48	P=.49	P=.50	n-X1
0	.0030	.0025	.0021	.0017	.0014	.0011	.0009	.0008	.0006	.0005	11
1	.0231	.0199	.0171	.0147	.0125	.0107	.0090	.0076	.0064	.0054	10
2	.0801	.0721	.0646	.0577	.0513	.0454	.0401	.0352	.0308	.0269	9
3	.1670	.1566	.1462	.1359	.1259	.1161	.1067	.0976	.0888	.0806	8
4	.2321	.2267	.2206	.2136	.2060	.1978	.1892	.1801	.1707	.1611	7
5	.2258	.2299	.2329	.2350	.2360	.2359	.2348	.2327	.2296	.2256	6
6	.1569	.1664	.1757	.1846	.1931	.2010	.2083	.2148	.2206	.2256	5
7	.0779	.0861	.0947	.1036	.1128	.1223	.1319	.1416	.1514	.1611	4
8	.0271	.0312	.0357	.0407	.0462	.0521	.0585	.0654	.0727	.0806	3
9	.0063	.0075	.0090	.0107	.0126	.0148	.0173	.0201	.0233	.0269	2
10	.0009	.0011	.0014	.0017	.0021	.0025	.0031	.0037	.0045	.0054	1
11	.0001	.0001	.0001	.0001	.0002	.0002	.0002	.0003	.0004	.0005	0

q=.59	q=.58	q=.57	q=.56	q=.55	q=.54	q=.53	q=.52	q=.51	q=.50

n = 12

X1	P=.01	P=.02	P=.03	P=.04	P=.05	P=.06	P=.07	P=.08	P=.09	P=.10	n-X1
0	.8864	.7847	.6938	.6127	.5404	.4759	.4186	.3677	.3225	.2824	12
1	.1074	.1922	.2575	.3064	.3413	.3645	.3781	.3837	.3827	.3766	11
2	.0060	.0216	.0438	.0702	.0988	.1280	.1565	.1835	.2082	.2301	10

X1											n−X1
3	.0002	.0015	.0045	.0098	.0173	.0272	.0393	.0532	.0686	.0852	9
4	.0000	.0001	.0003	.0009	.0021	.0039	.0067	.0104	.0153	.0213	8
5	.0000	.0000	.0000	.0001	.0002	.0004	.0008	.0014	.0024	.0038	7
6	.0000	.0000	.0000	.0000	.0000	.0000	.0001	.0001	.0003	.0005	6
7	.0000	.0000	.0000	.0000	.0000	.0000	.0000	.0000	.0000	.0000	5
8	.0000	.0000	.0000	.0000	.0000	.0000	.0000	.0000	.0000	.0000	4
9	.0000	.0000	.0000	.0000	.0000	.0000	.0000	.0000	.0000	.0000	3
10	.0000	.0000	.0000	.0000	.0000	.0000	.0000	.0000	.0000	.0000	2
11	.0000	.0000	.0000	.0000	.0000	.0000	.0000	.0000	.0000	.0000	1
12	.0000	.0000	.0000	.0000	.0000	.0000	.0000	.0000	.0000	.0000	0

q=.99   q=.98   q=.97   q=.96   q=.95   q=.94   q=.93   q=.92   q=.91   q=.90

X1	P=.11	P=.12	P=.13	P=.14	P=.15	P=.16	P=.17	P=.18	P=.19	P=.20	n−X1
0	.2470	.2157	.1880	.1637	.1422	.1234	.1069	.0924	.0798	.0687	12
1	.3663	.3529	.3372	.3197	.3012	.2821	.2627	.2434	.2245	.2062	11
2	.2490	.2647	.2771	.2863	.2924	.2955	.2960	.2939	.2897	.2835	10
3	.1026	.1203	.1380	.1553	.1720	.1876	.2021	.2151	.2265	.2362	9
4	.0285	.0369	.0464	.0569	.0683	.0804	.0931	.1062	.1195	.1329	8
5	.0056	.0081	.0111	.0148	.0193	.0245	.0305	.0373	.0449	.0532	7
6	.0008	.0013	.0019	.0028	.0040	.0054	.0073	.0096	.0123	.0155	6
7	.0001	.0001	.0002	.0004	.0006	.0009	.0013	.0018	.0025	.0033	5
8	.0000	.0000	.0000	.0000	.0001	.0001	.0002	.0002	.0004	.0005	4
9	.0000	.0000	.0000	.0000	.0000	.0000	.0000	.0000	.0000	.0001	3
10	.0000	.0000	.0000	.0000	.0000	.0000	.0000	.0000	.0000	.0000	2
11	.0000	.0000	.0000	.0000	.0000	.0000	.0000	.0000	.0000	.0000	1
12	.0000	.0000	.0000	.0000	.0000	.0000	.0000	.0000	.0000	.0000	0

q=.89   q=.88   q=.87   q=.86   q=.85   q=.84   q=.83   q=.82   q=.81   q=.80

X1	P=.21	P=.22	P=.23	P=.24	P=.25	P=.26	P=.27	P=.28	P=.29	P=.30	n−X1
0	.0591	.0507	.0434	.0371	.0317	.0270	.0229	.0194	.0164	.0138	12
1	.1885	.1717	.1557	.1407	.1267	.1137	.1016	.0906	.0804	.0712	11
2	.2756	.2663	.2558	.2444	.2323	.2197	.2068	.1937	.1807	.1678	10
3	.2442	.2503	.2547	.2573	.2581	.2573	.2549	.2511	.2460	.2397	9
4	.1460	.1589	.1712	.1828	.1936	.2034	.2122	.2197	.2261	.2311	8
5	.0621	.0717	.0818	.0924	.1032	.1143	.1255	.1367	.1477	.1585	7
6	.0193	.0236	.0285	.0340	.0401	.0469	.0542	.0620	.0704	.0792	6
7	.0044	.0057	.0073	.0092	.0115	.0141	.0172	.0207	.0246	.0291	5
8	.0007	.0010	.0014	.0018	.0024	.0031	.0040	.0050	.0063	.0078	4
9	.0001	.0001	.0002	.0003	.0004	.0005	.0007	.0009	.0011	.0015	3
10	.0000	.0000	.0000	.0000	.0000	.0001	.0001	.0001	.0001	.0002	2
11	.0000	.0000	.0000	.0000	.0000	.0000	.0000	.0000	.0000	.0000	1
12	.0000	.0000	.0000	.0000	.0000	.0000	.0000	.0000	.0000	.0000	0

q=.79   q=.78   q=.77   q=.76   q=.75   q=.74   q=.73   q=.72   q=.71   q=.70

X1	P=.31	P=.32	P=.33	P=.34	P=.35	P=.36	P=.37	P=.38	P=.39	P=.40	n−X1
0	.0116	.0098	.0082	.0068	.0057	.0047	.0039	.0032	.0027	.0022	12
1	.0628	.0552	.0484	.0422	.0368	.0319	.0276	.0237	.0204	.0174	11
2	.1552	.1429	.1310	.1197	.1088	.0986	.0890	.0800	.0716	.0639	10
3	.2324	.2241	.2151	.2055	.1954	.1849	.1742	.1634	.1526	.1419	9
4	.2349	.2373	.2384	.2382	.2367	.2340	.2302	.2254	.2195	.2128	8
5	.1688	.1787	.1879	.1963	.2039	.2106	.2163	.2210	.2246	.2270	7
6	.0885	.0981	.1079	.1180	.1281	.1382	.1482	.1580	.1675	.1766	6
7	.0341	.0396	.0456	.0521	.0591	.0666	.0746	.0830	.0918	.1009	5
8	.0096	.0116	.0140	.0168	.0199	.0234	.0274	.0318	.0367	.0420	4
9	.0019	.0024	.0031	.0038	.0048	.0059	.0071	.0087	.0104	.0125	3
10	.0003	.0003	.0005	.0006	.0008	.0010	.0013	.0016	.0020	.0025	2
11	.0000	.0000	.0000	.0001	.0001	.0001	.0001	.0002	.0002	.0003	1
12	.0000	.0000	.0000	.0000	.0000	.0000	.0000	.0000	.0000	.0000	0

q=.69   q=.68   q=.67   q=.66   q=.65   q=.64   q=.63   q=.62   q=.61   q=.60

X1	P=.41	P=.42	P=.43	P=.44	P=.45	P=.46	P=.47	P=.48	P=.49	P=.50	n−X1
0	.0018	.0014	.0012	.0010	.0008	.0006	.0005	.0004	.0003	.0002	12
1	.0148	.0126	.0106	.0090	.0075	.0063	.0052	.0043	.0036	.0029	11
2	.0567	.0502	.0442	.0388	.0339	.0294	.0255	.0220	.0189	.0161	10
3	.1314	.1211	.1111	.1015	.0923	.0836	.0754	.0676	.0604	.0537	9
4	.2054	.1973	.1886	.1794	.1700	.1602	.1504	.1405	.1306	.1208	8
5	.2284	.2285	.2276	.2256	.2225	.2184	.2134	.2075	.2008	.1934	7
6	.1851	.1931	.2003	.2068	.2124	.2171	.2208	.2234	.2250	.2256	6
7	.1103	.1198	.1295	.1393	.1489	.1585	.1678	.1768	.1853	.1934	5
8	.0479	.0542	.0611	.0684	.0762	.0844	.0930	.1020	.1113	.1208	4
9	.0148	.0175	.0205	.0239	.0277	.0319	.0367	.0418	.0475	.0537	3
10	.0031	.0038	.0046	.0056	.0068	.0082	.0098	.0116	.0137	.0161	2
11	.0004	.0005	.0006	.0008	.0010	.0013	.0016	.0019	.0024	.0029	1
12	.0000	.0000	.0000	.0001	.0001	.0001	.0001	.0001	.0002	.0002	0

q=.59   q=.58   q=.57   q=.56   q=.55   q=.54   q=.53   q=.52   q=.51   q=.50

X1	P=.01	P=.02	P=.03	P=.04	P=.05	P=.06	P=.07	P=.08	P=.09	P=.10	n-X1
0	.8775	.7690	.6730	.5882	.5133	.4474	.3893	.3383	.2935	.2542	13
1	.1152	.2040	.2706	.3186	.3512	.3712	.3809	.3824	.3773	.3672	12
2	.0070	.0250	.0502	.0797	.1109	.1422	.1720	.1995	.2239	.2448	11
3	.0003	.0019	.0057	.0122	.0214	.0333	.0475	.0636	.0812	.0997	10
4	.0000	.0001	.0004	.0013	.0028	.0053	.0089	.0138	.0201	.0277	9
5	.0000	.0000	.0000	.0001	.0003	.0006	.0012	.0022	.0036	.0055	8
6	.0000	.0000	.0000	.0000	.0000	.0001	.0001	.0003	.0005	.0008	7
7	.0000	.00C0	.0000	.0000	.0000	.0000	.0000	.0000	.0000	.0001	6
8	.0000	.0000	.0000	.0000	.0000	.0000	.0000	.0000	.0000	.0000	5
9	.0000	.0000	.0000	.0000	.0000	.0000	.0000	.0000	.0000	.0000	4
10	.0000	.0000	.0000	.0000	.0000	.0000	.0000	.0000	.0000	.0000	3
11	.0000	.0000	.0000	.0000	.0000	.0000	.0000	.0000	.0000	.0000	2
12	.0000	.0000	.0000	.0000	.0000	.0000	.0000	.0000	.0000	.0000	1
13	.0000	.0000	.0000	.0000	.0000	.0000	.0000	.0000	.0000	.0000	0
	q=.99	q=.98	q=.97	q=.96	q=.95	q=.94	q=.93	q=.92	q=.91	q=.90	

X1	P=.11	P=.12	P=.13	P=.14	P=.15	P=.16	P=.17	P=.18	P=.19	P=.20	n-X1
0	.2198	.1898	.1636	.1408	.1209	.1037	.0887	.0758	.0646	.0550	13
1	.3532	.3364	.3178	.2979	.2774	.2567	.2362	.2163	.1970	.1787	12
2	.2619	.2753	.2849	.2910	.2937	.2934	.2903	.2848	.2773	.2680	11
3	.1187	.1376	.1561	.1737	.1900	.2049	.2180	.2293	.2385	.2457	10
4	.0367	.0469	.0583	.0707	.0838	.0976	.1116	.1258	.1399	.1535	9
5	.0082	.0115	.0157	.0207	.0266	.0335	.0412	.0497	.0591	.0691	8
6	.0013	.0021	.0031	.0045	.0063	.0085	.0112	.0145	.0185	.0230	7
7	.0002	.0003	.0005	.0007	.0011	.0016	.0023	.0032	.0043	.0058	6
8	.0000	.0000	.0001	.0001	.0001	.0002	.0004	.0005	.0008	.0011	5
9	.0000	.0000	.0000	.0000	.0000	.0000	.0000	.0001	.0001	.0001	4
10	.0000	.0000	.0000	.0000	.0000	.0000	.0000	.0000	.0000	.0000	3
11	.0000	.0000	.0000	.0000	.0000	.0000	.0000	.0000	.0000	.0000	2
12	.0000	.0000	.0000	.0000	.0000	.0000	.0000	.0000	.0000	.0000	1
13	.0000	.0000	.0000	.0000	.0000	.0000	.0000	.0000	.0000	.0000	0
	q=.89	q=.88	q=.87	q=.86	q=.85	q=.84	q=.83	q=.82	q=.81	q=.80	

X1	P=.21	P=.22	P=.23	P=.24	P=.25	P=.26	P=.27	P=.28	P=.29	P=.30	n-X1
0	.0467	.0396	.0334	.0282	.0238	.0200	.0167	.0140	.0117	.0097	13
1	.1613	.1450	.1299	.1159	.1029	.0911	.0804	.0706	.0619	.0540	12
2	.2573	.2455	.2328	.2195	.2059	.1921	.1784	.1648	.1516	.1388	11
3	.2508	.2539	.2550	.2542	.2517	.2475	.2419	.2351	.2271	.2181	10
4	.1667	.1790	.1904	.2007	.2097	.2174	.2237	.2285	.2319	.2337	9
5	.0797	.0909	.1024	.1141	.1258	.1375	.1489	.1600	.1705	.1803	8
6	.0283	.0342	.0408	.0480	.0559	.0644	.0734	.0829	.0928	.1030	7
7	.0075	.0096	.0122	.0152	.0186	.0226	.0272	.0323	.0379	.0442	6
8	.0015	.0020	.0027	.0036	.0047	.0060	.0075	.0094	.0116	.0142	5
9	.0002	.0003	.0005	.0006	.0009	.0012	.0015	.0020	.0026	.0034	4
10	.0000	.0000	.0001	.0001	.0001	.0002	.0002	.0003	.0004	.0006	3
11	.0000	.0000	.0000	.0000	.0000	.0000	.0000	.0000	.0000	.0001	2
12	.0000	.0000	.0000	.0000	.0000	.0000	.0000	.0000	.0000	.0000	1
13	.0000	.0000	.0000	.0000	.0000	.0000	.0000	.0000	.0000	.0000	0
	q=.79	q=.78	q=.77	q=.76	q=.75	q=.74	q=.73	q=.72	q=.71	q=.70	

X1	P=.31	P=.32	P=.33	P=.34	P=.35	P=.36	P=.37	P=.38	P=.39	P=.40	n-X1
0	.0080	.0066	.0055	.0045	.0037	.0030	.0025	.0020	.0016	.0013	13
1	.0469	.0407	.0351	.0302	.0259	.0221	.0188	.0159	.0135	.0113	12
2	.1265	.1148	.1037	.0933	.0836	.0746	.0663	.0586	.0516	.0453	11
3	.2084	.1981	.1874	.1763	.1651	.1538	.1427	.1317	.1210	.1107	10
4	.2341	.2331	.2307	.2270	.2222	.2163	.2095	.2018	.1934	.1845	9
5	.1893	.1974	.2045	.2105	.2154	.2190	.2215	.2227	.2226	.2214	8
6	.1134	.1239	.1343	.1446	.1546	.1643	.1734	.1820	.1898	.1968	7
7	.0509	.0583	.0662	.0745	.0833	.0924	.1019	.1115	.1213	.1312	6
8	.0172	.0206	.0244	.0288	.0336	.0390	.0449	.0513	.0582	.0656	5
9	.0043	.0054	.0067	.0082	.0101	.0122	.0146	.0175	.0207	.0243	4
10	.0008	.0010	.0013	.0017	.0022	.0027	.0034	.0043	.0053	.0065	3
11	.0001	.0001	.0002	.0002	.0003	.0004	.0006	.0007	.0009	.0012	2
12	.0000	.0000	.0000	.0000	.0000	.0000	.0001	.0001	.0001	.0001	1
13	.0000	.0000	.0000	.0000	.0000	.0000	.0000	.0000	.0000	.0000	0
	q=.69	q=.68	q=.67	q=.66	q=.65	q=.64	q=.63	q=.62	q=.61	q=.60	

| P=.41 | P=.42 | P=.43 | P=.44 | P=.45 | P=.46 | P=.47 | P=.48 | P=.49 | P=.50 | |
X1										n-X1
0 .0010	.0008	.0007	.0005	.0004	.0003	.0003	.0002	.0002	.0001	13
1 .0095	.0079	.0066	.0054	.0045	.0037	.0030	.0024	.0020	.0016	12
2 .0395	.0344	.0298	.0256	.0220	.0188	.0160	.0135	.0114	.0095	11
3 .1007	.0913	.0823	.0739	.0660	.0587	.0519	.0457	.0401	.0349	10
4 .1750	.1653	.1553	.1451	.1350	.1250	.1151	.1055	.0962	.0873	9
5 .2189	.2154	.2108	.2053	.1989	.1917	.1838	.1753	.1664	.1571	8
6 .2029	.2080	.2121	.2151	.2169	.2177	.2173	.2158	.2131	.2095	7
7 .1410	.1506	.1600	.1690	.1775	.1854	.1927	.1992	.2048	.2095	6
8 .0735	.0818	.0905	.0996	.1089	.1185	.1282	.1379	.1476	.1571	5
9 .0284	.0329	.0379	.0435	.0495	.0561	.0631	.0707	.0788	.0873	4
10 .0079	.0095	.0114	.0137	.0162	.0191	.0224	.0261	.0303	.0349	3
11 .0015	.0019	.0024	.0029	.0036	.0044	.0054	.0066	.0079	.0095	2
12 .0002	.0002	.0003	.0004	.0005	.0006	.0008	.0010	.0013	.0016	1
13 .0000	.0000	.0000	.0000	.0000	.0000	.0001	.0001	.0001	.0001	0
q=.59	q=.58	q=.57	q=.56	q=.55	q=.54	q=.53	q=.52	q=.51	q=.50	

n = 14

| P=.01 | P=.02 | P=.03 | P=.04 | P=.05 | P=.06 | P=.07 | P=.08 | P=.09 | P=.10 | |
X1										n-X1
0 .8687	.7536	.6528	.5647	.4877	.4205	.3620	.3112	.2670	.2288	14
1 .1229	.2153	.2827	.3294	.3593	.3758	.3815	.3788	.3698	.3559	13
2 .0081	.0286	.0568	.0892	.1229	.1559	.1867	.2141	.2377	.2570	12
3 .0003	.0023	.0070	.0149	.0259	.0398	.0562	.0745	.0940	.1142	11
4 .0000	.0001	.0006	.0017	.0037	.0070	.0116	.0178	.0256	.0349	10
5 .0000	.0000	.0000	.0001	.0004	.0009	.0018	.0031	.0051	.0078	9
6 .0000	.0000	.0000	.0000	.0000	.0001	.0002	.0004	.0008	.0013	8
7 .0000	.0000	.0000	.0000	.0000	.0000	.0000	.0000	.0001	.0002	7
8 .0000	.0000	.0000	.0000	.0000	.0000	.0000	.0000	.0000	.0000	6
9 .0000	.0000	.0000	.0000	.0000	.0000	.0000	.0000	.0000	.0000	5
10 .0000	.0000	.0000	.0000	.0000	.0000	.0000	.0000	.0000	.0000	4
11 .0000	.0000	.0000	.0000	.0000	.0000	.0000	.0000	.0000	.0000	3
12 .0000	.0000	.0000	.0000	.0000	.0000	.0000	.0000	.0000	.0000	2
13 .0000	.0000	.0000	.0000	.0000	.0000	.0000	.0000	.0000	.0000	1
14 .0000	.0000	.0000	.0000	.0000	.0000	.0000	.0000	.0000	.0000	0
q=.99	q=.98	q=.97	q=.96	q=.95	q=.94	q=.93	q=.92	q=.91	q=.90	

| P=.11 | P=.12 | P=.13 | P=.14 | P=.15 | P=.16 | P=.17 | P=.18 | P=.19 | P=.20 | |
X1										n-X1
0 .1956	.1670	.1423	.1211	.1028	.0871	.0736	.0621	.0523	.0440	14
1 .3385	.3188	.2977	.2759	.2539	.2322	.2112	.1910	.1719	.1539	13
2 .2720	.2826	.2892	.2919	.2912	.2875	.2811	.2725	.2620	.2501	12
3 .1345	.1542	.1728	.1901	.2056	.2190	.2303	.2393	.2459	.2501	11
4 .0457	.0578	.0710	.0851	.0998	.1147	.1297	.1444	.1586	.1720	10
5 .0113	.0158	.0212	.0277	.0352	.0437	.0531	.0634	.0744	.0860	9
6 .0021	.0032	.0048	.0068	.0093	.0125	.0163	.0209	.0262	.0322	8
7 .0003	.0005	.0008	.0013	.0019	.0027	.0038	.0052	.0070	.0092	7
8 .0000	.0001	.0001	.0002	.0003	.0005	.0007	.0010	.0014	.0020	6
9 .0000	.0000	.0000	.0000	.0000	.0001	.0001	.0001	.0002	.0003	5
10 .0000	.0000	.0000	.0000	.0000	.0000	.0000	.0000	.0000	.0000	4
11 .0000	.0000	.0000	.0000	.0000	.0000	.0000	.0000	.0000	.0000	3
12 .0000	.0000	.0000	.0000	.0000	.0000	.0000	.0000	.0000	.0000	2
13 .0000	.0000	.0000	.0000	.0000	.0000	.0000	.0000	.0000	.0000	1
14 .0000	.0000	.0000	.0000	.0000	.0000	.0000	.0000	.0000	.0000	0
q=.89	q=.88	q=.87	q=.86	q=.85	q=.84	q=.83	q=.82	q=.81	q=.80	

| P=.21 | P=.22 | P=.23 | P=.24 | P=.25 | P=.26 | P=.27 | P=.28 | P=.29 | P=.30 | |
X1										n-X1
0 .0369	.0309	.0258	.0214	.0178	.0148	.0122	.0101	.0083	.0068	14
1 .1372	.1218	.1077	.0948	.0832	.0726	.0632	.0548	.0473	.0407	13
2 .2371	.2234	.2091	.1946	.1802	.1659	.1519	.1385	.1256	.1134	12
3 .2521	.2520	.2499	.2459	.2402	.2331	.2248	.2154	.2052	.1943	11
4 .1843	.1955	.2052	.2135	.2202	.2252	.2286	.2304	.2305	.2290	10
5 .0980	.1103	.1226	.1348	.1468	.1583	.1691	.1792	.1883	.1963	9
6 .0391	.0466	.0549	.0639	.0734	.0834	.0938	.1045	.1153	.1262	8
7 .0119	.0150	.0188	.0231	.0280	.0335	.0397	.0464	.0538	.0618	7
8 .0028	.0037	.0049	.0064	.0082	.0103	.0128	.0158	.0192	.0232	6
9 .0005	.0007	.0010	.0013	.0018	.0024	.0032	.0041	.0052	.0066	5
10 .0001	.0001	.0001	.0002	.0003	.0004	.0006	.0008	.0011	.0014	4
11 .0000	.0000	.0000	.0000	.0000	.0001	.0001	.0001	.0002	.0002	3
12 .0000	.0000	.0000	.0000	.0000	.0000	.0000	.0000	.0000	.0000	2
13 .0000	.0000	.0000	.0000	.0000	.0000	.0000	.0000	.0000	.0000	1
14 .0000	.0000	.0000	.0000	.0000	.0000	.0000	.0000	.0000	.0000	0
q=.79	q=.78	q=.77	q=.76	q=.75	q=.74	q=.73	q=.72	q=.71	q=.70	

X1	P=.31	P=.32	P=.33	P=.34	P=.35	P=.36	P=.37	P=.38	P=.39	P=.40	n−X1
0	.0055	.0045	.0037	.0030	.0024	.0019	.0016	.0012	.0010	.0008	14
1	.0349	.0298	.0253	.0215	.0181	.0152	.0128	.0106	.0088	.0073	13
2	.1018	.0911	.0811	.0719	.0634	.0557	.0487	.0424	.0367	.0317	12
3	.1830	.1715	.1598	.1481	.1366	.1253	.1144	.1039	.0940	.0845	11
4	.2261	.2219	.2164	.2098	.2022	.1938	.1848	.1752	.1652	.1549	10
5	.2032	.2088	.2132	.2161	.2178	.2181	.2170	.2147	.2112	.2066	9
6	.1369	.1474	.1575	.1670	.1759	.1840	.1912	.1974	.2026	.2066	8
7	.0703	.0793	.0886	.0983	.1082	.1183	.1283	.1383	.1480	.1574	7
8	.0276	.0326	.0382	.0443	.0510	.0582	.0659	.0742	.0828	.0918	6
9	.0083	.0102	.0125	.0152	.0183	.0218	.0258	.0303	.0353	.0408	5
10	.0019	.0024	.0031	.0039	.0049	.0061	.0076	.0093	.0113	.0136	4
11	.0003	.0004	.0006	.0007	.0010	.0013	.0016	.0021	.0026	.0033	3
12	.0000	.0000	.0001	.0001	.0001	.0002	.0002	.0003	.0004	.0005	2
13	.0000	.0000	.0000	.0000	.0000	.0000	.0000	.0000	.0000	.0001	1
14	.0000	.0000	.0000	.0000	.0000	.0000	.0000	.0000	.0000	.0000	0
	q=.69	q=.68	q=.67	q=.66	q=.65	q=.64	q=.63	q=.62	q=.61	q=.60	

X1	P=.41	P=.42	P=.43	P=.44	P=.45	P=.46	P=.47	P=.48	P=.49	P=.50	n−X1
0	.0006	.0005	.0004	.0003	.0002	.0002	.0001	.0001	.0001	.0001	14
1	.0060	.0049	.0040	.0033	.0027	.0021	.0017	.0014	.0011	.0009	13
2	.0272	.0233	.0198	.0168	.0141	.0118	.0099	.0082	.0068	.0056	12
3	.0757	.0674	.0597	.0527	.0462	.0403	.0350	.0303	.0260	.0222	11
4	.1446	.1342	.1239	.1138	.1040	.0945	.0854	.0768	.0687	.0611	10
5	.2009	.1943	.1869	.1788	.1701	.1610	.1515	.1418	.1320	.1222	9
6	.2094	.2111	.2115	.2108	.2088	.2057	.2015	.1963	.1902	.1833	8
7	.1663	.1747	.1824	.1892	.1952	.2003	.2043	.2071	.2089	.2095	7
8	.1011	.1107	.1204	.1301	.1398	.1493	.1585	.1673	.1756	.1833	6
9	.0469	.0534	.0605	.0682	.0762	.0848	.0937	.1030	.1125	.1222	5
10	.0163	.0193	.0228	.0268	.0312	.0361	.0415	.0475	.0540	.0611	4
11	.0041	.0051	.0063	.0076	.0093	.0112	.0134	.0160	.0189	.0222	3
12	.0007	.0009	.0012	.0015	.0019	.0024	.0030	.0037	.0045	.0056	2
13	.0001	.0001	.0001	.0002	.0002	.0003	.0004	.0005	.0007	.0009	1
14	.0000	.0000	.0000	.0000	.0000	.0000	.0000	.0000	.0000	.0001	0
	q=.59	q=.58	q=.57	q=.56	q=.55	q=.54	q=.53	q=.52	q=.51	q=.50	

n = 15

X1	P=.01	P=.02	P=.03	P=.04	P=.05	P=.06	P=.07	P=.08	P=.09	P=.10	n−X1
0	.8601	.7386	.6333	.5421	.4633	.3953	.3367	.2863	.2430	.2059	15
1	.1303	.2261	.2938	.3388	.3658	.3785	.3801	.3734	.3605	.3432	14
2	.0092	.0323	.0636	.0988	.1348	.1691	.2003	.2273	.2496	.2669	13
3	.0004	.0029	.0085	.0178	.0307	.0468	.0653	.0857	.1070	.1285	12
4	.0000	.0002	.0008	.0022	.0049	.0090	.0148	.0223	.0317	.0428	11
5	.0000	.0000	.0001	.0002	.0006	.0013	.0024	.0043	.0069	.0105	10
6	.0000	.0000	.0000	.0000	.0000	.0001	.0003	.0006	.0011	.0019	9
7	.0000	.0000	.0000	.0000	.0000	.0000	.0000	.0001	.0001	.0003	8
	q=.99	q=.98	q=.97	q=.96	q=.95	q=.94	q=.93	q=.92	q=.91	q=.90	

X1	P=.11	P=.12	P=.13	P=.14	P=.15	P=.16	P=.17	P=.18	P=.19	P=.20	n−X1
0	.1741	.1470	.1238	.1041	.0874	.0731	.0611	.0510	.0424	.0352	15
1	.3228	.3006	.2775	.2542	.2312	.2090	.1878	.1678	.1492	.1319	14
2	.2793	.2870	.2903	.2897	.2856	.2787	.2692	.2578	.2449	.2309	13
3	.1496	.1696	.1880	.2044	.2184	.2300	.2389	.2452	.2489	.2501	12
4	.0555	.0694	.0843	.0998	.1156	.1314	.1468	.1615	.1752	.1876	11
5	.0151	.0208	.0277	.0357	.0449	.0551	.0662	.0780	.0904	.1032	10
6	.0031	.0047	.0069	.0097	.0132	.0175	.0226	.0285	.0353	.0430	9
7	.0005	.0008	.0013	.0020	.0030	.0043	.0059	.0081	.0107	.0138	8
8	.0001	.0001	.0002	.0003	.0005	.0008	.0012	.0018	.0025	.0035	7
9	.0000	.0000	.0000	.0000	.0001	.0001	.0002	.0003	.0005	.0007	6
10	.0000	.0000	.0000	.0000	.0000	.0000	.0000	.0000	.0001	.0001	5
	q=.89	q=.88	q=.87	q=.86	q=.85	q=.84	q=.83	q=.82	q=.81	q=.80	

X1	P=.21	P=.22	P=.23	P=.24	P=.25	P=.26	P=.27	P=.28	P=.29	P=.30	n−X1
0	.0291	.0241	.0198	.0163	.0134	.0109	.0089	.0072	.0059	.0047	15
1	.1162	.1018	.0889	.0772	.0668	.0576	.0494	.0423	.0360	.0305	14
2	.2162	.2010	.1858	.1707	.1559	.1416	.1280	.1150	.1029	.0916	13
3	.2490	.2457	.2405	.2336	.2252	.2156	.2051	.1939	.1821	.1700	12
4	.1986	.2079	.2155	.2213	.2252	.2273	.2276	.2262	.2231	.2186	11
5	.1161	.1290	.1416	.1537	.1651	.1757	.1852	.1935	.2005	.2061	10
6	.0514	.0606	.0705	.0809	.0917	.1029	.1142	.1254	.1365	.1472	9
7	.0176	.0220	.0271	.0329	.0393	.0465	.0543	.0627	.0717	.0811	8

X1											n-X1
8	.0047	.0062	.0081	.0104	.0131	.0163	.0201	.0244	.0293	.0348	7
9	.0010	.0014	.0019	.0025	.0034	.0045	.0058	.0074	.0093	.0116	6
10	.0002	.0002	.0003	.0005	.0007	.0009	.0013	.0017	.0023	.0030	5
11	.0000	.0000	.0000	.0001	.0001	.0002	.0002	.0003	.0004	.0006	4
12	.0000	.0000	.0000	.0000	.0000	.0000	.0000	.0000	.0001	.0001	3
	q=.79	q=.78	q=.77	q=.76	q=.75	q=.74	q=.73	q=.72	q=.71	q=.70	

X1	P=.31	P=.32	P=.33	P=.34	P=.35	P=.36	P=.37	P=.38	P=.39	P=.40	n-X1
0	.0038	.0031	.0025	.0020	.0016	.0012	.0010	.0008	.0006	.0005	15
1	.0258	.0217	.0182	.0152	.0126	.0104	.0086	.0071	.0058	.0047	14
2	.0811	.0715	.0627	.0547	.0476	.0411	.0354	.0303	.0259	.0219	13
3	.1579	.1457	.1338	.1222	.1110	.1002	.0901	.0805	.0716	.0634	12
4	.2128	.2057	.1977	.1888	.1792	.1692	.1587	.1481	.1374	.1268	11
5	.2103	.2130	.2142	.2140	.2123	.2093	.2051	.1997	.1933	.1859	10
6	.1575	.1671	.1759	.1837	.1906	.1963	.2008	.2040	.2059	.2066	9
7	.0910	.1011	.1114	.1217	.1319	.1419	.1516	.1608	.1693	.1771	8
8	.0409	.0476	.0549	.0627	.0710	.0798	.0890	.0985	.1082	.1181	7
9	.0143	.0174	.0210	.0251	.0298	.0349	.0407	.0470	.0538	.0612	6
10	.0038	.0049	.0062	.0078	.0096	.0118	.0143	.0173	.0206	.0245	5
11	.0008	.0011	.0014	.0018	.0024	.0030	.0038	.0048	.0060	.0074	4
12	.0001	.0002	.0002	.0003	.0004	.0006	.0007	.0010	.0013	.0016	3
13	.0000	.0000	.0000	.0000	.0001	.0001	.0001	.0001	.0002	.0003	2
	q=.69	q=.68	q=.67	q=.66	q=.65	q=.64	q=.63	q=.62	q=.61	q=.60	

X1	P=.41	P=.42	P=.43	P=.44	P=.45	P=.46	P=.47	P=.48	P=.49	P=.50	n-X1
0	.0004	.0003	.0002	.0002	.0001	.0001	.0001	.0001	.0000	.0000	15
1	.0038	.0031	.0025	.0020	.0016	.0012	.0010	.0008	.0006	.0005	14
2	.0185	.0156	.0130	.0108	.0090	.0074	.0060	.0049	.0040	.0032	13
3	.0558	.0489	.0426	.0369	.0318	.0272	.0232	.0197	.0166	.0139	12
4	.1163	.1061	.0963	.0869	.0780	.0696	.0617	.0545	.0478	.0417	11
5	.1778	.1691	.1598	.1502	.1404	.1304	.1204	.1106	.1010	.0916	10
6	.2060	.2041	.2010	.1967	.1914	.1851	.1780	.1702	.1617	.1527	9
7	.1840	.1900	.1949	.1987	.2013	.2028	.2030	.2020	.1997	.1964	8
8	.1279	.1376	.1470	.1561	.1647	.1727	.1800	.1864	.1919	.1964	7
9	.0691	.0775	.0863	.0954	.1048	.1144	.1241	.1338	.1434	.1527	6
10	.0288	.0337	.0390	.0450	.0515	.0585	.0661	.0741	.0827	.0916	5
11	.0091	.0111	.0134	.0161	.0191	.0226	.0266	.0311	.0361	.0417	4
12	.0021	.0027	.0034	.0042	.0052	.0064	.0079	.0096	.0116	.0139	3
13	.0003	.0004	.0006	.0008	.0010	.0013	.0016	.0020	.0026	.0032	2
14	.0000	.0000	.0001	.0001	.0001	.0002	.0002	.0003	.0004	.0005	1
15	.0000	.0000	.0000	.0000	.0000	.0000	.0000	.0000	.0000	.0000	0
	q=.59	q=.58	q=.57	q=.56	q=.55	q=.54	q=.53	q=.52	q=.51	q=.50	

n = 16

X1	P=.01	P=.02	P=.03	P=.04	P=.05	P=.06	P=.07	P=.08	P=.09	P=.10	n-X1
0	.8515	.7238	.6143	.5204	.4401	.3716	.3131	.2634	.2211	.1853	16
1	.1376	.2363	.3040	.3469	.3706	.3795	.3771	.3665	.3499	.3294	15
2	.0104	.0362	.0705	.1084	.1463	.1817	.2129	.2390	.2596	.2745	14
3	.0005	.0034	.0102	.0211	.0359	.0541	.0748	.0970	.1198	.1423	13
4	.0000	.0002	.0010	.0029	.0061	.0112	.0183	.0274	.0385	.0514	12
5	.0000	.0000	.0001	.0003	.0008	.0017	.0033	.0057	.0091	.0137	11
6	.0000	.0000	.0000	.0000	.0001	.0002	.0005	.0009	.0017	.0028	10
7	.0000	.0000	.0000	.0000	.0000	.0000	.0000	.0001	.0002	.0004	9
8	.0000	.0000	.0000	.0000	.0000	.0000	.0000	.0000	.0000	.0001	8
	q=.99	q=.98	q=.97	q=.96	q=.95	q=.94	q=.93	q=.92	q=.91	q=.90	

X1	P=.11	P=.12	P=.13	P=.14	P=.15	P=.16	P=.17	P=.18	P=.19	P=.20	n-X1
0	.1550	.1293	.1077	.0895	.0743	.0614	.0507	.0418	.0343	.0281	16
1	.3065	.2822	.2575	.2332	.2097	.1873	.1662	.1468	.1289	.1126	15
2	.2841	.2886	.2886	.2847	.2775	.2675	.2554	.2416	.2267	.2111	14
3	.1638	.1837	.2013	.2163	.2285	.2378	.2441	.2475	.2482	.2463	13
4	.0658	.0814	.0977	.1144	.1311	.1472	.1625	.1766	.1892	.2001	12
5	.0195	.0266	.0351	.0447	.0555	.0673	.0799	.0930	.1065	.1201	11
6	.0044	.0067	.0096	.0133	.0180	.0235	.0300	.0374	.0458	.0550	10
7	.0008	.0013	.0020	.0031	.0045	.0064	.0088	.0117	.0153	.0197	9
8	.0001	.0002	.0003	.0006	.0009	.0014	.0020	.0029	.0041	.0055	8
9	.0000	.0000	.0000	.0001	.0001	.0002	.0004	.0006	.0008	.0012	7
10	.0000	.0000	.0000	.0000	.0000	.0000	.0001	.0001	.0001	.0002	6
	q=.89	q=.88	q=.87	q=.86	q=.85	q=.84	q=.83	q=.82	q=.81	q=.80	

	P=.21	P=.22	P=.23	P=.24	P=.25	P=.26	P=.27	P=.28	P=.29	P=.30	
X1											n−X1
0	.0230	.0188	.0153	.0124	.0100	.0081	.0065	.0052	.0042	.0033	16
1	.0979	.0847	.0730	.0626	.0535	.0455	.0385	.0325	.0273	.0228	15
2	.1952	.1792	.1635	.1482	.1336	.1198	.1068	.0947	.0835	.0732	14
3	.2421	.2359	.2279	.2185	.2079	.1964	.1843	.1718	.1591	.1465	13
4	.2092	.2162	.2212	.2242	.2252	.2243	.2215	.2171	.2112	.2040	12
5	.1334	.1464	.1586	.1699	.1802	.1891	.1966	.2026	.2071	.2099	11
6	.0650	.0757	.0869	.0984	.1101	.1218	.1333	.1445	.1551	.1649	10
7	.0247	.0305	.0371	.0444	.0524	.0611	.0704	.0803	.0905	.1010	9
8	.0074	.0097	.0125	.0158	.0197	.0242	.0293	.0351	.0416	.0487	8
9	.0017	.0024	.0033	.0044	.0058	.0075	.0096	.0121	.0151	.0185	7
10	.0003	.0005	.0007	.0010	.0014	.0019	.0025	.0033	.0043	.0056	6
11	.0000	.0001	.0001	.0002	.0002	.0004	.0005	.0007	.0010	.0013	5
12	.0000	.0000	.0000	.0000	.0000	.0001	.0001	.0001	.0002	.0002	4
	q=.79	q=.78	q=.77	q=.76	q=.75	q=.74	q=.73	q=.72	q=.71	q=.70	

	P=.31	P=.32	P=.33	P=.34	P=.35	P=.36	P=.37	P=.38	P=.39	P=.40	
X1											n−X1
0	.0026	.0021	.0016	.0013	.0010	.0008	.0006	.0005	.0004	.0003	16
1	.0190	.0157	.0130	.0107	.0087	.0071	.0058	.0047	.0038	.0030	15
2	.0639	.0555	.0480	.0413	.0353	.0301	.0255	.0215	.0180	.0150	14
3	.1341	.1220	.1103	.0992	.0888	.0790	.0699	.0615	.0538	.0468	13
4	.1958	.1865	.1766	.1662	.1553	.1444	.1333	.1224	.1118	.1014	12
5	.2111	.2107	.2088	.2054	.2008	.1949	.1879	.1801	.1715	.1623	11
6	.1739	.1818	.1885	.1940	.1982	.2010	.2024	.2024	.2010	.1983	10
7	.1116	.1222	.1326	.1428	.1524	.1615	.1698	.1772	.1836	.1889	9
8	.0564	.0647	.0735	.0827	.0923	.1022	.1122	.1222	.1320	.1417	8
9	.0225	.0271	.0322	.0379	.0442	.0511	.0586	.0666	.0750	.0840	7
10	.0071	.0089	.0111	.0137	.0167	.0201	.0241	.0286	.0336	.0392	6
11	.0017	.0023	.0030	.0038	.0049	.0062	.0077	.0095	.0117	.0142	5
12	.0003	.0004	.0006	.0008	.0011	.0014	.0019	.0024	.0031	.0040	4
13	.0000	.0001	.0001	.0001	.0002	.0003	.0003	.0005	.0006	.0008	3
14	.0000	.0000	.0000	.0000	.0000	.0000	.0000	.0001	.0001	.0001	2
	q=.69	q=.68	q=.67	q=.66	q=.65	q=.64	q=.63	q=.62	q=.61	q=.60	

	P=.41	P=.42	P=.43	P=.44	P=.45	P=.46	P=.47	P=.48	P=.49	P=.50	
X1											n−X1
0	.0002	.0002	.0001	.0001	.0001	.0001	.0000	.0000	.0000	.0000	16
1	.0024	.0019	.0015	.0012	.0009	.0007	.0005	.0004	.0003	.0002	15
2	.0125	.0103	.0085	.0069	.0056	.0046	.0037	.0029	.0023	.0018	14
3	.0405	.0349	.0299	.0254	.0215	.0181	.0151	.0126	.0104	.0085	13
4	.0915	.0821	.0732	.0649	.0572	.0501	.0436	.0378	.0325	.0278	12
5	.1526	.1426	.1325	.1224	.1123	.1024	.0929	.0837	.0749	.0667	11
6	.1944	.1894	.1833	.1762	.1684	.1600	.1510	.1416	.1319	.1222	10
7	.1930	.1959	.1975	.1978	.1969	.1947	.1912	.1867	.1811	.1746	9
8	.1509	.1596	.1676	.1749	.1812	.1865	.1908	.1939	.1958	.1964	8
9	.0932	.1027	.1124	.1221	.1318	.1413	.1504	.1591	.1672	.1746	7
10	.0453	.0521	.0594	.0672	.0755	.0842	.0934	.1028	.1124	.1222	6
11	.0172	.0206	.0244	.0288	.0337	.0391	.0452	.0518	.0589	.0667	5
12	.0050	.0062	.0077	.0094	.0115	.0139	.0167	.0199	.0236	.0278	4
13	.0011	.0014	.0018	.0023	.0029	.0036	.0046	.0057	.0070	.0085	3
14	.0002	.0002	.0003	.0004	.0005	.0007	.0009	.0011	.0014	.0018	2
15	.0000	.0000	.0000	.0000	.0001	.0001	.0001	.0001	.0002	.0002	1
16	.0000	.0000	.0000	.0000	.0000	.0000	.0000	.0000	.0000	.0000	0
	q=.59	q=.58	q=.57	q=.56	q=.55	q=.54	q=.53	q=.52	q=.51	q=.50	

n = 17

	P=.01	P=.02	P=.03	P=.04	P=.05	P=.06	P=.07	P=.08	P=.09	P=.10	
X1											n−X1
0	.8429	.7093	.5958	.4996	.4181	.3493	.2912	.2423	.2012	.1668	17
1	.1447	.2461	.3133	.3539	.3741	.3790	.3726	.3582	.3383	.3150	16
2	.0117	.0402	.0775	.1180	.1575	.1935	.2244	.2492	.2677	.2800	15
3	.0006	.0041	.0120	.0246	.0415	.0618	.0844	.1083	.1324	.1556	14
4	.0000	.0003	.0013	.0036	.0076	.0138	.0222	.0330	.0458	.0605	13
5	.0000	.0000	.0001	.0004	.0010	.0023	.0044	.0075	.0118	.0175	12
6	.0000	.0000	.0000	.0000	.0001	.0003	.0007	.0013	.0023	.0039	11
7	.0000	.0000	.0000	.0000	.0000	.0000	.0001	.0002	.0004	.0007	10
8	.0000	.0000	.0000	.0000	.0000	.0000	.0000	.0000	.0000	.0001	9
	q=.99	q=.98	q=.97	q=.96	q=.95	q=.94	q=.93	q=.92	q=.91	q=.90	

	P=.11	P=.12	P=.13	P=.14	P=.15	P=.16	P=.17	P=.18	P=.19	P=.20	
X1											n−X1
0	.1379	.1138	.0937	.0770	.0631	.0516	.0421	.0343	.0278	.0225	17
1	.2898	.2638	.2381	.2131	.1893	.1671	.1466	.1279	.1109	.0957	16
2	.2865	.2878	.2846	.2775	.2673	.2547	.2402	.2245	.2081	.1914	15

X1	q=.89	q=.88	q=.87	q=.86	q=.85	q=.84	q=.83	q=.82	q=.81	q=.80	n-X1
3	.1771	.1963	.2126	.2259	.2359	.2425	.2460	.2464	.2441	.2393	14
4	.0766	.0937	.1112	.1287	.1457	.1617	.1764	.1893	.2004	.2093	13
5	.0246	.0332	.0432	.0545	.0668	.0801	.0939	.1081	.1222	.1361	12
6	.0061	.0091	.0129	.0177	.0236	.0305	.0385	.0474	.0573	.0680	11
7	.0012	.0019	.0030	.0045	.0065	.0091	.0124	.0164	.0211	.0267	10
8	.0002	.0003	.0006	.0009	.0014	.0022	.0032	.0045	.0062	.0084	9
9	.0000	.0000	.0001	.0002	.0003	.0004	.0006	.0010	.0015	.0021	8
10	.0000	.0000	.0000	.0000	.0000	.0001	.0001	.0002	.0003	.0004	7
11	.0000	.0000	.0000	.0000	.0000	.0000	.0000	.0000	.0000	.0001	6

P=.21	P=.22	P=.23	P=.24	P=.25	P=.26	P=.27	P=.28	P=.29	P=.30		
X1											n-X1
0	.0182	.0146	.0118	.0094	.0075	.0060	.0047	.0038	.0030	.0023	17
1	.0822	.0702	.0597	.0505	.0426	.0357	.0299	.0248	.0206	.0169	16
2	.1747	.1584	.1427	.1277	.1136	.1005	.0883	.0772	.0672	.0581	15
3	.2322	.2234	.2131	.2016	.1893	.1765	.1634	.1502	.1372	.1245	14
4	.2161	.2205	.2228	.2228	.2209	.2170	.2115	.2044	.1961	.1868	13
5	.1493	.1617	.1730	.1830	.1914	.1982	.2033	.2067	.2083	.2081	12
6	.0794	.0912	.1034	.1156	.1276	.1393	.1504	.1608	.1701	.1784	11
7	.0332	.0404	.0485	.0573	.0668	.0769	.0874	.0982	.1092	.1201	10
8	.0110	.0143	.0181	.0226	.0279	.0338	.0404	.0478	.0558	.0644	9
9	.0029	.0040	.0054	.0071	.0093	.0119	.0150	.0186	.0228	.0276	8
10	.0006	.0009	.0013	.0018	.0025	.0033	.0044	.0058	.0074	.0095	7
11	.0001	.0002	.0002	.0004	.0005	.0007	.0010	.0014	.0019	.0026	6
12	.0000	.0000	.0000	.0001	.0001	.0001	.0002	.0003	.0004	.0006	5
13	.0000	.0000	.0000	.0000	.0000	.0000	.0000	.0000	.0001	.0001	4

q=.79 q=.78 q=.77 q=.76 q=.75 q=.74 q=.73 q=.72 q=.71 q=.70

P=.31	P=.32	P=.33	P=.34	P=.35	P=.36	P=.37	P=.38	P=.39	P=.40		
X1											n-X1
0	.0018	.0014	.0011	.0009	.0007	.0005	.0004	.0003	.0002	.0002	17
1	.0139	.0114	.0093	.0075	.0060	.0048	.0039	.0031	.0024	.0019	16
2	.0500	.0428	.0364	.0309	.0260	.0218	.0182	.0151	.0125	.0102	15
3	.1123	.1007	.0898	.0795	.0701	.0614	.0534	.0463	.0398	.0341	14
4	.1766	.1659	.1547	.1434	.1320	.1208	.1099	.0993	.0892	.0796	13
5	.2063	.2030	.1982	.1921	.1849	.1767	.1677	.1582	.1482	.1379	12
6	.1854	.1910	.1952	.1979	.1991	.1988	.1970	.1939	.1895	.1839	11
7	.1309	.1413	.1511	.1602	.1685	.1757	.1818	.1868	.1904	.1927	10
8	.0735	.0831	.0930	.1032	.1134	.1235	.1335	.1431	.1521	.1606	9
9	.0330	.0391	.0458	.0531	.0611	.0695	.0784	.0877	.0973	.1070	8
10	.0119	.0147	.0181	.0219	.0263	.0313	.0368	.0430	.0498	.0571	7
11	.0034	.0044	.0057	.0072	.0090	.0112	.0138	.0168	.0202	.0242	6
12	.0008	.0010	.0014	.0018	.0024	.0031	.0040	.0051	.0065	.0081	5
13	.0001	.0002	.0003	.0004	.0005	.0007	.0009	.0012	.0016	.0021	4
14	.0000	.0000	.0000	.0001	.0001	.0001	.0002	.0002	.0003	.0004	3
15	.0000	.0000	.0000	.0000	.0000	.0000	.0000	.0000	.0000	.0001	2

q=.69 q=.68 q=.67 q=.66 q=.65 q=.64 q=.63 q=.62 q=.61 q=.60

P=.41	P=.42	P=.43	P=.44	P=.45	P=.46	P=.47	P=.48	P=.49	P=.50		
X1											n-X1
0	.0001	.0001	.0001	.0001	.0000	.0000	.0000	.0000	.0000	.0000	17
1	.0015	.0012	.0009	.0007	.0005	.0004	.0003	.0002	.0002	.0001	16
2	.0084	.0068	.0055	.0044	.0035	.0028	.0022	.0017	.0013	.0010	15
3	.0290	.0246	.0207	.0173	.0144	.0119	.0097	.0079	.0064	.0052	14
4	.0706	.0622	.0546	.0475	.0411	.0354	.0302	.0257	.0217	.0182	13
5	.1276	.1172	.1070	.0971	.0875	.0784	.0697	.0616	.0541	.0472	12
6	.1773	.1697	.1614	.1525	.1432	.1335	.1237	.1138	.1040	.0944	11
7	.1936	.1932	.1914	.1883	.1841	.1787	.1723	.1650	.1570	.1484	10
8	.1682	.1748	.1805	.1850	.1883	.1903	.1910	.1904	.1886	.1855	9
9	.1169	.1266	.1361	.1453	.1540	.1621	.1694	.1758	.1812	.1855	8
10	.0650	.0733	.0822	.0914	.1008	.1105	.1202	.1298	.1393	.1484	7
11	.0287	.0338	.0394	.0457	.0525	.0599	.0678	.0763	.0851	.0944	6
12	.0100	.0122	.0149	.0179	.0215	.0255	.0301	.0352	.0409	.0472	5
13	.0027	.0034	.0043	.0054	.0068	.0084	.0103	.0125	.0151	.0182	4
14	.0005	.0007	.0009	.0012	.0016	.0020	.0026	.0033	.0041	.0052	3
15	.0001	.0001	.0001	.0002	.0003	.0003	.0005	.0006	.0008	.0010	2
16	.0000	.0000	.0000	.0000	.0000	.0000	.0001	.0001	.0001	.0001	1
17	.0000	.0000	.0000	.0000	.0000	.0000	.0000	.0000	.0000	.0000	0

q=.59 q=.58 q=.57 q=.56 q=.55 q=.54 q=.53 q=.52 q=.51 q=.50

n = 18

P=.01	P=.02	P=.03	P=.04	P=.05	P=.06	P=.07	P=.08	P=.09	P=.10		
X1											n-X1
0	.8345	.6951	.5780	.4796	.3972	.3283	.2708	.2229	.1831	.1501	18
1	.1517	.2554	.3217	.3597	.3763	.3772	.3669	.3489	.3260	.3002	17

X1											n-X1
2	.0130	.0443	.0846	.1274	.1683	.2047	.2348	.2579	.2741	.2835	16
3	.0007	.0048	.0140	.0283	.0473	.0697	.0942	.1196	.1446	.1680	15
4	.0000	.0004	.0016	.0044	.0093	.0167	.0266	.0390	.0536	.0700	14
5	.0000	.0000	.0001	.0005	.0014	.0030	.0056	.0095	.0148	.0218	13
6	.0000	.0000	.0000	.0000	.0002	.0004	.0009	.0018	.0032	.0052	12
7	.0000	.0000	.0000	.0000	.0000	.0000	.0001	.0003	.0005	.0010	11
8	.0000	.0000	.0000	.0000	.0000	.0000	.0000	.0000	.0001	.0002	10

q=.99 q=.98 q=.97 q=.96 q=.95 q=.94 q=.93 q=.92 q=.91 q=.90

P=.11	P=.12	P=.13	P=.14	P=.15	P=.16	P=.17	P=.18	P=.19	P=.20		
X1											n-X1
0	.1227	.1002	.0815	.0662	.0536	.0434	.0349	.0281	.0225	.0180	18
1	.2731	.2458	.2193	.1940	.1704	.1486	.1288	.1110	.0951	.0811	17
2	.2869	.2850	.2785	.2685	.2556	.2407	.2243	.2071	.1897	.1723	16
3	.1891	.2072	.2220	.2331	.2406	.2445	.2450	.2425	.2373	.2297	15
4	.0877	.1060	.1244	.1423	.1592	.1746	.1882	.1996	.2087	.2153	14
5	.0303	.0405	.0520	.0649	.0787	.0931	.1079	.1227	.1371	.1507	13
6	.0081	.0120	.0168	.0229	.0301	.0384	.0479	.0584	.0697	.0816	12
7	.0017	.0028	.0043	.0064	.0091	.0126	.0168	.0220	.0280	.0350	11
8	.0003	.0005	.0009	.0014	.0022	.0033	.0047	.0066	.0090	.0120	10
9	.0000	.0001	.0001	.0003	.0004	.0007	.0011	.0016	.0024	.0033	9
10	.0000	.0000	.0000	.0000	.0001	.0001	.0002	.0003	.0005	.0008	8
11	.0000	.0000	.0000	.0000	.0000	.0000	.0000	.0001	.0001	.0001	7

q=.89 q=.88 q=.87 q=.86 q=.85 q=.84 q=.83 q=.82 q=.81 q=.80

P=.21	P=.22	P=.23	P=.24	P=.25	P=.26	P=.27	P=.28	P=.29	P=.30		
X1											n-X1
0	.0144	.0114	.0091	.0072	.0056	.0044	.0035	.0027	.0021	.0016	18
1	.0687	.0580	.0487	.0407	.0338	.0280	.0231	.0189	.0155	.0126	17
2	.1553	.1390	.1236	.1092	.0958	.0836	.0725	.0626	.0537	.0458	16
3	.2202	.2091	.1969	.1839	.1704	.1567	.1431	.1298	.1169	.1046	15
4	.2195	.2212	.2205	.2177	.2130	.2065	.1985	.1892	.1790	.1681	14
5	.1634	.1747	.1845	.1925	.1988	.2031	.2055	.2061	.2048	.2017	13
6	.0941	.1067	.1194	.1317	.1436	.1546	.1647	.1736	.1812	.1873	12
7	.0429	.0516	.0611	.0713	.0820	.0931	.1044	.1157	.1269	.1376	11
8	.0157	.0200	.0251	.0310	.0376	.0450	.0531	.0619	.0713	.0811	10
9	.0046	.0063	.0083	.0109	.0139	.0176	.0218	.0267	.0323	.0386	9
10	.0011	.0016	.0022	.0031	.0042	.0056	.0073	.0094	.0119	.0149	8
11	.0002	.0003	.0005	.0007	.0010	.0014	.0020	.0026	.0035	.0046	7
12	.0000	.0001	.0001	.0001	.0002	.0003	.0004	.0006	.0008	.0012	6
13	.0000	.0000	.0000	.0000	.0000	.0000	.0001	.0001	.0002	.0002	5

q=.79 q=.78 q=.77 q=.76 q=.75 q=.74 q=.73 q=.72 q=.71 q=.70

P=.31	P=.32	P=.33	P=.34	P=.35	P=.36	P=.37	P=.38	P=.39	P=.40		
X1											n-X1
0	.0013	.0010	.0007	.0006	.0004	.0003	.0002	.0002	.0001	.0001	18
1	.0102	.0082	.0066	.0052	.0042	.0033	.0026	.0020	.0016	.0012	17
2	.0388	.0327	.0275	.0229	.0190	.0157	.0129	.0105	.0086	.0069	16
3	.0930	.0822	.0722	.0630	.0547	.0471	.0404	.0344	.0292	.0246	15
4	.1567	.1450	.1333	.1217	.1104	.0994	.0890	.0791	.0699	.0614	14
5	.1971	.1911	.1838	.1755	.1664	.1566	.1463	.1358	.1252	.1146	13
6	.1919	.1948	.1962	.1959	.1941	.1908	.1862	.1803	.1734	.1655	12
7	.1478	.1572	.1656	.1730	.1792	.1840	.1875	.1895	.1900	.1892	11
8	.0913	.1017	.1122	.1226	.1327	.1423	.1514	.1597	.1671	.1734	10
9	.0456	.0532	.0614	.0701	.0794	.0890	.0988	.1087	.1187	.1284	9
10	.0184	.0225	.0272	.0325	.0385	.0450	.0522	.0600	.0683	.0771	8
11	.0060	.0077	.0097	.0122	.0151	.0184	.0223	.0267	.0318	.0374	7
12	.0016	.0021	.0028	.0037	.0047	.0060	.0076	.0096	.0118	.0145	6
13	.0003	.0005	.0006	.0009	.0012	.0016	.0021	.0027	.0035	.0045	5
14	.0001	.0001	.0001	.0002	.0002	.0003	.0004	.0006	.0008	.0011	4
15	.0000	.0000	.0000	.0000	.0000	.0000	.0001	.0001	.0001	.0002	3

q=.69 q=.68 q=.67 q=.66 q=.65 q=.64 q=.63 q=.62 q=.61 q=.60

P=.41	P=.42	P=.43	P=.44	P=.45	P=.46	P=.47	P=.48	P=.49	P=.50		
X1											n-X1
0	.0001	.0001	.0000	.0000	.0000	.0000	.0000	.0000	.0000	.0000	18
1	.0009	.0007	.0005	.0004	.0003	.0002	.0002	.0001	.0001	.0001	17
2	.0055	.0044	.0035	.0028	.0022	.0017	.0013	.0010	.0008	.0006	16
3	.0206	.0171	.0141	.0116	.0095	.0077	.0062	.0050	.0039	.0031	15
4	.0536	.0464	.0400	.0342	.0291	.0246	.0206	.0172	.0142	.0117	14
5	.1042	.0941	.0844	.0753	.0666	.0586	.0512	.0444	.0382	.0327	13
6	.1569	.1477	.1380	.1281	.1181	.1081	.0983	.0887	.0796	.0708	12
7	.1869	.1833	.1785	.1726	.1657	.1579	.1494	.1404	.1310	.1214	11
8	.1786	.1825	.1852	.1864	.1864	.1850	.1822	.1782	.1731	.1669	10
9	.1379	.1469	.1552	.1628	.1694	.1751	.1795	.1828	.1848	.1855	9
10	.0862	.0957	.1054	.1151	.1248	.1342	.1433	.1519	.1598	.1669	8
11	.0436	.0504	.0578	.0658	.0742	.0831	.0924	.1020	.1117	.1214	7
12	.0177	.0213	.0254	.0301	.0354	.0413	.0478	.0549	.0626	.0708	6

X1											n-X1
13	.0057	.0071	.0089	.0109	.0134	.0162	.0196	.0234	.0278	.0327	5
14	.0014	.0018	.0024	.0031	.0039	.0049	.0062	.0077	.0095	.0117	4
15	.0003	.0004	.0005	.0006	.0009	.0011	.0015	.0019	.0024	.0031	3
16	.0000	.0000	.0001	.0001	.0001	.0002	.0002	.0003	.0004	.0006	2
17	.0000	.0000	.0000	.0000	.0000	.0000	.0000	.0000	.0000	.0001	1
18	.0000	.0000	.0000	.0000	.0000	.0000	.0000	.0000	.0000	.0000	0
	q=.59	q=.58	q=.57	q=.56	q=.55	q=.54	q=.53	q=.52	q=.51	q=.50	

n = 19

X1	P=.01	P=.02	P=.03	P=.04	P=.05	P=.06	P=.07	P=.08	P=.09	P=.10	n-X1
0	.8262	.6812	.5606	.4604	.3774	.3086	.2519	.2051	.1666	.1351	19
1	.1586	.2642	.3294	.3645	.3774	.3743	.3602	.3389	.3131	.2852	18
2	.0144	.0485	.0917	.1367	.1787	.2150	.2440	.2652	.2787	.2852	17
3	.0008	.0056	.0161	.0323	.0533	.0778	.1041	.1307	.1562	.1796	16
4	.0000	.0005	.0020	.0054	.0112	.0199	.0313	.0455	.0618	.0798	15
5	.0000	.0000	.0002	.0007	.0018	.0038	.0071	.0119	.0183	.0266	14
6	.0000	.0000	.0000	.0001	.0002	.0006	.0012	.0024	.0042	.0069	13
7	.0000	.0000	.0000	.0000	.0000	.0001	.0002	.0004	.0008	.0014	12
8	.0000	.0000	.0000	.0000	.0000	.0000	.0000	.0001	.0001	.0002	11
	q=.99	q=.98	q=.97	q=.96	q=.95	q=.94	q=.93	q=.92	q=.91	q=.90	

X1	P=.11	P=.12	P=.13	P=.14	P=.15	P=.16	P=.17	P=.18	P=.19	P=.20	n-X1
0	.1092	.0881	.0709	.0569	.0456	.0364	.0290	.0230	.0182	.0144	19
1	.2565	.2284	.2014	.1761	.1529	.1318	.1129	.0961	.0813	.0685	18
2	.2854	.2803	.2708	.2581	.2428	.2259	.2081	.1898	.1717	.1540	17
3	.1999	.2166	.2293	.2381	.2428	.2439	.2415	.2361	.2282	.2182	16
4	.0988	.1181	.1371	.1550	.1714	.1858	.1979	.2073	.2141	.2182	15
5	.0366	.0483	.0614	.0757	.0907	.1062	.1216	.1365	.1507	.1636	14
6	.0106	.0154	.0214	.0288	.0374	.0472	.0581	.0699	.0825	.0955	13
7	.0024	.0039	.0059	.0087	.0122	.0167	.0221	.0285	.0359	.0443	12
8	.0004	.0008	.0013	.0021	.0032	.0048	.0068	.0094	.0126	.0166	11
9	.0001	.0001	.0002	.0004	.0007	.0011	.0017	.0025	.0036	.0051	10
10	.0000	.0000	.0000	.0001	.0001	.0002	.0003	.0006	.0009	.0013	9
11	.0000	.0000	.0000	.0000	.0000	.0000	.0001	.0001	.0002	.0003	8
	q=.89	q=.88	q=.87	q=.86	q=.85	q=.84	q=.83	q=.82	q=.81	q=.80	

X1	P=.21	P=.22	P=.23	P=.24	P=.25	P=.26	P=.27	P=.28	P=.29	P=.30	n-X1
0	.0113	.0089	.0070	.0054	.0042	.0033	.0025	.0019	.0015	.0011	19
1	.0573	.0477	.0396	.0326	.0268	.0219	.0178	.0144	.0116	.0093	18
2	.1371	.1212	.1064	.0927	.0803	.0692	.0592	.0503	.0426	.0358	17
3	.2065	.1937	.1800	.1659	.1517	.1377	.1240	.1109	.0985	.0869	16
4	.2196	.2185	.2151	.2096	.2023	.1935	.1835	.1726	.1610	.1491	15
5	.1751	.1849	.1928	.1986	.2023	.2040	.2036	.2013	.1973	.1916	14
6	.1086	.1217	.1343	.1463	.1574	.1672	.1757	.1827	.1880	.1916	13
7	.0536	.0637	.0745	.0858	.0974	.1091	.1207	.1320	.1426	.1525	12
8	.0214	.0270	.0334	.0406	.0487	.0575	.0670	.0770	.0874	.0981	11
9	.0069	.0093	.0122	.0157	.0198	.0247	.0303	.0366	.0436	.0514	10
10	.0018	.0026	.0036	.0050	.0066	.0087	.0112	.0142	.0178	.0220	9
11	.0004	.0006	.0009	.0013	.0018	.0025	.0034	.0045	.0060	.0077	8
12	.0001	.0001	.0002	.0003	.0004	.0006	.0008	.0012	.0016	.0022	7
13	.0000	.0000	.0000	.0000	.0001	.0001	.0002	.0002	.0004	.0005	6
14	.0000	.0000	.0000	.0000	.0000	.0000	.0000	.0000	.0001	.0001	5
	q=.79	q=.78	q=.77	q=.76	q=.75	q=.74	q=.73	q=.72	q=.71	q=.70	

X1	P=.31	P=.32	P=.33	P=.34	P=.35	P=.36	P=.37	P=.38	P=.39	P=.40	n-X1
0	.0009	.0007	.0005	.0004	.0003	.0002	.0002	.0001	.0001	.0001	19
1	.0074	.0059	.0046	.0036	.0029	.0022	.0017	.0013	.0010	.0008	18
2	.0299	.0249	.0206	.0169	.0138	.0112	.0091	.0073	.0058	.0046	17
3	.0762	.0664	.0574	.0494	.0422	.0358	.0302	.0253	.0211	.0175	16
4	.1370	.1249	.1131	.1017	.0909	.0806	.0710	.0621	.0540	.0467	15
5	.1846	.1764	.1672	.1572	.1468	.1360	.1251	.1143	.1036	.0933	14
6	.1935	.1936	.1921	.1890	.1844	.1785	.1714	.1634	.1546	.1451	13
7	.1615	.1692	.1757	.1808	.1844	.1865	.1870	.1860	.1835	.1797	12
8	.1088	.1195	.1298	.1397	.1489	.1573	.1647	.1710	.1760	.1797	11
9	.0597	.0687	.0782	.0880	.0980	.1082	.1182	.1281	.1375	.1464	10
10	.0268	.0323	.0385	.0453	.0528	.0608	.0694	.0785	.0879	.0976	9
11	.0099	.0124	.0155	.0191	.0233	.0280	.0334	.0394	.0460	.0532	8
12	.0030	.0039	.0051	.0066	.0083	.0105	.0131	.0161	.0196	.0237	7
13	.0007	.0010	.0014	.0018	.0024	.0032	.0041	.0053	.0067	.0085	6
14	.0001	.0002	.0003	.0004	.0006	.0008	.0010	.0014	.0018	.0024	5
15	.0000	.0000	.0000	.0001	.0001	.0001	.0002	.0003	.0004	.0005	4
16	.0000	.0000	.0000	.0000	.0000	.0000	.0000	.0000	.0001	.0001	3
	q=.69	q=.68	q=.67	q=.66	q=.65	q=.64	q=.63	q=.62	q=.61	q=.60	

X1	P=.41	P=.42	P=.43	P=.44	P=.45	P=.46	P=.47	P=.48	P=.49	P=.50	n-X1
0	.0000	.0000	.0000	.0000	.0000	.0000	.0000	.0000	.0000	.0000	19
1	.0006	.0004	.0003	.0002	.0002	.0001	.0001	.0001	.0001	.0000	18
2	.0037	.0029	.0022	.0017	.0013	.0010	.0008	.0006	.0004	.0003	17
3	.0144	.0118	.0096	.0077	.0062	.0049	.0039	.0031	.0024	.0018	16
4	.0400	.0341	.0289	.0243	.0203	.0168	.0138	.0113	.0092	.0074	15
5	.0834	.0741	.0653	.0572	.0497	.0429	.0368	.0313	.0265	.0222	14
6	.1353	.1252	.1150	.1049	.0949	.0853	.0761	.0674	.0593	.0518	13
7	.1746	.1683	.1611	.1530	.1443	.1350	.1254	.1156	.1058	.0961	12
8	.1820	.1829	.1823	.1803	.1771	.1725	.1668	.1601	.1525	.1442	11
9	.1546	.1618	.1681	.1732	.1771	.1796	.1808	.1806	.1791	.1762	10
10	.1074	.1172	.1268	.1361	.1449	.1530	.1603	.1667	.1721	.1762	9
11	.0611	.0694	.0783	.0875	.0970	.1066	.1163	.1259	.1352	.1442	8
12	.0283	.0335	.0394	.0458	.0529	.0606	.0688	.0775	.0866	.0961	7
13	.0106	.0131	.0160	.0194	.0233	.0278	.0328	.0385	.0448	.0518	6
14	.0032	.0041	.0052	.0065	.0082	.0101	.0125	.0152	.0185	.0222	5
15	.0007	.0010	.0013	.0017	.0022	.0029	.0037	.0047	.0059	.0074	4
16	.0001	.0002	.0002	.0003	.0005	.0006	.0008	.0011	.0014	.0018	3
17	.0000	.0000	.0000	.0000	.0001	.0001	.0001	.0002	.0002	.0003	2
	q=.59	q=.58	q=.57	q=.56	q=.55	q=.54	q=.53	q=.52	q=.51	q=.50	

n = 20

X1	P=.01	P=.02	P=.03	P=.04	P=.05	P=.06	P=.07	P=.08	P=.09	P=.10	n-X1
0	.8179	.6676	.5438	.4420	.3585	.2901	.2342	.1887	.1516	.1216	20
1	.1652	.2725	.3364	.3683	.3774	.3703	.3526	.3282	.3000	.2702	19
2	.0159	.0528	.0988	.1458	.1887	.2246	.2521	.2711	.2818	.2852	18
3	.0010	.0065	.0183	.0364	.0596	.0860	.1139	.1414	.1672	.1901	17
4	.0000	.0006	.0024	.0065	.0133	.0233	.0364	.0523	.0703	.0898	16
5	.0000	.0000	.0002	.0009	.0022	.0048	.0088	.0145	.0222	.0319	15
6	.0000	.0000	.0000	.0001	.0003	.0008	.0017	.0032	.0055	.0089	14
7	.0000	.0000	.0000	.0000	.0000	.0001	.0002	.0005	.0011	.0020	13
8	.0000	.0000	.0000	.0000	.0000	.0000	.0000	.0001	.0002	.0004	12
9	.0000	.0000	.0000	.0000	.0000	.0000	.0000	.0000	.0000	.0001	11
	q=.99	q=.98	q=.97	q=.96	q=.95	q=.94	q=.93	q=.92	q=.91	q=.90	

X1	P=.11	P=.12	P=.13	P=.14	P=.15	P=.16	P=.17	P=.18	P=.19	P=.20	n-X1
0	.0972	.0776	.0617	.0490	.0388	.0306	.0241	.0189	.0148	.0115	20
1	.2403	.2115	.1844	.1595	.1368	.1165	.0986	.0829	.0693	.0576	19
2	.2822	.2740	.2618	.2466	.2293	.2109	.1919	.1730	.1545	.1369	18
3	.2093	.2242	.2347	.2409	.2428	.2410	.2358	.2278	.2175	.2054	17
4	.1099	.1299	.1491	.1666	.1821	.1951	.2053	.2125	.2168	.2182	16
5	.0435	.0567	.0713	.0868	.1028	.1189	.1345	.1493	.1627	.1746	15
6	.0134	.0193	.0266	.0353	.0454	.0566	.0689	.0819	.0954	.1091	14
7	.0033	.0053	.0080	.0115	.0160	.0216	.0282	.0360	.0448	.0545	13
8	.0007	.0012	.0019	.0030	.0046	.0067	.0094	.0128	.0171	.0222	12
9	.0001	.0002	.0004	.0007	.0011	.0017	.0026	.0038	.0053	.0074	11
10	.0000	.0000	.0001	.0001	.0002	.0004	.0006	.0009	.0014	.0020	10
11	.0000	.0000	.0000	.0000	.0000	.0001	.0001	.0002	.0003	.0005	9
12	.0000	.0000	.0000	.0000	.0000	.0000	.0000	.0000	.0001	.0001	8
	q=.89	q=.88	q=.87	q=.86	q=.85	q=.84	q=.83	q=.82	q=.81	q=.80	

X1	P=.21	P=.22	P=.23	P=.24	P=.25	P=.26	P=.27	P=.28	P=.29	P=.30	n-X1
0	.0090	.0069	.0054	.0041	.0032	.0024	.0018	.0014	.0011	.0008	20
1	.0477	.0392	.0321	.0261	.0211	.0170	.0137	.0109	.0087	.0068	19
2	.1204	.1050	.0910	.0783	.0669	.0569	.0480	.0403	.0336	.0278	18
3	.1920	.1777	.1631	.1484	.1339	.1199	.1065	.0940	.0823	.0716	17
4	.2169	.2131	.2070	.1991	.1897	.1790	.1675	.1553	.1429	.1304	16
5	.1845	.1923	.1979	.2012	.2023	.2013	.1982	.1933	.1868	.1789	15
6	.1226	.1356	.1478	.1589	.1686	.1768	.1833	.1879	.1907	.1916	14
7	.0652	.0765	.0883	.1003	.1124	.1242	.1356	.1462	.1558	.1643	13
8	.0282	.0351	.0429	.0515	.0609	.0709	.0815	.0924	.1034	.1144	12
9	.0100	.0132	.0171	.0217	.0271	.0332	.0402	.0479	.0563	.0654	11
10	.0029	.0041	.0056	.0075	.0099	.0128	.0163	.0205	.0253	.0308	10
11	.0007	.0010	.0015	.0022	.0030	.0041	.0055	.0072	.0094	.0120	9
12	.0001	.0002	.0003	.0005	.0008	.0011	.0015	.0021	.0029	.0039	8
13	.0000	.0000	.0001	.0001	.0002	.0002	.0003	.0005	.0007	.0010	7
14	.0000	.0000	.0000	.0000	.0000	.0000	.0001	.0001	.0001	.0002	6
	q=.79	q=.78	q=.77	q=.76	q=.75	q=.74	q=.73	q=.72	q=.71	q=.70	

X1	P=.31	P=.32	P=.33	P=.34	P=.35	P=.36	P=.37	P=.38	P=.39	P=.40	n−X1
0	.0006	.0004	.0003	.0002	.0002	.0001	.0001	.0001	.0001	.0000	20
1	.0054	.0042	.0033	.0025	.0020	.0015	.0011	.0009	.0007	.0005	19
2	.0229	.0188	.0153	.0124	.0100	.0080	.0064	.0050	.0040	.0031	18
3	.0619	.0531	.0453	.0383	.0323	.0270	.0224	.0185	.0152	.0123	17
4	.1181	.1062	.0947	.0839	.0738	.0645	.0559	.0482	.0412	.0350	16
5	.1698	.1599	.1493	.1384	.1272	.1161	.1051	.0945	.0843	.0746	15
6	.1907	.1881	.1839	.1782	.1712	.1632	.1543	.1447	.1347	.1244	14
7	.1714	.1770	.1811	.1836	.1844	.1836	.1812	.1774	.1722	.1659	13
8	.1251	.1354	.1450	.1537	.1614	.1678	.1730	.1767	.1790	.1797	12
9	.0750	.0849	.0952	.1056	.1158	.1259	.1354	.1444	.1526	.1597	11
10	.0370	.0440	.0516	.0598	.0686	.0779	.0875	.0974	.1073	.1171	10
11	.0151	.0188	.0231	.0280	.0336	.0398	.0467	.0542	.0624	.0710	9
12	.0051	.0066	.0085	.0108	.0136	.0168	.0206	.0249	.0299	.0355	8
13	.0014	.0019	.0026	.0034	.0045	.0058	.0074	.0094	.0118	.0146	7
14	.0003	.0005	.0006	.0009	.0012	.0016	.0022	.0029	.0038	.0049	6
15	.0001	.0001	.0001	.0002	.0003	.0004	.0005	.0007	.0010	.0013	5
16	.0000	.0000	.0000	.0000	.0000	.0001	.0001	.0001	.0002	.0003	4
	q=.69	q=.68	q=.67	q=.66	q=.65	q=.64	q=.63	q=.62	q=.61	q=.60	

X1	P=.41	P=.42	P=.43	P=.44	P=.45	P=.46	P=.47	P=.48	P=.49	P=.50	n−X1
0	.0000	.0000	.0000	.0000	.0000	.0000	.0000	.0000	.0000	.0000	20
1	.0004	.0003	.0002	.0001	.0001	.0001	.0001	.0000	.0000	.0000	19
2	.0024	.0018	.0014	.0011	.0008	.0006	.0005	.0003	.0002	.0002	18
3	.0100	.0080	.0064	.0051	.0040	.0031	.0024	.0019	.0014	.0011	17
4	.0295	.0247	.0206	.0170	.0139	.0113	.0092	.0074	.0059	.0046	16
5	.0656	.0573	.0496	.0427	.0365	.0309	.0260	.0217	.0180	.0148	15
6	.1140	.1037	.0936	.0839	.0746	.0658	.0577	.0501	.0432	.0370	14
7	.1585	.1502	.1413	.1318	.1221	.1122	.1023	.0925	.0830	.0739	13
8	.1790	.1768	.1732	.1683	.1623	.1553	.1474	.1388	.1296	.1201	12
9	.1658	.1707	.1742	.1763	.1771	.1763	.1708	.1708	.1661	.1602	11
10	.1268	.1359	.1446	.1524	.1593	.1652	.1700	.1734	.1755	.1762	10
11	.0801	.0895	.0991	.1089	.1185	.1280	.1370	.1455	.1533	.1602	9
12	.0417	.0486	.0561	.0642	.0727	.0818	.0911	.1007	.1105	.1201	8
13	.0178	.0217	.0260	.0310	.0366	.0429	.0497	.0572	.0653	.0739	7
14	.0062	.0078	.0098	.0122	.0150	.0183	.0221	.0264	.0314	.0370	6
15	.0017	.0023	.0030	.0038	.0049	.0062	.0078	.0098	.0121	.0148	5
16	.0004	.0005	.0007	.0009	.0013	.0017	.0022	.0028	.0036	.0046	4
17	.0001	.0001	.0001	.0002	.0002	.0003	.0005	.0006	.0008	.0011	3
18	.0000	.0000	.0000	.0000	.0000	.0000	.0001	.0001	.0001	.0002	2
	q=.59	q=.58	q=.57	q=.56	q=.55	q=.54	q=.53	q=.52	q=.51	q=.50	

n = 25

X1	P=.01	P=.02	P=.03	P=.04	P=.05	P=.06	P=.07	P=.08	P=.09	P=.10	n−X1
0	.7778	.6035	.4670	.3604	.2774	.2129	.1630	.1244	.0946	.0718	25
1	.1964	.3079	.3611	.3754	.3650	.3398	.3066	.2704	.2340	.1994	24
2	.0238	.0754	.1340	.1877	.2305	.2602	.2770	.2821	.2777	.2659	23
3	.0018	.0118	.0318	.0600	.0930	.1273	.1598	.1881	.2106	.2265	22
4	.0001	.0013	.0054	.0137	.0269	.0447	.0662	.0899	.1145	.1384	21
5	.0000	.0001	.0007	.0024	.0060	.0120	.0209	.0329	.0476	.0646	20
6	.0000	.0000	.0001	.0003	.0010	.0026	.0052	.0095	.0157	.0239	19
7	.0000	.0000	.0000	.0000	.0001	.0004	.0011	.0022	.0042	.0072	18
8	.0000	.0000	.0000	.0000	.0000	.0001	.0002	.0004	.0009	.0018	17
9	.0000	.0000	.0000	.0000	.0000	.0000	.0001	.0002	.0004	16	
10	.0000	.0000	.0000	.0000	.0000	.0000	.0000	.0000	.0000	.0001	15
	q=.99	q=.98	q=.97	q=.96	q=.95	q=.94	q=.93	q=.92	q=.91	q=.90	

X1	P=.11	P=.12	P=.13	P=.14	P=.15	P=.16	P=.17	P=.18	P=.19	P=.20	n−X1
0	.0543	.0409	.0308	.0230	.0172	.0128	.0095	.0070	.0052	.0038	25
1	.1678	.1395	.1149	.0938	.0759	.0609	.0486	.0384	.0302	.0236	24
2	.2488	.2283	.2060	.1832	.1607	.1392	.1193	.1012	.0851	.0708	23
3	.2358	.2387	.2360	.2286	.2174	.2033	.1874	.1704	.1530	.1358	22
4	.1603	.1790	.1940	.2047	.2110	.2130	.2111	.2057	.1974	.1867	21
5	.0832	.1025	.1217	.1399	.1564	.1704	.1816	.1897	.1945	.1960	20
6	.0343	.0466	.0606	.0759	.0920	.1082	.1240	.1388	.1520	.1633	19
7	.0115	.0173	.0246	.0336	.0441	.0559	.0689	.0827	.0968	.1108	18
8	.0032	.0053	.0083	.0123	.0175	.0240	.0318	.0408	.0511	.0623	17
9	.0007	.0014	.0023	.0038	.0058	.0086	.0123	.0169	.0226	.0294	16
10	.0001	.0003	.0006	.0010	.0016	.0026	.0040	.0059	.0085	.0118	15
11	.0000	.0001	.0001	.0002	.0004	.0007	.0011	.0018	.0027	.0040	14
12	.0000	.0000	.0000	.0000	.0001	.0002	.0003	.0005	.0007	.0012	13
13	.0000	.0000	.0000	.0000	.0000	.0000	.0001	.0001	.0002	.0003	12
14	.0000	.0000	.0000	.0000	.0000	.0000	.0000	.0000	.0000	.0001	11
	q=.89	q=.88	q=.87	q=.86	q=.85	q=.84	q=.83	q=.82	q=.81	q=.80	

X1	P=.21	P=.22	P=.23	P=.24	P=.25	P=.26	P=.27	P=.28	P=.29	P=.30	n−X1
0	.0028	.0020	.0015	.0010	.0008	.0005	.0004	.0003	.0002	.0001	25
1	.0183	.0141	.0109	.0083	.0063	.0047	.0035	.0026	.0020	.0014	24
2	.0585	.0479	.0389	.0314	.0251	.0199	.0157	.0123	.0096	.0074	23
3	.1192	.1035	.0891	.0759	.0641	.0537	.0446	.0367	.0300	.0243	22
4	.1742	.1606	.1463	.1318	.1175	.1037	.0906	.0785	.0673	.0572	21
5	.1945	.1903	.1836	.1749	.1645	.1531	.1408	.1282	.1155	.1030	20
6	.1724	.1789	.1828	.1841	.1828	.1793	.1736	.1661	.1572	.1472	19
7	.1244	.1369	.1482	.1578	.1654	.1709	.1743	.1754	.1743	.1712	18
8	.0744	.0869	.0996	.1121	.1241	.1351	.1450	.1535	.1602	.1651	17
9	.0373	.0463	.0562	.0669	.0781	.0897	.1013	.1127	.1236	.1336	16
10	.0159	.0209	.0269	.0338	.0417	.0504	.0600	.0701	.0808	.0916	15
11	.0058	.0080	.0109	.0145	.0189	.0242	.0302	.0372	.0450	.0536	14
12	.0018	.0026	.0038	.0054	.0074	.0099	.0130	.0169	.0214	.0268	13
13	.0005	.0007	.0011	.0017	.0025	.0035	.0048	.0066	.0088	.0115	12
14	.0001	.0002	.0003	.0005	.0007	.0010	.0015	.0022	.0031	.0042	11
15	.0000	.0000	.0001	.0001	.0002	.0003	.0004	.0006	.0009	.0013	10
16	.0000	.0000	.0000	.0000	.0000	.0001	.0001	.0002	.0002	.0004	9
17	.0000	.0000	.0000	.0000	.0000	.0000	.0000	.0000	.0001	.0001	8
	q=.79	q=.78	q=.77	q=.76	q=.75	q=.74	q=.73	q=.72	q=.71	q=.70	

X1	P=.31	P=.32	P=.33	P=.34	P=.35	P=.36	P=.37	P=.38	P=.39	P=.40	n−X1
0	.0001	.0001	.0000	.0000	.0000	.0000	.0000	.0000	.0000	.0000	25
1	.0011	.0008	.0006	.0004	.0003	.0002	.0001	.0001	.0001	.0000	24
2	.0057	.0043	.0033	.0025	.0018	.0014	.0010	.0007	.0005	.0004	23
3	.0195	.0156	.0123	.0097	.0076	.0058	.0045	.0034	.0026	.0019	22
4	.0482	.0403	.0334	.0274	.0224	.0181	.0145	.0115	.0091	.0071	21
5	.0910	.0797	.0691	.0594	.0506	.0427	.0357	.0297	.0244	.0199	20
6	.1363	.1250	.1134	.1020	.0908	.0801	.0700	.0606	.0520	.0442	19
7	.1662	.1596	.1516	.1426	.1327	.1222	.1115	.1008	.0902	.0800	18
8	.1680	.1690	.1681	.1652	.1607	.1547	.1474	.1390	.1298	.1200	17
9	.1426	.1502	.1563	.1608	.1635	.1644	.1635	.1609	.1567	.1511	16
10	.1025	.1131	.1232	.1325	.1409	.1479	.1536	.1578	.1603	.1612	15
11	.0628	.0726	.0828	.0931	.1034	.1135	.1230	.1319	.1398	.1465	14
12	.0329	.0399	.0476	.0560	.0650	.0745	.0843	.0943	.1043	.1140	13
13	.0148	.0188	.0234	.0288	.0350	.0419	.0495	.0578	.0667	.0760	12
14	.0057	.0076	.0099	.0127	.0161	.0202	.0249	.0304	.0365	.0434	11
15	.0019	.0026	.0036	.0048	.0064	.0083	.0107	.0136	.0171	.0212	10
16	.0005	.0008	.0011	.0015	.0021	.0029	.0039	.0052	.0068	.0088	9
17	.0001	.0002	.0003	.0004	.0006	.0009	.0012	.0017	.0023	.0031	8
18	.0000	.0000	.0001	.0001	.0001	.0002	.0003	.0005	.0007	.0009	7
19	.0000	.0000	.0000	.0000	.0000	.0000	.0001	.0001	.0002	.0002	6
	q=.69	q=.68	q=.67	q=.66	q=.65	q=.64	q=.63	q=.62	q=.61	q=.60	

X1	P=.41	P=.42	P=.43	P=.44	P=.45	P=.46	P=.47	P=.48	P=.49	P=.50	n−X1
0	.0000	.0000	.0000	.0000	.0000	.0000	.0000	.0000	.0000	.0000	25
1	.0000	.0000	.0000	.0000	.0000	.0000	.0000	.0000	.0000	.0000	24
2	.0003	.0002	.0001	.0001	.0001	.0000	.0000	.0000	.0000	.0000	23
3	.0014	.0011	.0008	.0006	.0004	.0003	.0002	.0001	.0001	.0001	22
4	.0055	.0042	.0032	.0024	.0018	.0014	.0010	.0007	.0005	.0004	21
5	.0161	.0129	.0102	.0081	.0063	.0049	.0037	.0028	.0021	.0016	20
6	.0372	.0311	.0257	.0211	.0172	.0138	.0110	.0087	.0068	.0053	19
7	.0703	.0611	.0527	.0450	.0381	.0319	.0265	.0218	.0178	.0143	18
8	.1099	.0996	.0895	.0796	.0701	.0612	.0529	.0453	.0384	.0322	17
9	.1442	.1363	.1275	.1181	.1084	.0985	.0886	.0790	.0697	.0609	16
10	.1603	.1579	.1539	.1485	.1419	.1342	.1257	.1166	.1071	.0974	15
11	.1519	.1559	.1583	.1591	.1583	.1559	.1521	.1468	.1404	.1328	14
12	.1232	.1317	.1393	.1458	.1511	.1550	.1573	.1581	.1573	.1550	13
13	.0856	.0954	.1051	.1146	.1236	.1320	.1395	.1460	.1512	.1550	12
14	.0510	.0592	.0680	.0772	.0867	.0964	.1060	.1155	.1245	.1328	11
15	.0260	.0314	.0376	.0445	.0520	.0602	.0690	.0782	.0877	.0974	10
16	.0113	.0142	.0177	.0218	.0266	.0321	.0382	.0451	.0527	.0609	9
17	.0042	.0055	.0071	.0091	.0115	.0145	.0179	.0220	.0268	.0322	8
18	.0013	.0018	.0024	.0032	.0042	.0055	.0071	.0090	.0114	.0143	7
19	.0003	.0005	.0007	.0009	.0013	.0017	.0023	.0031	.0040	.0053	6
20	.0001	.0001	.0001	.0002	.0003	.0004	.0006	.0009	.0012	.0016	5
21	.0000	.0000	.0000	.0000	.0001	.0001	.0001	.0002	.0003	.0004	4
22	.0000	.0000	.0000	.0000	.0000	.0000	.0000	.0000	.0000	.0001	3
	q=.59	q=.58	q=.57	q=.56	q=.55	q=.54	q=.53	q=.52	q=.51	q=.50	

X1	P=.01	P=.02	P=.03	P=.04	P=.05	P=.06	P=.07	P=.08	P=.09	P=.10	n−X1
0	.6050	.3642	.2181	.1299	.0769	.0453	.0266	.0155	.0090	.0052	50
1	.3056	.3716	.3372	.2706	.2025	.1447	.0999	.0672	.0443	.0286	49
2	.0756	.1858	.2555	.2762	.2611	.2262	.1843	.1433	.1073	.0779	48
3	.0122	.0607	.1264	.1842	.2199	.2311	.2219	.1993	.1698	.1386	47
4	.0015	.0145	.0459	.0902	.1360	.1733	.1963	.2037	.1973	.1809	46
5	.0001	.0027	.0131	.0346	.0658	.1018	.1359	.1629	.1795	.1849	45
6	.0000	.0004	.0030	.0108	.0260	.0487	.0767	.1063	.1332	.1541	44
7	.0000	.0001	.0006	.0028	.0086	.0195	.0363	.0581	.0828	.1076	43
8	.0000	.0000	.0001	.0006	.0024	.0067	.0147	.0271	.0440	.0643	42
9	.0000	.0000	.0000	.0001	.0006	.0020	.0052	.0110	.0203	.0333	41
10	.0000	.0000	.0000	.0000	.0001	.0005	.0016	.0039	.0082	.0152	40
11	.0000	.0000	.0000	.0000	.0000	.0001	.0004	.0012	.0030	.0061	39
12	.0000	.0000	.0000	.0000	.0000	.0000	.0001	.0004	.0010	.0022	38
13	.0000	.0000	.0000	.0000	.0000	.0000	.0000	.0001	.0003	.0007	37
14	.0000	.0000	.0000	.0000	.0000	.0000	.0000	.0000	.0001	.0002	36
15	.0000	.0000	.0000	.0000	.0000	.0000	.0000	.0000	.0000	.0001	35
	q=.99	q=.98	q=.97	q=.96	q=.95	q=.94	q=.93	q=.92	q=.91	q=.90	

X1	P=.11	P=.12	P=.13	P=.14	P=.15	P=.16	P=.17	P=.18	P=.19	P=.20	n−X1
0	.0029	.0017	.0009	.0005	.0003	.0002	.0001	.0000	.0000	.0000	50
1	.0182	.0114	.0071	.0043	.0026	.0016	.0009	.0005	.0003	.0002	49
2	.0552	.0382	.0259	.0172	.0113	.0073	.0046	.0029	.0018	.0011	48
3	.1091	.0833	.0619	.0449	.0319	.0222	.0151	.0102	.0067	.0044	47
4	.1584	.1334	.1086	.0858	.0661	.0496	.0364	.0262	.0185	.0128	46
5	.1801	.1674	.1493	.1286	.1072	.0869	.0687	.0530	.0400	.0295	45
6	.1670	.1712	.1674	.1570	.1419	.1242	.1055	.0872	.0703	.0554	44
7	.1297	.1467	.1572	.1606	.1575	.1487	.1358	.1203	.1037	.0870	43
8	.0862	.1075	.1262	.1406	.1493	.1523	.1495	.1420	.1307	.1169	42
9	.0497	.0684	.0880	.1068	.1230	.1353	.1429	.1454	.1431	.1364	41
10	.0252	.0383	.0539	.0713	.0890	.1057	.1200	.1309	.1376	.1398	40
11	.0113	.0190	.0293	.0422	.0571	.0732	.0894	.1045	.1174	.1271	39
12	.0045	.0084	.0142	.0223	.0328	.0453	.0595	.0745	.0895	.1033	38
13	.0016	.0034	.0062	.0106	.0169	.0252	.0356	.0478	.0613	.0755	37
14	.0005	.0012	.0025	.0046	.0079	.0127	.0193	.0277	.0380	.0499	36
15	.0002	.0004	.0009	.0018	.0033	.0058	.0095	.0146	.0214	.0299	35
16	.0000	.0001	.0003	.0006	.0013	.0024	.0042	.0070	.0110	.0164	34
17	.0000	.0000	.0001	.0002	.0005	.0009	.0017	.0031	.0052	.0082	33
18	.0000	.0000	.0000	.0001	.0001	.0003	.0007	.0012	.0022	.0037	32
19	.0000	.0000	.0000	.0000	.0000	.0001	.0002	.0005	.0009	.0016	31
20	.0000	.0000	.0000	.0000	.0000	.0001	.0002	.0003	.0006	30
21	.0000	.0000	.0000	.0000	.0000	.0000	.0000	.0000	.0001	.0002	29
22	.0000	.0000	.0000	.0000	.0000	.0000	.0000	.0000	.0000	.0001	28
	q=.89	q=.88	q=.87	q=.86	q=.85	q=.84	q=.83	q=.82	q=.81	q=.80	

X1	P=.21	P=.22	P=.23	P=.24	P=.25	P=.26	P=.27	P=.28	P=.29	P=.30	n−X1
0	.0000	.0000	.0000	.0000	.0000	.0000	.0000	.0000	.0000	.0000	50
1	.0001	.0001	.0000	.0000	.0000	.0000	.0000	.0000	.0000	.0000	49
2	.0007	.0004	.0002	.0001	.0001	.0000	.0000	.0000	.0000	.0000	48
3	.0028	.0018	.0011	.0007	.0004	.0002	.0001	.0001	.0000	.0000	47
4	.0088	.0059	.0039	.0025	.0016	.0010	.0006	.0004	.0002	.0001	46
5	.0214	.0152	.0106	.0073	.0049	.0033	.0021	.0014	.0009	.0006	45
6	.0427	.0322	.0238	.0173	.0123	.0087	.0060	.0040	.0027	.0018	44
7	.0713	.0571	.0447	.0344	.0259	.0191	.0139	.0099	.0069	.0048	43
8	.1019	.0865	.0718	.0583	.0463	.0361	.0276	.0207	.0152	.0110	42
9	.1263	.1139	.1001	.0859	.0721	.0592	.0476	.0375	.0290	.0220	41
10	.1377	.1317	.1226	.1113	.0985	.0852	.0721	.0598	.0485	.0386	40
11	.1331	.1351	.1332	.1278	.1194	.1089	.0970	.0845	.0721	.0602	39
12	.1150	.1238	.1293	.1311	.1294	.1244	.1166	.1068	.0957	.0838	38
13	.0894	.1021	.1129	.1210	.1261	.1277	.1261	.1215	.1142	.1050	37
14	.0628	.0761	.0891	.1010	.1110	.1186	.1233	.1248	.1233	.1189	36
15	.0400	.0515	.0639	.0766	.0888	.1000	.1094	.1165	.1209	.1223	35
16	.0233	.0318	.0417	.0529	.0648	.0769	.0885	.0991	.1080	.1147	34

X1											n-X1
17	.0124	.0179	.0249	.0334	.0432	.0540	.0655	.0771	.0882	.0983	33
18	.0060	.0093	.0137	.0193	.0264	.0348	.0444	.0550	.0661	.0772	32
19	.0027	.0044	.0069	.0103	.0148	.0206	.0277	.0360	.0454	.0558	31
20	.0011	.0019	.0032	.0050	.0077	.0112	.0159	.0217	.0288	.0370	30
21	.0004	.0008	.0014	.0023	.0036	.0056	.0084	.0121	.0168	.0227	29
22	.0001	.0003	.0005	.0009	.0016	.0026	.0041	.0062	.0090	.0128	28
23	.0000	.0001	.0002	.0004	.0006	.0011	.0018	.0029	.0045	.0067	27
24	.0000	.0000	.0001	.0001	.0002	.0004	.0008	.0013	.0021	.0032	26
25	.0000	.0000	.0000	.0000	.0001	.0002	.0003	.0005	.0009	.0014	25
26	.0000	.0000	.0000	.0000	.0000	.0001	.0001	.0002	.0003	.0006	24
27	.0000	.0000	.0000	.0000	.0000	.0000	.0000	.0001	.0001	.0002	23
28	.0000	.0000	.0000	.0000	.0000	.0000	.0000	.0000	.0000	.0001	22

q=.79 q=.78 q=.77 q=.76 q=.75 q=.74 q=.73 q=.72 q=.71 q=.70

P=.31 P=.32 P=.33 P=.34 P=.35 P=.36 P=.37 P=.38 P=.39 P=.40

X1											n-X1
4	.0001	.0000	.0000	.0000	.0000	.0000	.0000	.0000	.0000	.0000	46
5	.0003	.0002	.0001	.0001	.0000	.0000	.0000	.0000	.0000	.0000	45
6	.0011	.0007	.0005	.0003	.0002	.0001	.0001	.0000	.0000	.0000	44
7	.0032	.0022	.0014	.0009	.0006	.0004	.0002	.0001	.0001	.0000	43
8	.0078	.0055	.0037	.0025	.0017	.0011	.0007	.0003	.0003	.0002	42
9	.0164	.0120	.0086	.0061	.0042	.0029	.0019	.0013	.0008	.0005	41
10	.0301	.0231	.0174	.0128	.0093	.0066	.0046	.0032	.0022	.0014	40
11	.0493	.0395	.0311	.0240	.0182	.0136	.0099	.0071	.0050	.0076	39
12	.0719	.0604	.0498	.0402	.0319	.0248	.0189	.0142	.0105	.0076	38
13	.0944	.0831	.0717	.0606	.0502	.0408	.0325	.0255	.0195	.0147	37
14	.1121	.1034	.0933	.0825	.0714	.0607	.0505	.0412	.0330	.0260	36
15	.1209	.1168	.1103	.1020	.0923	.0819	.0712	.0606	.0507	.0415	35
16	.1188	.1202	.1189	.1149	.1088	.1008	.0914	.0813	.0709	.0606	34
17	.1068	.1132	.1171	.1184	.1171	.1133	.1074	.0997	.0906	.0808	33
18	.0880	.0976	.1057	.1118	.1156	.1169	.1156	.1120	.1062	.0987	32
19	.0666	.0774	.0877	.0970	.1048	.1107	.1144	.1156	.1144	.1109	31
20	.0463	.0564	.0670	.0775	.0875	.0965	.1041	.1098	.1134	.1146	30
21	.0297	.0379	.0471	.0570	.0673	.0776	.0874	.0962	.1035	.1091	29
22	.0176	.0235	.0306	.0387	.0478	.0575	.0676	.0777	.0873	.0959	28
23	.0096	.0135	.0183	.0243	.0313	.0394	.0484	.0580	.0679	.0778	27
24	.0049	.0071	.0102	.0141	.0190	.0249	.0319	.0400	.0489	.0584	26
25	.0023	.0035	.0052	.0075	.0106	.0146	.0195	.0255	.0325	.0405	25
26	.0010	.0016	.0025	.0037	.0055	.0079	.0110	.0150	.0200	.0259	24
27	.0004	.0007	.0011	.0017	.0026	.0039	.0058	.0082	.0113	.0154	23
28	.0001	.0003	.0004	.0007	.0012	.0018	.0028	.0041	.0060	.0084	22
29	.0000	.0001	.0002	.0003	.0005	.0008	.0012	.0019	.0029	.0043	21
30	.0000	.0000	.0001	.0001	.0002	.0003	.0005	.0008	.0013	.0020	20
31	.0000	.0000	.0000	.0000	.0001	.0001	.0002	.0003	.0005	.0009	19
32	.0000	.0000	.0000	.0000	.0000	.0000	.0001	.0001	.0002	.0003	18
33	.0000	.0000	.0000	.0000	.0000	.0000	.0000	.0000	.0001	.0001	17

q=.69 q=.68 q=.67 q=.66 q=.65 q=.64 q=.63 q=.62 q=.61 q=.60

P=.41 P=.42 P=.43 P=.44 P=.45 P=.46 P=.47 P=.48 P=.49 P=.50

X1											n-X1
8	.0001	.0001	.0000	.0000	.0000	.0000	.0000	.0000	.0000	.0000	42
9	.0003	.0002	.0001	.0001	.0000	.0000	.0000	.0000	.0000	.0000	41
10	.0009	.0006	.0004	.0002	.0001	.0001	.0001	.0000	.0000	.0000	40
11	.0024	.0016	.0010	.0007	.0004	.0003	.0002	.0001	.0001	.0000	39
12	.0054	.0037	.0026	.0017	.0011	.0007	.0005	.0003	.0002	.0001	38
13	.0109	.0079	.0057	.0040	.0027	.0018	.0012	.0008	.0005	.0003	37
14	.0200	.0152	.0113	.0082	.0059	.0041	.0029	.0019	.0013	.0008	36
15	.0334	.0264	.0204	.0155	.0116	.0085	.0061	.0043	.0030	.0020	35
16	.0508	.0418	.0337	.0267	.0207	.0158	.0118	.0086	.0062	.0044	34
17	.0706	.0605	.0508	.0419	.0339	.0269	.0209	.0159	.0119	.0087	33
18	.0899	.0803	.0703	.0604	.0508	.0420	.0340	.0270	.0210	.0160	32
19	.1053	.0979	.0893	.0799	.0700	.0602	.0507	.0419	.0340	.0270	31
20	.1134	.1099	.1044	.0973	.0888	.0795	.0697	.0600	.0506	.0419	30
21	.1126	.1137	.1126	.1092	.1038	.0967	.0884	.0791	.0695	.0598	29
22	.1031	.1086	.1119	.1131	.1119	.1086	.1033	.0963	.0880	.0788	28
23	.0872	.0957	.1028	.1082	.1115	.1126	.1115	.1082	.1029	.0960	27
24	.0682	.0780	.0872	.0956	.1026	.1079	.1112	.1124	.1112	.1080	26
25	.0493	.0587	.0684	.0781	.0873	.0956	.1026	.1079	.1112	.1123	25
26	.0329	.0409	.0497	.0590	.0687	.0783	.0875	.0957	.1027	.1080	24
27	.0203	.0263	.0333	.0412	.0500	.0593	.0690	.0786	.0877	.0960	23

	q=.59	q=.58	q=.57	q=.56	q=.55	q=.54	q=.53	q=.52	q=.51	q=.50	
28	.0116	.0157	.0206	.0266	.0336	.0415	.0502	.0596	.0692	.0788	22
29	.0061	.0086	.0118	.0159	.0208	.0268	.0338	.0417	.0504	.0598	21
30	.0030	.0044	.0062	.0087	.0119	.0160	.0210	.0270	.0339	.0419	20
31	.0013	.0020	.0030	.0044	.0063	.0088	.0120	.0161	.0210	.0270	19
32	.0006	.0009	.0014	.0021	.0031	.0044	.0063	.0088	.0120	.0160	18
33	.0002	.0003	.0006	.0009	.0014	.0021	.0031	.0044	.0063	.0087	17
34	.0001	.0001	.0002	.0003	.0006	.0009	.0014	.0020	.0030	.0044	16
35	.0000	.0000	.0001	.0001	.0002	.0003	.0005	.0009	.0013	.0020	15
36	.0000	.0000	.0000	.0000	.0001	.0001	.0002	.0003	.0005	.0008	14
37	.0000	.0000	.0000	.0000	.0000	.0000	.0001	.0001	.0002	.0003	13
38	.0000	.0000	.0000	.0000	.0000	.0000	.0000	.0000	.0001	.0001	12

n = 100

X1	P=.01	P=.02	P=.03	P=.04	P=.05	P=.06	P=.07	P=.08	P=.09	P=.10	n-X1
0	.3660	.1326	.0476	.0169	.0059	.0021	.0007	.0002	.0001	.0000	100
1	.3697	.2707	.1471	.0703	.0312	.0131	.0053	.0021	.0008	.0003	99
2	.1849	.2734	.2252	.1450	.0812	.0414	.0198	.0090	.0039	.0016	98
3	.0610	.1823	.2275	.1973	.1396	.0864	.0486	.0254	.0125	.0059	97
4	.0149	.0902	.1706	.1994	.1781	.1338	.0888	.0536	.0301	.0159	96
5	.0029	.0353	.1013	.1595	.1800	.1639	.1283	.0895	.0571	.0339	95
6	.0005	.0114	.0496	.1052	.1500	.1657	.1529	.1233	.0895	.0596	94
7	.0001	.0031	.0206	.0589	.1060	.1420	.1545	.1440	.1188	.0889	93
8	.0000	.0007	.0074	.0285	.0649	.1054	.1352	.1455	.1366	.1148	92
9	.0000	.0002	.0023	.0121	.0349	.0687	.1040	.1293	.1381	.1304	91
10	.0000	.0000	.0007	.0046	.0167	.0399	.0712	.1024	.1243	.1319	90
11	.0000	.0000	.0002	.0016	.0072	.0209	.0439	.0728	.1006	.1199	89
12	.0000	.0000	.0000	.0005	.0028	.0099	.0245	.0470	.0738	.0988	88
13	.0000	.0000	.0000	.0001	.0010	.0043	.0125	.0276	.0494	.0743	87
14	.0000	.0000	.0000	.0000	.0003	.0017	.0058	.0149	.0304	.0513	86
15	.0000	.0000	.0000	.0000	.0001	.0006	.0025	.0074	.0172	.0327	85
16	.0000	.0000	.0000	.0000	.0000	.0002	.0010	.0034	.0090	.0193	84
17	.0000	.0000	.0000	.0000	.0000	.0001	.0004	.0015	.0044	.0106	83
18	.0000	.0000	.0000	.0000	.0000	.0000	.0001	.0006	.0020	.0054	82
19	.0000	.0000	.0000	.0000	.0000	.0000	.0000	.0002	.0009	.0026	81
20	.0000	.0000	.0000	.0000	.0000	.0000	.0000	.0001	.0003	.0012	80
21	.0000	.0000	.0000	.0000	.0000	.0000	.0000	.0000	.0001	.0005	79
22	.0000	.0000	.0000	.0000	.0000	.0000	.0000	.0000	.0000	.0002	78
23	.0000	.0000	.0000	.0000	.0000	.0000	.0000	.0000	.0000	.0001	77
24	.0000	.0000	.0000	.0000	.0000	.0000	.0000	.0000	.0000	.0000	76

	q=.99	q=.98	q=.97	q=.96	q=.95	q=.94	q=.93	q=.92	q=.91	q=.90	

X1	P=.11	P=.12	P=.13	P=.14	P=.15	P=.16	P=.17	P=.18	P=.19	P=.20	n-X1
0	.0000	.0000	.0000	.0000	.0000	.0000	.0000	.0000	.0000	.0000	100
1	.0001	.0000	.0000	.0000	.0000	.0000	.0000	.0000	.0000	.0000	99
2	.0007	.0003	.0001	.0000	.0000	.0000	.0000	.0000	.0000	.0000	98
3	.0027	.0012	.0005	.0002	.0001	.0000	.0000	.0000	.0000	.0000	97
4	.0080	.0038	.0018	.0008	.0003	.0001	.0001	.0000	.0000	.0000	96
5	.0189	.0100	.0050	.0024	.0011	.0005	.0002	.0001	.0000	.0000	95
6	.0369	.0215	.0119	.0063	.0031	.0015	.0007	.0003	.0001	.0001	94
7	.0613	.0394	.0238	.0137	.0075	.0039	.0020	.0009	.0004	.0002	93
8	.0881	.0625	.0414	.0259	.0153	.0086	.0047	.0024	.0012	.0006	92
9	.1112	.0871	.0632	.0430	.0276	.0168	.0098	.0054	.0029	.0015	91
10	.1251	.1080	.0860	.0637	.0444	.0292	.0182	.0108	.0062	.0034	90
11	.1265	.1205	.1051	.0849	.0640	.0454	.0305	.0194	.0118	.0069	89
12	.1160	.1219	.1165	.1025	.0838	.0642	.0463	.0316	.0206	.0128	88
13	.0970	.1125	.1179	.1130	.1001	.0827	.0642	.0470	.0327	.0216	87
14	.0745	.0954	.1094	.1143	.1098	.0979	.0817	.0641	.0476	.0335	86
15	.0528	.0745	.0938	.1067	.1111	.1070	.0960	.0807	.0640	.0481	85
16	.0347	.0540	.0744	.0922	.1041	.1082	.1044	.0941	.0798	.0638	84
17	.0212	.0364	.0549	.0742	.0908	.1019	.1057	.1021	.0924	.0789	83
18	.0121	.0229	.0379	.0557	.0739	.0895	.0998	.1033	.1000	.0909	82
19	.0064	.0135	.0244	.0391	.0563	.0736	.0882	.0979	.1012	.0981	81
20	.0032	.0074	.0148	.0258	.0402	.0567	.0732	.0870	.0962	.0993	80
21	.0015	.0039	.0084	.0160	.0270	.0412	.0571	.0728	.0859	.0946	79

X1	q=.89	q=.88	q=.87	q=.86	q=.85	q=.84	q=.83	q=.82	q=.81	q=.80	n-X1
22	.0007	.0019	.0045	.0094	.0171	.0282	.0420	.0574	.0724	.0849	78
23	.0003	.0009	.0023	.0052	.0103	.0182	.0292	.0427	.0576	.0720	77
24	.0001	.0004	.0011	.0027	.0058	.0111	.0192	.0301	.0433	.0577	76
25	.0000	.0002	.0005	.0013	.0031	.0064	.0119	.0201	.0309	.0439	75
26	.0000	.0001	.0002	.0006	.0016	.0035	.0071	.0127	.0209	.0316	74
27	.0000	.0000	.0001	.0003	.0008	.0018	.0040	.0076	.0134	.0217	73
28	.0000	.0000	.0000	.0001	.0004	.0009	.0021	.0044	.0082	.0141	72
29	.0000	.0000	.0000	.0000	.0002	.0004	.0011	.0024	.0048	.0088	71
30	.0000	.0000	.0000	.0000	.0001	.0002	.0005	.0012	.0027	.0052	70
31	.0000	.0000	.0000	.0000	.0000	.0001	.0002	.0006	.0014	.0029	69
32	.0000	.0000	.0000	.0000	.0000	.0000	.0001	.0003	.0007	.0016	68
33	.0000	.0000	.0000	.0000	.0000	.0000	.0000	.0001	.0003	.0008	67
34	.0000	.0000	.0000	.0000	.0000	.0000	.0000	.0001	.0002	.0004	66
35	.0000	.0000	.0000	.0000	.0000	.0000	.0000	.0000	.0001	.0002	65
36	.0000	.0000	.0000	.0000	.0000	.0000	.0000	.0000	.0000	.0001	64
37	.0000	.0000	.0000	.0000	.0000	.0000	.0000	.0000	.0000	.0000	63

X1	P=.21	P=.22	P=.23	P=.24	P=.25	P=.26	P=.27	P=.28	P=.29	P=.30	n-X1
7	.0001	.0000	.0000	.0000	.0000	.0000	.0000	.0000	.0000	.0000	93
8	.0003	.0001	.0001	.0000	.0000	.0000	.0000	.0000	.0000	.0000	92
9	.0007	.0003	.0002	.0001	.0000	.0000	.0000	.0000	.0000	.0000	91
10	.0018	.0009	.0004	.0002	.0001	.0000	.0000	.0000	.0000	.0000	90
11	.0038	.0021	.0011	.0005	.0003	.0001	.0001	.0000	.0000	.0000	89
12	.0076	.0043	.0024	.0012	.0006	.0003	.0001	.0001	.0000	.0000	88
13	.0136	.0082	.0048	.0027	.0014	.0007	.0004	.0002	.0001	.0000	87
14	.0225	.0144	.0089	.0052	.0030	.0016	.0009	.0004	.0002	.0001	86
15	.0343	.0233	.0152	.0095	.0057	.0033	.0018	.0010	.0005	.0002	85
16	.0484	.0350	.0241	.0159	.0100	.0061	.0035	.0020	.0011	.0006	84
17	.0636	.0487	.0356	.0248	.0165	.0106	.0065	.0038	.0022	.0012	83
18	.0780	.0634	.0490	.0361	.0254	.0171	.0111	.0069	.0041	.0024	82
19	.0895	.0772	.0631	.0492	.0365	.0259	.0177	.0115	.0072	.0044	81
20	.0963	.0881	.0764	.0629	.0493	.0369	.0264	.0182	.0120	.0076	80
21	.0975	.0947	.0869	.0756	.0626	.0494	.0373	.0269	.0186	.0124	79
22	.0931	.0959	.0932	.0858	.0749	.0623	.0495	.0376	.0273	.0190	78
23	.0839	.0917	.0944	.0919	.0847	.0743	.0621	.0495	.0378	.0277	77
24	.0716	.0830	.0905	.0931	.0906	.0837	.0736	.0618	.0496	.0380	76
25	.0578	.0712	.0822	.0893	.0918	.0894	.0828	.0731	.0615	.0496	75
26	.0444	.0579	.0708	.0814	.0883	.0906	.0883	.0819	.0725	.0613	74
27	.0323	.0448	.0580	.0704	.0806	.0873	.0896	.0873	.0812	.0720	73
28	.0224	.0329	.0451	.0580	.0701	.0799	.0864	.0886	.0864	.0804	72
29	.0148	.0231	.0335	.0455	.0580	.0697	.0793	.0855	.0876	.0856	71
30	.0093	.0154	.0237	.0340	.0458	.0580	.0694	.0787	.0847	.0868	70
31	.0056	.0098	.0160	.0242	.0344	.0460	.0580	.0691	.0781	.0840	69
32	.0032	.0060	.0103	.0165	.0248	.0349	.0462	.0579	.0688	.0776	68
33	.0018	.0035	.0063	.0107	.0170	.0252	.0352	.0464	.0579	.0685	67
34	.0009	.0019	.0037	.0067	.0112	.0175	.0257	.0356	.0466	.0579	66
35	.0005	.0010	.0021	.0040	.0070	.0116	.0179	.0261	.0359	.0468	65
36	.0002	.0005	.0011	.0023	.0042	.0073	.0120	.0183	.0265	.0362	64
37	.0001	.0003	.0006	.0012	.0024	.0045	.0077	.0123	.0187	.0268	63
38	.0000	.0001	.0003	.0006	.0013	.0026	.0047	.0079	.0127	.0191	62
39	.0000	.0001	.0001	.0003	.0007	.0015	.0028	.0049	.0082	.0130	61
40	.0000	.0000	.0001	.0002	.0004	.0008	.0016	.0029	.0051	.0085	60
41	.0000	.0000	.0000	.0001	.0002	.0004	.0008	.0017	.0031	.0053	59
42	.0000	.0000	.0000	.0000	.0001	.0002	.0004	.0009	.0018	.0032	58
43	.0000	.0000	.0000	.0000	.0000	.0001	.0002	.0005	.0010	.0019	57
44	.0000	.0000	.0000	.0000	.0000	.0000	.0001	.0002	.0005	.0010	56
45	.0000	.0000	.0000	.0000	.0000	.0000	.0000	.0001	.0003	.0005	55
46	.0000	.0000	.0000	.0000	.0000	.0000	.0000	.0001	.0001	.0003	54
47	.0000	.0000	.0000	.0000	.0000	.0000	.0000	.0000	.0001	.0001	53
48	.0000	.0000	.0000	.0000	.0000	.0000	.0000	.0000	.0000	.0001	52

q=.79 q=.78 q=.77 q=.76 q=.75 q=.74 q=.73 q=.72 q=.71 q=.70

X1	P=.31	P=.32	P=.33	P=.34	P=.35	P=.36	P=.37	P=.38	P=.39	P=.40	n-X1
15	.0001	.0001	.0000	.0000	.0000	.0000	.0000	.0000	.0000	.0000	85
16	.0003	.0001	.0001	.0000	.0000	.0000	.0000	.0000	.0000	.0000	84
17	.0006	.0003	.0002	.0001	.0000	.0000	.0000	.0000	.0000	.0000	83

18	.0013	.0007	.0004	.0002	.0001	.0000	.0000	.0000	.0000	.0000	82
19	.0025	.0014	.0008	.0004	.0002	.0001	.0000	.0000	.0000	.0000	81
20	.0046	.0027	.0015	.0008	.0004	.0002	.0001	.0001	.0000	.0000	80
21	.0079	.0049	.0029	.0016	.0009	.0005	.0002	.0001	.0001	.0000	79
22	.0127	.0082	.0051	.0030	.0017	.0010	.0005	.0003	.0001	.0001	78
23	.0194	.0131	.0085	.0053	.0032	.0018	.0010	.0006	.0003	.0001	77
24	.0280	.0198	.0134	.0088	.0055	.0033	.0019	.0011	.0006	.0003	76
25	.0382	.0283	.0201	.0137	.0090	.0057	.0035	.0020	.0012	.0006	75
26	.0496	.0384	.0286	.0204	.0140	.0092	.0059	.0036	.0021	.0012	74
27	.0610	.0495	.0386	.0288	.0207	.0143	.0095	.0060	.0037	.0022	73
28	.0715	.0608	.0495	.0387	.0290	.0209	.0145	.0097	.0062	.0038	72
29	.0797	.0710	.0605	.0495	.0388	.0292	.0211	.0147	.0098	.0063	71
30	.0848	.0791	.0706	.0603	.0494	.0389	.0294	.0213	.0149	.0100	70
31	.0860	.0840	.0785	.0702	.0601	.0494	.0389	.0295	.0215	.0151	69
32	.0833	.0853	.0834	.0779	.0698	.0599	.0493	.0390	.0296	.0217	68
33	.0771	.0827	.0846	.0827	.0774	.0694	.0597	.0493	.0390	.0297	67
34	.0683	.0767	.0821	.0840	.0821	.0769	.0691	.0595	.0492	.0391	66
35	.0578	.0680	.0763	.0816	.0834	.0816	.0765	.0688	.0593	.0491	65
36	.0469	.0578	.0678	.0759	.0811	.0829	.0811	.0761	.0685	.0591	64
37	.0365	.0471	.0578	.0676	.0755	.0806	.0824	.0807	.0757	.0682	63
38	.0272	.0367	.0472	.0577	.0674	.0752	.0802	.0820	.0803	.0754	62
39	.0194	.0275	.0369	.0473	.0577	.0672	.0749	.0799	.0816	.0799	61
40	.0133	.0197	.0277	.0372	.0474	.0577	.0671	.0746	.0795	.0812	60
41	.0087	.0136	.0200	.0280	.0373	.0475	.0577	.0670	.0744	.0792	59
42	.0055	.0090	.0138	.0203	.0282	.0375	.0476	.0576	.0668	.0742	58
43	.0033	.0057	.0092	.0141	.0205	.0285	.0377	.0477	.0576	.0667	57
44	.0019	.0035	.0059	.0094	.0143	.0207	.0287	.0378	.0477	.0576	56
45	.0011	.0020	.0036	.0060	.0096	.0145	.0210	.0289	.0380	.0478	55
46	.0006	.0011	.0021	.0037	.0062	.0098	.0147	.0212	.0290	.0381	54
47	.0003	.0006	.0012	.0022	.0038	.0063	.0099	.0149	.0213	.0292	53
48	.0001	.0003	.0007	.0012	.0023	.0039	.0064	.0101	.0151	.0215	52
49	.0001	.0002	.0003	.0007	.0013	.0023	.0040	.0066	.0102	.0152	51
50	.0000	.0001	.0002	.0004	.0007	.0013	.0024	.0041	.0067	.0103	50
51	.0000	.0000	.0001	.0002	.0004	.0007	.0014	.0025	.0042	.0068	49
52	.0000	.0000	.0000	.0001	.0002	.0004	.0008	.0014	.0025	.0042	48
53	.0000	.0000	.0000	.0000	.0001	.0002	.0004	.0008	.0015	.0026	47
54	.0000	.0000	.0000	.0000	.0000	.0001	.0002	.0004	.0008	.0015	46
55	.0000	.0000	.0000	.0000	.0000	.0000	.0001	.0002	.0004	.0008	45
56	.0000	.0000	.0000	.0000	.0000	.0000	.0001	.0002	.0002	.0004	44
57	.0000	.0000	.0000	.0000	.0000	.0000	.0000	.0001	.0001	.0002	43
58	.0000	.0000	.0000	.0000	.0000	.0000	.0000	.0000	.0001	.0001	42
59	.0000	.0000	.0000	.0000	.0000	.0000	.0000	.0000	.0000	.0001	41

q=.69 q=.68 q=.67 q=.66 q=.65 q=.64 q=.63 q=.62 q=.61 q=.60

| | P=.41 | P=.42 | P=.43 | P=.44 | P=.45 | P=.46 | P=.47 | P=.48 | P=.49 | P=.50 | |
X1											n-X1
23	.0001	.0000	.0000	.0000	.0000	.0000	.0000	.0000	.0000	.0000	77
24	.0002	.0001	.0000	.0000	.0000	.0000	.0000	.0000	.0000	.0000	76
25	.0003	.0002	.0001	.0000	.0000	.0000	.0000	.0000	.0000	.0000	75
26	.0007	.0003	.0002	.0001	.0000	.0000	.0000	.0000	.0000	.0000	74
27	.0013	.0007	.0004	.0002	.0001	.0000	.0000	.0000	.0000	.0000	73
28	.0023	.0013	.0007	.0004	.0002	.0001	.0000	.0000	.0000	.0000	72
29	.0039	.0024	.0014	.0008	.0004	.0002	.0001	.0000	.0000	.0000	71
30	.0065	.0040	.0024	.0014	.0008	.0004	.0002	.0001	.0001	.0000	70
31	.0102	.0066	.0041	.0025	.0014	.0008	.0004	.0002	.0001	.0001	69
32	.0152	.0103	.0067	.0042	.0025	.0015	.0008	.0004	.0002	.0001	68
33	.0218	.0154	.0104	.0068	.0043	.0026	.0015	.0008	.0004	.0002	67
34	.0298	.0219	.0155	.0105	.0069	.0043	.0026	.0015	.0009	.0005	66
35	.0391	.0299	.0220	.0156	.0106	.0069	.0044	.0026	.0015	.0009	65
36	.0491	.0391	.0300	.0221	.0157	.0107	.0070	.0044	.0027	.0016	64
37	.0590	.0490	.0391	.0300	.0222	.0157	.0107	.0070	.0044	.0027	63
38	.0680	.0588	.0489	.0391	.0301	.0222	.0158	.0108	.0071	.0045	62
39	.0751	.0677	.0587	.0489	.0391	.0301	.0223	.0158	.0108	.0071	61
40	.0796	.0748	.0675	.0586	.0488	.0391	.0301	.0223	.0159	.0108	60
41	.0809	.0793	.0745	.0673	.0584	.0487	.0391	.0301	.0223	.0159	59
42	.0790	.0806	.0790	.0743	.0672	.0583	.0487	.0390	.0301	.0223	58
43	.0740	.0787	.0804	.0788	.0741	.0670	.0582	.0486	.0390	.0301	57
44	.0666	.0739	.0785	.0802	.0786	.0739	.0669	.0581	.0485	.0390	56
45	.0576	.0666	.0737	.0784	.0800	.0784	.0738	.0668	.0580	.0485	55
46	.0479	.0576	.0665	.0736	.0782	.0798	.0783	.0737	.0667	.0580	54
47	.0382	.0480	.0576	.0665	.0736	.0781	.0797	.0781	.0736	.0666	53
48	.0293	.0383	.0480	.0577	.0665	.0735	.0781	.0797	.0781	.0735	52
49	.0216	.0295	.0384	.0481	.0577	.0664	.0735	.0780	.0796	.0780	51
50	.0153	.0218	.0296	.0385	.0482	.0577	.0665	.0735	.0780	.0796	50
51	.0104	.0155	.0219	.0297	.0386	.0482	.0578	.0665	.0735	.0780	49
52	.0068	.0105	.0156	.0220	.0298	.0387	.0483	.0578	.0665	.0735	48
53	.0043	.0069	.0106	.0156	.0221	.0299	.0388	.0483	.0579	.0666	47
54	.0026	.0044	.0070	.0107	.0157	.0221	.0299	.0388	.0484	.0580	46

55	.0015	.0026	.0044	.0070	.0108	.0158	.0222	.0300	.0389	.0485	45
56	.0008	.0015	.0027	.0044	.0071	.0108	.0158	.0222	.0300	.0390	44
57	.0005	.0009	.0016	.0027	.0045	.0071	.0108	.0158	.0223	.0301	43
58	.0002	.0005	.0009	.0016	.0027	.0045	.0071	.0108	.0159	.0223	42
59	.0001	.0002	.0005	.0009	.0016	.0027	.0045	.0071	.0109	.0159	41
60	.0001	.0001	.0002	.0005	.0009	.0016	.0027	.0045	.0071	.0108	40
61	.0000	.0001	.0001	.0002	.0005	.0009	.0016	.0027	.0045	.0071	39
62	.0000	.0000	.0001	.0001	.0002	.0005	.0009	.0016	.0027	.0045	38
63	.0000	.0000	.0000	.0001	.0001	.0002	.0005	.0009	.0016	.0027	37
64	.0000	.0000	.0000	.0000	.0001	.0001	.0002	.0005	.0009	.0016	36
65	.0000	.0000	.0000	.0000	.0000	.0001	.0001	.0002	.0005	.0009	35
66	.0000	.0000	.0000	.0000	.0000	.0000	.0001	.0001	.0002	.0005	34
67	.0000	.0000	.0000	.0000	.0000	.0000	.0000	.0001	.0001	.0002	33
68	.0000	.0000	.0000	.0000	.0000	.0000	.0000	.0000	.0001	.0001	32
69	.0000	.0000	.0000	.0000	.0000	.0000	.0000	.0000	.0000	.0001	31

$q=.59$	$q=.58$	$q=.57$	$q=.56$	$q=.55$	$q=.54$	$q=.53$	$q=.52$	$q=.51$	$q=.50$

APPENDIX B   POISSON PROBABILITY DISTRIBUTION—VALUES OF $P(X) = (\lambda t)^X e^{-\lambda t}/X!$

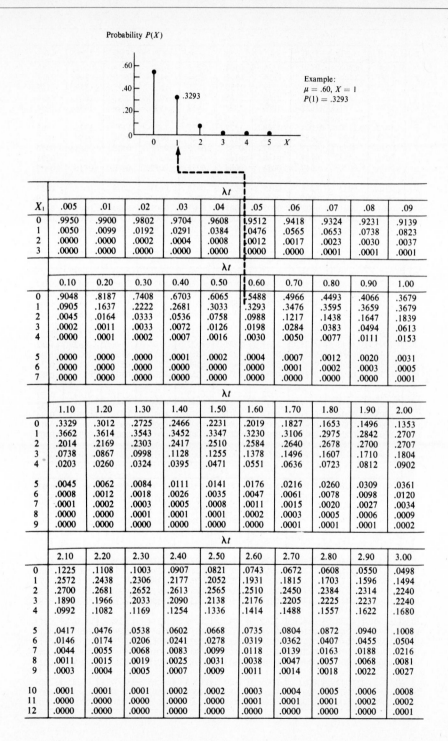

Probability $P(X)$

Example:
$\mu = .60$, $X = 1$
$P(1) = .3293$

X_1	.005	.01	.02	.03	.04	.05	.06	.07	.08	.09
					λt					
0	.9950	.9900	.9802	.9704	.9608	.9512	.9418	.9324	.9231	.9139
1	.0050	.0099	.0192	.0291	.0384	.0476	.0565	.0653	.0738	.0823
2	.0000	.0000	.0002	.0004	.0008	.0012	.0017	.0023	.0030	.0037
3	.0000	.0000	.0000	.0000	.0000	.0000	.0000	.0001	.0001	.0001

	0.10	0.20	0.30	0.40	0.50	0.60	0.70	0.80	0.90	1.00
					λt					
0	.9048	.8187	.7408	.6703	.6065	.5488	.4966	.4493	.4066	.3679
1	.0905	.1637	.2222	.2681	.3033	.3293	.3476	.3595	.3659	.3679
2	.0045	.0164	.0333	.0536	.0758	.0988	.1217	.1438	.1647	.1839
3	.0002	.0011	.0033	.0072	.0126	.0198	.0284	.0383	.0494	.0613
4	.0000	.0001	.0002	.0007	.0016	.0030	.0050	.0077	.0111	.0153
5	.0000	.0000	.0000	.0001	.0002	.0004	.0007	.0012	.0020	.0031
6	.0000	.0000	.0000	.0000	.0000	.0000	.0001	.0002	.0003	.0005
7	.0000	.0000	.0000	.0000	.0000	.0000	.0000	.0000	.0000	.0001

	1.10	1.20	1.30	1.40	1.50	1.60	1.70	1.80	1.90	2.00
					λt					
0	.3329	.3012	.2725	.2466	.2231	.2019	.1827	.1653	.1496	.1353
1	.3662	.3614	.3543	.3452	.3347	.3230	.3106	.2975	.2842	.2707
2	.2014	.2169	.2303	.2417	.2510	.2584	.2640	.2678	.2700	.2707
3	.0738	.0867	.0998	.1128	.1255	.1378	.1496	.1607	.1710	.1804
4	.0203	.0260	.0324	.0395	.0471	.0551	.0636	.0723	.0812	.0902
5	.0045	.0062	.0084	.0111	.0141	.0176	.0216	.0260	.0309	.0361
6	.0008	.0012	.0018	.0026	.0035	.0047	.0061	.0078	.0098	.0120
7	.0001	.0002	.0003	.0005	.0008	.0011	.0015	.0020	.0027	.0034
8	.0000	.0000	.0001	.0001	.0001	.0002	.0003	.0005	.0006	.0009
9	.0000	.0000	.0000	.0000	.0000	.0000	.0001	.0001	.0001	.0002

	2.10	2.20	2.30	2.40	2.50	2.60	2.70	2.80	2.90	3.00
					λt					
0	.1225	.1108	.1003	.0907	.0821	.0743	.0672	.0608	.0550	.0498
1	.2572	.2438	.2306	.2177	.2052	.1931	.1815	.1703	.1596	.1494
2	.2700	.2681	.2652	.2613	.2565	.2510	.2450	.2384	.2314	.2240
3	.1890	.1966	.2033	.2090	.2138	.2176	.2205	.2225	.2237	.2240
4	.0992	.1082	.1169	.1254	.1336	.1414	.1488	.1557	.1622	.1680
5	.0417	.0476	.0538	.0602	.0668	.0735	.0804	.0872	.0940	.1008
6	.0146	.0174	.0206	.0241	.0278	.0319	.0362	.0407	.0455	.0504
7	.0044	.0055	.0068	.0083	.0099	.0118	.0139	.0163	.0188	.0216
8	.0011	.0015	.0019	.0025	.0031	.0038	.0047	.0057	.0068	.0081
9	.0003	.0004	.0005	.0007	.0009	.0011	.0014	.0018	.0022	.0027
10	.0001	.0001	.0001	.0002	.0002	.0003	.0004	.0005	.0006	.0008
11	.0000	.0000	.0000	.0000	.0000	.0001	.0001	.0001	.0002	.0002
12	.0000	.0000	.0000	.0000	.0000	.0000	.0000	.0000	.0000	.0001

					λt					
X_1	3.10	3.20	3.30	3.40	3.50	3.60	3.70	3.80	3.90	4.00
0	.0450	.0408	.0369	.0334	.0302	.0273	.0247	.0224	.0202	.0183
1	.1397	.1304	.1217	.1135	.1057	.0984	.0915	.0850	.0789	.0733
2	.2165	.2087	.2008	.1929	.1850	.1771	.1692	.1615	.1539	.1465
3	.2237	.2226	.2209	.2186	.2158	.2125	.2087	.2046	.2001	.1954
4	.1734	.1781	.1823	.1858	.1888	.1912	.1931	.1944	.1951	.1954
5	.1075	.1140	.1203	.1264	.1322	.1377	.1429	.1477	.1522	.1563
6	.0555	.0608	.0662	.0716	.0771	.0826	.0881	.0936	.0989	.1042
7	.0246	.0278	.0312	.0348	.0385	.0425	.0466	.0508	.0551	.0595
8	.0095	.0111	.0129	.0148	.0169	.0191	.0215	.0241	.0269	.0298
9	.0033	.0040	.0047	.0056	.0066	.0076	.0089	.0102	.0116	.0132
10	.0010	.0013	.0016	.0019	.0023	.0028	.0033	.0039	.0045	.0053
11	.0003	.0004	.0005	.0006	.0007	.0009	.0011	.0013	.0016	.0019
12	.0001	.0001	.0001	.0002	.0002	.0003	.0003	.0004	.0005	.0006
13	.0000	.0000	.0000	.0000	.0001	.0001	.0001	.0001	.0002	.0002
14	.0000	.0000	.0000	.0000	.0000	.0000	.0000	.0000	.0000	.0001

					λt					
	4.10	4.20	4.30	4.40	4.50	4.60	4.70	4.80	4.90	5.00
0	.0166	.0150	.0136	.0123	.0111	.0101	.0091	.0082	.0074	.0067
1	.0679	.0630	.0583	.0540	.0500	.0462	.0427	.0395	.0365	.0337
2	.1393	.1323	.1254	.1188	.1125	.1063	.1005	.0948	.0894	.0842
3	.1904	.1852	.1798	.1743	.1687	.1631	.1574	.1517	.1460	.1404
4	.1951	.1944	.1933	.1917	.1898	.1875	.1849	.1820	.1789	.1755
5	.1600	.1633	.1662	.1687	.1708	.1725	.1738	.1747	.1753	.1755
6	.1093	.1143	.1191	.1237	.1281	.1323	.1362	.1398	.1432	.1462
7	.0640	.0686	.0732	.0778	.0824	.0869	.0914	.0959	.1002	.1044
8	.0328	.0360	.0393	.0428	.0463	.0500	.0537	.0575	.0614	.0653
9	.0150	.0168	.0188	.0209	.0232	.0255	.0280	.0307	.0334	.0363
10	.0061	.0071	.0081	.0092	.0104	.0118	.0132	.0147	.0164	.0181
11	.0023	.0027	.0032	.0037	.0043	.0049	.0056	.0064	.0073	.0082
12	.0008	.0009	.0011	.0014	.0016	.0019	.0022	.0026	.0030	.0034
13	.0002	.0003	.0004	.0005	.0006	.0007	.0008	.0009	.0011	.0013
14	.0001	.0001	.0001	.0001	.0002	.0002	.0003	.0003	.0004	.0005
15	.0000	.0000	.0000	.0000	.0001	.0001	.0001	.0001	.0001	.0002

					λt					
	5.10	5.20	5.30	5.40	5.50	5.60	5.70	5.80	5.90	6.00
0	.0061	.0055	.0050	.0045	.0041	.0037	.0033	.0030	.0027	.0025
1	.0311	.0287	.0265	.0244	.0225	.0207	.0191	.0176	.0162	.0149
2	.0793	.0746	.0701	.0659	.0618	.0580	.0544	.0509	.0477	.0446
3	.1348	.1293	.1239	.1185	.1133	.1082	.1033	.0985	.0938	.0892
4	.1719	.1681	.1641	.1600	.1558	.1515	.1472	.1428	.1383	.1339
5	.1753	.1748	.1740	.1728	.1714	.1697	.1678	.1656	.1632	.1606
6	.1490	.1515	.1537	.1555	.1571	.1584	.1594	.1601	.1605	.1606
7	.1086	.1125	.1163	.1200	.1234	.1267	.1298	.1326	.1353	.1377
8	.0692	.0731	.0771	.0810	.0849	.0887	.0925	.0962	.0998	.1033
9	.0392	.0423	.0454	.0486	.0519	.0552	.0586	.0620	.0654	.0688
10	.0200	.0220	.0241	.0262	.0285	.0309	.0334	.0359	.0386	.0413
11	.0093	.0104	.0116	.0129	.0143	.0157	.0173	.0190	.0207	.0225
12	.0039	.0045	.0051	.0058	.0065	.0073	.0082	.0092	.0102	.0113
13	.0015	.0018	.0021	.0024	.0028	.0032	.0036	.0041	.0046	.0052
14	.0006	.0007	.0008	.0009	.0011	.0013	.0015	.0017	.0019	.0022
15	.0002	.0002	.0003	.0003	.0004	.0005	.0006	.0007	.0008	.0009
16	.0001	.0001	.0001	.0001	.0001	.0002	.0002	.0002	.0003	.0003
17	.0000	.0000	.0000	.0000	.0000	.0001	.0001	.0001	.0001	.0001

X_1					λt					
	11.	12.	13.	14.	15.	16.	17.	18.	19.	20.
0	.0000	.0000	.0000	.0000	.0000	.0000	.0000	.0000	.0000	.0000
1	.0002	.0001	.0000	.0000	.0000	.0000	.0000	.0000	.0000	.0000
2	.0010	.0004	.0002	.0001	.0000	.0000	.0000	.0000	.0000	.0000
3	.0037	.0018	.0008	.0004	.0002	.0001	.0000	.0000	.0000	.0000
4	.0102	.0053	.0027	.0013	.0006	.0003	.0001	.0001	.0000	.0000
5	.0224	.0127	.0070	.0037	.0019	.0010	.0005	.0002	.0001	.0001
6	.0411	.0255	.0152	.0087	.0048	.0026	.0014	.0007	.0004	.0002
7	.0646	.0437	.0281	.0174	.0104	.0060	.0034	.0019	.0010	.0005
8	.0888	.0655	.0457	.0304	.0194	.0120	.0072	.0042	.0024	.0013
9	.1085	.0874	.0661	.0473	.0324	.0213	.0135	.0083	.0050	.0029
10	.1194	.1048	.0859	.0663	.0486	.0341	.0230	.0150	.0095	.0058
11	.1194	.1144	.1015	.0844	.0663	.0496	.0355	.0245	.0164	.0106
12	.1094	.1144	.1099	.0984	.0829	.0661	.0504	.0368	.0259	.0176
13	.0926	.1056	.1099	.1060	.0956	.0814	.0658	.0509	.0378	.0271
14	.0728	.0905	.1021	.1060	.1024	.0930	.0800	.0655	.0514	.0387
15	.0534	.0724	.0885	.0989	.1024	.0992	.0906	.0786	.0650	.0516
16	.0367	.0543	.0719	.0866	.0960	.0992	.0963	.0884	.0772	.0646
17	.0237	.0383	.0550	.0713	.0847	.0934	.0963	.0936	.0863	.0760
18	.0145	.0256	.0397	.0554	.0706	.0830	.0909	.0936	.0911	.0844
19	.0084	.0161	.0272	.0409	.0557	.0699	.0814	.0887	.0911	.0888
20	.0046	.0097	.0177	.0286	.0418	.0559	.0692	.0798	.0866	.0888
21	.0024	.0055	.0109	.0191	.0299	.0426	.0560	.0684	.0783	.0846
22	.0012	.0030	.0065	.0121	.0204	.0310	.0433	.0560	.0676	.0769
23	.0006	.0016	.0037	.0074	.0133	.0216	.0320	.0438	.0559	.0669
24	.0003	.0008	.0020	.0043	.0083	.0144	.0226	.0329	.0442	.0557
25	.0001	.0004	.0010	.0024	.0050	.0092	.0154	.0237	.0336	.0446
26	.0000	.0002	.0005	.0013	.0029	.0057	.0101	.0164	.0246	.0343
27	.0000	.0001	.0002	.0007	.0016	.0034	.0063	.0109	.0173	.0254
28	.0000	.0000	.0001	.0003	.0009	.0019	.0038	.0070	.0117	.0181
29	.0000	.0000	.0001	.0002	.0004	.0011	.0023	.0044	.0077	.0125
30	.0000	.0000	.0000	.0001	.0002	.0006	.0013	.0026	.0049	.0083
31	.0000	.0000	.0000	.0000	.0001	.0003	.0007	.0015	.0030	.0054
32	.0000	.0000	.0000	.0000	.0001	.0001	.0004	.0009	.0018	.0034
33	.0000	.0000	.0000	.0000	.0000	.0001	.0002	.0005	.0010	.0020
34	.0000	.0000	.0000	.0000	.0000	.0000	.0001	.0002	.0006	.0012
35	.0000	.0000	.0000	.0000	.0000	.0000	.0000	.0001	.0003	.0007
36	.0000	.0000	.0000	.0000	.0000	.0000	.0000	.0001	.0002	.0004
37	.0000	.0000	.0000	.0000	.0000	.0000	.0000	.0000	.0001	.0002
38	.0000	.0000	.0000	.0000	.0000	.0000	.0000	.0000	.0000	.0001
39	.0000	.0000	.0000	.0000	.0000	.0000	.0000	.0000	.0000	.0001

Source: Stephen P. Shao, *Statistics for Business and Economics*, 3rd ed. (Columbus, Ohio: Merrill Publishing Company, 1976), pp. 782–86. Used with permission.

To illustrate: 19.85 percent of the area under a normal curve lies between the mean, μ_x, and a point 0.52 standard deviation units away.

Example:
Z = 0.52 (or −0.52)
A(Z) = 0.1985 or 19.85%

Z	.00	.01	.02	.03	.04	.05	.06	.07	.08	.09
0.0	.0000	.0040	.0080	.0120	.0160	.0199	.0239	.0279	.0319	.0359
0.1	.0398	.0438	.0478	.0517	.0557	.0596	.0636	.0675	.0714	.0753
0.2	.0793	.0832	.0871	.0910	.0948	.0987	.1026	.1064	.1103	.1141
0.3	.1179	.1217	.1255	.1293	.1331	.1368	.1406	.1443	.1480	.1517
0.4	.1554	.1591	.1628	.1664	.1700	.1736	.1772	.1808	.1844	.1879
0.5	.1915	.1950	.1985	.2019	.2054	.2088	.2123	.2157	.2190	.2224
0.6	.2257	.2291	.2324	.2357	.2389	.2422	.2454	.2486	.2517	.2549
0.7	.2580	.2611	.2642	.2673	.2704	.2734	.2764	.2794	.2823	.2852
0.8	.2881	.2910	.2939	.2967	.2995	.3023	.3051	.3078	.3106	.3133
0.9	.3159	.3186	.3212	.3238	.3264	.3289	.3315	.3340	.3365	.3389
1.0	.3413	.3438	.3461	.3485	.3508	.3531	.3554	.3577	.3599	.3621
1.1	.3643	.3665	.3686	.3708	.3729	.3749	.3770	.3790	.3810	.3830
1.2	.3849	.3869	.3888	.3907	.3925	.3944	.3962	.3980	.3997	.4015
1.3	.4032	.4049	.4066	.4082	.4099	.4115	.4131	.4147	.4162	.4177
1.4	.4192	.4207	.4222	.4236	.4251	.4265	.4279	.4292	.4306	.4319
1.5	.4332	.4345	.4357	.4370	.4382	.4394	.4406	.4418	.4429	.4441
1.6	.4452	.4463	.4474	.4484	.4495	.4505	.4515	.4525	.4535	.4545
1.7	.4554	.4564	.4573	.4582	.4591	.4599	.4608	.4616	.4625	.4633
1.8	.4641	.4649	.4656	.4664	.4671	.4678	.4686	.4693	.4699	.4706
1.9	.4713	.4719	.4726	.4732	.4738	.4744	.4750	.4756	.4761	.4767
2.0	.4772	.4778	.4783	.4788	.4793	.4798	.4803	.4808	.4812	.4817
2.1	.4821	.4826	.4830	.4834	.4838	.4842	.4846	.4850	.4854	.4857
2.2	.4861	.4864	.4868	.4871	.4875	.4878	.4881	.4884	.4887	.4890
2.3	.4893	.4896	.4898	.4901	.4904	.4906	.4909	.4911	.4913	.4916
2.4	.4918	.4920	.4922	.4925	.4927	.4929	.4931	.4932	.4934	.4936
2.5	.4938	.4940	.4941	.4943	.4945	.4946	.4948	.4949	.4951	.4952
2.6	.4953	.4955	.4956	.4957	.4959	.4960	.4961	.4962	.4963	.4964
2.7	.4965	.4966	.4967	.4968	.4969	.4970	.4971	.4972	.4973	.4974
2.8	.4974	.4975	.4976	.4977	.4977	.4978	.4979	.4979	.4980	.4981
2.9	.4981	.4982	.4982	.4983	.4984	.4984	.4985	.4985	.4986	.4986
3.0	.4987	.4987	.4987	.4988	.4988	.4989	.4989	.4989	.4990	.4990

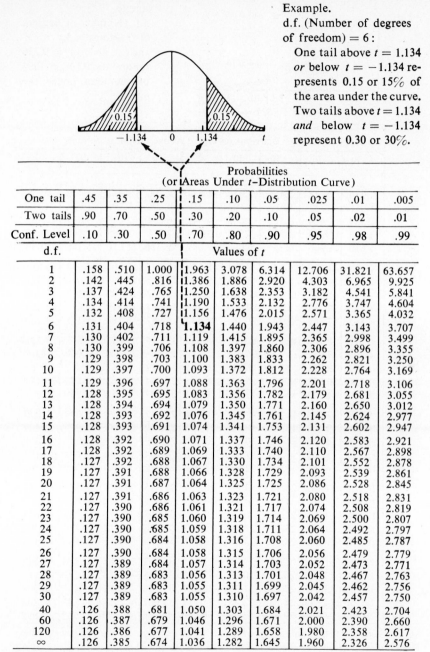

Example.
d.f. (Number of degrees
of freedom) = 6 :
One tail above $t = 1.134$
or below $t = -1.134$ represents 0.15 or 15% of
the area under the curve.
Two tails above $t = 1.134$
and below $t = -1.134$
represent 0.30 or 30%.

	Probabilities (or Areas Under t-Distribution Curve)								
One tail	.45	.35	.25	.15	.10	.05	.025	.01	.005
Two tails	.90	.70	.50	.30	.20	.10	.05	.02	.01
Conf. Level	.10	.30	.50	.70	.80	.90	.95	.98	.99
d.f.				Values of t					
1	.158	.510	1.000	1.963	3.078	6.314	12.706	31.821	63.657
2	.142	.445	.816	1.386	1.886	2.920	4.303	6.965	9.925
3	.137	.424	.765	1.250	1.638	2.353	3.182	4.541	5.841
4	.134	.414	.741	1.190	1.533	2.132	2.776	3.747	4.604
5	.132	.408	.727	1.156	1.476	2.015	2.571	3.365	4.032
6	.131	.404	.718	1.134	1.440	1.943	2.447	3.143	3.707
7	.130	.402	.711	1.119	1.415	1.895	2.365	2.998	3.499
8	.130	.399	.706	1.108	1.397	1.860	2.306	2.896	3.355
9	.129	.398	.703	1.100	1.383	1.833	2.262	2.821	3.250
10	.129	.397	.700	1.093	1.372	1.812	2.228	2.764	3.169
11	.129	.396	.697	1.088	1.363	1.796	2.201	2.718	3.106
12	.128	.395	.695	1.083	1.356	1.782	2.179	2.681	3.055
13	.128	.394	.694	1.079	1.350	1.771	2.160	2.650	3.012
14	.128	.393	.692	1.076	1.345	1.761	2.145	2.624	2.977
15	.128	.393	.691	1.074	1.341	1.753	2.131	2.602	2.947
16	.128	.392	.690	1.071	1.337	1.746	2.120	2.583	2.921
17	.128	.392	.689	1.069	1.333	1.740	2.110	2.567	2.898
18	.127	.392	.688	1.067	1.330	1.734	2.101	2.552	2.878
19	.127	.391	.688	1.066	1.328	1.729	2.093	2.539	2.861
20	.127	.391	.687	1.064	1.325	1.725	2.086	2.528	2.845
21	.127	.391	.686	1.063	1.323	1.721	2.080	2.518	2.831
22	.127	.390	.686	1.061	1.321	1.717	2.074	2.508	2.819
23	.127	.390	.685	1.060	1.319	1.714	2.069	2.500	2.807
24	.127	.390	.685	1.059	1.318	1.711	2.064	2.492	2.797
25	.127	.390	.684	1.058	1.316	1.708	2.060	2.485	2.787
26	.127	.390	.684	1.058	1.315	1.706	2.056	2.479	2.779
27	.127	.389	.684	1.057	1.314	1.703	2.052	2.473	2.771
28	.127	.389	.683	1.056	1.313	1.701	2.048	2.467	2.763
29	.127	.389	.683	1.055	1.311	1.699	2.045	2.462	2.756
30	.127	.389	.683	1.055	1.310	1.697	2.042	2.457	2.750
40	.126	.388	.681	1.050	1.303	1.684	2.021	2.423	2.704
60	.126	.387	.679	1.046	1.296	1.671	2.000	2.390	2.660
120	.126	.386	.677	1.041	1.289	1.658	1.980	2.358	2.617
∞	.126	.385	.674	1.036	1.282	1.645	1.960	2.326	2.576

Source: Stephen P. Shao, *Statistics for Business and Economics*, 3rd ed. (Columbus, Ohio: Merrill Publishing Company, 1976), p. 789. Used with permission.

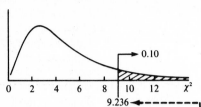

Example.
d.f. (Number of degrees of freedom) = 5, the tail above $\chi^2 = 9.236$ represents 0.10 or 10% of the area under the curve.

d.f	Probabilities (or Areas Under χ^2 Distribution Curve Above Given χ^2 Values)								
	.90	.70	.50	.30	.20	.10	.05	.02	.01
	Values of χ^2								
1	.016	.148	.455	1.074	1.642	2.706	3.841	5.412	6.635
2	.211	.713	1.386	2.408	3.219	4.605	5.991	7.824	9.210
3	.584	1.424	2.366	3.665	4.642	6.251	7.815	9.837	11.345
4	1.064	2.195	3.357	4.878	5.989	7.779	9.488	11.668	13.277
5	1.610	3.000	4.351	6.064	7.289	9.236	11.070	13.388	15.086
6	2.204	3.828	5.348	7.231	8.558	10.645	12.592	15.033	16.812
7	2.833	4.671	6.346	8.383	9.803	12.017	14.067	16.622	18.475
8	3.490	5.527	7.344	9.524	11.030	13.362	15.507	18.168	20.090
9	4.168	6.393	8.343	10.656	12.242	14.684	16.919	19.679	21.666
10	4.865	7.267	9.342	11.781	13.442	15.987	18.307	21.161	23.209
11	5.578	8.148	10.341	12.899	14.631	17.275	19.675	22.618	24.725
12	6.304	9.034	11.340	14.011	15.812	18.549	21.026	24.054	26.217
13	7.042	9.926	12.340	15.119	16.985	19.812	22.362	25.472	27.688
14	7.790	10.821	13.339	16.222	18.151	21.064	23.685	26.873	29.141
15	8.547	11.721	14.339	17.322	19.311	22.307	24.996	28.259	30.578
16	9.312	12.624	15.338	18.418	20.465	23.542	26.296	29.633	32.000
17	10.085	13.531	16.338	19.511	21.615	24.769	27.587	30.995	33.409
18	10.865	14.440	17.338	20.601	22.760	25.989	28.869	33.346	34.805
19	11.651	15.352	18.338	21.689	23.900	27.204	30.144	33.687	36.191
20	12.443	16.266	19.337	22.775	25.038	28.412	31.410	35.020	37.566
21	13.240	17.182	20.337	23.858	26.171	29.615	32.671	36.343	38.932
22	14.041	18.101	21.337	24.939	27.301	30.813	33.924	37.659	40.289
23	14.848	19.021	22.337	26.018	28.429	32.007	35.172	38.968	41.638
24	15.659	19.943	23.337	27.096	29.553	33.196	36.415	40.270	42.980
25	16.473	20.867	24.337	28.172	30.675	34.382	37.652	41.566	44.314
26	17.292	21.792	25.336	29.246	31.795	35.563	38.885	42.856	45.642
27	18.114	22.719	26.336	30.319	32.912	36.741	40.113	44.140	46.963
28	18.939	23.647	27.336	31.391	34.027	37.916	41.337	45.419	48.278
29	19.768	24.577	28.336	32.461	35.139	39.087	42.557	46.693	49.588
30	20.599	25.508	29.336	33.530	36.250	40.256	43.773	47.962	50.892

Source: Stephen P. Shao, *Statistics for Business and Economics*, 3rd ed. (Columbus, Ohio: Merrill Publishing Company, 1976), p. 790. Used with permission.

Upper 5% Probability
(or 5% Area under *F*-Distribution Curve)

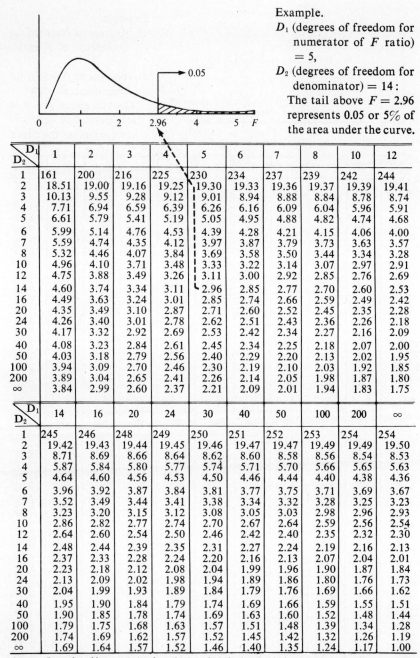

Example.
D_1 (degrees of freedom for numerator of F ratio) = 5,
D_2 (degrees of freedom for denominator) = 14:
The tail above $F = 2.96$ represents 0.05 or 5% of the area under the curve.

D_2 \ D_1	1	2	3	4	5	6	7	8	10	12
1	161	200	216	225	230	234	237	239	242	244
2	18.51	19.00	19.16	19.25	19.30	19.33	19.36	19.37	19.39	19.41
3	10.13	9.55	9.28	9.12	9.01	8.94	8.88	8.84	8.78	8.74
4	7.71	6.94	6.59	6.39	6.26	6.16	6.09	6.04	5.96	5.91
5	6.61	5.79	5.41	5.19	5.05	4.95	4.88	4.82	4.74	4.68
6	5.99	5.14	4.76	4.53	4.39	4.28	4.21	4.15	4.06	4.00
7	5.59	4.74	4.35	4.12	3.97	3.87	3.79	3.73	3.63	3.57
8	5.32	4.46	4.07	3.84	3.69	3.58	3.50	3.44	3.34	3.28
10	4.96	4.10	3.71	3.48	3.33	3.22	3.14	3.07	2.97	2.91
12	4.75	3.88	3.49	3.26	3.11	3.00	2.92	2.85	2.76	2.69
14	4.60	3.74	3.34	3.11	2.96	2.85	2.77	2.70	2.60	2.53
16	4.49	3.63	3.24	3.01	2.85	2.74	2.66	2.59	2.49	2.42
20	4.35	3.49	3.10	2.87	2.71	2.60	2.52	2.45	2.35	2.28
24	4.26	3.40	3.01	2.78	2.62	2.51	2.43	2.36	2.26	2.18
30	4.17	3.32	2.92	2.69	2.53	2.42	2.34	2.27	2.16	2.09
40	4.08	3.23	2.84	2.61	2.45	2.34	2.25	2.18	2.07	2.00
50	4.03	3.18	2.79	2.56	2.40	2.29	2.20	2.13	2.02	1.95
100	3.94	3.09	2.70	2.46	2.30	2.19	2.10	2.03	1.92	1.85
200	3.89	3.04	2.65	2.41	2.26	2.14	2.05	1.98	1.87	1.80
∞	3.84	2.99	2.60	2.37	2.21	2.09	2.01	1.94	1.83	1.75

D_2 \ D_1	14	16	20	24	30	40	50	100	200	∞
1	245	246	248	249	250	251	252	253	254	254
2	19.42	19.43	19.44	19.45	19.46	19.47	19.47	19.49	19.49	19.50
3	8.71	8.69	8.66	8.64	8.62	8.60	8.58	8.56	8.54	8.53
4	5.87	5.84	5.80	5.77	5.74	5.71	5.70	5.66	5.65	5.63
5	4.64	4.60	4.56	4.53	4.50	4.46	4.44	4.40	4.38	4.36
6	3.96	3.92	3.87	3.84	3.81	3.77	3.75	3.71	3.69	3.67
7	3.52	3.49	3.44	3.41	3.38	3.34	3.32	3.28	3.25	3.23
8	3.23	3.20	3.15	3.12	3.08	3.05	3.03	2.98	2.96	2.93
10	2.86	2.82	2.77	2.74	2.70	2.67	2.64	2.59	2.56	2.54
12	2.64	2.60	2.54	2.50	2.46	2.42	2.40	2.35	2.32	2.30
14	2.48	2.44	2.39	2.35	2.31	2.27	2.24	2.19	2.16	2.13
16	2.37	2.33	2.28	2.24	2.20	2.16	2.13	2.07	2.04	2.01
20	2.23	2.18	2.12	2.08	2.04	1.99	1.96	1.90	1.87	1.84
24	2.13	2.09	2.02	1.98	1.94	1.89	1.86	1.80	1.76	1.73
30	2.04	1.99	1.93	1.89	1.84	1.79	1.76	1.69	1.66	1.62
40	1.95	1.90	1.84	1.79	1.74	1.69	1.66	1.59	1.55	1.51
50	1.90	1.85	1.78	1.74	1.69	1.63	1.60	1.52	1.48	1.44
100	1.79	1.75	1.68	1.63	1.57	1.51	1.48	1.39	1.34	1.28
200	1.74	1.69	1.62	1.57	1.52	1.45	1.42	1.32	1.26	1.19
∞	1.69	1.64	1.57	1.52	1.46	1.40	1.35	1.24	1.17	1.00

Source: Reproduced by permission from *Statistical Methods,* 5th ed., by George W. Snedecor, © 1956 by the Iowa State University Press.

Upper 1% Probability
(or 1% Area under *F*-Distribution Curve)

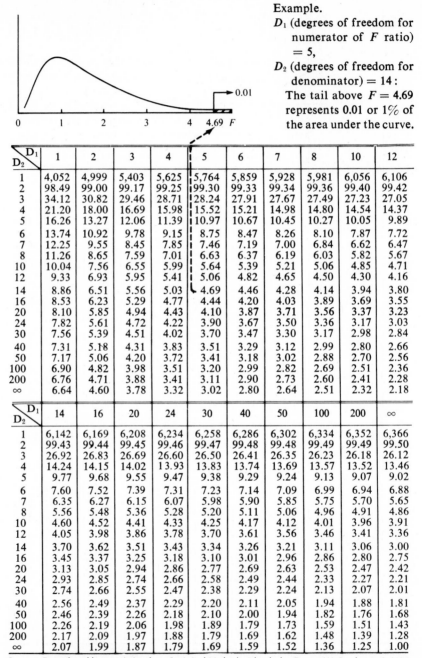

Example.

D_1 (degrees of freedom for numerator of F ratio) $= 5$,

D_2 (degrees of freedom for denominator) $= 14$: The tail above $F = 4.69$ represents 0.01 or 1% of the area under the curve.

D_1 / D_2	1	2	3	4	5	6	7	8	10	12
1	4,052	4,999	5,403	5,625	5,764	5,859	5,928	5,981	6,056	6,106
2	98.49	99.00	99.17	99.25	99.30	99.33	99.34	99.36	99.40	99.42
3	34.12	30.82	29.46	28.71	28.24	27.91	27.67	27.49	27.23	27.05
4	21.20	18.00	16.69	15.98	15.52	15.21	14.98	14.80	14.54	14.37
5	16.26	13.27	12.06	11.39	10.97	10.67	10.45	10.27	10.05	9.89
6	13.74	10.92	9.78	9.15	8.75	8.47	8.26	8.10	7.87	7.72
7	12.25	9.55	8.45	7.85	7.46	7.19	7.00	6.84	6.62	6.47
8	11.26	8.65	7.59	7.01	6.63	6.37	6.19	6.03	5.82	5.67
10	10.04	7.56	6.55	5.99	5.64	5.39	5.21	5.06	4.85	4.71
12	9.33	6.93	5.95	5.41	5.06	4.82	4.65	4.50	4.30	4.16
14	8.86	6.51	5.56	5.03	4.69	4.46	4.28	4.14	3.94	3.80
16	8.53	6.23	5.29	4.77	4.44	4.20	4.03	3.89	3.69	3.55
20	8.10	5.85	4.94	4.43	4.10	3.87	3.71	3.56	3.37	3.23
24	7.82	5.61	4.72	4.22	3.90	3.67	3.50	3.36	3.17	3.03
30	7.56	5.39	4.51	4.02	3.70	3.47	3.30	3.17	2.98	2.84
40	7.31	5.18	4.31	3.83	3.51	3.29	3.12	2.99	2.80	2.66
50	7.17	5.06	4.20	3.72	3.41	3.18	3.02	2.88	2.70	2.56
100	6.90	4.82	3.98	3.51	3.20	2.99	2.82	2.69	2.51	2.36
200	6.76	4.71	3.88	3.41	3.11	2.90	2.73	2.60	2.41	2.28
∞	6.64	4.60	3.78	3.32	3.02	2.80	2.64	2.51	2.32	2.18

D_1 / D_2	14	16	20	24	30	40	50	100	200	∞
1	6,142	6,169	6,208	6,234	6,258	6,286	6,302	6,334	6,352	6,366
2	99.43	99.44	99.45	99.46	99.47	99.48	99.48	99.49	99.49	99.50
3	26.92	26.83	26.69	26.60	26.50	26.41	26.35	26.23	26.18	26.12
4	14.24	14.15	14.02	13.93	13.83	13.74	13.69	13.57	13.52	13.46
5	9.77	9.68	9.55	9.47	9.38	9.29	9.24	9.13	9.07	9.02
6	7.60	7.52	7.39	7.31	7.23	7.14	7.09	6.99	6.94	6.88
7	6.35	6.27	6.15	6.07	5.98	5.90	5.85	5.75	5.70	5.65
8	5.56	5.48	5.36	5.28	5.20	5.11	5.06	4.96	4.91	4.86
10	4.60	4.52	4.41	4.33	4.25	4.17	4.12	4.01	3.96	3.91
12	4.05	3.98	3.86	3.78	3.70	3.61	3.56	3.46	3.41	3.36
14	3.70	3.62	3.51	3.43	3.34	3.26	3.21	3.11	3.06	3.00
16	3.45	3.37	3.25	3.18	3.10	3.01	2.96	2.86	2.80	2.75
20	3.13	3.05	2.94	2.86	2.77	2.69	2.63	2.53	2.47	2.42
24	2.93	2.85	2.74	2.66	2.58	2.49	2.44	2.33	2.27	2.21
30	2.74	2.66	2.55	2.47	2.38	2.29	2.24	2.13	2.07	2.01
40	2.56	2.49	2.37	2.29	2.20	2.11	2.05	1.94	1.88	1.81
50	2.46	2.39	2.26	2.18	2.10	2.00	1.94	1.82	1.76	1.68
100	2.26	2.19	2.06	1.98	1.89	1.79	1.73	1.59	1.51	1.43
200	2.17	2.09	1.97	1.88	1.79	1.69	1.62	1.48	1.39	1.28
∞	2.07	1.99	1.87	1.79	1.69	1.59	1.52	1.36	1.25	1.00

Source: Reproduced by permission from *Statistical Methods,* 5th ed., by George W. Snedecor, © 1956 by the Iowa State University Press.

APPENDIX G   DISTRIBUTION OF THE STUDENTIZED RANGE

$p = 0.95$

Percentage points of the studentized range,
$$q = (x_{D_1} - x_1)/s_{D_2}.$$

D_2 \ D_1	2	3	4	5	6	7	8	9	10
1	17·97	26·98	32·82	37·08	40·41	43·12	45·40	47·36	49·07
2	6·08	8·33	9·80	10·88	11·74	12·44	13·03	13·54	13·99
3	4·50	5·91	6·82	7·50	8·04	8·48	8·85	9·18	9·46
4	3·93	5·04	5·76	6·29	6·71	7·05	7·35	7·60	7·83
5	3·64	4·60	5·22	5·67	6·03	6·33	6·58	6·80	6·99
6	3·46	4·34	4·90	5·30	5·63	5·90	6·12	6·32	6·49
7	3·34	4·16	4·68	5·06	5·36	5·61	5·82	6·00	6·16
8	3·26	4·04	4·53	4·89	5·17	5·40	5·60	5·77	5·92
9	3·20	3·95	4·41	4·76	5·02	5·24	5·43	5·59	5·74
10	3·15	3·88	4·33	4·65	4·91	5·12	5·30	5·46	5·60
11	3·11	3·82	4·26	4·57	4·82	5·03	5·20	5·35	5·49
12	3·08	3·77	4·20	4·51	4·75	4·95	5·12	5·27	5·39
13	3·06	3·73	4·15	4·45	4·69	4·88	5·05	5·19	5·32
14	3·03	3·70	4·11	4·41	4·64	4·83	4·99	5·13	5·25
15	3·01	3·67	4·08	4·37	4·59	4·78	4·94	5·08	5·20
16	3·00	3·65	4·05	4·33	4·56	4·74	4·90	5·03	5·15
17	2·98	3·63	4·02	4·30	4·52	4·70	4·86	4·99	5·11
18	2·97	3·61	4·00	4·28	4·49	4·67	4·82	4·96	5·07
19	2·96	3·59	3·98	4·25	4·47	4·65	4·79	4·92	5·04
20	2·95	3·58	3·96	4·23	4·45	4·62	4·77	4·90	5·01
24	2·92	3·53	3·90	4·17	4·37	4·54	4·68	4·81	4·92
30	2·89	3·49	3·85	4·10	4·30	4·46	4·60	4·72	4·82
40	2·86	3·44	3·79	4·04	4·23	4·39	4·52	4·63	4·73
60	2·83	3·40	3·74	3·98	4·16	4·31	4·44	4·55	4·65
120	2·80	3·36	3·68	3·92	4·10	4·24	4·36	4·47	4·56
∞	2·77	3·31	3·63	3·86	4·03	4·17	4·29	4·39	4·47

D_2 \ D_1	11	12	13	14	15	16	17	18	19	20
1	50·59	51·96	53·20	54·33	55·36	56·32	57·22	58·04	58·83	59·56
2	14·39	14·75	15·08	15·38	15·65	15·91	16·14	16·37	16·57	16·77
3	9·72	9·95	10·15	10·35	10·52	10·69	10·84	10·98	11·11	11·24
4	8·03	8·21	8·37	8·52	8·66	8·79	8·91	9·03	9·13	9·23
5	7·17	7·32	7·47	7·60	7·72	7·83	7·93	8·03	8·12	8·21
6	6·65	6·79	6·92	7·03	7·14	7·24	7·34	7·43	7·51	7·59
7	6·30	6·43	6·55	6·66	6·76	6·85	6·94	7·02	7·10	7·17
8	6·05	6·18	6·29	6·39	6·48	6·57	6·65	6·73	6·80	6·87
9	5·87	5·98	6·09	6·19	6·28	6·36	6·44	6·51	6·58	6·64
10	5·72	5·83	5·93	6·03	6·11	6·19	6·27	6·34	6·40	6·47
11	5·61	5·71	5·81	5·90	5·98	6·06	6·13	6·20	6·27	6·33
12	5·51	5·61	5·71	5·80	5·88	5·95	6·02	6·09	6·15	6·21
13	5·43	5·53	5·63	5·71	5·79	5·86	5·93	5·99	6·05	6·11
14	5·36	5·46	5·55	5·64	5·71	5·79	5·85	5·91	5·97	6·03
15	5·31	5·40	5·49	5·57	5·65	5·72	5·78	5·85	5·90	5·96
16	5·26	5·35	5·44	5·52	5·59	5·66	5·73	5·79	5·84	5·90
17	5·21	5·31	5·39	5·47	5·54	5·61	5·67	5·73	5·79	5·84
18	5·17	5·27	5·35	5·43	5·50	5·57	5·63	5·69	5·74	5·79
19	5·14	5·23	5·31	5·39	5·46	5·53	5·59	5·65	5·70	5·75
20	5·11	5·20	5·28	5·36	5·43	5·49	5·55	5·61	5·66	5·71
24	5·01	5·10	5·18	5·25	5·32	5·38	5·44	5·49	5·55	5·59
30	4·92	5·00	5·08	5·15	5·21	5·27	5·33	5·38	5·43	5·47
40	4·82	4·90	4·98	5·04	5·11	5·16	5·22	5·27	5·31	5·36
60	4·73	4·81	4·88	4·94	5·00	5·06	5·11	5·15	5·20	5·24
120	4·64	4·71	4·78	4·84	4·90	4·95	5·00	5·04	5·09	5·13
∞	4·55	4·62	4·68	4·74	4·80	4·85	4·89	4·93	4·97	5·01

D_1: size of sample from which range obtained. D_2: degrees of freedom of independent s_{D_1}

$p = 0.99$

D_2 \ D_1	2	3	4	5	6	7	8	9	10
1	90·03	135·0	164·3	185·6	202·2	215·8	227·2	237·0	245·6
2	14·04	19·02	22·29	24·72	26·63	28·20	29·53	30·68	31·69
3	8·26	10·62	12·17	13·33	14·24	15·00	15·64	16·20	16·69
4	6·51	8·12	9·17	9·96	10·58	11·10	11·55	11·93	12·27
5	5·70	6·98	7·80	8·42	8·91	9·32	9·67	9·97	10·24
6	5·24	6·33	7·03	7·56	7·97	8·32	8·61	8·87	9·10
7	4·95	5·92	6·54	7·01	7·37	7·68	7·94	8·17	8·37
8	4·75	5·64	6·20	6·62	6·96	7·24	7·47	7·68	7·86
9	4·60	5·43	5·96	6·35	6·66	6·91	7·13	7·33	7·49
10	4·48	5·27	5·77	6·14	6·43	6·67	6·87	7·05	7·21
11	4·39	5·15	5·62	5·97	6·25	6·48	6·67	6·84	6·99
12	4·32	5·05	5·50	5·84	6·10	6·32	6·51	6·67	6·81
13	4·26	4·96	5·40	5·73	5·98	6·19	6·37	6·53	6·67
14	4·21	4·89	5·32	5·63	5·88	6·08	6·26	6·41	6·54
15	4·17	4·84	5·25	5·56	5·80	5·99	6·16	6·31	6·44
16	4·13	4·79	5·19	5·49	5·72	5·92	6·08	6·22	6·35
17	4·10	4·74	5·14	5·43	5·66	5·85	6·01	6·15	6·27
18	4·07	4·70	5·09	5·38	5·60	5·79	5·94	6·08	6·20
19	4·05	4·67	5·05	5·33	5·55	5·73	5·89	6·02	6·14
20	4·02	4·64	5·02	5·29	5·51	5·69	5·84	5·97	6·09
24	3·96	4·55	4·91	5·17	5·37	5·54	5·69	5·81	5·92
30	3·89	4·45	4·80	5·05	5·24	5·40	5·54	5·65	5·76
40	3·82	4·37	4·70	4·93	5·11	5·26	5·39	5·50	5·60
60	3·76	4·28	4·59	4·82	4·99	5·13	5·25	5·36	5·45
120	3·70	4·20	4·50	4·71	4·87	5·01	5·12	5·21	5·30
∞	3·64	4·12	4·40	4·60	4·76	4·88	4·99	5·08	5·16

D_2 \ D_1	11	12	13	14	15	16	17	18	19	20
1	253·2	260·0	266·2	271·8	277·0	281·8	286·3	290·4	294·3	298·0
2	32·59	33·40	34·13	34·81	35·43	36·00	36·53	37·03	37·50	37·95
3	17·13	17·53	17·89	18·22	18·52	18·81	19·07	19·32	19·55	19·77
4	12·57	12·84	13·09	13·32	13·53	13·73	13·91	14·08	14·24	14·40
5	10·48	10·70	10·89	11·08	11·24	11·40	11·55	11·68	11·81	11·93
6	9·30	9·48	9·65	9·81	9·95	10·08	10·21	10·32	10·43	10·54
7	8·55	8·71	8·86	9·00	9·12	9·24	9·35	9·46	9·55	9·65
8	8·03	8·18	8·31	8·44	8·55	8·66	8·76	8·85	8·94	9·03
9	7·65	7·78	7·91	8·03	8·13	8·23	8·33	8·41	8·49	8·57
10	7·36	7·49	7·60	7·71	7·81	7·91	7·99	8·08	8·15	8·23
11	7·13	7·25	7·36	7·46	7·56	7·65	7·73	7·81	7·88	7·95
12	6·94	7·06	7·17	7·26	7·36	7·44	7·52	7·59	7·66	7·73
13	6·79	6·90	7·01	7·10	7·19	7·27	7·35	7·42	7·48	7·55
14	6·66	6·77	6·87	6·96	7·05	7·13	7·20	7·27	7·33	7·39
15	6·55	6·66	6·76	6·84	6·93	7·00	7·07	7·14	7·20	7·26
16	6·46	6·56	6·66	6·74	6·82	6·90	6·97	7·03	7·09	7·15
17	6·38	6·48	6·57	6·66	6·73	6·81	6·87	6·94	7·00	7·05
18	6·31	6·41	6·50	6·58	6·65	6·73	6·79	6·85	6·91	6·97
19	6·25	6·34	6·43	6·51	6·58	6·65	6·72	6·78	6·84	6·89
20	6·19	6·28	6·37	6·45	6·52	6·59	6·65	6·71	6·77	6·82
24	6·02	6·11	6·19	6·26	6·33	6·39	6·45	6·51	6·56	6·61
30	5·85	5·93	6·01	6·08	6·14	6·20	6·26	6·31	6·36	6·41
40	5·69	5·76	5·83	5·90	5·96	6·02	6·07	6·12	6·16	6·21
60	5·53	5·60	5·67	5·73	5·78	5·84	5·89	5·93	5·97	6·01
120	5·37	5·44	5·50	5·56	5·61	5·66	5·71	5·75	5·79	5·83
∞	5·23	5·29	5·35	5·40	5·45	5·49	5·54	5·57	5·61	5·65

Source: Reprinted with permission from E. S. Pearson and H. O. Hartley, *Biometrika Tables for Statisticians* (New York: Cambridge University Press, 1954).

1260	5529	9540	3569	8381	9742	2590	2516	4243	8130
8979	2446	7606	6948	4519	2636	6655	1166	2096	1137
5470	0061	1760	5993	4319	0825	6874	3753	8362	1237
9733	0297	0804	4942	7694	9340	2502	3597	7691	5000
7492	6719	6816	7567	0364	2306	2217	5626	6526	6166
3715	2248	2337	6530	1660	7441	1598	0477	6620	1250
9491	4842	6210	9140	0180	5935	7218	4966	0537	4416
5192	7719	0654	4428	9771	4677	3291	4459	7432	2054
1714	3725	9397	9648	2550	0704	1239	5263	1601	5177
1052	8415	3686	4239	3272	7135	5768	8718	7582	8366
6998	3891	9352	6056	3621	5395	4551	4017	2405	0831
4216	4724	2898	1050	2164	8020	5274	6688	8636	2438
7115	2637	3828	0810	4598	2329	7953	4913	0033	2661
6647	4252	1869	9634	1341	7958	9460	1712	6060	0638
3475	2925	5097	8258	8343	7264	3295	8021	6318	0454
0415	1533	7670	0618	5193	9291	2205	2046	0890	6997
7064	4946	2618	7116	3784	2007	2326	4361	4695	8612
9772	4445	0343	5238	0317	7531	5916	8229	3296	2321
5365	4306	4036	9873	9669	8505	8675	3116	1484	9975
6395	4681	9319	6908	8154	5415	5728	1593	9452	8213
1554	0411	3436	1101	0966	5188	0225	5615	8568	5169
6745	7372	6984	0228	1920	6710	3459	0663	1407	9211
2217	3801	5860	1673	0264	6911	7623	7137	0774	5898
9255	9297	4305	5060	8312	9192	6016	7238	5193	4908
1615	9761	5744	2733	5314	6985	6670	0975	5487	6107
6679	4951	5716	5889	4413	1513	5023	7313	0317	0517
5221	3207	0351	2452	1072	3830	5518	5972	6111	9352
7720	5131	4867	6501	6970	4075	4869	4798	7104	5342
2767	6055	2801	7033	5305	9382	2354	4135	5975	7830
9202	6815	8211	5274	2303	1437	8995	2514	6515	0049
9359	2754	8587	2790	9524	5068	1230	4165	7025	4365
1078	7661	0999	4413	3446	2971	7576	3385	3308	0557
5732	4853	2025	1145	9743	8646	4918	3674	8049	1622
1596	0578	1493	4681	3806	8837	4241	4123	6513	3083
0602	8144	8976	9195	9012	7700	1708	5724	0315	8032
3624	8592	7942	4289	0736	4986	4839	4507	4997	7407
9328	3001	1462	1101	0804	9724	4082	2384	9631	8334
1981	1295	1963	3391	5757	4403	5857	4329	3682	3823
6001	4295	1488	6702	9954	6980	4027	8492	8195	7934
3743	0097	4798	6390	6465	6449	7990	3774	3577	3895

3343	6936	1449	2915	6668	8543	3147	1442	6022	0056
9208	3820	5165	3445	2642	2910	8336	1244	6346	0487
4581	3768	1559	7558	6660	0116	7949	5609	2887	4156
3206	5146	7191	8420	2319	4650	3734	0501	0739	2025
5662	8315	4226	8395	2931	1812	3575	9341	5894	3691
4631	6278	9444	4058	0505	4449	5959	7483	8641	1311
1046	6653	8333	5813	6586	9820	0190	9214	1947	9677
5231	2788	7198	5904	8370	8347	6599	7304	6430	3495
5349	6641	3234	8692	4424	9179	2767	9517	1173	4160
8363	9625	3329	5262	5360	8181	9298	6629	2433	9414
5967	1261	2470	8867	1962	1630	8360	6024	6232	8386
6716	3916	8712	6673	1156	0001	6760	6287	4546	5743
0323	3514	8550	3709	6614	5764	0600	7444	2795	4426
1765	0918	8972	9924	5941	0331	6909	4872	5693	8957
4345	6886	2032	4817	2725	9471	2443	9532	4770	1271
9614	8571	2174	0071	7824	0504	9600	6414	5734	1371
1291	8246	5019	6559	5051	5265	1184	9030	6689	2776
3867	3915	8311	2430	1235	7283	6481	2012	8487	0226
1056	1880	3610	7796	7192	6663	5810	3512	1572	2921
1691	2237	6713	4048	8865	5794	3419	4372	6996	8342
7920	8490	2822	2647	1700	5335	0732	9987	7501	1223
1646	4251	7732	2136	4339	0331	9293	1061	2663	4821
7928	2575	2139	2825	3806	2082	9285	7640	6166	5758
3563	9078	1979	1141	7911	6981	0183	7479	1146	8949
6546	3459	3824	2151	3313	0178	9143	7854	3935	7300
8315	8778	1296	3434	9420	3622	3521	0807	5719	7764
8442	4933	8173	6427	4354	3523	3492	2816	9191	6261
7446	1576	2520	6120	8546	3146	6084	1260	3737	1333
2619	1261	2028	7505	0710	4589	9632	2347	1975	6839
0814	8542	1526	1202	8091	9441	0456	0603	8297	1412

Source: Reprinted from Richard J. Hopeman, *Production and Operations Management,* 4th ed. (Columbus, Ohio: Merrill Publishing Company, 1980), pp. 569–70. Used with permission.

APPENDIX I DURBIN-WATSON TEST BOUNDS

Level of Significance $\alpha = 0.05$

n	$p-1=1$		$p-1=2$		$p-1=3$		$p-1=4$		$p-1=5$	
	d_L	d_U	d_L	d_U	d_L	d_U	d_L	d_U	d_L	d_U
15	1.08	1.36	0.95	1.54	0.82	1.75	0.69	1.97	0.56	2.21
16	1.10	1.37	0.98	1.54	0.86	1.73	0.74	1.93	0.62	2.15
17	1.13	1.38	1.02	1.54	0.90	1.71	0.78	1.90	0.67	2.10
18	1.16	1.39	1.05	1.53	0.93	1.69	0.82	1.87	0.71	2.06
19	1.18	1.40	1.08	1.53	0.97	1.68	0.86	1.85	0.75	2.02
20	1.20	1.41	1.10	1.54	1.00	1.68	0.90	1.83	0.79	1.99
21	1.22	1.42	1.13	1.54	1.03	1.67	0.93	1.81	0.83	1.96
22	1.24	1.43	1.15	1.54	1.05	1.66	0.96	1.80	0.86	1.94
23	1.26	1.44	1.17	1.54	1.08	1.66	0.99	1.79	0.90	1.92
24	1.27	1.45	1.19	1.55	1.10	1.66	1.01	1.78	0.93	1.90
25	1.29	1.45	1.21	1.55	1.12	1.66	1.04	1.77	0.95	1.89
26	1.30	1.46	1.22	1.55	1.14	1.65	1.06	1.76	0.98	1.88
27	1.32	1.47	1.24	1.56	1.16	1.65	1.08	1.76	1.01	1.86
28	1.33	1.48	1.26	1.56	1.18	1.65	1.10	1.75	1.03	1.85
29	1.34	1.48	1.27	1.56	1.20	1.65	1.12	1.74	1.05	1.84
30	1.35	1.49	1.28	1.57	1.21	1.65	1.14	1.74	1.07	1.83
31	1.36	1.50	1.30	1.57	1.23	1.65	1.16	1.74	1.09	1.83
32	1.37	1.50	1.31	1.57	1.24	1.65	1.18	1.73	1.11	1.82
33	1.38	1.51	1.32	1.58	1.26	1.65	1.19	1.73	1.13	1.81
34	1.39	1.51	1.33	1.58	1.27	1.65	1.21	1.73	1.15	1.81
35	1.40	1.52	1.34	1.58	1.28	1.65	1.22	1.73	1.16	1.80
36	1.41	1.52	1.35	1.59	1.29	1.65	1.24	1.73	1.18	1.80
37	1.42	1.53	1.36	1.59	1.31	1.66	1.25	1.72	1.19	1.80
38	1.43	1.54	1.37	1.59	1.32	1.66	1.26	1.72	1.21	1.79
39	1.43	1.54	1.38	1.60	1.33	1.66	1.27	1.72	1.22	1.79
40	1.44	1.54	1.39	1.60	1.34	1.66	1.29	1.72	1.23	1.79
45	1.48	1.57	1.43	1.62	1.38	1.67	1.34	1.72	1.29	1.78
50	1.50	1.59	1.46	1.63	1.42	1.67	1.38	1.72	1.34	1.77
55	1.53	1.60	1.49	1.64	1.45	1.68	1.41	1.72	1.38	1.77
60	1.55	1.62	1.51	1.65	1.48	1.69	1.44	1.73	1.41	1.77
65	1.57	1.63	1.54	1.66	1.50	1.70	1.47	1.73	1.44	1.77
70	1.58	1.64	1.55	1.67	1.52	1.70	1.49	1.74	1.46	1.77
75	1.60	1.65	1.57	1.68	1.54	1.71	1.51	1.74	1.49	1.77
80	1.61	1.66	1.59	1.69	1.56	1.72	1.53	1.74	1.51	1.77
85	1.62	1.67	1.60	1.70	1.57	1.72	1.55	1.75	1.52	1.77
90	1.63	1.68	1.61	1.70	1.59	1.73	1.57	1.75	1.54	1.78
95	1.64	1.69	1.62	1.71	1.60	1.73	1.58	1.75	1.56	1.78
100	1.65	1.69	1.63	1.72	1.61	1.74	1.59	1.76	1.57	1.78

Level of Significance $\alpha = 0.01$

n	$p-1=1$		$p-1=2$		$p-1=3$		$p-1=4$		$p-1=5$	
	d_L	d_U	d_L	d_U	d_L	d_U	d_L	d_U	d_L	d_U
15	0.81	1.07	0.70	1.25	0.59	1.46	0.49	1.70	0.39	1.96
16	0.84	1.09	0.74	1.25	0.63	1.44	0.53	1.66	0.44	1.90
17	0.87	1.10	0.77	1.25	0.67	1.43	0.57	1.63	0.48	1.85
18	0.90	1.12	0.80	1.26	0.71	1.42	0.61	1.60	0.52	1.80
19	0.93	1.13	0.83	1.26	0.74	1.41	0.65	1.58	0.56	1.77
20	0.95	1.15	0.86	1.27	0.77	1.41	0.68	1.57	0.60	1.74
21	0.97	1.16	0.89	1.27	0.80	1.41	0.72	1.55	0.63	1.71
22	1.00	1.17	0.91	1.28	0.83	1.40	0.75	1.54	0.66	1.69
23	1.02	1.19	0.94	1.29	0.86	1.40	0.77	1.53	0.70	1.67
24	1.04	1.20	0.96	1.30	0.88	1.41	0.80	1.53	0.72	1.66
25	1.05	1.21	0.98	1.30	0.90	1.41	0.83	1.52	0.75	1.65
26	1.07	1.22	1.00	1.31	0.93	1.41	0.85	1.52	0.78	1.64
27	1.09	1.23	1.02	1.32	0.95	1.41	0.88	1.51	0.81	1.63
28	1.10	1.24	1.04	1.32	0.97	1.41	0.90	1.51	0.83	1.62
29	1.12	1.25	1.05	1.33	0.99	1.42	0.92	1.51	0.85	1.61
30	1.13	1.26	1.07	1.34	1.01	1.42	0.94	1.51	0.88	1.61
31	1.15	1.27	1.08	1.34	1.02	1.42	0.96	1.51	0.90	1.60
32	1.16	1.28	1.10	1.35	1.04	1.43	0.98	1.51	0.92	1.60
33	1.17	1.29	1.11	1.36	1.05	1.43	1.00	1.51	0.94	1.59
34	1.18	1.30	1.13	1.36	1.07	1.43	1.01	1.51	0.95	1.59
35	1.19	1.31	1.14	1.37	1.08	1.44	1.03	1.51	0.97	1.59
36	1.21	1.32	1.15	1.38	1.10	1.44	1.04	1.51	0.99	1.59
37	1.22	1.32	1.16	1.38	1.11	1.45	1.06	1.51	1.00	1.59
38	1.23	1.33	1.18	1.39	1.12	1.45	1.07	1.52	1.02	1.58
39	1.24	1.34	1.19	1.39	1.14	1.45	1.09	1.52	1.03	1.58
40	1.25	1.34	1.20	1.40	1.15	1.46	1.10	1.52	1.05	1.58
45	1.29	1.38	1.24	1.42	1.20	1.48	1.16	1.53	1.11	1.58
50	1.32	1.40	1.28	1.45	1.24	1.49	1.20	1.54	1.16	1.59
55	1.36	1.43	1.32	1.47	1.28	1.51	1.25	1.55	1.21	1.59
60	1.38	1.45	1.35	1.48	1.32	1.52	1.28	1.56	1.25	1.60
65	1.41	1.47	1.38	1.50	1.35	1.53	1.31	1.57	1.28	1.61
70	1.43	1.49	1.40	1.52	1.37	1.55	1.34	1.58	1.31	1.61
75	1.45	1.50	1.42	1.53	1.39	1.56	1.37	1.59	1.34	1.62
80	1.47	1.52	1.44	1.54	1.42	1.57	1.39	1.60	1.36	1.62
85	1.48	1.53	1.46	1.55	1.43	1.58	1.41	1.60	1.39	1.63
90	1.50	1.54	1.47	1.56	1.45	1.59	1.43	1.61	1.41	1.64
95	1.51	1.55	1.49	1.57	1.47	1.60	1.45	1.62	1.42	1.64
100	1.52	1.56	1.50	1.58	1.48	1.60	1.46	1.63	1.44	1.65

Source: J. Durbin and G. S. Watson, "Testing for Serial Correlation in Least Squares Regression. II," *Biometrika,* vol. 38 (1951), pp. 159–78. Reprinted with permission.

ANSWERS TO SELECTED PROBLEMS

Chapter 2

7. a. 8 classes, $20 width

b. *Accounts Receivable*

Balance	Frequency
$ 0–19.99	15
20.00–39.99	11
40.00–59.99	8
60.00–79.99	9
80.00–99.99	8
100.00–119.99	4
120.00–139.99	2
140.00–159.99	3

9. 0.083, 0.292, 0.250, 0.125, 0.083, 0.083, 0.083

17. a. 9

b. Calculated width, 3217.33; more convenient width, 3300

c.

Size of Claim	Midpoint
0 to under 3,300	1,650
3,300 to under 6,600	4,950
6,600 to under 9,900	8,250
9,900 to under 13,200	11,550
13,200 to under 16,500	14,850
16,500 to under 19,800	18,150
19,800 to under 23,100	21,450
23,100 to under 26,400	24,750
26,400 to under 29,700	28,050

19. a. 152

c. 0.033, 0.132, 0.197, 0.178, 0.329, 0.132

d. Cumulative: 5, 25, 55, 82, 132, 152
Relative cumulative: 0.033, 0.164, 0.362, 0.539, 0.868, 1

21. a. 9

b. For check numbers: calculated width, 381.56; more convenient width, 400
For amount: calculated width, 11.647; more convenient width, 12

Chapter 3

1. Mean = 16.44; median = 16; mode = 16

3. Mean = 16.881; median = 17.26; no mode

5. Range = 15;
For population: variance = 19.621; standard deviation = 4.43
For sample: variance = 20.929; standard deviation = 4.57

7. Mean = 16.881; standard deviation = 4.07 Within one standard deviation, 60% of actual values; within two standard deviations, 100% of actual values; within three standard deviations, 100% of actual values

9. Mean = 14.11; median = 13.83

11. Mean = 51.82; median = 33.75; variance = 1999.72; standard deviation = 44.72

13. 20.91

15. Set A

21. **a.** 15.3 **b.** 14.5 **c.** 12
    d. Increases the mean **e.** Median

23. **a.** 70.425 **b.** 70 **c.** 70

27. Variance = 25.69; standard deviation = 5.07

29. Approximate standard deviation = 14.75; actual standard deviation = 14.4

31. **a.** Mean = 70.425; variance = 37.89; standard deviation = 6.16

33. Pine: mean = 1.93; standard deviation = 1.28
    Redwood: mean = 1.3; standard deviation = 1.06
    Cedar: mean = 2.43; standard deviation = 1.46

37. **a.** 41.26 **b.** 29.5
    c. Variance = 240.69; standard deviation = 15.51
    d.

Class	f	M
15 and under 25	10	20
25 and under 35	10	30
35 and under 45	11	40
45 and under 55	8	50
55 and under 65	5	60
65 and under 75	5	70
75 and under 85	1	80

   f. 41.4 **g.** 39.55
   h. Variance = 281.67; standard deviation = 16.78

39. **a** Seed type C
    b. $CV_A = 18.18$; $CV_B = 26.79$; $CV_C = 25$; seed type A

41. CV of height = 3.6; CV of weight = 6.78

Chapter 4

1. 30,240 **3.** 630,630 **5.** 10

7. **a.** .056 **b.** .167 **c.** .111
   d. .028 **e.** .019 **f.** .019

9. **a.** .4 **b.** .4 **c.** .04 **d.** .60
   e. .66 **f.** 0

11. **a.** .007 **b.** .115 **c.** .007
    d. .0063

19. **a.** .049 **b.** .40 **c.** .11

23. 60

25. 48

27. 252

29. **a.** 3,003 **b.** 10,897,286,400

33. Not independent

35. .2627

37. **a.** .44 **b.** .194 **c.** .927

39. **a.** .596 **b.** .087 **c.** Not independent

41. **a.** Tennis
    P(tennis/Jones won) = .727
    P(golf/Jones won) = .273
    b. Tennis

Chapter 5

1. Mean = 3; standard deviation = 1.254

3. Mean = expected value = 23.5; variance = 37.75; standard deviation = 6.144

5. **a.** 0.11, 0.1, 0.2, 0.275, 0.14, 0.1, 0.25, 0.05 **b.** 2.885 **c.** 1.773
   d. Between 0 and 6.431 calls

11. Mean = 1.8; standard deviation = 1.237

15. **a.** 0 **b.** 0 **c.** .0828 **d.** .0199

17. Mean = 22.5; standard deviation = 3.969

19. Mean = 175; variance = 52.5; standard deviation = 7.246; CV = 4.14

23. .6244

25. **a.** .0355 **b.** .0218 **c.** .0709

27. .1356

29. **a.** .9161 **b.** .744 **c.** .682

31. Mean = 10; standard deviation = 3.1623

33. More than 100

35. **a.** 1.1 **b.** .943 **c.** $7.29

37. **a.** $E(X) = 750$; $E(Y) = 100$

b. $SD(X) = 844.10$; $SD(Y) = 717.64$
c. $CV_X = 112.5$; $CV_Y = 717.6$
41. b. 3.5   **c.** .00243
43. b. $P(X \geq 4) = .087$ **c.** 1.9998
45. a. .2396
47. a. .4168   **b.** .4168   **c.** .0002
49. b. .0021   **c.** .0061
51. a. 40   **b.** 80   **c.** $1.80   **d.** 4
55. P(equally composed) $= .476$; P(all one party) $= .0476$
57. P(0 bad tapes) $= .1667$; P(3 bad tapes) $= .033$
59. .0816
61. .0076
63. a. .0681   **b.** .6376   **c.** .5438
65. a. .6065   **b.** .9856   **c.** .2231
     d. 0
67. a. .184   **b.** .0003
69. b. 3   **c.** Variance $= 3$; standard deviation $= 1.732$

Chapter 6

1. a. 40   **b.** 11.55   **c.** .25   **d.** 0
3. a. 11.5   **b.** .714   **c.** 2.021
5. b. 10,000   **c.** 1154.7   **d.** 11,600
7. a. .3707   **b.** .6293   **c.** .2514
     d. .1846
9. a. .1762   **b.** .3446   **c.** .4401
     d. .0548
11. 7.46
13. .5398
15. .8212
17. a. 10   **b.** 3.13   **c.** .7372
19. b. .2222   **c.** .4444   **d.** 4.75
     e. 1.299
21. a. .167   **b.** 60   **c.** 17.32
25. 4.2
27. a. .5   **b.** .5375   **c.** .0918
29. a. .3594   **b.** .9441   **c.** .7458
31. a. 12.96   **b.** 8.96
33. 10 feet 5.29 inches
35. $P(X < 40) = .0985$
37. 22.08

39. a. .1587   **b.** 0
41. a. .0336   **b.** .0237
43. a. .512   **b.** 1

Chapter 7

1. a. Mean $= 27.375$; standard deviation $= 7.78$ **b.** 70
3. a. 15,322.71   **b.** 35
5. a. Mean $= 245.5$; standard deviation $= 93.85$ **b.** 120
7. a. 58   **b.** 3.33   **c.** 2.236
9. a. .5   **b.** .86
11. Mean $= 36.7$; standard deviation $= .94$
13. a. .1469   **b.** .3156   **c.** .3212
     d. .6995
15. a. .0038   **b.** .9982
17. a. 400   **b.** .4   **c.** .015
     d. .9082   **e.** .0038   **f.** .7258
     g. .1587
35. a. 13,012.5   **b.** 28
45. Mean $= 45$; standard deviation $= 3.13$
55. .0106
57. 1.195
61. 0
65. .2389
67. a. .2643   **b.** .3752
69. a. .1112   **b.** .1112
71. a. 0   **b.** 0
73. 0
75. 0, 0

Chapter 8

1. a. 344.77 _____ 355.23
     b. 343.76 _____ 356.24
3. a. 171   **b.** 385
5. a. 1.131 _____ 1.269
     b. 1.142 _____ 1.258
7. 97
9. 1,209,067.53 _____ 1,297,932.47
11. a. .161 _____ .299
     b. .148 _____ .312
13. 423

17. .0815 _____ .1435
19. 3394
21. a. -6.56 _____ -3.44
   b. -7.21 _____ 2.79
23. a. $-.044$ _____ .104
   b. $-.058$ _____ .118
25. $-.0436$ _____ .0348
27. 1.6376 _____ 3.3624; yes
33. a. Mean   **b.** 2,250
   c. 2,215.1043 _____ 2,284.8957
35. a. 26,060.49 _____ 26,649.51
37. 13,879.91 _____ 14,530.09
45. 531
47. a. 52.92 _____ 58.68
   b. 127,060.85 _____ 140,779.16
49. a. Largest, sample 3; smallest, sample 2
   b. 97.4%   **c.** Sample 3
   d. SD(sample 1) = 33.28; SD(sample 2) = 36; SD(sample 3) = 24.2; sample size = 240   **e.** Sample 1
53. a. 897
55. .576 _____ .724
57. .122 _____ .158
59. a. 185   **b.** 71.02 _____ 298.98
61. a. .013 _____ .587   **b.** Yes
63. $-2,367.18$ _____ -148.82
65. a. .012 _____ .06
   b. $-.066$ _____ .010

Chapter 9

1. a. Reject H_0 if $Z > 1.645$, or reject H_0 if $\overline{X} > 305.23$
   b. $Z = 1.41$; accept H_0
3. a. Reject H_0 if $Z < -1.645$
   b. $Z = -.98$; accept H_0
5. a. Reject H_0 if $\overline{X} < 1383.15$ or if $\overline{X} > 1516.85$
   b. $\overline{X} = 1475.6$; accept H_0
7. a. $H_0: \mu_x \leq 5; H_A: \mu_x > 5$
   b. Reject H_0 if $Z > 1.41$; $Z = 4.33$; reject H_0
9. a. .6480
   b. Reject H_0 if $\overline{X} > 205.20$; $\overline{X} = 201.3$; accept H_0

11. a. .9192
   b. Reject H_0 if $\overline{X} < 1317.1$; $\overline{X} = 1337.5$; accept H_0
13. a. .0129
   b. Reject H_0 if $\overline{X} < 17.49$; $\overline{X} = 17.4$; reject H_0
15. a. 2771
   b. Reject H_0 if $\overline{X} > 3002.5$
17. a. 3860
   b. Reject H_0 if $\overline{X} < 196.68$
19. a. $H_0: \mu_x \geq \$1.00$
      $H_A: \mu_x < 1.00$
   b. 68
   c. Reject H_0 if $\overline{X} < .95$; $\overline{X} = .96$; accept H_0
25. a. $H_0: \mu_x \geq 62; H_A: \mu_x < 62$
   b. Reject H_0 if $Z < -1.645$
   c. $Z = -2.65$; reject H_0
29. $H_0: \mu_x \geq 200; H_A: \mu_x < 200$; reject H_0 if $Z < -1.645$; $Z = -1.31$; accept H_0
31. a. $H_0: \mu_x \geq 3.4; H_A: \mu_x < 3.4$
   b. Reject H_0 if $Z < -1.645$; $Z = -8$; reject H_0
   c. $Z = -2.4$; reject H_0
   d. $Z = -2.078$; reject H_0
33. a. .0228
35. a. $H_0: \mu_x = 70; H_A: \mu_x \neq 70$
   b. Reject H_0 if $\overline{X} > 72.53$ or if $\overline{X} < 67.47$; $\overline{X} = 68.75$; accept H_0
37. a. $H_0: \mu_x = 5; H_A: \mu_x \neq 5$
   b. Reject H_0 if $\overline{X} < 4.982$ or if $\overline{X} > 5.018$
   c. Accept H_0
39. a. $H_0: \mu_x \geq 5; H_A: \mu_x < 5$
   b. Reject H_0 if $Z < -1.645$; $Z = -2.3$; reject H_0
41. $H_0: \mu_x \geq 10; H_A: \mu_x < 10$; reject H_0 if $\overline{X} < 9.501$; $\overline{X} = 9.58$; accept H_0
43. a. $H_0: \mu_x \geq 20; H_A: \mu_x < 20$
   b. Reject H_0 if $\overline{X} < 19.91$
   c. .0119   **d.** .1977
45. a. $H_0: \mu_x \leq 10; H_A: \mu_x > 10$
   b. Reject H_0 if $\overline{X} > 10.329$
   c. .5577   **d.** .4424
   e. 0.8739, 0.7406, 0.5577, 0.3613, 0.1963, 0.0877

47. a. H_0: $\mu_x \geq 900$; H_A: $\mu_x < 900$
b. Reject H_0 if $\bar{X} < 863.796$
c. .6554
d. .5793

49. Sample size = 113; H_0: $\mu_x \geq 2.4$; H_A: $\mu_x < 2.4$; reject H_0 if $\bar{X} < 2.33$; $\bar{X} = 2.35$; accept H_0; Type II error

51. For constraints 1 and 2, sample size = 35; for constraints 1 and 3, sample size = 119
d. 268

Chapter 10

1. Reject H_0 if $Z > 1.645$; $Z = .675$; accept H_0

3. Reject H_0 if $\hat{p} < .12$ or $\hat{p} > .28$; $\hat{p} = .225$; accept H_0

5. H_0: $p \leq .01$; H_A: $p > .01$; reject H_0 if $\hat{p} > .022$; $\hat{p} = .03$; reject H_0

7. a. Reject H_0 if $Z < -1.645$ or if $Z > 1.645$
b. $Z = .77$; accept H_0

9. a. Reject H_0 if $Z < -1.645$
b. $Z = -.795$; accept H_0

11. a. H_0: $\mu_1 - \mu_2 = 0$; H_A: $\mu_1 - \mu_2 \neq 0$
b. Reject H_0 if $Z < -1.96$ or if $Z > 1.96$; $Z = -5.55$; reject H_0

13. Reject H_0 if $Z < -1.96$ or if $Z > 1.96$; $Z = -.61$; accept H_0

15. Reject H_0 if $Z < -1.645$; $Z = -.79$; accept H_0

17. H_0: $p_1 - p_2 = 0$; H_A: $p_1 - p_2 \neq 0$; reject H_0 if $Z < -1.96$ or if $Z > 1.96$; $Z = -.74$; accept H_0

19. a. H_0: $p \geq .75$; H_A: $p < .75$
b. Reject H_0 if $\hat{p} < .714$; $\hat{p} = .92$; accept H_0

21. a. H_0: $p \geq .4$; H_A: $p < .4$
b. Reject H_0 if $\hat{p} < .337$; $\hat{p} = .37$; accept H_0

23. a. H_0: $p \leq .65$; H_A: $p > .65$
b. Reject H_0 if $\hat{p} > .78$; $\hat{p} = .64$; accept H_0

25. a. H_0: $\mu_1 - \mu_2 = 0$
H_A: $\mu_1 - \mu_2 \neq 0$

b. Reject H_0 if $Z < -1.96$ or if $Z > 1.96$; $Z = -4.568$; reject H_0

27. a. H_0: $\mu_1 - \mu_2 \geq .4$; H_A: $\mu_1 - \mu_2 < .4$
b. Reject H_0 if $Z < -1.645$; $Z = 2.87$; accept H_0

29. a. H_0: $p_1 - p_2 = 0$; H_A: $p_1 - p_2 \neq 0$
b. Reject H_0 if $Z < -1.96$ or if $Z > 1.96$; $Z = .823$; accept H_0

31. a. H_0: $p_1 \leq p_2$; H_A: $p_1 > p_2$
b. Reject H_0 if $Z > 1.28$; $Z = 1.299$; reject H_0

33. H_0: $p_1 = p_2$; H_A: $p_1 \neq p_2$; reject H_0 if $Z < -1.96$ or if $Z > 1.96$; $Z = .717$; accept H_0

Chapter 11

1. a. 3.250   **b.** 1.734   **c.** 2.080
d. 1.860

3. $t = -11.18$

7. a. 112.752 _____ 134.248
b. 114.759 _____ 132.241

9. a. 3.637 _____ 4.823
b. 3.779 _____ 4.681

11. 2.629 _____ 4.271

13. 0.692 _____ 3.508

15. a. 36.15   **b.** 8.574 _____ 63.726

17. a. -0.476 _____ 1.176

19. -12.814 _____ 4.814

21. -1.055 _____ 1.331

25. -43.22 _____ -5.78

27. Reject H_0 if $t < 1.316$; $t = -0.72$; accept H_0

29. Reject H_0 if $t < -2.086$ or if $t > 2.086$; $t = -5.34$; reject H_0

31. Reject H_0 if $t > 2.528$; $t = 0.302$; accept H_0

33. H_0: $\mu_1 - \mu_2 = 0$; H_A: $\mu_1 - \mu_2 \neq 0$; reject H_0 if $t < -1.833$ or if $t > 1.833$; $t = -0.084$; accept H_0

35. H_0: $\mu_1 - \mu_2 = 0$; H_A: $\mu_1 - \mu_2 \neq 0$; reject H_0 if $t < -2.447$ or if $t > 2.447$; $t = -0.06$; accept H_0

41. a. 1.057 _____ 1.343
c. 1.027 _____ 1.373

43. a. 10.11 _____ 12.49

b. 10.54 _____ 12.06

45. a. 76.30 _____ 99.70

   b. 72.01 _____ 103.99

47. -0.121 _____ 0.721

49. b. -37.875 _____ 34.033

53. a. -0.476 _____ 1.876

   b. -0.80 _____ 2.20

   d. -2.102 _____ 3.502

55. -0.45 _____ 3.85

57. H_0: $\mu_x \le 1{,}800$; H_A: $\mu_x > 1{,}800$; reject H_0 if $t > 1.415$; $t = 1.06$; accept H_0

59. a. H_0: $\mu_x \le 1{,}000$; H_A: $\mu_x > 1{,}000$; reject H_0 if $t > 1.895$; $t = 1.479$; accept H_0

61. H_0: $\mu_x \ge 30$; H_A: $\mu_x < 30$; reject H_0 if $t < -1.833$; $t = -0.027$; accept H_0

63. a. H_0: $\mu_1 \ge \mu_2$; H_A: $\mu_1 < \mu_2$

   c. Reject H_0 if $t < -2.681$; $t = -0.45$; accept H_0

65. a. H_0: $\mu_1 - \mu_2 = 0$; H_A: $\mu_1 - \mu_2 \ne 0$

   b. Reject H_0 if $t < -1.796$ or if $t > 1.796$; $t = -1.383$; accept H_0

67. H_0: $\mu_1 - \mu_2 = 0$; H_A: $\mu_1 - \mu_2 \ne 0$; reject H_0 if $t < -2.447$ or if $t > 2.447$; $t = -0.192$; accept H_0

69. H_0: $\mu_1 \ge \mu_2$; H_A: $\mu_1 < \mu_2$; reject H_0 if $t < -1.476$; $t = -2.382$; reject H_0

Chapter 12

1. 16.919

3. 26.171

5. a. Reject H_0 if $\chi^2 > 16.919$; $\chi^2 = 11.025$; accept H_0

   b. Reject H_0 if $\chi^2 > 39.087$; $\chi^2 = 39.15$; reject H_0

7. a. Reject H_0 if $\chi^2 > 18.549$; $\chi^2 = 16$; accept H_0

   b. Reject H_0 if $\chi^2 > 42.557$; $\chi^2 = 50.75$; reject H_0

9. a. H_0: $\sigma^2 \le 64$
       H_A: $\sigma^2 > 64$

   b. Reject H_0 if $\chi^2 > 21.064$

   c. $\chi^2 = 23.233$; reject H_0

11. a. 3.62   **b.** 3.11   **c.** 3.05

13. a. Reject H_0 if $F > 2.86$

   b. $F = 1.20$; accept H_0

15. a. Reject H_0 if $F < 0.31$

   b. $F = 0.46$; accept H_0

17. a. H_0: $\sigma_1^2 \le \sigma_2^2$; H_A: $\sigma_1^2 > \sigma_2^2$

   b. Reject H_0 if $F > 1.98$; $F = 3.48$; reject H_0

   c. H_0: $\mu_1 - \mu_2 = 0$; H_A: $\mu_1 - \mu_2 \ne 0$; reject H_0 if $t < -2.021$ or $t > 2.021$; $t = 6.133$; reject H_0

19. b. 317.73   **c.** 163.72   **d.** Reject H_0 if $F > 3.16$; $F = 11.64$; reject H_0

21. b. Reject H_0 if $F > 5.49$; $F = 7.42$; reject H_0

25. b. 183   **c.** 89.44

   d. Reject H_0 if $F > 3.68$; $F = 15.35$; reject H_0

   e. Difference 1 and 2 $= 7.33$; difference 2 and 3 $= 6.00$; difference 1 and 3 $= 1.33$; T range $= 3.657$

27. b. 1178   **c.** 3148

   d. Reject H_0 if $F > 6.93$; $F = 2.25$; accept H_0

29. Reject H_0 if $F > 3.68$; $F = 22.33$; reject H_0; difference 1 and 2 $= 13.16$; difference 1 and 3 $= 19.16$; difference 2 and 3 $= 6.00$; T range $= 7.60$

31. b. TSS $= 1494.88$; SSBL $= 63.38$; SSB $= 1274.13$; SSW $= 157.37$

   c. F between groups $= 56.70$; F between blocks $= 1.21$; differences $= 3.5, 6.87, 12.87, 10.37, 16.37, 6.0$; LSD $= 2.846$

33. b. F between groups $= 11.91$; F between blocks $= 2.63$

35. H_0: $\sigma_x^2 \le (0.10)^2$; H_A: $\sigma_x^2 > (0.10)^2$; reject H_0 if $\chi^2 > 35.172$; $\chi^2 = 73.6$; reject H_0

37. H_0: $\sigma_1^2 \le 400$; H_A: $\sigma_1^2 > 400$; reject H_0 if $\chi^2 > 27.204$; $\chi^2 = 29.688$; reject H_0

39. a. H_0: $\mu_1 \ge \mu_2$
       H_A: $\mu_1 < \mu_2$

   c. Reject H_0 if $t < -2.681$; $t = 0.45$; accept H_0

   d. H_0: $\sigma_1^2 = \sigma_2^2$; H_A: $\sigma_1^2 \ne \sigma_2^2$; reject H_0 if $F > 8.47$; $F = 1.15$; accept H_0

41. a. H_0: $\sigma_1^2 \le \sigma_2^2$; H_A: $\sigma_1^2 > \sigma_2^2$

$-0.829.$

b. Reject H_0 if $F > 2.28$; $F = 1.45$; accept H_0

43. a. H_0: $\sigma_1^2 = \sigma_2^2$; H_A: $\sigma_1^2 \neq \sigma_2^2$; $F = 2.61$; accept H_0

47. Reject H_0 if $F > 8.105$; $F = 7.359$; accept H_0

49. Reject H_0 if $F > 4.43$; $F = 59.40$; reject H_0

53. Reject H_0 if $F > 2.74$; $F = 16.09$; reject H_0

55. a. Reject H_0 if $F > 2.585$; $F = 16.745$; reject H_0

b. Differences $= 2.6, 5.6, 12.7, 3.8, 3.0, 10.1, 1.2, 7.1, 1.8, 8.9$; T range $= 4.7$

57. a. Reject H_0 if $F > 2.79$; $F = 13.28$; reject H_0

b. Differences $= 4,400; 1,800; 3,100; 2,600; 1,300; 1,300$; T range $= 1,953.42$

59. a. Reject H_0 if $F > 2.745$; $F = 5.28$; reject H_0

b. Differences $= 4.9; 1.1; 6.7; 3.8; 1.8; 5.6$; T range $= 5.12$

61. a. Reject H_0 if $F > 3.685$; $F = 5.28$; reject H_0

b. Differences $= 8.92; 12.75; 3.83$; S range $= 5.57$

63. a. Reject H_0 if $F > 2.92$; $F = 6.53$; reject H_0

b. Difference between students over 18 and blue collar workers

67. F between groups $= 26.7$; F between blocks $= 10.95$

69. Differences $= 263; 555; 835; 818; 1,098; 280$; LSD $= 293.05$

71. a. F between groups $= 0.03$; accept H_0
b. F between blocks $= 1,209$; reject H_0
c. Reject H_0 if $F > 3.74$; reject H_0
d. LSD $= 254.66$; $\mu_1 \neq \mu_2$; $\mu_2 \neq \mu_3$

Chapter 13

7. b. .9239
c. Reject H_0 if $t < -2.306$ or $t > 2.306$; $t = 6.8295$; reject H_0

9. b. Reject H_0 if $t < -1.645$ or $t > 1.645$; $t = 7.303$; reject H_0

13. b. $-.289$; reject H_0 if $t < -2.365$ or $t > 2.365$; $t = -3.9219$; Reject H_0
c. $19.7547 - .0835X$

15. b. $-.5411$; reject H_0 if $t < -2.262$ or $t > 2.262$; $t = -1.9303$; accept H_0
c. $5.1568 - .07507X$
d. SSE $= 12.8580$; SS Y variable $= 18.1821$; SS residuals $= .0001$

17. a. Reject H_0 if $t < -2.069$ or $t > 2.069$; $t = 207.44$; reject H_0

19. b. Reject H_0 if $t < -1.96$ or $t > 1.96$; $t = 3.2436$; reject H_0

21. a. Reject H_0 if $t < -2.069$ or $t > 2.069$; $t = 13.4259$; reject H_0
c. 122.6548 _____ 167.3452

23. b. -16.3916 _____ -3.8488

25. a. 7400
b. 7399.3714 _____ 7400.6286
c. 7397.2636 _____ 7402.7364

27. a. 1242.144
b. $36,315.742$ _____ $36,324.2589$
c. $36,307.2234$ _____ $36,332.7766$

35. $r = -.567$; reject H_0 if $t < -1.833$ or $t > 1.833$; $t = -2.065$; reject H_0

39. b. $.891$
c. Reject H_0 if $t < -2.12$ or $t > 2.12$; $t = 7.85$; reject H_0

41. Reject H_0 if $t < -1.96$ or $t > 1.96$; $t = 1.908$; accept H_0

45. $166.46 + .0538$ (current \$); $239.66 + .0639$ (1977 \$)

47. b. $1735.9 + .1064X$
c. Reject H_0 if $F > 5.32$; $F = .536$; accept H_0 or reject H_0 if $t < -2.306$ or if $t > 2.306$; $t = .73$; accept H_0

49. Reject H_0 if $t < -1.86$ or $t > 1.86$; $t = 8.67$; reject H_0; standard error of slope $= .2486$

51. $F = 18.68$

55. TSS $= 550$; SSR $= 88$; SSE $= 462$; SEE $= 2.171$

57. 7.94 _____ 11.46

59. $.0002884$ _____ $.000768$

61. b. $\hat{y} = 1219.803 - 9.12x$

  c. -22.73 _____ 4.49

  d. $t = 1.23$

63. a. $t = 54.02$ **b.** 2.91 _____ 3.57

65. $\hat{y} = 3.464; 3.436$ _____ 3.492

Chapter 14

1. Reject H_0 if $t < -2.262$ or $t > 2.262$;
  (Y,X_1) $t = 2.12$; (Y,X_2) $t = 2.91$; (Y,X_3) t
  $= 1.83$; (X_1,X_2) $t = 2.55$; (X_1,X_3) $t = .81$;
  (X_2,X_3) $t = .09$

3. a. $-476 + .742X_1 + 1.31X_2 + .119X_3$

  b. $.735$

  c. Reject H_0 if $F > 4.35$; $F = 6.461$;
    reject H_0 **d.** X_2, X_3 **e.** $.621$

5. Reject H_0 if $t < -2.145$ or $t > 2.145$;
  (Y,X_1) $t = 6.01$; (Y,X_2) $t = 1.70$; (Y,X_3) t
  $= 2.80$; (Y,X_4) $t = -2.03$; (X_1,X_2) $t =$
  1.12; (X_1,X_3) $t = 2.65$; (X_1,X_4) $t = -1.31$;
  (X_2,X_3) $t = 1.65$; (X_2,X_4) $t = -1.87$;
  (X_3,X_4) $t = -2.46$

7. a. $14,122 + 63.2X_1 + 10.1X_2 + 31.5X_3$
    $- 55.5X_4$ **b.** $.775$

  c. Reject H_0 if $F > 3.36$; $F = 9.45$; reject
    H_0 **d.** X_1 **e.** $.693$

  f. X_1: 30.27 _____ 96.03; X_2: -21.40
    _____ 41.60; X_3: -358.30 _____
    421.30; X_4: -192.12 _____ 81.20

9. b. 3

13. b. $-774 + 66.2X_1$

  c. $-586.256 + 22.861X_1 + 2302.267X_2$
    $+ 1869.813X_3$; reject H_0 if $F > 4.35$; F
    $= 5.393$; reject H_0

  d. $-586.256 + 22.861X_1$

15. a. X_1 **b.** No other variables entered

  c. $11,392.04318 + 72.2163X_1$

  d. Reject H_0 if $F > 4.60$; $F = 36.07$;
    reject H_0; reject H_0 if $t < -2.16$ or $t >$
    2.16; $t = 6.006$; reject H_0

29. $A_L = -.5139$; $A_H = .5139$

33. Reject H_0 if $t < -2.201$ or $t > 2.201$; t for
  $X_1 = 1.99$; t for $X_2 = .86$; t for $X_3 =$
  1.52; accept H_0 for all variables

35. Reject H_0 if $t < -2.16$ or $t > 2.16$; (Y,X_1)
  $t = 2.877$; (Y,X_2) $t = 1.371$; (Y,X_3) $t =$
  2.85; (Y,X_4) $t = 2.0$

39. $.844$; reject H_0 if $F > 3.48$; $F = 13.607$;
  reject H_0

41. Reject H_0 if $t < -2.228$ or $t > 2.228$; X_1, t
  $= 4.422$; X_2, $t = -.788$; X_3, $t = 3.581$;
  X_4, $t = 2.581$

43. Reject H_0 if $t < -2.160$ or $t > 2.160$;
  (Y,X_5) $t = 7.266$; (Y,X_6) $t = 3.171$

45. Reject H_0 if $F > 3.58$; $F = 9.125$; reject
  H_0

51. $.00033$ _____ $.00365$

59. X_1; reject H_0 if $t < -2.069$ or $t > 2.069$; t
  $= 10.801$; reject H_0; $54,174.82 +$
  $36,241.53X_1$; $R^2 = .835$

Chapter 15

1. Reject H_0 if $\chi^2 > 7.815$; $\chi^2 = 65.206$;
  reject H_0

3. Reject H_0 if $\chi^2 > 18.307$; $\chi^2 = 33.4$; reject
  H_0

5. Reject H_0 if $\chi^2 > 15.507$; $\chi^2 = 8.19$;
  accept H_0

7. Reject H_0 if $\chi^2 > 12.592$; $\chi^2 = 23.17$;
  reject H_0

9. a. Reject H_0 if $t < -2.074$ or $t > 2.074$; t
    $= 1.27$; accept H_0

  b. Reject H_0 if $Z < -1.96$ or $Z > 1.96$; Z
    $= 1.21$; accept H_0

11. Reject H_0 if $Z > 1.645$; $Z = 2.18$; reject H_0

13. b. Reject H_0 if $H > 5.991$; $H = 5.416$;
    accept H_0

15. $H = 66.26$

17. $r_s = .876$; reject H_0 if $t < -2.228$ or $t >$
  2.228; $t = 5.74$; reject H_0

19. a. $r_s = .849$

  b. Reject H_0 if $t < -3.012$ or $t > 3.012$; t
    $= 5.79$; reject H_0

21. Reject H_0 if $\chi^2 > 11.34$; $\chi^2 = 6.625$;
  accept H_0

23. Reject H_0 if $\chi^2 > 12.592$; $\chi^2 = 25.4341$;
  reject H_0

25. $\overline{X} = 56.75$; $S_x = 17.32$; reject H_0 if $\chi^2 >$ 11.07; $\chi^2 = 80.944$; reject H_0

27. **b.** Reject H_0 if $\chi^2 > 3.84$; $\chi^2 = 3.338$; accept H_0

   c. Reject H_0 if $Z < -1.96$ or $Z > 1.96$; $Z = -1.828$; accept H_0

29. Reject H_0 if $\chi^2 > 10.644$; $\chi^2 = 38.08$; reject H_0

31. Reject H_0 if $Z < -1.645$ or $Z > 1.645$; $Z = .605$; accept H_0

33. Reject H_0 if $Z < -1.645$; $Z = -1.587$; accept H_0

35. Reject H_0 if $t < -2.845$ or $t > 2.845$; $t = -.252$; accept H_0

37. Reject H_0 if $\chi^2 > 4.61$; $H = 12.252$; reject H_0

39. Reject H_0 if $t < -2.228$ or $t > 2.228$; $t = -3.152$; reject H_0

41. $r_s = .915$; reject H_0 if $t < -1.782$ or $t > 1.782$; $t = 7.86$; reject H_0

Chapter 16

5. **a.** $101 + 1.9X$ **b.** .633

7. Centered moving averages: 163.25; 170.75; 178.75; 186.75; 194.88; 201.38; 204.88; 209.25; 214.63; 221.13; 228.88; 232.88
   Ratio to moving avg.: 96.17; 97.80; 101.82; 102.81; 98.01; 97.83; 105.92; 99.88; 94.12; 99.94; 103.11; 103.92
   Normalized avg. seasonal index: Qrt. 1: 103.502; Qrt. 2: 102.09; Qrt. 3: 95.994; Qrt. 4: 95.994

9. Norm. avg. seas. index (Jan.–Dec.): 95.89; 88.31; 88.80; 99.28; 102.74; 92.44; 97.76; 101.72; 104.89; 100.40; 111.16; 116.61

11. Normalized avg. seasonal index (Qtr. 1–4): 100.84; 92.89; 108.11; 98.16; $\hat{Y} = 222.375 + 1.353X$; $R^2 = .117$

13. Index numbers: 100.00; 116.49; 122.16; 131.44; 143.30; 144.85; 154.64; 165.98; 174.23; 181.96; 186.08; 200.52; 209.79

15. Radio index numbers: 100; 103.33; 110; 115.33; 120.67; 126.67; 132

Newspaper index numbers: 100; 105; 115; 130; 145; 160; 165

17. Laspeyres index: 100; 104.59; 113.78; 126.43; 139.08; 151.89; 156.97

19. 11.97; 11.86; 12.35; 14.03; 14.31; 15.38; 16.74

27. $-267.2 + 133.7t$; $R^2 = .913$; reject H_0 if $t < -2.145$ or $t > 2.145$; $t = 12.09$; reject H_0

29. $-1.4 + 1.5308t$; $R^2 = .939$; reject H_0 if $t < -2.228$ or $t > 2.228$; $t = 12.43$; reject H_0

31. **c.** Normalized avg. seasonal index (Jan.–Dec.): 85; 87; 79; 87; 93; 94; 96; 102; 108; 114; 125; 132

33. **a.** Normalized avg. seasonal index (Jan.–Dec.): 78.59; 51.90; 41.37; 94.87; 127.99; 60.72; 100.82; 96.04; 87.64; 120.22; 182.50; 157.29

   c. $\hat{Y} = 5.7155 + .0727t$; estimated interest amounts (Jan.–Dec.): 119,655; 79,575; 63,885; 147,540; 200,445; 95,760; 160,095; 153,555; 141,075; 194,835; 297,775; 258,345

39. Company 1: 1; 1.09148; 1.32264; 1.41679; 1.61838; 1.74292; 1.90958
   Company 2: 1; 1.04518; 1.14368; 1.22155; 1.40711

41. Labor index numbers: 100; 115.99; 132.34; 140.52; 149.44; 152.42; 161.34; 167.29; 178.44; 182.16; 186.61
   Materials index numbers: 100; 104; 108; 115.2; 124; 130.4; 134.93; 135.73; 136.53; 137.87; 138.8

43. 100; 104; 108.01; 115.21; 124.01; 130.41; 134.94; 135.74; 136.54; 137.88; 138.81

45. 100; 112.28; 125.67; 144.25; 162.83; 173.70; 185.9; 202.83

47. 3.41; 5.30; 4.48; 6.61; 7.38; 6.67; 9.11; 9.49; 10.87; 13.26; 15.29; 17.75; current dollars: $\hat{Y} = -1.4 + 1.53X$; $R^2 = .94$; deflated dollars: $\hat{Y} = 1.43 + 1.19X$; $R^2 = .93$

Chapter 17

1. $\hat{Y} = 243.875 + 5.463t$; $R^2 = .905$; 1988 forecast: 336.75; 342.21; 347.68; 353.14

3. 1988 forecast: 343.98; 348.72; 341.36; 352.65; $\hat{Y} = 242.4847 + 5.6362t$; $R^2 = .94$

5. **a.** $\hat{Y} = 54.837 + .633t$; $R^2 = .57$; 1988 forecast: 93.46; 94.10; 94.73; 95.36; 96; 96.63; 97.26; 97.90; 98.53; 99.16; 99.79; 100.43
   b. $\hat{Y} = 56.088 + .586t$; $R^2 = .663$; 1988 forecast: 88.07; 81.62; 82.59; 92.92; 96.76; 87.61; 93.22; 97.59; 101.25; 97.50; 108.60; 114.61

7. **a.** First-order lag: $\hat{Y} = 49.966 + .84357 Y_{t-1}$; $R^2 = .866$; second-order lag: $\hat{Y} = 91.8097 + .714629Y_{t-2}$; $R^2 = .706$; third-order lag: $\hat{Y} = 97.049 + .7157Y_{t-3}$; $R^2 = .716$; fourth-order lag: $\hat{Y} = 83.65979 + .782542Y_{t-4}$; $R^2 = .794$
   b. Fourth-order lag
   c. 338.77; 343.46; 334.86; 329.38

9. **a.** One-period lag; $\hat{Y} = 16.75520 + .790257Y_{t-1}$; $R^2 = .75$; twelve-period lag: $\hat{Y} = 46.441 + .457159Y_{t-12}$; $R^2 = .603$
   b. Twelve-period lag

11. **a.** 132.5   **b.** 133.3   **c.** 129.64
    d. 139.33   **e.** Weighted-moving average

13. **a.** $\hat{Y} = -0.5 + 0.2869t$; $R^2 = .919$; 4.09; 4.38; 4.66
    b. $\hat{Y} = 0.336 + 0.0176t^2$; $R^2 = .941$; 4.853; 5.435; 6.053
    c. Model in part b
    d. Part a; $D = 1.517$; Part b; $D = 1.80$; accept H_0 if $D > 1.36$; reject H_0 if $D < 1.08$

15. **c.** Normalized avg. seasonal index (July–June): 97.43; 101.25; 105.80; 110.84; 119.58; 125.09; 88.43; 89.53; 83.78; 89.74; 94.26; 94.77
    d. $\hat{Y} = 35.366 + .3365t$; $R^2 = .894$; forecast: 45.86; 46.73; 44.01; 47.44; 50.15; 50.74; 52.49; 54.89; 57.71; 60.56; 66.03; 69.50

17. **a.** Normalized avg. seasonal index (July–June): 123.62; 86.73; 79.20; 108.54; 165.08; 142.70; 71.66; 47.43; 37.69; 86.59; 116.50; 134.27
    c. $\hat{Y} = 7.2917 + 0.046768t$; $R^2 = .42$; seasonally-adjusted forecast: 7.27; 4.83; 3.86; 8.91; 12.04; 13.94; 12.89; 9.08; 8.33; 11.47; 17.52; 15.21

21. **a.** $\hat{Y} = 3.817 + .578Y_{t-1}$; $R^2 = .324$
    b. $\hat{Y} = .7569 + .9716Y_{t-12}$; $R^2 = .894$

23. 146.55; MAD $= 35.42$; MSE $= 1921.326$

25. 146.75; MAD $= 38.26$; MSE $= 2166.553$

27. **a.** 17,975.00; MAD $= 4240.63$; MSE $= 20,881,015$
    b. 18,673.24; MAD $= 3077.76$; MSE $= 13,675,133$
    c. 20,626.45; MAD $= 3000.20$; MSE $= 10,301,012$

29. **a.** alpha $= .2$; 1755.69; MAD $= 352.61$; MSE $= 184,633.9$
    alpha $= .5$; 1894.32; MAD $= 341.55$; MSE $= 186,996.6$
    alpha $= .8$; 2011.55; MAD $= 333.71$; MSE $= 165,594.7$
    b. alpha $= .2$, beta $= .2$; 1786.68; MAD $= 454.19$; MSE $= 249,136.0$
    alpha $= .5$, beta $= .4$; 1939.51; MAD $= 538.54$; MSE $= 341,951.6$
    alpha $= .8$, beta $= .6$; 2289.17; MAD $= 471.22$; MSE $= 311,351.5$

Chapter 18

1. 20; maximum payoff $= 15$

3.
Order Size	E(X)
15	10
16	10.85
17	11.40
18	11.35
19	10.10
20	8.40

Order 17 books

5. 500; payoff = 500
7. 2 lots; expected payoff = 60.00
9. Buy no lots; expected values = 0.0
11. 200; maximum payoff = 3000
13. Keep for two years, then sell if no increase in demand; expected value = $57,000
15. Expand; expected value = $34,500
17. Build the large resort; expected value = $1.95 million
23. .727
29. No homes; payoff = 0
31. For $60,000 home, 3; expected payoff = 20.00; for $80,000 home, 3; expected payoff = 34.88; for $100,000 home, 2; expected payoff = 31.91; best decision: build 3 of the $80,000 homes
33. 10; worst payoff = −490,000
35. 30; expected value = $386,000
37. Market the beer; expected value = $350,000
39. Market the beer; expected value = $555,000
41. 1,500 gallons; expected profits = $4,312.50
43. 3 or 4; payoffs = $9.49 and $9.50
45. Accept the offer; expected value = $47,280
47. Reject the offer; expected value = $27,360

Chapter 19

1. $P(A/D)$ = .5; $P(B/D)$ = .5; equally likely
3. $P(A/D)$ = .47619; $P(B/D)$ = .142857; $P(C/D)$ = .380952; Plant A = 4,761.90; Plant B = 1,428.57; Plant C = 3,809.52
5. $P(N/D)$ = .79; $P(O/D)$ = .21; new grower

7. E(machine A) = 8,500; E(machine B) = 9,500; choose machine B
9. E(machine A) = 19,360; E(machine B) = 17,770; choose machine A
11. North = .9606; south = .0394
13. E(sell) = 25,000; E(don't sell) = 22,000; sell business
15. $EVPI$ = 52,000 − 38,000 = 14,000
17. $EVPI$ = 725,000 − 650,000 = 75,000
19. $EVPI$ = 9800 − 1000 = 8800
21. $P(A/d)$ = .521; $P(B/d)$ = .375; $P(C/d)$ = .104; Plant A = 208,400; Plant B = 150,000; Plant C = 41,600
23. .69
25.

	Demand Levels				
	10,000	15,000	20,000	30,000	50,000
Old	14,700	23,450	32,200	49,700	84,700
New	11,500	22,750	34,000	56,500	101,500

27.

Demand	Posterior Prob.
10,000	.0057
15,000	.0343
20,000	.1371
30,000	.4571
50,000	.3657

29. .06
31. Same
33. Posterior prob. (good) = 0; posterior prob. (fair) = 1; posterior prob. (poor) = 0
35. Development project; expected value = $285,000
37. $EVPI$ = 530,000
39. $EVPI$ = 940,000 − 861,500 = 78,500
41. Value of sample = 78,500 − 88,780 = −10,280

INDEX

WE VALUE YOUR OPINION—PLEASE SHARE IT WITH US

Merrill Publishing and our authors are most interested in your reactions to this textbook. Did it serve you well in the course? If it did, what aspects of the text were most helpful? If not, what didn't you like about it? Your comments will help us to write and develop better textbooks. We value your opinions and thank you for your help.

Text Title _____ Edition _____

Author(s) _____

Your Name (optional) _____

Address _____

City _____ State _____ Zip _____

School _____

Course Title _____

Instructor's Name _____

Your Major _____

Your Class Rank _____ Freshman _____ Sophomore _____ Junior _____ Senior

_____ Graduate Student

Were you required to take this course? _____ Required _____ Elective

Length of Course? _____ Quarter _____ Semester

1. Overall, how does this text compare to other texts you've used?

_____ Superior _____ Better Than Most _____ Average _____ Poor

2. Please rate the text in the following areas:

	Superior	Better Than Most	Average	Poor
Author's Writing Style	_____	_____	_____	_____
Readability	_____	_____	_____	_____
Organization	_____	_____	_____	_____
Accuracy	_____	_____	_____	_____
Layout and Design	_____	_____	_____	_____
Illustrations/Photos/Tables	_____	_____	_____	_____
Examples	_____	_____	_____	_____
Problems/Exercises	_____	_____	_____	_____
Topic Selection	_____	_____	_____	_____
Currentness of Coverage	_____	_____	_____	_____
Explanation of Difficult Concepts	_____	_____	_____	_____
Match-up with Course Coverage	_____	_____	_____	_____
Applications to Real Life	_____	_____	_____	_____

3. Circle those chapters you especially liked:
   1   2   3   4   5   6   7   8   9   10   11   12   13   14   15   16   17   18   19   20
   What was your favorite chapter? _____
   Comments:

4. Circle those chapters you liked least:
   1   2   3   4   5   6   7   8   9   10   11   12   13   14   15   16   17   18   19   20
   What was your least favorite chapter? _____
   Comments:

5. List any chapters your instructor did not assign. _____

6. What topics did your instructor discuss that were not covered in the text?_____

   _____

7. Were you required to buy this book? _____ Yes _____ No

   Did you buy this book new or used? _____ New _____ Used

   If used, how much did you pay? _____

   Do you plan to keep or sell this book? _____ Keep _____ Sell

   If you plan to sell the book, how much do you expect to receive? _____

   Should the instructor continue to assign this book? _____ Yes _____ No

8. Please list any other learning materials you purchased to help you in this course (e.g., study guide, lab manual).

   _____

9. What did you like most about this text? _____

   _____

10. What did you like least about this text? _____

    _____

11. General comments:

    May we quote you in our advertising? _____ Yes _____ No

    Please mail to: Boyd Lane
                     College Division, Research Department
                     Box 508
                     1300 Alum Creek Drive
                     Columbus, Ohio 43216

    Thank you!

STANDARD NORMAL DISTRIBUTION TABLE

To illustrate: 19.85 percent of the area under a normal curve lies between the mean, μ_x, and a point 0.52 standard deviation units away.

Example:
$Z = 0.52$ (or -0.52)
$A(Z) = 0.1985$ or 19.85%

Z	.00	.01	.02	.03	.04	.05	.06	.07	.08	.09
0.0	.0000	.0040	.0080	.0120	.0160	.0199	.0239	.0279	.0319	.0359
0.1	.0398	.0438	.0478	.0517	.0557	.0596	.0636	.0675	.0714	.0753
0.2	.0793	.0832	.0871	.0910	.0948	.0987	.1026	.1064	.1103	.1141
0.3	.1179	.1217	.1255	.1293	.1331	.1368	.1406	.1443	.1480	.1517
0.4	.1554	.1591	.1628	.1664	.1700	.1736	.1772	.1808	.1844	.1879
0.5	.1915	.1950	.1985	.2019	.2054	.2088	.2123	.2157	.2190	.2224
0.6	.2257	.2291	.2324	.2357	.2389	.2422	.2454	.2486	.2517	.2549
0.7	.2580	.2611	.2642	.2673	.2704	.2734	.2764	.2794	.2823	.2852
0.8	.2881	.2910	.2939	.2967	.2995	.3023	.3051	.3078	.3106	.3133
0.9	.3159	.3186	.3212	.3238	.3264	.3289	.3315	.3340	.3365	.3389
1.0	.3413	.3438	.3461	.3485	.3508	.3531	.3554	.3577	.3599	.3621
1.1	.3643	.3665	.3686	.3708	.3729	.3749	.3770	.3790	.3810	.3830
1.2	.3849	.3869	.3888	.3907	.3925	.3944	.3962	.3980	.3997	.4015
1.3	.4032	.4049	.4066	.4082	.4099	.4115	.4131	.4147	.4162	.4177
1.4	.4192	.4207	.4222	.4236	.4251	.4265	.4279	.4292	.4306	.4319
1.5	.4332	.4345	.4357	.4370	.4382	.4394	.4406	.4418	.4429	.4441
1.6	.4452	.4463	.4474	.4484	.4495	.4505	.4515	.4525	.4535	.4545
1.7	.4554	.4564	.4573	.4582	.4591	.4599	.4608	.4616	.4625	.4633
1.8	.4641	.4649	.4656	.4664	.4671	.4678	.4686	.4693	.4699	.4706
1.9	.4713	.4719	.4726	.4732	.4738	.4744	.4750	.4756	.4761	.4767
2.0	.4772	.4778	.4783	.4788	.4793	.4798	.4803	.4808	.4812	.4817
2.1	.4821	.4826	.4830	.4834	.4838	.4842	.4846	.4850	.4854	.4857
2.2	.4861	.4864	.4868	.4871	.4875	.4878	.4881	.4884	.4887	.4890
2.3	.4893	.4896	.4898	.4901	.4904	.4906	.4909	.4911	.4913	.4916
2.4	.4918	.4920	.4922	.4925	.4927	.4929	.4931	.4932	.4934	.4936
2.5	.4938	.4940	.4941	.4943	.4945	.4946	.4948	.4949	.4951	.4952
2.6	.4953	.4955	.4956	.4957	.4959	.4960	.4961	.4962	.4963	.4964
2.7	.4965	.4966	.4967	.4968	.4969	.4970	.4971	.4972	.4973	.4974
2.8	.4974	.4975	.4976	.4977	.4977	.4978	.4979	.4979	.4980	.4981
2.9	.4981	.4982	.4982	.4983	.4984	.4984	.4985	.4985	.4986	.4986
3.0	.4987	.4987	.4987	.4988	.4988	.4989	.4989	.4989	.4990	.4990

SOURCE: From Stephen P. Shao, *Statistics for Business and Economics*, 3rd ed. (Columbus, Ohio: Charles E. Merrill, 1976), p. 788. Used with permission.